ANNUAL REVIEW OF PSYCHOLOGY

MARK R. ROSENZWEIG, *Editor*
University of California, Berkeley

LYMAN W. PORTER, *Editor*
University of California, Irvine

VOLUME 32

1981

ANNUAL REVIEWS INC.   4139 EL CAMINO WAY   PALO ALTO, CALIFORNIA 94306 USA

R ANNUAL REVIEWS INC.
Palo Alto, California, USA

REPRINTS   The conspicuous number aligned in the margin with the title of each article in this volume is a key for use in ordering reprints. Available reprints are priced at the uniform rate of $2.00 each postpaid. The minimum acceptable reprint order is 5 reprints and/or $10.00 prepaid. A quantity discount is available.

International Standard Serial Number: 0066-4308
International Standard Book Number: 0-8243-0232-X
Library of Congress Catalog Card Number: 50-13143

PRINTED AND BOUND IN THE UNITED STATES OF AMERICA

PREFACE

A few years have elapsed since the aims and practices of the *Annual Review of Psychology* have been published, so an up-to-date statement may be helpful to our readers. Each volume is planned to present selective and evaluative reviews of status and recent progress in several main areas of psychology. We do not intend to provide in a single volume an accurate representation of activity in each of the many subfields of psychology; space would not permit this. Rather, we try to follow (and frequently revise) a Master Plan according to which some topics appear each year, some every other year, and some less frequently. In this way, a few successive volumes, taken together, present an evaluative portrayal of the main recent findings and interpretations as they are viewed by the most expert judges who can be persuaded to contribute their critical and integrative skills to the task. We do not publish the Master Plan because some details are changed almost every year. The cumulative index of chapter titles published at the end of each volume shows the frequency of coverage of each main topic over the last five years.

The representation of chapters in different areas from volume to volume is not entirely a matter of planning by the Editorial Committee, but is also affected by circumstances beyond editorial control. Depending upon the availability of authors and upon their ability to meet deadlines, a particular field may show a chapter each year, or a gap one year may be followed by two chapters the next. Over a period of a few years, these fluctuations usually average out, and it is over such a span that the coverage should be judged.

The same span is useful in going beyond the personal choices of an individual author and in seeing what contributions are discussed by two or three successive reviewers. Authors of chapters are requested to make their reviews selective and evaluative rather than inclusive and merely descriptive. Here are some of the suggestions they receive:

> The best recent reviews have usually followed this model: After giving a general orientation to the subject, the review describes and evaluates significant advances on the cutting edge of research or theory; the main part of the review is focused on a few specific topics, but it is not restricted to the work of any one laboratory or group.
>
> The most important characteristic of successful chapters is that they evaluate research and theory rather than simply describing contributions. Beyond selecting the most important material, please tell the readers why you have selected it and how it contributes to clarifying knowledge and understanding of the subject. Please make clear in the introduction how the scope of your chapter is restricted and what main questions you will cover.

Try to keep the chapter readable, even if you get to rather specialized material. Define any specialized terms and concepts clearly and give concrete examples where they are useful and/or necessary. A dash of humor often helps.

Because the total page allotment for each volume is restricted, we ask that you limit your chapter to the assigned number of pages. We also urge you to make every effort to submit your manuscript on time. Publication of late manuscripts cannot be guaranteed and will be accepted only on a "space available" basis.

These objectives are not easy to achieve, and we must all be grateful that so many active investigators are willing to take the time and effort to survey their fields and share their insights and judgments with us.

* * *

The members of the Editorial Committee (with the exception of the Editors) serve for five-year terms. We regret that Norman D. Sundberg has now completed his period of service. The planning of five volumes has benefited from his wide knowledge of psychology and psychologists, and we will miss his genial comradeship at our meetings.

M.R.R.
L.W.P.

Annual Review of Psychology
Volume 32, 1981

CONTENTS

ERRATUM

Volume 31 (1980)

In "Evaluation Research," by Gene V. Glass and Frederick S. Ellett, Jr., A statement in the section headed DEFINITIONS OF EVALUATION on page 212 contained an error.

The statement should read:

Transactional evaluation . . . looks at the effects of changed programs—in schools and other institutions—on the incumbents of the roles in the system undergoing change.

(Rippey 1973, p. 3)

(In the statement as published in Volume 31, *"roles"* appeared incorrectly as *"rules."*)

SOME ARTICLES IN OTHER *ANNUAL REVIEWS* OF INTEREST
TO PSYCHOLOGISTS

From the *Annual Review of Anthropology,* Volume 9 (1980)

Some Anthropological Hindsights, Cora Du Bois

Human Growth, Stanley M. Garn

Sex Differences and Language, Susan U. Philips

Ecological Anthropology, Benjamin S. Orlove

Play in Species Adaptation, David F. Lancy

From the *Annual Review of Sociology,* Volume 6 (1980)

Models of Network Structure, Ronald S. Burt

The Comparative Evolutionary Biology of Social Behavior, Scott A. Boorman
  and Paul R. Levitt

Status Organizing Processes, Joseph Berger, Susan J. Rosenholtz,
  and Morris Zelditch, Jr.

Continuities in the Study of Total and Nontotal Institutions, C. A. McEwen

The Sociology of Cognitive Development, Miles Simpson

From the *Annual Review of Public Health,* Volume 2 (1981)

Behavioral Interventions and Compliance to Treatment Regimes, R. C. Benfari, E.
  Eaker, and S. G. Stoll

Maternal Behavior and Perinatal Risks: Alcohol, Smoking, and Drugs, I. M.
  Cushner

From the *Annual Review of Neuroscience,* Volume 4 (1981)

Changing Priorities, Roger Sperry

Plasticity in the Vestibulo-ocular Reflex: A New Hypothesis, F. A. Miles
  and S. G. Lisberger

Synaptic Plasticity in the Mammalian Central Nervous System,
  Nakaakira Tsukahara

Sleep and its Disorders, Elliot D. Weitzman and Charles Pollak

From the *Annual Review of Physiology,* Volume 43 (1981)

The Role of Nervous Systems in the Temperature Adaptation of Poikilotherms,
  C. Ladd Prosser and D. O. Nelson

Neural Activity and Development, William A. Harris

Leona E. Tyler

Ann. Rev. Psychol. 1981. 32:1–20

MORE STATELY MANSIONS— PSYCHOLOGY EXTENDS ITS BOUNDARIES

❖338

Leona E. Tyler

Professor Emeritus, Department of Psychology, University of Oregon, Eugene, Oregon 97403

CONTENTS

Psychology has a way of outgrowing its definitions. The complexity of human life makes this almost inevitable. Whatever aspect of it comes under observation, there are always other aspects that new generations of investigators view as more important. Recently, as psychologists have been looking back over the century since Wundt's laboratory was founded, there has been much thoughtful consideration of psychology's nature and mission, a questioning of overly restrictive concepts of what constitutes a science, and a legitimization of some sorts of research that were formerly considered unsound.

1

0066-4308/80/0201-0001$01.00

SPOKESMEN OF PAST YEARS

Statements about Past Challenges

Such a searching examination of what psychology is and should be is far from unprecedented. As one reads the recent collection of presidential addresses delivered to the American Psychological Association down through the years (Hilgard 1978), one finds that again and again these spokesmen for all of psychology used this opportunity to express their dissatisfaction with the way the boundaries of the discipline were being drawn. William James pointed out the inadequacy of the associationist concepts that psychology had taken over from British philosophers, arguing that unique compound entities could not be explained as simply combinations of sensory building blocks. A few years later, James R. Angell expressed profound dissatisfaction with structuralism, the orthodoxy of his day, and with trained introspection, the method by which it was being investigated, urging that attention be focused on what people or animals were *doing,* rather than on the contents of consciousness. John B. Watson carried this movement still further when he proposed that *behavior,* rather than any kind of experience, be taken as the province of psychology.

As time passed, behaviorism came to be viewed as too restrictive. Gordon Allport was one of the earliest presidents to put this dissatisfaction into words.

> So it comes about that after the initial takeoff we, as psychological investigators, are permanently barred from the benefit and counsel of our ordinary perceptions, feelings, judgments, and intuitions . . .
> The consequences of the raid on immediate experience have already been shown in the graphs, disbelief in the existence or approachability of mental processes as such, a flight from linguistic functions, loss of interest in the single case, as well as the historical background of psychology, and at the same time the development of a notable schism between the psychology constructed in a laboratory and the psychology constructed in the field of life . . . Methodism as the sole requirement of science means that all the faithful crowd onto a carpet of prayer, and with their logical shears cut more and more inches of the rug, permitting fewer and fewer aspirants to enjoy status (Hilgard 1978, p. 128).

Another quotation, this one from the presidential address given by Kohler in 1959 but harking back to the much earlier time when Gestalt psychology began, expresses the exhilarating sense of liberation that accompanied the outward extension of constricting boundaries.

> Gestalt psychologists were not satisfied with a quiet consideration of available facts . . . We were excited by what we found, and even more by the prospect of finding further revealing facts. Moreover, it was not only the stimulating newness of our enterprise which inspired us. There was also a great wave of relief—as though we were escaping from a prison. The prison was psychology as taught at the universities when we still were

students. At the time we had been shocked by the thesis that all psychological facts . . . consist of inert atoms and that almost the only factors which combine these atoms and thus introduce action are associations formed under the influence of mere contiguity. What had disturbed us was the utter senselessness of this picture, and the implication that human life, apparently so colorful and so intensely dynamic, is actually a frightful bore. This was not true of our new picture, and we felt that further discoveries were bound to destroy what was left of the old picture (Hilgard 1978, pp. 253–54).

Responses to the Challenges

The challenge that new ways of looking at the phenomena of life poses has been met in various ways. One, of course, is simply to ignore it, and to continue to do the kind of research one has been doing without regard to whether or not it is essential psychology. But many psychologists, especially those of the stature of APA presidents, seem unable or unwilling to take this path. They feel compelled to take note of the challenge. Their responses were often ahead of their time. It would be 20 years or more before Allport's ideas quoted above, for example, would be shared by a sizable proportion of psychologists.

Often these stated challenges have given rise to prolonged controversy. This has often focused on a definition of science as a criterion of what is and is not legitimate psychology. This was the prevailing strategy during the middle decades of our century, exemplified most clearly in the influential pronouncements of Clark Hull, setting up the hypothetico-deductive method as the sine qua non of proper science. The trouble with this solution is that science, like psychology, is impossible to define in a way that suits all sciences, all scientific epochs, and all scientists. For a time the Hullian thesis was agreed upon by perhaps the majority of psychologists, at least those active in research, as the established game plan, but eventually other rules, even other games, made it obsolete.

Another way to deal with the challenge of expanding boundaries is to fence off separate fields with boundaries of their own for the various psychological specialties. As the number and diversity of psychologists increases, specialization inevitably occurs, and boundaries tend to rigidify. One obvious example is the separation of experimental psychology from correlational psychology or individual differences. In the early days during and after World War I there was no such distinction. A person like Robert Yerkes, for example, could turn from the study of animal behavior to the construction of Army tests and back again without any difficulty. But with time the split widened and status differences appeared, with experimental psychology carrying more prestige. Cronbach's 1957 attempt to reunite the "two disciplines of scientific psychology" met with considerable approval but did not reverse the trend. Other kinds of psychology have also become encapsulated within their own boundaries, using their own theoretical con-

4   TYLER

cepts and research methods, defining psychology in their own ways. The most conspicuous example is psychoanalysis.

Strategies of ignoring new facts and questions, resorting to strict definitions of science, and confining separate groups of workers in separate cages, can be thought of as defense maneuvers designed to ward off challenges rather than to meet them head on. A more constructive way of responding is to attempt to assimilate the new ideas and to reorganize the total field to accommodate them. (Piaget's terms, assimilation and accommodation, are as useful here as in talking about individual development.) The process is never easy, but in every period some psychologists accomplish it. Thurstone was able to incorporate Spearman's g in a more complex theory of human abilities, and Guilford carried the process along. Tolman enlarged the learning theory of his day by incorporating concepts of purpose that had been viewed as foreign to an objective science. Examples of this kind of effort going on in our own time will be taken up in later sections.

CURRENT ENLARGEMENTS

Cognition

The period in which we are now living is characterized by major attempts to extend boundaries, assimilate, reorganize, synthesize. We see it going on in various branches of psychology—experimental, physiological, social, developmental, clinical. Of the many directions this effort is taking, probably the broadest and most significant is the construction of a *cognitive* psychology that will incorporate concepts originating in behaviorism, Gestalt work, and structuralism, as well as in the writings of prepsychological philosophers. Hilgard (1980) has told the story of this theoretical development, its roots, its course over the years, and its present status. When psychology began a century ago, conscious experience was considered to be its whole content. With the increasing popularity of behaviorism, the study of consciousness not only declined but for a time almost dropped out of psychological research and theory, as the passage from Allport's presidential address quoted above shows. Since World War II it has been resumed, and most psychologists now feel comfortable with definitions that include both behavior and experience, conscious and unconscious.

Hilgard analyzes some of the influences responsible for this change of direction. The one that probably carried most weight was the theory and technology of information processing. The replacement of the stimulus-response concept by the input-output concept, at first glance only a linguistic shift, actually entailed many consequences. The recognition that a complex *program* controlled the input-output sequence opened the way for new approaches to the study of cognitive processes. Suddenly it no longer appeared unscientific to investigate memory, attention, imagery, dreaming, and other subjective experiences. The computer provided a new analogy, and thus stimulated new techniques, new theories. A book by Miller, Galanter & Pribram (1960) marked an important turning point. In place of the stimulus-response units out of which so much of experimental psychology had been constructed, these authors proposed the TOTE unit, a cyclical feedback process by means of which an organism carries out purposeful action.

Since 1960 the new outlook has come to characterize more and more areas of research and practice. Posner (1978) has come up with innovative techniques for the study of attention and memory. Broadbent (1977) has made major contributions to research on attention, and has synthesized the results and clarified the stages in what has turned out to be a complex process that could not have been investigated until narrow behavioristic concepts had been superseded. Paivio's book (1971) brought visual imagery back into psychology after a long exile. Neisser (1976) organized the ideas that have emerged from recent research on perception and cognition. Simon (1979) performed the same service for the extensive work he and others have done on complex problem solving. The coalescence of experimental and psychometric research on intelligence (Resnick 1976) is bridging the gap between Cronbach's "two disciplines." The books and articles cited constitute only a small sample from what is becoming a very large "universe."

The broadening of viewpoint has proved highly stimulating to developmental psychology, bringing the experimental and developmental specialties closer to one another than they have been in the past. It seems important to everybody to find out how the programs controlling actions originate. New techniques have been invented to obtain evidence about what newborn infants perceive (Cohen 1979) and how preschool children think (Gelman 1978). Long-standing arguments over the stage theories of Piaget versus explanations on the basis of learning through reinforcement are being transcended. In clinical and counseling psychology similar convergences are occurring. Here one stream of thinking was derived from Freud, Rogers, and the existentialist thinkers, and emphasized anxiety reduction, the resolution of inner conflicts, and self-knowledge. The other flowed from behavioral research on learning, especially Skinner's demonstration of behavior modification through contingent reinforcement. Dealing with external inputs and internal programs together has made it possible for Bandura (1977), Lazarus (1971), and others to demonstrate that one need not line up on one side or the other of this argument.

Context

Enlargement of the content of psychological science is occurring on other fronts as well. One is certainly the increasing attention being given to the larger context of individual behavior, its ecology, the total environment in which it occurs. What began with the tiny trickle of interest Roger Barker initiated in the 1950s when he and his coworkers set out to map the total ecology of a small midwestern town (Barker & Wright 1955) has become a torrent. Barker's (1968) comprehensive text on ecological psychology was followed by many others, culminating in Bronfenbrenner's closely knit theoretical synthesis (1979), to be summarized later in this paper. Much of the research on behavior settings, defined as sets of time-space boundaries generating recurring patterns of behavior, has focused on children, but in recent years adults have also been studied (Stokols 1978, p. 277).

Ecological psychology is one branch of a very large and rapidly growing tree of *environmental psychology*. Stokols (1978) cited 497 references, published over a five-year period. They represented a wide variety of research topics and an even wider variety of research methods. There are studies of cognitive representations of spatial environments, of relative contributions to behavior of environments and personality, of environmental attitudes, of crowding, and of territoriality, to mention just a few.

Offshoots of this concern for context can be identified. Cross-cultural psychology is receiving increasing emphasis, and the research being done is increasingly sophisticated and discriminating (Laboratory for Comparative Human Cognition 1979). Field as well as laboratory experiments and non-experimental observational techniques are being recognized as legitimate vehicles for scientific work.

Multiplicity-Pluralism

Another extension of psychology's boundaries arises not from the inclusion of new kinds of content but from the recognition of the complexity of all of the phenomena being studied. Experiments in which single dependent variables are related to single independent variables are being criticized on the grounds that causal principles derived from such experiments cannot be generalized to the real world. In experimental psychology, complex multifactorial designs have become the rule rather than the exception. Factor analysis and multidimensional scaling have transformed measurement theory and practice.

But such changes still seem inadequate to many observers of complex psychological realities. The trouble with even the most complicated factorial design is that the experimenter is still assuming that causation works in one direction, that the independent variables are causes and the dependent variables effects. It now seems obvious to developmental psychologists that such reasoning does not tell the whole story. Parents' actions, for example, certainly have causative effects on children's behavior, but at the same time what children do affects the parents (Bell & Harper 1977). The arrows of causation point in both directions in any social interchange, between experimenter and subject, between teacher and student, between therapist and patient. Psychologists have discovered *reciprocity.*

Awareness of multiplicity and reciprocity has given rise to new ways of conceptualizing human action not based on the stimulus-response units that have dominated psychology for so long. Psychologists are attempting to replace the concept of "response" or "reaction" with "interaction" or "transaction." A book edited by Pervin & Lewis (1978) reflects the varied forms this attempt is taking. One problem is that the term "interaction" has taken on a number of different meanings. The statistical definition assumed in analysis of variance is not adequate to describe the way in which genetic and experiential factors are linked in the development of intelligence, for example, or the way in which personality traits and situations interact in the production of behavior. Pervin (1978) suggests that "transaction" is a better term. Overton & Reese (1973) have formulated a process model of development based on this central concept. It assumes that variables do not act singly, that their relationships need not be additive or linear, and that causal influences are not unidirectional. One salient characteristic of this and other process models is that *time* is an essential component. Bandura (1978) is building into his social learning theory a concept of "reciprocal determinism" to replace previous treatments of interaction processes. The long-standing controversy over the relative contributions of heredity and environment to human development is giving way to similar process conceptions. Carter-Saltzman (1978) provides a recent discussion of this trend, an outgrowth of Waddington's (1966) theory.

An interesting example of the movement in a long-continued research program from the independent-dependent variable orientation to a transactional-reciprocal orientation is the account given by Lazarus & Launier (1978) of the changes in their research on stress. They have now developed a complex theory in which several aspects of cognitive appraisal combine with several varieties of coping process to produce actions in stressful situations, actions which become parts of both person and situation. Putting this complex research plan into operation has involved moving from the laboratory to real life settings.

Uniqueness

Another change that is enlarging the boundaries of psychology is that the uniqueness of each individual is at last being recognized (Tyler 1978). Allport (1937) argued years ago for a psychology that would be *idiographic* as well as *nomothetic* and would study the unique as well as the common features of personality. Many agreed with him, but few until recently made any attempt to follow his prescription. Experimenters typically base their conclusions on differences between the means of groups undergoing differential treatments. Differences in the reactions of individuals within each group are reflected only in the error term of statistical formulas. It is becoming apparent in many places that idiosyncratic effects are not simply random error. In drug research, for example, one individual may be soothed by a medication that excites another.

The branch of psychology labeled "individual differences" has not dealt adequately with individuality either. Here it has been assumed that all human beings share the same traits, and that differences between them are only quantitative. Intelligence, for example, is the same characteristic for everyone, but some persons are endowed with more of it than others are. The possibility that important differences may be *qualitative* rather than quantitative has not received much consideration.

Here again the picture is changing. Some lines of research are leading to classifications or typologies of persons who react in qualitatively different ways to standard situations. Witkin and his associates (Witkin 1978) several decades ago initiated the study of cognitive styles when they discovered that some persons, the *field dependent,* when placed in a tilted chair within a tilted room, judged themselves to be in an upright position when the chair was aligned visually with the walls of the room, whereas others, the *field independent,* ignored the visual cues and used instead kinesthetic cues from their own muscles as a basis for judgment as to whether or not they were in an upright position. This experiment was the first step in a long series that has produced a rich harvest of knowledge about this and other cognitive styles, including techniques for assessing them, evidence about how they develop, and demonstrations of their significance in many areas of life.

Another landmark event in the opening toward individuality was the publication of George Kelly's (1955) book, *The Psychology of Personal Constructs.* Although it took a number of years for the full significance of Kelly's theory to become apparent, there is now a worldwide network of communicating investigators who are developing and extending Kelly's theory and techniques, applying them in clinical and environmental psychology, anthropology, criminology, urban planning, and many other research areas (Fransella & Bannister 1977).

Possibilities-Alternatives-Choice

Another kind of expansion, one with a strong grounding in evolutionary biology (Mayr 1976), is our increasing awareness of the significance of alternative possibilities and choices in human affairs. The phenomena we observe constitute only a small fraction of possible phenomena. In the long course of evolution, the millions of species that have been cataloged still constitute only a fraction of the species that might have developed—and that perhaps did appear and become extinct. Only a very small fraction of the egg-sperm combinations that are possible ever occur. Only a fraction of the kinds of behavior possible for any one human individual ever make an appearance. On many fronts, evidence of the richness of life's possibilities and the inevitability of selection pours in upon us. Marine biologists find strange new species not dependent upon the sun's energies in deep vents in the ocean floor. Anthropologists and cross-cultural psychologists observe diverse ways in which human intelligence manifests itself. Creative people continue to astonish us with ideas nobody ever thought of before. Awareness of the multiplicity of possibilities for action and for development has brought with it an increasing realization of the importance of *choice,* conscious or unconscious, in human life. (The neuroscientist, J. Z. Young 1978, shows that choice characterizes all living things, from the single-celled to the most complex.) Few, if any, human beings are limited to a single line of development, a single destiny. Families, communities, and nations face alternative possibilities for action and must choose which to embark upon.

The emphasis on alternatives and choices has not as yet been fully assimilated into psychological thinking and practice. Few experimenters consider alternate theoretical explanations of the phenomena they study and deliberately design experiments that will facilitate a comparison of alternatives rather than the acceptance or rejection of a single hypothesis. Counseling psychologists often fail to examine the considerable array of possible courses of action an individual life presents. But the concepts of possibility, alternatives, and choice have now become a part of the psychologist's intellectual world, and an expanded science must find a place for them.

TWO DOUBTFUL EXTENSIONS

On the margins of the territory psychologists regard as their legitimate area are two kinds of effort about which there is much less consensus than there would be about the topics discussed in the previous section. One might be described as the radical wing of humanistic psychology, the interest in spiritual, mystical experience, esoteric religions, and unusual states of consciousness. The other is the separate discipline of parapsychology. The two fields are somewhat related. Psychologists interested in unusual states of consciousness are often interested in extrasensory perception as well. There is some evidence that mainstream psychologists are becoming more hospitable than they once were to both sets of ideas.

Humanistic and Religious Psychology
Humanistic psychology, defined as the study of persons viewed as they normally see themselves rather than as animals or machines, has been a part

of psychology from the beginning, and became popular after the publication of Maslow's (1962) book. As existentialist concepts spread through the intellectual world during post-World War II years, they were incorporated into the developing humanistic psychology (May 1961). The scientific wing of this movement, represented by APA Division 32, now has an established place. The fringe areas, represented by so-called growth centers such as the Esalen Institute, are less generally accepted as legitimate psychology.

Child (1973) undertook to show how the progress of research is bringing experimental and humanistic psychology closer together. In one specialty area after another he points out how researchers' own findings have been forcing them to attach more and more importance to the ways in which their subjects interpret what is going on and incorporate their own values and purposes into what they say and do in research situations. The "self" turns out to be an indispensable component of research on aesthetics, hypnosis, attitude change, and a number of other topics. Psychological interest in religious experience has also been legitimized with the formation of APA Division 36. Such experience is, of course, a fundamental aspect of human life down through the centuries, going back through history and prehistory to the time of our remote ancestors. Anthropologists and philosophers have done research on it. There seems no good reason for psychologists to avoid it. Because moral codes, patterns of social organization, attitudes and self concepts are linked to religious beliefs, knowledge about them seems important when we try to understand a society that is foreign to us. But it is more difficult to study religion in our diverse, highly secularized society. The fact that Freud and many other influential thinkers considered religion to be an illusion that should be outgrown as rapidly as possible in our scientific age also contributes to the reluctance psychologists have felt to deal with it.

It seems obvious that supernatural phenomena as such cannot be incorporated into a natural science. Psychologists can hardly be expected to validate or invalidate visions, miracles, or answers to prayer. But much of the content of the world's religions is clearly amenable to scientific study. In recent years we have seen considerable research on values, culminating in Rokeach's (1973) demonstration that different segments of the population can be distinguished by the way they rank 18 terminal values (end states of existence) and 18 instrumental values (modes of conduct by means of which desirable end-states are attained). We have also seen significant research on the nature and origins of moral concepts and behavior (Hoffman 1979). Among factors analyzed are aspects of child rearing, peer influences, and the effects of television. Kohlberg (1969) postulated six stages of moral reasoning correlated with increasing cognitive competence, a formulation that has served as a framework for a considerable number of research investigations. Other workers are interested in how children learn to feel empathy and to experience guilt over transgressions. Not much has been done to link values, moral behavior, and the development of conscience to religious beliefs, but perhaps such links should be explored. Moral codes and value systems arose in the first place as aspects of deeply rooted religious systems. It is possible that a new large branch of psychology comprising humanistic, religious, and moral studies is in the making. Whether it can be stretched to cover metaphysical and mystical experience as well is still uncertain. Pelletier's (1978) book, *Toward a Science of Consciousness,* points in this direction.

Parapsychology

Research on phenomena like extrasensory perception, psychokinesis, and precognition, some of it by reputable psychologists, has been going on for decades without ever being assimilated into the main body of psychology. Some recent evidence suggests that there may be developing an increasing willingness to consider the findings. It may be significant that in 1979 one of the most prestigious universities in the world, Cambridge, awarded a PhD to Carl Sargent for research on a parapsychological problem (Evans 1980). It is interesting that the editor entitled this news item "The Fringes of Orthodoxy."

One reason for the continuing lack of acceptance may well be that the phenomena studied are difficult if not impossible to demonstrate to skeptics. People differ in their Psi abilities, and a belief in the reality of ESP and PK seems to be necessary for their occurrence. Since a measure of skepticism is fundamental to the scientific spirit, the majority of psychologists decade after decade have remained unconvinced. The assumption referred to in a previous section that every human characteristic is possessed to some extent by every individual has also made it difficult to accept skills that only some persons seem able to acquire.

A more important reason for the continuing stalemate is probably the lack of any comprehensive theory that would make sense of parapsychological processes in a framework that would also include the other processes psychologists have studied. During most of the history of parapsychology investigators have been more interested in proving that the effects occur than in exploring the processes underlying them. Recently there have been some attempts to change this. Child (1973) in the book referred to above includes a chapter on ESP research in which he reports some impressive findings and attempts to incorporate them in the system of humanistic psychology he espouses. Tart (1978), after carefully screening out the dependable findings that need to be explained, stresses the need for an explanatory theory and makes a start toward the construction of one. Bowles et al (1978) also present the results of an intensive effort to separate the sound from the unsound evidence, and stress the need for both theory and technology. "Like Franklin's electricity, Psi may be awaiting its Edison. But even now, we have clues that its possible significance for our lives could be enormous" (p. 138).

It would appear, then, that parapsychology is closer to incorporation in the main body of psychological knowledge now than it has been in any previous period. A report prepared for the American Association for the Advancement of Science (Mauskopf 1979) includes it as one of four case studies on the reception of unconventional science. The others are causal quantum mechanics, continental drift theory, and acupuncture. Eventually the definition of science itself seems to broaden sufficiently to accommodate material that is at first unacceptable.

BEYOND MECHANISM—APPROACHES TO THEORY

As one considers the significance of all of these actual, probable, and possible enlargements of the territory psychologists are staking out for themselves, it becomes apparent that many theories serving us well in the past will no longer be capable of organizing the new kinds of knowledge. For decades the investigation of problems in perception, learning, and motivation has rested on certain basic assumptions, assumptions that constitute what might be called the metaphysics of psychological thinking. It is assumed that the human being (as well as other behaving organisms) is a *machine,* the components of which can be identified, and the functioning of which is ultimately reducible to the laws of physics and chemistry. Along with this assumption goes the faith that actions of living creatures are *in principle* completely determined by outer and inner circumstances and thus in principle predictable. Psychologists have remained loyal to the metaphor of the machine long after most biologists and even many physicists have given it up. It now seems clear that we will never be able to describe the phenomena of adaptation to environment, multiplicity and reciprocity, individuality and choice, to say nothing of altered states of consciousness and extrasensory perception, in these terms. Thus, there has been initiated in recent years a search for other assumptions, other basic metaphors, on which scientific psychology might be grounded.

It would be overly simplistic to contend that all significant research of the last several decades rested on this foundation of mechanism and strict determinism. The Gestalt psychologists, with their emphasis on wholeness, field forces, and inherent organization, have been a continuous counterforce to the behaviorists. The influence of Kurt Lewin, especially in social psychology, has been considerable and lasting. Others might be mentioned. However, there appears to be now a more concerted effort to build a new theoretical structure than there has been in the past. The emphasis being placed on *evolutionary* as distinguished from *functional* biology (Mayr 1976) is a related shift of perspective probably related to the shift in psychological thinking.

Probabilistic Functionalism

One of the directions the search for adequate theories is taking involves a new look at a theory proposed by Brunswik (1956), subjected to searching analysis and criticism (Hammond 1966), and then largely lost sight of, although particular components of it, such as situation sampling, from time to time were mentioned. Petrinovich (1979) has resurrected the system, adding some useful modifications of his own, and shown how it differs from predominant patterns of thinking.

Brunswik replaced prevailing definitions of psychology as the science of behavior, behavior and experience, or mental life, with the statement that psychology is the science of organism-environment relationships. Its basic unit, a unit in time as well as space, is the *behavioral episode*. This is conceptualized graphically in what is called the *lens model*. Brunswik distinguished in this model between proximal and distal stimuli and proximal and distal actions. The distal ends of the behavioral episode are in the environment, and are molar rather than molecular in character—perceived objects on the stimulus side, accomplished achievements on the action side. From distal objects, a number of separate kinds of energy are transmitted to a sense organ that constitutes a lens focusing them on a central area. From this center a number of specific movement impulses are directed to another lens that focuses them on the distal goal. For an organism, the important relationship is between distal stimulus and distal accomplishment. This is what is meant by molar as opposed to molecular behavior. Brunswik felt strongly that limiting psychological research to the process linking proximal responses to proximal stimuli, as is often done in laboratory experiments, kept psychology irrelevant to the business of living.

Hammond (1966) summarized very clearly what the main features of Brunswik's theory are. First, both the cues on the input side and the relationships between proximal actions and distal goals on the output side are inherently ambiguous. Thus, the process of adapting to the environment is inherently *probabilistic*. Second, not all cues coming in need be or are used, and some are always more dependable than others. Similarly, on the action side, not all specific responses leading toward the distal goal need be or are employed, and some are always more promising than others. Some cues may be used on one occasion, others on another; the same is true for responses. This is what Brunswik meant by *vicarious functioning,* a fundamental concept in his theory. Cues can substitute for one another. Responses can substitute for one another. In any behavior episode there are more possibilities than are utilized. The organism is constantly engaged in an active process of weighing the dependability of cues, compromising between conflicting conclusions about what they mean, and judging the probable efficacy of different molecular responses. Adaptive behavior is inherently active, inherently variable.

Brunswik argued that if psychologists wish to generalize about any kind of behavior they study, it is incumbent upon them to obtain a representative sample, not only of subjects, but also of situations. This is the most widely discussed concept in the system, but very difficult to put into practice. It would seem, however, that the current advances in environmental psychology and the current efforts to produce a workable taxonomy of situations may make it more feasible to do this now than it was in the past.

In summary, Brunswik replaced the metaphor of the machine with the metaphor of the living creature adapting to its environment. It may serve to liberate investigators working in psychology's expanded area from some of the self-imposed limitations that have prevailed in the past. With his broader view of psychology, Brunswik also held a broader view of science than many of his contemporaries, getting away from "the reductionistic-nomothetic-systematic syndrome which some psychologists have adopted under the spell of a somewhat stereotyped image of science" (Brunswik 1956, p. 144).

The Theory of Living Systems

The most conspicuous of the attempts to replace prevailing mechanistic theories with a broader, more inclusive framework is *general systems theory.* First proposed during the 1940s by Bertalanffy, it has been developed during the following decades by Bertalanffy himself (1968), Laszlo (1972), and many others, culminating in a monumental work by Miller (1978). In systems theory the entity to be studied is a set of interacting units rather than separate objects, bits of behavior, or cause-effect linkages. Everything in a system is related to everything else, and these internal relationships are different from those between any of the parts and things outside the system's boundary. Change in one part of a system changes this whole pattern of relationships. A cell is a system; so is a person, a family, or a nation. Miller (1978) hypothesizes that the same principles hold at all levels.

The characteristics Miller lists as common to all living systems are as follows:

1. They are always *open* systems with inputs, throughputs, and outputs of matter, energy, and information.
2. For a time they *counteract entropy,* the universal tendency of matter to move toward a dispersed, static state.
3. They have some degree of *complexity* or differentiation of parts.
4. They contain basic *blueprints* controlling their functioning, DNA in individuals, a charter of some sort in the case of groups.
5. They are made up of *macromolecules* and may include nonliving components within their boundaries.
6. They contain subsystems, the most critical of which is a *decider.*
7. They carry on essential processes mainly through their own subsystems, but sometimes make use of nonliving material outside their boundaries.
8. Subsystems are integrated into the self-regulating, developing system as a whole, which manifests purposes and goals.
9. Every system requires a particular environment for its maintenance.

Miller distinguishes 19 critical subsystems a living system must have for processing matter and energy, information, or both. The most essential of these is the *decider* where information is received and from which information controlling the whole system is transmitted. In a simple organism this may be a neural or chemical component. In a person it is a complex, multilevel subsystem with the cerebral cortex at its apex.

All systems theorists stress the importance of *feedback* and the maintenance of *steady states,* including both homeostatis and constant growth rates even when environmental conditions change.

Systems theory seems capacious enough to include most if not all of the expanded content of psychology considered in this chapter. Gray et al (1975) show, for example, that it is compatible with their emotional cognitive structure theory of personality. Laszlo (1972) finds a place for consciousness in human systems, and makes a case for formulating the goals of humanism in systems terms as "reorientation of cultural values in reference to the norms of individual fulfillment in a flexible and dynamic social system" (p. 117). Emphases on content, multiplicity and diversity, reciprocity, purposive action, and choice are readily incorporated into the systems framework.

Not all thinkers are as certain as Miller is, however, that systems theory is what psychology and the other social sciences need. Whether the same principles govern all systems from the amoeba to the multinational corporation has not been settled, as Lilienfeld (1978) points out. Miller (1978, Chap.

5) presents evidence for the conclusion that systems at all levels react in the same way to one kind of environmental challenge, information overload, but there are hundreds of other stress-producing conditions that have not been studied. A more serious question for psychologists may be whether tying things together in this way can generate new research strategies and techniques. How do we characterize particular systems if we do not single out separate parts to be measured? How do we identify system change in response to changes in the environment? How do we test the significances of differences between systems if linear combinations of single variables are ruled out? In order to reap the benefits of general systems theory, psychologists must apply it to specified research domains, formulate hypotheses applicable to the kind of phenomena they are studying, and then come up with ways of obtaining evidence bearing upon these hypotheses. It is encouraging to find that at least one psychologist has done this.

Bronfenbrenner's (1979) impressive book entitled *The Ecology of Human Development* demonstrates both the utility and the feasibility of a systems approach. Out of careful examination of a broad spectrum of research findings he generates 9 basic propositions and 50 hypotheses. For some of the hypotheses research findings of the past provide some evidence. For others the evidence is incomplete or nonexistent—but obtainable. Evidence Bronfenbrenner considers relevant must include data on all participants and the situation in which they are embedded.

Contextualism

A set of philosophical ideas first proposed by Pepper (1942) lay fallow for a long time, but is now being picked up and developed as a basis for psychological theory (Sarbin 1977). During recent years there has been an increasing realization of the importance of *metaphor* in human thinking (Mair 1977), and this has caused Pepper's analysis to take on new relevance. His basic proposition is that there is only a limited number of world hypotheses, each based on a different root metaphor. The first two of these, *animism* (control by spirits that inhabit all of the things that we observe in the world) and *mysticism* (all-pervasive spiritual reality that human beings are able to tune in to), Pepper considered to be incompatible with science and to a large extent outmoded. (Both have reappeared, however, in the decades since his book appeared.) The third, *formism,* going back to the Greek philosophers, has predominated during most of the modern era. The root metaphor is classification by similarity, and the business of science is considered to be the careful observation and classification of phenomena. The fourth world hypothesis is *mechanism.* The root metaphor is the machine, in which all the parts, intricate as they are, are linked together in cause-effect relationships that can be discovered by isolating and manipuling the components. *Contextualism* is the fifth world hypothesis. Its root metaphor is the historical event, complex, unique, unrepeatable. Through careful observation it can be understood but never predicted except in general terms, because of the fact that contexts are constantly changing. Pepper called his sixth world hypothesis *organicism,* in which the root metaphor is the integrated organism within which everything is related to everything else. Coming before the extensive development of general systems theory, discussed in the previous section, Pepper's consideration of this world hypothesis has been largely superseded by the later developments.

Each of the world hypotheses generates its own set of categories and its own criteria for truth. For contextualism the categories are change and novelty, quality and texture, each of which is further subdivided. It is the categories that govern scientific work by their control over what is to be observed about events being studied. The criteria of truth for contextualism are the successful working out of the plans based on the observations, the verification of hypotheses, and qualitative confirmation of the conclusions drawn from the observations. As Pepper indicates, contextualism is actually the same system as *pragmatism.*

Sarbin (1977), applying the contextual approach more specifically to psychology, considers the *dramatic event* to be the basic unit. The psychologist's task is to understand its changing shape, quality, and texture. This approach makes a large place for idiographic research, and techniques such as those based on Kelly's personal construct theory come into their own. Measurement of traits common to all does not assume much importance, but Sarbin thinks that classifications or taxonomies of the plots or scenarios manifested in individual lives may be useful. Contextualism is essentially pluralistic. It makes no assumptions about whether everything and everybody can be explained according to the same principles.

As in the case of general systems theory, the contextual approach needs to be translated into explicit propositions and hypotheses relevant to particular research domains. It is interesting to note that what looks like a contextual sort of theory is in the process of superseding the prevailing mechanistic theory in a field where it has long been dominant. *Event perception* is the name that has been given to this new line of research (Johansson et al 1980), and Gibson (1979) is a prominent representative. What it involves is the replacement of the image-and-cue model of perception with a flow model to explain how three-dimensional objects and motion are perceived. Because of the motion of objects in the environment and the movements of the perceiver, the visual stimulus is a constantly changing flow of light rather than a series of static images. The transformation of perspective that characterizes the flow can be expressed mathematically using projective geometry. Theories of this type are being applied in the investigation of a wide range of perceptual problems.

Pepper (1942) did not believe that any of the six systems could be combined because of differences in their basic categories and criteria. But he considered it quite possible for scientists to shift from one to another according to the nature of their materials and the problems they were working on. They are, after all, hypotheses about the world and its inhabitants, and if a person avoids dogmatism, there is no reason not to accept different hypotheses at different times. This attitude makes Pepper's ideas especially relevant when we think about how to deal with psychology's expanded content. Neither formism nor mechanism is obsolete. Some phenomena call for observation and classification. Factor analytic studies of abilities constitute one example. Some problems lend themselves to experimental manipulation and mechanistic conclusions. But to be able to shift to a contextual or organic orientation when it is needed is an advantage for the scientist.

Gilmore (1980, paper prepared for the International Round Table for the Advancement of Counseling, meeting at the University of Thessaloniki, Greece) has been constructing a comprehensive theory for eclectic intervention from a contextual point of view, a detailed theoretical formulation to undergird the efforts clinical and counseling psychologists make to help individuals and groups, to evaluate their work, and to do research on the process.

FINAL COMMENTS

During scientific psychology's first hundred years, each attempt to define it in an exact way has failed. New generations of psychologists pose questions about aspects of life that do not fit the definition. Eventually the accepted theories catch up with these questions. There is inevitably much waste motion in this process, much conflict and controversy. But through it psychological knowledge has grown. Perhaps a realization that definitions and boundaries are not permanent will enable the mature scientists of psychology's second century to settle down to the task of building and furnishing the "more stately mansions" for which the initial blueprints have appeared.

Literature Cited

Allport, F. 1937. *Personality: A Psychological Interpretation.* New York: Holt, Rinehart & Winston

Bandura, A. 1977. *Social Learning Theory.* Englewood Cliffs, NJ: Prentice-Hall

Bandura, A. 1978. The self system in reciprocal determinism. *Am. Psychol.* 33:344–58

Barker, R. G. 1968. *Ecological Psychology.* Stanford: Stanford Univ. Press

Barker, R. G., Wright, H. F. 1955. *Midwest and Its Children.* Evanston, Ill: Row, Peterson

Bell, R. Q., Harper, L. V. 1977. *The Effect of Children on Parents.* Hillsdale, NJ: Erlbaum

Bertalanffy, L. von. 1968. *General System Theory.* New York: Braziller

Bowles, N., Hynds, F., Maxwell, J. 1978. *Psi Search: The New Investigation of Psychic Phenomena that Separates Fact from Fiction.* San Francisco: Harper & Row

Broadbent, D. E. 1977. The hidden preattentive process. *Am. Psychol.* 32:109–18

Bronfenbrenner, U. 1979. *The Ecology of Human Development: Experiments by Nature and Design.* Cambridge: Harvard Univ. Press

Brunswik, E. 1956. *Perception and the Representative Design of Experiments.* Berkeley: Univ. Calif. Press

Carter-Saltzman, L. 1978. Behavior genetics from an interactional point of view. See Pervin & Lewis 1978, pp. 171–200

Child, I. L. 1973. *Humanistic Psychology and the Research Tradition: Their Several Virtues.* New York: Wiley

Cohen, L. B. 1979. Our developing knowledge of infant perception and cognition. *Am. Psychol.* 34:894–99

Evans, P. 1980. The fringes of orthodoxy. *APA Monitor,* Jan., p. 16

Fransella, F., Bannister, D. 1977. *A Manual for Repertory Grid Technique.* New York: Academic

Gelman, R. 1978. Cognitive development. *Ann. Rev. Psychol.* 29:297–332

Gibson, J. J. 1979. *The Ecological Approach to Visual Perception.* Boston: Houghton Mifflin

Gray, W., Gray, L. R., Gray, N. 1975. A systems view of emotional cognitive structure theory. In *Interdisciplinary Aspects of General Systems Theory,* pp. 82–89. Washington DC: Soc. Gen. Syst. Res.

Hammond, K. R. 1966. Probabilistic functionalism: Egon Brunswik's integration of the history, theory, and method of psychology. In *The Psychology of Egon Brunswik,* ed. K. R. Hammond, pp. 15–80. New York: Holt, Rinehart & Winston

Hilgard, E. R., ed. 1978. *American Psychology in Historical Perspective.* Washington: Am. Psychol. Assoc.

Hilgard, E. R. 1980. Consciousness in contemporary psychology. *Ann. Rev. Psychol.* 31:1–26

Hoffman, M. L. 1979. Development of moral thought, feeling, and behavior. *Am. Psychol.* 34:958–66

Johansson, G., von Hofsten, C., Jansson, G. 1980. Event perception. *Ann. Rev. Psychol.* 31:27–63

Kelly, G. S. 1955. *The Psychology of Personal Constructs.* New York: Norton

Kohlberg, L. 1969. The cognitive-developmental approach. In *Handbook of Socialization Theory and Research,* ed. D. A. Goslin. Chicago: Rand McNally

Laboratory of Comparative Human Cognition. 1979. What's cultural about cross-cultural psychology? *Ann. Rev. Psychol.* 30:145–72

Landfield, A. W., ed. 1977. *Nebraska Symposium on Motivation, 1976.* Lincoln: Univ. Nebr. Press

Laszlo, E. 1972. *The Systems View of the World.* New York: Braziller

Lazarus, A. 1971. *Behavior Therapy and Beyond.* New York: McGraw-Hill

Lazarus, R. S., Launier, R. 1978. Stress-related transactions between person and environment. See Pervin & Lewis 1978, pp. 287–327

Lilienfeld, R. 1978. *The Rise of Systems Theory.* New York: Wiley Interscience

Mair, J. M. M. 1977. Metaphors for living. See Landfield 1977, Vol. 24

Maslow, A. 1962. *Toward a Psychology of Being.* New York: Van Nostrand

Mauskopf, S. H., ed. 1979. *The Reception of Unconventional Science.* Boulder: Westview Press (for the AAAS)

May, R. 1961. *Existential Psychology.* New York: Random House

Mayr, E. 1976. *Evolution and the Diversity of Life.* Cambridge: Harvard Univ. Press

Miller, G. A., Galanter, E., Pribram, K. H. 1960. *Plans and the Structure of Behavior.* New York: Holt, Rinehart & Winston

Miller, J. G. 1978. *Living Systems.* New York: McGraw-Hill

Neisser, U. 1976. *Cognition and Reality.* San Francisco: Freeman

Overton, W. F., Reese, H. W. 1973. Models of development: methodological implications. In *Life Span Developmental Psychology,* ed. J. R. Nesselroade, H.

20   TYLER

W. Reese, pp. 65–86. New York: Academic

Paivio, A. 1971. *Imagery and Verbal Processes.* New York: Holt, Rinehart & Winston

Pelletier, K. R. 1978. *Toward a Science of Consciousness.* New York: Dell

Pepper, S. C. 1942. *World Hypotheses: A Study in Evidence.* Berkeley: Univ. Calif. Press

Pervin, L. A. 1978. Theoretical approaches to the analysis of individual-environment interaction. See Pervin & Lewis 1978, pp. 67–85

Pervin, L. A., Lewis, M., eds. 1978. *Perspectives in Interactional Psychology.* New York: Plenum

Petrinovich, L. 1979. Probabilistic functionalism: a conception of research method. *Am. Psychol.* 34:373–90

Posner, M. I. 1978. *Chronometric Explorations of Mind: The Third Paul M. Fitts Lectures Delivered at the University of Michigan, Sept. 1976.* Hillsdale, NJ: Erlbaum

Resnick, L. B., ed. 1976. *The Nature of Intelligence.* Hillsdale, NJ: Erlbaum

Rokeach, M. 1973. *The Nature of Human Values.* New York: Free Press

Sarbin, T. R. 1977. Contextualism: a world view for psychology. See Landfield 1977, pp. 1–41

Simon, H. A. 1979. Information processing models of cognition. *Ann. Rev. Psychol.* 30:363–96

Stokols, D. 1978. Environmental psychology. *Ann. Rev. Psychol.* 29:253–95

Tart, C. T. 1978. *Psi: Scientific Studies of the Psychic Realm.* New York: Dutton

Tyler, L. E. 1978. *Individuality: Human Possibilities and Personal Choice in the Psychological Development of Men and Women.* San Francisco: Jossey-Bass

Waddington, C. H. 1966. *Principles of Development and Differentiation.* New York: Macmillan

Witkin, H. A. 1978. *Cognitive Styles in Personal and Cultural Adaptation.* Worcester: Clark Univ. Press

Young, J. Z. 1978. *Programs of the Brain.* New York: Oxford

Ann. Rev. Psychol. 1981. 32:21–52

HUMAN LEARNING
AND MEMORY

❖339

Wayne A. Wickelgren[1]

Department of Psychology, University of Oregon, Eugene, Oregon 97403

CONTENTS

[1]Preparation of this article was supported in part by NSF grant BNS78-08878.

21

0066-4308/80/0201-0021$01.00

Do you admire the insights into the nature of the human mind that have
been achieved by theoretical and empirical research on learning and memory? More times than I care to remember, I have heard my colleagues
denigrate our understanding of human learning and memory. Many of the
best known researchers in this field claim that we understand very little
about learning and memory—that at best we have made some progress in
improving our experimental methods for studying learning and memory, or
at worst that we have merely been amusing ourselves at the taxpayer's
expense. This pessimistic view is totally and tragically wrong. Its persistence
in the minds of so many eminent researchers in cognitive psychology serves,
for these individuals and those who listen to them, as a self-fulfilling
prophecy. Because they believe it to be impossible, they do not strive for
precise and general theories that accurately integrate the welter of specific
facts we know regarding learning and memory and that bestow understanding as a consequence. The overall purpose of this article is to demonstrate that a very high level of integrative theoretical understanding of
human learning and memory is possible today. Many aspects of this theoretical understanding will change in the future. Indeed, the pace of change will
quicken as a consequence of taking the best present-day theories seriously.
However, the future changes in our theoretical understanding of learning
and memory will be evolutionary, incorporating the wisdom of the past with
the wisdom of the future, not revolutionary in the sense of ignoring the
wisdom of the past for an ever changing succession of fads.

MEMORY CODING

Associative Memory

Koffka (1935) proposed a nonassociative theory of human long-term memory according to which the mind lays down a continuous record of experience (trace column), much like a videotape. Popular accounts often talk
about memory in this nonassociative way, and even sophisticated cognitive
psychologists sometimes give credence to such nonassociative theories. This
is a shame, because one of the important successes of cognitive psychology
is that we can confidently assert that this nonassociative theory of LTM is
false (Wickelgren 1972a; 1977a, pp. 233–47).

DIRECT ACCESS   From a functional standpoint, the most critical defining
feature of an associative memory is the capacity for direct access retrieval
of traces without search. In artifical intelligence, associative memories are

often called content-addressable when they have this direct access property that the most common location-addressable computer memories lack. In a location-addressable computer memory, one must serially search through all memory locations to find the one containing a stored (trace) pattern matching the input pattern. However, if the properties of an input pattern determine exactly where in the memory that pattern will be stored, then the memory is content-addressable, that is, associative. One is directly addressing the contents of the memory location, not just addressing the location number. Present-day computers can be programmed to achieve a very limited degree of associativity (direct access to information), but in the future, computers with large parallel processing capacity may achieve associative memories closer to human capacity (Fahlman 1979).

The main argument against human memory retrieval being a random serial search of a location-addressable store is the incredible speed that would be required—on the order of ten million locations searched per second. Since synaptic transmission appears to be the most basic functional time unit in the brain, and that is on the order of 1 msec per synapse, it is plausible to assume that searching one memory location would require at least 1 msec. This yields an upper limit on search speed of 1000 locations per second, which is at least 10,000 times too slow.

Another retrieval theory that can be rejected is the hybrid search/direct access theory that postulates direct access to a category of memory locations, e.g. those storing species of birds, followed by serial search at modest speeds (tens of milliseconds per location) through this much smaller set of locations. Corbett & Wickelgren (1978) obtained evidence contrary to the versions of this theory that have been proposed by Rosch (1973) and Rips et al (1973). Furthermore, it is very unparsimonious to postulate a direct access process that does most of the retrieval work and then have some slow search process finish the job. If you can have fast, accurate direct access to all of the bird storage locations, you should be able to have at least equally fast and accurate direct access to the hummingbird location(s).

The most plausible alternative to direct access is the hierarchical search theory in which search occurs first for the correct high-level category of locations, then within this set for a correct subordinate category of locations, and so on until the correct individual location is searched for and found (e.g. Greeno et al 1978, pp. 24–27). If searching among categories of memory locations was on the order of 10 msec per alternative category, then a seven-stage hierarchical serial search process with an average of ten alternatives at each stage would result in the capacity to search ten billion locations in 700 msec. However, the information necessary to accomplish an hierarchical search process could be used more simply and efficiently to implement a direct access retrieval process.

With direct access, the features of the input signal are processed in parallel to intersect at the locations (nodes in memory that represent each feature, segment, concept, and proposition signaled by the input. With any serial search process, one must either possess an independent means of accurately segmenting temporally distributed input (which has proved to be an intractable problem for speech recognition by serial computers) or else try potentially thousands or millions of alternative parsings into phonemes and words of even short phrases, for example. An analogous problem exists for grouping (parsing) spatially distributed input (e.g. determining the form constituents of a complex picture). The more one considers the difficulties of serial search retrieval processes for recognition of any of the tens of millions of things humans beings can recognize in a matter of seconds, the more one appreciates the power of parallel processing, direct access retrieval systems (Fahlman 1979).

Retrieval speed considerations argue strongly that the basic human long-term memory retrieval process is direct access. Furthermore, the phenomenon of redundancy gain—e.g. faster discrimination of a large bright circle from a small dim circle than of either a large from a small circle or a bright from a dim circle (Biederman & Checkosky 1970)—argues compellingly for parallel processing of retrieval cues.

SPECIFIC NODE ENCODING   I have emphasized direct access as the defining property of an associative memory from a processing standpoint. From a structural standpoint, direct access appears to require the property I call specific node encoding or specific element representation (Wickelgren 1977a, 1979a), after Johannes Müller's similar neurophysiological doctrine of specific nerve energies. For every idea (feature, segment, word, image, concept, proposition, etc) that we can represent in our minds, there is assumed to be a particular set of elements that represents (encodes, stands for) the idea. Call this set of elements the node representing the idea. More generally, a node is a fuzzy set of elements, that is, a vector of weights between zero and one ($\ldots w_i \ldots$) representing the degree to which each element in the memory participates in representing that particular idea (e.g. Anderson 1973). The difference between specific localization and more global theories of mental representation concerns what percentages of the w entries in the vector for any particular idea are zero. Global theories assume few zero entries. Specific localization theories assume that almost all (e.g. 99% or more) of the entries for a particular node are zero. One way to add inhibition to such a specific node encoding theory is to allow w_i entries to have negative values as well as positive values, e.g. from −1 to 1.

Psychologically, a node means nothing more than "whatever represents an idea." There must be at least one node representing any idea we have

There is no point in having a code in a node unless you could have any of several different codes representing different ideas. This makes the memory nonassociative to a greater or lesser degree depending upon the variety of possible codes in each node.

TYPES OF LINKS   Until quite recently, nodes in associative memory were usually assumed to be connected by only one type of excitatory link (association), and there has been very little theoretical use of inhibitory links among memory nodes outside of the perceptual and neural areas. Prior to Quillian's (1966) thesis, people occasionally discussed the possibility of labeled associations (different types of links), but, with the notable exception of inhibitory links in neural net theories, nobody did anything with it. However, beginning with Quillian, an ever increasing number of associative network models of human and artificial semantic memory have been invented, virtually all of which use a large variety of link types to express a large variety of relations between concepts (e.g. Rumelhart, Lindsay & Norman 1972, Anderson & Bower 1973, Anderson 1976, Findler 1979). Virtually all semantic memory nets, whether designed to be artificial intelligence models or models of human memory, are considered by their inventors to be associative memory networks to a greater or lesser degree, contingent upon the degree of direct access capability, but irrespective of the variety of link types. Anyone who asserts that a critical defining property of an associative memory is the assumption of a single type of link between idea nodes (e.g. Greeno et al 1978, p. 21) is behind the times. Direct access (sometimes marching under the name of "content-addressable memory") has been recognized by computer scientists as the defining property of an associative memory, at least since the early 1960s. In cognitive psychology, Wickelgren (1965; 1972a; 1977a, pp. 11–22, 220–25, 233–51; 1979a, pp. 6–11) has repeatedly pointed out that the critical defining features of an associative memory are specific node encoding and the direct access retrieval such coding makes possible.

The number of different types of links is an important and as yet unsettled theoretical issue, but the issue concerns the specific type of associative memory we have, not whether or not human memory is characterized by specific node encoding and direct access retrieval, which are widely accepted as the critical defining properties of an associative memory in the fields of computer science and semantic memory and should be so considered in all of cognitive psychology. Cognitive psychology should recognize that a major theoretical problem has been largely solved, namely, the definition of the concept of associative memory, and that a great truth has been established regarding how the mind works, namely, that it is associative.

Links bond idea nodes together to encode more complex sets and sequences of ideas. One day we will know how many distinct types of bonds there are, like the electrovalent and covalent bonds that hold atoms together to form molecules or the four types of force that hold the nucleus together. Psychology has as much potential for intellectual beauty as any other science. Some of that beauty can be appreciated today if you have the eye for it. A great deal more can be created in the near future if psychologists have the will to do it.

Chunking and Vertical Associative Memory

In a horizontal (nonhierarchical) associative memory, the set of idea nodes is fixed after maturation is complete, not growing with experience. Learning changes the strengths of the links connecting these nodes to each other, but does not add any new nodes to the memory (e.g. Hebb 1949). In a vertical associative memory, this horizontal associative learning process is supplemented by a vertical associative learning process, chunking, that adds new nodes to associative memory, specifying new chunk nodes to stand for combinations of old nodes. George Miller (1956) originated the concept of chunking, and its meaning was extended by many others (e.g. Estes 1972, Johnson 1972, Anderson & Bower 1973, Wickelgren 1969a, 1976a,b, 1977a,b, 1979a,b). Of course, the new chunk nodes do not appear out of thin air. From a physical standpoint, new nodes are probably added by strengthening synaptic connections to neurons that have not previously been functionally connected to associative memory, though the anatomical connections might already exist prior to the chunking learning process. From a psychological standpoint, new nodes have been added to memory by the chunking process. Intuitively, it is clear that as we acquire concepts for ever more complex combinations of simpler ideas, we are not finding it ever more difficult to think with these concepts. The new higher-level concept nodes allow us to think about complex subject matter just about as easily and efficiently as we could previously think about simpler subject matter using lower-level concepts. This is a remarkable accomplishment. It is surely an important reason for the seemingly boundless potential of the human mind to understand ever more about anything.

Concepts

CONCEPTS AND WORDS A typical word probably has thousands of different meanings (e.g. "house" can refer to any particular house you ever experienced). Dictionaries list several meanings for the typical word, but each of these refers to a large family of different specific meanings. The modern word for any particular meaning of a word or phrase is "concept." Because words do not have unique meanings, words cannot be the atomic elements of semantic memory. The atoms of semantic memory are either concepts or semantic features. Words are high-level structural units representing ordered sets of phonetic and graphic segments.

Understanding the relation between concepts and words and that concepts, not words, are the atoms of semantic memory clarifies thinking about many problems. For example, consider the phenomenon of synonymity (Herrmann 1978). It is of no interest whether there are any "true" synonyms for any given speaker of a language, that is, pairs of words (or phrases) which are associated to exactly the same set of concepts. If there are any, they are rare. The interesting point is that any given concept can be expressed by so many different words or phrases. What could be the purpose of such duplication? One plausible answer derives from the multiplicity of concepts associated with each word and consideration of a likely role of short-term memory in understanding speech and text. What should you do in writing a paragraph when you have used the same word to refer to two different concepts? Use a synonym in place of one of the occurrences of the word. Otherwise, the reader may mistakenly retrieve the former concept to the second occurrence of the word, because its strength of association to the word was temporarily increased by the prior pairing of word and concept. Synonyms probably exist to minimize the short-term memory interference problem that derives from our efficient use of tens of thousands of words to refer to millions of concepts.

CONCEPTS AND IMAGES   Concept nodes not only receive input from words, but, at least for concrete concepts, also from nonverbal stimulus cues, e.g. the feel of fur, the shape of a cat, a meow, etc as cues to activate the cat concept. The combination of features that make up each of these cues constitutes an image. It seems clear and accurate to regard concept nodes as the first level of nodes that integrate verbal and nonverbal stimuli. The constituents of concept nodes are the chunk nodes for the words and images that cue them.

CONSTITUENT VS PROPOSITIONAL AND PROCEDURAL MEANING
The meaning of a concept is given partly by the constituent words and images that activate it from below and partly by the propositions and procedures of which it is a constituent, which can activate it from above (Woods 1975, Wickelgren 1979a). Propositional and procedural meaning are equivalent to what linguistic philosophers refer to as intensional meaning. Constituent meaning is a generalized and more psychological analog of the philosophical notion of extensional (referential) meaning. Both are essential components of the meaning of concepts.

CONCEPTS VS SEMANTIC FEATURES   The two principal theoretical approaches to semantic memory are the associative network theory used
throughout this article and the semantic feature theory developed by Katz
& Fodor (1963), Schaeffer & Wallace (1969, 1970), Meyer (1970), Clark
(1973), Rips et al (1973), and Smith et al (1974). As Smith (1978, p. 23)
describes these semantic feature models, "Each word is represented by a set
of attributes, called semantic features . . . 'bird' would include as defining
features . . . animate and feathered . . . and as characteristic features . . . a
particular size . . ." "Robin" has many features in common with "bird" plus
such features as "red-breasted."

The experimental testing of semantic feature theories has focused on
verification and contradiction of category-example relations between concepts, e.g. a robin is a bird (high feature similarity true), a chicken is a bird
(low similarity true), a bat is a bird (high similarity false), and a rat is a bird
(low similarity false). Some network theories have had trouble explaining
why high similarity trues are verified faster than low similarity trues, but
high similarity falses are contradicted more slowly than low similarity
falses. The assumption that is rejected by these data is that semantic judgment times depend entirely or primarily upon the number of links separating the concepts whose relation is being judged. If one assumes that there
are two processes, verification and contradiction, initiated in parallel by
these tasks, each with a characteristic asymptotic strength, and that judgments are made when the difference in retrieved strength of the two processes exceeds some critical value, then network theories account for
category-example judgment findings better than existing feature theories
(e.g. the results of Holyoak & Glass 1975 and Corbett & Wickelgren 1978).
Such a two-process retrieval assumption, married to the associative network
theory, can doubtless account for the recent antonym judgment results as
well (Glass et al 1979, Herrmann et al 1979). However, a feature theory can
be easily married to the same two-process retrieval theory and account just
as well for these results. Indeed, McCloskey & Glucksberg (1979) suggest
just such a model, although the mathematical formulation leaves a bit to
be desired.

What can be concluded concerning semantic features vs concept networks? First, almost all of the semantic features anyone has discussed
would be considered concepts in semantic memory. No reasonable person
could deny that there are nodes encoding these features somewhere in
memory. From a coding standpoint there are two issues: (a) Are semantic
feature concepts the most basic concepts of semantic memory, that is, the
lowest level concepts, which serve as the constituents of higher-level concepts and/or the first concepts learned by children? (b) Are concepts other
than semantic feature concepts represented by unitary nodes at all, or are

these concepts represented only as sets of semantic feature nodes? I believe that we can draw firm conclusions on both of these issues.

Although the above two questions are best posed in the order I used, they are best answered in the opposite order. There is a great deal of evidence supporting the chunking capacity of the human mind, as discussed earlier. If other modalities of memory form new chunk nodes to represent combinations of more elementary constituents, it would be peculiar indeed if semantic memory did not. Semantic memory is just where we need chunking the most to avoid the enormous associative interference problem that would result from associating concepts only by associating their featural constituents, each of which participates in thousands of other concepts and so would have thousands of competing associations. If the mind represented concepts only as sets of semantic features, retrieval of information by experts would be less efficient than by amateurs and retrieval by adults would be less efficient than by children, contrary to fact.

With respect to whether semantic features are the basic concepts of semantic memory, the answer is also clear. They are not. Semantic features are necessarily superordinate concepts with wide referential generality (large sets of examples), such as physical object, animate, white, living, male, feathered, etc. The research of Rosch et al (1976) and Rosch (1977) makes it quite clear that these very general superordinate categories are not the basic level of concepts in adult semantic memory, nor are they typically the first concepts learned by children. Neither are the basic concepts highly specific (narrow referential generality), e.g. ball peen hammer, delicious apple, or collie. As Rosch demonstrates, the basic concepts are of intermediate referential generality, namely, hammer, apple, or dog (see also Piaget 1954; Brown 1958; Anglin 1977; de Villiers & de Villiers 1978, pp. 126–32). Clark & Clark (1977, p. 500) have already pointed out this fundamental contradiction to the semantic feature theory.

Rejection of the semantic feature theory in favor of the more general concept-node-and-link network theory does not mean that the general concepts referred to as "semantic features" do not exist in semantic memory. They surely do. However, they do not appear to be more simply coded nor developmentally prior to other concepts. Indeed, on the average, these general concepts are probably coded more complexly and are certainly acquired later than concepts of intermediate referential generality.

Besides the general failure of psychologists to try to decide theoretical issues, there is probably a more specific reason for the persistence of this inadequate semantic feature theory. Some of these alleged semantic features refer to sensory attributes of the stimuli that activate concepts from below. These attributes are part of the constituent meaning of a concept, and they are certainly coded at levels below the concepts they activate in semantic memory. However, such sensory features and semantic features are very different beasts. In the first place, most of the alleged semantic features are much too abstract to be considered elementary sensory features. In the second place, the concept red is activated by the word "red" as well as by red light. The concept red is not coded in the lower levels of the visual system where the sensory feature red is first encoded. We represent red at several levels of coding in the mind. Failure to realize this causes confusion. Consistent terminology might help. I propose that we use the otherwise synonymous terms "feature" and "attribute" differentially to help remind us of the distinction between sensory features and conceptual attributes. What more appropriate way to bury the semantic feature theory than to take away part of its name?

FUZZY LOGIC   Fuzzy logic (Zadeh 1965) is a generalization of standard logic that is more applicable to human thinking. Instead of assuming that the degree of membership of some instance in any concept (category) is limited to the extreme values zero or one, fuzzy logic assumes any degree between zero and one. Fuzzy logic can express various relations between different concepts, more generally, between any idea nodes in the mind. For example, Kay & McDaniel (1978) discuss a couple of different alternative rules for fuzzy intersection (C = A AND B), using the example of ORANGE = RED AND YELLOW. They reject the standard minimum rule for fuzzy intersection, namely, that the degree of membership of an event in the intersection of two categories is the minimum of the degree of membership in either constituent category. They also discuss the standard maximum law for fuzzy union (C = A OR B), lising the example of GRUE = GREEN OR BLUE, namely, that the degree of membership in the union equals the maximum of the degree of membership in either constituent category.

Zadeh's invention of fuzzy logic is an important intellectual accomplishment both for artificial intelligence and for cognitive psychology. However, there are a great variety of possible fuzzy logics yet to be invented, especially if one relaxes the restriction that fuzzy logic be a simple extension of classical logic, including it as a special case. Bellman & Zadeh (1970) suggest a multiplicative rule for intersection (C = AB) and an additive rule for union (C = A + B − AB), that also include classical logic as a special case. However, it seems to me that in describing the mind we ought not to restrict ourselves to logics that include classical logic. Whatever the value of classical logic to mathematics, it is a multifaceted failure as a description of the "laws of thought" (Wason & Johnson-Laird 1972, Wickelgren 1979a, pp. 360–68). Fuzzy logic corrects one of the flaws of classical logic as a theory of human thought: the restriction to two-valued set membership functions. The various fuzzy logical operators that have been suggested are interesting to consider, probably as a point of departure, rather than being satisfactory as they stand.

So far, most psychological applications of fuzzy set theory by cognitive psychologists have been banal or vague, but I am hopeful this will change. For a striking exception, see the superb application of fuzzy logic to speech recognition by Oden & Massaro (1978), which uses the multiplicative rule for combining the featural constituents of a speech segment after power function weighting of each featural constituent. The weights can be considered to be the associative strength of each feature to each segment. In general, fuzzy logic is completely compatible with the assumption of graded strengths of associations between nodes in the mind, which is a very strong point in its favor. Oden has done a number of other pioneering studies on the application of fuzzy logic to semantic memory, speech, and reading (e.g. Oden 1979).

FAMILY RESEMBLANCE   Frequently, only a tiny subset of all the characteristic attributes of a concept will be sufficient to cause us to think of that concept. There is nothing common to all of the sufficient cue sets for a given concept (Wickelgren 1969a), but there are many attributes that appear frequently in these cue sets. Following Wittgenstein (1953), we say that the cue sets for a given concept have a family resemblance to each other.

PROTOTYPES   The prototype hypothesis is that a concept can be characterized by an ideal set of attributes (Evans 1967, Posner & Keele 1968, Reed 1972). If we include both verbal and nonverbal constituent, propositional, and procedural meaning as constituting the entire set of ideal attributes characteristic of a concept, then clearly no single example of most concepts, and certainly no single cue set, will contain all of the ideal attributes. Thus, it is probably correct to assert that for most natural concepts, the prototype is an ideal that can never be experienced at one time. In any case, the prototype hypothesis in no way depends upon whether a real example of a concept or possible cue set for a concept actually matches the prototype.

What does the prototype hypothesis add to our characterization of concepts as family resemblances with fuzzy boundaries from other concepts? This is not entirely clear (Neumann 1977). If it were true that activating a concept from a cue set involved matching that cue set to the ideal set (prototype) for each concept (Reed 1972), then the prototype hypothesis would have importance. However, this is almost certainly not what we do. Instead, any cue set will have some strength of association to every concept node in memory, and the strongest association will win most of the time, subject to random error. The most compelling reason to prefer this associative strength hypothesis to the prototype matching hypothesis is that the strength hypothesis is exactly what an associative memory with direct access predicts. A second reason to prefer the strength hypothesis is that a theory with predictions that are probably very similar to it, namely, the context theory of Medin & Schaffer (1978), has been shown by them to account better for transfer from concept learning to classification of new instances than the independent cue type of prototype matching theory. A third reason to prefer the strength hypothesis derives from consideration of the abstraction process by which concepts are learned.

ABSTRACTION   Abstraction is the process by which the input links to a chunk node from other nodes are selectively strengthened and weakened through repeated experience with different instances of the concept. These input links should include the specification of constituent, propositional, and procedural meaning of concepts, since the relations between concepts often appear to be learned very early (e.g. chairs are to sit on). This strength learning hypothesis is both reasonable and consistent with associative network theory.

It would be highly unparsimonious to opt for some prototype learning theory that cannot be incorporated easily within the more general associative network theory. For example, one way to store an average prototype without storing examples is to add the value of each attribute dimension to a counter, add its square to another counter, and add one to a number-of-instances counter. This permits determining the average value and the variance on each feature dimension. When people speak of storing the average prototype without storing the examples, this must be the sort of process they have in mind. An associative computer could be built to do this, but it is a less accurate way to record the regions in a multidimensional attribute space that are associated with any given concept than the strength mechanism previously described. Such an average prototype abstraction mechanism could learn concepts whose examples cluster about a single prototype, such as "apple" or "cat," but would be quite inadequate to learn superordinate concepts such as "fruit" and "mammal" that do not cluster about a single prototype. Furthermore, the more adequate instance strength abstraction mechanism is also more natural for an associative memory, while the prototype abstraction mechanism would be much more complex to implement.

Recently, evidence has accumulated to support the hypothesis that for adults the best example of a concept is sometimes composed of the modal (most frequently occurring) values on each attribute dimension rather than the average values (Goldman & Homa 1977, Neumann 1977, Strauss 1979), though so far infants have been demonstrated to abstract only averages

(Strauss 1979). Whether adults abstract modes or averages depends on the discriminability of the values on a dimension—highly discriminable values cause the mode to have the greatest strength of association to the concept, less discriminable values cause the average value to have the greatest strength of association to the concept. As Neumann (1977) and Wickelgren (1979a, p. 310) point out, this can be accounted for by old-fashioned stimulus generalization in an associative network theory. No other unified theory, to my knowledge, explains the abstraction of averages when discriminability is low and modes when discriminability is high. Starting most recently with Brooks (1978), there is increasing acceptance of the hypothesis that the learning of a concept derives from encoding each instance more or less faithfully, subject to selective attention in learning and to the interference and facilitation in learning, storage, and retrieval that inevitably results from encoding in an associative memory. The most plausible theory at present is that the abstracted constituent structure of a concept is the result of accumulated association of the attributes of events that cued that concept.

In addition, inhibition is also involved in some manner so that the attributes that have the strongest association to a concept are those that discriminate best between this concept and other concepts (Rosch & Mervis 1975). See also Wickelgren (1979a, pp. 311–12) for an associative explanation of this using the Spencian overlapping excitatory and inhibitory generalization gradients mechanism.

BASIC CONCEPTS   If it hadn't been so sad it would have been funny to hear psychologists at one time asserting that the earliest concepts learned by children were the most general ones followed by increasing conceptual differentiation, and at other times asserting that the earliest learned concepts were the most specific ones followed by concepts of increasingly greater generality. Brown (1958) pointed out that neither extreme was true and that the earliest concepts learned by children are of intermediate referential generality, and, as discussed earlier, subsequent research has confirmed this conclusion. Brown suggested that the reason for this was greater frequency of use of these concepts by other humans in the child's environment, and this is surely an important component of the explanation for why concepts like "cat" and "apple" are basic instead of "mammal" or "fruit" on the one hand or "Siamese cat" or "Jonathan apple" on the other. However, it was not until the elegant insight of Rosch (Rosch et al 1976, Rosch 1977) that we understood this phenomenon adequately. According to Rosch, basic concepts are the most general concepts whose examples are sufficiently similar that they hover around a single prototype. This high degree of example similarity means extensive strength generalization in the integrative learning of separate examples, which, in effect, increases the frequency of pairing each attribute node with the concept node. On the average, the basic level concepts are those where the two factors contributing to associative strength, example frequency and example similarity, typically hit the maximum in their combined effect on speed of concept learning. Hence these concepts are typically learned first. At the same time, this explanation makes it clear how exceptions could occur when a child has a great deal of experience with a more general or less general concept than the corresponding basic level concept. I have taken a little license with Rosch's idea to make it compatible with the associative-strength, instance-learning theory of abstraction advocated in the prior section.

EPISODIC AND SEMANTIC MEMORY   If you accept the instance memory theory of abstraction presented earlier, you have the best extant explanation of the relation between episodic and semantic (generic) memory. There is no reason to believe that these are two different forms of memory with either different coding structure or different cognitive processes. Unique experiences will by definition not be merged with subsequent experiences via the abstraction process. As a consequence, unique experiences will generally be forgotten unless they are frequently recalled. When they are recalled, they become subject to integration and abstraction with the recall experience. Thus, except for the first recall of a unique experience, there is no episodic memory, only various degrees of generic memory.

Propositions

UNITS OF SEMANTIC MEMORY   A proposition contains a relational concept (verb) and one or more argument concepts (agent, object, etc). The cognitively correct definition of a proposition is not known, but people have a very high degree of agreement concerning the analysis of sentences into component propositions, so it has been possible to establish that propositions are units of coding above concepts in semantic memory (Wickelgren 1979a, pp. 317–21).

CONSTITUENT STRUCTURE   A proposition is a set of concepts, but what kind of set is unclear at the present time. Neither predicate nor case constituent structure has proved completely satisfactory (Dosher 1976). Given that concept nodes and phonetic and graphic segment nodes are fuzzy combinations of their constituents, it is parsimonious to assume that propositions are fuzzy combinations of their concept constituents as well (Oden 1978, Wickelgren 1979a, pp. 321–25). Although it probably does not apply to networks with redundant link paths between nodes, Cunningham (1978) has devised a very interesting scaling method for determining network structure from dissimilarity data.

Plans and the Coding of Order

Propositions are units of declarative knowledge. Plans are units of procedural knowledge. It may not be useful to distinguish these two types of knowledge, but in agreement with Anderson (1976), I currently believe it is. My theory is that propositions are unordered sets of concepts, while plans are ordered (most generally, partially ordered) sets of concepts. While propositions can encode all knowledge, including knowledge about actions and the temporal sequence of events, this knowledge is not in the proper form for the temporal control of human action (by which I mean all mental actions, not just those mental actions that directly control obvious physical actions by the muscles). Plans achieve this control of sequences of mental actions contingent upon internal and external events. Plans have been described using augmented transition networks (Woods 1970), production systems (Newell 1973, Anderson 1976), and context-sensitive coding (Wickelgren 1979a, pp. 357–60; 1979c). As a theory of the coding of order in phonetic and graphic segments in words, context-sensitive coding is incomparably superior to any other theory (Wickelgren 1969b,c, 1972b, 1976c, 1979a), but it is far too early to conclude anything about its application to the encoding of syntax and other higher-order procedural knowledge.

Schemata

Some people believe that there is a level in the mind above propositions and plans that integrates sets of these into single units called schemata. A more parsimonious alternative is that a schema is a mental set of primed (partially activated) nodes (and links?) that results automatically from spreading activation from the activation of nodes representing prior thoughts (Wickelgren 1979a, pp. 325–27). Priming via spreading activation is a natural part of an associtive memory, and there is considerable evidence supporting such a hypothesis (Collins & Loftus 1975, Wickelgren 1979a). There is no evidence supporting the hypothesis of unitary schema nodes, although they could exist.

MEMORY DYNAMICS

Memory has three temporal phases: learning, storage (consolidation and forgetting), and retrieval (recall or recognition). Widespread understanding and acceptance of the learning, storage, and retrieval distinction has greatly facilitated scientific research on memory. Another basic and obvious distinction is sorely needed, that between the macro and micro levels in the cognitive analysis of learning, storage, and retrieval. This distinction is analogous to that between macroeconomics and microeconomics.

Microlearning is concerned with the learning of a single association or a small set of associations encoding a single chunk or a small set of chunks. Microstorage is concerned with the subsequent consolidation and forgetting of such small atoms or molecules of learned information. Microretrieval is concerned with a single elementary act of recalling or recognizing some unit of information (e.g. word, concept, proposition).

To explicate the distinction, let us consider the retrieval process in more detail. One elementary act of microretrieval takes about one second, varying from .2 to 2 sec depending upon the coding level (Wickelgren 1979a, pp. 270–78). Fortunately, because of chunking, one elementary act of microretrieval can be of a very complex chunk of information with numerous constituents. Furthermore, under many conditions, several separate (unchunked) traces can be retrieved in parallel, within the attention span. Basically, if the retrieval takes place in a couple of seconds or less, you are studying microretrieval. If the retrieval is extended over tens of seconds, minutes, or longer, as in free or ordered recall of lists or text, this is a complex retrieval process consisting of a sequence of elementary acts of recall and recognition, and perhaps some inference processes as well. Such tasks are studying macroretrieval. The study of single inference operations or small sets or sequences of inference, recall, and recognition operations is at the micro level, but problem solving, creativity, and comprehension of large units of text are at the macro level. This review is only concerned with the micro level of learning, storage, and retrieval. Accordingly, I tend to ignore all multiple recall (especially free recall) studies, where there is little control over the control processes, retrieval cues, and retrieval time for each elementary act of retrieval.

Learning

REPETITION "Practice makes perfect"—or, in any case, it makes memory traces stronger. It is still possible that memory traces are composed of varying numbers of component traces each of which is learned, consolidated, forgotten, and/or retrieved in an all-or-none manner, but no evidence compels this assumption. To study memory dynamics independently from coding, it is simpler to characterize traces by continuous strengths, given that forgetting and retrieval functions are always continuous incremental functions of storage and retrieval time, and learning curves are almost always continuous incremental functions of study time. There do appear to be sudden jumps in strength during learning, which probably result from insights regarding good ways to code material (e.g. integrating the to-be-learned material with related already-learned material). However, even when a single jump in learning boosts retrieval from chance to 100% accuracy, subsequent learning will further increase strength, as shown by increases in strength ratings and in retrieval speed (Corbett 1977, Wickelgren 1977a, p. 320). Further support for the incremental nature of memory traces comes from Nelson (1977), who found that repetition at the same phonetic level of coding, even with the same question each time (does the word have an r sound), produced increased learning, contrary to the assertion that increased learning results only from adding traces at higher levels of processing.

SPACING Spaced repetitions almost always benefit memory more than massed repetitions. Progress has been made in understanding the reasons for this phenomenon. We can classify theories of the spacing effect into three categories: encoding variability, deficient consolidation or rehearsal of the first presentation, and deficient learning of the second presentation. Hintzman (1976) argued that the first two categories of theories could be ruled out on the basis of prior evidence, and since then an ingenious study by Ross & Landauer (1978) provides more evidence against all encoding varability explanations. A novel experiment by Jacoby (1978) further supports the deficient second-trial learning hypothesis. Jacoby suggests that subjects do not go through the same recognition and other coding processes for a massed second trial as for a first trial or a spaced second trial. With a massed second trial, the end product of these processes can be activated without all of the preliminary coding required by first or spaced-second trials. This deficient coding hypothesis is doubtless the explanation of Jacoby's results, which were obtained using an unusual learning task. However, in more standard learning tasks, the levels (types) of coding and processing may be identical, but the speed of achieving the encoding is much faster for massed second trials. If increases in degree of learning are closely tied to the encoding process and not to the period of maintained activation after encoding, then faster encoding may necessarily produce less learning.

One of the persistent problems with almost all research on spacing effects is the failure to separately assess the effects of spacing on learning and retention. This can only be done by obtaining retention functions for the single-trial learning condition and for each two-trial learning condition (Wickelgren 1972c, Reed 1977). The increment to the memory trace contributed by second-trial learning can be estimated by subtracting the memory strength due to the first learning trial at the appropriate retention interval from the total learning strength obtained with two learning trials. This can be done at a variety of retention intervals following the second learning trial. Thus, not only can the second trial learning increment be estimated, but also the retention function for the second-trial learning increment can be determined for comparison across spacing conditions and to the first-trial retention function. This makes the assumption that the second trial does not destroy or alter in any way the memory trace resulting from the first trial. The evidence reviewed by Hintzman (1976) and the results of Wickelgren (1972c) are in agreement with this assumption.

Retention function analyses of the spacing effect produce the following conclusions: (*a*) Second-trial learning increases monotonically with spacing, perhaps indefinitely, though the maximum increases are achieved during the first 10 to 30 minutes after first-trial learning (Wickelgren 1972c and unpublished data). (*b*) The memory trace for the first trial is probably unaffected by second trial learning (Wickelgren 1972c, Hintzman 1976). (*c*) Consolidation and forgetting of the second-trial's trace is probably identical to that for the first trial; certainly, retention of the second-trial trace is at least as good as that of the first trial (Wickelgren 1972c and unpublished data).

All of this tends to produce a beneficial effect of greater spacing between learning trials under many circumstances. However, shorter spacings have the advantage of shorter retention intervals for the first learning trial at any given retention interval following the second trial. This can produce advantages for shorter over longer spacings. It is foolish to do research on such a complex quantitative problem as the spacing effect without a mathematical modeling approach and without obtaining complete retention functions.

LEVELS OF CODING AND PROCESSING   The levels of processing fad is over in the field of learning and memory. Of course, the concept of levels of coding (and processing) existed long before the fad started and will continue to be an essential, though not yet completely specified, concept for understanding the structure of the mind. One of the criticisms of the levels fad was that it failed to add to the precise theoretical specification of the levels concept in either coding or processing domains. Another flaw with the faddish conception was that its specific claims about learning and memory turned out to be almost entirely false. First, it is clearly not the level of processing that matters for degree of learning and retention, but the trace code that results from this processing. Semantic processing by itself is no guarantee of a high level of learning. For example, deciding that an ostrich is not a geographical location results in very little memory for having processed "ostrich," compared to deciding that an ostrich is a living thing (Schulman 1971). Second, high levels of performance on memory tests are not guaranteed by a semantic coding level either. What counts most is the relation between the information stored and the information questioned in retrieval. Phonetic traces are what will help you perform best on a phonetic retrieval test, semantic on a closely related semantic test, etc (Morris, Bransford & Franks 1977; McDaniel, Friedman & Bourne 1978; Stein 1978). Third, substantial learning takes place at lower structural levels of coding and, as mentioned earlier, repetition of processing at lower structural levels further increases degree of learning; it is not necessary to process at semantic levels to achieve further increases in degree of learning (Nelson 1977). Fourth, despite the plausibility of the hypothesis that coding is more distinctive at semantic than at structural levels and thus less subject to interference, forgetting of many structural traces is not especially rapid and often there has been no difference in forgetting rate between structural and semantic traces (Nelson & Vining 1978). For all these reasons, the levels of processing framework has been largely abandoned. However, I believe it left a useful legacy of facts and ideas generated in its disproof, and it generated interest in levels of coding and processing, which is surely a critically important concept in understanding the mind. At least, now no knowledgeable cognitive psychologist should have trouble explaining to students what it means to read a page of words and suddenly realize that you haven't been processing the meanings at all.

ELABORATION AND DISTINCTIVENESS   Two other explanations of the variability in learning are the elaboration hypothesis (Craik & Tulving 1975, Anderson & Reder 1979) and the distinctiveness hypothesis (Klein & Saltz 1976, Wickelgren 1977a, Eysenck 1979, Jacoby & Craik 1979). The elaboration hypothesis is that traces with many constituents or many associations to other traces are well learned and well remembered. The distinctiveness hypothesis has two principal variants, which are complete opposites, though no one seems to have realized this before: (a) Elaborate traces are more distinctive and therefore have more effective possible retrieval cues and are also less subject to interference in storage and retrieval. (b) Traces whose constituents have few interfering associations to other traces are more distinctive and thus remembered better because they are less subject to interference. The latter conception of what makes a trace less subject to interference is clearly the correct one, so the former conception appears to be left with only the multiple retrieval cues explanation for the effectiveness of elaboration-distinctiveness.

Choosing between these alternatives is difficult. On the one side is all the evidence from decades of verbal learning research and more recently from semantic memory research (e.g. Anderson 1974, King & Anderson 1976, Bower 1978) that learning multiple associations to the same nodes causes interference. On the other side is the evidence that elaboration often aids learning and memory, despite the fact that embedding the material in a sentence or image, relating the new material to schemata from existing knowledge, etc. appears to be increasing the potential for proactive and retroactive interference. Such interference has been demonstrated (Owens et al 1979). To add to the problems with the elaboration hypothesis, elaboration has not always been found to provide a net benefit to memory (Nelson et al 1978, Stein et al 1978, Morris et al 1979). Nelson et al found that interactive images were superior to noninteractive images for learning word pairs, but that multiple interactive images produced no better memory than a single interactive image. Of course, we know for certain that multiple associations are important for making a piece of knowledge related to all that it should be related to in memory, but these results demonstrate that there is no huge benefit to redundant multiple associations connecting the same nodes. The Stein et al and Morris et al studies indicate that certain kinds of elaboration increase memorability more than other kinds. Elaboration that merely adds to what must be learned does not increase the memorability of the other material and often decreases it. Elaboration that increases the amount of the other material that can be encoded using already learned schemata is beneficial to learning. This means that elaboration of the stimulus input may be benefitting memory because it is requiring a *less* elaborate addition to memory than nominally simpler stimulus input.

CHUNKING   Of course, it would be wrong to go overboard on what could be called the reduction hypothesis, that we learn best when we have the least to add to what is already in memory. In the extreme, when everything in some input material is already encoded in memory, we often do further strengthen the existing associations, but this is not when the greatest amount of learning occurs. Learning curves always indicate diminishing returns after an earlier period of positive acceleration, though only studies measuring learning on an unbounded strength scale are relevant for establishing such diminishing returns without ceiling artifact (e.g. Wickelgren & Norman 1971, Wickelgren 1972c). Information that is in the part of a sentence that the syntax signals to be new is better learned than information in the part the syntax signals to be given (Hornby 1974, Singer 1976). Nickerson & Adams (1979) discovered that people have extraordinarily poor recall and recognition memory for the visual details of a very familiar object, a United States penny. Thousands of experiences recognizing pennies clearly led to little learning of its features once it became highly familiar on the basis of some subset of features. All of these observations support the hypothesis that learning is maximal at intermediate degrees of prior chunking (integration) of the material to be learned (Wickelgren 1979a, pp. 119–20).

Probably the primary reason that maximal learning occurs for material with intermediate degrees of prior integration into chunks is that this is where maximal new chunking (specification of new nodes) occurs. When the current experience is already integrated under one top chunk node, as in recognizing a penny, little or no further chunking occurs. When the experience is an unfamiliar combination of too many separate (ungrouped or unrelated) parts, as with some of my lectures, the entire experience is too complex to be integrated into one chunk at that time. Chunking may occur, but it will be of only one or a few subsets of the component features of the complex unfamiliar experience. Such partial chunking is under the control of the subject's attentional and grouping strategies, and as a consequence may be difficult for an experimenter to measure.

According to this theory of chunking, one way to obtain further chunking of a highly familiar entity would be to focus attention on subsets of features and the relations between them. This may explain why learning of familiar words and pictures has often been enhanced by increasing the difficulty of processing the material: presenting incomplete pictures (Kunen et al 1979), requiring completion of incomplete sentences or recognition of inverted text (Kolers & Ostry 1974, Masson & Sala 1978), presenting misspelled words for error correction (Jacoby et al 1979). Along the same line, Tyler et al (1979) found that greater difficulty in finding the correct word to complete a sentence or solve an anagram led to better memory for the target words.

The chunking and consolidation theory proposed by Wickelgren (1979b) can be extended in an elegant way to account for a variety of learning phenomena. The theory assumes the following: (*a*) There are two (fuzzy) sets of nodes in cortical associative memory, bound and free. Bound nodes have strong input and output links to other nodes in cortical memory and weak links to the hippocampal chunking arousal system. Free nodes have weak input and output links to other cortical nodes and strong input links from, and possibly to, the hippocampal chunking arousal system. (*b*) In chunking, the chunking arousal system primes the free nodes so that they can compete successfully for activation against other bound nodes to which the set of bound nodes to be chunked may already be associated. The node or set of nodes maximally activated (by the weak links from the bound nodes to be chunked) will increase in activation so that by standard nodal contiguity conditioning (Hebb 1949), the links associating the new chunk node to its constituent nodes will be strengthened. This binds the formerly free chunk node to represent the set of its constituent nodes. (*c*) Lateral inhibition among cortical nodes limits the total number of nodes (free or bound) that can be fully activated at any one time, preventing epilepsy (Milner 1957). Activating a set of bound nodes that is already well integrated under a bound top chunk node produces a very high level of activation of these nodes. This inhibits the activation of all other nodes, including free nodes, thus preventing further chunking. Activating less strongly associated sets produces less inhibition, permitting some further integration of these bound nodes by strengthening associations from various combinations of these bound nodes to free chunk nodes. (*d*) Binding a chunk node to its constituents initiates a consolidation process that cumulatively disconnects the now bound chunk node from the chunking arousal system, preventing it from being recruited to represent some other combination of constituents.

Storage: Consolidation and Forgetting

The theory of consolidation and forgetting described in Wickelgren (1972c; 1974; 1977a, pp. 362–94; 1979b) is, in my opinion, much more general, accurate, and elegant than any other, and, except for the modifications concerning chunking and spacing effects in learning discussed in the last section, I have nothing to add to the theory at this time.

Retrieval

SPEED-ACCURACY TRADEOFF FUNCTIONS   The study of the dynamics of memory retrieval, and indeed of all cognitive processes, has been given a powerful new experimental tool comparable in significance to the invention of the microscope. A. V. Reed (1973, 1976) had the insight that the phenomenon of speed-accuracy tradeoff in reaction time could be used to study the time course of all mental information processing (all of which is memory retrieval in the broadest sense). Speed-accuracy tradeoff functions have three major advantages over reaction-time measures (even accompanied by an accuracy measure): (*a*) It is not possible to meaningfully compare the difficulty of two conditions when one condition has a shorter reaction time, but a lower accuracy level, than another condition. Obtaining the entire speed-accuracy tradeoff function for each condition avoids this problem and permits comparison of two conditions without the possibility of an invalidating speed-accuracy tradeoff (Wickelgren 1977c). (*b*) Obtaining the entire speed-accuracy tradeoff function provides much more extensive information concerning the time course of retrieval dynamics than does a reaction-time experiment, which provides the equivalent of a single point of such a function, typically at a point near the asymptote, where retrieval dynamics is over (Wickelgren 1977c). (*c*) Speed-accuracy tradeoff functions permit separate estimation of the strength of a memory trace in storage and its retrieval dynamics parameters and functional form. Reaction-time measures completely confound storage and retrieval. A variety of phenomena, most obviously subject's ratings of trace strength, establish that there are many levels of trace strength above the minimum level necessary to yield 100% correct performance at asymptote (unlimited retrieval time). Unless those asymptotic (stored) strength differences are estimated and factored out using speed-accuracy tradeoff methods and, if necessary, incremental scaling (Wickelgren 1978, Wickelgren et al 1980), one cannot study retrieval dynamics, because storage and retrieval are confounded. Thus, in particular, just because subjects always respond correctly that "a robin is a bird" and "a chicken is a bird" does not mean that these traces have equal strength in storage. Indeed, subject's ratings of trace strength establish that they do not. Virtually all reaction-time studies of memory are uninterpretable with respect to retrieval dynamics because of this confounding of storage and retrieval.

WHAT DO WE KNOW? Since the thousands of reaction-time studies of memory retrieval dynamics tell us very little that is definitive, and there have been only a few tens of speed-accuracy tradeoff studies, we know much less about retrieval dynamics than we ought to know. Nevertheless, we can draw some conclusions about memory retrieval dynamics with varying degrees of certainty: (a) Microretrieval in both recall and recognition is a simple direct-access process, not a search process (Corbett & Wickelgren 1978, Dosher 1976, Remington 1977, Wickelgren & Corbett 1977). Since this conclusion is supported by the arguments for associative memory described earlier, we can be quite confident of it. (b) Tentatively, microretrieval in recall is identical in dynamics to recognition (Wickelgren & Corbett 1977). (c) Within the span of attention, we can process several retrieval cues in parallel with little or no loss in efficiency (Dosher 1976, Wickelgren & Corbett 1977). The major uncertainty is just how little the loss is, what the span of attention is, and how each is affected by various conditions. (d) Retrieval of each link in a chain of links occurs, not strictly serially, but in a partially overlapping manner, such that partial retrieval at a lower level initiates retrieval at the next higher level and continually updates its input to the next level as its own retrieval becomes more complete. Retrieval of many, and sometimes all, levels is occurring in parallel. Turvey (1973) calls this parallel-contingent processing, Wickelgren (1976a) calls it chain-parallel processing, and McClelland (1979) probably has the best name for it, cascade processing. There is quite a lot of evidence supporting cascade processing. (e) Despite cascade processing, coding level is perhaps the most important determinant of retrieval dynamics. Higher-level traces (longer associative chains from input to output) have slower retrieval dynamics (Wickelgren 1979a, pp. 273–76). (f) Repeated retrieval of an associative chain in some cases can result, not only in increased strength, but also in a short-circuiting of the chain, speeding retrieval dynamics (Corbett 1977). Thus, both theories of automatization are correct (Wickelgren 1979a, pp. 276–78).

Finally, one of the most important accomplishments in the study of retrieval is purely conceptual. Some of us now clearly understand that memory traces should be considered to have at least two extreme states: retrieved (on our minds, conscious, in active memory) and unretrieved (not on our minds, unconscious, in passive memory). This must be true, because we are not thinking all thoughts simultaneously, at least not to the same degree. Speed-accuracy tradeoff functions are most simply interpreted as indicating that the transition from the unretrieved state to the retrieved state is an incremental rather than an all-or-none process, but we have yet to establish this definitively. Persistence in the retrieved (active memory) state is one type of short-term memory.

Short-Term Memory

I will use "short-term memory" to refer to any rapidly forgotten memory, regardless of whether the trace on which the memory is based is the same or different from associative long-term memory. It is clear that one form of short-term memory is different from long-term memory, namely, active (primary) memory. I believe that this is the only distinct form of short-term memory. There is long-term associative memory (passive memory) and there is the subset of this passive memory that is currently in various states of activation. Such active memory is the only true form of short-term memory, and active memory is limited to the trace(s) currently being thought of and, to a lesser extent, the traces associated to this attentional focus. Active memory is equivalent to the span of attention, modified to include both a focus and an associative halo of decreasing activation. The focus is what is being consciously attended to, and the halo includes the entire attentional set of traces primed (partially activated) by the traces in the attentional focus.

Because we are not thinking all thoughts simultaneously and because time is required to retrieve new thoughts, it is clear that there is one kind of short-term memory, namely, active memory. In bridging the gap from active memory to the sort of memory that every cognitive psychologist agrees is long-term memory, there are three principal theoretical alternatives: (a) There is only active short-term memory and associative long-term memory. Active memory is limited to the currently activated thought and its associative halo (the span of attention). Previously activated thoughts, even the immediately previous one, are not in active memory. So-called short-term memory for short lists is just long-term associative memory under conditions where forgetting is rapid, presumably due to high levels of interference. (b) There is only active short-term memory and associative long-term memory. Active memory extends to encompass short lists of items (the span of immediate memory). (c) There are three dynamically distinct types of traces: active memory, short-term memory, and long-term memory. Active memory is limited to the span of attention. Short-term memory mediates the span of immediate memory. Long-term memory accounts for everything else.

The third alternative simply cannot be supported at the present time because all of the known memory phenomena can be accounted for more parsimoniously with but two traces, active memory and long-term memory (Wickelgren 1973, 1974, 1975, 1979b). I supported the second alternative for a time (Wickelgren 1979a), but a recent experiment (Wickelgren et al 1980) definitively rules out the second alternative in favor of the first. Wickelgren et al reasoned that since retrieval converts traces from the passive to the active state, traces that are still in active memory to some extent (primed or partially activated) should have faster retrieval dynamics. Accordingly, if the basis of short-term memory for lists (probe memory span) is active memory, then the decline in asymptotic recognition accuracy with more intervening items should have the same dynamics as the decline in the priming effect on retrieval dynamics. What we found was that the priming effect on retrieval dynamics was strictly limited to the very last item in the list. The retrieval dynamics of all other items in the list were identical, despite massive changes in asymptotic recognition memory accuracy. It appears that active memory is confined to the very last thought (and whatever it is associated to in long-term memory, to a lesser extent). The rest of the span of immediate memory is most parsimoniously attributed to associative long-term memory.

A very remarkable property of the retention function for long-term memory is that it automatically includes a rapidly decaying short-term memory buffer without the need for a separate short-term memory system. The reason for this is that the rate of forgetting in long-term memory is initially very rapid and continually slowing down with increasing trace age. This initially rapid fall in trace strength means that it is impossible to push the strength of long-term memory traces up to their maxima for more than a fraction of a second, and this, in turn, means that there is always room at the top of the current levels of long-term memory to add a short-lasting increment. This short-lasting increment to the long-term memory trace functions as a short-term memory buffer and is the basis for the span of immediate memory. Besides allowing us to dial telephone numbers without continually looking at the phone book, this short-term aspect of associative memory doubtless plays an important role in speech recognition, articulation, and reading.

It is also what accounts for "warm-up" effects when we sit down to think and write. At first we have trouble getting our thoughts to flow until we have retrieved some associations and strengthened them. As we all know, this strengthening dissipates to a large extent with time and interference. Hence, if our thinking on a particular problem is too fragmented in time, we find ourselves spending a large fraction of our time warming up our minds reviewing old thoughts and not enough time producing new thoughts. However, it is clear that such short-term memory is not as rapidly lost as list memory in a typical probe memory span experiment. The difference is presumably due to differences in the susceptibility of the traces to interference (Wickelgren 1974, 1975), but there may also be important differences in the degree of learning that account for some of the differences in how long the memory lasts as well.

Another remarkable property of long-term retention is that modest differences in degree of learning are amplified to produce enormous differences in trace longevity, even with no difference in forgetting rate (Wickelgren 1977a, pp. 371–72). For example, a factor of two in learning can increase trace longevity by a factor of 100. Hence, what appears to be a difference in "forgetting rate" is very often merely a difference in degree of learning. When initial degree of learning in two conditions is sufficient to produce nearly perfect performance on immediate retention tests, people often erroneously assume that initial degree of learning is equal, when the differences could be quite substantial. With the large amplification factor that prevails between degree of learning and trace longevity, failing to control degree of learning has often led to wrong conclusions. In any case, judging by trace longevity, there are not just two categories of memories, short-term and long-term. There are memories that last seconds, memories that last minutes, memories that last hours, memories that last days, and memories that last months and years. Although we may find evidence for some biological separation into several stages of memory storage, there is currently no psychological reason to peel off the memories that last seconds and call them a different kind of memory trace. Associative long-term memory has solved the whole problem of having memories last for widely varying times, presumably because such limited longevity is functional. Functionally, there is a continuous spectrum of trace lifetimes. Theoretically, except for active memory, they all derive from the same remarkable associative memory. Even active memory is but a change of state for traces in the same associative memory system, but this state change is a dynamically different trace from passive long-term memory.

Literature Cited

Anderson, J. A. 1973. A theory for the recognition of items from short memorized lists. *Psychol. Rev.* 80:417–38

Anderson, J. R. 1974. Retrieval of propositional information from long-term memory. *Cognit. Psychol.* 4:451–74

Anderson, J. R. 1976. *Language, Memory, and Thought.* Hillsdale, NJ: Erlbaum. 546 pp.

Anderson, J. R., Bower, G. H. 1973. *Human Associative Memory.* Washington DC: Winston. 524 pp.

Anderson, J. R., Reder, L. M. 1979. An elaborative processing explanation of depth of processing. See Eysenck 1979, pp. 385–403

Anglin, J. M. 1977. *Word, Object, and Conceptual Development.* New York: Norton. 302 pp.

Bellman, R. E., Zadeh, L. A. 1970. Decision-making in a fuzzy environment. *Manage. Sci.* 17:141–64

Biederman, I., Checkosky, S. F. 1970. Processing redundant information. *J. Exp. Psychol.* 83:486–90

Bower, G. H. 1978. Interference paradigms for meaningful propositional memory. *Am. J. Psychol.* 91:575–85

Brooks, L. 1978. Nonanalytic concept formation and memory for instances. In *Cognition and Categorization*, ed. E. Rosch, B. B. Lloyd, pp. 169–211. Hillsdale, NJ: Erlbaum. 328 pp.

Brown, R. 1958. *Words and Things.* New York: Free Press, 315 pp.

Clark, E. V. 1973. What's in a word? On the child's acquisition of semantics in his first language. In *Cognitive Development and the Acquisition of Language*, ed. T. E. Moore. New York: Academic. 308 pp.

Clark, H. H., Clark, E. J. 1977. *Psychology and Language.* New York: Harcourt. 608 pp.

Collins, A. M., Loftus, E. F. 1975. A spreading-activation theory of semantic processing. *Psychol. Rev.* 82:407–28

Corbett, A. T. 1977. Retrieval dynamics for rote and visual image mnemonics. *J. Verb. Learn. Verb. Behav.* 16:233–46

Corbett, A. T., Wickelgren, W. A. 1978. Semantic memory retrieval: Analysis by speed accuracy tradeoff functions. *Q. J. Exp. Psychol.* 30:1–15

Craik, F. I. M., Tulving, E. 1975. Depth of processing and the retention of words in episodic memory. *J. Exp. Psychol.–Gen.* 104:268–94

Cunningham, J. P. 1978. Free trees and bidirectional trees as representations of psychological distance. *J. Math. Psychol.* 17:165–88

de Villiers, J. G., de Villiers, P. A. 1978. *Language Acquisition.* Cambridge, Mass: Harvard. 312 pp.

Dosher, B. A. 1976. The retrieval of sentences from memory: a speed-accuracy study. *Cognit. Psychol.* 8:291–310

Estes, W. K. 1972. An associative basis for coding and organization in memory. In *Coding Processes in Human Memory*, ed. A. W. Melton, E. Martin, pp. 161–90. New York: Wiley. 448 pp.

Evans, S. H. 1967. A brief statement of schema theory. *Psychon. Sci.* 8:87–88

Eysenck, M. W. 1979. Depth, elaboration, and distinctiveness. In *Levels of Processing in Human Memory*, ed. L. S. Cermak, F. I. M. Craik, pp. 89–118. Hillsdale, NJ: Erlbaum. 479 pp.

Fahlman, S. E. 1979. *NETL: A System for Representing and Using Real-World Knowledge.* Cambridge, Mass: MIT. 278 pp.

Findler, N. V., ed. 1979. *Associative Networks.* New York: Academic. 462 pp.

Flexser, A. J., Bower, G. H. 1974. How frequency affects recency judgments: A model for recency discrimination. *J. Exp. Psychol.* 103:706–16

Glass, A. L., Holyoak, K. J., Kiser, J. I. 1979. Role of antonymy relations in semantic judgments. *J. Exp. Psychol.–Hum. Learn. Mem.* 5:598–606

Goldman, D., Homa, D. 1977. Integrative and metric properties of abstracted information as a function of category discriminability, instance variability, and experience. *J. Exp. Psychol.–Hum. Learn. Mem.* 3:375–85

Greeno, J. G., James, C. T., DaPolito, F. J., Polson, P. G. 1978. *Associative Learning: A Cognitive Analysis.* Englewood Cliffs, NJ: Prentice-Hall. 241 pp.

Hebb, D. O. 1949. *The Organization of Behavior.* New York: Wiley. 335 pp.

Herrmann, D. J. 1978. An old problem for the new psychosemantics: synonymity. *Psychol. Bull.* 85:490–512

Herrmann, D. J., Chaffin, R. J. S., Conti, G., Peters, D., Robbins, P. H. 1979. Comprehension of antonymy and the generality of categorization models. *J. Exp. Psychol.–Hum. Learn. Mem.* 5:585–97

Hintzman, D. L. 1976. Repetition and memory. In *The Psychology of Learning and Motivation*, ed. G. H. Bower, 10:47–91. New York: Academic. 247 pp.

Hintzman, D. L., Block, R. A. 1971. Repetition and memory: Evidence for a multiple-trace hypothesis. *J. Exp. Psychol.* 88:297–306

Holyoak, K. J., Glass, A. L. 1975. The roles of contradictions and counterexamples in the rejection of false sentences. *J. Verb. Learn. Verb. Behav.* 14:215–39

Hornby, P. A. 1974. Surface structure and presupposition. *J. Verb. Learn. Verb. Behav.* 13:530–38

Jacoby, L. L. 1978. On interpreting the effects of repetition: solving a problem versus remembering a solution. *J. Verb. Learn. Verb. Behav.* 17:649–67

Jacoby, L. L., Craik, F. I. M. 1979. Effects of elaboration of processing at encoding and retrieval: trace distinctiveness and recovery of initial context. See Eysenck 1979, pp. 1–21

Jacoby, L. L., Craik, F. I. M., Begg, I. 1979. Effects of decision difficulty on recognition and recall. *J. Verb. Learn. Verb. Behav.* 18:585–600

Johnson, N. F. 1972. The role of chunking and organization in the process of recall. In *The Psychology of Learning and Motivation*, ed. G. H. Bower, 4:171–247. New York: Academic. 315 pp.

Katz, J. J., Fodor, J. A. 1963. The structure of a semantic theory. *Language* 39:170–210

Kay, P., McDaniel, C. K. 1978. The linguistic significance of the meanings of basic color terms. *Language* 54:610–46

King, D. R. W., Anderson, J. R. 1976. Long-term memory search: an intersecting activation process. *J. Verb. Learn. Verb. Behav.* 15:587–605

Klein, K., Saltz, E. 1976. Specifying the mechanisms in a levels-of-processing approach to memory. *J. Exp. Psychol.–Hum. Learn. Mem.* 2:671–79

Koffka, K. 1935. *Principles of Gestalt Psychology.* New York: Harcourt. 485 pp.

Kolers, P. A., Ostry, D. J. 1974. Time course of loss of information regarding pattern analyzing operations. *J. Verb. Learn. Verb. Behav.* 13:599–612

Kunen, S., Green, D., Waterman, D. 1979. Spread of encoding effects within the nonverbal domain. *J. Exp. Psychol.–Hum. Learn. Mem.* 5:574–84

Masson, M. E. J., Sala, L. S. 1978. Interactive processes in sentence comprehension and recognition. *Cognit. Psychol.* 10:244–70

McClelland, J. L. 1979. On the time relations of mental processes: an examination of systems of processes in cascade. *Psychol. Rev.* 86:287–330

McCloskey, M., Glucksberg, S. 1979. Decision processes in verifying category membership statements: Implications for models of semantic memory. *Cognit. Psychol.* 11:1–37

McDaniel, M. A., Friedman, A., Bourne, L. E. 1978. Remembering the levels of information in words. *Mem. Cognit.* 6:156–64

Medin, D. L., Schaffer, M. M. 1978. Context theory of classification learning. *Psychol. Rev.* 85:207–38

Meyer, D. E. 1970. On the representation and retrieval of stored semantic information. *Cognit. Psychol.* 1:242–99

Miller, G. A. 1956. The magical number seven, plus or minus two: some limits on our capacity for processing information. *Psychol. Rev.* 63:81–97

Milner, P. M. 1957. The cell assembly: Mark II. *Psychol. Rev.* 64:242–52

Morris, C. D., Bransford, J. D., Franks, J. J. 1977. Levels of processing versus transfer appropriate processing. *J. Verb. Learn. Verb. Behav.* 16:519–33

Morris, C. D., Stein, B. S., Bransford, J. D. 1979. Prerequisites for the utilization of knowledge in the recall of prose passages. *J. Exp. Psychol.–Hum. Learn. Mem.* 5:253–61

Nelson, T. O. 1977. Repetition and depth of processing. *J. Verb. Learn. Verb. Behav.* 16:151–71

Nelson, T. O., Greene, G., Ronk, B., Hatchett, G., Igl, V. 1978. Effect of multiple images on associative learning. *Mem. Cognit.* 6:337–41

Nelson, T. O., Vining, S. K. 1978. Effect of semantic versus structural processing on long-term retention. *J. Exp. Psychol.–Hum. Learn. Mem.* 4:198–209

Neumann, P. G. 1977. Visual prototype formation with discontinuous representation of variability. *Mem. Cognit.* 5:187–97

Newell, A. 1973. Production systems: models of control structures. In *Visual Information Processing,* ed. W. G. Chase, pp. 463–526. New York: Academic. 555 pp.

Nickerson, R. S., Adams, M. J. 1979. Long-term memory for a common object. *Cognit. Psychol.* 11:287–307

Norman, D. A., Rumelhart, D. E., eds. 1975. *Explorations in Cognition.* San Francisco: Freeman. 430 pp.

Oden, G. C. 1978. Semantic constraints and judged preference for interpretations of ambiguous sentences. *Mem. Cognit.* 6:26–37

Oden, G. C. 1979. A fuzzy logical model of letter identification. *J. Exp. Psychol.: Hum. Percept. Perform.* 5:336–52

Oden, G. C., Massaro, D. W. 1978. Integration of featural information in speech perception. *Psychol. Rev.* 85:172–91

Owens, J., Bower, G. H., Black, J. B. 1979. The "soap opera" effect in story recall. *Mem. Cognit.* 7:185–91

Piaget, J. 1954. *The Construction of Reality in the Child.* New York: Basic Books. 315 pp.

Posner, M. I., Keele, S. W. 1968. On the genesis of abstract ideas. *J. Exp. Psychol.* 77:353–63

Quillian, M. R. 1966. *Semantic memory.* PhD thesis. Carnegie-Mellon Univ., Pittsburg, Pa. (Reprinted in part in *Semantic Information Processing,* ed. M. Minsky, pp. 227–70. Cambridge, Mass: MIT Press, 1968. 440 pp.

Reed, A. V. 1973. Speed-accuracy trade-off in recognition memory. *Science* 181:574–76

Reed, A. V. 1976. List length and the time course of recognition in immediate memory. *Mem. Cognit.* 4:16–30

Reed, A. V. 1977. Quantitative prediction of spacing effects in learning. *J. Verb. Learn. Verb. Behav.* 16:693–98

Reed, S. K. 1972. Pattern recognition and categorization. *Cognit. Psychol.* 3:382–407

Remington, R. 1977. Processing of phonemes in speech: A speed-accuracy study. *J. Acoust. Soc. Am.* 62:1279–90

Rips, L. J., Shoben, E. J., Smith, E. E. 1973. Semantic distance and the verification of semantic relations. *J. Verb. Learn. Verb. Behav.* 12:1–20

Rosch, E. H. 1973. On the internal structure of perceptual and semantic categories. In *Cognitive Development and the Acquisition of Language*, ed. T. E. Moore, pp. 111–44. New York: Academic. 308 pp.

Rosch, E. H. 1977. Human categorization. In *Advances in Cross-Cultural Psychology*, ed. N. Warren, 1:1–49. New York: Academic. 212 pp.

Rosch, E. H., Mervis, C. B. 1975. Family resemblances: Studies in the internal structure of categories. *Cognit. Psychol.* 7:573–605

Rosch, E. H., Mervis, C. B., Gary, W. D., Johnson, D. M., Boyes-Braem, P. 1976. Basic objects in natural categories. *Cognit. Psychol.* 8:382–439

Ross, B. H., Landauer, T. K. 1978. Memory for at least one of two items: test and failure of several theories of spacing effects. *J. Verb. Learn. Verb. Behav.* 17:669–80

Rumelhart, D. E., Lindsay, P. H., Norman, D. A. 1972. In *Organization of Memory*, ed. E. Tulving, W. Donaldson, pp. 197–246. New York: Academic. 423 pp.

Schaeffer, B., Wallace, R. 1969. Semantic similarity and the comparison of word meanings. *J. Exp. Psychol.* 82:343–46

Schaeffer, B., Wallace, R. 1970. The comparison of word meanings. *J. Exp. Psychol.* 86:144–52

Schulman, A. I. 1971. Recognition memory for targets from a scanned word list. *Br. J. Psychol.* 62:335–46

Singer, M. 1976. Thematic structure and the integration of linguistic information. *J. Verb. Learn. Verb. Behav.* 15:549–58

Smith, E. E. 1978. Theories of semantic memory. In *Handbook of Learning and Cognitive Processes*, ed. W. K. Estes, 6:1–56. Hillsdale, NJ: Erlbaum. 311 pp.

Smith, E. E., Shoben, E. J., Rips, L. J. 1974. Structure and process in semantic memory: A featural model for semantic decisions. *Psychol. Rev.* 81:214–41

Stein, B. S. 1978. Depth of processing reexamined: the effects of the precision of encoding and test appropriateness. *J. Verb. Learn. Verb. Behav.* 17:165–74

Stein, B. S., Morris, C. D., Bransford, J. D. 1978. Constraints on effective elaboration. *J. Verb. Learn. Verb. Behav.* 17:707–14

Strauss, M. S. 1979. Abstraction of prototypical information by adults and 10-month-old infants. *J. Exp. Psychol.– Hum. Learn. Mem.* 5:618–32

Turvey, M. 1973. On peripheral and central processes in vision: inferences from an information-processing analysis of masking with patterned stimuli. *Psychol. Rev.* 80:1–52

Tyler, S. W., Hertel, P. T., McCallum, M. C., Ellis, H. C. 1979. Cognitive effort and memory. *J. Exp. Psychol.–Hum. Learn. Mem.* 5:607–17

Wason, P. C., Johnson-Laird, P. N. 1972. *Psychology of Reasoning: Structure and Content*, Cambridge, Mass: Harvard. 264 pp.

Wickelgren, W. A. 1965. Short-term memory for repeated and non-repeated items. *Q. J. Exp. Psychol.* 17:14–25

Wickelgren, W. A. 1969a. Learned specification of concept neurons. *Bull. Math. Biophys.* 31:123–42

Wickelgren, W. A. 1969b. Context-sensitive coding, associative memory, and serial order in (speech) behavior. *Psychol. Rev.* 76:1–15

Wickelgren, W. A. 1969c. Context-sensitive coding in speech recognition, articulation, and development. In *Information Processing in the Nervous System*, ed. K. N. Leibovic, pp. 85–96. New York: Springer. 315 pp.

Wickelgren, W. A. 1972a. Coding, retrieval, and dynamics of multitrace associative memory. In *Cognition in Learning and Memory*, ed. L. W. Gregg, pp. 19–50. New York: Wiley. 315 pp.

Wickelgren, W. A. 1972b. Context-sensitive coding and serial vs. parallel processing in speech. In *Speech and Cortical Functioning*, ed. J. H. Gilbert, pp. 237–62. New York: Academic. 272 pp.

Wickelgren, W. A. 1972c. Trace resistance and the decay of long-term memory. *J. Math. Psychol.* 9:418–55

Wickelgren, W. A. 1973. The long and the short of memory. *Psychol. Bull.* 80:425–38

Wickelgren, W. A. 1974. Single-trace fragility theory of memory dynamics. *Mem. Cognit.* 2:775–80

Wickelgren, W. A. 1975. More on the long and short of memory. In *Short-Term Memory*, ed. D. Deutsch, J. A. Deutsch, pp. 65–72. New York: Academic. 411 pp.

Wickelgren, W. A. 1976a. Network strength theory of storage and retrieval dynamics. *Psychol. Rev.* 83:466–78

Wickelgren, W. A. 1976b. Subproblems of semantic memory: A review of *Human*

Associative Memory by J. R. Anderson, G. H. Bower. *J. Math. Psychol.* 13:243–68

Wickelgren, W. A. 1976c. Phonetic coding and serial order. In *Handbook of Perception,* ed. E. C. Carterette, M. P. Freidman, 7:227–64. New York: Academic. 501 pp.

Wickelgren, W. A. 1977a. *Learning and Memory.* Englewood Cliffs, NJ: Prentice-Hall. 448 pp.

Wickelgren, W. A. 1977b. Concept neurons: A proposed developmental study. *Bull. Psychon. Soc.* 10:232–34

Wickelgren, W. A. 1977c. Speed-accuracy tradeoff and information processing dynamics. *Acta Psychol.* 41:67–85

Wickelgren, W. A. 1978. Wickelgren's neglect. *Acta Psychol.* 42:81–82

Wickelgren, W. A. 1979a. *Cognitive Psychology.* Englewood Cliffs, NJ: Prentice-Hall. 436 pp.

Wickelgren, W. A. 1979b. Chunking and consolidation: A theoretical synthesis of semantic networks, configuring in conditioning, S-R vs Cognitive Learning, normal forgetting, the amnesic syndrome, and the hippocampal arousal system. *Psychol. Rev.* 86:44–60

Wickelgren, W. A. 1979c. I liked the postcard you sent Abe and I: Context-sensitive coding of syntax and other procedural knowledge. *Bull. Psychon. Soc.* 13:61–63

Wickelgren, W. A., Corbett, A. T. 1977. Associative interference and retrieval dynamics in yes-no recall and recognition. *J. Exp. Psychol.–Hum. Learn. Mem.* 3:189–202

Wickelgren, W. A., Corbett, A. T., Dosher, B. A. 1980. Priming and retrieval from short-term memory: a speed accuracy tradeoff analysis. *J. Verb. Learn. Verb. Behav.* In press

Wickelgren, W. A., Norman, D. A. 1971. Invariance of forgetting rate with number of repetitions in verbal short-term recognition memory. *Psychon. Sci.* 22:363–64

Wittgenstein, L. 1953. *Philosophical Investigations.* New York: Macmillan

Woods, W. A. 1970. Transition network grammars for natural language analysis. *Commun. ACM* 13:591–606

Woods, W. A. 1975. What's in a link: Foundations for semantic networks. In *Representation and Understanding,* ed. D. G. Bobrow, A. Collins, pp. 35–82. New York: Academic. 427 pp.

Zadeh, L. A. 1965. Fuzzy sets. *Inf. Control.* 8:338–53

Ann. Rev. Psychol. 1981. 32:53–88

BEHAVIORAL DECISION THEORY: PROCESSES OF JUDGMENT AND CHOICE

♦340

Hillel J. Einhorn and Robin M. Hogarth

Center for Decision Research, Graduate School of Business, University
of Chicago, Chicago, Illinois 60637

CONTENTS

INTRODUCTION

Why are normative theories so prevalent in the study of judgment and choice, yet virtually absent in other branches of science? For example, imagine that atoms and molecules failed to follow the laws supposed to describe their behavior. Few would call such behavior irrational or suboptimal. However, if people violate expected utility axioms or do not revise probabilities in accord with Bayes' theorem, such behavior is considered suboptimal and perhaps irrational. What is the difference, if any, between

53

the two situations? In the latter we implicitly assume that behavior is purposive and goal-directed while this is less obvious (if at all) in the former. (It is problematic how one might treat plant and animal behavior according to a descriptive–normative dichotomy.) Therefore, if one grants that behavior is goal-directed, it seems reasonable to assume that some ways of getting to the goal are better, in the sense of taking less time, making fewer errors, and so on, than others. Indeed, much of decision research concerns evaluating and developing ways for improving behavior, thereby reflecting a strong engineering orientation (Edwards 1977; Hammond, Mumpower & Smith 1977; Keeney & Raiffa 1976). Moreover, comparison of actual behavior with normative models has been important in focusing attention on the discrepancies between them, and this in turn has raised important questions about the causes of such discrepancies.

Central to normative theories are the concepts of rationality and optimality. Recently Simon (1978) has argued for different types of rationality, distinguishing between the narrow economic meaning (i.e. maximizing behavior) and its more general dictionary definition of "being sensible, agreeable to reason, intelligent." Moreover, the broader definition itself rests on the assumption that behavior is functional. That is,

> Behaviors are functional if they contribute to certain goals, where these goals may be the pleasure or satisfaction of an individual or the guarantee of food or shelter for the members of society. . . . It is not necessary or implied that the adaptation of institutions or behavior patterns of goals be conscious or intended. . . . As in economics, evolutionary arguments are often adduced to explain the persistence and survival of functional patterns and to avoid assumptions of deliberate calculation in explaining them (pp. 3–4).

Accordingly, Simon's concept of "bounded rationality," which has provided the conceptual foundation for much behavioral decision research, is itself based on functional and evolutionary arguments. However, although one may agree that evolution is nature's way of doing cost/benefit analysis, it does not follow that all behavior is cost/benefit efficient in some way. We discuss this later with regard to misconceptions of evolution, but note that this view: (a) is unfalsifiable (see Lewontin 1979, on "imaginative reconstructions"); (b) renders the concept of an "error" vacuous; (c) obviates the distinction between normative and descriptive theories. Thus, while it has been argued that the difference between bounded and economic rationality is one of degree, not kind, we disagree.

The previous review of this field (Slovic, Fischhoff & Lichtenstein 1977) described a long list of human judgmental biases, deficiencies, and cognitive illusions. In the intervening period this list has both increased in size and influenced other areas of psychology (Bettman 1979, Mischel 1979, Nisbett

& Ross 1980). Moreover, in addition to cataloging the types of errors induced by the manner in which people make judgments and choices, concern has now centered on explaining the causes of both the existence and persistence of such errors. This is exemplified by examination of a basic assumption upon which adaptive and functional arguments rest, namely the ability to learn (Einhorn & Hogarth 1978, Hammond 1978a, Brehmer, 1980). However, if the ability to learn is seriously deficient, then dysfunctional behavior can not only exist but persist, thus violating the very notion of functionality. It is therefore essential to delimit the conditions under which this can occur. Indeed, the *general* importance of considering the effects of specific conditions on judgment and choice is emphasized by the following irony: the picture of human judgment and choice that emerges from the literature is characterized by extensive biases and violations of normative models whereas in work on lower animals much choice behavior seems consistent with optimizing principles (e.g. Killeen 1978, Rachlin & Burkhard 1978, Staddon & Motheral 1978). The danger of such pictures is that they are often painted to be interesting rather than complete. In the next section we consider the complexities involved in evaluating discrepancies between optimal models and human responses, and how persistent dysfunctional behavior is consistent with evolutionary concepts.

ARE OPTIMAL DECISIONS REASONABLE?

How are discrepancies between the outputs of optimal models and human responses to be evaluated? First, consider the latter to be generated through a cognitive model of the task and note the different possibilities: 1. Both models could inadequately represent the task, but in different ways; 2. the optimal model is a more adequate representation than that of the person. Indeed, this is the assumption upon which most decision research is predicated; and 3. the person's model is more appropriate than the optimal model —a hypothesis suggested by March (1978). Furthermore, in the absence of discrepancies, neither model could be appropriate if they misrepresent the environment in similar ways. Therefore, before one compares discrepancies between optimal models and human judgments, it is important to compare each with the environment.

Task vs Optimal Model of Task

We begin by offering a definition of optimality; namely, decisions or judgments that maximize or minimize some explicit and measurable criterion (e.g. profits, errors, time) *conditional on certain environmental assumptions and a specified time horizon.* The importance of this definition is that it stresses the conditional nature of optimality. For example, Simon (1979) points out that because of the complexity of the environment, one has but two alternatives: either to build optimal models by making simplifying environmental assumptions, or to build heuristic models that maintain greater environmental realism (also see Wimsatt 1980). Unfortunately, the conditional nature of optimal models has not been appreciated and too few researchers have considered their limitations. For instance, it has been found that people are insufficiently regressive in their predictions (Kahneman & Tversky 1973). While this is no doubt true in stable situations, extreme predictions are not suboptimal in nonstationary processes. In fact, given a changing process, regressive predictions are suboptimal. The problem is that extreme responses can occur at random or they can signal changes in the underlying process. For example, if you think that Chrysler's recent large losses are being generated by a stable process, you should predict that profits will regress up to their mean level. However, if you take the large losses as indicating a deteriorating quality of management and worsening market conditions, you should be predicting even more extreme losses. Therefore, the optimal prediction is conditional on which hypothesis you hold.

The above is not an isolated case. For example, Lopes (1980) points out that the conclusion that people have erroneous conceptions of randomness (e.g. Slovic, Kunreuther & White 1974) rests on the assumption that well-defined criteria of randomness exist. She convincingly demonstrates that this is not the case. Or consider the work on probability revision within the Bayesian framework (e.g. Slovic & Lichtenstein 1971). Much of this work makes assumptions (conditional independence, perfectly reliable data, well-defined sample spaces) that may not characterize the natural environment. Moreover, alternative normative models for making probabilistic inferences have been developed based on assumptions different from those held by Bayesians (Shafer 1976, Cohen 1977; also see Schum 1979 for a discussion of Cohen). In fact, Cohen's model rests on a radically different system that obeys rules quite different from the standard probability calculus. Competing normative models complicate the definition of what is a "bias" in probability judgment and has already led to one debate (Cohen 1979, Kahneman & Tversky 1979b). Such debate is useful if for no other reason than it focuses attention on the conditionality of normative models. To consider human judgment as suboptimal without discussion of the limitations of optimal models is naive. On the other hand, we do not imply that inappropriate optimal models always, or even usually, account for observed discrepancies.

The definition of optimality offered above deals with a single criterion or goal. However, actual judgments and choices typically are based on multiple goals or criteria. When such goals conflict, as when they are negatively correlated (e.g. quantity and quality of merchandise, cf Coombs & Avrunin 1977), there can be no optimal solution in the same sense as the single criterion case (Shepard 1964). That is, the most one can do is to execute the trade-offs or compromises between the goals that reflect one's values. Therefore, the imposition of (subjective) values for resolving conflicts leads to rejecting "objective" optimality and replacing it with the criterion of consistency with one's goals and values. Furthermore, even the single goal situation is transformed into a multiple goal case when judgments and choices are considered over time. For example, consider the single goal of maximizing profit. Conflicts between short-run and longer-run strategies can exist even with a single well-defined criterion. Therefore, unless a time horizon is specified, optimality can also be problematic in what might seem to be simple situations.

Environment vs Problem Space

The importance to behavior of the cognitive representation of the task, i.e. "problem space," has been emphasized by Newell & Simon (1972). It is now clear that the process of representation, and the factors that affect it, are of major importance in judgment and choice. Illustrations of the effects of problem representation on behavior are found in work on estimating probabilities via fault trees (Fischhoff, Slovic & Lichtenstein 1978); response mode effects inducing preference reversals (Grether & Plott 1979); coding processes in risky choice (Kahneman & Tversky 1979a); "problem isomorphs" in problem solving (Simon & Hayes 1976); context effects in choice (Aschenbrenner 1978, Tversky & Sattath 1979) and agenda setting (Plott & Levine 1978); purchasing behavior (Russo 1977); and causal schemas in probability judgments (Tversky & Kahneman 1980a).

It is essential to emphasize that the cognitive approach has been concerned primarily with *how* tasks are represented. The issue of *why* tasks are represented in particular ways has not yet been addressed. However, given functional arguments, this is a crucial issue in view of the way minor contextual changes can lead to the violation of the most intuitively appealing normative principles, e.g. transitivity.

The reconciliation of persistent errors and biases with functional arguments has taken two forms. First, it has been claimed that such effects can be overcome by increasing incentives (through higher payoffs and/or punishments). In one sense, this argument is irrefutable since it can always be claimed that the incentive wasn't high enough. However, direct evidence shows that increased payoffs do not necessarily decrease extreme overconfidence (Fischhoff, Slovic & Lichtenstein 1977) nor prevent preference reversals (Grether & Plott 1979). Furthermore, the indirect evidence from clinical judgment studies in naturally occurring settings, where payoffs are presumably high enough to be motivating, continues to indicate low validity and inferiority to statistical models (Dawes 1979). In addition, claims that people will seek aids and/or experts when the stakes are high (Edwards 1975) are predicated on the assumptions that: (*a*) people know that they don't know; and (*b*) they know (or believe) that others do. On the other hand, it is foolish to deny that payoffs, and thus motivation, have no effect on processes of judgment and choice. Indeed, one only needs to recall the fundamental insight of signal detection theory (Green & Swets 1966), which is that both cognitive and motivational components affect judgment (also see Killeen 1978).

A second way of reconciling biases with functional arguments involves enlarging the context in which performance is evaluated. This has taken four forms: 1. One view of evolutionary theory (as espoused by the sociobiologists; for example, Wilson 1978) could lead to the belief that the human system represents the optimal design for a complex environment. Heuristics exist because they serve useful functions and their benefits outweigh their costs. While this view is often espoused, there is surprisingly little evidence to support it. An important exception is the simulation study by Thorngate (1980), where it was shown how heuristics can often pick the best of several alternatives across a range of tasks. However, neither this study nor any other that we are aware of has considered the distribution of tasks in the natural environment in which heuristics would work well or poorly. 2. Hogarth (1980a) has argued that most judgments and choices occur sequentially and that many biases reflect response tendencies which are functional in dynamic environments. Furthermore, the static tasks typically investigated reflect a preoccupation with those relatively simple situations for which optimal models can be constructed. 3. Toda (1962) has claimed that it is the coordination of behavior that reflects an organism's efficiency, not individual and thus isolated actions. Furthermore, coordination between functions requires trade-offs and these can be facilitated by limitations (e.g. a limited memory facilitates efficient forgetting of needless detail). 4. Cost/benefit analyses can be expanded to include "the cost of thinking" (Shugan 1980), which seems compatible with notions of bounded rationality.

While there is much merit in the above arguments, care must be taken since they can easily become tautological; i.e. costs and benefits can be defined post hoc in accord with a presumption of optimality. However, can there be actual dysfunctional behavior (rather than seeming dysfunctional behavior) that persists, and if so, by what mechanism(s)?

Since functional arguments rest on evolutionary theory, it is easy to overlook the fact that nonadaptive behavior can also be compatible with principles of natural selection: 1. Biological evolution is directly related to the amount of variance in the genotype (Lewontin 1979). For example, the development of wings could be functional for humans on many occasions. However, without an appropriate mutation (the chance of which is miniscule), such evolution cannot take place. While it is evident that physical limitations preclude certain types of behavior regardless of incentives to the contrary, biological limitations can also preclude certain cognitive operations (Russo 1978). For example, the study of memory indicates limitations on short-term storage and retrieval. Furthermore, Seligman (1970) has explicated biological limitations in the learning process itself. Cognitive limitations can therefore persist and be dysfunctional (relative to given goals) for the same reasons that account for physical limitations. 2. The time-frame of human biological evolution is such that it can be considered constant over many generations. It is thus difficult to determine whether any current trait or mechanism is becoming more or less adaptive, or is a vestige without apparent function (e.g. the human appendix: see also Skinner 1966). Therefore, without denying general cost/benefit considerations over the very long run, dysfunctional behaviors may persist for extremely long periods by human standards. The demise of the dinosaur, for example, is popularly cited as an example of the effectiveness of natural selection. However, it is easy to forget that dinosaurs existed for about 160 million years. So far, humans are a mere 2.5 million years old (Sagan 1977). 3. Humans adapt the environment to their own needs as well as adapting to the environment. For example, poor eyesight is certainly dysfunctional, yet a major judgment aid, eye glasses, has been invented to deal with this problem. Furthermore, note that this aid actually works against natural selection, i.e. those with poor vision will not be selected against since their survival chances are now equal to those without the need for glasses. In fact, if poor eyesight were correlated with higher reproductive rates, there would be an increase in the aggregate level of this deficiency. 4. The analogy has been drawn between learning and evolution (e.g. Campbell 1960). However, the attempt to link individual learning with species level survival is problematic (Lewontin 1979). For example, consider whether response competition within an organism can be viewed as identical to competition between organisms. While the latter can and has been analyzed via game theoretic ideas of zero-sum payoffs and conflicting interests, such an approach seems foreign to intraindividual response competition.

Intuitive Responses and Optimal Models

The above arguments leave us on the horns of a dilemma. Given the complexity of the environment, it is uncertain whether human responses or optimal models are more appropriate. Furthermore, we know of no theory or set of principles that would resolve this issue. Indeed, the optimal-intuitive comparison presents the following paradox: Optimal models have been suggested to overcome intuitive shortcomings. However, in the final analysis the outputs of optimal models are evaluated by judgment, i.e. do we like the outcomes, do we believe the axioms to be reasonable, and should we be coherent?

If the assessment of rationality ultimately rests on judgment, what are its components? To discuss this, imagine being a juror in a trial and having to decide whether someone who has committed a heinous crime acted "rationally." The prosecution argues that the crime was meticulously planned and carried out, thus demonstrating that the person was in complete control of what he/she was doing. Note that this argument defines rationality by the efficiency with which means are used to attain ends. Moreover, this manner of defining rationality is exactly what decision theorists have stressed, that is, given one's goals, what is the best way of attaining them. However, the defense argues that the goal of committing such a crime is itself evidence of irrationality. That is, rationality is to be judged by the goals themselves. Moreover, the argument is made that the deliberative way such despicable goals were reached is itself an indication of irrationality. Finally, the defense argues that when one understands the background of the defendant (the poverty, lack of parental love, etc), the irrational goals are, in fact, reasonable. This last point emphasizes that goals can only be understood within the person's task representation. Moreover, this argument highlights a crucial problem; namely, to what extent *should* one be responsible for one's task representation (cf Brown 1978)?

What are the implications of the above for behavioral decision theory? First, judgments of rationality can be conceptualized as forming a continuum which can be dichotomized by imposing a cutoff when actions must be taken. This idea has been advanced by Lopes (1980) with respect to judging randomness. Moreover, she suggests that the placement of the cutoff can be viewed within a signal-detection framework; i.e. payoffs and costs are reflected by the cutoff point. Second, judged rationality is a mixture of the efficiency of means to ends (called "instrumental rationality," Tribe 1973) and the "goodness" of the goals themselves (cf Brown 1978). While the former is familiar to decision theorists, the latter is the concern of moral philosophers, theologians, and the like. However, at a practical level it is of concern to all. In fact, it may well be that the efficacy of decision aids comes from structuring tasks so that the nature of one's goals is clarified (Humphreys & McFadden 1980). Third, the importance of *behavioral* decision theory lies in the fact that even if one were willing to accept instrumental rationality as the sole criterion for evaluating decisions, knowledge of how tasks are represented is crucial since people's goals form part of their models of the world. Moreover, their task representation may be of more importance in defining errors than the rules they use within that representation. For example, imagine a paranoid who processes information and acts with remarkable coherence and consistency. Such coherence of beliefs and actions is likely to be far greater than in so-called "normal" people (when does coherence become rigidity?) Thus, the representation of the world as a place where others persecute one is the source of difficulty, and not necessarily the incorrect or inconsistent use of inferential rules or decision strategies.

STRATEGIES AND MECHANISMS OF JUDGMENT AND CHOICE

The inescapable role of intuitive judgment in decision making underscores the importance of descriptive research concerned with how and why processes operate as they do. Moreover, the most important empirical results in the period under review have shown the sensitivity of judgment and choice to seemingly minor changes in tasks. Such results illustrate the importance of context in understanding behavior in the same way that the context of a passage affects the meaning of individual words and phrases. We consider context to refer to *both* the formal structure and the content of a task. On the other hand, normative models gain their generality and power by ignoring content in favor of structure and thus treat problems out of context (cf Shweder 1979). However, content gives meaning to tasks and this should not be ignored in trying to predict and evaluate behavior. For example, consider the logical error of denying the antecedent; i.e. "if A, then B", does not imply "if not-A, then not-B." However, as discussed by Harris & Monaco (1978), the statement: "If you mow the lawn (A), I'll give you $5 (B)", does imply that if you don't mow the lawn (not-A) you won't get the $5 (not-B). Or consider a choice between a sure loss of $25 and a gamble with 3 : 1 odds in favor of losing $100 vs $0. Compare this with the decision to buy or not buy an insurance policy for a $25 premium to protect you against a .75 chance of losing $100. Although the two situations are structurally identical, it is possible for the same person to prefer the gamble in the first case yet prefer the insurance policy in the second (for experimental results, see Hershey & Schoemaker 1980a). Such behavior can be explained in several ways: (*a*) the person may not perceive the tasks as identical since content can hide structure (Einhorn 1980); and (*b*) even if the two situations are seen as having identical structure, their differing content could make their meaning quite different. For example, buying insurance may be seen as the purchase of protection (which is good) against the uncertainties of nature, while being forced to choose between two painful alternatives is viewed as a no-win situation.

While context has typically been defined in terms of task variables, it is clear from the above examples that it is also a function of what the person brings to the task in the way of prior experience via learning, and biological limitations on attention, memory, and the like, that affect learning. Therefore, the elements of a psychological theory of decision making must include a concern for task structure, the representation of the task, and the information processing capabilities of the organism.

In order to discuss specific findings in the literature, we artificially decompose processes of judgment and choice into several subprocesses, namely, information acquisition, evaluation, action, and feedback/learning. We are well aware that these subprocesses interact and that their interaction is of great importance in the organization and coordination of decision making. Accordingly, we consider these issues within subsections where appropriate.

The Role of Acquisition in Evaluation

Much work in judgment and choice involves the development and testing of algebraic models that represent strategies for evaluating and combining information (see Slovic & Lichtenstein 1971). Although work in this tradition continues (e.g. Anderson 1979), it has been accompanied by increasing dissatisfaction in that processes are treated in a static manner; i.e. judgments and choices are considered to be formed on the basis of information that is given. In contrast, the process of information search and acquisition should also be considered (cf Elstein, Shulman & Sprafka 1978) since evaluation and search strategies are interdependent. In fact, the evaluation strategies proposed in the literature imply various search processes either explicitly (e.g. Tversky & Sattath 1979) or implicitly (Payne 1976). Of great importance is the fact that the concern for how information is acquired raises questions about the role of attention and memory in decision making that have received relatively little concern (however, see Hogarth 1980b, Rothbart 1980). Furthermore, concern for the dynamics of information search has necessitated the use of different methodologies; e.g. process-tracing approaches such as verbal protocols and eye movements, as well as information display boards (Payne 1976). However, these methods need not replace more general modeling efforts and may in fact be complementary to them (Payne, Braunstein & Carroll 1978; Einhorn, Kleinmuntz & Kleinmuntz 1979).

The importance of considering the interdependence of evaluation and acquisition can be seen in considering the issue of whether people lack insight into the relative importance they attach to cues in their judgment policies. The literature contains conflicting evidence and interpretations (Nisbett & Wilson 1977, Schmitt & Levine 1977). However, the use of weights in models as reflecting differential cue importance ignores the importance of attention in subjective weight estimates and illustrates our emphasis on understanding persons and tasks. Correspondence between subjective and statistical weights requires that people attend to and evaluate cues and that such cues contain both variance and low intercorrelations. Disagreement between subjective and statistical weights can thus occur for three reasons: 1. people indeed lack insight; 2. people attend to, but cannot use, cues that lack variance (Einhorn et al 1979); 3. cues to which attention is not paid are correlated with others such that the nonattended cues receive inappropriate statistical weights. Both process-tracing methods and statistical modeling are necessary to untangle these competing interpretations.

Acquisition

Acquisition concerns the processes of information search and storage—both in memory and the external environment. Central to acquisition is the role of attention since this necessarily precedes the use and storage of information. We discuss attention by using an analogy with the perceptual concept of figure-ground noting that, as in perception, the cognitive decomposition of stimuli can be achieved in many ways. Accordingly, different decompositions may lead to different task representations (cf Kahneman & Tversky 1979a). Indeed, context can be thought of as the meaning of figure in relation to ground.

In an insightful article, Tversky (1977) analyzed the psychological basis of similarity judgments, and in so doing emphasized the importance of context and selective attention in judgmental processes. He first noted that our knowledge of any particular object "is generally rich in content and complex in form. It includes appearance, function, relation to other objects, and any other property of the object that can be deduced from our general knowledge of the world" (p. 329). Thus, the process of representing an object or alternative by a number of attributes or features depends on prior processes of selective attention and cue achievement. Once features are achieved, the similarity between objects a and b, $s(a,b)$, is defined in terms of feature sets denoted by A and B, respectively. Thus,

$$s(a,b) = \theta\ f(A \cap B) - \alpha\ f(A\text{-}B) - \beta\ f(B\text{-}A) \quad 1.$$

where $A \cap B$ = features that a and b have in common; A-B, B-A = distinctive features of a and b, respectively; f = salience of features; and θ, α, and β are parameters. Note that Equation 1 expresses $s(a,b)$ as a weighted linear function of three variables thereby implying a compensatory combining rule. The importance of Equation 1 lies in the concept of salience (f) and the role of the parameters. Tversky first defines salience as the intensity, frequency, familiarity, or more generally the signal-to-noise ratio of the features. Thereafter, the way in which the f scale and the parameters depend on context are discussed. We consider three important effects: asymmetry and focus, similarity vs difference, diagnosticity and extension.

Asymmetry in similarity judgments refers to the fact that the judged similarity of a to b may not be equal to the similarity of b to a. This can occur when attention is focused on one object as subject and the other as referent. For example, consider the statements, "a man is like a tree" and "a tree is like a man." It is possible to judge that a man is more like a tree than vice versa, thus violating symmetry (and metric representations of similarity). The explanation is that in evaluating $s(a,b)$ vs $s(b,a)$, $\alpha > \beta$ in 1; i.e. the distinct features of the subject are weighted more heavily than those of the referent. Hence, the focusing of attention results in differential weighting of features such that symmetry is violated.

The similarity/difference effect occurs when $\alpha = \beta$ and $s(a,b) = s(b,a)$. In judging similarity, people attend more to common features, while in judging difference, they attend more to distinctive features. This leads to the effect in which "a pair of objects with many common and many distinctive features may be perceived as both more similar and more different than another pair of objects with fewer common and fewer distinctive features" (Tversky 1977, p. 340).

The first effect results from a shift in attention due to focusing on an anchoring point (the subject). The second is caused by a shift in attention induced by different response modes. The third effect, diagnosticity and extension, involves changes in the salience of the features in an object due to the specific object set being considered. For example, consider the feature "four wheels" in American cars. Such a feature is not salient since all American cars have four wheels. However, a European car with three wheels on an American road would be highly salient. Therefore, salience is a joint function of intensity and what Tversky calls diagnosticity, which is related to the variability of a feature in a particular set (cf Einhorn & McCoach 1977). An important implication of diagnosticity is that the similarity between objects can be changed by adding to (or subtracting from) the set. For example, consider the similarity between Coca-Cola and Pepsi-Cola. Now add 7-Up to the set and note the increased similarity of the colas.

Although Tversky's paper is of great importance for judgment and choice, it has not been linked to earlier concepts such as representativeness, anchoring and adjusting, or availability. However, the question of context and the figure-ground issues which underlie similarity would seem to be of great importance in understanding these heuristics and their concomitant biases as well as a wide range of phenomena in the literature. To illustrate, we first discuss work on base rates.

Earlier work (reviewed in Slovic et al 1977) indicated that subjects ignore base rates, and it was postulated that this resulted from use of the representativeness heuristic and/or the apparent salience of concrete or vivid information (Nisbett et al 1976). However, a base rate can only be defined conditional on some population (or sample space). Whereas many might agree that the base rates defined by experimenters in laboratory tasks make the sample space clear, the definition of the population against which judgments should be normalized in the natural ecology is unclear. Consider an inference concerning whether someone has a particular propensity to heart disease. What is the relevant population to which this person should be compared? The population of people in the same age group? The population of the United States? Of Mexico? There is no generally accepted normative way of defining the appropriate population. Thus, for naturally occurring phenomena it is neither clear whether people do or do not ignore base rates, nor whether they should (see also Goldsmith 1980, Russell 1948).

Even in the laboratory, base rates are not always ignored. Indeed, Tversky & Kahneman (1980a) have argued that base rates will be used to the extent that they can be causally linked to target events. Their data supported this hypothesis, and Ajzen (1977) independently reached similar results and conclusions. A further implication of causal thinking concerns asymmetries in the use of information; i.e. information that receives a causal interpretation is weighted more heavily in judgment than information that is diagnostic (although probability theory accords equal weight to both). Whether such judgments are biased or not depends on whether one believes that causality should be ignored in a normative theory of inference (as is the case in standard probability theory; see Cohen 1977, 1979 for a different view).

Bar-Hillel (1980) further explicated the conditions under which base rates are used. She argued that people order information by its perceived degree of relevance to the target event (with high relevant dominating low relevant information). Causality, Bar-Hillel argued, is but one way of inducing relevance (it is sufficient but not necessary). Relevance can also be induced by making target information more specific, which is tantamount to changing the figure-ground relationship between targets and populations. We believe that further elucidation of the role of causality in judgment is needed (Mowrey, Doherty & Keeley 1979) and note that the notion of causality, like probability, is conditional on the definition of a background or "causal field" (Mackie 1965).

Central to the distinction between figure and ground is the concept of cue redundancy. As Garner (1970) has stated, "good patterns have few alternatives," i.e. cue redundancy helps achievement of the object and thus sharpens figure from ground. Tversky (1977) makes the point that for familiar, integral objects there is little contextual ambiguity; however, this is not the case for artificial, separable stimuli. For example, consider the differential effects of acquiring information from intact or decomposed stimuli (the former being more representative of the natural ecology, the latter of experimental tasks). Phelps & Shanteau (1978) have shown that when expert livestock judges are presented with information in the form of 11 decomposed, orthogonal attributes of sows, they are capable of using all the information in forming their judgment; however, when presented with intact stimuli (photographs), their judgments can be modeled by a few cues. These results illustrate that people can handle more information than previously thought; moreover, they can be interpreted as indicating that cue redundancy in the natural ecology reduces the need for attending to and evaluating large numbers of cues. Redundancy in the natural ecology also implies that cues can indicate the presence of other cues and can thus lead one to expect cue co-occurrences. For example, in a study of dating choice, Shanteau & Nagy (1979) showed that subjects used cues not presented by the experimenters. That is, when choosing between potential dates from photographs, subjects' choices were influenced by the probability that their requests for dates would be accepted even though this cue was not explicitly given.

The importance of redundancy in acquisition has been discussed by Einhorn et al (1979), who note the following benefits: "(a) Information search is limited without large losses in predictive accuracy; (b) attention is highly selective; (c) dimensionality of the information space is reduced, thereby preventing information overload; (d) intersubstitutability of cues is facilitated; and (e) unreliability of cues is alleviated by having multiple measures of the same cue variable" (p. 466). Studies and models that fail to consider cue redundancy in search processes are thus incomplete. For example, consider risky choice in the natural ecology vs the laboratory (for reviews of risk see Libby & Fishburn 1977, Vlek & Stallen 1980). In the former, probabilities are typically not explicit and must be judged by whatever environmental cues are available. A particularly salient cue is likely to be the size of the payoff itself, especially if people have beliefs about the co-occurrence of uncertainty and reward (e.g. large payoffs occur with small probabilities). Thus, payoff size can be used as a cue to probability (cf Shanteau & Nagy 1979). Moreover, the degree of perceived redundancy may also be important in understanding issues of ambiguity in decision making (cf Yates & Zukowski 1976). That is, one's uncertainty about a probability estimate (so-called second order probability) may be related to a variety of cues, including payoff size. In fact, Pearson (1897) noted that although means and variances of distributions are usually treated as independent, in the natural ecology they tend to be correlated and can thus be used as cues to each other. The analogy to means and variances of payoff distributions from gambles seems useful.

The temporal order of information acquisition can also affect salience, both by creating shifts in figure-ground relations and differential demands on attention and memory. Consider, for example, the effects of simultaneous vs sequential information display. In a study of supermarket shopping, Russo (1977) found that when unit prices were presented to shoppers in organized lists (ordered by relative size of unit prices, hence simultaneous presentation), purchasing behavior was changed relative to the situation where shoppers either did not have unit price information or such information was simply indicated next to products on the shelves (the latter implying sequential acquisition). An interesting aspect of this study is that it represents a form of decision aiding quite different from those proposed in earlier work. That is, instead of helping people to evaluate information that has already been acquired (e.g. through bootstrapping or multiattribute models), one eases strain on memory and attention by aiding the acquisition process itself. However, that greater understanding of attention and memory processes is necessary for this approach to be successful was underscored in a study by Fischhoff et al (1978) on the use of "fault trees." Fault trees are diagnostic check lists represented in tree-like form. The task studied by Fischhoff et al (1978) involved automobile malfunction and had both experts (i.e. automobile mechanics) and novices as subjects. The results indicated that the apparently comprehensive format of the fault tree blinded both expert and novice subjects to the possibility of missing causes of malfunction.

Since information is normally acquired in both intact form and across time (i.e. sequentially), determining the manner and amount of information to be presented in acquisition aids is a subject of great importance. It raises issues of both how external stimuli cue memory and the organization of memory itself (Broadbent, Cooper & Broadbent 1978; Estes 1980). Different ways of organizing information, for example by attributes or by alternatives in a choice situation, could have implications for task representation. In addition, several recent studies of the "availability" heuristic (Tversky & Kahneman 1973) have further emphasized how ease of recall from memory has important effects on judgment (Kubovy 1977). Moreover, experimenters should be aware that subjects interpret stimuli rather than respond to them. For example, Tversky & Kahneman (1980a) show that when information is presented in a manner involving an ambiguous time sequence, intuitive interpretations may reflect a reordering of that information to conform to the time dependence of naturally occurring phenomena.

That the figure-ground relation at a particular point in time affects judgment and choice has been demonstrated in a number of studies. A particularly compelling example is given by Tversky & Kahneman (1980b): It is expected that a certain flu will kill 600 people this year and you are faced with two options: option 1 will save about 200 people; option 2 will save about 600 people with probability of ⅓ and no people with probability of ⅔. Now consider a re-wording of the alternatives: option 1 will result in about 400 people dying; option 2 gives a ⅓ probability that none will die and a ⅔ chance that about 600 people will die. By a simple change in the reference point induced by formulating the same problem in terms of lives lost or saved, cognitive figure and ground are reversed, as were the choices of a majority of subjects. Similar preference reversals can be obtained through the isolation effect where sequential presentation of information can isolate and hence highlight the common components of choice alternatives. Aspects seen to be common to alternatives are cancelled out and the choice process determined by comparing the distinctive features of the alternatives.

Payne, Laughhunn & Crum (1979) have linked reference effects to the dynamic concept of aspiration level and further illustrated how this affects the encoding of outcomes as losses or gains relative to a standard (rather than considering the overall wealth position implied by different end states). Sequential effects in choice have also been demonstrated by Levine & Plott (1977) and Plott & Levine (1978) in both field and laboratory studies. The structure of an agenda was shown to affect the outcomes of group choice by sequencing the comparisons of particular subsets of alternatives. Tversky & Sattath (1979) have further considered implications of these effects within individuals when sequential elimination strategies of choice are used. That judgment should be affected in a relative manner by momentary reference points should, however, come as no surprise (cf Slovic & Fischhoff 1977). Weber's law predicts just this, and the prevalence of "adjustment and anchoring" strategies in dynamic judgmental tasks is congruent with these findings (Hogarth 1980a).

Cognitive figure-ground relations vary considerably on the ease with which they can be reversed. On the one hand, the tendency not to seek information that could disconfirm one's hypotheses (Mynatt, Doherty & Tweney 1977, 1978) illustrates strong figure-ground relations where confirming evidence is attracted to the figure and possible disconfirming evidence remains in the ground. Consider also the difficulty of reformulating problem spaces in creative efforts where inversion of figure and ground is precisely what is required. On the other hand, situations also arise where figure and ground can invert themselves with minor fluctuations in attention, as in the case of "reversible figures" in perception. Whereas the analogy one could draw between "preference reversals" and "reversible figures" is possibly tenuous, both do emphasize the role of attention. In particular, its fluctuating nature implies that for certain types of stimulus configurations, task representations can be unstable. Both choice and the application of judgmental rules have often been stated to be inherently inconsistent and hence probabilistic (Brehmer 1978, Tversky & Sattath 1979). However, the effects of fluctuating attention in producing such inconsistencies has not been explored.

Lest it be thought that the importance of attention in acquisition is limited to descriptive research, Suppes (1966) has stated: "What I would like to emphasize . . . is the difficulty of expressing in systematic form the mechanisms of attention a rationally operating organism should use" (p. 64). Furthermore, Schneider & Shiffrin (1977) have raised the possibility that attention is not completely under conscious control. Thus the normative problem posed by Suppes takes on added difficulty.

Evaluation/Action

Imagine that you are faced with a set of alternatives and have at your disposal the following evaluation strategies: conjunctive, disjunctive, lexicographic, elimination by aspects, additive, additive difference, multiplicative, majority of confirming instances, or random. Furthermore, you could also use combinations of any number of the above. How do you choose? The wide range of strategies one can use in any given situation poses important questions about how one decides to choose (Beach & Mitchell 1978, Svenson 1979, Wallsten 1980). For example, what environmental cues "trigger" particular strategies? What affects the switching of rules? Are strategies organized in some way (e.g. hierarchically), and if so, according to what principles? Although there has been concern for meta-strategies, most notably in Abelson's "script" theory (1976), the need for general principles is acute. This can be illustrated in the following way: each evaluation strategy can be conceptualized as a multidimensional object containing such attributes as speed of execution, demands on memory (e.g. storage and retrieval), computational effort, chance of making errors, and the like. However, each strategy could also be considered as a metastrategy for evaluating itself and others. For example, an elimination by aspects metastrategy would work by eliminating strategies sequentially by distinctive attributes. However, the choice of a metastrategy would imply a still higher level choice process thereby leading to an infinite regress.

The above emphasizes the need for finding principles underlying choice processes at all levels. One appealing possibility suggested by Christensen-Szalanski (1978, 1980) is that of an over-riding cost/benefit analysis, which can induce suboptimal behavior in particular circumstances. However, this raises several issues: 1. The meaning of costs and benefits is necessarily dependent on task representation, and thus context. For example, a tax cut can be viewed as a gain or a reduced loss (Kahneman & Tversky 1979a; also see Thaler 1980 for an illuminating discussion of how this affects economic behavior). 2. Cost/benefit "explanations" can always be applied after the fact and thus become tautological (see earlier discussion). 3. The very notion of balancing costs and benefits indicates that conflict is inherent in judgment and choice. For instance, consider our earlier example of the options of insuring against a possible loss versus facing a no-win situation. The former can be conceptualized as an approach-avoidance conflict, the latter as an avoidance-avoidance conflict. In fact, Payne et al (1979) have demonstrated the importance of considering the perceived conflict in choice in the following way: Subjects first made choices between pairs of gambles. A constant amount of money was then added or subtracted from the payoffs such that, for example, an approach-avoidance gamble was changed to an approach-approach situation. With gambles altered in this manner, systematic preference reversals were found. Hence, while the structure of the gambles remained unchanged, the nature of the conflict and the choices did not.

The importance of conflict in choice has been emphasized by Coombs & Avrunin (1977), who considered the joint effects of task structure and the nature of pleasure and pain. They begin by noting the prevalence of single-peaked preference functions (i.e. nonmonotonic functions relating stimulus magnitude to preference) in a wide variety of situations. For example, consider the usual belief that more money is always preferred to less. While this violates single-peakedness, note that great wealth increases the risk of being kidnapped, of social responsibility to spend wisely, of lack of privacy, and so on. Thus, if one also considered these factors, it may be that there is some optimal level beyond which more money is not worth the increased trouble. Hence, there is an approach-avoidance conflict between the "utility for the good" and the "utility for the bad." The nature of this conflict eventuates in a single-peaked function, given the behavioral assumption that "Good things satiate and bad things escalate" (p. 224). Therefore, at some point, the bad becomes greater than the good and overall utility decreases. (In the single object case, it is not central that the bad escalate, only that it satiate at a slower rate than the good.)

The theory becomes more complex when objects are characterized on multiple dimensions. For example, consider a number of alternatives that vary on price and quality and suppose that some are both higher in price and lower in quality than others. Such dominated alternatives would seem to be eliminated quickly from further consideration. Indeed, the second principle in the theory is just this; dominated options are ignored. Hence, the alternatives that remain form a Pareto optimal set. While single-peakedness requires stronger conditions than this, from our perspective the important point is that the remaining set of alternatives highlights the basic conflict; that is, higher quality can only be obtained at a higher cost.

While the role of conflict in choice has received earlier attention (Miller 1959), its usefulness for elucidating psychological issues in decision making has not been fully exploited (however, see Janis & Mann 1977). We consider some of these issues by examining the role of conflict in, respectively, judgments of worth or value, deterministic predictions, and probabilistic judgments. Subsequently, conflict in taking action is discussed.

Conflict in Judgment

Consider the conflict between subgoals or attributes when one is judging overall value or worth. If dominated alternatives are eliminated, this will result in negative correlations between the attributes of objects in the nondominated set, thereby insuring that one has to give up something to obtain something else. The resolution of the conflict can take several forms, the most familiar being the use of compensatory strategies (usually of additive form, although multiplicative models have also been used, cf Anderson 1979). Psychologically, this approach can be thought of as conflict "confronting" since conflict is faced and resolution achieved through compromise. Of crucial concern in executing one's compromise strategy is the issue of judgmental inconsistency (Hammond & Summers 1972). While the origin of such inconsistency is not well understood (cf Brehmer 1978), it has often been considered as reflecting environmental uncertainty (Brehmer 1976). However, inconsistency may exist in the absence of environmental uncertainty. For example, price and quality can each be perfectly correlated with overall worth, yet one could argue that this highlights the conflict and thus contributes to inconsistency. Although the theoretical status of conflict and inconsistency needs further development, it should be noted that methods for aiding people to both recognize and reduce conflict through compensatory compromise have been developed, and several applications are particularly noteworthy (Hammond & Adelman 1976; Hammond, Mumpower & Smith 1977).

Alternatively, conflict in judging overall worth can be resolved by avoiding direct confrontation and compromise. Specifically, noncompensatory strategies allow evaluation to proceed without facing the difficulties (computational and emotional) of making trade-offs. As indicated above, the conditions in both task and person that control strategy selection remain relatively unchartered. However, in addition to the error/effort trade-offs thought to influence such decisions (Russo 1978), the existence of conflict per se and the need to take it into account makes this issue problematic.

The evaluation of information in making predictions from multiple cues raises further questions concerning conflict in judgment. In particular, when a criterion is available for comparison one can consider conflict and uncertainty to arise from several sources: uncertainty in the environment due to equivocal cue-criterion relations; inconsistency in applying one's information combination strategy; and uncertainty regarding the weighting of cues appropriate to their predictiveness. These three aspects and their effects on judgmental accuracy have been considered in great detail within the lens model framework (Hammond et al 1975). Moreover, the integration of uncertain and contradictory evidence, which is at the heart of prediction, can be seen as an attempt to establish "compensatory balance in the face of comparative chaos in the physical environment" (Brunswik 1943, p. 257). Brunswik called this process "vicarious functioning," and Einhorn et al (1979) have expanded on this to show that the compensatory process captured in linear models can also be seen in the fine detail of process-tracing models developed from verbal protocols. Furthermore, they argued that linear models represent cognitively complex and sophisticated strategies for information integration. However, the continued predictive superiority of bootstrapping, and even equal-weight linear models over clinical judgment (Dawes 1979), attests to the difficulty of establishing the correct compensatory balance (also see Armstrong 1978a, 1978b and Dawes 1977 for further work on the statistical vs clinical prediction controversy).

The basic issues involved in studying deterministic predictive judgment also underlie interest in probability judgment. That is, both are concerned with the making of inferences from uncertain and conflicting data/evidence. However, the different terminologies used in each approach reflect different historical antecedents; the psychology of inference on the one hand, and a formal theory of evidence (de Finetti, Savage) on the other. Formal approaches are concerned with developing general structures for inferential tasks independent of specific content. However, as noted previously, the psychology of inference is intimately concerned with both content and structure. This distinction is central for understanding the discrepancies between the outputs of formal models and intuitive processes found in recent research. To illustrate, whereas causality has no role in probability theory, it is important in human inference (Tversky & Kahneman 1980a). Moreover, the existence of causal schemas can lead to the reinforcement of a person's cognitive model after receiving contradictory evidence, rather than its revision. Schum (1980) has demonstrated the enormous statistical intricacies involved in the Bayesian modeling of inferences made from unreliable data. Indeed, one interpretation of this work is that a purely formal approach cannot handle the evaluation of evidence in any relatively complex task (such as a trial). The role of content, however, in simplifying these tasks has not been explored. For example, the use of a heuristic such as representativeness, which depends on content via similarity, takes on added importance in a normative sense (cf Cohen 1979). That is, in the face of great complexity, the use of heuristics and content may be necessary to induce structure.

The importance of heuristics in making inferences has long been recognized (Polya 1941, 1954), and current interest in them seems well justified. However, their present psychological status requires more specification (cf Olson 1976). For example, the use of the same heuristic can lead to opposite predictions (for an example concerning "availability," see Einhorn 1980). In addition, the ease with which heuristics can be brought to mind to explain phenomena can lead to their nonfalsifiability. For example, if representativeness accounts for the nonregressiveness of extreme predictions, can adjustment and anchoring explain predictions that are too regressive?

As in deterministic predictions, there has been much concern with the accuracy of probabilistic judgment. However, measurement of accuracy raises issues of defining criteria and the adequacy of samples. Moreover, in the Bayesian framework subjective probabilities represent statements of personal belief and therefore have no objective referent. Nonetheless, Bayesian researchers have borrowed relative frequency concepts to measure how well probabilistic judgment is calibrated, i.e. the degree to which probability judgments match empirical relative frequencies (Lichtenstein, Fischhoff & Phillips 1977) and what variables affect calibration (Lichtenstein & Fischhoff 1977). Calibration has therefore become the accuracy criterion for probabilistic judgment similar to the achievement index in the lens model. Moreover, the research findings in the two paradigms are also similar; that is, most people are poorly calibrated and even the effectiveness of training is limited for generalizing to other tasks (Lichtenstein & Fischhoff 1980).

Judgment = Choice?

Is judgment synonymous with choice? The normative model treats them as equivalent in that alternative x will be chosen over y if and only if $u(x) > u(y)$; i.e evaluation is necessary and sufficient for choice. However, from a psychological viewpoint, it may be more accurate to say that while judgment is generally an aid to choice, it is neither necessary nor sufficient for choice. That is, judgments serve to reduce the uncertainty and conflict in choice by processes of deliberative reasoning and evaluation of evidence. Moreoever, taking action engenders its own sources of conflict (see below) so that judgment may only take one so far; indeed, at the choice point, judgment can be ignored. The distinction between judgment and choice, which is blurred in the normative model, is exemplified in common language. For example, one can choose in spite of one's better judgment whereas the reverse makes little sense.

The distinction made above should not be construed to mean that judgment and choice are unrelated. In many situations they are inseparable. For example, consider diagnostic and prognostic judgments and the choice of treatment in clinical situations. It seems unthinkable that the choice of treatment could proceed without prior diagnosis and prognosis. More generally, this example illustrates several further points: 1. since judgment is deliberative, there must be sufficient time for its formation; 2. deliberation can itself be affected by the size of payoffs—e.g. people may invest in judgment to insure against accusations of irresponsibility from others and from oneself in the event of poor outcomes (cf Hogarth 1980b); 3. when alternatives are ordered on some continuum, a quantitative judgment may be necessary to aid choice, as when choosing a therapy that varies in intensity. These examples point to the importance of considering the conditions under which judgment and choice are similar or different, a crucial question that has barely been posed.

Conflict in Action

The conflict inherent in taking action, as distinct from conflict in judgment, occurs because action implies greater commitment (cf Beach & Mitchell 1978, Janis & Mann 1977). Such commitment induces conflict in several ways: 1. Whereas the existence of alternatives implies freedom to choose, the act of choice restricts that very freedom. Hence, keeping "one's options open" is in direct conflict with the need to take action. 2. Given a set of nondominated alternatives, Shepard (1964) has stated, " . . . at the moment when a decision is required the fact that each alternative has both advantages and disadvantages poses an impediment to the attainment of the most immediate sub-goal; namely, escape from the unpleasant state of conflict induced by the decision problem itself" (p. 277). Thus, conflict is inherent in choice as an attribute of the choice situation. 3. Unlike judgments, actions are intimately tied to notions of regret and responsibility. For example, consider the decision to have children faced by married career women. An important component in this choice may involve imagining the regret associated with both alternatives later in life. Or imagine the conflict involved in choosing a place to live and work where the responsibility to oneself and one's family do not coincide.

As with the resolution of conflict in judgment, conflict resolution in action can involve either avoidance or confrontation. One important form of avoidance is to not choose. Corbin (1980) has recognized the importance of the "no choice" option noting that it can take three forms: refusal, delay, and inattention. Moreover, she notes that attraction to the status quo has two advantages: it involves less uncertainty, and there may be "less responsibility associated with the effects of 'doing nothing' than with some conscious choice" (Corbin 1980). Toda (1980a) points out that people often make "meta-decisions" (e.g. to smoke), to avoid the conflict of having to continually decide on each of many future occasions. Thaler & Shiffrin (1980) further point out the importance of developing and enforcing self-imposed rules (rather than allowing oneself discretion) in avoiding conflicts in self-control problems.

Although choice involves considerable conflict, the mode of resolution typically considered in the literature is a confronting, compensatory strategy embodied in the expected utility model. This model is based on the following tenets: 1. The expected utility, E(U), of a gamble whose payoffs are x and y with probabilities p and q ($p + q = 1.0$), is given by E(U) = $p\, u(x) + q\, u(y)$. Note from the formulation that: (a) the rule says that the evaluation of a gamble is a weighted average of future pleasures and pains, where the weights are probabilities of attaining these outcomes; (b) the evaluation is solely a function of utility and probability, there being no utility or disutility for gambling per se; (c) the rule assumes that payoffs are independent of probabilities, i.e. wishful thinking (optimism) or pessimism are not admissible; (d) there is no inconsistency or error in executing the rule. Thus, although the rule specifically deals with the uncertainty of future events, it does not consider the evaluation process itself to be probabilistic (however, see Luce 1977). Moreover, choice is assumed to follow evaluation by picking the alternative with the highest E(U). 2. The theory assumes that the utility of payoffs is integrated into one's current asset position. Hence, final asset positions determine choice, not gains and/or losses. 3. Although not central to E(U), it is generally assumed that people are risk averse, i.e. utility is marginally decreasing with payoff size.

Whereas the E(U) model has been proposed as a prescriptive theory, much confusion exists in that it has been used extensively to both explain and predict behavior. However, while the descriptive adequacy of E(U) has been challenged repeatedly (Anderson & Shanteau 1970, Slovic et al 1977), Kahneman & Tversky's "prospect theory" (1979a) represents a major attempt at an alternative formulation. Since elements of this theory are discussed throughout this review, we only consider the proposed evaluation model. Prospect theory superficially resembles the E(U) model in that the components involve a value function, v; decision weights, $\pi(p)$; and a compensatory combining rule. However, the value function differs from utility in that: 1. It is defined on deviations from a reference point [where $v(0) = 0$] rather than being defined over total assets. Furthermore, the reference point may be either identical to or different from the asset position depending on a number of factors (somewhat akin to Helson's adaptation level). 2. It is concave for gains but convex for losses inducing "reflection effects" via risk aversion for gains and risk seeking for losses. For example, consider the choice between $3000 and a .50 chance at $6000 or 0. While many would prefer the sure gain of $3000 to the gamble (thus exhibiting risk aversion), if the sign of the payoff is changed, e.g. –$3000 or a .50 chance at –$6000 or 0, they might prefer the gamble to the sure loss. Note that the reflection effect contradicts the widely held belief that people generally abhor and seek to avoid uncertainty (Hogarth 1975, Langer 1977). 3. It is steeper for losses than gains, i.e. the pain of losing is greater than the pleasure of winning an equal amount.

Although decision weights are not subjective probabilities as such, they reflect the impact of uncertainty on the evaluation of prospects (gambles) and are transformations of probabilities. They have several interesting properties; for example, the sum of complementary decision weights does not sum to one (subcertainty), and small probabilities are overweighted. These properties, when combined with those of the value function in bilinear form induce overweighting of certainty (thus resolving Allais' paradox), violations of the substitution axiom, and avoidance of probabilistic insurance. Karmarkar (1978, 1979) was also able to explain many similar violations of the E(U) model by transforming probabilities into weights (using a single parameter) and then incorporating them in what he called a subjectively weighted utility model.

Although the above models are an important step in analyzing choice behavior, March (1978) has made a penetrating analysis of the deficiencies in conceptualizing tastes/preferences in such models. He points out that people are often unsure about their preferences (see also Fischhoff, Slovic & Lichtenstein 1980) and that uncertainty concerning future preferences complicates the modeling of choice. For example, how does one model the knowledge that one's tastes will change over time but in unpredictable ways? Moreover, although instability and ambiguity of preferences are treated as deficiencies to be corrected in normative approaches and as random error in descriptive models, March (1978) points out that ". . . goal ambiguity like limited rationality, is not necessarily a fault in human choice to be corrected but often a form of intelligence to be refined by the technology of choice rather than ignored by it" (p. 598).

The management of conflict induced by unstable preferences over time is also central to self-control (Thaler 1980). The recognition that one's tastes can change, and that such changes are undesirable, leads to precommitment strategies to prevent the harm that follows such changes. For example, consider saving money in Christmas clubs which pay no interest but which restrict the freedom to withdraw money before Christmas in order to protect one against one's self. Such behavior is difficult to explain without resort to a multiple-self model (Freud 1923, Sagan 1977, Toda 1980b). Conceptualizing decision conflict as the clash between multiple selves is a potentially rich area of investigation and could provide useful conceptual links between phenomena of individual and group behavior. For example, individual irrationality might be seen as similar to the various voting paradoxes found in group decision making (Plott 1976).

LEARNING/FEEDBACK

The beginning of this review indicated a questioning of the basic assumption upon which functional and adaptive arguments rest, namely, the ability to learn. We now consider this in light of our discussion of heuristic and other rule-based behavior. For example, how are rules tested and maintained (or not) in the face of experience? Under what conditions do we fail to learn about their quality? Are we aware of our own rules?

Hammond (1978a) and Brehmer (1980) have discussed a number of important issues bearing on the ability to learn from experience. The former paper considers six "modes of thought" for learning relations between variables which include: true experiments, quasi-experiments, aided judgment, and unaided intuitive judgment. Moreover, these modes vary on six factors, including the degree to which variables can be manipulated and controlled, feasiblity of use, and covertness of the cognitive activity involved in each. Hammond points out that the most powerful modes (involving experimentation) are least feasible and thus not likely to be implemented. Unfortunately, the least powerful modes are most feasible and hence most common. Thus, correct learning will be exceptionally difficult since it will be prey to a wide variety of judgmental biases (Campbell 1959). The seriousness of this is further emphasized by the seeming lack of awareness of the inadequacy of unaided judgment. Brehmer (1980) has further considered the difficulties inherent in learning from experience by contrasting such learning with laboratory studies (and formal learning through teaching). The former is far more difficult in that: 1. we don't necessarily know that there *is* something to be learned; 2. or if we do, it is not clear *what* is to be learned; and 3. there is often much ambiguity in judging *whether* we have learned (e.g. what, if anything, did the U.S. learn from the Viet Nam war?).

The general difficulties of learning from experience have also been demonstrated in specific areas. For example, Shweder (1977) has analyzed the ability of adults to learn environmental contingencies and points out that: 1. Whereas adults are capable of correlational reasoning, they frequently use cognitive strategies that can result in the genesis and perpetuation of myths, magic, and superstitious behavior. 2. Judgments of contingency are frequently based on likeness and similarity. For example, the treatment of ringworm by fowl excrement in primitive societies is based on the similarity of symptoms to "cure." 3. Contingencies provide the links in structuring experience by implying meaning through context. For example, "the trip was not delayed because the bottle shattered" can be understood when speaking of "launching a ship."

The learning of contingencies between actions and outcomes is obviously central for survival. Moreover, contiguity of actions and outcomes is an important cue for inferring causality (Michotte 1963) and thus for organizing events into "causal schemas" (Tversky & Kahneman 1980a). A particularly important type of contingent learning that has received little attention involves the learning and changing of tastes and preferences. For example, consider the unpleasant affect felt by a child after eating a particular vegetable, and the ensuing negative utility so learned; or imagine the changes in the same child's taste for members of the opposite sex as he or she grows older. Concern with the normative model, in which tastes are fixed, has obscured important psychological questions about the nature of tastes/preferences (cf March 1978).

The learning of action-outcome connections illustrates an obvious but essential point, that is, learning occurs through outcome feedback (cf Powers 1973). Moreover, since multiple actions must be taken over time, judgment is often required to predict which actions will lead to specified outcomes. Thus, feedback from outcomes is used to evaluate both judgments and actions. This assumes that the quality of decisions can be assessed by observing outcomes. Nonetheless, decision theorists have pointed out that outcomes also depend on factors that people cannot control; hence, decisions should be evaluated by the process of deciding. While there is much merit in this argument, the distinction between good/bad decisions and good/bad outcomes is strongly counterintuitive and may reflect several factors: (a) people have a lifetime of experience in learning from outcomes; (b) whereas process evaluation is complex, outcomes are visible, available, and often unambiguous; and (c) evaluation of process is conditional upon an appropriate representation of the task (see above). People cannot ignore outcomes in evaluating decisions.

The role of outcome feedback has been studied extensively within a number of probability learning paradigms. However, Estes (1976a,b) has emphasized the importance of considering what is learned in such tasks. In a series of experiments using simulated public opinion polls, he found that subjects coded outcomes as frequencies rather than probabilities. Indeed, as the history of probability indicates, the notion of probability was late in developing, a key difficulty being the specification of the sample space (such problems persist, see Bar-Hillel & Falk 1980). Einhorn & Hogarth (1978) note that the transformation of frequency into probability requires paying attention to nonoccurrences of the event of interest as well as the event itself. This added burden on attention and memory may thus favor the coding of outcomes as frequencies rather than probabilities. Moreover, the tendency to ignore nonoccurrences is intimately related to the lack of search for disconfirming evidence (Wason & Johnson-Laird 1972, Mynatt et al 1977, 1978). Furthermore, attempts to alter this tendency have been generally unsuccessful, although Tweney et al (1980) have reported some success. Whether or not this tendency can be modified, we note that it is not limited to scientific inference; e.g. how many people seek disconfirming evidence to test their political, religious, and other beliefs by reading newspapers and books opposed to their own views?

The implications of the above for learning from experience were explored by Einhorn & Hogarth (1978). They specifically considered how confidence in judgment is learned and maintained despite low (and or even no) judgmental validity. The tasks analyzed are those in which actions are based on an overall evaluative judgment and outcome feedback is subsequently used to assess judgmental accuracy. However, the structure of this task makes learning difficult in that: 1. When judgment is assumed to be valid, outcomes that follow action based on negative judgment, cannot typically be observed. For example, how is one to assess the performance of rejected job applicants? 2. Given limited feedback (which can also result from a lack of search for disconfirming evidence), various task variables such as base rates, selection ratios, and the self-fulfilling treatment effects of taking action per se can combine to produce reinforcement through positive outcome feedback. Thus, one can receive positive feedback in spite of, rather than because of, one's judgmental ability. A formal model of this process was developed in which outcomes were generated by combining various task variables with the validity of judgment. The results indicated a wide range of conditions where overconfidence in poor judgment can be learned and maintained.

Of great importance to the issue of learning from experience is the role of awareness of the task factors that can influence outcomes. This includes the probabilistic nature of the task itself (cf Brehmer 1980), as well as other task variables discussed in multiple-cue probability learning studies (Hammond et al 1975). Einhorn (1980) has discussed this issue within the concept of outcome-irrelevant-learning-structures (OILS). This refers to the fact that in certain tasks positive outcome feedback can be irrelevant or even harmful for correcting poor judgment when knowledge of task structure is missing or seriously in error. This concept is obviously similar to the notion of "superstitious" behavior (Skinner 1948, Staddon & Simmelhag 1971). However, the concept of OILS raises the issue of what is reinforced (Wickelgren 1979). For example, consider a consumer who uses a conjunctive rule when purchasing a wide range of products. It could be argued that positive outcomes following purchases reinforce the use of the rule, the specific behaviors, or both. This is a complex issue that would seem to depend on the extent to which people are aware of their own judgmental rules (Hayek 1962, Nisbett & Wilson 1977, Smith & Miller 1978). That is, to what extent are judgmental rules reinforced without awareness, and can inappropriate rules be *un*learned? The importance of this question is that it raises the issue of whether, or to what extent, procedures for correcting judgmental deficiencies can be developed.

It is important to stress that awareness of task structure does not necessarily lead to learning (see Castellan 1977). Furthermore, it is possible to choose not to learn. For example, consider a waiter in a busy restaurant who believes he can predict those customers most likely to leave generous tips, and the quality of his service reflects this prediction. If the quality of service has a treatment effect on the size of the tip, the outcomes confirm the prediction. With awareness of the task structure, the waiter could perform an experiment to disentangle the treatment effects of quality of service from his predictions; i.e. he could give poor service to some of those judged to leave good tips and good service to some of those judged to leave poor tips. Note that the waiter must be willing to risk the possible loss of income if his judgment is accurate, against learning that his judgment is poor. Therefore, there is conflict between short-run strategies for action that result in reasonably good outcomes vs long-run strategies for learning that have potential short-run costs. That is, would you be willing to risk the loss of income by doing a real experiment in order to learn? This dilemma is quite frequent, yet it is not clear that awareness of it would lead to the choice to learn.

METHODOLOGICAL CONCERNS

The substantive matters discussed in this review raise various issues regarding the methodology of decision research. We consider some of these by posing the following questions: 1. How can we know whether applications of decision aids improve the quality of decisions? 2. How prevalent are judgmental biases in the natural environment? 3. What methods are most likely to provide insight into decision processes?

The review by Slovic et al (1977) reported a growing number of applications of decision aids in a wide variety of fields and this growth continues (see e.g. Jungermann 1980 and references). However, it is appropriate to ask whether such applications work and how one can know this. While care in applying basic principles of experimental design involving consideration of threats to internal and external validity are recognized in some applications (cf Russo 1977), many more can be characterized as one-shot case studies where the experimental treatment is the decision aid or procedure. Although painful, it might be remembered that such a design is scientifically useless for assessing treatment efficacy. Moreover, the fact that clients are likely to seek aid from decision analysts (broadly defined) when things are not going well renders evaluation of pretest-posttest designs lacking control groups particularly susceptible to regression effects.

The difficulties in evaluating decision aids have been noted by Fischhoff (1980), who draws an analogy between decision analysis and psychotherapy. He writes that, "like psychotherapy, decision analysis is advocated because the theory is persuasive, because many clients say that it helps them, because many practitioners are extremely talented and because the alternative seems to be to sink back into an abyss (seat-of-the-pants decision making)." Indeed, we note that decision analysis might be called "rational therapy" if that term were not similar to one already in use (see Ellis 1977 on "rational-emotive therapy"). The importance of Fischhoff's analogy is twofold: it raises basic questions regarding the evaluation of decision aids, and it provides some necessary (if not sufficient) motivation to do something about it.

The issue concerning the prevalence of judgmental biases in the natural environment raises familiar questions of external validity (Brunswik 1956). Ebbesen & Konečni (1980) have studied several judgment tasks within laboratory and natural settings (e.g. setting of bail, driving a car) and have found major differences in results. In reviewing these and other studies they conclude:

> There is considerable evidence to suggest that the external validity of decision making research that relies on laboratory simulations of real-world decision problems is low. Seemingly insignificant features of the decision task and measures cause people to alter their decision strategies. The context in which the decision problem is presented, the salience of alternatives, the number of cues, the concreteness of the information, the order of presentation, the similarity of cue to alternative, the nature of the decomposition, the form of the measures, and so on, seem to affect the decisions that subjects make.

Given the above, the issue of external validity is not liable to be resolved without recourse to theory that attempts to answer how tasks vary between the laboratory and the natural environment and what kinds of effects can be expected from such differences. Howell & Burnett (1978) have taken a first step in this direction by proposing a cognitive taxonomy based on task variables and response demands that affect judgments of uncertainty. However, greater concern with how people's experience influences their judgment is needed. For example, Bar-Hillel (1979) has pointed out that although people ignore sample size in certain laboratory studies, they seem to judge sample accuracy by the ratio of sample size to population. Furthermore, she emphasizes that such a rule can be justified in the natural environment since one typically samples without replacement. For example, "When dining out, one samples, without replacement, some dishes from a menu and generalizes about the restaurant's quality. When shopping in a new store, one samples, without replacement, the price of several items and judges how expensive the store is" (p. 250).

Lacking theoretical guidance, one has no recourse but to judge the prevalence of judgmental biases. There are two extreme views. The most optimistic asserts that biases are limited to laboratory situations which are unrepresentative of the natural ecology. However, Slovic et al (1977) point out that in a rapidly changing world it is unclear what the relevant natural ecology will be. Thus, although the laboratory may be an unfamiliar environment, lack of ability to perform well in unfamiliar situations takes on added importance. The pessimistic viewpoint is that people suffer from "cognitive conceit" (Dawes 1976); i.e. our limited cognitive capacity is such that it prevents us from being aware of its limited nature. Even in a less pessimistic form, this view is highly disturbing and emphasizes the importance of further research on the factors which foster or impede awareness of the quality of one's judgmental rules.

Both of the above positions presuppose the internal validity of the experimental evidence concerning judgmental biases. However, Hammond (1978b) has criticized much of this research by pointing out the inadequacy of exclusive reliance on between-subjects-designs for studying cognition. For example, he notes that many experimental demonstrations of "illusory correlation" rest on the incorrect specification of the sampling unit; i.e. the sampling unit should be defined by the stimuli judged (within each person), not the people doing the judging. Thus, while group data may indicate large effects unless sufficient stimuli are sampled, no single individual can be shown to exhibit the bias (see also Hershey & Schoemaker 1980b). However, within-subjects designs can also be problematic in that effects due to memory when responding to stimuli across time (e.g. anchoring and carry-over) may distort the phenomenon being studied (Greenwald 1976). This is particularly important when considering possible biases in judgment made in unique circumstances. Hence, the temporal spacing between administration of stimuli is a crucial variable in within-subjects designs and its effects also need to be studied.

While there is controversy regarding the appropriateness of different experimental designs for studying decision processes, there is more agreement on the need for multimethod approaches (Payne et al 1978). Such approaches, which can use methods as diverse as statistical modeling and verbal protocols or eye movements, not only provide much needed evidence on convergent validity, but may also be necessary to discriminate between strategies that can result in identical outcomes (Einhorn et al 1979, Tversky & Sattath 1979). Furthermore, in addition to positive scientific effects, multimethod approaches may have the salutary effect of convincing researchers that "truth" can be shared.

CONCLUSION

Decision making is a province claimed by many disciplines, e.g. economics, statistics, management science, philosophy, and so on. What then should be the role of psychology? We believe this can be best illustrated by the economic concept of "comparative advantage." For example, how much typing should the only lawyer in a small town perform (Samuelson 1948)? Even if the lawyer is an excellent typist, it is to both his/her and the town's advantage to concentrate on law, provided that typing is not a rare skill. Similarly, we believe that psychologists can best contribute to decision research by elucidating the basic psychological processes underlying judgment and choice. Indeed, this review has tried to place behavioral decision theory within a broad psychological context, and in doing so we have emphasized the importance of attention, memory, cognitive representation, conflict, learning, and feedback. Moreover, the interdependence and coordination of these processes suggest important challenges for understanding complex decision making. In order to meet these, future research must adopt a broader perspective (cf Carroll 1980) by not only investigating the topics discussed here, but also those not usually treated in the decision literature (e.g. creativity, problem solving, concept formation, etc). Indeed, given the ubiquity and importance of judgment and choice, no less a perspective will do.

ACKNOWLEDGMENT

We wish to thank Jay Russo for his many incisive comments on an earlier draft of this review. We also wish to thank the following people for their suggestions and support: Maya Bar-Hillel, Nick Dopuch, Baruch Fischhoff, Paul Hirsch, Ed Joyce, John Payne, Paul Schoemaker, Rick Shweder, and Paul Slovic. The superb abilities of Charlesetta Nowels in handling the preparation of this chapter are gratefully acknowledged.

Literature Cited

Abelson, R. P. 1976. Script processing in attitude formation and decision making. In *Cognition and Social Behavior,* ed. J. S. Carroll, J. W. Payne, pp. 33–46. Hillsdale, NJ: Erlbaum. 290 pp.

Ajzen, I. 1977. Intuitive theories of events and the effects of base-rate information on prediction. *J. Pers. Soc. Psychol.* 35:303–14

Anderson, N. H. 1979. Algebraic rules in psychological measurement. *Am. Sci.* 67:555–63

Anderson, N. H., Shanteau, J. C. 1970. Information integration in risky decision making. *J. Exp. Psychol.* 84:441–51

Armstrong, J. S. 1978a. *Long Range Forecasting.* New York: Wiley. 612 pp.

Armstrong, J. S. 1978b. Forecasting with econometric methods: Folklore versus fact. *J. Bus.* 51:549–64

Aschenbrenner, K. M. 1978. Single-peaked risk preferences and their dependability on the gambles' presentation mode. *J. Exp. Psychol.–Hum. Percept. Perform.* 4:513–20

Bar-Hillel, M. 1979. The role of sample size

in sample evaluation. *Organ. Behav. Hum. Perform.* 24:245–57

Bar-Hillel, M. 1980. The base-rate fallacy in probability judgments. *Acta Psychol.* In press

Bar-Hillel, M., Falk, R. 1980. *Some teasers concerning conditional probabilities.* Presented at 18th Conf. Bayesian Inference and Decision Making, Univ. South. Calif.

Beach, L. R., Mitchell, T. R. 1978. A contingency model for the selection of decision strategies. *Acad. Manage. Rev.* 3:439–49

Bettman, J. R. 1979. *An Information Processing Theory of Consumer Choice.* Reading, Mass: Addison-Wesley. 402 pp.

Brehmer, B. 1976. Note on clinical judgment and the formal characteristics of clinical tasks. *Psychol. Bull.* 83:778–82

Brehmer, B. 1978. Response consistency in probabilistic inference tasks. *Organ. Behav. Hum. Perform.* 22:103–15

Brehmer, B. 1980. In one word: Not from experience. *Acta Psychol.* 45. In press

Broadbent D. E., Cooper, P. J., Broadbent, M. H. P. 1978. A comparison of hierarchical and matrix retrieval schemes in recall. *J. Exp. Psychol.–Hum. Learn. Mem.* 4:486–97

Brown, H. I. 1978. On being rational. *Am. Philos. Q.* 15:241–48

Brunswik, E. 1943. Organismic achievement and environmental probability. *Psychol. Rev.* 50:255–72

Brunswik, E. 1956. *Perception and the Representative Design of Experiments.* Berkeley: Univ. Calif. Press. 154 pp. 2nd ed.

Campbell, D. T. 1959. Systematic error on the part of human links in communication systems. *Inf. Control* 1:334–69

Campbell, D. T. 1960. Blind variation and selective retention in creative thought as in other knowledge processes. *Psychol. Rev.* 67:380–400

Carroll, J. S. 1980. Analyzing decision behavior: The magician's audience. In *Cognitive Processes in Choice and Decision Behavior,* ed. T. S. Wallsten. Hillsdale, NJ: Erlbaum. In press

Castellan, N. J. Jr. 1977. Decision making with multiple probabilistic cues. In *Cognitive Theory,* ed. N. J. Castellan, D. B. Pisoni, G. R. Potts, 2:117–47. Hillsdale, NJ: Erlbaum. 342 pp.

Christensen-Szalanski, J. J. J. 1978. Problem solving strategies: A selection mechanism, some implications, and some data. *Organ. Behav. Hum. Perform.* 22:307–23

Christensen-Szalanski, J. J. J. 1980. A further examination of the selection of problem-solving strategies: The effects of deadlines and analytic aptitudes. *Organ. Behav. Hum. Perform.* 25:107–22

Cohen, L. J. 1977. *The Probable and the Provable.* Oxford: Clarendon. 272 pp.

Cohen, L. J. 1979. On the psychology of prediction: Whose is the fallacy? *Cognition* 7:385–407

Coombs, C. H., Avrunin, G. S. 1977. Single-peaked functions and the theory of preference. *Psychol. Rev.* 84:216–30

Corbin, R. M. 1980. Decisions that might not get made. See Carroll 1980. In press

Dawes, R. M. 1976. Shallow psychology. See Abelson 1976, pp. 3–11

Dawes, R. M. 1977. Case-by-case versus rule-generated procedures for the allocation of scarce resources. In *Human Judgment and Decision Processes in Applied Settings,* ed. M. F. Kaplan, S. Schwartz, pp. 83–94. New York: Academic. 281 pp.

Dawes, R. M. 1979. The robust beauty of improper linear models in decision making. *Am. Psychol.* 34:571–82

Ebbesen, E. B., Konečni, V. J. 1980. On the external validity of decision-making research: What do we know about decisions in the real world? See Carroll 1980. In press

Edwards, W. 1975. Comment. *J. Am. Stat. Assoc.* 70:291–93

Edwards, W. 1977. Use of multiattribute utility measurement for social decision making. In *Conflicting Objectives in Decisions,* ed. D. E. Bell, R. L. Keeney, H. Raiffa, pp. 247–75. New York: Wiley. 442 pp.

Einhorn, H. J. 1980. Learning from experience and suboptimal rules in decision making. See Carroll 1980. In press

Einhorn, H. J., Hogarth, R. M. 1978. Confidence in judgment: Persistence of the illusion of validity. *Psychol. Rev.* 85:395–416

Einhorn, H. J., Kleinmuntz, D. N., Kleinmuntz, B. 1979. Linear regression *and* process-tracing models of judgment. *Psychol. Rev.* 86:465–85

Einhorn, H. J., McCoach, W. P. 1977. A simple multiattribute utility procedure for evaluation. *Behav. Sci.* 22:270–82

Ellis, A. 1977. The basic clinical theory of rational-emotive therapy. In *Handbook of Rational-Emotive Therapy,* ed. A. Ellis, R. Grieger, pp. 3–34. New York: Springer. 433 pp.

Elstein, A. S., Shulman, L. E., Sprafka, S. A. 1978. *Medical Problem Solving: An Analysis of Clinical Reasoning.* Cambridge, Mass: Harvard Univ. Press. 330 pp.

Estes, W. K. 1976a. The cognitive side of probability learning. *Psychol. Rev.* 83:37–64

Estes, W. K. 1976b. Some functions of memory in probability learning and choice behavior. In *The Psychology of Learning and Motivation: Advances in Research and Theory,* ed. G. H. Bower, 10:1–45. New York: Academic. 247 pp.

Estes, W. K. 1980. Is human memory obsolete? *Am. Sci.* 68:62–69

Fischhoff, B. 1980. Decision analysis: Clinical art or clinical science? In *Human Decision Making,* Vol. I, ed. L. Sjöberg, T. Tyszka, J. A. Wise. Bodafors, Sweden: Doxa. In press

Fischhoff, B., Slovic, P., Lichtenstein, S. 1977. Knowing with certainty: The appropriateness of extreme confidence. *J. Exp. Psychol.–Hum. Percept. Perform.* 3:552–64

Fischhoff, B., Slovic, P., Lichtenstein, S. 1978. Fault trees: Sensitivity of estimated failure probabilities to problem representation. *J. Exp. Psychol.–Hum. Percept. Perform.* 4:330–44

Fischhoff, B., Slovic, P., Lichtenstein, S. 1980. Knowing what you want: Measuring labile values. See Carroll 1980. In press

Freud, S. 1960. *The Ego and the Id.* New York: Norton. Orginally published 1923. 67 pp.

Garner, W. R. 1970. Good patterns have few alternatives. *Am. Sci.* 58:34–42

Goldsmith, R. W. 1980. Studies of a model for evaluating judicial evidence. *Acta Psychol.* 45. In press

Green, D. M., Swets, J. A. 1966. *Signal Detection Theory and Psychophysics.* New York: Wiley. 455 pp.

Greenwald, A. G. 1976. Within-subjects designs: To use or not to use? *Psychol. Bull.* 83:314–20

Grether, D. M., Plott, C. R. 1979. Economic theory of choice and the preference reversal phenomenon. *Am. Econ. Rev.* 69:623–38

Hammond, K. R. 1978a. Toward increasing competence of thought in public policy formation. In *Judgment and Decision in Public Policy Formation,* ed. K. R. Hammond, pp. 11–32. Denver: Westview. 175 pp.

Hammond, K. R. 1978b. *Psychology's Scientific Revolution: Is It in Danger?* Univ. Colo. Inst. Behav. Sci. Cent. Res. Judgment and Policy, Rep. No. 211

Hammond, K. R., Adelman, L. 1976. Science, values and human judgment. *Science* 194:389–96

Hammond, K. R., Mumpower, J. L., Smith, T. H. 1977. Linking environmental models with models of human judgment: A symmetrical decision aid. *IEEE Trans. Syst. Man Cybern.* (SMC)5:358–67

Hammond, K. R., Stewart, T. R., Brehmer, B., Steinmann, D. O. 1975. Social judgment theory. In *Human Judgment and Decision Processes,* ed. M. Kaplan, S. Schwartz, pp. 271–312. New York: Academic. 325 pp.

Hammond, K. R., Summers, D. A. 1972. Cognitive control. *Psychol. Rev.* 79:58–67

Harris, R. J., Monaco, G. E. 1978. Psychology of pragmatic implication: Information processing between the lines. *J. Exp. Psychol.* 107:1–22

Hayek, F. A. 1962. Rules, perception, and intelligibility. *Proc. Br. Acad.* 48:321–44

Hershey, J. C., Schoemaker, P. J. H. 1980a. Risk taking and problem context in the domain of losses: An expected utility analysis. *J. Risk Insur.* 46:111–32

Hershey, J. C., Schoemaker, P. J. H. 1980b. Prospect theory's reflection hypothesis: A critical examination. *Organ. Behav. Hum. Perform.* 25:395–418

Hogarth, R. M. 1975. Cognitive processes and the assessment of subjective probability distributions. *J. Am. Stat. Assoc.* 70:271–94

Hogarth, R. M. 1980a. *Beyond static biases: Functional and dysfunctional aspects of judgmental heuristics.* Univ. Chicago, Grad. Sch. Bus., Cent. Decis. Res.

Hogarth, R. M. 1980b. *Judgement and Choice: The Psychology of Decision.* Chichester, England: Wiley. In press

Howell, W. C., Burnett, S. A. 1978. Uncertainty measurement: A cognitive taxonomy. *Organ. Behav. Hum. Peform.* 22:45–68

Humphreys, P., McFadden, W. 1980. Experience with MAUD: Aiding decision structuring through reordering versus automating the composition rule. *Acta Psychol.* In press

Janis, I. L., Mann, L. 1977. *Decision Making: A Psychological Analysis of Conflict, Choice, and Commitment.* New York: Free Press. 488 pp.

Jungermann, H. 1980. 'Decisionectics': The art of helping people to make personal decisions. *Acta Psychol.* 45. In press

Kahneman, D., Tversky, A. 1973. On the psychology of prediction. *Psychol. Rev.* 80:251–73

Kahneman, D., Tversky, A. 1979a. Prospect theory: An analysis of decision under risk. *Econometrica* 47:263–91

Kahneman, D., Tversky, A. 1979b. On the interpretation of intuitive probability. A reply to Jonathan Cohen. *Cognition* 7:409–11

Karmarkar, U. S. 1978. Subjectively weighted utility: A descriptive extension of the expected utility model. *Organ. Behav. Hum. Perform.* 21:61–72

Karmarkar, U. S. 1979. Subjectively weighted utility and the Allais paradox. *Organ. Behav. Hum. Perform.* 24:67–72

Keeney, R. L., Raiffa, H. 1976. *Decisions with Multiple Objectives: Preferences and Value Tradeoffs.* New York: Wiley. 569 pp.

Killeen, P. R. 1978. Superstition: A matter of bias, not detectability. *Science* 199:88–90

Kubovy, M. 1977. Response availability and the apparent spontaneity of numerical choices. *J. Exp. Psychol.–Hum. Percept. Perform.* 3:359–64

Langer, E. J. 1977. The psychology of chance. *J. Theory Soc. Behav.* 7:185–207

Levine, M. E., Plott, C. R. 1977. Agenda influence and its implications. *Va. Law Rev.* 63:561–604

Lewontin, R. C. 1979. Sociobiology as an adaptationist program. *Behav. Sci.* 24:5–14

Libby, R., Fishburn, P. C. 1977. Behavioral models of risk-taking in business decisions. *J. Account. Res.* 15:272–92

Lichtenstein, S., Fischhoff, B. 1977. Do those who know more also know more about how much they know? *Organ. Behav. Hum. Perform.* 20:159–83

Lichtenstein, S., Fischhoff, B. 1980. Training for calibration. *Organ. Behav. Hum. Perform.* In press

Lichtenstein, S., Fischhoff, B., Phillips, L. D. 1977. Calibration of probabilities: The state of the art. In *Decision Making and Change in Human Affairs*, ed. H. Jungermann, G. de Zeeuw, pp. 275–324. Dordrecht-Holland: Riedel. 527 pp.

Lopes, L. L. 1980. *Doing the impossible: A note on induction and the experience of randomness.* Dep. Psychol., Univ. Wis., Madison

Luce, R. D. 1977. The choice axiom after twenty years. *J. Math. Psychol.* 15:215–33

Mackie, J. L. 1965. Causes and conditions. *Am. Philos. Q.* 2:245–64

March, J. G. 1978. Bounded rationality, ambiguity, and the engineering of choice. *Bell J. Econ. Manage. Sci.* 9:587–608

Michotte, A. 1963. *The Perception of Causality.* London: Methuen. 425 pp.

Miller, N. E. 1959. Liberalization of basic S-R concepts: Extensions to conflict behavior, motivation, and social learning. In *Psychology: A Study of a Science,* ed. S. Koch, 2:196–292. New York: McGraw Hill. 706 pp.

Mischel, W. 1979. On the interface of cognition and personality: Beyond the person-situation debate. *Am. Psychol.* 34:740–54

Mowrey, J. D., Doherty, M. E., Keeley, S. M. 1979. The influence of negation and task complexity on illusory correlation. *J. Abnorm. Psychol.* 88:334–37

Mynatt, C. R., Doherty, M. E., Tweney, R. D. 1977. Confirmation bias in a simulated research environment: An experimental study of scientific inference. *Q. J. Exp. Psychol.* 29:85–95

Mynatt, C. R., Doherty, M. E., Tweney, R. D. 1978. Consequences of confirmation and disconfirmation in a simulated research environment. *Q. J. Exp. Psychol.* 30:395–406

Newell, A., Simon, H. A. 1972. *Human Problem Solving.* Englewood Cliffs, NJ: Prentice-Hall. 920 pp.

Nisbett, R. E., Borgida, E., Crandall, R., Reed, H. 1976. Popular induction: Information is not necessarily informative. See Abelson 1976, pp. 113–33

Nisbett, R. E., Ross, L. 1980. *Human Inference: Strategies and Shortcomings of Social Judgment.* Englewood Cliffs, NJ: Prentice-Hall. 334 pp.

Nisbett, R. E., Wilson, T. D. 1977. Telling more than we can know: Verbal reports on mental processes. *Psychol. Rev.* 84:231–59

Olson, C. L. 1976. Some apparent violations of the representativeness heuristic in human judgment. *J. Exp. Psychol.–Hum. Percept. Perform.* 2:599–608

Payne, J. W. 1976. Task complexity and contingent processing in decision making: An information search and protocol analysis. *Organ. Behav. Hum. Perform.* 16:366–87

Payne, J. W., Braunstein, M. L., Carroll, J. S. 1978. Exploring predecisional behavior: An alternative approach to decision research. *Organ. Behav. Hum. Perform.* 22:17–44

Payne, J. W., Laughhunn, D. J., Crum, R. 1979. *Levels of aspiration and preference reversals in risky choice.* Grad. Sch. Bus., Duke Univ., Durham, NC

Pearson, K. 1897. On the scientific measure of variability. *Nat. Sci.* 11:115–18

Phelps, R. H., Shanteau, J. 1978. Livestock judges: How much information can an expert use? *Organ. Behav. Hum. Perform.* 21:209–19

Plott, C. R. 1976. Axiomatic social choice theory: An overview and interpretation. *Am. J. Polit. Sci.* 20:511–96

Plott, C. R., Levine, M. E. 1978. A model of agenda influence on committee decisions. *Am. Econ. Rev.* 68:146–60

Polya, G. 1941. Heuristic reasoning and the theory of probability. *Am. Math. Mon.* 48:450–65

Polya, G. 1954. *Patterns of Plausible Inference,* Vol. 2. Princeton, NJ: Princeton Univ. Press. 190 pp.

Powers, W. T. 1973. Feedback: Beyond behaviorism. *Science* 179:351–56

Rachlin, H., Burkhard, B. 1978. The temporal triangle: Response substitution in instrumental conditioning. *Psychol. Rev.* 85:22–47

Rothbart, M. 1980. Memory processes and social beliefs. In *Cognitive Processes in Stereotyping and Intergroup Perception,* ed. D. Hamilton. Hillsdale, NJ:Erlbaum. In press

Russell, B. 1948. *Human Knowledge: Its Scope and Limits.* New York: Simon & Schuster. 524 pp.

Russo, J. E. 1977. The value of unit price information. *J. Mark. Res.* 14:193–201

Russo, J. E. 1978. Comments on behavioral and economic approaches to studying market behavior. In *The Effect of Information on Consumer and Market Behavior,* ed. A. A. Mitchell, pp. 65–74. Chicago: Am. Mark. Assoc. 112 pp.

Sagan, C. 1977. *The Dragons of Eden.* New York: Random House. 263 pp.

Samuelson, P. A. 1948. *Economics, An Introductory Analysis.* New York: McGraw Hill. 622 pp.

Schmitt, N., Levine, R. L. 1977. Statistical and subjective weights: Some problems and proposals. *Organ. Behav. Hum. Perform.* 20:15–30

Schneider, W., Shiffrin, R. M. 1977. Controlled and automatic human information processing: I. Detection, search, and attention. *Psychol. Rev.* 84:1–66

Schum, D. A. 1979. A review of a case against Blaise Pascal and his heirs. *Univ. Mich. Law Rev.* 77:446–83

Schum, D. A. 1980. Current developments in research on cascaded inference processes. See Carroll 1980. In press

Seligman, M. E. P. 1970. On the generality of the laws of learning. *Psychol. Rev.* 77:406–18

Shafer, G. 1976. *A Mathematical Theory of Evidence.* Princeton, NJ: Princeton Univ. Press. 297 pp.

Shanteau, J., Nagy, G. F. 1979. Probability of acceptance in dating choice. *J. Pers. Soc. Psychol.* 37:522–33

Shepard, R. N. 1964. On subjectively optimum selections among multi-attribute alternatives. In *Human Judgments and Optimality,* ed. M. W. Shelly, G. L. Bryan, pp. 257–81. New York: Wiley. 436 pp.

Shugan, S. M. 1980. The cost of thinking. *J. Consum. Res.* 7: In press

Shweder, R. A. 1977. Likeness and likelihood in everyday thought: Magical thinking in judgments about personality. *Curr. Anthropol.* 18:637–58

Shweder, R. A. 1979. Rethinking culture and personality theory. Part II: A critical examination of two more classical postulates. *Ethos* 7:279–311

Simon, H. A. 1978. Rationality as process and as product of thought. *Am. Econ. Rev.* 68:1–16

Simon, H. A. 1979. Rational decision making in business organizations. *Am. Econ. Rev.* 69:493–513

Simon, H. A., Hayes, J. R. 1976. The understanding process: Problem isomorphs. *Cogn. Psychol.* 8:165–90

Skinner, B. F. 1948. "Superstition" in the pigeon. *J. Exp. Psychol.* 38:168–72

Skinner, B. F. 1966. The phylogeny and ontogeny of behavior. *Science* 153:1205–13

Slovic, P., Fischhoff, B. 1977. On the psychology of experimental surprises. *J. Exp. Psychol.–Hum. Percept. Perform.* 3:544–51

Slovic, P., Fischhoff, B., Lichtenstein, S. 1977. Behavioral decision theory. *Ann. Rev. Psychol.* 28:1–39

Slovic, P., Kunreuther, H., White, G. F. 1974. Decision processes, rationality and adjustment to natural hazards. In *Natural Hazards, Local, National, and Global,* ed. G. F. White, pp. 187–205. New York: Oxford Univ. Press. 288 pp.

Slovic, P., Lichtenstein, S. 1971. Comparison of Bayesian and regression approaches to the study of information processing in judgment. *Organ. Behav. Hum. Perform.* 6:649–744

Smith, E. R., Miller, F. D. 1978. Limits on perception of cognitive processes: A reply to Nisbett and Wilson. *Psychol. Rev.* 85:355–60

Staddon, J. E. R., Motheral, S. 1978. On matching and maximizing in operant choice experiments. *Psychol. Rev.* 85:436–44

Staddon, J. E. R., Simmelhag, V. L. 1971. The "superstitious" experiment: A re-examination of its implications for the principles of adaptive behavior. *Psychol. Rev.* 78:3–43

Suppes, P. 1966. Probabilistic inference and the concept of total evidence. In *Aspects of Inductive Logic,* ed. J. Hintikka, P. Suppes, pp. 49–65. Amsterdam: North-Holland. 320 pp.

Svenson, O. 1979. Process descriptions of decision making. *Organ. Behav. Hum. Perform.* 23:86–112

Thaler, R. 1980. Toward a positive theory of consumer choice. *J. Econ. Behav. Organ.* In press

Thaler, R., Shiffrin, H. M. 1980. *An economic theory of self-control.* Grad. Sch. Bus., Cornell Univ.

Thorngate, W. 1980. Efficient decision heuristics. *Behav. Sci.* 25:219–25

Toda, M. 1962. The design of a fungus-eater: A model of human behavior in an unsophisticated environment. *Behav. Sci.* 7:164–83

Toda, M. 1980a. What happens at the moment of decision? Meta decisions, emotions and volitions. In *Human Decision Making,* Vol. 2, ed. L. Sjöberg, T. Tyszka, J. A. Wise. Bodafors, Sweden: Doxa. In press

Toda, M. 1980b. Emotion and decision making. *Acta Psychol.* 45. In press

Tribe, L. H. 1973. Technology assessment and the fourth discontinuity: The limits of instrumental rationality. *South. Calif. Law Rev.* 46:617–60

Tversky, A. 1977. Features of similarity. *Psychol. Rev.* 84:327–52

Tversky, A., Kahneman, D. 1973. Availability: A heuristic for judging frequency and probability. *Cogn. Psychol.* 5:207–32

Tversky, A., Kahneman, D. 1980a. Causal schemas in judgments under uncertainty. In *Progress in Social Psychology,* ed. M. Fishbein, 1:49–72. Hillsdale, NJ:Erlbaum. 240 pp.

Tversky, A., Kahneman, D. 1980b. *The framing of decisions and the rationality of choice.* Dep. Psychol., Stanford Univ.

Tversky, A., Sattath, S. 1979. Preference trees. *Psychol. Rev.* 86:542–73

Tweney, R. D., Doherty, M. E., Worner, W. J., Pliske, D. B., Mynatt, C. R., Gross, K. A., Arkkelin, D. L. 1980. Strategies of rule discovery in an inference task. *Q. J. Exp. Psychol.* 32:109–23

Vlek, C., Stallen, P. 1980. Rational and personal aspects of risk. *Acta Psychol.* In press

Wallsten, T. S. 1980. Processes and models to describe choice and inference. See Carroll 1980. In press

Wason, P. C., Johnson-Laird, P. N. 1972. *Psychology of Reasoning. Structure and Content.* London: Batsford. 264 pp.

Wickelgren, W. A. 1979. Chunking and consolidation: A theoretical synthesis of semantic networks, configuring in conditioning, S-R versus cognitive learning, normal forgetting, the amnesic syndrome, and the hippocampal arousal system. *Psychol. Rev.* 86:44–60

Wilson, E. O. 1978. *On Human Nature.* Cambridge, Mass: Harvard Univ. Press. 260 pp.

Wimsatt, W. C. 1980. Reductionistic research strategies and their biases in the units of selection controversy. In *Scientific Discovery,* Vol. 2, ed. T. Nickles. Dordrecht, Holland: Reidel. In press

Yates, J. F., Zukowski, L. G. 1976. Characterization of ambiguity in decision making. *Behav. Sci.* 21:19–25

Ann. Rev. Psychol. 1981. 32:89–115

CATEGORIZATION OF ❖341
NATURAL OBJECTS

Carolyn B. Mervis

Department of Psychology, University of Illinois, Champaign, Illinois 61820

Eleanor Rosch

Department of Psychology, University of California, Berkeley, California 94720

CONTENTS

A category exists whenever two or more distinguishable objects or events are treated equivalently. This equivalent treatment may take any number of forms, such as labeling distinct objects or events with the same name, or performing the same action on different objects. Stimulus situations are unique, but organisms do not treat them uniquely; they respond on the basis of past learning and categorization. In this sense, categorization may be considered one of the most basic functions of living creatures.

The last chapters on concept formation in the *Annual Review of Psychology* (Neimark & Santa 1975, Erickson & Jones 1978) treated concepts (categories) as part of the study of problem solving within the general field of psychological learning theory. Meanwhile, an essentially new field of research and theory concerning concepts and categories has emerged, fed

89

0066-4308/81/0201-0089$01.00

by two major trends: 1. The study of naturalistic categories (for example, "red," "chair") particularly as influenced by input from anthropology, philosophy, and developmental psychology. 2. The modeling of natural concepts in the field called semantic memory, an area greatly influenced by artificial intelligence. This chapter is a selective review of these newer developments.

First a word about the historical context of this work. In the usual way of thinking, people distinguish objects (material things in space and time) from the attributes, properties, or qualities of those objects (such as color, shape, function, or parts). In the history of thought, there have been many ideas about the nature of objects, of qualities, of their relation to one another, and of their relation to the ideas which people have of them. British empiricist philosophy had one such view. In British empiricism (for example, Locke 1690), the ideas that people have of objects (concepts) consist of an intension (meaning) and an extension (the objects in the class). The intension is a specification of those qualities that a thing must have to be a member of the class; the extension consists of things that have those qualities. Thus, qualities (attributes) connect concepts to the world. Concept formation research within learning theory, by the very nature of its research paradigm, presupposes a British empiricist stand on these issues (e.g. see Fodor 1981).

In a classical concept formation experiment, stimuli are typically sets of items varying orthogonally on a limited number of sensory qualities such as color and form. Concepts are complexes composed of and decomposable into the defining qualities and logical relations between those qualities (e.g. red and square) which are their elements. Originally, the passive and gradual learning of common defining elements was emphasized in research (Hull 1920). However, since Bruner (Bruner et al 1956), research has concentrated on subjects' active hypothesis testing in the learning of relevant features and the logical rules combining them (see Bourne et al 1979).

The newer categorization research has raised for debate at least six empirical and theoretical issues, none of which had been considered debatable by the earlier approach. They are listed below, beginning with the somewhat more concrete structural problems.

1. Arbitrariness of categories. Are there any a priori reasons for dividing objects into categories, or is this division initially arbitrary?
2. Equivalence of category members. Are all category members equally representative of the category, as has often been assumed?
3. Determinacy of category membership and representation. Are categories specified by necessary and sufficient conditions for membership? Are boundaries of categories well defined?

4. The nature of abstraction. How much abstraction is required—that is, do we need only memory for individual exemplars to account for categorization? Or, at the other extreme, are higher-order abstractions of general knowledge, beyond the individual categories, necessary?
5. Decomposability of categories into elements. Does a reasonable explanation of objects consist in their decomposition into elementary qualities?
6. The nature of attributes. What are the characteristics of these "attributes" into which categories are to be decomposed?

Below we consider work bearing on each of these issues.

THE NONARBITRARY NATURE OF CATEGORIES

In the stimulus sets of the classical concept formation paradigm, attributes are combined arbitrarily to form items. This view has been echoed in related disciplines ". . . the physical and social environment of a young child is perceived as a continuum. It does not contain any intrinsically separate 'things' " (Leach 1964, p. 34).

However, the contention that the division of real world objects into categories is originally arbitrary would make sense only if the attributes in the world formed a total set (in Garner's 1974 sense); that is, if all combinations of attribute values were equally likely to occur. For example, consider some of the qualities ordinarily treated as attributes in classifying animals: "coat" (fur, feathers), "oral opening" (mouth, beak), and "primary mode of locomotion" (flying, on foot). If animals were created according to the total set model, then there would be eight different types:

(*a*) those with fur and mouths, which move about primarily on foot;
(*b*) those with fur and mouths, which move about primarily by flying;
(*c*) those with fur and beaks, which move about primarily on foot;
(*d*) those with fur and beaks, which move about primarily by flying;
(*e*) those with feathers and mouths, which move about primarily on foot;
(*f*) those with feathers and mouths, which move about primarily by flying;
(*g*) those with feathers and beaks, which move about primarily on foot;
(*h*) those with feathers and beaks, which move about primarily by flying.

It is not immediately obvious how to assign these (hypothetical) creatures to categories; any of several schemes (e.g. by coat type, by oral opening type) would be equally plausible, and none seems particularly reasonable a priori. Thus, given the total set type of organization, it makes sense that category assignments should be originally arbitrary. However, it hardly requires research to demonstrate that the perceived world of objects is *not* structured in this manner. Just two of the eight theoretically possible combinations of attribute values, types *a* and *h* (mammals and birds, respectively), comprise the great majority of existent species in the world that are possible based on this total set. This correlated attribute structure of the perceived world has been used as the basis for several programs of research concerning natural category structure.

Basic Level Categories

Any object may be categorized at each of several different hierarchical levels. When the levels are related to each other by class inclusion, they form a taxonomy. Anthropologists working with botanical and zoological categories (Berlin et al 1973, C. H. Brown et al 1976) have suggested, on the basis of linguistic and cultural evidence, that one of these levels is more fundamental than the others. Psychologists (Rosch et al 1976a) have argued that the most cognitively efficient, and therefore the most basic level of categorization, is that at which the information value of attribute clusters is maximized. This is the level at which categories maximize within-category similarity relative to between-category similarity.

Several studies have investigated hierarchical levels of abstraction. Rosch et al (1976a) performed attribute analyses for three-level hierarchies of common concrete objects (e.g. furniture, chair, easy chair) and found the level corresponding to the level of "chair" to possess the characteristics of basic level categories. Cantor et al (1980) have confirmed that a basic level also exists for psychiatric category hierarchies. Using somewhat different measures, Tversky (1977) and Hunn (1976) have found the same level to be basic.

If this level of categorization is really the most fundamental, one would expect categories at this level to have special properties. In fact, several such properties have been identified. Rosch et al (1976a) have shown that the basic level is the most general level at which (*a*) a person uses similar motor actions for interacting with category members, (*b*) category members have similar overall shapes, and (*c*) a mental image can reflect the entire category. Hunn (1975) has argued that the basic level is the only level at which category membership can be determined by an overall Gestalt perception without an attribute analysis. Rosch et al (1976a) have shown that objects are recognized as members of basic level categories more rapidly than as members of categories at other levels. In language, the basic level is the one at which adults spontaneously name objects, whether for adults (Rosch et al 1976a) or for young children (R. Brown 1958, 1976; Anglin 1977). Cruse (1977) has argued that labels for basic level categories are unmarked linguistically—that is, words at this level are used in normal everyday conversation. In American Sign Language basic level categories are generally denoted by single signs, while superordinate and subordinate categories are almost always denoted by multiple sign sequences (Newport & Bellugi 1978).

One of the most pervasive research findings is that basic level categories are acquired before categories at other hierarchical levels. Rosch et al (1976a) and Daehler et al (1979) found that young children can solve simple sorting problems at the basic level before solving them at the superordinate level. Mervis & Crisafi (1981), using artificial category hierarchies, found that 2½-year-olds were able to sort basic level triads correctly, but could not sort either superordinate or subordinate level triads. With regard to language acquisition, Stross (1973) and Dougherty (1978) have both shown that the first botanical labels that children learn are names for basic level categories. Other studies have yielded similar results for selected nonbotanical taxonomies (Rosch et al 1976a, Anglin 1977). Taking a historical perspective, Berlin (1972) has shown that languages first encode basic level biological categories, and only later (if at all) encode categories superordinate or subordinate to the basic level ones.

All of these studies have concerned naturally occurring hierarchies, and it could be argued that the basic level effects are due to linguistic factors (e.g. shorter names, greater frequency, learned first) rather than to perceptual-cognitive structural factors. Two recent studies, using artificial categories whose hierarchical structure mirrored the naturally occurring structure, have suggested that the perceptual-cognitive explanation is more appropriate.

Murphy & E. E. Smith (1981) taught subjects to label stimuli at each of three levels. Order of learning was counterbalanced, and word frequency and length were controlled. After learning the labels, subjects participated in a verification task. Response times to verify labels for basic level categories were significantly shorter than response times to verify labels for subordinate or superordinate level categories. Mervis & Crisafi (1981) controlled for potential linguistic confounds by never naming the stimuli for their subjects. One group of subjects was asked to sort the stimuli however it made sense to them. A second group of subjects was told that a particular stimulus had been given a certain name, and they should decide which of the other stimuli should also be given that name. For both tasks, virtually all of the responses corresponded to the predicted basic level categories.

The principles underlying the determination of which hierarchical level is basic are expected to be universal. However, for a given domain, the particular level which is found to be basic may not be universal. This level can vary as a function of both the cultural significance of the domain and the level of expertise of the individual (Rosch et al 1976a, Dougherty 1978). These two factors are important because they influence which attributes of an object are noticed (perhaps constructed) by an observer; psychological measures of basicness rely on analyses of perceived attribute structures. Dougherty and Rosch et al both provide examples of the relativity of the basic level.

Basic Level Categorization as a Basic Process

Flavell & Wellman (1976, Flavell 1977) have proposed that memory phenomena be divided into four types: basic processes, knowledge (semantic memory), strategies, and metamemory. Might basic level categorization be included as a basic process?

Flavell & Wellman have described two important characteristics of basic processes. First, a person is not conscious of the actual working of the process. Second, the process undergoes no significant development (other than that due to maturation) with age; development is complete by the end of the sensorimotor period (age 1½ to 2 years). They provide three examples of basic processes: 1. the processes by which an object is recognized; 2. the processes of representation underlying recall of absent objects or events; 3. the process of cueing or associating. They also point out that the four types of memory phenomena are not mutually exclusive.

Why should basic level categorization be included as a basic process? Without any categorization an organism could not interact profitably with the infinitely distinguishable objects and events it experiences. Therefore, even infants should be able to categorize. Nevertheless, until recently there was little motivation to consider infant categorization abilities, since it was widely believed (see Gelman 1978) that children could not categorize until they reached the stage of concrete operations (when they are 5 to 7 years old). However, once simple categorization abilities were demonstrated in preschool children, research with infants began in earnest. Most of these studies have taken advantage of an infant's predictable preference for novel stimuli over familiar ones (L. B. Cohen & Gelber 1975). The studies use the same general procedure. First, the infant is given several familiarization trials with different category members. Then he is shown either a novel member of the same category, a novel member of a different category, or both at once. If the infant has formed a category, then he should spend significantly more time looking at a stimulus from a novel category than from the familiar one. Using this format, G. Ross (1977) demonstrated that 12-month-old infants were able to form a variety of basic level categories. L. B. Cohen demonstrated that much younger infants (30-week-olds) were able to form the categories "female face" (L. B. Cohen & Strauss 1979) and "stuffed animal" (L. B. Cohen & Caputo 1978). Strauss (1979), using schematic faces, demonstrated that 10-month-olds were able to categorize an average prototype after familiarization with other category members.

Three additional studies have used different techniques. Husaim & L. B. Cohen (1980), using a discrete trial discrimination learning paradigm, found that ten-month-olds could form two noncriterially defined categories (of schematic animals). The infants attended to more than one attribute, and the same models that predict adult categorization behavior were able to predict infant behavior. Ricciuti (1965) examined the behavior of 12-, 18-, and 24-month-olds who were given two types of toys to play with, and found considerable evidence of categorization abilities in even the 12-month-olds. K. Nelson (1973), using 20-month-olds, has replicated this result for other basic level categories. In summary, then, there is now substantial evidence that basic level categorization should be considered a basic process.

NONEQUIVALENCE OF CATEGORY MEMBERS

In a classical concept formation experiment, any one stimulus which fits the definition of the concept (possesses the relevant attributes in the correct combination) is as good an example of the concept as any other. More generally, if categories are seen as determinately established by necessary and sufficient criteria for membership (and if, in addition, the role of rationality is to abstract out what is essential to a situation while ignoring what is inessential; see e.g. James 1890a,b), then any member of a category should be cognitively equivalent qua the category to any other member. However, there is now a growing amount of empirical evidence that all members are not equally representative of their category.

The first domain for which nonequivalence was proposed was that of color. Berlin & Kay (1969) showed that many apparent contradictions reported in the anthropological literature on color naming could be clarified by distinguishing focal from nonfocal colors. Focal colors are points in the color space which speakers of diverse languages agree represent the best examples of the 11 basic color categories. While the number of color terms in a language and the boundaries of color categories vary widely across cultures, colors most representative of basic color categories appear to be universal. These results actually provide cross-linguistic confirmation of well-established effects in the physiological literature on color naming functions (see Cornsweet 1970). The best exemplars of the four primary colors correspond to the physiologically determined unique hue points for these colors (De Valois & Jacobs 1968, Kay & McDaniel 1978). Standard psychological variables such as memory accuracy and ease of learning have been shown to co-vary with representativeness of the color in question (Heider 1972, Rosch 1974). Findings similar to those with color categories have also been demonstrated for geometric shape categories (Rosch 1973a,b). For recent reviews of research on color categories see R. Brown (1976) and Witkowski & C. H. Brown (1978).

Gradients of representativeness have been found not only for color and geometric shape categories but also for many common semantic categories (e.g. "dog," "furniture"). The great majority of psychological studies of representativeness have focused on such categories. Representativeness is here defined operationally by means of subjects' ratings of how good an example an item is of its category (Rosch 1975b). Consistency in such ratings has been obtained. Individual subjects agree that some exemplars of a category are more representative than others, and different subjects consistently choose the same examples as most representative of the category. The overall scale that is obtained is robust under differing conditions of instruction and stimulus presentation (Rips et al 1973; Rosch 1973b, 1975a,b; Rosch & Mervis 1975; E. E. Smith et al 1974; Whitfield & Slatter 1979). Two recent studies have found similar gradients for other types of categories: locatives (Erreich & Valian 1979) and psychiatric classifications (Cantor et al 1980). Gradients of representativeness for various linguistic categories have also been widely reported (see e.g. J. Ross 1972; Fillmore 1975, 1977; Lakoff 1977; Bowerman 1978; Bates & MacWinney 1980; deVilliers 1980; Maratsos & Chalkley 1980; Coleman & Kay 1981).

Representativeness of items within a category has been shown to affect virtually all of the major dependent variables used as measures in psychological research. In this section we consider speed of processing, free production of exemplars, natural language use of category terms, asymmetries in similarity relationships between category exemplars, and learning and development.

Speed of processing (reaction time) has been extensively investigated in category verification tasks. Subjects are usually asked to verify statements of the form "An [exemplar] is a [category name]" as rapidly as possible. Response times are shorter for verification of the category membership of representative exemplars than nonrepresentative exemplars; these effects are robust and appear in a variety of experimental paradigms (see reviews in E. E. Smith et al 1974, E. E. Smith 1978, Hampton 1979, Danks & Glucksberg 1980, Kintsch 1980). Rosch et al (1976b) have also demonstrated this effect for three types of artificial categories, where representativeness was defined by family resemblance, by mean values of attributes, or by degree of distortion from the prototype (random dot pattern). These differences in response times are amplified when a prime (prior mention of the category name) is provided. Priming reduces response times to verify the category membership of representative exemplars but increases response times to verify the membership of nonrepresentative exemplars. This result has been obtained for colors (Rosch 1975c), superordinate semantic categories (Rosch 1975b, MacKenzie & Palermo 1981), and for the artificial categories just described (Rosch et al 1976b).

Order and probability of exemplar production have been investigated primarily for superordinate semantic categories. Battig & Montague (1969) asked subjects to list exemplars of each of 56 superordinate categories. Frequency of mention of an exemplar was found to be significantly correlated with degree of representativeness (Mervis et al 1976). Posnansky (1973) replicated this result using elementary school children. Both Rosch et al (1976b) and Erreich & Valian (1979) found that when subjects were asked to sketch an exemplar of a particular category, they were most likely to depict the most representative exemplar.

Natural languages possess mechanisms for coding gradients of representativeness. For example, languages generally include qualifying terms ("hedges") such as "true" or "technically." Lakoff (1973) has shown that a given hedge is applicable to only a subset of category exemplars; this subset is determined by degree of representativeness. For instance, it is acceptable to say "A sparrow is a true bird," but not "A penguin is a true bird." Correspondingly, the sentence "A penguin is technically a bird" is acceptable, but "A sparrow is technically a bird" is not. Similarly, Rosch (1975a) has shown that when subjects are given sentence frames such as "[x] is virtually [y]," they reliably place the more representative member of a pair in the referent (y) slot. In addition, representativeness ratings for members of superordinate categories predict the extent to which the member term is substitutable for the superordinate word in sentences (Rosch 1977). Finally, Newport & Bellugi (1978) have shown that in American Sign Language, when superordinate terms are denoted by a short list of exemplars only the more representative exemplars may be used.

Asymmetry in similarity ratings between members that vary in representativeness is another way in which members of a category fail to be equivalent. Tversky & Gati (1978) and Rosch (1975a) have shown that less representative exemplars are often considered more similar to more representative exemplars than vice versa. For example, subjects felt that Mexico was more similar to the United States than the United States was to Mexico. This phenomenon helps to explain the asymmetries which Whitten et al (1979) found in similarity ratings of pairs of "synonyms." It also helps to explain Keller & Kellas's (1978) finding that release from proactive inhibition is significantly greater if the change is from typical to atypical members of a category than if the change is from atypical to typical members. In addition, asymmetry in similarity ratings has implications for inductive reasoning. Rips (1975) found that new information about a category member was generalized asymmetrically; for example, when told that the robins on an island had a disease, subjects were more likely to decide that ducks would catch it than that robins would catch a disease which the ducks had.

In the *learning and development* of categories, representativeness appears to be a major variable. Representativeness gradients have two basic implications for category acquisition (Mervis & Pani 1980). The first implication is that category membership is established (for the set of exemplars to which a person has been exposed) first for the most representative exemplars and last for the least representative exemplars. One of the most robust findings from research using statistically generated categories is that correct classification of novel exemplars is strongly negatively correlated with degree of distortion of the exemplar from the prototype pattern. This result has been obtained using both random dot pattern categories (e.g. Posner & Keele 1968, Homa et al 1973, Homa & Vosburgh 1976) and random polygon categories (e.g. Aiken & Williams 1973, Williams et al 1977). Similarly, when subjects are asked to indicate which of a series of categorically related stimuli have been seen previously, percentage of false recognition responses and degree of confidence that the (novel) pattern has been seen previously are both negatively correlated with degree of distortion from the prototype (e.g. Franks & Bransford 1971; Neumann 1974, 1977; Posnansky & Neumann 1976). When subjects are given explicit feedback concerning the correctness of their classifications, categories consisting of low distortions are learned significantly faster than categories consisting of either high distortions or both low and high distortions (e.g. Posner et al 1967, Homa & Vosburgh 1976). For categories including both low and high distortions, the low distortions are learned first (Mirman 1978). Similarly, Rosch (1973a,b) found that focal (representative) colors and forms were learned more rapidly than nonfocal colors and forms by persons whose language did not contain explicit labels for these categories. In a study of 5-year-olds learning artificial categories modeled after natural categories, Mervis & Pani (1980) found that more representative exemplars were learned first; in this study, no feedback was provided during learning.

The developmental research relevant to this issue has concentrated primarily on the acquisition of superordinate semantic categories. K. E. Nelson & K. Nelson (1978) have argued that as children learn about a category, their criteria for assigning an object to that category shift back and forth between generous and conservative, until finally the adult criteria (which themselves vary according to cognitive style; see Kogan 1971) are used. This pendulum theory predicts that category membership of representative exemplars should be firmly established at a young age, while membership of less representative exemplars will vascillate. Although no single study has considered a wide enough age range to test the theory conclusively, it appears, based on the combined results from several sorting studies using children of different ages (Saltz et al 1972, Neimark 1974, Anglin 1977), that the theory may be correct. Two studies of children's production of category exemplars (K. Nelson 1974, Rosner & Hayes 1977) provided additional support. Research with basic color categories (Mervis et al 1975) and with basic object categories (Saltz et al 1977) support the finding of the superordinate sorting studies.

The second major implication of representativeness is that categories are learned more easily and more accurately if initial exposure to the category is through only representative exemplars. Two studies have shown that initial exposure to only representative exemplars is more effective than initial exposure to only nonrepresentative exemplars; the stimuli were dot patterns (Mirman 1978) and multimodal artificial stimuli with natural category structure (Mervis & Pani 1980).

Results are somewhat more equivocal when initial exposure to both representative and nonrepresentative examples is compared with initial exposure to only representative examples. Two studies (Homa & Vosburgh 1976, Goldman & Homa 1977) found that for categories with certain characteristics initial exposure to the full range of category membership was not worse than exposure to good examples only. However, three other studies found training on good examples superior to training on a range of examples (Mervis & Pani 1980, Hupp & Mervis 1981, Mervis & Mirman 1981).

What might make some objects more representative of their category than others? It may be useful to consider once more the previous section in which we discussed clusters of correlated attributes. These correlations are not perfect—for example, in our hypothetical set of creatures (p. 91), besides the two main correlated clusters (birds and mammals), there are many types of flightless birds, a few flying mammals (bats), and the duck-billed platypus. It has been argued that the logic of attribute structures associated with gradients of representativeness within categories is parallel to the logic (described in the previous section) that predicts which level in a taxonomy will be the basic level (Rosch 1978, Mervis 1980).

Rosch & Mervis (1975) have shown that category members differ in the extent to which they share attributes with other category members. They call this variable family resemblance (after Wittgenstein 1953). Items which have the highest family resemblance scores are those with the most shared attributes. Rosch & Mervis (1975) have also shown that the exemplars with the highest family resemblance scores are those which share few (if any) attributes with members of related categories. In other words, given the nature of real-world attribute clusters, the items that have most attributes in common with other members of their own category also have fewest attributes in common with related contrast categories. Both family resemblance and dissimilarity from contrast categories are highly correlated with ratings of representativeness for superordinate and basic level natural categories and for artificial categories (Rosch & Mervis 1975). The within-category correlations have been confirmed using different measures (Neumann 1977, Tversky 1977, Tversky & Gati 1978). Studies with various artificial categories have shown that when within-category similarity and between-category dissimilarity are dissociated, either factor is sufficient to produce a representativeness gradient (Rosch et al 1976b, E. E. Smith & Balzano 1977). (Note that the family resemblance idea does not indicate that category members must have no attributes common to all members—

in fact, insofar as category members are the same higher level "sort of thing" they will share such higher level, and therefore necessary, attributes as "animate" or "solid object"; see Keil 1979, E. E. Smith & Medin 1981.)

We can now see how a family resemblance structure of categories might make sense of the findings that the most representative members of categories are established first as category members and are the most useful basis for learning categories. Because basic level categories maximize within-category similarity relative to between-category similarity, it is reasonable that they were found to be learned first—before categories subordinate and superordinate to them. Correspondingly, the most representative exemplars of a category have maximal within-category and minimal between-category similarity. Therefore, category membership is most obvious for the highly representative exemplars, and generalization based on similarity to these will be the most accurate.

The above findings on the nonequivalence of natural category members have been mirrored in research on social phenomena. Relying on the correlated attribute cluster as a basis for assigning category membership serves to make the world seem more orderly than it really is (Rosch 1978, Mervis 1980). Lippmann (1922) has argued that social stereotypes serve exactly this purpose. Kahneman & Tversky (1973) have shown that when subjects are asked to predict a person's occupation based on a description of the person, the person is assigned to the occupation for which the best match between personal description and occupational stereotype is obtained. C. E. Cohen (1976) found that occupational and role stereotypes are used as a basis for inferring a person's characteristics. Cantor & Mischel (1979) showed the usefulness of a family resemblance stereotype notion for determining attribution of personality trait categories such as "introvert" and "extrovert." McCauley & Stitt (1978) have presented a Bayesian method for determining which attributes should be included in a stereotype; their method is reminiscent of family resemblances. In fact, McCauley & Stitt have argued that their method is also applicable to concrete object representations, since stereotypes of groups and representations of object categories serve the same function. For reviews of research concerning stereotypes, see Brigham (1971) and McCauley et al (1980).

INDETERMINACY OF CATEGORY MEMBERSHIP AND REPRESENTATION

That category members vary in degree of representativeness is essentially a set of empirical findings. What does it imply about the nature of categories? There are two separable issues: the relatively empirical question of whether the boundaries of categories are determinate (well defined) or fuzzy, and the theoretical issue of how well defined one wants to consider the category "representation" itself.

Two experimental approaches have been used to demonstrate that category boundaries are not well defined. The first involves demonstrations that there are between-subject disagreements concerning which categories certain (poor) exemplars belong to. Berlin & Kay (1969) found substantial disagreement among subjects concerning the location of color category boundaries, even when native language was controlled. This result has been replicated by Labov (1973), using schematic drawings of cups, by McCloskey & Glucksberg (1978), using superordinate semantic categories, by Cantor et al (1980), using subordinate psychiatric categories, and by Kempton (1978) using drinking vessels in a cross-cultural setting.

The demonstration of between-subject disagreement is suggestive, but this disagreement could possibly be an artifact stemming from the combining of data from different subjects, each of whose categories had a different well-defined cutoff. Therefore, a demonstration of within-subject disagreement is also important. Berlin & Kay (1969) noted substantial within-subject disagreement across testing sessions concerning color category boundaries. McCloskey & Glucksberg (1978) found the same result for multiple within-subject judgments concerning superordinate category assignments of potential poor exemplars. They also demonstrated that their results could not be explained simply by reference to polysemous superordinate category labels.

Another empirical consideration points to the reasonableness of nondefinite boundaries of categories. Poorer members of categories are likely to contain attributes from the correlated attribute clusters of other categories (see e.g. Rosch & Mervis 1975). Sokal (1974) has provided an elegant demonstration of this point for biological categories (see also Simpson 1961, Sneath & Sokal 1973).

The controversy over the determinacy of categories, however, extends beyond empirical evidence. In present cognitive psychology it has become almost obligatory to explain and model phenomena in terms of cognitive representations and processes which act on them. If one believes that categories consist of determinate necessary and sufficient criteria, one can develop a model which attempts to explain representativeness and indeterminate boundary effects by means of processes operating on a determinate representation. For example, Wanner (1979) reported the finding that mathematical concepts such as "odd number" show the same representativeness effects described in the Nonequivalence section. He argued that since mathematical concepts are the archetype of concepts "true by definition alone," one may interpret these results to imply that the "real meaning" of a concept consists of a criterial definition; representativeness effects would be produced by separate processing heuristics. [It is interesting to note in this context that a major contemporary school of mathematics (the constructivist school) does not consider mathematical concepts to be either true by definition alone or necessarily criterial; see Calder 1979.] Glass & Holyoak (1975) have developed a model in which concepts are represented by semantic markers (Katz 1972) which contain the essential features of the concept. These markers are nodes in semantic memory connected by pathways; representativeness effects are modeled by means of variation in length and directness of these pathways. Another strategy is used in the fuzzy set (Zadeh 1965) model of Caramazza (1979). In this model noun concepts are represented by determinate specification of defining attributes, but the attributes (which are presumed not to be concepts) are treated as fuzzy. E. E. Smith & Medin (1981) provide a general characterization of such models. They argue that such models cannot account for a variety of empirical findings.

Other models incorporate greater indeterminacy into the representation itself. In the two-stage model of E. E. Smith et al (1974) and the single-stage models of McClosky & Glucksberg (1979) and Hampton (1979), concepts are represented by sets of weighted non-necessary features. Processing decisions about category membership are made on a probabilistic basis. Collins & Loftus's (1975) model also includes a probabilistic decision process, but it is allowed to operate on more varied types of structural information than simply attributes.

The issue of determinacy has been approached in a slightly different fashion in research on context effects. Both Collins & Loftus (1975) and McClosky & Glucksberg (1979) invoke Bayesian inference procedures specifically to deal with context; however, all of the probabilistic models have an unchanging (and, in that sense, determinate) representation of some sort. Context has been employed to criticize just this sort of assumption. In the psychological literature, changes in meaning, comprehension, or memory of particular terms as a function of differing contexts have been used to question the adequacy of semantic memory models (see e.g. Barclay et al 1974, R. C. Anderson & Ortony 1975, R. C. Anderson et al 1976, Potter & Faulconer 1979). These studies tend to be primarily critical rather than to offer formulations of their own. In addition, context has been used as the basis of more far reaching criticisms of determinate views; for authors in the hermeneutic tradition, context becomes the basis of arguments against representations and other noninteractive accounts of meaning (see for example the papers in Rabinow & Sullivan 1979).

THE NATURE OF ABSTRACTION

In the classic concept formation paradigm, a concept is an abstraction consisting of a set of defining features and the relationship between them.

Contemporary views have argued both that concepts may be conceived as less abstract or must be conceived as more abstract than this formulation. There are, of course, also accounts that posit intermediate levels of abstraction.

On the one hand, it has been asserted that we need only memory for individual exemplars in order to account for categorization. In a sense, from the time of Pavlov, "strength theory" models of stimulus generalization have been of this type (see Riley & Lamb 1979). In human categorization research, Reber (1976) and Brooks (1978) have demonstrated cases where learning of instances can occur without the learning of rules or abstractions; in fact, where telling a subject the rule may retard performance. If only specific exemplars are stored in memory, categorization of novel items could occur by matching the new instance to the most similar item in memory. Formal exemplar ("nearest neighbor") models which incorporate this type of processing have been tested against various abstraction models; in all cases, exemplar models were inferior to the abstraction models (Reed 1972, Hyman & Frost 1975, Hayes-Roth & Hayes-Roth 1977). In addition, in order to account for hierarchical relationships, exemplar models must require that the names of all possible superordinate categories be stored with each exemplar. Meyer (1970) has discussed problems with this approach.

Given the state of present cognitive modeling, exemplar models are also theoretically anomalous for two reasons. First, if beyond learning items cognitive representations of them are required, instances must either be coded by first order isomorphism (the representation of "green square" as green and square; Shepard & Chipman 1970, Palmer 1978) or undergo some kind of abstractive process. Second, nearest neighbor models require an account of similarity judgments; presently such accounts all involve abstractions (Tversky 1977).

Virtually all models of categorization involve abstraction—that is, ways in which the cognitive system acts "creatively" on input during learning of categories and uses the resultant categorical information to classify novel items. The creativity is of two types: determining which elements of a situation are "essential" and which irrelevant; and the creation of new higher order information which was not given in any particular exemplar. In the classical concept formation paradigm, abstraction of essential elements is involved in learning which attributes are relevant, and creation of higher order information is involved in learning the logical relationship between these attributes. Any model that includes representation of features (whether defining or characteristic) posits creativity of the first type. The type of novel higher order information generated varies for different models. The most minimal computation is required by prototype models based on central tendency: e.g. on means (Posner et al 1967, Posner & Keele 1968, Reed 1972, Reed & Friedman 1973), modes (Neumann 1974, 1977; Hayes-

Roth & Hayes-Roth 1977) or ideal values based on perceptual characteristics (Kay & McDaniel 1978, Oden & Massaro 1978). Some models posit that category representations include both summary information and exemplar information (Medin & Schaffer 1978, Smith & Medin 1981). For their summary information, these models require abstraction of "essential" elements to generate features and the creation of new information in the form of weights for the features (computed, in general, on the basis of the usefulness of the feature for determining category membership).

Abstraction models involving simple attributes, rules, or prototypes (such as any of the above) are criticized by those who feel that higher order abstractions and general knowledge more extensive than that of individual categories are required in any account of categorization. For example, Pittenger & Shaw (1975, Pittenger et al 1979) argue that higher order knowledge about transformations serves as the perceptual invariant underlying certain types of categorization. In the tradition of constructive memory research (e.g. Bartlett 1932, Bransford & McCarrell 1974), categories are treated as part of very general schemas. Finally, large scale computer models (Collins & Loftus 1975, Schank & Abelson 1977, Winograd 1972) treat categories and categorization processes as inseparable from world knowledge and the inference processes used in such knowledge.

DECOMPOSABILITY OF CATEGORIES INTO ELEMENTS

Virtually all accounts of the representation and processing of categories assume that categories are decomposable into more elementary qualities. This is not surprising: as Dreyfus (1979) has pointed out, since the time of Plato one of the major aspects of what has been meant by an explanation has been the decomposition of the thing to be explained into its elements. In psychology, however, arguments against the indiscriminate use of explanation-by-decomposition have been with the field since its inception (see e.g. James 1890a on the unitary nature of a single complex thought). The issue of decomposability was the focus of the debate in the early part of this century between the structuralists, who saw all experience as built out of primitive meaningless sensations, and the Gestaltists, who emphasized irreducible emergent properties of wholes (see Boring 1950).

At present, while decomposition is the unmarked assumption in model building, the possible need for less analytic factors is periodically acknowledged. For example, in the pattern recognition literature, analysis into features and holistic matching to a template are generally presented as the two major types of alternative models (Reed 1973), although for good reasons templates are usually treated as straw men (see Palmer 1978).

Various empirical developments have brought the nature and role of decomposition into current debate. First, categorization has been investigated for types of stimuli that do not have obvious elements at a cognitive level. The most notable of these are color (Rosch 1973b, 1974) and overall configuration (e.g. Attneave 1957, Posner 1969, Lockhead 1972—but see also Barresi et al 1975, Homa & Vosburgh 1976). It is not surprising that such stimuli do not strike us as obviously decomposible, since they are themselves normally treated as attributes, i.e. the qualities into which more complex objects are decomposed. There has also been considerable disagreement as to whether faces should be considered special holistically perceived objects (Hochberg & Galper 1967, Yin 1969, Rock 1973, Bradshaw 1976). A second development which has offered the opportunity to view categories as wholes is the possibility for spatial representation of within- and between-category structures through techniques such as multidimensional scaling. For example, Hutchinson & Lockhead (1977) have argued that categories can best be conceived as unanalyzed points in metric multidimensional space. A third trend has been use of the concept of a prototype and the facts of gradients of representativeness to suggest holistic processing (e.g. Rosch 1973b, Dreyfus 1979).

The great majority of arguments over decomposition concern specifying the level of abstraction at which a particular kind of decomposition can or cannot be said to occur. While most categorization models include decomposition, it is never to the point of infinite regress. Some elements are included as the primitives, although usually by default, rather than by explicit labeling as primitives.

Because some elements are not decomposed, many accounts of categorization include an explicit holistic component. For example, this can be introduced by means of a (relatively) holistic processing stage (E. E. Smith et al 1974). Another possibility is that a given level of abstraction may be a basic and (potentially) holistically perceived level, even if other levels require more analytic mechanisms (Rosch et al 1976a). Perceptual processing of figures (such as a large letter constructed of smaller letters) has been shown to proceed from global to local analysis under some stimulus conditions (Navon 1977) but to proceed from local to global under others (e.g. Kinchla & Wolf 1979). In the perception models of Palmer (1975) and Winston (1975), the decomposition of a visual scene is viewed as a hierarchical network of subscenes, and it is claimed that higher-order properties are processed first, followed by lower-order properties. Depending on the circumstances, however, a given aspect of a scene might be either the higher- or the lower-order property. The controversy over lexical decomposition in linguistics and artificial intelligence (does "kill" really mean "cause to die") can be seen as largely an issue of which linguistic level to consider a whole and which to consider the elements (Fodor 1970; McCawley 1971,

1978; Schank 1973; Fodor et al 1980). The recent suggestion that the capacity to match figures holistically may be a cognitive strategy which shows individual differences (Cooper 1976, Cooper & Podgorny 1976) is intriguing; for contrasting work on individual differences see Day (1976).

Two important points have been made in this discussion of decomposability. First, although the tendency in cognitive models is to decompose almost automatically, the evidence of holistic processing of some stimuli or at some stages suggests that we be more thoughtful about decompositional models. Second, findings concerning decomposition appear to be dependent on the level under consideration. Some general principles of decomposition are needed.

THE NATURE OF ATTRIBUTES

In the British empiricist account, attributes correspond to elementary sensations. However, in modern cognitive psychology, almost anything has been used as an attribute at one time or another. This produces some anomalies, particularly in the use of parts, relations, and functions as attributes (Rosch 1978). Indeed, as pointed out in the previous section, what is considered a category and what are called its attributes depend on the level one is describing; the same item (e.g. "red" or "circular") can be what is to be explained (category) or what is referred to as part of the explanation (attribute). Appropriately, therefore, there have recently been a number of discussions of the nature of attributes and the manner in which they combine.

The first controversy in the field involves use of features vs use of dimensions in the representation of categories. Features generally designate qualitative properties (e.g. legs, wooden, you sit on it) and so need not be applicable to all objects in the same domain. Large numbers of features may be included in a single representation. There are many different types of feature representations, such as feature lists and structural descriptions; for an extensive discussion see Palmer (1978). Explanations using features are overtly decompositional.

In contrast, dimensions are usually employed to describe quantitative properties (e.g. size); therefore, every object in a given domain is assigned some value on each of the dimensions used to describe the domain. An ideal dimensional representation includes only a small number of dimensions. There are two different types of dimensional representation, metric and nonmetric; for a discussion of their use in categorization models see E. E. Smith & Medin (1981). Dimensional descriptions often use a spatial metaphor (encouraged by the availability of multidimensional scaling techniques) and thus may appear to be relatively holistic representations of categories.

However, as Palmer (1978) and E. E. Smith & Medin (1981) have pointed out, the difference between features and dimensions may apply more to the surface form of the representation than to the underlying information that is represented. It can be shown that features may be extended to handle quantitative properties, and dimensions may be extended to handle most (but perhaps not all; see Beals et al 1968) qualitative properties. (But note that missing values communicate different information for features vs for dimensions; see Garner 1978a,b.) Features, transformations, and nonmetric dimensions can be integrated reasonably into the same representation.

One of the first psychologists to question the nature of attributes (whether features or dimensions) was Garner (1970, 1974). Garner was concerned not with the form by which attributes should be represented in cognitive models, but rather with a proposed difference in kind among perceptual attributes. This difference is concerned with how types of attributes combine with each other. Garner distinguished two types of attribute combinations: those that are separable (e.g. form and size) and those that are integral (e.g. brightness and saturation). Attribute combinations are considered separable if they are perceived in terms of their separate attributes; similarity is therefore judged by comparing the relevant stimuli with regard to their values on each of the component attributes. Attribute combinations are considered integral if the two attributes are not treated separately, that is, if a change in one attribute appears to produce a stimulus which is different as a whole rather than different for that one attribute. For integral attributes, similarity is judged holistically, according to how much the relevant stimuli are alike.

This distinction between types of attributes appeared temporarily to have major developmental implications. For adults, certain combinations of attributes are separable, while others are integral; however, young children appeared to treat virtually all attribute combinations as though they were integral (see e.g. Shepp & Swartz 1976, Shepp 1978). Clarification of the developmental data results from a further consideration of the nature of integral combinations. It has been suggested (e.g. Lockhead 1972, Garner 1974) that there are actually two types of integral combinations: those which seem to be mandatorily perceived holistically, and those which people prefer to process holistically, but which can also be processed dimensionally if such processing is advantageous. Recently, there have been several demonstrations (e.g. L. B. Smith & Kemler 1977, 1978; Kemler & L. B. Smith 1978) that young children treat those attribute combinations which are separable for adults as though they corresponded to the second type of integral combination. Thus, children are in fact able to perceive each of the attributes and to treat them as though they were separable; young children simply prefer to attend to holistic relationships. Young children are especially likely to consider separable dimensions separately if the required task is conceptual rather than perceptual (Kemler & L. B. Smith 1979).

The question arises as to what makes some attributes combine in an integral fashion and others in a separable fashion. Aside from some initial speculation (Garner 1974), this question has not been pursued. It may be pointed out, however, that integral and separable attributes appear to be at different levels of abstraction. When stimulus dimensions are considered at the level at which one normally calls something an attribute (e.g. at the level of colors and forms), the attributes are separable. Integral attributes are further decompositions of that level (e.g. hue and brightness are further decompositions of color). Thus separability and integrality of attributes, like other issues in decomposition, appear to depend on the level of abstraction considered.

Integrality and separability of attributes may be considered part of the general issue of information integration. Even given separable attributes, there remains the question of how to model the way in which they combine. The main choice in formal models has been between additive and multiplicative. Additive models treat attributes as though they were independent. These models appear to work best when relevant information is presented sequentially and correlations between attributes are absent or not apparent. Multiplicative models treat attributes as though they were nonindependent, and therefore work best when relevant information is presented simultaneously and correlations between attributes are apparent. (For a review of information integration see N. H. Anderson 1974.) In categorization research, additive and multiplicative models may make very similar predictions for real-world categories, since the attributes which are correlated are generally also most frequent.

Let us return to the original role of attributes in categorization theory. In empiricist philosophy, attributes were used to connect concepts to the real world; that is, to connect the meaning (intension) of a concept with the objects (extension) which fit that meaning. In the psychology of categorization, attributes are often used for this purpose. These attributes are generally of four types: parts, physical characteristics such as color and shape, relational concepts such as taller, and functional concepts. However, these types of attributes as represented in categorization models are all categories themselves; therefore, they can themselves be examined as a categorization problem (see Rosch 1979).

Note that one major psychological theory takes a different approach to the origin of attributes. A constructivist approach to logical classification (Piaget 1970, 1972) takes as its unit of analysis the *interaction* of persons and objects. Attributes are developed out of this interaction. Perhaps the closest analogy to such an approach in non-Piagetian cognitive psychology is the current interest in modeling categories by means of procedures. At present, this work is largely confined to formal systems (Miller & Johnson-Laird 1976) and to artificial intelligence (see Winograd 1975).

SUMMARY

New trends in categorization research have brought into investigation and debate some of the major issues in conception and learning whose solution had been unquestioned in earlier approaches. Empirical findings have established that: (*a*) categories are internally structured by gradients of representativeness; (*b*) category boundaries are not necessarily definite; (*c*) there is a close relation between attribute clusters and the structure and formation of categories. This appears to be a particularly promising approach for future research.

These findings challenge determinate definitions of categories and provide constraints on alternative views. Other issues that research and theory in the modeling of categorization have brought into focus are the nature of the abstractive process, the question of decomposition of categories into elements, and the nature of the attributes into which categories are often decomposed. In short, current research on categories could be said to represent a kind of experimental epistemology.

ACKNOWLEDGMENTS

We would like to thank Doug Medin, Elissa Newport, Emilie Roth, and especially John Pani for their thoughtful criticisms of previous drafts of this paper. Preparation of the manuscript was supported by grant No. BNS79-15120 from the National Science Foundation and by grant No. 6-400-76-0116 from the National Institutes of Education, both to the University of Illinois, Urbana-Champaign; and by grant No. 1 RO1 MH24316-03 from the National Institutes of Mental Health to the University of California, Berkeley.

Literature Cited

Aiken, L. S., Williams, T. M. 1973. A developmental study of schematic concept formation. *Dev. Psychol.* 8:162–67
Anderson, N. H. 1974. Algebraic models in perception. In *Handbook of Perception*, ed. E. C. Carterette, M. P. Friedman, 2:215–99. New York: Academic. 556 pp.
Anderson, R. C., Ortony, A. 1975. On putting apples into bottles—A problem of polysemy. *Cognit. Psychol.* 7:167–80
Anderson, R. C., Pichert, J. W., Goetz, E. T., Schallert, D. L., Stevens, K. V., Trollip, S. R. 1976. Instantiation of general

terms. *J. Verb. Learn. Verb. Behav.* 15:667–79
Anglin, J. M. 1977. *Word, Object and Conceptual Development.* New York: Norton. 302 pp.
Attneave, F. 1957. Transfer of experience with a class-schema to identification-learning of patterns and shapes. *J. Exp. Psychol.* 54:81–88
Barclay, J. R., Bransford, J. D., Franks, J. J., McCarrell, N. S., Nitsch, K. 1974. Comprehension and semantic flexibility. *J. Verb. Learn. Verb. Behav.* 13:471–81

Barresi, J., Robbins, D., Shain, K. 1975. Role of distinctive features in the abstraction of related concepts. *J. Exp. Psychol.– Hum. Learn. Mem.* 104:360–68

Bartlett, F. C. 1932. *Remembering: A Study in Experimental and Social Psychology.* Cambridge: Cambridge Univ. Press. 317 pp.

Bates, E., MacWinney, B. 1980. Functionalist approaches to grammar. In *Language Acquisition: The State of the Art*, ed. L. Gleitman, E. Wanner. Cambridge: Cambridge Univ. Press. In press

Battig, W. F., Montague, W. E. 1969. Category norms for verbal items in 56 categories: A replication and extension of the Connecticut category norms. *J. Exp. Psychol. Monogr.* 80:1–46

Beals, R., Krantz, D., Tversky, A. 1968. Foundations of multidimensional scaling. *Psychol. Rev.* 75:127–42

Berlin, B. 1972. Speculations on the growth of ethnobotanical nomenclature. *Lang. Soc.* 1:51–86

Berlin, B., Breedlove, D. E., Raven, P. H. 1973. General principles of classification and nomenclature in folk biology. *Am. Anthropol.* 75:214–42

Berlin, B., Kay, P. 1969. *Basic Color Terms: Their Universality and Evolution.* Berkeley: Univ. Calif. Press. 178 pp.

Boring, E. G. 1950. *A History of Experimental Psychology.* New York: Appleton-Century-Crofts. 777 pp. 2nd ed.

Bourne, L. E. Jr., Dominowski, R. L., Loftus, E. F. 1979. *Cognitive Processes.* Englewood Cliffs, NJ: Prentice-Hall. 408 pp.

Bowerman, M. 1978. The acquisition of word meaning: An investigation into some current conflicts. In *Development of Communication: Social and Pragmatic Factors in Language Acquisition*, ed. N. Waterson, C. Snow, pp. 263–87. New York: Wiley. 498 pp.

Bradshaw, M. 1976. An investigation of stimulus integrality in the perception of schematic faces. *Tech. Rep. 82, Dep. Psychol., Johns Hopkins Univ.*

Bransford, J. D., McCarrell, N. S. 1974. A sketch of a cognitive approach to comprehension: Some thoughts about understanding what it means to comprehend. In *Cognition and the Symbolic Processes*, ed. W. B. Weimer, D. S. Palermo, pp. 189–229. New York: Wiley. 450 pp.

Brigham, J. C. 1971. Ethnic stereotypes. *Psychol. Bull.* 76:15–38

Brooks, L. 1978. Nonanalytic concept formation and memory for instances. In *Cognition and Categorization*, ed. E. Rosch, B. B. Lloyd, pp. 169–215. Hillsdale, NJ: Erlbaum. 328 pp.

Brown, C. H., Kolar, J., Torrey, B. J., Truong-Quang, T., Volkman, P. 1976. Some general principles of biological and non-biological folk classification. *Am. Ethnol.* 3:73–85

Brown, R. 1958. How shall a thing be called? *Psychol. Rev.* 65:14–21

Brown, R. 1976. Reference: In memorial tribute to Eric Lenneberg. *Cognition* 4:125–53

Bruner, J. S., Goodnow, J. J., Austin, J. G. 1956. *A Study of Thinking.* New York: Wiley. 330 pp.

Calder, A. 1979. Constructive mathematics. *Sci. Am.* 241:146–69

Cantor, N., Mischel, W. 1979. Prototypes in person perception. In *Adv. Exp. Soc. Psychol.* 12:3–52

Cantor, N., Smith, E. E., French, R. D., Mezzich, J. 1980. Psychiatric diagnosis as prototype categorization. *J. Abnorm. Psychol.* 89:181–93

Caramazza, A. 1979. *Are concepts ill-defined or vague?* Presented at Conf. Word & Concept, Stanford, Calif.

Cohen, C. E. 1976. *Cognitive basis of stereotyping: An information-processing approach to social perception.* PhD dissertation. Univ. Calif., San Diego

Cohen, L. B., Caputo, N. F. 1978. *Instructing infants to respond to perceptual categories.* Presented at Midwestern Psychol. Assoc. Conv., Chicago

Cohen, L. B., Gelber, E. R. 1975. Infant visual memory. In *Infant Perception: From Sensation to Cognition: Basic Visual Processes*, ed. L. B. Cohen, P. Salapatek, 1:347–403. New York: Academic. 426 pp.

Cohen, L. B., Strauss, M. S. 1979. Concept acquisition in the human infant. *Child Dev.* 50:419–24

Coleman, L., Kay, P. 1981. Prototype semantics: The English word *lie*. *Language*, Vol. 57. In press

Collins, A. M., Loftus, E. F. 1975. A spreading activation theory of semantic processing. *Psychol. Rev.* 82:407–28

Cooper, L. A. 1976. Individual differences in visual comparison processes. *Percept. Psychophys.* 19:433-44

Cooper, L. A., Podgorny, P. 1976. Mental transformations and visual comparison processes: Effects of complexity and similarity. *J. Exp. Psychol.–Hum. Percept. Perform.* 2:503–14

Cornsweet, T. N. 1970. *Visual Perception.* New York: Academic. 475 pp.

Cruse, D. A. 1977. The pragmatics of lexical specificity. *J. Ling.* 13:153–64

Daehler, M. W., Lonardo, R., Bukatko, D. 1979. Matching and equivalence judgments in very young children. *Child Dev.* 50:170–79

Danks, J. H., Glucksberg, S. 1980. Experimental psycholinguistics. *Ann. Rev. Psychol.* 31:391–417

Day, R. 1976. *Language-bound and language-optional processing.* Presented at Psychon. Soc., St. Louis

DeValois, R. L., Jacobs, F. H. 1968. Primate color vision. *Science* 162:533–40

deVilliers, J. 1980. The process of rule learning in child speech: A new look. In *Children's Language,* ed. K. E. Nelson, Vol. 2. New York: Gardner. In press

Dougherty, J. W. D. 1978. Salience and relativity in classification. *Am. Ethnol.* 5: 66–80

Dreyfus, H. L. 1979. *What Computers Can't Do: A Critique of Artificial Reason.* New York: Harper & Row. 354 pp. 2nd ed.

Erickson, J. R., Jones, M. R. 1978. Thinking. *Ann. Rev. Psychol.* 29:61–90

Erreich, A., Valian, V. 1979. Children's internal organization of locative categories. *Child Dev.* 50:1071–77

Fillmore, C. D. 1975. An alternative to checklist theories of meaning. *Proc. 1st Ann. Meet. Berkeley Ling. Soc.* 1: 123–31

Fillmore, C. D. 1977. Topics in lexical semantics. In *Current Issues in Linguistic Theory,* ed. R. W. Cole, pp. 76–138. Wilmington, Ind: Indiana Univ. Press. 303 pp.

Flavell, J. H. 1977. *Cognitive Development.* Englewood Cliffs, NJ: Prentice Hall. 286 pp.

Flavell, J. H., Wellman, H. M. 1976. Metamemory. In *Perspectives on the Development of Memory and Cognition,* ed. R. V. Kail Jr., J. W. Hagen, pp. 3–33. Hillsdale, NJ: Erlbaum. 498 pp.

Fodor, J. 1970. Three reasons for not deriving 'kill' from 'cause to die'. *Ling. Inq.* 1:429–38

Fodor, J. 1981. The current status of the innateness controversy. In *Representations,* ed. J. Fodor. Vermont: Bradford Books. In press

Fodor, J., Garrett, M., Walker, E., Parkes, R. 1980. Against definitions. *Cognition* Vol. 8. In press

Franks, J. J., Bransford, J. D. 1971. Abstraction of visual patterns. *J. Exp. Psychol.* 90:65–74

Garner, W. R. 1970. The stimulus in information processing. *Am. Psychol.* 25: 350–58

Garner, W. R. 1974. *The Processing of Infor-*

mation and Structure. New York: Wiley. 203 pp.

Garner, W. R. 1978a. Aspects of a stimulus: Features, dimensions, and configurations. See Brooks 1978, pp. 99–133

Garner, W. R. 1978b. Selective attention to attributes and to stimuli. *J. Exp. Psychol.–General* 107:287–308

Gelman, R. 1978. Cognitive development. *Ann. Rev. Psychol.* 29:297–332

Glass, A. L., Holyoak, K. J. 1975. Alternative conceptions of semantic memory. *Cognition* 3:313–39

Goldman, D., Homa, D. 1977. Integrative and metric properties of abstracted information as a function of category discriminability, instance variability, and experience. *J. Exp. Psychol.–Hum. Learn. Mem.* 3:375–85

Hampton, J. A. 1979. Polymorphous concepts in semantic memory. *J. Verb. Learn. Verb. Behav.* 18:441–61

Hayes-Roth, B., Hayes-Roth, F. 1977. Concept learning and the recognition and classification of exemplars. *J. Verb. Learn. Verb. Behav.* 16:321–38

Heider, E. R. 1972. Universals in color naming and memory. *J. Exp. Psychol.* 93: 10–20

Hochberg, J., Galper, R. E. 1967. Recognition of faces I: An exploratory study. *Bull. Psychon. Soc.* 9:619–20

Homa, D., Cross, J., Cornell, D., Goldman, D., Shwartz, S. 1973. Prototype abstraction and classification of new instances as a function of number of instances defining the prototype. *J. Exp. Psychol.* 101:116–22

Homa, D., Vosburgh, R. 1976. Category breadth and the abstraction of prototypical information. *J. Exp. Psychol.–Hum. Learn. Mem.* 2:322–30

Hull, C. L. 1920. Quantitative aspects of the evolution of concepts. *Psychol. Monogr.* Vol. 28 (whole No. 123). 86 pp.

Hunn, E. 1975. Cognitive processes in folk ornithology: The identification of gulls. *Work. pap. No. 42. Lang. Behav. Res. Lab.,* Univ. Calif., Berkeley

Hunn, E. 1976. Toward a perceptual model of folk biological classification. *Am. Ethnol.* 3:508–24

Hupp, S. C., Mervis, C. B. 1981. *Acquisition of Basic Object Categories by Severely Handicapped Children.* Submitted for publication.

Husaim, J. S., Cohen, L. B. 1980. *Infant learning of ill-defined categories.* Presented at Int. Conf. Infant Stud. New Haven

Hutchinson, J. W., Lockhead, G. R. 1977. Similarity as distance: A structural principle for semantic memory. *J. Exp. Psychol.–Hum. Learn. Mem.* 3:660–78

Hyman, R., Frost, N. H. 1975. Gradients and schema in pattern recognition. In *Attention and Performance,* ed. P. M. A. Rabbit, S. Dornig, 5:630–54. New York: Academic. 732 pp.

James, W. 1890a. *The Principles of Psychology,* Vol. 1. New York: Dover. 689 pp.

James, W. 1890b. *The Principles of Psychology,* Vol. 2. New York: Dover. 688 pp.

Kahneman, D., Tversky, A. 1973. On the psychology of prediction. *Psychol. Rev.* 80:237–51

Katz, J. J. 1972. *Semantic Theory.* New York: Harper & Row. 464 pp.

Kay, P., McDaniel, C. K. 1978. The linguistic significance of the meanings of basic color terms. *Language* 54:610–46

Keil, F. C. 1979. *Semantic and Conceptual Development: An Ontological Perspective.* Cambridge, Mass: Harvard Univ. Press. 214 pp.

Keller, D., Kellas, G. 1978. Typicality as a dimension of encoding. *J. Exp. Psychol.–Hum. Learn. Mem.* 4:78–85

Kemler, D. G., Smith, L. B. 1978. Is there a developmental trend from integrality to separability in perception? *J. Exp. Child Psychol.* 26:498–507

Kemler, D. G., Smith, L. B. 1979. Accessing similarity and dimensional relations: Effects of integrality and separability on the discovery of complex concepts. *J. Exp. Psychol.–General* 108:133–50

Kempton, W. 1978. Category grading and taxonomic relations: A mug is a sort of a cup. *Am. Ethnol.* 5:44–65

Kinchla, R. A., Wolf, J. M. 1979. The order of visual processing: "Top-down," "bottom-up," or "middle-out." *Percept. Psychophys.* 25:225–31

Kintsch, W. 1980. Semantic memory: A tutorial. In *Attention and Performance VIII,* ed. R. S. Nickerson. Hillsdale, NJ: Erlbaum. In press

Kogan, N. 1971. Educational implication of cognitive styles. In *Psychology and Educational Practice,* ed. G. Lesser, pp. 242–92. Glenview, Ill: Scott, Foresman. 580 pp.

Labov, W. 1973. The boundaries of words and their meanings. In *New Ways of Analyzing Variation in English,* ed. C. J. Bailey, R. Shuy, pp. 340–73. Washington: Georgetown Univ. Press. 373 pp.

Lakoff, G. 1973. Hedges: A study in meaning criteria and the logic of fuzzy concepts. *J. Philos. Logic* 2:458–508

Lakoff, G. 1977. On linguistic gestalts. *Chicago Ling. Soc. Pap.* 13:236–87

Leach, E. 1964. Anthropological aspects of language: Animal categories and verbal abuse. In *New Directions in the Study of Language,* ed. E. H. Lenneberg, pp. 23–63. Cambridge, Mass: MIT Press. 194 pp.

Lippmann, W. 1922. *Public Opinion.* New York: Harcourt, Brace. 427 pp.

Locke, J. 1690. *An Essay Concerning Human Understanding.* Annotated by A. C. Fraser, 1959. New York: Dover. 495 pp.

Lockhead, G. R. 1972. Processing dimensional stimuli: A note. *Psychol. Rev.* 79:410–19

MacKenzie, D. L., Palermo, D. S. 1981. *The Effect of Context on Semantic Categorization.* Submitted for publication

Maratsos, M. P., Chalkley, M. A. 1980. The internal language of children's syntax: The ontogenesis and representation of syntactic categories. See deVilliers 1980. In press

McCauley, C., Stitt, C. L. 1978. An individual and quantitative measure of stereotypes. *J. Pers. Soc. Psychol.* 36:929–40

McCauley, C., Stitt, C. L., Segal, M. 1980. Stereotyping: From prejudice to prediction. *Psychol. Bull.* 87:195–208

McCawley, J. 1971. Prelexical syntax. *Georgetown Univ. Monogr. Ser. Lang. Ling.* 23:19–33

McCawley, J. 1978. Conversational implicature and the lexicon. In *Syntax and Semantics,* ed. P. Cole, 9:245–59. New York: Academic. 340 pp.

McCloskey, M. E., Glucksberg, S. 1978. Natural categories: Well defined or fuzzy sets? *Mem. Cognit.* 6:462–72

McCloskey, M. E., Glucksberg, S. 1979. Decision processes in verifying category membership statements: Implications for models of semantic memory. *Cognit. Psychol.* 11:1–37

Medin, D. L., Schaffer, M. M. 1978. Context theory of classification learning. *Psychol. Rev.* 85:207–38

Mervis, C. B. 1980. Category structure and the development of categorization. In *Theoretical Issues in Reading Comprehension,* ed. R. Spiro, B. C. Bruce, W. F. Brewer. Hillsdale, NJ: Erlbaum. In press

Mervis, C. B., Catlin, J., Rosch, E. 1975. Development of the structure of color categories. *Dev. Psychol.* 11:54–60

Mervis, C. B., Catlin, J., Rosch, E. 1976. Relationships among goodness-of-example, category norms, and word frequency. *Bull. Psychon. Soc.* 7:283–84

Mervis, C. B., Crisafi, M. A. 1981. *The Perceptual-Cognitive Primacy of Basic Level Categories.* In preparation

Mervis, C. B., Mirman, M. C. 1981. *The Effects of Category Size and Distortion Level on Concept Abstraction.* In preparation

Mervis, C. B., Pani, J. R. 1980. Acquisition of basic object categories. *Cognit. Psychol.* Vol. 12. In press

Meyer, D. E. 1970. On the representation and retrieval of stored semantic information. *Cognit. Psychol.* 1:242–300

Miller, G. A., Johnson-Laird, P. N. 1976. *Language and Perception.* Cambridge, Mass: Harvard Univ. Press. 760 pp.

Mirman, M. C. 1978. *The Effects of Number and Distortion Level of Category Exemplars on Concept Abstraction.* Honors BS thesis. Univ. Illinois, Urbana-Champaign

Murphy, G., Smith, E. E. 1981. *Levels of Categorization and Object Identification.* In preparation

Navon, D. 1977. Forest before trees: The precedence of global features in visual perception. *Cognit. Psychol.* 9:353–83

Neimark, E. D. 1974. Natural language concepts: Additional evidence. *Child Dev.* 45:508–11

Neimark, E. D., Santa, J. L. 1975. Thinking and concept attainment. *Ann. Rev. Psychol.* 26:173–205

Nelson, K. 1973. Some evidence for the cognitive primacy of categorization and its functional basis. *Merrill-Palmer Q.* 19:21–39

Nelson, K. 1974. Variations in children's concepts by age and category. *Child Dev.* 45:577–84

Nelson, K. E., Nelson, K. 1978. Cognitive pendulums and their linguistic realization. In *Children's Language,* ed. K. E. Nelson, 1:223–85. New York: Gardner. 567 pp.

Neumann, P. G. 1974. An attribute frequency model for the abstraction of prototypes. *Mem. Cognit.* 2:241–48

Neumann, P. G. 1977. Visual prototype formation with discontinuous representation of dimensions of variability. *Mem. Cognit.* 5:187–97

Newport, E. L., Bellugi, U. 1978. Linguistic expression of category levels in a visual-gestural language: A flower is a flower is a flower. See Brooks 1978, pp. 49–71

Oden, G. C., Massaro, D. W. 1978. Integration of featural information in speech perception. *Psychol. Rev.* 85:172–91

Palmer, S. E. 1975. Visual perception and world knowledge: Notes on a model of sensory-cognitive interaction. In *Exploration in Cognition,* ed. D. A. Norman, D. E. Rumelhart, LNR Research Group, pp. 279–307. San Francisco: Freeman. 430 pp.

Palmer, S. E. 1978. Fundamental aspects of cognitive representation. See Brooks 1978, pp. 259–303

Piaget, J. 1970. Piaget's theory. In *Carmichael's Manual of Child Psychology,* ed. P. H. Mussen, 1:703–32. New York: Wiley. 1519 pp. Piaget, J. 1972. *The Principles of Genetic Epistemology.* New York: Basic Books. 98 pp.

Pittenger, J. B., Shaw, R. E. 1975. Aging faces as visual-elastic events: Implications for a theory of nonrigid shape perception. *J. Exp. Psychol.–Hum. Percept. Perform.* 1:374–82

Pittenger, J. B., Shaw, R. E., Mark, L. S. 1979. Perceptual information for the age level of faces as a higher order invariant of growth. *J. Exp. Psychol.–Hum. Percept. Perform.* 5:478–93

Posnansky, C. J. 1973. *Category norms for verbal items in 25 categories for children in grades 2-6.* Prog. Cognit. Factors Hum. Learn. Mem., Rep. 7, Univ. Colo., Boulder

Posnansky, C. J., Neumann, P. G. 1976. The abstraction of visual prototypes by children. *J. Exp. Child Psychol.* 21:367–79

Posner, M. I. 1969. Abstraction and the process of recognition. In *The Psychology of Learning and Motivation,* ed. G. H. Bower, J. T. Spence, 3:44–96. New York: Academic. 398 pp.

Posner, M. I., Goldsmith, R., Welton, K. E., Jr. 1967. Perceived distance and the classification of distorted patterns. *J. Exp. Psychol.* 73:28–38

Posner, M. I., Keele, S. W. 1968. On the genesis of abstract ideas. *J. Exp. Psychol.* 77:353–63

Potter, M. C., Faulconer, B. A. 1979. Understanding noun phrases. *J. Verb. Learn. Verb. Behav.* 18:509–21

Rabinow, P., Sullivan, W. M., eds. 1979. *Interpretive Social Science: A Reader.* Berkeley: Univ. Calif. Press. 367 pp.

Reber, A. S. 1976. Implicit learning of synthetic languages: The role of instructional set. *J. Exp. Psychol.–Hum. Learn. Mem.* 2:88–94

Reed, S. K. 1972. Pattern recognition and categorization. *Cognit. Psychol.* 3:382–407

Reed, S. K. 1973. *Psychological Processes in Pattern Recognition.* New York: Academic. 244 pp.

Reed, S. K., Friedman, M. P. 1973. Perceptual vs. conceptual categorization. *Mem. Cognit.* 1:157–63

114   MERVIS & ROSCH

Ricciuti, H. N. 1965. Object grouping and selective ordering behavior in infants 12 to 24 months old. *Merrill-Palmer Q.* 11:129–48

Riley, D. A., Lamb, M. R. 1979. Stimulus generalization. In *Perception and Its Development: A Tribute to Eleanor J. Gibson,* ed. A. D. Pick, pp. 7–37. Hillsdale, NJ: Erlbaum. 258 pp.

Rips, L. J. 1975. Inductive judgments about natural categories. *J. Verb. Learn. Verb. Behav.* 14:665–81

Rips, L. J., Shoben, E. J., Smith, E. E. 1973. Semantic distance and the verification of semantic relations. *J. Verb. Learn. Verb. Behav.* 12:1–20

Rock, I. 1973. *Orientation and Form.* New York: Academic Press. 165 pp.

Rosch, E. H. 1973a. Natural categories. *Cognit. Psychol.* 4:328–50

Rosch, E. 1973b. On the internal structure of perceptual and semantic categories. In *Cognitive Development and the Acquisition of Language,* ed. T. E. Moore, pp. 111–44. New York: Academic. 308 pp.

Rosch, E. 1974. Linguistic relativity. In *Human Communication: Theoretical Explorations,* ed. A. Silverstein, pp. 95–121. Hillsdale, NJ: Erlbaum. 264 pp.

Rosch, E. 1975a. Cognitive reference points. *Cognit. Psychol.* 7:532–47

Rosch, E. 1975b. Cognitive representations of semantic categories. *J. Exp. Psychol.–General* 104:192–233

Rosch, E. 1975c. The nature of mental codes for color categories. *J. Exp. Psychol.–Hum. Percept. Perform.* 1:303–22

Rosch, E. 1977. Human categorization. In *Studies in Cross-Cultural Psychology,* ed. N. Warren, 1:3–49. London: Academic. 212 pp.

Rosch, E. 1978. Principles of categorization. See Brooks 1978, pp. 27–48

Rosch, E. 1979. *Attributes.* Presented at Conf. Word & Object, Stanford, Calif.

Rosch, E., Mervis, C. B. 1975. Family resemblances: Studies in the internal structure of categories. *Cognit. Psychol.* 7:573–605

Rosch, E., Mervis, C. B., Gray, W. D., Johnson, D. M., Boyes-Braem, P. 1976a. Basic objects in natural categories. *Cognit. Psychol.* 8:382–439

Rosch, E., Simpson, C., Miller, R. S. 1976b. Structural bases of typicality effects. *J. Exp. Psychol.–Hum. Percept. Perform.* 2:491–502

Rosner, S. R., Hayes, D. S. 1977. A developmental study of category item production. *Child Dev.* 48:1062–65

Ross, G. 1977. *Concept categorization in 1 to 2 year olds.* Presented at Bien Meet. Soc. Res. Child Dev., New Orleans

Ross, J. 1972. The category squish: Endstation Hauptwort. *Chicago Ling. Soc. Pap.* 8:316–29

Saltz, E., Dixon, D., Klein, S., Becker, G. 1977. Studies of natural language concepts: III. Concept overdiscrimination in comprehension between two and four years of age. *Child Dev.* 48:1682–85

Saltz, E., Soller, E., Sigel, I. E. 1972. The development of natural language concepts. *Child Dev.* 43:1191–1202

Schank, R. C. 1973. Identification of conceptualizations underlying natural language. In *Computer Models of Thought and Language,* ed. R. C. Schank, K. M. Colby, pp. 187–247. San Francisco: Freeman. 454 pp.

Schank, R. C., Abelson, R. P. 1977. *Scripts, Plans, Goals and Understanding: An Inquiry into Human Knowledge Structures.* Hillsdale, NJ:Erlbaum. 248 pp.

Shepard, R. N., Chipman, S. 1970. Second-order isomorphism of internal representations: Shapes of states. *Cognit. Psychol.* 1:1–17

Shepp, B. E. 1978. From perceived similarity to dimensional structure: A new hypothesis about perceptual development. See Brooks 1978, pp. 135–67

Shepp, B. E., Swartz, K. B. 1976. Selective attention and the processing of integral and nonintegral dimensions: A developmental study. *J. Exp. Child Psychol.* 22:73–85

Simpson, G. G. 1961. *Principles of Animal Taxonomy.* New York: Columbia Univ. Press. 247 pp.

Smith, E. E. 1978. Theories of semantic memory. In *Handbook of Learning and Cognitive Processes,* ed. W. K. Estes, 6:1–56. Hillsdale, NJ: Erlbaum. 311 pp.

Smith, E. E., Balzano, G. 1977. *Concepts and prototypes.* Colloquium, Harvard Univ.

Smith, E. E., Medin, D. L. 1981. *The Psychology of Conceptual Processes.* Cambridge, Mass: Harvard Univ. Press. In press

Smith, E. E., Rips, L. J., Shoben, E. J. 1974. Semantic memory and psychological semantics. In *The Psychology of Learning and Motivation,* ed. G. H. Bower, 8:1–45. New York: Academic. 305 pp.

Smith, L. B., Kemler, D. G. 1977. Developmental trends in free classification: Evidence for a new conceptualization of perceptual development. *J. Exp. Child Psychol.* 24:279–98

Smith, L. B., Kemler, D. G. 1978. Levels of experienced dimensionality in children and adults. *Cognit. Psychol.* 10:502–32

Sneath, P. H. A., Sokal, R. R. 1973. *Numerical Taxonomy.* San Francisco: Freeman. 573 pp.

Sokal, R. R. 1974. Classification: Purposes, principles, progress, prospects. *Science* 185:1115–23

Strauss, M. S. 1979. Abstraction of prototypical information by adults and 10-month-old infants. *J. Exp. Psychol.–Hum. Learn. Mem.* 5:618–32

Stross, B. 1973. Acquisition of botanical terminology by Tzeltal children. In *Meaning in Mayan Languages,* ed. M. Edmonson, pp. 107–42. The Hague: Mouton. 256 pp.

Tversky, A. 1977. Features of similarity. *Psychol. Rev.* 84:327–52

Tversky, A., Gati, I. 1978. Studies of similarity. See Brooks 1978, pp. 79–98

Wanner, E. 1979. *Discussion of prototypes.* Presented at Meet. Soc. Philos. Psychol., New York

Whitfield, T. W. A., Slatter, P. E. 1979. The effects of categorization and prototypicality on aesthetic choice in a furniture selection task. *Br. J. Psychol.* 70:65–75

Whitten, W. B. II, Suter, W. N., Frank, M. L. 1979. Bidirectional synonym ratings of 464 noun pairs. *J. Verb. Learn. Verb.*

Behav. 18:109–27

Williams, T. M., Fryer, M. L., Aiken, L. S. 1977. Development of visual pattern classification in preschool children: Prototypes and distinctive features. *Dev. Psychol.* 13:577–84

Winograd, T. 1972. Understanding natural language. *Cognit. Psychol.* 3:1–191

Winograd. T. 1975. Frame representations and the declarative-procedural controversy. In *Representation and Understanding: Studies in Cognitive Science,* ed. D. G. Bobrow, A. Collins, pp. 185–210. New York: Academic. 427 pp.

Winston, P. H. 1975. Learning structural description from examples. In *The Psychology of Computer Vision,* ed. P. H. Winston, pp. 157–210. New York: McGraw-Hill. 282 pp.

Witkowski, S. R., Brown, C. H. 1978. Lexical universals. *Ann. Rev. Anthropol.* 7:427–51

Wittgenstein, L. 1953. *Philosophical Investigations.* New York: Macmillan. 232 pp.

Yin, R. K. 1969. Looking at upside-down faces. *J. Exp. Psychol.* 81:141–45

Zadeh, L. A. 1965. Fuzzy sets. *Inf. Control* 8:338–53

Ann. Rev. Psychol. 1981. 32:117–51

DEVELOPMENTAL PSYCHOLOGY

♦342

John C. Masters[1]

Institute for Public Policy Studies, Vanderbilt University, Nashville, Tennessee 37235

CONTENTS

INTRODUCTION

In many ways developmental psychology is a microcosm of psychology in general. Most, if not all, of the subareas within psychology are represented within developmental psychology, usually by their typical labels with the

[1]My sincere thanks to the following colleagues who provided thoughtful commentary and bibliographic direction: Leslie Cohen, John Flavell, Wyndol Furman, John Hagen, Willard Hartup, Lewis Lipsitt, Michael Maratsos, Herbert Pick, Robert Plomin, Richard Odom, Sandra Scarr, Ronald Wilson.

117

0066-4308/81/0201-0117$01.00

qualifier "developmental" appended initially. Thus, there is developmental: behavioral genetics, cognitive, social, personality and language, and so on. Each of these specialties has become reasonably complex and encompasses a large literature of contemporary theory and research that would require its own individual review to provide any degree of depth. In fact, a recent review in this series focuses singularly upon cognitive development (Gelman 1978).

The present review is neither an anomoly nor an anachronism in the face of the appropriate trend to subdivide developmental psychology, for it remains a worthwhile endeavor to attempt a review of the field in breadth. Such reviews will surely become rarer, however. When accomplished they will also of necessity sacrifice depth for breadth, but the trade seems a fair one. In this review I attempt to identify the important or innovative work that has been accomplished most recently in a number of readily identifiable subareas of developmental psychology—subareas defined in large part by commonly shared divisions such as those used to segment faculty groups in psychology departments and, perhaps more in the past than currently, areas of preliminary examination in doctoral programs. If the field of developmental psychology has become meaningfully divided into subareas, so have the competencies of developmental psychologists become focused into one or a small number of such subareas. In preparing this review I have enlisted the able assistance of colleagues across the country whose expertise lies in the various subareas of developmental psychology here identified. Their suggestions and comments helped focus this review on what seem to be the most salient issues and developments in the various subareas.

DEVELOPMENTAL BEHAVIORAL GENETICS

Behavioral genetics seeks to specify and explain genetic sources for variance in behavior and abilities. Within the realm of developmental behavioral genetics, two domains of behavior and ability have generally been the focus of attention: intelligence or assessed aspects of cognitive functioning, and patterns of social behavior or dimensions of personality. However, although particular studies and specific conclusions may address one or the other general domain, larger issues are frequently addressed. Currently these include the equivalence of genetic and environmental impact on different behavioral or ability variables (Park et al 1978; Wilson, Johnson, Vandenberg, McClearn & Wilson, unpublished), the degree to which the family, as a social unit of genetic and environmental variance, is more remarkable for the induction of similarities or differences among family members (Willerman & Fiedler 1977, Plomin & DeFries 1980, Willerman 1979); or the degree to which development is best construed as an orchestrated and varying interaction between the variables of heredity, environment, and maturational status (Wilson 1978).

A procedure used increasingly to study behavioral genetics in humans is the adoption study in which similarities and differences between parents and children in adoptive homes are contrasted with those between biologically related parents and children. Many recent research reports have come from three adoption studies, a short-term one conducted at the University of Minnesota (Scarr & Weinberg 1976, 1977, 1978), and continuing ones at the University of Texas (Willerman 1979; Horn, Loehlin & Willerman 1979) and the University of Colorado (Plomin & DeFries, unpublished).

While it is common to assume that environmental factors salient to the development of behavior and abilities vary between families, thus making family members more similar to one another than to members of other families, recently it has been emphasized how much variance there is among family members despite the apparently common environment. This has been concluded by investigators studying intellectual (Willerman 1979, Plomin & DeFries 1980, Scarr & Weinberg 1978) as well as social (Plomin & Rowe 1979) behavior. It has been proposed, for example, that within the SES range of the middle class family, environmental differences have little impact on the intellectual performance of adolescents (Scarr & Weinberg 1978), and many of the nongenetic biological events that affect individual family members and which can influence intellectual functioning may not be systematic—i.e. they may be random and nearly unpredictable, such as infections, nutritional disorders, or seemingly minor and unnoticed injuries.

There is repeated concern in this literature with the understanding of environmental contributors to behavioral development, particularly as they are articulated with genetic determinants (Willerman 1979; R. Plomin, personal communication; Scarr-Salapatek 1976). The general conclusion is that we know little in this area, especially with respect to the development of intellectual functioning (Willerman 1979). Wilson et al (unpublished) found that different environmental variables had differing degrees of relationship to a variety of cognitive abilities, and these differing relative influences were reasonably consistent across ethnic groups. Willerman & Fiedler (1977) report data suggesting that boys' intellectual development may be more responsive to environmental influences than that of girls. An emerging rule of thumb seems to be that the more specific the behavior assessed, the less the demonstrable role of genetic factors. Thus, although Willerman, Horn & Loehlin (1977) report an inability to distinguish achievement from intelligence tests on the basis of their heritabilities, Scarr & Yee (1979) conclude that "the more a test samples what is recently and explicitly taught in school, the more that differences in adolescents' social environments account for differences in performance (p. 1)." They point out that while

Scarr & Weinberg (1978) found little effect of family background on IQ, there was substantial variance due to social (family) environment on school achievement.

Recent studies of the developmental behavioral genetics of social behavior have rather consistently concluded that the influence of genetic factors appears to be less than that for intellectual development (Wilson 1978; A. P. Matheny, Jr., unpublished) or remarkably small compared to the influence of environmental factors (Plomin, Foch & Rowe 1980; Plomin & Rowe 1979). It may be that only when measures that summarize different specific behaviors/abilities are used do common threads of genetic influence appear. Thus, measures of intelligence are more summary in nature than are frequency counts for a particular social behavior in a constant, controlled situation.

While it is no longer stressed, the question of the relative influence of heredity and environment is not absent even from the most recent literature. Often, however, the presentation of amounts-of-variance-accounted-for is not intended competitively but rather to clarify a more basic point, such as variance in the degree of environmental contribution from one behavior/ability category to another (Wilson et al, unpublished). Nevertheless, it seems reasonable to propose that the nature of the constructs used in research— their breadth and hence the use of summary variables for assessment as opposed to behavioristic specificity—may contribute to some aspects of findings, especially those contrasting proportions of variance accounted for. While Loehlin & Nichols (1976) reported moderate heritabilities for paper-and-pencil measures of personality variables, Plomin and his colleagues (Plomin, Foch & Rowe 1980; Plomin & Rowe 1979) found little genetic influence using objective measures such as actometer assessment or activity level or behavioral measures of selective attention. Plomin & Rowe (1979) found evidence of heritable influence in infants' social responsiveness toward strangers but not toward their mothers. This may indicate that under some circumstances (e.g. little prior social learning for behavior patterns toward strangers) even specific behavioral measures may show genetic influences.

INFANCY

Although chronological aspects of development are clearly important, there has been a tendency in recent years to parse the field of developmental psychology in terms of substantive or topical areas of development rather than chronological periods—much as the present chapter is organized. There are some exceptions, however, and infancy is one chronological period that has survived the move to topical organization. In 1978, the journal *Infant Behavior and Development* was born, and Lewis Lipsitt entitled his foreword "A coming out occasion for infants." And come out they did, to participate in studies of early perception, cognition, memory, emotional development, social development, genetic contributions to early behavior, and more. As developmental psychology is a microcosm of psychology, focusing upon developmental aspects of many different substantive areas, so is infancy a microcosm of developmental psychology, but one where the chronological developmental level of the organism provides a continuing thread.

Widespread interest in infancy in recent years has produced reviews of the literature in specific areas such as perception (Cohen & Salapatek 1975), and a wide-ranging handbook as well (Osofsky 1979). Several recent contributions to an issue of the *American Psychologist* celebrating the year of the child (Scarr 1979, Cohen 1979a, Lipsitt 1979, Sroufe 1979a) provide briefer summaries of research and theory.

As Gelman (1978) has argued for older children, the cognitive competency of infants is also being touted. By 30 weeks of age infants can be shown to conceptualize and recognize a given female face regardless of its orientation and to respond to female faces in general (Cohen & Strauss 1979). Two to 4-week-old infants can learn to recognize a word that their mothers repeat to them over a period of time (2 weeks) and will remember the word up to 42 hours without intervening presentations (Ungerer, Brody & Zelazo 1978). A finding that by 15 weeks of age infants will search visually for a parent whose voice they hear indicates that intermodal search patterns already exist and visual and acoustic information about persons (and objects) in the environment has been conceptually coordinated (Spelke & Owsley 1979).

The notion of prototypes has also found its way into the domain of early infant cognition. Strauss (1979) found that infants who are familiarized primarily to extremes of facial dimensions (narrow vs wide noses; eyes widely vs narrowly separated) generalized their responding to a face with average dimensions more than to one with extreme values. Strauss concluded that the infants had formed an internal, prototypic representation of feature categories by averaging feature values.

Infant cognitive processing, both concept formation and memory, thus can be demonstrated at very early ages and appears to be more sophisticated and robust than earlier has been thought (Cohen & Gelber 1975, Cohen, DeLoache & Pearl 1977). Similar conclusions are being drawn for early infant perception (Cohen, DeLoach & Strauss 1979). Newborn infants can turn toward a stimulus in their periphery (Aslin & Salapatek 1975, Lewis & Maurer 1977). They can see both high contrast edges and angles (Maurer & Salapatek 1976, Milewski 1976). By 3 months of age or so patterns can be recognized (Milewski 1979) and infants begin to respond to relationships between elements of a stimulus (Schwartz & Day 1979). Seemingly slight increases in age, experience, and physiological maturity are accompanied by remarkable increases in perceptual competence and proficiency (Cohen et al 1979).

A burgeoning area of theoretical and research interest in infancy is that of early social behavior and the role the infant plays in determining the behavior of others. Not surprisingly, caring for an infant increases its attractiveness to the caretaker (Corter et al 1978). It also appears that initial ratings of attractiveness for given infants tend to be similar for different adults making the ratings (Corter et al 1978). The speech of mothers to year-old infants is also influenced by the infants' behavior (West & Rheingold 1978), with social and exploratory behaviors being associated with 70% of mothers' utterances to their infants. Mothers also adjust the categories of their speech in accord with infant behavior, thus providing information to the infants about the environment and providing associations between acts and words.

One-year-old infants have been shown to adjust their behavior according to whether one or both parents are present (Lamb 1978a), and infants tend to direct more affiliative and attachment behaviors to a parent when she or he is alone with the child. Peers are also coming to be recognized as a reality in the infant's social world. Field (1978) has reported that 3-month-old infants show longer fixations of preschool peers than they do of their mothers. In another study, Field (1979b) found that 3-month-old infants facing a mirror or a peer looked longer at the mirror but showed rudimentary social responsiveness such as smiling, vocalizing, reaching, and squirming when faced with a peer. In yet another investigation, Field (1979a) found that year-old infants behaved in a more social fashion toward their peers in their mother's absence than in her presence, and that repeated exposure to peers increased social responding. While it is not surprising that age and social experience increase social behavior, it is becoming even more clear that even the very young infant participates in, and to some extent controls, her or his social environment, and the role of peers in social development is not one reserved for the years beyond infancy.

An important area of research on infancy deserves special mention, although it has received enough recent attention to make sustained attention here redundant. This is the area of psychobiology, which is concerned with the contribution of hereditary, congenital, perinatal stress, drugs, and other biological/constitutional variables to early behavioral development and learning. A herald of this emerging concern was a volume edited by Lipsitt (1976) entitled *Developmental Psychobiology: The Significance of Infancy.* Lipsitt has further elaborated on this topic in his contribution to the Year of the Child issue of the *American Psychologist* (Scarr 1979, Lipsitt 1979). An important contribution in this area has been the emerging interrelationship between scientists concerned with early behavioral development and those in the biomedical professions whose concerns also extend to the physical well-being of infants. A particularly salient case in point is research on the Sudden Infant Death Syndrome (SIDS) (Steinschneider 1977; Black, Steinschneider & Sheehe 1979; Lipsitt, Sturner & Burke 1979). Although there is some dispute as to the particular type of anomoly, agreement seems to exist that some sort of early respiratory disorder is indicative, if not causal, of subsequent crib death. Lipsitt (1979, Lipsitt et al 1979) proposes that infants who do not have an adequate *reflexive* response to early respiratory distress, typically a rage or postural response that is likely to clear respiratory passages, may fail to *learn* to perform these responses habitually to respiratory distress so that they will continue after the reflex is no longer operative. When weak but effective early reflexive responses fade from the infant's repertoire, the absence of a learned response to take their place will put the infant at risk for severe consequences from subsequent respiratory disorders (e.g. a cold), a vulnerability now mediated by a failure in the learning process. This hypothesis has not been fully explored, but it is illustrative of the recognition of interplay between biological and psychological factors in early infant development.

PERCEPTUAL DEVELOPMENT

Most stimuli are necessarily complex and may be analyzed into specific components. These components, in turn, are typically dimensions of stimuli, and a certain value within a given dimension characterizes a particular stimulus—the specific hue or brightness of a color chip, for example. Garner (1970, 1974) has proposed that stimulus dimensions may be more or less separable from one another or, in other words, nonintegral or integral in character. Integral dimensions such as hue and brightness are not separable and are perceived as unitary, while nonintegral dimensions such as area (e.g. the size of a circle) and angle (the tilt of a straight line) (for adults) or the color vs the form of a stimulus drawing (for children) are separate and perceived as independent and distinct.

In a series of investigations, Shepp (1978, Shepp & Swartz 1976) and Smith and Kemler (Kemler & Smith 1978, Smith 1979, Smith & Kemler 1977) have provided evidence that developmental differences in the perceived structure of stimuli mirror differences found for adults between integral and nonintegral stimulus dimensions: younger children perceive different stimulus dimensions as integral and nonseparable which older children and adults perceive as nonintegral and separable. For example, in free classifications, young children group stimuli varying in size and brightness according to similarity, which is the way that adults classify integral dimensions (Handel & Imai 1972). Compatible with Gibson's theory of perceptual learning (1969) and Lewin's (1955) general theory of developmental differentiation, it is proposed that one aspect of perceptual learning is the differentiation of separable dimensions of stimuli or, in other words, that there is a developmental trend from perceived similarity to perceived dimensional structure. If this is the case, limits on young children's perceptual learning would not be due to failures in selective attention when aspects of stimuli that seem separable to adults are perceived as integral, and children would need to perceive dimensional structure in stimuli before being able to acquire the skill of selective attention.

Although an argument has not yet developed in the literature, there is at least one alternative approach to the questions addressed by those exploring the developmental relevance of Garner's theory. This is the proposal by Odom (Odom & Guzman 1972) for varying degrees of salience in stimulus dimensions. The argument here would be that the level of distinctiveness between the values representing the component dimensions of stimuli affects the salience of those dimensions and therefore the likelihood that they will be conceptually evaluated. Older children may be more perceptually sensitive than younger children to overall differences between dimensional values and therefore be more likely to reject them as "going together" or being similar. A comparative evaluation of the perceptual structure and dimensional salience approaches to perceptual learning has not yet been undertaken.

In an ordered progression of investigations, Bornstein (1979, 1980; Bornstein, Kessen & Weiskopf 1976) has explored the concept of prototypicality in the categorization of hues. This work finds remarkable concordance in the categories of hue that are perceived by infants and adults, humans and other primates, primates and other color-perceiving organisms (e.g. bees). Basic hue categories of blue, green, yellow, and red and the wavelength boundaries between adjoining categories are commonly perceived by infants and adults, in the former case prior to any opportunity for perceptual learning or the use of language for color naming. Since color names in language parallel categories already discriminated by infants, the perception of the physical world leads the nominal classification system inherent in languages for color designation. The question is raised concerning the possibility of prototypicality in perception for other categorizations of experience, and this term has already been adapted to the area of person perception (Mischel & Cantor 1979).

Questions of categorization, the perception of similarities as well as differences, lead to inquiry regarding whether or how early infants can perceive relations among stimuli. In a series of experiments, Schwartz & Day (1979) presented infants with simple figures or geometric forms and through a habituation paradigm determined whether the infants perceived a difference when the form was rotated, with no other changes, or when angles within the form were altered. It was found that infants classed rotated forms as similar, but changes in the angles between constituent lines were perceived as different. Responding, perhaps, to evidence such as that from Bornsteins's (1980) work that characteristics of perception may be innate, Schwartz & Day (1979) argued that the perception of relations is also an innate capability. Cohen (1979a) has taken issue with this conclusion. Drawing on work by Salapatek (1975), Bower (1966), Fantz (Fantz, Fagan & Miranda 1975) and himself (Cohen & Gelber 1975), Cohen argues that the perception of relations can be found even in very young infants, but the types of relations that can be perceived change markedly over the first few months of life. Under 1 1/2 or 2 months of age, infants are able to perceive high contrast edges, but probably not until 2–4 months can they perceive relations among such edges or among angles. Not until 4 or 5 months of age are they able to perceive relationships among forms. Developmental changes of this sort imply that perceptual learning processes interact significantly with any innate capabilities and should not be neglected. Cohen (1979b) proposes that infant perceptual development be viewed from a constructivistic stance, looking for successive levels of perceptual ability stemming from infant-environment interaction in addition to capabilities that may well be innate. While the climate may not be a particularly heated one, the nature-nurture controversy seems far from dead within the area of perceptual development, primarily that of infant perceptual development.

There has been fairly broad interest recently in the development of spatial localization abilities, spatial coding, and, on a broader level, cognitive maps. It has become clear that children become able to identify landmarks and use them to understand and remember the environment. Acredolo (1977) found that 3 and 4-year-old children were less accurate than 5-year-olds when confronted with a large-scale environment containing no landmarks (e.g. a small room), while a small-scale space (2 by 2 feet) revealed no differences between children at the two ages. In a subsequent study with infants, she (1979) found that 9-month-old infants were egocentric and used their own body as a base for a spatial-reference system when external landmarks were unavailable. In this experiment infants watched while an object was hidden under a cloth to their left or right and then allowed to search for it after being moved to the opposite side of the table. An egocentric solution was to continue to look to the infant's *own* left or right after repositioning. When the same task was presented in the home environment, infants did not depend upon their body as a reference base. It was also found that infants used an egocentric reference base when tested in a landmark-filled but unfamiliar environment. Thus, both availability and familiarity affect infants' use of landmarks to achieve accurate spatial localization, but as early as 9 months of age infants are able to use either personal (egocentric) or external reference bases.

In the construction of cognitive maps from either direct or vicarious (pictorialized) experience, there seems to be very clear developmental improvement in accuracy. In a study with second grade children, fifth grade children, and adults, Siegel, Allen & Kirasic (1979) found systematic improvement in the accuracy with which subjects were able to represent the distances between sequentially encountered landmarks. Feldman & Acredolo (1979) found that preschool children's accuracy in spatial location was greater if they had actively traversed the general environment than if their experience was more constrained. In the active exploration condition children proceeded on their own through an unfamiliar hallway in search of a hidden object, while in the passive condition an adult held the child's hand. Free exploration did not improve the performance of 9–10 year old children, who were consistently more accurate than the younger children. It is proposed that for the younger children active, unfettered exploration increased their attention to the environment, thus improving their ability to relocate the hidden object.

Just as there is developmental improvement in the creation of cognitive maps from experience, improvement is found in children's ability to decode maps that are presented to them. Bluestein & Acredolo (1979) presented 3-, 4-, and 5-year-old children with maps describing the location of an object. The maps were presented in alignment with the coordinates of the room containing the object or out of alignment, in the room or outside it, and vertically or horizontally. Even the youngest children could read an aligned map, but only the oldest children could compensate for a rotation. Location of the map inside or outside the room made little difference, and most children were also able to read a vertical map with ease, indicating that even young children can interchange up and down with near and far.

Some of the recent work on the development of spatial abilities has focused on the role of cerebral lateralization as a determining factor. Flanery & Balling (1979) found that fifth grade children and adults were more accurate in tracing a previously explored nonsense form when they used their left hand (right hemisphere) than when they used their right (left hemisphere), but there was no significant difference between hands for first grade children. They concluded that the right hemisphere becomes progressively more specialized for tactile spatial ability with age. In dichotic listening tasks, a right ear advantage (REA) is typically found, presumably due to the left hemisphere localization of language. This advantage can be overcome with selective attention strategies in adults (Morais 1975, Treisman & Geffen 1968), but there is little evidence this is true for children (Geffen 1978, Hiscock & Kinsbourne 1977). In fact, recent work (Geffen & Wale 1979) has found that the REA may stay constant with age or, under some conditions such as rapid presentation rates, show a decrease. Developmental consequences of laterality for perception thus appear to vary with the perceptual mode. This possibility is consistent with a study of visual lateralization (Carter & Kinsbourne 1979) which found no evidence for the progressive lateralization for either the verbal identification (right hemisphere) of tachistoscopically presented numbers or for accuracy given spatial priming (which should invoke left hemisphere function) in children from 5 to 12 years of age. Another hypothesis is, of course, that lateralization in general is not progressive with age and results such as those reported by Flanery & Balling (infant of 1979) are invalid or due to extraneous factors that are thus far unidentified.

One aspect of emerging spatial abilities that has received attention recently is the ability of infants to engage in visually directed reaching. Early work on visual pursuit confirmed that infants demonstrate predictive reactions to stimulus motion through their visual orientation as early as 6–8 weeks of age (White, Castle & Held 1964), but reaching requires both motor capability and visual-motor coordination. Reaching succeeds the capability for visual pursuit, developmentally, beginning to occur about 3–5 months of age. The question that arises, then, is the age at which visually directed reaching can be observed and what, if any, are the factors accelerating or impeding its development.

One impediment to reaching is the difficulty experienced by infants in reaching across the midline of their body in order to contact an object. The development of the ability to cross the body midline has been construed to be important in the development of manual complementarity and coordination (Bruner 1969, 1971). Provine & Westerman (1979) found that infants do indeed show a progressive capability to reach contralaterally. From 9–17 weeks of age infants' success at touching objects presented at midline rose from 33% to 93% and success in contacting objects across the midline from the reaching hand rose from 0% to 71%. By 20 weeks of age all infants were able to reach contralaterally.

A second developmental accomplishment is the ability to grasp objects that are actually moving. This capability would seem to follow directly from the ability for accurate visual pursuit, when combined with skills in visual-motor coordination and motor coordination alone. Von Hofsten & Lindhagen (1979) studied the static and motile reaching abilities of 11 infants from between 12 and 24 weeks of age up to 36 weeks of age. They found that the ability to reach moving objects was apparent at approximately the same time that the ability to reach a static object was observed, and 18-week-old infants were able to catch an object moving at the rate of 30 cm/sec. Acknowledging the need for replication, these results nevertheless indicate a remarkable and to some extent unforeseen competence in infants for active intervention in their environment, one containing both static and moving objects. The absence of a lag between the onset of an ability to apprehend still and moving objects may also be interpreted to indicate capability to coordinate one's movement (behavior) with that of external objects that is basic (innate) or developed through early learning that does not involve reaching for objects (von Hofsten & Lindhagen 1979).

If infants show an already sophisticated ability to adjust the motor extension response of reaching in accord with visual feedback so as to apprehend a still or moving object, it stands to reason that other motor activities may be guided by visual feedback. Another area of visually guided control that has been investigated of late is that of postural stability by young infants. In an ingenious experiment, Lee & Aronson (1974) demonstrated that infants who have just learned to walk use visual information to assess postural sway so that motor adjustments can be made to retain a standing posture. In this work a room with movable walls was constructed so that while the floor remained still, the walls could move as if the infant were falling toward or away from them. When the walls were moved, visual information was placed in conflict with vestibular information which still indicated that a vertical posture ws being maintained. It was argued, however, that in early postural control proprioceptive feedback such as vestibular may not be adequate to the task and other input, i.e. exteroceptive visual, may be required to augment or may replace other sources of control. In fact, it was found that infants showed a significant tendency to fall backward when the room walls moved such that it must have appeared subjectively to the infant that she was falling forward or backward. In a follow-up investigation, Butterworth & Hicks (1977) showed that the visual feedback was specific to postural control. While falling backward when the far wall of a room moves towards you might just be a response to a looming stimulus, children also swayed or fell forward when the far wall of the room receded, as it would appear to if they were falling backward, and viewing the side of the room pass by also induced postural adjustment (although not as clearly as viewing a wall loom or recede). Butterworth & Hicks also examined the question of whether learning to walk, and the accompanying postural instability, promotes the salience of visual information or whether infants who have learned to sit but not walk would show a similar reliance on visual cues. When the postural responses to the moving room were examined for sitting infants, both younger infants who could not yet walk and older ones who could showed a dependence on visual information to maintain sitting posture, and there was a slight tendency for the *younger* infants to show a greater response. However, the impact of visual information on sitting posture appeared to be distinctly less than it was for the delicate act of balancing on one's feet. The thrust of this work has been to clarify the role of sensory functions in the direction of behavior. While vision has classically been construed as an exteroceptive sense, this work indicates quite clearly that it serves proprioceptive functions as well.

COGNITIVE DEVELOPMENT

Recently in this series, Gelman (1978) reviewed the cognitive development literature. In that review she concentrated on the thesis that the cognitive competencies of children have perhaps been underestimated, or at least not well appraised, and proposed that an appropriate stance for researchers would be to determine not merely what the young child *can't* do relative to the older child but rather what the young child *can* do. Gelman's case was well made with respect to children's competencies in cognitive invariance concepts, classification abilities, sensitivity to order and causal relationships, and perspective-taking abilities.

It is surely fair to say that one of the more influential conceptual developments in cognition during the last decade has been the notion of metacognition, which highlights the individual's own awareness and consideration of her or his cognitive processes and strategies (Flavell 1976a,b; 1978a,b; Kreutzer, Leonard & Flavell 1975; Flavell & Wellman 1977). While this concept initially dealt with children's knowledge of memory processes (Kreutzer et al 1975), it has been broadened considerably to include awareness of comprehension (Markman 1978, Brown 1979, Brown & Smiley 1979), the effectiveness of one's attempts to persuade others (Howie-Day 1977), problem solving (Flavell 1976b, Brown 1978, Flavell 1978a, Hayes 1976), communication (Flavell 1976a), attention (Miller & Bigi unpublished), memory (A. L. Brown 1978, Flavell & Wellman 1977), social cognition (Flavell 1978a,b,c, 1979), and has even been integrated into conceptualizations of cognitive behavior modification (Meichenbaum & Asarnow 1979).

There is a sufficient diversity in metacognitive research, as illustrated above, to prevent a rich and detailed description here of the various findings. A good review has been provided elsewhere by Flavell (1978a). The general developmental picture is not surprising: with increasing age, children engage in more metacognitive efforts and activity and show a growing awareness of strategies to improve cognitive performances of various types, including the strategic use of metacognitive behavior per se, such as the cognitive monitoring of comprehension during referential communication

(Cosgrove & Patterson 1978; Ironsmith & Whitehurst 1978; Patterson, Massad & Cosgrove 1978; Markman 1978). For example, when faced with an ambiguous message in a communication interaction, young children may fail to seek clarification (all references noted above apply here) because they do not recognize that alternative interpretations exist. On the other hand, very young children have a metacognitive awareness of some memory strategies, and if they are instructed to remember the spatial location of an object, they will show intentional strategies to keep track of the object and remember its location (Wellman, Ritter & Flavell 1975).

Flavell & Wellman (1977) have proposed a classification of metamemory dimensions which has proved helpful in systematizing the broader concept of metacognition (Flavell 1978c). In this conceptualization, there is first a sensitivity category characterizing the acquisition of metacognitive knowledge about the depth and type of cognitive processing that is appropriate in various circumstances—the understanding, for example, that performance in certain types of memory tasks will benefit from a strategy, e.g. rehearsal, which others will not. The second major category concerns the variables whose cognitive appraisal may be important to direct the selection or implementation of strategies. There are several types of variables with relevance, including person variables (Am I smart enough to learn this? Can the person listening to me understand what I am attempting to communicate?); task variables (Is what I am trying to learn well organized or should I impose organization upon it? Am I faced with distracting circumstances that I should work to overcome?); and strategy variables (I should organize this material I am trying to learn. That person did not understand what I said (person variable) so I should rephrase it (strategy variable)). The area of metacognitive skills and competencies continues to generate interest, and a theoretical structure has evolved from the growing pool of research findings about metacognitive behavior as well.

Related to research and theory on metacognition has been work on the teaching of cognitive and metacognitive strategies, particularly those likely to influence learning and memory (Brown & Barclay 1976; Brown & Campione 1977, 1978; Brown et al 1973; Brown, Campione & Murphy 1974, Campione & Brown 1977). In addition to practical, educational utility, knowledge about the design and effectiveness of training programs for learning and memory is also informative about cognitive processes themselves and the efficacy of specific classes of strategies, such as metacognitive ones, for the immediate and sustained enhancement of cognitive processing. Most training studies begin with a task analysis to identify the cognitive strategy(ies) most likely to improve performance (Brown & Campione 1978). The results of training studies are often impressive. Butterfield (Butterfield, Wambold & Belmost 1973) trained retarded adolescents in a memory-retrieval strategy, achieving a final performance level that was in *excess* of that by nonretarded adolescents who received no strategy training.

In addition to evidence that strategy training can produce impressive improvements in cognitive performance, there are other findings that indicate some longevity of training procedures. Brown, Campione & Murphy (1974) retested subjects trained by Brown et al (1973) some 6 months earlier and found that 80% of the subjects continued to use the earlier trained rehearsal strategy. Brown, Campione & Barclay (1979) followed up subjects from an earlier study (Brown & Barclay 1976). They found that after a year, younger, educably retarded children (MA=6 years) failed to retain earlier trained memory strategies of anticipation and rehearsal, but slightly older children (MA=8 years) not only retained the strategies when faced with the original task but also generalized the strategies to a new learning situation and task. This research does not reveal the extent to which metacognitive strategies may be acquired during naturally occurring experiences of cognitive socialization or even by spontaneous trial and error; nevertheless, the potency of such strategies to influence learning and memory on an immediate and continuing basis has clearly been demonstrated.

There are many other areas of cognitive development in which interesting developments are taking place. Researchers are active in elucidating the schemata of stories, the units that are expected to comprise stories, and the way they are sequenced (Mandler & DeForest 1979, Poulsen et al 1980, Stein & Glenn 1977). These schemata have been found to influence comprehension as well as memory (Mosenthal 1979). Attention is being given to staple components of cognitive developmental theory such as Piaget's stages, with the result that criticism of their explanatory power (Brainerd 1978) as well as praise (Gelman 1978) has been forthcoming. It is probably safe to say that the area of cognitive development is to some extent in a period of self-appraisal, and new directions include some very different aspects of cognitive activity (metacognition) and a critical review of some old ones.

LANGUAGE DEVELOPMENT

There are three features of language that generally define areas of inquiry regarding language development. These are semantics, the encoding of meaning, grammar, or syntax; the way meaningful elements (e.g. words) are combined into communicative units such as sentences; and phonology, the production of spoken utterances. Most recent work has concentrated on syntax and semantics.

Following the remarkable impact of transformational grammar theory in the late 1950s and mid 1960s (Chomsky 1957, 1965), little attention was paid to the continued viability of nontransformational descriptions of language. More recently, there has been serious consideration of the utility of syntactic descriptions that do not rely on transformations emanating from deep structures and are more "close-to-surface" in nature (deVilliers & deVilliers 1978, Maratsos & Kuczaj 1978, Maratsos 1978). The sort of evidence used to support a move away from transformational grammars is exemplified in the evaluation of the hypothesis of derivational cumulative complexity. This hypothesis proposes that during development a child's use of language, as it becomes more complex, mirrors the complexity of transformations required to go from a deep structure kernel sentence (or sentences) to a final utterance. For example, a sentence like "The wagon is red" is closer to a deep structure form (it *is* a deep structure form) than a sentence such as "push the red wagon." According to the derivational hypothesis, children should be observed to use sentences of the first type earlier than those of the second. However, both types of sentences tend to occur even in very early speech and there is no preferential tendency that can be demonstrated (deVilliers & deVilliers 1978).

This argument is not yet concluded. It can be argued that evidence of the sort cited above does not necessarily indicate that transformational accounts per se are incorrect since it could also be posssible that merely the exact grammar which specifies the presumed transformations is incorrect, in this case Chomsky's 1965 grammar (Maratsos 1978).

The interaction of cognitive and linguistic development characterizes several different areas of concern within the domain of language development. Children's acquisition of syntactic rules is a good case in point. Two important aspects of such rules are their degree of specificity and of generality. It has been proposed that rules are initially specific and through development become more generalized. When this happens overgeneralization is likely to occur as the rule is applied in inappropriate instances, as when the regular past tense ending (-ed) is added to an irregular verb incorrectly (e.g., goed). Research on the acquisition of the regular past tense suffix *-ed* (Brown 1973, Kuczaj 1977) as well as other aspects of syntax such as the construction of passive sentences (Maratsos et al 1979) or the formation of *wh* questions (why? who? when? where?) (Kuczaj & Brannick 1979) has shown such overgeneralization. An even more obvious fusion of cognitive and language concerns is evident in some research on semantics operations of hypothetical reference, the ability to refer to nonpresent objects and occurrences. Studies of language acquisition (Bates 1976, Paris 1975) have reported late occurrence of the conditional, as would have been expected from studies of children's cognitive abilities to decenter (Cromer 1971, Piaget 1969). Most recently, Kuczaj & Daly (1979) report that future hypothetical reference is an earlier acquisition than past, and reference to single hypothetical events occurs earlier to that of sequences of hypothetical events.

An important cognitive aspect of language is its acquisition per se. During the latter 1970s a consistent body of work developed concerning the "learnability" of language. In this work, an attempt was made to provide a formal model of what must be learned in mastering a language by considering the linguistic information that is available to a learner (typically a child). The proponents of this approach use logical and mathematical analysis to conclude that a transformational grammar as proposed by Chomsky (1965) is indeed descriptive of the basic language process and structure onto which the specific lexicon and syntax of a given language is mapped (Hamburger & Wexler 1975; Culicover & Wexler 1977; Wexler, Culicover & Hamburger 1975; Wexler 1978). The intricacies of this analysis are remarkable and cannot be reproduced here. It should be noted, however, that the acceptance of this model or acknowledgment of its contribution to the understanding of language development is not undisputed. Questions may be raised about some assumptions that underlie the analysis, such as the prototypicality or innateness of deep structure representation in the child prior to hearing grammatical utterances in her/his native language, or the adequacy of Chomsky's 1965 model of transformational grammar as opposed to other models. One goal of such a theory is simply to provide a representation and source of hypotheses regarding language and language acquisition that can lead to empirical work (Wexler 1978), and as such the validity of the theory is not an evaluative concern but rather its heurism. The data on that point are not yet in.

Notions of prototype similar to those in research on perceptual development (Bornstein 1980) or cognitive development (e.g. Rosch 1975, Rosch & Lloyd 1978) have also been considered in recent research on semantic development (Kuczaj, unpublished; Bowerman 1978). It is being argued that word acquisition is a complex interaction between children's own predispositions to categorize objects and events and categorizations provided by words in a language (Bowerman 1978). Cognitive or linguistic prototypicality theory proposes that categories are not necessarily populated by referents all of which share one or several criterial attributes. Rather, for each category there may be one or more prototypical exemplars, accompanied by other members of the category that are progressively less exemplary and which may not all share attributes with one another (Rosch 1975, Smith, Shoben & Rips 1974). Bowerman (1978) has concluded that children's prototypes will tend to be the *first* referent the child has for a particular word, following which the word will be used to name or classify new objects/experiences according to some perceived similarity, not always the same in each instance nor perhaps always recognized or understood by the child. Errors of overgeneralization or overinclusion may thus be productive and intentional, representing a *non*inadvertent extension of a category boundary as in an intentional metaphor. Bloom (1973) anticipated this conceptualization in the following speculation: "It is almost as if the child were reasoning, 'I know about dogs, that thing is not a dog, I don't know what to call it, but it is like a dog'" (Bloom 1973, p. 79).

Research on the role of prototypicality in semantic development is a combination of the compilation of examples and, to a lesser extent, experimental research. Kuczaj (unpublished) reports that overextension of concepts can be demonstrated in comprehension as well as in production, which had been the primary type of evidence. In this research, when children are given a number of choices on a comprehension task, while the initial choice is almost always an appropriate exemplar of the target, successive choices for the same target will commonly involve overextensions of some other, not altogether unrelated category, indicating a tendency and willingness to elaborate a category. Bowerman (1978) has marshalled examples of the way perceptual dimensions such as spatial orientation or parts of the body guide the application of words (concepts) to new referents and has proposed that the directions of such generalizations are not random but guided by universally shared categorizational propensities. Feedback from the environment as to whether the new labeling is acceptable then cues the child about properties of the language (and culture) that she/he is acquiring. This model is provocative as it brings together cognitive, perceptual, and linguistic factors in a common pattern of development.

PERSONALITY AND SOCIAL DEVELOPMENT AND SOCIAL COGNITION

The area of personality and social development is broad, and recent integrations of cognitive and social/personality development have extended this breadth significantly (Collins 1980, Mischel 1973, Sroufe 1979b). There is a continuing increase in the use of sophisticated observational and analytic techniques for the analysis of social behavior (Furman & Masters 1980a,b; Lamb, Suomi & Stephenson 1979). Greater emphasis is being placed on social behavior and the development of a social psychological or social systems approach to family and peer socialization (Hartup 1980, Feiring & Lewis 1978). Emotion, often relegated solely to the domain of psychopathology, is now a legitimate and avidly pursued topic of concern as a component of personality and social development (e.g. Sroufe 1979a,b; Sroufe & Waters 1977; Masters, Barden & Ford 1979; Rosenhan, Underwood & Moore 1974). With these introductory comments, let us turn to some representative findings in several commonly defined subareas of personality, social, and social-cognitive development.

Attachment

Since a major upsurge of interest in the early 1970s (Maccoby & Masters 1970), research appears to be concentrated on attempts to validate qualitative dimensions of attachment [e.g. secure vs anxious attachment (Sroufe 1979a, Ainsworth 1979)] and to determine more clearly what relationships exist between attachment relations in infancy and subsequent, more general social relations in the peer group. Infants are classified as securely attached when they spontaneously and energetically seek proximity and contact on reunion but then renew an interest in play. On the other hand, an infant who seems ambivalent during reunion or even actively avoids the caregiver is said to be insecurely or anxiously attached (Ainsworth et al 1978). There seem to be a number of differences in infants falling into these two classifications. Infants judged to be securely attached are more obedient, responsive, and likely to explore in the presence of the mother using her as a secure base (Ainsworth et al 1978; Bretherton et al 1978; Londerville 1977; Matas, Arend & Sroufe 1978). Mothers of securely attached infants are rated to be more sensitive, accepting, and affectively expressive than those of insecurely attached infants who, in turn, are rated as more angry (Main, Tomasini & Tolan 1979). Findings of this sort do not indicate whether parent/caretaker behaviors induce the attachment relationship directly, but Lamb (1978a) has argued that they do since security of attachment toward one parent is not a perfect predictor of attachment toward the other, indicating that different parental behavior patterns may induce different attachment relations.

Several recent studies have indicated relationships between patterns of infant attachment and current or future patterns of peer relations. Blanchard & Main (1979) found that 1- to 2-year old infants who had more lengthy day-care experiences showed reduced levels of avoidance during reunion and greater social-emotional adjustment in the day-care setting. Easterbrooks & Lamb (1979) found systematic variations in peer relations even within the category of secure attachment, with more securely attached infants showing more frequent and sophisticated peer interactions than less securely attached infants who, in turn, sought proximity and contact with their mothers even in the presence of peers (as well as in the reunion situation). Waters, Wippman & Sroufe (1979) studied the relationship between attachment assessed at 15 months of age and peer relations at 42 months. They found that securely attached children were more socially active, sought out by other children, peer leaders, and sympathetic to peer distress. The emerging picture is clearly one of increased social competence in children whose attachment is rated to be secure.

Aggression

The most remarkable aspect of current research on aggression is its general absence. In an extensive review of articles published in developmental psychology journals during 1979, only two articles were found (Messer & Brodzinsky 1979; Brodzinsky, Messer & Tew 1979). The meaning of this change in interest is difficult to discern. It is perhaps most likely that interest in the competencies of children for prosocial interaction has led researchers away from aggression as a topic of concern. Whatever the case, there is clearly little emphasis in this area, and a recent review of current issues in social development (Hartup 1979) did not even mention the topic of aggression despite the fact that the writer had himself concentrated upon it but a few years earlier (Hartup & DeWit 1978, DeWit & Hartup 1974).

Sex typing

The sex-typing literature is rather sprawling, not in terms of sheer numbers of research reports but in terms of the diversity of subtopics within the area that are studied. Some research seems merely to confirm prior findings about sex differences in areas such as anxiety (Douglas & Rice 1979), sex-role liberation (Spence & Helmreich 1979), attitudes toward cooperation and competition (Ahlgren & Johnson 1979), or aggression (Brodzinsky, Messer & Tew 1979).

Two recent studies focused upon the conditions under which a given sex difference will or will not be evident. Thus, Brodzinsky et al (1979) found that while boys may show more direct aggression than girls, no sex differences pertain for indirect (fantasy) aggression. These results were interpreted to indicate sex-related socialization pressures for overt aggressive behavior. Serbin et al (1979) found that sex-typed play behavior was more prevalent in the presence of an opposite-sex peer and interpreted this to indicate differential reinforcement for sex-typed play in the presence of peers.

Several studies have focused upon children's sex-role stereotyping. Davidson, Yasuna & Tower (1979) found that low-stereotyped television content reduces the degree of sex-role stereotype in girls. Cordua, McGraw & Drabman (1979), however, described children's resistance to information (films, in this case) that is contrary to established sex-role stereotypes. In this study, children shown counterstereotypical portrayals of female doctors and male nurses were prone to relabel the occupations of the characters. Maternal employment and exposure to real male nurses tended to promote relabeling.

If these studies may be taken as an indication, there is some movement to explore the cognitive aspects of sex differences and to describe the conditions under which sex differences in preferential and social behavior are under cognitive control or, contrariwise, influence cognition. An exception to this generalization is a study by Maccoby et al (1979) investigating the relations of sex hormones at birth to infants' sex and ordinal position. They found greater testosterone concentrations in males than females, but no sex differences in the concentrations of four other sex hormones. Hormonal differences also characterized firstborns as opposed to laterborns of both sexes, and reduced concentrations of hormones in laterborns were more greatly reduced if their birth was more closely spaced in relation to their next older sibling. These findings are discussed in terms of physiological as opposed to psychological determinants of early sex differences and ordinal position effects on behavior determinants.

Moral Judgment and Behavior

In addition to studies investigating hypotheses relating to Kohlberg's theory of moral development in invariant stages (Larson & Kurdek 1979, Moran & Joniak 1979, Eisenberg-Berg 1979, Walker & Richards 1979), there appears to be a developing focus of research interest on the component dimensions of situations that may provoke a moral judgment and the role these dimensions play in determining that judgment. Suls and his colleagues (Suls, Gutkin & Kalle 1979; Suks & Kalle 1979) have studied the role of intentions, damage, and personal or social consequences in the formation of moral judgments. During grade school, the use of social consequence information decreases with age, while damage cues remain important (Suls et al 1979). Not surprisingly, the use of intent cues increased with age, but there was a tendency for even very young children (kindergartners) to use intent cues when social reactions were positive (Suls et al 1979). Wellman, Larkey & Somerville (1979) report clear developmental changes in children's ability to take specific moral criteria into account. Thus, children understand the relevance of an apology in a moral judgment situation even before they totally understand damage cues. These results indicate that research looking primarily at cues such as intention or damages have not tapped the full complement of moral criteria children use in making judgments. To underscore once again the point made by Gelman (1978), the competence of young children has not been fully acknowledged or explored.

At least one recent study has reawakened the question of the interaction between moral judgment or cognition and moral or prosocial behavior (Eisenberg-Berg & Hand 1979). It was found that moral reasoning was differentially related to several types of prosocial behavior. For example, hedonistic reasoning was negatively related to sharing, while needs-oriented reasoning showed a positive relationship. The increasing concern with cognitive aspects of personality and social behavior should lead to more inquiry about the ways that cognition and behavior are and are not related, not just in the area of moral judgment and behavior.

Affective Processes and Development

An emerging area of work during the last several years has involved the experimental induction of emotional states. Rosenhan and his colleagues (Moore, Underwood & Rosenhan 1973; Underwood, Moore & Rosenhan 1973; Rosenhan, Underwood & Moore 1974) demonstrated that positive affective states increase self-gratification and altruism in young children, while negative states increase self-gratification but decrease altruism. Subsequent research has demonstrated that emotional states influence social behaviors such as aggression (Harris & Siebel 1975) as well as aspects of cognition such as problem solving (Masters, Barden & Ford 1979) and memory (Barden et al 1980, Bartlett & Santrock 1979). Not surprisingly, it is found that positive states facilitate cognitive endeavors and negative states interfere.

Thus far it has been the cognitive aspect of emotion that has been most studied. It is found, for example, that when an affective state is induced through thinking about experiences that happened to another person, altruism is greater than follows a state induced by thoughts about one's own experiences (Barnett, King & Howard 1979). It has also been found that children understand that apparent emotion, such as that indicated by facial expression, may not be a true index of an internal state and that people have "display rules" regulating expressive behavior in different contexts (Saarni 1979). Nevertheless, young children may have difficulty in regulating their own facial expressions to the point where they can deceive an adult observer (Feldman, Jenkins & Popoola 1979). Finally, although cognitive manipulations such as thinking about happy or sad events may induce emotional states (Masters, Barden & Ford 1979; Bugental & Moore 1979), there is some evidence that similar manipulations may *not* be able to alter existing affective states (Barden et al 1980).

Social Relations

The two major social contexts of child development that have received the greatest attention are those of family and the peer group. Whereas normally these contexts are considered separately, there has been a thrust of late (e.g. Hartup 1979) to consider them jointly, noting similarities in the two systems as well as differences. They will be considered together here because there is also an emerging literature of studies relating the two contexts in their effects on children and children's effects on them (reciprocal causality) (Klein, Jorgensen & Miller 1978).

When parents interact with a child in a socializing fashion, the child's responsiveness influences the parents' continued socialization practices. It has been argued, for example, that when children's behavior improves after use of punishment by parents, this negatively reinforces that use of punishment and makes it more likely in the future (Parke & Collmer 1975). There is some evidence to support this contention (Mulhern & Passman 1979). Furthermore, there is some evidence that abused children may behave in ways that not only are the product of abuse but may subsequently contribute to it. For example, George & Main (1979) report that abused toddlers more frequently physically assault their peers and harass their caregivers verbally and nonverbally. They are also less likely to approach caregivers in response to friendly overtures and show some tendency to avoid peers and caregivers making friendly gestures.

Within the peer group, sociometric status is enjoying a new burst of interest. Friendship among children is being examined as a cause, not a consequence of behavior. Newcomb, Brady & Hartup (1979) report, for example, that in a cooperative task friends and nonfriends did not differ in terms of performance outcome, but friendship did facilitate the expressive and cooperative components of social interaction during the task performance. Positive, socially reinforcing interactions of the type likely to be common among friends have been shown to have affective consequences for peers (Furman & Masters 1980a). Self-regulatory behavior, such as resistance to deviation, has been shown to be sensitive to peer processes. It is found, for example, that a prohibition that is endorsed by a peer is less likely to be obeyed by children who are more frequently punished by their peers, but the frequency of peer reinforcement does not increase resistance to deviation given a peer-endorsed prohibition (Furman & Masters 1980b).

An important emerging area of interest concerns the relationship between the peer and parent (family) contexts of socialization. Conformity to peer norms tends to be curvilinear, peaking between the sixth and ninth grades, while conformity to parents decreases steadily with age (Berndt 1979). Toddlers who have playgroup experiences change in the ways they interact with parents, becoming more active and more responsive to the interaction initiations of parents (Vandell 1979). Parents change too, becoming less dominant. A group setting encourages interaction and reciprocal smiling with adults in infants (18 months old), while the home environment seems to encourage greater responsiveness to maternal talking, greater frequency of crying, and more restrictiveness on the part of mothers (Rubenstein & Howes 1979). When the developmental level of play is assessed, a peer setting seems faciliatory (Rubenstein & Howes 1979). Children from families disrupted by divorce are more immature, ineffective, and negative in their social interactions than are children from intact families (Hetherington, Cox & Cox 1980). In short, not only do family and peer contexts influence development, not only do infants and children influence the behavior of adult caretakers and peers, but there is also a reciprocity between the family and peer contexts themselves as they influence the behavior of all participants.

Social Cognition and the Interaction Between Cognition and Social Behavior

A decade ago this section would not have appeared in this review. Today the interaction and reciprocity between the social and cognitive spheres of behavior is not merely recognized but is becoming more and more frequently the target of investigation. This investigation has taken a variety of forms. There is inquiry into the cognitive correlates and determinants of behavior. Investigators have inquired into the child's recognition that behavior is multiply caused. Erwin & Kuhn (1979) found, for example, that not until adolescence do children appear to understand that there may be multiple determining factors underlying human behavior. It has been suggested that at least some developmental findings regarding moral judgment may reflect not differing judgmental behavior but rather a different understanding of the vignette (dilemma) that is presented to the child. Sedlak (1979) reports that children may disagree with the interpretations adults place on stories and are likely to impute intentionality where adults do not.

On the other hand, social experiences may influence cognitions. Newcomb & Collins (1979) studied the influence of SES on children's processing of the content of television programs. They found that middle class children comprehend plot content and infer more about the causes of actions and the feelings and emotions of characters than do lower class children when the content of the program concerns a white, middle class family, while the reverse is true when the program concerns a black working-class family. Similarly, children's previewing level of aggressive behavior moderates the effects of televised violence and the effectiveness of procedures designed to mitigate the effects of viewing aggression. Stories depicting adults rewarding children for prosocial conflict resolution or punishing them for aggression decreased the effects of aggressive television for children whose initial level of aggression was low but resulted in high postviewing aggression by initially high aggressive children (Collins 1980, Gouze & Collins unpublished).

Finally, there is a growing body of evidence that early social interaction experiences have consequences for later cognitive and social competence. It is found, for example, that for preterm infants the frequency of social transactions during the first year predicts the competence at age 2 on such cognitive measures as the Bayley Mental Scale, the Gesell Developmental Schedules, and other indicators such as a sensorimotor scale or a measure of receptive language (Cohen & Beckwith 1979). Mother-infant interactions and maternal attitudes are predictive of children's IQ at 3 years of age (Ramey, Farran & Campbell 1979) and of general competency indicators such as IQ, language level, and sociability to adults (Clarke-Stewart, VanderStoep & Killian 1979). There is some evidence, however, that relationships such as these are peculiar to the influence of early social interaction on cognitive development, and that during the later preschool years the relationship is reversed, with cognitive processes facilitating social adaptation (Emmerich, Cocking & Sigel 1979). Other evidence indicates that the cutoff for early social effects may be rather early. Stevenson & Lamb (1979) found that at 12 months there were no relationships between measures of home environment and cognitive competence except among firstborn children. It may also be that the early social determinants of competence are specifically behavioral—interactional—in nature and more global assessments of the home environment are not sensitive to the factors of greatest importance. This awaits clarification.

DEVELOPMENTAL PSYCHOPATHOLOGY

While there is not yet a great deal of contemporary research to review in the developmental psychopathology domain, the topic itself illustrates the melding of developmental and clinical concerns toward a common goal, the elucidation of developmental processes germane to disordered behavior, its development and change.

More and more frequently a developmental perspective is being brought to the understanding of behavior problems and procedures for their remediation. It is being argued strongly that a dimension of competence, largely social competence, is important in attempts to construe the behavior disorders of children (Achenbach 1978; Gesten 1976; Achenbach & Edelbrock 1978, 1979; Furman 1980), and therapeutic intervention may both address the dimension of competence and employ the orchestration of naturally occurring socialization experiences, such as interactions with peers (Furman 1980; Furman, Rahe & Hartup 1979). Furman et al, for example, identified socially withdrawn preschool children and provided 10 play sessions with a same-age peer or a younger peer. Compared to a notreatment group, social experience with peers tended to eliminate social withdrawal, with younger peers being more effective "therapists" than same-age peers. Studies with infrahuman primates reared in isolation (e.g. Novak 1979) confirm the effectiveness of "peer therapy" and support the competence-deficit approach to at least some categories of behavior problems such as social isolation.

There is increasing attention in the literature to problems of nondisturbed children which are nevertheless stressful and likely to have adverse effects on behavior and behavioral development. Perhaps foremost among the factors at the moment is that of divorce (Hetherington 1979; Magrab 1978; Hetherington, Cox & Cox 1978; Santrock & Tracy 1978). Developmental factors are realized to influence the child's interpretation of the divorce experience and her or his adaptation to it (Tessman 1978, Hetherington 1979). Child abuse is another area of concern, although at the moment the research literature is impoverished at best (e.g. Starr 1979; Burgess & Conger 1978; Disbrow, Doerr & Caulfield 1977), and current efforts seem concentrated on defining strategies of research and dimensions of the problem more than upon actual research per se. Strong arguments are heard, however, for the use of a developmental perspective and dimensions of behavior such as competence in conceptualizing the psychological aspects of abuse (Garbarino 1978).

ADOLESCENCE

Within developmental psychology, adolescence is the one age period other than infancy which provides a grouping rubric for diverse topics in behavioral development. Interestingly, at about the same time that a journal on infancy was introduced, a different set of pressures promoted the introduction of a journal on adolescence. However, the similarity between these two areas of interest generally ceases at this point. While infancy research, like that in developmental psychology in general, can be divided into conceptual domains of perception, cognition, etc., research on adolescence may be systematized best by reference to theories of adolescence rather than conceptual dimensions of psychology (e.g. Erikson 1950).

One factor directing research in this area is that of social problems relating to adolescents. Attention is given to such topics as drug use (Gonzalez 1979, Levine & Kozak 1979), adolescent pregnancy (Kaplan, Smith & Pokorny 1979; Mednick, Baker & Sutton-Smith 1979), runaways (Adams & Munro 1979), or personality characteristics of minority young (Jones 1979). The range of topics such as these is so great that incremental threads of knowledge are not readily apparent, especially given the small body of research available.

However, there are some that receive repeated attention, although from such varying perspectives that, again, general conclusions are not easy. One important variable in adolescent research is that of ego development (Steward, Bryant & Steward 1979; Adams & Shea 1979; Redmore & Loevinger

1979; Meilman 1979; Adams, Shea & Fitch 1979; Waterman & Archer 1979; St. Clair & Day 1979). Another topic of direct relevance for adolescent development is sensitivity to peers and the use of peers as a reference group (Young & Ferguson 1979, Finney 1979, Elkind & Bowen 1979). For both of these topics a multitude of conceptual and methodological definitions of the concepts prevent any general summary of findings.

It should be noted that some topics of developmental concern, such as social cognition, have relevance for adolescent development but are often studied in investigations that include children, adolescents, and sometimes even adults (e.g. Collins 1980). Since neither the theoretical focus of these studies nor the empirical results involve the notion of continuity in development within narrow developmental periods, adolescence per se as a distinct developmental period is not singled out.

One is tempted to declare that despite a history of theoretical concern of some longevity, research on adolescence is in its infancy. Certainly, the organization of knowledge and ongoing research topics in adolescence is different from that characterizing other domains of developmental psychology, and it does not lend itself to concise summarizations or integration into the rest of the field as of yet.

CONCLUSION

It is both hazardous and difficult to attempt a summary of work in an area as diverse as that embraced by developmental psychology. Nevertheless, certain threads of continuity or common interest and interpretation seem discernible. The thrust toward viewing the young child as competent, noted first in the area of cognition (Gelman 1978), is apparent in many sectors of concern now, including competency-based assessments of psychopathology (e.g. Furman et al 1979, Furman 1980), recognition of the early social competencies of infants and children in family and peer contexts (e.g. Vandell 1979, Lamb 1978b), and demonstration of the remarkable perceptual and conceptual competencies of very young infants (e.g. Cohen, De-Loache & Strauss 1979), to name but a few.

Another commonality across many subareas of developmental psychology today is the interpretation of results in terms of the prototype notion. Prototypes have been invoked to account for findings in the areas of infancy (Strauss 1979), cognition (Rosch 1975, Rosch & Lloyd 1978), perception (Bornstein et al 1976; Bornstein 1979, 1980), personality (Mischel & Cantor 1979), and language (Kuczaj 1979, Bowerman 1978). Perhaps related to this is an increased interest in the interplay between biological and experiential/environmental factors in development. This is seen in the area of developmental behavioral genetics through the increased interest in environmental factors (e.g. Willerman 1979, Scarr-Salapatek 1976), in infancy research through hypotheses relating the occurrence of reflex behavior to subsequent learned responding (Lipsitt 1979), in perceptual development through research on topics such as perceptual dominance (Flanery & Balling 1979, Geffen & Wale 1979, Carter & Kinsbourne 1979), and in the area of personality development through research such as that on hormonal factors in early behavioral development (Maccoby et al 1979).

Despite the ability to find some common threads in the recent fabric of research in developmental psychology, the impression most salient to this reviewer is the diversity of the field and the richness of research within definable subareas such as those used to classify sections within this review. Global reviews should perhaps give way to less frequent but more specifically focused reviews of individual areas of developmental research. And perhaps this is the most appropriate final conclusion: the current scope and depth of developmental psychology is simply remarkable.

Literature Cited

Achenbach, T. M. 1978. The child behavior profile: I. boys aged 6–11. *J. Consult. Clin. Psychol.* 46:478–88

Achenbach, T. M., Edelbrock, C. S. 1978. The classification of child psychopathology: A review and analysis of empirical efforts. *Psychol. Bull.* 85:1275–1301

Achenbach, T. M., Edelbrock, C. S. 1979. The child behavior profile: II. Boys aged 12–16 and girls aged 6–11 and 12–16. *J. Consult. Clin. Psychol.* 47:223–33

Acredolo, L. P. 1977. Developmental changes in the ability to coordinate perspectives of a large-scale space. *Dev. Psychol.* 13:1–8

Acredolo, L. P. 1979. Laboratory versus home: The effect of environment on the 9-month-old infant's choice of spatial reference system. *Dev. Psychol.* 15:666–67

Adams, G. R., Munro, G. 1979. Portrait of the North American runaway: A critical review. *J. Youth Adolesc.* 8:359–73

Adams, G. R., Shea, J. A. 1979. The relationship between identity status, locus of control, and ego development. *J. Youth Adolesc.* 8:81–89

Adams, G. R., Shea, J. A., Fitch, S. A. 1979. Toward the development of an objective assessment of ego-identity status. *J. Youth Adolesc.* 8:223–37

Ahlgren, A., Johnson, D. W. 1979. Sex differences in cooperative and competitive attitudes from the 2nd through the 12th grades. *Dev. Psychol.* 14:45–49

Ainsworth, M. D. S. 1979. Infant-mother attachment. *Am. Psychol.* 34:932–37

Ainsworth, M. D. S., Blehar, M. C., Waters, E., Wall, S. 1978. *Patterns of Attachment.* Hillsdale, NJ: Erlbaum

Aslin, R. N., Salapatek, P. 1975. Saccadic localization of peripheral targets by the very young human infant. *Percept. Psychophys.* 17:292–302

Barden, R. C., Garber, J., Duncan, S. W., Masters, J. C. 1980. Cumulative effects of induced affective states in children: Accentuation, inoculation, and remediation. *J. Pers. Soc. Psychol.* In press

Barnett, M. A., King, L. M., Howard, J. A. 1979. Inducing affect about self or other: Effects on generosity in children. *Dev. Psychol.* 15:164–67

Bartlett, J. C., Santrock, J. W. 1979. Affect-dependent episodic memory in young children. *Child Dev.* 50:513–18

Bates, E. 1976. *Language and Context: The Acquisition of Pragmatics.* New York: Academic

Berndt, T. J. 1979. Developmental changes in conformity to peers and parents. *Dev. Psychol.* 15:608–16

Black, L., Steinschneider, A., Sheehe, P. R. 1979. Neonatal respiratory instability and infant development. *Child Dev.* 50:651–64

Blanchard, M., Main, M. 1979. Avoidance of the attachment figure and social-emotional adjustment in day-care infants. *Dev. Psychol.* 15:445–46

Bloom, L. 1973. *One Word at a Time: The Use of Single Word Utterances Before Syntax.* The Hague: Mouton. 261 pp.

Bluestein, N., Acredolo, L. 1979. Developmental changes in map-reading skills. *Child Dev.* 50:691–97

Bornstein, M. H. 1979. Effects of habituation experience on posthabituation behavior in young infants: Discrimination and generalization among colors. *Dev. Psychol.* 15:348–49

Bornstein, M. H. 1980. *Minnesota Symposia on Child Psychology,* Vol. 14. Hillsdale, NJ:Erlbaum. In press

Bornstein, M. H., Kessen, W., Weiskopf, S. 1976. Categories of hue in infancy. *Science* 191:201–2

Bower, T. G. R. 1966. Heterogeneous summation in human infants. *Anim. Behav.* 14:395–98

Bowerman, M. 1978. Fundamentals of symbolism. In *Symbol as Sense: New Approaches to the Analysis of Meaning,* ed. E. L. Foster, S. Brandis. New York: Academic

Brainerd, C. J. 1978. The stage question in cognitive-developmental theory. *Behav. Brain Sci.* 2:173–213

Bretherton, L., Bates, E., Benigni, L., Camioni, L., Volterra. 1978. *Relationships between cognition, communication and quality of attachment: What are we measuring?* Presented at Int. Conf. Infant Stud., Providence, RI

Brodzinsky, D. M., Messer, S. B., Tew, J. D. 1979. Sex differences in children's expression and control of fantasy and overt aggression. *Child Dev.* 50:372–79

Brown, A. L. 1978. Knowing when, where, and how to remember: A problem of metacognition. In *Advances in Instructional Psychology,* ed. R. Glaser. New York: Halsted

Brown, A. L. 1979. *Theoretical Issues in Reading Comprehension,* ed. R. J. Spiro, B. Bruce, W. F. Brewer. Hillsdale, NJ: Erlbaum. In press

Brown, A. L., Barclay, C. R. 1976. The effects of training specific mnemonics on the mentamnemonic efficiency of retarded children. *Child Dev.* 47:70–80

Brown, A. L., Campione, J. C. 1977. Training strategic study time apportionment in educable retarded children. *Intelligence* 1:94–107

Brown, A. L., Campione, J. C. 1978. Memory strategies in learning. Training children to study strategically. In *Psychology: Research to Practice,* ed. H. L. Pick Jr. New York: Plenum. 390 pp.

Brown, A. L., Campione, J. C., Barclay, C. R. 1979. Training self-checking routines for estimating test readiness: Generalization from list learning to prose recall. *Child Dev.* 40:501–12

Brown, A. L., Campione, J. C., Bray, N. W., Wilcox, B. L. 1973. Keeping track of changing variables: Effects of rehearsal training and rehearsal prevention in normal and retarded adolescents. *J. Exp. Psychol.* 101:123–31

Brown, A. L., Campione, J. C., Murphy, M. D. 1974. Keeping track of changing variables: Long-term retention of trained rehearsal strategy by retarded adolescents. *Am. J. Ment. Defic.* 78:446–53

Brown, A. L., Smiley, S. S. 1979. *Child Dev.* In press

Brown, R. 1973. *A First Language: The Early Stages.* Cambridge: Harvard. 437 pp.

Bruner, J. S. 1969. Eye, hand and mind. In *Studies in Cognitive Development: Essays in Honor of Jean Piaget,* ed. D. Elkind, J. H. Flavell, pp. 223–35. New York: Oxford. 503 pp.

Bruner, J. S. 1971. The growth and structure of skill. In *Motor Skills in Infancy,* ed. K. J. Connolly. New York: Academic

Bugental, D. B., Moore, B. S. 1979. Effects of induced moods on voice affect. *Dev. Psychol.* 15:664–65

Burgess, R. L., Conger, R. D. 1978. Family interaction in abusive, neglectful and normal families. *Child Dev.* 49:1163–73

Butterfield, E. C., Wambold, C., Belmont, J. M. 1973. On the theory and practice of improving short-term memory. *Am. J. Ment. Defic.* 77:654–69

Butterworth, G., Hicks, L. 1977. Visual proprioception and postural stability in infancy. A developmental study. *Perception* 6:255–62

Campione, J. C., Brown, A. L. 1977. Memory and metamemory development in educable retarded children. In *Perspectives on the Development of Memory and Cognition,* ed. R. V. Kail Jr., J. W. Hagen. Hillsdale, NJ: Erlbaum

Carter, G. L., Kinsbourne, M. 1979. The ontogeny of right cerebral lateralization of spatial mental set. *Dev. Psychol.* 15:241–45

Chomsky, N. 1957. *Syntactic Structures.* The Hague: Mouton. 116 pp.

Chomsky, N. 1965. *Aspects of the Theory of Syntax.* Cambridge: MIT. 251 pp.

Clarke-Stewart, K. A., VanderStoep, L. P., Killian, G. A. 1979. Analysis and replication of mother-child relations at two years of age. *Child Dev.* 50:777–93

Cohen, L. B. 1979a. Our developing knowledge of infant perception and cognition. *Am. Psychol.* 34:894–99

Cohen, L. B. 1979b. Commentary in *Monogr. Soc. Res. Child Dev.,* ed. M. Schwartz, R. H. Day, 44:Ser. 182, pp. 59–63

Cohen, L. B., DeLoache, J. S., Pearl, R. A. 1977. An examination of interface effects in infant's memory for faces. *Child Dev.* 48:88-96

Cohen, L. B., DeLoache, J. S., Strauss, M. S. 1979. Infant visual perception.In *The Handbook of Infant Development,* ed. J. D. Osofsky, II, pp. 393-429. New York: Wiley. 945 pp.

Cohen, L. B., Gelber, E. R. 1975. Infant visual memory. See Cohen & Salapatek 1975, pp. 347-99

Cohen, L. B., Salapatek, P., eds. 1975. *Infant Perception: From Sensation to Cognition, Vol. 1: Basic Visual Processes.* New York: Academic. 415 pp.

Cohen, L. B., Strauss, M. S. 1979. Concept acquisition in the human infant. *Child Dev.* 50:419-24

Cohen, S. E., Beckwith, L. 1979. Preterm infant interaction with the caregiver in the first year of life and competence at age two. *Child Dev.* 50: 767-76

Collins, W. A. 1980. Social antecedents, cognitive processing, and comprehension of social portrayals on television. In *Social Cognition and Social Behavior: Developmental Perspectives,* ed. E. T. Higgins, D. N. Ruble, W. W. Hartup. New York: Cambridge. In press

Cordua, G. D., McGraw, K. O., Drabman, R. S. 1979. Doctor or nurse: Children's perception of sex typed occupations. *Child Dev.* 50:590-93

Corter, C., Trehub, S., Boukydis, C., Ford, L., Celhoffer, L., Minde, K. 1978. Nurses' judgments of the attractiveness of premature infants. *Behav. Dev.* 1:373-80

Cosgrove, J. M., Patterson, C. J. 1978. Generalization of training for children's listener skills. *Child Dev.* 49:513-16

Cromer, R. 1971. The development of the ability to decenter in time. *Br. J. Psychol.* 62:353-65

Culicover, P. W., Wexler, K. 1977. Some syntactic implications of a theory of language learnability. In *Formal Syntax,* ed. P. Culicover, T. Wasow, A. Akmajian. New York: Academic. 55 pp.

Davidson, E. S., Yasuna, A., Tower, A. 1979. The effects of television cartoons on sex-role stereotyping in young girls. *Child Dev.* 50:597-600

deVilliers, J. G., deVilliers, P. A. 1978. *Language Acquisition.* Cambridge: Harvard

DeWit, J., Hartup, W. W., eds. 1974. *Determinants or Origins of Aggressive Behavior.* The Hague: Mouton

Disbrow, M. A., Doerr, H. O., Caulfield, C. 1977. *Measures to predict child abuse.* Final rep. submitted to Off. Matern. Child Health, Educ. Welfare

Douglas, J. D., Rice, K. M. 1979. Sex differences in children's anxiety and defensiveness measures. *Dev. Psychol.* 15:223-24

Easterbrooks, M. A., Lamb, M. E. 1979. The relationship between quality of infant-mother attachment and infant peer competence. *Child Dev.* In press

Eisenberg-Berg, N. 1979. Development of children's prosocial moral judgment. *Dev. Psychol.* 15:128-37

Eisenberg-Berg, N., Hand, M. 1979. The relationship of preschoolers' reasoning about prosocial moral conflicts to prosocial behavior. *Child Dev.* 50:356-63

Elkind, D., Bowen, R. 1979. Imaginary audience behavior in children and adolescents. *Dev. Psychol.* 15:38-44

Emmerich, W., Cocking, R. R., Sigel, I. E. 1979. Relationships between cognitive and social functioning in preschool children. *Dev. Psychol.* 15:485-504

Erikson, E. 1950. *Childhood and Society.* New York: Norton. 444 pp.

Erwin, J., Kuhn, D. 1979. Development of children's understanding of the multiple determination underlying human behavior. *Dev. Psychol.* 15:352-53

Fantz, R. L. Fagan, J. F., Miranda, S. B. 1975. Early visual selectivity. See Cohen & Salapatek 1975, pp. 249-341

Feiring, C., Lewis, M. 1978. The child as a member of the family system. *Behav. Sci.* 23:225-33

Feldman, A., Acredolo, L. 1979. The effect of active versus passive exploration on memory for spatial location in children. *Child Dev.* 50:689-704

Feldman, R. S., Jenkins, L., Popoola, O. 1979. Detection of deception in adults and children via facial expressions. *Child Dev.* 50:350-55

Field, T. 1978. Interaction patterns of high risk and normal infants. In *Infants Born at Risk,* ed. T. Field, A. Sostek, S. Goldberg, H. H. Shuman. New York: Spectrum

Field, T. 1979a. Infant behaviors directed toward peers and adults in the presence and absence of mother. *Infant Behav. Dev.* 2:47-54

Field, T. 1979b. Differential behavioral and cardiac responses of 3-month-old infants to a mirror and peer. *Infant Behav. Dev.* 2:179-84

Finney, J. W. 1979. Friends; interests: A cluster-analytic study of college student peer environments, personality, and behavior. *J. Youth Adolesc.* 8:299–315

Flanery, R. C., Balling, J. D. 1979. Developmental changes in hemispheric specialization for tactile spatial ability. *Dev. Psychol.* 15:364–72

Flavell, J. H. 1976a. *The development of metacommunication.* Presented at 21st Int. Congr. Psychol., Paris

Flavell, J. H. 1976b. Metacognitive aspects of problem solving. In *The Nature of Intelligence,* ed. L. B. Resnick. Hillsdale, NJ: Erlbaum

Flavell, J. H. 1978a. Metacognitive development. In *Structural/Process Theories of Complex Human Behavior,* ed. J. M. Scandura, C. J. Brainerd, pp. 213–45. Alphen a. d. Rijn, The Netherlands: Stijthoff & Noordhoff

Flavell, J. H. 1978b. Metacognition. In *Current Perspectives on Awareness and Cognitive Processes.* Symp. presented at APA meet., Toronto, Chair. E. Langer

Flavell, J. H. 1978c. *Cognitive monitoring.* Paper (revised) prepared for Conf. Children's Oral Commun. Skills, Univ. Wis.

Flavell, J. H. 1979. Metacognition and cognitive monitoring. *Am. Psychol.* 34:906–11

Flavell, J. H., Wellman, H. M. 1977. Metamemory. See Campione & Brown 1977

Furman, W. 1980. Promoting appropriate social behavior: A developmental perspective. *Adv. Clin. Child Psychol.,* Vol. 3. In press

Furman, W., Masters, J. C. 1980a. Affective consequences of social reinforcement, punishment, and neutral behavior. *Dev. Psychol.* 16:100–4

Furman, W., Masters, J. C. 1980b. Peer interactions, sociometric status and resistance to deviation in young children. *Dev. Psychol.* In press

Furman, W., Rahe, D. F., Hartup, W. W. 1979. Rehabilitation of socially-withdrawn preschool children through mixed-age and same-age socialization. *Child Dev.* In press

Garbarino, J. 1978. The elusive "crime" of emotional abuse. *Child Abuse Neglect* 2:89–100

Garner, W. R. 1970. The stimulus in information processing. *Am. Psychol.* 25:350–58

Garner, W. R. 1974. *The Processing of Information and Structure.* Potomac, Md: Erlbaum. 203 pp.

Geffen, G. 1978. The development of the right ear advantage in dichotic listening with focussed attention. *Cortex* 14:11–17

Geffen, G., Wale, J. 1979. Development of selective listening and hemispheric asymmetry. *Dev. Psychol.* 15:138–46

Gelman, R. 1978. Cognitive development. *Ann. Rev. Psychol.* 29:297–332

George, C., Main, M. 1979. Social interactions of young abused children: Approach, avoidance, and aggression. *Child Dev.* 50:306–18

Gesten, E. L. 1976. A health resources inventory: The development of a measure of the personal and social competence of primary-grade children. *J. Consult. Clin. Psychol.* 5:775–86

Gibson, E. J. 1969. *Principles of Perceptual Learning and Development.* New York: Appleton-Century-Crofts. 537 pp.

Gonzalez, R. M. 1979. Hallucinogenic dependency during adolescence as a defense against homosexual fantasies: A reenactment of the first separation-individuation phase in the course of treatment. *J. Youth Adolesc.* 8:63–71

Hamburger, H., Wexler, K. 1975. A mathematical theory of learning transformational grammar. *J. Math. Psychol.* 12:137–77

Handel, S., Imai, S. 1972. The free classification of analyzable and unanalyzable stimuli. *Percept. Psychophys.* 2:333–48

Harris, M. B., Siebel, C. E. 1975. Affect, aggression, and altruism. *Dev. Psychol.* 11:623–27

Hartup, W. W. 1979. *Current issues in social development.* Presented at bienn. meet. Soc. Res. Child Dev., San Francisco

Hartup, W. W. 1980. Toward a social psychology of childhood: Trends and issues. *Minn. Symp. Child Psychol.* 13: In press

Hartup, W. W., DeWit, J., eds. 1978. *Origins of Aggression.* The Hague: Mouton

Hayes, J. R. 1976. It's the thought that counts: New approaches to educational theory. In *Cognition and Instruction,* ed. D. Klahr. Hillsdale, NJ: Erlbaum

Hetherington, E. M. 1979. Divorce: A child's perspective. *Am. Psychol.* 34:851–58

Hetherington, E. M., Cox, M., Cox, R. 1978. The aftermath of divorce. In *Mother-Child, Father-Child Relations,* ed. J. H. Stevens, M. Matthews. Washington DC: Natl. Assoc. Educ. Young Child.

Hetherington, E. M., Cox, M., Cox, R. 1980. Play and social interaction in children following divorce. *J. Soc. Issues.* In press

Hiscock, M., Kinsbourne, M. 1977. Selective listening asymmetry in preschool children. *Dev. Psychol.* 13:217–24

Horn, J. M., Loehlin, J. C., Willerman, L. 1979. Intellectual resemblance among adoptive and biological relatives: The Texas adoption project. *Behav. Genet.* 9:177–207

Howie-Day, A. M. 1977. *Metapersuasion: The development of reasoning about persuasive strategies.* PhD thesis. Univ. Minn., Minneapolis

Ironsmith, M., Whitehurst, G. J. 1978. The development of listener abilities in communication: How children deal with ambiguous information. *Child Dev.* 49:348–52

Jones, E. E. 1979. Personality characteristics of black youth: A cross-cultural investigation. *J. Youth Adolesc.* 8:149–59

Kaplan, H. B., Smith, P. B., Pokorny, A. D. 1979. Psychosocial antecedents of unwed motherhood among indigent adolescents. *J. Youth Adolesc.* 8:181–207

Kemler, D. G., Smith, L. B. 1978. Is there a developmental trend from integrality to separability in perception? *J. Exp. Child Psychol.* 26:498–507

Klein, D. M., Jorgensen, S. R., Miller, B. C. 1978. Research methods and developmental reciprocity in families. In *Child Influences on Marital and Family Interaction,* ed. R. M. Lerner, G. B. Spanier. New York: Academic. 360 pp.

Kreutzer, M. A., Leonard, C., Flavell, J. H. 1975. An interview study of children's knowledge about memory. *Monogr. Soc. Res. Child Dev.* 40:Ser. 159

Kuczaj, S. A. II. 1977. The acquisition of regular and irregular past tense forms. *J. Verb. Learn. Verb. Behav.* 16:589–600

Kuczaj, S. A. II 1979. *Young children's overextensions of object words in comprehension and/or production: Support for a prototype theory of early object word meaning.* Presented at SRCD Meet.

Kuczaj, S. A. II, Brannick, N. 1979. Children's use of the *Wh* question modal auxiliary placement rule. *J. Exp. Child Psychol.* 28:43–67

Kuczaj, S. A. II, Daly, M. J. 1979. The development of hypothetical reference in the speech of young children. *J. Child Lang.* 6:563–79

Lamb, M. E. 1978a. Infant social cognition and "second-order" effects. *Behav. Dev.* 1:1–10

Lamb, M. E. 1978b. Qualitative aspects of mother- and father-infant attachments. *Infant Behav. Dev.* 1:265–75

Lamb, M. E., Suomi, S. J., Stephenson, G. R., eds. 1979. *Social Interaction Analysis: Methodological Issues,* pp. 11–32. Madison: Univ. Wis.

Larson, S., Kurdek, L. A. 1979. Intratask and intertask consistency of moral judgment indices in first-, third-, and fifth-grade children. *Dev. Psychol.* 15:462–63

Lee, D. N., Aronson, E. 1974. Visual proprioceptive control of standing in human infants. *Percept. Psychophys.* 15:529–32

Levine, E. M., Kozak, C. 1979. Drug and alcohol use, delinquency, and vandalism among upper middle class pre- and post- adolescents. *J. Youth Adolesc.* 8:91–101

Lewin, K. 1955. *A Dynamic Theory of Personality.* Transl. D. K. Adams, K. E. Zerner. New York: McGraw. 286 pp.

Lewis, T. L., Maurer, D. 1977. *Newborns' central vision: Whole or hole?* Presented at Meet. Soc. Res. Child Dev., New Orleans

Lipsitt, L. P., ed. 1976. *Developmental Psychobiology: The Significance of Infancy.* Hillsdale, NJ: Erlbaum

Lipsitt, L. P. 1979. Critical conditions in infancy: A psychological perspective. *Am. Psychol.* 34:973–80

Lipsitt, L. P., Sturner, W. Q., Burke, P. 1979. Perinatal indicators and subsequent crib death. *Infant. Behav. Dev.* 2:325–28

Loehlin, J. C., Nichols, R. C. 1976. *Heredity, Environment and Personality.* Austin: Univ. Tex. 202 pp.

Londerville, S. 1977. *Socialization in toddlers.* Presented at bienn. meet. Soc. Res. Child Dev., New Orleans

Maccoby, E. E., Doering, C. H., Jacklin, C. N., Kraemer, H. 1979. Concentrations of sex hormones in umbilical-cord blood: Their relation to sex and birth order of infants. *Child Dev.* 50:632–42

Maccoby, E. E., Masters, J. C. 1970. Attachment and dependency. In *Carmichael's Manual of Child Psychology,* ed. P. H. Mussen, pp. 73–157. New York: Wiley

Magrab, P. 1978. For the sake of the children: A review of the psychological effects of divorce. *J. Divorce* 1:233–45

Main, M., Tomasini, L., Tolan, W. T. 1979. Differences among mothers of infants judged to differ in security. *Dev. Psychol.* 15:472–73

Mandler, J. M., DeForest, M. 1979. Is there more than one way to recall a story? *Child Dev.* 50:886–89

Maratsos, M. 1978. New models in language and language acquisition. In *Linguistic Theory and Psychological Reality,* ed. M. A. Halle, J. Bresnan, G. A. Miller. Cambridge:MIT. 329 pp.

Maratsos, M., Kuczaj, S. A. II. 1978. Against the transformationalist hypothesis: A simpler account of redundant tense markings. *J. Child Lang.* 5:337–46

Marastos, M., Kuczaj, S. A. II, Fox, D. E. C., Chalkley, M. A. 1979. Some empirical studies in the acquisition of transformational relations. *Minn. Symp. Child Psychol.* 12

Markman, E. 1978. *Comprehension monitoring.* Presented at Conf. Children's Oral Commun. Skills. Madison: Univ. Wis.

Masters, J. C., Barden, R. C., Ford, M. E. 1979. Affective states, expressive behavior and learning in children. *J. Pers. Soc. Psychol.* 37:380–90

Matas, L., Arend, R. A., Sroufe, L. A. 1978. Continuity of adaptation in the second year: The relationship between quality of attachment and later competence. *Child Dev.* 49:547–56

Maurer, D., Salapatek, P. 1976. Developmental changes in the scanning of faces by young infants. *Child Dev.* 47:523–27

Mednick, B. R., Baker, R. L., Sutton-Smith, B. 1979. Teenage pregnancy and perinatal mortality. *J. Youth Adolesc.* 8:343–57

Meichenbaum, D., Asarnow, J. 1979. Cognitive-behavior modification and metacognitive development: Implications for the classroom. In *Cognitive-Behavioral Interventions: Theory, Research and Procedures,* ed. P. Kendall, S. Hollon. New York: Academic. In press

Meilman, P. W. 1979. Cross-sectional age changes in ego identity status during adolescence. *Dev. Psychol.* 15:230–31

Messer, S. B., Brodzinsky, D. M. 1979. The relation of conceptual tempo to aggression and its control. *Child Dev.* 50:758–66

Milewski, A. E. 1976. Infants' discrimination of internal and external pattern elements. *J. Exp. Child Psychol.* 22:229–46

Milewski, A. E. 1979. Visual discrimination and detection of configurational invariance in 3-month infants. *Dev. Psychol.* 15:357–63

Mischel, W. 1973. Toward a cognitive social learning reconceptualization of personality. *Psychol. Rev.* 80:252–83

Mischel, W., Cantor, N. 1979. Prototypicality and personality: Effects on free recall and personality impressions. *J. Res. Pers.* 13:187–205

Moore, B. S., Underwood, B., Rosenhan, D. L. 1973. Affect and altruism. *Dev. Psychol.* 8:99–104

Morais, J. 1975. The effects of ventriloquism on the right side advantage for verbal material. *Cognition* 3:127–39

Moran, J. J., Joniak, A. J. 1979. Effect of language on preference for respoɪ.ses to a moral dilemma. *Dev. Psychol.* 15:337–38

Mosenthal, P. 1979. Three types of schemata in children's recall of cohesive and noncohesive text. *J. Exp. Child Psychol.* 27:129–42

Mulhern, R. K. Jr., Passman, R. H. 1979. The child's behavioral pattern as a determinant of maternal punitiveness. *Child Dev.* 50:815–20

Newcomb, A. F., Brady, J. F., Hartup, W. W. 1979. Friendship and incentive condition as determinants of children's task-oriented social behavior. *Child Dev.* 50:878–81

Newcomb, A. F., Collins, W. A. 1979. Children's comprehension of family role portrayals in televised dramas: Effects of socioeconomic status, ethnicity, and age. *Dev. Psychol.* 15:417–23

Novak, M. A. 1979. Social recovery of monkeys isolated for the first year of life: II. long-term assessment. *Dev. Psychol.* 15:50–61

Odom, R. D., Guzman, R. D. 1972. Development of hierarchies of dimensional salience. *Dev. Psychol.* 6:271–87

Osofsky, J. D., ed. 1979. *The Handbook of Infant Development.* New York: Wiley

Paris, S. 1975. *Propositional Logical Thinking and Comprehension of Language Connectives.* The Hague: Mouton. 101 pp.

Park, J., Johnson, R. C., DeFries, J. C., McClearn, G. E., Mi, M. P., Rashad, M. N., Vandenberg, S. G., Wilson, J. R. 1978. Parent-offspring resemblance for specific cognitive abilities in Korea. *Behav. Genet.* 8:43–52

Parke, R. D., Collmer, C. W. 1975. Child abuse: An interdisciplinary analysis. In *Review of Child Development Research,* ed. E. M. Hetherington, pp. 509–90. Chicago: Univ. Chicago. 615 pp.

Patterson, C. J., Massad, C. M., Cosgrove, J. M. 1978. Children's referential communication: Components of plans for effective listening. *Dev. Psychol.* 14:401–6

Piaget, J. 1969. *The Child's Conception of Time.* New York: Ballantine

Plomin, R., DeFries, J. C. 1980. Genetics and intelligence: Recent data. *Intelligence* 4:15–24

Plomin, R., Foch, T. T., Rowe, D. C. 1980. Bobo clown aggression in childhood: Environment, not genes. *J. Res. Pers.* In press

Plomin, R., Rowe, D. C. 1979. Genetic and environmental etiology of social behavior in infancy. *Dev. Psychol.* 15:62–72

Poulsen, D., Kintsch, E., Kintsch, W., Premack, D. 1980. Children's comprehension and memory for stories. *J. Exp. Child Psychol.* In press

Provine, R. R., Westerman, J. A. 1979. Crossing the midline: Limits of early eye-hand behavior. *Child Dev.* 50:437–41

Ramey, C. T., Farran, D. C., Campbell, F. A. 1979. Predicting IQ from mother-infant interactions. *Child Dev.* 50:804–14

Redmore, C. D., Loevinger, J. 1979. Ego development in adolescence: Longitudinal studies. *J. Youth Adolesc.* 8:1–20

Rosch, E. 1975. Universals and cultural specifics in human categorization. In *Cross-cultural Perspectives on Learning,* ed. R. Brislin, S. Bochner, W. Lonner. New York: Halsted. 335 pp.

Rosch, E., Lloyd, B., eds. 1978. *Cognition and Categorization.* Hillsdale, NJ: Erlbaum. 328 pp.

Rosenhan, D. L., Underwood, B., Moore, B. S. 1974. Affect moderates self-gratification and altruism. *J. Pers. Soc. Psychol.* 30:546–52

Rubenstein, J. L., Howes, C. 1979. Caregiving and infant behavior in day care and in homes. *Dev. Psychol.* 15:1–24

Saarni, C. 1979. Children's understanding of display rules for expressive behavior. *Dev. Psychol.* 15:424–29

Salapatek, P. 1975. Pattern perception in early infancy. See Cohen & Salapatek 1975, pp. 133–234

Santrock, J., Tracy, R. 1978. The effects of children's family structure status on the development of stereotypes by teachers. *J. Educ. Psychol.* 70:754–57

Scarr, S. 1979. Psychology and children: Current research and practice. *Am. Psychol.* 34:809–1039

Scarr-Salapatek, S. 1976. Comments on "heart rate: A sensitive tool for the study of emotional development in the infant." In *Developmental Psychobiology: The Significance of Infancy,* ed. L. P. Lipsitt, pp. 32–34. Hillsdale, NJ: Wiley, 143 pp.

Scarr, S., Weinberg, R. A. 1976. IQ test performance of black children adopted by white families. *Am Psychol.* 31:726–39

Scarr, S., Weinberg, R. A. 1977. Intellectual similarities within families of both adopted and biological children. *Intelligence* 1:170–91

Scarr, S., Weinberg, R. A. 1978. The influence of "family background" on intellectual attainment. *Am. Sociol. Rev.* 43:674–92

Scarr, S., Yee, D. 1979. *Heritability and educational policy: Genetic and environmental effects on IQ, aptitude and achievement.* Presented at APA, annual meet. New York City

Schwartz, M., Day, R. H. 1979. Visual shape perception in early infancy. *Monogr. Soc. Res. Child Dev.* 44:Ser 182. 57 pp.

Sedlak, A. J. 1979. Developmental differences in understanding plans and evaluation actors. *Child Dev.* 50:536–60

Serbin, L. A., Connor, J. M., Burchardt, C. J., Citron, C. C. 1979. Effects of peer presence on sex-typing of children's play behavior. *J. Exp. Child Psychol.* 27:303–9

Shepp, B. E. 1978. From perceived similarity to dimensional structure: A new hypothesis about perceptual development. See Rosch & Lloyd 1978, pp. 133–66

Shepp, B. E., Swartz, K. B. 1976. Selective attention and the processing of integral and nonintegral dimensions: A developmental study. *J. Exp. Child Psychol.* 22:73–85

Siegel, A. W., Allen, G. L., Kirasic, K. C. 1979. Children's ability to make bidirectional distance comparisons: The advantage of thinking ahead. *Dev. Psychol.* 15:656–57

Smith, E., Shoben, E., Rips, L. 1974. Structure and process in semantic memory; A featural model for semantic decisions. *Psychol. Rev* 81:214–41

Smith, L. B. 1979. Perceptual development and category generalization. *Child Dev.* 50: 705-15

Smith, L. B., Kemler, D. G. 1977. Developmental trends in free classification: Evidence for a new conceptualization of perceptual development. *J. Exp. Child Psychol.* 24:279–98

Spelke, E. S., Owsley, C. J. 1979. Intermodal exploration and knowledge in infancy. *Behav. Dev.* 2:13–27

Spence, J. T., Helmreich, R. L. 1979. Comparison of masculine and feminine personality attributes and sex-role attitudes across age groups. *Dev. Psychol.* 14:583–84

Sroufe, L. A. 1979a. The coherence of individual development: Early care, attachment, and subsequent development issues. *Am. Psychol.* 34:834–40

Sroufe, L. A. 1979b. Socioemotional development. See Osofsky 1979

Sroufe, L. A., Waters, E. 1977. Attachment as an organizational construct. *Child Dev.* 48:1184–99

Starr, R. H. Jr. 1979. Child abuse. *Am. Psychol.* 34:872–78

St. Clair, S., Day, H. D. 1979. Ego identity status and values among high school females. *J. Youth Adolesc.* 8:317–26

Stein, N. L., Glenn, C. G. 1977. An analysis of story comprehension in elementary school children. In *Multi-disciplinary Approaches to Discourse Comprehension*, ed. R. O. Freedle. Hillsdale, NJ: Ablex

Steinschneider, A. 1977. Prolonged sleep apnea and respiratory instability: A discriminative study. *Pediatrics* 59:962–70

Stevenson, M. B., Lamb, M. E. 1979. Effects of infant sociability and the caretaking environment on infant cognitive performance. *Child Dev.* 50:340–49

Steward, M. S., Bryant, B. K., Steward, D. S. 1979. Adolescent women's developing identity: A study of self-definition in the context of family relationships. *J. Youth Adolesc.* 8:209–22

Strauss, M. S. 1979. The abstraction of prototypical information by adults and 10-month-old infants. *J. Exp. Psychol.–Hum. Learn. Mem.* 5:618–35

Suls, J., Gutkin, D., Kalle, R. J. 1979. The role of intentions, damage, and social consequences in the moral judgment of children. *Child Dev.* 50:784–87

Suls, J., Kalle, R. J. 1979. Children's moral judgments as a function of intention, damage, and an actor's physical harm. *Dev. Psychol.* 15:93–94

Tessman, L. H. 1978. *Children of Parting Parents.* New York: Aronson

Treisman, A., Geffen, G. 1968. Selective attention and cerebral dominance in perceiving and responding to speech message. *Q. J. Exp. Psychol.* 20:139–50

Underwood, B., Moore, B. S., Rosenhan, D. L. 1973. Affect and self-gratification. *Dev. Psychol.* 8:209–14

Ungerer, J. A., Brody, L. R., Zelazo, P. R. 1978. Long-term memory for speech in 2 to 4 week-old infants. *Behav. Child Dev.* 1:177–86

Vandell, D. L. 1979. Effects of a playgroup experience on mother-son and father-son interaction. *Dev. Psychol.* 15:379–85

von Hofsten, C., Lindhagen, K. 1979. Observations on the development of reaching for moving objects. *J. Exp. Child Psychol.* 28:158–73

Walker, L. J., Richards, B. S. 1979. Stimulating transitions in moral reasoning as a function of stage of cognitive development. *Dev. Psychol.* 15:95–103

Waterman, A. S., Archer, S. 1979. Ego identity status and expressive writing among high school and college students. *J. Youth Adolesc.* 8:327–41

Waters, E., Wippman, J., Sroufe, L. A. 1979. Social competence in preschool children as a function of the security of earlier attachment to the mother. *Child Dev.* In press

Wellman, H. M., Larkey, C., Somerville, S. C. 1979. The early development of moral criteria. *Child Dev.* 50:869–73

Wellman, H. M., Ritter, K., Flavell, J. H. 1975. Deliberate memory behavior in the delayed reactions of very young children. *Dev. Psychol.* 11:780–87

West, M. J., Rheingold, H. L. 1978. Infant stimulation of maternal instruction. *Behav. Dev.* 1:205–15

Wexler, K. 1978. Empirical questions about developmental psycholinguistics raised by a theory of language acquisition. In *Recent Advances in the Psychology of Language*, ed. R. N. Campbell, P. T. Smith. New York: Plenum

Wexler, K., Culicover, P., Hamburger, H. 1975. Learning-theoretical foundations of linguistic universals. *Theor. Ling.* 2:3, 215–53

White, B. L., Castle, P., Held, R. 1964. Observation on the development of visually-directed reaching. *Child Dev.* 35:349–64

Willerman, L. 1979. Effects of families on intellectual development. *Am. Psychol.* 34:923–29

Willerman, L., Fiedler, M. F. 1977. Intellectually precocious preschool children: Early development and later intellectual accomplishments. *J. Genet. Psychol.* 131:13–20

Willerman, L., Horn, J. M., Loehlin, J. C. 1977. The aptitude-achievement test distinction: A study of unrelated children reared together. *Behav. Genet.* 7:465–69

Wilson, R. S. 1978. Synchronies in mental development: An epigenetic perspective. *Science* 202:939–48

Young, J. W., Ferguson, L. R. 1979. Developmental changes through adolescence in the spontaneous nomination of reference groups as a function of decision content. *J. Youth Adolesc.* 8:239–45

Ann. Rev. Psychol. 1981. 32:153–90

COCHLEAR PHYSIOLOGY   ♦343

Peter Dallos[1]

Auditory Physiology Laboratory, Northwestern University, Evanston, Illinois 60201

CONTENTS

INTRODUCTION

Cochlear physiology is in a state of revolution. The validity of long cherished concepts that seemed secure as bases of our understanding of hearing is now questioned. Thus the traveling wave of von Békésy (1960) may not be the general mediator of frequency analysis as it once was thought. The

[1]The preparation of this manuscript was supported in part by grants NS 08635 and NS 06730 from the NINCDS, NIH. I thank my colleagues M. A. Cheatham, K. Dennis, E. Relkin and K. Wolff for their help.

153

resistance-modulation scheme of hair cell function (Davis 1965) may require substantial modification. The notion that the cochlea is a fundamentally linear system is now all but abandoned. Striking new observations were made during the 1970s with some of the most dramatic ones taking place in the waning years of the decade. Being in the midst of feverish activity does not permit one the long view or the luxury of simple synthesis. I am afraid this review is merely a glimpse at an array of issues whose resolution will be reported by a luckier colleague, some 3 to 5 years hence.

This review covers journal articles and compendia from January 1976 to the beginning of 1980. Material is restricted to vertebrate hearing. The physiology of the external and middle ear is not covered and neither is that of the central auditory system. I did not include material on development, or results obtained from tissue or organ cultures. Clinical material is not considered; under this heading I include issues pertaining to the cochlear prosthesis and electrocochleography. Finally, the review is biased toward experimental work. During the past few years there has been a veritable explosion of modeling, with only a few of the model makers attempting to make their creations conform to anything beyond a few favorite experimental results. Von Békésy's admonition of 1966 seems equally valid today; to paraphrase him: we need more and better experiments and probably fewer theories.

GENERAL

Several books published during the review period deserve mention here. E. G. Wever's long awaited monograph on the reptilian ear became available in 1978. This is a monumental book that covers decades of work, providing an almost comprehensive coverage of the structure of inner ears of various orders within this most important class. The book gives gross anatomy of the cochleas of multitudes of species as determined by light microscopy. The anatomical data are supplemented with limited electrophysiological material in the form of gross cochlear microphonic responses recorded from the round window. Since these measures most strongly reflect the transfer characteristics of the middle ear, the data are of rather limited value.

Volume 4 of the *Handbook of Perception* is entitled *Hearing* (Carterette & Friedman 1978). It contains a now somewhat outdated chapter on cochlear biophysics by this author and a rather cursory exposition of the "neural code" by Whitfield. The remainder of the book is largely devoted to psychophysics, but thoughtful chapters on the history of research on hearing by Carterette and Schubert should be of great interest. A compendium on research methods (Smith & Vernon 1976) contains some very fine chapters.

A *festschrift* honoring Hallowell Davis' 80th birthday (Hirsh et al 1976) has contributions of mixed quality from his many students and associates. Three basic texts worthy of note have appeared recently. These are by Green (1976), Durrant & Lovrinic (1977), and Yost & Nielsen (1977). All three of these are excellent textbooks, the first being the most advanced and the last one the least demanding.

Two important conference proceedings are edited by Ruben et al (1976) and by Naunton & Fernández (1978). Both meetings focused on electrocochleography and evoked response audiometry. Aside from a wealth of significant clinical material, both books contain valuable new data by respected investigators. The latter book is particularly outstanding in this respect, and many of its chapters are reviewed below on an individual basis. Davis's (1976) monograph on electric response audiometry is also highly recommended.

The last book to be noted, *Psychophysics and Physiology of Hearing* (Evans & Wilson 1977), contains presentations and comments made at a symposium held in Keele. Again, many of the relevant articles are considered in the main body of this review.

Finally, one should mention the appearance of a new journal, *Hearing Research,* which may become an important forum for the dissemination of results from basic investigations of various facets of hearing.

MECHANICS AND MICROMECHANICS

The primary consequence of the absorption of sound energy by the fluid that fills the bony cochlea is a wave propagation sustained by the contents of the cochlear partition. The partition is the membranous cochlea, delimited by the basilar membrane on the scala tympani side and by Reissner's membrane on the scala vestibuli side. The partition is endolymph-filled and within it is the sensory organ for hearing, the organ of Corti. When discussing gross cochlear mechanics, one refers to the movement pattern of the partition or more restrictively to that of the basilar membrane. Micromechanics refers to motions within the partition, specifically movements at the level of sensory cell cilia and the immediate precursors of ciliary displacement. The principal motion pattern of the cochlear partition is a traveling wave (TW) which was described on the basis of experimental observations by von Békésy (1960). He noted that, at least up to moderately high frequencies, the basilar and Reissner's membranes moved in phase, and thus that the TW described the motion pattern of the entire partition. All contemporary measurements are from the basilar membrane, except the recent work of Rhode (1978), who also obtained some limited data from Reissner's membrane. While a comparison between the two measurement sites is not simple, about the only striking difference is an apparent absence of nonlinear motion of Reissner's membrane in the presence of prominent nonlinearity of the basilar membrane.

The TW is a disturbance that propagates away from the window-region of the cochlea with decreasing wavelength and velocity. Its amplitude rises with distance, reaches a distinct peak, and then rapidly diminishes. The spatial extent of the wave, and the position of the maximum, are frequency dependent. Frequencies are mapped along the partition in a high- (basal) to low-frequency (apical) progression. It has become one of the basic tenets of hearing science that this spatial mapping, due to hydromechanical characteristics of the cochlea, forms the basis of spectral analysis by the ear. It has been recognized all along, however, most prominently by von Békésy himself, that the mechanical spectral selectivity of the TW is seemingly inadequate to account for the psychophysically measured resolving capability of the auditory system. This inadequacy was forcefully emphasized by Evans (1975a) and Evans & Wilson (1973), who asserted that the frequency resolving capability of the ear was already present at the cochlear output, but that the real discrepancy resided in the sharpness of tuning of single auditory nerve fibers and the basilar membrane. Based on the previous notions of others (J. L. Goldstein 1967, Pfeiffer 1970), Evans postulated the presence of a "second filter" in the cochlea, following the first filter represented by the TW mechanism. The existence of this second filter is controversial and some feel that, at least for the mammalian cochlea, the mechanical properties of the basilar membrane are sufficient to explain most known phenomena. Before considering the second filter below, let us review the new developments about the first filter, the traveling wave.

The Traveling Wave

The demonstration of more pronounced frequency selectivity of basilar membrane motion by contemporary measurements (Johnstone & Boyle 1967, Rhode 1971, Wilson & Johnstone 1972) and the discovery of a significant nonlinearity (Rhode 1971) are the cornerstones of any argument against an independent second filter. The nonlinearity is apparently confined to the best frequency region of the measuring location, and it is reflected in the pronounced saturation of vibratory amplitude with increasing intensity. The same basilar membrane spot apparently vibrates linearly for frequencies both above and below the characteristic frequency. The nonlinearity is apparent in the impulse response of the membrane (Robles & Rhode 1974), is manifest in two-tone suppression and the generation of some distortion products (Rhode 1977), and appears to be physiologically vulnerable (Rhode 1973). All measurements that indicated that the basilar membrane vibrates nonlinearly were obtained in squirrel monkeys with the

Mössbauer method. When used with guinea pigs, the same method yielded linear results (Johnstone & Yates 1974, Rhode 1978). It is now suggested, however, that nonlinearities may also be detected in the movement of guinea pig basilar membranes (LePage & Johnstone 1980). If so, then one major objection to nonlinear basilar membrane mechanics, an unlikely species specificity, may have been eliminated.

The probable explanation for this long-standing controversy resides in the apparent sensitivity of the nonlinearity to interference with cochlear function. It has been shown that mechanical tuning characteristics change postmortem (Rhode 1973) and that the nonlinearity disappears. The sharpness of neural tuning is also a function of the integrity and health of the cochlea (Evans 1975a, Robertson & Manley 1974). In addition, the propensity of the ear to generate nonlinear distortion processes can be altered by either temporary or permanent damage to the organ of Corti (Robertson 1976, Dallos 1977, Siegel et al 1977, Kim et al 1978). It is thus a plausible notion that nonlinearities are a normal part of mammalian cochlear mechanics and that they are suppressed by some, possibly even subtle, experimental manipulations of the ear. Nonlinear basilar membrane motion does have great potential advantages. One of these is that if one estimates the amplitude of motion at threshold at the best frequency by extrapolating along the nonlinear response curve, one obtains a much larger displacement than hitherto assumed. Rhode (1978) estimates the displacement to be around 0.1 nm. From some of his curves one gets a value as high as 2.0 nm. Linear estimates from older data yielded about 10^{-4} nm, a value that troubled a great many people. The other advantage is that the nonlinearity allows for progressively sharper tuning with the lowering of input level.

Comparison of the sharpest mechanical tuning curves with neural tuning characteristics (Geisler et al 1974, Rhode 1978) still leaves a significant discrepancy. It is conceivable that the "sharpness gap" may be closed if mechanical measurements could be made at lower sound levels. This remains to be accomplished. Meanwhile, the trend is for newer, and presumably better, mechanical measurements to reflect more accurately the neural response characteristics, thus conceivably obviating the need for invoking a second filter. Several problems with utilizing the nonlinearity as a sharpening mechanism are summarized below. First, however, one particular discrepancy between mechanical and neural tuning, which almost forces the acceptance of additional filtering beyond the TW, needs to be mentioned. In mechanical measurements amplitude and phase plateaus are seen above the best frequency. These are conspicuously absent in neural tuning curves, indicating suppression of the high-frequency input to the neuron (actually, to inner hair cells). This significant discrepancy has not received any attention to date.

Two-tone suppression, the interference with the response to one tone by the presence of another, is generally prominent both above and below the characteristic frequency (CF) of a nerve fiber, even though the characteristics of the suppression may differ (Sachs & Abbas 1974). Rhode (1977, 1978), however, could not show convincingly that two-tone suppression exists below the CF. When measured in the cochlear microphonic (CM) response the only prominent frequency-dependent two-tone suppression effect is seen above the CF (Dallos et al 1974, Legouix et al 1976) in spite of some earlier claims (Legouix et al 1973). Since the CM is assumed to reflect basilar membrane displacement (Dallos 1973a, Wilson & Johnstone 1975, Schmiedt & Zwislocki 1977), a band-limited low-frequency suppression should be reflected in it. A more significant consideration, one whose importance is not yet generally appreciated, is that many of the phenomena in question—sharp neural tuning, two-tone suppression, and distortion component generation—are possible without obvious mechanical precursors on the basilar membrane. In fact, some are possible even without a basilar membrane. Let us examine these situations.

Tuning Without Traveling Waves

In anurans all auditory nerve fibers show V-shaped tuning curves, generally grouped into two or three frequency ranges and showing the first appearance of spatial-frequency mapping among vertebrates (Capranica 1976, Lewis 1977, Capranica & Moffat 1980). Low-frequency fibers that originate from the rostral pole of the amphibian papilla are distinguished in that their responses can be suppressed by the addition of a second tone, and they also respond at the difference frequency $(f_2\text{-}f_1)$ (Capranica & Moffat 1980). These are remarkable observations if one considers that there is no basilar membrane in the amphibian papilla, the receptor cells being incorporated in an immobile epithelial lining of the inner ear cavity. Thus frequency analysis and nonlinear mechanical interactions originating in a "conventional" TW must be ruled out. These papillae, however, possess tectorial membranes, and it is conceivable that this structure could be responsible for the frequency analysis and some other related phenomena.

The tectorial membrane is also an element of apparently great importance in the analysis of signals by the lizard's cochlea. Wever (1978) describes a great variety of forms of tectorial structures among species of lizards. One species, the alligator lizard, served as the subject for one of the most significant experimental series of the decade. Weiss and his colleagues examined the anatomy and physiology of this ear and found, along with other results to be discussed below, that there is no mechanical tuning of the basilar membrane (aside from that attributable to gross middle ear mechanics) in spite of a clear-cut tonotopic arrangement and V-shaped tuning curves for all auditory nerve fibers (Weiss et al 1976, 1978a; Peake & Ling 1980). The apical, low-frequency region of the papilla is covered with a tectorial membrane, whereas the cilia of the hair cells in the basal, high-frequency segment of the papilla are free-standing. Low-frequency fibers show much sharper tuning than high-frequency ones, and the driven discharge of all low-frequency fibers is suppressible by the addition of a second tone to the stimulus (Holton & Weiss 1978, Weiss et al 1978b, Holton 1980). Sharp tuning and the presence of two-tone suppression thus correlate with the presence of tectorial covering (and maybe incidentally with efferent innervation) in this papilla. In the basal region of the papilla an unmistakable tonotopic arrangement is also seen, however, In other words, the CF of fibers is correlated with their location along the papilla. Recall that in this region the basilar membrane shows no graded tuning and there is no tectorial membrane. Weiss and colleagues suggest that the change in CF may be related to the change in ciliary height along the papilla (Weiss et al 1978b). The latter vary from about 12 μm to 31 μm (Mulroy 1974). An interesting aside is that in the amphibian ear, when two-tone suppression is present, it is seen only above the CF. An additional item to note is that Moffat & Capranica (1976) showed tuning in frog sacculus nerve fibers in the obvious absence of a TW or a tectorial membrane (the otolithic membrane is unlikely to possess mechanical properties akin to the tectorial membrane).

It is apparent that a TW or a basilar membrane or even a tectorial membrane is not a necessary prerequisite for tuning and tonotopic organization. A gradation of ciliary height along some spatial dimension of the papilla is indicated as a conceivable basis of frequency analysis. Such gradation is well established for mammals (Lim 1980), birds (Saunders & Tilney 1980), some reptiles (Mulroy 1974), and some amphibians (Lewis 1977). Another possibility is that the receptor cells themselves possess tuned bioelectric characteristics (Fettiplace & Crawford 1978). This mechanism will be considered later in the text. While the various mechanisms that conceivably provide tuning could substitute for the conventional traveling wave type of frequency analysis, it is likely that, when present, the TW provides at least a preanalysis of the signal, and it cannot be ruled out that it may be responsible for the entire analysis process. It is at least conceivable that we will have to learn to live with the unappealing notion that nature developed several solutions for the spectral analysis problem. Thus in more primitive ears a TW-type analysis may have no importance, while in more advanced hearing organs (birds, mammals) TWs in combination with a second filter, or even alone, could be responsible for spectral processing.

Unequivocal indication of the overriding importance of mechanical factors in advanced ears is seen in the structure and physiology of the ear of the greater horseshoe bat. This creature has an orientation cry that consists of a constant frequency (83 kHz) portion followed by an FM-glide. Significant dimensional changes underlie a profound variation in stiffness over the 4.3–4.6 mm segment of this 16 mm cochlea. The result is that the all important 83–86 kHz region (0.05 octave) is expanded onto a length that normally subtends a full octave (Bruns 1976a,b). In addition, the sharpness of tuning of nerve fibers in this frequency region is much greater than what is seen for other mammals (Suga et al 1976, Neuweiler & Vater 1977). This type of mechanical specialization at the basilar membrane level, coupled with conspicuously high frequency selectivity, emphasizes the possibility of a purely mechanical solution of the frequency analysis problem. Apparently this type of mechanical specialization is more common among mammalia than hitherto appreciated (Bruns 1979).

The response of the basilar membrane is primarily determined by its spatial pattern of stiffness. This variable has not been remeasured since von Békésy's original investigations. In a related experiment, however, Voldrich (1978) reassessed the symmetry of the basilar membrane by deforming it with fine probes. He found in fresh preparations that the deformation was elliptical with the long axis in the radial direction. These results are in contrast with von Békésy's circular deformations and admit the possibility of membrane resonance. Voldrich attributes the discrepancies to a change in mechanical properties due to fixation. It should be mentioned, however, that at least some of von Békésy's measurements were made on live specimens (1960, p. 544).

While it is conceivable that with further advances in measuring methods the discrepancies between sharpness of tuning of basilar membrane motion and single nerve fibers may be eliminated, it is worth repeating that the evidence is quite compelling that simple membrane mechanics is insufficient to account for all observed phenomena. Moreover, in some submammalian species, basilar membrane or tectorial membrane properties cannot be responsible for tuning. It is thus imperative that we consider the speculative realm of "second filters."

Second Filters

Many suggestions have been advanced about the nature of the "second filter." A sampling of these may be found in Zwicker & Terhardt (1974) and Evans & Wilson (1977). Newer work is included in *Supplement* No. 9 of *Scandinavian Audiology* (1979) and *Supplement* No. 1 of *Hearing Research* (1980). Experimenters and modelers tend to seek the second filter in one of four general classes of mechanisms. Some consider passive mechanical processes involving the micromechanics of the organ of Corti and the tectorial membrane (Allen 1977, Hall 1977, Zwislocki & Kletsky 1979,

Zwislocki 1980). One of the most ingenuous of these is the model of Duifhuis (1976), who invoked the directional sensitivity of hair cells as a possible
contributor to the sharpening of frequency selectivity.

Another class of models, originating with Lynn & Sayers (1970), invokes
interactions between the two groups of receptor cells of the cochlea: outer
hair cells (OHC) and inner hair cells (IHC). Contemporary versions assume
that OHCs influence IHCs either via electrical interaction or by a modification of organ of Corti micromechanics. The former possibility is exemplified
by Manley's (1978) suggestions. The latter scheme has not been formally
developed, but several authors allude to its conceivable existence. OHC-
IHC interaction hypotheses receive indirect support from experiments that
demonstrate altered auditory function in the absence of OHCs (Ryan &
Dallos 1975, Kiang et al 1976a, Dallos & Harris 1978, Harrison & Evans
1979b, Dallos et al 1980).

A third class of sharpening scheme assumes the presence of active processes in the organ of Corti. Gold (1948) originally suggested that a positive
feedback of the electrical output (CM) to the vibratory structures of the
cochlea could be conceived. More contemporary versions of such an active
process have been mentioned by several authors, one example of this approach being the model of Kim et al (1980b). The impetus for incorporating
active processes into cochlear models is found in various experimental
observations. Important among these is the emission of detectable tones by
the ear that accompany certain forms of tinnitus (Kemp 1979). Other
findings are compatible with active processes but do not necessarily require
them. These are the physiological vulnerability of basilar membrane tuning
and nonlinearity (Rhode 1973, Robles et al 1976), of acoustic emissions at
distortion frequencies (Kim et al 1980a), and of stimulated acoustic emissions themselves (Kemp 1978).

Stimulated acoustic emissions from the ear are a curious class of phenomena (Kemp 1978, Anderson & Kemp 1979, Kemp & Chum 1980) which
may be a byproduct of cochlear function but unlikely to represent an
essential feature. The basic observation is that a brief transient delivered to
the ear evokes a delayed acoustic echo in the form of damped oscillations
The mechanism of echo generation is highly nonlinear, with relative magnitude of the reflected signal increasing toward lower input levels. Its presence
signifies that reverse transmission of acoustic energy is possible when the
source is in the cochlear partition, a fact evident from earlier experiments
on subharmonic generation (Dallos 1966).

Acoustic echoes may be as sharply tuned as neural responses (Kemp &
Chum 1980), implying that generation occurs at the level of the second
filter. A bidirectional coupling between this site and the preceding mechanical stage may also be inferred from the finding that nonlinear response

components (such as $2f_1-f_2$) are also detectable in the earcanal but disappear upon interference with the organ of Corti (Kim et al 1980a). There is a rapidly growing literature on acoustic emissions; the following are some examples: Kemp (1978), Anderson & Kemp (1979), Wit & Ritsma (1979, 1980), Wilson (1980).

The fourth mechanism suggested for the second filter is a tuned hair cell-first order neuron system (J. R. Johnstone 1977). Here it is simply assumed, in analogy with some electroreceptors (for a good summary see Bennett & Clusin 1979), that the receptor cell-synapse combination is inherently frequency-specific. We will discuss this in more detail below.

Before considering various aspects of cochlear electrophysiology, two additional matters need to be mentioned. It is apparent that the tectorial membrane (TM) plays a pivotal role in hair cell excitation, and consequently its relationship to the reticular lamina and to the hair cell cilia is of fundamental importance. Conventional wisdom has it that both IHC and OHC cilia contact the TM. Actually, the bulk of experimental evidence shows that while there is a firm contact between the tallest row of OHC cilia and TM, the relationship between IHC cilia and TM is unclear. Such contact was not seen by Kimura (1966), Lindeman et al (1971), or Lim (1972, 1977), but others feel that some contact exists (Ross 1974, Hoshino & Kodama 1977, Engström & Engström 1978). Even if there is some contact between IHC cilia and TM, it appears less firm than that seen for OHC cilia. The latter are inserted into shallow pits on the underside of the TM and are fixed there with some glue-like substance. This fixation is certainly missing from IHC cilia (Lim 1977, Engström & Engström 1978). The strongest evidence for some attachment, the appearance of pits or grooves on the underside of the TM in the area of IHCs, may simply be a remnant of close apposition between IHC and TM during embryonic development (Lim 1977). A lack of firm attachment of IHC cilia of course implies a different mode of stimulation for IHCs and OHCs (Dallos et al 1972).

A second matter concerning the TM is its general relation and attachment to the organ of Corti. It has been generally accepted that a subtectorial space corresponding to the height of the tallest cilia exists and that the fluid in this space is endolymph which is in free communication with the scala media via the open marginal net that attaches the TM to the organ of Corti in the region of the Hensen's cells (Lim 1972). Support for free communication comes from experiments in which the ion content of the subtectorial fluid was determined with X-ray microanalysis (Flock 1977a, Ryan et al 1980) and the electrophysiological work of Tanaka et al (1977). The results indicate high K and low Na concentration. Opposing such open endolymph channels are the results of Kronester-Frei (1978, 1979a,b) and Manley & Kronester-Frei (1980). Using anatomical and electrophysiological techniques, these workers conclude that the marginal net is closed, that the subtectorial fluid is unlikely to be endolymph, and that the probable boundary of the positive endocochlear potential (EP) is the underside of the TM. These conclusions are reminiscent of Lawrence's (1967) suggestions, except that he placed the EP boundary at the scala media side of the TM. Burgio & Lawrence (1980) have even proposed that the subtectorial space does not exist and that the TM extends to the reticular lamina, in the fashion of otolithic membranes in the vestibular system. The TM is a notoriously difficult substance to work with; it shrinks or expands depending on its ionic environment (Kronester-Frei 1979b). Consequently, it is safe to say that no unassailable work is available on the subject. If newer contentions are found to be correct, then the entire conventionally accepted scheme for hair cell excitation (Davis 1965) must be reevaluated, since conceivably neither the high K^+-concentration endolymph nor the high positive EP would be available to the apical surfaces of the receptor cells.

From the above considerations we can naturally shift to the second major topic of this review.

CHEMICAL AND ELECTRICAL ENVIRONMENT OF THE ORGAN OF CORTI

Anatomical Considerations

It has been the consensus of the hearing science community that both the high K^+ content of the endolymph and the positive polarization of the endolymphatic space (EP) are of significance for the functioning of the organ of Corti. Thus it is not surprising that a great deal of attention is paid to the origins of ionic concentration gradients and the EP. A delineation of electrical conductance paths within the cochlea is also of interest. The morphological substrate of electrical boundaries has been studied with conventional transmission electron microscopy and with freeze-fracture techniques. Good summaries of recent work are those of C. A. Smith (1978) and Iurato et al (1976a). It seems clear that there are two separate compartments in the cochlea that are bounded by zonulae occludentes. First, the stria vascularis is separated from both the endolymphatic and perilymphatic spaces by tight junctions among the marginal and basal cells respectively. Second, the scala media space is entirely closed by tight junctions among the cells of Reissner's membrane, marginal cells of stria vascularis, cells of inner and outer sulci, and between all cells that compose the reticular lamina (Jahnke 1975, Reale et al 1975, Iurato et al 1976a, Gulley & Reese 1976, Nadol et al 1976, Nadol 1979). These occluding junctions are thought to present extremely low conductance pathways to ion flow and thus effectively insulate the scala media space. In contrast, the basilar membrane and spiral ligament appear to be fully permeable to small ions and thus the fluid spaces within the organ of Corti are in communication with perilymphatic compartments (C. A. Smith 1978, Nadol 1979). The junctions in the reticular lamina appear to be "very tight" and of exceptionally high insulating quality (Iurato et al 1976a).

Supporting cells within the organ of Corti are also joined by junctional complexes, but these are of the gap junction variety (Jahnke 1975, Gulley & Reese 1976, Iurato et al 1976b, Hama & Saito 1977). In the mammalian ear such gap junctions are prevalent between all adjoining supporting cells, whether they are of the same or different cell types. Thus the implication is that all supporting cells of the organ have their cytoplasms electrically and metabolically coupled. In the ear of the lizard, Nadol et al (1976) found gap junctions between hair cells and supporting cells. This controversial finding is supported by the intracellular measurement of Mulroy et al (1974), who found well-developed receptor potentials in supporting cells. No similar junctional complexes have been seen in mammalian organs of Corti or in another species of lizard (Bagger-Sjöbäck & Flock 1977).

Endocochlear Potential and Ionic Concentrations

Ever since its discovery in 1950 by von Békésy, the endocochlear potential (EP) has been the subject of an unabating stream of investigations. The finding by Konishi et al (1961) that in anoxic animals the EP becomes negative raised the question about the origin of the two varieties of resting potential: EP^+ and EP^-. It was also noted by many that electrodes within the organ of Corti often recorded a larger negative resting potential which was christened the organ of Corti potential (OCP). The latter is now clearly understood to be a reflection of the intracellular negativity of supporting and probably receptor cells arising from injury or artifacts (Sohmer et al 1971; Dallos 1973b, pp. 223–28). Recent mapping of the fluid spaces within the organ with microelectrodes (Manley & Kronester-Frei 1980, Dallos & Flock 1980) shows that the potentials do not depart significantly from zero. Yet the notion persists that an entity, OCP, does exist and some experimenters use the "OCP" to assess the state of the organ (e.g. Sitko et al 1976).

The measured EP is thought to arise as the sum of two or three components. There is general agreement that there exists in the marginal cells of the stria vascularis an electrogenic K^+ pump which is responsible for contributing a positive component to the EP (Kuijpers & Bonting 1970, Sellick & Bock 1974). Sellick & Johnstone (1974) proposed the existence of a second Na^+-K^+ exchange pump which is also electrogenic but produces a negative potential in the endolymph. The first pump is inhibited by ouabain and by etharcrynic acid (EA) and it is sensitive to anoxia. The presumed second pump is inhibited by both ouabain and anoxia, but does not immediately respond to EA. Thus after administration of EA, the EP^+ changes to EP^- and the magnitude of this EP^- can be further affected by anoxia (Sellick & Johnstone 1974, Kusakari & Thalmann 1976, Kusakari et al 1978). In an elegant experiment, using IV instead of perilymphatic perfusion of EA, Bosher (1979) failed to find a negative electrogenic component of the EP. These well-controlled experiments are likely to hold up, and at this time it may be most parsimonious to consider the resting potential to be the sum of only two components. The first, positive, component is due to an electrogenic K^+–Na^+ pump, as originally proposed by Kuijpers & Bonting (1970). When anoxia, ouabain, or EA are applied to the cochlea, the pump is inhibited and the EP rapidly moves to a value of approximately –40 mV. The nature of this negative potential has been disputed. Most assume that it is a K^+ diffusion potential between perilymph and endolymph (Kuijpers & Bonting 1970, B. M. Johnstone 1970, Melichar & Syka 1977, Konishi et al 1979). Others propose that the negative component is due to a leakage current from cells of the organ of Corti (Honrubia et al 1976). Recent work (exemplified by that of Bosher 1979) strongly supports the K^+ diffusion hypothesis.

High K^+ concentration and the presence of a positive potential at the hair-bearing surface of the receptor cells are not phenomena restricted to the mammalian cochlea. Russell & Sellick (1976) showed these conditions to exist in the cupula of the lateral line organ of the frog. High K^+ is also evident in the ampulla of Lorenzini (Okitsu et al 1978). In the lizard endolymph the K content is apparently high as well. However, in fish the situation may be different (Peterson et al 1978). The last result notwithstanding, there is a great deal of evidence that under normal conditions K^+ is important for the function of receptor cells in the acoustico-lateralis systems (Valli et al 1979).

A great deal of interesting work, utilizing contemporary methodologies with ion-selective microelectrodes and radioactive tracers, has provided new information on ion fluxes and concentrations in the cochlea: Melichar & Syka (1977), Bosher & Warren (1978), Konishi & Hamrick (1978), Konishi et al (1978), Peterson et al (1978), Asakuma et al (1979), Konishi (1979), Marcus & Thalmann (1980).

Ions other than K^+ and Na^+ have also been sampled in endolymph and perilymph, Cl^- and Ca^{2+} receiving the greatest attention (Bosher & Warren 1978, Peterson et al 1978). The interesting result emerges that while endolymphatic Ca^{2+} concentration is unusually low, it is still higher than the expected equilibrium concentration. Bosher & Warren (1978) propose that active transport mechanisms may be responsible for the disequilibrium of this cation. Konishi & Hamrick (1978), using chloride isotopes to measure flux, explained the normal Cl^- concentration in endolymph as a result of passive flux due to the EP and the presence of an active transport mechanism that moves chloride out of the scala media.

The strial energy metabolism was studied by recording adenine nucleotide levels in the normal state and during ischemia (Marcus et al 1978a,b; Thalmann et al 1978, 1979). Another approach to the study of energy metabolism in the inner ear is represented by the work of Prazma et al (1978), who measured endolymphatic oxygen tension under various conditions.

Transmitters

To close this segment, let us consider recent work on the identification of neural transmitters in the cochlea. There is overwhelming evidence (reviewed by Guth et al 1976) that ACh is the efferent transmitter. Recent work (Robertson & Johnstone 1978) showed that intracochlear perfusion with Ringer's solution containing ACh and eserine caused a frequency-dependent change in the sensitivity of primary afferents. The change mimicked that seen with electrical activation of the crossed olivocochlear bundle (Wiederhold 1970).

The identity of the afferent transmitter has not yet been determined, although the possibility of the amino acids glutamate or aspartate cannot be ruled out (Godfrey et al 1976, Klinke & Oertel 1977c). In contrast, there is some evidence against ACh (reviewed by Klinke & Galley 1974, Guth et al 1976), catecholamines (Klinke & Evans 1977), GABA (Fex & Wenthold 1976, Klinke & Oertel 1977a), and serotonin (Klinke & Oertel 1977b). Support for glutamate or aspartate as putative afferent transmitters also derives from the work of Bobbin (1979) and Bobbin & Morgan (1979).

HAIR CELL PHYSIOLOGY

Up to the year 1970 when the first intracellular recordings from lateral line hair cells were obtained (G. G. Harris et al 1970), all information about hair cell physiology was derived by indirect means. The primary method of assessing hair cell function was the study of gross receptor potentials, cochlear microphonic (CM) and summating potential (SP). Even after 1970, until the appearance of the work of Russell and Sellick (1977a,b, 1978), gross potentials provided most of the information about mammalian hair cell physiology. The extrapolation of results from gross recording to the unit level is a difficult process but the information can be most valuable when carefully interpreted (Dallos 1973b, 1975). During this period strides were made in the study of hair cells at lower levels of the acoustico-lateralis system (Flock et al 1973, Weiss et al 1974, Sand et al 1975).

New and significant information about the general physiology of hair cells was provided primarily by the laboratories of Flock and Hudspeth. The former concentrated on the properties of stereocilia while the latter investigated the transduction process as well.

Nature of Cilia

Flock et al (1977) micromanipulated the hairs in the frog's crista and found them to be stiff and brittle. When displaced at their tips, they pivoted around their insertion into the cuticular plate without bending. Apparently the entire ciliary tuft of a given hair cell moves together, indicating strong lateral coupling among adjacent cilia. Stiffness is due to the filamentous structure of the hairs, and it is unaltered when the cilia are demembranated. Flock (1977b) and Flock & Cheung (1977) found that when crista stereocilia are demembranated and incubated with myosin subfragment–1, the ciliary filaments, the rootlets and the filaments of the cuticular plate became serrated, reflecting the binding of the S–1 to the filaments. The periodicity of attachment was 35 nm and the angle 45°. This arrangement is similar to that seen in intestinal microvilli (Mooseker & Tilney 1975) which are known to contain actin filaments. Since F-actin's paracrystalline state can be altered physiologically, Flock & Cheung's discovery opened the theoretical possibility that the stiffness of stereocilia may be altered with the conceivable result of influencing organ of Corti micromechanics. Numerous investigators have referred to this possibility in their considerations of second filters and active cochlear processes. While they do not explicitly mention it, the scheme of Zwislocki & Kletsky (1979) would be well augmented by a controllable coupling between reticular lamina and tectorial membrane via changing ciliary stiffness. Unfortunately, the recent work of Tilney et al (1980) may dampen enthusiasm for an active ciliary process. In an extensive study of stereocilia from the alligator lizard's basilar papilla, these authors confirm Flock's finding that S-1 decoration indicates unidirectional polarity of the actin filaments toward the cell's center. They, however, find a random polarity in the cuticular plate. In addition, they find that the packing of filaments is not altered by fixation in different media or by incubation in media containing Ca^{2+}, ATP, EGTA, etc. It is concluded that in contrast to the cilia in the brush border, these cilia are not likely to be contractile. While contraction of the cilia may be unlikely, their stiffness conceivably could still be altered with a concomitant modification of the TM-reticular lamina coupling. The extensive network of endoplasmic reticulum of OHCs could, in such a scheme, serve to sequester Ca^{2+} which may mediate the process.

Electrophysiology: General

Significant information derives from the work of Hudspeth & Corey (1977), who recorded intracellularly from hair cells in bullfrog saccular maculae. Large (up to 15 mV) receptor potentials were noted, in contrast with all earlier intracellular studies. The low-frequency response characteristic of the cells indicated depolarization with hair bundle displacement toward the kinocilium and hyperpolarizatin for the opposite direction. Displacement of the hairs was accompanied by a change in membrane resistance—a decrease for movements toward the kinocilium. The approximately 200 $M\Omega$ resting membrane resistance could be modulated by up to 50 $M\Omega$. Occasional intracellular spikes were seen, most likely due to the high Ca^{2+} content of the bathing medium. Nevertheless, their presence indicates a voltage sensitive conductance mechanism operational in the cell membrane. Hudspeth & Jacobs (1979) micromanipulated individual cilia and ciliary bundles. They found that kinocilia participate in the transduction process only passively; in other words, they may transmit movements from the otolithic membrane to the stereocilia. In order for transduction to take place, stereocilia themselves must be displaced. Corey & Hudspeth (1979a) studied voltage clamped hair cells in their in vitro frog sacculus preparation. The I-V characteristic has a slope of 200–300 $M\Omega$ between membrane voltages of –100 to –50 mV. For greater depolarizations, the slope decreases to about 6 $M\Omega$. This region seems to represent a voltage-dependent K^+-conductance. For hyperpolarizations beyond –100 mV there is a secondary anomalous resistance decrease. This I-V pattern indicates that injured cells with membrane potentials less than –50 mV could be expected to produce small receptor potentials which may explain previous data. This characteristic, however, is unlikely to have general numerical validity since in mammalian inner hair cells Russell & Sellick (1977a,b) find membrane potentials of –40 mV or less along with large receptor potentials.

It was noted that the reversal potential of these cells was around 0 mV, suggesting that the transducer mechanism relies on a nonspecific stimulus-dependent conductance. Crawford & Fettiplace (1979) also report a near zero reversal potential in turtle receptor cells. It was further found by Corey and Hudspeth (1979a) that all alkali cations supported the receptor current, as did Ca^{2+}. Thus it may be concluded that the ion channels appear to be nonspecific and that in vivo the receptor current is carried by whatever ion species are available. This would normally by K^+ which is the dominant ion of endolymph. A final significant finding is that Ca^{2+} is a necessary cofactor in transduction; if it was reduced in concentration below 10 μM the receptor current was abolished. Corey & Hudspeth (1979b) also determined that the response latency of these hair cells was less than 40 μsec.

In contrast with the above findings, Valli et al (1979), using techniques similar to those of Hudspeth and Corey, noted that discharges from the ampullary nerve could be completely suppressed if K^+ was removed from the bathing medium irrespective of its ionic content. This finding intimates that only K^+ can carry the receptor current. They also noted that the receptor remained excitable with electrical, but not mechanical, stimulation if Ca^{2+} was eliminated from the bath. This suggests that the mechanical transduction in the receptor is mediated by Ca^{2+}-sensitive potassium channels. This conclusion about the importance of Ca^{2+} is in harmony with the findings of Sand (1975) and Cory & Hudspeth (1979a) but is opposed by the somewhat peculiar results of Katsuki (1976), who noted an inhibitory effect by divalent cations upon current carried by monovalent cations.

Weiss et al (1978a) assessed the various resting potentials, endolymphatic and intracellular, of the reptilian ear. Fettiplace & Crawford (1978), in an elegant study on the cochlea of the turtle, recorded intracellular responses from receptor cells. With membrane potentials of –40 to –50 mV, they found receptor potentials of ± 20 mV. Response characteristics were strongly nonlinear, saturation having been seen at high sound levels for all driving frequencies. All cells were tuned with asymmetrical V-shaped response curves and clearly defined best frequencies. Responses from supporting cells were very small in contrast with the findings of Mulroy et al (1974) from the alligator lizard's basilar papilla. By manipulating nonlinear response characteristics obtained at various driving frequencies, the authors derived hypothetical shapes for two cascaded filters that could be responsible for the observed response patterns. A potentially significant observation is that with low-frequency acoustic stimulation or with injected rectangular current pulses a ringing response was seen. The frequency of these oscillations corresponded approximately to the best frequency of the cell. The ringing could be eliminated by hyperpolarizing the cell to about –70 mV. Thus it is conceivable that a voltage-sensitive potassium conductance underlies the oscillatory response and, by implication, some of the frequency selectivity of these cells. Although similar "electrical tuning" is not apparent in recordings from other hair cell systems (Flock et al 1973, Mulroy et al 1974, Hudspeth & Corey 1977, Russell & Sellick 1977a,b), Manley (1979) finds that many primary auditory neurons of the starling discharge in the absence of any stimulus at preferred intervals that are the reciprocal of their best frequency. This self-oscillation may be the result of an intrinsic filtering mechanism of the receptor cell-synapse system.

Electrophysiology: Mammalian

Probably the single most significant achievement of the past few years has been the accomplishment of intracellular recording from mammalian IHCs by Russell & Sellick (1977a,b, 1978). Data were obtained in guinea pig cochleas from IHCs located at the high-frequency (17–18 kHz) region. Results revealed relatively low membrane potentials (up to –43 mV) coupled with large receptor potentials. The latter were primarily DC responses, roughly reflecting the envelope of the stimulating sound and not unlike the familiar extracellular SP. The DC receptor potentials could reach magnitudes of 20 mV and were always of the depolarizing polarity. AC receptor potentials (analogous to the extracellular CM) were also recorded, but their magnitude was subject to frequency-dependent attenuations due to the cell's membrane capacitance and the low-pass characteristics of the recording electrodes. How big these AC responses were, and how well the experimenters were capable of correcting for various filter effects across frequency, is not entirely clear. Both DC and AC responses showed strong saturating nonlinearity around the best frequency, with much more linear growth at lower frequencies. Isoresponse curves, both AC and DC, resembled (qualitatively and quantitatively) single fiber tuning curves showing very sharp frequency selectivity. This result clearly indicates that cochlear filtering is accomplished at or before the hair cell level. DC resistance changes elicited by stimulation were proportional to the receptor potential magnitude. In these experiments AC resistance changes were not measured. For information on these one needs to rely on the indirect methods utilized to good advantage by Geisler et al (1977).

Preliminary data on intracellular recording from positively identified OHCs in the guinea pig's cochlea reveal predominantly AC receptor potentials of small magnitude (1–2 mV) coupled with relatively high membrane potentials (up to –70 mV). The tuning of these cells is not significantly sharper than that seen in the extracellular spaces around them (Dallos & Flock, unpublished data).

In subsequent experiments on IHCs, Sellick & Russell (1979) demonstrated the presence of two-tone suppression at the receptor potential level. They also noted (Sellick & Russell 1980) that at low frequencies (<200 Hz) the receptor potential seems to reflect the velocity of basilar membrane motion as was predicted from gross CM measurements in IHC-only regions of the cochlea (Dallos et al 1972). These findings lend support to the notion that IHC cilia do not make intimate contact with the tectorial membrane and thus are deflected by viscous fluid drag.

Gross CM and impedance measurements utilized by Geisler et al (1977) and Hubbard et al (1979a,b) also provide insights about basic transducer mechanisms. While the overall qualitative changes in resistance are similar to CM responses, the spectral structure of the CM appears incompatible with a model (Davis' 1965 scheme) in which a simple time-varying resistance gives rise to the receptor current. Similarly incompatible with the

Davis model is the observation that CM and resistance changes are not proportional to one another when the EP is altered by anoxia. Extensive data are provided on the harmonic structure of the CM, and distinctions are made between components generated by the nonlinearity of the transducer and those due to the inherently nonlinear nature of the cochlear circuit itself (Honrubia & Ward 1970; Dallos 1973b, pp. 278–83). The former nonlinearity is shown to be dominant.

Other contributors to the gross CM literature are Schmiedt & Zwislocki (1977, 1978), who showed extensive data for the mongolian gerbil indicating correlations with middle ear transfer characteristics and basilar membrane displacement.

Denton & Gray (1979) recorded microphonics from the sprat utricle and found the frequency-doubled responses commonly associated with epithelia having groups of hair cells of morphologically opposing polarity (Flock 1971). With two inputs the response was dependent on the phase between the two, which led the authors to the remarkable conclusion that this organ behaved unlike the mammalian ear. Why they assume that mammalian CM waveforms would not similarly reflect phase differences between stimulus sounds is unfathomable.

ROLE OF INNER AND OUTER HAIR CELLS

Obvious morphological differences (reviewed by, e.g., C. A. Smith 1975, 1978) and striking differences in innervation (reviewed by Spoendlin 1978) suggest that the role of the two types of cochlear receptor should be distinct. Newer work on the subject includes morphological, anatomical, physiological, and behavioral studies. The intracellular recordings from IHCs of Russell & Sellick, reviewed above, constitute one of the cornerstones of our developing understanding.

Morphology and Innervation
There have been numerous contributions to the literature further delineating the striking differences in morphology and innervation between IHCs and OHCs. C. A. Smith (1975, 1978), in splendid summaries, discusses the differences between OHC and IHC morphology with special attention to the conspicuous and well-organized smooth endoplasmic reticulum adjacent to the plasmalemma in OHCs. Differences between presynaptic zones of the two types of hair cell have received ample attention. Dunn & Morest (1975), Gulley & Reese (1977a), and Spoendlin (1978, 1979) all emphasize the lack of synaptic ribbons and vesicle aggregates in the infranuclear zone of OHCs. In contrast, Angelborg & Engström (1973), C. A. Smith (1975), and most recently Siegel & Brownell (1980) note that synaptic bodies are often seen

in OHCs adjacent to afferent endings. The latter investigators state that in appropriately fixed material they are invariably present. Gulley & Reese (1977a) found very different particle distributions in freeze-fractured material on IHC and OHC afferent postsynaptic membranes, indicating the possibility of different transmitters for the two types of synapse. In the same experimental series they also showed striking differences between the accumulation of particles on cytoplasmic leaflets of efferent contacts on OHCs and on IHC afferents. Here again, the structural dissimilarity of postsynaptic membranes may signal the presence of different receptors or even of different transmitters. Gulley & Reese (1977b) also found a variety of structural dissimilarities and regional specializations in IHC and OHC membrane structures, indicating different physiological mechanisms for the two receptor types. Gulley & Bagger-Sjöbäck (1979), on the basis of freeze-fracture preparations, also emphasize considerable differences in the presynaptic zones of Types I and II vestibular hair cells. Based on this work it appears possible that the two cell types function with different neurotransmitters or, conceivably, that Type I cells may have a mode of mixed chemical-electrical transmission. These findings are interesting because of the homology between Type I–Type II vestibular receptors and the corresponding IHC-OHC cochlear receptors.

In other interesting new work, Nadol (1980) found reciprocal synapses between OHCs and "afferent" terminals in human material, whereas Kimura et al (1980), again in human cochleas, noted synaptic contacts on spiral ganglion cells of conceivably parasympathetic or efferent origin.

Spoendlin (1978, 1979) restates and expands his findings on radically different degeneration patterns of IHC and OHC afferents. He notes that OHC destruction has no effect on neuron count, a finding which does not completely agree with Hunter-Duvar & Mount's (1978) results. The fascinating possibility is entertained that OHC afferents may not possess central nervous system terminations. These unmyelinated fibers apparently are not present in the internal meatus where the myelinated (presumably IHC afferent) fibers constitute 95–98% and the remaining extremely thin unmyelinated axons may well be autonomic. A contrasting view is that of Webster & Webster (1978) and Morest & Bohne (1980), who show degenerative debris in the cochlear nucleus after OHC destruction.

Physiology and Function

It has been stated often that OHCs are responsible for producing the gross receptor potentials in normal cochleas (Davis et al 1958; Dallos 1973a, 1978). The basis of such assertions was that in cochleas showing predominant OHC damage due to some intervention, the CM is severely diminished. The necessary counterexperiment was performed by Dallos & Cheatham

(1976a), in which CM and SP were recorded from cochlear regions devoid of IHCs. The responses were nearly normal, indicating the probable validity of the notion that OHCs control the gross receptor potentials. This finding is puzzling in light of the large receptor potentials seen intracellularly in IHCs and the relatively small ones in OHCs. Thus the gross responses may be even more affected by electroanatomical influences than hitherto assumed (Dallos 1973b, Strelioff 1973).

The effect of OHC loss on behavior threshold was studied by Prosen et al (1978) in kanamycin-poisoned guinea pigs. Their results support Ryan & Dallos' (1975) finding in the chinchilla that this type of pathology induces a high-frequency threshold deficit of 40–55 dB, the extent of which correlates well with the destruction of OHCs. In contrast, Ehret (1979), working with the mouse, concluded that OHC loss has no effect on thresholds as long as IHCs are undamaged. The recent provocative finding of Deol & Glueck-sohn-Waelsch (1979) of no hearing in mutant mice having only OHCs is attuned to much current thinking about the roles of the two receptor cell types. This work utilized the notoriously imprecise Preyer's reflex and will certainly be repeated with more contemporary methods. The question of how hair cell loss affects the audiogram clearly requires further elucidation, utilizing more rigorous behavioral techniques than employed by some previous workers.

Other behavioral manifestations of OHC loss have also been studied. Psychophysical tuning curves are elevated in proportion to the threshold shift but maintain their shape as long as IHCs are presumably normal (Dallos et al 1977, Ryan et al 1979). Psychophysical tuning curves, however, may not be a relevant measure of frequency selectivity (Pickles 1979a, Johnson-Davies & Patterson 1979). Other measures of frequency selectivity, such as the frequency DL, also remain unchanged in experimental animals after the elimination of OHCs (Nienhuys & Clark 1978, Ryan 1978). Intensity DLs appear to be similarly impervious to OHC deficit (Prosen et al 1980).

For a while it appeared that auditory nerve fibers were unresponsive if OHCs were absent from the region of their origin (Kiang et al 1970, 1976a). It is now clear that they in fact respond and that many of their response characteristics are unaltered (Dallos & Harris 1978, Harrison & Evans 1979a,b). The ability of fibers to phase lock at low frequencies and their properties of adaptation appear unchanged (Harrison & Evans 1979a), as does the distribution of spontaneous rates, latency to click stimuli, and Q_{10} (sharpness of tuning) (Dallos & Harris 1978). The latter finding is highly controversial in that only Dallos & Harris (1978) found a significant portion of their tuning curves (FTC) to possess a sharply tuned tip whereas others have obtained FTCs that have their tip section missing (Kiang et al

1970, 1976a; Liberman & Kiang 1978; Harrison & Evans 1979b; Robertson & Johnstone 1979). Supporting the contention that sharp tips in the absence of OHCs can be found are the fragmentary data of Markuszka (1977) and material from Romahn & Boerger (1977). The latter authors claim that OHC lesions do not affect the FTCs at all, a contention not substantiated by any other investigator. It is likely that Romahn & Boerger misestimated the position of their normal fibers and that they in fact originated from outside the lesion. Whether FTCs of fibers that originate from the IHC-only segment do in fact possess sharp tips (as contended by Dallos & Harris 1978 and Ryan et al 1979 for the cases when ICHs are unaffected by the lesion) remains uncertain. It is clear, however, that it is invariably the sharply tuned tip region of the FTCs that is altered by insults to the cochlea. It is the lability of the sharply tuned tip segment that prompted Evans (1972, 1975a) to propose a physiologically vulnerable second filter. It is apparent that the tip and tail segments of FTCs can be modified separately, and they may reflect different modes of transduction (Kiang & Moxon 1974, Kiang et al 1976a, Schmiedt 1977).

Another significant effect of OHC damage is the interference with nonlinear phenomena generated in the cochlea. Strongly affected are two-tone suppression and the generation of distortion frequencies such as $2f_1\text{-}f_2$ (Schmiedt 1977, Siegel 1978, Dallos et al 1980). It seems that the generation of pronounced cochlear distortion may be intimately tied to the OHC system.

Finally, Sokolich et al (1976) and Schmiedt (1977), on the basis of data from kanamycin- or noise-damaged gerbils, assert that fibers originating from IHC-only regions respond on opposite polarities of the stimulus from normal fibers. This provocative notion of phase opposition is weakened by highly variable lesion patterns and the difficulty of unequivocally assigning fibers to IHC-only or normal regions. The excitatory phase of basilar membrane motion is worth considering further. The data of Zwislocki & Sokolich (1973) and Konishi & Nielsen (1978) indicate that the majority of nerve fibers show excitation when basilar membrane displacement is inferred to be toward scala tympani. This finding is in contrast with earlier results (Tasaki 1954, Peake & Kiang 1962), as well as with expectations based on the known excitatory direction of displacement of cilia (Flock 1971, Hudspeth & Corey 1977). This matter and the conditions under which fibers show velocity sensitivity require additional studies.

Various lines of evidence (well summarized by Manley 1978) indicate the necessity for interaction between IHC and OHC groups. The prevailing notion is that IHCs control the outflow of afferent information from the cochlea and that OHCs influence the IHCs either directly or via the microenvironment in which they operate. In contrast with these schemes, which we have considered in more detail in a previous section, are the notions of Tumarkin (1978, 1979), arguing on a paleontological basis that the IHC and OHC systems are distinct and evolved for different purposes. He considers that the latter is a part of a hypothesized acoustico-spinal arousal mechanism. Anatomical evidence for such a tract is lacking at present.

Pierson & Møller (1980) demonstrated that under certain circumstances two populations of generators contribute to the gross CM. They suggested that the two populations are likely to be OHCs and IHCs. It appears more probable, however, that their two populations correspond to two spatially separated groups of OHCs that respond in very different fashion depending on their relative positions vis-à-vis the TW.

SINGLE FIBER AND COMPOUND RESPONSES OF THE AUDITORY NERVE

Single Fiber Response

The auditory nerve is like a window to the cochlea. The properties and functioning of the end organ may be deduced from carefully interpreted data on the discharge characteristics of auditory nerve fibers. This endeavor has engaged a very significant fraction of auditory physiologists active today. A comprehensive and well-written review on the subject by Evans (1975b) is recommended as background to this section.

Since 90–95% of the afferent fibers in the mammal innervate IHCs and the remaining small fraction OHCs, there is a perpetual quest to identify physiologically two populations of nerve fibers belonging to these two groups. It is fair to say that to date this quest remains unsuccessful. There does not appear to be any general physiological criterion which would identify the small segment of fibers that originate from OHCs. It is thus likely that all information in the literature is derived from IHC afferents. This is reinforced by the striking results of Klinke & Pause (1977, 1980), who could find only a single physiologically identifiable neural population in the caiman in spite of the fact that in this animal the innervation ratio of IHC-OHC is 60%–40%. The OHC afferents are either silent, nonexistent at the recording site (see above), or cannot be "picked up" with existing recording techniques (discriminated against by usual recording methods). Reports that claim to have identified an appropriate proportion of OHC afferents on the basis of some salient response characteristic have not received wide currency (Pfeiffer & Kim 1972, Romahn & Boerger 1978). One interesting dichotomy in auditory nerve fibers is their spontaneous rate. Almost distinct distributions between low ($<$10–20/sec) and high ($>$10–20/sec) rates are seen in all species examined recently (cat: Liberman 1978, Kim & Molnar 1979; guinea pig: Evans 1972; chinchilla: Dallos & Harris

1978; caiman: Klinke & Pause 1980). None of these distributions, however, match the proportion of IHC-OHC afferents.

Liberman (1978) studied the response characteristics of fibers from kittens that were raised in an exceptionally low-noise environment. He broke down the low spontaneous rate population into two groups, one that he called medium rate (between 0.5 and 18 spikes/sec) and a very low rate group (<0.5/sec). Thresholds of medium and high spontaneous units clustered within a narrow 10–15 dB range, whereas the very low rate units had thresholds over a 50 dB range. These fibers also had different tuning curve shapes and different rate-level functions. It is not clear whether these generally high threshold, exceptionally low spontaneous units, comprising 16% of the fibers seen, constitute a normal or subtly pathological population.

Even if Liberman's peculiar low spontaneous rate population is taken into account, the vast majority of fibers have thresholds that are closely clustered. In addition, the dynamic range at the best frequency (CF) is almost always less than 40 dB. Thus the question of intensity coding in the auditory nerve is a serious one and has received increasing attention in the past few years. The general tenor of these studies is that while the driven rate of a fiber may saturate at relatively low sound levels, the time structure of discharges is essentially maintained up to the highest intensities. Thus, for example, the FTC of a fiber may be derived with the reverse correlation method of de Boer & Kuyper (1968), or other transform techniques, from the time structure of rate-saturated responses with virtually no change in shape with stimulus level (Evans 1977, Bilsen & ten Kate 1977, Møller 1977a,b). Møller (1977b) attributed the maintenance of stimulus waveform in the response pattern of discharges above average rate saturation to the operation of an amplitude-compression nonlinearity. However, de Jongh (1977) and de Boer & de Jongh (1978) demonstrate that a linear transform of basilar membrane displacement (and to some extent velocity) controls the temporal pattern of firing probability. De Jongh (1977) also emphasized the importance of using pseudorandom noise stimuli with caution, a point that was beautifully developed by Swerup (1978).

Kim & Molnar (1979) recorded from large fiber populations in cats with standardized stimuli to establish the spatial pattern (response measure as a function of CF) of responses. Various response measures were derived from the Fourier analysis of period histograms. It was found that phase-locking response measures better reflected the stimulus than measures that did not take synchronization into account. Spatial patterns of second and third harmonic distortion components reflected those of the primaries, indicating local generation (no traveling wave type propagation). This demonstration supports the findings of Dallos and Sweetman (1969).

In a significant study, Young & Sachs (1979) obtained population responses from many fibers in response to synthesized vowels. The spectra of
period histograms was obtained and compared with that of the stimulus.
The rate at each harmonic component was averaged over all fibers whose
CF surrounded (±½ octave) the frequency of the harmonic. Thus a localized, synchronized population response was derived. Frequency plots
derived from this measure reflected the spectrum of the stimulus and were
insensitive to level. In contrast, simple rate measures saturated at low levels
and all spectral information was lost. The data revealed that smaller harmonic peaks between the formant frequencies were diminished, probably as
a consequence of two-tone suppression (2TS). Thus nonlinear processing
contributed significantly to the preservation of the stimulus spectrum in the
response pattern. It appears, therefore, that the auditory nerve preserves
information about the input in a combination of place and temporal pattern,
at least at relatively low frequencies. It is well to remember that recent
demonstrations on the importance of temporal patterning of discharges had
their origin in the pioneering work of Hind et al (1971).

Auditory nonlinearities as reflected in single unit discharge patterns were
studied by several investigators: Smoorenburg et al (1976), Greenwood et
al (1976), Buunen & Rhode (1978), and Kim et al (1978). The general
conclusion is that responses to the distortion component $2f_1-f_2$ behave as
if a tone at that frequency would be introduced in the sound stimulus along
with the primaries f_1 and f_2. The other important nonlinear phenomenon,
2TS, also received considerable attention (Abbas & Sachs 1976, Sachs &
Abbas 1976, Javel et al 1978, Rhode et al 1978, Harris 1979, Holton 1980).
Temporal patterning, processes of adaptation, and forward masking were
examined in several studies (R. L. Smith 1977, 1979; Bauer 1978; Harris
& Dallos 1979).

Compound Response

The compound response of the auditory nerve (AP) has enjoyed a renaissance during the past few years. This stems partly from its utility in electrocochleography and partly from its now realized ability to provide an
adequate representation of the underlying neural activity. In an ingenious
study, Kiang et al (1976b) determined the contribution of a given fiber to
the recorded gross AP. As expected from theoretical considerations (Teas
et al 1962), the unit response was a negative-positive biphasic voltage of
approximately 0.25 μV in magnitude. Actual measurement of the unit
responses places the various schemes on a firm basis in which the AP is
computed as the summed convolutions between the unit responses and
firing probabilities of the contributing neurons (M. H. Goldstein & Kiang

1958, Teas et al 1962, de Boer 1975, Elberling 1976) or those in which the firing pattern is derived from the AP by deconvolution (Elberling 1976, Hoke et al 1979).

The principal factor that assures the utility of the AP is the finding that near threshold the response is contributed to by only a small group of neurons, and thus it shows pronounced frequency specificity (de Boer 1975, Özdamar & Dallos 1976). Two experimental techniques for determining frequency-specific AP have been favored. With click-evoked responses the contributions of neurons from various CF regions can be isolated by selective high-pass masking techniques (Teas et al 1962, Eggermont et al 1974). Alternatively, using tone burst stimuli and tonal maskers, so-called AP tuning curves can be generated (Dallos & Cheatham 1976b, Eggermont 1977, Harris 1979). Correlations between unit discharge poststimulus time histograms and AP waveforms were measured for tone-burst stimuli by Özdamar & Dallos (1978) and for click stimuli by Antoli-Candela & Kiang (1978). The relationship between AP threshold obtained with shaped tone bursts and single unit thresholds was established in the studies of Dallos et al (1978) and J. R. Johnstone et al (1979). With appropriate masking techniques even such complex single fiber response phenomena as 2TS can be shown to possess clearcut analogs in the AP (Dallos & Cheatham 1977, Harris 1979).

MISCELLANY AND COMMENTS

A selection of references that defy easy classification is included in this section.

The anatomy of the efferent system was reevaluated by Warr (1975, 1978) and Warr & Guinan (1979) using axonal transport of HRP and labeled protein. The olivocochlear bundle (OCB) of the cat seems to consist of about 1800 neurons, or about three times the number that was hitherto assigned to this system. Approximately 42% of the fibers originate in large stellate neurons in the region of the medial and ventral nuclei of the trapezoid body and the dorso-medial periolivary nucleus. These cells send their axons to OHCs, 69% in the crossed OCB, 31% in the uncrossed. About 58% of the OCB fibers originate in small fusiform neurons located dorsal to the lateral superior olive. The axons go to IHCs, 86% uncrossed, 14% crossed. Altogether, 63% of the fibers comprise the uncrossed OCB and 37% make up the crossed. While the IHC and OHC systems are clearly separated, the previous notion of the crossed OCB supplying only OHCs and the uncrossed only IHCs, no longer appears tenable. Ross et al (1977), however, have criticized some of this work.

The ever elusive efferent system was also investigated in a series of behavioral studies by Igarashi et al (1979a,b). They noted that neither intensity nor frequency discrimination was affected by the transection of the crossed OCB. Stopp & Comis (1979) report that some cholinergic efferent fibers that disappear after sectioning of the OCB innervate Hensen's cells. These fibers appear to be the same as those studied by Wright & Preston (1976). The latter authors, however, could find no synaptic contacts with supporting cells. C. A. Smith et al (1976) also note the presence of long lateral branches among apical afferents that terminate among Deiters' cells. They saw no synaptic specializations, but concede the possibility that these fibers maintain a trophic relationship with the supporting cells. It is thus possible that the supporting cell matrix, known to be interconnected by gap junctions, does possess some pattern of innervation in certain vertebrate ears.

Several studies dealt with a quantitative description of the longitudinal properties of elements in the cochlear partition. Thus Ehret & Frankenreiter (1977) provided morphometry for the mouse, Bruns (1976a,b) for the horseshoe bat, Ramprashad et al (1979) for the little brown bat, Bohne & Carr (1979) for the chinchilla, while Miller (1978) gave us an extensive survey of lizard ears from seven different families.

Pickles (1979b) investigated the effect of lesions of the superior cervical ganglion and sympathetic trunk upon absolute and masked behavioral thresholds in cats. He found no effect due to the sympathectomy.

The old issue whether the curvature of the cochlea is of significance has reliably surfaced again. Viergever (1978) assures us that it is not, while Barrett (1978) and Kohllöffel (1979) think that it is.

Finally, in what must rate as the experimental series with the most peculiar results, Aran and colleagues (Aran et al 1979, Cazals et al 1979) find that after destroying essentially all cochlear hair cells with ototoxic drugs, a clearly distinguishable AP-like response can be observed. This AP can be elicited with inputs between 0.5–4kHz. It is maskable, but shows no adaptation. Most significantly its latency is extremely short, 0.2–0.5 msec. It may be of vestibular origin, but if so, it is mysterious why it would not be seen in normal ears.

It should be apparent that the past few years have been productive ones for devotees of cochlear physiology. Refinements in technology and skill allowed for more accurate measurement of gross vibratory motion patterns of the basilar membrane. Further advances are anticipated with the utilization of laser interferometry which should allow measurements down to near threshold levels. This should finally determine the degree of mechanical nonlinearity at threshold. Significant advances have also been made in observations of ciliary properties and mechanics. The next major advance is anticipated to be actual measurements of organ of Corti and tectorial membrane micromechanics. At this time we have little more than speculations on these critical subjects. Recent trends to emphasize time-domain and dynamic measures instead of, or in addition to, steady-state frequency domain analysis will certainly continue. Intracellular recording accomplishments from both mammalian and other types of hair cells have been among the most significant developments. It is anticipated that these techniques will become more productive, although probably not routine without some entirely new technology. The realization that frequency selectivity (tuning) and tonotopicity are possible without traveling waves and tectorial membranes should force a major rethinking of long cherished concepts. A heterogeneity of auditory mechanisms, even among vertebrates, may have to be entertained. However, for the most highly developed ears, mammalian and avain, problems posed by the function of outer hair cells will surely be solved in the near future. A closely linked part of this problem is the mode of operation and function of the efferent system. A solution to the OHC issue may also yield the solution to the efferent puzzle. Good times are ahead.

Literature Cited

Abbas, P. J., Sachs, M. B. 1976. Two-tone suppression in cat auditory nerve fibers: Extension of response relationship. *J. Acoust. Soc. Am.* 59:112–22

Allen, J. B. 1977. Cochlear micromechanics —A mechanism for transforming mechanical to neural tuning within the cochlea. *J. Acoust. Soc. Am.* 62:930–39

Anderson, S. D., Kemp, D. T. 1979. The evoked cochlear mechanical response in laboratory primates. *Arch. Otorhinolaryngol.* 224:47–54

Angelborg, C., Engström, H. 1973. The normal organ of Corti. In *Basic Mechanisms in Hearing,* ed. A. Møller, pp. 125–82. New York: Academic. 941 pp.

Antoli-Candela, F. Jr., Kiang, N.Y.S. 1978. Unit activity underlying the N₁ potential. See Naunton & Fernández, pp. 165–91

Aran, J.-M., Cazals, Y., Erre, J.-P., Guilhaume, A. 1979. Conflicting electrophysiological and anatomical data from drug impaired guinea pig cochlea. *Acta Otolaryngol.* 87:300–9

Asakuma, S., Lowry, L. D., Snow, J. B. Jr. 1979. Effect of kanamycin sulfate on the endocochlear dc potential of guinea pigs. *Arch. Otolaryngol.* 105:145–48

Bagger-Sjöbäck, D., Flock, Å. 1977. Freeze-fracturing of the auditory basilar papilla

in the lizard *Calotes versicolor. Cell Tissue Res.* 177:431–41

Barrett, T. W. 1978. The transfer function of the cochlea. *Q. Rev. Biophys.* 11:1–38

Bauer, J. W. 1978. Tuning curves and masking function of auditory-nerve fibers in cats. *Sens. Processes* 2:156–72

Bennett, M. V. L., Clusin, W. T. 1979. Transduction at electroreceptors: Origins of sensitivity. In *Membrane Transduction Mechanisms,* ed. R. A. Cone, J. E. Dowling, pp. 91–116. New York: Raven. 236 pp.

Bilsen, F. A., ten Kate, J. H. 1977. Preservation of the internal spectrum of complex signals at high intensities. See Evans & Wilson 1977, pp. 193–95

Bobbin, R. P. 1979. Glutamate and aspartate mimic the afferent transmitters in the cochlea. *Exp. Brain Res.* 34:389–93

Bobbin, R. P., Morgan, D. N. 1979. Actions of glutamate, aspartate, and related substances on the spontaneous activity of afferent nerve in the toad (*Xenopus laevis*) lateral line. *Proc. Assoc. Res. Otolaryngol., 2nd, St. Petersburg,* p. 3

Bohne, B. A., Carr, C. D. 1979. Location of structurally similar areas in chinchilla cochleae of different lengths. *J. Acoust. Soc. Am.* 66:411–14

Bosher, S. K. 1979. The nature of the negative endocochlear potentials produced by anoxia and ethacrynic acid in the rat and guinea-pig. *J. Physiol.* 293:329-45

Bosher, S. K., Warren, R. L. 1978. Very low calcium content of cochlear endolymph, an extracellular fluid. *Nature* 273:377-78

Bruns, V. 1976a. Peripheral auditory tuning for fine frequency analysis by the CF-FM bat, *Rhinolophus ferrumequinum.* I. Mechanical specialization of the cochlea. *J. Comp. Physiol.* 106:77-86

Bruns, V. 1976b. Peripheral auditory tuning for fine frequency analysis by the CF-FM bat, *Rhinolophus ferrumequinum.* II. Frequency mapping in the cochlea. *J. Comp. Physiol.* 106:87-97

Bruns, V. 1979. Functional anatomy as an approach to frequency analysis in the mammalian cochlea. *Verh. Dtsch. Zool. Ges.* 72:141-54

Burgio, P. A., Lawrence, M. 1980. A new technique to determine the attachments of tectorial membrane and chemical composition of the fluids of the inner sulcus and tunnel of Corti. *Proc. Assoc. Res. Otolaryngol., 3rd, St. Petersburg,* p. 22

Buunen, T. J. F., Rhode, W. S. 1978. Responses of fibers in the cat's auditory nerve to the cubic difference tone. *J. Acoust. Soc. Am.* 64:772-81

Capranica, R. R. 1976. Morphology and physiology of the auditory system. In *Frog Neurobiology,* ed. R. Llinás, W. Precht, pp. 551-75. Berlin: Springer-Verlag. 1046 pp.

Capranica, R. R., Moffat, A. J. M. 1980. Nonlinear properties of the peripheral auditory system. In *Comparative Studies of Hearing in Vertebrates,* ed. A. Popper, R. Fay. Berlin: Springer-Verlag. In press

Carterette, E. C., Friedman, M. P., eds. 1978. *Handbook of Perception,* Vol. 4. *Hearing.* New York: Academic. 717 pp.

Cazals, Y., Aran, J.-M., Erre, J.-P., Guilhaume, A., Hawkins, J. E. Jr. 1979. "Neural" responses to acoustic stimulation after destruction of cochlear hair cells. *Arch. Otorhinolaryngol.* 224: 61-70

Corey, D. P., Hudspeth, A. J. 1979a. Ionic basis of the receptor potential in a vertebrate hair cell. *Nature* 281:675-77

Corey, D. P., Hudspeth, A. J. 1979b. Response latency of vertebrate hair cell. *Biophys. J.* 26:499-506

Crawford, A. C., Fettiplace, R. 1979. Reversal of hair cell responses by current. *J. Physiol.* 295:66P

Dallos, P. J. 1966. On the generation of odd-fractional subharmonics. *J. Acoust. Soc. Am.* 40:1381-91

Dallos, P. 1973a. Cochlear potentials and cochlear mechanics. See Angelborg & Engström 1973, pp. 335-72

Dallos, P. 1973b. *The Auditory Periphery: Biophysics and Physiology.* New York: Academic. 566 pp.

Dallos, P. 1975. Cochlear potentials. In *The Nervous System,* ed. D. B. Tower. Vol. 3: *Human Communication and Its Disorders,* ed. E. L. Eagles, pp. 69-80. New York: Raven. 564 pp.

Dallos, P. 1977. Comments on: "Some observations on two-tone interactions measured with the Mössbauer effect," W. S. Rhode. See Evans & Wilson 1977, p. 39

Dallos, P. 1978. Cochlear electrophysiology. See Naunton & Fernández 1978, pp. 141-47

Dallos, P., Billone, M. C., Durrant, J. D., Wang, C.-Y., Raynor, S. 1972. Cochlear inner and outer hair cells: Functional differences. *Science* 177:356-58

Dallos, P., Cheatham, M. A. 1976a. Production of cochlear potentials by inner and outer hair cells. *J. Acoust. Soc. Am.* 60:510-12

Dallos, P., Cheatham, M. A. 1976b. Compound action potential (AP) tuning curves. *J. Acoust. Soc. Am.* 59:591-97

Dallos, P., Cheatham, M. A. 1977. Analog of two-tone suppression in whole-nerve responses. *J. Acoust. Soc. Am.* 62:1048-51

Dallos, P., Cheatham, M. A., Ferraro, J. 1974. Cochlear mechanics, nonlinearities, and cochlear potentials. *J. Acoust. Soc. Am.* 55:597-605

Dallos, P., Flock, Å. 1980. Comment on: "The electrophysiological profile of the organ of Corti," by G. A. Manley & A. Kronester-Frei. In *Psychophysical, Physiological and Behavioural Studies in Hearing,* ed. F. A. Bilsen, B. van den Brink, p. 32. Delft: Delft Univ.

Dallos, P., Harris, D. 1978. Properties of auditory nerve responses in the absence of outer hair cells. *J. Neurophysiol.* 41: 365-83

Dallos, P., Harris, D., Özdamar, Ö., Ryan, A. 1978. Behavioral, compound action potential, and single unit thresholds: Relationship in normal and abnormal ears. *J. Acoust. Soc. Am.* 64:151-57

Dallos, P., Harris, D. M., Relkin, E., Cheatham, M. A. 1980. Two-tone suppression and intermodulation distortion in the cochlea: Effect of outer hair cell lesions. See Dallos & Flock 1980, pp. 242-49

Dallos, P., Ryan, A., Harris, D., McGee, T., Özdamar, Ö. 1977. Cochlear frequency selectivity in the presence of hair cell damage. See Evans & Wilson 1977, pp. 249–78

Dallos, P., Sweetman, R. H. 1969. Distribution pattern of cochlear harmonics. *J. Acoust. Soc. Am.* 45:37–46

Davis, H. 1965. A model for transducer action in the cochlea. *Cold Spring Harbor Symp. Quant. Biol.* 30:181–90

Davis, H. 1976. Principles of electric response audiometry. *Ann. Otol. Rhinol. Laryngol. Suppl.* 28:1–96

Davis, H., Deatherage, B. H., Rosenblut, B., Fernández, C., Kimura, R., Smith, C. A. 1958. Modification of cochlear potentials produced by streptomycin poisoning and by extensive venous obstructions. *Laryngoscope* 68:596–627

de Boer, E. 1975. Synthetic whole nerve action potential for the cat. *J. Acoust. Soc. Am.* 58:1030–45

de Boer, E., de Jongh, H. R. 1978. On cochlear encoding: Potentialities and limitations of the reverse-correlation technique. *J. Acoust. Soc. Am.* 63:115–35

de Boer, E., Kuyper, P. 1968. Triggered correlation. *IEEE Trans. Biomed. Eng.* 15:169–79

de Jongh, H. R. 1977. Which stimulus transform controls firing probability of an auditory nerve fibre? See Evans & Wilson 1977, pp. 150–52

Denton, E. J., Gray, J. A. B. 1979. The analysis of sound by the sprat ear. *Nature* 282:406–7

Deol, M.S., Glueeksohn-Waelsch, S. 1979. The role of inner hair cells in hearing. *Nature* 278:250–52

Duifhuis, H. 1976. Cochlear nonlinearity and second filter: Possible mechanism and implications. *J. Acoust. Soc. Am.* 59:408–23

Dunn, R. A., Morest, D. K. 1975. Receptor synapses without synaptic ribbons in the cochlea of the cat. *Proc. Natl. Acad. Sci. USA* 72:3599–3603

Durrant, J. D., Lovrinic, J. H. 1977. *Bases of Hearing Science.* Baltimore: Williams & Wilkins. 185 pp.

Eggermont, J. J. 1977. Compound action potential tuning curves in normal and pathological human ears. *J. Acoust. Soc. Am.* 62:1247–51

Eggermont, J. J., Odenthal, D. W., Schmidt, P. H., Spoor, A. 1974. Electrocochleography. Basic principles and clinical application. *Acta Otolaryngol. Suppl.* 316:1–84

Ehret, G. 1979. Correlations between cochlear hair cell loss and shifts of masked and absolute behavioral auditory thresholds in the house mouse. *Acta Otolaryngol.* 87:28–38

Ehret, G., Frankenreiter, M. 1977. Quantitative analysis of cochlear structures in the house mouse in relation to mechanisms of acoustical information processing. *J. Comp. Physiol.* 122:65–85

Elberling, C. 1976. Simulation of cochlear action potentials recorded from the ear canal in man. See Ruben et al 1976, pp. 151–68

Engström, H., Engström, B. 1978. Structure of the hairs on cochlear sensory cells. *Hearing Res.* 1:49–66

Evans, E. F. 1972. Does frequency sharpening occur in the cochlea? *Symp. Hearing Theory,* IPO, Eindhoven, The Netherlands, pp. 27–34

Evans, E. F. 1975a. The sharpening of cochlear frequency selectivity in normal and abnormal cochlea. *Audiology* 14:419–44

Evans, E. F. 1975b. Cochlear nerve and cochlear nucleus. In *Handbook of Sensory Physiology* Vol. V/2. *Auditory System,* ed. W. D. Keidel, W. D. Neff, pp. 1–108. Berlin: Springer-Verlag. 526 pp.

Evans, E. F. 1977. Frequency selectivity at high signal levels of single units in cochlear nerve and nucleus. See Evans & Wilson 1977, pp. 185–92

Evans, E. F., Wilson, J. P. 1973. Frequency selectivity of the cochlea. See Angelborg & Engström 1973, pp. 519–51

Evans, E. F., Wilson, J. P., eds. 1977. *Psychophysics and Physiology of Hearing.* London: Academic. 525 pp.

Fettiplace, R., Crawford, A. C. 1978. The coding of sound pressure and frequency in cochlear hair cells of the terrapin. *Proc. R. Soc. London Ser. B* 203:209–18

Fex, J., Wenthold, R. J. 1976. Choline acetyltransferase, glutamate decarboxylase and tyrosine hydroxylase in the cochlea and cochlear nucleus of the guinea pig. *Brain Res.* 109:575–85

Flock, Å. 1971. Sensory transduction in hair cells. In *Handbook of Sensory Physiology* Vol 1. *Principles of Receptor Physiology.* ed. W. R. Lowenstein, pp. 396–441. Berlin: Springer-Verlag. 600 pp.

Flock, Å. 1977a. Electron probe determination of relative ion distribution in the inner ear. *Acta Otolaryngol.* 83:239–44

Flock, Å. 1977b. Physiological properties of sensory hairs in the ear. See Evans & Wilson 1977, pp. 15–25

Flock, Å., Cheung, H. C. 1977. Actin filaments in sensory hairs of inner ear receptor cells. *J. Cell Biol.* 75:339–43

Flock, Å., Flock, B., Murray, E. 1977. Studies on the sensory hairs of receptor cells in the inner ear. *Acta Otolaryngol.* 83:85–91

Flock, Å., Jørgensen, J. M., Russell, I. J. 1973. The physiology of individual hair cells and their synapses. See Angelborg & Engström 1973, pp. 272–306

Geisler, C. D., Mountain, D. C., Hubbard, A. E., Adrian, H. O., Ravindran, A. 1977. Alternating electrical-resistance changes in the guinea-pig cochlea caused by acoustic stimuli. *J. Acoust. Soc. Am.* 51:1557–66

Geisler, C. D., Rhode, W. S., Kennedy, D. T. 1974. Responses to tonal stimuli of single auditory nerve fibers and their relationship to basilar membrane motion in the squirrel monkey. *J. Neurophysiol.* 37:1156–72

Godfrey, D. A., Carter, J. A., Berger, S. J., Matschinsky, F. M. 1976. Levels of putative transmitter amino acids in the guinea pig cochlea. *J. Histochem. Cytochem.* 24:468–70

Gold, T. 1948. Hearing II. The physical basis of action of the cochlea. *Proc. R. Soc. Edinburgh, Sect. B* 135:492–98

Goldstein, J. L. 1967. Auditory nonlinearity. *J. Acoust. Soc. Am.* 41:676–88

Goldstein, M. H. Jr., Kiang, N. Y. S. 1958. Synchrony of neural activity in electric responses evoked by transient acoustic stimuli. *J. Acoust. Soc. Am.* 30:107–14

Green, D. M. 1976. *An Introduction to Hearing.* Hillsdale, NJ: Erlbaum. 353 pp.

Greenwood, D. D., Merzenich, M. M., Roth, G. L. 1976. Some preliminary observations on the interrelations between two-tone suppression and combination-tone driving in the anteroventral cochlear nucleus of the cat. *J. Acoust. Soc. Am.* 59:607–33

Gulley, R. L., Bagger-Sjöbäck, D. 1979. Freeze-fracture studies on the synapse between type I hair cell and the calyceal terminal in the guinea-pig vestibular system. *J. Neurocytol.* 8:591–60

Gulley, R. L., Reese, T. S. 1976. Intercellular junctions in the reticular lamina of the organ of Corti. *J. Neurocytol.* 5:479–507

Gulley, R. L., Reese, T. S. 1977a. Freeze-fracture studies on the synapses in the organ of Corti. *J. Comp. Neurol.* 171:517–43

Gulley, R. L., Reese, T. S. 1977b. Regional specialization of the hair cell plasmalemma in the organ of Corti. *Anat. Rec.* 189:109–23

Guth, P. S., Norris, C. H., Bobbin, R. P. 1976. The pharmacology of transmission in the peripheral auditory system. *Ann. Rev. Pharmacol.* 28:95–125

Hall, J. L. 1977. Spatial differentiation as an auditory "second filter": Assessment on a nonlinear model of the basilar membrane. *J. Acoust. Soc. Am.* 61:520–24

Hama, K., Saito, K. 1977. Gap junctions between the supporting cells in some acoustico-vestibular receptors. *J. Neurocytol.* 6:1–12

Harris, D. M. 1979. Action potential suppression, tuning curves and thresholds: comparison with single fiber data. *Hearing Res.* 1:133–54

Harris, D. M., Dallos, P. 1979. Forward masking of auditory nerve fiber responses. *J. Neurophysiol.* 42:1083–1107

Harris, G. G., Frishkopf, L. S., Flock, Å. 1970. Receptor potentials from hair cells of the lateral line. *Science* 167:76–79

Harrison, R. V., Evans, E. F. 1979a. Some aspects of temporal coding by single cochlear fibres from regions of cochlear hair cell degeneration in the guinea pig. *Arch. Otorhinolaryngol.* 224:71–78

Harrison, R. V., Evans, E. F. 1979b. Cochlear fibre responses in guinea pigs with well defined cochlear lesions. *Scand. Audiol. Suppl.* 9:83–92

Hind, J. E., Rose, J. E., Brugge, J.F., Anderson, D. J. 1971. Some effects of intensity on the discharge of auditory-nerve fibers. In *Physiology of the Auditory System*, ed. M. B. Sachs, pp. 101–11. Baltimore: Natl. Educ. Consult. 392 pp.

Hirsh, S. K., Eldredge, D. H., Hirsh, I. J., Silverman, S. R., eds. 1976. *Hearing and Davis.* St. Louis: Washington Univ. 476 pp.

Hoke, M., Elberling, C., Hieke, D., Bappert, E. 1979. Deconvolution of compound PST histograms. *Scand. Audiol. Suppl.* 9:141–54

Holton, T. 1980. Relations between frequency selectivity and two-tone rate suppression in lizard cochlear-nerve fibers. *Hearing Res.* 2:21–38

Holton, T., Weiss, T. F. 1978. Two-tone rate suppression in lizard cochlear nerve fibers, relation to receptor organ morphology. *Brain Res.* 159:219–22

Honrubia, V., Strelioff, D., Sitko, S. T. 1976. Physiological basis of cochlear transduction and sensitivity. *Ann. Otol. Rhinol. Laryngol.* 85:697–710

Honrubia, V., Ward, P. H. 1970. Mechanism of production of cochlear microphonics. *J. Acoust. Soc. Am.* 47:498–503

Hoshino, T., Kodama, A. 1977. The contact between the cochlear sensory cell hairs and the tectorial membrane. *Scanning Electron Microsc.* 2:409–13

Hubbard, A. E., Geisler, C. D., Mountain, D. C. 1979a. Comparison of the spectra of the cochlear microphonic and of the sound-elicited electrical impedance changes measured in scala media of the guinea pig. *J. Acoust. Soc. Am.* 66:431–45

Hubbard, A. E., Mountain, D. C., Geisler, C. D. 1979b. The spectral content of the cochlear microphonic measured in scala media of the guinea pig cochlea. *J. Acoust. Soc. Am.* 66:415–30

Hudspeth, A. J., Corey, D. P. 1977. Sensitivity, polarity, and conductance change in the response of vertebrate hair cells to controlled mechanical stimuli. *Proc. Natl. Acad. Sci. USA* 74:2407–11

Hudspeth, A. J., Jacobs, R. 1979. Stereocilia mediate transduction in vertebrate hair cells. *Proc. Natl. Acad. Sci. USA* 76:1506–9

Hunter-Duvar, I. M., Mount, R. J. 1978. The organ of Corti following ototoxic antibiotic treatment. *Scanning Electron Microsc.* 2:423–30

Igarashi, M., Cranford, J. L., Allen, E. A., Alford, B. R., 1979a. Behavioral auditory function after transection of crossed olivo-cochlear bundle in the cat. V. Pure-tone intensity discrimination. *Acta Otolaryngol.* 87:429–33

Igarashi, M., Cranford, J. L., Nakai, Y., Alford, B. R. 1979b. Behavioral auditory function after transection of crossed olivo-cochlear bundle in the cat. IV. Study on pure-tone frequency discrimination. *Acta Otolaryngol.* 87:79–83

Iurato, S., Franke, K., Luciano, L., Wermbter, G., Pannese, E., Reale, E. 1976a. Fracture faces of the functional complexes in the reticular membrane of the organ of Corti. *Acta Otolaryngol.* 81:36–47

Iurato, S., Franke, K., Luciano, L., Wermbter, G., Pannese, E., Reale, E. 1976b. Intercellular junctions in the organ of Corti as revealed by freeze fracturing. *Acta Otolaryngol.* 82:57–69

Jahnke, K. 1975. The fine structure of freeze-fractured intercellular junctions in the guinea pig inner ear. *Acta Otolaryngol. Suppl.* 336:1–140

Javel, E., Geisler, C. D., Ravindran, A. 1978. Two-tone suppression in auditory nerve of the cat: Rate-intensity and temporal analyses. *J. Acoust. Soc. Am.* 63:1093–1104

Johnson-Davies, D., Patterson, R. D. 1979. Psychophysical tuning-curves: Restricting the listening band to the signal region. *J. Acoust. Soc. Am.* 65:765–70

Johnstone, B. M. 1970. Ion fluxes in the cochlea. In *Membranes and Ion Transport,* ed. E. E. Bittar, 3:167–84. New York: Wiley. 382 pp.

Johnstone, B. M., Boyle, A. J. T. 1967. Basilar membrane vibration examined with the Mössbauer technique. *Science* 158:389–90

Johnstone, B. M., Yates, G. K. 1974. Basilar membrane tuning curves in the guinea pig. *J. Acoust. Soc. Am.* 55:584–87

Johnstone, J. R. 1977. Properties of ganglion cells from the extreme basal region of guinea pig cochlea. See Evans & Wilson 1977, pp. 89–98

Johnstone, J. R., Alder, V. A., Johnstone, B. M., Robertson, D., Yates, G. K. 1979. Cochlear action potential threshold and single unit thresholds. *J. Acoust. Soc. Am.* 65:254–57

Katsuki, Y. 1976. The origin of the microphonic potential. See Hirsh el al 1976, pp. 25–35

Kemp, D. T. 1978. Stimulated acoustic emissions from within the human auditory system. *J. Acoust. Soc. Am.* 64:1386–91

Kemp, D. T. 1979. Evidence of mechanical nonlinearity and frequency selective wave amplification in the cochlea. *Arch. Otorhinolaryngol.* 224:37–45

Kemp, D. T., Chum, R. A. 1980. Observations on the generation mechanism of stimulated acoustic emissions—two-tone suppression. See Dallos & Flock 1980, pp. 34–41

Kiang, N. Y. S., Liberman, M. C., Levine, R. A. 1976a. Auditory nerve activity in cats exposed to ototoxic drugs and high intensity sounds. *Ann. Otol. Rhinol. Laryngol.* 75:752–79

Kiang, N. Y. S., Moxon, E. C., Kahn, A. R. 1976b. The relationship of gross potentials recorded from the cochlea to single unit activity in the auditory nerve. See Ruben et al 1976, pp. 95–115

Kiang, N. Y. S., Moxon, E. C. 1974. Tails of tuning curves of auditory-nerve fibers. *J. Acoust. Soc. Am.* 55:620–30

Kiang, N. Y. S., Moxon, E. C., Levine, R. A. 1970. Auditory nerve activity in cats with normal and abnormal cochleas. In *Sensorineural Hearing Loss,* ed. G. E. W. Wolstenholme, J. Knight, pp. 241–73. London: Churchill. 358 pp.

Kim, D. O., Molnar, C. E. 1979. A population study of cochlear nerve fibers: Comparisons of the spatial distributions of average-rate and phase locking measures of responses to single tones. *J. Neurophysiol.* 42:16–30

Kim, D. O., Molnar, C. E., Matthews, J. W. 1980a. Cochlear mechanics: Nonlinear behavior in two-tone responses as reflected in cochlear nerve fiber responses and in ear-canal sound pressure. *J. Acoust. Soc. Am.* 67:1736–45

Kim, D. O., Neely, S. T., Molnar, C. E., Matthews, J. W. 1980b. An active cochlear model with negative damping in the partition: Comparison with Rhode's ante- and post-mortem observations. See Dallos & Flock 1980, pp. 7–14

Kim, D. O., Siegel, J. H., Molnar, C. E. 1978. Cochlear nonlinear phenomena in two-tone responses. *Scand. Audiol. Suppl.* 9:63–81

Kimura, R. 1966. Hairs of the cochlear sensory cells and their attachment to the tectorial membrane. *Acta Otolaryngol.* 61:55–72

Kimura, R. S., Ota, C., Takahasi, T. 1980. Nerve fiber synapses on spiral ganglion cells in the human cochlea. See Burgio & Lawrence 1980, p. 6

Klinke, R., Evans, E. F. 1977. Evidence that catecholamines are not the afferent transmitter in the cochlea. *Exp. Brain Res.* 28:315–24

Klinke, R., Galley, N. 1974. Efferent innervation of vestibular and auditory receptors. *Physiol. Rev.* 54:316–57

Klinke, R., Oertel, W. 1977a. Evidence that GABA is not the afferent transmitter in the cochlea. *Exp. Brain Res.* 28:311–14

Klinke, R., Oertel, W. 1977b. Evidence that 5-HT is not the afferent transmitter in the cochlea. *Exp. Brain Res.* 30:141–43

Klinke, R., Oertel, W. 1977c. Amino-acids—putative afferent transmitter in the cochlea. *Exp. Brain Res.* 30:145–48

Klinke, R., Pause, M. 1977. The performance of a primitive hearing organ of the cochlea. See Evans & Wilson 1977, pp. 101–11

Klinke, R., Pause, M. 1980. Discharge properties of primary auditory fibers in *Caiman crocodilus:* Comparisons and contrasts to the mammalian auditory nerve. *Exp. Brain Res.* 38:137–50

Kohllöffel, L. U. E. 1979. The inner ear of mammals: Sound in spirals. *Naturwissenschaften* 66:114–14

Konishi, T. 1979. Some observations of negative endocochlear potential during anoxia. *Acta Otolaryngol.* 87:506–16

Konishi, T., Butler, R. A., Fernández, C. 1961. Effect of anoxia on cochlear potentials. *J. Acoust. Soc. Am.* 33:349–56

Konishi, T., Hamrick, P. E. 1978. Ion transport in the cochlea of guinea pig. II. Chloride transport. *Acta Otolaryngol.* 86:176–84

Konishi, T., Hamrick, P. E., Walsh, P. J. 1978. Ion transport in guinea pig cochlea. I. Potassium and sodium transport. *Acta Otolaryngol.* 86:22–34

Konishi, T., Nielsen, D. 1978. The temporal relationship between basilar membrane motion and nerve impulse initiation in auditory nerve fibers of guinea pigs. *Jpn. J. Physiol.* 28:291–307

Konishi, T., Salt, A. N., Hamrick, P. E. 1979. Effects of exposure to noise on ion movement in guinea pig cochlea. *Hearing Res.* 1:325–42

Kronester-Frei, A. 1978. Ultrastructure of the different zones of the tectorial membrane. *Cell Tissue Res.* 193:11–23

Kronester-Frei, A. 1979a. Localization of the marginal zone of the tectorial membrane in situ, unfixed, and with in vivo-like ionic milieu. *Arch. Otorhinolaryngol.* 224:3–9

Kronester-Frei, A. 1979b. The effect of changes in endolymphatic ion concentrations on the tectorial membrane. *Hearing Res.* 1:81–94

Kuijpers, W., Bonting, S. L. 1970. The cochlear potentials. II. The nature of the cochlear endolymphatic resting potential. *Pfleugers Arch.* 320:359–72

Kusakari, J., Ise, I., Comegys, T. H., Thalmann, I., Thalmann, R. 1978. Effect of ethacrynic acid, furosemide, and ouabain upon the endolymphatic potential and upon high energy phosphates of the stria vascularis. *Laryngoscope* 88:12–37

Kusakari, J., Thalmann, R. 1976. Effects of anoxia and ethacrynic acid upon high energy phosphates in ampullar wall. *Laryngoscope* 86:132–47

Lawrence, M. 1967. Electric polarization of the tectorial membrane. *Ann. Otol. Rhinol. Laryngol.* 76:287–312

Legouix, J. P., Remond, M. C., Greenbaum, H. B. 1973. Interference and two-tone inhibition. *J. Acoust. Soc. Am.* 53:409–19

Legouix, J. P., Remond, M. C., Harrison, J. 1976. Interference, its functional significance. See Hirsh et al 1976, pp. 53–63

LePage, E. L., Johnstone, B. M. 1980. Basilar membrane mechanics in the guinea pig cochlea. Details of nonlinear frequency response characteristics. *J. Acoust. Soc. Am.* 67:S45

Lewis, E. R. 1977. Structural correlates of function in the anuran amphibian papilla. *Scanning Electron Microsc.* 2:429–35

Liberman, M. C. 1978. Auditory-nerve response from cats raised in a low-noise chamber. *J. Acoust. Soc. Am.* 63:442–55

Liberman, M. C., Kiang, N. Y. S. 1978. Acoustic trauma in cats. *Acta Otolaryngol. Suppl.* 358:1–63

186   DALLOS

Lim, D. J. 1972. The fine morphology of the tectorial membrane—Its relationship to the organ of Corti. *Arch. Otolaryngol.* 96:199–215

Lim, D. J. 1977. Fine morphology of the tectorial membrane—Fresh and developmental. *INSERM* 68:47–60

Lim, D. J. 1980. Cochlear anatomy related to cochlear micromechanics. A review. *J. Acoust. Soc. Am.* 67:1686–95

Lindeman, H. H., Ades, H. W., Bredberg, G., Engström, H. 1971. The sensory hairs and the tectorial membrane in the development of the cat's organ of Corti—A scanning electron microscope study. *Acta Otolaryngol.* 72:229–42

Lynn, P. A., Sayers, B. McA. 1970. Cochlear innervation, signal processing, and their relation to auditory time-intensity effects. *J. Acoust. Soc. Am.* 47:525–33

Manley, G. A. 1978. Cochlear frequency sharpening—a new synthesis. *Acta Otolaryngol.* 85:167–76

Manley, G. A. 1979. Preferred intervals in the spontaneous activity of primary auditory neurons. *Naturwissenschaften* 66:582–83

Manley, G. A., Kronester-Frei, A. 1980. The electrophysiological profile of the organ of Corti. See Dallos & Flock 1980, pp. 24–31

Marcus, D. C., Thalmann, R. 1980. Comments concerning a possible independent potassium pump in the cochlear duct. *Hearing Res.* 2:163–65

Marcus, D. C., Thalmann, R., Marcus, N. Y. 1978a. Respiratory rate and ATP content of stria vascularis of guinea pig in vitro. *Laryngoscope* 88:1825–35

Marcus, D. C., Thalmann, R., Marcus, N. Y. 1978b. Respiratory quotient of stria vascularis of guinea pig in vitro. *Arch. Otorhinolaryngol.* 221:97–103

Markuszka, J. 1977. *The relative contributions of inner and outer hair cells to cochlear potentials and the discharge pattern of auditory nerve fibers in the guinea pig.* PhD thesis. Princeton Univ., Princeton, NJ. 126 pp.

Melichar, I., Syka, J. 1977. Time course of anoxia-induced K^+ concentration changes in the cochlea measured by K^+ specific microelectrodes. *Pfleugers Arch.* 372:207–13

Miller, M. R. 1978. Further scanning electron microscope studies of lizard auditory papillae. *J. Morphol.* 156:381–418

Moffat, A. J. M., Capranica, R. R. 1976. Auditory sensitivity of the saccule in the American toad (Bufo americanus). *J. Comp. Physiol.* 105:1–8

Møller, A. R. 1977a. Frequency selectivity of the basilar membrane revealed from discharges in auditory nerve fibers. See Evans & Wilson 1977, pp. 197–205

Møller, A. R. 1977b. Frequency selectivity of single auditory-nerve fibers in response to broadband noise stimuli. *J. Acoust. Soc. Am.* 62:135–42

Mooseker, M. S., Tilney, L. G. 1975. Organization of an actin filament-membrane complex. Filament polarity and membrane attachment in the microvilli of intestinal epithelial cells. *J. Cell Biol.* 67:725–43

Morest, D. K., Bohne, B. A. 1980. Differential degeneration in the brain of chinchillas following outer hair cell damage by cochlear stimulation. See Burgio & Lawrence 1980, p. 11

Mulroy, M. J. 1974. Cochlear anatomy of the alligator lizard. *Brain Behav. Evol.* 10:69–87

Mulroy, M. J., Altmann, D. W., Weiss, T. F., Peake, T. W. 1974. Intracellular electric response to sound in a vertebrate cochlea. *Nature* 249:482–85

Nadol, J. B. Jr. 1979. Intercellular fluid pathways in the organ of Corti of cat and man. *Ann. Otol. Rhinol. Laryngol.* 88:2–11

Nadol, J. B. Jr. 1980. Reciprocal synapses at the base of outer hair cells in the organ of Corti of man. See Burgio & Lawrence 1980, p. 6

Nadol, J. B. Jr., Mulroy, M. J., Goodenough, D. A., Weiss, T. F. 1976. Tight and gap junctions in a vertebrate inner ear. *Am. J. Anat.* 147:281–301

Naunton, R. F., Fernández, C., eds. 1978. *Evoked Electrical Activity in the Auditory Nervous System.* New York: Academic. 588 pp.

Neuweiler, G., Vater, M. 1977. Response patterns to pure tones of cochlear nucleus units in the CF-FM bat, *Rhinolophus ferrumequinum. J. Comp. Physiol.* 115:119–33

Nienhuys, T. G., Clark, G. M. 1978. Frequency discrimination following the selective destruction of cochlear inner and outer hair cells. *Science* 199:1356–57

Okitsu, S., Umekita, S., Obara, S. 1978. Ionic compositions of the media across the sensory epithelium in the ampullae of Lorenzini of the marine catfish, *Plotosus. J. Comp. Physiol.* 126:115–21

Özdamar, Ö., Dallos, P. 1976. Input-output functions of cochlear whole-nerve action potentials: Interpretation in terms of one population of neurons. *J. Acoust. Soc. Am.* 59:143–47

Özdamar, Ö., Dallos, P. 1978. Synchronous responses of the primary auditory fibers to the onset of tone bursts and their relation to compound action potentials. *Brain Res.* 155:169–75

Peake, W. T., Kiang, N.Y.S. 1962. Cochlear responses to condensation and rarefaction clicks. *Biophys. J.* 2:23–34

Peake, W. T., Ling, A. Jr. 1980. Basilar membrane motion in the alligator lizard: Its relation to tonotopic organization and frequency selectivity. *J. Acoust. Soc. Am.* 67:1736–45

Peterson, S. K., Frishkopf, L. S., Lechéne, C., Oman, C. M., Weiss, T. F. 1978. Element composition of inner ear lymphs in cats, lizards, and skates determined by electron probe microanalysis of liquid samples. *J. Comp. Physiol.* 126:1–14

Pfeiffer, R. R. 1970. A model for two-tone inhibition of single cochlear-nerve fibers. *J. Acoust. Soc. Am.* 48:1373–78

Pfeiffer, R. R., Kim, D. O. 1972. Response patterns of single cochlear nerve fibers to click stimuli: descriptions for cat. *J. Acoust. Soc. Am.* 52:1669–77

Pickles, J. O. 1979a. Psychophysical frequency resolution in the cat as determined by simultaneous masking and its relation to auditory-nerve resolution. *J. Acoust. Soc. Am.* 66:1725–32

Pickles, J. O. 1979b. An investigation of sympathetic effects on hearing. *Acta Otolaryngol.* 87:69–71

Pierson, M., Møller, A. 1980. Some dualistic properties of the cochlear microphonic. *Hearing Res.* 2:135–50

Prazma, J., Fischer, N. D., Biggers, W. P., Ascher, D. 1978. A correlation of the effects of normoxia, hyperoxia and anoxia on PO2 of endolymph and cochlear potentials. *Hearing Res.* 1:3–9

Prosen, C. A., Moody, D. B., Stebbins, W. C., Hawkins, J. E. Jr. 1980. Absolute and intensity difference thresholds in the guinea pig after cochlear injury by kanamycin and amikacin. See Burgio & Lawrence 1980, p. 36

Prosen, C. A., Petersen, M. R., Moody, D. B., Stebbins, W. C. 1978. Auditory thresholds and kanamycin-induced hearing loss in the guinea pig assessed by a positive reinforcement procedure. *J. Acoust. Soc. Am.* 63:559–66

Ramprashad, F., Landolt, J. P., Money, K. E., Clark, D., Laufer, J. 1979. A morphometric study of the cochlea of the Little Brown bat (*Myotis lucifugus*). *J. Morphol.* 160:345–58

Reale, E., Luciano, L., Franke, K., Pannese, E., Wermbter, G., Iurato, S. 1975. Intercellular junctions in the vascular stria and spiral ligament. *J. Ultrastruct. Res.* 53:284–97

Rhode, W. S. 1971. Observations of the vibration of the basilar membrane in squirrel monkeys using the Mössbauer technique. *J. Acoust. Soc. Am.* 49:1218–31

Rhode, W. S. 1973. An investigation of postmortem cochlear mechanics using the Mössbauer effect. See Angelborg & Enström 1973, pp. 49–63

Rhode, W. S. 1977. Some observations on two-tone interaction measured with the Mössbauer effect. See Evans & Wilson 1977, pp. 27–38

Rhode, W. S. 1978. Some observations on cochlear mechanics. *J. Acoust. Soc. Am.* 64:158–76

Rhode, W. S., Geisler, C. D., Kennedy, D. T. 1978. Auditory nerve fiber responses to wide-band noise and tone combinations. *J. Neurophysiol.* 41:692–704

Robertson, D. 1976. Correspondence between sharp tuning and two-tone inhibition in primary auditory neurones. *Nature* 259:477–78

Robertson, D., Johnstone, B. M. 1978. Efferent transmitter substance in the mammalian cochlea: Single neuron support for acetylcholine. *Hearing Res.* 1:31–34

Robertson, D., Johnstone, B. M. 1979. Aberrant tonotopic organization in the inner ear damaged by kanamycin. *J. Acoust. Soc. Am.* 66:466–69

Robertson, D., Manley, G. A. 1974. Manipulation of frequency analysis in the cochlear ganglion of the guinea pig. *J. Comp. Physiol.* 91:363–75

Robles, L., Rhode, W. S. 1974. Nonlinear effects in the transfer response of the basilar membrane. See Zwicker & Terhardt, pp. 287–98

Robles, L., Rhode, W. S., Geisler, C. D. 1976. Transient response of the basilar membrane measured in squirrel monkeys using the Mössbauer effect. *J. Acoust. Soc. Am.* 59:926–39

Romahn, G., Boerger, G. 1977. Filter function of the guinea pig cochlea after degeneration of outer hair cells. *Arch. Otorhinolaryngol.* 215:223–39

Romahn, G., Boerger, G. 1978. Influence of a low-frequency tone on the sensitivity of primary auditory neurons: two fiber populations. *Exp. Brain Res.* 32:423–28

Ross, M. D. 1974. The tectorial membrane of the rat. *Am. J. Anat.* 139:449–82

Ross, M. D., Nuttall, A. L., Wright, C. G. 1977. Horseradish peroxidase acute ototoxicity and the uptake and movement of the peroxidase in the auditory system of the guinea pig. *Acta Otolaryngol.* 84:187–201

188   DALLOS

Ruben, R. J., Elberling, C., Salomon, G., eds. 1976. *Electrocochleography.* Baltimore: Univ. Park. 506 pp.

Russell, I. J., Sellick, P. M. 1976. Measurement of potassium and chloride ion concentrations in the cupulae of the lateral lines of *Xenopus laevis. J. Physiol.* 257:245–55

Russell, I. J., Sellick, P. M. 1977a. Tuning properties of cochlear hair cells. *Nature* 267:858–60

Russell, I. J., Sellick, P. M. 1977b. The tuning properties of cochlear hair cells. See Evans & Wilson 1977, pp. 71–87

Russell, I. J., Sellick, P. M. 1978. Intracellular studies of hair cells in the mammalian cochlea. *J. Physiol.* 284:261–90

Ryan, A. 1978. Behavioral correlates of outer and inner hair cell damage in the chinchilla and mongolian gerbil. *Proc. Assoc. Res. Otolaryngol., 1st, St. Petersburg,* pp. 46–47

Ryan, A., Dallos, P. 1975. Absence of cochlear outer hair cells: Effect on behavioural auditory threshold. *Nature* 253:44–46

Ryan, A., Dallos, P., McGee, T. 1979. Psychophysical tuning curves and auditory thresholds after hair cell damage in the chinchilla. *J. Acoust. Soc. Am.* 66: 370–78

Ryan, A. F., Wickham, M. G., Bone, R. C. 1980. Studies of ion distribution in the inner ear: Scanning electron microscopy and X-ray microanalysis of freeze-dried cochlear specimens. *Hearing Res.* 2:1–20

Sachs, M. B., Abbas, P. J. 1974. Rate versus level functions for auditory-nerve fibers in cats: Tone burst stimuli. *J. Acoust. Soc. Am.* 56:1835–47

Sachs, M. B., Abbas, P. J. 1976. Phenomenological model for two-tone suppression. *J. Acoust. Soc. Am.* 60:1157–63

Sand, O. 1975. Effects of different ionic environments on the mechano-sensitivity of lateral line organs in the mudpuppy. *J. Comp. Physiol.* 102:27–42

Sand, O., Ozawa, S., Hagiwara, S. 1975. Electrical and mechanical stimulation of hair cells in the mudpuppy. *J. Comp. Physiol.* 102:13–26

Saunders, J. C., Tilney, L. G. 1980. The relation between frequency selectivity of tuning curves and stereocilia height along the basilar papilla of neonatal chicks. See Burgio & Lawrence 1980, p. 8

Schmiedt, R. A. 1977. *Single and two-tone effects in normal and abnormal cochleas: A study of cochlear microphonics and auditory-nerve units.* PhD thesis.

Syracuse Univ., Syracuse, NY. 158 pp.

Schmiedt, R. A., Zwislocki, J. J. 1977. Comparison of sound-transmission and cochlear-microphonic characteristics in Mongolian gerbil and guinea pig. *J. Acoust. Soc. Am.* 61:133–49

Schmiedt, R. A., Zwislocki, J. J. 1978. Low-frequency neural and cochlear-microphonic tuning curves in the gerbil. *J. Acoust. Soc. Am.* 64:502–7

Sellick, P. M., Bock, G. R. 1974. Evidence for an electrogenic potassium pump as the origin of the positive component of the endocochlear potential. *Pfleugers Arch.* 352:351–61

Sellick, P. M., Johnstone, B. M. 1974. Differential effects of ouabain and ethacrynic acid on the labyrinthine potentials. *Pfleugers Arch.* 352:339–50

Sellick, P. M., Russell, I. J. 1979. Two-tone suppression in cochlear hair cells. *Hearing Res.* 1:227–36

Sellick, P. M., Russell, I. J. 1980. The responses of inner hair cells to basilar membrane velocity during low frequency auditory stimulation in the guinea pig cochlea. *Hearing Res.* 2:439–45

Siegel, J. H. 1978. *Effects of altering the organ of Corti on cochlear distortion products (f_2-f_1) and $(2f_1-f_2)$.* PhD thesis. Washington Univ. St. Louis. Mo. 119 pp.

Siegel, J. H., Brownell, W. E. 1980. Synaptic bars in outer hair cells of the chinchilla cochlea. See Burgio & Lawrence 1980, p. 5

Siegel, J. H., Kim, D. O., Molnar, C. E. 1977. Cochlear distortion products: Effects of altering the organ of Corti. *J. Acoust. Soc. Am.* 61:S1

Sitko, S. T., Strelioff, D., Honrubia, V. 1976. Source and maintenance of the endocochlear potential. *Trans. Am. Acad. Ophthalmol. Otolaryngol.* 82:328–35

Smith, C. A. 1975. The inner ear: Its embryological development and microstructure. See Dallos 1975, pp. 1–18

Smith, C. A. 1978. Structure of the cochlear duct. See Naunton & Fernández 1978, pp. 3–19

Smith, C. A., Cameron, S., Richter, R. 1976. Cochlear innervation: Current status and new findings by use of the Golgi stain. See Hirsh et al 1976, pp. 9–24

Smith, C. A., Vernon, J. A., eds. 1976. *Handbook of Auditory and Vestibular Research Methods.* Springfield, Ill: Thomas. 600 pp.

Smith, R. L. 1977. Short-term adaptation in single auditory nerve fibers: Some poststimulatory effects. *J. Neurophysiol.* 40:1098–1112

Smith, R. L. 1979. Adaptation, saturation, and physiological masking in single auditory-nerve fibers. *J. Acoust. Soc. Am.* 65:166–78

Smoorenburg, G. F., Gibson, M. M., Kitzes, L. M., Rose, J. E., Hind, J. E. 1976. Correlates of combination tones observed in the response of neurons in the anteroventral cochlear nucleus of the cat. *J. Acoust. Soc. Am.* 59:945–62

Sohmer, H. S., Peake, W. T., Weiss, T. F. 1971. Intracochlear potential recorded with micropipets. I. Correlation with micropipet location. *J. Acoust. Soc. Am.* 50:572–86

Sokolich, W. G., Hamernik, R. P., Zwislocki, J. J., Schmiedt, R. A. 1976. Inferred response polarities of cochlear hair cell. *J. Acoust. Soc. Am.* 59:963–74

Spoendlin, H. 1978. The afferent innervation of the cochlea. See Naunton & Fernández 1978, pp. 21–41

Spoendlin, H. 1979. Neural connections of the outer haircell system. *Acta Otolaryngol.* 87:381–87

Stopp, P. E., Comis, S. D. 1979. Relationship of centrifugal fibres to "supporting" cells. *Arch. Otorhinolaryngol.* 224: 11–15

Strelioff, D. 1973. A computer simulation of the generation and distribution of cochlear potentials. *J. Acoust. Soc. Am.* 54:620–29

Suga, N., Neuweiler, G., Moller, J. 1976. Peripheral auditory tuning for fine frequency analysis by the CF-FM bat, *Rhinolopus ferrumequinum.* IV. Properties of peripheral auditory neurons. *J. Comp. Physiol.* 106:111–25

Swerup, C. 1978. On the choice of noise for the analysis of the peripheral auditory system. *Biol. Cybern.* 29:97–104

Tanaka, Y., Asanuma, A., Yanagisawa, K., Katsuki, Y. 1977. Electrical potentials of the subtectorial space in the guinea pig cochlea. *Jpn. J. Physiol.* 27:539–49

Tasaki, I. 1954. Nerve impulses in individual auditory nerve fibers of guinea pigs. *J. Neurophysiol.* 17:97–122

Teas, D. C., Eldredge, D. H., Davis, H. 1962. Cochlear responses to acoustic transients: An interpretation of whole-nerve action potential. *J. Acoust. Soc. Am.* 34:1438–89

Thalmann, I., Marcus, N. Y., Thalmann, R. 1979. Adenine nucleotides of the stria vascularis. *Arch. Otorhinolaryngol.* 224:89–95

Thalmann, R., Marcus, N. Y., Thalmann, I. 1978. Adenylate energy charge, energy status, and phosphorylation state of stria vascularis under metabolic stress. *Laryngoscope* 88:1985–98

Tilney, L. G., DeRosier, D. J., Mulroy, M. J. 1980. The organization of actin filaments in the sterocilia of cochlear hair cells. *J. Cell Biol.* 86:244–59

Tumarkin, A. 1978. A new theory of cochlear function based on quasi quantum considerations. *Br. J. Audiol.* 12:119–22

Tumarkin, A. 1979. A new theory of cochlear function, part II. *Br. J. Audiol.* 13:15–18

Valli, P., Zucca, G., Casella, C. 1979. Ionic composition of the endolymph and sensory transduction in labyrinthine organs. *Acta Otolaryngol.* 87:466–71

Viergever, M. A. 1978. Basilar membrane motion in a spiral-shaped cochlea. *J. Acoust. Soc. Am.* 64:1048–53

Voldrich, L. 1978. Mechanical properties of basilar membrane. *Acta Otolaryngol.* 86:331–35

von Békésy, G. 1960. *Experiments in Hearing.* New York: McGraw-Hill. 745 pp.

Warr, W. B. 1975. Olivocochlear and vestibular efferent neurons in the feline brain stem: Their location, morphology and number determined by retrograde axonal transport and acetylcholinesterase histochemistry. *J. Comp. Neurol.* 161:159–82

Warr, W. B. 1978. The olivocochlear bundle: Its origins and terminations in the cat. See Naunton & Fernández 1978, pp. 43–65

Warr, W. B., Guinan, J. J. Jr. 1979. Efferent innervation of the organ of Corti: Two separate systems. *Brain Res.* 173: 152–55

Webster, M., Webster, D. B. 1978. Cochlear nuclear projections from outer hair cells. *Soc. Neurosci. Abstr.* 4:11

Weiss, T. F., Mulroy, M. J., Altmann, D. W. 1974. Intracellular responses to acoustic clicks in the inner ear of the alligator lizard. *J. Acoust. Soc. Am.* 55:606–21

Weiss, T. F., Mulroy, M. J., Turner, R. G., Pike, C. L. 1976. Tuning of single fibers in the cochlear nerve of the alligator lizard: Relation to receptor morphology. *Brain Res.* 115:71–90

Weiss, T. F., Altmann, D. W., Mulroy, M. J. 1978a. Endolymphatic and intracellular resting potential in the alligator lizard cochlea. *Pfleugers Arch.* 373:77–84

Weiss, T. F., Peake, W. T., Ling, A. Jr., Holton, T. 1978b. Which structures determine frequency selectivity and tonotopic organization of vertebrate nerve fibers? See Naunton & Fernández 1978, pp. 91–112

Wever, E. G. 1978. *The Reptile Ear.* Princeton: Princeton Univ. 1024 pp.

Wiederhold, M. L. 1970. Variations in the effects of electric stimulation of the crossed olivocochlear bundle on cat single auditory-nerve-fiber responses to tone bursts. *J. Acoust. Soc. Am.* 48:966–77

Wilson, J. P. 1980. The combination tone, 2 f_1-f_2, in psychophysics and ear-canal recording. See Dallos & Flock 1980, pp. 43–50

Wilson, J. P., Johnstone, J. R. 1972. Capacitive probe measures of basilar membrane vibrations. See Evans 1972. pp. 172–81

Wilson, J. P., Johnstone, J. R. 1975. Basilar membrane and middle ear vibration in guinea pig measured by capacitive probe. *J. Acoust. Soc. Am.* 57:705–23

Wit, H. P., Ritsma, R. J. 1979. Stimulated acoustic emissions from the human ear. *J. Acoust. Soc. Am.* 66:91–13

Wit, H. P., Ritsma, R. J. 1980. On the mechanism of the evoked cochlear mechanical response. See Dallos & Flock 1980, pp. 53–60

Wright, C. G., Preston, R. E. 1976. Efferent nerve fibers associated with the outermost supporting cells of the organ of Corti in the guinea pig. *Acta Otolaryngol.* 82:41–47

Yost, W. A., Nielsen, D. W., 1977. *Fundamentals of Hearing.* New York: Holt, Rinehart & Winston. 240 pp.

Young, E. D., Sachs, M. B. 1979. Representation of steady-state vowels in the temporal aspects of the discharge patterns of populations of auditory-nerve fibers. *J. Acoust. Soc. Am.* 66:1381–1403

Zwicker, E., Terhardt, E., eds. 1974. *Facts and Models in Hearing.* Berlin: Springer-Verlag. 360 pp.

Zwislocki, J. J. 1980. Five decades of research on cochlear mechanics. *J. Acoust. Soc. Am.* 67:1679–85

Zwislocki, J. J., Kletsky, E. J. 1979. Tectorial membrane: A possible effect on frequency analysis in the cochlea. *Science* 204:639–41

Zwislocki, J. J., Sokolich, W. G. 1973. Velocity and displacement responses in auditory nerve fibers. *Science* 182: 64–66

Ann. Rev. Psychol. 1981. 32:191–241

GRAPHICAL DATA ANALYSIS ♦344

Howard Wainer[1]

Bureau of Social Science Research, Washington, D.C. 20036, and Educational Testing Service, Princeton, New Jersey 08540

David Thissen

Department of Psychology, University of Kansas, Lawrence, Kansas 66044

CONTENTS

[1]Research for this chapter was supported in part by a grant from the National Science Foundation (SOC-76-17768), Albert D. Biderman and Howard Wainer, principal investigators.

191

0066-4308/81/0201-0191$01.00

INTRODUCTION

Psychology is full of a facile complexity. Physical sciences gain in truth when most quantitative, whereas psychology, when most quantitative is of least scope, though the sweetness of elegance lingers on. Over the century since Wundt's laboratory started modern experimental psychology, its characteristic paradigms have emerged in fits and starts. In an attempt to deal with the frequent crudeness of its data, psychology has adopted, adapted, and polished a set of statistical procedures and models that are second in sophistication and complexity only to those employed by Carlyle's "dismal science." The often self-conscious attempt to make paradigms statistically rigorous when experimental controls lacked rigor was in keeping with comments of statisticians such as Wallis (1949), who argued that "So-called 'high-powered,' 'refined,' or 'elaborate' statistical techniques are generally called for when the data are crude and inadequate—exactly the opposite, if I may be permitted an *obiter dictum,* of what crude and inadequate statisticians usually think."

Of course, there were many reasons other than self-conscious defensiveness for the development and use of "high-powered" statistical techniques. Often such techniques were desperately required. This need provided the impetus for the development of rigorous, formal statistical models, but deemphasized the need for descriptive methods: methods whose aims were exploratory rather than confirmatory.

The past 10 years have seen a vigorous development of methods, by the foremost of statisticians, which have as their very nature an informality that was unheard of in the social sciences for a half century. These techniques are primarily graphical in form, flexible and robust in character, and informative in a wide variety of problems and so are of general applicability. It is toward a review of these techniques that this chapter is directed.

The signal event in this area was the 1977 publication of Tukey's *Exploratory Data Analysis* (EDA). Prepublication versions of this document abounded, and so dating the start of the movement of informal data analysis by that book's publication is a bit misleading. Consequently we shall refer to Tukey as the modern progenitor of the movement which dates back at least to 1962 and the publication of Tukey's prophetic "Future of data analysis."

Other recent works of importance on this topic include: Everitt (1978), Gnanadesikan (1977), Hartwig & Dearing (1979), Monkhouse & Wilkinson (1971), Mosteller & Tukey (1968, 1977), and Wang (1978).

Limits of this Chapter

In this chapter we shall not discuss directly issues of robustness, although that is one aim of many of the procedures which will be discussed. Sometimes graphical methods allow the easy computation of a statistical test (e.g. binomial probability paper, Mosteller & Tukey 1949) or a statistic (computing a robust correlation graphically, Sandiford 1932; or model parameters, Bock and Jones 1968); we shall generally not discuss this aspect, although occasional reference toward such things will be made. Further, although we recognize that graphics have many uses, we shall generally limit ourselves to data analysis. Graphs for communicative purposes or nomographs for computational ones we shall leave to other accounts. Occasionally some rules for good exploratory graphs carry over into presentational rules, and when this occurs we shall make mention of it.

We view this chapter as didactic, and so it will contain many examples of the sorts of plots we will be discussing. This will avoid the anomalous situation of a chapter on graphs describing its subject in prose. We intend to "show" rather than "tell" whenever possible. We shall exclude color for purely economic reasons.

It is the purpose of a review article to start where the last review article left off and to contain as much of the intervening work as space permits. This allows the researcher to read the most recent review and be more or less current with the work done at the time that review was written. Since this is the first review of graphics to appear in the *Annual Review of Psychology,* we will have to go back a bit further than most such chapters and have a bit spottier coverage. We shall attempt to increase the depth of coverage as the work becomes more current.

The role of graphs in theory development is often misunderstood. Tilling (1975), in a recent history of experimental graphs, restates this misconception:

> Clearly an ability to plot an experimental graph necessarily precedes an ability to analyse it. However, although any map may be considered as a graph, and carefully constructed maps had been in use long before the eighteenth century, we do not expect the shape of a coast-line to follow a mathematical law. Further, although there are a great many physical phenomena that we do expect to follow mathematical laws, they are in general so complex in nature that direct plotting will reveal little about the nature of those laws ... (p. 193)

Attitudes like these have hindered appropriately serious regard for such theories as that of continental drift, whose initial evidence (noticed by every school child) is solely graphical.

The point of this chapter is to introduce many of the developments in graphical data analysis to psychology, as well as to aid in their legitimization for theory construction within a scholarly context. This is done in the ardent belief that graphs can aid us in the discovering and understanding of psychological phenomena. Although science (following Chamberlain) may be the "holding of multiple working hypotheses," the picturing of data allows us to be sensitive "not only to the multiple hypotheses we hold, but to the many more we have not yet thought of, regard as unlikely or think impossible" (Tukey 1974, p. 526).

HISTORY[2]

The use of visual displays to present quantitative material is very old indeed. As Shakespeare noted (Henry VI, Act IV), "Our forefathers had no other books but the score and tally." Both score and tally represented an advance to the concept of abstract number from more literally iconic predecessors. Our use of "graphic" here is the opposite of "graphic" in the sense of literal life-likeness. Historical development displays both the replacement of iconic aspects of representation by progressively more abstract (and potentially more logically elaborate) forms as well as the development of signs and sign systems progressively stripped of their iconic features and adapted instead to the grammar and syntax of linearly configured, written counterparts to spoken language. For most human purposes, the alphanumerical system proved infinitely more useful and largely displaced graphic devices as means of recording, reordering, manipulating, comprehending, and analyzing symbolic representations of quantitative aspects of phenomena. The principal exception to the preponderant alphanumerical form uses the scalar representation of space, and objects concretely located in space, on a graphic plane. The earlier-to-evolve form of schematic spatial representation is the map; the more highly abstract form is the geometric diagram. Cartography and geometry, in both their terrestrial and astronomical applications, have been the most important areas of graphic development. Geometry also evolved to treat space as pure abstraction equivalent to number. The movement of objects in space made for ready extension to include time in the graphic spatial plane. Certain other graphic systems, including mechanical and architectural drawing, musical notation, astrological and alchemical or scientific chemical symbol systems, were all partially diagrammatic in character. The systematization of the spatial diagrammatic forms by Descartes in 1637 in the Cartesian coordinate system and his integration of the geometric and the algebraic systems established what until the present day remains the most intellectually important and useful of diagrammatic graphic systems.

As Biderman (1978) has noted, the Cartesian system so dominated intellectual conceptions of what graphs were and what they were for—i.e. the depiction of the mathematical functions governing the behavior of objects

---

[2]The first two paragraphs of this section are taken almost verbatim from an unpublished paper by Albert D. Biderman. A fuller account of Playfair's role in the development of the schematic representation of statistics was given by Biderman (1980a) in a recent AAAS talk. Copies of that talk (less the color graphics) are available from him.

in space and time—that it took more than a century and a half before it occurred to anyone that graphs could be used for anything else. Furthermore, as Biderman also notes, the Cartesian tradition was so strong that it misled those who were using graphs in altogether different ways for altogether different intellectual tasks into the belief that they were doing Cartesian geometric analysis. In truth, they were engaged in something quite different, involving no geometry more complex than that well known even in pre-Classical antiquity. What they were doing was, however, an important intellectual departure from Cartesianism—that is, graphic methods were being applied to exploratory analysis of empirical statistics. Eventually, with d'Alembert, Gauss, et al, a method of joining the Cartesian and the statistical graphic approaches developed, but, in application, curve-fitting remained on an intellectually separate track until very late in the nineteenth century. Cartesian curve-fitting uses data to determine (comprehend) the structure (curves = laws) governing the universe. The statistical orientation uses curves (regularities) to determine (comprehend) the structure of concrete sets of data—data about phenomena that are important to understand in their own right.

A major conceptual breakthrough in graphical presentation came in 1786 with the publication of Playfair's *Political Atlas* in which spatial dimensions were used to represent nonspatial, quantitative, idiographic, empirical data. Although it now seems natural to represent, for example, rising and falling imports over time as a rising and falling line, it does not seem to have been done before that time and was quite an accomplishment. Notably, in addition to the statistical line chart, Playfair at one fell swoop single-handedly invented most of the remaining forms of the statistical graphic repertoire used today—the bar chart and histogram, the surface chart, and the circle diagram or "pie chart."

In addition to Biderman's account above, an extensive history of graphical developments is provided by Funkhouser (1937), in which he reviews the use of graphic display in the physical and social sciences from early picture writing to uses during the 1930s. It contains many examples, but, because of economic and technical reasons, spends many pages describing color graphs rather than reproducing them. A similar problem confronts the authors of this review, as will be evident in the section on multivariate display.

A useful tool for the study of the history, development, and applications of the graphical method is the annotated bibliography prepared by Feinberg & Franklin (1975). For other reviews the interested reader is referred to Beniger & Robyn (1978), Brinton (1939), Chambers (1977, Chap. 8), Cox (1978), Fienberg (1979), Fisher (1979), Huggins & Entwisle (1974) and Macdonald-Ross (1978).

GRAPHICS FOR DATA ANALYSIS

In the sections to follow, we describe a variety of procedures judged useful for data analysis. These methods display the data and thus in a real sense describe them. They aid in analysis and interpretation, summarize what we know about the data, and expose what we do not know. The usefulness of any particular display is determined by comparison with a list of desirable characteristics (proposed by Gnanadesikan 1980). These are their: (*a*) descriptive capacity, (*b*) versatility, (*c*) data orientation, (*d*) potential for internal comparisons, (*e*) aid in focussing attention, (*f*) degree to which they are self critical of assumptions, and (*g*) adaptability to large volumes of data.

We shall not go through this list of desiderata for each display technique, but the reader should remember these and compare each technique with the others on these bases. Further, this list forms a basis of comparisons for other techniques that we do not mention but which the reader might find available. For many purposes some of these desiderata are not crucial, and so a method which is not, say, versatile, may be very useful for a narrow purpose of a particular investigation. These criteria are general ones, meant for the overall evaluation of a data analytic technique.

One-Way Displays of One-Way Data

Such is the current renaissance of the development of statistical graphics that even the graphics associated with counting are being altered. While numerals are useful for the storage of numbers and their presentation in tabular form, the act of counting may be aided by other graphic devices; and entirely graphic displays are often superior to tables for data analytic purposes.

Even now, when calculating machines as powerful as the room-sized computers of past decades are pocket-sized, and when general-purpose computers cost less than color televisions, much counting is still done by hand. A prerequisite to efficient data analysis is the ability to count quickly and accurately. Tukey (1977) complains that the traditional tallying procedure,

$$/ \quad // \quad /// \quad //// \quad \cancel{||||}$$

is slow and "treacherous" since one can accidently make completed figures of four or six ($\cancel{|||}$ or $\cancel{|||||}$). He suggests another tallying procedure, using dots and lines to form a square figure, as in Figure 1. Successive dots (representing the counts one to four) form a square; lines connecting the dots represent five to eight, and the diagonals are nine and ten. A series of such figures is easy to total: completed figures are multiplied by ten, and the rest are added (i.e. there are 22 sophomore boys in the two-way example in part C of Figure 1).

Tallying by tens variously illustrated

A) TALLY

TALLY	COUNT
.	1
∴ or ..	2
∴ or ∴. (etc.)	3
::	4
⊓ or I: (etc.)	5
⌐. or L: (etc.)	6
⊓ or ⊏ (etc.)	7
□	8
◨ or ◪	9
⊠	10
⊠ ⊠ ⊓	27
⊠ ⊠ ⊠ ⊠ ·	42

B) A SIMPLE EXAMPLE

0	⊠ ⊠ □
1	⊠ ⊠ ∴
2	⊠ ◩
3	⊠ ⌐.
4	⊠ ·
5	⊠ ⊠ ∴˙
6	◩
7	⊓
8	I ∶
9	∴˙
10	·

C) A TWO-WAY EXAMPLE

	Freshmen	Sophs	Juniors	Seniors
Boys	⊠ ⊠ ⊠ ⊠ ˙˙	⊠ ⊠ ∴	⊠ ⌐.	⊠ ·
Girls	⊠ ⊠ ⌐.	⊠ ⊠ ⊠ ∷	⊠ ∴˙	⊠ ⊠ ∴

Figure 1   Tallying by tens variously illustrated, from Tukey (1977). Used by permission.

The square figures are so easily read as numbers that it is frequently unnecessary to translate them into numerals; see, e.g., part B of Figure 1, which gives a kind of bar chart for scores from zero to ten, and part C of Figure 1, which is a two-way table. While the new figures are not universally praised, they have come into fairly widespread use since they were introduced 10 years ago in the preliminary edition of *EDA* because they have been found useful by many in practical data analysis.

While Tukey has been improving the way people represent counts when a computer is not doing the work, Roberto Bachi (1968, 1976, 1978a,b) has been improving the way computers represent numbers to people. Bachi's work makes heavy use of variations on a theme he calls the "graphic rational pattern" (GRP). The basic square GRP is shown in Figure 2; patterns of small squares represent the units and larger squares represent the tens—the result is a system which graphically represents amount (the more, the darker) and precisely represents numbers at the same time (each figure can be read as an exact count). The figures must, for practical purposes, be computer-generated, of course; but currently available computer

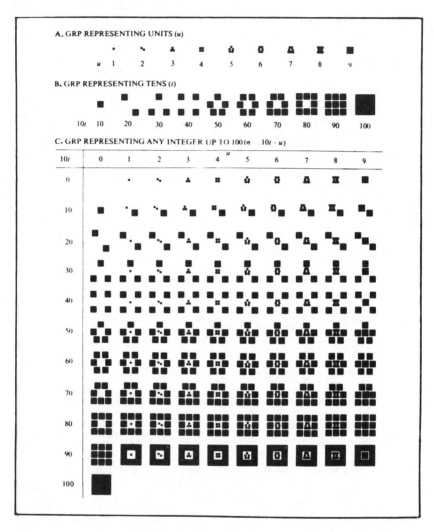

Figure 2   The basic scale of graphic rational patterns (GRP) showing integers from 1 to 100, from Bachi (1978b). Used by permission.

graphic systems can easily produce patterns like those in Figure 2, or the various circular variants (using several circles or fractions of circles to represent digits) Bachi has designed variants for use in a wide variety of contexts. The displays in Figure 3 show one use for the GRP: a traditional bar chart is replaced by a set of the little clusters of squares. Display by the GRP method of the seven counts requires much less space and is probably as informative as the "diagrammatic" representation, or bar chart, given

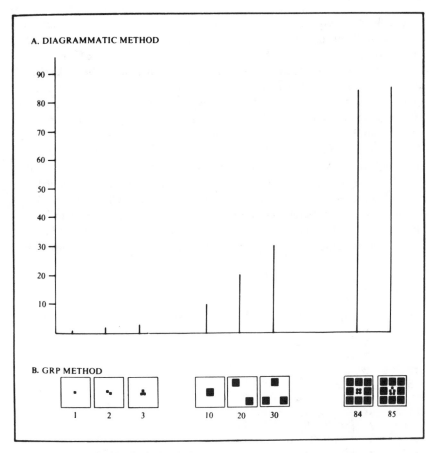

Figure 3   A comparison of GRP and diagrammatic methods, from Bachi (1978b). Used by permission.

above. Bachi's GRP method also may be used in bivariate and multivariate displays; these will be discussed in later sections of this review.

Two-Way Displays of One-Way Data

STEM-AND-LEAF DIAGRAMS   The stem-and-leaf display is the most important device for the analysis of small batches of numbers to appear since the t-test. In one sense, a stem-and-leaf display is simply a labeled bar chart. In a more important sense, however, the stem-and-leaf display permits the data analyst to examine the distributional properties of a batch of data, check for outliers, and compute a collection of useful order statistics, all for the price of writing down the data (once) and counting a bit.

The horticulture associated with stem-and-leaf diagrams is described most completely in Tukey's (1977) volume, but abridged treatments are included in Tukey (1972), Andrews (1978) and Leinhardt & Wasserman (1979). A set of tips for prospective gardeners is also included here. A robust and healthy stem-and-leaf diagram, plucked from Tukey's (1977) greenhouse, is shown in Figure 4. The data displayed are the populations of the 50 states as determined by the 1960 census, in units of 10,000 people.

The numbers in boldface on the left side of the vertical bar are the "stems" (the top one is 1*; the bottom one is 2), and the numbers on the right side of the vertical bar are the "leaves." Each state is represented by a leaf, which is made up of the trailing digits of that state's 1960 population in units of 10,000; each leaf is attached to a stem, which is the first digit of that state's population. Thus, the least populated state is on stem 2, has leaf 3, and had a population in 1960 of 23 × 10,000 = 230,000. For convenience, some states of special interest (the most and least populous,

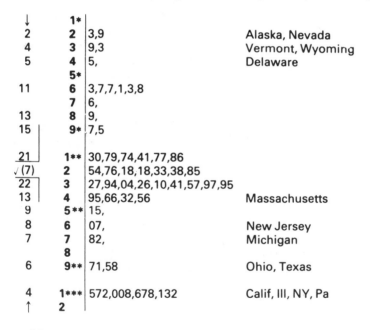

	1*		
↓	1*		
2	2	3,9	Alaska, Nevada
4	3	9,3	Vermont, Wyoming
5	4	5,	Delaware
	5*		
11	6	3,7,7,1,3,8	
	7	6,	
13	8	9,	
15	9*	7,5	
21	1**	30,79,74,41,77,86	
√(7)	2	54,76,18,18,33,38,85	
22	3	27,94,04,26,10,41,57,97,95	
13	4	95,66,32,56	Massachusetts
9	5**	15,	
8	6	07,	New Jersey
7	7	82,	Michigan
	8		
6	9**	71,58	Ohio, Texas
4	1***	572,008,678,132	Calif, Ill, NY, Pa
↑	2		

50 populations in tens of thousands				50 populations in millions		
M25h		246		M25h		2.5
H13	89		432	H13	0.89	4.3
1	23		1678	1	0.23	17

Figure 4 A stem-and-leaf display of the 1960 populations of the 50 states, from Tukey (1977). Used by permission.

and the author's home state) are named at the right of the display, providing us with the information that the least populated state is Alaska. Nevada is clearly next, with 290,000. At the other end of the distribution, New York was most populous, with 16,780,000 inhabitants (its stem was 1*** and its leaf 678).

The asterisks to the right of the stems and to the left of the bar might be called "buds"; they are place-holders, indicating the number of digits in each leaf. In this essentially logarithmic stem-and-leaf display, the states with populations between 100,000 and 990,000 are represented by one-digit stems in the upper segment; states which had populations in the millions are represented (with equal precision) by two-digit or three-digit leaves in the lower segments of the plot. The asterisks are reminders of the scale-shifts associated with increasing values of the stems, and the corresponding increase in the size of the leaves. (There could be asterisks next to each stem; some are omitted in Figure 4 for typographical clarity.)

To the left of the stems in Figure 4 are numbers—the cumulative counts from the top to the middle and from the bottom to the middle. Once a stem-and-leaf display has been made, the data have been partially ordered and a number of useful order statistics may be computed. Since there are 50 states, the median is the average of the 25th and the 26th states, or the 25h (for 25-and-a-halfth) entry on the plot. So the median is computed by counting in (either from the top or the bottom) to 25 and 26 and averaging those entries. The median is 246 (10,000s) and is recorded next to the code "M25h" in the box at the bottom of the stem-and-leaf.

Tukey calls the 25th and 75th percentiles of the distribution "hinges." The hinges, i.e. 25th and 75th percentiles, are the 13th numbers counting in (have a "depth" of 13), are 89 and 432 (10,000s) in the present example, and are recorded next to "H13" in the box below the stem-and-leaf. That box is filled by including the numbers whose depth is one (the extremes). The numbers in the box make up what Tukey calls a "five-number summary" of the batch. A number of Tukey's (1977) robust procedures for estimating the location and width of the distribution, as well as for identifying outliers, are based on the information in the five-number summary.

Tukey also makes heavy use of five-number summaries when considering transformations, or "re-expressions," of batches of data, especially when it is desirable to achieve symmetry in the distribution for some further analysis. It is clear that the population data of Figure 4 are markedly asymmetrical. If the larger populations were not compressed by changing the stems from 100,000s to millions and then to tens of millions, the stem-and-leaf display would be more than 200 lines long, and there would be only four states in the last 100 lines. So the data were (impicitly) log-transformed in Figure 4.

Figure 5 includes two stem-and-leaf displays of the population data after they have really been transformed to be log (population in 10,000s). The stem-and-leaf display on the left gives the log data with three-significant-digit accuracy "for storage"; but it is too spread out to show the form of the distribution well. The stem-and-leaf on the right "squeezes" the leaves onto shorthand stems (* for zero or one, "t" for two or three, "f" for four or five, "s" for six or seven, and "." for eight or nine); the form of the distribution is clarified. The distribution of the logs is fairly symmetrical, with no extreme values; we will use log population data for other examples later in the chapter.

Stem-and-leaf displays may be made with one-digit or two-digit or more-digit stems, or leaves, or both, or the leaves may be labels rather than digits; they may be made with or without asterisks or commas or upside-down or rightside-up by a computer or by hand. The distributions of data from two groups may be compared with "back-to-back" stem-and-leaf displays; these have a common set of stems in the middle of the page and leaves on both sides—showing one group on the left and the other on the right. Or several may use a common stem on the left, for an even more elaborate plot (see Inside-Out plots on page 221). This short discussion is meant to indicate that there are many ways to look at data as a stem-and-leaf display. Some of those ways may be useful.

1	13*	6		1*		
2	14	6	1	t	3	Alaska
4	15	29	4	f	455	
5	16	5	6	s	67	
6	17*	9	15	1·	888888999	
12	18	003338	17	2*	11	Ariz, Nebr
15	19	589	√ 25	t	22223333	
	20		25	f	444445555	
17	21*	15	16	s	666666677	
21	22	4557	7	2·	899	
25	23	4478	4	3*	00	Ill, Pa
＼ 25	24	04589	2	t	22	Cal, NY
20	25*	1135				
16	26	0004679				
9	27	18				
7	28	9				
6	29*	89				
4	30	05				
	31					
2	32	02				
	33*					

Figure 5 Stem-and-leaf displays of the log-transformed populations of the 50 states, from Tukey (1977). Used by permission.

BOX PLOTS   The five-number summary associated with the stem-and-leaf display provides the seeds for Tukey's next-most-useful display, the box plot. A set of basic box plots is shown in Figure 6, giving the distribution of telephone bills (in $) for groups with varying lengths of residence in Chicago. For each of the six groups, the box encloses the middle 50% of

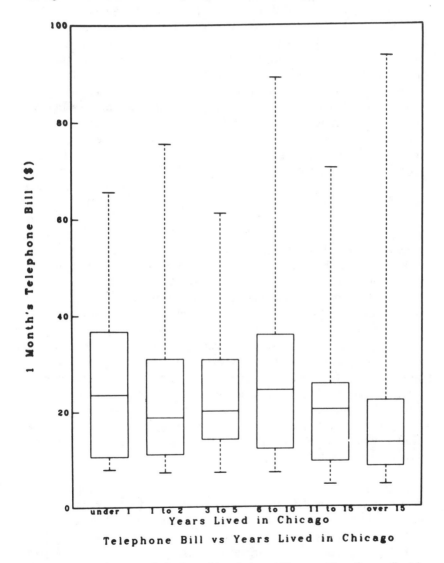

Figure 6 A "regular box plot" of monthly telephone bills vs number of years lived in Chicago, from McGill et al (1978). Used by permission.

the data: the top of the box is at the upper hinge (75th percentile) and the bottom of the box is at the lower hinge (25th percentile). The line across the middle of the box is the median, and the dotted lines (frequently called whiskers) extend to the extremes.

The regular box plots of Figure 6 give an informative display of six distributions. They are all skewed upward (note the long upper whiskers), and the "under 1" and "6 to 10" year group receives lower ones. McGill, Tukey & Larsen (1978) provide a number of intriguing elaborations on the basic box plot. These include the plots in Figure 7, which show the same data as are displayed in Figure 6. The data have been log-transformed to approximate symmetry; the width of each box is proportional to root group size; and a lack of overlap of the obvious "notches" indicates a significant difference at a "rough 95% level." Formulas for the size of the notches and other technical details are given in McGill et al (1978); this example represents one of the few expressions of hypothesis testing ideas in the new graphics. Figure 7, showing the entire distributions, represents a marked improvement over the classical "mean with standard error bars." These plots follow in the tradition of "range charts" (Schmid 1954).

Tukey (1977) distinguishes between "schematic plots" for which he provides precise rules about the treatment of outliers and such, and regular box plots which may be drawn quite flexibly. Tufte (1979) has proposed yet another class of box-plot variants called "mid-gap" plots: they are box plots with the top, bottom, and sides of the box omitted. Mid-gap plots increase the comprehensible density of such displays for multiple group comparisons; but the sides of the box can no longer be used to convey information.

The psychologist interested in comparing groups will undoubtedly find a favorite graph in the box plot or a variant. But the statisticians who have been designing data analytic graphics betray their own concerns with the detailed analysis of single distributions (instead of the gross analysis of several distributions) by providing a plethora of distributional displays. Tukey, of course, is an innovator and adaptor in the area of distributional display, with a variety of contributions besides the essential, all-purpose stem-and-leaf display.

SUSPENDED ROOTOGRAMS   In his pioneering comments on graphics in data analysis, Tukey (1972) questioned a number of assumptions implicit in the traditional use of the histogram to compare empirical and theoretical distributions. Tukey argued that histograms need not be drawn with area proportional to count; he also argued (following Jevons 1884) that comparisons are best made between data and fitted straight lines. An example of a better "-gram" following Tukey's first argument is his proposed "rootogram," in which area is proportional to the square root of the count—on

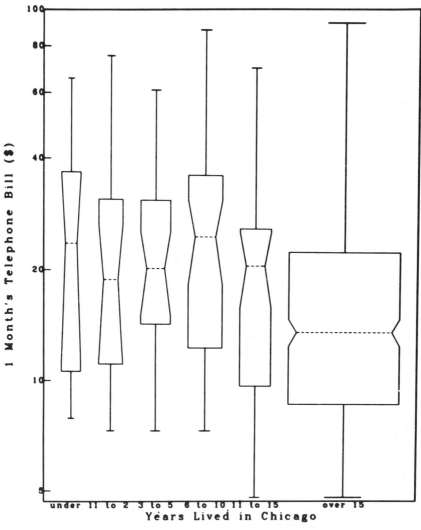

Figure 7 A "variable width notched box plot" of the data in Figure 6, from McGill et al (1978). Used by permission.

the grounds that the roots of counts are usually better behaved statistically than are the counts themselves. A traditional histogram of the height of some 218 volcanoes is shown in Figure 8; in Figure 9, the same data are displayed as a rootogram of the square roots of the heights.

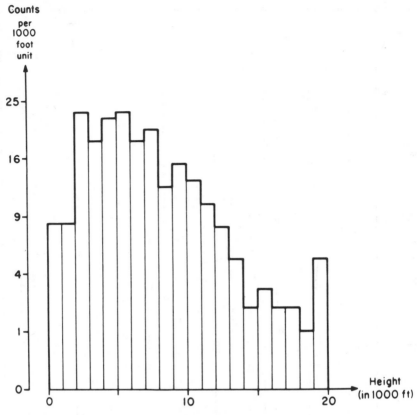

Figure 8   A rootogram of the heights of 218 volcanoes, from Tukey (1972). Used by permission.

Figure 9, of course, suggests a normal distribution. That distribution could be superimposed on Figure 9, and the goodness-of-fit examined by comparing the curve to the tops of the histobars; but using a curve as a standard of comparison is always poor graphical practice. Instead, Tukey provides the "hanging rootogram" shown in Figure 10, in which the rootobars of Figure 9 have been hung from the fitted normal distribution, leaving the discrepancies at the bottoms as deviations around a horizontal line. An even better display might be the "suspended rootogram" of Figure 11 in which the hanging rootogram is turned upside-down, suspending the normal curve from the axis; and the deviations, not the data, are plotted as excess or deficit root counts. In this example, Tukey concludes that the "fit of the normal curve to the square roots of these volcano heights is very good indeed"; that conclusion was not strongly suggested by the traditional display in Figure 8. Wainer (1974), in one of the rare experimental evaluations of the new graphics, validated the usefulness of hanging rootograms.

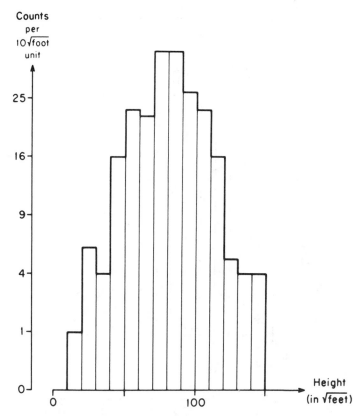

Figure 9   A rootogram of the square roots of the heights of 218 volcanoes, from Tukey (1972). Used by permission.

P-P AND Q-Q PLOTS   The classical alternative to the histogram for distributional display has been the probability plot, at least since the invention of normal probability paper, suggested by Galton in 1899 and created by Hazen a decade later (Funkhouser 1937). Normal probability paper is ruled with the quantiles of the normal distribution (usually in z-score units) on the abscissa, with the intervals chosen so that a plot of a cumulative normal distribution is a straight line. Thus, when a scatterplot is made on such a grid, with the ordered data on the ordinate and the quantiles associated with each observation's percentile on the abscissa, the plot resembles a straight line to the extent that the data are normally distributed. Deviations from linearity are diagnostic of non-normality. The plot, once made, provides an easy way to make a detailed analysis of the shape of the distribution. However, since normal probability paper has always been a bit hard to find (and paper ruled for any other distributions even harder), and probability plots have been tedious to make even when the paper is at hand, such plots

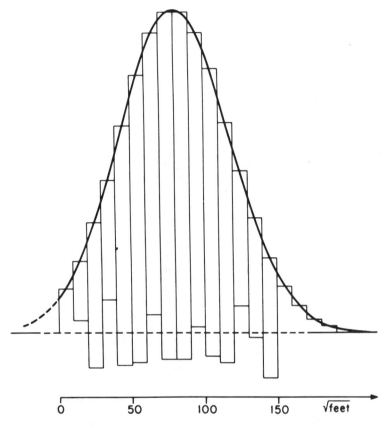

Figure 10   A hanging rootogram of the heights of 218 volcanoes, from Tukey (1972). Used by permission.

have not been used often. The computer has changed all of that. Probability plots made by computer graphic systems, line printers, or even on type-writer terminals, are now as easily made as any two-way plot; and the scale may be set to be appropriate for any distribution: a gamma plot is no more difficult to make than a normal one.

Wilk & Gnanadesikan (1968) and Gnanadesikan (1977) offer a number of suggestions for the use of both quantile (Q-Q) and percentile (P-P) plots. The name "Q-Q plot" refers to all possible elaborations of the traditional probability plot: the ordered data may be plotted against the quantiles of a theoretical distribution, or the quantiles of one empirical distribution may be plotted against another, or two theoretical distributions may be displayed together. The goal is always to compare two distributions; "the same" is always a straight line. An example of a Q-Q plot taken from Wilk &

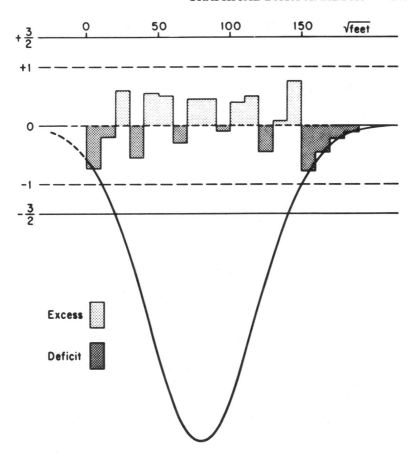

Figure 11   A suspended rootogram of the data in Figure 10, from Tukey (1972). Used by permission.

Gnanadesikan (1968) is shown in Figure 12. The data plotted make up a distribution of log energies associated with an individual repeatedly speaking a single word. The display is far superior to a list of the several hundred data points; from it, it is clear that the distribution is bimodal with one mode at the lower extreme and another around 1.0 on the normal quantile (z-score) scale. Both modes are represented by positive deviations from the (imaginary) straight line which would appear if the data were normal. The plot begins high (in the lower left-hand corner), indicating that the distribution of the data does not have a tail, as a normal distribution should, but rather has a large number of tied values at the lower extreme. The second mode is indicated by the "hump" above the imaginary 45° line about two-thirds of the way up the plot. Such displays can be more useful than

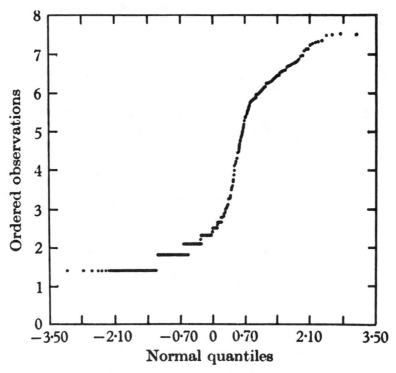

Figure 12   A normal Q-Q plot from Wilk & Gnanadesikan (1968). Used by permission.

histograms, as there are no potential artifacts of categorization. They do require some practice to read skillfully, but Wilk & Gnanadesikan provide much helpful advice, and Daniel & Wood (1971) provide a large section of computer-generated examples of Q-Q plots as an aid in acquiring skills in interpretation. P-P plots are plots of percentiles rather than quantiles, but are otherwise similar to Q-Q plots However, they have different properties than Q-Q plots; P-P plots emphasize differences in the middles of distributions, whereas Q-Q plots emphasize the tails. And P-P plots are affected by linear transformations of the data, whereas Q-Q plots are not. P-P plots have been studied relatively little.

Wilk and Gnanadesikan discuss in detail the different virtues of Q-Q and P-P plots, and offer several original suggestions for their use. Two of the most interesting proposals in Gnanadesikan's (1977) book [from Gnanadesikan (1973) and Wilk & Gnanadesikan (1968)] are the use of Q-Q plots as an aid in the evaluation of dimensionality in principal component analysis and the use of normal and gamma Q-Q plots to analyze effects and variance components in experimental data. While those techniques are too complex to be reviewed in detail here, the investigator confronted, with complex multidimensional data or complex experimental designs would do well to consider those procedures. Daniel & Wood (1971) also make heavy use of Q-Q plots in their treatment of regression as a data-analytic tool; Q-Q plots of residuals are an important part of their analyses. But much of their work is concerned with plots of two or more variables, and that brings us to the next topic.

Two-Way Displays of (Mostly) Two-Way Data

In the April 1963 issue of *The American Statistician,* Bradley (1963) described an early procedure for producing a scatterplot with the assistance of computational machinery. It works like this: beginning with a computer card deck on which are punched the values of X and Y, use a card-sorter to order the cards on X; then draw a diagonal line across the top of the deck and reorder the cards, this time on Y. The result is a scatterplot of the order statistics of X and Y, made of the (reordered) pieces of the diagonal line on top of the cards. The plot may be photographed for permanent storage.

Bertin (1977, 1980) uses a similar but much more general scheme for the graphical analysis of data matrices using an array in which the entries are shaded proportionally to the observation in that cell. The rows and columns are then permuted in his "domino" apparatus to yield a visual cluster structure. The obtained structure is then interpreted. In Figure 13 there are three versions of the same data with the one on the right being the preferred display indicating the structure of meat production in Western Europe.

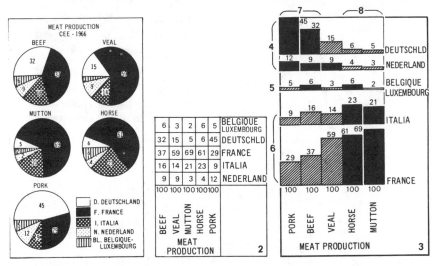

Figure 13   A comparison of three methods of displaying meat production in Western Europe, from Bertin (1980). The pie chart is included as an example of poor practice, with the profile (3) preferred.

Figure 14 shows the similarity of Bertin's "graphical matrix" to Bradley's scatterplot in its method of construction. Such displays, reminiscent of Guttman scalograms, are useful for multivariate data and are discussed in the next section.

Fortunately, considering the love affair of psychologists with both correlational analysis and the scatterplot, techniques for mechanically producing such plots have matured considerably in the past two decades. Many of the major software packages which perform correlation or regression analysis, like SPSS (Nie, Bent & Hull 1975), the Linear Least Squares Curve-Fitting Program (Daniel & Wood 1971), and BMDP-R series of programs (Dixon & Brown 1979) to name a few, and countless local special purpose programs produce pages of line-printed scatterplots easily. Some of the packaged programs add ingenious and useful features to their scatterplots. For in-

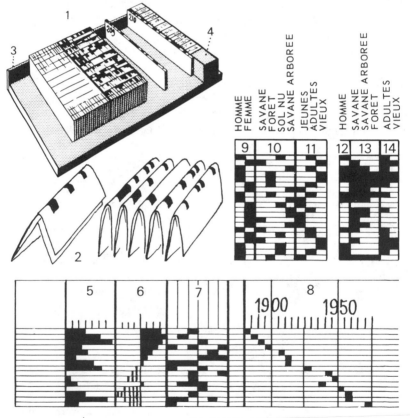

Figure 14   A simplified version of Bertin's "Domino Apparatus" for the manipulation of a graphical data matrix (Bertin 1977).

stance, the BMDP programs include markers (Xs and Ys) on the borders of X-Y plots at the points at which the regression lines cross the edges, thus allowing the user to pencil in the least squares fit. The line printer cannot draw oblique lines well, but this trick solves the problem. But line printers do make satisfactory scatterplots for many purposes. So, since the machine is doing the work, the question is no longer "Shall we plot?" but rather it is "What shall we plot?"

DIAGNOSTIC PLOTS   In the context of regression analysis, the answer given by Daniel & Wood (1971, Wood 1973) to that question is "Plot everything." Besides advocating quantile plots of residuals from regression equations, they discuss the usefulness and interpretation of plots of residuals against the fitted dependent variable, the residuals against independent variables (both those included and excluded from the equation), and "component-plus-residual plots." The BMDP (Dixon & Brown 1979) programs permit similarly prolific production of scatterplots, uses of which have been described in their technical report series (Hill 1979).

And the data, fit, and residuals are no longer the only candidates for plotting regression analysis. Recent advances in regression methods make use of a number of different kinds of "diagnostic plots" which are designed to assist the data analyst in fitting the model. The choice of the best regression equation in "all possible subsets" regression, as performed by the Linear Least Squares Curve-Fitting program of Daniel & Wood (1971) and BMDP9R (Dixon & Brown 1979), is usually made with the help of the "C_p plot" (Gorman & Toman 1966, Daniel & Wood 1971; Furnival & Wilson 1974). Such plots use Colin Mallow's C_p statistic to compare the goodness-of-fit of large numbers of regression equations, considering simultaneously the number of predictors in the equation and the residual variance. These plots are extremely useful; indeed, without them, all possible subsets regression might be an algebraic nightmare rather than a practical tool in data analysis.

While one major advance of the past decade in multiple regression has been the replacement of stepwise procedures with all possible subset searches for model selection, served by the C_p plot, another has been a proliferation of procedures for robust regression analysis. Denby & Mallows (1977) have suggested a solution to the problem of selecting the "trimming" parameter for Huber's (1972) extremely robust "trimmed M-estimators" of multiple regression weights; that solution is based on a series of diagnostic plots. Basically, the residuals and all of the weights are plotted against the trimming parameter; then the data analyst picks the result that makes sense.

Gnanadesikan (1977) suggests yet another variety of diagnostic plotting, based on a creative choice of variables to be placed on a scatterplot. The idea is to detect multivariate outliers in datasets containing several variables. It is done by plotting the values of the several variables on the last two principal components (those associated with the smallest eigenvalues), the opposite of the usual procedure in principal components analysis. Since variation on those components is usually essentially random, any outliers on such a scatterplot probably consist of highly unusual data and should be inspected closely.

ENHANCED SCATTERPLOTS   In addition to these sophisticated procedures, there have been numerous suggestions to improve the performance of the traditional bivariate scatterplot by enhancing it. One of the easiest ways to enhance a scatterplot is to mark the points with something more informative than dots. Some line printer scatter plots have identified the points either by sequence number, as in the KYST/INDSCAL plotting routines (Kruskal, Young & Seery 1977; Pruzansky 1975) or by real labels, as in EXPAK (Thissen & Wainer 1977). It is nice to be able to figure out which point is which, but some data analysts have done much better than that.

Bickel, Hammel & O'Connell (1975) analyzed the relationship between admission rate and the proportion of women applying to the various academic departments at the University of California at Berkeley. When those data are plotted, as they are in Figure 15, with the relative number of applicants determining the size of the box plotted for each department, it is clear that there is a negative correlation. That negative correlation is due almost exclusively to a trend for the large departments. While group size does not always merit such prominence in data display, in this case the enhanced plot provides vital information about the relationship in question. A simpler scatterplot, with identical points for each department, would not show the substantively crucial trend.

Even more elaborate enhancements in the form of informative plotting characters are now easy to find. The scatterplot in Figure 16 appears to be a plot of ozone concentration against solar radiation (each point represents one day's weather and pollution data). But the "weathervanes" plotted instead of points by Bruntz et al (1974) actually reflect three more variables. The size of the circle is temperature, the angle of the line is wind direction, and its length is inversely proportional to wind speed. (High ozone levels are associated with hot, calm days with lots of sunshine.) Bachi (1978b) provides a number of similar graphics; many of them depend on color for their effect and cannot be reproduced effectively here.

But the graphic rational pattern joins the scatterplot (or the two-way table) in Figure 17, which is an unusually precise presentation of data on ages at marriage in the United States. Since the data were categorized on

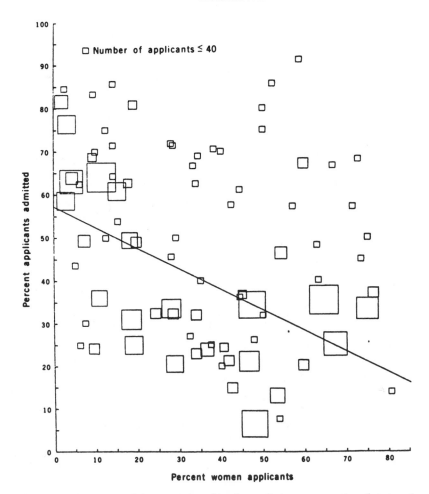

Figure 15 Scatter plot of the proportion of applicants that are women plotted against the proportion of applicants admitted for 85 departments at the University of California, Berkeley; from Bickel et al. (1975). Used by permission.

both the X and Y variables to begin with, the GRPs provide a highly informative way to plot the relationship; the graphic is as precise as a table about the counts and as informative as a scatterplot about the relationship. Any scatterplot which would be more useful if information about counts were added for each data point may be enhanced by plotting GRPs instead of dots. (Imagine Figure 15, the Berkeley data, with the appropriate GRP in place of each square. Is it better?)

The points need not be the entire content of a scatterplot; there are also lines, and some enhancements add more lines. Devlin, Gnandesikan &

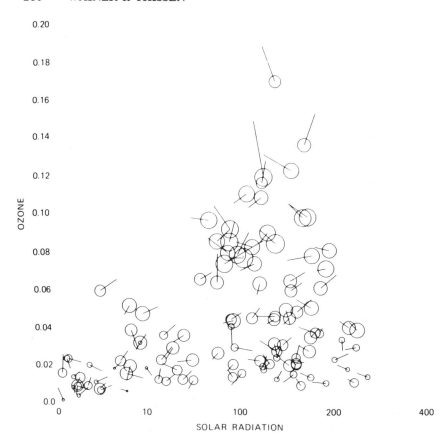

Figure 16   Scatter plot of ozone concentration against solar radiation, from Bruntz et al (1974).

Kettenring (1975) and Gnanadesikan (1977) suggest the addition of "influence function contours" to scatterplots as an aid in the interpretation of correlations and as a technique for spotting outliers. Figure 18 shows such an enhanced scatterplot with several points identified. The "influence contours" are, numerically, the "effect" of any point on that line on the correlation: the number associated with each line is the amount the correlation would change if a point on that line were deleted from the data. In the figure, points numbered 16 and 23 have substantial (opposite) effects on the value of the correlation, which would be more or less unchanged if both were removed but which would change by about 0.025 if only one were deleted. The point marked 42, however much it may seem to be an outlier, is an inconsequential one, having only a negligible effect on the correlation.

Tukey (1972, 1977) generalizes his concept of the box plot into two

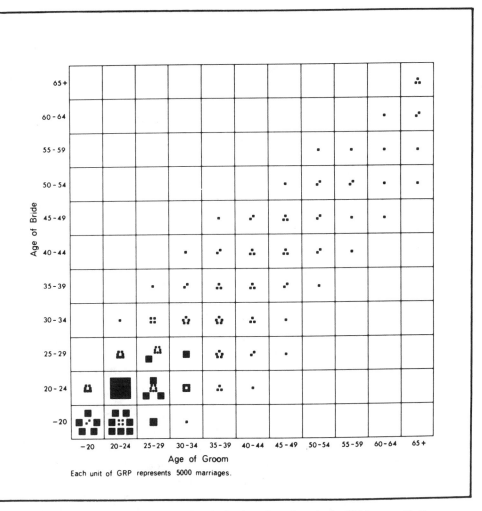

Figure 17   A display of the frequency distribution of marriages in the U.S. by age of brides and grooms, from Bachi (1978b). Used by permission.

dimensions to derive a "schematic (x, y) plot" which may be used to detect outliers and describe the general form of a two-way relationship with few assumptions about the distributional behavior of the data. Cleveland (1979) has proposed the use of robust locally weighted regression lines to enhance the visual impression of the overall trend in a bivariate plot.

There are special techniques—scatterplots which actually represent time-series or trend data; both Tukey (1977) and Cleveland & Kleiner (1975) emphasize the usefulness of lines drawn through moving statistics of one

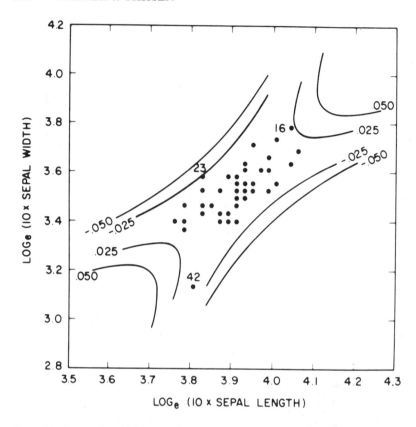

Figure 18 Scatter plot with influence function contours for natural logarithms of sepal length and width of 50 iris setosa, from Gnanadesikan (1977). Used by permission.

sort or another. Figure 19 uses some of those techniques to show that some of the ozone pollution in Ancora, N. J., comes from Philadelphia. While the unadorned scatterplot of ozone concentrations at Ancora against wind direction in Philadelphia shows only a few high points near the vertical line which marks the Philadelphia - Ancora wind direction, the superimposed moving averages show a clear peak and place the blame for the bad air on Philadelphia Tukey (1972) suggested that sometimes this plot should be extended to two cycles (of 360°) so that any effect can be seen in context.

More can be done with scatterplots than was discussed here. But some situations are too complex for even the most enhanced scatterplot, or are not organized well for presentation on coordinate axes. The next section deals with those situations.

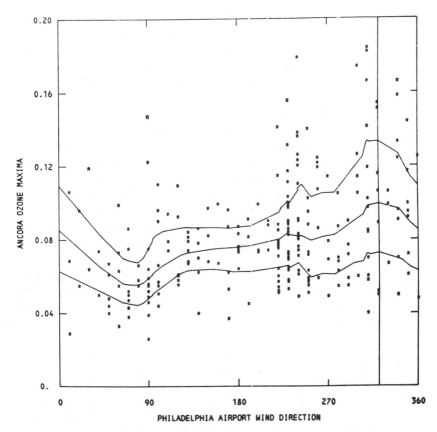

Figure 19 Scatter plot of ozone concentration at Ancora, NJ against wind direction at Philadelphia, enhanced with moving averages, from Cleveland & Kleiner (1975). Used by permission.

Two-Way Displays of Multivariate Data

Until recently, most common display methodologies had to confine themselves to the two dimensions of the plane. Attempts to represent three or more dimensions on a surface involved such devices as multiple-bar charts, subdivided bilateral frequency diagrams, perspective drawings, contour plots, shading variations, etc. These schemes are well known in cartography and their advantages and disadvantages are fully described in Bertin's classic treatise (Bertin 1973). Depiction of more than three dimensions by these techniques was difficult, and the results of some attempts left much to be desired. For example, one attempt to display four dimensions is the Two-Variable Color Map (U. S. Bureau of the Census 1976).

In this display, two statistical variables are represented on top of two geographic ones. One variable is represented on the geographic background by increasing saturations of blue, with the lowest level yellow; the second, with increasing saturations of red, the lowest level again being yellow. Bivariate events are represented by overlaying one color scheme on the other, thus yielding various color mixtures of yellow, green, orange, and purple—in different saturations.

This sort of map, though difficult to describe, is still more difficult to comprehend when viewed. This criticism was leveled by Fienberg (1979) and shown experimentally to be valid by Wainer & Francolini (1980). They reported that a similar conception was published a century earlier by Mayr (1874), who obtained a more evocative image by using the more natural visual metaphor of white (maximally unsaturated) instead of yellow.

Nevertheless, the search for effective multivariate displays was not exhausted by this discovery; not even for just four variables. The last 20 years has seen increased interest in this area by statisticians concomitant with the development and use of multivariate statistical procedures, and a number of interesting suggestions have been made. What follows are some brief descriptions of some of these suggestions, after which we will illustrate them on a sample data set.

TABLES   The initial collection, and hence display, of most data sets begins with a data table. Thus any discussion of multivariate display should start with the table as the most basic construction. Rules for table construction are often misguided, aimed at the use of a table for data storage rather than data exploration or communication. The computer revolution of the past 20 years has reduced the need for archiving of data in tables, but rules for table preparation have not been revised apace with this change in purpose.

Ehrenberg (1977) suggests some very specific preparation rules to allow tables to serve as an effective multivariate display. Among them are: 1. rounding heavily, 2. ordering rows and columns by some aspect of the data, 3. spacing to aid perception, and 4. flanking the display with suitable summary statistics. Chakrapani & Ehrenberg (1976) illustrate this advice on correlation matrices and such matrices as are usually found in factor analysis output. They provide convincing evidence of the efficacy of one digit correlation matrices, omitting values that are sufficiently small. Ramsay (1980) notes that the structure of correlation matrices is exposed better by omitting as much visual clutter as possible (omit decimal points). He generates a series of such matrices, omitting all correlations below a particular size, and then increasing the allowable appearance threshold in each generation. Not only does this increase the readability of the correlation matrix, but often more accurately reflects the precision of the correlation as well. McGill (1978) describes other changes that can be made in tables when they are printed to increase their ability to expose structure. His suggestions center around the notion of making the physical size and/or darkness of the numbers displayed relate to their importance. In some circumstances he emphasizes the especially large ones, in others, the small ones. For other schemes for looking at correlation matrices see Taguri et al (1976). Wainer, Groves & Lono (1980) show that in certain kinds of tasks, for data sets of only modest size and complexity, tables do very well indeed in comparison to other graphical forms. Wainer (1980a) shows that tables are quite effective with young children as well.

Bertin (1977) suggests the use of a "graphical matrix" in which the cells of a matrix representing the observations-by-variables are shaded in by amounts which vary as a function of the size of that cell's data. The rows and columns are then permuted until a simple structure is obtained.

GLYPHS   Anderson (1960) suggested the use of a star-like glyph consisting of a central circle with rays coming out of it, in which each ray corresponded to a variable to be displayed, and the length of the ray to the value of that variable. Variations on this theme abound. For example, one could connect the ends of each of the rays, omitting the rays themselves, preserving only the outline and compare the shapes of the resulting polygons (Siegel, Goldwyn & Friedman 1971). These polygons were used extensively to communicate multivariate health and demographic information for the state of Arkansas (Walls & Epley 1975). Another adaptation of this sort of procedure, the "weathervane" plot (mentioned earlier), was used (with the wind speed represented somewhat backwards) by Bruntz et al (1974) to try to depict the complex dependence of ambient atmospheric ozone on a variety of meteorological variables.

Kleiner & Hartigan (1980) piece together line segments, proportional in length to the variables they represent, to form variable size tree diagrams much like those so commonly used in hierarchical cluster analysis (Gruvaeus & Wainer 1972) to depict multivariate data. This technique capitalizes on the correlational structure among the variables to yield the background against which to display the values of each variable. This technique shows explicitly what the others only suggest. Wakimoto (1977b) proposes another variation on the use of tree diagrams for display, as well (in Wakimoto & Taguri, 1978) as other sorts of special schemes for different purposes.

INSIDE-OUT PLOTS   Ramsay (1980) uses multiple stem-and-leaf diagrams in his "Inside-Out" plots to yield another interesting technique. In an "Inside-Out" plot one arranges the data in a matrix so that the rows are the observations and the columns are the variables (much as is done in Bertin's and Ehrenberg's methods). Next the columns are robustly centered and scaled. This matrix is then row centered by subtracting out row effects, and the residual matrix is examined "Inside-Out."

"Inside-Out" plotting of the residual matrix is Ramsay's principal contribution. We first note that the rows are labeled OUTSIDE the matrix, and the standardized and doubly centered data are INSIDE. We turn this inside-out by preparing a stem representing the data on the outside, and next to the stem (under the appropriate variable name) we plot the label inside. The observations of interest are those which are extreme in one or more of the columns which indicate an unusual interaction between variable and observation.

The contention is that one may be interested, superficially, in the column effects and scales, but they only reflect on the scaling of the variable and are frequently of no more than secondary importance. The row effects reflect the overall level of each observation and are again not of primary interest, especially since such things are easily examined with traditional display methods (e.g. stem-and-leaf diagrams). The data matrix must, of course, be transformed initially to be reasonably symmetric and all the variables should be oriented so that, as much as possible, they form a positive manifold. If this is not done, the row summaries are not very meaningful. What is of interest is the structure of the residuals, which is difficult to see in the ordinary tabular representation. Tukey (1977, Chap. 11-12) presents alternative plots for two-way tables.

FACES   An ingenious method of display, relying on human ability to perceive and remember even small variation in the structure of human faces, was developed and tested by Chernoff (1973, Chernoff & Rizvi 1975). This scheme involves letting the size, shape, or orientation of each feature of a cartoon face represent a particular variable. Thus one might let the size of the eyes represent one variable, the width of the mouth another, the length of the nose a third, and so on. Programs have been developed which will allow the representation of up to 18 variables. How well this scheme performs is not fully explored, although Jacob et al (1976) and Wainer (1979a) have found that human judgment of relative distance between faces is rather good. That is, the clusters of faces produced perceptually correspond closely to those of formal analyses.

FACES have been criticized because the affect associated with a particular variable configuration may work against the message the data structure is trying to convey. For example, if each aspect of the face was being used to represent a subscore on some personality inventory, it would be indeed unfortunate if a depressive was represented by a happy smiling face. Of course, a wisely chosen featural representation restricts this possibility, but care must be taken. Jacob (1976) utilized a careful scaling experiment to allow experts to assign features to variables in such a way so as to optimize the extent to which the hypothetical face described above resembled the personality condition it depicted. Alternative meta-iconic displays based upon Chernoff faces have been proposed for special purposes which do not have this particular problem. Wakimoto (1977a) suggests using whole body graphs, whereas Wainer (1979b) proposed the use of a cartoon rabbit.

OTHER SUGGESTIONS   Andrews (1972) suggested representing each variable as a Fourier component of a periodic function, and thus one could then group variables by the similarity of the observed cyclic function.

There have also been some special purpose displays devised for multivariate contingency tables. One such method, the "floating fourfold circular display" (or 3FCD for short) was described by Fienberg (1975), and is reminiscent of "coxcombs" used by Florence Nightingale (1858). 3FCDs are often helpful for the examination of those discrete multivariate models described in Bishop, Fienberg & Holland (1975). Bachi's (1968) GRPs (mentioned earlier) can also be adapted for such use, as can Wainer & Reiser's (1978) "Cartesian rectangles." Other approaches are described and discussed in Cox & Lauh (1967), Fienberg (1969), and Snee (1974).

A MULTIVARIATE EXAMPLE: THE WORST AMERICAN STATE REVISITED

> Just what such words as progress and civilization mean is often disputed, but no one doubts that such things exist. Holland is obviously a more progressive country than Portugal, and equally obviously France is more civilized than Albania. It is when concrete criteria are set up that dispute begins, for every man tries to measure the level of a given culture by his own yardstick (Angoff & Mencken 1931, p. 1)

Fifty years ago Angoff and Mencken began their comparative study of social indicators in search of "The Worst American State." Having started out with the basic premise that some places are better to live in than others, they go on to quote Todd that,

> We shall have to agree that life on the whole is better than death, that health is better than sickness, that freedom is better than slavery, that control over fate is better than ignorance, that moderate provision for human need is better than chronic lack, that broad interests and moderate desires are better than narrowness and enforced asceticism—

In an effort to reexamine Angoff and Mencken's conclusions half a century later, and to illustrate some of the multivariate display techniques described previously, we gathered recent data for seven of the same variables (from the *Statistical Abstract of the United States: 1977*).

Table 1 shows data on ten states for the seven variables indicated. The form of the table is not a recommended one, but is done in a manner that

Table 1 Excerpted from "Worst American State: Revisited" data

State	Population (1,000s)	Average per capita income ($)	Illiteracy rate (% popul.)	Life expectancy	Homicide rate (1,000)[a]	Percent high school graduates	Average no. days per year below freezing
Alabama	3,615	3,624	2.1	69.05	15.1	41.3	20
California	21,198	5,114	1.1	71.71	10.3	62.6	20
Iowa	2,861	4,628	.5	72.56	2.3	59.0	140
Mississippi	2,341	3,098	2.4	68.09	12.5	41.0	50
New Hampshire	812	4,281	.7	71.23	3.3	57.6	174
Ohio	10,735	4,561	.8	70.82	7.4	53.2	124
Oregon	2,284	4,660	.6	72.13	4.2	60.0	44
Pennsylvania	11,860	4,449	1.0	70.43	6.1	50.2	126
South Dakota	681	4,167	.5	72.08	1.7	53.3	172
Vermont	472	3,907	.6	71.64	5.5	57.1	168

a"Homicide rate per 1,000" is actually combined murders and non-negligent manslaughter per 1,000 population.

Table 2 Table 1 rounded with rows and columns reordered

State	Life expectancy	Homicide rate	Income (100s)	High school grads (%)	Illiteracy rate	Population (100,000s)	No. days of freezing
A. Iowa	73	2	46	59	.5	29	140
B. Oregon	72	4	47	60	.6	23	44
C. South Dakota	72	2	42	53	.5	7	172
D. Calfornia	72	10	51	63	1.1	212	20
E. Vermont	72	6	39	57	.6	5	168
F. New Hampshire	71	3	43	58	.7	8	174
G. Ohio	71	7	46	53	.8	107	124
H. Pennsylvania	70	6	44	50	1.0	119	126
I. Alabama	69	15	36	41	2.1	36	20
J. Mississippi	68	12	31	41	2.4	31	50
Medians	72	6	44	55	.8	26	125

is probably most common. The states are ordered alphabetically; the numbers are given in varying accuracy [population is given to the nearest thousand, life expectancy to the hundreth of a year (4 days)]. It is clear that although the accuracy represented may be justified by the data, it is not the most useful way to show the data for communicative nor exploratory purposes.

Following Ehrenberg's (1977) suggestions, the data were rounded, states were reordered by an aspect of the data (life expectancy), the variables were reordered, and column medians were calculated and shown. In addition, space was used to demarcate Alabama and Mississippi from the rest, which an examination of the data indicates is justified.

Viewing Table 2 tells us much more than was immediately evident from the original data table—that the two southern states are substantially inferior to the other eight on the first five social indicators. We see that California seems to have a relatively high homicide rate and per capita income. Further we get an impression of the overall levels of each of these indicators from the summaries at the bottom of the table, thus adding meaning to any particular entry. We lose the ability to immediately locate any particular state, which does not seem too important in a short list, but which may become more important with larger tables. Ehrenberg (1977) argues that most tables are looked at by individuals who are not naive with respect to their contents, and so have a reasonably good idea about the approximate position of each member. Thus if one looked at the bottom of a list for a state one expected to find there, and only later discovered that it was somewhere else, this would be useful and surprising information. He claims that the losses associated with not having the table in alphabetical order are modest (for most applications) compared to the gains in potential for internal comparisons. The Statistical Atlases of the U. S. published in the latter part of the 19th century presented the data ordered by some meaningful ranking along with some indexing device.

To apply Ramsay's inside-out procedure we rescaled the data in Table 2 so that all variables "pointed in the same direction." Thus illiteracy rate was transformed (by an inverse square root) to a measure of literacy rate, homicide rate became [through –logit (homicide rate)] a function of its complement. Population became log (population) and the square root of income was used. Then we standardized by columns robustly and obtained row effects, which are shown in Figure 20. These are only the main effects, which reaffirm our original observation (from the revamped table) that the two southern states are different. The matrix of residuals was then examined "inside-out" to yield the picture in Figure 21.

We note that despite Iowa's generally high showing in this competition, it has a still higher position on life expectancy than anticipated; and the

STEM & LEAF DISPLAY OF STATE EFFECTS

IOWA, OREGON, CALIFORNIA	1.5	IA OR CA
SOUTH DAKOTA	1.0	SD
VERMONT, NEW HAMPSHIRE, PENNSYLVANIA	0.5	VT NH PA
OHIO	0.0	OH
	-0.5	
	-1.0	
	-1.5	
	-2.0	
ALABAMA	-2.5	AL
MISSISSIPPI	-3.0	MS

Figure 20 Stem-and-leaf display of state effects using the data in Table 1 after column standardizing.

southern states and Pennsylvania seem to have lower life expectancies than would be predicted from their overall showing. Further, we see that California has a higher homicide rate than would be expected as well as a higher income and lower literacy rate. These latter findings are also visible in Table 2, now that we know to look for them. The low literacy rate in California suggests an interpretation based upon its large Spanish speaking population. The reader is invited to further pore over this display for additional information. The stem (scale) is in robust z-scores, and can be approximately interpreted that way. This display has the added advantage of getting better as the data set (number of observations) gets larger. We are typically only interested in observations with large residuals, and so when data bunch up in the middle (as would be the case with a larger data set) we can safely ignore them. Further, this display method works well when data are not scored in the same way, though it does take some preprocessing to get the data reading for plotting. That includes a variety of two-way scatter plots to determine the best orientation of each variable. In this instance we ordered "number of days below freezing" in the same direction as literacy, not because of any love for cold weather, but rather because it was in this direction that it related to all the variables that are easily oriented. (Angoff and Mencken ordered "number of Baptists" as "more = worse" partially because of its high correlation with "number of lynchings" in that orientation).

Shown in Figures 22 and 23 are STARs and Andrews' curves of these same data. Once again we see much the same structure. Both STARS and Andrews' curves show the similarity and isolation of Mississippi and Alabama. STARS seems to show other distinctive features more clearly than

	Life Expectancy	Non-Homicide Rate	Income	% HS Grads	Literacy Rate	Population	# Days Below 0° C
4.0							
3.6							
3.2						AL	
2.8						MS	
2.4	IA		CA				
2.0		MS					
1.6		AL	OH			OH	MS
1.2		SD				PA	AL
0.8	VT	IA NH	PA				
0.4	SD CA OR	PA OH	IA OR AL	CA	SD IA VT	CA	NH VT
0.0		OR		NH OR MS VT	AL OH NH OR		OH PA SD
-0.4	OH	VT		AL OH IA			
-0.8			NH			MS	IA
-1.2	NH		SD	PA		IA OR	
-1.6	AL	CA	MS VT	SD		NH	
-2.0					CA	VT	
-2.4						SD	
-2.8	PA						OR
-3.2							CA
-3.6	MS						
-4.0							

Figure 21   Inside-out plot of the residuals after row and column effects have been removed from the data in Table 1.

do the Andrews' curves. They also allow easier identification of the variables which cause the display to take on a particular shape. Andrews' curves could have accommodated many more variables but not too many more states, whereas STARS could easily have accommodated more states, albeit one would have needed a more clever display format to keep them all identifiable. Also the STAR glyph cannot handle many variables, for even with seven it is hard to remember which is which and thus be able to interpret why a particular state looks as it does. Both of these techniques may be helpful in allowing a visual clustering of the data, although they do not necessarily provide a memorable picture. Both techniques present some difficulties to the observer in the relating of visual features to variables.

As the last example of multivariate display let us consider the use of Chernoff FACES. Before doing this we must assign each variable to a facial feature. This is not always easy, nor is it unimportant. After several tries we arrived at the following scheme:

1. Population → the number of faces/state—The number of faces is proportional to the log of the population. We used one large face in each state for easier identification and as many identical small faces as required. The size of these latter faces was kept small so as to allow us to fit them within the confines of the state boundaries.
2. Literacy rate → size of the eyes (bigger = higher).
3. % HS graduates → slant of the eyes (the more slanted the better).
4. Life expectancy → the length of the mouth (the longer the better).

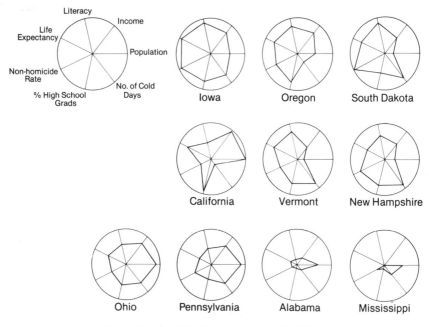

Figure 22   A STAR display of the data in Table 1.

5. Homicide rate → the width of the nose (the wider the nose the lower the homicide rate).
6. Income → the curvature of the mouth (the bigger the smile the higher the income).
7. Temperature → the shape of the face (the more like a peanut the warmer, the more like a football the colder).
8,9. Longitude and latitude → The X and Y position of the face on the cooridinate axes of the paper represent the position of the state.

Thus we tried to use sensible visual metaphors for representing each variable; "bigger = better" was the general rule when normative direction was clear. In the case of a variable (such as weather) where desirability could not be determined easily, we used an aspect of the face that is not ordered. To show the adaptability of the FACE scheme to larger data sets, we prepared a plot involving all 50 states. Similar plots could have been prepared for most other meta-iconic schemes (STARs, TREEs, etc). The resulting plot is shown in Figure 24.

A viewing of the map reveals many things. First, we can see the relative density of population in the East at a glance. Next note the temperature gradient as one goes south from North Dakota to Texas. The Pacific current is also evident. Looking more closely we see that the Deep South looks very

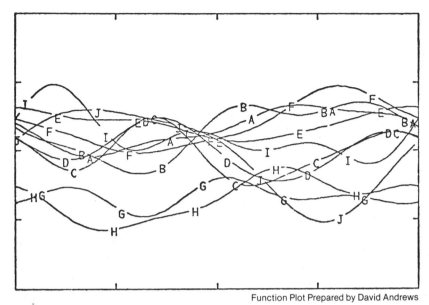

Function Plot Prepared by David Andrews

Legend

A New Hampshire
B Vermont
C Pennsylvania
D Ohio
E Iowa
F South Dakota
G Alabama
H Mississippi
I Oregon
J California

Figure 23 A function plot of the data in Table 1.

homogeneous and low on all variables of quality of life used. Thus we can
see that Angoff and Mencken's finding of Mississippi as the "Worst American State," followed closely by Alabama, South Carolina, Georgia, Arkansas, Tennessee, North Carolina, and Louisiana, is still essentially valid
almost a half century later (at least with these variables). Note further that
New England states (Vermont, New Hampshire, and Maine) look the same:
they are generally high on education variables, as well as having low homicide rates, but seem to have low incomes. Massachusetts seems to have a
somewhat lower literacy rate but a higher per capita income. Connecticut
and New Jersey seem remarkably similar with higher incomes still. We also
see a clustering of mideastern states on all variables (Pennsylvania, Ohio,
Michigan, and Indiana) with the border states of Virginia, West Virginia,

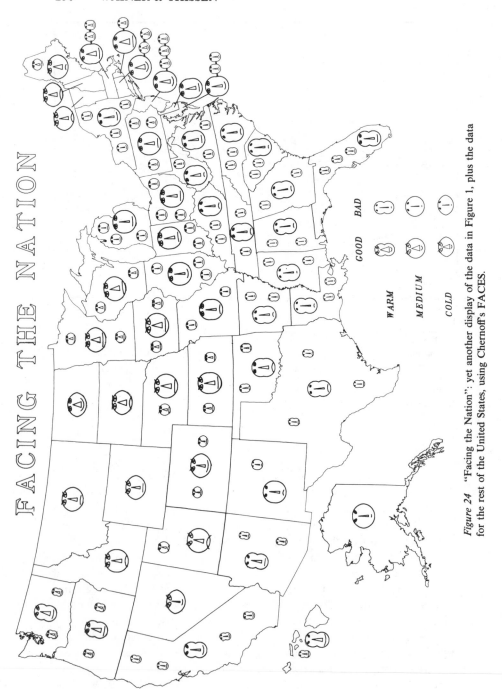

Figure 24 "Facing the Nation": yet another display of the data in Figure 1, plus the data for the rest of the United States, using Chernoff's FACES.

and Kentucky falling somewhere between their rural southern neighbors and their more industrial northern ones.

The Midwest looks homogeneous with the rather surprising difference between North and South Dakota in income. A check back to the original data indicates that this is not a data entry mistake, and there is a substantial difference between these two neighbors. We also note that except for the cold weather, North Dakota seems a pleasant place to live. Utah has an interesting structure, being very high on all variables except income which may reflect the influence of the Mormon church on the state. There are many other interesting similarities that might be noted, and the reader is invited to study the map more closely. As a last comment we draw the reader's attention to the similarity between California and Hawaii. We see benign weather, long life, a high income, low homicide rate, high proportion of high school graduates, but a low literacy rate. This reflects either their high proportion of non-English speaking inhabitants, or a propensity for lotus eating so common in paradise.

Three-and-More-Way Displays of Multivariate Data

Thus far we have restricted ourselves to the description of display methodologies confined to two dimensions of the plotting medium. This was due primarily to the widespread availability of paper and blackboards, and because of the restraints imposed upon us by publication media. Technology is changing, so that in the near future other display modes will be common and will allow the use of more general techniques. Standard graphics terminals running at low baud rates focus attention on the graph as it is generated. There has been some work on the display of data in three-or-more-way displays which is worth mentioning for their future application.

The capturing of complex data structures by adapting dynamic media to the needs of data presentation has been called *kinostatistics* (Biderman 1971). Biderman argues that the communication of such things as changes in rates through time, multidimensional relationships, statistical variance, measures of association, and other complex functions of data can be more efficiently done in a dynamic medium. This was illustrated in a film by Feinberg (1973).

The differences between a display technique designed to communicate with others and one for communication with oneself (data exploration) are small. Thus perhaps Biderman's notion of kinostatistics was formed partially by exploratory suggestions like that of Barnard (1969), who proposed a dynamic four-dimensional display in which one starts with a two-dimensional perspective drawing of a surface y as a function of variables x_1 and

x_2, then by moving the display one can introduce a third variable x_3. He hypothesized further that if one changes with respect to x_3 slowly, one might be able to add another variable x_4 on a much faster cycle. This would present the viewer with [in Kruskal's (1975, p. 32) words], "a pictured surface that heaves (for x_3) and quivers (for x_4)."

A realization of such a scheme was devised by Friedman, Tukey & Tukey (1979) under the general name of PRIM-9. PRIM-9 is a computer based display system which will take a multivariate data set and allow the user to display a scatter plot of any two variables in a traditional way and then rotate, in real time, that plot through any third dimension. To gain some understanding of what this does for the data explorer, consider a three-dimensional set of points in the shape of a donut projected into two-space from the side. A rotation around the X-axis shows the appearance and disappearance of the hole and gives the viewer a strong impression of the shape of the data distribution. With similar kinds of manipulations the experienced PRIM-9 analyst can explore complex data efficiently. PRIM-9 has other features which allow the isolation of certain areas, changes in scale, etc. For a fuller description of this exciting new technique the interested reader can borrow a film from Friedman (at the Stanford Linear Accelerator) which shows PRIM-9 in action.

An extraordinary tour de force of twentieth century display technology was developed by Geoffry Dutton of Harvard, and discussed and displayed at the First General Conference on Social Graphics. This display was a four-dimensional statistical graphic called "Manifested Destiny." The data being displayed were the population distributions of the United States from 1790 until 1970. This was done by generating a contour map of the U. S. in which the heights of the mountains were proportional to the population at that point. One can look at a map of the U. S. from any point of view; usually it is from below Texas, but that is merely convention. In his map Dutton generates one view (from off the coast of Massachusetts) which reflects the 1790 population distribution; another from, say New Jersey, from the 1800 census, and so around the country, until the 1970 census is seen from off the California coast. He then interpolates both geographically and in time to yield many, many views in a relatively smooth set of changes across time and around the country. Next these many pictures were put together into a film strip (one picture/frame), and the film made into a hologram. The hologram image floats inside of what looks like a lampshade and turns before the viewer. As it turns one sees the mountains of population grow westward. The effect is very dramatic indeed.

A useful bibliography of dynamic graphical aids has been compiled by Posten (1976) and subsequently updated (1977).

EVERYTHING ELSE

In the foregoing sections of this review we tried to give the reader a flavor of the exciting developments in the field of graphical data analysis, with an eye toward both the future and the past. In doing so the chapter reads like Stephen Leacock's young man who ran out of his house, jumped on his horse, and galloped off in all directions at once. The sketchy nature of this review is due principally to the vast nature of the topic and the sensible space restrictions under which the authors labored. There are many areas left unmentioned. In this section we shall try to touch a few of these, but will discuss them in far less detail than they merit.

Complexity vs Simplicity

There is a substantial difference in epistemology between the multihued-multidimensioned graphs favored by such organizations as Census (Barabba 1980) and the mass media (Wainer 1980b) and the simple diagrams suggested by the sophisticated statisticians at Bell Labs (Gnanadesikan 1977, 1980). In the former case, an important role of the graphic is to attract attention as well as to inform. In the latter the assumption is that the analyst is already interested, and the motivations are well described by the desiderata at the beginning of the third section (p. 196). The determination of what display methodology should be used must be made by a careful examination of the displayer's purpose. Often a plot will have several purposes and so the displayer must order priorities. Tufte (1977) and Wainer (1977, 1978) warn against trying to do too much; trying to make an exploratory graph a data archive can destroy much of the graph's effectiveness in its primary role.

Tufte (1978) tries to provide a theoretical basis for the development of graphical standards. His basic tenet (although by no means universally accepted) is the same as the architectural one of "less is more." Tufte states (and illustrates) that if a particular piece of a graph can be removed without losing information, then the resulting graph is better than the original. This rule bodes ill for pseudo-perspectival plots often found in newspapers. Tufte calls such extra stuff "chartjunk." From this point of view he defines a measure of the quality of a graph by its "data-ink ratio." This is the ratio of the amount of ink used to depict the data divided by the total amount of ink in the graph. As this ratio approaches unity, so the graph's quality increases. Graphs with a low D-I ratio Tufte dubs "boutique graphics" suitable only for the purpose of decoration.

Much of what Tufte has discovered has its basis in the work of Bertin (1973, 1977), who provides a thorough if idiosyncratic theory of graphic display. Bertin's work has remained largely inaccessible to English reading audiences but will shortly be available in translation (Bertin 1980).

Standards

We have not dealt with the complex issues of graphical standards, although much has been written about them. Graphical standards were a concern in the mid-nineteenth century, and several abortive attempts to develop rules and standards were made in sessions of the International Statistical Institute at the beginning of the twentieth century. In 1914 a joint committee of a number of national associations presented their preliminary report. These rules were published in the *Journal of the American Statistical Association* in 1915 (Joint Committee on Standards for Graphic Presentation, 1915). More recent versions were published in 1979 by the American National Standards Institute, as well as another version by the U. S. Army (1966).

Even though there have been several attempts to revise these rules and standards, for the most part they have stood the test of time rather well. This is partially due to the wisdom of those who originally formulated them and partially because the necessary empirical evidence to challenge these standards has not been gathered. A carefully prepared description of graphical standards and their application was prepared by Schmid & Schmid (1979) which is a revision of Schmid's (1954) first *Handbook*. Although an excellent effort in most regards, even the revision spends a great deal of time (as the 1915 Standards) talking about T-squares and pen nibs and relatively little about Raster scans, refresh tubes, and other output devices of modern technology. This field is vast, but a brief introduction is provided by Teicholz (1976).

Experimental Evidence

Paraphrasing Margerison (1965) [quoted by Kruskal (1975)], "Drawing graphs, like motor-car driving and love-making, is one of those activities which almost every Psychologist thinks he can do well without instruction. The results are of course usually abominable." How do we know that the rules specified by the experts are in fact correct? Bertin provides the rudiments of a theory, as does Bowman (1968), but there is no large body of cohesive evidence to support them. Most work is done piecemeal on one small problem or other without any careful attempt to integrate the findings within the broader context of perceptual and cognitive psychology. In the late 1920s and early 1930s a series of papers explored the relative merits of bar charts, pie charts, etc (Eells 1926, Croxton & Stryker 1927, Huhn 1927, Croxton & Stein 1932). More recently Wainer, Groves & Lono (1978, 1980) continued this in a somewhat broader sense. Wainer (1974) tested some of Tukey's notions about hanging histograms, and Chernoff & Rizvi (1975) conducted some experiments on the stability of the perceptual clusters of faces when the variable-feature assignments were permuted. In cartography there is a more widespread tradition of the testing of new ideas (see for example Castner & Robinson 1969; Crawford 1976; Wainer & Biderman 1977, 1978; Wainer & Francolini 1980). A very extensive and thoughtful review of this area prepared by Macdonald-Ross (1977) is a sensible place for the interested reader to start.

Little formal work has been done on the perceptual efficacy of the techniques that we have described here. For example, there have been some experiments on the use of the scatter plot to visually estimate a correlation (e.g. Strahan & Hansen 1978), but except for Wainer & Thissen's (1979) paper, the bivariate distributions were always Gaussian, and so the Pearson r is always better. In Wainer & Thissen (1979) we showed that when the data were not Gaussian the scatter plot allowed even naive viewers to disregard the outliers to some extent and still accurately estimate the underlying correlation. It is hypothesized that the augmentations to scatter plots mentioned earlier would aid still more, but these were not tested. Relles & Rogers (1977) also looked into the use of a graphical aid for the discovery of outliers. Despite the very poor quality of their graphs, they concluded that their subjects became "fairly robust estimators of location."

Ehrenberg has done some experiments testing his own recommendations, but the results would be more persuasive coming from an independent source. Wainer (1980a) found that children do well with good tables (confirming Ehrenberg's findings), and Wainer, Groves & Lono (1978) found similar results with adults. Yet none of these answers the fundamental question of data graphics. A good graph "forces us to notice what we never expected to see" (Tukey 1977, p. vi). Yet how do we test the extent to which a graph does this? This aspect of graphics research seems to be a perfect question for psychologists—an area that requires a deep knowledge of perception and its associated experimental paradigms. Perhaps this area is one where psychometricians can usefully contribute. Certainly the need of this area is well expressed by the late labor leader John L. Lewis, who when asked what the labor movement wanted replied "More."

We need more experimentation with the innovations developed, we need more careful training in the use of graphs for our students, more integration of results from a variety of disciplines, more flexible graphics software to utilize the astonishing variety of new equipment being produced, and greater acceptance of graphical presentation of data in professional publications.

It is on this last note that we wish to conclude. We began this review noting that the use of graphics by psychologists has lagged far behind their use of elegant statistical procedures. Part of the blame for this appears to be peer pressure suggesting that it is not the work of the scientist to draw little pictures. A second part is economic, which forces journals to warn authors to "limit their use of figures to only those essential for presentation." (Note "essential" not "useful." One rarely gets such a caveat for prose—"use only those words essential.") We are warned that the publication of figures is expensive, yet who is to say that for the conveyance of ideas a figure is not "em for em" (Biderman 1980b) cheaper than the requisite prose.

Are things changing? This chapter represents one change, but it seems clear that the changes were in the wind well before we were invited to prepare this essay. Fienberg (1979) surveyed the statistical literature for graphs in the course of preparing his excellent paper. He found that the use of graphs in the journal *Biometrika* for the display of data hit a peak in the early 1930s and had dropped substantially to remain essentially constant thereafter. The same was true for the *Journal of the American Statistical Association.* We did a similar survey of several psychology journals and found quite a different picture. A smoothed summary of some of what we found is shown in Figure 25, and it is clear that while the use of graphs to communicate data has undergone a sharp renaissance over the past 30 years, there is evidence of a recent decline. We hope that the renewal of interest among statisticians will spark a similar revival in the use of graphs in psychology, for we strongly support Yogi Berra's observation that: "You can see a lot just by lookin'." This chapter has been an attempt to review some new ways to look.

SUMMARY

"Getting information from a table is like
extracting sunlight from a cucumber"
Farquhar & Farquhar, 1891

The disdain shown by the two 19th century economists quoted above reflected a minority opinion at that time. Since then the use of graphs for data analysis and communication has increased in fits and starts. Strangely, we find that the quality of graphs used has not increased since the time of Playfair's invention, and the tables, spoken of so disparagingly by the Farquhars, remain, to a large extent, worthy of contempt. This chapter has been a review of methods, new and old, which improve the way that graphs

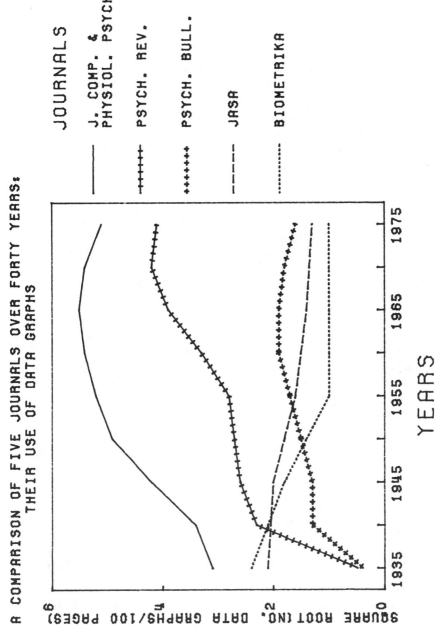

Figure 25 Smoothed plot of the trends in the use of graphs for data display by psychological and statistical journals over the last 40 years.

and tables can be used to aid in the depiction, exploration, summarization, and communication of data.

ACKNOWLEDGMENTS

This chapter owes a great deal of its substance and thought to the help provided by the many colleagues who responded to our initial letters with bibliographies, reprints, preprints, advice, and criticism. We thank you all. Of special help were Albert D. Biderman, William H. Kruskal, Frederick Mosteller, and John W. Tukey, who provided help and advice and supported the notion that research on graphics is a proper pursuit for a scholar, and is not merely the drawing of pictures.

Literature Cited

American National Standards Institute. 1979. *American National Standard Time-Series Charts.* ANSI Y15.2M. New York: Am. Soc. Mech. Eng.

American National Standards Institute. 1979. *American National Standard Illustrations for Publication and Projection.* ANSI Y15.1M. New York: Am. Soc. Mech. Eng.

Anderson, E. 1960. A semi-graphical method for the analysis of complex problems. *Technometrics* 2:387–92

Andrews, D. F. 1978. Exploratory data analysis. *International Encyclopedia of Statistics,* pp. 97–107. New York: Free Press

Andrews, D. F. 1972. Plots of high-dimensional data. *Biometrics* 28:125–36

Angoff, C., Mencken, H. L. 1931. The worst American state. *Am. Mercury* 31:1–16, 175–88, 355–71

Bachi, R. 1968. *Graphical Rational Patterns.* Jerusalem: Israeli Univ.

Bachi, R. 1976. Graphical methods for presenting statistical data: Chairman's comments. *Am. Stat. Assoc. Proc. Soc. Stat. Sect.,* pp. 72–73. Washington DC: Am. Stat. Assoc.

Bachi, R. 1978a. *Graphical statistical methodology in the automation era.* Graphic Presentation of Stat. Inf.: Presented at 136th Ann. Meet. Am. Stat. Assoc., Soc. Stat. Sect. Sess. Graphical Meth. Stat. Data, Boston, 1976. Tech. Rep. 43, pp. 4–6. Washington DC: Census Bureau

Bachi, R. 1978b. Proposals for the development of selected graphical methods. See Bachi 1978a pp. 23–68

Barabba, V. 1980. *The revolution in graphic technology.* Presented at Ann. Meet. Am. Assoc. Adv. Sci., San Francisco

Barnard, G. 1969. Summary remarks. In *New Developments in Survey Sampling,* ed. N. L. Johnson, H. Smith Jr., pp. 696–711. New York: Wiley Interscience

Beniger, J. R., Robyn, D. L. 1978. Quantitative graphics in statistics: A brief history. *Am. Stat.* 32:1–11

Bertin, J. 1973 *Semiologie Graphique.* The Hague: Mouton-Gautier. 2nd ed.

Bertin, J. 1977. *La Graphique et Le Traitement Graphique de L'Information.* Paris: Flammarion

Bertin, J. 1980. *Graphics and the Graphical Analysis of Data,* transl. W. Berg, Tech. Ed. H. Wainer. Berlin: De Gruyter

Bickel, P. J., Hammel, E. A., O'Connell, J. W. 1975. Sex bias in graduate admissions: Data from Berkeley. *Science* 187:398–404

Biderman, A. D. 1971. Kinostatistics for social indicators. *Educ. Broadcast. Rev.* 5:13–19

Biderman, A. D. 1978. *Intellectual impediments to the development and diffusion of statistical graphics, 1637–1980.* Presented at 1st Gen. Conf. Soc. Graphics, Leesburg, Va.

Biderman, A. D. 1980a. *The Playfair Enigma: Toward understanding the development of the schematic representation of statistics from origins to the present day.* Presented at Ann. Meet. Am. Assoc. Adv. Sci., San Francisco

Biderman, A. D. 1980b. The graph as a victim of adverse discrimination and segregation. *Inf. Des. J.* In press

Bishop, Y., Fienberg, S. E., Holland, P. 1975. *Discrete Multivariate Analysis.* Boston: MIT Press

Bock, R. D., Jones, L. V. 1968. *The Measurement and Prediction of Judgement and Choice.* San Francisco: Holden-Day

Bowman, W. J. 1968. *Graphic Communication*. New York: Wiley

Bradley, J. V. 1963. Rank-order correlation scatter diagrams without plotting points. *Am. Stat.* 17:14–15

Brinton, W. C. 1939. *Graphic Presentation*. New York: Brinton

Bruntz, S. M., Cleveland, W. S., Kleiner, B., Warner, J. L. 1974. The dependence of ambient ozone on solar radiation, wind, temperature, and mixing height. In *Preprint vol.: Symp. Atmos. Diffus. Air Pollut. Santa Barbara, Calif.,* pp. 9–13. Boston: Am. Meteorol. Soc.

Castner, H. W., Robinson, A. H. 1969. *Dot Area Symbols in Cartography: The Influence of Pattern on Their Perception.* Am. Congr. Surv. Mapp., Cartogr. Div., Tech. Monogr. CA-4

Chakrapani, T. K., Ehrenberg, A. S. C. 1976. *Factor Analysis or BGA?* Unpublished manuscript Multivar. Study Group of R. Stat. Soc.

Chambers, J. M. 1977. *Computational Methods for Data Analysis*. New York: Wiley

Chernoff, H. 1973. The use of faces to represent points in k-dimensional space graphically. *J. Am. Stat. Assoc.* 68: 361–68

Chernoff, H., Rizvi, H. M. 1975. Effect on classification error of random permutations of features in representing multivariate data by faces. *J. Am. Stat. Assoc.* 70:548–54

Cleveland, W. 1979. Robust locally weighted regression and smoothing scatterplots. *J. Am. Stat. Assoc.* 74:829–36

Cleveland, W., Kleiner, B. 1975. A graphic technique for enhancing scatter plots with moving statistics. *Technometrics* 17:447–54

Cox, D. R. 1978. Some remarks on the role in statistics of graphical methods. *Appl. Stat.* 29:4–9

Cox, D. R., Lauh, E. 1967. A note on the graphical analysis of multidimensional contingency tables. *Technometrics* 9: 481–88

Crawford, P. V. 1976. Optimal spatial design for thematic maps. *Cartogr. J.* 13:145–55

Croxton, F. E., Stein, H. 1932. Graphic comparisons by bars, squares, circles and cubes. *J. Am. Stat. Assoc.* 27:54–60

Croxton, F. E., Stryker, R. E. 1927. Bar charts versus circle diagrams. *J. Am. Stat. Assoc.* 22:473–82

Daniel, C., Wood, F. S. 1971. *Fitting Equations to Data*. New York: Wiley

Denby, L., Mallows, C. L. 1977. Two diagnostic displays for robust regression analysis. *Technometrics* 19:1–13

Devlin, S., Gnanadesikan, R., Kettenring, J. 1975. Robust estimation and outlier detection with correlation coefficients. *Biometrika* 62:531–45

Dixon, W. J., Brown, M. B. 1979. *BMDP: Biomedical Computer Programs, P-series.* Berkeley: Univ. Calif. Press

Dutton, G. 1978. *Manifested destiny: A graphic account of the settlement and growth of America 1790–1970.* Presented at 1st Gen. Conf. Soc. Graphics, Leesburg, Va.

Eells, W. C. 1926. The relative merits of circles and bars for representing component parts. *J. Am. Stat. Assoc.* 21: 119–32

Ehrenberg, A. S. C. 1977. Rudiments of numeracy. *J. R. Stat. Soc. Ser. A* 140: 277–97

Everitt, B. 1978. *Graphical Techniques for Multivariate Data.* London: Heinemann

Farquhar, A. B., Farquhar, H. 1891. *Economic and Industrial Delusions: A Discourse of the Case for Protection.* New York: Putnam

Feinberg, B. M. 1973. *Approaches to Kinostatistics.* 16mm sound/color, 15 min. BSSR

Feinberg, B. M., Franklin, C. A. 1975. *Social Graphics Bibliography.* Washington DC BSSR

Fienberg, S. E. 1969. Graphical analysis of contingency tables. *Appl. Stat.* 18: 153–68

Fienberg, S. E. 1975. PERSPECTIVE CANADA as a social report. *Soc. Indic. Res.* 2:153–74

Fienberg, S. E. 1979. Graphical methods in statistics. *Am. Stat.* 33:165–78

Fisher, N. I. 1979. *Graphical methods in nonparametric statistics: An annotated bibliography.* Tech. Rep. 141, Dep. Math., Univ. Aukland, NZ

Friedman, J., Tukey, J. W., Tukey, P. A. 1979. Approaches to analysis of data that concentrate near higher-dimensional manifolds. *Proc. 2nd IRIA Symp. Data Anal. Informatics,* Versailles, France

Funkhouser, H. G. 1937. Historical development of the graphical representation of statistical data. *Osiris* 3:269–404

Furnival, G. M., Wilson, R. W. 1974. Regression by leaps and bounds. *Technometrics* 16:499–511

Gnanadesikan, R. 1973. Graphical methods for informal inference in multivariate data analysis. *Proc. Int. Stat. Inst. Bull.* 45:195–206

Gnanadesikan, R. 1977. *Methods for Statisti-*

cal Data Analysis of Multivariate Observations. New York: Wiley

Gnanadesikan, R. 1980. *Graphic data analysis: Issues, tools and examples.* Presented at Ann. Meet. Am. Assoc. Adv. Sci., San Francisco

Gorman, J. W., Toman, R. J. 1966. Selection of variables for fitting equations to data. *Technometrics* 8:27–51

Gruvaeus, G. T., Wainer, H. 1972. Two additions to hierarchical cluster analysis. *Br. J. Math. Stat. Psychol.* 25:200–6

Hartwig, F., Dearing, B. D. 1979. *Exploratory Data Analysis,* London: Sage

Hill, M. A. 1979. *Annotated computer output for regression analysis.* Los Angeles: Univ. Calif. Health Sci. Comput. Facil. Tech. Rep. 48

Huber, P. 1972. Robust statistics: A review. *Ann. Math. Stat.* 43:1041–67

Huggins, W. H., Entwisle, D. 1974. *Iconic Communication: An Annotated Bibliography.* Baltimore: Johns Hopkins Univ. Press

Huhn, R. von 1927. Further studies in the graphic use of circles and bars I: A discussion of the Eell's experiment. *J. Am. Stat. Assoc.* 22:31–36

Jacob, R. J. K. 1976 *Computer-produced faces as an iconic display for complex data.* PhD Thesis. Johns Hopkins Univ., Batimore, MD.

Jacob, R. J. K., Egeth, H. E., Bevan, W. 1976. The face as a data display. *Hum. Factors* 18:189–200

Jevons, W. S. 1884. *Investigations in Currency and Finance.* London: Macmillan

Joint Committee on Standards for Graphic Presentation. 1915. Preliminary report. *J. Am. Stat. Assoc.* 14:790–97

Kleiner, B., Hartigan, J. 1980. Representing points in many dimensions by trees and castles. *J. Am. Stat. Assoc.* 75: In press

Kruskal, J. B., Young, F. W., Seery, J. B. 1977. *How to Use KYST 2: A very flexible program to do multidimensional scaling and unfolding.* Murray Hill: Bell Telephone Labs

Kruskal, W. H. 1975. Visions of maps and graphs. In *Auto Carto II: Proc. Int. Symp. Computer-Assisted Cartogr.* Washington DC: Census Bureau

Leinhardt, S., Wasserman, S. S. 1979. Exploratory data analysis: An introduction to selected methods. In *Sociological Methodology,* ed. K. Schussler. San Francisco: Jossey-Bass

Macdonald-Ross, M. 1978. *Research in graphic communication, IET Monogr. 7.* Reprint of "Graphics in texts," in *Rev. Res. Educ.* Vol. 5, 1977: and "How numbers are shown: A review of re-

search on the presentation of quantitative data in texts." *Audio-Vis. Commun. Rev.* 1977, 25:459–509. United Kingdom: Inst. Educ. Tech., Open Univ.

Margerison, T. 1965. Review of *Writing Technical Reports,* by Bruce M. Cooper, *SUNDAY TIMES,* 3 January. Quoted on p. 49 of *A Random Walk in Science,* R. L. Weber, compiler, E. Mendoza, ed. London: Inst. Physics; New York: Crane, Russak

Mayr, G. von. 1874. *Gutachten uber die Anwendung der graphischen and geographischen Methode in der Statistik,* Munich

McGill, R. 1978. *Printing tables to expose structure.* Presented at Ann. Meet. Stat. Assoc., San Diego

McGill, R., Tukey, J. W., Larsen, W. 1978. Variations of box plots. *Am. Stat.* 32(1):12–16

Monkhouse, F. J., Wilkinson, H. R. 1971. *Maps and Diagrams.* London: Methuen

Mosteller, F., Tukey, J. W. 1949. The uses and usefulness of binomial probability paper. *J. Am. Stat. Assoc.* 44:174–212

Mosteller, F., Tukey, J. W. 1968. Data analysis: Including statistics. In *The Handbook of Social Psychology,* ed. G. Lindsey, E. Aronson, pp. 80–203. Reading, Mass: Addison-Wesley

Mosteller, F., Tukey, J. W. 1977. *Data Analysis and Regression.* Reading, Mass: Addison-Wesley

Nie, N. H., Bent, D. H., Hull, C. H. 1975. *SPSS: Statistical Package for the Social Sciences.* New York: McGraw-Hill

Nightingale, F. 1858. *Notes on Matters Affecting Health, Efficiency, and Hospital Administration of the British Army, Founded Chiefly on the Experience of the Late War.* London: Harrison

Playfair, W. 1786. *The Commercial and Political Atlas.* London: Corry

Posten, H. O. 1976. A bibliography on audiovisual materials for statistical education. *Am. Stat.* 30:91–96

Posten, H. O. 1977. Supplement to a bibliography on audiovisual materials for statistical education. *Am. Stat.* 31:163–65

Pruzansky, S. 1975. *How to Use SINDSCAL: A computer program for individual differences in multidimensional scaling.* Murray Hill, NJ: Bell Telephone Labs

Ramsay, J. O. 1980. *Inside-out displays and more.* Presented at Symp. Multivar. Data Display, Psychometric Soc. Meet., Iowa City

Relles, D., Rogers, W. 1977. Statisticians are fairly robust estimators of location. *J. Am. Stat. Assoc.* 72:107–11

Sandiford, P. 1932. *Educational Psychology,* Appendix A. London: Longman's, Green

Schmid, C. F. 1954. *Handbook of Graphic Presentation.* New York: Ronald

Schmid, C. F., Schmid, S. E. 1979. *Handbook of Graphic Presentation.* New York:Wiley. 2nd ed.

Siegel, J. H., Goldwyn, R. M., Friedman, H. P. 1971. Pattern and process in the evolution of human septic shock. *Surgery* 70:232–45

Snee, R. D. 1974. Graphical display of two-way contingency tables. *Am. Stat.* 28:9–12

Strahan, R. F., Hansen, C. J. 1978. Underestimating correlation from scatterplots. *Appl. Psychol. Meas.* 2:543–50

Taguri, M., Hiramatsu, M., Kittaka, T., Wakimoto, K. 1976. Graphical representation of correlation analysis of ordered data by linked vector patterns. *J. Jpn. Stat. Soc.* 6:17–25

Teicholz, E. 1976. Computer graphics: A perspective. Reprint from *Biosciences Communications.* Basel, Switzerland: Karger

Thissen, D. M., Wainer, H. 1977. EXPAK: A computer program for exploratory data analysis. *Appl. Psychol. Meas.* 1:49–50

Tilling, L. 1975. Early experimental graphs. *Br. J. Hist. Sci.* 8:193–213

Tufte, E. R. 1977. Improving data display. Dep. Stat., Univ. Chicago

Tufte, E. R. 1978. Data graphics. First Gen. Conf. Soc. Graphics, Leesburg, Va.

Tufte, E. R. 1979. Personal communication

Tukey, J. W. 1962. The future of data analysis. *Ann. Math. Stat.* 33:1–67

Tukey, J. W. 1972. Some graphic and semigraphic displays. In *Statistical Papers in Honor of George W. Snedecor,* ed. T. A. Bancroft, pp. 293–316. Ames: Iowa State Univ. Press

Tukey, J. W. 1974. Mathematics and the picturing of data. *Proc. Int. Congr. Math., Vancouver*

Tukey, J. W. 1977. *Exploratory Data Analysis.* Reading, Mass: Addison-Wesley

U.S. Bureau of the Census. 1976. *STATUS, A Monthly Chartbook of Social and Economic Trends* (August issue)

U.S. Department of the Army. 1966. *Standards of Statistical Presentation.* Washington DC: GPO

Wainer, H. 1974. The suspended rootogram and other visual displays: An empirical validation. *Am. Stat.* 28:143–45

Wainer, H. 1977. *Data Display—Graphical and Tabular.* Hackensack, NJ: NCCD

Wainer, H. 1978. *Graphical display.* Presented at Eur. Math. Psychol. Assoc., Uppsala, Sweden

Wainer, H. 1979a. About faces in factor analysis. BSSR Tech. Rep. 547–791

Wainer, H. 1979b. The Wabbit: An alternative icon for multivariate data display. BSSR Tech. Rep. 547–792

Wainer, H. 1980a. A test of graphicacy in children. *Appl. Psychol. Meas.* 4:In press

Wainer, H. 1980b. Making newspaper graphs fit to print. In *Processing of Visible Language,* Vol. 2, ed. P. A. Kolers, M. A. Wrolsted. New York: Plenum

Wainer, H., Biderman, A. D. 1977. Some methodological comments on evaluating maps. *Cartogr. J.* 14:109–14

Wainer, H., Biderman, A. D. 1978. Reply to Noyes. *Cartogr. J.* 15:104–5

Wainer H., Francolini, C. 1980. An empirical inquiry into human understanding of 'two variable color maps'. *Am. Stat.* 34:81–93

Wainer, H., Groves, C., Lono, M. 1978. *Some experiments in graphical comprehension.* Presented at Ann. Meet. Am. Stat. Assoc., San Diego

Wainer, H., Groves, C., Lono, M. 1980. On the display of data: Some empirical findings. In preparation

Wainer, H., Reiser, M. 1978. Assessing the efficacy of visual displays. See Bachi 1978a

Wainer, H., Thissen, D. 1979. On the robustness of a class of naive estimators. *Appl. Psychol. Meas.* 4:543–51

Wakimoto, K. 1977a. A trial of modification of the face graph proposed by Chernoff: Body graph. *Quant. Behav. Sci., Kodo Keiryogaku* 4:67–73

Wakimoto, K. 1977b. Tree graph method for visual representation of multi-dimensional data. *J. Jpn. Stat. Soc.* 7:27–34

Wakimoto, K., Taguri, M. 1978. Constellation graphical method for representing multi-dimensional data. *Ann. Inst. Math. Stat.* 30:97–104

Wallis, W. A. 1949. Statistics of the Kinsey Report. *J. Am. Stat. Assoc.* 44:463–84

Walls, R. C., Epley, E. A. 1975. *Ark. Health Graphics,* pp. 15–135. Little Rock: Univ Ark.

Wang, P. C. C. 1978. *Graphical Representation of Multivariate Data.* New York: Academic

Wilk, M. B., Gnanadesikan, R. 1968. Probability plotting methods for the analysis of data. *Biometrika* 55:1–17

Wood, F. 1973. The use of individual effects and residuals in fitting equations to data. *Technometrics* 15:677–95

Ann. Rev. Psychol. 1981. 32:243–78

CHILD PSYCHOPATHOLOGY   ❖345

Alan O. Ross

Department of Psychology, State University of New York, Stony Brook,
New York 11794

William E. Pelham

Department of Psychology, Florida State University, Tallahassee, Florida 32306

CONTENTS

243

0066-4308/81/0201-0243$01.00

Although a great deal of research has been conducted in the area of child psychopathology in the past 15 years, most of the major questions regarding the etiology, nature, treatment, and prognosis of childhood psychological disorders remain unanswered. They remain unanswered for several reasons. Foremost among these are difficulties involved in classifying childhood disorders. When a classification system yields categories which are heterogenous and overlapping, the conclusions which can be drawn from even carefully designed studies are limited. The current state of nomenclature and diagnostic criteria in the field of adult psychopathology is barely more than one of organized confusion, but compared to the chaos that reigns in the realm of child psychopathology it is one of rigorous exactitude.

Secondly, psychopathology in childhood is confounded with the development of cognitive and social behavior. Much child behavior which is viewed as deviant at one age is nonpathological when it occurs at a different developmental stage. There are qualitative age-related changes in the way children process information. The changing nature of behavior and cognition in children makes the study of child psychopathology a more complex task than the study of psychopathology based on the relatively static behavior of adults. Additionally, research in child psychopathology is limited by the state of knowledge about child development. For example, it is difficult to formulate a comprehensive and theoretically solid theory regarding the cause of reading disabilities when so little is known about the development of information processing and the acquisition of reading skills in nondisabled children.

A third reason for the dearth of knowledge in child psychopathology is that children are dependent on environments over which they have little influence and less choice. The reactions of the significant adults in a child's life both determine the child's behavior and influence the identification of the child as disordered. This interaction between adult observers and child behavior thus further complicates research into the nature of child psychopathologies. Finally, interest in conducting research in child psychopathology is relatively new. There have long been speculations regarding the nature of child psychopathology, but the systematic investigation which has characterized the study of adult psychopathology for many years is a relatively recent phenomenon with children. Significant advances in child psychopathology can be expected as programmatic research continues.

For these reasons knowledge about the psychopathology of children is ill defined and poorly understood. A chapter devoted to a review of that field is thus bound to be more a call for much-needed research than an outline of well-established knowledge. Rather than attempt to provide a comprehensive overview of the entire field of child psychopathology, we have chosen to discuss two disorders as illustrative examples. Of the many topics that might have been chosen for elaboration, from aggression and delinquency to fears, phobias, or psychophysiological disorders, we have decided to focus this discussion on one of the most prevalent and one of the rarest of psychological disorders of children: hyperactivity and early infantile autism. These disorders are two of the most widely researched types of child psychopathology, and both the state of knowledge and the problematic issues regarding these disorders are representative of most other categories of the psychological disorders of childhood.

Although they are quite dissimilar on dimensions of incidence, severity, prognosis, and response to treatment, autism and hyperactivity share with other forms of child psychopathology the ambiguity of definition we have just discussed. Thus the children one finds bearing one or the other of these diagnostic labels comprise a heterogeneous group. Given the heterogeneity, it is not at all unlikely that each of the various assertions made about the etiology, nature, and treatment of hyperactive or autistic children may be correct about some of the children who bear one or the other of these labels. By the same token, anyone claiming to have the definitive answer about any one of these aspects for either of these groups of children is more likely wrong than right, as shall become apparent below.

HYPERACTIVITY

Hyperactivity is said to affect approximately 3% to 5% of the elementary-aged population of North America (80% to 90% of them are boys), and these children constitute the largest category of child psychological referrals to mental health and pediatric facilities (Ross & Ross 1976). Although widely used and generally accepted as a label, the term *hyperactivity,* focused as it is on activity level, does not provide an accurate description of the problems of these children. Most contemporary investigators focus more on the cognitive aspects of the disorder than on a child's activity level. Indeed, the disorder is now formally referred to as *attention deficit disorder* (ADD) *with hyperactivity.* Listed below are the diagnostic criteria for this disorder (American Psychiatric Association 1980).

Diagnostic Criteria for ADD with Hyperactivity

The child displays for his or her mental and chronological age signs of developmentally inappropriate inattention, impulsivity, and hyperactivity. The signs must be reported by adults in the child's environment, such as parents and teachers. Because the symptoms are typically variable, they may not be observed directly by the clinician. When the reports of teachers and parents conflict, primary consideration should be given to the teacher reports because of greater familiarity with age-appropriate norms. Symptoms typically worsen in situations that require self-application, as in the classroom. Signs of the disorder may be absent when the child is in a new or a one-to-one situation. The number of symptoms specified is for children between the ages of 8 and 10, the peak age range for referral. In younger children, more severe forms of the symptoms and a greater number of symptoms are usually present. The opposite is true of older children.

A. *Inattention*. At least three of the following:
1. often fails to finish things he or she starts;
2. often doesn't seem to listen;
3. easily distracted;
4. has difficulty concentrating on schoolwork or other tasks requiring sustained attention;
5. has difficulty sticking to a play activity.

B. *Impulsivity*. At least three of the following:
1. often acts before thinking;
2. shifts excessively from one activity to another;
3. has difficulty organizing work (this not being due to cognitive impairment);
4. needs a lot of supervision;
5. frequently calls out in class;
6. has difficulty awaiting turn in games or group situations.

C. *Hyperactivity*. At least two of the following:
1. runs about or climbs on things excessively;
2. has difficulty sitting still or fidgets excessively;
3. has difficulty staying seated;
4. moves about excessively during sleep;
5. is always "on the go" or acts as if "driven by a motor."

D. Onset before the age of 7.
E. Duration of at least 6 months.
F. Not due to schizophrenia, affective disorder, or severe or profound mental retardation.

Problems of Definition

Although this definition is a substantial improvement over previous attempts to define the disorder, there is still considerable work to be done before a reliable and valid definition of hyperactivity is finalized. Consider for example the criterion, "difficulty sitting still or fidgets excessively." Although there have been many attempts to define fidgeting, none has resulted in a scheme which provides reliable data and has sufficient discriminating power to yield useful information regarding individual differences.

Regarding the criteria for inattention, although "easily distracted" is listed as one of the criteria, one of the few consistent findings concerning the attention deficits of hyperactive children is that they do *not* appear to be more easily distracted than nonhyperactive children (Douglas & Peters 1979). As we shall discuss in greater detail below, the exact nature of the attention deficit in hyperactive children is not yet known. It is worth noting that there is widespread disagreement among experimental psychologists regarding the nature of the hypothetical construct of attention (cf Kahneman 1973, Posner 1978). A more precise operationalization of attention deficits in hyperactive children is clearly needed.

An important aspect of hyperactivity is that it is a developmental disorder (Werry 1968), and deviation from age-appropriate norms is thus a criterion for diagnosis. Unfortunately, comprehensive normative information on most of the behaviors described above is lacking. What normative data exist suggest that these behaviors are perceived as relatively common in young, elementary-aged children. Thus teachers of 8-year-old boys view 43% of them as having short attention spans, 44% as restless, 31% as overactive, and 45% as inattentive to directions (Werry & Quay 1971). Clearly the development of solid normative data for the operational criteria of hyperactivity should be a priority for future research. Two available rating scales, the Abbreviated Conners Teacher and Parent Rating Scale (Goyette et al 1978) and the Werry-Weiss-Peters Activity Scale (Routh et al 1974), measure some of the behaviors described earlier as diagnostic criteria, and normative data have been generated for each. Rating scales, however, are particularly susceptible to idiosyncratic interpretation of behavior. Although any one person's rating of a child's behavior may be reliable over time, differences in tolerance across individual raters may reduce the validity of rating scale measures.

Normative data that would provide more reliable and valid diagnostic information than rating scales would come from direct observation of behavior in natural or standardized situations. For example, to obtain reliable information regarding the criterion, "difficulty awaiting turn in games or group situations," it would first be necessary to develop comprehensive sets of norms from many hours of observations of children playing on school playgrounds, using a reliable observational code. Only then could one gather reliable observations on the specific child under diagnostic consideration to determine his or her degree of deviation from the norm. Alternatively, one could develop a standard set of tasks in which a tester and child (or two children) could interact, generate normative data as reliable as those which have been obtained with standardized tests of intelligence, for example, and then use this set of tasks to determine whether a particular criterion for hyperactivity has been met.

Such a process must be completed before we can be very confident that hyperactivity is a valid diagnostic category. During the brief history of the term there has been considerable debate regarding its validity as a diagnostic syndrome. Some research has demonstrated that when different observers rate the presence of behaviors similar to the criteria listed earlier, and the resulting data are factor analyzed, items load on factors which describe the source of the rating rather than a homogeneous diagnostic category which could be labeled *hyperactive* or *hyperkinetic* (Langhorne et al 1976). Other studies have shown that a factor which can be labeled *hyperactivity* emerges when the item pool includes a wide range of relevant descriptors (Lahey et al 1978). Other factor analytic research shows that two subtypes of hyperactive children can be identified: those who present with aggressive symptomatology and those whose problems are primarily attentional in nature (Loney et al 1978). These subtypes appear to be more diagnostically homogeneous than the global syndrome of hyperactivity, and continued research on subgroups will most likely be necessary before reliable etiologic and prognostic correlates of hyperactivity can be identified.

Associated Problems

The symptoms listed as diagnostic criteria provide a definition for hyperactivity, but they do not provide an adequate description of the problems exhibited by the children. The actual problems which result in referral and which are treated are not activity level and inattention, but difficulties in life functioning which result from these behaviors. Presumably as a result of their attention problems, for example, 50% of children labeled hyperactive exhibit significant problems in academic learning severe enough to result in school failure (Safer & Allen 1976). The great majority of hyperactives have difficulty getting along with their parents and teachers, usually because they fail to comply with adult requests or commands (e.g. Barkley & Cunningham 1979). Finally, hyperactive children have seriously disturbed peer relationships. They are nominated as disliked much more often than peers on classroom peer nomination inventories (Pelham & Bender, in press).

These secondary symptoms of hyperactivity have increasingly come to be viewed as critical dimensions of the problem. The interpersonal aggressiveness characteristic of many hyperactives, for example, has been shown to be a better predictor of poor outcome than any of the primary symptoms of attention, impulsivity, or activity (Milich & Loney 1979). As we shall discuss below, the emphasis in treatment has recently shifted from a focus on the primary to a focus on these secondary symptoms.

Prognosis

For many years the clinical lore has been that hyperactive children outgrow their problems when they reach puberty, but a large body of research fails to support this expectation. Given the stormy, conflict-laden childhood and the academic difficulties that are often associated with hyperactivity, it would be surprising if these youngsters' behavior were to be entirely unremarkable once they reached their adolescent and adult years. Several studies have followed hyperactive children into adolescence. They reveal that 50% to 70% of hyperactives have failed at least one grade in school with half of them having failed two grades by the time they reach adolescence (Huessy & Cohen 1976). Twenty-five to 60% of these individuals drop out of school before high school graduation (Huessy et al 1974), while two-thirds of adolescent hyperactives have serious discipline problems at home and at school, with resulting higher rates of school suspensions and expulsions than nonhyperactive controls (Mendelson et al 1971). From 25% to 60% have had contact with legal authorities (Weiss et al 1971), and more hyperactive than comparison adolescents are prone to excessive use of alcohol (Blouin et al 1978). Finally, the most widely cited finding is that a majority of adolescent hyperactives suffer from a chronically low level of self esteem (Weiss et al 1971).

While considerable research is available that attests to the fate of hyperactive children once they reach adolescence, less is known about what happens when they become adults. Long-term follow-up studies have not yet been conducted, and retrospective studies are handicapped by the fact that the term hyperactivity was not in diagnostic usage 20 or 30 years ago. For example, it is not clear that children who were labeled as aggressive and who grew up to manifest sociopathic tendencies (Robins 1979) are the same as those we would now designate as hyperactive. Until children who are clearly diagnosed as hyperactive are followed into adulthood, the issue of long-range prognosis remains unresolved. At a somewhat shorter range, data are becoming available that show that as young adults former hyperactive children have a variety of deficits in the area of social skills and social perception that cause them difficulties in interpersonal relationships (Weiss et al 1979). In any case, it is clear that hyperactive children are at risk for a variety of problems in their later years so that the development of effective treatment methods for this disorder represents an urgent need.

Etiology

During the 1950s and 1960s the prevailing assumption was that hyperactivity was a result of brain damage. This belief resulted from the logical error made when research revealed that WWI combat veterans with confirmed brain injury often exhibited difficulties in abstract thinking, attentional processes, and emotional lability. Because some children with a variety of learning and behavior problems, particularly those labeled *hyperactive* or *learning-disabled,* exhibited similar behaviors, the conclusion was reached that their disturbances also resulted from brain damage (Hallahan & Kauffman 1976), and this notion prevailed for several decades. When it became clear that no evidence of gross brain damage could be demonstrated in the majority of children with these behavioral and learning problems (Ross 1976), the term *minimal brain damage* came into prominence. Because it had no more validity in this application than the term (nonminimal) *brain damage,* this descriptor eventually gave way to *minimal brain dysfunction,* which, together with its abbreviation "MBD," continues to have currency.

The implications involved in applying a label such as *minimal brain dysfunction* to a child with behavior problems of undetermined origin deserve careful consideration (see Ross 1976 for a discussion). In itself the term *minimal brain dysfunction* is innocuous, and if it were used only among professionals to denote their speculations about the state of functioning of a problem child's central nervous system, one would have no need to question it. To the lay public, however, and particularly to a child's parents and teachers, a diagnostic label containing the word *brain* has connotations that are far more dismal and profound than those intended by the professions. Given this state of affairs, we deem it best to limit our terminology to *hyperactivity* in its descriptive sense when talking about the children here under discussion, although it is not unlikely that some type of subtle CNS dysfunction may be involved in an unknown number of cases.

PERINATAL VARIABLES   Since the late 1950s there have been frequent suggestions that behavioral and learning problems often resulted from a variety of biological disturbances in pregnancy and birth (e.g. bleeding in pregnancy, anoxia at birth). The term "continuum of reproductive casualty" has been used to imply not only that *severe* biological disturbances result in profound psychological problems (for example, children with birthweights below 1500 g are often mentally retarded), but also that less serious deviations of pregnancy can result in a variety of less serious behavior disorders.

Because the postulated perinatal disruptions are thought to result in damage to the central nervous system (CNS), they have been considered likely causes of disorders where there is some evidence of neurological dysfunction. Studies which have compared hyperactive children to normal children and to children with other types of behavior disorders often report that on the average hyperactive children have a greater number of "soft" neurological signs than comparison children (Safer & Allen 1976). Research has thus been directed at discovering whether hyperactive children were more likely than controls to have been exposed to a variety of perinatal disturbances. Studies in which mothers were interviewed to provide retrospective information on perinatal disturbances revealed that many such disturbances were reported more frequently for hyperactives than for controls (Werry et al 1964). When Minde et al (1968) reanalyzed the data from the Werry et al (1964) study using medical records rather than parental report, however, they found that the differences between hyperactives and controls were reduced markedly. Objective records of perinatal disturbances generally show few differences between hyperactives and normals. In addition, because perinatal disturbances cannot be identified for *all* children in a hyperactive sample, at the least they must interact with other variables if they are to result in hyperactivity.

Two prospective studies with very large samples have studied the relationship between perinatal disturbances and a variety of later behavior and learning disorders in children including hyperactivity. The Kauai study (Werner 1971) followed 1000 children from pregnancy to the age of 10. No relationship was found between (*a*) 60 selected complications or events which could have occurred during prenatal, labor, delivery, and neonatal periods, and (*b*) teacher-rated presence of symptoms associated with hyperkinesis at age 10 years. The Collaborative Project of the National Institute of Neurologic Diseases and Stroke (NINDS) followed 50,000 pregnancies from the mother's first missed period until the children were 7 years old. From these cases Nichols (1976) examined the relationship between a large number of perinatal factors and "hyperactivity," based on clinic ratings and judgments. Although he found a number of weak relationships, none of the perinatal factors increased the likelihood of "hyperactivity" at age 7 by more than 5%. Support for these findings came from a project which is following 1600 of the children originally included in the NINDS Collaborative Project (Rubin & Balow 1977). A multiple regression analysis revealed that 7 subclasses of 72 perinatal factors accounted for only 13% of the variance of teacher-identified behavior problems (not just hyperactivity) at age 10. Eight percent of the total variance was accounted for solely by the SES of the family and related variables.

In summary, the literature suggests that there are mean differences between hyperactive and control children in the frequency with which a variety of perinatal disturbances occurred. These mean differences, however, are small, and as Rubin & Balow (1977) concluded, except in extreme cases do *not* provide an adequate basis for prediction of school achievement or behavior problems.

MINOR PHYSICAL ANOMALIES   Several investigators have examined a set of neurologically related variables different from the perinatal factors already discussed. There are 17 minor physical anomalies (e.g. epicanthus, low-set ears, curved fifth finger, elongated middle toe) that are formed in early fetal development, known to be affected by genetic, toxic, and other environmental factors, and apparently related more closely to CNS dysfunction than to other types of physical disorders (Rapoport et al 1979). These congenital anomalies are often found in children with Down's syndrome and a wide variety of other behavior disorders (Rubin & Balow 1977). They are presumed to be caused by whatever agent causes the neurological dysfunction assumed to be later manifested in behavior problems.

The relationship between these anomalies and behavior in the school setting has been examined in several samples of children, and results generally reveal a moderate correlation between anomaly score and teacher or peer ratings of behaviors characteristic of hyperactivity and other behavior problems. The most striking finding was reported by Waldrop et al (1978), who measured anomalies in 30 males at birth and 3 years later and in 36 additional boys at age 3 years. All of the boys were then attending a nursery school where observations of play behavior and peer interactions were conducted. Scores from factors representing short attention span, peer aggression, and impulsivity were highly correlated ($r=.67$) with newborn anomaly scores. Inexplicably, however, the correlation dropped to .35 when the entire sample, including those children in whom anomalies were measured only at age 3, was examined. This lower value is closer to that reported in other studies when anomalies and behavior have been measured concurrently (e.g. Halverson & Victor 1976). The higher of the two correlations Waldrop reported may have been a function of the particular sample studied, and replication of their results is needed before they can be accepted without qualification.

Rapoport and her colleagues (Rapoport et al 1979) have conducted series of studies in which they have examined minor physical anomalies in clinically hyperactive children. They have reported that (a) hyperactive children had a higher average anomaly score than nonhyperactive comparison children, (b) the number of anomalies was positively correlated with the degree of teacher-rated problem behaviors, (c) the high-anomaly children were more likely than low-anomaly children to have had a father who remembered himself to have been hyperactive as a child, (d) mothers of high-anomaly children were more likely than mothers of low-anomaly children to have had obstetrical complications during pregnancy (especially bleeding during the first trimester), and (e) anomaly score was *unrelated* to the presence of neurological signs and EEG abnormalities.

Although Rapoport argues that these data point to a major biologic subgroup of hyperactive children, additional research is needed before such a conclusion should be drawn. The fact that no relationship has been identified between anomaly scores and signs of neurological dysfunction contradicts the basic assumption underlying the study of the anomalies. In addition, although the hyperactives studied by Rapoport had higher than average anomaly scores, the mean score reported for the hyperactive group in one early study, 3.58, was lower than the mean anomaly score obtained by a nonhyperactive, conduct disordered group (Quinn & Rapoport 1974) and was apparently obtained by more than 30% of the male infants examined in a normative study (Rapoport et al 1979). The fact that anomalies have been shown to relate to behavior disorders ranging from retardation to "childhood schizophrenia" means that the burden is on researchers to offer a basis for arguing that anomalies are specifically associated with hyperactivity. Though the results reported thus far show some promise, if this line of research is to prove fruitful, it will be necessary to postulate and then demonstrate a theoretical relationship linking specific anomalies, specific genetic or teratogenic mechanisms, specific resulting neurological dysfunction, and specific later behavior patterns and diagnostic categories. Additional research on the significance of the minor physical anomalies is clearly warranted.

DIET   Feingold (1975) hypothesized that hyperactivity is a result of hypersensitivity to artificial colors, artificial flavorings, preservatives BHA and BHT, and naturally occurring salicylates. He suggested that elimination of these substances from hyperactive children's diets would result in remission of their problems. Feingold's hypothesis has not fared well under the scrutiny of scientific inquiry, however.

For example, Conners (1976) used a crossover design in which 15 hyperactive children were placed on the Feingold diet, from which the suspected substances had been eliminated, and on a placebo diet, from which a variety of food types had been randomly selected for elimination. The averaged groups results showed that parent and teacher ratings failed to discriminate reliably between effects of the two diets. Individual data revealed that 1 of the 15 children was rated as showing dramatic improvement and 4 children were rated as moderately improved on the Feingold diet relative to the placebo diet. In a larger study Harley et al (1978b) reported even fewer differences between the Feingold and a placebo diet.

In challenge studies children rated by parents and/or teachers as having shown improved behavior on the Feingold diet are maintained on the diet and then given either active or placebo challenges (single doses) of a blend of food dyes (Harley et al 1978a, Weiss et al 1980). The results of the Weiss et al (1980) study are representative in that only 1 of 22 children was found to show an adverse response to the blend of food dyes. Such results suggest that for the majority of children placed on the Feingold diet the reported improvement in behavior is *unrelated* to the elimination of artificial colors from their diets. Such improvements may either be illusory or the result of parental expectations or attributable to the increased attention given the child as the diet is implemented.

In contrast to these results, Swanson & Kinsbourne (1980) reported dye-induced performance decrements on a paired-associates learning task in 17 of 20 hyperactive children. These children had been given a much larger dose of the color blend, 100 or 150 mg, than those in previous studies. Weiss et al (1980), for example, had used only 35 mg. Swanson & Kinsbourne's results could be a function of (*a*) the higher dosages used compared to other studies, (*b*) the sensitivity of the dependent measure, which was also different from all other studies, (*c*) careful selection of subjects who had been all diagnosed as hyperactive and were responders to methylphenidate. In contrast, none of the subjects in the Weiss et al (1980) study was clinically hyperactive. The results of the Swanson and Kinsbourne study are intriguing and their work calls for replication.

Finally, recent studies have investigated the effect of the food dyes on central or peripheral nervous system functioning in animal subjects. One study showed that the blend of dyes used in human research inhibited neurotransmitter uptake in rat brain homogenate (Logan & Swanson 1979), and further investigation suggested that the effect could have been accounted for by one dye, Red No. 3 or erythrosin (Logan & Swanson 1979). Although other research has shown that erythrosin facilitates release of acetylcholine in frog neuromuscular synapse (Augustine & Levitan 1980) and attenuates the suppressive effects of punishment in rats (Mailman et al 1980), the exact mechanism through which the dye exerts its effect is unknown (Mailman et al 1980), and thus far erythrosin has not been shown to adversely affect hyperactive children (Swanson & Logan 1979).

It appears that from 5% to 10% of hyperactive children exhibit a toxic behavioral response to artificial colors, although neither the exact neural mechanism of this response nor which color is responsible is clear. Very large doses of color apparently increase the percentage of children affected. Further research should focus on three areas: 1. investigation of the other dyes and substances which Feingold has implicated; 2. dose-response studies on the behavioral effects of the dyes; 3. replication and extension of the neurophysiological work which has been done with animals. The challenge design appears to offer most potential for the human studies, especially if objective laboratory and observational measures of behavior are employed.

SUMMARY   We have not been able to review all theories and research into the etiology of hyperactivity. Theories such as Kinsbourne's (1973) theory of developmental lag have not been discussed because, although they are heuristically valuable, there is very little research base on which they can be evaluated. Other areas, such as the recently proposed and theoretically interesting animal models of hyperactivity (see Rosenthal & Allen 1978 or Ferguson & Pappas 1979 for reviews) were omitted because they are less directly related to hyperactivity in children than the research we chose to discuss. Genetics, no doubt an extremely important variable in etiology of hyperactivity, was not covered because at present the research in the area is at an embryonic stage. Although there is preliminary evidence that genetic factors play a role in hyperactivity (Cantwell 1975), the mechanism involved is unclear and definitive studies remain to be done.

Finally, several researchers (Wender 1978, Shaywitz et al 1978) have hypothesized that hyperactive children differ from nonhyperactive comparison children in brain levels of one of the neurotransmitters: serotonin, dopamine, or norepinephrine. When measurement technology in neurochemistry improves, this area of research will be quite critical. Currently brain levels of neurotransmitters can only be inferred from peripheral levels, and the relationship between central and peripheral levels is not well established. There currently is no evidence that hyperactive children differ from nonhyperactive children in brain levels of neurotransmitters (Ferguson & Pappas 1979).

A discussion of the etiology of a problem as poorly defined and as lacking in a generally agreed-upon diagnostic criterion as hyperactivity will of necessity be fraught with ambiguity. Investigators have pursued hypotheses dealing with central nervous system defects, perinatal factors, dietary influences, and other contributing causes. Two points should be apparent. One is that these various hypotheses are not mutually exclusive, and the proposed etiological mechanisms most probably interact. For example, genetic predispositions may set the occasion for an environmental (physiological or psychological) effect on the developing fetus, which results in minor physical anomalies *and* a biochemical imbalance in the central nervous system which manifests itself as a toxic response to food dyes. The second point is that, given the heterogeneous nature of the group of children labeled *hyperactive,* each of these hypothesized causal factors may—alone or in combination with others—be correct for some but not all of these children. The one conclusion that one can draw from the work here reviewed is that further research is essential.

Mediating Variables

A great deal of research has examined the nature of the underlying cognitive and physiological variables which are present in children who demonstrate hyperactivity. Most of the research we shall discuss focuses on the constructs of attention and physiological arousal. As others have noted (Ferguson & Pappas 1979), these are two of the most poorly understood concepts in psychology. It is thus to be expected that there are very few conclusions which can be drawn with conviction regarding this body of research.

PHYSIOLOGICAL AROUSAL   The nature of the behavioral disturbances exhibited by hyperactive children led to early speculation that they suffered from a chronic state of overarousal, while more recent theorists have argued that at least a subgroup of hyperactive children are in a chronic state of underarousal (Satterfield et al 1974). The arousal level of these children has been studied in both the autonomic and the central nervous systems.

Investigators who examined electrodermal measures of arousal compared hyperactive and nonhyperactive children on basal skin conductance level (SCL) and nonspecific galvanic skin responses (GSRs), but none of these studies reported hyperactive children to be overaroused on these measures. An early study reported that hyperactives had lower arousal levels on these measures than comparison children (Satterfield & Dawson 1971), but subsequent research failed to replicate this result (Spring et al 1974, Zahn et al 1975, Ferguson et al 1976). Studies which measured heart rate as an indicator of autonomic arousal also failed to document differences between hyperactives and controls (Zahn et al 1975, Ferguson et al 1976).

Other studies examined arousal differences during task performance, and here the results are more conflicting. In some studies hyperactives showed lower frequencies and lower amplitudes of specific GSR responses to tones or reaction time (RT) stimuli (Zahn et al 1975), but others failed to replicate those findings (Ferguson et al 1976). On another measure of autonomic responsivity, heart rate deceleration, hyperactives have not been shown to be different from comparison children in two studies (Zahn et al 1975, Ferguson et al 1976). In contrast, one study showed that hyperactives exhibited less deceleration than control children (Zahn et al 1978), and one study that did not include controls revealed that hyperactives exhibited a reliable and significant deceleration during a RT foreperiod (Porges et al 1975). Most reviews of the literature conclude that hyperactive children are autonomically less responsive than comparison children (Hastings & Barkley 1978, Ferguson & Pappas 1979), although this conclusion should be viewed as tentative.

Cortical arousal has been examined in several studies. In general, with the majority of hyperactive children differences in tonic or background EEG have not been found when they were compared to appropriate controls (Dubey 1976), although excessive slow wave activity has been reported in a minority of hyperactive children across a number of different experimental samples (Hastings & Barkley 1978). Because control groups have usually *not* included a deviant control, and because there is a 10% to 12% base rate of these abnormalities in normal children (Hastings & Barkley 1978), the significance of these findings is unclear (Dubey 1976). More recent studies have measured cortical arousal by comparing hyperactive and control children on their averaged evoked cortical responses (AERs or EPs) to auditory or visual stimuli. The relationships between the various components of the AER and other physiological and behavioral measures of arousal and attention are not clear, a fact that makes interpretation of these data difficult. Satterfield et al (1974) and Buchsbaum & Wender (1973) obtained results which they interpreted as indicating cortical immaturity and a lower cortical responsivity than age-matched nonhyperactive children. In a study which included an initial and a replication sample, however, Hall et al (1976) completely failed to replicate those results. A subsequent study by Satterfield & Braley (1977) suggested that the discrepant results from a number of previous studies were due to differences in the ages of the samples studied. The investigators studied three age groups of hyperactive and control children (72–84 months, 96–108 months, and 120–144 months) and examined auditory evoked potentials which occurred from 50 msec to 330 msec after auditory clicks. They reported that control children showed no developmental change in the amplitude of an early EP component but did show a decrease in amplitude of a later component with increasing age. In contrast, hyperactive children showed an age-related increase in amplitude of the early component and no age-related changes in amplitude of the later component. On both late and early components, young hyperactive subjects had lower amplitudes than controls, the middle groups did not differ, and older hyperactives had higher amplitudes than controls. Although Satterfield and Braley do not explain how these differences in the early components relate to arousal and attention, they suggest that the late component differences indicate that young hyperactive children are overaroused while the older hyperactives have normal or slightly lower than normal levels of arousal.

In summary, the evidence regarding differences between hyperactive and control children in neurophysiological arousal is conflicting. Most studies fail to find differences between hyperactives and normals. Very few investigators report hyperactive children to be overaroused compared to controls, while a fair number report that hyperactive children exhibit lower responsivity to stimuli, especially in task situations. Ferguson & Pappas (1979) note that the concept of arousal may be too broad to yield meaningful information in this area. The more general theories of over- and underarousal appear to be yielding to theories which are more circumscribed in their hypotheses regarding neurophysiological arousal (e.g. Porges 1976, Rosenthal & Allen 1977). With careful subject definition and selection and with examination of interactions between diagnosis and developmental changes, the more recent theories may yield useful information.

ATTENTION DEFICITS   The change in focus from activity level to attention as the central problem in hyperactivity resulted from a large number of laboratory studies which presumed to demonstrate that hyperactive children have deficits in attention. Yet despite these studies and the consequent adoption of the term *attention deficit disorder,* relatively little is known about the nature of the attention deficit which is presumably found in hyperactive children (Rosenthal & Allen 1977).

The shift in focus from observable activity level to inferred attentional processes began with research in the mid-1960s that was conducted largely by Virginia Douglas and her colleagues in Montreal (reviewed in Douglas 1972). Unfortunately, much of this work entailed a confound that complicates interpretation of these findings as well as most others to date. As Safer & Allen (1976) have pointed out, approximately 50% of the children diagnosed as hyperactive also manifest severe deficits in academic performance so that a substantial number of them are also diagnosed as learning disabled. A good deal of research has demonstrated that learning-disabled children may have some form of attention deficit (Hallahan & Kauffman 1976, Ross 1976, Douglas & Peters 1979, Pelham 1979). Findings on children selected for participation in a study on the basis of their hyperactivity may thus be related to their learning problems unless children with learning problems are screened out so that the sample represents only hyperactive children. Since this was not done in any of the studies to be cited below, it is impossible to interpret their findings in terms of the cognitive factors correlated with hyperactivity per se.

The early work of the Montreal group compared the performance of hyperactive and control children on a number of different laboratory tasks with results that have been widely replicated They were that hyperactive children showed poorest performance on tasks in which attention had to be maintained over a period of time and in which impulsive responding interfered with performance. Thus hyperactives had longer and more variable simple RTs following preparatory intervals (Cohen & Douglas 1972) and made more errors of omission on a continuous performance test of vigilance (Sykes et al 1973). In contrast, hyperactives performed as well as controls in choice RT tasks or self-paced serial RT tasks (Sykes et al 1971). In addition, hyperactives performed more poorly than controls on the Matching Familiar Figures Test, a task which measures the child's ability to match a sample figure with an identical standard and in which careful visual scanning and impulse control are important performance-facilitating characteristics (Campbell et al 1971). Finally, Douglas and her colleagues found no evidence that hyperactive children were more distracted than controls when irrelevant stimuli are present during task performance (Sykes et al 1971, 1973; Campbell et al 1971).

Douglas concluded (a) that hyperactive children have a constitutional inability to sustain attention and to inhibit responding in situations which require focused, directed, and organized effort, and (b) that due to these underlying cognitive deficits, hyperactive children fail to apply sufficient strategic effort in processing information in task settings (Douglas & Peters 1979). This failure is presumed to account for the problems that the children exhibit in a wide variety of academic and social situations.

While the above is the principal contemporary formulation that is meant to account for the attention deficit exhibited by hyperactive children, it is evident that additional research is necessary before the notion of a deficit in sustained attention can be invoked with confidence as the explanation for hyperactivity. For example, clinical observations reveal that the great majority of children diagnosed as hyperactive do pay very careful attention for a substantial period of time in high interest situations, such as watching favorite television shows or playing video games. If a well-designed study were to reveal that the same hyperactive children who show deficient sustained attention in a standard vigilance task maintain attention when watching an interesting television show, it would not be valid to conclude that their problem is a deficit in the *ability* to sustain attention.

Two other aspects of attention which are invoked as important basic cognitive processes more often than vigilance and which therefore might offer more insight into the nature of the cognitive deficit in hyperactivity are selective attention and attentional capacity (Posner 1978). Conners (1976) has hypothesized that hyperactive children exhibit a basic deficit in selective attention. When selective attention is defined as the degree to which performance is disrupted by the presence of irrelevant stimuli, however, no differences in such distractibility have been detected between hyperactive and control children (Douglas & Peters 1979). Further study with more precise measures of selective attention (cf Pelham 1979) than have been used with hyperactives is required before Conners' hypothesis should be rejected, however.

Attentional capacity is a construct that refers to the amount of attentional effort which is allocated to a task or available for allocation. Hyperactive children have difficulties in a variety of complex tasks in which cognitive strategies such as rehearsal would facilitate performance (Douglas & Peters 1979, Weingartner et al 1980). Although Douglas supposed that these processes were disrupted by failure to sustain attention, they would also be disrupted by a limit in the capacity which hyperactives had available for allocation to the task. An analysis of attention deficits which focuses not only on sustained attention but also on selective attention and attentional capacity should help resolve the currently vague and imprecise theorizing regarding attention deficits in hyperactive children.

Treatment

PSYCHOPHARMACOLOGICAL INTERVENTION Pharmacological intervention with one of the CNS psychostimulants is the most common treatment and the current medical treatment of choice for hyperactivity. Approximately 2.5% of all elementary-aged children in North America (600,000 children) are currently receiving stimulant medication for treatment of learning and behavior problems (Weiss & Hechtman 1979).

A very large number of investigations have shown that the psychostimulants dextroamphetamine, methylphenidate, and pemoline are effective in the short-term management of hyperactivity. In approximately 70% of medicated children, the psychostimulants are effective in improving classroom behavior, such as reduced disruptiveness and increased task-relevant, compliant activity (see Sroufe 1975 for a review). The remaining children either fail to show a positive response to psychostimulants or show an adverse response or side effects sufficient to terminate medication (Swanson et al 1978). The improvement which is seen, however, lasts only for as long as the medication is administered. When the effect of the medication wears off, the child's behavior immediately returns to the premedication baseline. This occurs within three to eight hours after ingestion, depending on the type of stimulant, its dosage, and the individual child. In other words, psychostimulant medication does not "cure" hyperactivity, but merely alleviates the primary symptomatology as long as it is exerting a pharmacological effect.

In addition, a number of limitations in the effectiveness of psychostimulants have become apparent. For example, the use of psychostimulants does not appear to be associated with either short-term or long-term improvement in academic performance (Barkley & Cunningham 1978, Rie & Rie 1977) or with long-term improvement of social behavior (Weiss et al 1975). Concern about potentially adverse and dosage-related side effects such as reduction in the rate of weight gain (Safer & Allen 1976; but see also Satterfield et al 1979b) has led clinicians to use dosages smaller than those used in many of the earlier studies. Although there is some evidence that the smaller dosages are clinically useful (Werry & Sprague 1974), it is not abundant. The same concerns over side effects have resulted in a curtailment in the use of medication in the home setting, with the result that when medication is the only treatment given, improvement in the home situation often does not occur (e.g. Sleator & von Neumann 1974). Approximately

10% of hyperactive children (Sleator & von Neumann 1974) respond so positively to a psychostimulant regimen that their behavior reaches the normative range.

A very important recent study showed that the most commonly used psychostimulant, methylphenidate, has different dose-response curves for performance on cognitive tasks and improvement in classroom behavior. The dose which maximized improvement in teacher-rated behavior impaired performance on the cognitive task (Sprague & Sleator 1977). In conjunction with the finding that the short-term benefits of psychostimulants may be state dependent (Swanson & Kinsbourne 1976), this result suggests that psychostimulants should be used in treatment only after very careful consideration. It is worth noting that the stimulants have never been recommended as a sufficient treatment for hyperactivity. Rather they are to be used as an adjunct to educational and psychological interventions.

Finally, although the common belief is that psychostimulants exert a paradoxical effect on hyperactive children, two recent studies suggest that psychostimulant effects on normal children are similar to those seen in hyperactive children (Rapoport et al 1978, Weingartner et al 1980). A great deal of additional research is necessary before complete information about the effects of psychostimulants in hyperactive children is available and their utility in treatment is clear.

BEHAVIORAL INTERVENTIONS   The principal alternative to pharmacological intervention with hyperactivity has been behavior therapy or behavior modification, terms herein used interchangeably.

Although research in the area is relatively recent and thus not abundant, there are strong indications that behavior therapy is an effective form of treatment for hyperactive children. The standard form of behavior therapy used in these studies is characterized by an emphasis on teacher and parent training in contingency management, including the contingent use of attention, consistency of response, incentive systems, daily report cards, and time out from positive reinforcement (see Pelham 1978 for a more extensive description of the standard behavioral approach).

Studies have shown that behavioral interventions result in improvement on a number of dimensions both at home and in school. In the classroom it has been demonstrated (a) that some hyperactive children treated with behavior therapy show the same degree of improvement on standard teacher rating scales and classroom observations of on-task behavior as medicated children (O'Leary & Pelham 1978); (b) that they improve more on these measures than untreated controls (O'Leary et al 1976); and (c) that a behavioral intervention results in a significant decrease in negative nominations on a classroom peer nomination inventory (Pelham et al 1979).

Regarding parent training, it has been shown that parents rate their children as improved following behavioral intervention (Pelham et al 1979) and that observed parent-child interactions improve with behavioral intervention (Pelham et al 1980).

As is the case with medication, however, it has become apparent that while the effects of behavioral intervention with hyperactives are positive, they are not sufficient to bring hyperactive behavior into the normal range. Hyperactive children are usually a standard deviation above the norm on most measures even after behavioral interventions. The failure of standard behavioral interventions to provide maximally effective treatments has led to a search for adjunctive treatments that could be combined with a behavioral treatment to yield a more effective intervention. Studies investigating the effects of training in self-control, or verbal self-instruction, and social skills as adjunctive treatments, however, have thus far yielded data that are equivocal (Hobbs et al 1980; Pelham & Bender, in press).

If behavior therapy alone is to be sufficient treatment, it must be carried out in an intensive fashion over a long period of time by dedicated, well-trained, and consistent parents and teachers. Additional research on the nature of behavioral interventions with hyperactive children is required. Careful research in the functional analytic model relating specific procedures to specific behavior changes is needed, and special attention must be paid to how parents and teachers can be persuaded to implement behavioral procedures with consistency and maintain them over time without ongoing professional help.

COMBINED PROCEDURES   Although it has long been recommended, the combination of pharmacological and behavioral interventions has only been studied recently. Pelham et al (1980) treated eight children with a behavioral intervention and examined the incremental value of low and high doses of methylphenidate by giving medication probes before behavioral intervention began and after it had been implemented for 13 weeks. Maximum improvement on all measures was reached only during the final medication probe when the low or high dose was given; in other words, when the children were receiving both medication and behavioral intervention. For some of the children, the combination of the low dose and behavior therapy resulted in maximum improvement, while for others the higher dose was necessary.

A second study (Pelham et al 1979) examined whether children receiving a low dose of methylphenidate (.3 mg/kg b.i.d.) for the duration of a behavioral intervention lasting 4 months would show greater improvement than those receiving placebo with the behavioral intervention. Results revealed that children improve significantly on all dependent measures relative to no-treatment and contrast treatment groups, but those in the medication group failed to show greater improvement than children in the placebo group. Teacher ratings made midway through treatment when children were still receiving active medication or placebo revealed a main effect of medication.

These results suggest that it is not the effect of medication to facilitate the acquisition of information taught in the behavioral programs, since one would expect that such an effect would be maintained (relative to a placebo group) after medication is terminated. Instead, it seems that the medication simply exerts a main effect which disappears when medication is discontinued. This finding thus contradicts the basic rationale offered for the combination treatment, that medication facilitates the implementation of therapy. The results of the Pelham et al (1979) study must be explained before it can be claimed that children treated with a combination approach will have a better outcome than children not so treated (cf Satterfield et al 1979a). In fact, the state-dependent learning effects discussed above would seem to argue that a combination treatment, while offering the best short-term results, may have serious long-term disadvantages. Further research on the combination treatment is clearly warranted.

EARLY INFANTILE AUTISM

The term early infantile autism is used to describe children who exhibit three primary characteristics; 1. profound and general failure to develop social relationships; 2. profound impairment in the acquisition and use of language for communication, including peculiar speech patterns such as echolalia and pronominal reversal when speech is present; and 3. bizarre and ritualistic responses to various aspects of the environment, such as insistence on the preservation of sameness and peculiar attachment to objects. It is now generally agreed that the onset of the disorder must be before the age of 30 months in order for a child to be diagnosed as a case of early infantile autism (Rutter 1978a, American Psychiatric Association 1980). This is a rare disorder that affects only approximately 4 or 5 out of 10,000 children. As is the case in most disorders of childhood, the frequency of occurrence is higher in males than in females, the ratio of males to females being approximately 3 or 4 to 1 (Rutter & Lockyer 1967, Werry 1979).

Prognosis
Autism falls in the general category of psychotic disorders. For our purpose, the term *psychotic* simply means that disorders so labeled are profound disturbances in functioning. Children labeled autistic display generalized pervasive deficits that usually preclude their functioning outside of an insti-

tutional or otherwise very structured setting. The profound nature of the disorder extends to prognosis. Thus far, only a small proportion of autistic children have ever reached a level of functioning that enables them to live independent lives. In one follow-up study, 63 children were examined from 5 to 15 years after initial hospital contact (Rutter et al 1967, Rutter & Lockyer 1967). Only 5 of these children were found to be in a regular school or occupational setting. Similar outcomes are reported from other follow-up studies (Lotter 1978).

Problems of Definition

It is important to stress that autism and childhood schizophrenia are separate disorders, although both are psychoses. The onset of psychotic disorders in children shows a bimodal distribution. One peak occurs in early infancy, the other in early adolescence. It is relatively rare to find children whose symptoms begin between those modes, though some children do exhibit onset in early or middle childhood (Kolvin 1971a,b). The types of children in these two groups of peak onset are very different. Those with the early onset display the symptoms outlined above for autism while the other group displays symptoms more typical of schizophrenia, so that it is presumed to be related to adult schizophrenia. Little agreement exists regarding the nature of the disorder which begins between the two peak periods (Werry 1979). There is agreement, however, that there is a difference between autism and adult schizophrenia. For example, autistic children generally do not have hallucinations, nor do they develop them in adulthood (Rutter 1978a). The incidence of autism is considerably lower than the incidence of schizophrenia. The incidence of psychotic disorders is not higher in the families of autistic children than in the general population, while it is raised in the families of schizophrenics (Kolvin 1971a,b). Finally, the time course of autism does not show the episodic pattern characteristic of schizophrenia (Rutter 1978a). Although some researchers and clinicians persist in labeling as childhood schizophrenics all children exhibiting psychotic behavior, the consensus is that the two disorders are unrelated (Rutter 1978a, Werry 1979).

One problem in interpreting and comparing studies such as the follow-ups discussed above and those reviewed below is that autistic children and children with other profound disorders have often been grouped together. Differentiation between these disorders must be made if their nature, prognosis, and causes are to be discovered. In view of this we shall attempt to focus our discussion primarily on studies that have separated children labeled *autistic* from those with other psychoses of childhood. Because reliable diagnostic instruments and normative data have not yet been developed, however, it is not always easy to make this discrimination. There is critical need for development of such tools, not only so that one can differentiate autistic from other psychotic children, but also in order to discriminate reliable subgroups within the broader category of autistic children. The same recommendations we made above for development of measures of hyperactivity apply here.

Etiology

ENVIRONMENTAL EXPLANATIONS   Much attention has been devoted to the notion that autism can be explained on the basis of various environmental factors. Although most of these formulations focus on the nature of the parent-child relationship, they have diverse theoretical bases. Ferster (1961) emphasized the reinforcement history of autistic children. He argued that autistic children emit behaviors at a very low frequency, and that those behaviors are not maintained by appropriate responses from the significant adults, especially parents, in the child's life. He further speculated that secondary or generalized reinforcers fail to acquire value for autistic children. In contrast, Bettelheim (1967) posited a dynamic explanation involving negative maternal feelings toward the child, and a resulting lack of mother-child warmth and love, which gives rise to the child's autistic behavior.

One of the telling arguments against the validity of these theories is the relatively low incidence of autism in the siblings of autistic children. If parental psychopathology or parenting style always resulted in autism, siblings would be expected to be affected. As we note below, however, the incidence of autism in siblings of autistics is only 2%. In addition, a large number of empirical findings have failed to provide support for these environmental hypotheses. For example, such formulations depend on the demonstration that the parents of autistic children differ from the parents of nonautistic children. Presenting data consisting of detailed interviews and extensive direct observation and analysis of behavior in the home setting, however, Cantwell et al (1979) showed that parent-autistic child interactions did not differ from parent-dysphasic child interactions.

Reasoning that relatively severe parental psychopathology would be necessary to result in as severe a disorder as autism, McAdoo & DeMyer (1978) compared the MMPI (Minnesota Multiphasic Personality Inventory) profiles of three groups of parents: 1. parents of autistic children; 2. parents of nonpsychotic children who were attending a child guidance clinic for help with various psychological disorders; and 3. parents who were themselves attending an adult outpatient clinic for help with a variety of psychopathological conditions. The results showed no difference on subtest and profile scores between the parents of the autistic and other-disordered children. In addition, scores for both of these groups were significantly lower than were the scores obtained by the adult outpatients. Similar results have been reported by other investigators. There is thus little support for the hypotheses that parents of autistic children are different from parents of other children with severe psychological problems and that they contribute in some unique and sufficient manner to the development of the disorder (Werry 1979).

GENETIC EXPLANATIONS   As noted above, the incidence of autism in the siblings of autistic children is approximately 2%, 50 times greater than the population incidence of autism (Rutter 1967). This fact raises the possibility that there might be a genetic aspect of the etiology of the disorder. Even though the incidence in siblings is higher than expected, however, the fact that it is only 2% means that any hypothesized genetic pathway must be exceedingly complex. The best examination of the possible genetic involvement in autism was reported by Folstein & Rutter (1977). Through an extensive search, they identified an almost exhaustive sample of all twins in Great Britain in which one member of the pair was autistic. Because of the low prevalence of the disorder, the number of pairs finally studied was only 21. Results revealed that 4 of the 11 monozygotic pairs were concordant for autism, while none of the dizygotic pairs showed such concordance. Further, 5 of the 7 monozygotic twins who were *not* concordant for autism did exhibit what Folstein and Rutter called a cognitive/linguistic deficit, characterized by a marked delay in the acquisition of speech and (in three cases) low intelligence. In contrast, only one of the dizygotic twins showed evidence of a cognitive/linguistic deficit. These authors made a strong case for the heritability of some type of cognitive/linguistic impairment, the most severe instances of which result in autism. As discussed in greater detail below, Folstein and Rutter noted that genetic factors appeared to play a clear role in some cases of autism.

In a cautionary note regarding interpretation of these findings, however, Ornitz (1978) pointed out that damage to genetic material which occurs very early in the organism's development can result in the pattern of concordance-discordance found by Folstein and Rutter. Ornitz argued that their results are supportive of genetic damage, though not necessarily of inherited dysfunction. Data which would resolve this question remain to be generated.

NEUROPHYSIOLOGICAL FACTORS   A great deal of evidence suggests that many autistic children have accompanying neurophysiological conditions or stigmata suggestive of CNS damage (Werry 1979). Additionally, a large number of autistic children in whom no neurological disorder is noted in childhood develop seizure activity in adolescence and adulthood, suggesting that some type of CNS dysfunction or damage existed in childhood even though none was noted (Rutter et al 1967). Both early and more recent reviews, however, have noted that research has not reached the point where the precise nature of the mechanism of neurophysiological involvement can be specified (Hingtgen & Bryson 1972, Werry 1979).

Studies of neurophysiological factors have addressed several different issues. For example, in the study discussed above, Folstein & Rutter (1977) had also examined the relationship between severe biological hazards primarily birth-related and concordance/discordance rates. They found a pattern suggesting that biological hazards appeared to be related to autism *only* in twin pairs *discordant* for autism, and further, that biological hazards did not appear to be related to cognitive/linguistic disorder. In other words, they found that the biological hazards studied, each of which had been known to be associated with brain damage, were related to autism in some of the children, while autism in other children was apparently associated only with genetic factors. Genetic and biological factors appeared to operate separately.

The role of biochemical factors in autism was recently reviewed by Ritvo et al (1978). They covered a number of studies that had examined blood and urinary levels of neurotransmitters and their metabolites in autistic and comparison children and concluded that the research has been complicated by a variety of methodological difficulties but that several promising directions have emerged. It would seem, however, that methodological problems preclude even that limited optimism. As Ritvo et al noted, there are two types of problems which must be addressed. First, as we noted above, there exists an insufficient knowledge base, especially with children, regarding the normative relationship between (*a*) blood levels of neurotransmitters and their metabolites, and (*b*) CNS level and function of the transmitters. This knowledge base must be expanded before reliable biochemical studies can be conducted with autistics. Secondly, and also as previously noted, much of the confusion in the literature results from the heterogeneity of the subject population examined. It would seem that not all children who show the behavioral symptoms of autism share the same underlying etiology (Werry 1979). Results from biochemical studies which are averaged over a heterogeneous group of autistic children are not likely to yield a homogeneous explanation. Autistic children should be divided into subgroups based on such factors as type and severity of behavioral and cognitive symptomatology, age, presence of mental retardation, and likely etiology (e.g. genetic vs biological hazard). Only when this is done are biochemical investigations likely to provide information critical to the explanation of autism.

Mediating Variables

LANGUAGE   As noted above, severe deficits in language are a critical aspect of autism, and much research has focused on the nature of this linguistic deficit. One direction which has been taken to study the nature of the autistic language deficit has been to compare linguistic skills in autistic children and nonautistic, dysphasic children (Bartak et al 1975, 1977). These studies have shown not only that autistic children are differentiated from dysphasic children by the behavioral symptoms used to define autism but also that autistic children have a different pattern of linguistic disturbances than dysphasic children. For example, autistics exhibited fewer defects of articulation than dysphasics but more instances of pronominal reversal, echolalia, and other linguistic abnormalities. In addition, autistics showed deficits in the spontaneous use of language compared to the dysphasics, and they also used fewer gestures for the purpose of communication. In fact, Bartak et al (1977) found that a variety of linguistic and cognitive measures differentiated between autistic and dysphasic children as well as the standard behavioral definition of autism. Rutter (1978b) concluded that linguistic disturbances constitute a central feature of the cognitive deficits shown by autistic children, and argued that the deficit was more severe, more extensive, and qualitatively different from the language deficits shown by children with developmental receptive dysphasia.

The exact nature or source of the language deficits shown by autistic children are not known. The successful language training programs developed by some investigators (e.g. Lovaas, see below) seem to suggest that a tightly structured operant approach is quite effective in teaching language to autistic children. Their success implies that whatever the nature of the language block is, it is not so profound that it cannot be overcome with appropriate teaching strategies. In contrast, Churchill (1978) has argued that the language deficit of some autistic children cannot be overcome through the use of operant approaches to language instruction. He reported on two children who could be taught to respond discriminatively to each word of a nine word experimental language (including three nouns, three adjectives, and three verbs), but whose performance broke down when relatively simple levels of grammatical complexity were reached. One child, for example, could discriminate and name objects *or* discriminate and describe position, but was unable to perform both tasks simultaneously.

Although Churchill does not speculate on the underlying cause of the deficit he described, his data would appear to suggest that the language problem results from some permanent CNS dysfunction or damage. While anatomical defects in speech areas of the brain have been reported for some autistic children (DeLong 1978), the nature and locus of presumed CNS damage/dysfunction has not yet been reliably identified. As Werry (1979) notes, if the defects are presumed to have primary impact on language functions, the areas of the brain in which to search for damage are well known.

MEMORY AND ATTENTION   Other investigators have studied the hypothesis that underlying deficits in information processing may be the mediating factors in the language deficits and other cognitive dysfunctions of autistic children. In a review of early literature, Hingtgen & Bryson (1972) suggested that autistic children appeared to have severe deficits in short-term memory, and recent data reported by Lovaas & Newsom (1976) support this conclusion. They found that autistic children apparently exhibited severe performance deficits in a successive matching to sample task when the interval between offset of the first stimulus and onset of the stimuli to be matched was from .5 to 2.0 seconds. Working with an older group of autistics with a higher level of functioning, Hermelin & O'Connor conducted a series of studies (summarized in Hermelin 1978) but failed to find deficits on short-term memory tasks as severe as those reported by Lovaas and Newsom. They did, however, find that autistics did not use memory coding strategies as efficiently as nonautistic children. For example, unlike normal children, the autistic children (as well as deaf comparison children) were unable to recode visually presented stimuli into verbal codes in order to maximize performance. Both of the studies suggest that autistic children have some type of memory deficit, but additional research is needed to clarify the nature of this deficit.

An extensive series of studies examining possible selective attention deficits in autistic children has been conducted by Lovaas and his associates (see Lovaas et al 1979 for a review). Beginning with hypotheses derived from their clinical work in teaching language to autistic children, they found that autistic children's responding came under the functional control of only one or a few of multiple stimuli presented during a variety of discrimination learning tasks. Thus when a stimulus complex consisting of a light, a tactile stimulus, and a white noise was used as the discriminative stimulus, subsequent testing revealed that autistic children had apparently attended to only one of the three stimuli. Retarded comparison children had attended to two stimuli, while normal control children attended to all three (Lovaas et al 1971). Lovaas labeled this behavior "overselective attention" or "stimulus overselectivity." Because most stimuli present in a learning setting are actually irrelevant to establishing a functional, stimulus-response relationship, autistic children's overselectivity makes them likely to focus on irrelevant stimuli in such situations, resulting in the extreme performance deficits and teaching failures so often found. The Lovaas group has demonstrated overselectivity in autistics across a number of settings, spanning different experimental tasks and teaching situations, and they have argued that the notion can be used to explain many of the common behavioral deficits of autistic children. Although Lovaas does not speculate on the nature of a possible underlying neurological substrate for overselectivity, there have been recent speculations attempting to relate attentional dysfunctions to central and peripheral arousal mechanisms in autistics (Porges 1976). In contrast, Lovaas has preferred to view overselectivity as a changeable aspect of an autistic learning deficit. Ross (1976) and Lovaas et al (1979) have both noted that overselectivity is characteristic of very young children and that it changes developmentally. Lovaas and his group have thus focused on developing teaching strategies that can be used to overcome the difficulties imposed by the autistic tendency to overselectivity. A number of quite effective strategies have been discovered (e.g. Schreibman 1975). In general the approach taken has been to emphasize the salience of the relevant stimulus and to decrease both the salience and the number of irrelevant stimuli present during discrimination training. As training proceeds, the salience of the relevant stimulus is gradually faded to its "normal" state, while irrelevant stimuli are concurrently increased in salience and number.

The work of the Lovaas group has been a model of clinical research. Having observed difficulties in the clinical setting, they developed hypotheses about basic processing dysfunctions. They then investigated the nature of the processing deficit in detailed laboratory studies, where more work clearly remains to be done. Finally, they went back and applied in the clinical arena the information developed in the laboratory analyses of the processing problem. This model should be encouraged and imitated in other areas of clinical research.

In addition to the studies of attention and memory just mentioned, an aspect of information processing by autistic children which calls for investigation is their processing capacity (Posner 1978). Churchill's (1978) results suggested that autistic children's language problems were most apparent when the load on the child's processing capacity was increased. Others have noted that autistic children seem to attempt to escape from teaching situations when the demands become great (Carr 1977). Limitations in attentional capacity could result in a variety of the cognitive dysfunctions noted and research is therefore warranted.

While more research is necessary, it appears that the nature of the cognitive deficit in autism involves memory or attention or both. Further studies in this area could draw on the notions currently being investigated in the literature on information processing in adults (Posner 1978). In addition, the research in the area of attention and memory deficits in learning-disabled children (e.g. Pelham 1979, Torgesen & Kail 1980) and mentally retarded children (Brown 1974) provide interesting directions which might be taken in further investigations of cognitive deficit in autism. Careful attention should be paid to methodological issues, as the severe performance deficits of autistic children make it difficult to design, implement, and interpret necessary experiments. Appropriate control subjects must be employed (Hermelin 1978). In addition, simply showing that autistic children perform more poorly than controls in a task does not contribute much to our knowledge of the precise nature of the cognitive deficit. The appropriate experimental design should include manipulation of tasks or task variables with the purpose of demonstrating a group X task interaction (Chapman & Chapman 1974). Only that kind of data will provide precise information regarding cognitive deficits in a target group.

Treatment

PHARMACOLOGICAL INTERVENTIONS   A variety of drugs, ranging from antipsychotics to CNS stimulants, have been administered to autistic children (see Campbell 1978 for a review). Although an abysmal lack of rigorous methodology makes interpretation of this literature difficult, there is no evidence from well-controlled, doubled-blind studies that pharmacological agents are more effective than a placebo in the treatment of autism (Campbell 1978). Some feel that the major tranquilizers are helpful in the management of psychotic children, but the same researchers agree that pharmacological intervention fails to affect the psychotic behavior and severe developmental deviations which constitute the most serious problems for autistic children (Gittleman-Klein et al 1978, Winsberg & Yepes 1978). There is a great need for methodologically more sophisticated research in this area. On the basis of present evidence it appears that pharmacotherapy will prove to be considerably less useful with autistic children than it has with hyperactive children.

TRADITIONAL PSYCHOTHERAPIES   As Werry (1979) notes, the methodology employed in most studies investigating treatment effects of the traditional forms of psychotherapy with autistic children is so deficient that no study can be taken to indicate that such treatment is effective. Untreated control or other comparison groups are rarely included, and treatment gains are rarely quantified. Treatment descriptions are so vague that conclusions about causal relationships between treatment manipulations and behavior change are difficult to determine, and replication is virtually impossible. When traditional psychotherapies, such as play therapy, insight therapy, or other analytically derived techniques, have been compared with other treatments, the more structured, behaviorally oriented forms have been found to produce the greatest behavior change (Ney et al 1971, Schopler et al

1971, Bartak & Rutter 1973, Rutter & Bartak 1973). Until carefully documented research demonstrates otherwise, we must conclude that no approach to psychotherapy with autistic children other than the behavioral one has shown effects which could not be accounted for on the basis of improvement with the passage of time alone.

BEHAVIOR THERAPY   By far the greatest success in treating autistic children has been reported by those researchers who used behavior therapy or behavior modification as the mode of treatment. Several recent and comprehensive reviews of behavioral approaches to treatment of autism are available (Lovaas & Newsom 1976, Rincover & Koegel 1977). In general, these approaches have employed standard operant procedures and other experimentally derived methods to teach these children appropriate behaviors, most notably language, self-help skills, and social interaction, and to decrease the frequency of inappropriate behaviors, such as self-stimulation, self-mutilation, tantruming, and echolalia. The procedures and techniques that have been used included prompting, successive approximation, modeling, differential reinforcement of other behavior (DRO schedules), time out from positive reinforcement, contingent use of positive reinforcement, and punishment. Behavioral approaches have been implemented by trained professionals in laboratory, clinic, and school settings, as well as in home settings by parents who were trained by professionals. The results from many studies with a large number of autistic children are in agreement. Behavior therapy is extremely effective in three domains of autistic behavior: 1. teaching language, 2. increasing the repertoire of appropriate self-help and social behaviors, and 3. decreasing the frequency of inappropriate behaviors. It would be difficult to deny that behavior modification is at this time the treatment of choice for autism.

While careful research has documented the virtues of behavioral approaches to the treatment of autism, it has also revealed their limitations. Early proponents of behavior modification generated the expectation that it could make autistic children behave normally. It is now quite clear that this is not the case. Although treated children develop behaviors that enable them to achieve a higher level of functioning, only those who start treatment very early and at a relatively high level of functioning come to approach behavior which would be considered normal. The remainder are improved but still clearly autistic (Lovaas et al 1973). Nowadays the goal of treatment with the most severely disturbed autistic children often is to help them reach a level of functioning that will enable them to be cared for at home or in community group homes, rather than in large institutional settings.

A second limitation of behavior modification is that its effects are often quite specific to the situations in which treatment was conducted. That is, behaviors trained in one setting by one teacher often fail to generalize to other settings and other persons. Thus children treated in an intensive inpatient program may show lasting treatment gains only if individuals in the setting to which they are returned after discharge continue to employ the same treatment approaches under which the children initially learned (Lovaas et al 1973). We should note that this is a limitation only in the sense that a time-limited treatment does not result in a "cure." If generalization is carefully programmed across both settings and time, it can be expected to occur. If parents are taught to use behavior modification on an ongoing basis, treatment effects will maintain (e.g. Lovaas et al 1973). With continuing, detailed functional analyses of behavior (e.g. Carr 1977) and applications of ingenious and innovative treatments (Rincover & Koegel 1977), additional progress in the behavioral treatment of autism can be expected.

CONCLUDING COMMENT

The research we have discussed regarding autism and hyperactivity is representative of that in other areas of child psychopathology. Reviews of learning disabilities or conduct disorders, for example, would have revealed similar problems of diagnostic heterogeneity, inconsistent experimental findings, and severely limited conclusions regarding etiology, nature, and treatment. Of all recent developments, it would appear that attempts to isolate and study subgroups of diagnostic categories are most likely to contribute to knowledge. In addition, as our knowledge of the normal course of development of information processing, peer relationships, and biochemical and neurological functions increases, we shall be able to formulate and test more useful hypotheses in the study of child psychopathology. These developments and the suggestions we have made should result in major advances in our understanding of child psychopathology. There are currently many more unanswered questions than there are answers.

Literature Cited

American Psychiatric Association. 1980. *Diagnostic and Statistical Manual of Mental Disorders.* Washington DC: Am. Psychiatric Assoc. 494 pp. 3rd ed.

Augustine, G. J., Levitan, H. 1980. Neurotransmitter release from a vertebrate neuromuscular synapse affected by a food dye. *Science* 207:1489–90

Barkley, R. A., Cunningham, C. E. 1978. Do stimulant drugs improve the academic performance of hyperactive children? A review of outcome research. *Clin. Pediatr.* 17:85–93

Barkley, R. A., Cunningham, C. E. 1979. The effects of methylphenidate on the moth-er-child interactions of hyperactive children. *Arch. Gen. Psychiatry* 36:201–11

Bartak, L., Rutter, M. 1973. Special education treatment of autistic children: A comparative study. I. Design of study and characteristics of units. *J. Child Psychol. Psychiatry* 14:161–79

Bartak, L., Rutter, M., Cox, A. A. 1975. A comparative study of infantile autism and specific developmental receptive language disorder. I. The children. *Br. J. Psychiatry* 126:127–45

Bartak, L., Rutter, M., Cox, A. 1977. A comparative study of infantile autism and specific developmental receptive language disorder. III. Discriminant functions analysis. *J. Autism Child. Schizophr.* 7:383–96

Bettelheim, B. 1967. *The Empty Fortress.* New York: Free Press. 484 pp.

Blouin, A. G. A., Bornstein, R. A., Trites, R. L. 1978. Teenage alcohol abuse among hyperactive children: A five-year follow-up study. *J. Pediatr. Psychol.*

Brown, A. L. 1974. The role of strategic behavior in retardate memory. In *International Review of Research in Mental Retardation,* ed. N. R. Ellis, 5:55–111. New York: Academic. 301 pp.

Buchsbaum, M., Wender, P. H. 1973. Averaged evoked responses in normal and minimally brain dysfunctioned children treated with amphetamine. *Arch. Gen. Psychiatry* 29:764–70

Campbell, M. 1978. Pharmacotherapy. See Churchill 1978, pp. 337–56

Campbell, S. B., Douglas, V. I., Morgenstern, G. 1971. Cognitive styles in hyperactive children and the effect of methylphenidate. *J. Child. Psychol. Psychiatry* 12:55–67

Cantwell, D. P. 1975. Familial-genetic research with hyperactive children. In *The Hyperactive Child: Diagnosis, Management, Current Research,* ed. D. P. Cantwell, pp. 93–108. Hollywood, NY: Spectrum. 209 pp.

Cantwell, D. P., Baker, L., Rutter, M. 1979. Families of autistic and dysphasic children. *Arch. Gen. Psychiatry* 36:682–90

Carr, E. G. 1977. The motivation of self-injurious behavior: A review of some hypotheses. *Psychol. Bull.* 84:800–16

Chapman, L. J., Chapman, J. P. 1974. Alternatives to the design of manipulating a variable to compare retarded and nonretarded subjects. *Am. J. Ment. Defic.* 79:404–11

Churchill, D. W. 1978. Language: The problem beyond conditioning. In *Autism: A Reappraisal of Concepts and Treatment,* ed. M. Rutter, E. Schopler, pp. 71–84. New York: Plenum. 540 pp.

Cohen, N. J., Douglas, V. I. 1972. Characteristics of the orienting response in hyperactive and normal children. *Psychophysiology* 9:238–45

Conners, C. K. 1976. Learning disabilities and stimulant drugs in children: Theoretical implications. In *The Neuropsychology of Learning Disorders,* ed. R. M. Knights, D. J. Bakker, pp. 389–404. Baltimore: Univ. Park. 532 pp.

DeLong, G. R. 1978. A neuropsychologic interpretation of infantile autism. See Churchill 1978, pp. 207–18

Douglas, V. I. 1972. Stop, look and listen: The problem of sustained attention and impulse control in hyperactive and normal children. *Can. J. Behav. Sci.* 4:259–82

Douglas, V. I., Peters, K. G. 1979. Toward a clearer definition of the attentional deficit of hyperactive children. In *Attention and the Development of Cognitive Skills,* ed. G. A. Hale, M. Lewis, pp. 173–247. New York: Plenum. 366 pp.

Dubey, D. R. 1976. Organic factors in hyperkinesis: A critical evaluation. *Am. J. Orthopsychiatry* 46:353–66

Feingold, B. F. 1975. *Why Your Child is Hyperactive.* New York: Random. 211 pp.

Ferguson, H. B., Pappas, B. A. 1979. Evaluation of psychophysiological, neurochemical and animal models of hyperactivity. In *Hyperactivity in Children: Etiology, Measurement and Treatment Implications,* ed. R. L. Trites, pp. 61–92. Baltimore: Univ. Park. 241 pp.

Ferguson, H. B., Simpson, S., Trites, R. L. 1976. See Conners 1976, pp. 89–98

Ferster, C. B. 1961. Positive reinforcement and behavioral deficits of autistic children. *Child Dev.* 32:437–56

Folstein, S., Rutter, M. 1977. Infantile autism: A genetic study of 21 twin pairs. *J. Child Psychol. Psychiatry* 18:297–321

Gittleman-Klein, R., Spitzer, R. L., Cantwell, D. P. 1978. Diagnostic classifications and psychopharmacological indications. In *Pediatric Psychopharmacology: The Use of Behavior Modifying Drugs with Children,* ed. J. S. Werry, pp. 136–70. New York: Bruner/Mazel. 416 pp.

Goyette, C. H., Conners, C. K., Ulrich, R. F. 1978. Normative data on revised Conners parent and teacher rating scales. *J. Abnorm. Child Psychol.* 6:221–36

Hall, R. A., Griffin, R. B., Moyer, D. L., Hopkins, K. H., Rapoport, M. 1976. Evoked potential, stimulus itensity and drug treatment in hyperkinesis. *Psychophysiology* 13:405–18

Hallahan, D. P., Kauffman, J. M. 1976. *Introduction to Learning Disabilities: A Psycho-behavioral Approach.* Englewood Cliffs, NJ: Prentice-Hall. 310 pp.

Halverson, C. F., Victor, J. B. 1976. Minor physical anomalies and problem behavior in elementary school children. *Child Dev.* 47:281–85

Harley, J. P., Matthews, C. G., Eichman, P. 1978a. Synthetic food colors and hyperactivity in children: A double-blind challenge experiment. *Pediatrics* 62:975–83

Harley, J. P., Ray, R. S., Tomasi, L., Eichman, P. L., Matthews, C. G., Chun, R., Cleeland, C. S., Traisman, E. 1978b. Hyperkinesis and food additives: Testing the Feingold hypothesis. *Pediatrics* 61:818–28

Hastings, J. E., Barkley, R. A. 1978. A review of psychophysiological research with hyperactive children. *J. Abnorm. Child Psychol.* 6:413–48

Hermelin, B. 1978. Images and language. See Churchill 1978, pp. 141–54

Hingtgen, J. N., Bryson, C. Q. 1972. Recent developments in the study of early childhood psychoses: Infantile autism, childhood schizophrenia and related disorders. *Schizophr. Bull.* 5:8–53

Hobbs, S. A., Moguin, L. E., Tyroler, M., Lahey, B. B. 1980. Cognitive behavior therapy with children: Has clinical utility been demonstrated? *Psychol. Bull.* 87:147–65

Huessy, H., Cohen, A. 1976. Hyperkinetic behaviors and learning disabilities followed over seven years. *Pediatrics* 57:4–10

Huessy, H., Metoyer, M., Townsend, M. 1974. Eight-ten year follow-up of 84 children treated for behavioral disorder in rural Vermont. *Acta Paedopsychiatr.* 40:230–35

Kahneman, D. 1973. *Attention and Effort.* Englewood Cliffs, NJ: Prentice-Hall. 246 pp.

Kinsbourne, M. 1973. Minimal brain dysfunction as a neurodevelopmental lag. *Ann. NY Acad. Sci.* 205:263–73

Kolvin, I. 1971a. Psychoses in childhood—a comparative study. In *Infantile Autism: Concepts, Characteristics and Treatment,* ed. M. Rutter, pp. 7–26. London: Churchill-Livingstone. 328 pp.

Kolvin, I. 1971b. Studies in childhood psychoses. I. Diagnostic criteria and classification. *Br. J. Psychiatry* 118:381–84

Lahey, B. B., Stempniak, M., Robinson, E. J., Tyroler, M. 1978. Hyperactivity and learning disabilities as independent dimensions of child behavior problems. *J. Abnorm. Psychol.* 87:333–40

Langhorne, J. E., Loney, J., Paternite, C. E., Bechtoldt, H. P. 1976. Childhood hyperkinesis: A return to the source. *J. Abnorm. Psychol.* 85:201–9

Logan, W. J., Swanson, J. M. 1979. Erythrosin B. inhibition of neurotransmitter accumulation by rat brain homogenate. *Science* 206:363–64

Loney, J., Langhorne, J. E., Paternite, C. E. 1978. An empirical basis for subgrouping the hyperkinetic/minimal brain dysfunction syndrome. *J. Abnorm. Psychol.* 87:431–41

Lotter, V. 1978. Follow-up studies. See Churchill 1978, pp. 475–95

Lovaas, O. I., Koegel, R. L., Schreibman, L. 1979. Stimulus overselectivity in autism: A review of research. *Psychol. Bull.* 86:1236–54

Lovaas, O. I., Koegel, R. L., Simmons, J. Q., Long, J. S. 1973. Some generalization and follow-up measures on autistic children in behavior therapy. *J. Appl. Behav. Anal.* 6:131–66

Lovaas, O. I., Newsom, C. D. 1976. Behavior modification with psychotic children. In *Handbook of Behavior Modification and Behavior Therapy,* ed. H. Leitenberg, pp. 303–60. Englewood Cliffs, NJ: Prentice-Hall. 671 pp.

Lovaas, O. I., Schreibman, L., Koegel, R. L., Rehm, R. 1971. Selective responding by autistic children to multiple sensory input. *J. Abnorm. Psychol.* 77:211–22

Mailman, R. B., Ferris, R. M., Tang, F. L. M., Vogel, R. A., Kilts, C. D., Lipton, M. A., Smith, D. A., Mueller, R. A., Breese, G. R. 1980. Erythrosin (Red No. 3) and its nonspecific biochemical actions: What relation to behavioral changes? *Science* 207:535–37

McAdoo, W. G., DeMyer, M. K. 1978. Personality characteristics of parents. See Churchill 1978, pp. 251–67

Mendelson, W., Johnson, N., Stewart, M. A. 1971. Hyperactive children as teenagers: A follow-up study. *J. Nerv. Ment. Dis.* 153:273–79

Milich, R., Loney, J. 1979. The role of hyperactive and aggressive symptomatology in predicting adolescent outcome among hyperactive children. *J. Pediatr. Psychol.* 4:93–112

Minde, K., Webb, G., Sykes, D. 1968. Studies on the hyperactive child. VI. Prenatal and paranatal factors associated with hyperactivity. *Dev. Med. Child Neurol.* 10:355–63

Ney, P., Palvesky, A., Markely, J. 1971. Relative effectiveness of operant conditioning and play therapy in childhood schizophrenia. *J. Autism Child. Schizophr.* 1:337–49

Nichols, P. 1976. *Minimal brain dysfunction: Associations with perinatal complications.* Presented at Bienn. Meet. Soc. Res. Child Dev., New Orleans

O'Leary, K. D., Pelham, W. E., Rosenbaum, A., Price, G. 1976. Behavioral treatment of hyperkinetic children: An experimental evaluation of its usefulness. *Clin. Pediatr.* 15:511–15

O'Leary, S. G., Pelham, W. E. 1978. Behavior therapy and withdrawal of stimulant medication with hyperactive children. *Pediatrics* 61:217–21

Ornitz, E. M. 1978. Biological homogeneity or heterogeneity? See Churchill 1978, pp. 243–50

Pelham, W. E. 1978. Hyperactive children. *Psychiatr. Clin. North Am.* 1:217–42

Pelham, W. E. 1979. Selective attention deficits in poor readers? Dichotic listening, speeded classification, and auditory and visual central and incidental learning tasks. *Child Dev.* 50:1050–61

Pelham, W. E., Bender, M. E. 1981. Peer interactions in hyperactive children: assessment and treatment. In *Advances in Learning and Behavioral Disabilities,* Vol. 1, ed. K. D. Gadow, I. Bialer. Greenwich, Conn: JAI Press. In press

Pelham, W. E., Schnedler, R. W., Bologna, N. C., Contreras, J. A. 1980. Behavioral and stimulant treatment of hyperactive children: A therapy study with methylphenidate probes in a within-subject design. *J. Appl. Behav. Anal.* 13:221–36

Pelham, W. E., Schnedler, R. W., Miller, J., Ronnei, M., Paluchowski, C., Budrow, M. S., Marks, D. A., Nilsson, D. E., Bender, M. E. 1979. *The combination of behavior therapy and psychostimulant medication in the treatment of hyperactive children: A therapy outcome study.* Presented at Ann. Meet. Assoc. Adv. Behav. Ther., 13th, San Francisco

Porges, S. W. 1976. Peripheral and neurochemical parallels of psychopathology: A psychophysiological model relating autonomic imbalance to hyperactivity, psychopathy and autism. *Adv. Child Dev. Behav.* 11:36–67.

Porges, S. W., Walter, G. F., Korb, R. J., Sprague, R. L. 1975. The influences of methylphenidate on heart rate and behavioral measures of attention in hyperactive children. *Child Dev.* 46:727–33

Posner, M. I. 1978. *Chronometric Explorations of Mind.* Hillsdale, NJ: Erlbaum. 271 pp.

Quinn, P. O., Rapoport, J. L. 1974. Minor physical anomalies and neurologic status in hyperactive boys. *Pediatrics* 53:742–47

Rapoport, J. L., Buchsbaum, M. S., Zahn, T. P., Weingartner, H., Ludlow, C., Mikkelsen, E. J. 1978. Dextroamphetamine: Cognitive and behavioral effects in normal prepubertal boys. *Science* 199: 560–63

Rapoport, J. L., Quinn, P. O., Burg, C., Bartley, L. 1979. Can hyperactives be identified in infancy? See Ferguson 1979, pp. 103–15

Rie, E. D., Rie, H. E. 1977. Recall, retention and Ritalin. *J. Consult. Clin. Psychol.* 44:250–60

Rincover, A., Koegel, R. L. 1977. Research on the education of autistic children: recent advances and future directions. In *Advances in Child Clinical Psychology,* ed. B. B. Lahey, A. E. Kazdin, 1:329–61

Ritvo, E. R., Rabin, K., Yuwiler, A., Freeman, B. J., Geller, E. 1978. Biochemical and hematologic studies: A critical review. See Churchill 1978, pp. 163–84

Robins, L. N. 1979. Follow-up studies. In *Psychopathological Disorders of Childhood,* ed. H. C. Quay, J. S. Werry, pp. 483–513. New York: Wiley. 542 pp. 2nd ed.

Rosenthal, R., Allen, T. 1978. An examination of the attention, arousal and learning dysfunctions of hyperactive children. *Psychol. Bull.* 85:689–716

Ross, A. O. 1976. *Psychological Aspects of Learning Disabilities and Reading Disorders.* New York: McGraw-Hill, 191 pp.

Ross, D., Ross, S. 1976. *Hyperactivity: Research, Theory, and Action.* New York: Wiley. 385 pp.

Routh, D. K., Schroeder, C. S., O'Tuama, L. A. 1974. Development of activity level in children. *Dev. Psychol.* 10:163–68

Rubin, R. A., Balow, B. 1977. Perinatal influences on the behavior and learning problems of children. See Rincover 1977, pp. 119–60

Rutter, M. 1967. Psychotic disorders in early childhood. In *Recent Developments in Schizophrenia: A Symposium,* ed. A. Coppen, A. Walk, pp. 133–58. Ashford, Kent: Headley. 158 pp.

Rutter, M. 1978a. Diagnosis and definition. See Churchill 1978, pp. 1–26

Rutter, M. 1978b. Language disorder and infantile autism. See Churchill 1978, pp. 85–104

Rutter, M., Bartak, L. 1973. Special educational treatment of autistic children: A comparative study. II. Follow-up findings and implications for services. *J. Child Psychol. Psychiatry* 14:241–70

Rutter, M., Greenfeld, D., Lockyer, L. 1967. A five to fifteen year follow-up study of infantile psychosis. II. Social behavioral outcome *Br. J. Psychiatry* 113:1183–99

Rutter, M., Lockyer, L. 1967. A five to fifteen year follow-up study of infantile psychosis. I. Description of sample. *Br. J. Psychiatry* 113:1169–82

Safer, D. J., Allen, R. P., 1976. *Hyperactive Children: Diagnosis and Management.* Baltimore: Univ. Park. 239 pp.

Satterfield, J. H., Braley, B. W. 1977. Evoked potentials and brain maturation in hyperactive and normal children. *Electroencephalogr. Clin. Neurophysiol.* 43: 43–51

Satterfield, J. H., Cantwell, D. P., Satterfield, B. T. 1974. Pathophysiology of the hyperactive child syndrome. *Arch. Gen. Psychiatry* 31:839–844

Satterfield, J. H., Cantwell, D. P., Satterfield, B. T. 1979a. Multimodality treatment. *Arch. Gen. Psychiatry* 36:965–78

Satterfield, J. H., Cantwell, D. P., Schell, A., Blaschke, T. 1979b. Growth of hyperactive children treated with methylphenidate. *Arch. Gen. Psychiatry* 36:212–17

Satterfield, J. H., Dawson, M. E. 1971. Electrodermal correlates of hyperactivity in children. *Psychophysiology* 8:191–97

Schopler, E., Brehm, S., Kinsbourne, M., Reichler, R. J. 1971. Effect of treatment structure on development in autistic children. *Arch. Gen. Psychiatry* 24: 415–21

Schreibman, L. 1975. Effects of within-stimulus and extra-stimulus prompting on discrimination learning in autistic children. *J. Appl. Behav. Anal.* 8:91–112

Shaywitz, S. E., Cohen, D. J., Shaywitz, B. A. 1978. The biochemical basis of minimal brain dysfunction. *J. Pediatr.* 92:179–87

Sleator, E. K., von Neumann, A. 1974. Methylphenidate in the treatment of hyperactive children. *Clin. Pediatr.* 13:19–24

Sprague, R. L., Sleator, E. K. 1977. Methylphenidate in hyperactive children: Differences in dose effects on learning and social behavior. *Science* 198: 1274–76

Spring, C., Greenberg, L., Scott, J., Hopwood, J. 1974. Electrodermal activity in hyperactive boys who are methylphenidate responders. *Psychophysiology* 11: 436–42

Sroufe, L. A. 1975. Drug treatment of children with behavior problems. In *Review of Child Development Research,* ed. F. Horowitz, 4:347–407. Univ. Chicago Press

Swanson, J. M., Kinsbourne, M. 1976. Stimulant-related state dependent learning in hyperactive children. *Science* 192:1754–55

Swanson, J. M., Kinsbourne, M. 1980. Food dyes impair the performance of hyperactive children on a laboratory learning test. *Science* 207:1485–87

Swanson, J. M., Kinsbourne, M., Roberts, W., Zucker, K. 1978. A time-response analysis of the effect of stimulant medication on the learning ability of hyperactive children. *Pediatrics* 61:21–29

Swanson, J. M., Logan, W. J. 1979. *Effects of erythrosin B (FD & C Red Dye No. 3) on the uptake of neurotransmitters in rat brain homogenate and the behavior of hyperactive children.* Presented at Sci. Symp. Food Drug Adm., 5th, Washington DC

Sykes, D. H., Douglas, V. I., Morgenstern, G. 1973. Sustained attention in hyperactive children. *J. Child Psychol. Psychiatry* 14:213–30

Sykes, D. H., Douglas, V. I., Weiss, G., Minde, K. K. 1971. Attention in hyperactive children and the effect of methylphenidate (Ritalin). *J. Child Psychol. Psychiatry* 12:129–39

Torgesen, J. K., Kail, R. V. 1980. Memory processes in exceptional children. In *Advances in Special Education,* Vol. 1, ed. B. Keogh. Greenwich, Conn: JAI Press. In press

Waldrop, M. F., Bell, R. Q., McLaughlin B., Halverson, C. F. 1978. Newborn minor physical anomalies predict short attention span, peer aggression, and impulsivity at age 3. *Science* 199:563–65

Weingartner, H., Rapoport, J. L., Buchsbaum, M. S., Bunney, W. E., Ebert, M. H., Mikkelsen, E. J., Caine, E. D. 1980. Cognitive processes in normal and hyperactive children and their responses to amphetamine treatment. *J. Abnorm. Psychol.* 89:25–37

Weiss, B., Williams, J. H., Margen, S., Abrams, B., Caan, B., Citron, L. J., Cox, C., McKibben, J., Ogar, D., Schultz, S. 1980. Behavioral response to artificial food colors. *Science* 207: 1487–89

Weiss, G., Hechtman, L. 1979. The hyperactive child syndrome. *Science* 206: 309–14

Weiss, G., Hechtman, L., Perlman, T. 1978. Hyperactives as young adults: School employer and self-rating scales obtained during the ten-year follow-up evaluation. *Am. J. Orthopsychiatry* 48: 439–45

Weiss, G., Hechtman, L., Perlman, T., Hopkins, J., Werner, A. 1979. Hyperactives as young adults. *Arch. Gen. Psychiatry* 36:675–81

Weiss, G., Kruger, E., Danielson, U., Elman, M. 1975. Effect of long-term treatment of hyperactive children with methylphenidate. *Can. Med. Assoc. J.* 112:159–65

Weiss, G., Minde, K., Werry, J. S., Douglas, V. I., Nemeth, E. 1971. Studies on the hyperactive child. VIII. Five-year follow-up. *Arch. Gen. Psychiatry* 24: 409–14

Wender, P. H. 1978. Minimal brain dysfunction: An overview. In *Psychopharmacology: A Generation of Progress,* ed. M. A. Lipton, A. DiMascio, K. F. Killan, pp. 1429–36. New York: Raven. 1731 pp.

Werner, E. E. 1971. *The Children of Kauai.* Honolulu: Univ. Hawaii Press. 199 pp.

Werry, J. S. 1968. Developmental hyperactivity. *Pediatr. Clin. North Am.* 15:581–99

Werry, J. S. 1979. The childhood psychoses. See Robin 1979, pp. 43–89

Werry, J. S., Quay, H. C. 1971. The prevalence of behavior symptoms in younger elementary school children. *Am. J. Orthopsychiatry* 41:136–43

Werry, J. S., Sprague, R. L. 1974. Methylphenidate in children: effect of dosage. *Aust. NZ J. Psychiatry* 8:9–19

Werry, J. S., Weiss, G., Douglas, V. 1964. Studies on the hyperactive child; I—Some preliminary findings. *Can. Psychiatr. Assoc. J.* 9:120–30

Winsberg, B. G., Yepes, L. E. 1978. Antipsychotics (major tranquilizers, neuroleptics). See Gittleman-Klein 1978, pp. 234–73

Zahn, T. P., Abate, F., Little, B. C., Wender, P. H. 1975. Minimal brain dysfunction, stimulant drugs and autonomic nervous system activity. *Arch. Gen. Psychiatry* 32:381–87

Zahn, T. P., Little, B. C., Wender, P. H. 1978. Pupillary and heart rate reactivity in children with minimal brain dysfunction. *J. Abnorm. Child Psychol.* 6:135–48

Ann. Rev. Psychol. 1981. 32:279–305
Copyright © 1981 by Annual Reviews Inc. All rights reserved

COUNSELING PSYCHOLOGY: CAREER INTERVENTIONS, RESEARCH, AND THEORY

◆346

John L. Holland[1]

Department of Social Relations, John Hopkins University, Baltimore, Maryland 21218

Thomas M. Magoon

Counseling Center and Departments of Counseling and Personnel Services and Psychology, University of Maryland, College Park, Maryland 20742

Arnold R. Spokane

Department of Counseling and Personnel Services, University of Maryland, College Park, Maryland 20742

CONTENTS

[1]We gratefully acknowledge the reference assistance provided by Susan R. Spencer and the exceptional manuscript typing by Deloris Holmes, Diane Lewis, and Barbara Germann.

279

0066-4308/81/0201-0279$01.00

Only 15 years ago the study of careers was confined largely to the work of counseling and industrial psychologists and a small cadre of sociologists. In 1980, the study of careers is now on the agenda of every social science: economics, education, political science, sociology, and psychology. Within psychology, careers are now studied by clinical, aging, developmental, educational, personality psychologists and others. At the same time, counseling and industrial psychologists have become more interested in social psychology, learning theory, sociology, and clinical psychology.

This great expansion of interest has led to new knowledge, new perspectives, and also some unintegrated and uninformed effort. This diffuse effort has also made reviews like this one more and more an arbitrary task and less and less the review of a well-defined field that enjoys a consensus about its goals and subject matter. Fields represented by terms such as counseling psychology (formerly counseling and guidance) or career development are now too amorphous and extensive for even a selective review. Other familiar terms such as vocational counseling—if considered narrowly—are too limited to represent the increasing diversity of vocational treatments.

To cope with these ambiguities we have focused our review on career interventions or the multiple forms of vocational assistance: vocational counseling, self-help devices, career courses, occupational information, interest inventories, and vocational card sorts. Career interventions, and the related research and theory, represent one of the core elements of counseling psychology in the past and perhaps the most productive area of practice, research, and theory in more recent years. Unlike some special fields, diverse research and speculation are coming together in substantial and reinforcing ways. This is good news. In addition, career interventions are the most sought after services by college students (Carney et al 1979), and are given a high priority by high school students (Prediger et al 1974). These signs of interest and need are also indicated by the great popularity of self-help vocational books for adults (Bolles 1975) and by national surveys (Kerr & Rosnow 1979). In short, this topic is timely, has been productive, and forms a major and coherent area within the field of counseling psychology. As we indicate above, it spills over into other areas of psychology and social science. Our review is limited almost entirely to the work of psychologists. The integration of the same work for the social sciences calls for another review.

Our review covers the period 1978–1979, but we have also included a few older publications that have gone unappreciated in earlier reviews. For closely related chapters in the *Annual Review of Psychology,* the reader should see Krumboltz et al (1979) and Super & Hall (1978). Likewise, the most recent annual review in the *Journal of Vocational Behavior* has a substantial overlap with our review (Walsh 1979); and Rehberg & Hotchkiss (1979) provide a review of career counseling that entails a more sociological orientation to career counseling, their term for career interventions.

Finally, we have tried to soften our prejudices and to increase the quality of this review by asking 30 colleagues (journal editors, training directors, recent authors of related annual reviews, practitioners, test authors and others) to nominate the most useful articles and books in 1978–1979. This strategy produced more sensible material than APA's all-knowing PASAR.

The review is organized in four main sections: career interventions, vocational research, speculation, and theory. A final section outlines some achievements and directions for new work.

CAREER INTERVENTIONS

The forms of career assistance for people of all ages have undergone a rapid perhaps explosive growth in the 1970s. Before 1970, career assistance was focused principally on high school and college students; in 1980, it is aimed at almost everyone. Before 1970, career assistance was delivered largely through individual counseling and a few large-scale testing programs; in 1980, career assistance is delivered via multiple techniques and treatments: traditional materials and formal courses, computer-assisted career and information systems, tests and inventories, and self-help materials.

The proliferation of materials and techniques has not been accompanied by a similar interest in evaluation. Like the growth of projective devices in another era, new or revised forms of career assistance are easily created; their evaluation comes harder.

Forms of Career Assistance

The distribution of research about the many forms of career assistance is uneven. Regardless of their popularity, the majority of old and new treatments have generated little evaluation or research.

CAREER COUNSELING   Individual counseling is a popular but generally unevaluated technique. The most recent work implies that PhD level career counselors are no more helpful than interest inventories. Three experiments found that the effects of the Self-Directed Search equaled those of counselors (Avallone 1974, Nolan 1974, Krivatsy & Magoon 1976). These unexpected results, the logistic and technical difficulties involved in performing such experiments, and the cost benefit implications of the outcomes may have dimmed interest in further work.

GROUP TREATMENTS   Although no national survey is available, group treatments of all kinds (courses, seminars, workshops, job finding and interviewing, values clarification, special courses for women, retirees, blacks and others) are flourishing. They range from one or two group meetings with simple role-playing activity to semester courses with elaborate materials, texts, and teacher guides.

The most popular form of group treatment is a seminar, course, or workshop. The developers use a wide range of materials, and theoretical orientations and evaluations suggest that diverse treatments have a useful impact (College Entrance Examination Board 1978, Evans & Rector 1978, National Consortium 1978, Bartsch & Hackett 1979, Heppner & Krause 1979, Super & Harris-Bowlsbey 1979, Winefordner 1979). The evaluations also suggest new treatment ideas, but like psychotherapy evaluations, it is difficult to attribute outcomes to a specific experience or to generalize from one course to the next.

INSTRUCTIONAL MATERIALS   This may be the decade of workbooks, texts and related printed materials written to help people find jobs, create resumes, decide on what job, and cope with interviewers and vocational crises (Bartsch & Sandmeyer 1979, Figler 1979). These materials are produced by amateurs, professionals, school systems, colleges, and entrepreneurs. With a few exceptions, evaluations usually entail enthusiastic endorsements by authors. However, the use of some materials in courses and workshops has received repeated positive student ratings (Evans & Rector 1978, Lawler 1979).

This is an area of research and development that has been neglected by psychologists yet needs comprehensive and hard-headed evaluation. Some evaluations imply that insightful amateurs have some ideas that warrant attention, testing, and perhaps greater use and extension (Atlas et al 1977).

OCCUPATIONAL INFORMATION   The organization and use of occupational information for decision making has become an almost lively topic after many years of disinterest. The *Dictionary of Occupational Titles* has been evaluated by a select committee (Miller et al 1980). The Department of Labor has prepared a special volume to simplify and stimulate occupational exploration (U.S. Department of Labor 1979) and has prepared a compatible interest inventory to accompany the *Guide to Occupational Exploration* (GOE).

Along with these national efforts, there are some promising research beginnings concerned with either what people know about occupations (Loesch et al 1978, Loesch & Sampson 1978) or techniques for stimulating occupational exploration (Bostaph & Moore 1979, Fifield & Petersen 1978, Harris & Wallin 1978, Young 1979). Until recently there were no published data about the amount of occupational information possessed by any segment of the population (Tiedeman et al 1978). Harris & Wallin (1978) and Malett et al (1978) demonstrate how a person's vocational aspirations can be manipulated by the amount and kind of information provided. Haase et al (1979) show experimentally that the presentation of both positive and negative occupational information increases the cognitive complexity of a person's occupational perceptions. In contrast, the presentation of only positive information increases the simplicity of perceptions. These beginnings may make it possible to dispense occupational information in more compatible and beneficial ways. This work may also provide one of the keys to the understanding of treatment effects.

INTEREST INVENTORIES   Interest inventories remain perhaps the most popular form of vocational assistance. This popularity is manifested in the publication of new inventories, the rapid revision of old inventories and manuals (Gottfredson et al 1978, Holland 1979, Kuder & Diamond 1979, Lamb & Prediger 1979, Lunneborg 1979), and the stimulation of much research, speculation, and controversy.

Validity studies   Like recent trends in advertising, the comparison of interest inventories is in. Because four inventories use Holland's model of six types of interest, more estimates of the relative concurrent or predictive validities of inventories developed by divergent scaling techniques, formats, and items have become available, although such comparisons are usually flawed by divergent sampling procedures. Nevertheless, like the prediction of grades by divergent tests and past records, using a wide range of samples, the prediction of current aspiration, future aspiration, or occupation entered appears to have reached a limit. In a six-category system, most inventories have a hit rate of about 40% plus or minus 5%.

For example, a 4-year longitudinal study (Spokane 1979) of 618 college students (freshman to senior year) who took the SCII before entrance yields hit rates of 34.4% and 39.7% for women and men. In a similar 4-year longitudinal analysis, Hanson et al (1977), using the ACT Interest Inventory, obtained hit rates of between 33% and 44% for another sample of 4419 college students. Related investigations by Lamb & Prediger (1979), O'Neil et al (1978a), Gottfredson & Holland (1975), and Wiggins & Weslander (1977) provide similar hit rates for other inventories.

Parenthetically, it is also clear that substantial increases in predictive efficiency can be obtained by combining a person's vocational aspiration and an inventory (Borgen & Seling 1978, Holland & Gottfredson 1975, Touchton & Magoon 1977). This evidence is summarized in the research section. In short, psychometric theory may have had its day as a dominant force in interest inventory or treatment development. In the future the development of new treatments rather than the honing of old inventories may be a more productive strategy.

Inventory effects and controversy   The controversy about the influence of interest inventories on males and females dominated the research on interest inventories in the 1970s. Perhaps the most valuable outcomes of that controversy have been a better understanding of how interest inventories affect a client's vocational aspirations, self-understanding, and confidence, and a realization of the virtues of experimental evaluations for all vocational interventions.

These experiments typically have demonstrated that changing the directions or language of an inventory has no important effect on the test taker (Boyd 1976, Gottfredson 1976, Siebel & Walsh 1977, Lawler 1979); also, inventories using different norms, scaling procedures, and interpretative materials have similar if not identical impact on the test taker (Zener & Schnuelle 1976, Prediger & Noeth 1979), much to the surprise of authors, practitioners, and publishers.

The most recent experiments continue to close the door on the belief that interest inventories maintain the status quo by reinforcing only traditional options for females and males. Five of six investigations (Cooper 1976, Slaney 1978, Lawler 1979, Takai & Holland 1979, Talbot & Birk 1979, Atanasoff & Slaney 1980), using high school or college samples, indicate that use of a vocational card sort in which there is no keying or structure does not yield more options than a structured interest inventory. Both produce more options, but card sorts lack any quality control; any option stimulated by the use of a vocational card sort is counted as a valid option —occupational alternatives that are consistent or inconsistent with a person's measured interests. In contrast, interest inventories suggest only options that are consistent with a person's measured interests.

Other studies (Prediger & Noeth 1979, Zener & Schnuelle 1976) indicate that inventories, using norms so that a uniform distribution of occupational alternatives is presented to high school and college females, are no more effective in stimulating options than the influence of an inventory that uses raw scores and presents an uneven distribution of options. In addition, Keeling & Tuck (1978) demonstrated experimentally that high school boys and girls were more attracted toward job descriptions (not occupational titles) that were congruent with their highest interest inventory raw as opposed to standard interest score.

Still other analytical experiments vitiate other plausible hypotheses about the relation of inventory characteristics and reported effects. Holland and associates (1978) found that the influence of the SDS disappears after two months and that presenting the SDS in eight different forms (with and without an Occupations Finder, an interpretative booklet or not, structured or randomized items) makes little or no difference. Finally, two simple experiments indicate that the goal of more vocational options for everyone is not an outcome that all people want. Slaney (1978) found that college women wanted more or fewer options to about an equal degree. Power et al (1979) found that high school boys and girls wanted to find out what career to follow more than they wanted to increase the range of jobs they might consider. Girls want more or fewer options to about the same degree; boys want to reduce their options rather than have more.

Prediger and his colleagues (Prediger & Lamb 1979, Hanson et al 1977) continue to demonstrate that inventories with more versus less balanced items usually have similar concurrent and predictive validities. No direct tests of the influence of these versions have been performed.

Some Interpretations

The experimental evaluations of counselors, courses, career programs, card sorts, interest inventories, workshops, and related treatments imply that the beneficial effects are due to the common elements in these divergent treatments: (a) exposure to occupational information; (b) cognitive rehearsal of vocational aspirations; (c) acquisition of some cognitive structure for organizing information about self, occupations, and their relations; and (d) social support or reinforcement from counselors or workshop members. In addition, the strong tendency to find some positive effects for both diffuse interventions (Brenner & Gazda-Grace 1979, Snodgrass & Healy 1979, Young 1979) and specific interventions (Galassi & Galassi 1978, Dixon et al 1979, Hollandsworth & Sandifer 1979, Speas 1979) occurs because the average client knows so little about career decision making and career problems that a small amount of new information and support makes a difference.

At the same time, the general failure to find different effects for different treatments demonstrates a large hole in our understanding of client-treatment interactions and indicates the need for more analytical and less shot-gun evaluation.

The more analytical experiments about the effects of interest inventories and career courses suggest that clients have different expectations for an inventory (Power et al 1979), that clients with a clear sense of identity benefit more than those with a diffuse sense of identity (Power et al 1979), and that clients with well-defined interests benefit more than those with poorly defined interests (Schenk et al 1979). Likewise, there is a wide variation in student ratings of treatments that is often divergent from professional opinion (Evans & Rector 1978). Finally, there is a growing realization among practitioners that potential clients want to invest different amounts of time and money, although professionals are prone to lay on a favorite treatment rather than providing a cafeteria of motivating possibilities.

Another provocative finding—the failure to produce larger effects by piling similar or diverse treatments together (Miller & Cochran 1979, Takai & Holland 1979, Talbot & Birk 1979)—also implies the need to develop integrated treatment chains that are more beneficial than the individual links. In addition, we need some explanation of why many brief treatments appear to be as effective as long-term treatments (cf course outcomes with counselors).

Diagnostic Assessments

Diagnostic schemes or scales for assessing a client's vocational competencies, difficulties, or knowledge have formed a relatively moribund area. The period 1940–1970 produced numerous schemes and revisions (Crites 1969) that were greeted with interest but received almost no research evaluation and only modest use by practitioners. The 1970s have been characterized by a resurgence of interest that flows from theoretical thinking, from the experience of practitioners and researchers, and from the experimental evaluations of vocational treatments.

The most comprehensive theoretically oriented scheme to appear in 1978–1979 is Harren's (1978) Assessment of Career Decision Making (ACDM), which implements Tiedeman's speculations (Tiedeman & O'Hara 1963) about the stages in decision making: exploration, crystallization, choice, and clarification. The ACDM has attracted more positive research evidence than any other diagnostic scheme (Evans & Rector 1978, Harren et al 1978, Moreland et al 1979).

Super & Thompson (1979) recently have reported a new inventory to assess adolescent vocational maturity. This six-scale inventory resembles Crites' Career Maturity Inventory (Crites 1978) and has similar uses: criteria for evaluation studies, assessment of individual and group guidance needs. Osipow and his colleagues (Osipow et al 1976) have developed a brief scale to assess educational-vocational undecidedness for college and high school students that has been revised to use with graduate students (Hartman et al 1979). The original validation of this scale is impressive (Osipow et al 1976), and this recent extension adds to the earlier work. Also, a diagnostic scheme composed of Identity, Information, and Barrier scales has been developed by Holland and associates (1980) to assess a client's difficulties and to select suitable treatments. This scheme grew out of the vocational treatment experiments, and its initial validation is promising.

The next hurdle for this diverse collection of new diagnostic schemes is to learn if they increase the compatibility of client-treatment interactions and the level of attainment on one or more outcome measures.

VOCATIONAL RESEARCH

Researchers have been most concerned with biases in career interventions, followed by lesser concerns with occupational classification, career histories, vocational aspirations, origins of interests, and vocational decision making. Many of these topics are enjoying a heyday of successful replication, usefulness, and stimulation.

Origins and Life Histories

Most attempts to trace the origins of vocational interests have been plagued by negative, weak, or ambiguous outcomes. Nevertheless, the studies of twins old and new have consistently suggested that vocational interests have a small inherited component.

Two recent studies move the field ahead. Grotevant et al (1977) assessed 114 biologically related families and 109 adoptive families by administering the SCII to each family member. Using the six theme scales, they found that parent-child correlations for biological families are more closely related than the same correlations for adoptive families. In an elaborate profile analysis, they also found that the *shape* of an interest profile may have an inherited component.

In a second investigation, Grotevant (1979), using the same data, examined family influence by hypothesizing that parents with similar interests would have more impact on their children than parents with divergent interests. Using regression analysis, he found that both genetic and environmental sources contributed to the development of vocational interests.

These recent investigations are valuable because the results are consistent with one another and with the major trends in earlier studies both twin (Roberts & Johansson 1974) and nontwin (Dewinne et al 1978). Equally important, the methodologies provide models for more analytical and stronger designs.

Several related studies show the power of using garden variety life history data to predict vocational preferences, needs, or work performance. Using a large sample of high school students, Kelso (1976) predicted with substantial efficiency the category of a student's vocational aspiration from clusters of personal, family, and peer data. The cross-validated outcomes were similar for both females and males. Rounds, Davis & Lofquist (1979) used a biographical information form to predict a woman's scores on the Minnesota Importance Questionnaire (20 vocational needs scales). Their double cross-validation procedure revealed that vocational needs are explicitly and moderately related to a person's life history.

Perhaps the application of a personal history key (Brown 1978), developed on a 1933 sample of 10,111 life insurance agents and reevaluated on samples of 857 and 14,738 agents in 1939 and 1967–1971 should receive the annual award for hard-headed success. Brown used expectancy tables to show that little if any predictive validity was lost over the 6- and 18-year cross-validation periods.

Despite the demonstrated validity of biographical keys and scales, psychologists, except for industrial types, show little interest in exploiting the data from life histories. Both Owens (1976) and Baird (1976) have provided comprehensive reviews of this work.

Occupational Classification

At this time, interest-oriented occupational classification systems are enjoying multiple applications and nearly always with a moderate degree of success. L. S. Gottfredson (1978) has tested the construct validity of Holland's system by comparing it with prestige, census, Department of Labor (DOT), and other systems. Although these comparisons indicate that the Holland system has validity for describing work activities, rewards, and general training requirements, these comparisons are also valuable because they demonstrate the marked overlap among divergent systems. Earlier, Dawis & Lofquist (1974) had shown similar overlap between the Minnesota Occupational Classification System. They classify occupations according to and the Holland system.

Dawis et al (1979) have provided a major revision of the Minnesota Occupational Classification System. They classify occupations according to both aptitude (GATB) and reinforcer patterns (supervisor ratings) into 77 categories. This complex system provides considerable information and has marked face validity. Like many systems, some pragmatic tests to demonstrate its usefulness would be helpful, although its overlap with other systems provides impressive construct validity.

Owens & Schoenfeldt (1979) have produced a classification of persons. This preliminary scheme of 18 and 23 types of females and males was derived by assessing the life histories of college freshmen via autobiographical data and by applying various clustering procedures. Next, the clusters were tested in numerous ways to learn if the assignment to a cluster led to predictable behaviors. It does. The extensive validation suggests that this system has an auspicious beginning and many potential applications to career counseling and personnel research.

Expressed and Measured Interests

This period saw the capstone placed on the validity of vocational aspirations versus interest measures. Borgen & Seling (1978) followed a sample of 795 high scholastic aptitude males from freshmen year in college to 3 years after college. The predictive accuracy for 10 occupational areas was 52% and 40% for expressed and measured interests (SVIB-M). If a person's aspiration and inventory profiles were congruent, the prediction jumped to 70%, and if aspiration and inventory were incongruent, the predictions fell to 41% for aspiration and only 22% for the inventory. This pattern of results also holds in a similar longitudinal study (Bartling 1979) for an 11-year interval—college freshmen to seventh year out in which large samples of females and males had taken the female or male forms of the Strong Vocational Interest Blank. In addition, this pattern of results closely parallels the earlier investigations reviewed by Borgen & Seling (1978).

In an analytical, 4-year longitudinal study, Spokane et al (1978) demonstrate that congruence of measured and expressed interests is associated with fewer curricular changes in college. Holcomb & Anderson (1978) obtained similar results using the SVIB with agricultural students. O'Neil et al (1978a), using a small sample of men with scientific interests, found that a freshman's vocational aspiration forecast the category of job entered 7 years later as well as did the high point code of the SDS. In short, it is now clear that vocational aspirations are as predictive as inventories, and their joint use leads to more efficient predictions.

In several studies using nationally representative samples, L. S. Gottfredson has examined the predictive value of vocational aspirations and current job and the trajectories of successive aspirations and jobs in the careers of young men. In the first longitudinal study, L. S. Gottfredson (1979) shows how aspiration and job held become more congruent with age. In a second analysis, Gottfredson & Becker (1979) found that congruence of category of work and aspiration is achieved more often by changing aspirations to match jobs rather than vice versa. And when aspirations are categorized by prestige level, middle class men, as opposed to lower class men, have higher aspirations, but most important these differences are *stable* over the age range 15 to 27. These outcomes challenge the traditional optimism of practitioners and indicate the need to develop a more explicit picture of the origins of aspirations at a much earlier age.

Career Patterns and Processes

There is now a wealth of data and speculation about the career development of young and old. The National Assessment of Educational Progress (Aubrey 1978, Miller 1978, Mitchell 1978, Tiedeman et al 1978, Westbrook 1978) has provided status reports about the career preparation, knowledge, planning, competencies, attitudes, and related topics for nationally representative samples of 13- and 17-year-olds and adults. These vast, eclectic archives should provide useful background data for more focused investigations.

At the other extreme, Jordaan & Heyde (1979) have provided another volume of the Career Pattern studies. Their elaborate analyses of the vocational maturity of 103 high school boys to adulthood are a rich source of theoretical ideas and data. However, this report appears to provide only ambiguous and weak support for the Super formulations (Super et al 1963). Using a large high school sample, Noeth & Prediger (1978) provide persuasive evidence that career development as expressed in occupational knowledge and planning increases from the ninth to the twelfth grade.

Longitudinal studies of careers are rare. The 25-year follow-up of clinical psychology graduate students by Kelly & associates (1978) provides a wide range of educational and occupational data. For example, the best predictor of professional specialization in 1973 was actual specialization in 1957, and the worse predictor was 1957 preference. This finding is consistent with the Gottfredson & Becker work (1979) reviewed earlier.

The stability found in these recent longitudinal studies is consistent with the stability found in more comprehensive investigations. G. D. Gottfredson's (1977) analysis of the 1970 census data makes clear that career stability increases for both sexes from ages 21 to 70. Without exception, each successive increase in age is associated with an increase in stability—the percentage of people remaining within one of six occupational categories. Other work using census or large samples provides similar evidence of stability (Brousseau 1976). Careers do have a lawful quality. Likewise, a person's aspirations from childhood to adulthood appear to have a similar regularity (McLaughlin & Tiedeman 1974, Holland & Gottfredson 1975).

Interest in midcareer change has become strong, but this interest has not been associated with an equally strong research interest. So far most investigations use small and unrepresentative samples. Two investigations support Holland's formulations (Vaitenas & Wiener 1977, Wiener & Vaitenas 1977) as opposed to developmental formulations; two other investigations fail to support his speculations (Robbins et al 1978, Thomas & Robbins 1979), and one study (Snyder et al 1978) found Vroom's theory of preference useful for explaining a professor's decision to become an administrator—something that still puzzles most of us.

Career Decision Making

Despite its importance, research about career decision making has been infrequent. Most work has been concerned with either characterizing decision makers according to style or stage (Lunneborg 1978, Harren 1979), or according to miscellaneous descriptive variables—sex, age, interest, and indecision (Lunneborg 1978, Niece & Bradley 1979, Slaney 1980).

These studies indicate that it is now possible to characterize people with different degrees of indecision (Osipow et al 1976, Holland & Holland 1977) with moderate efficiency and to characterize decision-making styles (Lunneborg 1978, Harren 1979). On the other hand, rare are the experiments in which decision-making ideas or models are used to accelerate the process or quality of decision making.

The major contribution in this area is an elaborate correlational-experimental project by Krumboltz and his students (Krumboltz 1979b) whose goal was to discover whether the *methods* people use to make career decisions affect the outcomes. The correlational analyses identified four decision-making styles: intuitive, impulsive, fatalistic, and dependent. "Rational" items did not form a single factor. Contrary to expectation, no single style was associated with more positive outcomes than any other style.

The experimental study tested the effects of teaching a systematic "rational" procedure. The outcomes of this elaborate experiment were mixed: (*a*) training in decision making failed to increase knowledge of decision-making practices; (*b*) borderline sex and age interactions occurred—rational training helped females of all ages and younger males; (*c*) subjects with impulsive and intuitive styles made poorer decisions after the "rational" training. These and other outcomes imply that different people will benefit from different treatments and that the rational assumption underlying many treatment plans may be unwarranted for a large proportion of clients.

We should not be discouraged. Janis & Mann (1977) have concluded in their comprehensive summary of decision making that "we have no dependable way of objectively assessing the success of a decision . . ." (p. 11), but they provide as an alternative some criteria for examining the *quality of the procedures* used by the decision maker. Most of the proposed criteria (Janis & Mann 1977) are the goals of many vocational treatments. Perhaps more explicit attempts to orient programs around these goals via multiple treatments will be more effective than an adherence to a particular model or treatment plan.

Biases, Barriers, and Interventions

A large proportion of research is still devoted to the biases that affect careers
—age, sex, physical characteristics, and race. Most investigations document
the origins and prepetuation of barriers and biases that interfere with career
choosing and achievement, but relatively little research is concerned with
the development and examination of proposed remedies, especially experimental evaluations. The extensive evaluation of interest inventories is the
exception to this observation.

ORIGINS AND PERPETUATION   The documentation of how society creates and perpetuates sex differences that lead in turn to divergent vocational
aspirations and achievement for females and males is now extensive. Similar
but much smaller literatures are accruing for other kinds of bias—age and
race.

The recent volume by Spence & Helmreich (1978) has become a major
resource for measuring masculinity and femininity and for understanding
the origins of these characteristics. Although this work is not focused on
vocational problems, the research, speculation, and assessment scales are
already a major influence in vocational research.

Other researchers continue to fill in the blank spaces in our knowledge
of sex role socialization. McDaniel et al (1978), using a survey of spatial
experience, found that differences in estimated spatial ability were related
more to experiences that foster spatial ability than to gender. This provocative but soft analysis needs replication with a more valid criterion. Frost &
Diamond (1979), in a large-scale survey of fourth, fifth, and sixth grade
children, found more evidence for both sex and ethnic differences in occupational stereotyping.

Still other investigators have provided more evidence of the influence or
bias present in a wide range of informational materials. Heilman (1979) has
demonstrated experimentally that information about the sexual composition of a field can be used to manipulate a high school student's aspirations.
For example, projections of more balanced sex ratios for a field encouraged
greater interest in females, but a totally balanced sex ratio reduced the
degree of interest expressed by males. In a related report, Krefting et al
(1978) show that the base rate of females and males in an occupation is the
most efficient predictor of job sex typing, accounting for 48 to 70% of the
variance. They found little support for the relation of job content to sex
typing.

This rediscovery—you can manipulate people with occupational information, especially the sex ratio in each occupation—leads to the dilemma
enunciated by Birk et al (1979). If occupational materials show the status
quo via sex ratios and illustrations, they probably serve to maintain the

status quo with all of its inequities; and if the same materials report and depict a future ideal status, they probably mislead some indeterminate proportion of aspirants. Birk et al (1979) summarize this discussion and recommend "access to a process" for exploring all options. This strategy appears too diffuse. Just how occupational information should be presented to people who differ in age, sex, and race remains a dilemma. In addition, if the reporting of sex ratios is as powerful as it appears to be (Krefting et al 1978), then future studies need to isolate that information from other less influential information. For instance, the influence of language and illustrations may be of minor importance relative to the influence of reported sex ratios. This disparity in influence may clarify some of the results found in recent work (Yanico 1978, Krefting & Berger 1979).

REMEDIES AND EVALUATIONS   Unfortunately, only a few remedies have undergone any rigorous evaluation, and the effectiveness of individual interventions has usually been small or negligible. Several evaluations illustrate some of the values and problems entailed in counseling and educational interventions.

Wirtenberg (1979) has conducted a comprehensive, long-term evaluation of the sex-desegregation of industrial arts and home economics at the seventh grade level. Her goal was to measure the impact of desegregation on the occupational potential of females over one school year. She found that the effects of sex-desegregation were most apparent at the beginning rather than the end of the year—girls saw themselves as more competent in male domains, saw fewer sex differences, and attributed more male characteristics to themselves. The failure of these initial effects to increase over the school year can be attributed to multiple contradictory influences: teachers treated boys differently than girls within the desegregated classes, and parental expectations for children were at variance with treatment goals.

Fox and her colleagues (1979) have evaluated the impact of early intervention programs developed to get more women into mathematics and science by increasing the enrollment of bright females in mathematics courses and by changing attitudes about mathematical and scientific careers. These elaborate evaluations of diverse programs have produced mixed but useful results. Special programs for mathematically talented females had a positive impact on course-taking and vocational aspirations. Females who received career awareness treatments and exposure to female role models expressed higher levels of educational aspirations than did females receiving no treatment.

O'Neil and his colleagues (O'Neil et al 1978b) have devised a training program to reduce sexism in the career planning of females. O'Neil et al (1979) performed an experimental evaluation of this 4-week career workshop and obtained positive outcomes. Workshop females spent more time thinking about careers, described themselves as more masculine, and reported more scientific, social, and enterprising careers as appropriate choices than did control females. Parenthetically, this program increased interest in traditional occupations as well as nontraditional occupations and perhaps should be relabeled as a self-exploration treatment that does not attempt to affect particular kinds of aspirations and may be equally helpful for males.

In the evaluation of a special summer program to stimulate interest in engineering among high school blacks and females, Richards & colleagues (1978) also obtained a twofold effect. The students who had the most potential for engineering were the students whose interest in engineering was strengthened by the minority introduction to engineering programs; whereas the students with the least potential were affected in the opposite direction—became more certain that engineering was not for them. The special program appeared to function like a brief work experience—attracting some and repelling others.

SPECULATION AND THEORY

This 2-year period has yielded a wide range of speculation and theory. The speculation is especially difficult to characterize, for it ranges from brief notes to books, from origins of interest to maintenance of vitality, and from good old idle speculation to carefully reasoned formulation with an extensive marshalling of evidence. The theory is dominated by theories or typologies that grew out of differential psychology. Theories concerned with development are no longer in ascendance, and a social learning theory of career decision making is the most promising new development.

Speculation

Perhaps Tyler's (1978) call for looking at an individual as a special "sequence of selective acts" (so that only a few of many developmental possibilities are chosen and organized) is the most persuasive new formulation for amending our methods for explaining careers and for understanding individuality in general. The implications of her speculations call for a reexamination of the conventional experiment and a concern with the horizontal as well as the vertical differences between individuals—lifestyles, cognitive styles, and strategies for decision making. The keys to improved understanding lie in "the examination of repertoires and priorities rather than single types of variables" (p. 232). Possibility theory, like personal construct theory, is appealing, but its successful implementation requires both a relaxation of old attitudes and habits and some original thinking.

Other speculation about the origins of children's interests (Travers 1978), the complexity of vocational choice (Roe 1979), the meaning of radical career change (Krantz 1978), and ways to optimize adult development (Fozzard & Popkin 1978)—including life at work—are stimulating but have rarely been accompanied by persuasive evidence. At the same time, these diverse speculations suggest the potential of seeing careers from multiple perspectives—even a few that appear odd.

Speculation about the future of work and the role of counseling psychologists in old and new forms of research and service appear somewhat predictable from long-term trends. Magoon (1980) outlines his concerns with the dangers of over-guildism and insensitivity to the consumer of psychological services. He visualizes a continued increase in group work, consultation, and a decrease in one-to-one interviewing. Along with these trends he anticipates "the creation of tiers of services along a continuum of time and work expected of the help-seeker . . ." In contrast, present services offer too few alternatives, require a high level of motivation to expect much benefit, and offer the client too limited a role in selecting a treatment. In a similar effort Hilton and his colleagues (1979) outline a conceptual framework for secondary school guidance and the necessary research and development for more effective programs. These comprehensive speculations should serve as useful beginnings for the planning of research or the organization of a program of treatments. Some will quarrel with their priorities for research and wonder why most guidance plans for high schools must resemble a Hollywood production, but everyone will benefit from a careful reading of this monograph.

Theory

Formulations about the origins and patterning of careers are now numerous and varied. Krumboltz (1979a) has provided a social learning theory analysis of career decision making. Developmentally oriented formulations have multiplied and undergone revision (Knefelkamp & Slepitza 1976, Knefelkamp et al 1979, Super & Kidd 1979). The Minnesota theory of work adjustment (Lofquist & Dawis 1969) and Holland's (1973) typology that grew out of the differential psychology and person-environment traditions continue to enjoy most of the research attention.

Krumboltz's (1979a) formulations appear to be the most appealing of the new models. Many have advocated the application of learning theory to vocational problems, but the task required someone who was knowledgeable about learning theory *and* vocational behavior. Krumboltz (1979a) shows how learning theory is applicable to a wide range of vocational questions and clinical problems throughout the life span. Equally important, social learning principles are congenial with the other forms of speculation about vocational life. This model appears to supplement rather than to supplant other formulations. In short, whenever another theory of careers uses words like "change," "learn," or "develop" (to come degree), Krumboltz's suggestions can be applied like a microscope to show an enlarged and more detailed account of the person-environment interaction.

Developmental theories of careers continue to be characterized more by appealing but vague statements and weak data rather than by explicit statements and strong data. We have new formulations about the vocational development of college students (Knefelkamp et al 1979, Harren 1979), engineers (Kopelman 1977), older males (Levinson 1978), older males and females (Super & Kidd 1979), and development over the whole career (Schein 1978).

Two formulations have been accompanied by strong and convincing data. Hershenson's programmatic testing (Hershenson & Lavery 1978) of his life-stage model continues to receive positive results but not the attention it warrants. In another strong study using 376 engineers, Kopelman (1977) applied expectancy theory with substantial success. Expectancies and values declined with the passage of time, and expectancies declined prior to a change in values. Despite some ambiguities, these and other findings are among the most substantial anyone has obtained.

Despite the scientific deficiencies of developmental formulations, they have a strong appeal to the majority of clients, practitioners, and researchers. For a comprehensive eclectic overview for working with clients, practitioners will find Schein's (1978) text an exemplar.

Finally, the Minnesota theory of work adjustment (Lofquist & Dawis 1969) and Holland's (1973) theory of careers continued to undergo reformulation and to grind out empirical studies. Both models have now stimulated a substantial array of research over a long period. For the period 1964 to 1979, the Minnesota and Holland views are associated with approximately 150 and 300 articles.

The Minnesota view (Lofquist & Dawis 1969) has been elaborated to include the concepts of work personality style and work environment style. In a subsequent article, Dawis & Lofquist (1978) present the process of vocational adjustment in a system-type model in order to integrate old and new propositions. These revisions are appealing and plausible ideas for coping with person-work interactions and their outcomes that everyone has difficulty predicting. This group also continues to examine and revise the instrumentation (Shubsachs et al 1978), the related occupational classification (Dawis et al 1979), and the hypotheses in the theory (Stickney 1978, Murray 1979, Sloan 1979).

The future of the formulations and descriptive materials on the dynamics and processes of work adjustment may lie in intervention programs or studies planned to help clients or workers achieve a higher level of fulfillment. The Minnesota work is one of only a few programmatic efforts to comprehend a major element of vocational life. Both practitioners and researchers can benefit from a reading of perhaps the most analytical and hard-headed analysis of person-job interactions.

Holland's theory of careers continued to generate research on a wide range of populations and for diverse problems, but the theoretical formulations have undergone only minor revision since 1973 (Holland & Gottfredson 1976). In general, the strongest support for this person-environment typology has been obtained in tests of its organizing properties—testing the formulations about the types and by organizing vocational aspirations or work histories according to the classification. It is now clear that the instruments used to assign people to occupational categories have moderate validity for nonprofessional workers (Matthews & Walsh 1978, Salomone & Slaney 1978), females and males (Doty & Betz 1979), blacks and whites (Bingham & Walsh 1978, Walsh et al 1979), professionals and nonprofessionals (Spokane & Walsh 1978), and that the classification scheme provides some simple techniques for organizing aspirations (Gottfredson 1977) so that their regularity or coherence becomes apparent.

The evidence for the secondary constructs in this formulation continues to be mixed—some clearly positive and some clearly negative evidence. For example, Mount & Muchinsky (1978), using a sample of 362 workers, found strong support for the importance of congruence of person and job but no support for the hexagonal arrangement of occupations. Others (Rounds, Davison & Dawis 1979) found that the interest inventory data for males and females produce somewhat different hexagons.

In a 7-year longitudinal study, Peiser & Meier (1978) reported positive evidence for the usefulness of congruence, consistency, and differentiation, but the results hold largely for males rather than for females. And a 7-year study of males with investigative interests (O'Neil et al 1978a) revealed that the construct of consistency had substantial predictive value in accord with the theoretical formulations—consistent interests were associated with career stability.

Testings of the personality formulations are now few in number. Helson's (1978) analysis of the two subtypes—authors and critics—is an exception to this trend. It is noteworthy, because the comparison of subtypes put the theory to a severe test but with positive outcomes, and because she suggests how the theory might be helpfully modified by the application of systems theory.

At this point, the Holland and Minnesota formulations have a set of predictable problems. Like most typological formulations, Holland's scheme has been most successful in organizing personal and occupational data. In contrast, it has been least successful in accounting for person-environment interactions and related problems that call for more analytical and more positive evidence. The formulations about consistency and differentiation require clarification and revision. Congruence seems in good health relative to similar concepts used to account for the same phenomena.

The Minnesota group has continued to develop a more and more analytical theory and to revise the associated occupational classification system. These revisions now have displaced tests of the ability of these formulations to organize personal and occupational data, or to direct more successful empirical analyses of the outcomes that the authors are most concerned with—job satisfaction, performance, and more recently personality style and the influence of work and organizational behavior.

ACHIEVEMENTS AND POSSIBILITIES

The research and theory about career interventions has culminated in some practical, substantive, and theoretical achievements. Although it has become fashionable to report that your speciality, methodology, or theoretical perspective has dead-ended, the work in this area has resulted in some important accomplishments. These positive outcomes are summarized next and are followed by some promising possibilities for new work that are foreshadowed by these recent developments.

1. The number and variety of career interventions has greatly increased so that researchers and practitioners have a larger pool of treatments to draw from.

2. Multiple evaluations suggest that divergent treatments (counselors, inventories, workshops, special techniques, workbooks, and so on) usually have positive effects on clients. These positive outcomes usually hold for a wide range of evaluations that use divergent populations and designs which range from elegant to ugly. We appear to have some beneficial treatments. Those outcomes are remarkable in view of the relatively brief period of evaluation—less than 10 years. There is considerable merit in the study of standard or highly structured treatments, especially because under certain conditions some structured treatments are as helpful as professional counselors.

3. We have a rough understanding of how career interventions work. An ideal intervention or a series of related interventions would include (a) occupational information organized by a comprehensible method and easily accessible to a client; (b) assessment materials and devices that clarify a client's self-picture and vocational potentials; (c) individual or group activities that require the rehearsal of career plans or problems; (d) counselors, groups, or peers that provide support; and (e) a comprehensible cognitive structure for organizing information about self and occupational alternatives.

4. Our understanding of the development of vocational interests and career pathways is more complete. In particular, the extensive examination of sex-role socialization and interests shows in considerable detail how occupational goals are probably formed, how they are maintained, and how they can be modified. Parenthetically, the search for the origins of interest at some unspecified young age is a scientific wild goose chase, for the origins are taking place now and at every other time in a person's life history.

5. The development and revision of occupational classification systems have had a pervasive substantive and theoretical impact. On the one hand, these systems have greatly facilitated the use of occupational data for clients, counselors, and researchers. They have demonstrated that both aspiration and work histories have a lawful character from childhood through adulthood. In addition, different systems have a relatively rational and substantial overlap. The predictive efficiency obtained by the application of these systems to a person's vocational aspiration or current job is high—so much so that more elaborate techniques are usually less efficient. Finally, the use of parallel but independent assessment and classification schemes (Lofquist & Dawis 1969, Holland 1979) has led to new knowledge.

A review of the recent progress and some speculation about new and old theorizing implies some promising possibilities for research, theory, and practice. The following suggestions are offered for discussion and debate. For purposes of clarity and succinctness the traditional qualifications and weasel words have been omitted.

In evaluative research, several directions appear desirable: (*a*) More rigorous evaluations of all forms of vocational intervention are still required. It is surprising that we have come so far with so little. (*b*) More analytical evaluations in which client goals are linked to treatments via goal attainment scaling (Cytrynbaum et al 1979) or diagnostic procedures are needed to acquire a comprehensive knowledge of client treatment interactions and related outcomes. This research may be unsuccessful, but at this time there has been very little exploration of these ideas. (*c*) More potent treatments should be developed by incorporating the influential characteristics of past treatments. (*d*) The ordering effects of treatment chains should be investigated.

The analysis of how interventions work needs to be continued and to be reexamined in the context of instructional technology, decision making, and information processing. The experiments by Bodden & his colleagues (Haase et al 1979) have culminated in some valuable principles of decision making that parallel some of those reviewed by Janis & Mann (1977). Counseling psychology, like other specialities, could occasionally profit by looking around for intellectual help rather than by trying to do it all.

In vocational research, some redirection of effort is warranted. The neglected but painfully relevant topics of job finding, placement strategies, and vocational adaptation require more attention (Becker 1977). They should not be left almost entirely to entrepreneurs and writers. These topics encompass perhaps the major portion of a person's career behavior.

The classification research should be more completely exploited. The first stage has demonstrated that these schemes can organize the vocational world efficiently and in many useful ways. The next stage might include attempts to track careers in two directions simultaneously—by level and kind of work. The typology of persons, proposed by Owens & Schoenfeldt (1979), may prove to be a powerful way to illuminate occupational classification systems and career behavior.

The new formulations deserve vigorous trials. Tyler's (1978) possibility theory implies not only new directions but also some ideas for revising older formulations. For instance, her call for the examination of "repertoires and priorities" could be tested by using interest or needs profiles within the context of other formulations (Holland 1973, Lofquist & Dawis 1969).

Finally, the road to continued progress in this area may be a road that is paved more with perseverance, reading, and thinking rather than worrying about methodological perspectives. The tools, theories, and substantive advances in this field owe very little to method and very much to a relatively small number of good ideas vigorously followed for long periods of time.

Literature Cited

Atanasoff, G., Slaney, R. B. 1980. Three approaches to counselor free career exploration among college women. *J. Couns. Psychol.* In press

Atlas, J. W., Minor, J. H., Minor, B. J. 1977. Effects of Crystal and Bolles' life work —planning process on selected factors related to vocational choice. *J. Employment Couns.* 14:14–22

Aubrey, R. F. 1978. *Career Development Needs of Thirteen-year-olds.* Washington DC: Am. Pers. Guid. Assoc. 81 pp.

Avallone, V. L. 1974. *A comparative study of the effects of two vocational guidance systems.* PhD thesis. Univ. North Colo., Greeley

Baird, L. L. 1976. *Using self-reports to predict student performance.* New York: Coll. Entrance Exam. Board. 90 pp.

Bartling, H. C. 1979. *An eleven year follow-up study of measured interest and inventoried choice.* PhD thesis. Univ. Iowa, Iowa City. 155 pp.

Bartsch, K., Hackett, G. 1979. Effect of a decision-making course on locus of control, conceptualization, and career planning. *J. Coll. Stud. Pers.* 20:230–35

Bartsch, K., Sandmeyer, L. 1979. *Skills in Life Career Planning.* Monterey, Calif: Brooks Cole. 184 pp.

Becker, H. J., 1977. *How young people find career entry jobs: A review of the literature. Tech. Rep. 241,* Cent. Soc. Organ. Sch., Johns Hopkins Univ. 61 pp.

Bingham, R. P., Walsh, W. B. 1978. Concurrent validity of Holland's theory for college-degreed black women. *J. Vocat. Behav.* 13:242–50

Birk, J. M., Tanney, M. F., Cooper, J. F. 1979. A case of blurred vision: Stereotyping in career information illustrations. *J. Vocat. Behav.* 15:247–57

Bolles, R. N. 1975. *What Color is Your Parachute?* Berkeley, Calif: Ten Speed. 229 pp.

Borgen, F. H., Seling, M. J. 1978. Expressed and inventoried interests revisited: Perspicacity in the person. *J. Couns. Psychol.* 25:536–43

Bostaph, C., Moore, M. 1979. Using alumni as career consultants. *J. Coll. Stud. Pers.* 20:83

Boyd, V. S. 1976. Neutralizing sexist titles in Holland's Self-Directed Search: What difference does it make? *J. Vocat. Behav.* 9:191–99

Brenner, D., Gazda-Grace, P. A. 1979. Career decision making in women as a function of sex composition of career planning groups. *Meas. Eval. Guid.* 12:8–13

Brousseau, K. R. 1976. *Effects of job experience on personality.* PhD thesis. Yale Univ., New Haven, Conn. 207 pp.

Brown, S. H. 1978. Long-term validity of a personal history item scoring procedure. *J. Appl. Psychol.* 63:673–76

Carney, C. G., Savitz, C. J., Weiskott, G. N. 1979. Students' evaluations of a university counseling center and their intentions to use its programs. *J. Couns. Psychol.* 26:242–49

College Entrance Examination Board. 1978. *Career Skills Assessment Program.* New York: Coll. Board

Cooper, J. F. 1976. Comparative impact of the SCII and the Vocational Card Sort on career salience and career exploration of women. *J. Couns. Psychol.* 23:348–52

Crites, J. O. 1969. *Vocational Psychology.* New York: McGraw-Hill. 704 pp.

Crites, J. O. 1978. *Career Maturity Inventory.* Monterey, Calif: McGraw-Hill

Cytrynbaum, S., Ginath, Y., Birdwell, J., Brandt, C. 1979. Goal attainment scaling. *Eval. Q.* 3:5–40

Dawis, R. V., Lofquist, L. H. 1974. *Minnesota Occupational Classification System.* Univ. Minn. Dep. Psychol. 153 pp.

Dawis, R. V., Lofquist, L. H. 1978. A note on the dynamics of work adjustment. *J. Vocat. Behav.* 12:76–79

Dawis, R. V., Lofquist, L. H., Henly, G. A., Rounds, J. B. 1979. *Minnesota Occupational Classification System II.* Univ. Minn. Dep. Psychol. 170 pp.

Dewinne, R. F., Overton, T. D., Schneider, L. J. 1978. Types produce types—especially fathers. *J. Vocat. Behav.* 12:140–44

Dixon, D. N., Heppner, P. P., Peterson, C. H., Ronning, R. R. 1979. Problem-solving workshop training. *J. Couns. Psychol.* 26:133–39

Doty, M. S., Betz, N. E. 1979. Comparison of the concurrent validity of Holland's theory for men and women in an enterprising occupation. *J. Vocat. Behav.* 15:207–16

Evans, J. R., Rector, A. P. 1978. Evaluation of a college course in career decision-making. *J. Coll. Stud. Pers.* 19:163–68

Fifield, M., Petersen, L. 1978. Job simulation: A method of vocational exploration. *Vocat. Guid. Q.* 26:326–33

Figler, H. 1979. *The Complete Job Search Handbook.* New York: Holt Rinehart

Fox, L. H., Brody, L., Tobin, D. 1979. *Women and mathematics: The impact of early intervention programs upon course-taking and attitudes in high school.* Final rep., No. NIE-G-77-0062, Johns Hopkins Univ.

Fozzard, J. L., Popkin, S. J. 1978. Optimizing adult development: Ends and means of an applied psychology of aging. *Am. Psychol.* 33:975–89

Frost, F. D., Diamond, E. E. 1979. Ethnic and sex differences in occupational stereotyping by elementary school children. *J. Vocat. Behav.* 15:43–54

Galassi, J. P., Galassi, M. D. 1978. Preparing individuals for interviews: Suggestions from more than 60 years of research. *Pers. Guid. J.* 57:188–92

Gottfredson, G. D. 1976. A note on sexist wording in interest measurement. *Meas. Eval. Guid.* 8:221–23

Gottfredson, G. D. 1977. Career stability and redirection in adulthood. *J. Appl. Psychol.* 62:436–45

Gottfredson, G. D., Holland, J. L. 1975. Vocational choices of men and women: A comparison of predictors from the Self-Directed Search. *J. Couns. Psychol.* 22:28–34

Gottfredson, G. D., Holland, J. L., Holland, J. E. 1978. The seventh revision of the Vocational Preference Inventory. *JSAS Cat. Sel. Doc. Psychol.* 8:98, No. 1783

Gottfredson, L. S. 1978. *The construct validity of Holland's occupational classification system in terms of prestige, census, Department of Labor and other classification systems.* Tech. Rep. 260, Cent. Soc. Organ. Sch., Johns Hopkins Univ. 70 pp.

Gottfredson, L. S. 1979. Aspiration-job match: Age trends in a large nationally representative sample of young white men. *J. Couns. Psychol.* 26:319–28

Gottfredson, L. S., Becker, H. J. 1979. *A challenge to vocational psychology: How important are aspirations in determining career development?* Tech. Rep. 294, Cent. Soc. Organ. Sch., Johns Hopkins Univ. 44 pp.

Grotevant, H. D. 1979. Environmental influences on vocational interest development in adolescents from adoptive and biological families. *Child Dev.* 50:854–60

Grotevant, H. D., Scarr, S., Weinberg, R. A. 1977. Patterns of interest similarity in adoptive and biological families. *J. Pers. Soc. Psychol.* 35:667–76

Haase, R. F., Reed, C. F., Winer, J. L., Bodden, J. L. 1979. Effects of positive, negative and mixed occupational information on cognitive and affective complexity. *J. Vocat. Behav.* 15:294–302

Hanson, G. R., Noeth, R. J., Prediger, D. J. 1977. Validity of diverse procedures for reporting interest scores: An analysis of longitudinal data. *J. Couns. Psychol.* 24:487–93

Harren, V. A. 1978. *Assessment of Career Decision-Making (ACDM): Counselor/Instructor Guide.* Unpublished manuscript, Psychol. Dep., Southern Ill. Univ.

Harren, V. A. 1979. A model of career decision-making for college students. *J. Vocat. Behav.* 14:119–35

Harren, V. A., Kass, R. A., Tinsley, H. E. A., Moreland, J. R. 1978. Influence of sex role attitudes and cognitive styles on career decision-making. *J. Couns. Psychol.* 25:390–98

Harris, T. L., Wallin, J. S. 1978. Influencing career choices of seventh-grade students. *Vocat. Guid. Q.* 27:244–49

Hartman, B. W., Utz, P. W., Farnum, S. O. 1979. Examining the reliability and validity of an adopted scale of educational-vocational undecidedness in a sample of graduate students. *J. Vocat. Behav.* 15:224–30

Heilman, M. E. 1979. High school students' occupational interest as a function of projected sex ratios in male-dominated occupations. *J. Appl. Psychol.* 64:275–79

Helson, R. 1978. Writers and critics: two types of vocational consciousness in the art system. *J. Vocat. Behav.* 12:351–63

Heppner, P. P., Krause, J. B. 1979. A career seminar course. *J. Coll. Stud. Pers.* 20:300–5

Hershenson, D. B., Lavery, G. J. 1978. Sequencing of vocational development stages: Further studies. *J. Vocat. Behav.* 12:102–8

Hilton, T. L. 1979. *Confronting the Future: A Conceptual Framework for Secondary School Guidance.* New York: Coll. Entrance Exam. Board. 148 pp.

Holcomb, W. R., Anderson, W. P. 1978. Expressed and inventoried interests as predictors of college graduation and vocational choice. *J. Vocat. Behav.* 12:290–96

Holland, J. L. 1973. *Making Vocational Choices: A Theory of Careers.* Englewood Cliffs, NJ: Prentice Hall. 150 pp.

Holland, J. L. 1979. *The Self-Directed Search: Professional Manual.* Palo Alto: Calif. Consult. Psychol. Press. 96 pp.

Holland, J. L., Daiger, D. C., Power, P. G. 1980. Some diagnostic scales for research in decision-making and personality: Identity, information, and barriers. *J. Pers. Soc. Psychol.* In press

Holland, J. L., Gottfredson, G. D. 1975. Predictive value and psychological meaning of vocational aspirations. *J. Vocat. Behav.* 6:349–63

Holland, J. L., Gottfredson, G. D. 1976. Using a typology of persons and environments to explain careers. *Couns. Psychol.* 6:20–29

Holland, J. L., Holland, J. E. 1977. Vocational indecision: More evidence and speculation. *J. Couns. Psychol.* 24:404–14

Holland, J. L., Takai, R., Gottfredson, G. D., Hanau, C. 1978. A multivariate analysis of the effects of the Self-Directed Search on high school girls. *J. Couns. Psychol.* 28:384–89

Hollandsworth, J. G., Sandifer, B. A. 1979. Behavioral training for increasing effective job-interview skills: Follow-up and evaluation. *J. Couns. Psychol.* 26:448–50

Janis, I. L., Mann, L. 1977. *Decision-Making: A Psychological Analysis of Conflict, Choice and Commitment.* New York: Free Press. 489 pp.

Jordaan, J. P., Heyde, M. B. 1979. *Vocational Maturity During the High School Years.* New York: Teachers Coll. Press. 236 pp.

Keeling, B., Tuck, B. F. 1978. Raw scores versus same-sex normed scores: An experimental study of the validity of Holland's SDS with adolescents of both sexes. *J. Vocat. Behav.* 13:263–71

Kelly, E. L., Goldberg, L. R., Fiske, D. W., Kilkowski, J. M. 1978. Twenty-five years later: A follow-up study of the graduate students in clinical psychology assessed in the V. A. selection research project. *Am. Psychol.* 33:746–55

Kelso, G. I. 1976. *Explorations of the developmental antecedents of Holland's occupational types.* PhD thesis. Johns Hopkins Univ., Baltimore, Md.

Kerr, C., Rosnow, J. M., eds. 1979. *Work in America.* New York: Van Nostrand. 288 pp.

Knefelkamp, L. L., Slepitza, R. 1976. A cognitive developmental model of career development—an adaptation of the Perry scheme. *Couns. Psychol.* 6:53–58

Knefelkamp, L. L., Widick, C., Parker, C. A., eds. 1979. *Applying New Developmental Findings.* San Francisco: Jossey-Bass. 125 pp.

Kopelman, R. E. 1977. Psychological stages of careers in engineering: An expectancy theory taxonomy. *J. Vocat. Behav.* 10:270–80

Krantz, D. L. 1978. *Radical Career Change.* New York: Free Press. 157 pp.

Krefting, L. A., Berger, P. K. 1979. Masculinity-femininity perceptions of job-sex stereotypes. *J. Vocat. Behav.* 15: 164–74

Krefting, L. A., Berger, P. K., Wallace, M. J. 1978. The contribution of sex distribution, job content, and occupational classification to sextyping: Two studies. *J. Vocat. Behav.* 13:181–91

Krivatsy, S. E., Magoon, T. M. 1976. Differential effects of three vocational counseling treatments. *J. Couns. Psychol.* 43: 112–18

Krumboltz, J. D. 1979a. A social learning theory of career decision-making. In *Social Learning and Career Decision Making,* ed. A. Mitchell, G. Jones, J. Krumboltz, pp. 19–49. Cranston, RI: Carroll. 244 pp.

Krumboltz, J. D. 1979b. *The effect of alternative career decision-making strategies on the quality of resulting decision.* Final rep. U.S. Off. Educ. Grant No. G007605241: Sch. Educ., Stanford Univ.

Krumboltz, J. D., Becker-Haven, J. F., Burnett, K. F. 1979. Counseling psychology. *Ann. Rev. Psychol.* 30:555–602

Kuder, F., Diamond, E. E. 1979. *Kuder DD: Occupational Interest Survey, General Manual.* Chicago: Sci. Res. Assoc. 64 pp.

Lamb, R. R., Prediger, D. J. 1979. Criterion-related validity of sex-restrictive and unisex interest scales: A comparison. *J. Vocat. Behav.* 15:231–46

Lawler, A. C. 1979. Career exploration with women using the non-sexist Vocational Card Sort, the SDS, and the Vocational Exploration and Insight Kit. *Meas. Eval. Guid.* 12:87–97

Levinson, D. J. 1978. *The Seasons of a Man's Life.* New York: Knopf. 363 pp.

Loesch, L. C., Rucker, B. B., Shub, P. A. 1978. A field test of an instrument for assessing job knowledge. *Meas. Eval. Guid.* 11:26–33

Loesch, L. C., Sampson, J. P. 1978. Job knowledge and vocational preferences. *Vocat. Guid. Q.* 27:55–60

Lofquist, L. H., Dawis, R. N. 1969. *Adjustment to Work.* Englewood Cliffs, NJ: Prentice Hall. 185 pp.

Lunneborg, P. W. 1978. Sex and career decision-making styles. *J. Couns. Psychol.* 25:299–305

Lunneborg, P. W. 1979. The Vocational Interest Inventory: Development and vali-dation. *Educ. Psychol. Meas.* 39:445–51

Magoon, T. M. 1980. The eye of a beholder. *Couns. Psychol.* 8:26–28

Malett, S. D., Spokane, A. R., Vance, F. L. 1978. Effects of vocationally relevant information on the expressed and measured interests of freshman males. *J. Couns. Psychol.* 25:292–98

Matthews, D. F., Walsh, W. B. 1978. Concurrent validity of Holland's theory for non college-degreed working women. *J. Vocat. Behav.* 12:371–79

McDaniel, E., Guay, R., Ball, L., Kolloff, M. 1978. *A spatial experience questionnaire and some preliminary findings.* Presented at Ann. Meet. Am. Psychol. Assoc., Toronto

McLaughlin, D. H., Tiedeman, D. V. 1974. Eleven-year career stability and change as reflected in project talent data through the Flanagan, Holland, and Roe Occupational Classification systems. *J. Vocat. Behav.* 5:177–96

Miller, A. R., Treiman, D. J., Cain, P. S., Roos, P. A., Eds. 1980. *The Dictionary of Occupational Titles: A Critical Review.* Final rep. Comm. Occup. Classif. Anal. To US Dep. Labor. Washington DC: Natl. Acad. Sci.

Miller, J. V. 1978. *Career development needs of nine-year olds.* Washington DC: Am. Pers. Guid. Assoc. 53 pp.

Miller, M. J., Cochran, J. R. 1979. Comparison of the effectiveness of four methods of reporting interest inventory results. *J. Couns. Psychol.* 26:263–66

Mitchell, A. M. 1978. *Career development needs of seventeen-year olds.* Washington DC: Am. Pers. Guid. Assoc. 97 pp.

Moreland, J. R., Harren, V. A., Krimsky-Montague, E., Tinsley, H. E. A. 1979. Sex role self-concept and career decision-making. *J. Couns. Psychol.* 26: 329–74

Mount, M. K., Muchinsky, P. M. 1978. Concurrent validation of Holland's hexagonal model with occupational workers. *J. Vocat. Behav.* 13:348–54

Murray, S. G. 1979. *Work personality characteristics of adult women low and high profiles on the SCII or SVIB occupational scales.* PhD thesis. Univ. Minn., Minneapolis

National Consortium on Competency-Based Staff Development. 1978. Module series. Palo Alto, Calif: Am. Inst. Res. 52 modules

Niece, D. E., Bradley, R. W. 1979. Relationship of age, sex, and educational groups to career decisiveness. *J. Vocat. Behav.* 14:271–78

Noeth, R. J., Prediger, D. J. 1978. Career development over the high school years. *Vocat. Guid. Q.* 26:244–54

Nolan, J. J. 1974. *The effectiveness of the Self-Directed Search compared with group counseling in promoting information seeking behavior and realism of vocational choices.* PhD thesis. Univ. Maryland, College Park. 110 pp.

O'Neil, J. M., Magoon, T. M., Tracey, T. J. 1978a. Status of Holland's investigative personality types and their consistency levels seven years later. *J. Couns. Psychol.* 25:530–35

O'Neil, J. M., Meeker, C. H., Borgers, S. B. 1978b. A developmental preventative and consultative model to reduce sexism in the career planning of women. *JSAS Cat. Select. Doc. Psychol.* 8:1684

O'Neil, J. M., Ohlde, C., Barke, C. 1979. Research on a career workshop to reduce sexism with women. Presented at Ann. Meet. Am. Psychol. Assoc., 87th, New York

Osipow, S. H., Carney, C. G., Barak, A. 1976. A scale of educational-vocational undecidedness: A typological approach. *J. Vocat. Behav.* 9:223–43

Owens, W. A. 1976. Background data. In *Handbook of Industrial and Organizational Psychology,* ed. M. D. Dunnette. Chicago: Rand McNally. 1740 pp.

Owens, W. A., Schoenfeldt, L. F. 1979. Toward a classification of persons. *J. Appl. Psychol. Monogr.* 65:568–607

Peiser, C., Meier, E. I. 1978. Congruency, consistency, and differentiation of vocational interests as predicters of vocational satisfaction and preference stability. *J. Vocat. Behav.* 12:270–78

Power, P. G., Holland, J. L., Daiger, D. C., Takai, R. T. 1979. The relation of student characteristics to the influence of the Self-Directed Search. *Meas. Eval. Guid.* 12:98–107

Prediger, D. J., Lamb, R. R. 1979. The validity of sex-balanced and sex-restrictive vocational interest reports: A comparison. *Vocat. Guid. Q.* 28:16–24

Prediger, D. J., Noeth, R. J. 1979. Effectiveness of a brief counseling intervention in stimulating vocational exploration. *J. Vocat. Behav.* 14:352–68

Prediger, D. J., Roth, J. D., Noeth, R. J. 1974. Career development of youth: A nationwide study. *Pers. Guid. J.* 53:97–104

Rehberg, R., Hotchkiss, L. 1979. Career counseling in contemporary U.S. high schools. In *Review of Research in Education,* ed. D. C. Berliner, 7:92–150

Richards, J. M., Williams, G. D., Holland, J. L. 1978. *An evaluation of the 1977 minority introduction to engineering summer program. Tech. Rep. 270.* Cent. Soc. Organ. Sch., Johns Hopkins Univ. 90 pp.

Robbins, P. I., Thomas, L. E., Harvey, D. W., Kandefer, C. 1978. Career change and congruence of personality type: An examination of DOT derived work environment designations. *J. Vocat. Behav.* 13:15–25

Roberts, C. A., Johansson, C. B. 1974. The inheritance of cognitive interest styles among twins. *J. Vocat. Behav.* 4:237–43

Roe, A. 1979. Confronting complexity. *Acad. Psychol. Bull.* 1:19–21

Rounds, J. B., Davison, M. L., Dawis, R. V. 1979. The fit between Strong-Campbell Interest Inventory general occupational themes and Holland's hexagonal model. *J. Vocat. Behav.* 15:303–15

Rounds, J. B., Dawis, R. V., Lofquist, L. H. 1979. Life history correlates of vocational needs for a female adult sample. *J. Couns. Psychol.* 26:487–96

Salomone, P. R., Slaney, R. B. 1978. The applicability of Holland's theory to non-professional workers. *J. Vocat. Behav.* 13:63–74

Schein, E. H. 1978. *Career Dynamics: Matching Individual and Organizational Needs.* Reading, Mass: Addison-Wesley. 276 pp.

Schenk, G. E., Johnston, J. A., Jacobsen, K. 1979. The influence of a career group experience on the vocational maturity of college students. *J. Vocat. Behav.* 14:284–96

Shubsachs, A. P., Rounds, J. B., Dawis, R. V., Lofquist, L. H. 1978. Perception of work reinforcer systems: Factor structure. *J. Vocat. Behav.* 13:54–62

Siebel, C. E., Walsh, W. B. 1977. A modification of the instructions to Holland's Self-Directed Search. *J. Vocat. Behav.* 11:282–90

Slaney, R. B. 1978. Expressed and inventoried vocational interests: A comparison of instruments. *J. Couns. Psychol.* 25:520–29

Slaney, R. B. 1980. Expressed vocational choice and vocational indecision. *J. Couns. Psychol.* 27:122–29

Sloan, E. B. 1979. *An investigation of relationships between vocational needs and personality.* PhD thesis. Univ. Minn., Minneapolis

Snodgrass, G., Healy, C. C. 1979. Developing a replicable career decision-making counseling procedure. *J. Couns. Psychol.* 26:210–16

Snyder, R. A., Howard, A., Hammer, T. H. 1978. Mid career change in academia: The decision to become an administrator. *J. Vocat. Behav.* 13:229–41

Speas, C. M. 1979. Job-seeking interview skills training: A comparison of four instructional techniques. *J. Couns. Psychol.* 26:405–12

Spence, J. T., Helmreich, R. L. 1978. *Masculinity and Femininity: Their Psychological Dimensions, Correlates and Antecedents.* Austin: Univ. Texas Press. 297 pp.

Spokane, A. R. 1979. Validity of Holland's categories for college women and men. *J. Coll. Stud. Pers.* 20:335–40

Spokane, A. R., Malett, S. D., Vance, F. L. 1978. Consistent curricular choice and congruence of subsequent changes. *J. Vocat. Behav.* 13:45–53

Spokane, A. R., Walsh, W. B. 1978. Occupational level and Holland's theory for employed men and women. *J. Vocat. Behav.* 12:145–54

Stickney, P. D. 1978. *Vocational needs, occupational reinforcers, job satisfaction, and job turnover among work adjustment specialists.* MA thesis. Univ. Minn., Minneapolis

Super, D. E., Hall, D. T. 1978. Career development: Exploration and planning. *Ann. Rev. Psychol.* 29:333–72

Super, D. E., Harris-Bowlsbey, J. 1979. *Guided Career Exploration.* New York: Psychol. Corp. 79 pp.

Super, D. E., Kidd, J. M. 1979. Vocational maturity in adulthood: Toward turning a model into a measure. *J. Vocat. Behav.* 14:225–70

Super, D. E., Starishevsky, R., Matlin, N., Jordaan, J. P. 1963. *Career Development: Self-concept Theory.* Princeton, NJ: Coll. Entrance Exam. Board. 95 pp.

Super, D. E., Thompson, A. S. 1979. A six-scale, two-factor measure of adolescent career or vocational maturity. *Vocat. Guid. Q.* 28:6–15

Takai, R., Holland, J. L. 1979. Comparison of the Vocational Card Sort, The SDS, and the Vocational exploration and Insight Kit. *Vocat. Guid. Q.* 27:312–18

Talbot, D. B., Birk, J. M. 1979. Does the Vocational Exploration and Insight Kit equal the sum of its parts?: A comparison study. *J. Couns. Psychol.* 26:359–62

Thomas, L. E., Robbins, P. I. 1979. Personality and work environment congruence of mid-life career changers. *J. Occup. Psychol.* 52:177–83

Tiedeman, D. V., Katz, M. R., Miller-Tiedeman, A., Osipow, S. H. 1978. *The Cross Sectional Story of Early Career Develop-ment.* Washington DC: Am. Pers. Guid. Assoc. 183 pp.

Tiedeman, D. V., O'Hara, R. P. 1963. *Career Development: Choice and Adjustment.* Princeton, NJ: Coll. Entrance Exam. Board. 108 pp.

Touchton, J. B., Magoon, T. M. 1977. Occupational daydreams as predictors of vocational plans for college women. *J. Vocat. Behav.* 10:156–66

Travers, R. M. 1978. *Children's Interests.* Kalamazoo: West. Mich. Univ. 146 pp.

Tyler, L. E. 1978. *Individuality.* San Francisco: Jossey-Bass. 274 pp.

U.S. Department of Labor. 1979. *Guide for Occupational Exploration.* Washington DC: GPO. 715 pp.

Vaitenas, R., Wiener, Y. 1977. Developmental, emotional and interest factors in voluntary mid-career change. *J. Vocat. Behav.* 11:291–304

Walsh, W. B. 1979. Vocational behavior and career development, 1978: A review. *J. Vocat. Behav.* 15:119–54

Walsh, W. B., Bingham, R., Horton, J. A., Spokane, A. 1979. Holland's theory and college-degreed working black and white women. *J. Vocat. Behav.* 15:217–23

Westbrook, B. W. 1978. *Career Development Needs of Adults.* Washington DC: Am. Pers. Guid. Assoc. 36 pp.

Wiener, Y., Vaitenas, R. 1977. Personality correlates of voluntary mid-career change in enterprising occupations. *J. Appl. Psychol.* 62:706–12

Wiggins, J. D., Weslander, D. 1977. Expressed vocational choices and later employment compared with Vocational Preference Inventory and Kuder Preference Record—Vocational Scores. *J. Vocat. Behav.* 11:158–65

Winefordner, D. W. 1979. *AEL Career Planning and Decision-Making.* Bloomington, Ill: McKnight

Wirtenberg, J. T. 1979. *The impact of a sex-desegregated practical arts course on maximization of occupational potential in seventh grade girls.* PhD thesis. Univ. Calif., Los Angeles

Yanico, B. J. 1978. Sex bias in career information: Effects of language on attitudes. *J. Vocat. Behav.* 13:26–34

Young, R. A. 1979. The effects of value confrontation and reinforcement counseling on the career planning attitudes and behavior of adolescent males. *J. Vocat. Behav.* 15:1–11

Zener, T. B., Schnuelle, L. 1976. Effects of the Self-Directed Search on high school students. *J. Couns. Psychol.* 23:353–59

Ann. Rev. Psychol. 1981. 32:307–56

MASS COMMUNICATION EFFECTS

❖347

Donald F. Roberts and Christine M. Bachen[1]

Institute for Communication Research, Stanford University, Stanford, California 94305

CONTENTS

INTRODUCTION AND OVERVIEW

It is appropriate to describe the state of mass communication research at the end of the 1970s as resurgent. By the end of the 1950s the field was limping along under the burden of the "law of minimal effects"—the generalization that the dominant influence of the mass media was reinforcement

[1]Preparation of this review was aided by a grant from the John and Mary R. Markle Foundation.

0066-4308/81/0201-0307$01.00

of the status quo, an effect viewed by many as having little import (Katz 1977, Comstock et al 1978). The past decade, however, has witnessed a revival of the view that the mass media exert powerful influences on the way people perceive, think about, and ultimately act in their world.

The field's resurgence is manifested in various ways. One is the presence in our bibliography of a number of communication journals and annuals that simply did not exist when the decade began. In addition, a number of major syntheses of the effects of mass media on different aspects of human behavior have appeared (Kraus & Davis 1976, Lerner & Nelson 1977, Comstock et al 1978, Murray & Kippax 1979). A third indicator of the field's revival is the emergence (in some cases reemergence) of an array of new and important dependent variables—a broadening of the meaning of the term "mass media effect." The earlier focus on persuasion and attitude change has given way to a belief that the media exert important influences on the consciousness and world view of the audience (Gerbner & Gross 1976a, Katz 1980). Concern with cognitive effects, with mass communication's influence on how people perceive and organize their world, is becoming more the rule than the exception. Moreover, "cognitive" effects are being conceptualized more broadly, extending beyond traditional knowledge indexes to include such outcomes as perceptions of reality, issue salience, information holding, message discrimination, and so forth (Clarke & Kline 1974, Chaffee 1977). Other healthy trends include increased attention to contingent conditions underlying media effects (McLeod & Reeves 1980), a return to a concern with entertainment fare and its impact on consciousness and cognitions (Gerbner et al 1979, Tannenbaum 1980), and growing attention to *processing* of mass mediated information including: examinations of how social and cognitive factors affect comprehension of narrative plots (Collins 1979a), of the role of cognitive development in children's comprehension of television messages (Wackman & Wartella 1977, Roberts et al 1978), and of whether "meaning" is extracted from print and television in the same way (Salomon 1979a). Finally, the field is beginning to spawn a number of lively theoretical and methodological debates. Special issues of journals, entire annuals, and a number of syntheses and "reconsiderations" debate whether "there is any there, there . . ." in terms of such issues as uses and gratifications research (Blumler & Katz 1974, Swanson 1979a), the impact of television violence (Comstock et al 1978, Eysenck & Nias 1978), the role of mass communication in economic and social development (Rogers 1976a, Schramm & Lerner 1976), and the significance for broadcasting of social research (Carey 1978, Halloran 1978, Katz 1978a,b).

All this is not to say that characterizations of mass communication research applied by earlier reviewers—descriptions of the field as a potpourri, a borrowing area, lacking in unifying theory, a collection of suburbs in search of a city (Schramm 1962, Tannebaum & Greenberg 1968, Weiss 1971, Liebert & Schwartzberg 1977)—are no longer accurate. They remain as valid today as they were then. But this should not be surprising given the sheer ubiquity of the mass media in everyday aspects of contemporary U.S. society, hence the "problem orientation" of the field. Almost every dimension of social behavior is at least potentially influenced by mass communication (Weiss 1969, Comstock et al 1978, Chaffee 1979). Politics, health, prosocial and antisocial behavior, attitudes toward almost every definable group within society, occupational knowledge, education, consumer behavior, all these and more have been pointed to by parents, educators, policy makers, and the media themselves as being influenced, for better or ill, by mass communication. In the face of such an array of concerns, researchers from a variety of fields with a variety of theoretical orientations contribute to the mass communication research literature in order to "solve problems." Small wonder that so many of these contributions maintain an applied tenor, and that "communication variables" seem to proliferate faster than does our understanding (Foley 1979).

This problem orientation is one of the factors that for so long led researchers to concentrate on attitude and behavior change as *the* important media effect. At bottom, public concern with media portrayals of sex or violence, or with the role of television in political campaigns, is based on assumptions of direct effects of media content on behavior. And given the dominant view of the 1950s and 1960s that attitudes directly mediated behavior, it was reasonable to focus on the impact of media on behavior when convenient (e.g. votes, fights in the schoolyard) and on attitudes when less convenient (e.g. whom do you like or dislike?). It was only as the gradual accumulation of evidence made the causal linkages among knowledge, attitude, and behavior highly ambiguous that the media's impact on various cognitive indicators began to receive more attention (Chaffee 1977). Thus, current research and theorizing indicate that the cognitive outcomes of mass communication, whether from informational or entertainment content, are no longer taken for granted or deemed less important than attitudinal or behavioral outcomes (Chaffee 1977, Dennis 1978). Rather, various cognitive effects have gained at least conceptual equality, and in some areas, conceptual dominance.

This is not to imply that concern with how specific kinds of media content affect people's behavior or with how special groups of people might be affected is waning. Mass communication research continues to respond to problems articulated by various interest groups and/or funding sources because the media continue to impinge on most areas of social behavior. Thus, much of the literature organizes itself around various "problems" defined in terms of the particular kind of behavior mass communication content is presumed to influence (e.g. politics, violence, health) or in terms of special audiences presumed to be particularly vulnerable (e.g. children, the poor, women, the aging) (Comstock 1978, Comstock et al 1978).

To some extent this review reflects that problem orientation because it is convenient and it indicates the kinds of research that have been emphasized. For example, we continue to deal with children and youth as a special audience, a practice which certainly mirrors current literature. Nevertheless, organization of empirical findings in terms of special topics or groups can be dysfunctional to the development of more general, middle-range theories of the process and effects of mass communication. To the extent that studies of political campaigns, product campaigns, health campaigns, and so forth are conceptualized and dealt with separately, the benefits of comparison are lost. We give up the advantage of sharpened contrast between differences, we risk overlooking important similarities, and we sometimes assume nonexistent differences. Comstock et al (1978) provide an example of the benefits to be gained from handling the results of two types of campaign—political and product oriented—within the same framework. The following pages attempt to overlay the more common problem areas with a somewhat more general, process-oriented framework.

A few caveats are necessary. The literature search concentrated on work published between 1975 and early 1980, but some reference to earlier literature is made in order to provide a context for current research. The review does not pretend to be comprehensive. Given the eclectic nature of the field, our strategy was to emphasize work particularly relevant to psychologists. This we interpreted to mean primarily work concerned with the influence on individuals of exposure to media content. Hence, these pages contain little consideration of the various sociological and institutional studies that take a more macroscopic view of mass media processes and organizations. Finally, even in those topic areas that are covered, we make no claim to be all-inclusive. We attempted to provide a sense of the conceptual issues that have received research attention and to detail many, but not all, of the relevant empirical studies. We believe that the following pages fairly represent the mainstream of mass communication research over the past 5 years, at least insofar as the effects of mass communication on individuals are concerned.

PATTERNS OF USE

Exposure to the various media is a necessary precondition for any effect of content on people to occur. Exposure is a function of a number of environmental, social, and psychological conditions that influence the availability of various media and types of media content, the communication skills and information needs of people, and the psychosocial gratifications related to media use. The picture emerging from work reported during the past 5 years does not differ greatly from earlier findings. There has been a tendency for television use to increase; the evidence is that newspaper use is decreasing, patterns of radio and magazine use continue to receive short shrift in the academic literature; there is increasing attention to children's use of news media; there has been a great deal of activity in the area of uses and gratifications research.

Television

An extensive analysis of Nielsen data through 1976 indicates that the trend in amount of television viewing since the early 1960s has been upward. Although there are wide variations depending on which segment of the audience is surveyed, the trend holds across most demographic classifications but is most pronounced among groups which viewed less a decade ago. For example, from 1970 to 1976 the average hours per day that the household television set was on increased from 6.5 hours to over 6.8 hours. However, for that part of the sample in which the head of household had less than one year of college education the increase was only two tenths of an hour (from 6.8 to 7.0). But in households indexed by one or more years of college, the increase was almost eight tenths of an hour [from 5.6 to 6.39 (Comstock et al 1978)]. Moreover, over 25% of mothers in a recent national sample of families reported that the TV set was on for at least 9 hours per day (Newspaper Advertising Bureau 1978), and over 35% of a sample of California families were classified as "constant television households," households in which the set was on most of the afternoon, during dinner, and most of the evening (Medrich 1979). Amount of time the set is on, of course, is quite different from the amount of time that any particular individual views. Nevertheless, to the extent that an operating television set is a relatively constant feature of the environment, individuals tend to view more.

The most frequently examined predictors of individual television use continue to be gender, various socioeconomic status indicators, and age, with the latter receiving the greatest emphasis. Purposive television viewing begins between 2 and 3 years of age (Anderson et al 1979, von Feilitzen 1976). Several syntheses of a large number of U.S. studies describe the age progression in amount of viewing as one of gradual increase to a peak in early adolescence, followed by a sharp decline in late adolescence, relatively low amounts of viewing during adulthood, and then a gradual increase through later adulthood to the heaviest period of use after the age of 50 years (Bower 1973, Chaffee & Wilson 1975, Comstock et al 1978). A review of international studies of television viewing patterns generally accords with these findings (Murray & Kippax 1979).

The relationship between amount of television viewing and age can be largely attributed to variations in available time which occur as a function of competing activities located by different periods in the life cycle. This is illustrated by such phenomena as the temporary decrease in children's amount of viewing at about 5 or 6 years of age, when school begins to compete for their time (Comstock et al 1978), and by the dramatic increase in all media use among older people who, subsequent to retirement, have a good deal of time to view, listen, and read (Chaffee & Wilson 1975, Danowski 1975, Atkin 1976).

Studies continue to indicate that adult women view more than men (again, probably due to available time) and that amount of viewing is inversely related to education, income, and occupational status, although all of these relationships tend to be somewhat weaker than they were some years ago (Bower 1973, Comstock et al 1978). The data are also relatively consistent in the finding that blacks view more than whites even after controls for socioeconomic status and education are applied. More interesting is the evidence that patterns of television use among blacks depart rather dramatically from patterns revealed by whites. Younger black adults view more than do older blacks, and better educated blacks view more than do lesser educated blacks (Comstock et al 1978). Allen & Bielby (1979) point to the dangers in comparative studies that conceive of blacks as a relatively homogeneous group, and demonstrate wide variations in media behavior within a black sample.

The role ascribed to television in our society is that of light entertainer; hence, most people are content to "watch television" as opposed to watching particular programs (Comstock et al 1978). Probably the best indicator of what types of television content are viewed, then, is inherent in the distribution of programs in any TV log. Of course, various demographic and personality variables have been shown to relate to viewing of different types of television content. However, with the exception of a number of studies of children's exposure to news programming examined below, little has appeared to change the general patterns reported in earlier reviews (Liebert & Schwartzberg 1977, Comstock et al 1978).

Newspapers

Recent evidence suggests that daily newspaper readership is in a period of real decline. According to National Opinion Research Center surveys, the proportion of adults who claimed to read a newspaper every day declined from 73% in 1967, to 66% in 1975, to only 57% in 1978 (Robinson & Jeffres 1979).

Attempts to explain the decrease have ranged from examinations of increased television news programming (Bogart 1975a) to sociological phenomena such as the decline in home ownership, the increase in single person households, the increase of women in the labor force, changes in amount of available time, and fractionation of the cities (Bogart 1975b, Denbow 1975, Robinson & Jeffres 1979), to such psychological constructs as "traditional values," "satisfaction with life" (Bryant et al 1976), and various civic attitudes (McCombs & Poindexter 1978). Stamm & Fortini-Campbell (1977) report strong positive correlations between individuals' sense of belonging to a community and newspaper subscriptions and readership.

Most of the same demographic variables that predict television use also predict newspaper readership. However, several of the relationships are reversed. Two recent, large-scale studies (Newspaper Advertising Bureau 1978, 1980a,b,c, Robinson & Jeffres 1979) continue to find that daily newspaper reading is positively related to income and education, that whites read more than blacks, and that there is less newspaper availability in single parent households and in households with younger children.

Newspaper readership is directly related to age (Robinson & Jeffres 1979), the relationship appearing as early as the elementary school years (Newspaper Advertising Bureau 1980a). Large proportions of younger people, however, do not have the newspaper habit. Robinson & Jeffres (1979) found that over 85% of a national sample of people over 60 years reported "using a newspaper yesterday," but just 51% of adults under the age of 29 years did so. A particularly noteworthy dimension of this finding is that it represents an increase in the age differences found a decade earlier. That is, there is a striking trend toward decreasing newspaper use across age cohorts; young adults who do not manifest a newspaper habit are less likely than earlier generations to develop that habit as they grow older (Jennings & Niemi 1975, Robinson & Jeffres 1979). Conversely, each succeeding generation is more likely than its predecessor to cite television over newspapers as its major news source (Roper Organization 1977). These findings take on particular significance in light of research (reported later) on the relationship between media use and public affairs knowledge.

Children and the News Media

Interest in the role of the mass media in the political socialization of children has sparked increased attention to children's exposure to news and public affairs media. Not surprisingly, most children's introduction to the world of politics and public affairs comes through television. Although much of the evidence is based on nonrandom samples of children, and it is often difficult to determine just what "news viewing" consists of, several studies converge in their finding that children are exposed to television news at much younger ages than had been previously assumed (Hawkins et al 1975, Roberts et al 1975, Rubin 1978, Prisuta 1979). Indeed, news viewing occurs among significant numbers of early elementary school and even kindergarten children (Atkin 1978, Egan 1978). Most studies find that news viewing increases with age throughout the childhood and adolescent years to the point that almost all adolescents report at least minimal television news exposure. Atkin (1978) found that over half of a sample of elementary school children watched Saturday morning children's news programming "a lot." There is also evidence that self-reported liking for news programs predicts amount of news viewing even among young children (Atkin 1978, Prisuta 1979), although these data suffer from problems of correlated response error.

Newspaper use, of course, depends on the development of reading skills. The newspaper, as well as other print media, begins to be relatively comprehensible after the age of 9 years, which is also about the time that school-related newspaper use begins. By late adolescence half of the 15- to 17-year-olds responding reported regular newspaper reading (Newspaper Advertising Bureau 1980a). The importance of the newspaper as a source of information increases throughout the school years (Conway et al 1975, Newspaper Advertising Bureau 1980a,b). In spite of the increase in newspaper use, however, the data are quite clear that children continue to prefer television over newspapers as a source of information during both the elementary school years (Egan 1978) and the high school years (Atkins & Elwood 1978), a trend which we have already noted now continues into adulthood. High school students also label television as the most believable news medium (Atkins & Elwood 1978).

Attention has also focused on how the family context influences children's use of the news media. There is evidence for a modeling effect in that children whose parents view television news are more likely to view, and for an effect of direct stimulation in that children whose parents discuss the news with them are more likely to view (Atkin 1978, Egan 1978). Similarly, the availability of a daily newspaper in the household, parental newspaper behavior, and parental discussion of newspaper content all predict children's newspaper use (Newspaper Advertising Bureau 1980a,c). Finally, the family communication system typology described by Chaffee et al (1977) indicates how the norms inherent in a family interactions influence children's public affairs media use. Children from homes stressing independent thinking and self-expression on potentially controversial topics continue to report more exposure to the news media (Jackson-Beeck & Chaffee 1975, Roberts et al 1975).

Given the evidence that parents and the environment they create are important mediators of children's future news media behavior, and that successive cohorts of young adults use newspapers less and television news more, the decline in newspaper readership and increased dependence on television for news and information seems likely to continue at an increasing pace.

Uses and Gratifications

Although recent claims that uses and gratifications research has become the most popular and important approach to the study of mass communication (Swanson 1979a,b) seem a bit overstated, the amount of empirical activity and theoretical debate focusing on the uses and gratifications approach certainly supports Blumler & Katz's (1974) contention that "it is well and truly launched on a third major phase of its development . . ." (p. 13). Uses and gratifications research is audience centered, asking what people do with media rather than what the media do to people. It has been summarized as "concerned with 1. the social and psychological origins of 2. needs, which generate 3. expectations of 4. the mass media or other sources, which lead to 5. differential patterns of media exposure (or engagement in other activities), resulting in 6. need gratifications and 7. other consequences, perhaps mostly unintended ones" (Katz et al 1974, p. 20). Blumler & Katz (1974) characterize early uses and gratifications studies (1940s and 50s) as primarily descriptive, and the second phase (1960s) as mainly concerned with operationalizing the needs presumed to mediate different patterns of media consumption. Current work they see as more explanatory in nature—concerned with relating media consumption to systematic formulations of social and psychological needs and, ultimately, with understanding the relationship between patterns of gratifications sought and obtained and media effects. Palmgreen & Rayburn (1979) argue that it is just this emphasis on the "active" audience and concern with how need-related gratification activities mediate effects that underlies the burgeoning popularity of the approach. Certainly current work expresses these concerns, but empirical demonstrations of the genesis of basic needs presumed to underlie consumption, or of how gratifications sought and/or obtained mediate more "traditional" effects, or that the audience is indeed active, are more the exception than the rule.

Not surprisingly, increased interest in uses and gratifications research has spawned critical voices. Several point to the tautological shortcomings of functional theories in general (Carey & Kreiling 1974, Elliott 1974, Anderson & Meyer 1975), and comment on the problems inherent in uses and gratifications' concentration on the individual-as-system rather than the individual-within-a-system (Elliot 1974, Messaris 1977). The approach is also taken to task as fundamentally "atheoretical," as being more a research strategy or hueristic than a theory (Elliot 1974, Weiss 1976, Swanson 1977, Becker 1979), and as failing to provide any systematic linkages between media gratifications and their social and psychological origins (Katz et al 1974, Levy 1977). Swanson (1976, 1977, 1979b) scores the approach for lack of conceptual clarity, noting that terms such as "function," "use," "gratification," "need," and "motive" are rarely defined, let alone explicated. Similarly, Blumler (1979) notes a number of problems with the notion of the "active" audience, including a great deal of variance in meaning for the term, a tendency to treat activity as an either/or matter, and failure to recognize that activity might vary across both media and time. Swanson (1979b) argues that audience activity should be defined only in terms of the assignment of meaning—selectivity during interpretation as opposed to selective exposure or selective attention (Katz 1979)—and contends that the typical research strategy of relating exposure patterns to gratifications precludes the possibility of demonstrating an active audience.

Critics have also focused on the approach's reliance on self-report data. This method, it is argued, forces respondents to treat all exposure as the result of deliberate choice (ignoring possible roles of habit, social expectations, casual encounters, etc), risks eliciting conventional beliefs about media use because it demands a degree of awareness and analytical ability that respondents may not have, is subject to distortion because of its retrospective nature, and provides no independent evidence for the existence or importance of respondent-identified needs or gratifications (Elliot 1974, Messaris 1977, Becker 1979).

Recent empirical work reveals that although much of the criticism is deserved, issues raised by the critics are being addressed (Katz 1979). For example, consider the extensive list of needs that adults report they seek to gratify through the mass media: surveillance, excitement, reinforcement, guidance, anticipated communication, relaxation, alienation, information acquisition, interpretation, tension reduction, social integration, social and parasocial interaction, entertainment, affective guidance, behavioral guidance, social contact, self and personal identity, reassurance, escape, and so on (McLeod & Becker 1974, Peled & Katz 1974, Canadian Broadcasting Corporation 1975, Kippax & Murray 1977, Levy 1977, Wenner 1977, Nordlund 1978, Becker 1979). Needs articulated by children and adolescents show some differences, but many more similarities (Brown et al 1974, Greenberg 1974, Johnstone 1974, von Feilitzen 1976, Lometti et al 1977, Rubin 1979). And needs articulated by a sample of elderly people look very much the same (Danowski 1975, Wenner 1976). Such profusion can be frustrating, but may be due more to the kind of looseness of terminology noted earlier than to any legitimate proliferation of needs. That is, just as Murray & Kippax (1979) found in a survey of cross-national studies, a general picture of four basic clusters of needs into which most of the foregoing can be fitted tends to emerge: self and personal identity, social contact, diversion and entertainment, and information and knowledge about the world. Blumler (1979) argues for reduction to three fundamental orientations toward the media: cognitive, diversion, and personal. But regardless of whether one settles on three, four, or five clusters of needs, the point is that there is a high degree of similarity in the various lists, a convincing convergence for the very reason that it emerges from such profusion (Katz 1979).

Other trends in current uses and gratifications research also speak to some of the criticisms. Studies have been concerned with validating various gratifications measures and with examining the notion of communication avoidances—reasons for not reading, viewing, or listening (McLeod & Becker 1974, Levy 1977, Becker 1979). Research has tested the assumption that individuals differentiate among channels on the basis of expected gratifications and that different media do indeed fulfill different needs (Lometti et al 1977, Stroman & Becker 1978, Adoni 1979). Palmgreen and his associates (Palmgreen & Rayburn 1979; Palmgreen et al 1980) have begun to examine the relationship between gratifications sought from the media and gratifications obtained. They find important differences between the two dimensions which argues against the teleological criticism that any gratification sought must be obtained, and raises several new theoretical issues. Finally, following the lead of Blumler & McQuail (1969) and attempting to support the active audience assumption, a few studies report evidence linking gratifications (or avoidances) to such traditional "effects" measures as political information, political attitudes, and perceptions of issue salience (McLeod & Becker 1974, McLeod et al 1974, Becker 1976).

The predominant "cognitive" or "instrumental" flavor of most of the studies cited above bears comment. There is a striking tendency for uses and gratifications researchers to concentrate on the utilitarian aspects of media consumption. They concentrate on political communication (Becker 1979) or news (Levy 1977, 1978) or on public television (Palmgreen & Rayburn 1979). They ask where adolescents obtain useful family planning information (Kline et al 1974) and political values (Adoni 1979). They focus on media use during significant sociopolitical events such as wars (Dotan & Cohen 1976) or political scandals (Becker 1976). Of course, even studies of the news generate mention of entertainment, of diversion, of escape, but it is striking how seldom uses and gratifications researchers examine the entertainment function in and of itself. When one considers that most people use most media most of the time for entertainment (Comstock et al 1978, Tannenbaum 1980), the relative absence of research on this central function of mass communication is disconcerting to say the least. It is to be hoped that Tannenbaum's (1980) recent volume signals the emergence of more concern with the entertainment function per se.

EFFECTS ON ADULTS

To the extent that concern focuses on how individuals respond to media content, the fundamental effects of mass communication are cognitive. Regardless of whether influence is direct or indirect, immediate or delayed, short-term or long-term, regardless of whether ultimate concern is with emotions, attitudes, or behavior, any "effect" of media content on individuals originates with whether and how people interpret and incorporate information transmitted by the media into their existing conceptualizations of the world (Roberts 1971). Thus, the basic link between media content and human social behavior is forged in the interaction between information transmitted by the media on the one hand and human information processing on the other. This implies that differences in responses to mass communication may derive from variations in exposure to media or types of media content—the kinds of variations touched on in preceding paragraphs. Or, more important to the present section, differences in response may derive from variations in how similar messages are interpreted by different people or by similar people under differing conditions. Hence, one trend of recent mass communication research has been to specify the various conditions under which people respond to mass-mediated information (McLeod & Reeves 1980).

Recent work has also begun to assess the cognitive effects of media in more audience-centered terms. Attention has been focused on the media's role in determining what issues people think about—the public's agenda— quite independent of how much they might know about any one of those issues. Measures of information "holding" as distinct from knowledge have been used. Other work takes what can be called a cultural perspective, attempting to assess the relationship between media use and the cultivation of major dimensions of belief systems—how people conceive of power or roles or norms within a given society. And, of course, there is continued fascination with communication campaigns, with the role of the mass media in planned change programs. The following pages review those areas that have received more than passing research attention over the past 5 years.

Transmission of Knowledge and Information

Typically the media's ability to transmit information is examined in the context of news and public affairs content. This practice reflects the view, articulated by communication scholars (Schramm 1971) and media practitioners (Halberstam 1979) alike, that the primary function of the news media is to provide information. Clearly the effects of public affairs content, the avowed purpose of which is to inform, deserve close scrutiny. Nevertheless, it is also clear that content designed to fulfill other functions (e.g. entertainment) also conveys a great deal of information.

People perceive themselves as acquiring a great deal of information from the mass media. When the Roper Organization (1977) asked a national sample of adults where they get most of their information about "what's going on in the world," over 95% answered in terms of the mass media.

Often such self-perceptions are tested by relating media exposure to scores on various knowledge indices, usually comprised of specific questions about current political figures or issues. Work in this vein conducted prior to 1975 is reviewed by Becker et al (1975) and by Kraus & Davis (1976). More recent studies using respondents ranging from black adolescents (Tan & Vaughn 1976), to adults from various different nations (Chaffee & Izcaray 1975, Feigert 1976), to a variety of U.S. samples continue to find moderate positive relationships between public affairs media use and current affairs knowledge (Atkin et al 1976, Atkin & Heald 1976, Patterson & McClure 1976, Palmgreen 1979, Quarles 1979, Becker & Whitney 1980). In many of these studies the relationship has withstood controls for education, although education itself is more often than not found to be a stronger predictor of knowledge than is media use.

Partly in response to what they feel may be a premature acceptance of the generalization that education is vastly more important than media use for current affairs knowledge acquisition, Clarke & Kline (1974) have called for new approaches to measuring both media exposure and knowledge. Their reconsideration of media effects argues against the normative, intrusive nature of knowledge items based on the kinds of "textbook" information that, although salient to educators and researchers, may not be at all relevant knowledge to the public. They advocate more audience centered measures of "information holding," based on "problems" articulated by respondents and the number of solutions and actors that are mentioned in relation to those problems. Similarly, they propose to abandon media use indices for measures of "message discrimination" based on asking people whether they have seen, read, or heard anything about the self-nominated problems, and obtaining descriptions of the content and channel of these "discriminated" messages. A trend toward employing measures of information holding and message discrimination has begun to emerge in the literature. As with the traditional approaches, studies using such audience-centered measures also find positive relationships between levels of information and both media exposure and message discrimination (Edlestein 1974, Palmgreen et al 1974, Clarke & Fredin 1978, Becker et al 1979a). Moreover, at least under some conditions message discrimination has been found to be more strongly related to information holding than is either media use (Palmgreen 1979) or education (Clarke & Kline 1974).

A number of findings elaborate and modify these first-order relationships between media use and information. Perhaps most striking among them is that the term "media use" is too general. Contrary to popular conceptions of the dominance of television news, much of this work indicates that it is more accurate to talk about a relationship between print use and knowledge. In those studies where newspaper vs television comparisons were made, only two instances of even moderate positive relationships between television use and knowledge appeared (Atkin et al 1976, Atkin & Heald 1976); in most studies the television-knowledge relationship hovered near zero (Patterson & McClure 1976, Tan & Vaughn 1976, Clarke & Fredin 1978, Becker et al 1979b, Quarles 1979, Becker & Whitney 1980). These findings are somewhat disturbing given the evidence reviewed earlier indicating a general decline in regular newspaper use with each succeeding generation.

One explanation offered for the superior power of newspaper use vs television exposure to predict knowledge levels is based on differences between the media in format and content. That television's search for exciting visuals often leads to a focus on peripheral aspects of the news, on action and events rather than issues and policies, is well documented (Robinson 1975, Carey 1976, Hofstetter & Zukin 1979). Hence, it is argued, people who depend on television for their news obtain a fragmented, nonrepresentative view of the world which mediates against the acquisition of substantive current events information. Patterson & McClure (1976) write: "Network news may be fascinating. It may be highly entertaining. But it is simply not informative" (p. 54). The implicit value judgment in this argument, of course, is that the corpus of information found in newspapers is more substantive, more "central" than that found in television. A second explanation posits that the superiority of print for imparting knowledge stems from differences in people's skill at processing information from the two media which, in turn, stems from differences in training. This argument notes that in our society both the current educational system and norms developed prior to the advent of broadcasting emphasize and train people to deal with print for information acquisition. Hence the obtained differences in predictive power are hypothesized to reflect differences in training or other information processing variables (Becker & Whitney 1980). But in at least one experiment literate adults acquired far more information from television news than did adult nonreaders, indicating that the skills necessary for reading also enhance the ability to decode audiovisual information (Stauffer et al 1978).

All this, of course, is not to say that people do not acquire information from television. Indeed they do, as is demonstrated when the measure of information acquisition is specific to observed television content and viewers and nonviewers are compared. Recent examples of this approach in the area of current events information are found in studies of the impact of the Carter-Ford debates. These found that debate viewing led to increased information about the candidates, the differences between them, and their stands on various issues (Morrison et al 1977, Bishop et al 1978, Wald &

Lupfer 1978, Dennis et al 1979, Miller & MacKuen 1979). Results of these and other studies of the debates are fully discussed in several overview papers (Chaffee 1978, Chaffee & Dennis 1979, Sears & Chaffee 1979). In addition, studies report that exposure to televised political commercials is related to increased information about issues and candidates (Atkin & Heald 1976, Patterson & McClure 1976).

The studies cited above have examined a number of other variables that, depending on conditions, influence the media use-information level relationship. These include consideration of such factors as whether concern is with local or national affairs and amount and quality of media coverage (Clarke & Fredin 1978, Palmgreen 1979, Becker & Whitney 1980), and of such social and psychological factors as group membership, number of coorientation peers and discussion partners, interest in politics, motivations for using news media, degree of black nationalism, age, education, and so on (Chaffee & Izcaray 1975, Atkin et al 1976, Tan & Vaughn 1976, Genova & Greenberg 1979, Palmgreen 1979, Quarles 1979). The relationships are anything but simple, and recent work makes it abundantly clear that one of the more important tasks facing the field is careful specification of the conditions under which various media effects do and do not occur.

The Gap Hypothesis

Work concerned with the knowledge gap hypothesis exemplifies why such elaboration of contingent conditions is necessary. As initially formulated in communication research, the gap hypothesis simply states that higher socioeconomic segments of a population acquire information from the mass media faster than do lower socioeconomic segments, thus increasing the difference in the amount of knowledge held by the two segments (Tichenor et al 1970). Stated thus, the hypothesis implies that any attempt to use media to equalize the distribution of knowledge within a social system seems doomed not just to fail, but to increase inequities. Moreover, the initial hypothesis fails to specify any factors mediating the knowledge gap. However, several recent studies find conditions under which knowledge gaps (as well as other communication effects gaps) narrow (Tichenor et al 1973, Donohue et al 1975, Shingi & Mody 1976, Maccoby et al 1977, McLeod et al 1979), calling the initial implication of the hypothesis into question and emphasizing the need to construct and elaborate a theoretical model to explain knowledge gap phenomena.

Several recent papers have attempted the latter task. Ettema & Kline (1977) list a number of factors that have been posited, usually as post hoc explanations, to account for widening and narrowing of the knowledge gap. These, they argue, can be reduced to three categories of causal factors that may account for knowledge gap phenomena: 1. transitational deficits (lack of communication skills) on the part of one of the population segments under consideration; 2. between-group differences in perceived relevance and/or motivation to acquire the information under study; 3. ceiling effects imposed either by message content or by the information of concern. Although there have been no direct tests of the three models, the tenor of the Ettema and Kline paper tends to favor a difference interpretation because in most instances in which a widening of the gap has been demonstrated, factors that might reduce the motivation of lower socioeconomic segments of the population to acquire information seem to have been operating. Moreover, findings that the knowledge gap narrowed when concern focused on local community issues about which there was conflict also points to a motivational interpretation (Donohue et al 1975). Conflict, it is argued, increases both information salience and the likelihood of interpersonal discussion among various population segments, as well as the functionality of acquiring such information. Genova & Greenberg (1979) also argue that interest in an issue is a better predictor of a knowledge gap than is socioeconomic status.

Additional evidence that motivational differences are important mediators of gap phenomena comes from an imaginative study of "equivalences" in use of and response to the Carter-Ford debates and communication about the debates (McLeod et al 1979). This work moves the gap literature forward on several fronts: it is based on a longitudinal design permitting examination of change; it includes exposure to several different information sources; it measures involvement, decision making, participation, and attachment to system values as well as knowledge; it divides the sample not only in terms of education but also on the basis of age and interest in politics. Moreover, the study makes an important distinction between "equivalence of exposure" and "equivalence of effect" and examines whether obtained differences on a given criterion are more strongly related to differences in exposure or to predictive strength given equal exposure (the latter indicating differences in communication skills). Their finding that less educated, younger, and less interested people were less exposed to the debates and to information about them, but gained as much as did better educated, older, and more interested people per *unit of exposure,* supports a motivational as opposed to a deficit interpretation of gap phenomena. Their finding that a gap was more likely to occur on measures other than knowledge is also important, given that most "gap" research has focused on knowledge.

Agenda Setting

Research on the agenda-setting hypothesis has increased dramatically. We suspect that some of the popularity of the approach stems from its assertion of the power of the media in conjunction with its simultaneous affirmation of the independence of the individual—a promise of both cake and consumption.

Agenda setting refers to the ability of the mass media to influence the level of the public's awareness of issues as opposed to their specific knowledge about those issues—in Cohen's (1963) terms, what to think about as opposed to what to think. As initially put forth, the hypothesis deals with aggregate phenomena and proposes a main effect. It states that the degree to which the media attend to a given issue determines the degree to which the public ascribes importance to that issue. The strength of the causal hypothesis varies from a weak version that predicts simply an overlap between media and public agendas with little regard to their respective ordering of issues, to a moderate version that predicts similar rankings of issues, to a strong version that posits similar weightings of issues across the two agendas (McCombs 1977). Adequate tests of the hypothesis, then, depend on careful conceptualization and measurement of both the media and the public agenda and the execution of research designs that allow causal inferences. Unfortunately, the literature in this area is not marked by consistency in either area.

Media agendas have been measured via straightforward counts of the number of articles concerning various issues appearing in major news magazines (Funkhouser 1973, MacKuen 1979), enumeration of issues covered by newspapers and TV and then identified as salient by respondents (Palmgreen & Clarke 1977), counts of issue categories weighted by airtime or column inches over some specific period of time (Williams & Semlak 1978), and counts of stories referring to specific problems or controversies that were covered on the front page or editorial page of at least four of five selected newspapers (Gormley 1975). Similarly, there is variation in terms of whether the media agenda is examined in terms of a single, short-term event such as a presidential visit to a local city (Kaid et al 1977) or the presidential debates (Becker et al 1979b), a longer-term event such as a presidential campaign (McCombs & Shaw 1972), a single issue such as Watergate (Weaver et al 1975b), or an array of major issues that captured media attention across several decades (MacKuen 1979). Other variations in the operationalization of the media agenda which make comparisons difficult include the duration of the interval across which the index is constructed (Eyal et al 1979), the use of local vs national issues (Palmgreen & Clarke 1977) and other variations in the nature of issues (Eyal 1979), and the level of generality at which an "issue" is defined (Gormley 1975). The ease with which the agenda-setting effect is demonstrated increases the more broadly an issue area is defined.

Similar diversity is found in operationalizations of the public agenda. Measurement strategies have included importance ratings of a list of issues on closed-ended scales (Gormley 1975) and nominations of important problems in response to open-ended questions. The latter approach requests nominations of problems perceived to be personally important (McCombs & Shaw 1972), important to the community or country (MacKuen 1979), or issues most often talked about, or some combination of the preceding (Becker et al 1975, Williams & Semlak 1978, Becker et al 1979b).

Some investigators have been content to assume that the direction of causality is from media to public, making no attempt to eliminate the alternative possibilities that either the media respond to the public's agenda, or that both media and public agenda are simply reflections of an environment in which events set the agenda. Nevertheless, in spite of the lack of consistency across studies and the various methodological weaknesses in some of the research, there has been enough activity to permit some tentative generalizations and to indicate that the agenda-setting function of the media deserves close attention.

Fortunately, some work has introduced at least some of the controls necessary to permit causal inferences. Time-lagged correlational designs have been used to eliminate the possibility that the public agenda establishes the media agenda (Tipton et al 1975, McCombs 1977, Sohn 1978). And although for certain economic issues the public does seem to respond to the environment independently of media treatment (MacKuen 1979), there is mounting evidence that media emphasis on certain issues fluctuates from "objective" indicators of those issues in the environment and that public concern follows media emphases (Funkhouser 1973, MacKuen 1979). Overall, evidence supporting a causal influence of the media on the public's agenda, at least under some conditions, is beginning to accumulate.

Some work has attempted to go beyond the main effect prediction to specify both media related and audience related factors conditioning the agenda-setting effect. One of the most frequently examined conditioning factors is the nature of the medium. Both print and television have been shown to influence the public agenda. McCombs & Shaw's (1972) seminal work found effects for both media and no difference between them, several studies based exclusively on broadcast news have demonstrated the phenomenon (Siune & Borre 1975, Zucker 1978), and there is evidence that televised political commercials can raise the salience of issues (Patterson & McClure 1976). However, the many studies which compare the agenda setting function of TV and newspapers generally give the nod to print (Tipton et al 1975, Benton & Frazier 1976, McClure & Patterson 1976, McCombs 1977, McCombs & Weaver 1977, Mullins 1977, Weaver 1977, Williams & Larsen 1977). McClure & Patterson (1976) contend that television's role as an agenda setter improves for certain dramatic, highly pictorial events which are uncomplicated and which sustain intense and extended coverage, but Becker et al (1979b) found no agenda-setting impact of the televised presidential debates. On the other hand, Palmgreen & Clarke (1977) report that although newspapers exercised a stronger agenda-setting influence in terms of local issues, network television news was dominant for national issues. Two studies also report at least a minimal agenda-setting impact of radio (Siune & Borre 1975, Williams & Larsen 1977). There is also evidence that the agenda-setting impact of each medium may differ over time. McCombs (1977) found that television's influence increased over the course of an election campaign, although it never surpassed that of local newspapers. Eyal et al (1979) discuss the importance of the time frame within which the agenda-setting function of each medium might occur and be measured, and Eyal (1979) considers a variety of additional possible theoretical and methodological factors that might explain the apparent superiority of newspapers over television as agenda setters.

Among the various audience attributes that have been examined, fairly consistent results concern amount of media exposure. The strength of the agenda-setting phenomenon is directly related to amount of news exposure (Weaver et al 1975a,b, McClure & Patterson 1976). Weaver et al (1976) found that the agenda people held differed as a function of whether they reported relying primarily on television, on newspapers, or on both for political information, a result that Winter (1979) cites in his call for future work examining the nature as well as quantity of media exposure. Chaffee & Wilson's (1977) imaginative study of diversity in public agenda as a function of the number of newspapers available in a given community also supports the exposure-agenda relationship.

There have been few consistent findings on other audience related characteristics. Several studies have employed a measure of "need for orientation" —an index of "inherent curiosity about the environment" (Weaver et al 1975b)—as a predictor of agenda holding. This index has included measures of interest in or perceived relevance of a campaign, degree of certainty about a candidate or issue, party affiliation, and political participation. Work employing such indexes finds that higher levels of need for orientation locate greater acceptance of the media agenda (Weaver et al 1975a,b, Weaver 1977). However, it is difficult to determine just what the mediating factor is. Interest in the campaign is an important part of the index, but studies measuring interest alone have found positive relationships (MacKuen 1979) and negative relationships (McLeod et al 1974). Moreover, there has been enough variety in the way that various components of the need for orientation index have been operationalized to lead to some confusion. Williams & Semlak (1978), for example, listed eight variables that might be used in such an index and obtained different results depending on whether the media agenda was defined in terms of newspapers or television.

Other audience attributes examined in relation to the agenda-setting phenomenon include age (McLeod et al 1974), education (Mullins 1977, MacKuen 1979), respondents' amount of political information (Williams & Larsen 1977), and respondents' preference for one medium over another as a source of news (Williams & Larsen 1977, Williams & Semlak 1978).

Finally, there has been attention to the relationship between interpersonal communication and the agenda-setting effect, but the matter remains in dispute. Recent work has shown that interpersonal communication reduces the agenda-setting impact of the media (Weaver et al 1975a) and that it facilitates the impact (Atwood et al 1976). Winter (1979) examines these and earlier studies in terms of methodological differences that may account for the conflicting results. Given the evidence for a reciprocal relationship between mass communication behavior and interpersonal communication behavior, and Chaffee's (1979) convincing analysis of the futility of thinking in terms of competition between mass media and interpersonal channels, the role of interpersonal communication in agenda setting demands further investigation.

Cultivation of Beliefs

Ironically, several proponents of a return to the view that mass communications exert powerful influences argue for a return to the idea that the dominant effect is reinforcement. However, the rather innocent tone of Klapper's (1960) conclusion that the media serve primarily to reinforce existing attitudes has changed to "excursions and alarums" about the media's cultivation of a consciousness that seldom differs from an establishment view of the status quo. Klapper's work, of course, must be seen in an historical context of fear that the media had immense power to manipulate people immediately and directly—to change the status quo. More recent concern with the power of the media to affect belief systems derives from the revival of conflict theory and social criticism during the 1960s (Katz 1980). Katz calls what has emerged theories of "ideological effects" based on a view that the latent structure of mass media messages distorts (or selectively presents) reality in ways that perpetuate the interests of the existing power structure. These theories view media as the handmaidens of the establishment, arguing that news programming legitimizes managerial power (Glasgow group 1976), that current affairs programs advocate parlimentarianism (Hall 1977), that routine news practices perpetuate existing norms, conventions, and sociopolitical relationships (Tuchman 1977), that the fundamental message of television drama is the definition of the nature of power—a power that tends to reside in white, middle-class males who operate within established norms and conventions (Gerbner et al 1978, 1979).

Whether and how such latent messages are perceived by mass media audiences, and how they are responded to if they are perceived, are the critical questions to be asked if the validity of such theories is to be tested. Katz (1978b, 1980) voices optimism when he notes a progression in this work from surface to "deep" content analysis, to comparisons of media reality with independent measures of reality, and finally to recent attempts to operationalize measures of "consciousness" in order to examine how the audience might be affected. This move toward empirical tests of the powerful effects hypothesis is exemplified in the work of Noelle-Neumann and Gerbner.

Noelle-Neumann (1973, 1974) contends that because people avoid social isolation, they tend to voice opinions that support what they perceive to be dominant opinions and to suppress perceived "unpopular" opinions. This, in turn, changes the "opinion environment" such that it reinforces the perceived dominance of the majority opinion, which leads to further suppression of minority opinion, and so on, creating a "spiral of silence." She also notes that the mass media play a large role in defining the opinion environment. Because of their ubiquity, the repetitiveness of their messages, and the relative unanimity among journalists in how they view and report the world (a unanimity that tends to support the establishment), the media are viewed as operating to limit individual selective perception, hence to limit independent judgment. Thus, the opinion environment created by the mass media cannot but help to create a spiral of silence for all but the establishment opinion. A combination of rigorous content analyses and measures of public opinion compared *over time* has provided a method for testing the spiral of silence theory (Noelle-Neumann 1977). The results indicate that the media may restrict individual selective perception, and that the more they do so the more silent minority voices become and the more the dominant voice of the status quo is reinforced. In short, Noelle-Neumann appears to be developing a solid empirical basis for her call to return to a concept of at least one powerful media effect.

Reinforcement is also the dominant effect of television in the view of George Gerbner and his colleagues, but reinforcement of the most fundamental kind in that it is synonomous with enculturation. They assert that "television is the central cultural arm of American Society," and argue that the medium socializes people into standardized roles and behaviors not so much by affecting specific opinions and attitudes as through the "cultivation" of more basic assumptions about the nature of social reality (Gerbner & Gross 1976a,b). The ability of television to do this derives from: (*a*) the uniformity of its message system which acts to maintain and reinforce conventional values and behaviors, (*b*) the reach and scope of the medium and the nonselective use made of it, and (*c*) the realism with which it presents its view of the world, a realism that hides the synthetic, selective nature of television drama (Gerbner & Gross 1976a, Gerbner et al 1979).

The basic procedure for testing the cultivation model requires periodic analyses of large aggregates of programming in order to obtain comprehensive descriptions of the symbolic world of television. Among other things, these analyses reveal dimensions on which television's world differs from the real world. This, in turn, allows comparison of heavy and light television viewers' conceptions of reality on those dimensions where the real and symbolic worlds differ. Comparisons of this type have consistently demonstrated a stable relationship between patterns of television content and heavy viewers' conceptions of reality. For example, adults averaging four or more hours of televiewing per day were more likely than adults averaging two or less hours per day to overestimate both the proportion of people in the U.S. employed in law enforcement occupations and their own chances of being involved in a violent incident. Heavy viewers were also less likely to feel that most people can be trusted. In all cases, the responses of heavy viewers revealed a conception of the world that differs from reality but that is characteristic of television's world. Moreover, the responses withstood controls for age, education, gender, and amount of newspaper reading (Gerbner & Gross 1976a,b). Similar findings have been reported with samples of children (Gerbner et al 1978) and adolescents (Gerbner et al 1979). The 1979 article concludes: "The most significant and recurring conclusion of our long-range study is that one correlate of television viewing is a heightened and unequal sense of danger and risk in a mean and selfish world" (p. 196). Although interesting, the conclusion fails to satisfy the promise of the model. Given that these studies have extended over several years, it is disappointing that time-lagged procedures or some other form of causal analysis has not been applied to the data. The obtained synchronous relationships appear strong, but the critical test of the causal implication of the cultivation model remains to be conducted. Moreover, several recent studies raise doubts about some of the synchronous relationships used to support the model. Doob & Macdonald (1979) found no relationship between amount of television viewing and fear of the environment when the actual incidence of crime in respondents' neighborhoods was controlled. Even more fundamental questions are raised by Hirsch's (1980) extensive reanalysis of the National Opinion Research Center data set which Gerbner and his colleagues used to support much of the cultivation model. Hirsch finds "remarkably little support" for a cultivation effect, and warns that acceptance of the hypothesis at this time is premature and unwarranted. We suspect that the next few years will witness a healthy debate over the cultivation hypothesis.

Other studies have demonstrated television's impact on cultural images. Caron (1979) controlled Eskimo children's first experience with television and found that exposure to a TV series devoted to the portrayal of a variety of cultures had a significant impact on their images and evaluations of other cultural groups, particularly those close to them. Coldevin (1979) reports that the introduction of television into a previously isolated area of northern Canada accelerated adolescents' acculturation to Euro-Canadian structures and values, and increased the culture replacement gap between them and their more traditional parents.

Campaigns and Development

A long-standing debate in communication research concerns the ability of mass communication campaigns to produce change. The "minimal effects" position was largely based on early studies that found little change following campaigns conducted in the U.S. (Weiss 1969). On the other hand, an extensive literature on the role of communication in economic and social development, particularly in third world countries, presented a rather optimistic view of what mass media could do (Lerner & Schramm 1967, Rogers & Shoemaker 1971). Over the past decade, however, positions have changed. Development communication scholars have become much less sanguine about the potential of mass communication, acting alone, to engender meaningful change directly, at least in the third world (Rogers 1976a,b), while several health related campaigns have encouraged optimism among some U.S. researchers (Farquhar et al 1977, McAlister et al 1980).

The Stanford Heart Disease Prevention Program's (SHDPP) three community study exemplifies a successful U.S. campaign (Farquhar et al 1977, Maccoby et al 1977). This project used a community-based quasi-experimental field design (Farquhar 1978) to examine the potential of media to influence people's dietary, smoking, and exercise habits in order to reduce the risk of heart disease. Two communities received a two-year campaign using television, radio, newspapers, direct mail, billboards, and posters. In one of these communities, media were augmented with intensive face-to-face instruction of a subsample of "high risk" individuals. A third community served as a no-treatment control. At the end of a year, individuals in the treatment communities showed dramatic increases in knowledge about risk factors associated with heart disease. Moreover, there were significant decreases in saturated fat intake, numbers of cigarettes smoked, plasma-cholesterol levels, and systolic blood pressure. Overall, the probability of heart disease was reduced within campaign community samples while it actually increased in the control community. Finally, by the end of the second year of the campaign, the community receiving the media-only treatment manifested as much change as did the community augmented by face-to-face instruction

Several other health related media campaigns have also achieved significant change. Rogers (1976b) describes several successful radio-based public health and nutrition projects in Tanzania. In spite of its reputation as a failure, the televised experimental health program "Feeling Good" engendered a number of behavior changes among the few who saw it (Mielke & Swinehart 1976). A small-scale study in New York (Dubren 1977) and a nationwide program in Finland (McAlister et al 1980) successfully used television to counsel smokers on cessation procedures. Not all such health related projects are as effective, however (Atkin 1979).

Maccoby & Alexander (1979, 1980) describe several key features of the three-community project, many of which appear to have operated in other successful campaigns. Some, such as extensive use of formative evaluation in message design and utilization of creative media scheduling, pertain primarily to the campaign's communication components. However, others such as development of specific objectives for each component of the campaign and stimulation of interpersonal networks, recognize that a change campaign requires more than communication. Indeed, an important feature of this study is that it conceptualized communication as necessary but not sufficient to engender meaningful change. The project's emphasis on "community-based" intervention reflects the belief that change occurs within a social structure and that characteristics of that structure facilitate or impede change independent of the communication aspects of the campaign. Thus, a critical dimension of this project was its concern with elements of the social structure. Both the goals and the communication components of the campaign were designed with that structure in mind, and there were a number of attempts to use the structure to facilitate and maintain both communication and change.

The need to adapt the communication components of change efforts to the realities of the social structure in which change is to be achieved is a central issue in the current reassessment of the role of communication in economic and social development. Many of the "failures" pointed to in recent criticisms of both the general role of mass communication and the specific role of diffusion models in development attempts articulate the position that "Western" communication paradigms failed to account for the realities of non-Western social structures (Beltran S. 1975, 1976; Diaz Bordenave 1976; Roling et al 1976). And indeed, numerous examples of the benefits of various communication and change campaigns accruing to the already more advantaged segments of the population (Rogers 1976b, Roling et al 1976) certainly point to a failure of many campaigns to account for structural factors. However, given our preceding discussion of the gap hypothesis and the evidence that various U.S. campaigns (presumably conducted using Western paradigms) have also increased inequities in the distribution of knowledge and goods, it seems reasonable to wonder whether the fault lies as much with the communication models as with the way in which the models are put into practice. Rogers' (1976a) insightful examination of the history of development efforts and the suggestions for future research it leads to, as well as the new directions suggested by such critics as Diaz Bordenave (1976), strike us more as remedies for ethnocentric operationalizations of fundamentally sound theoretical concepts than as lethal blows to either the diffusion model or our fundamental belief that mass communication has an important role to play in development.

Indeed, recent attempts to respond to one form of structural constraints by merging network analysis with the diffusion model (Rogers 1976c, 1977) and to use findings from earlier diffusion studies for formative and predictive purposes (Roling et al 1976, Shingi & Mody 1976) indicate that researchers are beginning to respond to the complexities of development in third world countries with appropriately more complex methodologies. Similarly, Whiting's (1976) analysis of communication as it both facilitates and impedes change, and the various alternative conceptions of the role of communication in change emerging in China (Chu 1976) and elsewhere (Rogers 1976b), lead us to view future research on development communication with a good deal of anticipation. Finally, several scholars (Nordenstreng & Schiller 1979) have begun to develop yet another paradigm for national development which calls for examination of dimensions of individual action and intranational structure within an international economic framework that influences both.

Space precludes fuller consideration of the current debate over just what development means, let alone how it can be achieved. However, the philosophical and scientific issues being raised in that debate appear to be having a profound and healthy impact on the entire field of mass communication research.

EFFECTS ON CHILDREN AND ADOLESCENTS

Given the "special status" accorded children in the U.S. (Roberts et al 1980), it would be surprising if attention to how children use and respond to television had not remained one of the liveliest areas of mass communication research, or if many of the "problems" addressed did not continue to reflect current social issues. The impact of violent programming on children continues to be of concern, but at a reduced level from 10 years ago. There has been a moderate increase in work on the prosocial effects of the medium. Concern with the effects of advertising and with political socialization has burgeoned, and research on the potential role of the medium in sex-role stereotyping has begun to appear.

More interesting than the ebb and flow of categories of "effects" are changes in the way various problems are being addressed. Ten years ago questions tended to be posed in terms of main effects (Does TV violence facilitate aggressive behavior?) and to be guided by social learning theory (Liebert & Schwartzberg 1977). Currently there is movement toward considering television as just one element, albeit an important one, in a larger system of influences acting on the developing child (Comstock et al 1978). This has led to less concern with main effects and more attempts to identify and elaborate contingent conditions. Social learning remains a primary theoretical framework for much of the work, but it has begun to share the spotlight with other approaches, including information processing, social scripts, attribution theory, and so on. Finally, much recent work on children and television has adopted a long overdue developmental perspective. Recognition of both the policy-related and the scientific importance of ontogenetic changes in the child/television/social-system relationship has brought a heretofore missing richness to the area. Attempts to examine age-related change in attention to and comprehension of television content in terms of various approaches to cognitive and social development have begun to produce findings related to children's *processing* of television-mediated information, a promising extension of emphases on effects.

Attention and Comprehension

Pragmatic questions raised during the initial production stages of *Sesame Street* (Lesser 1974) as well as recent more theoretical attempts to understand children's information processing have engendered a rapidly growing body of work on the development of attention to television content. Hollenbeck & Slaby (1979) report that infants begin to respond differentially to various sound-picture conditions as early as 6 months. However, most studies find that age-related changes in attentional strategies occur somewhat later, paralleling changes in children's cognitive abilities.

Comstock et al's (1978) interpretation of earlier work on children's attention to TV in terms of cognitive development receives support from recent studies. Purposive viewing begins as early as 2½ years (Anderson & Levin 1976, Levin & Anderson 1976), along with attentional strategies foreshadowing those of adults. For example, changes in concrete symbolic content begin to mediate changes in attention. This is about the age at which children move from sensorimotor operations to concrete operations, and marks the beginning of attempts to internalize events symbolically. Hence, attentional variations linked to changes in concrete stimulus characteristics suggest that attention to television content is closely tied to cognitive abilities necessary to engage in symbolic activities (Anderson et al 1979). Similarly, several studies have varied the complexity and/or comprehensibility of program content in order to look at differences in attention (Krull & Husson 1979, Lorch et al 1979, Anderson et al 1980). Results of this work indicate that, among older children, program comprehensibility and visual attention conform to an inverted U curve where attention is optimal if content is neither too simple nor too complex. Failure to find strong differences as a function of content complexity among the youngest children provides another indicator of the importance of cognitive capacities in mediating attention.

The development of a continuous rating procedure that enables researchers to match the onset and termination of any number of program attributes to the onset and termination of children's visual attention (Levin & Anderson 1976) has added to information about how different program attributes elicit, maintain, and terminate attention. Among preschool children, "bit changes," transition points from one segment of programming to another, continue to be strong predictors of changes in attention, both in terms of elicitation and termination (Wartella & Ettema 1974, Anderson et al 1979, Alwitt et al 1980). Other program factors found to elicit and maintain attention within this age group include the visual and auditory presence of women, children's voices, and sound effects such as laughter and applause. Indeed, the data emphasize the importance of sound in attentional behavior to the point that certain visual attributes seem compelling only to the extent that they are associated with sound. Attributes negatively related to attention include male voices, animals, slow music, extended zooms and pans, and still photos (Anderson et al 1979). All of this fits nicely with Wartella & Ettema's (1974) findings that younger children's attention is highly responsive to perceptual variations in content but less so to conceptual variations, while conceptual changes are more important to older children. Unfortunately, recent work has not been extended to older children, precluding a more complete developmental examination of the results.

Anderson et al (1979) have also located a phenomenon they call "attentional inertia." This is the tendency for viewers to continue looking at the TV screen as a function of the preceding amount of time that attention has been maintained, irrespective of content or formal attributes. They speculate that such inertia is a result of processing information at progressively higher conceptual units of content. That is, the longer a look continues, the higher the probability that a viewer treats content in successively larger units, thus reducing the number of opportunities to break out of the attentional sequence. The phenomenon has been found with children and adults, but controlled age comparisons have not been reported. Nevertheless, earlier findings of continual increases across age in the duration of attention

(Levin & Anderson 1976) indicate that attentional inertia may also be a function of cognitive development insofar as changes in cognitive capabilities locate the capacity to process increasingly larger conceptual units.

The few early studies of television's influence on social behavior which included children of several ages uncovered striking differences in magnitude of effect as a function of age, leading to conjecture that there were age differences in processing the same content (Roberts 1973, Collins 1975). Collins (1979a) conceptualizes "mature" comprehension in terms of *selection* of essential information from the program, *ordering* the essential scenes according to some organizational scheme, and making *inferences* that go beyond what is explicitly presented to relate discrete units of information into a meaningful whole. He proceeds from the assumption that age-related differences in cognitive capabilities and accumulated experiences locate differences in how children comprehend a television program.

In order to test these notions, dramatic television programs were "parsed" to identify units of information as central or peripheral and explicit or implicit; entire programs were then edited into simple or complex versions in which scenes were presented in an ordered or randomized sequence. Subsequent to viewing a version of these programs, second, fifth and eighth graders were tested for recall of implicit and explicit content and ability to make inferences regarding that content (Collins et al 1978). This kind of approach has produced evidence that younger children select different information from dramatic presentations than do their older counterparts, fail to use the dramatic framework to organize and understand the narrative scenes, and make fewer inferences about implicit content and relationships among program elements, be they the linkage among the motives, acts, and consequences, or the simple insight that two scenes are temporally related (Collins et al 1974, Collins et al 1978, Collins 1979a,b). Newcomb & Collins (1979) also found that children understand programs as a function of the degree to which the portrayed context is similar to or different from their own backgrounds, but that the influence is greater among younger children. Collins (1979b) interprets these findings in terms of Schank & Abelson's (1977) notion of scripts. He argues that younger children's comprehension is dominated by personal scripts while older children are more able to apply a wider variety of scripts which depart from their personal social circumstances. This explanation dovetails nicely with several other discussions of children's comprehension of television content (Worth & Gross 1974, Comstock et al 1978).

Concern with how model characteristics influence children's observational learning has led to work on how children perceive television characters. Several studies explore the attributes children use to differentiate among TV characters and the bases on which they would choose to be like TV characters. The important judgmental dimensions appear to be humor, attractiveness, activity, and some kind of strength-dominated sex difference. Boys and girls use the same dimensions to distinguish among TV characters, but there are large sex differences in the criteria they use to determine whom they would most like to be like. Girls rely on the attractiveness dimension, boys use the activity and strength dimensions (Reeves & Greenberg 1977, Reeves & Miller 1978, Reeves & Lometti 1979). Reeves (1979) examines these and earlier findings in a developmentally based person perception framework and notes that the findings for TV characters differ from those for real people in terms of both the dimensions employed by children and the way that those dimensions are organized. He speculates that a model of TV character perception will have to differ from one of person perception.

Empirical work on the development and role of perceived reality in children's comprehension of and response to television has also begun to accumulate. Younger children, children with lower IQ scores, children who view a great deal of television, and children who manifest little understanding of the medium or its production techniques attribute more reality to television content, with the phenomenon increasing the more specifically the questions regarding the "realness" of television content are worded (Leifer et al 1974, Greenberg & Reeves 1976, Quarfoth 1979). Several studies have demonstrated that reality-fantasy distinctions are multidimensional, that various developmental trends may depend on the particular dimension the child is using when making a judgment, and that the spontaneous application of the ability to make reality-fantasy distinctions comes somewhat later than the ability itself (Hawkins 1977, Morison et al 1979). Assumptions that perceived reality would be a straightforward mediator of subsequent behavior are also being questioned. Reeves (1978) found that the degree to which portrayed prosocial behavior was perceived to be real predicted subsequent prosocial and antisocial behavior, but that the perceived reality of portrayed antisocial behavior had no effect.

Finally, in a reversal of much of the developmental work on children's comprehension of television, work on how different media influence the development of different cognitive behaviors is being reported. Salomon (1979a,b) argues that different media employ different symbol systems, that different symbol systems structure the world differently, and that different types of symbols not only require the use of different age-related cognitive skills, but also that they cultivate different cognitive skills. We expect the next decade to witness a great deal of work in this area.

Responses to Advertising

Over the past 5 years, questions about children's special vulnerability to television advertising raised by the Federal Communications Commission (1974) and the Federal Trade Commission (1978) brought the "problem" of television advertising and children to the center of the research arena. Much of the work is highly applied in that it is designed to address questions concerning the potentially misleading or unfair influence of specific advertising practices such as premium offers, separation of commercial and programs, and disclaimers (Adler 1977). However, the FTC decision to consider whether young children even understand the nature of commercials and the degree to which any lack of understanding might render all commercials unfair or misleading to children gave research a more theoretical tone, if only because it addressed the question in terms of various developmental models of cognition, information processing, and social behavior (Dorr 1978, Roberts et al 1978, Wackman et al 1978).

Children are exposed to a great many commercials—over 20,000 per year (Adler 1977). Those explicitly designed for children, the Saturday morning ads, dramatically over-represent toys and sugared food products (Council on Children, Media, and Merchandising 1977) and employ techniques usually appealing, sometimes confusing, and often not very informative to young children (Adler 1977, FTC 1978). For example, Atkin & Heald (1977) found that toy ads seldom present relevant substantive attributes of the products.

There is also evidence that children are influenced by commercials. Comstock et al (1978) review various studies which indicate that young children often request advertised products, that such requests tend to decrease as the child grows older, that there are some signs of a relationship between amount of exposure to commercials and purchase requests, and that teenagers report being at least somewhat influenced by commercials. Adler (1977) also cites evidence that commercials are moderately successful at fostering positive attitudes toward products. Galst & White (1976) demonstrated that young children's willingness to expend effort to see television commercials in an experimental situation was positively related to subsequent attempts to influence mothers' purchases in a supermarket. Goldberg & Gorn (1977) found that exposure to toy commercials influenced preschool children to make more "materialistic" as opposed to "social" choices in a test situation. Robertson & Rossiter (1974) report that the barrage of toy commercials antecedent to the Christmas holidays overcame the defenses of even initially skeptical children.

The important question, however, is not so much whether children are influenced by commercials, as whether whatever influence there is occurs because of failure to comprehend the commercial appeal. For example, there is little evidence that children comprehend typical commercial disclaimers much before the age of 7 (D. E. Liebert et al 1977, Roberts & Bachen 1978). However, rewording disclaimers into language appropriate to young children dramatically increases comprehension. Clearly ads can be designed so that even very young children understand their discrete elements in the same way that they understand discrete elements of dramatic narratives (Collins 1979a). Certainly the *Sesame Street* experience supports this (Lesser 1974).

A more fundamental question concerns children's understanding of the nature of commercials per se—that they differ from informational and entertainment messages, that they are intended to persuade and they use biased appeals, that they require different information processing strategies than other types of messages (Roberts et al 1978). The bulk of evidence indicates that understanding of this type does not occur much before the age of 7 years. An indirect approach to comprehension is found in several early studies that noted a lack of differentiation in visual attention across the transition from program to commercial, and little decline in attention to clustered commercials much before the age of 7 or 8 years, and interpreted this as indicating a failure to understand that commercials are different from program material (Ward et al 1972, Ward & Wackman 1973). However, more recent work finds attentional variations among younger as well as older children (Zuckerman et al 1978), and the evidence is mounting that perceptual as opposed to conceptual attributes mediate young children's attentional shifts as they relate to commercials (Wartella & Ettema 1974, Anderson et al 1979). Moreover, the connection between visual attention patterns and comprehension of complex concepts remains to be established (Dorr 1978).

A more direct approach is to interview children concerning the difference between commercials and programs or the purpose of commercials. Some early work found that children under 7 or 8 years of age expressed confusion regarding the program-commercial distinction (Ward et al 1977), but much of this confusion could be attributed to age differences in verbal ability. Similarly, data derived from interviews concerned with children's ability to explain the selling intent of commercials is open to such criticism. Nevertheless, there is rather consistent agreement that before the age of 7 fewer than half of the children interviewed comprehend the intent of commercials (Robertson & Rossiter 1974, Ward et al 1977). Moreover, Dorr (1978) reports preliminary data from a three-item multiple-choice test, demanding less sophisticated language skills, that indicates the majority of a sample of 8- and 9-year-olds did not understand commercials' selling intent. Roberts et al (1978) go further to raise the question of whether comprehension of selling intent is sufficient, on the grounds that it is possible to understand that a commercial intends to sell a product but be totally oblivious to the fact that this implies that biased informational strategies may be used to achieve such intent.

There is also general agreement across studies that children's understanding of the nature of commercials increases with age. Similarly, recall of the content of commercials and the ability to integrate message elements into a meaningful and integrated framework increases with age (Ward et al 1977) although here, too, recognition as opposed to verbal measures indicate better memory at earlier ages (Wartella et al 1979). There is also a good deal of evidence that trust in commercials is negatively related to age (Robertson & Rossiter 1974, Adler 1977, Ward et al 1977, Comstock et al 1978, Roberts et al 1980). Whether age-related distrust is due to more sophisticated understanding of the nature of commercials, or to past experience with advertised products, or to peer pressures, or to some other factor remains to be established.

Underlying concern with whether children comprehend the nature of commercials is the assumption that the better children understand them the less susceptible to manipulation they will be (Christenson 1980). However, the relationship between comprehension of intent to persuade and resistance to persuasive appeals remains uncertain. Several recent studies have demonstrated that it is possible to increase even very young children's understanding of the selling intent of commercials. Dorr (1978) reports that training children about the production process and economic basis of the television industry dramatically increased kindergarten and second and third grade children's understanding of the selling intent of commercials. Roberts et al (1980) found that an instructional film concerned with teaching children about commercials and persuasive techniques engendered significant increases in skepticism toward commercials, particularly among the initially less skeptical viewers. Several other studies have found that television shows or public service announcements concerned with either commercials or products advertised on commercials can influence children's product choices and expressed attitudes toward products (Goldberg et al 1978, Roberts & Bachen 1978, Christenson 1980). Nevertheless, questions remain. Rossiter & Robertson (1974) found that even older children with relatively strong defenses against commercial appeals eventually succumbed to a barrage of toy commercials, and Adler (1977) notes a number of studies that indicate older children—those presumed to better understand commercial appeals—are frequently more influenced than their younger counterparts.

Finally, as with so many other areas of communication research, a good deal of work on contingent conditions has begun to appear. Such factors as peer and parent influences as well as a number of family context variables have been shown to condition or mediate children's responsiveness to commercials (Robertson & Rossiter 1977, Sheikh & Moleski 1977, Wackman et al 1977, Ward et al 1977).

Political Socialization

If an informed citizenry is important to the functioning of a participatory democracy, then how children learn to acquire the appropriate information is a critical outcome in the political socialization process. Hence, the development of patterns of exposure to mass-mediated political information—patterns such as those covered earlier—has recently become a legitimate political socialization criterion variable in and of itself (Chaffee et al 1977). More typically, however, communication researchers have concerned themselves with the degree to which media use is related to such outcomes as political and civic knowledge and attitudes on the assumption that these form the foundation of adult political behavior. Several reviews detail work conducted prior to 1975 (Kraus & Davis 1976, Chaffee et al 1977, Comstock et al 1978).

Evidence continues to mount that, relative to such other socialization agents as parents, schools, and peers, the mass media play an important role in the acquisition of political information. When asked to name the "best" source of information on a variety of political topics or to state where they get most of their political information, children ranging from 7 years upward give the media a lion's share of the nominations. Television is preferred overall, but reliance on newspapers increases as the child enters adolescence (Chaffee et al 1977, Atkins & Elwood 1978, Egan 1978, Rubin 1978, Newspaper Advertising Bureau 1980a). One sample of seventh graders simultaneously voiced reliance on the media and skepticism about the wisdom of such a choice (Rubin 1976).

The degree to which exposure to the media is related to children's level of political knowledge depends on both the age of the children and the way in which media use is operationalized. Among both elementary school children and adolescents there is a negative relationship between overall television viewing and political knowledge. When measures of television news viewing are used, however, the relationships tend to become relatively strong, at least among the younger children (Conway et al 1975, Atkin 1977, Atkin & Gantz 1978). Among adolescents the picture is somewhat clouded; studies find political information to be positively (Rubin 1978) and negatively (Chaffee et al 1977, Jackson-Beeck 1979) associated with public affairs news viewing. As with adults, the evidence is relatively consistent that newspaper use is strongly and positively related to various measures of political information regardless of age (Conway et al 1975, Chaffee et al 1977, Jackson-Beeck 1979, Newspaper Advertising Bureau 1980a). The importance of age in specifying any relationship between mass media use and political knowledge is further illustrated by the consistent finding that the strength of association between public affairs media use and political knowledge tends to increase with age (Roberts et al 1975, Hawkins et al 1975, Atkin & Gantz 1978, Rubin 1978). This, along with the age-related switch in predictive power from television use to print use, probably indicates an increase in the kinds of skills necessary to integrate politically relevant media content into a developing structure of political knowledge.

The question of causality, of course, underlies most examinations of the relationship between public affairs media use and political knowledge. Several studies have addressed this question using time-lagged correlation techniques with samples of both elementary school children (Atkin & Gantz 1978) and adolescents (Chaffee et al 1977). In both cases the evidence indicates that use of public affairs media causes subsequent increases in levels of political knowledge. Similarly, Hawkins et al (1975) found that preadolescents high in public affairs media use during the 1972 presidential campaign knew substantially more about Watergate the following spring than did those low in such media use.

Other indicators of political socialization have also been considered. Rubin (1978) reports that younger children high in public affairs viewing have more favorable attitudes toward government, and Atkin (1977) found that exposure to campaign advertisements predicted both liking for and information about presidential candidates among third through sixth graders. Chaffee et al (1977) found that adolescents who engaged in little print use were low in political efficacy while the reverse was true for high print users. Several studies have also reported positive relationships between public affairs media use and interpersonal discussion about politics (Hawkins et al 1975, Roberts et al 1975, Atkin & Gantz 1978, Jackson-Beeck 1979). Other variables considered in the preceding studies include interest in politics, willingness to declare partisan identity, ability to name parents' political affiliation, and engaging in political activities at school.

In general, the thrust of recent work on the role of media in political socialization has been toward multivariate designs that conceive of the media as just one influence in a total system of political socialization agents. Multivariate models presented in path analysis form demonstrate both the importance of media to any complete understanding of political socialization and the necessity of examining the media in a context of other socialization agents and background variables. Chaffee et al (1977) provide a thoughtful discussion of the problems inherent in relating mass communication research to political socialization, and encourage optimism that inquiry in this particular problem area will flourish.

Antisocial Behavior

Research on television and children has been dominated by concern with the impact of viewing portrayals of violence. Empirical studies focusing on this "problem" outweigh work in all other problem areas by more than four to one (Comstock et al 1978). Studies continue to mount, although at a much reduced rate from that of the early 1970s.

Several recent correlational studies continue to examine various contingent conditions that mediate the violence viewing-aggression relationship.

For example, in one large sample of children ranging from 6 through 18 years, violence viewing was negatively related to various demographic indicators of family education and income and to the child's degree of isolation, and positively related to measures of aggression such as amount of conflict with parents, frequency of fighting, and delinquent behavior (McCarthy et al 1975). A panel survey of fourth, sixth, and eighth graders found evidence that aggressive attitudes are strong predictors of later violence viewing, but that parental restrictions on exposure to certain programs can moderate such selective exposure (Atkin et al 1979). Edgar (1977) found that Australian children low in self-esteem were less likely to understand film violence and less likely to take action to preclude real violence. She also reports that it is the context rather than the nature of the portrayed violence that is important, children being most disturbed by portrayals of contexts that could easily be related to their own lives. Haynes (1978) points out that children may perceive and evaluate violence differently than do adults and that differences in perceptions can be expected to mediate different responses. In this vein, Collins & Zimmerman (1975) showed that experimentally manipulated perceptions engendered different responses to an aggressive film. Children who saw violence portrayed in a context of consistently negative motives and consequences inhibited subsequent violent responses. Children who viewed the same violent portrayal surrounded by mixed cues, some positive and some negative, were subsequently more aggressive. The authors suggest that divergent cues resulted in perceptions of the portrayed aggression as relatively positive.

Several large-scale field experiments have addressed some of the criticisms concerning the lack of ecological validity of work in this area. A Canadian study (Joy et al 1977) took advantage of the introduction of television into a previously isolated community by observing the changes in aggressive behavior of children in three towns over a period of 2 years. At the beginning of the study one town had no television, one town had one channel, and one town had multiple channels, including the U.S. networks. Longitudinal data indicate no differences in the aggressive behavior of elementary school children across the three towns at the beginning of the study, but a significant increase in such behavior among children in the town into which television was introduced. Cross-sectional data also indicate a dramatic increase in aggressiveness among children just receiving television, an outcome interpreted by the authors as possibly due to a "disinhibiting" effect rather than to the cumulative impact of viewing.

Finally, three field experiments are reported by Parke et al (1977). The studies, conducted in the U.S. and Belgium, exposed groups of adolescent boys living in minimum security institutions to unedited, feature-length films that were either aggressive or nonaggressive. Measures of aggressive behavior were derived from naturalistic observations made in the institutional setting before, during, and after the exposure periods. Results indicate that exposure to films portraying violence increased aggressive behavior, and that the effect was greatest among boys who were initially predisposed to be more aggressive. One study also produced support for a cumulative effect, viewers of five movies over the course of a week manifesting more aggressive behavior than viewers of a single movie. Taken together, these field experiments, in conjunction with those conducted prior to 1975 (Comstock et al 1978), provide relatively convincing evidence that television violence can have an antisocial impact.

Although publication of the Surgeon General's Scientific Advisory Committee's (1972) report on television and social behavior appears to have marked the crest of the wave of television and aggression research, efforts to review and integrate an almost bewildering array of studies using different methodologies, testing different hypotheses, focusing on different age groups, and producing what often seem to be conflicting results, continue to appear (Kaplan & Singer 1976, Andison 1977, Murray & Kippax 1979). At least one review finds little or no effect of television on the "level of violence in society" (Howitt & Cumberbatch 1975). However, the general consensus seems to be that there is a positive, causal relationship between viewing television violence and subsequent aggressive behavior. Of course, the relationship is conditioned by a host of environmental, individual, and content-related variables. Moreover, the strength with which the relationship has been demonstrated varies with the general empirical method and the specific operationalizations used in the various studies. Nevertheless, it is just this multiplicity of approaches and findings that led one major review to characterize the area of violence viewing and aggression as the one problem in television research in which there is enough diversity to instill great confidence in a causal interpretation (Comstock et al 1978).

Prosocial Effects

Research in this area grew out of recognition that the same principles underlying learning and performance of television-mediated antisocial behavior should also operate for more positive behavior. Fortunately, the large theoretical literature on observational learning and the available empirical data on television and children's aggressive behavior has enabled research on the medium's prosocial effects to move rapidly away from laboratory studies conducted with specially prepared stimuli toward field experiments conducted with naturally occurring television programs.

Children have little trouble recognizing the prosocial themes in entertainment programs. Interviews with hundreds of elementary school children who had viewed episodes of various programs with prosocial themes revealed that, regardless of whether the children viewed the program in a captive situation or under natural viewing conditions, approximately 90% of all viewers recalled at least one prosocial message—up to 5 hours after viewing (Columbia Broadcasting System 1977). Similarly, several studies have found significant levels of understanding of prosocial messages among kindergarten children (Silverman 1977).

Prosocial programs also influence behavior. One study found that second and third grade children were more cooperative on verbal problem-solving measures and on a behavioral helping measure subsequent to viewing an episode of *The Waltons* which emphasized a problem-solving theme (Baran et al 1979). Another found that fourth through tenth grade children who viewed an action-adventure program in which the protagonist coped constructively with an interpersonal conflict were subsequently more likely to help a peer than were children who viewed an aggressive or neutral program (Collins & Getz 1976). Still other work found that an episode of *Lassie* which emphasized helping behavior encouraged first graders to help a dog perceived to be in trouble at a cost to themselves (Sprakfin et al 1975), and that segments of *Sesame Street* depicting nonwhite children as primary characters made 3- to 5-year-olds more willing to select nonwhite playmates (Gorn et al 1976).

Several researchers have examined the impact of extended viewing of series of either neutral or prosocial programs by coding subsequent behavior in school settings. Coates et al (1976) observed children's frequency of social contacts and of giving positive reinforcement and punishment to peers in the nursery school before, during, and after a week of exposure to either *Sesame Street* or *Mister Rogers' Neighborhood*. Murray & Ahammer (1977) showed preschool children either a prosocial or a neutral television diet over a 4-week period and examined changes in helping behavior. Both studies report increases in prosocial behavior as a function of prosocial program content.

Work on the effect of combining television and various kinds of supplemental treatment such as verbal labeling or role playing has also begun to appear (Friedrich & Stein 1975, Ahammer & Murray 1979). Results indicate that preschool children are influenced by prosocial television content and that the influence can be increased significantly with the kinds of supplementary training that could logically be carried out in the nursery school setting.

Not all results are quite so straightforward or positive, however. Silverman (1977) showed 3-, 5-, and 7-year-olds *Sesame Street* segments edited to emphasize either resolution of conflict via cooperation or just cooperation. The treatment films influenced the cognitions of 5- and 7-year-olds, but not their behavior. Among 3-year-olds the conflict-cooperation program had a negative effect, reducing cooperative behavior to below that of children who viewed a control film. In addition, some of the studies cited above found that the impact of prosocial programs depends on characteristics of the child such as initial levels of prosocial behavior, age, the specific type of behavior being examined, and so forth (Friedrich & Stein 1975, Coates et al 1976, Baran et al 1979). Finally, Sprafkin & Rubinstein (1979) report a correlational study that found second, third, and fourth graders' viewing of prosocial television programs accounted for no more than 1% of the variance in an index of prosocial behavior exhibited in school. They speculate that some of this lack of effect can be attributed to early overlearning of prosocial behavior which implies that such content functions more as a reinforcer than a source of new information, a possibility that fits nicely with the idea that in controlled experimental and measurement situations the effect of prosocial content can be explained in terms of its cueing or eliciting function (Baran et al 1979).

Speculation that some of the differences among children in response to prosocial content is due both to presentation factors and to the particular prosocial behavior being portrayed (Coates et al 1976, Sprafkin & Rubinstein 1979) points to a major problem with work in this area. There is an obvious need to be more precise about what "prosocial content" means. Effects categorized under this rubric have ranged across helping, kindness, altruism, empathy, friendliness, creativity, stereotyping—almost any behavior with positive social value seems fair game. Little attention has been paid to conceptual differences among such "prosocial" effects. Yet it is quite reasonable to expect qualitative differences in the way television would portray helping or task persistence as opposed to creativity or lack of prejudice. And given what we know about differences in comprehension as a function of differences in both presentation factors and the child viewer, differences in response are also predictable.

Sex-Role Socialization

Concern with the status of women, in combination with the pervasiveness of sex-role stereotypes in mass media content (Butler & Paisley 1980), has led to the emergence of the media's role in sex-role socialization as a "problem" area in its own right. Five years ago, research consisted almost entirely of content analyses and speculation concerning the potential impact of stereotypic sex-role portrayals (Busby 1975). Today, empirical studies of children's responses to sex-role content are appearing. Pingree & Hawkins (1980) note that it is difficult to test the degree to which media content affects children's sex-role attitudes or behavior because representative, unexposed control groups are impossible to find and because nontraditional, nonsexist portrayals of male/female roles are rare. Nevertheless, it is possible to establish partial answers by determining whether there is any relationship between viewing and sex-role attitudes, and by testing whether exposure to nonstereotypic portrayals influences children to change from some presumed stereotypic baseline.

There appears to be a relationship between amount of television viewing and stereotypic responses to sex-role questions. Among children between 3 and 12 years, those who view more television give more traditional responses on various sex-role measures (Beuf 1974, Freuh & McGhee 1975). The relationship survives controls for age and sex, although older children and boys tend to be more stereotyped in their responses. Moreover, grade school children who viewed more nonsex stereotyped programs were more likely to accept the nontraditional role as appropriate (Miller & Reeves 1976). Of course, a difficulty with these studies is that children we would expect to give more traditional responses on a variety of issues tend to be heavier viewers (Comstock et al 1978). Still, demonstrating a relationship is a necessary first step in determining whether media affect sex-role expectations.

Several experiments have explored the impact of commercials portraying more or less traditional sex-role behavior. Tan (1979) reports a "cultivation effect" in that adolescent girls exposed to an "artificially heavy dose" of beauty commercials were more likely than a control group to respond that beauty characteristics were necessary to be popular with men and were personally important characteristics. Atkin & Miller (1975) and Pingree (1978) obtained tentative evidence that, under some conditions, young children exposed to commercials portraying women in nontraditional occupations give less traditional responses to questions about appropriate sex-role behavior. The weakness of their findings might be attributable to the use of commercials as stimuli. When, for example, children were exposed to inherently more appealing cartoons selected for stereotypic, neutral, or nonstereotypic sex-role content, 5- and 6-year-old girls who saw the nontraditional cartoon produced significantly lower sex-role stereotype scores (Davidson et al 1979).

The most encouraging work on television and sex-role socialization is presented in an extensive evaluation of *Freestyle,* a television series designed to reduce sex-role stereotypes among 9- through 12-year-olds and to expand career awareness for girls within that age range (Johnston et al 1980). Although the program had little effect in altering individual interest patterns, relative to control groups, viewers from seven different U.S. sites became more approving of girls in nontraditional roles and less stereotypic in their perceptions of what was "real" concerning the nontraditional sex-role behavior of both males and females. These effects were greatly facilitated when the program was viewed in a school setting and accompanied by classroom discussion, a combination that led to persistence of over 60% of the original effect up to 9 months after exposure (Johnston & Davidson 1980).

As with so many studies in other problem areas, then, work on sex-role socialization supports a cultivation effect interpretation. The media appear to contribute to the continuance of sex-stereotyped perceptions, but are capable of establishing new perceptual sets when nonstereotypic content is introduced.

RETROSPECT

Our sense at the end of the search conducted for this review is that mass communication research has entered its adolescence. On the one hand, the field is experiencing a period of rapid growth marked by a tremendous outpouring of empirical studies. Many of these have attempted to use new techniques and to adopt new perspectives. We also found conscious—indeed, self-conscious—efforts to assert independence from such parent disciplines as psychology and sociology.

On the other hand, a kind of consolidation of what has gone before is also beginning to emerge. The optimism of the early years and the pessimism of the 1950s have given way to recognition that mass communication plays an important role in our social system, but that it is just one element in that system. Moreover, we found the beginning of a good deal of higher level conceptual development. The field's problem orientation probably means that it will always be marked by some degree of brute empiricism, and there remains some truth to Nordenstreng's (1968) characterization of U.S. communication research as long on empirical technique and short on thinking. Nevertheless, one of the more pleasant surprises connected with this review was the discovery that a great deal of conceptual development has begun to emerge. The straightforward listing of studies and results typical of many reviews of several decades ago has begun to give way to critical syntheses of research in the service of formulating higher level generalizations about the communication process. Even more encouraging, many of the higher level statements that have begun to appear are solidly grounded in empirical data.[2] In short, we believe that the trends in the field will make the task of the next reviewer of mass communication effects particularly exciting.

[2]Some of our thinking about this issue derives from discussions with E. M. Rogers, who plans to discuss the importance to communication research of such "meta-research" in his Presidential Address to the 1981 Conference of the International Communication Association.

Literature Cited

Adler, R., ed. 1977. *Research on the effects of television advertising on children.* Washington DC: GPO

Adoni, H. 1979. The functions of mass media in the political socialization of adolescents. *Commun. Res.* 6:84–106

Ahammer, I. M., Murray, J. P. 1979. Kindness in the kindergarten: the relative influence of role playing and prosocial television in facilitating altruism. *Int. J. Behav. Dev.* 2:133–57

Allen, R. L., Bielby, W. T. 1979. Blacks' attitudes and behaviors toward television. *Commun. Res.* 6:437–62

Alwitt, L. F., Anderson, D. R., Lorch, E. P., Levin, S. R. 1980. Preschool children's visual attention to attributes of television. *Hum. Commun. Res.* In press

Anderson, D. R., Alwitt, L. F., Lorch, E. P., Levin, S. R. 1979. Watching children watch television. In *Attention and Cognitive Development*, ed. G. A. Hale, M. Lewis, pp. 331–61. New York: Plenum. 366 pp.

Anderson, D. R., Levin, S. R. 1976. Young children's attention to "Sesame Street." *Child Dev.* 47:806–11

Anderson, D. R., Lorch, E. P., Field, D. E., Sanders, J. 1980. The effects of TV program comprehensibility on preschool children's visual attention to television. *Child Dev.* In press

Anderson, J. A., Meyer, T. P. 1975. Functionalism and the mass media. *J. Broadcast.* 19:11–22

Andison, F. S. 1977. TV violence and viewer aggression: a cumulation of study results. *Public Opin. Q.* 41:314–31

Atkin, C. K. 1975. Communication and political socialization. *Polit. Commun. Rev.* 1:2–7

Atkin, C. K. 1976. Mass media and the aging. In *Aging and Communication*, ed. H. J. Oyer, E. H. Oyer, pp. 99–118, Baltimore. Md: Univ. Park Press. 302 pp.

Atkin, C. K. 1977. Effects of campaign advertising and newscasts on children. *Journ. Q.* 54:503–8

Atkin, C. K. 1978. Broadcast news programming and the child audience. *J. Broadcast.* 22:47–61

Atkin, C. K. 1979. Research evidence on mass mediated health communication campaigns. In *Communication Yearbook*, ed. D. Nimmo, 3:655–68. New Brunswick, NJ: Int. Commun. Assoc. 704 pp.

Atkin, C. K., Galloway, J., Nayman, O. 1976. News media exposure, political knowledge, and campaign interest. *Journ. Q.* 53:231–37

Atkin, C. K., Gantz, W. 1978. Television news and political socialization. *Public Opin. Q.* 42:183–98

Atkin, C. K., Greenberg, B., Korzenny, F., McDermott, S. 1979. Selective exposure to televised violence. *J. Broadcast.* 23:5–13

Atkin, C. K., Heald, G. 1976. Effects of political advertising. *Public Opin. Q.* 40:216–28

Atkin, C. K., Heald, G. 1977. The content of children's toy and food commercials. *J. Commun.* 27(1):107–14

Atkin, C. K., Miller, M. 1975. *The effects of television advertising on children: experimental evidence.* Presented at Ann. Meet. Int. Commun. Assoc., Chicago

Atkins, P. A., Elwood, H. 1978. TV news is first choice in survey of high schools. *Journ. Q.* 55:596–99

Atwood, L. E., Sohn, A., Sohn, H. 1976. *Community discussion and newspaper content.* Presented at Ann. Meet. Assoc. Educ. Journ., College Park, Md.

Baran, S. J., Chase, L. J., Courtright, J. A. 1979. Television drama as a facilitator of prosocial behavior: "The Waltons." *J. Broadcast.* 23:277–85

Becker, L. B. 1976. Two tests of media gratifications: Watergate and the 1974 election. *Journ. Q.* 53:29–33, 87

Becker, L. B. 1979. Measurement of gratifications. *Commun. Res.* 6:54–73

Becker, L. B., McCombs, M. E., McLeod, J. M. 1975. The development of political cognitions. In *Political Communication: Issues and Strategies for Research,* ed. S. H. Chaffee, pp. 21–63. Beverly Hills: Sage. 319 pp.

Becker, L. B., Sobowale, I. A., Casey, W. E. 1979a. Newspaper and television dependencies: effects on evaluations of public officials. *J. Broadcast.* 23:465–75

Becker, L. B., Weaver, D. H., Graber, D. A., McCombs, M. E. 1979b. Influence on public agendas. In *The Great Debates: Carter vs. Ford, 1976,* ed. S. Kraus, pp. 418–28. Bloomington: Indiana Univ. Press. 553 pp.

Becker, L. B., Whitney, D. C. 1980. Effects of media dependencies: audience assessment of government. *Commun. Res.* 7:95–120

Beltran S., L. R. 1975. Research ideologies in conflict. *J. Commun.* 25(2):187–93

Beltran S., L. R. 1976. Alien premises, objects, and methods in Latin American communication research. *Commun. Res.* 3:107–34

Benton, M., Frazier, P. J. 1976. The agenda-setting function of mass media at three levels of information holding. *Commun. Res.* 3:261–74

Beuf, A. 1974. Doctor, lawyer, household drudge. *J. Commun.* 24(2):142–45

Bishop, G. F., Oldendick, R. W., Tuchfarber, A. J. 1978. Debate watching and the acquisition of political knowledge. *J. Commun.* 28(4):99–113

Blumler, J. G. 1979. The role of theory in uses and gratifications studies. *Commun. Res.* 6:9–36

Blumler, J. G., Katz, E. 1974. Forward. In *The Uses of Mass Communications: Current Perspectives on Gratifications Research,* ed. J. G. Blumler, E. Katz. Beverly Hills: Sage. 318 pp.

Blumler, J. G., McQuail, D. 1969. *Television in Politics: Its Uses and Influences.* Chicago: Univ. Chicago Press. 379 pp.

Bogart, L. 1975a. How the challenge of television news affects the prosperity of daily newspapers. *Journ. Q.* 52:403–10

Bogart, L. 1975b. The future of the metropolitan daily. *J. Commun.* 25(2):30–43

Bower, R. T. 1973. *Television and the Public.* New York: Holt, Rinehart & Winston. 205 pp.

Brown, J. R., Cramond, J. K., Wilde, R. J. 1974. Displacement effects of television and the child's functional orientation to media. See Blumler & Katz 1974, pp. 93–112

Bryant, B., Currier, F., Morrison, A. 1976. Relating life style factors of a person to his choice of newspaper. *Journ. Q.* 53:74–79

Busby, L. J. 1975. Sex-role research on the mass media. *J. Commun.* 25(4):107–31

Butler, M., Paisley, W. 1980. *Women and the Mass Media: Sourcebook for Research and Action.* New York: Hum. Sci. Press. 432 pp.

Canadian Broadcasting Corporation. 1975. *Dimensions of audience response to television programs in Canada.* Toronto: CBC

Carey, J. W. 1976. How media shape campaigns. *J. Commun.* 26(2):50–57

Carey, J. W. 1978. The ambiguity of policy research. *J. Commun.* 28(2):114–19

Carey, J. W., Kreiling, A. L. 1974. Popular culture and uses and gratifications: notes toward an accommodation. See Blumler & Katz 1974, pp. 225–48

Caron, A. H. 1979. First-time exposure to television: effects on Inuit children's cultural images. *Commun. Res.* 6:135–54

Chaffee, S. H. 1977. Mass media effects: new research perspectives. See Lerner & Nelson 1977, pp. 210–41

Chaffee, S. H. 1978. Presidential debates— are they helpful to voters? *Commun. Monogr.* 45:330–53

Chaffee, S. H. 1979. *Mass media vs. interpersonal channels: The synthetic competition.* Presented at Ann. Meet. Speech Commun. Assoc., San Antonio

Chaffee, S. H., Dennis, J. 1979. Presidential debates: an empirical assessment. In *The Past and Future of Presidential Debates,* ed. A. Ranney, pp. 75–106. Washington DC: Am. Enterp. Inst. 236 pp.

Chaffee, S. H., Izcaray, F. 1975. Mass communication functions in a media rich developing society. *Commun. Res.* 2:367–95

Chaffee, S. H., Jackson-Beeck, M., Durall, J., Wilson, D. 1977. Mass communication in political communication. In *Handbook of Political Socialization: Theory and Research,* ed. S. A. Renshon, pp. 223–58. New York: Free Press. 547 pp.

Chaffee, S. H., Wilson, D. G. 1975. *Adult life cycle changes in mass media use.* Presented at Ann. Meet. Assoc. Educ. Journ., Ottawa, Ontario, Canada

Chaffee, S. H., Wilson, D. G. 1977. Media rich, media poor: two studies of diversity in agenda-holding. *Journ. Q.* 54:466–76

Christenson, P. G. 1980. *The effects of consumer information processing announcements on children's perceptions of commercials and products.* PhD thesis. Stanford Univ., Stanford, Calif. 107 pp.

Chu, G. C. 1976. Group communication and development in mainland China—the functions of social pressure. See Schramm & Lerner 1976, pp. 119–33

Clarke, P., Fredin, E. 1978. Newspapers, television and political reasoning. *Public Opin. Q.* 42:143–60

Clarke, P., Kline, F. G. 1974. Media effects reconsidered: some new strategies for communication research. *Commun. Res.* 1:224–40

Coates, B., Pusser, H. E., Goodman, I. 1976. The influence of "Sesame Street" and "Mister Rogers' Neighborhood" on children's social behavior in the preschool. *Child Dev.* 47:138–44

Cohen, B. C. 1963. *The Press and Foreign Policy.* Princeton: Princeton Univ. Press. 228 pp.

Coldevin, G. A. 1979. Satellite television and cultural replacement among Canadian Eskimos: adults and adolescents compared. *Commun. Res.* 6:115–34

Collins, W. A. 1975. The developing child as viewer. *J. Commun.* 25(4):35–44

Collins, W. A. 1979a. Children's comprehension of television content. In *Children Communicating: Media and Development of Thought, Speech, Understanding*, ed. E. Wartella, pp. 21–52. Beverly Hills: Sage. 286 pp.

Collins, W. A. 1979b. *Social antecedents, cognitive processing, and comprehension of social portrayals on television.* Presented at Soc. Sci. Res. Counc. Conf. on Soc. Cognit. Soc. Behav., London, Ont. Canada

Collins, W. A., Berndt, T., Hess, V. 1974. Observational learning of motives and consequences for television aggression: a developmental study. *Child Dev.* 45:799–802

Collins, W. A., Getz, S. K. 1976. Children's social responses following modeled reactions to provocation: prosocial effects of a television drama. *J. Pers.* 44:488–500

Collins, W. A., Wellman, H., Keniston, A. H., Westby, S. D. 1978. Age-related aspects of comprehension and inference from a televised dramatic narrative. *Child Dev.* 49:389–99

Collins, W. A., Zimmermann, S. A. 1975. Convergent and divergent social cues: effects of televised aggression on children. *Commun. Res.* 2:331–46

Columbia Broadcasting System. 1977. *Communicating With Children Through Television: Studies of Messages and Other Impressions Conveyed by Five Children's Programs.* New York: CBS Econ. Res. 534 pp.

Comstock, G. 1978. The impact of television on American institutions. *J. Commun.* 28(2):12–28

Comstock, G., Chaffee, S., Katzman, N., McCombs, M., Roberts, D. 1978. *Television and Human Behavior.* New York: Columbia Univ. Press. 581 pp.

Conway, M. M., Stevens, A. J., Smith, R. G. 1975. The relation between media use and children's civic awareness. *Journ. Q.* 52:531–38

Council on Children, Media and Merchandising. 1977. *Edible TV: Your Child and Food Commercials.* Prepared for Senate Select Comm. Hum. Needs, 95th Congr., 1st session. Washington DC: GPO. 105 pp.

Danowski, J. 1975. *Informational aging: interpersonal and mass communication patterns in a retirement community.* Presented at Gerontol. Soc. Conv., Louisville, Ky.

Davidson, E. S., Yasuna, A., Tower, A. 1979. The effects of television cartoons on sex-role stereotyping in young girls. *Child Dev.* 50:597–600

Denbow, C. 1975. A test of predictors of newspaper subscribing. *Journ. Q.* 52:744–48

Dennis, E. E. 1978. *The Media Society: Evidence about Mass Communication in America.* Dubuque, Iowa: Brown. 166 pp.

Dennis, J., Chaffee, S. H., Choe, S. Y. 1979. Impact on partisan, image, and issue voting. See Becker et al 1979b, pp. 314–30

Diaz Bordenave, J. 1976. Communication of agricultural innovations in Latin America: the need for new models. *Commun. Res.* 3:135–54

Donohue, G. A., Tichenor, P. J., Olien, C. N. 1975. Mass media and the knowledge gap: a hypothesis reconsidered. *Commun. Res.* 2:3–23

Doob, A. N., Macdonald, G. E. 1979. Television viewing and fear of victimization: is the relationship causal? *J. Pers. Soc. Psychol.* 37:170–79

Dorr, A. 1978. *Children's advertising rulemaking comment.* Testimony to the Federal Trade Commission's Rulemaking Hearings on Television Advertising and Children, San Francisco, Calif., Nov. 31 pp.

Dotan, J., Cohen, A. A. 1976. Mass media use in the family during war and peace. *Commun. Res.* 3:393–402

Dubren, R. 1977. Evaluation of a televised stop-smoking clinic. *Public Health Rep.* 92:81–84

Edelstein, A. S. 1974. *The Uses of Communication in Decision-Making: A Comparative Study of Yugoslavia and the United States.* New York: Praeger. 270 pp.

Edgar, P. 1977. *Children and Screen Violence.* St. Lucia, Queensland, Aust: Univ. Queensland Press. 275 pp.

Egan, L. M. 1978. Children's viewing patterns for television news. *Journ. Q.* 55:337–42

Elliot, P. 1974. Uses and gratifications research: a critique and a sociological alternative. See Blumler & Katz 1974, pp. 249–68

Ettema, J. S., Kline, F. G. 1977. Deficits, differences, and ceilings: contingent conditions for understanding the knowledge gap. *Commun. Res.* 4:179–202

Eyal, C. H. 1979. *The roles of newspapers and television in agenda-setting.* Presented at Ann. Meet. Am. Assoc. Public Opin. Res., Buck Hills Falls, Pa.

Eyal, C. H., Winter, J. P., DeGeorge, W. F. 1979. *Time frame for agenda-setting.*

Presented at Ann. Meet. Am. Assoc. Public Opin. Res., Buck Hills Falls, Pa.

Eysenck, H. J., Nias, D. K. B. 1978. *Sex, Violence and the Media.* New York: St. Martin's. 306 pp.

Farquhar, J. W. 1978. The community-based model of life style intervention trials. *Am. J. Epidemiol.* 108:103–11

Farquhar, J. W., Wood, P. D., Breitrose, H., Haskell, W. L., Meyer, A. J., Maccoby, N., Alexander, J. K., Brown, B. W., McAlister, A. L., Nash, J. D., Stern, M. 1977. Community education for cardiovascular health. *Lancet* 1:1192–95

Federal Communications Commission. Children's Television Programs: Report and Policy Statement, 39 Fed. Reg. 39396, 39401; 50 F.C.C. 2nd 1,11

Federal Trade Commission. 1978. *FTC staff report on television advertising to children.* Washington DC: Fed. Trade Comm. 346 pp.

Feigert, F. B. 1976. Political competence and mass media use. *Public Opin. Q.* 40: 234–38

Foley, J. M. 1979. Mass communication theory and research: an overview. See Atkin 1979, pp. 263–70

Freuh, T., McGhee, P. E. 1975. Traditional sex role development and amount of time spent watching television. *Dev. Psychol.* 11:109

Friedrich, L. K., Stein, A. H. 1975, Prosocial television and young children: the effects of verbal labeling and role playing on learning and behavior. *Child Dev.* 46:27–38

Funkhouser, G. R. 1973. Trends in media coverage of the issues of the 60's. *Journ. Q.* 50:533–38

Galst, J. P., White, M. A. 1976. The unhealthy persuader: the reinforcing value of television and children's purchase-influencing attempts at the supermarket. *Child Dev.* 47:1089–96

Genova, B. K. L., Greenberg, B. S. 1979. Interests in news and the knowledge gap. *Public Opin. Q.* 43:79–91

Gerbner, G., Gross, L. 1976a. Living with television: the violence profile. *J. Commun.* 26(2):173–99

Gerbner, G., Gross, L. 1976b. The scary world of television. *Psychol. Today,* April: 41–45, 89

Gerbner, G., Gross, L., Jackson-Beeck, M., Jeffries-Fox, S., Signorielli, N. 1978. Cultural indicators: violence profile No. 9 *J. Commun.* 28(3):176–207

Gerbner, G., Gross, L., Signorielli, N., Morgan, M., Jackson-Beeck, M. 1979. The demonstration of power: violence profile No. 10. *J. Commun.* 29(3):177–96

Glasgow University Media Group. 1976. *Bad News.* London: Routledge

Goldberg, M. E., Gorn, G. 1977. *Material vs. social preferences, parent-child relations and the child's emotional responses: three dimensions of responses to children's TV advertising.* Presented at 5th Ann. Telecommun. Policy Res. Conf., Airlie House, Va.

Goldberg, M. E., Gorn, G., Gibson, W. 1978. TV messages for snack and breakfast foods: do they influence children's preferences? *J. Consum. Res.* 5:73–81

Gormley, W. T. Jr. 1975. Newspaper agendas and political elites. *Journ. Q.* 52:30–38

Gorn, G. J., Goldberg, M. E., Kanungo, R. N. 1976. The role of educational television in changing the intergroup attitudes of children. *Child Dev.* 47:277–80

Greenberg, B. S. 1974. Gratifications of television viewing and their correlates for British children. See Blumler & Katz 1974, pp. 71–92

Greenberg, B. S., Reeves, B. 1976. Children and the perceived reality of television. *J. Soc. Issues* 32:86–97

Halberstam, D. 1979. *The Powers That Be.* New York: Knopf. 771 pp.

Hall, S. 1977. Culture, the media and the 'ideological effect.' In *Mass Communication and Society,* ed. J. Curran, M. Gurevitch, J. Woollacott, pp. 315–48. London: Arnold. 479 pp.

Halloran, J. D. 1978. Further development—or turning the clock back. *J. Commun.* 28(2):120–32

Hawkins, R. P. 1977. The dimensional structure of children's perceptions of television reality. *Commun. Res.* 4:299–320

Hawkins, R. P., Pingree, S. H., Roberts, D. F. 1975. Watergate and political socialization: the inescapable event. *Am. Politics Q.* 3:406–22

Haynes, R. B. 1978. Children's perceptions of "comic" and "authentic" cartoon violence. *J. Broadcast.* 22:63–70

Hirsch, P. M. 1980. *The "scary world" of the nonviewer and other anomalies: a reanalysis of Gerbner et al's findings on cultivation analysis.* Presented at Ann. Meet. Am. Assoc. Public Opin. Res., King's Island, Ohio

Hirsch, P. M., Miller, P. V., Kline, F. G., eds. 1977. *Strategies for Communication Research.* Beverly Hills: Sage. 288 pp.

Hofstetter, C. R., Zukin, C. 1979. TV network political news and advertising in the Nixon and McGovern campaigns. *Journ. Q.* 56:106–15, 152

Hollenbeck, A. R., Slaby, R. G. 1979. Infant visual and vocal responses to television. *Child Dev.* 50:41–45

Howitt, D., Cumberbatch, G. 1975. *Mass Media, Violence and Society.* London: Elek. 167 pp.

Jackson-Beeck, M. 1979. Interpersonal and mass communication in children's political socialization. *Journ. Q.* 56:48–53

Jackson-Beeck, M., Chaffee, S. H. 1975. *Family communication, mass communication, and differential political socialization.* Presented at Ann. Meet. Int. Commun. Assoc., Chicago

Jennings, M. K., Niemi, R. G. 1975. Continuity and change in political orientations: a longitudinal study of two generations. *Am. Polit. Sci. Rev.* 69:1316–35

Johnston, J., Davidson, T. 1980. *The persistence of effects—a supplement to "An evaluation of 'Freestyle': a television series to reduce sex role stereotypes."* Ann Arbor: Inst. Soc. Res., Univ. Mich. 29 pp.

Johnston, J., Ettema, J., Davidson, T. 1980. *An evaluation of "Freestyle": a television series to reduce sex role stereotypes.* Ann Arbor: Inst. Soc. Res., Univ. Mich. 297 pp.

Johnstone, J. W. C. 1974. Social integration and mass media use among adolescents: a case study. See Blumler & Katz 1974, pp. 35–47

Joy, L. A., Kimball, M., Zabrack, M. L. 1977. *Television exposure and children's aggressive behavior.* Presented at Ann. Meet. Can. Psychol. Assoc., Vancouver, BC

Kaid, L. L., Hale, K., Williams, J. A. 1977. Media agenda setting of a specific political event. *Journ. Q.* 54:584–87

Kaplan, R. M., Singer, R. D. 1976. Television violence and viewer aggression: a re-examination of the evidence. *J. Soc. Issues* 32:35–70

Katz, E. 1977. *Social Research on Broadcasting: Proposals for Further Development.* London: British Broadcast. Corp. 116 pp.

Katz, E. 1978a. Looking for trouble. *J. Commun.* 28(2):90–95

Katz, E. 1978b. Of mutual interest. *J. Commun.* 28(2):133–41

Katz, E. 1979. The uses of Becker, Blumler, and Swanson. *Commun. Res.* 6:74–83

Katz, E. 1980. On conceptualizing media effects. In *Communications Studies: Decade of Dissent,* ed. T. MacCormak. Greenwich, Conn: JAI Press. In press

Katz, E., Blumler, J. G., Gurevitch, M. 1974. Utilization of mass communication by the individual. See Blumler & Katz 1974, pp. 19–32

Kippax, S., Murray, J. P. 1977. Using television: programme content and need gratification. *Politics* 12:56–69

Klapper, J. T. 1960. *The Effects of Mass Communication.* Glencoe, Ill: Free Press. 302 pp.

Kline, F. G., Miller, P. V., Morrison, A. J. 1974. Adolescents and family planning information: an exploration of audience needs and media effects. See Blumler & Katz 1964, pp. 113–36

Kraus, S., Davis, D. 1976. *The Effects of Mass Communication on Political Behavior.* University Park: Penn. State Univ. Press. 308 pp.

Krull, R., Husson, W. 1979. Children's attention: the case of TV viewing. See Collins 1979, pp. 83–114

Leifer, A. D., Gordon, N. J., Graves, S. B. 1974. Children's television: more than mere entertainment. *Harv. Educ. Rev.* 44:213–45

Lerner, D., Nelson, L. M., eds. 1977. *Communication Research—a Half Century Appraisal.* Honolulu: Univ. Press Hawaii. 348 pp.

Lerner, D., Schramm, W., eds. 1967. *Communication and Change in the Developing Countries.* Honolulu: East-West Center Press. 333 pp.

Lesser, G. S. 1974. *Children and Television: Lessons from Sesame Street.* New York: Random House. 290 pp.

Levin, S. R., Anderson, D. R. 1976. The development of attention. *J. Commun.* 26(2):126–35

Levy, M. R. 1977. Experiencing television news. *J. Commun.* 27:112–17

Levy, M. R. 1978. Opinion leadership and television news uses. *Public Opin. Q.* 42:402–6

Liebert, D. E., Sprafkin, J. N., Liebert, R. M., Rubinstein, E. A. 1977. Effects of television disclaimers on the product expectations of children. *J. Commun.* 27(1):118–24

Liebert, R. M., Schwartzberg, N. S. 1977. Effects of mass media. *Ann. Rev. Psychol.* 28:141–73

Lometti, G. E., Reeves, B., Bybee, C. R. 1977. Investigating the assumptions of uses and gratifications research. *Commun. Res.* 4:321–38

Lorch, E. P., Anderson, D. R., Levin, S. R. 1979. The relationship of visual attention to children's comprehension of television. *Child Dev.* 50:722–27

Maccoby, N., Alexander, J. 1979. Field experimentation in community intervention. In *Research in Social Contexts: Bringing About Change,* ed. R. F. Munoz, L. R. Snowden, J. G. Kelley, pp. 69–100. San Francisco: Jossey Bass. 394 pp.

Maccoby, N., Alexander, J. 1980. Use of media in lifestyle programs. In *Behavioral Medicine: Changing Health Lifestyles,* ed. P. O. Davidson, S. M. Davidson, pp. 351–70. New York: Brunner/Mazel. 474 pp.

Maccoby, N., Farquhar, J. W., Wood, P. D., Alexander, J. 1977. Reducing the risk of cardiovascular disease: effects of a community-based campaign on knowledge and behavior. *J. Community Health* 3:100–14

MacKuen, M. B. 1979. *Social communication and the mass policy agenda.* PhD thesis. Univ. Mich., Ann Arbor. 175 pp.

McAlister, A., Puskaa P., Koskele, K., Pallonen, U., Maccoby, N. 1980. Mass communication and community organization for public health education. *Am. Psychol.* 35:375–79

McCarthy, E. D., Langner, T. S., Gersten, J. C., Eisenberg, J. G., Orzeck, L. 1975. Violence and behavior disorders. *J. Commun.* 25(4):71–85

McClure, R. D., Patterson, T. E. 1976. Setting the political agenda: print vs. network news. *J. Commun.* 26(2):23–28

McCombs, M. E. 1977. Newspapers versus television: mass communication effects across time. In *The Emergence of American Political Issues: The Agenda-Setting Function of the Press,* ed. D. L. Shaw, M.E. McCombs, pp. 89–105. St. Paul: West. 208 pp.

McCombs, M. E., Poindexter, P. 1978. *Civic attitudes and newspaper readership.* Presented at Ann. Meet. Midwest Assoc. Public Opin Res., Chicago

McCombs, M. E., Shaw, D. L. 1972. The agenda-setting function of mass media. *Public Opin. Q.* 36:176–87

McCombs, M. E., Weaver, D. H. 1977. *Voters and the mass media: information seeking, political interest, and issue agendas.* Presented at Ann. Meet. Am. Assoc. Public Opin. Res., Buck Hills Falls, Pa.

McLeod, J. M., Becker, L. B. 1974. Testing the validity of gratification measures through political effects analysis. See Blumler & Katz 1974, pp. 137–64

McLeod, J. M., Becker, L. B., Byrnes, J. E. 1974. Another look at the agenda setting function of the press. *Commun. Res.* 1:131–66

McLeod, J. M., Bybee, C. R., Durall, J. A. 1979. Equivalence of informed political participation: the 1976 presidential debates as a source of influence. *Commun. Res.* 6:463–87

McLeod, J. M., Reeves, B. 1980. On the nature of mass media effects. In *Television and Social Behavior: Beyond Violence and Children,* ed. S. B. Withey, R. P. Ables, pp. 17–54. Hillsdale, NJ: Erlbaum. 356 pp.

Medrich, E. A. 1979. Constant television: a background to daily life. *J. Commun.* 29(3):171–76

Messaris, P. 1977. Biases of self-reported functions and gratifications of mass media use. *Et cetera: A Review of General Semantics* 34:316–29

Mielke, K. W., Swinehart, J. W. 1976. *Evaluation of the "Feeling Good" Television Series.* New York: Child. Telev. Workshop. 362 pp.

Miller, A. H., MacKuen, M. 1979. Informing the electorate: a national study. See Becker *et al* 1979b, pp. 269–97

Miller, M. M., Reeves, B. 1976. Linking dramatic TV content to children's occupational sex-role stereotypes. *J. Broadcast.* 20:35–50

Morison, P., McCarthy, M., Gardner, M. 1979. Exploring the realities of television with children. *J. Broadcast.* 23:453–63

Morrison, A. J., Steeper, F., Greendale, S. C. 1977. *The first 1976 presidential debate: the voters win.* Presented at Ann. Meet. Am. Assoc. Public Opin. Res., Buck Hills Falls, Pa.

Mullins, M. E. 1977. Agenda-setting and the young voter. See McCombs 1977, pp. 133–48

Murray, J. P., Ahammer, I. M. 1977. *Kindness in the kindergarten: a multidimensional program for facilitating altruism.* Presented at Bienn. Meet. Soc. Res. Child Dev., New Orleans

Murray, J. P., Kippax, S. 1979. From the early window to the late night show: international trends in the study of television's impact on children and adults. *Adv. Exp. Soc. Psychol.* 12:253–320

Newcomb, A. F., Collins, W. A. 1979. Children's comprehension of family role portrayals in televised dramas: effects of socioeconomic status, ethnicity, and age. *Dev. Psychol.* 15:417–23

Newspaper Advertising Bureau. 1978. *Children, Mothers and Newspapers.* New York: Newspaper Advert. Bur. 13 pp.

Newspaper Advertising Bureau. 1980a. *Children and Newspapers: Changing Patterns of Readership and Their Effects.* New York: Newspaper Advert. Bur. 96 pp.

Newspaper Advertising Bureau. 1980b. *Daily Newspapers in American Classrooms: A National Study of Their Impacts on Stu-*

dent *Attitudes, Readership and Political Awareness.* New York: Newspaper Advert. Bur. 46 pp.

Newspaper Advertising Bureau. 1980c. *Mass Media in the Family Setting: Social Patterns in Media Availability and Use by Parents.* New York: Newspaper Advert. Bur. 60 pp.

Noelle-Neumann, E. 1973. Return to the concept of powerful mass media. In *Studies of Broadcasting,* ed. H. Eguchi, K. Sata, 9:67–112. Tokyo: Nippon Hoso Kyokai

Noelle-Neumann, E. 1974. The spiral of silence: a theory of public opinion. *J. Commun.* 24(2):43–51

Noelle-Neumann, E. 1977. Turbulences in the climate of opinion: methodological applications of the spiral of silence theory. *Public Opin. Q.* 41:143–58

Nordenstreng, K. 1968. Communications research in the United States. *Gazette* 14(3):207–16

Nordenstreng, K., Schiller, H. I., eds. 1979. *National Sovereignty and International Communication.* New Jersey: Ablex. 286 pp.

Nordlund, J. 1978. Media interaction. *Commun. Res.* 5:150–75

Palmgreen, P. 1979. Mass media use and political knowledge. *Journ. Monogr.* 61. 39 pp.

Palmgreen, P., Clarke, P. 1977. Agenda-setting with local and national issues. *Commun. Res.* 4:435–52

Palmgreen, P., Kline, F. G., Clarke, P. 1974. *Message discrimination and information-holding about political affairs.* Presented at Ann. Meet. Int. Commun. Assoc., New Orleans

Palmgreen, P., Rayburn, J. D. 1979. Uses and gratifications and exposure to public television: a discrepency approach. *Commun. Res.* 6:181–202

Palmgreen, P., Wenner, L. A., Rayburn, J. D. 1980. Relations between gratifications sought and gratifications obtained: a study of television news. *Commun. Res.* 7:161–92

Parke, R. D., Berkowitz, L., Leyens, J. P., West, S., Sebastian, R. J. 1977. Some effects of violent and nonviolent movies on the behavior of juvenile delinquents. *Adv. Exp. Soc. Psychol.* 10:135–72

Patterson, T. E., McClure, R. D. 1976. *The Unseeing Eye: The Myth of Television Power in National Elections.* New York: Putnam. 218 pp.

Peled, T., Katz, E. 1974. Media functions in wartime: the Israel home front in October 1973. See Blumler & Katz 1974, pp. 49–69

Pingree, S. 1978. The effects of nonsexist television commercials and perceptions of reality on children's attitudes about women. *Psychol. Women Q.* 2:262–77

Pingree, S., Hawkins, R. P. 1980. Children and media. See Butler & Paisley 1980, pp. 279–99

Prisuta, R. H. 1979. The adolescent and television news: a viewer profile. *Journ. Q.* 56:277–82

Quarfoth, J. M. 1979. Children's understanding of the nature of television characters. *J. Commun.* 29(3):210–18

Quarles, R. C. 1979. Mass media use and voting behavior: the accuracy of political perceptions among first-time and experienced voters. *Commun. Res.* 6: 407–36

Reeves, B. 1978. Perceived TV reality as a predictor of children's social behavior. *Journ. Q.* 55:682–95

Reeves, B. 1979. Children's understanding of television people. See Collins 1979, pp. 115–56

Reeves, B., Greenberg, B. S. 1977. Children's perceptions of television characters. *Hum. Commun. Res.* 3:113–27

Reeves, B., Lometti, G. E. 1979. The dimensional structure of children's perceptions of television characters: a replication. *Hum. Commun. Res.* 5:247–56

Reeves, B., Miller, M. M. 1978. A multidimensional measure of children's identification with television characters. *J. Broadcast.* 22:71–85

Roberts, D. F. 1971. The nature of communication effects. In *The Process and Effects of Mass Communication,* ed. W. Schramm, D. F. Roberts, pp. 349–87. Urbana: Univ. Ill. Press. 997 pp.

Roberts, D. F. 1973. Communication and children: a developmental approach. In *Handbook of Communication,* ed. I. de Sola Pool, W. Schramm, pp. 174–215. Chicago: Rand McNally. 1011 pp.

Roberts, D. F., Bachen, C. M. 1978. *The impact of within-ad disclosures vs. supplemental nutrition messages on children's understanding of the concept of a "balanced breakfast."* Testimony to the Federal Trade Commission's Rulemaking Hearings on Television Advertising and Children, San Francisco, Nov. 21 pp.

Roberts, D. F., Bachen, C. M., Christenson, P. 1978. *Children's information processing: perceptions of and cognitions about television commercials and supplemental consumer information.* Testimony to the Federal Trade Commission's Rulemaking Hearings on Television Advertising and Children, San Francisco, Nov. 123 pp.

Roberts, D. F., Christenson, P., Gibson, W. A., Mooser, L., Goldberg, M. E. 1980. Developing discriminating consumers. *J. Commun.* 30(3):94–105

Roberts, D. F., Hawkins, R. P., Pingree, S. P. 1975. Do the mass media play a role in political socialization? *Aust. NZ J. Sociol.* 11:37–43

Robertson, T. S., Rossiter, J. R. 1974. Children and commercial persuasion: an attribution theory analysis. *J. Consum. Res.* 1:13–20

Robertson, T. S., Rossiter, J. R. 1977. Children's responsiveness to commercials. *J. Commun.* 27(1):101–5

Robinson, J. P., Jeffres, L. W. 1979. The changing role of newspapers in the age of television. *Journ. Monogr.* 63, 31 pp.

Robinson, M. J. 1975. American political legitimacy in an era of electronic journalism: reflections on the evening news. In *Television as a Social Force: New Approaches to TV Criticism,* ed. D. Cater, R. Adler, pp. 97–139. New York: Praeger. 171 pp.

Rogers, E. M. 1976a. Communication and development: the passing of the dominant paradigm. *Commun. Res.* 3:213–40

Rogers, E. M. 1976b. New perspectives on communication and development: overview. *Commun. Res.* 3:99–106

Rogers, E. M. 1976c. Where are we in understanding the diffusion of innovations? See Schramm & Lerner 1976, pp. 204–22

Rogers, E. M. 1977. Network analysis of the diffusion of innovations: family planning in Korean villages. See Lerner & Nelson 1977, pp. 117–47

Rogers, E. M., Shoemaker, F. F. 1971. *Communication of Innovations: A Cross-Cultural Approach.* New York: Free Press. 476 pp.

Roling, N. G., Ashcroft, J., Chege, F. W. 1976. The diffusion of innovations and the issue of equity in rural development. *Commun. Res.* 3:155–70

Roper Organization. 1977. *Changing Public Attitudes toward Television and Other Media.* New York: Telev. Inf. Off.

Rossiter, J. R., Robertson, T. S. 1974. Children's TV commercials: testing the defenses. *J. Commun.* 24(4):137–44

Rubin, A. M. 1976. Television in children's political socialization. *J. Broadcast.* 20:51–60

Rubin, A. M. 1978. Child and adolescent television use and political socialization. *Journ. Q.* 55:125–29

Rubin, A. M. 1979. Television use by children and adolescents. *Hum. Commun. Res.* 5:109–20

Salomon, G. 1979a. *Interaction of Media, Cognition and Learning.* San Francisco: Jossey-Bass. 282 pp.

Salomon, G. 1979b. Shape, not only content: how media symbols partake in the development of abilities. See Collins 1979, pp. 53–82

Schank, R., Abelson, R. 1977. *Scripts, Plans, Goals and Understanding: An Inquiry into Human Knowledge Structures.* Hillsdale, NJ: Erlbaum. 248 pp.

Schramm, W. 1962. Mass communication. *Ann. Rev. Psychol.* 13:251–84

Schramm, W. 1971. The nature of communication between humans. See Roberts 1971, pp. 3–53

Schramm, W., Lerner, D., eds. 1976. *Communication and Change: The Last Ten Years—And the Next.* Honolulu: Univ. Press Hawaii. 372 pp.

Sears, D. O., Chaffee, S. H. 1979. Uses and effects of the 1976 debates: an overview of empirical studies. See Becker et al 1979b, pp. 223–61

Sheikh, A. A., Moleski, L. M. 1977. Conflict in the family over commericals. *J. Commun.* 27(1):152–57

Shingi, P. M., Mody, B. 1976. The communication effects gap: a field experiment on television and agricultural ignorance in India. *Commun. Res.* 3:171–90

Silverman, L. T. 1977. *Effects of "Sesame Street" programming on the cooperative behavior of preschoolers.* PhD thesis. Stanford Univ., Stanford, Calif. 140 pp.

Siune, K., Borre, O. 1975. Setting the agenda for a Danish election *J. Commun.* 25(1):65–73

Sohn, A. B. 1978. A longitudinal analysis of local non-political agenda-setting effects. *Journ. Q.* 55:325–33

Sprafkin, J. N., Liebert, R. M., Poulos, R. W. 1975. Effects of a prosocial televised example on children's helping. *J. Exp. Child Psychol.* 20:119–26

Sprafkin, J. N., Rubinstein, E. A. 1979. Children's television viewing habits and prosocial behavior: a field correlational study. *J. Broadcast.* 23:265–76

Stamm, K. R., Fortini-Campbell, L. 1977. *Readership and community identification.* Presented at Ann. Meet. Assoc. Educ. Journ., Houston

Stauffer, J., Frost, R., Rybolt, W. 1978. Literacy, illiteracy, and learning from television news. *Commun. Res.* 5:221–32

Stroman, C. A., Becker, L. B. 1978. Racial differences in gratifications. *Journ. Q.* 55:767–71

Surgeon General's Scientific Advisory Committee. 1972. *Television and Growing Up: The Impact of Televised Violence.* Washington DC: GPO. 169 pp.

Swanson, D. L. 1976. *Some theoretic approaches to the emerging study of political communication: a critical assessment.* Presented at Ann. Meet. Int. Commun. Assoc., 26th, Portland, Ore.

Swanson, D. L. 1977. The uses and misuses of uses and gratifications. *Hum. Commun. Res.* 3:214–21

Swanson, D. L. 1979a. The continuing evolution of the uses and gratifications approach. *Commun. Res.* 6:3–7

Swanson, D. L. 1979b. Political communication research and the uses and gratifications model: a critique. *Commun. Res.* 6:37–53

Tan, A. S. 1979. TV beauty ads and role expectations of adolescent female viewers. *Journ. Q.* 56:283–88

Tan, A. S., Vaughn, P. 1976. Mass media exposure, public affairs knowledge, and black militancy. *Journ. Q.* 53:271–79

Tannenbaum, P. H. 1980. An unstructured introduction to an amorphous area. In *The Entertainment Functions of Television*, ed. P. H. Tannenbaum, pp. 1–12. Hillsdale, NJ: Erlbaum. 262 pp.

Tannenbaum, P. H., Greenberg, B. S. 1968. Mass communication. *Ann. Rev. Psychol.* 19:351–86

Tichenor, P. J., Donohue, G. A., Olien, C. N. 1970. Mass media and differential growth in knowledge. *Public Opin Q.* 34:158–70

Tichenor, P. J., Rodenkirchen, J. M., Olien, C. N., Donohue, G. A. 1973. Community issues, conflict and public affairs knowledge. In *New Models for Communication Research,* ed. P. Clarke, pp. 45–79. Beverly Hills: Sage. 307 pp.

Tipton, L. P., Haney, R. D., Baseheart, J. R. 1975. Media agenda-setting in city and state election campaigns. *Journ. Q.* 52:15–22

Tuchman, G. 1977. The exception proves the rule: the study of routine news practice. See Hirsch et al 1977, pp. 43–62

von Feilitzen, C. 1976. The functions served by the media. In *Children and Television,* ed. R. Brown, pp. 90–115. Beverly Hills: Sage. 368 pp.

Wackman, D. B., Ward, S., Wartella, E. 1978. *Comments on 'FTC staff report on television advertising to children.'* Testimony to the Federal Trade Commission's Rulemaking Hearings on Television Advertising and Children, Washington DC, Nov. 24 pp.

Wackman, D. B., Wartella, E. 1977. A review of cognitive development theory and research and the implications for research on children's responses to television. *Commun. Res.* 4:203–24

Wackman, D. B., Wartella, E., Ward, S. 1977. Learning to be consumers: the role of the family. *J. Commun.* 27:138–51

Wald, K. D., Lupfer, M. B. 1978. The presidential debate as a civics lesson. *Public Opin. Q.* 42:342–53

Ward, S., Levinson, D., Wackman, D. 1972. Children's attention to television advertising. In *Television and Social Behavior.* Vol 4: *Television in Day-to-Day Life: Patterns of Use,* ed. E. A. Rubinstein, G. A. Comstock, J. P. Murray, pp. 432–51. Washington DC: GPO. 603 pp.

Ward, S., Wackman, D. B. 1973. Children's information processing of television advertising. See Tichenor et al 1973, pp. 119–46

Ward, S., Wackman, D., Wartella, E. 1977. *How Children Learn to Buy: The Development of Consumer Information-Processing Skills.* Beverly Hills: Sage. 271 pp.

Wartella, E., Ettema, J. S. 1974. A cognitive developmental study of children's attention to television commercials. *Commun. Res.* 1:69–88

Wartella, E., Wackman, D. B., Ward, S., Shamir, J., Alexander, A. 1979. The young child as consumer. See Collins 1979, pp. 251–79

Weaver, D. H. 1977. Political issues and voter need for orientation. See McCombs 1977, pp. 107–19

Weaver, D. H., Auh, T. S., Stehla, T., Wilhoit, C. 1975a. *A path analysis of individual agenda-setting during the 1974 Indiana senatorial campaign.* Presented at Ann. Meet. Assoc. Educ. Journ., Ottawa, Canada

Weaver, D. H., Becker, L. B., McCombs, M. E. 1976. *Influence of the mass media on issues, images, and political interest: the agenda-setting function of mass communication during the 1976 campaign.* Presented at Ann. Meet. Midwest Assoc. Public Opin. Res., Chicago

Weaver, D. H., McCombs, M. E., Spellman, C. 1975b. Watergate and the media: a case study of agenda-setting. *Am. Politics Q.* 3:458–72

Weiss, W. 1969. Effects of the mass media of communication. In *The Handbook of Social Psychology,* ed. G. Lindzey, E. Aronson, 5:77–195. Reading, Mass: Addison Wesley, 786 pp.

Weiss, W. 1971. Mass communication. *Ann. Rev. Psychol.* 22:309–36

Weiss, W. 1976. Review of *The Uses of Mass Communications: Current Perspectives on Gratifications Research.* ed. J. G. Blumler, E. Katz. *Public Opin. Q.* 40:132–33

Wenner, L. A. 1976. Functional analysis of TV viewing for older adults. *J. Broadcast.* 20:77–88

Wenner, L. A. 1977. *Political news on television: a uses and gratifications study.* PhD thesis. Univ. Iowa, Iowa City

Whiting, G. C. 1976. How does communication interface with change? *Commun. Res.* 3:191–212

Williams, W. Jr., Larsen, D. C. 1977. Agenda-setting in an off-election year. *Journ. Q.* 54:744–49

Williams, W. Jr., Semlak, W. 1978. Campaign 76: agenda-setting during the New Hampshire primary. *J. Broadcast.* 22:531–40

Winter, J. P. 1979. *Contingent conditions and the agenda-setting function.* Presented at Ann. Meet. Am. Assoc. Public Opin. Res., Buck Hills Falls, Pa.

Worth, S., Gross, L. 1974. Symbolic strategies. *J. Commun.* 24(4):27–39

Zucker, H. G. 1978. The variable nature of news media influence. In *Communication Yearbook 2,* ed. B. D. Ruben, 225–40. New Brunswick, NJ: Transaction. 587 pp.

Zuckerman, P., Ziegler, M., Stevenson, H. W. 1978. Children's viewing of television and recognition memory of commercials. *Child Dev.* 48:96–104

Ann. Rev. Psychol. 1981. 32:357-404

ATTITUDE AND ATTITUDE CHANGE[1]

♦348

Robert B. Cialdini

Department of Psychology, Arizona State University, Tempe, Arizona 85281

Richard E. Petty

Department of Psychology, University of Missouri, Columbia, Missouri 65211

John T. Cacioppo[2]

Department of Psychology, University of Iowa, Iowa City, Iowa 52242

CONTENTS

[1]This review concerns itself principally with the published material appearing between January 1, 1977, and January 1, 1980.

[2]We are grateful to Robert M. Arkin, Bruce J. Biddle, and Robert S. Baron for critical readings of an earlier version of this chapter.

357

INTRODUCTION

In the last such review of attitude research, Eagly & Himmelfarb (1978) noted that after a decade of diminished attention, psychologists were showing renewed interest in attitudinal phenomena. Three years later, our own perspective on the intervening literature allows us to report that the revival has continued and is likely to remain steady for a time. Fueling the resurgence have been developments in three major areas. First has been the growing concern with and support for cognitive responses as mediators of attitude effects. Extending earlier information-processing formulations that focused on the processing of attitude-related information (e.g. message arguments), the cognitive response approach emphasizes the mediating influence of the specific cognitive *reactions* (e.g. counterarguments, favorable thoughts, etc) elicited by such information. Second, the prevailing view of the ability of attitudes to predict and cause behavior has rarely been more positive. The consequence has been and will continue to be the enhanced use of attitude measurement and models in applied settings. Third, consistency is back. Following recent demonstrations of the vitality of a pair of consistency theories whose stars had been in decline—balance and dissonance—the consistency principle is once more being given substantial explanatory weight in the interpretation of attitude effects. Interestingly, even the most active present rival of dissonance theory offers a consistency motive of sorts. It contends that the results of typical dissonance studies occur not from a subject's desire to be consistent, but from a desire to look consistent.

Each of these three major areas of work will be treated more fully in the initial portion of this chapter. The second half of the chapter, however, will involve a consideration of developments in six traditional areas of investigation that continued to stimulate attitude research during the period of our review.

THREE AREAS OF SPECIAL EMPHASIS

Cognitive Response Analysis of Attitude Effects

A theme of much of the attitude change research reported in the last 3 years has been that the information people generate themselves is a more important determinant of the direction and amount of persuasion than is information provided by others. When people generate new favorable information about an issue, attitudes are likely to become more positive, but when people generate new unfavorable information about an issue, attitudes are likely to become more negative.

ROLE-PLAYING AND THE EFFECTS OF MERE THOUGHT   One of the earliest demonstrations of the importance of self-persuasion came from Janis & King's (1954, King & Janis 1956) studies of improvisational role playing. Janis (1968) argued that when a person agrees to espouse a discrepant position, a "biased scanning" of the arguments on the issue occurs. The person temporarily becomes motivated to think up favorable information about the side to be advocated and suppress thoughts unfavorable to the issue. This biased information search presumably increases the likelihood of attitude change. In a test of the biased scanning hypothesis, O'Neill & Levings (1979) told high school students which side of a debate they were going to be on either before or after they were given 40 minutes to think about the issue. Students who knew at the outset of the 40 minute period which side they would have to defend engaged in a biased generation of arguments favorable to the assigned side and expressed more agreement with the assigned side of attitude measures taken both immediately before and right after the actual debate. Cunningham & Collins (1977) tested for biased scanning by giving subjects who were about to role-play a chance to listen to tapes that either supported or contradicted the discrepant positions they were about to advocate. When there was only enough time to listen to one tape completely, role-play subjects spent more time listening to the tape that was consistent with their role-playing assignment. However, when there was enough time to listen to both tapes completely, role-play subjects first chose to listen to the tape that was inconsistent with their role-play assignment, but consistent with their original attitudes. Perhaps this was done to bolster their original attitude, or perhaps to help generate counterarguments which would facilitate their role-playing. Eiser & Ross (1977) attempted to bias the kind of information that people would generate by requiring them to write essays that used certain words that were associated with either a pro or an anti position. As expected, subjects using the pro words became more favorable and those using the anti words became less favorable to the issue (see also Eiser & Pancer 1979). Interestingly, in a second study subjects were given explicit arguments containing the biasing words to use in their essays, but this did not affect subjects' attitudes. This highlights the importance of the subjects' *own* generation of the arguments. Finally, in another role-playing study, Watts (1977) attempted to account for the failure of previous research to find that high intelligence facilitates role-playing effects (e.g. Elms 1966, Kelman 1953). Increased intelligence would presumably render a person more able to generate convincing arguments on the issue. Watts varied the amount of improvisation required in the role-playing (subjects either were or were not given help in generating arguments), and found that intelligence enhanced attitude change only when total improvisation was required. He concluded that the failure of past studies to find facilitating effects of intelligence was due to the fact that these studies did not require *total* improvisation (and thus the person's intelligence was less important).

In role-playing research, people are specifically requested to generate arguments on a particular side of an issue. Tesser (1978) has investigated the effects of simply asking people to think about an attitude object and has found that "mere thought" can cause attitudes to become more extreme. Polarization is only likely with increased thought, however, when the person has a *schema* (a structure of preexisting information about the issue) that biases the thoughts generated in a schema-consistent direction. In a prototypical study (Tesser & Leone 1977) men and women were either instructed to think about or were distracted from thinking about videotaped sequences of football tackles and women's fashions. For men, attitudes toward the football tackles (but not fashions) became more polarized with thought than with distraction, but for women, attitudes toward fashions (but not tackles) become more polarized with thought than with distraction. The men presumably had a schema about football tackles and the women about fashions that guided thinking and produced the polarization. These polarization effects appear to be quite robust and have been shown with a wide variety of different issues and schemas (Clary, Tesser & Downing 1978, Tesser & Danheiser 1978).

COGNITIVE RESPONSES TO PERSUASIVE MESSAGES   The basic tenet of the cognitive response approach is that when a person anticipates or receives a persuasive message, an attempt is made to relate the information in the message (or the expected message) to the preexisting knowledge that the person has about the issue. In so doing, the person will generate a number of issue-relevant beliefs that may support the advocated position (proarguments) or may oppose it (counterarguments). If the elicited thoughts (cognitive responses) are primarily favorable, persuasion will be the likely result, but if the thoughts are primarily unfavorable, resistance will be more likely (cf Greenwald 1968; Petty, Ostrom & Brock 1980).

Inducing resistance to persuasion   One of the earliest demonstrations of the importance of counterarguments in producing resistance to persuasion came from McGuire's (1964) work on inoculation theory. McGuire demonstrated that a person's belief on a cultural truism could be made highly resistant to attack by exposing the person to sample opposing arguments and showing the person how to refute them (refutational defense). In McGuire's work, this inoculation strategy was generally more effective in inducing resistance to a later attack than exposing the person to supportive information only. Using a cultural truism topic, Suedfeld & Borrie (1978) replicated McGuire's finding that a refutational defense was superior to a supportive defense in producing resistance to a subsequent attacking message. Two studies not employing cultural truisms, however, found that refutational and supportive defenses were equal in inducing resistance (Adams & Beatty 1977, Pryor & Steinfatt 1978). McGuire has argued that refutational defenses are particularly effective with cultural truisms because people have probably never heard the truism attacked and may not even be able to conceive of it being attacked. The refutational defense disabuses people of this notion, motivating them to bolster their belief and giving them practice in defending it. When the issue employed is not a cultural truism, and people are not operating under the assumption that their belief is invulnerable, the refutational defense should not have any unique motivating power, and thus would not necessarily be any more effective than a supportive defense.

Inoculation defenses are particularly effective in inducing resistance on cultural truisms because people are not initially very able to defend these beliefs. For issues that are more involving and that people have more information about, simply forewarning them that they are about to receive a discrepant message is sufficient to motivate people to generate their own defenses. Evidence of the spontaneous thinking (primarily counterarguing) that occurs when a person anticipates receiving an involving discrepant communication has been measured using both thought listings (Petty & Cacioppo 1977) and facial EMG activity (Cacioppo & Petty 1979a).

A third way to increase resistance to persuasion by enhancing counterarguing is to forewarn the message recipients of the speaker's persuasive intent. Consistent with reactance theory (Brehm 1966), Petty & Cacioppo (1979a) found that a forewarning of persuasive intent elicited more counterarguments and greater resistance to persuasion on involving than uninvolving issues. The more involving the issue, the more motivated people would be to demonstrate their freedom to hold their attitudes by counterarguing opposing messages. Watts & Holt (1979) found that a forewarning of persuasive intent reduced persuasion only when no distraction accompanied the message presentation. When distraction was present, the counterarguing that would have been elicited by the forewarning would presumably be disrupted (cf Petty & Brock 1980). M. J. Smith (1977) investigated the effects of manipulating persuasive intent within a message rather than prior to it. She found that persuasive intent increased source derogation and tended to reduce persuasion only when the subjects disagreed with the position advocated. When subjects agreed with the message no effects were observed. Presumably, the persuasive intent is not as threatening if the person agrees with what is being said. Additionally, Smith (1979) showed that the persuasion inhibiting effects of a message with explicit persuasive intent could be eliminated if the message recipients were given a chance to bolster their attitudes prior to message exposure. This preliminary cognitive bolstering presumably obviates the person's need to counterargue *during* the message rendering the person more susceptible (see also Snyder & Wicklund 1976).

Variables affecting the ability to process a message   The variables that we discussed above are ones that enhance the likelihood that a person will process a message in a *biased* manner. Some variables appear to affect a person's ability to process a message in a more objective manner. For example, Lammers & Becker (1980) obtained support for the dominant thought disruption explanation for the effects of distraction on persuasion (Petty, Wells & Brock 1976). When subjects were distracted during the presentation of a message that predominantly elicited counterarguments, they saw the message as closer to their own view than nondistracted subjects, but when the subjects were distracted during the presentation of a message that predominantly elicited proarguments, they tended to see the message as being further from their own view than nondistracted subjects. Romer (1979a), employing a message that predominantly elicited counterarguments, found a curvilinear effect (increasing then decreasing persuasion) with increasing distraction. The decline in persuasion under the highest distraction levels in this study was probably due to the dramatic drop in message comprehension that was observed. The cognitive response interpretation of distraction effects assumes that the message arguments are encoded but just not evaluated (Festinger & Maccoby 1964).

Just as distraction decreases message elaboration, Cacioppo & Petty (1979b) reasoned that message repetition would *increase* a person's opportunity to elaborate the content of an advocacy. If the content contained compelling arguments of some complexity, increased favorable thoughts and decreased counterarguments should be observed as the message was considered (i.e. repeated). This effect was observed at low levels of repetition, but at high levels subjects began to counterargue the message and persuasion declined. Cacioppo and Petty suggested that at low to moderate levels of message repetition, processing is of a fairly objective nature. The greater opportunity for elaboration should lead to more favorable thoughts and persuasion if the arguments are cogent, but to more counterarguments and less persuasion if the arguments are weak (cf Cacioppo & Petty 1980). When the repetition reaches tedious levels, however, objective processing ceases and the person becomes motivated to reject the message regardless of its quality (cf Sawyer 1980). Gorn & Goldberg (1980) and Miller (1976) also reported curvilinear effects of message repetition on persuasion. Swinyard & Coney (1978) found a curvilinear effect with relatively familiar stimuli but a linear effect with relatively unfamiliar stimuli. Presumably, tedium would set in earlier the more familiar the repeated stimulus was.

Variables affecting the motivation to process a message   Like ability variables, motivational variables can also affect the manner in which a message is processed. Perhaps the most researched variable was issue-involvement. Halverson & Pallak (1978) argued that typical manipulations of commitment (cf Kiesler 1971) elevated involvement with an issue although Sherif (1976) suggested that this effect would only be temporary. Most studies on issue involvement, though, manipulated the personal relevance or importance of the attitude topic. For example, Petty & Cacioppo (1979b) found that, contrary to the traditional social judgment theory view that involvement invariably reduces persuasion (Sherif & Sherif 1967), increased involvement could enhance persuasion if the message contained cogent arguments. Petty and Cacioppo argued that increasing issue involvement increased a person's motivation to process the content of an advocacy. Thus, they found that increasing the personal relevance of a message containing good arguments led to more persuasion, but increasing the personal relevance of a message with poor arguments led to less persuasion. Lord, Ross & Lepper (1979) found evidence to suggest that when a person is involved with an attitude issue, but the communication presents inconclusive or mixed data rather than data that are clearly strong or weak, attitude polarization will occur. Apparently, when the arguments presented in a message are inconclusive, the recipients' thoughts are guided more by their preexisting attitudes than by the content of the communication.

Personal involvement with an issue was manipulated in different ways in different studies, but the results were generally consistent with the view that increasing involvement enhances issue-relevant thinking (cf Crano 1977, Webb 1979). On the other hand, a way to decrease motivation to engage in issue-relevant thinking is to lead people to believe that they are part of a large group of individuals who are responsible for evaluating the message (Petty, Harkins & Williams 1980; Petty et al 1977).

Sternthal, Dholakia & Leavitt (1978) provided a cognitive response analysis of the effects of source expertise. They argued that when the message presented a counterattitudinal position, people would generate fewer counterarguments to high than low expert sources (since experts can be trusted) and this would produce greater persuasion for high than low experts. When a message presented a proattitudinal position, however, they argued that people would be more motivated to generate proarguments to a low than a high expert communicator (presumably to ensure that their side was adequately represented). This should lead to more persuasion for the low than high expert source. The available data appear to support these propositions for low involving issues (Sternthal, Phillips & Dholakia 1978). For highly involving issues, however, Hass (1980) has argued that high expert sources elicit more counterarguing than low. Because the data are limited at present, the effects of source expertise on cognitive responses must await future research.

The persistence of persuasion   Just as the thoughts elicited at the time of message exposure determine the amount of initial attitude change according to the cognitive response approach, Greenwald (1968) proposed that the persistence of persuasion depends on the extent to which these thoughts remain salient over time. In a test of this hypothesis, Love & Greenwald (1978) had subjects read a message and write their thoughts about it. One week later, the subjects indicated their attitudes and were asked to recall the message arguments and the thoughts that they had listed the previous week. Subjects' ability to recall their cognitive responses was a better predictor of the delayed attitude measure (with initial attitudes partialed out) than was their ability to recall the message arguments.

From a cognitive response perspective, an important question concerns the determinants of whether or not one's initial cognitive responses will be salient at some later point in time (Perloff & Brock 1980, Petty 1977). Presumably, then, all inductions (e.g. moderate message repetition) that increase the opportunity to generate and rehearse cognitive responses, or increase the motivation to generate and rehearse cognitive responses (e.g. high issue-involvement) would enhance the likelihood that any initially produced persuasion would be relatively enduring. Cook & Flay's (1978) comprehensive literature review of the persistence of experimentally induced attitude change generally supports this view. Studies in which subjects were motivated and able to think about and elaborate upon the information provided to them generally evidenced persisting persuasion effects, but studies in which subjects' motivation and/or ability to think about the message was low demonstrated relatively short-lived attitude changes. For instance, Ronis et al (1977) found that although it was more difficult to change attitudes on relatively involving issues (e.g. school integration), these changes persisted longer than changes induced on less involving topics (e.g. the statesmanship of President Polk).

CENTRAL AND PERIPHERAL ROUTES TO PERSUASION   The cognitive response approach to attitude change can be criticized on the grounds that it emphasizes a too thoughtful picture of persuasion. People are not always able and motivated to engage in effortful cognitive activity, but attitude changes occur nonetheless (cf Miller et al 1976). Petty and Cacioppo (in press) mapped two basic routes to persuasion—a *central route* which occurs when the person is motivated and able to think about the issue, and a *peripheral route* which occurs when either motivation or ability is low. The central route emphasizes a thoughtful consideration of the attitude issue whereas the peripheral route emphasizes aspects of the persuasion situation that are clearly tangential to the issue under consideration (e.g. the rewards available for advocating a certain view; the attractiveness of the message's source, etc).[3] The accumulated literature on persuasion indicates that persuasion via the central route is likely to produce an enduring attitude change, but persuasion via the peripheral route is likely to produce a change that lasts only if the change is subsequently bolstered by supportive cognitive argumentation (cf Cialdini et al 1976).

   In a study that clearly demonstrates the importance of these two routes, Chaiken (in press) exposed subjects to a message containing either two or six arguments that came from either a likeable or dislikeable source. Half of the subjects expected to be interviewed on the issue at a later time (high consequences condition), and half expected to be interviewed on an irrelevant issue (low consequences). Under the high consequences conditions, attitude change was determined primarily by the number of arguments presented; the likeability manipulation had no significant effect. Under low consequences, however, change was determined primarily by the likeability of the source; the number of arguments presented made little difference. Furthermore, on a measure of opinion taken about 10 days later, the changes of the high consequences subjects (whose changes were determined primarily by thinking about the arguments central to the issue) showed

[3]The distinction between central and peripheral processing has much in common with the distinctions between deep versus shallow processing (Craik & Lockhart 1972), controlled versus automatic processing (Schneider & Shiffrin 1977), systematic versus heuristic processing (Chaiken, in press), and thoughtful versus mindless or scripted processing (Abelson 1976, Langer et al 1978).

greater stability than the changes of the low consequences subjects (whose shifts were determined primarily by considerations peripheral to the issue).

It is instructive to note that much of the early research on attitude change specifically employed attitude issues that were relatively uninvolving and about which subjects knew very little (cf Hovland, Janis & Kelley 1953; Hovland 1959). This may have predisposed the observed persuasion effects to be rather temporary.

The Attitude-Behavior Relationship

PREDICTING OVERT BEHAVIORS FROM ATTITUDES   The attitude-behavior problem has continued to generate a great deal of research, but no longer are researchers questioning *if* attitudes predict behaviors (e.g. Wicker 1969), they are investigating *when* attitudes predict behaviors. Two cross-lagged panel analyses of the attitude-behavior relationship provided an optimistic answer to an old but important question—do attitudes cause behaviors, or do behaviors lead to attitudes? Kahle & Berman (1979) and Andrews & Kandel (1979) both found that attitudes had causal predominance over behaviors which suggests that attitudes have an important degree of *predictive* utility. In the remaining sections on the predictive utility of attitudes, we will discuss measurement issues that affect the attitude-behavior relationship and attempts to improve behavioral prediction by including variables other than attitudes.

Measurement issues   The most influential paper on the attitude-behavior problem during this review period was probably Ajzen & Fishbein's (1977) extensive literature review in which they concluded that attitudes were good predictors of behavior only when the attitudinal and behavioral measures showed a high degree of *correspondence.*

Attitude and behavior measures are said to correspond when they match on action, target, context, and time dimensions. Thus, an investigator should not expect to measure attitudes toward an action element (e.g. driving), and predict whether a person will drive a two-ton truck (target) on a snowy highway (context) on New Year's Eve (time). In three studies demonstrating this point, Jaccard, King & Pomazal (1977) attempted to predict a single behavior from attitude measures that varied in their level of specificity. The more the attitude measure corresponded to the behavioral criterion, the better was prediction.

The failure of some studies to find significant attitude-behavior relationships can probably be attributed to a lack of correspondence in the measures. Thus, Anderson & Lipsey (1978) found that reports of efforts to reduce energy consumption were not related to general attitudes about technology, and Fox (1977) found that general sex-role attitudes did not predict contraceptive use (except for women with an internal locus of control). On the other hand, a lack of correspondence does not guarantee that attitudes will be unrelated to behaviors. For example, McGuinness, Jones & Cole (1977) found that general attitudes toward ecology predicted specific recycling behavior over a 7 week period, and Schriesheim (1978) found that general attitudes toward unions predicted whether or not production employees would vote for the union in a local election (see also Hamner & Smith 1978, Mirvis & Lawler 1977, Seligman et al 1979, F. J. Smith 1977). In a variation of Milgram's (1969) lost letter technique for assessing attitudes in a disguised manner, Howitt & McCabe (1978) attempted to validate the *misdirected letter technique* (Howitt et al 1977) in which wrongly addressed letters are sent to households and the return rates are used as a behaviorally based measure of attitude toward the addressee. Letters with English or Irish names were sent to English households where attitudes toward the Irish had previously been assessed. There were no differences in attitudes toward the Irish between those who returned the letters addressed to an Englishman and those who did not, but those who returned the letters addressed to an Irishman had significantly more pro-Irish attitudes than those who did not return them. In sum, even though general attitudes may relate to specific behaviors in some instances, it is now clear that the attitude-behavior correlation can be improved by measuring attitudes and behaviors at corresponding levels of specificity.

In addition to the level of specificity at which attitudes and behaviors are measured, several other measurement factors can increase the attitude-behavior correlation. For example, Davidson & Jaccard (1979) and Schwartz (1978) found higher attitude-behavior correlations the closer in time the attitude and behavior measures were taken. The greater the time period separating the two measures, the greater the likelihood that attitudes will change in the interval, decreasing the utility of the initial (old) attitude measures as a predictor. Gabrenya & Arkin (1979) found that attitudes were better predictors of interracial behaviors when the measures were taken under high commitment conditions (i.e. subjects thought they would have to perform the behaviors).

Measuring attitudes and/or behaviors under conditions of objective self-awareness (Duval & Wicklund 1972) appears to enhance attitude-behavior consistency. Pryor et al (1977), for example, had subjects rate their attitudes toward various puzzles either in the presence of a mirror (self-awareness condition) or not (control). The attitude measure taken under self-awareness conditions predicted the actual proportion of time that subjects spent playing with the puzzles significantly better than the attitudes measured under control conditions. Similarly, Gibbons (1978) found that male subjects' attitudes toward erotica predicted their ratings of pictures of nude women better when the ratings were taken in the presence of a mirror than when they were not. The self-attention produced by the mirror presumably causes the person to be more introspective and accurate in reporting internal states. This greater accuracy enhances the consistency between attitudes and behaviors. As a final measurement concern, we note Bagozzi & Burnkrant's (1979) finding that affectively oriented attitude scales (e.g. semantic differential) predicted behaviors better than more cognitively oriented scales (e.g. Thurstone).

Even though it is now clear that respectable attitude-behavior correlations can be obtained when appropriate measures are taken, many investigators have attempted to enhance behavioral prediction still further by taking variables other than attitudes into account. We discuss the various approaches that have developed below.

Normative influences   The approach that has received the most attention is Fishbein & Ajzen's (1975, 1980) "theory of reasoned action." According to the theory, the best predictor of behavior is the actor's *intention* to perform the behavior. The intention is based on the person's *attitude* toward the behavior and the *subjective norm* regarding the behavior (the extent to which the person feels that significant others think that the behavior should be performed). A number of studies employing the Fishbein and Ajzen model found that behavioral intentions showed strong correlations with behaviors, and behavioral intentions were related to both attitudinal and normative influences. The model was generally successful in accounting for such things as family planning behavior (Davidson & Jaccard 1979, Vinokur-Kaplan 1978), adult (Kilty 1978) and adolescent alcohol use (Schlegel, Crawford & Sanborn 1977), reenlistment in the National Guard (Hom, Katerberg & Hulin 1979), and voting on a nuclear power plant initiative (Bowman & Fishbein 1978). Although both attitudes and norms significantly contributed to intentions in these studies, the impact of attitudes was generally greater than that of norms.

The norm concept was also the subject of more controversy than the attitude concept. For example, there is not yet widespread agreement on whether the components of the subjective norm concept (normative beliefs X motivation to comply) should both be measured on bipolar scales (Hom et al 1979), both on unipolar scales (Davidson & Jaccard 1979), or one on a bipolar and the other on a unipolar scale (Bowman & Fishbein 1978). Each of these procedures imparts a different meaning to the subjective norm. There appears to be particular dissatisfaction with the motivation to comply concept. Schlegel et al (1977) report that, regardless of whether motivation to comply was measured on a bipolar or a unipolar scale, inclusion of this variable in the model decreased the ability to predict behavioral intentions. Miniard & Cohen (1979) complained that the motivation to comply concept incorporated attitudinal influences, and they called for establishing discriminant validity between the attitude and norm measures. In a study of parental and peer influence on adolescent drinking behavior, Biddle, Bank & Marlin (1980) distinguished between normative pressures that resulted from what significant others said versus pressures that resulted from the behaviors that significant others modeled. They found that the norms modeled by peers and the norms verbally expressed by parents significantly affected adolescents' own attitudes toward alcohol use which in turn influenced reported drinking behavior. Biddle et al argued that rather than norms and attitudes separately affecting behaviors, norms affected behaviors through attitudes. In any case, it is clear that neither the best way to measure normative influences on behavior nor the causal sequence among attitudes, norms, and behaviors has been firmly established. Ajzen & Fishbein (1980) have agreed that their procedure for measuring norms may not be the best one, and have further noted that their "theory of reasoned action" is still developing.

Effects of habit   Fishbein & Ajzen (1975, 1980) have argued that all variables affect behavior only through their effects on behavioral intentions. In a test of this notion against alternative causal paths, Bentler & Speckart (1979) found that college students' previous drug and alcohol use (past behavior) accounted for a significant degree of variability in present drug and alcohol use that was not mediated by behavioral intentions (see also Bearden & Woodside 1977). This finding is consistent with the behavioral prediction model of Triandis (1977, 1980). Triandis proposed that future behaviors could be predicted from a combination of *intentions* (which are based on attitudes and norms) and *habits* (which refer to past behaviors) weighted by the person's *psychological arousal* (arousal enhances the likelihood of behavior) and *facilitating conditions* in the environment (whether conditions are favorable or unfavorable for the act's performance). According to Triandis, the more a person has engaged in a behavior previously, the less important is intention in predicting future behavior and the more important is habit. In a test of this model, Landis, Triandis & Adamopoulos (1978) measured the intentions of teachers to engage in various social behaviors with black and white male and female pupils (e.g. intentions to praise, command, etc). Two months later, classroom observations were taken with the first two-thirds of the observations being used as the measure of habit. The habit measure (past behavior) predicted the last one-third of the observations better than the intention measure. Of course, since intentions were measured 2 months prior to the behavioral observation, the intentions may have changed in the interim. Brinberg (1979) directly compared the Triandis model with that of Fishbein and Ajzen in an attempt to predict the church attendance of college students. The Fishbein and Ajzen model (predicting from intentions alone) proved superior to the Triandis model (including the habit component) in accounting for the students' church attendance. Unfortunately, in this study the measure of habit ("How often have you gone to church in the past?") may have assessed the students' *old* habits (i.e. when they lived at home) and not their newly acquired habits at college. A strong test of these two approaches is still needed.

Logical models Just as Wyer (1974) and McGuire (1960, 1980) have shown that linkages among beliefs could be described adequately by the laws of probability, Jaccard & King (1977) demonstrated that behavioral intentions could be viewed as the logical conclusion of a belief syllogism. For example, $p(I)$, the probability that Jones intends to vote for Smith, equals $p(B) p(I/B) + p(\bar{B}) p(I/\bar{B})$, where, for example, $p(B)$ = the probability that Smith favors school busing, $p(I/B)$ = the probability that Jones will vote for Smith given that Smith favors busing, $p(\bar{B})$ = the probability that Smith does not favor busing, and $p(I/\bar{B})$ = the probability that Jones will vote for Smith given that Smith does not favor busing. Jaccard and King found that predicted behavioral intentions (from the equation) and obtained behavioral intentions correlated highly. Also, induced changes in the component beliefs of the model led to the predicted changes in behavioral intentions.

Jaccard, Knox & Brinberg (1979) used the model to predict successfully presidential voting behavior in the 1976 election from various beliefs. Although the model is very successful in predicting intentions and voting from beliefs, it does not appear to matter what beliefs are measured. For example, when the belief is irrelevant to voting behavior [i.e. $p(I/B) = p(I/\bar{B})$], then these conditional probabilities simply serve as another measure of $p(I)$. Although the assessment of any one belief is sufficient for prediction of behavioral intentions in the model, the assessment of one belief cannot provide information about the *causes* of the intention. For the latter purpose, many different beliefs would have to be assessed. The quantity $p(I/B) - p(I/\bar{B})$ would provide an indication of the relevance of each belief for the behavior under investigation.

Direct experience with the attitude object Attitudes formed on the basis of direct experience with the attitude object are better predictors of behavior than are attitudes formed without such experience (Regan & Fazio 1977, Songer-Nocks 1976). Also, an attitude formed by merely watching and *empathizing* with a person who is having a direct experience with the attitude object can increase the attitude-behavior correlation for people who have no direct experience themselves (Fazio, Zanna & Cooper 1978). Several reasons for this phenomenon have been suggested. Fazio & Zanna (1978a,b) emphasized the effect of direct experience on the confidence, certainty, and clarity with which the attitude is held. Fazio and Zanna (in press) further suggested that attitudes based on direct experience are more salient in memory. Presumably, the more confidence in an attitude or the more salient the attitude is in memory, the more likely it is that the attitude can and will be acted upon. The focus on the confidence with which an attitude is held may help to explain Werner's (1978) finding that general attitudes toward abortion predicted abortion-relevant behaviors better for females than males. Ajzen & Fishbein (1980) suggested that the effect of direct experience toward abortion predicted abortion-relevant behaviors better for females than males. Ajzen & Fishbein (1980) suggested that the effect of direct experience on attitude-behavior consistency may be due to the differential reliabilities of the two kinds of attitudes. This explanation was tested by Fazio and Zanna (in press); however, they found that internal reliability coefficients did not vary as a function of direct experience, but attitude-behavior consistency did. Furthermore, not attitude extremity, variability, nor past behaviors per se (as predictors of future behaviors) accounted for the effects of past experience on the attitude-behavior relation.

Personality mediators   Zuckerman, Siegelbaum & Williams (1977) found support for Schwartz's (1973) notion that people high in *ascription of responsibility* (measuring the tendency to assign responsibility to the self) would be more likely to act on their behavioral intentions (as assessed by personal norms) than those who were low in their ascription of responsibility. Zuckerman & Reis (1978) compared Schwartz's ascription of responsibility model, Snyder's (1974, 1979) self-monitoring model, and Fishbein and Ajzen's intention model in an attempt to predict blood donations. The self-monitoring notion is that people who are low self-monitors will show stronger attitude-behavior correlations than high self-monitors because they tend to guide their behavioral choices mainly on the basis of salient inner states rather than situational information. Zuckerman and Reis found that the ascription of responsibility and self-monitoring variables added nothing to the predictability already afforded by attitudes and behavioral intentions; attitudes and intentions did add predictability to the personality constructs, however. In another test of the self-monitoring model, Zanna, Olson & Fazio (1980) found that low self-monitors had stronger attitude-behavior correspondence than high self-monitors only when the two groups reported that their past behaviors toward the attitude object had been relatively consistent (see Bem & Allen 1974). This is presumably due to the fact that when past behaviors toward an object are quite variable, low self-monitors are unable to infer a clear attitude that can influence their subsequent behavior.

ATTITUDES AND COVERT BEHAVIORS   So far we have discussed the research on attitudes and overt behaviors. We now turn to the study of attitudes and concomitant physiological reactions (PRs). This research ranges from the study of the effects of bogus feedback on attitudes to explorations of the attitudinal effects of undetected physiological responses. We begin the review of this research with the work on PRs as *measures* of attitudes and attitudinal processes.

Attitude measurement   Physiological processes have been of interest in attitude measurement because they may reflect subtle cognitive or affective responses to an attitude object that the individual is either unable or unwilling to report accurately. In a review of this research, Cacioppo & Sandman (1980) characterized three distinct approaches: (*a*) *Emotional response approach*—Naturally occurring physiological responses are monitored to obtain information about the intensity and/or direction of an affective or attitudinal response (e.g. Mewborn & Rogers 1979, Schwartz et al 1978, White & Maltzman 1978); (*b*) *Classical conditioning approach*—An induced (classically conditioned) physiological response is used to measure the intensity and/or direction of the attitudinal response (Tursky, Lodge & Reeder 1979); and (*c*) *Cognitive response approach*—Naturally occurring physiological responses are monitored to obtain evidence regarding the cognitive processes underlying attitude change (Cacioppo & Petty 1979a, Kroeber-Riel 1979).

Although these approaches are conceptually distinct, two or more of them can be used in combination to supplement and/or validate simpler, more economical assessment procedures. For instance, Cacioppo & Petty (1979a) employed both the emotional and cognitive response approaches, which involved measuring two different sets of PRs, to obtain convergent validity for retrospective self-report measures of cognitive responses and to examine the conditions under which anticipatory cognitive preparation for a persuasive communication occurs. Tursky et al (1979) used psychophysiological and psychophysical assessment procedures. They compared the data obtained using a classically conditioned physiological response (electrodermal activity) with that secured by magnitude estimation and category scaling. Overall, Tursky et al obtained correspondence between the psychophysical and psychophysiological measures. These experiments represent an increasing trend in social psychophysiological studies to employ a set of measures (e.g. multiple PRs, PRs and verbal judgments) to assess a person's attitude. Discrepancies between measures, for instance between psychophysiological and the more easily controlled verbal measures, do arise though. Whether the discrepancies reflect unique aspects of the attitude or artifacts in one or more of the measures is at present uncertain.

Perspectives on the role of bodily responses in attitude change   Most research on attitude change pertains to situations in which there are neither significant physiological reactions arising within one's body nor salient external information about one's physiological reactions. Nevertheless, Cacioppo & Petty (in press) have noted that a surprising number of recent studies can be characterized by one of the following perspectives on the role of bodily responses in attitude change: (*a*) *PRs that are detected internally* —The subject becomes aware of internal (proprioceptive) sensations; (*b*) *PRs that are detected externally*—The subject contains information (usually bogus) through exteroceptive channels regarding the status of his or her bodily reactions while the sensations obtained through internal channels are absent, weak, or ambiguous; and (*c*) *PRs that are undetected*—The attitudinal effects of actual bodily reactions of which the subject is unaware are investigated.

PRs that are detected internally   Most research on bodily responses and attitude change falls within the first classification: PRs that are "felt." This includes the work on perceived and actual arousal of the viscera (internal organs) during fear appeals (Mewborn & Rogers 1979) and on the misattribution of unexplained arousal (Marshall & Zimbardo 1979, Maslach 1979, Schachter & Singer 1979). Dissonance theorists, too, have utilized this general perspective to explore the phenomenology (Cooper, Fazio & Rhodewalt 1978a; Cooper, Zanna & Taves 1978b; Higgins, Rhodewalt & Zanna 1979; Rhodewalt & Comer 1979) and domain (Fazio, Zanna & Cooper 1977; cf Fazio et al 1979, Ronis & Greenwald 1979) of cognitive dissonance. Typically, a misattribution paradigm has been employed in which subjects are either exposed or not to treatments that are believed to arouse cognitive dissonance and are either exposed or not to a possible external cause for their felt internal sensations. Several studies hinted that dissonance might feel "arousing" (e.g. Cooper et al 1978a,b), but the results could be explained as parsimoniously if dissonance simply felt "unpleasant." Higgins et al (1979) conducted a study to determine which or if both of these phenomenological reactions characterized a dissonant state. They found that the most salient aspect of cognitive dissonance was the feeling of unpleasantness (see also Rhodewalt & Comer 1979). Of course, *there may be large discrepancies between the fact and the phenomenology of one's bodily reactions.* Cognitive dissonance, therefore, may have "arousing" motivational properties (cf Kiesler & Pallak 1976) even though it does not *feel* arousing.

A misattribution paradigm was used also by Fazio et al (1977) to test their resolution of the controversy between cognitive dissonance and self-perception theory. They reasoned that cognitive dissonance theory, which postulates that dissonance produces a tension that people feel, applies to the realm of attitude-discrepant behavior, whereas self-perception theory, which postulates that internal sensations are either unperceived or so ambiguous as to have no role in change (Bem 1972), applies to the realm of attitude-congruent behavior. Consistent with their hypotheses, Fazio et al (1977) observed that the opportunity to misattribute a feeling of unpleasant arousal to the experimental booth in which subjects were seated eliminated the attitude change that was otherwise observed following a chosen attitude-discrepant behavior, whereas the opportunity to misattribute unpleasant internal sensations to the booth had no effect on the changes in attitude that were obtained following a chosen attitude-congruent behavior. (See Ronis & Greenwald 1979 and Fazio et al 1979 for more detail on Fazio et al's 1977 procedures and analysis.) Our reading of the literature suggests that internal sensations may play a role in certain self-inference processes (see Comer & Rhodewalt 1979), but that the inclusion of these sensations would necessitate a major revision of Bem's original formulation of the attitude-inference process.

Yet another line of research that pertains to felt bodily reactions is the work on self-attention (Carver 1979, Scheier & Carver 1980). There is increasing evidence that self-attention compared to environment attention enhances the intensity of attitudes, feelings, and emotions. The notion is that self-attention increases one's hypothesis awareness of bodily states and enhances self-relevant thinking. Support for this hypothosis has been obtained in studies of the arousing properties of female nudes and the perception of taste (Scheier, Carver & Gibbons 1979); the affective reactions to pleasant and unpleasant pictures and the induction of moods (Scheier & Carver 1977); and the arousal of psychological reactance (Carver 1977, Carver & Scheier, in press). The program of research on self-attention suggests that there are individual differences in people's sensitivity to internal cues (i.e. interoceptive and proprioceptive feedback) and, in addition, that fairly common environmental stimuli (e.g. cameras, mirrors) can alter people's sensitivity to their internal sensations.

PRs that are detected externally   The second general perspective on the role of bodily responses in attitude change ascribes little importance to a person's bodily reactions per se (Valins 1966). According to this view, felt bodily reactions are influential only insofar as they cue a person that she or he has responded unexpectedly to a stimulus. The bodily reactions need not be felt, but rather can be perceived through exteroceptive channels, such as by viewing an "arousal" meter. Several experiments were conducted recently that measured actual physiological activity (e.g. heart rate, electrodermal activity) while subjects received bogus physiological feedback (Hirschman & Hawk 1978, Kerber & Coles 1978). These studies indicate that bogus feedback often alters actual physiological activity, but the former rather than the latter influences affective ratings (cf Hirschman, Clark & Hawk 1977).

Liebhart (1979) provides a comprehensive review of the past research on bogus physiological feedback. He suggests that unexpected information about one's bodily reactions to a stimulus leads one to inspect more closely the attributes of the stimulus to discern the cause which leads to attitude polarization.

PRs that are undetected   Finally, the complement of research on PRs that are detected (by whatever means) is the study of the effects on attitudes of unperceived bodily reactions. For instance, Cacioppo (1979) momentarily altered the heart rates of outpatients while they performed intellective tasks and while they were exposed to a counterattitudinal message. In this research, the subjects were unable to discriminate between the trials on which their heart rate was maintained at the basal level of 72 bpm and those on which it increased to 88 bpm. Nevertheless, message comprehension (Experiment 1) and message elaboration (Experiment 2) were enhanced when cardiac pacing was momentarily accelerated (cf Cacioppo, Sandman & Walker 1978).

The study of the role of unperceived bodily reactions on attitudes and persuasion has heretofore been largely neglected (cf McGuire, in press), but now appears to be expanding to include cardiac activity, facial feedback (e.g. Cacioppo & Petty 1979a,c; Izard 1977; but see Comer & Rhodewalt 1979, Tourangeau & Ellsworth 1979), and interhemispheric patterns of alpha brain wave activity (Cacioppo, Petty & Snyder 1979).

The Consistency Model

Interest in the effects on attitudes of motivational forces and psychological processes waned in the early to mid 1970s as researchers explored instead the implications of viewing people as rational problem solvers (cf Bem 1972). More recently, however, attitude-inference processes are again being viewed as flawed by strains for consistency of both the intrapersonal (e.g. balance, dissonance) and interpersonal (e.g. image management) varieties.

BALANCE   Balance theory has been used recently to account for revolutionary behavior (Opello 1977), attitudes toward political candidates (Kinder 1978, Van Jones 1977), confidence of jurors in their verdicts (Fischoff 1979), and attitudes among people of different nations (Moore 1979). The near impossible task of disconfirming balance theory has also been registered; Insko (1980) noted that the phenomenological nature of balance raises the possibility that subjects "balance" some combination of experimenter-specified and *subject generated* elements and relations that were previously unrecognized by researchers.

Nevertheless, the view that subjects are using self-generated elements and relations has led to several tests of specific balance interpretations for the attraction and agreement effects that are so common in research using *p-o-x* triads. (Mower-White 1979 provides a review of the previous research.) Insko & Adewole (1979) reasoned that the attraction effect could be conceived as an agreement effect regarding *p* that involved the specified *p-o* relation and subject-generated relations between *o-p* and *p-p* (where people are presumed to like themselves). As expected by this reasoning, subjects assumed reciprocal liking and disliking between *p* and *o*. Thus, Insko and Adewole argued that attraction effects can be viewed as agreement effects.

Therefore, specifying the agreement effect in terms of the balance bias becomes the key to a comprehensive balance theory. Two possible accounts have been suggested (Insko & Adewole 1979; Tashakkori & Insko 1979 and unpublished manuscript). This first is based upon the social comparison notion that subjects assume *o* is similar to themselves (*p*), thereby constituting a positive *p-o* unit relation. When there is agreement between *p-x* and *o-x*, balance exists since the positive *p-o* unit relation is presumed to complete the subjects' phenomenological triad. The second account holds that subjects assume that disagreement regarding *x* causes *o* to dislike *p*, that they (*p*) nevertheless are similar to *o*, and that they like themselves (*p-p*). This set of elements also is balanced when there is agreement and imbalanced when there is disagreement between *p* and *o* regarding *x*.

These accounts are intriguing and testable. They have not, however, been well supported by empirical research. First, Insko & Adewole (1979) manipulated the similarity between *p* and *o* and failed to find the predicted impact on the agreement effect. The alternative account for the agreement effect suggests that subjects view *o-p* as bonded negatively when there is disagreement regarding *x*, but the hypothesis for the attraction effect states that *o-p* relation is positive as long as the *p-o* sentiment relation is positive. Thus, balance interpretations of the agreement and the attraction effects appear contradictory where there is disagreement and the *p-o* sentiment relation is positive. Finally, Sentis & Burnstein (1979) employed the Sternberg reaction time paradigm and found that balanced triads were accessed fastest as a unit, whereas the opposite was true for the imbalanced triads. These results held for probes for which the answer was "true"; "false" responses did not differ according to structural balance.

An alternative perspective on attraction, agreement, and balance effects casts them as consequences of distinct biases in information processing. The balance effect, Heider (1946) argued, was attributable to gestaltic forces toward cognitive consistency. Data provided by Sentis & Burnstein (1979) strongly support the notion that balanced traids are "chunked" rather than stored as separate pieces of information. The attraction and agreement effects, on the other hand, might be explained in terms of alternative biases. For instance, the attraction effect might be a special case of the positivity bias, which is the tendency for people to remember, prefer, and expect positive rather than negative relations between elements, particularly between individuals, as exemplified by the high regard people express for public figures (Lau, Sears & Centers 1979; Rook et al 1978). The agreement effect, on the other hand, might be due simply to a motive to be correct in one's judgments of persons, places, and things. Alternatively, agreement may be more pleasant than disagreement because the former has been associated with more rewards than the latter (Byrne & Clore 1970).

In sum, despite the reemergence of sophisticated mathematical analyses of balance (see the section on Mathematical Models), in some ways the more revealing research about psychological processes is that designed to assess the storage and retrieval of balanced information and to discern eliciting conditions for balance, attraction, and agreement effects. Advances have been made by Insko and his colleagues in specifying potential accounts of attraction and agreement effects, by Tyler & Sears (1977) on identifying the conditions that do and do not lead to a balance effect when anticipating an interaction with an obnoxious person, and by Gerbing & Hunter (1979) in demonstrating that the inferences that people report when judging p-o-x triads are not completely explicable by balance theory.

COGNITIVE DISSONANCE THEORY   In 1957, Festinger described in general terms a set of conditions that would evoke a "dissonance effect": when insufficient compared to sufficient justification for acting contrary to an initial attitude leads to greater attitude change.

Alternative accounts have been suggested for this counterhedonic effect; twice as many alternative accounts existed in 1977 as in 1967 (Möntmann 1979). But dissonance theory appears to be thriving, having weakened the threat posed by its archnemesis, self-perception theory, as we noted above (Fazio et al 1977, Frey et al 1979). Indeed, statistical analysis of the characteristics of and trends in dissonance research is one of the newer offsprings of cognitive dissonance theory (Johnson & Watkins 1977, Möntmann 1979).

The initial formulation of dissonance theory was general. Empirical studies and theoretical statements since 1957, but particularly in the last decade, have aimed toward specifying the antecedent conditions for the dissonance effect. As of 1977, dissonance was thought to result when people accepted personal responsibility for an attitude-discrepant behavior that they foresaw producing unwanted consequences (Eagly & Himmelfarb 1978, Wicklund & Brehm 1976). Some doubt lingered, however, about the necessity of these preconditions since evidence also suggested that the unwanted consequences need not be foreseen in all circumstances. Data from Goethals, Cooper & Naficy (1979) suggest that dissonance can be aroused when the conditions that exist at decision time either clearly predict unwanted consequences resulting from the chosen alternative or create clear *retrospective foreseeability* of the unwanted consequences. Furthermore, Goethals et al (1979) demonstrated that these two sets of conditions have distinguishable temporal characteristics for dissonance arousal and reduction. If the unwanted consequences are foreseen as likely at the time of a decision, dissonance reduction begins immediately following the decision (see demonstrations also by Davis 1979; Younger, Walker & Arrowood 1977); if the unwanted consequences are not foreseen at the time of a decision but are viewed retrospectively as having been foreseeable, then dissonance reduction begins when subjects are informed of the unwanted consequences of their action; if the unwanted consequences are neither foreseen nor foreseeable at the time of the decision, then information regarding the negative consequences of the decision does not induce dissonance (Goethals et al 1979).

The mitigating influence of *vigilant predecisional* information processing on dissonance arousal was suggested in a study by Converse & Cooper (1979). An inconsistent body of data has accumulated regarding the relationship between the importance of a decision and the extent of the postdecisional spreading of chosen and unchosen alternatives. Converse & Cooper (1979) have proposed that this relationship is in the form of an inverted-U. Specifically, they suggested that moderate compared to low decisional importance induced greater postdecisional dissonance as subjects were faced with foregoing the desirable attributes of the unchosen alternative and accepting the undesirable attributes of the chosen alternative. Furthermore, they argued that high relative to moderate decisional importance caused the subjects to "exercise considerably more care in coming to their attitude judgments" (p. 51), which, they suggested, attenuates the arousal of cognitive dissonance. Though the authors provided no independent evidence that bore directly upon this latter notion, their reasoning is supported by Janis & Mann's (1977) analysis of predecisional information processing and by Petty & Cacioppo's (1979b) study of involvement and cognitive response.

A major problem that has plagued research on dissonance effects is that no "manipulation check" for the arousal of dissonance has existed. In the past one could tell if dissonance was aroused only by observing whether or not the predicted mode of dissonance reduction occurred. When predictions were disconfirmed, it was unclear whether dissonance in that particular circumstance was not aroused, failed to have the predicted consequence, or was reduced through some other mode. These various possibilities, and the problems they create, can be illustrated in the area of dissonance and selective exposure/learning. Repeated failures in the past to obtain a consistent relationship between dissonance arousal and selective exposure led to a rejection of the dissonance hypothesis (e.g. Greenwald & Ronis 1978). This hypothesis recently experienced a rebirth, however, as Frey & Wicklund (1978) observed that supportive compared to nonsupportive information was favored particularly when an unpleasant task was selected under conditions of choice. Nevertheless, much of the data suggest that the dissonance hypothesis regarding selective exposure/learning is still unclear. In two additional experiments, Frey (1979) demonstrated a *curvilinear* relationship between the amount of dissonance and the selective search for consonant information. He suggested that the attentuation of selective exposure at high levels of dissonance was due to the increased use of an alternative mode of dissonance reduction. In studies of the role of personality dimensions on selective exposure (Olson & Zanna 1979a) and on selective learning (Olson & Zanna 1979b), it was demonstrated that "repressors" in contrast to "sensitizers" exhibit the dissonance effect (see also Innes 1978). To what extent are these data in accord with dissonance theory? Manipulation checks regarding dissonance *arousal* would assist greatly in answering this question.

Advocates of disconfirmable theories might be frustrated by the speed with which dissonance theory has evolved to accommodate empirical results (Greenwald & Ronis 1978, Ronis & Greenwald 1979), whereas advocates of theoretical refinements applaud these developments (e.g. Fazio et al 1979). Greenwald & Ronis (1978), for instance, argue that the present preconditions for "dissonance arousal" suggest a theory "focused on cognitive changes occurring in the service of ego defense, or self-esteem maintenance, rather than in the interest of preserving psychological consistency" (p. 55). They raise the possibility but provide no empirical evidence that a cognitive dissonance theory focused on the latter, as the initial version was, may be correct but less powerful than ego maintenance processes (cf Colman & Olver 1978). They suggest, too, that dissonance theory is evolving at such a rapid pace that this convergence of dissonance and self theory may only be temporary. Indeed, as we shall describe below, the newest competitor to dissonance theory focuses on the image maintenance processes serving one's social identity. If Greenwald & Ronis (1978) are correct, then dissonance theory may survive this challenge by redefining the necessary preconditions for the arousal of dissonance.

We should note that despite the conceptual problems inherent in dissonance theory, the theory has repeatedly provided nonobvious insights into human behavior. Most recently, studies of the role of effort justification in increasing assertiveness, reducing snake phobia, and inducing weight loss (Axsom & Cooper 1979, Cooper in press) and of the differential use of alcohol by moderate and heavy drinkers to reduce tension (C. M. Steele, R. Croyle & B. Morasch, unpublished) have been guided by dissonance theory. These studies raise interesting questions regarding the traditional views of psychotherapy and maladaptive behavior and suggest that dissonance theory may have numerous practical applications.

IMPRESSION MANAGEMENT   In addition to one's tendency for intrapersonal consistency, there exists a desire to *appear* consistent in the eyes of observers. Thus, evidence for attitude-related consistency must be examined in light of possible self-presentational goals. Recent reviews (Schlenker 1980, Tedeschi in press) have documented the workings of image management influences over a large range of human action. Within the domain of attitude research, three primary areas of contact with impression management notions have emerged.

Admissions of attitude change   It appears that admissions of opinion shifts are used strategically for self-presentational purposes. A statement of attitude can be seen as an interpersonal communication (Schlenker 1978) and, like any other such communication, can be employed to enhance public image. One type of attitude statement particularly relevant to image management involves the declaration of attitude *change.* Early research indicated that a target person who admits opinion change after receiving a persuasive message is viewed more positively by the persuader than by a witness to the successful persuasive attack; further, this persuader-witness difference has been shown to occur for perceptions of the target's intelligence (Cialdini, Braver & Lewis 1974) and general attractiveness (Cialdini & Mirels 1976). In a pair of subsequent studies, Braver et al (1977) found that (*a*) subjects were aware of the differing evaluations directed at persuaded individuals by persuaders and witnesses and (*b*) subjects structured their own admissions of attitude change to produce the most positive evaluations from the audience. That is, subjects admitted to the most opinion change when the persuader was their only audience, and they admitted to the least change when a witness was their only audience, and they admitted to an intermediate amount of change when both persuader and witness were present. Attitude researchers would be well advised to take account of this image management tactic in the design and interpretation of their studies.

Anticipatory shifts   Although the great tradition of attitude change research has been to examine the degree of persuasion resulting from the receipt of a communication, certain work (e.g. McGuire & Millman 1965) has demonstrated that the mere expectation of persuasive attack can produce movement in the direction of the communication. In a recent review of such effects, Cialdini & Petty (1980) concluded that a large self-presentational component is involved in their occurrence. Their conclusion was based on three features of the effects: (*a*) the shifts appear to be attempts to move toward the defensible and admirable moderate positions of the attitude scale; (*b*) subjects "snap back" to their preexperimental positions when they no longer expect to receive the communication; and (*c*) shifts in the direction of the expected communication only occur when the issue is not a personally important one for the subjects. Within the period of the present review, results consistent with a strategic view of anticipatory shifts have been obtained in experiments employing typical laboratory attitude topics (Gaes & Tedeschi 1978), causal attributions (Wells et al 1977), judicial judgments (Saltzstein & Sandberg 1979), and personality factors (Turner 1977).

Image management explanations of dissonance/self-perception effects   Just when it seemed that the dissonance/self-perception controversy of the last 15 years had been mostly resolved, or at least that the attitude effects under contention had been appropriately allocated to one or another of the formulations (Fazio, Zanna & Cooper 1977), a new challenger has risen to claim explanatory superiority over both other theories. Although some skirmishing has occurred in the area of proattitudinal behavior (e.g. Goldman & Schlenker 1977, Schlenker & Riess 1979), the forced compliance experiment remains the traditional battlesite.

The first shot was fired a decade ago when Tedeschi, Schlenker & Bonoma (1971) postulated an impression management theory to account for attitude effects previously interpreted in dissonance theory terms. They argued that the active agent underlying the attitude shifts seen in forced compliance situations is the subject's motive to appear consistent in the eyes of others, especially the experimenter, rather than the motive to be consistent within one's own actions and cognitions. Although the basic impression management formulation has been expanded and modified somewhat

(Gaes, Kalle & Tedeschi 1978), the fundamental difference between it and dissonance or self-perception approaches remains that the latter theories contend that the influence of forced compliance procedures occurs upon subjects' true opinions, while impression management theory contends that only the opinion reporting process is influenced.

Recognizing this central area of disagreement, researchers disposed toward the impression management view have conducted a series of studies comparing forced compliance attitude effects as assessed by standard measurement devices and the bogus pipeline procedure. Arguing that the bogus pipeline provides a valid measure of subjects' genuine feelings, undistorted by self-presentational pressures (Quigley-Fernandez & Tedeschi 1978), these researchers have found support for impression management theory in that typical forced compliance effects did not appear via the bogus pipeline but did appear on the standard paper and pencil attitude measures (Gaes, Kalle & Tedeschi 1978; Malkis, Kalle & Tedeschi, unpublished; Riess, Kalle & Tedeschi, in press; Rivera & Tedeschi, unpublished). One problem with the bogus pipeline procedure in this regard, however, lies in the negative arousal it produces in subjects (Gaes, Kalle & Tedeschi 1978). The possibility exists that any discomfort generated by cognitive dissonance would be misattributed by subjects to the unpleasant bogus pipeline experience and for this reason would fail to create typical forced compliance effects. Although one study has attempted to disconfirm the misattribution explanation (Riess, Kalle & Tedeschi, in press), it appears to us to remain tenable until additional and stronger evidence is produced against it. Nonetheless, we do support the general strategy of differentiating between impression management and dissonance/self-perception predictions through the use of measurement devices that vary in their vulnerability to image-related tactics. It would be informative, for instance, to examine the effects of forced compliance procedures upon opinions measured by unobtrusive techniques.

Overall, there is little question that image maintenance concerns are an important source of influence upon the results of typical attitude change studies. Within the forced compliance paradigm, it may well be that such concerns sometimes lead to the simulation of genuine effects upon the attitude process. However, we would not agree with the claim that self-presentational influences are the sole mediators of traditional forced compliance results. It would be difficult to explain the outcomes of the brace of "placebo" studies discussed earlier in this review, for example, in impression management theory terms. Our feeling is that future work will find an image enhancement strategy to be a determining but not necessary condition for the occurrence of standard opinion effects in the forced compliance situation. A promising approach in this direction is offered by Schlenker (Schlenker 1980; Schlenker et al, in press).

CONSISTENCY-BASED COMPLIANCE   In addition to its influence on attitude change, the consistency principle can be argued to mediate changes in overt behavior, such as compliance with a request. The best known consistency-based technique for producing compliance is the foot-in-the-door procedure (Freedman & Fraser 1966). It proceeds by advancing from a small request (that is commonly granted by the target person) to a larger, related request. Although the evidence is not unequivocal (e.g. Foss & Dempsey 1979), a recent review of the literature (DeJong 1979) indicates that this procedure reliably increases the target's compliance with the larger request. Further, the review favored a consistency-based explanation of the foot-in-the-door effect over several alternatives. That is, after assenting to the initial request, the target is said to view him or herself as more of a complier with such requests than before. In order to be consistent with this revised self-perception, then, the target becomes more willing to comply with subsequent, larger requests. Oddly, however, the modification-of-self-perception feature of this explanation has never been directly documented. Thus, it remains feasible that compliance with the initial request serves as a commitment and that subsequent compliance occurs through a strain for consistency with the earlier form of action without the mediating influence of self-image change.

Another compliance tactic employing consistency pressures is the low-ball technique, long practiced by car salesmen but only recently put to experimental study (Cialdini et al 1978). The low-ball phenomenon is that an active decision to take action tends to perservere, even after the costs of performing the action have been increased. In three experiments, a requester who induced subjects to make a voluntary initial decision to perform a target behavior and who then made performance of the behavior more costly obtained greater final compliance than a requester who informed subjects of the full costs of the target behavior from the outset (Cialdini et al 1978). These authors argued that the freely-made initial decision committed subjects to the target action and rendered them reluctant to change, even in the face of newly unfavorable circumstances. Data consistent with this interpretation have been collected in a field study of energy conservation that produced strikingly large compliance effects (Pallak et al 1980). It also appears that the basic effect is importantly enhanced when the initially committing action is public (Pallak & Sullivan 1979).

SIX CONTINUING AREAS OF ATTITUDE RESEARCH

Mere Exposure

Since the initial publication of Zajonc's "mere exposure" hypothesis (1968), there has been a considerable and continuing experimental interest in the effects of repeated stimulus exposure on affect toward the stimulus (cf Harrison 1977). The years falling within the province of the present review have been no exception.

Grush (Grush 1980; Grush, McKeough & Ahlering 1978) documented the influence of a mere exposure factor on voting preferences within American congressional and presidential primary elections. The amount of variance in election outcomes due to the exposure factor was surprisingly large. With the use of a virtually demand-free paradigm, a clever pair of experiments by Mita, Dermer & Knight (1977) seem to have laid to rest the possibility that the mere exposure effect in humans is attributable to demand characteristics. Subjects rated their preferences for facial photographs that depicted either a mirror image or a true image. When subjects were presented with photographs of themselves, they preferred a mirror image print; however, when presented with photographs of close friends or lovers, they preferred a true image print. The results were interpreted to support the mere exposure hypothesis, as the preferred perspectives were those with which the subjects would be naturally more familiar. Finally, research on negative stimuli reaffirmed the applicability of the exposure-attraction relationship to stimuli that are initially disliked (Bukoff & Elman 1979); however, the relationship did not hold for stimuli that themselves caused negative outcomes for an observer (Swap 1977).

An interesting controversy has been stimulated by Moreland & Zajonc (1977), who have taken the position that stimulus recognition on a conscious level is not a necessary condition for exposure effects. Independent experimental evidence consistent with their argument has been provided by Wilson (1979). The Moreland and Zajonc contention is an intriguing one for a pair of reasons. First, it runs counter to most traditional explanations of the exposure-attraction effect whose mediators depend on cognitive recognition of the stimulus. Second, it presents the possibility that a *direct* influence of exposure upon affect may exist and thus that there may be prior changes in affect which help mediate the oft-observed relationship between stimulus frequency and recognition. Birnbaum & Mellers (1979a) have disputed the Moreland and Zajonc position and have proposed a one-factor, "subjective recognition" model to account for the data of Moreland & Zajonc (1977). The debate is presently turning on some fairly technical statistical issues (cf Birnbaum & Mellers 1979b, Moreland & Zajonc 1979); nonetheless, its point is conceptually important and researchers in the area would be well advised to watch for its resolution.

Mathematical Models

The use of mathematical models to describe attitude formation and change has advanced along three distinct theoretical fronts, and the utility of these models in explaining the attitudinal impact of antecedents has been demonstrated in a number of applications including mass communication (Danes, Hunter & Woelfel 1978), consumer preference (Sheluga, Jaccard & Jacoby 1979), and juridic/moralistic judgments (Kaplan, Steindorf & Iervolino 1978). If mathematical modeling has fallen short of its potential, it is in modeling the persuasion process per se so that predictions of new effects can be derived in advance of data collection (Anderson & Shanteau 1977).

QUANTITATIVE BALANCE THEORY   Mathematical modeling of balance theory was in its heyday in the late 1960s and early 1970s. As we enter the 1980s, there appears to be a renewed interest in testing and developing the tetrahedronic equal-weights and unequal-weights models and Feather's composite model of balance theory. In three experiments (Tashakkori & Insko 1979 and unpublished manuscript, Experiment 1; Wellens 1979), two or more of these models were contrasted by specifying all but the p-o relation, which subjects were left to specify. Tashakkori and Insko used p-o-x triads and sentiment measures, whereas Wellens used p-o-q triads and both sentiment and unit measures. These studies generally favored the tetrahedonic models. Tashakkori and Insko (unpublished, Experiment 2) found that the equal-weights tetrahedronic model was the most plausible and indicated that the support for the other models was the most plausible and indicated that the support for the other models was due to cognitive biases other than the three-sign p-o-x/q balance bias. Thus, the earlier support obtained for the composite and unequal-weights tetrahedonic models of triadic balance seems to have been more apparent than real.

INFORMATION INTEGRATION THEORY   Anderson's influential information integration theory is tested by giving people pieces of information and obtaining measurements of their overall judgments by integrating information in some algebraic fashion [e.g. adding, multiplying, averaging (cf Anderson 1980)]. Though the theory has not developed to the point where it can predict a priori new persuasion effects (cf Ostrom & Davis 1979), it has done an admirable job these past 3 years of providing accounts for the effects of source credibility (Birnbaum & Stegner 1979), product attributes (Lutz & Bettman 1977), group discussion (Kaplan & Miller 1977), and juror biases (Kaplan & Miller 1978; Ostrom, Werner & Saks 1978).

EXPECTANCY VALUE MODELS   Research has continued to examine the utility of Fishbein and Ajzen's expectancy value model for predicting attitudes (Lutz 1977, Olson & Dover 1978). One interesting new finding from this research is that the model's predictiveness increases as prior information about the topic increases (Olson & Dover 1978; see also Lutz 1978).

MISCELLANEOUS If there were a fourth focus of interest in math models in the past 3 years, it would concern the untested assumptions and analytic procedures employed in math models. Included here are the debates on the use of correlational analyses for model testing (Anderson & Shanteau 1977, Lutz 1977), the problem of indeterminacy (Anderson 1977, 1979; Gollob 1979), and the existence of meaning shifts (Zanna & Hamilton 1977). In our view, these debates are a healthy sign for this increasingly sophisticated and useful approach.

Group Polarization of Position

What began two decades ago as a Masters thesis investigation into the risk decisions of group members has become one of the most persistent single lines of research of its time. Much of that perserverance can be attributed to the remarkable generality of the basic finding. It is quite clear now that the implications of this work transcend the boundaries of group research. We now know that all sorts of initial positions (opinions, judgments, preferences, etc) become more polarized as a result of relevant group discussion or simple exposure to the positions of others (cf Lamm & Myers 1978, Myers 1980). We can safely substitute the term "polarization of position" for the originally coined "risky shift." A second reason for continued interest in the phenomenon has been the unsettled state of knowledge concerning its mediation. During the span of the present review, most of the work on group polarization shifts has involved this mediational issue.

GENERALITY A number of studies have examined the continuing question of generality. Several researchers have investigated the applicability of polarization shifts to jury-like settings (e.g. Bray & Noble 1978; Kaplan & Miller 1977; Rumsey, Allgeier & Castore 1978) and have found a good fit. Examining applicability in another context, Myers, Wojcicki & Aardema (1977) exposed church members to the averaged, rather than the individual, opinions of others in the form of opinion poll information; reliable polarization effects were observed as a result. Paicheler (1979) discovered that certain groups, in which members can be easily identified as subscribing to different norms, can polarize *prior* to discussion as soon as group members are in one another's presence. Finally, Hong (1978) showed that some issues that produce shifts toward risk in group discussions among American subjects will produce consistent shifts toward caution in Chinese subjects.

MEDIATION Although quite a number of processes have been hypothesized to mediate the group polarization effect, only two enjoy much currency—social comparison and persuasive argumentation. Recently evolved forms of the social comparison explanation argue that group discussion allows members to compare their issue-positions and/or abilities with those of the other members. The effect of this comparison is to drive most group members in the initially valued direction, via a desire to place themselves either publicly (Jellison & Arkin 1977) or privately (Sanders & Baron 1977) in an esteemed position relative to the others. The persuasive arguments approach (e.g. Burnstein & Vinokur 1977), however, suggests that issues that produce polarization do so because group discussion generates a preponderance of arguments supportive of the group's predisposition; the result is an average shift in the direction of the predisposition.

The major issue in the controversy is not whether persuasive argumentation significantly influences group polarization effects, as much recent work has proved congenial with that formulation (e.g. Kaplan & Miller 1977, Madsen 1978, Vinokur & Burnstein 1978a,b). Rather, the issue seems to be the validity of Burnstein & Vinokur's (1977) contention that "social comparison is neither a necessary nor a sufficient condition for polarization." We suspect that considerable future work will be directed toward the disconfirmation of Burnstein and Vinokur's provocative claim, as any assertion of the null offers an attractive research target (e.g. Goethals & Zanna 1979).

Judgmental Effects

Perhaps the best known judgmental phenomena are assimilation and contrast effects. Although there were some demonstrations of attitudinal assimilation during the review period (cf Olson & Dover 1979), far more attention was paid to attitudinal contrast. A contrast effect occurs when the judgment of some "target" stimulus is displaced away from the "contextual" stimuli that accompany it. For example, Dermer et al (1979) found that people who had just finished writing about hedonically positive events judged their present life satisfaction to be lower than people who had just written about hedonically negative events. Similarly, Brickman et al (1978) found that people who had recently won money in the Illinois state lottery (an extremely positive hedonic event) judged the pleasure that they derived from several common life events (e.g. watching television) as lower than that of people who had entered the lottery but did not win. Interestingly though, the lottery winners did not judge their overall life satisfaction as any different from the losers. Brickman et al argued that this occurred because the increased happiness from the lottery win was offset by the devaluation of the ordinary life events.

Some particular features of contrast effects also received attention during the review period. In typical demonstrations of contrast effects, the contextual stimuli are presented *prior* to the target stimulus to be judged. Manis

& Moore (1978) found that a contrast effect could also be obtained if the contextual stimuli were presented immediately *after* the target stimulus. Marsh & Parducci (1978) found that when dealing with dimensions of judgment that have a natural neutral point, the ratings of neutral stimuli are not affected by the accompanying contextual stimuli. Sherman et al (1978) found that judgments that were the result of a contrast effect could influence subsequent behavior if the distorted ratings were made salient prior to the behavior. Finally, there was some evidence that people anticipated the judgmental distortions made by others (Alexander 1977) and that politicians sometimes distorted their positions to match that of the audience they were addressing (Miller & Sigelman 1978). It may be that, as suggested by Newtson & Czerlinsky (1974), people sometimes shift their positions to correct for expected contrast effects.

The contrast effects that have been found in the studies described above were explained with a wide variety of judgmental theories, and it is not yet clear which theoretical framework provides the most comprehensive account of the contrast phenomena. The two judgmental theories that generated the most attention during this period, however, were perspective theory and accentuation theory.

PERSPECTIVE THEORY   Perspective theory emphasizes how the range of content positions that a person considers (one's perspective) affects attitude judgments (cf Upshaw 1969). Harkins & Becker (1979) applied the theory to the attitude-behavior problem and argued that people may employ different perspectives when rating their attitudes and the behaviors that they would engage in. This implies that what may appear to be an attitude-behavior discrepancy to an observer may appear quite consistent to the actor. Perhaps the most important development in perspective theory, though, was Upshaw's (1978) disavowal of previous procedures for distinguishing the attitude "content" from the attitude "rating" (cf Ostrom & Upshaw 1968). Unfortunately, this leaves the theory without a standard procedure for assessing attitude content, although there have been some recent suggestions for assessing attitude content by measuring subjects' idiosyncratic beliefs with free response measures (Judd & DePaulo 1979).

ACCENTUATION THEORY   Accentuation theory (cf Eiser & Stroebe 1972) emphasizes the effects on attitude judgments of the evaluative connotations of the particular words used to label the extremes of the attitude rating scale. Researchers using the accentuation theory framework have found that judges will give more polarized ratings on a given scale when the subjects' own evaluations are congruent with the value connotations of the scale labels (Eiser & Mower-White 1974, Van der Plight & Van Dijk 1979). Furthermore, subjects' attitude ratings may be more polarized when the scales are anchored by two positive (e.g. thrifty-generous) rather than two negative (e.g. stingy-extravagant) labels, presumably because the negative labels imply more extreme positions than do the positive labels (Eiser & Osmon 1978). Finally, in judging attitude statements, subjects' attitude ratings will be more polarized on scales that are relevant to the aspect of the issues emphasized by the attitude statement than on irrelevant scales (Osmon & Mower-White 1977).

Attributional Processes

As the single most pervasive influence upon social psychology in the past decade (cf Kelley & Michela 1980), it is not surprising that the effects of Attribution Theory have been recently felt within the study of attitudes.

ATTRIBUTIONS OF CREDIBILITY   One approach designed to link attributional analysis directly to the persuasion process has been taken by Eagly and her co-workers (cf Eagly, Chaiken & Wood 1981), who propose that message recipients are best viewed as rational problem-solvers attempting to maximize the validity of their opinions. According to this model, a key factor in the persuasion process is the message recipient's presumption about the likely position that a communicator will espouse. This expectancy is formed from premessage cues regarding the communicator's traits and the extant situational pressures. If the presumption is subsequently confirmed by the message, little attitude change results because the recipient attributes the communicator's position to the action of the traits or pressures that initially generated the presumption. Thus, when the recipient's prior message expectancy holds true, the validity of the message arguments is discounted and the communicator is viewed as a biased and therefore noncredible source of information. However, when the premessage expectancy is disconfirmed, these discounting factors (i.e. personal traits and situational pressures) cannot be invoked. Under such conditions, the communicator is seen as credible and attitude change results. Although this model has predicted well in the test situations designed by Eagly and colleagues (e.g. Eagly, Wood & Chaiken 1978), it would seem to have limited applicability to attitude effects that occur when very little is known about the communicator's traits and circumstances or when no external communication is presented. For example, various role-playing effects, especially those involving advocacy that is consonant with the subject's initial attitude (e.g. Jellison & Mills 1969), would be difficult to explain according to this model, as would opinion change produced prior to receipt of any communication (cf Cialdini & Petty 1980). Nonetheless, the formulation offers a promising way to integrate attribution principles into many attitude change contexts.

UNDERMINING OF INTEREST   A second area of linkage between attribution and attitude that has captured interest is less directly related to the persuasion process. "Overjustification" or, alternately, "undermining" effects have proven both fascinating and controversial since they began to attract attention in the early 1970s. Although the phenomenon continues to be a delicate one (e.g. Kiesler 1977), it does appear that favorability toward an activity can be reliably reduced through the application of certain forms of reward to performance of the activity (cf Lepper & Greene 1978). Condry (1977) specified a variety of features of such rewards that seem to be required for the undermining of intrinsic interest (e.g. the rewards should be salient, anticipated, and positive). More recently, evidence has begun to accumulate to suggest, in support of Deci's (1975) formulation, that it is the *controlling* character of reward that generates undermining effects while its *informational* aspect may have the opposite results (Anderson, Manoogian & Reznick 1976; Boggiano & Ruble 1979; Dollinger & Thelen 1978; Enzle & Ross 1978; Folger, Rosenfield & Hays 1978; Harackiewicz 1979; Pittman et al 1980). In keeping with this work, other procedures shown to produce undermining effects have also involved the factor of constraint (i.e. threat, surveillance, and time deadlines).

Most recent research has supported an attributional account of undermining effects (e.g. Pittman, Cooper & Smith 1977; Scott & Yalch 1978; Smith & Pittman 1978). According to this interpretation, the presence of external pressures (like rewards) for task performance can cause individuals to attribute their subsequent performance of the task to the action of these external pressures rather than to an inherent interest in the task; consequently, these individuals will see themselves as less intrinsically favorable to the task activity. However, because of the seeming necessity of the constraint factor in the generation of undermining effects, at least one nonattributional formulation appears plausible as well—reactance theory (Brehm 1966). Although we have not seen such a suggestion in the literature to date, it might be argued that all of the procedures for creating undermining effects (rewards, threats, surveillance, deadlines, etc) can be conceptualized as restrictions of an individual's freedom to decide whether and how to perform an activity. The resultant reactance from such restrictions may then produce the traditional undermining effects of reduced task favorability and interest. Thus, the undermining phenomenon may not be due to the "cool" process of causal attribution, but to the "hot" process of motivational arousal that is brought about by external constraint. Such a distinction between possible mediators seems closely akin to that of the self-perception/dissonance controversy treated elsewhere in this chapter. As such, a test of the attribution vs reactance interpretations of undermining might well employ the "arousal placebo" procedures that have proved so informative in the earlier controversy.

Source Effects

Source factors subsume a diverse number of variables whose effects on attitudes are neither homogeneous (cf Birnbaum & Stegner 1979, Chaiken et al 1978, Romer 1979b) nor necessarily additive with the effects of other factors (e.g. channel, message, cf Andreoli & Worchel 1978). For instance, Liska (1978) argued that the attributes that characterized a "credible" source varied across topics, whereas Andreoli & Worchel (1978) found that trustworthy sources were particularly more persuasive than untrustworthy sources when the persuasive message was delivered through an audiovisual rather than an audio or print medium.

Research also focused on the communication skills that characterized various sources. Chaiken (1979), for instance, found that physically attractive sources were more persuasive and possessed a set of personal competencies (i.e. rapid speech, high S.A.T. scores) that predisposed them to be more influential than physically unattractive sources. In addition, several studies were based upon previous reports that high relative to low status people use a "powerful" form of speech (e.g. fluent speech). Results indicated that "powerful" compared to "powerless" speech elicited higher judgments of credibility and agreement from recipients even when the source and substantive content of the message were held constant (Conley, O'Barr & Lind 1979; Erickson et al 1978; Lind & O'Barr 1979). Finally, several studies identified gaze direction (Hemsley & Doob 1978) and the language variables of intensity (i.e. affectivity), verbal immediacy (i.e. the strength of association between the source and topic), and lexical density [i.e. the range of vocabulary (Bradac, Desmond & Murdock 1977; cf Bradac, Bowers & Courtright 1979)] as determinants of judgments of credibility and agreement.

Recent comprehensive reviews of attitudinal persistence are now available and provide an informative backdrop against which to view contemporary research on the temporal characteristics of source effects (cf Cook & Flay 1978, Cook et al 1979). For instance, Cook et al (1979) argued that the past searches for the elusive (absolute) sleeper effect were theoretically misdirected. In an empirical study, they demonstrated a sleeper effect could be found when the conditions specified by the discounting cue hypothesis were provided (Gruder et al 1978).

The Gruder et al study was somewhat unusual in that the discounting cue followed rather than preceded the presentation of the message. Though uncommon, the procedure had been used previously and, according to the discounting cue hypothesis, this procedural detail should make little difference (cf Kelman & Hovland 1953). Greenwald, Baumgardner & Leippe (unpublished), however, demonstrated that the sleeper effect was obtained when the discounting cue followed but not when it preceded the message. The Greenwald et al results suggest that the discounting cue may alter the interpretation and attitudinal effects of the message unless much of its processing and acceptance precedes the introduction of the discounting cue (see Craik 1979 for a review of evidence for a similar finding in the area of thematic cues and text comprehension). Hence, future research may hold a revision or rejection of the original discounting cue hypothesis.

CONCLUSION

If there is a new theme within the reviewed literature that is likely to affect importantly the conception of attitudinal phenomena, it is the emerging awareness of two separate categories of persuasion processes. The first, which Petty and Cacioppo (in press) have termed persuasion via the central route, involves the cognitive (but not necessarily rational) assessment of the validity of information fundamentally related to the attitude issue at hand. These changes tend to be relatively enduring. The second, called persuasion via the peripheral route, incorporates the action of factors (e.g. habits, self-presentation) extrinsic to the validity of issue-related information. These changes tend to be rather temporary.

The central/peripheral distinction suggests a continuum of attitude change phenomena. At one end of the continuum we have what has been viewed traditionally as "genuine attitude change," in that it involves affective changes that are relatively enduring and consistent within the affective, cognitive, and behavioral domains. Perhaps the best example of this type of change is the persuasion produced by role-playing. These changes are the result of considerable issue-relevant thinking, tend to be quite long-lasting, and have predictable behavioral implications (Cook & Flay 1978, Janis & Mann 1977). On the other end of the continuum we have what might best be labeled "temporary position shifts." Studies by Cialdini and co-workers (1973, 1976) and by Hass (1975, Hass & Mann 1976) seem to have identified the anticipatory opinion change paradigm, wherein subjects' feelings are measured while they anticipate the receipt of a persuasive message, as one prototypical setting for the examination of position shifts. Their evidence suggests that the position shifts appeared automatically without conscious processing of issue-related argumentation, and were transitory in that they disappeared when subjects no longer expected to receive a message.

We suspect that a crucial variable in determining whether an instance of attitude change is likely to occur principally through the central or peripheral route is the personal relevance of the issue under consideration (cf Petty & Cacioppo 1979b). When an individual's personal concerns are closely related to the attitude issue itself, change on the issue will likely come about primarily via the central rather than the peripheral route. For example, when issues have been personally involving (or some manipulation has forced the cognitive processing of issue-related arguments), persuasion has tended to be enduring. However, when the issues have been uninvolving, the attitude changes have tended to be transitory and situation specific (cf Chaiken, in press). Personal importance also appears relevant to attitude-behavior prediction. When issues have been personally relevant (or some manipulation has caused subjects to be more thoughtful in completing the attitude scales), attitudes have been better predictors of behaviors than when the issues were relatively uninvolving or the attitude scales were completed without much thought (cf Fazio & Zanna, in press; Pryor et al 1977).

In sum, it now appears that attitude changes that occur through the central versus peripheral routes take place for different proximal reasons, through different psychological processes, and have different long-term consequences. Accordingly, we suggest that they might best be viewed as distinct phenomena. Both phenomena will be of considerable interest to social psychologists. In fact, we believe that much of the natural interaction with certain issues involves no enduring attitude changes, but the tactical and temporary shifting about of one's position. It will be valuable for persuasion researchers to study both kinds of processes and to differentiate clearly between them in the future.

Literature Cited

Abelson, R. P. 1976. Script processing in attitude formation and decision making. In *Cognition and Social Behavior,* ed. J. Carroll, J. Payne, pp. 33–46. Hillsdale, NJ: Erlbaum. 290 pp.

Adams, W. C., Beatty, M. J. 1977. Dogmatism, need for social approval and the resistance to persuasion. *Commun. Monogr.* 44:321–25

Ajzen, I., Fishbein, M. 1977. Attitude-behavior relations: A theoretical analysis and review of empirical research. *Psychol. Bull.* 84:888–918

Ajzen, I., Fishbein, M. 1980. *Understanding Attitudes and Predicting Social Behavior.* Englewood Cliffs, NJ: Prentice-Hall. 278 pp.

Alexander, C. N. 1977. Role-taking processes in constructing social realities. *Pers. Soc. Psychol. Bull.* 3:654–57

Anderson, N. H. 1977. Some problems in using analysis of variance in balance theory. *J. Pers. Soc. Psychol.* 35:140–58

Anderson, N. H. 1979. Indeterminate theory: Reply to Gollob. *J. Pers. Soc. Psychol.* 37:950–52

394   CIALDINI, PETTY & CACIOPPO

Anderson, N. H. 1980. Integration theory applied to cognitive responses and attitudes. In *Cognitive Responses in Persuasion,* ed. R. E. Petty, T. M. Ostrom, T. C. Brock. Hillsdale, NJ: Erlbaum. 512 pp.

Anderson, N. H., Shanteau, J. 1977. Weak inference with linear models. *Psychol. Bull.* 84:1155–70

Anderson, R., Manoogian, S. T., Reznick, J. S. 1976. The undermining and enhancing of intrinsic motivation in preschool children. *J. Pers. Soc. Psychol.* 34:915–22

Anderson, R. W., Lipsey, M. W. 1978. Energy conservation and attitudes toward technology. *Public Opin. Q.* 42:17–30

Andreoli, V., Worchel, S. 1978. Effects of media, communicator, and position of message on attitude change. *Public Opin. Q.* 42:59–70

Andrews, K. H., Kandel, D. B. 1979. Attitude and behavior: A specification of the contingent consistency hypothesis. *Am. Sociol. Rev.* 44:298–310

Axsom, D., Cooper, J. 1979. *Reducing weight by reducing dissonance: The role of effort justification in inducing.* Presented at Am. Psychol. Assoc., 87th, New York

Bagozzi, R. P., Burnkrant, R. E. 1979. Attitude organization and the attitude-behavior relationship. *J. Pers. Soc. Psychol.* 37:913–29

Bearden, W. O., Woodside, A. G. 1977. The effect of attitudes and previous behavior on consumer choice. *J. Soc. Psychol.* 103:129–37

Bem, D. J. 1972. Self-perception theory. *Adv. Exp. Soc. Psychol.* 6:1–62

Bem, D. J., Allen, A. 1974. On predicting some of the people some of the time: The search for cross-situational consistencies in behavior. *Psychol. Rev.* 81:506–20

Bentler, P. M., Speckart, G. 1979. Models of attitude-behavior relations. *Psychol. Rev.* 86:452–64

Biddle, B. J., Bank, B. J., Marlin, M. M. 1980. What they think, what they do, and what I think and do: Social determinants of adolescent drinking. *J. Stud. Alcohol.* 41:215–41

Birnbaum, M. H., Mellers, B. A. 1979a. Stimulus recognition may mediate exposure effects. *J. Pers. Soc. Psychol.* 37:391–94

Birnbaum, M. H., Mellers, B. A. 1979b. One-mediator model of exposure effects is still viable. *J. Pers. Soc. Psychol.* 37:1090–96

Birnbaum, M. H., Stegner, S. E. 1979. Source credibility in social judgment: Bias, expertise, and the judge's point of view. *J. Pers. Soc. Psychol.* 37:48–74

Boggiano, A. K., Ruble, D. N. 1979. Competence and the overjustification effect: A developmental study. *J. Pers. Soc. Psychol.* 37:1462–68

Bowman, C. H., Fishbein, M. 1978. Understanding public reaction to energy proposals: An application of the Fishbein model. *J. Appl. Soc. Psychol.* 8:319–40

Bradac, J. J., Bowers, J. W., Courtright, J. A. 1979. Three language variables in communication research: Intensity, immediacy, and diversity. *Hum. Commun. Res.* 5:257–69

Bradac, J. J., Desmond, R. J., Murdock, J. I. 1977. Diversity and density: Lexically determined evaluative and informational consequences of linguistic complexity. *Commun. Monogr.* 44:273–83

Braver, S. L., Linder, D. E., Corwin, T. T., Cialdini, R. B. 1977. Some conditions that affect admissions of attitude change. *J. Exp. Soc. Psychol.* 13:565–76

Bray, R. M., Noble, A. M. 1978. Authoritarianism and decisions of mock juries: Evidence of jury bias and group polarization. *J. Pers. Soc. Psychol.* 36:1424–30

Brehm, J. W. 1966. *A Theory of Psychological Reactance.* New York: Academic. 135 pp.

Brickman, P., Coates, D., Janoff-Bulman, R. 1978. Lottery winners and accident victims: Is happiness relative? *J. Pers. Soc. Psychol.* 36:917–27

Brinberg, D. 1979. An examination of the determinants of intention and behavior: A comparison of two models. *J. Appl. Soc. Psychol.* 9:560–75

Bukoff, A., Elman, D. 1979. Repeated exposure to liked and disliked social stimuli. *J. Soc. Psychol.* 107:133–34

Burnstein, E., Vinokur, A. 1977. Persuasive argumentation and social comparison as determinants of attitude polarization. *J. Exp. Soc. Psychol.* 13:315–32

Byrne, D., Clore, G. L. 1970. A reinforcement model of evaluative responses. *Pers. Int. J.* 1:103–28

Cacioppo, J. T. 1979. The effects of exogenous changes in heart rate on the facilitation of thought and resistance to persuasion. *J. Pers. Soc. Psych.* 37:487–96

Cacioppo, J. T., Petty, R. E. 1979a. Attitudes and cognitive response: An electrophysiological approach. *J. Pers. Soc. Psychol.* 37:2181–99

Cacioppo, J. T., Petty, R. E. 1979b. Effects of message repetition and position on cognitive response, recall, and persuasion. *J. Pers. Soc. Psychol.* 37:97–109

Cacioppo, J. T., Petty, R. E. 1979c. Neuromuscular circuits in affect-laden information processing. *Pavlovian J. Biol. Sci.* 14:177–85

Cacioppo, J. T., Petty, R. E. 1980. Persuasiveness of commercials is affected by exposure frequency and communication cogency. A theoretical and empirical analysis. In *Current Issues and Research in Advertising*, ed. J. H. Leigh, C. R. Martin. Ann Arbor: Grad. Sch. Bus. Adm., Univ. Mich. In press

Cacioppo, J. T., Petty, R. E. 1981. A biosocial model of attitudes and bodily responses. In *Focus on Cardiovascular Psychophysiology*, ed. J. T. Cacioppo, R. E. Petty. New York: Guilford. In press

Cacioppo, J. T., Petty, R. E., Snyder, C. W. 1979. Cognitive and affective response as a function of relative hemispheric involvement. *Int. J. Neurosci.* 9:81–89

Cacioppo, J. T., Sandman, C. A. 1980. Psychophysiological functioning, cognitive responding, and attitudes. See Anderson 1980

Cacioppo, J. T., Sandman, C. A., Walker, B. B. 1978. The effects of operant heart rate conditioning on cognitive elaboration and attitude change. *Psychophysiology* 15:330–38

Carver, C. S. 1977. Self-awareness, perception of threat, and the expression of reactance through attitude change. *J. Pers.* 45:501–12

Carver, C. S. 1979. A cybernetic model of self-attention processes. *J. Pers. Soc. Psychol.* 37:1251–81

Carver, C. S., Scheier, M. F. 1980. Self-consciousness and reactance. *J. Pers. Soc. Psychol.* In press

Chaiken, S. 1979. Communicator physical attractiveness and persuasion. *J. Pers. Soc. Psychol.* 37:1387–97

Chaiken, S. 1980. Heuristic versus systematic information processing and the use of source versus message cues in persuasion. *J. Pers. Soc. Psychol.* In press

Chaiken, S., Eagly, A. H., Sejwacz, D., Gregory, W. L. 1978. Communicator physical attractiveness as a determinant of opinion change. *JSAS* 8:9–10

Cialdini, R. B., Braver, S. L., Lewis, S. K. 1974. Attributional bias and the easily persuaded other. *J. Pers. Soc. Psychol.* 30:613–37

Cialdini, R. B., Cacioppo, J. T., Basset, R., Miller, J. A. 1978. Low-ball procedure for producing compliance: Commitment then cost. *J. Pers. Soc. Psychol.* 36:463–76

Cialdini, R. B., Levy, A., Herman, C. P., Evenbeck, S. 1973. Attitudinal politics: The strategy of moderation. *J. Pers. Soc. Psychol.* 25:100–8

Cialdini, R. B., Levy, A., Herman, C. P., Kozlowski, L. T., Petty, R. E. 1976. Elastic shifts of opinion: Determinants of direction and durability. *J. Pers. Soc. Psychol.* 34:663–72

Cialdini, R. B., Mirels, H. 1976. Sense of personal control and attributions about yielding and resisting persuasion targets. *J. Pers. Soc. Psychol.* 33:395–402

Cialdini, R. B., Petty, R. E. 1980. Anticipatory opinion effects. See Anderson 1980

Clary, E. G., Tesser, A., Downing, L. L. 1978. Influence of a salient schema on thought-induced cognitive change. *Pers. Soc. Psychol. Bull.* 4:39–43

Colman, A. M., Olver, K. R. 1978. Reactions to flattery as a function of self-esteem: Self-enhancement and cognitive consistency theories. *Br. J. Clin. Psychol.* 17:25–29

Comer, R., Rhodewalt, F. 1979. Cue utilization in the self-attribution of emotions and attitudes. *Pers. Soc. Psychol. Bull.* 5:320–24

Condry, J. 1977. Enemies of exploration: Self-initiated versus other-initiated learning. *J. Pers. Soc. Psychol.* 35:459–77

Conley, J. M., O'Barr, W. M., Lind, E. A. 1979. *Duke Law J.* 1978:1375–99

Converse, J. Jr., Cooper, H. 1979. The importance of decisions and free-choice attitude change: A curvilinear finding. *J. Exp. Soc. Psychol.* 15:48–61

Cook, T. D., Flay, B. R. 1978. The persistence of experimentally induced attitude change. *Adv. Exp. Soc. Psychol.* 11:1–57

Cook, T. D., Gruder, C. L., Hennigan, K. M., Flay, B. R. 1979. History of the sleeper effect: Some logical pitfalls in accepting the null hypothesis. *Psychol. Bull.* 35:140–58

Cooper, J. 1980. Reducing fears and increasing assertiveness: The role of dissonance reduction. *J. Exp. Soc. Psychol.* In press

Cooper, J., Fazio, R. H., Rhodewalt, F. 1978a. Dissonance and humor: Evidence for the undifferentiated nature of dissonance arousal. *J. Pers. Soc. Psychol.* 36:280–85

Cooper, J., Zanna, M. P., Taves, P. A. 1978b. Arousal as a necessary condition for attitude change following induced compliance. *J. Pers. Soc. Psychol.* 36:1101–6

Craik, F. I. M. 1979. Human memory. *Ann. Rev. Psychol.* 30:63–102

Craik, F. I. M., Lockhart, R. S. 1972. Levels of processing: A framework for memory research. *J. Verb. Learn. Verb. Behav.* 11:671–84

Crano, W. D. 1977. Primacy versus recency in retention of information and opinion change. *J. Soc. Psychol.* 101:87–96

Cunningham, J. D., Collins, B. E. 1977. The role of biased scanning in counterattitudinal advocacy. *Soc. Behav. Pers.* 5:263–71

Danes, J. E., Hunter, J. E., Woelfel, J. 1978. Mass communication and belief change: A test of three mathematical models. *Hum. Commun. Res.* 4:243–52

Davidson, A. R., Jaccard, J. J. 1979. Variables that moderate the attitude-behavior relation: Results of a longitudinal survey. *J. Pers. Soc. Psychol.* 37:1364–76

Davis, M. H. 1979. Changes in evaluative beliefs as a function of behavioral commitment. *Pers. Soc. Psychol. Bull.* 5:177–87

Deci, E. 1975. *Intrinsic Motivation.* New York: Plenum. 324 pp.

DeJong, W. 1979. An examination of self-perception mediation of the foot-in-the-door effect. *J. Pers. Soc. Psychol.* 37:2221–39

Dermer, M., Cohen, S. J., Jacobsen, E., Anderson, E. A. 1979. Evaluative judgments of aspects of life as a function of vicarious exposure to hedonic extremes. *J. Pers. Soc. Psychol.* 37:247–60

Dollinger, S. J., Thelen, M. H. 1978. Overjustification and children's intrinsic motivation: Comparative effects of four rewards. *J. Pers. Soc. Psychol.* 36:1259–69

Duval, S., Wicklund, R. A. 1972. *A Theory of Objective Self-Awareness.* New York: Academic. 283 pp.

Eagly, A. H., Chaiken, S., Wood, W. 1981. An attributional analysis of persuasion. In *New Directions in Attribution Research,* Vol. 31, ed. J. H. Harvey, W. J. Ickes, R. F. Kidd. Hillsdale, NJ: Erlbaum. In press

Eagly, A. H., Himmelfarb, S. 1978. Attitudes and opinions. *Ann. Rev. Psychol.* 29:517–54

Eagly, A. H., Wood, W., Chaiken, S. 1978. Causal inferences about communicators and their effect on opinion change. *J. Pers. Soc. Psychol.* 36:424–35

Eiser, J. R., Mower-White, C. J. 1974. Evaluative consistency and social judgment. *J. Pers. Soc. Psychol.* 30:349–59

Eiser, J. R., Osmon, B. E. 1978. Judgmental perspective and value connotations of response scale labels. *J. Pers. Soc. Psychol.* 36:491–97

Eiser, J. R., Pancer, S. M. 1979. Attitudinal effects of the use of evaluative biased language. *Eur. J. Soc. Psychol.* 9:39–47

Eiser, J. R., Ross, M. 1977. Partisan language, immediacy, and attitude change. *Eur. J. Soc. Psychol.* 7:477–89

Eiser, J. R., Stroebe, W. 1972. *Categorization and Social Judgment.* London: Academic. 235 pp.

Elms, A. C. 1966. Influence of fantasy ability on attitude change through role playing. *J. Pers. Soc. Psychol.* 4:36–43

Enzle, M. E., Ross, J. M. 1978. Increasing and decreasing intrinsic interest with contingent rewards: A test of cognitive evaluation theory. *J. Exp. Soc. Psychol.* 14:588–97

Erickson, B., Lind, E. A., Johnson, B. C., O'Barr, W. M. 1978. Speech style and impression formation in a court setting: The effects of "powerful" and "powerless" speech. *J. Exp. Soc. Psychol.* 14:266–79

Fazio, R. H., Zanna, M. P. 1978a. Attitudinal qualities relating to the strength of the attitude-behavior relationship. *J. Exp. Soc. Psychol.* 14:398–408

Fazio, R. H., Zanna, M. P. 1978b. On the predictive validity of attitudes: The roles of direct experience and confidence. *J. Pers.* 46:228–43

Fazio, R. H., Zanna, M. P. 1980. Direct experience and attitude-behavior consistency. *Adv. Exp. Soc. Psychol.* In press

Fazio, R. H., Zanna, M. P., Cooper, J. 1977. Dissonance and self-perception: An integrative view of each theory's proper domain of application. *J. Exp. Soc. Psychol.* 13:464–79

Fazio, R. H., Zanna, M. P., Cooper, J. 1978. Direct experience and attitude-behavior consistency: An information processing analysis. *Pers. Soc. Psychol. Bull.* 4:48–51

Fazio, R. H., Zanna, M. P., Cooper, J. 1979. On the relationship of data to theory: A reply to Ronis and Greenwald. *J. Exp. Soc. Psychol.* 15:70–76

Festinger, L. 1957. *A Theory of Cognitive Dissonance.* Stanford, Calif: Stanford Univ. Press. 291 pp.

Festinger, L., Maccoby, N. 1964. On resistance to persuasive communications. *J. Abnorm. Soc. Psychol.* 68:359–66

Fischoff, S. 1979. "Recipe for a jury" revisited: A balance theory prediction. *J. Appl. Soc. Psychol.* 9:335–49

Fishbein, M. 1980. A theory of reasoned action: Some applications and implications. *Nebr. Symp. Motiv.* In press

Fishbein, M., Ajzen, I. 1975. *Belief, Attitude, Intention, and Behavior: An Introduc-*

tion to Theory and Research. Reading, Mass: Addison-Wesley. 578 pp.

Fishbein, M., Ajzen, I. 1980. Acceptance, yielding, and impact: Cognitive processes in persuasion. See Anderson 1980

Folger, R., Rosenfield, D., Hays, R. P. 1978. Equity and intrinsic motivation: The role of choice. *J. Pers. Soc. Psychol.* 36:557–64

Foss, R. D., Dempsey, C. B. 1979. Blood donation and the foot-in-the-door technique: A limiting case. *J. Pers. Soc. Psychol.* 37:580–90

Fox, G. L. 1977. Sex-role attitudes as predictors of contraceptive use among unmarried university students. *Sex Roles* 3:265–83

Freedman, J. L., Fraser, S. C. 1966. Compliance without pressure: The foot-in-the-door technique. *J. Pers. Soc. Psychol.* 4:195–202

Frey, D. 1979. *Experimental investigations in selective exposure to information.* Presented at Am. Psychol. Assoc., 87th, New York

Frey, D., Ochsmann, R., Kumpf, M., Sauer, C., Irle, M. 1979. The effects of discrepant or congruent behavior and reward upon attitude and task attractiveness. *J. Soc. Psychol.* 108:63–73

Frey, D., Wicklund, R. A. 1978. A clarification of selective exposure. *J. Exp. Soc. Psychol.* 14:132–39

Gabrenya, W. K., Arkin, R. M. 1979. The effect of commitment on expectancy value and expectancy weight in social decision making. *Pers. Soc. Psychol. Bull.* 5:86–90

Gaes, G. G., Kalle, R. J., Tedeschi, J. T. 1978. Impression management in the forced compliance situation. *J. Exp. Soc. Psychol.* 14:493–510

Gaes, G. G., Tedeschi, J. T. 1978. An evaluation of self-esteem and impression management theories of anticipatory belief change. *J. Exp. Soc. Psychol.* 14:579–87

Gerbing, D. W., Hunter, J. E. 1979. Phenomenological bases for the attribution of balance to social structure. *Pers. Soc. Psychol. Bull.* 5:299–302

Gibbons, F. X. 1978. Sexual standards and reactions to pornography: Enhancing behavioral consistency through self-focused attention. *J. Pers. Soc. Psychol.* 36:976–87

Goethals, G. R., Cooper, J., Naficy, A. 1979. Role of foreseen, foreseeable, and unforeseeable behavioral consequences in the arousal of cognitive dissonance. *J. Pers. Soc. Psychol.* 37:1179–85

Goethals, G. R., Zanna, M. P. 1979. The role of social comparison in choice shifts. *J. Pers. Soc. Psychol.* 37:1469–76

Goldman, H., Schlenker, B. R. 1977. *Proattitudinal behavior, impression management, and attitude change.* Presented at Ann. Meet. Am. Psychol. Assoc., 85th, San Francisco

Gollob, H. F. 1979. A reply to Norman H. Anderson's critique of the subject-verb-object approach to social cognition. *J. Pers. Soc. Psychol.* 37:931–49

Gorn, G. J., Goldberg, M. E. 1980. Children's responses to repetitive television commercials. *J. Consum. Res.* 6:421–24

Greenwald, A. G. 1968. Cognitive learning, cognitive response to persuasion, and attitude change. In *Psychological Foundations of Attitudes,* ed. A. G. Greenwald, T. C. Brock, T. M. Ostrom, pp. 147–70. New York: Academic. 407 pp.

Greenwald, A. G., Ronis, D. L. 1978. Twenty years of cognitive dissonance: A case study of the evolution of a theory. *Psychol. Rev.* 85:53–57

Gruder, C. L., Cook, T. D., Hennigan, K. M., Flay, B. R., Halamaj, J. 1978. Empirical tests of the absolute sleeper effect predicted from the discounting cue hypothesis. *J. Pers. Soc. Psychol.* 36:1061–74

Grush, J. E. 1980. The impact of candidate expenditures, regionality, and prior outcomes on the 1976 Democratic Presidential primaries. *J. Pers. Soc. Psychol.* 38:337–47

Grush, J. E., McKeough, K. L., Ahlering, R. F. 1978. Extrapolating laboratory exposure research to actual political elections. *J. Pers. Soc. Psychol.* 36:257–70

Halverson, R. R., Pallak, M. S. 1978. Commitment, ego-involvement, and resistance to attack. *J. Exp. Soc. Psychol.* 14:1–12

Hamner, W. C., Smith, F. J. 1978. Work attitudes as predictors of unionization activity. *J. Appl. Psychol.* 63:415–21

Harackiewicz, J. M. 1979. The effects of reward contingency and performance feedback on intrinsic motivation. *J. Pers. Soc. Psychol.* 37:1352–63

Harkins, S. G., Becker, L. A. 1979. A psychological perspective interpretation of the attitude-behavior relationship. *J. Exp. Soc. Psychol.* 15:197–208

Harrison, A. A. 1977. Mere exposure. *Adv. Exp. Soc. Psychol.* 10:39–83

Hass, R. G. 1975. Persuasion or moderation? Two experiments on anticipatory belief change. *J. Pers. Soc. Psychol.* 31:1155–62

Hass, R. G. 1980. Effects of source characteristics on the cognitive processing of persuasive messages and attitude change. See Anderson 1980

Hass, R. G., Mann, R. W. 1976. Anticipatory belief change: Persuasion or impression management. *J. Pers. Soc. Psychol.* 34:105–11

Heider, F. 1946. Attitudes and cognitive organization. *J. Psychol.* 21:107–12

Hemsley, G. D., Doob, A. N. 1978. The effect of looking behavior on perceptions of a communicator's credibility. *J. Appl. Soc. Psychol.* 8:136–44

Higgins, E. T., Rhodewalt, F., Zanna, M. P. 1979. Dissonance motivation: Its nature, persistence, and reinstatement. *J. Exp. Soc. Psychol.* 15:16–34

Hirschman, R., Clark, M., Hawk, G. 1977. Relative effects of bogus physiological feedback and control stimuli on autonomic and self report indicants of emotional attribution. *Pers. Soc. Psychol. Bull.* 3:270–75

Hirshman, R., Hawk, G. 1978. Emotional responsivity to nonveridical heart rate feedback as a function of anxiety. *J. Res. Pers.* 12:235–42

Hom, P. W., Katerberg, R., Hulin, C. L. 1979. Comparative examination of three approaches to the prediction of turnover. *J. Appl. Psychol.* 64:280–90

Hong, L. K. 1978. Risky shift and cautious shift: Some direct evidence on the cultural-value theory. *Soc. Psychol.* 41:342–46

Hovland, C. I. 1959. Reconciling conflicting results derived from experimental and survey studies of attitude change. *Am. Psychol.* 14:8–17

Hovland, C. I., Janis, I. L., Kelley, H. H. 1953. *Communication and Persuasion.* New Haven: Yale Univ. Press. 315 pp.

Howitt, D., Craven, G., Iveson, C., Kremer, J., McCabe, J., Rolph, T. 1977. The misdirected letter. *Br. J. Soc. Clin. Psychol.* 16:285–86

Howitt, D., McCabe, J. 1978. Attitudes do predict behavior—In mails at least. *Br. J. Soc. Clin. Psychol.* 17:285–86

Innes, J. M. 1978. Selective exposure as a function of dogmatism and incentive. *J. Soc. Psychol.* 106:261–65

Insko, C. A. 1980. Balance theory and phenomenology. See Anderson 1980

Insko, C. A., Adewole, A. 1979. The role of assumed reciprocation of sentiment and assumed similarity in the production of attraction and agreement effects in *p-o-x* triads. *J. Pers. Soc. Psychol.* 37:790–808

Izard, C. 1977. *Human Emotions.* New York: Plenum. 495 pp.

Jaccard, J., King, G. W. 1977. A probabilistic model of the relationship between beliefs and behavioral intentions. *Hum. Commun. Res.* 3:332–42

Jaccard, J., King, G. W., Pomazal, R. 1977. Attitudes and behavior: An analysis of specificity of attitudinal predictors. *Hum. Relat.* 30:817–24

Jaccard, J., Knox, R., Brinberg, D. 1979. Prediction of behavior from beliefs: An extension and test of a subjective probability model. *J. Pers. Soc. Psychol.* 37:1239–48

Janis, I. L. 1968. Attitude change via role playing. In *Theories of Cognitive Consistency: A Sourcebook,* ed. R. P. Abelson, E. Aronson, W. J. McGuire, T. M. Newcomb, M. J. Rosenberg, P. H. Tannenbaum, pp. 810–18. Chicago: Rand McNally. 901 pp.

Janis, I. L., King, B. T. 1954. The influence of role-playing on attitude change. *J. Abnorm. Soc. Psychol.* 49:211–18

Janis, I. L., Mann, L. 1977. *Decision Making: A Psychological Analysis of Conflict, Choice, and Commitment.* New York: Free Press. 488 pp.

Jellison, J. M., Arkin, R. 1977. Social comparison of abilities: A self-presentational approach to decision making in groups. In *Social Comparison Processes: Theoretical and Empirical Perspectives,* ed. J. M. Suls, R. L. Miller, Pp. 235–57. Washington: Hemisphere. 371 pp.

Jellison, J. M., Mills, J. 1969. Effects of public commitment upon opinions. *J. Exp. Soc. Psychol.* 5:340–46

Johnson, H. H., Watkins, T. 1977. Trends in dissonance research and the Chapanis' criticisms. *Pers. Soc. Psychol. Bull.* 3:244–47

Judd, C. M., DePaulo, B. M. 1979. The effect of perspective differences on the measurement of involving attitudes. *Soc. Psychol. Q.* 42:185–89

Kahle, L. R., Berman, J. J. 1979. Attitudes cause behaviors: A cross-lagged panel analysis. *J. Pers. Soc. Psychol.* 37: 315–21

Kaplan, M. F., Miller, C. E. 1977. Judgments and group discussion: Effect of presentation and memory factors on polarization. *Sociometry* 40:337–43

Kaplan, M. F., Miller, L. E. 1978. Reducing the effect of juror bias. *J. Pers. Soc. Psychol.* 36:1443–55

Kaplan, M. F., Steindorf, J., Iervolino, A. 1978. Courtrooms, politics, and morality: Toward a theoretical integration. *Pers. Soc. Psychol. Bull.* 4:1555–60

Kelley, H. H., Michela, J. L. 1980. Attribution theory and research. *Ann. Rev. Psychol.* 31:457–501

Kelman, H. C. 1953. Attitude change as a function of response restriction. *Hum. Relat.* 6:185–214

Kelman, H. C., Hovland, C. I. 1953. "Reinstatement" of the communicator in delayed measurement of opinion change. *J. Abnorm. Soc. Psychol.* 48:326–35

Kerber, K. W., Coles, M. G. 1978. The role of perceived physiological activity in affective judgments. *J. Exp. Soc. Psychol.* 14:419–33

Kiesler, C. A. 1971. *The Psychology of Commitment: Experiments Linking Behavior to Belief.* New York: Academic. 190 pp.

Kiesler, C. A. 1977. Sequential events in commitment. *J. Pers.* 45:65–78

Kiesler, C. A., Pallak, M. S. 1976. Arousal properties of dissonance manipulations. *Psychol. Bull.* 83:1014–25

Kilty, K. M. 1978. Attitudinal and normative variables as predictors of drinking behavior. *J. Stud. Alcohol* 39:1178–94

Kinder, D. R. 1978. Political person perception: The asymmetrical influence of sentiment and choice on perceptions of presidential candidates. *J. Pers. Soc. Psychol.* 36:859–71

King, B. T., Janis, I. L. 1956. Comparison of the effectiveness of improvised versus non-improvised role-playing in producing opinion changes. *Hum. Relat.* 9:177–86

Kroeber-Riel, W. 1979. Activation research: Psychobiological approaches in consumer research. *J. Consum. Res.* 5:240–50

Lamm, H., Myers, D. G. 1978. Group-induced polarization of attitudes and behavior. *Adv. Exp. Soc. Psychol.* 11:145–95

Lammers, H. B., Becker, L. A. 1980. Distraction effects on the perceived extremity of a communication and on cognitive responses. *Pers. Soc. Psychol. Bull.* 6:261–66

Landis, D., Triandis, H. C., Adamopoulos, J. 1978. Habit and behavioral intentions as predictors of social behavior. *J. Soc. Psychol.* 106:227–37

Langer, E., Blank, A., Chanowitz, B. 1978. The mindlessness of ostensibly thoughtful action: The role of "placebic" information in interpersonal interaction. *J. Pers. Soc. Psychol.* 36:635–42

Lau, R. R., Sears, D. O., Centers, R. 1979. The "positivity bias" in evaluations of public figures: Evidence against instrument artifacts. *Public Opin. Q.* 347–58

Lepper, M. R., Greene, D., eds. 1978. *The Hidden Costs of Reward.* Hillsdale, NJ: Erlbaum. 262 pp.

Liebhart, E. H. 1979. Information search and attribution: Cognitive processes mediating the effect of false autonomic feedback. *Eur. J. Soc. Psychol.* 9:19–37

Lind, E. A., O'Barr, W. M. 1979. The social significance of speech in the courtroom. In *Language and Social Psychology,* ed. H. Giles, R. St. Clair, pp. 66–87. Oxford, England: Blackwell. 261 pp.

Liska, J. 1978. Situational and topical variations in credibility criteria. *Commun. Monogr.* 45:85–92

Lord, C. G., Ross, L., Lepper, M. R. 1979. Biased assimilation and attitude polarization: The effects of prior theories on subsequently considered evidence. *J. Pers. Soc. Psychol.* 37:2098–2109

Love, R. E., Greenwald, A. G. 1978. Cognitive responses to persuasion as mediators of opinion change. *J. Soc. Psychol.* 104:231–41

Lutz, R. J. 1977. An experimental investigation of causal relations among cognitions, affect, and behavioral intention. *J. Consum. Res.* 3:197–208

Lutz, R. J. 1978. Rejoinder. *J. Consum. Res.* 4:276–78

Lutz, R. J., Bettman, J. R. 1977. Multiattribute models in marketing: A bicentennial review. In *Consumer and Industrial Buying Behavior,* ed. A. G. Woodside, J. N. Sheth, P. D. Bennet, pp. 137–49. New York: North-Holland. 523 pp.

Madsen, D. B. 1978. Issue importance and group choice shifts: A persuasive arguments approach. *J. Pers. Soc. Psychol.* 36:1118–27

Manis, M., Moore, J. C. 1978. Summarizing controversial messages: Retroactive effects due to subsequent information. *Soc. Psychol. Q.* 41:62–68

Marsh, H. W., Parducci, A. 1978. Natural anchoring at the neutral point of category rating scales. *J. Exp. Soc. Psychol.* 14:193–204

Marshall, G. D., Zimbardo, R. P. 1979. Affective consequences of inadequately explained physiological arousal. *J. Pers. Soc. Psychol.* 37:970–88

Maslach, C. 1979. Negative emotional biasing of unexplained arousal. *J. Pers. Soc. Psychol.* 37:953–69

McGuinness, J., Jones, A. P., Cole, S. G. 1977. Attitudinal correlates of recycling behavior. *J. Appl. Psychol.* 62:376–84

McGuire, W. J. 1960. A syllogistic analysis of cognitive relationships. In *Attitude Organization and Change,* ed. C. Hovland, M. Rosenberg, pp. 65–111. New Haven: Yale Univ. Press. 239 pp.

McGuire, W. J., 1964. Inducing resistance to persuasion: Some contemporary approaches. *Adv. Exp. Soc. Psychol.* 1:192–229

McGuire, W. J. 1980. The probabiological model of cognitive structure and attitude change. See Anderson 1980

McGuire, W. J. 1980. Communication and social influence processes. In *The Social Psychology of Psychological Problems*, ed. M. Feldman, J. Orford. Essex: Wiley. In press

McGuire, W. J., Millman, S. 1965. Anticipatory belief lowering following forewarning of a persuasive attack. *J. Pers. Soc. Psychol.* 34:105–11

Mewborn, C. R., Rogers, R. W. 1979. Effects of threatening and reassuring components of fear appeals on physiological and verbal measures of emotion and attitudes. *J. Exp. Soc. Psychol.* 15:242–53

Milgram, S. 1969. The lost-letter technique. *Psychol. Today* 3:30–33, 66, 68

Miller, L. W., Sigelman, L. 1978. Is the audience the message? A note on LBJ's Vietnam statements. *Public Opin. Q.* 42:71–80

Miller, N., Maruyama, G., Beaber, R., Valone, K. 1976. Speed of speech and persuasion. *J. Pers. Soc. Psychol.* 31:615–24

Miller, R. C. 1976. Mere exposure, psychological reactance, and attitude change. *Public Opin. Q.* 40:229–33

Miniard, P. W., Cohen, J. B. 1979. Isolating attitudinal and normative influences in behavioral intention models. *J. Mark. Res.* 16:102–10

Mirvis, P. H., Lawler, E. E. 1977. Measuring the financial impact of employee attitudes. *J. Appl. Psychol.* 62:1–8

Mita, T. H., Dermer, M., Knight, J. 1977. Reversed facial images and the mere-exposure hypothesis. *J. Pers. Soc. Psychol.* 35:597–601

Möntmann, V. 1979. *Cognitive dissonance: A statistical analysis of its development 1957–1977.* Presented at Am. Psychol. Assoc., 87th, New York

Moore, M. 1979. Structural balance and international relations. *Eur. J. Soc. Psychol.* 9:323–26

Moreland, R. L., Zajonc, R. B. 1977. Is stimulus recognition a necessary condition for the occurrence of exposure effects? *J. Pers. Soc. Psychol.* 35:191–99

Moreland, R. L., Zajonc, R. B. 1979. Exposure effects may not depend on stimulus recognition. *J. Pers. Soc. Psychol.* 37:1085–89

Mower-White, C. J. 1979. Factors affecting balance, agreement, and positivity biases in POQ and POX triads. *Eur. J. Soc. Psychol.* 9:129–48

Myers, D. G. 1980. Polarizing effects of social interaction. In *Contemporary Problems in Group Decision Making*, ed. H. Brandstätter, J. H. Davis, G. Stocker-Kreichgauer. New York: Academic

Myers, D. G., Wojcicki, S. B., Aardema, B. 1977. Attitude comparison: Is there ever a bandwagon effect? *J. Appl. Soc. Psychol.* 7:341–47

Newtson, D., Czerlinksy, T. 1974. Adjustment of attitude communications for contrasts by extreme audiences. *J. Pers. Soc. Psychol.* 30:829–37

Olson, J. C., Dover, P. A. 1978. Attitude maturation: Changes in related belief structures over time. *Adv. Consum. Res.* 5:333–42

Olson, J. C., Dover, P. A. 1979. Disconfirmation of consumer expectations through product trial. *J. Appl. Psychol.* 64:179–89

Olson, J. M., Zanna, M. P. 1979a. A new look at selective exposure. *J. Exp. Soc. Psychol.* 15:1–15

Olson, J. M., Zanna, M. P. 1979b. *Opinions and memory: Individual differences in selective learning.* Presented at Am. Psychol. Assoc., 87th, New York

O'Neill, P., Levings, D. E. 1979. Inducing biased scanning in a group setting to change attitudes toward bilingualism and capital punishment. *J. Pers. Soc. Psychol.* 37:1432–38

Opello, W. C. Jr. 1977. Cognitive inconsistency among some Mozambican revolutionaries. *J. Soc. Psychol.* 102:73–77

Osmon, B. E., Mower-White, C. J. 1977. The importance of both judgmental scales and aspects of an attitudinal issue for dimensional salience. *Br. J. Soc. Clin. Psychol.* 16:123–29

Ostrom, T. M., Davis, D. 1979. Idiosyncratic weighting of trait information in impression formation. *J. Pers. Soc. Psychol.* 37:2025–43

Ostrom, T. M., Upshaw, H. S. 1968. Psychological perspective and attitude change. See Greenwald 1968, pp. 217–42

Ostrom, T. M., Werner, C., Saks, M. J. 1978. An integration theory of jurors' presumptions of guilt or innocence. *J. Pers. Soc. Psychol.* 36:436–50

Paicheler, G. 1979. Polarization of attitude in homogeneous and heterogeneous groups. *Eur. J. Soc. Psychol.* 9:85–96

Pallak, M. S., Cook, D. A., Sullivan, J. J. 1980. Commitment and energy conservation. *Appl. Soc. Psychol. Ann.* 1:235–53

Pallak, M. S., Sullivan, J. J. 1979. The effect of commitment, threat, and restoration of freedom on attitude change and action-taking. *Pers. Soc. Psychol. Bull.* 5:307–10

Perloff, R. M., Brock, T. C. 1980. And thinking makes it so: Cognitive responses to persuasion. In *Persuasion: New Directions in Theory and Research,* ed. M. E. Roloff, G. R. Miller, pp. 67–99. Beverly Hills: Sage. 311 pp.

Petty, R. E. 1977. The importance of cognitive responses in persuasion. *Adv. Consum. Res.* 4:357–62

Petty, R. E., Brock, T. C. 1980. Thought disruption and persuasion: Assessing the validity of attitude change experiments. See Anderson 1980

Petty, R. E., Cacioppo, J. T. 1977. Forewarning, cognitive responding, and resistance to persuasion. *J. Pers. Soc. Psychol.* 35:645–55

Petty, R. E., Cacioppo, J. T. 1979a. Effects of forewarning of persuasive intent and involvement on cognitive responses and persuasion. *Pers. Soc. Psychol. Bull.* 5:173–76

Petty, R. E., Cacioppo, J. T. 1979b. Issue-involvement can increase or decrease persuasion by enhancing message-relevant cognitive responses. *J. Pers. Soc. Psychol.* 37:1915–26

Petty, R. E., Cacioppo, J. T. 1980. *Attitudes and Persuasion. Classic and Contemporary Approaches.* Dubuque: Brown. In press

Petty, R. E., Harkins, S. G., Williams, K. D. 1980. The effects of group diffusion of cognitive effort on attitudes: An information processing view. *J. Pers. Soc. Psychol.* 38:81–92

Petty, R. E., Harkins, S. G., Williams, K. D., Latane, B. 1977. The effects of group size on cognitive effort and evaluation. *Pers. Soc. Psychol. Bull.* 3:579–82

Petty, R. E., Ostrom, T. M., Brock, T. C. 1980. Historical foundations of the cognitive response approach to attitudes and persuasion. See Anderson 1980

Petty, R. E., Wells, G. L., Brock, T. C. 1976. Distraction can enhance or reduce yielding to propaganda: Thought disruption versus effort justification. *J. Pers. Soc. Psychol.* 34:874–84

Pittman, T. S., Cooper, E. E., Smith, T. W. 1977. Attribution of causality and the overjustification effect. *Pers. Soc. Psychol. Bull.* 3:280–83

Pittman, T. S., Davey, M. E., Alafat, K. A., Wetherill, K. V., Wirsul, N. A. 1980. Informational vs. controlling verbal rewards, levels of surveillance, and intrinsic motivation. *Pers. Soc. Psychol. Bull.* 6:238–43

Pryor, B., Steinfatt, T. M. 1978. The effects of initial belief level on inoculation theory and its proposed mechanisms. *Hum. Commun. Res.* 4:217–30

Pryor, J. B., Gibbons, F. X., Wicklund, R. A., Fazio, R. H., Hood, R. 1977. Self-focused attention and self-report validity. *J. Pers.* 45:513–27

Quigley-Fernandez, B., Tedeschi, J. T. 1978. The bogus pipeline as lie detector: Two validity studies. *J. Pers. Soc. Psychol.* 36:247–56

Regan, D. T., Fazio, R. H. 1977. On the consistency between attitudes and behavior: Look to the method of attitude formation. *J. Exp. Soc. Psychol.* 13:28–45

Rhodewalt, F., Comer, R. 1979. Induced-compliance attitude change: Once more with feeling. *J. Exp. Soc. Psychol.* 15:35–47

Riess, M., Kalle, R. J., Tedeschi, J. T. 1980. The bogus pipeline and attitude moderation following forced compliance: Misattribution of dissonance arousal on impression management inhibition. *J. Soc. Psychol.* In press

Romer, D. 1979a. Distraction, counterarguing, and the internalization of attitude change. *Eur. J. Soc. Psychol.* 9:1–17

Romer, D. 1979b. Internalization versus identification in the laboratory: A causal analysis of attitude change. *J. Pers. Soc. Psychol.* 37:2171–80

Ronis, D. L., Baumgardner, M. H., Leippe, M. R., Cacioppo, J. T., Greenwald, A. G. 1977. In search of reliable persuasion effects: I. A computer-controlled procedure for studying persuasion. *J. Pers. Soc. Psychol.* 35:548–69

Ronis, D. L., Greenwald, A. G. 1979. Dissonance theory revised again: Comment on the paper by Fazio, Zanna, and Cooper. *J. Exp. Soc. Psychol.* 15:62–69

Rook, K. S., Sears, D. O., Kinder, D. R., Lau, R. R. 1978. The "positivity bias" in evaluations of public figures: Evidence against interpersonal artifacts. *Polit. Methodol.* 5:469–99

Rumsey, M. G., Allgeier, E. R., Castore, C. H. 1978. Group discussion, sentencing judgments and the leniency shift. *J. Soc. Psychol.* 105:249–57

Saltzstein, H. D., Sandberg, L. 1979. Indirect social influence: Change in judgmental process or anticipatory conformity? *J. Exp. Soc. Psychol.* 15:209–16

Sanders, G. S., Baron, R. S. 1977. Is social comparison irrelevant for producing choice shifts? *J. Exp. Soc. Psychol.* 13:303–14

Sawyer, A. G. 1980. Repetition, cognitive responses, and persuasion. See Anderson 1980

Schachter, S., Singer, J. E. 1979. Comments on the Maslach and Marshall-Zimbardo experiments. J. Pers. Soc. Psychol. 37:989–95

Scheier, M. F., Carver, C. S. 1977. Self-focused attention and the experience of emotion: Attraction, repulsion, elation, and depression. J. Pers. Soc. Psychol. 35:625–36

Scheier, M. F., Carver, C. S. 1980. Individual differences in self-concept and self-process. In The Self in Social Psychology, ed. D. M. Wegner, R. R. Vallacher, pp. 229–51. New York: Oxford Univ. Press. 300 pp.

Scheier, M. F., Carver, C. S., Gibbons, F. X. 1979. Self-directed attention, awareness of bodily states, and suggestibility. J. Pers. Soc. Psychol. 37:1576–88

Schlegel, R. P., Crawford, C. A., Sanborn, M. D. 1977. Correspondence and mediational properties of the Fishbein model: An application to adolescent alcohol use. J. Exp. Soc. Psychol. 13:421–30

Schlenker, B. R. 1978. Attitudes as actions: Social identity theory and consumer research. Adv. Consum. Res. 5:352–59

Schlenker, B. R. 1980. Impression Management: The Self-Concept, Social Identity, and Interpersonal Relations. Belmont, Calif: Brooks/Cole

Schlenker, B. R., Forsyth, D. R., Leary, M. R., Miller, R. S. 1980. A self-presentational analysis of the effects of incentives on attitude change following counterattitudinal behavior. J. Pers. Soc. Psychol. In press

Schlenker, B. R., Riess, M. 1979. Self-presentation of attitudes following commitment to proattitudinal behavior. Hum. Commun. Res. 5:325–34

Schneider, W., Shiffrin, R. M. 1977. Controlled and automatic human information processing. I. Detection, search, and attention. Psychol. Rev. 84:1–66

Schriescheim, C. A. 1978. Job satisfaction, attitudes toward unions, and voting in a union representation election. J. Appl. Psychol. 63:548–52

Schwartz, G. E., Fair, P. L., Mandel, M. R., Salt, P., Mieske, M., Klerman, G. L. 1978. Facial electromyography in the assessment of improvement in depression. Psychosom. Med. 40:355–60

Schwartz, S. H. 1973. Normative explanations of helping behavior: A critique, proposal, and empirical test. J. Exp. Soc. Psychol. 9:349–64

Schwartz, S. H. 1978. Temporal instability as a moderator of the attitude-behavior relationship. J. Pers. Soc. Psychol. 36:715–24

Scott, C. A., Yalch, R. F. 1978. A test of the self-perception explanation of rewards on intrinsic interest. J. Exp. Soc. Psychol. 14:180–92

Seligman, C., Kriss, M., Darley, J. M., Fazio, R. H., Becker, L. J., Pryor, J. B. 1979. Predicting summer energy consumption from homeowners' attitudes. J. Appl. Soc. Psychol. 9:70–90

Sentis, K. P., Burnstein, E. 1979. Remembering schema-consistent information: Effects of a balance schema on recognition memory. J. Pers. Soc. Psychol. 37:2200–11

Sheluga, D. A., Jaccard, J., Jacoby, J. 1979. Preference, search, and choice: An integrative approach. J. Consum. Res. 6:166–76

Sherif, C. W. 1976. Orientation in Social Psychology. New York: Harper & Row. 441 pp.

Sherif, M., Sherif, C. W. 1967. Attitude as the individual's own categories: The social judgment-involvement approach to attitude and attitude change. In Attitude, Ego-involvement and Change, ed. C. W. Sherif, M. Sherif, pp. 105–39. New York: Wiley. 316 pp.

Sherman, S. J., Ahlm, K., Berman, L., Lynn, S. 1978. Contrast effects and their relationship to subsequent behavior. J. Exp. Soc. Psychol. 14:340–50

Smith, F. J. 1977. Work attitudes as predictors of attendence on a specific day. J. Appl. Psychol. 62:16–19

Smith, M. J. 1977. the effects of threats to attitudinal freedom as a function of message quality and initial receiver attitude. Commun. Monogr. 44:195–206

Smith, M. J. 1979. Extreme disagreement and the expression of attitudinal freedom. Commun. Monogr. 46:112–18

Smith, T. W., Pittman, T. S. 1978. Reward, distraction and the overjustification effect. J. Pers. Soc. Psychol. 36:565–72

Snyder, M. 1974. The self-monitoring of expressive behavior. J. Pers. Soc. Psychol. 30:526–37

Snyder, M. 1979. Self-monitoring processes. Adv. Exp. Soc. Psychol. 12:85–128

Snyder, M. L., Wicklund, R. A. 1976. Prior exercise of freedom and reactance. J. Exp. Soc. Psychol. 12:120–29

Songer-Nocks, E. 1976. Situational factors affecting the weighting of predictor component in the Fishbein model. J. Exp. Soc. Psychol. 12:56–69

Sternthal, B., Dholakia, R., Leavitt, C. 1978. The persuasive effect of source credibility: Tests of cognitive response. *J. Consum. Res.* 4:252–60

Sternthal, B., Phillips, L. W., Dholakia, R. 1978. The persuasive effect of source credibility: A situational analysis. *Public Opin. Q.* 42:285–314

Suedfeld, P., Borrie, R. A. 1978. Sensory deprivation, attitude change, and defense against persuasion. *Can. J. Behav. Sci.* 10:16–27

Swap, W. C. 1977. Interpersonal attraction and repeated exposure to rewarders and punishers. *Pers. Soc. Psychol. Bull.* 3:248–51

Swinyard, W. R., Coney, K. A. 1978. Promotional effects on a high versus low-involvement electorate. *J. Consum. Res.* 5:41–48

Tashakkori, A., Insko, C. A. 1979. Interpersonal attraction and the polarity of similar attitudes: A test of three balanced models. *J. Pers. Soc. Psychol.* 37: 2262–77

Tedeschi, J. T., ed. 1981. *Impression Management Theory and Social Psychological Research.* New York: Academic. In press

Tedeschi, J. T., Schlenker, B. R., Bonoma, T. V. 1971. Cognitive dissonance: Private ratiocination or public spectacle? *Am. Psychol.* 26:685–95

Tesser, A. 1978. Self-generated attitude change. *Adv. Exp. Soc. Psychol.* 11:289–338

Tesser, A., Danheiser, P. 1978. Anticipated relationship, salience of partner, and attitude change. *Pers. Soc. Psychol. Bull.* 4:35–38

Tesser, A., Leone, C. 1977. Cognitive schemas and thought as determinants of attitude change. *J. Exp. Soc. Psychol.* 13:340–56

Tourangeau, R., Ellsworth, P. C. 1979. The role of facial response in the experience of emotion. *J. Pers. Soc. Psychol.* 37:1519–31

Triandis, H. C. 1977. *Interpersonal Behavior.* Monterey: Brooks/Cole. 329 pp.

Triandis, H. C. 1980. Values, attitudes, and interpersonal behavior. *Nebr. Symp. Motiv.* In press

Turner, R. G. 1977. Self-consciousness and anticipatory belief change. *Pers. Soc. Psychol. Bull.* 3:438–41

Tursky, B., Lodge, M., Reeder, R. 1979. Psychophysical and psychophysiological evaluation of the direction, intensity, and meaning of race-related stimuli. *Psychophysiology* 16:452–62

Tyler, T. R., Sears, D. O. 1977. Coming to like obnoxious people when we must live with them. *J. Pers. Soc. Psychol.* 35:200–11

Upshaw, H. S. 1969. The personal reference scale: An approach to social judgment. *Adv. Exp. Soc. Psychol.* 4:315–71

Upshaw, H. S. 1978. Social influence on attitudes and on anchoring of cogeneric attitude scales. *J. Exp. Soc. Psychol.* 14:327–39

Valins, S. 1966. Cognitive effects of false heart-rate feedback. *J. Pers. Soc. Psychol.* 4:400–8

Van der Plight, J., Van Dijk, J. A. 1979. Polarization of judgment and preference for judgmental labels. *Eur. J. Soc. Psychol.* 9:233–41

Van Jones, B. 1977. Attitude change toward the winner and the loser of the 1976 presidential election. *J. Psychol.* 96: 213–15

Vinokur, A., Burnstein, E. 1978a. Depolarization of attitudes in groups. *J. Pers. Soc. Psychol.* 36:872–85

Vinokur, A., Burnstein, E. 1978b. Novel argumentation and attitude change: The case of polarization following group discussion. *Eur. J. Soc. Psychol.* 8:335–48

Vinokur-Kaplan, D. 1978. To have- or not to have-another child: Family planning attitudes, intentions, and behavior. *J. Appl. Soc. Psychol.* 8:29–46

Watts, W. A. 1977. Intelligence and opinion change through active participation as a function of requirements for improvisation and time of opinion measurement. *Soc. Behav. Pers.* 5:171–76

Watts, W. A., Holt, L. E. 1979. Persistence of opinion change induced under conditions of forewarning and distraction. *J. Pers. Soc. Psychol.* 37:778–89

Webb, P. H. 1979. Consumer initial processing in a difficult media environment. *J. Consum. Res.* 6:225–36

Wellens, A. R. 1979. Quantitative balance theory and the interpersonal liking-proximity relationship: A replication and extension of previous findings. *J. Psychol.* 101:237–39

Wells, G. L., Petty, R. E., Harkins, S. G., Kagehiro, D., Harvey, J. H. 1977. Anticipated discussion of interpretation eliminates actor-observer differences in the attribution of causality. *Sociometry* 40:247–53

Werner, P. D. 1978. Personality and attitude-activism correspondence. *J. Pers. Soc. Psychol.* 36:1375–90

White, G. L., Maltzman, I. 1978. Pupillary activity while listening to verbal passages. *J. Res. Pers.* 12:361–69

Wicker, A. W. 1969. Attitudes versus action: The relationship of verbal and overt behavioral responses to attitude objects. *J. Soc. Issues* 25:41–78

Wicklund, R. A., Brehm, J. W. 1976. *Perspectives on Cognitive Dissonance.* Hillsdale, NJ: Erlbaum. 349 pp.

Wilson, W. R. 1979. Feeling more than we can know: Exposure effects without learning. *J. Pers. Soc. Psychol.* 37:811–21

Wyer, R. S. 1974. *Cognitive Organization and Change.* Potomac, MD: Erlbaum. 502 pp.

Younger, J. C., Walker, L., Arrowood, A. J. 1977. Postdecision dissonance at the fair. *Pers. Soc. Psychol. Bull.* 3:284–87

Zajonc, R. 1968. Attitudinal effects of mere exposure. *J. Pers. Soc. Psychol.* 9:1–27

Zanna, M. P., Hamilton, D. L. 1977. Further evidence for meaning change in impression formation. *J. Exp. Soc. Psychol.* 13:224–38

Zanna, M. P., Olson, J. M., Fazio, R. H. 1980. Attitude-behavior consistency: An individual difference perspective. *J. Pers. Soc. Psychol.* 38:432–40

Zuckerman, M., Reis, H. T. 1978. Comparison of three models for predicting altruistic behavior. *J. Pers. Soc. Psychol.* 36:498–510

Zuckerman, M., Siegelbaum, H., Williams, R. 1977. Predicting helping behavior: Willingness and ascription of responsibility. *J. Appl. Soc. Psychol.* 7:295–99

Ann. Rev. Psychol. 1981. 32:405–38

CLINICAL PSYCHOLOGY: INDIVIDUAL METHODS[1]

❖349

Jeanne S. Phillips and Karen Linn Bierman

Department of Psychology, University of Denver, Denver, Colorado 80208

CONTENTS

[1]The most recent review of individual therapies for adults appeared in Volume 29, by Gomes-Schwartz, Hadley & Strupp (1978). Therefore, we concentrate on literature for the period 1976 to early 1980 to update their review. Excluded for the most part are single-subject designs and research on marital, family, and group therapy. Because we believe there is a shift toward blurred demarcations and more eclectic treatment packages in the field, and also to avoid redundancy, we do not discuss traditional psychotherapies and behavior therapies separately; some sections are concerned more with one or the other because of differing preoccupations of investigators in traditional or behavioral modes.

Our special thanks go to Dr. Roberta Ray for her help and counsel.

0066-4308/81/0201-0405$01.00

Authors for these volumes typically apologize in distress because of the impossibility of constructing a comprehensive, systematic review that acknowledges all important work. We are relieved of this burden by the recent publication of Garfield & Bergin's (1978) revised *Handbook of Psychotherapy and Behavior Change,* which does all that and more. Other comprehensive recent sources include a report prepared at NIMH for the President's Commission on Mental Health (Parloff et al 1978), volumes by Claghorn (1976), Gurman & Razin (1977), Frank et al (1978), Lambert (1979), and Kanfer & Goldstein (1980). Developments in behavioral therapies are documented in an annual series edited by Hersen, Eisler & Miller (1975–80) and in a multitude of texts.

INFLUENCES: URGENCY AND ACCOUNTABILITY

"Psychotherapy Faces Test of Worth: Therapists may become eligible for direct federal reimbursement if they prove psychotherapy works" (headline in *Science,* 4 January 1980).

"A host of idiosyncratic studies of poorly defined populations with vaguely described therapies and exceedingly variable outcome criteria will not produce findings of any substance" (Garfield 1978, p. 225).

These two quotations illustrate the paradoxical status of psychotherapy research today. While policy makers demand rapid substantive answers to practical questions, production of usable knowledge has been flawed and slow. From this viewpoint, one of the most significant recent publications is Parloff's (1979) sobering discussion of the implications of having research reports interpreted not by sophisticated investigators but by political decision makers. His perspective argues the necessity of large-scale clinical trials to produce persuasive data. Opponents believe we should stay with long-range goals of explicating issues basic to therapeutic change while fending off pressures to certify this cure for that ill (Strupp 1980). The possibility that psychotherapy soon may undergo efficacy tests and regulation by a federal agency is only one example of how public events define the operational arena of psychotherapy and set its research priorities. Psychotherapy is big business and as such cannot escape the general social-economic-political movements in this country, for each of which accountability is a central theme.

In the fiscal arena, shrinking resources have steadily reduced federal support of psychotherapy research, pressed public sector therapists toward short-term therapy, and curtailed training funds for core mental health disciplines in favor of "primary providers," that is, physicians in general practice whose suitability for delivering psychotherapeutic care is questionable. Third-party payment policies and the prospects for national health insurance have enormous implications, ranging from who will receive care to the qualifications of providers and the range of services attracted by or permitted in this newly lucrative marketplace (Meltzer 1975, Gross 1978, Edwards et al 1979). Nowhere is the link between funding and pressures on research more clear than in the monitoring of care by professional standards review organizations whose charts will perforce define "proper" treatment, whatever data may or may not be available.

Consumer protection, landmark court decisions, and the growth of public law are equally important influences. Here accountability is in humane terms, the well-being and rights of patients (Hare-Mustin et al 1979). The impact of consumerism is illustrated by promulgation of patients' bills of rights, regulations governing behavioral treatments, and the development of a new profession in health advocacy. Ethical limits on forming control groups are more critical. Informed consent protects patients but may bias samples (Spohn & Fitzpatrick 1980). Therapeutic contracting and consumer education and choice are becoming mandatory, epitomized by publication of a Consumer's Union guide for selecting one's therapist (Park & Shapiro 1976, Bloom & Asher 1980). Research demonstrating negative effects of therapy (Strupp et al 1977) makes the link between ethical concerns and efficacy research all the more paramount.

Credentialling of professionals as competent is another aspect of public accountability, although its major impetus may have more to do with eligibility for third-party payments. Until psychotherapy research can offer far more solid guidance about the components of success, failure, or harm to specified classes of clients, it is difficult to see what criteria credentialling authorities can apply beyond those of usual and accepted practice. NIMH has proposed a new thrust of research on psychosocial treatments in order to build the required knowledge base. Training sufficient numbers of well-prepared researchers ready to conduct the slow, complex work will be a first hurdle, however. A second obstacle is the receptivity of clinical field settings to the massive amount of needed research; yet without their participation, generalization of results is limited to specialized settings and samples.

TRENDS AND ISSUES

Jerome Frank (1979), in summarizing the present status of outcome studies, labels the amount of well-established, clinically relevant knowledge as disappointingly meager and intuitively obvious. He concludes that while answers are sparse, we are becoming able to ask more cogent questions. Rather than organizing this review around knowledge gained about customary variables, we emphasize instead trends in the questions being asked and the methods used to address them.

Refinement and Complexity of Questions Addressed

Happily continuing the trend noted by Bergin & Suinn (1975), almost no one any longer asks generically: "Does psychotherapy work?" Smith & Glass's (1977) novel method of meta-analysis of all available literature is an exception, made in part to support global assertions of political consequence but controversial in method and conclusions (Agras et al 1979). The general movement is toward specificity: specificity of patient problems even within broad diagnostic groups, of therapeutic operations, of targeted outcomes, and of constructs within orienting conceptualizations. Comparative studies are less often between two generic brands than between specific components or packages and usually entail asking not just whether several methods differ in outcome, but also whether they differentially affect different aspects of outcome. Thus the models in which specific variables are embedded are more complex and research is shifting to examinations of multidimensional combinations of interactive variables. Outcome assessment, for example, is in terms of multiple measures tapping different perspectives within multiple domains.

Changes in the way therapist and patient variables and nonspecific effects are construed and studied document this shift. Largely abandoned are searches for single therapist or patient characteristics correlated with outcome; patient perceptions and satisfaction are better predictors (Garfield 1978, Lambert et al 1978). Nonspecific factors such as expectancy, placebo effects, or demand characteristics are also difficult to manipulate singly since they cannot be empirically discriminated (Bernstein & Nietzel 1977, Wilkins 1978). Investigators therefore have moved to interactional models, checking for characteristics by treatment technique by pathology interactions, and to matching strategies. Matching patient and therapist has largely failed, perhaps because of methodological weaknesses and reliance on simplistic matching variables (Kilmann et al 1979). In consequence, efforts have been renewed to dissect and influence the therapeutic relationship or alliance since there, perhaps, resides the common meeting ground of patient and therapist characteristics, nonspecific effects, and the search for characteristics common to all effective interventions (Luborsky 1976, Strupp & Hadley 1979).

Advances in Design, Method, and Assessment

Methodological critiques are having a cumulative positive effect (Kiesler 1966, Paul 1969, Bergin & Strupp 1972, Kazdin & Wilson 1978). The desiderata of psychotherapy research have not changed much. Luborsky et al (1975) used 13 criteria by which to grade the quality of comparative outcome studies. In summary these were: *subjects* should be reasonably large numbers of real patients, matched on important dimensions including severity, adequately and completely diagnosed, and assigned to groups in a controlled fashion; *therapists* should be experienced and equally competent across treatments; *treatments* should be equally valued by therapists and patients, monitored to insure that they are conducted as prescribed, conducted for equal and adequate durations and/or frequencies; other *concurrent* treatments should be controlled for; *outcome measures* should be multiple and in part standardized, take account of target goals, be applied by independent evaluators, and include an adequate follow-up period.

Additional criteria are suggested by frequent errors: inadequate description and restricted populations of patients sampled; biased selection procedures; confounding of therapists and treatment; absence of treatment manuals; and failure of the design to take account of nonspecific and relationship factors and of sample attrition, correlations among measures, and practical significance.

The average level of adequacy attained seems not to have changed much: many small studies contain so many flaws that they simply confuse the literature with unsound results. The important change is in the number of large studies that exemplify increasingly sophisticated methodology. Use of complex designs is one element in this trend: dismantling and parametric designs, studies of interaction effects, prediction and discrimination of effects in different domains by different interventions. Single-subject designs have been more thoroughly elaborated (Barlow & Hayes 1979) while behavioral researchers have at the same time become more discriminating about the relative utilities of single-subject and group designs (Kazdin 1978, Kratochwill 1978).

Methodological articles are more frequent in clinical journals. Particularly significant are those dealing with innovative applications of sophisticated statistical approaches. For example, multivariate and discriminant analyses are advocated to handle multiple behavioral outcome measures (Kaplan & Litrownik 1977, Turner 1978). Time-series analyses and other quasi-experimental designs, path analyses, advanced methods for estimating size of effects, and empirical methods for selection of matching factors are all appearing more frequently (Gottman & Markman 1978).

The methodology of assessment is advancing particularly rapidly. Standardization of outcome measures is occurring, in part as a consequence of an important NIMH publication (Waskow & Parloff 1975). Generalizability theory is finding promising applications in evaluating outcome measures, particularly single-subject and observational data (Jones 1977, Mitchell 1979). Construct validity of outcome measures is receiving more attention, especially in the behavioral literature which heretofore has more assumed than discussed the validity of its performance measures (Cone 1977, Drabman & Furman 1980). Wolf (1978) has drawn particular attention to the importance of social validity of outcome measures.

Individually tailored outcome measures which still permit group comparisons have been developed in the form of dynamic assessment, problem-oriented records, goal-attainment scaling, and quantified target complaints. Kiesler (1977) and Mintz (1977), in reviewing individualized measures, identify unresolved issues in their measurement properties and application but conclude that they may provide the optimal combination of nomothetic and idiographic approaches.

Shapiro & Morris (1978), in a masterful review, warn that the history of psychological treatment is largely a history of placebo effects. One approach to dealing with nonspecific effects has been to operationalize them and to document factors which influence them, an effort which still has far to go (Kazdin 1979a,b). Attention-expectancy-placebo groups have become a standard design feature in order to insure that outcome can be attributed to specific interventions rather than nonspecific effects. Unfortunately, such pseudotreatments often are not very credible and hence elicit lower expectancy of benefit than do active treatments (Kazdin & Wilcoxon 1976). Ideally, then, groups should be equated for credibility, patient and therapist expectancies, and perhaps a number of other stylistic variables (Jacobson & Baucom 1977). Extensive control procedures may at times be unethical, impractical, or methodologically unsound for long-term research in clinical settings (O'Leary & Borkovec 1978). One solution may be techniques which minimize demand characteristics, such as counterdemand instructions and unobtrusive measures. Attention-placebo groups may not always be necessary, or even the control group of choice, as a function of the problem being studied and the questions being asked.

Renewed Interest in Diagnosis and Models of Psychopathology

Psychotherapy research has gone through a number of phases. The 1950s were marked by molecular studies of process, an overwhelming effort that has almost died away for lack of substantive results (but see Howard et al 1976, Orlinsky & Howard 1978). Research of the 1960s focused especially on testing the limits of new models of treatment and target definition, particularly behavioral ones. Large outcome and comparative studies were featured in the 1970s, but that decade also saw the reemergence of dominant cognitive and biological models. At the start of the 1980s, advocates of these approaches are led back to consideration of the nature of psychological disorder and the mechanisms of individual change. Outcome studies, particularly analog and disassembly designs, are used to test models of etiology and of processes of pathology as well as of therapy (thereby risking grave logical error). The revolution in biological psychiatry has given impetus to research establishing more descriptive and concrete patient typologies, a direction paralleled by the functional descriptions of behavioral assessment (Kanfer & Grimm 1977). Prognostic distinctions are proposed on the basis of specific symptom clusters or predominant dysfunction, with surprising convergence of different theoretical camps in goals and often in content (Beutler 1979, Craighead 1980).

In all of these developments, psychotherapy models are increasingly responsive to the theories and research of experimental psychology, in part as a legacy of the behavior therapies and harkening back to the pioneering suggestions of Goldstein et al (1966). Cognitive therapies are the most obvious example, springing from the cognitive revolution in psychology generally and effecting new integrations of behavioral and traditional treatment approaches (Lazarus 1977, Murray & Jacobson 1978). Equally important if less pervasive are influences by and adoptions from social psychology, social learning theory, epidemiology and stress research, and psychobiology (Dohrenwend & Dohrenwend 1974, Moos 1974, Rosenthal & Bandura 1978, Schwartz 1978, Strong 1978, Heller 1979).

Prominence of Self-Control Therapies

New cognitive emphases are evident even in traditional psychotherapies (Singer & Pope 1978) but far more so in the behavior therapies, albeit not without debate (Mahoney 1977, Rachlin 1977, Ledwidge 1978). Self-regulation, how it develops and is exercised, and the strategies people naturally use to control their own behavior have become prominent areas of cognitive social learning research (Mischel 1979). Therapeutic instruction in self-management methods is in consequence a rapidly developing field (Kanfer 1980). Self-regulatory models are also invoked to understand why people fail to maintain behaviors of presumed utility and desirability.

Kanfer's (1971) heuristic model, the basis for much of the research, identifies three components: self-monitoring, self-evaluation, and self-consequation. Affective arousal may be an additional essential component since as a corollary of self-evaluation it affects performance (Kirschenbaum & Karoly 1977). The effects of manipulating each of the components are examined in a very large literature (Kanfer 1977, Nelson 1977). Much of the outcome research has concentrated on habit disorders, for obvious reasons, but has included the full gamut of clinical problems from anxiety and stress to sexual problems, insomnia, and depression (Thoresen & Coates 1976). The proliferation of self-help manuals, distributed as popular trade books, similarly cover a gamut of problems from habit disorders to assertiveness to anxiety and depression. The manuals remain almost totally unevaluated (Glasgow & Rosen 1978).

As Mahoney & Arnkoff (1978) point out, other cognitive therapies such as rational emotive therapy (RET), self-instruction, or problem solving are largely self-regulatory in nature even though they entail different technical operations and different theoretical parentage. Each entails elements that the patient practices and carries out on his/her own, with therapy primarily aimed at instigating and training these self-regulatory techniques. Bandura (1977) has postulated that psychological procedures, whatever their format, act to create and strengthen expectations of one's personal effectiveness. Analog studies suggest that attribution and experience of choice do affect outcome (Kanfer & Grimm 1978) and that perceived self-efficacy is a sensitive indicator of level of improvement at different phases of treatment (Bandura & Adams 1977).

Developing Areas of Therapeutic Innovation

Maintenance of therapeutic gains over a reasonable period of time and their transfer to ordinary life settings are in one sense an aspect of outcome assessment. However, they are no longer viewed as by-products of ordinary treatment, but rather as specific targets in their own right. Karoly & Steffen (1980) and Goldstein & Kanfer (1979) summarize relevant literature and describe innovative proposals for enhancement of transfer and maintenance. A number of authors have suggested that while comparative studies of outcome often find little difference in short-term effects, treatments may differ in the durability and transfer they promote (Liberman 1978), an hypothesis yet to be well examined because adequate follow-up is so rare. Imber and his associates (1980) have synthesized literature on attribution, mastery, life events, and active change maintenance behaviors by the patient, to form a standardized set of procedures for "anticipatory maintenance." This approach and others like it reflect a growing sense of the importance of cognitive-social and environmental variables in influencing maintenance (Price 1979, Patterson & Fleischman 1979).

A second trend is planned short-term therapy, advocated by many as the treatment of choice for most patients (Bloom 1980, Strupp 1978). Impetus comes not only from efficiency, economy, and changing concepts of the nature and goals of psychotherapy, but also from social policy developments. Snow & Newton (1976) provide a sociopolitical description of the development of CMHCs, showing how their mandate guarantees that short-term individual therapy will be their major function. Most therapy today is, in fact, brief, both in research studies and in practice. The innovative element is in constructing models of change that not only justify brief therapy as best fitting the way people learn, but also prescribe the steps and phases of brief therapy and who most benefits from it.

Reviewers consistently conclude that treatments structured at the outset as time-limited appear to do as well as traditional time-unlimited therapies but that there is no evidence for the superiority of one variety over another (Butcher & Koss 1978). Empirical research in support of the models which structure short-term therapies is still sparse and weak, not so much because of inadequate science as because of conceptual and measurement difficulties inherent in process variables. The role of heightened emotional arousal in accentuating openness to change, or of awareness of temporal limits in promoting a goal focus and more rapid change are examples of key concepts yet to be subjected to thorough study.

In a related development, social and cultural influences on psychopathology form a literature large enough now to merit regular reviews in this series (King 1978). Prevention strategies rely heavily on stress models to identify at-risk populations and possible intervention targets, as for example in the growing literature on marital disruption (Bloom et al 1978). Stress and other environmental factors now figure importantly in estimating prognosis (Clum 1976, Vaughn & Leff 1976) and draw notice to coping and adaptive behaviors, social support systems, and social climate as vital in the recovery process (Cobb 1976, Dean & Lin 1977, Mechanic 1977). Measures of support and life events should be included as moderator variables in most outcome studies (Sarason et al 1978, Pilkonis 1979), just as extraorganizational factors must be taken into account in evaluating treatment programs more broadly.

When account is taken of environmental influences, the internal processing by the individual of these events also comes into greater prominence. Thus an environmental emphasis is accompanied by models which incorporate such internal cognitive variables as locus of control, attribution, and predictability of stress as moderators of the effects of stress (Miller 1980). There are ethical implications as well, when goals of treatment shift from self-fulfillment to individual success in social coping to perhaps the prosocial functioning of groups (Wolfe 1977, Kanfer 1979).

Therapeutic innovations are ongoing to discover and adapt to presumed special needs of subcultural groups. Next to nothing is known about the cognitive, affective, and behavioral characteristics of subgroups which could be used in devising group-specific treatments. Ethnic and socioeconomic parameters and perhaps sex do relate epidemiologically to high incidence and prevalence rates of psychopathology and to underutilization of services. Low SES and minority clients receive more severe diagnoses, receive differential treatment, more often terminate prematurely, and obtain poorer outcomes (Vail 1978, Sue 1977). On the other hand, some reviewers argue that minority and other disadvantaged groups are prematurely excluded from traditional therapies that would benefit them (Tischler et al 1975a,b). This discouraging picture, well summarized in Lorion's (1978) review, makes clear why NIMH priorities emphasize these disadvantaged groups, and at the same time why specialized training programs are struggling with the absence of knowledge by which to tailor their curricula (Anderson et al 1977, Bernal 1980).

Role induction and other pretherapy procedures can prepare disadvantaged clients for traditional therapies, and clinicians can be trained for more sensitive handling of cultural diversity (Heitler 1976). Another strategy has been to develop particular modifications of technique matched to client characteristics (Goldstein 1973, LeVine & Padilla 1980). Unhappily, in these areas too, validating research is poor or nonexistent. For example, feminist therapies are designed to counter sex biases in traditional therapies (Waskow 1976, Loeffler & Fiedler 1979), but it is uncertain whether sex bias is real or more an artifact of analog studies. Research on the nature and extent of sex bias in therapy is not yet adequate to guide professional and public policy-making (Stricker 1977, Whitley 1979). NIMH recently sponsored a conference on the psychotherapy of women (Brodsky & Hare-Mustin 1980), in part to stimulate more of the needed research.

TREATMENT OF DEPRESSION: AN ILLUSTRATION OF TRENDS AND ISSUES

The exploding literature on psychosocial treatment of depression exemplifies many of the current trends and issues of psychotherapy research as a whole. The boom has produced a number of comprehensive volumes summarizing the status of the field (Becker 1974, Gallant & Simpson 1976, Usdin 1977, Depue 1979, Rehm 1980).

Influences

A major influence on psychotherapy research of depression has come, paradoxically, from developments within the biologically oriented, research-based wing of psychiatry which grew out of the psychopharmacological discoveries of the 1950s. NIMH has been a catalyst throughout, shaping the directions and speed of work (Katz et al 1979). In the late 1960s the Psychopharmacology Branch sponsored a multicenter study of maintenance trials of drugs and psychotherapy for the prevention of relapse after drug reduction of acute symptoms. Results were consistent across centers: maintenance medication prevented symptom return; the psychotherapies had little effect on relapse but positive effects on social functioning, attitudes, and interpersonal behaviors (Weissman 1979). Until this initiative by psychopharmocologists, there were no adequately controlled studies of traditional psychotherapy efficacy with large homogeneous samples of depressives (Lieberman 1975), although research on behavioral treatments of depression was well underway.

In the same period, NIMH's Clinical Research Branch stimulated work on the psychobiology of depression. Important methodological and conceptual advances in nosology were one result. Strict research criteria for homogeneous groups were necessary for all types of investigation, and controlled drug trials, as well as other findings, provided partial evidence for subtypes of depression with different etiologies, mechanisms, and therapeutic responses (Feighner et al 1972, Spitzer et al 1977, Endicott & Spitzer 1978). Thus, while much of psychology and psychiatry were moving away from traditional diagnostic concerns, biologically oriented investigators were developing constructs and measures that were to become essential ingredients of more effective psychotherapy outcome research.

By the early 1970s, NIMH was concerned that whereas the majority of depressed patients received psychosocial therapies, little basic or clinical research existed to support those efforts. To rectify this imbalance, NIMH sponsored a conference to forecast research directions in the psychology of depression (Friedman & Katz 1974). Funding continued to support work on descriptive psychopathology and diagnosis, longitudinal studies of the natural course of depression, and epidemiological and clinical studies of social-cultural variations in depression. NIMH contracted for literature surveys summarizing the state of the art of psychotherapy and of assessment and outcome measurement for depression (Lieberman 1975, Rehm 1978). A 1979 conference again charged participants to recommend desirable research initiatives to NIMH, this time on behavioral treatments (Rehm 1980).

Most recently, NIMH determined that the time is finally ripe to invite contracts for a collaborative research program on psychotherapy. As the target they chose depression. This project, historic for our field, was influenced to a degree by legislative and financial pressures to produce efficacy data. More importantly, it was guided by the often proposed scientific strategy that gradual acquisition of *cumulative* knowledge requires coordinated planning and large scale efforts to assure standardized samples, measures, and interventions across investigators (NIMH 1980). The depression project is intended to be a stimulus to the field to initiate similar undertakings for other patient problems and therapies. The interplay of scientific, professional, financial, and personal factors in production of psychotherapy research is superbly illustrated in the vicissitudes of this project (Waskow 1979).

The psychopathological work in depression and mood changes excited general interest of psychotherapists. Psychodynamic formulations and treatment have become more detailed (Bemporad 1976). The big explosion in the last 10 years has been in cognitive and behavioral therapies. A behavioral view of depression as extinction had been in place for years but little studied (Ferster 1965). Laboratory studies, long a preferred source of behavioral models, produced experimental analogs of depression. Behaviorists' growing interest in self-control expanded the domain of legitimate models and intervention targets to more complex and covert phenomena.

Psychopathological Models and Research Strategies

For a long period, traditional and behavioral therapies operated with only relatively loose ties to general notions of the nature and etiology of psychopathology. Current work on depression stands in marked contrast. Relatively cohesive, comprehensive models of depression now identify points of intervention and suggest why the interventions should work. The models often offer clearly competing formulations: do depressed persons view actions and consequences as causally unrelated, as Seligman's helplessness model suggests, or do they overestimate their own causal responsibility for negative but not positive events, as Beck's scheme proposes (Abramson & Sackeim 1977, Rizley 1978); is the deficit in availability of reinforcement, as Lewinsohn assumes, or in reinforcer effectiveness, according to Beck and others (Nelson & Craighead 1977)? The components, mediators, and critical variables affected by therapy that are proposed in each model are being studied in designs more sophisticated than the earlier outcome studies. There is still risk that the models are overly simple and that overly simple tests of them will be done (Costello 1978). Some of the research may smack of cheap-and-quick, paralleling the hundreds of theses using minor variations of systematic desensitization or test anxiety as a handy analog. On the other hand, not only are treatment packages proving to have promising effectiveness, but this return to a complex integration of psychopathology, assessment, and treatment is essential to discover not only how to treat but what to treat in defined subgroups of patients.

Theoretical boundaries are to a degree blurred among the models on which major controlled outcome studies have been done. Particular operations appear in a number of models just as models under the same label often have quite varied operations. Other implicit elements overlap most of the models (e.g. high degree of structure, self-directed homework, instilled hopefulness). Such implicit elements are "nonspecific" or "indirect," but only in the sense that they may be by-products of those operations deemed crucial by the models' inventor, and may operate on variables not selected as primary by the model. Excellent reviews of the models are available: Kovacs (1979), Rehm & Kornblith (1979), Hollon (1980).

BEHAVIORAL MODELS   Two treatment systems comprise this category, those of Lewinsohn (1975) and of McLean (1976). Building on Lewinsohn's early programmatic research, both focus on the role of social skills in acquisition of positive reinforcement; have viewed behavior change as the precursor of change in mood, cognition, and somatic complaints; prescribe increased activity level; and intervene on communication patterns believed to maintain social isolation and depressive symptomology through loss of positive reinforcement. There are important differences between the two models as well, however. Lewinsohn and his associates (Lewinsohn et al 1976) hypothesize that low rate of response-contingent positive reinforcement constitutes a sufficient causal basis for parts of the depressive syndrome. A large number of studies have examined and mainly confirmed separate aspects of Lewinsohn's formulation. In a recent outcome study (Zeiss et al 1979) patient groups treated by interpersonal skills training, increase in pleasant activities, or cognitive change procedures all showed improvement in depressive symptoms, and outcome in different areas was not differentially dependent on the kind of therapy received. The authors suggest that reduced depression in the absence of specific therapy impact on matched target behaviors may be evidence for Bandura's (1977) self-efficacy model.

McLean's model (McLean et al 1973) assumes that depression is the consequence of ineffective coping techniques. A functional analysis of patient deficits and of personal and social environmental resources is combined with data from ongoing treatment response to guide explicit selections among available treatment components. A complex comparative outcome study (McLean & Hakstian 1979) demonstrated the superiority of this approach to short-term dynamic psychotherapy, drug therapy, and relaxation training. Behavior therapy produced the best outcome overall. The different treatments again did not produce differential effects on the outcome measures selected to match each treatment.

COGNITIVE-ATTRIBUTION MODELS   Seligman's learned helplessness model has attracted so much attention that an entire issue of the *Journal of Abnormal Psychology* (1978, 87, Number 1) was devoted to it. That issue contains a reformulation of the model incorporating aspects of attribution theory (Abramson et al 1978). According to the model, learning that consequences are noncontingent results in motivational, cognitive, and emotional deficits; the expectation of noncontingency produces helplessness. Depression is construed as a manifestation of learned helplessness (Seligman 1975). Laboratory studies of depressed and nondepressed subjects have tested treatment implications in analog situations. Early work on this and other models was flawed by reliance on mildly depressed college students as subjects (Hammen 1980). Critical reviews of the learned-helplessness model conclude that the attributions of depressed persons are not consistent with Seligman's theory (but partially supportive of Beck's attribution model) and that as it has been reformulated, the model lacks predictive precision and is not readily tested empirically (Rippere 1977, Depue & Monroe 1978, Rizley 1978, Wortman & Dintzer 1978).

Beck's (1976) model also emphasizes the role of cognitions in causing and maintaining depression: rigid automatic cognitive schemas of the depression-vulnerable person, activated by stress, produce distorted perceptions and interpretations that perpetuate unrealistic pessimism about the self, the world, and the future. Beck began with observed clinical phenomena for which he then constructed and tested laboratory analogs, whereas Seligman tried to relate previously obtained laboratory variables to clinical phenomena (Buchwald et al 1978). Efficacy of Beck's cognitive-behavioral therapy is comparatively strongly supported by high quality studies. A treatment manual facilitates replication studies (Beck et al 1979). Encouraged by early tentative results, Rush et al (1977) compared cognitive therapy with a tricyclic antidepressant. Both treatments significantly decreased depression, but cognitive therapy resulted in greater improvement, more cases of marked or complete remission, and fewer dropouts. These gains persisted at one year follow-up (Kovacs et al 1980). This is the only well controlled study to find a psychosocial treatment superior to drugs for depression.

SELF-CONTROL   Others have viewed depression within a self-control paradigm, but Rehm (1977) and his colleagues have performed the most systematic controlled research with this model. In an early study, their program produced more improvement than did a nonspecific therapy condition or a wait list control (Fuchs & Rehm 1977). In a later comparison with behavioral assertion training, self-control subjects gained more on self-control dependent measures and on indices of depression, while assertion training subjects showed greater gains on social skills outcome measures (Rehm et al 1979), an instance in which different treatments did produce differentiated outcomes on variables related to treatment type as well as differences in overall effect on syndrome depression. At one year follow-up, however, few between-group differences remained (Romano & Rehm 1979). Later studies examined contributions to outcome of individual components of the treatment package, with contradictory and puzzling results (Kornblith et al 1979). We have here, then, a somewhat cautionary tale in which an innovative package based on an etiologic-therapeutic model first shows very promising success, then in replications has somewhat less effectiveness, and finally in dismantling tests produces results quite at variance with the model although still therapeutically useful. Lewinsohn's model, as described above, has made a similar journey; the other two or three contenders for most effective psychosocial interventions have not yet been subjected to component analysis to see how they will fare.

Kanfer & Hagerman (1980) have extended the self-control model to improve its predictive utility and its heuristic value. Their differentiated model moves back toward individual functional analysis as the basis for intervention. They suggest that a variety of therapies may disrupt the cycle of depression at different points and hence all be equally effective.

INTERPERSONAL MODEL   While skill and social reinforcement deficit models suggest an interpersonal locus for much of the difficulty in depression, psychodynamic theories give greater importance to interactional processes as the core of depression. Klerman & Weissman's Interpersonal Therapy (IPT) uses a here-and-now approach to clarifying and modifying the patients' relationships, maladaptive perceptions, and social contingencies (Klerman et al 1979). In a series of studies comparing IPT with medication, IPT enhanced social adjustment, drug therapy reduced relapse, while the combination of both produced marginally superior additive effects (Klerman et al 1974, Weissman et al 1979). Additional evidence for the importance of interpersonal relationships in depression comes from data relating marital difficulties to symptom ebb and flow in depressed women (Weissman & Paykel 1974, Weissman & Klerman 1977).

Arieti & Bemporad (1978) present a psychoanalytic formulation of the depressive as a person incapable of autonomous gratification, self-direction, or self-definition separate from immediate external input, and who therefore looks to a "dominant other" person as the major source of direction, gratification, and self-esteem; when these unrealistic needs and expectations fail, depression results. Ilfeld (1977) concludes from epidemiological data that persistent difficulties with primary adult relationships are more strongly associated with depression than are conflicts in other relationships, a notion consistent with Arieti & Bemporad's stress on the "dominant other" and at variance with therapeutic training in general social skills. Coyne (1976a,b) has found that people tend to react with avoidance and ambiguous or deceptive messages when conversing with depressed persons. One implication is that cognitions of depressed persons may be far more consistent with the information (and misinformation) they are given by the behavior of others than is assumed in models emphasizing cognitive distortions.

MODULAR APPROACHES   Several of the models discussed above provide for matching subgroups of patients to treatment by selection of a specified set of targets and training components. Others hope to cover individual needs through multimodal treatment packages. Liberman (1980) at the extreme holds that any ideal goal of matching patient subgroups to treatment type is "fatuous" because it ignores the overarching importance of individual differences. Liberman proposes a modular approach as more efficient and effective. A flow chart guides each treatment decision by linking results of intensive individual assessment to a treatment module, e.g. brief support, drugs, self-control training, family-social network therapy, desensitization. The mammoth task of research on the modular approach would require validation of the assessment process, each separate component module, the sequencing of modules, and the decision-rules governing their application. Liberman's approach is basically a pragmatic stepwise outcome-based method, probably close to what therapists actually do but more explicit in its heuristics of decision-rules and sequencing.

OTHER MODELS   Affect-mediated interventions assume that depression is a function of inhibition by conditioned anxiety responses of potentially satisfying behaviors (Wolpe 1979). Typically interventions have been systematic desensitization and relaxation training. Many commentators agree that anxiety is an important ingredient in some depressive behavior (Gersh & Fowles 1979), but there is little research support for anxiety reduction therapies.

The life stress model is gradually influencing other formulations, even though it offers little direct guidance to therapeutic interventions. Depression is preceded by more than the usual number of stressful events, especially those representing losses and exits (Paykel 1979). Continuing stress is associated with continuation of symptoms. Measures of life events are appearing as predictors or covariates in comparative studies with useful results. McLean and Hakstian (1979), for example, found life stress events among the few important predictors of outcome for depressed patients, regardless of type of therapy. The stress model is also evident within psychodynamic formulations. Horowitz (1976) proposes that stress produces changes in states of mind, which in turn produce depressive symptoms. He and his colleagues are using process studies of brief psychotherapy to test his model and the effectiveness of the interventions (Horowitz 1979). Stress and life event models also have interesting ties to attribution, social support systems, and social roles (Brown & Harris 1978, Hammen & Cochran 1980). Defining vulnerability and linking it to precipitating factors and mechanisms for producing depression is a major challenge for current stress research (Radloff & Rae 1979). Since all other models incorporate stressful events to a degree, mechanisms they propose may be joined with life event research to produce a more detailed and comprehensive system.

Methodological Issues

The usual litany of complaints applies to depression research, some of them especially pointedly. Until far more is known about the relationship between mild and severe affective complaints, treatment research is on very thin ice when it employs nonclinical samples. To insure treatment relevance and comparability across samples, subjects should meet research diagnostic criteria for affective disorder as well as reasonable cutoff scores on multiple measures of symptom severity. Samples need to be large enough to allow powerful tests of null hypotheses as well as to make a beginning on the matching issue using more powerful designs. No outcome study can warrant much confidence until investigators not associated with the originator of the model have replicated it. There should be some basis for believing that the frequency and duration of treatment are adequate; ten or so sessions is the norm, if not the upper limit, in most studies, without data tracking change over time to support arbitrary termination limits. Since the more effective treatments are complex packages, disassembly designs are necessary early on, both to test the conceptual model and to streamline treatment. Given the vagaries of sample composition, untreated control groups still seem to be mandatory in one form or another (e.g. unscheduled treatment). Need is great for measures less dependent on self-report and more applicable to naturalistic studies, attentive to social-environmental and stress factors, and more differentiated and balanced in tapping the different dimensions of depression. Attention should be given to the *magnitude* of benefit on each dimension since some problems seem to endure after acute symptoms wane and since statistically significant change does not necessarily denote reestablishment of a happy or even normative lifestyle.

A Common Theme and Surprising Omission

All models of depression in one way or another emphasize deficit in positive reinforcement but differ in their prescriptions of necessary and sufficient points of intervention. Can scheduled pleasant events be salutory as long as one "dominant other" possesses all self-enhancing goods? Can self-evaluation and self-reinforcement training overcome aversive or avoidant reactions from others, or major disputes with a spouse? Can analysis of the roots of dependency provide social skills to broaden the range of potential reinforcing others?

Wachtel (1977) has urged behavioral therapists to operate more often on *content* suggested by psychodynamic clinical studies. One content item seemingly largely ignored by the cognitive and behavioral models, probably because it is encased in such a loose construct as "dependency," is the nature and range of persons who are major sources of reinforcement for a patient, as determined in part by the person's own perception. More broadly put, behavioral theories and interventions to a surprising degree neglect the person's functional social *environment.* Klein & Gurman (1980) argue that matching control and treatment samples or measuring outcome cannot be valid unless the ecological context of depression is taken into account. Only rarely have there been attempts to assess directly the primary social environment, or to develop interactional behavioral models comparable to Patterson's coercion hypothesis for marital or parent-child interactions (Patterson & Reid 1970). Such data are likely to be revealing since the behavior of depressed persons seems to be highly situation specific (Libet & Lewinsohn 1973). Naturalistic, longitudinal studies are the best route to addressing not only situational variability and possible deficits in the interpersonal behavior of depressed persons, but also such questions as what they do when they are not depressed (within or between episodes), and how untreated episodes come to an end (Jacobson 1980). It is notable that in this area as in others (e.g. the assertiveness literature), behavior therapy researchers increasingly omit the hallmarks of their approach: emphasis on person-environment interaction, observational data, micro-analyses of the elements of a functional analysis in specific situations. If more naturalistic, longitudinal studies are done, taking account of findings from the stress and epidemiological literatures, behavioral models may yet be restored to their natural posture.

STATUS OF THERAPIES FOR SPECIFIC PROBLEMS

The trends described earlier and illustrated by the depression literature characterize work on other target problems as well. In the following sections we point out examples of this along with summaries of the status of research in each problem area.

Neuroses

In addition to the standard techniques of systematic desensitization (SDS), progressive relaxation (PR), and flooding, current treatments of anxiety include training in biofeedback and anxiety management. Anxiety-management programs instruct clients in how to identify the indices of their anxiety and to execute anxiety-reducing skills, such as relaxation, cue-controlled SDS, or cognitive restructuring, which are applicable across problem situations and thus should enhance generalization. Although these treatments are usually superior to no-treatment controls, modeling, supportive psychotherapy, and even credible placebo treatments may be as effective in reducing anxiety at least on self-report measures (Barrios & Shigetomi 1979).

Phobias are effectively treated by SDS, cognitive restructuring, flooding, and participant modeling (Rosenthal & Bandura 1978). Implosion with vivid, horrifying images is used less frequently now, since prolonged exposure to the feared stimulus under benign conditions appears a more comfortable and more effective treatment (Foa et al 1977). Understanding the differential effects of these treatments perhaps must await progress in multidimensional models of the fear response and in corresponding multiple measures (Mineka 1979).

Cognitive interventions, including thought stopping, covert conditioning, rational-emotive therapy, and self-instruction are utilized with obsessive-compulsive disorders. Investigators hope that such procedures will improve upon the standard treatments of flooding and response prevention by including associated problems such as depression and interpersonal difficulties, as well as eliminating the primary symptoms (Heppner 1978, Foa & Steketee 1979).

Methodological deficiencies continue to limit the conclusions that can be drawn regarding treatments of neuroses (Barrios 1979). Nonspecific expectancy factors remain an alternative explanation in many studies (Lick & Bootzin 1975). Furthermore, reliance on mildly fearful or anxious college students as subjects and on laboratory tests as dependent variables makes questionable the applicability of this research to clinical populations (Mathews 1978).

Behavioral Medicine

The application of psychological measures and treatments to a variety of health care problems is a rapidly growing field. In the area of biofeedback alone, for example, national and state societies have been developed, national conferences held, and specialized journals, training programs, and certification examinations established (Schwartz & Weiss 1978, Stachnik 1980). Comprehensive reviews are provided by Schwartz & Beatty (1977), Epstein et al (1979), McNamara (1979), and the volumes edited by Ferguson & Taylor (1980). Only a few major trends are described here.

New models of comprehensive health care stress the role of a wide variety of psychological factors, including stress, lifestyle habits, abilities and skills, defensive techniques, and motivational factors in maintaining health and coping with illness (Schwartz 1978). Techniques ranging from desensitization and operant conditioning to self-control and problem solving are used to complement medical treatments for a variety of disorders. Seizures, tics, asthma, and insomnia, for example, are common targets (Knapp et al 1976, Mostofsky & Balaschak 1977, Knapp & Wells 1978). By far the most active area of publication is the use of biofeedback for muscular tension and migraine headaches and for hypertension (Blanchard & Miller 1977). Despite continuing debate concerning the role of muscle contractions in the etiology of headaches, treatments utilizing frontalis EMG or finger temperature biofeedback appear effective in reducing both tension and migraine headaches (Bakal 1975). Biofeedback techniques may also reduce blood pressure, but usually only temporarily. It remains unclear, however, whether biofeedback significantly improves upon relaxation alone, and what role placebo effects may play (Seer 1979). Biofeedback procedures apparently are most effective when applied to the specific physiological responses that comprise a disorder. For example, heart rate feedback can control premature ventricular contractions, and skin temperature biofeedback may reduce the painful vascular constriction in the extremities caused by Raynauld's Disease (Blanchard & Miller 1977). Multicomponent packages which teach coping skills as well as relaxation may be more effective for multiply determined disorders such as hypertension and headaches (Holroyd et al 1977).

A variety of methods are used to control pain (Sanders 1979, Turk & Genest 1979, Turk et al 1979). Preexposure to medical procedures and participant modeling may reduce stress, and cognitive-imaginal strategies may heighten tolerance of pain (Beers & Karoly 1979). Stress innoculation programs, involving such components as relaxation, cognitive skill training, and environmental manipulations, show promise (Horan et al 1977, Weisenberg 1977).

Sexual Dysfunctions and Preferences

Recent reviews on treatment of sexual dysfunctions include: Ascher & Clifford (1976), Adams & Sturgis (1977), and McConaghy (1977). Methodological inadequacies characterize much of the research—samples are typically small, heterogeneous, and biased, and outcome criteria often unsubstantiated (Farkas 1978).

Investigators are now questioning the propriety of reorientation programs for homosexual males and lesbians in the belief that such programs reflect discriminatory social practices. Recommended instead is research on gay lifestyles in recognition of the heterogeneity of homosexual populations, including studies of the dynamics of gay relationships, ingredients of positive gay identity, and advantages and disadvantages of varying degrees of gay identification and commitment (Morin 1977, Davison 1978).

Aversive conditioning, once the stock in trade for reducing the arousal properties of stimuli considered to be deviant, has been challenged because it does not promote appropriate sexual arousal. Alternative or adjunctive techniques that target heterosexual arousal and general social adjustment include orgasmic reconditioning, assertiveness training, operant interventions, and cognitive restructuring.

Multiple component packages have dominated treatment of sexual dysfunctions since Masters and Johnson's first program (Masters & Johnson 1970). Critics have asserted that the standard packages may neglect crucial interpersonal factors which often affect sexual interaction. Communication training, behavior exchange contracts, and assertiveness training target such factors and may promote treatment maintenance. Newly developed individual, group, and conjoint behavioral programs for nonorgasmic women show promise (Sotile & Kilmann 1977).

Problems in Social Adjustment and Social Skill Deficits

Social skill models of interpersonal adjustment have become more elaborate and precise as training programs have been expanded and applied to more diverse clinical populations. Comprehensive reviews include: Heimberg et al (1977), Rich & Schroeder (1976), Curran (1977), and Twentyman & Zimering (1979).

Assessment of skill deficits is central. Behavioral ratings and self-report inventories have been criticized for their simplicity and questionable validity (Bellack et al 1979, Hersen & Bellack 1977). Skill models are becoming more complex by taking account of interactional variables such as situational appropriateness, sense of timing, and interpersonal consequences, and of covert mediators like self-efficacy (Fischetti et al 1977). Clinically relevant social skills and their discrete behavioral components may be identified by a number of methods: discrete behavioral ratings may be compared with global skill ratings (social-criterion validation method); significant others may be asked to identify behaviors they value (critical other method); and responses of subgroups with high global skill ratings may be contrasted with those of low-rated persons (competent subgroup method). Particularly useful and popular is a two-step process of social validation in which discrete behavioral skill components are identified by one of these methods and then taught to a low rated group. Any resultant improvements in social interaction abilities, measured by an independent criterion such as judges' ratings, suggest that the behaviors selected were valid skill components (Kupke et al 1979).

Training programs typically combine several components, each of which theoretically facilitates a different aspect of skill acquisition. For example, instructions and modeling provide a cognitive representation of the desired behavior, while rehearsal and performance feedback enable successive approximations. Cognitive restructuring may reduce anxiety and enhance self-efficacy, thereby promoting generalization to naturalistic settings (Phillips 1978, Rosenthal & Bandura 1978, Ladd 1979). A lack of systematic application of techniques and the diversity of treatment components studied, however, have made it difficult to substantiate this model empirically. The research base is narrow—samples are usually either mildly anxious college students or chronic psychiatric patients, and dating and assertiveness are grossly overrepresented skill areas. At the same time the usefulness of various training components may depend on the client population and the nature of their skill deficits. Modeling, for example, can add significantly to the effects of coaching assertiveness with schizophrenic inpatients, who may lack an adequate understanding of what constitutes an assertive response, or who have difficulties integrating appropriate verbal and nonverbal behaviors. Neurotic inpatients, on the other hand, who may have less severe deficits, may benefit from practice and instructions alone (Eisler et al 1978). Given such patient by problem by treatment technique interactions, empirical advances require more broadly based, applied research.

Chronic Psychiatric Disorders

As Mosher & Keith (1979) summarize in their review, treatment of schizophrenia and other chronic psychiatric disorders has been revolutionized in the last 15 years. Extended hospitalization has given way to early release, since brief hospitalization may be as effective as longer stays in fostering community adjustment and preventing relapse (Penk et al 1978). The consequence is that community programs bear the brunt of providing the social support and competence building basic to posthospital adjustment. A range of services is offered which seem to reduce recidivism and raise patient satisfaction, among them family therapy, skill training, companion programs, and halfway or day care. Because the typical program entails a melange of poorly specified components assessed by global outcome measures that are confounded with many other influences (e.g. recidivism), available research offers no clear evaluation of their effectiveness (Iscoe 1977). Probably only by incorporating specifically tailored skill training can aftercare programs achieve changes in the social skill deficits common in psychiatric populations (Trower et al 1978). Several projects report success in doing this (Goldsmith & McFall 1975).

Research on psychosocial treatment within the hospital itself largely comprises token economies and milieu therapy. Outcomes of token economies run from extremely to moderately successful, to only equivocally better than traditional programs (Hall et al 1977, Miller & Dermer 1979). In a definitive large-scale clinical study, Paul & Lentz (1977) found a comprehensive token economy significantly more effective than either a milieu therapy program or a traditional hospital program. The token economy fostered higher levels of functioning, achieved greater numbers of institutional releases, and was more cost-effective. Maintenance and generalization of treatment gains, however, are still central concerns with token economies (Hersen 1976). The use of deprivation to facilitate token economies continues to be embroiled in ethical and legal debate (American Bar Association 1977).

Habit Disorders

Obesity, smoking, alcoholism, and drug abuse are behavior excesses that comprise a large volume of research. Their appeal to investigators may be a function of their discrete response topography, which reduces the ambiguity in goal setting and outcome measurement that plagues other areas of outcome research. The result is a relatively broad base of methodologically sound, often replicated findings which serve to illustrate many trends we have discussed. Comprehensive review articles include Abramson (1977), Bellack (1977), and Leon (1976) on eating; Lichtenstein & Danaher (1976) and McFall (1978) on smoking; and Briddell & Nathan (1976), Lovibond (1977), and Marlatt (1979) on alcoholism. Bemis (1978) and Kellerman (1977) review anorexia nervosa, and Callner (1975) reviews current therapies for drug abusers.

While aversive conditioning and covert sensitization procedures have generally failed to produce behavior change or weight loss in the obese (Abramson 1977), these procedures have shown some utility in suppressing smoking and drinking. Rapid smoking, in particular, is effective, although some debate exists concerning its potential health risks for persons with cardiovascular disease (Hall et al 1979). The most effective aversive strategy for alcoholics may be self-administered shock (Wilson & Tracey 1976). Unless aversion techniques are embedded in a comprehensive treatment package, however, maintenance should not be expected.

Self-control techniques are becoming prominent for all the habit disorders. Stimulus control, for example, while rarely effective by itself, may significantly add to package programs in changing eating and smoking habits. Self-monitoring can be effective for obesity, particularly when it is completed prior to food intake, is focused on rate of food consumption, and is combined with self-reward (Green 1978). Self-monitoring of blood alcohol level is frequently included in the treatment of alcoholism when controlled drinking rather than abstinence is the goal (Briddell & Nathan 1976). Self-directed contingency management may be as effective as externally controlled contingencies in changing eating and smoking habits, and is consistently superior to control treatments and insight-oriented therapies (Hall et al 1977). When individuals are trained in self-standard setting and problem solving, self-control treatments for obesity may be more effective

(Loro et al 1979). Relaxation techniques, problem solving skills, and assertiveness training may similarly help clients deal with problematic smoking and drinking situations (Intagliata 1978, Marlatt 1979).

Methods to enhance maintenance are the single biggest need in dealing with habit disorders, since most successfully treated patients return to pretreatment levels within months after termination. Initial investigations of therapist fading and booster sessions show some promise for weight control (Kingsley & Wilson 1977), but have not been effective for smoking (Elliott & Denney 1978). Jeffery & Coates (1978) suggest that improving maintenance may require greater attention to a number of variables, including stress management, interpersonal and coping skills to resist urges to smoke, drink, or eat too much. Social support can also be a crucial factor in preventing relapse and promoting maintenance. In treatments for smoking and eating, spouses or families may be involved (Wilson & Brownell 1978), while for alcohol abusers, comprehensive aftercare, including peer support, group counseling, family involvement, and occupational counseling may be necessary (Azrin 1976).

To date, since no one treatment has emerged as clearly superior for any of the habit disorders, most reviewers recommend broad treatment packages with three basic kinds of components. First, some components must suppress or establish environmental control over the problematic responses, e.g. aversive procedures, stimulus control, or self-monitoring. Second, it is important to provide skill training to remediate any functionally related problems, such as deficits in self-regulation, problem solving, interpersonal or other coping skills. Finally, provisions for environmental support should be included to facilitate maintenance. While such packages have produced marked gains, their superiority over simpler, more cost-effective methods is not established (Miller 1978).

IN CLOSING

Psychotherapy research is an active, exciting place to be these days. Integration among treatment models and with other areas of psychology is adding intellectual zest. Enthusiasm for any data set, construct, or model must be tempered, however, by Meehl's (1978) cautionary note that "in soft psychology theories rise and decline, come and go, more as a function of baffled boredom than anything else" (p. 807). Reading Frank's (1974) recounting of 25 years of pioneering research on psychotherapy is a poignant experience; the fruits of that labor seem to have had so little influence on what therapists do (although a great deal on what they think about what they do); many of the results have just faded away. Frank and Meehl reach parallel conclusions: that statistically significant group differences do not readily translate into clinical importance. If those who write about psychotherapy research find it difficult to make sense of disparate results, often drawn from poor science, they can offer little clear direction to practitioners or policy makers.

Discontent grows within each therapeutic school as their limits become evident; too much research has dealt with detailed perusal of trivia or with supposed advantages of one form over another, to the neglect of common elements which may be the bases for effectiveness of all (Anonymous 1980). There is another point as well: Kuhn (1977) locates the "essential tension" of science within the scientist, who must be thoroughly trained in a line of convergent thinking in order to use divergent results creatively, who must have "a thoroughgoing commitment to the tradition with which, if he is successful, he will break" (p. 235). For psychotherapy research, the solution may be a new convergence on common clinical intervention strategies, robust phenomena derived from common observations by clinicians of varying orientations. Alternatively, it may be that psychotherapy researchers, under the societal pressures of accountability, economic access, and political value choices, are to be seen more accurately as applied scientists or inventors whose cognitive tools and models are quite different from those of the basic scientist. For Kuhn (1977), the distinction is that basic science practitioners choose their own problems

> characteristically ... selected in areas where paradigms were clearly applicable but where exciting puzzles remained about how to apply them and how to make nature conform to the results of the application. Clearly, the inventor and applied scientist are not generally free to choose puzzles of this sort. Often the decision to seek a cure ... must be made with little reference to the state of the relevant science (p. 238).

The applied scientist, to whose problems no paradigm need be fully relevant, is a divergent thinker whose requisite personality and training may be quite different from the basic scientist.

It may be that psychotherapy research must for now follow the path of the applied scientist, conducting large clinical trials based on eclectic strategies or techniques in order to find supportable remedies for specified maladies. At the same time others of a more paradigmatic bent may be pursuing the intriguing puzzles which may someday transform the field into a science. It is a truism that clinical psychology is the application of the basic science of psychology. Yet the distinctions Kuhn is making have been lost when applied problems are approached as if one paradigm is fully relevant, or when efforts to find practical answers to what works best for now are attacked as if merit belongs solely to the more basic questions of underlying processes governing pathology and change.

Literature Cited

Abramson, E. E. 1977. Behavioral approaches to weight control: An updated review. *Behav. Res. Ther.* 15:355–63

Abramson, L. Y., Sackeim, H. A. 1977. A paradox in depression: Uncontrollability and self-blame. *Psychol. Bull.* 84:838–51

Abramson, L. Y., Seligman, M. E. P., Teasdale, J. D. 1978. Learned helplessness in humans: Critique and reformulation. *J. Abnorm. Psychol.* 87:49–74

Adams, H. E., Sturgis, E. T. 1977. Status of behavioral reorientation techniques in the modification of homosexuality: A review. *Psychol. Bull.* 84:1171–88

Agras, W. S., Kazdin, A. E., Wilson, G. T. 1979. *Behavior Therapy: Toward an Applied Clinical Science.* San Francisco: Freeman. 173 pp.

American Bar Association, Commission on the Mentally Disabled. 1977. Mental health standards and human rights. *Ment. Disab. Law Rep.* 2:291–303

Anderson, G., Bass, B. A., Munford, P. R., Wyatt, G. E. 1977. A seminar on the assessment and treatment of Black patients. *Prof. Psychol.* 8:340–48

Anonymous. 1980. Toward the delineation of therapeutic change principles. *Am. Psychol.* In press

Arieti, S., Bemporad, J. 1978. *Severe and Mild Depression: The Psychotherapeutic Approach.* New York: Basic Books. 453 pp.

Ascher, L. M., Clifford, R. E. 1976. Behavioral considerations in the treatment of sexual dysfunction. *Prog. Behav. Modif.* 3:242–93

Azrin, N. H. 1976. Improvements in the community-reinforcement approach to alcoholism. *Behav. Res. Ther.* 14:339–48

Bakal, D. A. 1975. Headache: A biopsychological perspective. *Psychol. Bull.* 82:369–82

Bandura, A. 1977. Self efficacy: Towards a unifying theory of behavioral change. *Psychol. Rev.* 84:191–215

Bandura, A., Adams, N. E. 1977. Analysis of self-efficacy theory of behavioral change. *Cognit. Ther. Res.* 1:287–310

Barlow, D. H., Hayes, S. C. 1979. Alternating treatments design: One strategy for comparing the effects of two treatments in a single subject. *J. Appl. Behav. Anal.* 12:199–210

Barrios, B. A. 1979. Publication trends in behavior therapy analogue research on phobias. *J. Behav. Ther. Exp. Psychiatry* 10:203–5

Barrios, B. A., Shigetomi, C. C. 1979. Coping-skills training for the management of anxiety: A critical review. *Behav. Ther.* 10:491–522

Beck, A. T. 1976. *Cognitive Therapy and the Emotional Disorders.* New York: Int. Univ. Press. 356 pp.

Beck, A. T., Rush, A. J., Shaw, B. F., Emery, G. 1979. *Cognitive Therapy of Depression.* New York: Guilford. 425 pp.

Becker, J. 1974. *Depression: Theory and Research.* New York: Wiley. 239 pp.

Beers, T. M. Jr., Karoly, P. 1979. Cognitive strategies, expectancy, and coping style in the control of pain. *J. Consult. Clin. Psychol.* 47:179–80

Bellack, A. S. 1977. Behavioral treatment for obesity: Appraisal and recommendations. *Prog. Behav. Modif.* 4:1–38

Bellack, A. S., Hersen, M., Lamparski, D. 1979. Role-play tests for assessing social skills: Are they valid? Are they useful? *J. Consult. Clin. Psychol.* 47:335–42

Bemis, K. M. 1978. Current approaches to the etiology and treatment of anorexia nervosa. *Psychol. Bull.* 85:593–617

Bemporad, J. 1976. Psychotherapy of the depressive character. *J. Am. Acad. Psychoanal.* 4:347–72

Bergin, A. E., Strupp, H. H. 1972. *Changing Frontiers in the Science of Psychotherapy.* Chicago: Aldine-Atherton. 468 pp.

Bergin, A. E., Suinn, R. M. 1975. Individual psychotherapy and behavior therapy. *Ann. Rev. Psychol.* 26:509–56

Bernal, M. E. 1980. Hispanic issues in curriculum and training in psychology. *Hisp. J. Behav. Sci.* In press

Bernstein, D. A., Nietzel, M. T. 1977. Demand characteristics in behavior modification: The natural history of a "nuisance." *Prog. Behav. Modif.* 4:119–62

Beutler, L. E. 1979. Toward specific psychological therapies for specific conditions. *J. Consult. Clin. Psychol.* 47:882–97

Blanchard, E. B., Miller, S. T. 1977. Psychological treatment of cardiovascular disease. *Arch. Gen. Psychiatry* 34:1402–13

Bloom, B. L. 1980. Social and community interventions. *Ann. Rev. Psychol.* 31:111–42

Bloom, B. L., Asher, S. J., eds. 1980. *Psychiatric Patient Rights and Patient Advocacy: Issues and Evidence.* New York: Human Sci. Press

Bloom, B. L., Asher, S. J., White, S. W. 1978. Marital disruption as a stressor: A review and analysis. *Psychol. Bull.* 85:867–94

Briddell, D. W., Nathan, P. E. 1976. Behavior assessment and modification with alcoholics: Current status and future trends. *Prog. Behav. Modif.* 2:2–52

Brodsky, A. M., Hare-Mustin, R., eds. 1980. *Women in Psychotherapy: Assessment of Research and Practice.* New York: Guilford. 410 pp.

Brown, G. W., Harris, T. 1978. *Social Origins of Depression: A Study of Psychiatric Disorder in Women.* New York: Free Press. 399 pp.

Buchwald, A. M., Coyne, J. C., Cole, C. S. 1978. A critical evaluation of the learned helplessness model of depression. *J. Abnorm. Psychol.* 87:180–93

Butcher, J. N., Koss, M. P. 1978. Research on brief and crisis-oriented psychotherapies. See Garfield & Bergin 1978, pp. 725–68

Callner, D. A. 1975. Behavioral treatment approaches to drug abuse: A critical review of the research. *Psychol. Bull.* 82:143–64

Claghorn, J. L., ed. 1976. *Successful Psychotherapy.* New York: Brunner/Mazel. 208 pp.

Clum, G. A. 1976. Role of stress in the prognosis of mental illness. *J. Consult. Clin. Psychol.* 44:54–60

Cobb, S. 1976. Social support as a moderator of life stress. *Psychosom. Med.* 38:300–14

Cone, J. D. 1977. The relevance of reliability and validity for behavioral assessment. *Behav. Ther.* 8:411–26

Costello, C. G. 1978. A critical review of Seligman's laboratory experiments on learned helplessness and depression in humans. *J. Abnorm. Psychol.* 87:21–31

Coyne, J. C. 1976a. Toward an interactional description of depression. *Psychiatry* 39:28–40

Coyne, J. C. 1976b. Depression and the response of others. *J. Abnorm. Psychol.* 85:186–93

Craighead, W. E. 1980. Away from a unitary model of depression. *Behav. Ther.* 11:122–28

Curran, J. P. 1977. Skills training as an approach to the treatment of heterosexual-social anxiety: A review. *Psychol. Bull.* 84:140–57

Davison, G. C. 1978. Not can but ought: The treatment of homosexuality. *J. Consult. Clin. Psychol.* 46:170–72

Dean, A., Lin, N. 1977. The stress-buffering role of social support: Problems and prospects for systematic investigation. *J. Nerv. Ment. Dis.* 165:403–17

Depue, R. A., ed. 1979. *The Psychobiology of the Depressive Disorders: Implications for the Effects of Stress.* New York: Academic. 446 pp.

Depue, R. A., Monroe, S. M. 1978. Learned helplessness in the perspective of the depressive disorders: Conceptual and definitional issues. *J. Abnorm. Psychol.* 87:3–20

Dohrenwend, B. S., Dohrenwend, B. P., eds. 1974. *Stressful Life Events: Their Nature and Effects.* New York: Wiley. 340 pp.

Drabman, R. S., Furman, W. 1980. Behavioral procedures in the classroom. In *Behavioral Community Psychology,* ed. D. Glenwick, L. Jason, pp. 81–107. New York: Praeger. 495 pp.

Edwards, D. W., Greene, L. R., Abramowitz, S. I., Davidson, C. V. 1979. National health insurance, psychotherapy, and the poor. *Am. Psychol.* 34:411–19

Eisler, R. M., Blanchard, E. B., Fitts, H., Williams, J. G. 1978. Social skill training with and without modeling for schizophrenic and non-psychotic hospitalized psychiatric patients. *Behav. Modif.* 2:147–72

Elliott, C. H., Denney, D. R. 1978. A multiple-component treatment approach to smoking reduction. *J. Consult. Clin. Psychol.* 46:1330–39

Endicott, J., Spitzer, R. L. 1978. A diagnostic interview: The Schedule for Affective Disorders and Schizophrenia. *Arch. Gen. Psychiatry* 35:837–44

Epstein, L. H., Katz, R. C., Zlutnick, S. 1979. Behavioral medicine. *Prog. Behav. Modif.* 7:117–71

Farkas, G. M. 1978. Comments on Levin et al. and Rosen and Kopel: Internal and external validity issues. *J. Consult. Clin. Psychol.* 46:1515–16

Feighner, J. P., Robins, E., Guze, S. B., Woodruff, R. A., Winokur, G., Munoz, R. 1972. Diagnostic criteria for use in psychiatric research. *Arch. Gen. Psychiatry* 26:57–63

Ferguson, J. M., Taylor, C. B., eds. 1980. *The Comprehensive Handbook of Behavioral Medicine,* Vols. 1–3. Jamaica, NY: SP Med. Sci. Books. 1050 pp.

Ferster, C. B. 1965. Classification of behavioral pathology. In *Research in Behavior Modification,* ed. L. Krasner, L. P. Ullmann, pp. 6–26. New York: Holt, Rinehart & Winston. 403 pp.

Fischetti, M., Curran, J. P., Wessberg, H. W. 1977. Sense of timing: A skill deficit in heterosexual-socially anxious males. *Behav. Modif.* 1:179–94

Foa, E. B., Blau, J. S., Prout, M., Latimer, P. 1977. Is horror a necessary component of flooding (implosion)? *Behav. Res. Ther.* 15:397–402

Foa, E. B., Steketee, G. S. 1979. Obsessive-compulsives: Conceptual issues and treatment interventions. *Prog. Behav. Modif.* 8:1–54

Frank, J. D. 1974. Therapeutic components of psychotherapy: A 25-year progress report of research. *J. Nerv. Ment. Dis.* 159:325–42

Frank, J. D. 1979. The present status of outcome studies. *J. Consult. Clin. Psychol.* 47:310–16

Frank, J. D., Hoehn-Saric, R., Imber, S. D., Liberman, B. L., Stone, A. R. 1978. *Effective Ingredients of Successful Psychotherapy.* New York: Brunner/Mazel. 224 pp.

Friedman, R. J., Katz, M. M., eds. 1974. *The Psychology of Depression: Contemporary Theory and Research.* New York: Wiley. 318 pp.

Fuchs, C. Z., Rehm, L. P. 1977. A self-control behavior therapy program for depression. *J. Consult. Clin. Psychol.* 45:206–15

Gallant, D. M., Simpson, G. M., eds. 1976. *Depression: Behavioral, Biochemical, Diagnostic and Treatment Concepts.* New York: Spectrum. 351 pp.

Garfield, S. L. 1978. Research on client variables in psychotherapy. See Garfield & Bergin 1978, pp. 191–232

Garfield, S. L., Bergin, A. E., eds. 1978. *Handbook of Psychotherapy and Behavior Change: An Empirical Analysis.* New York: Wiley. 1024 pp. 2nd ed.

Gersh, F. S., Fowles, D. C. 1979. Neurotic depression: The concept of anxious depression. See Depue 1979, pp. 81–104

Glasgow, R. E., Rosen, G. M. 1978. Behavioral bibliotherapy: A review of self-help behavior therapy manuals. *Psychol. Bull.* 85:1–23

Goldsmith, J. B., McFall, R. M. 1975. Development and evaluation of an interpersonal skill-training program for psychiatric inpatients. *J. Abnorm. Psychol.* 84:51–58

Goldstein, A. P. 1973. *Structured Learning Therapy: Toward a Psychotherapy for the Poor.* New York: Academic. 421 pp.

Goldstein, A. P., Heller, K., Seechrest, L. B., eds. 1966. *Psychotherapy and the Psychology of Behavior Change.* New York: Wiley. 472 pp.

Goldstein, A. P., Kanfer, F. H., eds. 1979. *Maximizing Treatment Gains: Transfer Enhancement in Psychotherapy.* New York: Academic. 487 pp.

Gomes-Schwartz, B., Hadley, S. W., Strupp, H. H. 1978. Individual psychotherapy and behavior therapy. *Ann. Rev. Psychol.* 29:435–71

Gottman, J. M., Markman, H. J. 1978. Experimental designs in psychotherapy research. See Garfield & Bergin 1978, pp. 23–62

Green, L. 1978. Temporal and stimulus factors in self-monitoring by obese persons. *Behav. Ther.* 9:328–41

Gross, S. J. 1978. The myth of professional licensing. *Am. Psychol.* 33:1009–16

Gurman, A. S., Razin, A. M., eds. 1977. *Effective Psychotherapy: A Handbook of Research.* Oxford: Pergamon. 628 pp.

Hall, J. N., Baker, R. D., Hutchinson, K. 1977. A controlled evaluation of token economy procedures with chronic schizophrenic patients. *Behav. Res. Ther.* 15:261–83

Hall, R. G., Sachs, D. P. L., Hall, S. M. 1979. Medical risk and therapeutic effectiveness of rapid smoking. *Behav. Ther.* 10:249–59

Hall, S. M., Hall, R. G., DeBoer, G., L'Kulitch, P. 1977. Self and external management compared with psychotherapy in the control of obesity. *Behav. Res. Ther.* 15:89–95

Hammen, C. L. 1980. Depression in college students: Beyond the Beck Depression Inventory. *J. Consult. Clin. Psychol.* 48:126–28

Hammen, C. L., Cochran, S. D. 1980. Cognitive correlates of life stress and depression in college students. *J. Abnorm. Psychol.* In press

Hare-Mustin, R. T., Marecek, J., Kaplan, A. G., Liss-Levinson, N. 1979. Rights of clients, responsibilities of therapists. *Am. Psychol.* 34:3–16

Heimberg, R. G., Montgomery, D., Madsen, C. H. Jr., Heimberg, J. S. 1977. Assertion training: A review of the literature. *Behav. Ther.* 8:953–71

Heitler, J. B. 1976. Preparatory techniques in initiating expressive psychotherapy with lower-class unsophisticated patients. *Psychol. Bull.* 83:339–52

Heller, K. 1979. The effects of social support: Prevention and treatment implications. See Goldstein & Kanfer 1979, pp. 353–82

Heppner, P. P. 1978. The clinical alteration of covert thoughts: A critical review. *Behav. Ther.* 9:717–34

Hersen, M. 1976. Token economies in institutional settings: Historical, political, deprivation, ethical, and generalization issues. *J. Nerv. Ment. Dis.* 162:206–11

Hersen, M., Bellack, A. S. 1977. Assessment of social skills. In *Handbook for Behavioral Assessment,* ed. A. R. Ciminero, K. S. Calhoun, H. E. Adams, pp. 509–54. New York: Wiley. 751 pp.

Hersen, M., Eisler, R. M., Miller, P. M., eds 1975–80. *Progress in Behavior Modification,* Vols. 1–9. New York: Academic

Hollon, S. D. 1980. Comparisons and combinations with alternative approaches. See Rehm, 1980

Holroyd, K. A., Andrasik, F., Westbrook, T. 1977. Cognitive control of tension headache. *Cognit. Ther. Res.* 1:121–33

Horan, J. J., Hackett, G., Buchanan, J. D., Stone, C. I., Demchik-Stone, D. 1977. Coping with pain: A component analysis of stress inoculation. *Cognit. Ther. Res.* 1:211–21

Horowitz, M. J. 1976. *Stress Response Syndromes.* New York: Aronson

Horowitz, M. J. 1979. *States of Mind: Analysis of Change in Psychotherapy.* New York: Plenum. 282 pp.

Howard, K. I., Orlinsky, D. E., Perilstein, J. 1976. Contribution of therapists to patients' experiences in psychotherapy: A components of variance model for analyzing process data. *J. Consult. Clin. Psychol.* 44:520–26

Ilfeld, F. W. Jr. 1977. Current social stressors and symptoms of depression. *Am. J. Psychiatry* 134:161–66

Imber, S. D., Pilkonis, P. A., Harway, N. I., Klein, R. H., Rubinsky, P. A. 1980. Maintenance of change in the psychotherapies. In press

Intagliata, J. C. 1978. Increasing the interpersonal problem-solving skills of an alcoholic population. *J. Consult. Clin. Psychol.* 46:489–96

Iscoe, I. 1977. Issues in the evaluation of community and hospital mental health and mental retardation facilities. *Prof. Psychol.* 8:573–82

Jacobson, N. S. 1980. The assessment of overt behavior in depression. See Rehm 1980

Jacobson, N. S., Baucom, D. H. 1977. Design and assessment of nonspecific control groups in behavior modification research. *Behav. Ther.* 8:709–19

Jeffery, R. W., Coates, T. J. 1978. Why aren't they losing weight? *Behav. Ther.* 9:856–60

Jones, R. R. 1977. Conceptual vs. analytic uses of generalizability theory in behavioral assessment. In *Behavioral Assessment: New Directions in Clinical Psychology,* ed. J. D. Cone, R. P. Hawkins, pp. 330–43. New York: Brunner/Mazel. 440 pp.

Kanfer, F. H. 1971. The maintenance of behavior by self-generated stimuli and reinforcement. In *The Psychology of Private Events,* ed. A. Jacobs, L. B. Sachs, pp. 39–59. New York: Academic. 201 pp.

Kanfer, F. H. 1977. The many faces of self-control, or behavior modification changes its focus. In *Behavioral Self-management: Strategies, Techniques, and Outcomes,* ed. R. B. Stuart, pp. 1–48. New York: Brunner/Mazel. 366 pp.

Kanfer, F. H. 1979. Personal control, social control, and altruism: Can society survive the age of individualism? *Am. Psychol.* 34:231–39

Kanfer, F. H. 1980. Self-management methods. See Kanfer & Goldstein 1980, pp. 334–89

Kanfer, F. H., Goldstein, A. P., eds. 1980. *Helping People Change: A Textbook of Methods.* New York: Pergamon. 600 pp. 2nd ed.

Kanfer, F. H., Grimm, L. G. 1977. Behavioral analysis: Selecting target behaviors in the interview. *Behav. Modif.* 1:7–28

Kanfer, F. H., Grimm, L. G. 1978. Freedom of choice and behavioral change. *J. Consult. Clin. Psychol.* 46:873–78

Kanfer, F. H., Hagerman, S. 1980. The role of self-regulation in depression. See Rehm 1980

Kaplan, R. M., Litrownik, A. J. 1977. Some statistical methods for the assessment of multiple outcome criteria in behavioral research. *Behav. Ther.* 8:383–92

Karoly, P., Steffen, J. 1980. *Improving the Long-term Effects of Psychotherapy.* New York: Halsted. 450 pp.

Katz, M. M., Secunda, S. K., Hirschfeld, R. M. A., Koslow, S. H. 1979. NIMH Clinical Research Branch Collaborative Program on the Psychobiology of Depression. *Arch. Gen. Psychiatry* 36:765–71

Kazdin, A. E. 1978. Methodological and interpretive problems of single-case experimental designs. *J. Consult. Clin. Psychol.* 46:629–42

Kazdin, A. E. 1979a. Nonspecific treatment factors in psychotherapy outcome research. *J. Consult. Clin. Psychol.* 47:846–51

Kazdin, A. E. 1979b. Therapy outcome questions requiring control of credibility and treatment-generated expectancies. *Behav. Ther.* 10:81–93

Kazdin, A. E., Wilcoxon, L. A. 1976. Systematic desensitization and non-specific treatment effects: A methodological evaluation. *Psychol. Bull.* 83:729–58

Kazdin, A. E., Wilson, G. T. 1978. *Evaluation of Behavior Therapy: Issues, Evidence, and Research Strategies.* Cambridge, Mass: Ballinger. 227 pp.

Kellerman, J. 1977. Anorexia nervosa: The efficacy of behavior therapy. *J. Behav. Ther. Exp. Psychiatry* 8:387–90

Kiesler, D. J. 1966. Some myths of psychotherapy research and the search for a paradigm. *Psychol. Bull.* 65:110–36

Kiesler, D. J. 1977. *Use of Individualized Measures in Psychotherapy and Mental Health Program Evaluation Research: A Review of Target Complaints, Problem-oriented Record, and Goal Attainment Scales.* Washington DC: Clin. Res. Branch, NIMH. 150 pp.

Kilmann, P. R., Scovern, A. W., Moreault, D. 1979. Factors in the patient-therapist interaction and outcome: A review of the literature. *Comp. Psychiatry* 20:132–46

King, L. M. 1978. Social and cultural influences on psychopathology. *Ann. Rev. Psychol.* 29:405–33

Kingsley, R. G., Wilson, G. T. 1977. Behavior therapy for obesity: A comparative investigation of long-term efficacy. *J. Consult. Clin. Psychol.* 45:288–98

Kirschenbaum, D. S., Karoly, P. 1977. When self-regulation fails: Tests of some preliminary hypotheses. *J. Consult. Clin. Psychol.* 45:1116–25

Klein, M. H., Gurman, A. S. 1980. Ritual and reality: Some clinical implications of experimental designs for behavior therapy of depression. See Rehm 1980

Klerman, G. L., DiMascio, A., Weissman, M. M., Prusoff, B., Paykel, E. S. 1974. Treatment of depression by drugs and psychotherapy. *Am. J. Psychiatry* 131:186–91

Klerman, G. L., Rounsaville, B., Chevron, E., Neu, C., Weissman, M. 1979. *Manual for Short-term Interpersonal Psychotherapy (IPT) of Depression.* 4th draft. New Haven: Yale Univ. 72 pp.

Knapp, T. J., Downs, D. L., Alperson, J. R. 1976. Behavior therapy for insomnia: A review. *Behav. Ther.* 7:614–25

Knapp, T. J., Wells, L. A. 1978. Behavior therapy for asthma: A review. *Behav. Res. Ther.* 16:103–15

Kornblith, S. J., Rehm, L. P., O'Hara, M. W., Lamparski, D. 1979. Unpublished data described in L. P. Rehm 1979. *Outcome studies of behavioural therapy for depression.* Presented at Soc. Psychother. Res., Oxford, England

Kovacs, M. 1979. Treating depressive disorders: The efficacy of behavior and cognitive therapies. *Behav. Modif.* 3:496–517

Kovacs, M., Rush, A. J., Beck, A. T., Hollon, S. D. 1980. A one year follow-up of depressed outpatients treated with cognitive therapy or pharmacotherapy. *Arch. Gen. Psychiatry.* In press

Kratochwill, T. R., ed. 1978. *Single-subject Research: Strategies for Evaluating Change.* New York: Academic. 316 pp.

Kuhn, T. S. 1977. *The Essential Tension: Selected Studies in Scientific Tradition and Change.* Chicago: Univ. Chicago Press. 366 pp.

Kupke, T. E., Calhoun, K. S. Hobbs, S. A. 1979. Selection of heterosocial skills: II. Experimental validity. *Behav. Ther.* 10:336–46

Ladd, G. 1979. *Social skills and peer acceptance: Effects of a social learning method for training verbal and social skills.* Presented at Soc. Res. Child Dev., San Francisco

Lambert, M. J. 1979. *The Effects of Psychotherapy.* Montreal: Eden. 158 pp.

Lambert, M. J., DeJulio, S. S., Stein, D. M. 1978. Therapist interpersonal skills: Process, outcome, methodological considerations, and recommendations for future research. *Psychol. Bull.* 85:467–89

Lazarus, A. A. 1977. Has behavior therapy outlived its usefulness? *Am. Psychol.* 32:550–54

Ledwidge, B. 1978. Cognitive behavior modification: A step in the wrong direction? *Psychol. Bull.* 85:353–75

Leon, G. R. 1976. Current directions in the treatment of obesity. *Psychol. Bull.* 83:557–78

LeVine, E. S., Padilla, A. M. 1980. *Crossing Cultures in Therapy: Pluralistic Counseling for the Hispanic.* Monterey, Calif: Brooks/Cole. 303 pp.

Lewinsohn, P. M. 1975. The behavioral study and treatment of depression. *Prog. Behav. Modif.* 1:19–65

Lewinsohn, P. M., Biglan, A., Zeiss, A. M. 1976. Behavioral treatment of depression. In *The Behavioral Management of Anxiety, Depression and Pain,* ed. P. O. Davidson, pp. 91–146. New York: Brunner/Mazel. 197 pp.

Liberman, B. L. 1978. The maintenance and persistence of change: Long-term follow-up investigations of psychotherapy. See Frank et al 1978, pp. 107–29

Liberman, R. P. 1980. To each his own: Individualizing treatment strategies for depressed persons. See Rehm 1980

Libet, J. M., Lewinsohn, P. M. 1973. The concept of social skill with special reference to the behavior of depressed persons. *J. Consult. Clin. Psychol.* 40:304–12

Lichtenstein, E., Danaher, B. G. 1976. Modification of smoking behavior: A critical analysis of theory, research, and practice. *Prog. Behav. Modif.* 3:79–132

Lick, J., Bootzin, R. 1975. Expectancy factors in the treatment of fear: Methodological and theoretical issues. *Psychol. Bull.* 82:917–31

Lieberman, M. A. 1975. *Survey and Evaluation of the Literature on Verbal Psychotherapy of Depressive Disorders.* Washington DC: Clin. Res. Branch, NIMH

Loeffler, D., Fiedler, L. 1979. Women—a sense of identity: A counseling intervention to facilitate personal growth in women. *J. Couns. Psychol.* 26:51–57

Lorion, R. P. 1978. Research on psychotherapy and behavior change with the disadvantaged: Past, present, and future directions. See Garfield & Bergin 1978, pp. 903–38

Loro, A. D. Jr., Fisher, E. B. Jr., Levenkron, J. C. 1979. Comparison of established and innovative weight-reduction treatment procedures. *J. Appl. Behav. Anal.* 12:141–55

Lovibond, S. H. 1977. Behavioral control of excessive drinking. *Prog. Behav. Modif.* 5:63–110

Luborsky, L. 1976. Helping alliances in psychotherapy. See Claghorn 1976, pp. 92–116

Luborsky, Lester, Singer, B., Luborsky, Lisa. 1975. Comparative studies of psychotherapies: Is it true that "everybody has won and all must have prizes?" *Arch. Gen. Psychiatry* 32:995–1008

Mahoney, M. J. 1977. Reflections on the cognitive-learning trend in psychotherapy. *Am. Psychol.* 32:5–13

Mahoney, M. J., Arnkoff, D. 1978. Cognitive and self-control therapies. See Garfield & Bergin 1978, pp. 689–722

Marlatt, G. A. 1979. Alcohol use and problem drinking: A cognitive-behavioral analysis. In *Cognitive-Behavioral Interventions: Theory, Research, and Procedures*, ed. P. C. Kendall, S. D. Hollon, pp. 319–55. New York: Academic. 481 pp.

Masters, W. H., Johnson, V. E. 1970. *Human Sexual Inadequacy.* Boston: Little, Brown. 467 pp.

Mathews, A. 1978. Fear-reduction research and clinical phobias. *Psychol. Bull.* 85:390–404

McConaghy, N. 1977. Behavioral treatment in homosexuality. *Prog. Behav. Modif.* 5:310–80

McFall, R. M. 1978. Smoking-cessation research. *J. Consult. Clin. Psychol.* 46:703–12

McLean, P. D. 1976. Therapeutic decision-making in the behavioral treatment of depression. See Lewinsohn, Biglan & Zeiss 1976, pp. 54–90

McLean, P. D., Hakstian, A. R. 1979. Clinical depression: Comparative efficacy of outpatient treatments. *J. Consult. Clin. Psychol.* 47:818–36

McLean, P. D., Ogston, K., Grauer, L. A. 1973. A behavioral approach to the treatment of depression. *J. Behav. Ther. Exp. Psychiatry* 4:323–30

McNamara, J. R., ed. 1979. *Behavioral Approaches in Medicine: Applications and Analysis.* New York: Plenum. 290 pp.

Mechanic, D. 1977. Illness behavior, social adaptation, and the management of illness. *J. Nerv. Ment. Dis.* 165:79–87

Meehl, P. E. 1978. Theoretical risks and tabular asterisks: Sir Karl, Sir Ronald, and the slow progress of soft psychology. *J. Consult. Clin. Psychol.* 46:806–34

Meltzer, M. L. 1975. Insurance reimbursement: A mixed blessing. *Am. Psychol.* 30:1150–56

Miller, H. R., Dermer, S. W. 1979. Quasi-experimental follow-up of token-economy and conventional treatment graduates. *J. Consult. Clin. Psychol.* 47:625–27

Miller, S. M. 1980. The stress reducing effects of uncontrollability. In *Human Helplessness: Theory and Application*, ed. J. Garber, M. Seligman. New York: Academic

Miller, W. R. 1978. Behavioral treatment of problem drinkers: A comparative outcome study of three controlled drinking therapies. *J. Consult. Clin. Psychol.* 46:74–86

Mineka, S. 1979. The role of fear in theories of avoidance learning, flooding, and extinction. *Psychol. Bull.* 86:985–1010

Mintz, J. 1977. *Tailoring Psychotherapy Outcome Measures to Fit the Individual Case: A Review.* Washington DC: Clin. Res. Branch, NIMH. 69 pp.

Mischel, W. 1979. On the interface of cognition and personality: Beyond the person-situation debate. *Am. Psychol.* 34:740–54

Mitchell, S. K. 1979. Interobserver agreement, reliability, and generalizability of data collected in observational studies. *Psychol. Bull.* 86:376–90

Moos, R. H. 1974. *Evaluating Treatment Environments: A Social Ecological Approach.* New York: Wiley. 388 pp.

Morin, S. F. 1977. Heterosexual bias in psychological research on lesbianism and male homosexuality. *Am. Psychol.* 32:629–37

Mosher, L. R., Keith, S. J. 1979. Research on the psychosocial treatment of schizophrenia: A summary report. *Am. J. Psychiatry* 136:623–31

Mostofsky, D. I., Balaschak, B. A. 1977. Psychobiological control of seizures. *Psychol. Bull.* 84:723–50

Murray, E. J., Jacobson, L. I. 1978. Cognition and learning in traditional and behavioral therapy. See Garfield & Bargin 1978, pp. 661–87

National Institute of Mental Health. 1980. *Revised Research Plan: Psychotherapy of Depression Collaborative Research Program.* Washington DC: NIMH. 53 pp.

Nelson, R. E., Craighead, W. E. 1977. Selective recall of positive and negative feedback, self-control behaviors, and depression. *J. Abnorm. Psychol.* 86:379–88

Nelson, R. O. 1977. Assessment and therapeutic functions of self-monitoring. *Prog. Behav. Modif.* 5:264–309

O'Leary, K. D., Borkovec, T. D. 1978. Conceptual, methodological, and ethical problems of placebo groups in psychotherapy research. *Am. Psychol.* 33:821–30

Orlinsky, D. E., Howard, K. I. 1978. The relation of process to outcome in psychotherapy. See Garfield & Bergin 1978, pp. 283–329

Park, C. C., Shapiro, L. N. 1976. *You Are Not Alone: Understanding and Dealing with Mental Illness.* Boston: Little, Brown. 496 pp.

Parloff, M. B. 1979. Can psychotherapy research guide the policy-maker? A little knowledge may be a dangerous thing. *Am. Psychol.* 34:296–306

Parloff, M. B., Wolfe, B., Hadley, S., Waskow, I. E. 1978. *Assessment of Psychosocial Treatment of Mental Disorders: Current Status and Prospects.* Washington DC: NIMH. NTIS #PB-287640. 324 pp.

Patterson, G. R., Fleischman, M. J. 1979. Maintenance of treatment effects: Some considerations concerning family systems and follow-up data. *Behav. Ther.* 10:168–85

Patterson, G. R., Reid, J. B. 1970. Reciprocity and coercion: Two facets of social systems. In *Behavior Modification in Clinical Psychology,* ed. C. Neuringer, J. L. Michael, pp. 133–77. New York: Appleton-Century-Crofts. 261 pp.

Paul, G. L. 1969. Behavior modification research: Design and tactics. In *Behavior Therapy: Appraisal and Status,* ed. C.M. Franks, pp. 29–62. New York: McGraw-Hill. 730 pp.

Paul, G. L., Lentz, R. J. 1977. *Psychosocial Treatment of Chronic Mental Patients: Milieu versus Social Learning Programs.*

Cambridge, Mass: Harvard Univ. Press. 528 pp.

Paykel, E. S. 1979. Recent life events in the development of the depressive disorders. See Depue 1979, pp. 245–63

Penk, W. E., Charles, H. L., Van Hoose, T. A. 1978. Comparative effectiveness of day hospital and inpatient psychiatric treatment. *J. Consult. Clin. Psychol.* 46:94–101

Phillips, E. L. 1978. *The Social Skills Basis of Psychopathology: Alternatives to Abnormal Psychology and Psychiatry.* New York: Grune & Stratton. 281 pp.

Pilkonis, P. A. 1979. *An experimental study of life events and psychotherapy: Preliminary results.* Presented at Soc. Psychother. Res., Oxford, England

Price, R. H. 1979. The social ecology of treatment gain. See Goldstein & Kanfer 1979, pp. 383–426

Rachlin, H. 1977. Reinforcing and punishing thoughts. *Behav. Ther.* 8:659–65

Radloff, L. S., Rae, D. S. 1979. Susceptibility and precipitating factors in depression: Sex differences and similarities. *J. Abnorm. Psychol.* 88:174–81

Rehm, L. P. 1977. A self-control model of depression. *Behav. Ther.* 8:787–804

Rehm, L. P. 1978. *The Assessment of Depression in Therapy Outcome Research: A Review of Instruments and Recommendations for an Assessment Battery.* Washington DC: Clin. Res. Branch, NIMH. 124 pp.

Rehm, L. P., ed. 1980. *Behavior Therapy for Depression: Current Status and Future Directions.* New York: Academic

Rehm, L. P., Fuchs, C. Z., Roth, D. M., Kornblith, S. J., Romano, J. M. 1979. A comparison of self-control and assertion skills treatments of depression. *Behav. Ther.* 10:429–42

Rehm, L. P., Kornblith, S. J. 1979. Behavior therapy for depression: A review of recent developments. *Prog. Behav. Modif.* 7:277–320

Rich, A. R., Schroeder, H. E. 1976. Research issues in assertiveness training. *Psychol. Bull.* 83:1081–96

Rippere, V. 1977. Comments on Seligman's theory of helplessness. *Behav. Res. Ther.* 15:207–9

Rizley, R. 1978. Depression and distortion in the attribution of causality. *J. Abnorm. Psychol.* 87:32–48

Romano, J. M., Rehm, L. P. 1979. *Self-control treatment of depression: One year followup.* Presented at East. Psychol. Assoc., Philadelphia

Rosenthal, T., Bandura, A. 1978. Psychologi-

CLINICAL PSYCHOLOGY   437

cal modeling: Theory and practice. See
Garfield & Bergin 1978, pp. 621–58
Rush, A. J., Beck, A.T., Kovacs, M., Hollon,
S. I. 1977. Comparative efficacy of cognitive therapy and pharmacotherapy in
the treatment of depressed outpatients.
Cognit. Ther. Res. 1:17–37
Sanders, S. H. 1979. Behavioral assessment
and treatment of clinical pain: Ap-
praisal of current status. *Prog. Behav.
Modif.* 8:249–92
Sarason, I. G., Johnson, J. H., Siegel, J. M.
1978. Assessing the impact of life chan-
ges: Development of the Life Experiences Survey. *J. Consult. Clin. Psychol.*
46:932–46
Schwartz, G. E. 1978. Psychobiological foundations of psychotherapy and behavior
change. See Garfield & Bergin 1978, pp.
63–99
Schwartz, G. E., Beatty, J., eds. 1977.
Biofeedback: Theory and Research.
New York: Academic. 467 pp.
Schwartz, G. E., Weiss, S. M., eds. 1978. *Proceedings of Yale Conference on Behavioral Medicine.* Washington DC: GPO.
DHEW No. (NIH) 78-1424
Seer, P. 1979. Psychological control of essen-
tial hypertension: Review of the litera-
ture and methodological critique. *Psy-
chol. Bull.* 86:1015–43
Seligman, M. E. P. 1975. *Helplessness: On
Depression, Development, and Death.*
San Francisco: Freeman. 250 pp.
Shapiro, A. K., Morris, L. A. 1978. Placebo
effects in medical and psychological
therapies. See Garfield & Bergin 1978,
pp. 369–410
Singer, J. L., Pope, K. S., eds. 1978. *The
Power of Human Imagination: New
Methods in Psychotherapy.* New York:
Plenum. 405 pp.
Smith, M. L., Glass, G. V. 1977. Meta-anal-
ysis of psychotherapy outcome studies.
Am. Psychol. 32:752–60
Snow, D. L., Newton, P. M. 1976. Task, so-
cial structure, and social process in the
community mental health center movement. *Am. Psychol.* 31:582–94
Sotile, W. M., Kilmann, P. R. 1977. Treatments of psychogenic female sexual dysfunctions. *Psychol. Bull.* 84:619–33
Spitzer, R. L., Endicott, J., Woodruff, R. A.
Jr., Andreasen, N. 1977. Classification
of mood disorders. In *Depression: Clinical, Biological, and Psychological Perspectives,* ed. G. Usdin, pp. 70–103.
New York: Brunner/Mazel. 346 pp.
Spohn, H. E., Fitzpatrick, T. 1980. Informed
consent and bias in samples of schizophrenic subjects at risk for drug withdrawal. *J. Abnorm. Psychol.* 89:79–92

Stachnik, T. J. 1980. Priorities for psy-
chology in medical education and
health care delivery. *Am. Psychol.*
35:8–15
Stricker, G. 1977. Implications of research
for psychotherapeutic treatment of
women. *Am. Psychol.* 32:14–22
Strong, S. R. 1978. Social psychological ap-
proach to psychotherapy research. See
Garfield & Bergin 1978, pp. 101–35
Strupp, H. H. 1978. Psychotherapy research
and practice: An overview. See Garfield
& Bergin 1978, pp. 3–22
Strupp, H. H. 1980. Letters: Psychotherapy:
Assessing methods. *Science* 207:590
Strupp, H. H., Hadley, S. W. 1979. Specific
vs. nonspecific factors in psychother-
apy: A controlled study of outcome.
Arch. Gen. Psychiatry 36:1125–36
Strupp, H. H., Hadley, S. W., Gomes-
Schwartz, B. 1977. *Psychotherapy for
Better or Worse: The Problems of Negative Effects.* New York: Aronson.
354 pp.
Sue, S. 1977. Community mental health services to minority groups: Some optimism, some pessimism. *Am. Psychol.*
32:616–24
Thoresen, C. E., Coates, T. J. 1976. Behavioral self-control: Some clinical concerns. *Prog. Behav. Modif.* 2:308–52
Tischler, G. L., Henisz, J. E., Myers, J. K.,
Boswell, P. C. 1975a. Utilization of
mental health services. I: Patienthood
and the prevalence of symptomatology
in the community. *Arch. Gen. Psychiatry* 32:411–15
Tischler, G. L., Henisz, J. E., Myers, J. K.,
Boswell, P. C. 1975b. Utilization of
mental health services. II: Mediators of
service allocation. *Arch. Gen. Psychiatry*
32:416–18
Trower, P., Bryant, B., Argyle, M., Marzil-
lier, J. 1978. *Social Skills and Mental
Health.* Pittsburgh: Univ. Pittsburgh
Press. 306 pp.
Turk, D. C., Genest, M. 1979. Regulation of
pain: The application of cognitive and
behavioral techniques for prevention
and remediation. See Marlatt 1979, pp.
287–318
Turk, D. C., Meichenbaum, D. H., Berman,
W. H. 1979. Application of biofeedback
for the regulation of pain: A critical review. *Psychol. Bull.* 86:1322–38
Turner, R. M. 1978. Multivariate assessment
of therapy outcome research. *J. Behav.
Ther. Exp. Psychiatry* 9:309–14
Twentyman, C. T., Zimering, R. T. 1979. Behavioral training of social skills: A critical review. *Prog. Behav. Modif.* 7:321–
400

Usdin, G., ed. 1977. *Depression: Clinical, Biological, and Psychological Perspectives.* New York: Brunner/Mazel. 346 pp.

Vail, A. 1978. Factors influencing lower-class black patients remaining in treatment. *J. Consult. Clin. Psychol.* 46:341

Vaughn, C.E., Leff, J. P. 1976. The influence of family and social factors on the course of psychiatric illness: A comparison of schizophrenic and depressed neurotic patients. *Br. J. Psychiatry* 129:125–37

Wachtel, P. L. 1977. *Psychoanalysis and Behavior Therapy: Toward an Integration.* New York: Basic Books. 315 pp.

Waskow, I. E. 1976. Research on psychotherapy with women: A workshop introduction. *Psychother. Theory Res. Pract.* 13:64–65

Waskow, I. E. 1979. *Presidential address.* Presented at Soc. Psychother. Res., Oxford, England

Waskow, I. E., Parloff, M. B., eds. 1975. *Psychotherapy Change Measures.* Washington DC: GPO-DHEW No. (ADM) 74-120. 327 pp.

Weisenberg, M. 1977. Pain and pain control. *Psychol. Bull.* 84:1008–44

Weissman, M. M. 1979. The psychological treatment of depression: Evidence for the efficacy of psychotherapy alone, in comparison with, and in combination with pharmacotherapy. *Arch. Gen. Psychiatry* 36:1261–69

Weissman, M. M., Klerman, G. L. 1977. Sex differences and the epidemiology of depression. *Arch. Gen. Psychiatry* 34:98–111

Weissman, M. M., Paykel, E. S. 1974. *The Depressed Woman: A Study of Social Relationships.* Chicago: Univ. Chicago Press. 289 pp.

Weissman, M. M., Prusoff, B. A., DiMascio, A., Neu, C., Goklaney, M., Klerman, G.

L. 1979. The efficacy of drugs and psychotherapy in the treatment of acute depressive episodes. *Am. J. Psychiatry* 136:555–58

Whitley, B. E. Jr. 1979. Sex roles and psychotherapy: A current appraisal. *Psychol. Bull.* 86:1309–21

Wilkins, W. 1978. Expectancy effects versus demand characteristics: An empirically unresolvable issue. *Behav. Ther.* 9:363–67

Wilson, G. T., Brownell, K. 1978. Behavior therapy for obesity: Including family members in the treatment process. *Behav. Ther.* 9:943–45

Wilson, G. T., Tracey, D. A. 1976. An experimental analysis of aversive imagery versus electrical aversive conditioning in the treatment of chronic alcoholics. *Behav. Res. Ther.* 14:41–51

Wolf, M. M. 1978. Social validity: The case for subjective measurement or how applied behavior analysis is finding its heart. *J. Appl. Behav. Anal.* 11:203–14

Wolfe, B. E. 1977. Moral transformations in psychotherapy. In *Science and Psychotherapy,* ed. S. Stern, L. S. Horowitz, J. Lynes, pp. 177–89. New York: Haven. 288 pp.

Wolpe, J. 1979. The experimental model and treatment of neurotic depression. *Behav. Res. Ther.* 17:555–65

Wortman, C. B., Dintzer, L. 1978. Is an attributional analysis of the learned helplessness phenomenon viable?: A critique of the Abramson-Seligman-Teasdale reformulation. *J. Abnorm. Psychol.* 87:75–90

Zeiss, A. M., Lewinsohn, P. M., Munoz, R. F. 1979. Nonspecific improvement effects in depression using interpersonal skills training, pleasant activity schedules, or cognitive training. *J. Consult. Clin. Psychol.* 47:427–39

Ann. Rev. Psychol. 1981. 32:439–76

CREATIVITY, INTELLIGENCE, AND PERSONALITY ◆350

Frank Barron and David M. Harrington[1]

Department of Psychology, University of California,
Santa Cruz, California 95064

CONTENTS

[1]The authors wish to acknowledge the very substantial contributions of UCSC psychology graduate student Teresa Zembower to this review, especially in the culling of important findings from dissertation abstracts and from articles in the *Journal of Creative Behavior*. She also undertook the onerous task of preparing the bibliography and reconciling it with the text. We are also grateful to Wallace B. Hall for many helpful comments and corrections. Financial costs were met by a faculty research grant from the Santa Cruz campus.

0066-4308/81/0201-0439$01.00

INTRODUCTION

Divergent thinking; creativity in women; hemispheric specialization opposing right brain to left as the source of intuition, metaphor, and imagery; the contribution of altered states of consciousness to creative thinking; an organismic interpretation of the relationship of creativity to personality and intelligence; new methods of analysis of biographical material and a new emphasis on psychohistory; the relationship of thought disorder to originality; the inheritance of intellectual and personal traits important to creativity; the enhancement of creativity by training; these have been the main themes emerging in research on creativity since the last major reviews of the field (Stein 1968; Dellas & Gaier 1970; Freeman, Butcher & Christie 1971; Gilchrist 1972).

Much indeed has happened in the field of creativity research since 1950, when J. P. Guilford in his parting address as president of the American Psychological Association pointed out that up to that time only 186 out of 121,000 entries in *Psychological Abstracts* dealt with creative imagination. By 1956, when the first national research conference on creativity was organized by C. W. Taylor at the University of Utah (under the sponsorship of the National Science Foundation), this number had doubled. By 1962, when *Scientific Creativity* (compiled by C. W. Taylor and F. Barron) went to press with a summary of the first three biennial Utah-NSF conferences, approximately 400 references post-1940, mostly of an empirical research character, were found for citation. In 1965, the comprehensive bibliography of the Creative Education Foundation (Razik 1965), which includes articles and books outside the professional field of psychology, contained 4176 references, nearly 3000 of them dated later than 1950. This almost exponential increase has leveled off to a stream of approximately 250 new dissertations, articles, or books every year since 1970.

New journals attest to the vigor of this still growing field of study. *The Journal of Creative Behavior,* under the editorship of Angelo Biondi, has proved to be much more than a house organ of the Foundation for Creative

Education, with whose sponsorship it was founded. Its listing of creativity-related dissertations and theses is an invaluable scholarly resource. *The Gifted Child Quarterly,* both in its publication of research on the relationship of the various forms of giftedness to creativity in general and in its attentive book reviews, has kept a professional readership up to date on new developments in a socially important movement in education. Other new journals of general importance to the field are: *Intelligence, Journal of Mental Imagery, The Psychocultural Review,* and *The Journal of Altered States of Consciousness.* Several important publications emerged from conferences and symposia involving creativity during this period (Steiner 1965; Roslansky 1970; Taylor 1972; Stanley, Keating & Fox 1974; Keating 1976; Stanley, George & Solano 1977) along with a collection of pieces by investigators invited to take stock of the field 25 years after Guilford's 1950 APA address (Taylor & Getzels 1975).

Scholarship was also facilitated by the publication of two major reference works by Rothenberg & Greenberg—*Creative Men and Women* (1974) and *The Index of Scientific Writings on Creativity: General, 1566–1974* (1976). Torrance's impressively lengthy cumulative bibliography on the *Torrance Tests of Creativity and Thinking* (1979) and an unpublished cumulative bibliography of research at the University of California's Institute of Personality Assessment and Research (IPAR) containing more than 600 references (and available from the Institute) are valuable guides to significant lines of research during the past 15 years.

In addition to the comprehensive reviews cited above and the many more specialized reviews noted later in this chapter, particularly useful surveys and analyses of the field include those by Chambers (1969), Bloomberg (1973), Taylor (1975), and Rothenberg & Hausman (1976).

The Varieties of "Creativity"

The term creativity stands in need of precise distinctions among the referents it has acquired. Commonly used definitions of creativity vary in several ways. First of all, some definitions require socially valuable *products* if the act or person is to be called creative, while others see creativity itself as being intrinsically valuable, so that nothing of demonstrable social value need be produced; dreams thus may be creative, or unexpressed thoughts or simply the imaginative expressiveness or curiosity of a child. Definitions may vary also in terms of the level of accomplishment recognized as creative: difficulty of the problem seen or solved, e.g., or elegance or beauty of the product or the nature of the impact. A third kind of distinction is between creativity as achievement, creativity as ability, and creativity as disposition or attitude.

By way of illustration, let us take the two main categories of definition of a criterion of creativity actually used in large bodies of research: 1. creativity as socially recognized achievement in which there are novel products to which one can point as evidence, such as inventions, theories, buildings, published writings, paintings and sculptures and films; laws; institutions; medical and surgical treatments, and so on; and 2. creativity as an ability manifested by performance in critical trials, such as tests, contests, etc, in which one individual can be compared with another on a precisely defined scale.

The first category may lead to a definition of a field of activity and its products as intrinsically creative: all inventors, e.g., or all artists or all poets. This has led to a certain amount of research in which practitioners of a creative activity are compared with people in general, leading to a portrait of "the creative person" in terms of intellectual and personality differences between the criterion group and the generality. But these intrinsically creative products may differ among themselves in qualities such as originality, elegance, impact, and far-reachingness. Studies of individual differences as to creativity *among* members of such groups (architects, artists, mathematicians, and writers in the IPAR studies, for example) give a different picture of the components of creativity than do "field vs the generality" studies. A good example is measured intelligence. Creative architects do not score higher than comparison groups in architecture on standardized intelligence tests, but *all* architects studied scored an average of about two standard deviations higher than the general population (MacKinnon & Hall 1971). What does one then conclude about the relationship of creativity to intelligence?

Many such examples could be given, not just in relationship to intelligence but to personality, interests, values, life history. The point is that results will appear confusing and contradictory unless the implications of the adopted definition of creativity and the assumptions of the methods are kept clearly in mind.

Creativity as an ability manifested by performance on tests is dogged by even more formidable difficulties. What kind of test is it? What abilities is it tapping? What effect do different methods of scoring it (and different, usually anonymous, scorers) have upon its correlates? How does timing affect the test? How do the instructions themselves affect performance in defining the implicit work schedule? The literature since 1970 reflects increasing sophistication about these difficulties as will be seen below.

Let us take divergent thinking (DT) tests as a prime example. There is a certain uncriticalness of analysis embedded in DT tests and their scoring methods. High scores on the Consequences test, e.g., are considered evidence of divergent thinking, although in fact the criterion of high quality is remoteness, perhaps combined with cleverness and aptness. Remoteness implies a process of going a distance from the obvious, but does it rule out the process of thought by which one *converges,* sometimes by occasional divergence, on an idea or result? Divergent thinking in fact goes hand in glove with convergent thinking in every thought process that results in a new idea. The aha! comes when the process reaches a conclusion. But process is precisely what is invisible in the usual DT test used in creativity research. A problem is set, and a written answer is obtained. What happens in between is anybody's guess, except the respondent's, who hasn't been asked.

Short, closely timed tests in which a problem is set and a brief response is required are ideal for use in a battery of tests destined for factor analysis. Has this requirement, which deliberately excludes scrutiny and analysis of process, been more of a bane than a blessing to research on creativity? Has the distinction between convergent and divergent, though real enough in the life of thought, been a mischievous one? We have for this review surveyed hundreds of reports on DT tests and are left wondering.

The actual sampling of persons, using either criterion of creativity, may also confound the search for commonalities of "the creative person." Creative women may be quite different from creative men, e.g., and different too in each field of endeavor. Age and level of training must also enter the picture. While this review cites many studies which individually respect the distinctions noted here (ability vs achievement, sex of person, etc), we believe the field needs a comprehensive catalog of empirical studies and a set of conceptual categories and dimensions with which a meta-analysis of results in the entire domain of creativity could be conducted. Though such an analysis was beyond the scope of this review, we urge its undertaking and refer colleagues to exemplary meta-analytic efforts in other domains (e.g. Block 1976, Smith & Glass 1977, Cooper 1979).

Before turning to our review of 15 years' work, a few comments regarding our space- and self-imposed restrictions are in order. In general we have emphasized empirical rather than theoretical work and studies employing achievement- rather than ability-based criteria. For some important topics we have only been able to recommend other reviews to the interested reader. Regarding creativity enhancement, e.g., we refer the reader to Stein's (1974) definitive two-volume work, *Stimulating Creativity.* Prentky's (1979) lengthy review and theoretical analysis of some of the psychobiological questions, "Creativity and Psychopathology: a neurocognitive approach," gives a full picture of relevant work in the neurosciences, including cerebral lateralization and cortical arousal. For the latter topic, see the very interesting work of Martindale (1977–1978) and Martindale & Hasenfus (1978). An excellent analytical treatment of laterality has appeared recently (Corballis 1980).

CREATIVITY AND INTELLIGENCE

Intelligence itself is a term with many meanings and referents. While an analysis of this construct is beyond the scope of this chapter (see Resnick 1976 and numerous articles in the new journal *Intelligence* for some current perspectives), we would like to note that creativity investigators have used the term "intelligence" variously to refer to (*a*) that which IQ tests measure; (*b*) the entire multifactorial domain of human cognitive abilities (including such creativity-related components as DT abilities, problem-finding abilities, special talents such as musical and artistic abilities, and the ability to access primary process modes of thought by regressing in the service of the ego); and (*c*) that which qualified observers (peers, teachers, etc) describe as "intelligence" on the basis of repeated observations of behavior in many situations. Our brief review of research of the past 15 years regarding creativity and intelligence will deal briefly with each of these perspectives.

Models of Intellect, Old and New

Though Guilford's Structure-of-Intellect (SI) model has continued to dominate discussions of the relationship between intelligence and creativity, the SI model has been increasingly criticized on technical and conceptual grounds. (See Butcher 1973, Horn 1977, and Vernon 1979 for summaries and evaluations of such criticism.) Critics object to the alleged subjectivity of the underlying rotational procedures, to Guilford's insistence upon orthogonal rather than oblique factors, to some possible narrowness in the 120 (!) SI abilities, to the alleged psychological superficiality of the SI's "product" category, and to the tendency of the model to suggest that the operations (cognition, memory, evaluation, convergent production, and divergent production) are mutually exclusive and isolatable. Despite these criticisms, the SI model has spurred the development of interesting new tests [e.g. Lang & Ryba's (1976) SI-inspired tests of auditory abilities which nicely discriminated musicians, artists, and controls] and provided a conceptual framework for many investigators.

During this same period, Cattell continued to develop his alternative model of fluid and crystalized intelligence. In its radically elaborated 1971 form, this appeared to involve about 500 sub-abilities (Cattell 1971, Butcher 1973). A study by Rossman & Horn (1972) found modest positive *r*s between indices of creative achievement or reputation and a broad "fluency" factor, but insignificant and very small *r*s with "fluid" and "crystalized" intelligence factors. While Cattell's model of intellect will surely receive much deserved attention, and while the thirteenth chapter ("Genius and the processes of creative thought") of Cattell's 1971 book is must reading for serious students of creativity, the links between Cattell's model of intellect and achievement-based creativity are primarily speculative at this point.

The emergence of what one might term "differential cognitive psychology" in recent years also holds enormous potential for future research involving the cognitive underpinnings of creativity. This approach, which involves the simultaneous attempt to understand test performances and intellectual abilities in terms of underlying cognitive processes and the reciprocal effort to view cognitive processes in terms of potentially measurable subskills and component abilities, may lead to a much needed blending of the process and ability approaches to the study of creativity. Recent efforts by Carroll (1976), for example, to identify and characterize DT abilities in terms of underlying information-processing components have obvious implications for creativity research. (See also the review by Stankov 1980, the effort by Mendelsohn 1976 to understand Remote Association Test (RAT) performance in terms of attentional abilities, and the attempt by Sternberg 1977 to analyze analogical thinking skills into component abilities.) In our view, differential cognitive psychology has the potential to deepen our understanding of creative processes and abilities quite substantially. For further introductions to this perspective, the reader is referred to Resnick (1976), to a series of articles appearing in the second volume of *Intelligence* (1978), to Carroll & Maxwell (1979), to Pellegrino & Glaser (1979), to Sternberg (1979), and to Royce (1980).

Creativity and Traditional Measures of Intelligence

Findings in the last 15 years have tended to confirm the picture which earlier research had suggested. Studies of creative adult artists, scientists, mathematicians, and writers find them scoring very high on tests of general intelligence (e.g. Barron 1969; Bachtold & Werner 1970; Helson & Crutchfield 1970b; Cattell 1971; Helson 1971; Bachtold & Werner 1973; Gough 1976a), though rs between tested intelligence and creative achievement in these samples range from insignificantly negative ($r = -.05$, Gough 1976a) to mildly and significantly positive ($r = +.31$, Helson 1971). In other studies, often involving nonprofessional samples, measures of tested intelligence and indices of creative achievement or reputation are often insignificantly or only very weakly positive (e.g. Helson & Crutchfield 1970b; Rotter, Langland & Berger 1971; Davis & Belcher 1971; Rossman & Horn 1972; R. M. Milgram, Yitzhak & N. A. Milgram 1977; Frederiksen & Ward 1978; and Hocevar 1980) and sometimes modestly positive (e.g. McDermid

1965; Helson 1971; Vernon 1972b; Torrance 1972b; Schmidt 1973; Kogan & Pankove 1974; Gough 1976a; and Hocevar 1980). Though a curvilinear relationship between intelligence and creativity has often been suggested (with intelligence presumably becoming less and less influential as one moves into higher and higher levels of intelligence), the only formal test (with negative results) of this hypothesis we are aware of was conducted by Simonton (1976a) in a reanalysis of Cox's historical geniuses—a sample quite probably too rarified to be a particularly good test of the curvilinear hypothesis.

Creativity and Rated or Perceived Intelligence

It should be noted that creative people are often perceived and rated as more intelligent than less creative people even in samples where no corresponding correlations between tested intelligence and creativity obtain. Despite an r of $-.08$ between Terman's Concept Mastery Test and professionally rated creativity among the top 40 IPAR architects (MacKinnon 1962a), e.g., staff *ratings* of the single adjective "intelligent" correlated $+.39$ with the index of creativity (MacKinnon 1966).

While such an r may reflect some spurious halo effects, it may also tell us something about the true overlap in meaning of these terms in the natural language. Popular criteria for "intelligence" are much broader than those tested by standard "intelligence" tests. It is also possible that such rs partially reflect the presence of a set of personality characteristics and processes which influence the degree to which raw talent or aptitude of almost any form is translated into effective and socially impressive behavior. It is conceivable, for example, that factors making for success (such as forcefulness of character, self-confidence, etc) facilitate effective behavior of many forms (including behavior having an "intelligent" and a "creative" look about it) and thereby produce a degree of correlation between "effective creativity" and "effective intelligence" which is higher than the correlation between "raw creative ability" and "raw intelligence." After all, creativity is a social outcome, and so is intelligent action. We believe that this distinction between "raw (or best-measured) intelligence" and "effective intelligence" and between "raw creative ability" and "effective creativity" is certainly one worth making.

Creativity and Divergent Thinking Abilities

Binet began the development of open-ended, multiple-solution measures (e.g. "Sentence Invention" and "Ink Blots") of the type we now call divergent thinking (DT) tests (Binet & Henri 1896). Upon such tests, much of modern research on creativity depends and is focused. Though DT tests were essentially excluded from Binet's subsequent batteries (see Guilford

1967, chapter 1, for an interesting discussion of this point), the open-ended, multiple-solution format assumed by Binet to facilitate the measurement of imaginative abilities was quickly adopted by early creativity investigators. Indeed, the proliferation of studies involving such tests was so great that by 1915 Whipple was able to devote an entire chapter in the second edition of his *Manual of Mental and Physical Tests* (1915) to "Tests of Imagination and Invention" in which he cites the work of at least 19 investigators actively exploring this domain.

The development and use of DT tests continued quite steadily up to 1950, at which time Guilford's (1950) presidential address to the American Psychological Association introduced many psychologists to his own research group's new efforts in a research tradition already half a century old. The impact of Guilford's address upon the field of creativity was, of course, catalytic and long term.

Wallach and Kogan's influential book, *Modes of Thinking in Young Children,* which contained a battery of highly intercorrelated DT tests influenced by Guilford's earlier work, was published in 1965. These tests [and Ward's (1968) modification of them for use with much younger children], together with the Torrance Tests of Creative Thinking (TTCT) (Torrance 1966) and a few of the early measures produced by Guilford's group (Alternate Uses, Consequences, Plot Titles), have dominated the DT test scene for the past 15 years.

THE QUESTION OF VALIDITY   Despite the 80-year history of such measures of productive imagination, the vitally important question of whether divergent thinking tests measure abilities actually involved in creative thinking is not at all easy to answer in satisfying detail. Nevertheless, an imprecisely qualified answer does seem justified by the evidence gathered thus far: some divergent thinking tests, administered under some conditions and scored by some sets of criteria, do measure abilities related to creative achievement and behavior in some domains. Our own extensive review of the literature reveals more than 70 studies in which positive and statistically significant relationships have apparently been observed between various divergent thinking test scores and reasonably acceptable nontest indices of creative behavior or achievement. In addition to the more than 50 studies cited elsewhere and earlier (Harrington 1972, pp. 30–32), validating evidence for DT tests has been reported at the elementary school level (Rotter, Langland & Berger 1971; Schaefer 1971a; Torrance 1974; Wallbrown & Huelsman 1975; Wallbrown, Wallbrown & Wherry 1975); at the junior high school level (Vernon 1971, 1972b); and at the high school level (Lynch 1970; Anastasi & Schaefer 1971; Kogan & Pankove 1972, 1974; Milgram & Milgram 1976). At the undergraduate and graduate levels, significant positive relationships have been reported by Khatena 1971b; Harrington 1972; Rossman & Horn 1972; Domino 1974; Torrance 1974; Lang & Ryba 1976; Holloway & Torrance 1977; Forisha 1978a; Frederiksen & Ward 1978; Hocevar 1980. Significant results with nonstudent adults have also been reported by Tan-Willman 1974; Getzels & Csikszentmihalyi 1976; Gough 1976a.

Two comments are immediately in order. It should first be noted that DT test scores have often failed to correlate significantly positively with plausible indices of creative achievement and behavior. While there are probably many reasons for this, one factor undoubtedly involves the field-specific relevance of many DT abilities and the primitive state of knowledge regarding the abilities underlying creative behavior in any given field. Because the DT abilities presumably underlying creative achievements probably vary from field to field, there is little reason to expect any randomly selected DT test to correlate with creative achievement in any randomly selected domain. Until greater attention is paid to the matching of DT tests to relevant domains, attempts to validate DT tests will proceed in an essentially shotgun fashion. It is therefore particularly encouraging to note that several investigators have demonstrated substantial sensitivity to this issue in recent years. Efforts by Cunnington & Torrance (1965) and Lang & Ryba (1976) to develop measures involving auditory stimuli for studies in the domain of musical creativity (Torrance 1969, Khatena 1971b, Holloway & Torrance 1977) and by Gough (1975, 1976a) and Frederiksen & Ward (1978) to develop DT tests particularly relevant to scientific creativity clearly reflect a heightened awareness of this issue. Similar efforts by Hall (1972) and Lunneborg & Lunneborg (1969) to study architectural creativity using tests involving visual stimuli also reflect a growing desire to match ability measures to creative process and product.

The second point involves the possible role of general intelligence in the DT "validity" coefficients reported above. Though most of the studies cited did not report the data necessary to determine whether DT tests are measuring creativity-related variance beyond that measured by intelligence tests, a few did. On the basis of those few studies one can say that some DT tests, administered to some samples, under some conditions and scored according to some criteria, measure factors relevant to creativity criteria beyond those measured by indices of general intelligence (see Harrington 1972, pp. 39–40). As investigators begin including measures of general intelligence in DT validation studies routinely and begin to approach their data using the most appropriate analytic techniques (such as the multiple regression methods used by Cronbach 1968 and Hocevar 1980), evidence relevant to this critical issue should accumulate much more rapidly than it has to date.

THE QUESTIONS OF SCORING, INSTRUCTIONS, AND TEST ADMINIS-
TRATION   A great deal of attention has been devoted in the last several
years to the question of optimal DT test instructions and test conditions (see
Hattie 1977, 1980 for recent reviews). Most of this work has focused on
conditions needed to generate DT scores which are as weakly correlated
with general intelligence measures as possible or on conditions which maximize raw fluency or uniqueness scores. Though less attention has been
directed to the development of test instructions and scoring procedures
which, when coordinated, maximize the construct-validity of DT tests, at
least two studies (Datta 1963 and Harrington 1975) found that when DT
instructions to "be creative" were coordinated with scoring procedures
sensitive to creative quality, correlations with indices of creativity were
significantly improved. A recent report by Katz & Poag (1979) replicating
some aspects of these studies for men but not for women calls attention to
the need for much more extensive work in this generally neglected area.

Because the question of optimal scoring methods for DT tests deserves
lengthier treatment than we can give it, the reader is referred to useful
discussions and illustrations of various scoring methods by Vernon (1971),
Harrington (1972, 1975), and Frederiksen & Ward (1978).

DIVERGENT THINKING ABILITIES AND TRADITIONAL MEASURES
OF INTELLIGENCE   For those who believe that DT abilities are the key
to (and perhaps even an appropriate operational definition of) creative
thinking ability, the relationship between DT abilities and traditional measures of intelligence has been a topic of great interest and the subject of
much investigation. (See Butcher 1973, Horn 1976, and Vernon, Adamson
& Vernon 1977 for some useful reviews.) In general it seems best to summarize these studies by saying that DT X intelligence rs vary widely (from zero
upward) depending upon the DT tests, the heterogeneity of the sample, and
the testing conditions. In a much-cited review, Torrance (1967) summarized 388 rs involving intelligence measures and the Torrance Tests of
Creative Thinking (TTCT) and reported a median r of +.06 for his figural
DT tests and +.21 for his verbal DT tests. Guilford (1967) reported average
rs of +.22 for his figural DT tests, +.40 for symbolic DT tests, and +.37
for semantic DT tests in a sample of 204 ninth graders but a *range* of DT
X IQ rs from −.04 to +.70. Such wide variations in DT X IQ rs are not
uncommon; Bennett (1972, as reported by Butcher 1973) obtained aggregate DT X IQ rs in the +.5 to +.6 range in a sample of approximately 1000
United Kingdom youngsters, whereas Magnusson & Backteman (1978)
reported aggregate DT X IQ rs in the range of +.2 to +.3 in a sample of
approximately 1000 Swedish teenagers. (The Magnusson and Backteman

study was also noteworthy for having demonstrated substantial temporal stability over a 2-year period for these DT tests which were largely independent of traditional intelligence measures.)

While the average figure of approximately +.3 sometimes referred to in reviews (e.g. Horn 1976 and Richards 1976) is a reasonable estimate of central tendency, it must be recalled that the actual DT X IQ rs vary widely depending upon the nature of the DT tests, the heterogeneity of the sample, and apparently the nature of the testing situation. (For reviews of research dealing with this latter point, see Hattie 1977, 1980.)

The possibility that IQ may be a prerequisite to DT performance was proposed by Guilford (1967) and studied by examining relevant scatterplots for triangularity (Guilford 1967, Guilford & Christensen 1973, Schubert 1973, Richards 1976). While this line of investigation is far from conclusive, some DT and IQ scatterplots do seem to form a quasi-triangle compatible with Guilford's hypothesis.

Creativity and Other Special Abilities

ASSOCIATIONAL ABILITIES   The idea that creativity involves the ability or tendency to form numerous and unusual associations is, of course, a very old and sturdy one in the history of psychology. It is therefore not surprising that considerable effort was devoted to examining relationships between creativity and associative abilities and tendencies during the past 15 years. Much of this work centered on the Mednicks' Remote Associates Test (Mednick & Mednick 1967). Rather than attempt a superficial review of the substantial work using this measure, we refer the reader to test reviews by Baird (1972), Bennett (1972), Vernon (1972a), and Backman & Tuckman (1978), to Worthen & Clark (1971) for a critique of the RAT and a possibly improved measure of remote associational ability, to Mendelsohn (1976) for a good review of his studies of attentional processes presumably underlying RAT performance, to Noppe & Gallagher (1977) for a cognitive-style approach to the RAT, and to Sobel (1978) for a very recent review of 18 studies examining the remote associates theory of creativity.

Interesting new work in the associationistic tradition was also reported by Rothenberg (1973a,b), who found evidence supporting his Janusian thinking theory of creativity (Rothenberg 1979) in the fact that opposite-responding on word association tests was significantly and positively related to indices of creativity, and by MacKinnon (1962a) and Gough (1976a), who found that *moderately* unusual associations were positively correlated with rated creativity in their samples of architects, research scientists, and engineering students.

ACCESS TO MORE PRIMITIVE MODES OF THOUGHT   The idea that creativity is facilitated by access to relatively primitive modes of cognition is a fundamental aspect of the psychoanalytic theory of creativity, and as such has been a focus of considerable research for many years. The past 15 years have seen a steady stream of research by Child (1965), Wild (1965), Dudek (1968), Taft (1971), Schaefer (1971b, 1972a), Holland & Baird (1968), Rogolsky (1968), Gray (1969), Raychaudhuri (1971, 1972), Aronow (1972), Barron (1972), Schmidt (1973), Eiduson (1974), Dudek (1975), Del Gaudio (1976), Domino (1976), Loshak & Reznikoff (1976), Schaefer, Diggens & Millman (1976), and Frank (1979). Recently this topic has been reviewed comprehensively by Suler (1980).

This line of research has also produced several new measures of relevance to creativity: Singer's Regression in the Service of the Ego (RISE) scale (as reported in Child 1965); Fitzgerald's Experience Inquiry (1966) (which also attempts to measure RISE, among other interesting characteristics); a Preconscious Activity Scale by Holland & Baird (1968); an "Ego-Permissiveness" scale by Taft (1971); and Coan's Experience Inventory (as described in Schaefer et al 1976).

ANALOGICAL AND METAPHORICAL ABILITIES   During the past 15 years investigators have actively examined the possible role of analogical and metaphorical thinking in creativity (e.g. Gordon 1966; Dreistadt 1968, 1974; Arieti 1976; Khatena 1975; Harrington 1979, 1981). This interest had earlier led to the development of Barron's Symbol Equivalents Test (1969), in use since 1951 at IPAR, and Schaefer's Similes Test (1971a), both of which measure abilities involved in the production of analogical and metaphorical images. Other tests in this domain include Khatena's Onomatopoeia and Images Test (Khatena 1969, Khatena & Torrance 1976), and Kogan's Metaphoric Triads Task (Kogan et al 1980). Winner & Gardner (1977) developed a "metaphoric competence" measure with which to study laterality effects in the thinking of brain-damaged patients. It seems very likely that the 1980s will see a vigorous exploration of the role played in creative thinking by analogical and metaphorical processes and abilities.

IMAGERY ABILITIES   Spurred by developments in cognitive psychology which "re-legitimized" the topic and partly spurred by a new journal (*Journal of Mental Imagery*), several creativity investigators have also returned to a topic of long-standing interest in this field: imagery. We refer the reader to recent overviews by Lindauer (1977), Forisha (1978a,b), Khatena (1978), and a very interesting piece of earlier work by Juhasz (1972) which has not received the attention we think it deserves.

PROBLEM FINDING ABILITIES   One of the most interesting developments of the past 15 years was the emergence of problem finding as an
important topic of investigation. Significant contributions included Mackworth's paper on problem-finding in science (1965), Csikszentmihalyi and
Getzels' interest in problem finding in art (Getzels & Csikszentmihalyi
1976) and life (Csikszentmihalyi & Beattie 1979) and Arlin's attempts to
develop and explore problem finding within a neo-Piagetian developmental
perspective (1975, 1977). Recent studies by Kasperson (1978) and Glover
(1979) of relationships between creativity and question asking and information obtaining behaviors represent further extensions of this new interest in
what is clearly a crucial aspect of creative behavior and one which will
almost surely be studied very seriously in the 1980s.

CREATIVITY AND PERSONALITY

A Proliferation of Studies in Many Fields

The search for personality characteristics associated with creative achievement and activity has been carried on in many domains and at many age
levels by investigators using a variety of procedures and approaching the
task from both the intra- and inter-field perspectives described above. Let
us first look at the scope of the studies by field before seeking a common
core in the diverse findings.

ART   Studies of personality characteristics associated with artistic activity
and creative achievement involved preschool children (Harrington, Block
& Block 1974, Trowbridge & Charles 1966); elementary school children
(Trowbridge & Charles 1966, Ellison et al 1976, Milgram et al 1977); high
school students (Trowbridge & Charles 1966, Schaefer & Anastasi 1968,
Holland & Baird 1968, Anastasi & Schaefer 1969, Schaefer 1969a,b, Walberg 1969a, Ellison et al 1976); undergraduates and students in art schools
(Cross, Cattell & Butcher 1967, Barron 1972, Rossman & Horn 1972, Gotz
& Gotz 1973, Csikszentmihalyi & Getzels 1973, Schaefer 1973, Zeldow
1973, Getzels & Csikszentmihalyi 1976, Rossman 1976, Korb & Frankiewicz 1979, Shelton & Harris 1979); professional artists (Cross et al 1967,
Bachtold & Werner 1973, Amos 1978, Gotz & Gotz 1979a,b). Personality
correlates of architectural creativity were studied using students of architecture (Karlins, Schuerhoff & Kaplan 1969, Schmidt 1973) and professional
architects (Hall & MacKinnon 1969, Gough 1979). The personality characteristics of undergraduate cinematographers were also examined (Domino
1974).

LITERATURE   Investigators studied personality characteristics associated with creative writing among elementary school children (Milgram et al 1977); high school students (Schaefer & Anastasi 1968, Holland & Baird 1968, Anastasi & Schaefer 1969, Schaefer 1969a,b); college students (Korb & Frankiewicz 1979); and professional writers (Helson 1970, 1973a,b, Bachtold & Werner 1973, Helson 1977, 1977–1978).

MUSIC   Personality characteristics of creative musicians in India were studied (Raychaudhuri 1966, 1967) as were characteristics associated with musical composition grades in a sample of music students (Khatena 1971b).

SCIENCE AND TECHNOLOGY   Personality correlates of scientific achievement and creativity were studied in elementary school children (Milgram et al 1977); high school students (Schaefer & Anastasi 1968, Parloff et al 1968, Anastasi & Schaefer 1969, Schaefer 1969a,b, Walberg 1969a); undergraduates, young adults, and graduate students (Rossman & Horn 1972, Schaefer 1973, Gough 1979, Korb & Frankiewicz 1979); psychologists (Chambers 1964, Wispe 1965, Bachtold & Werner 1970); inventors (Bergum 1975, Albaum 1976, Albaum & Baker 1977); mathematicians (Helson 1967b, 1968a; Parloff et al 1968; Helson & Crutchfield 1970a,b; Helson 1971; Gough 1979); chemists (Chambers 1964); and assorted engineers and research scientists (McDermid 1965, Owens 1969, Bachtold & Werner 1972, Bergum 1973, Eiduson 1974, Gough 1979).

MULTIPLE DOMAINS   Personality correlates of global or multiple field indices of creative achievement, activity, and reputation were studied using elementary school children (Sussman & Justman 1975); undergraduates and young adults (Helson 1967a, Domino 1970, Taft & Gilchrist 1970, Elton & Rose 1974); college professors (Chambers 1973, Bergum 1974); and adults living in Calcutta (Raychaudhuri 1971).

The Emergence of Core Characteristics

The empirical work of the past 15 years on the personality characteristics of creative people brought few surprises. In general, a fairly stable set of core characteristics (e.g. high valuation of esthetic qualities in experience, broad interests, attraction to complexity, high energy, independence of judgment, autonomy, intuition, self-confidence, ability to resolve antinomies or to accommodate apparently opposite or conflicting traits in one's self-concept, and, finally, a firm sense of self as "creative") continued to emerge as correlates of creative achievement and activity in many domains.

One manifestation of this apparent emergence of core characteristics was the development of several empirically keyed "creative personality" scales for Gough's *Adjective Check List* (Smith & Schaefer 1969; Domino 1970; Yarnell 1971a,b; Harrington 1972, 1975; Gough 1979). Reasonably encouraging evidence of the construct validity of these scales has subsequently emerged (Domino 1974, Welsh 1975, Albaum & Baker 1977, Domino 1977, Ironson & Davis 1979). A 5-year follow-up (Schaefer 1972c) has demonstrated the temporal stability of one of these scales, and studies (Harrington 1972; unpublished manuscript, 1979) have revealed very high interscale correlations. The magnitude of these correlations (typically in the .70s and .80s after statistical removal of general adjective-endorsing tendencies) establishes the existence of a set of core characteristics associated with creative achievement and activity in a fairly wide range of domains. The adjectives in the Composite Creative Personality scale (Harrington 1972, 1975) provide a good sense of these scales: active, alert, ambitious, argumentative, artistic, assertive, capable, clear thinking, clever, complicated, confident, curious, cynical, demanding, egotistical, energetic, enthusiastic, hurried, idealistic, imaginative, impulsive, independent, individualistic, ingenious, insightful, intelligent, interests wide, inventive, original, practical, quick, rebellious, reflective, resourceful, self-confident, sensitive, sharp-witted, spontaneous, unconventional, versatile, and *not* conventional and *not* inhibited.

Because the scales are embedded in a set of 300 extremely diverse adjectives, they are not transparent (and thus unduly face valid) in their naturally administered form. Recent evidence regarding their vulnerability to conscious attempts to "fake creative" (Ironson & Davis 1979), however, suggests that application of the ACL to subjects sensitive to the issue of creativity should be avoided when these scales are used. For example, they would probably be very poor measures to use in evaluating the effectiveness of creativity workshops or training programs.

The apparent emergence of core characteristics also prompted several investigators to survey the pattern of consistent correlates and to construct their own creative personality scales and inventories on a rational, aposteriori basis. Creative personality scales were thus developed for use with elementary school children by Schaefer (see Schaefer & Bridges 1970; Schaefer 1971c; and reviews by Vernon 1978 and Yamamoto 1978); Rookey 1971, 1974; Rimm 1976; Rimm & Davis 1976; Davis & Rimm 1977) and for use with adolescents and adults by Torrance and Khatena (Torrance 1970; Khatena 1971a; Khatena & Torrance 1976) and by Davis (1975). Evidence regarding the construct validity of several of these instruments was presented by Rekdal (1977) and is routinely updated in *Gifted Child Quarterly*.

The consistent emergence of certain correlates of creative achievement and activity also led to the development of an empirically based "creativity equation" by Cattell for his widely used 16 PF (Cattell, Eber & Tatsuoka 1970, pp. 129, 241–42). In a partial validation of this equation, Csikszentmihalyi & Getzels (1973) applied Cattell's equation to a sample of student artists and found those students' average creativity scores to be at the eighty-ninth percentile using college norms. Though the 16PF equation was offered as an index of the global creative personality, hope was held out that further research would provide evidence by which different equation weights could be developed for specific types of creativity and situations. Similar indices or composites were developed by the IPAR group for several widely used inventories (Hall & MacKinnon 1969). Which of these "core" personality characteristics facilitate effective social behavior of almost any form? Which specifically facilitate *creative* behavior? Which are by-products of social achievement and recognition of almost any form? Which are specifically by-products of creative achievement and recognition? Which are merely noncausally related correlates of creative achievement? These are questions that deserve careful attention from investigators of the 1980s. We suspect that longitudinal studies and systematic cross-field comparisons may be particularly helpful in illuminating these unresolved issues.

Increased Attention to Age- and Field-Related Differences

While evidence of a set of core characteristics associated with creative achievement and activity in many domains grew stronger, several investigators became increasingly sensitive to the possibility that the picture of the creative person might vary as a function of age, sex, and field of creative activity.

AGE   The proliferation of studies of creativity involving adolescents and young adults made possible an expanded search for age-related changes in the picture of the creative person. In an analysis of personality correlates associated with creativity in adolescent and adult men, Parloff et al (1968), for example, identified a factor they called "Disciplined Effectiveness" which correlated positively with indices of creative achievement in their adolescent males and negatively with indices of creative achievement in their adult males. This reversal was discussed at some length in terms of the relative importance of impulse control at certain stages of personal and professional development. Somewhat similar evidence of possible age-related correlational reversal involving the CPI Responsibility scale (slightly positively correlated with creativity among undergraduate cinematographers and significantly negatively correlated with creativity among professional architects) appeared in evidence reported by Domino (1974), who also commented upon apparent age-related correlational differences involving confidence in interpersonal interactions. In a similar vein, change in the apparent role of self-regulatory capacities regarding "creative" artistic achievement was also noted in a longitudinal study of preschool children (Harrington et al 1974) where indices of self-regulation were positively correlated with creative artistic achievement at 3-1/2 and negatively correlated at 5-1/2. This is an important point; the search for taxonomic simplicity has all too often ignored the phenomenon of developmental ebb and flow in many traits.

FIELD OF CREATIVITY   As the number of studies in any given area has increased, it has become easier to detect and view with confidence the apparent field specificity of certain characteristics associated with creativity. It has become increasingly clear, for example, that creative scientists tend to be more emotionally stable, venturesome, and self-assured than the average individual, whereas creative artists and writers tend to be less stable, less venturesome, and more guilt prone (Cattell 1971, p. 411). As the studies of Getzels & Csikszentmihalyi (1976) make clear, it may also be necessary to draw distinctions *within* domains (e.g. fine artists vs applied artists) lest intradomain differences cancel one another out and badly obscure overall findings. Important studies in which the role of domain has been explicitly considered have also been reported by Parloff et al (1968); Anastasi & Schaefer 1969; Schaefer 1969a,b,c and 1972b,c, 1973; Schaefer & Anastasi 1968; Helson 1968a; Rossman & Horn 1972; Korb & Frankiewicz 1979. It should be noted in this context that Schaefer's studies of biographical inventory correlates of creativity led him to develop field-specific creativity scales (Schaefer 1970a) for his inventory.

The search for field-specific correlates and characteristics is in no way incompatible with the search for a set of core characteristics associated with creativity in fairly diverse domains. The 1980s will surely see a tendency to develop increasingly field-specific pictures of the creative person.

Creativity in Men and Women: A New Focus on Sex-Related Differences

Led by the pioneering efforts of Ravenna Helson (1966a,b, 1967a,b, 1968a,b, 1970, 1971, 1973a,b, 1974, 1977, 1977–1978, 1978a,b), many creativity investigators turned their attention to the psychology of creativity in women, to the possibility that different stories must be told about creative men and creative women, and to the possible roles played by such constructs as "psychological masculinity," "matriarchal consciousness," and "psychological androgyny."

STUDIES OF CREATIVE WOMEN   Studies and reviews of creative women focused on women engaged in art (Nochlin 1971, 1979; Greer, 1979);

writing (Olsen 1970, 1978; Spacks 1972; Showalter 1971; Helson 1973b); art and literature (Anastasi & Schaefer 1969; Schaefer 1969a,b, 1970b, 1971b, 1972b,c, 1973; Bachtold & Werner 1973); science (Walberg 1969b; Bachtold & Werner 1972); mathematics (Helson 1971); psychology (Bachtold & Werner 1970); elementary school teaching (Torrance, Tan & Allman 1970); college teaching (Groth 1975); and other assorted activities (Helson 1966a,b, 1967a, 1968b; Torrance 1972a; Suter & Domino 1975; Yu 1977; Blaubergs 1978; Morse & Bruch 1978; Lemkau 1979). It is clear that those wishing to examine the psychology of creative women have far more empirical evidence to look at today than they did 15 years ago. Very helpful reviews of this work can be found in Blaubergs (1978), Helson (1978b), and Lemkau (1979).

TWO TYPES OF SEX DIFFERENCES

Mean differences   Because investigators increasingly included sex as a variable in their analysis, studies comparing males and females on creativity-related indices are simply too numerous to cite. For integrations of these studies the reader is referred to useful reviews by Kogan (1974), Forisha (1978b), and Helson (1978b).

Correlational differences   Investigators have also become increasingly sensitive to the possibility of sex differences involving correlational patterns or interactions involving sex. For example, investigators have reported and commented upon different patterns of results for males and females related to creative working styles (Helson 1967b, 1968a) and products (Helson 1977); relationship of DT test performances to indices of psychological androgyny (Jones, Chernovetz & Hansson 1978); personality characteristics associated with barrier resourcefulness in preschool children (Block, Block & Harrington 1975); personality correlates of artistic achievement and status (Schaefer 1969b, Barron 1972, Getzels & Csikszentmihalyi 1976); cognitive-perceptual correlates of artistic achievement (Getzels & Csikszentmihalyi 1976); correlations among creative activity-achievement checklist scores (Hocevar 1976); correlations between imagery and creativity indices (Forisha 1978b); correlates of RAT scores (Gall & Mendelsohn 1967, Mendelsohn & Covington 1972, Mendelsohn 1976); validities of divergent thinking test scores (Vernon 1972b); behavioral correlates of DT test scores among kindergarteners (Singer & Rummo 1973); correlations between defensiveness and DT scores in children (Wallach & Kogan 1965, Kogan & Morgan 1969); reliabilities of DT test scores (Kogan & Pankove 1972, Torrance & Alliotti 1969); correlations between biographical inventory scales of creativity and indices of openness to experience and sensation seeking (Schaefer et al 1976); and effects of explicit instructions to "be creative" on divergent thinking tests (Katz & Poag 1979).

In some of these studies correlational differences were tested for statistical significance and in many they were not. As differences between correlational and regression patterns become of greater interest, investigators will presumably grow more sophisticated in their analysis.

PSYCHOLOGICAL FEMININITY, MASCULINITY, AND ANDROGYNY Studies of the relationship between various indices of creativity (sometimes defined as achievement and sometimes as ability) and indices of psychological masculinity ("patriarchal consciousness"), psychological femininity ("matriarchal consciousness"), and psychological androgyny were reported by Helson 1966a, 1967b, 1968a, 1970, 1971, 1973b; Littlejohn 1967; Stringer 1967; Hall & MacKinnon 1969; Urbina et al 1970; Domino 1974; Barron 1972; Suter & Domino 1975; Welsh 1975; Kanner 1976; Milgram et al 1977; Jones et al 1978; Harrington & Anderson 1979 and unpublished manuscript, 1980). The results of these studies cannot be summarized briefly. Suffice it to say that indices of psychological femininity, masculinity, and androgyny were sometimes positively and sometimes negatively associated with indices of creative achievement, ability, or self-concept. This area of research is simply too new for a clear picture to have emerged.

In addition to focusing attention upon creative women as such and thereby enormously broadening our picture of creative people, the study of creativity in women called the field's attention to the critical role which social context, expectation, and pressure play in determining whether creative talent is fostered and, if so, how it is directed. We suspect the benefits of this redirection of attention will be felt increasingly as the 1980s progress.

Development of New Measures of Personality

In addition to the creative personality scales described above, a number of interesting new personality measures relevant to creativity research were introduced. Based on the early work by Gough & Woodworth (1960) with research scientists, by MacKinnon & Hall (MacKinnon 1963) with architects, and by Barron & Egan (1968) with business managers, Helson (1967b, 1973a,b) developed a Mathematician's Q-set and a Writer's Q-set by which individuals in these fields could describe their own work styles, relationships to their work, and other factors rarely tapped by standard personality assessment devices. By including formally similar items in field-specific Q-sets, Helson is obviously creating the possibility for very interesting studies across fields. Evidence reported thus far suggests that self-descriptions generated with these Q-sets are very useful in drawing connections between personality and process.

Kirton's Adaptation-Innovation Inventory (Kirton 1976, 1977a,b) was designed to measure an individual's tendency to direct creativity either toward innovation or toward creative adaptation. Though validity information is meager at this point, the idea of measuring such a creativity style seems quite intriguing.

Pursuing his five-level definition of creativity, I. A. Taylor (Taylor, Sutton & Haworth 1974) developed the Creative Behavior Disposition Scale to assess dispositions toward expressive, technical, inventive, innovative, and emergentive creativity. Again, though validity data are meager, the concept underlying this instrument is promising.

New personality inventories containing scales of potential relevance to creativity investigators included Jackson's *Personality Research Form* (particularly his scales for autonomy, change, cognitive structure, sentience, and understanding) (Jackson 1967) and the *Jackson Personality Inventory* (Jackson 1976, 1978) (especially the scales for breadth of interest, complexity, conformity, energy level, and innovation).

A fine review of recent progress in the assessment of curiosity has also appeared (Maw & Maw 1978). Reviews of recent methodological and theoretical progress with respect to such potentially relevant dimensions as achievement striving, field dependence, locus of control, and sensation seeking have also appeared recently in an edited collection by London & Exner (1978).

New Efforts to Link Personality to Process and Product

Extremely interesting attempts have been made in the last few years to link personality characteristics to facets of the creative process and to characteristics of creative products.

In her studies of writers of children's fiction, Helson (1973a,b) has made some progress in relating the placement of her Writers Q-set items to consensually rated characteristics of the children's books themselves. More recently Helson (1977–78) has begun to link personality characteristics of the writers to characteristics of their products via the writers' recollected experiences during the writing process. Dudek & Hall's (1978–79) effort to relate personal style in architecture to personality characteristics of the architect via qualitative analysis of Rorschach responses is another example of this interesting new line of inquiry. Fraught with the difficulties of pioneering efforts as they are, these initial studies seem very promising.

In an intriguingly similar enterprise, Atwood & Tomkins (1976) and Stolorow & Atwood (1979) have attempted to draw clear connections between personality characteristics of personality theorists and the character of their personality theories. The formal similarity to Helson's work is obvious and interesting.

Krantz & Wiggins (1973) have also undertaken a study linking personality characteristics of highly creative psychologists (Hull, Skinner, Spence, and Tolman) to their impact on the field by examining their direct relationships with their students. Implications of this work for a sociology of knowledge have been discussed by Campbell (1979).

These efforts to connect personality, process, and product strike us as extraordinarily exciting and deserving of encouragement and emulation.

THOUGHT DISORDER AND CREATIVITY

Disorders of thinking may occur in clinical syndromes such as schizophrenia, manic depressive psychosis, and brain damage. Reasoning and realistic observation may also be diminished in certain readily reversible altered states of consciousness, such as extreme emotion, mystical states, reveries, temporary alcoholic- or drug-induced derangements, dreams, and domination by unconscious motives in more or less ordinary individuals.

Meehl (1962) in his APA presidential address saw thought disorder as one of four hypothesized components in schizophrenia (the other three being anhedonia, ambivalence, and personal aversiveness). He proposed that it is necessary to distinguish among *schizotaxia, schizotypia,* and *schizophrenia. Schizotaxia* is an inherited specific etiology, "an aberration in some parameter of a single-cell function," and is essentially a neural integrative defect; the *schizotype* is a form of personality organization arising from schizotaxia but conditioned by social learning and including as dispositional tendencies the four components of schizophrenia; *schizophrenia* is the clinical manifestation of a process of decompensation in a subset of schizotypic personalities.

This seems to us an important clarification of the difference between an inherited disposition and a social outcome. By analogy, divergent thinking at the neurological (single cell or not) level is *originotaxic;* the *originotype* is a form of personality organization in which the disposition toward originality, itself having several discernible components (Barron 1955), are present and capable of expression depending upon the presence of other factors, both in the environment and in the personality; *creativity* is a social outcome, certainly not a decompensation but quite possibly an overcompensation, if one employs those terms.

Let us back up a bit and look at the problem of the relationship of divergent thinking (originality) and thought disorder once again.

Studies of "normal" relatives of persons diagnosed as schizophrenic have shown a markedly higher incidence of thought disorder than one finds in the general population. At the same time, among the relatives of such patients there is a higher proportion of individuals who have achieved eminence through creative activities (see Karlsson 1978 for a summary of the evidence from his own and others' researches).

Dobzhansky (1964) has argued that schizophrenia is strongly hereditary and may be inherited according to a simple Mendelian model but that incomplete penetrance of the gene is common, so that there may be as many as ten undetected carriers to one who develops a florid psychosis. Furthermore, the percentage of carriers may range from 10 to 20% of the general population. The implication is that an unusual cognitive condition, with a single-gene, single-cell base and sometimes clinically evident as thought disorder, is relatively common. In the presence of certain crucially ameliorative factors or moderator variables (high intelligence, e.g., or high ego strength) could this condition manifest itself as originality of thought, or creativity? Jarvik & Chadwick (1973) point out that a condition so detrimental to survival as schizophrenia, with a highly probable genetic component, should have declined by natural selection unless it had positive, adaptive aspects.

In a study by Al-issa (1972), 50 schizophrenics were administered ten of the Guilford tests, including Impossibilities, Consequences scored for remoteness, and Alternative Uses. All tests proved to have a high positive correlation with vocabulary. However, Remote Consequence and Alternative Uses were significantly negatively related to a measure of overinclusion, traditionally a sign of thought disorder. (Overinclusion may be a misleading term, a name given by the test interpreter to the respondent's tendency to use, or at least attend to, more and seemingly irrelevant information than is necessary for the solution of the problem at hand. But sometimes that is a very useful habit for the creative problem solver to have; overinclusion today may yield tomorrow's fresh insight.) The (complex) W score on the Rorschach, which reflects the respondent's effort to include many aspects of the blot in a single synthesizing image, has been shown by Barron (1955, 1957) to be highly positively correlated with a composite score for originality, including many DT tests; moreover, a substantial correlation of W with originality survives the partialling out of measured intelligence.

Several studies support this line of reasoning. McConaghy & Clancy (1968) showed that "allusive" thinking on object-sorting tasks is common though not so pronounced in the normal population as in schizophrenics, and they showed familial transmission in schizophrenics and nonschizophrenics. Dykes & McGhie (1976) showed that highly creative normal subjects score as high on the Loviband object sorting test as do schizophrenics. Woody & Claridge (1977), using Guilford DT tests and the Eysenck Personality Inventory (EPI) with a group of 100 university students, found "psychoticism" strongly related to divergent thinking. Farmer (1974) (cited by Woody & Claridge 1977) showed that EPI Psychoticism was very highly correlated with Originality on the Consequences test.

In an analysis of the Schizophrenia scale of the MMPI to discover how hospitalized "schizophrenics" differed from at-large "artists" matched for Sc score, age, sex, and education, it was discovered that the two groups clearly earned their identical Sc elevations in very different ways; the analysis yielded a subset of 18 items significantly differentiating the groups (Barron 1972). The item content for the 18-item subscale seems to express mostly a positive hedonic tone in the artists as contrasted with anhedonia in the patients; items on which schizophrenics and artists were similar are reports of odd sensory and perceptual experiences, a preference for solitude, rejection of common social values, and feelings of restlessness leading at times to impulsive outbursts. Claridge (1972) showed that divergent thinking tests were significantly related to an index of psychoticism based on a principal components analysis of a wide range of psychophysiological parameters known to discriminate psychotics from normal controls.

For an incisive analysis of these questions and a selected brief but excellent review of the literature, see Hasenfus & Magaro (1976), "Creativity and schizophrenia: An equality of empirical constructs." As they show, the research evidence supports the thesis that ideational fluency and "overinclusion" are facets of the same cognitive propensity, and that a tendency to introduce complexity in perception goes both with creativity and with schizophrenia. Yet the core characteristics of the creative person as summarized above are certainly not those of someone in the throes of a bout with schizophrenia, nor even of the schizotypic personality. Here we are badly in need of thoughtful research. The question itself may contain an important key to the psychological and genetic connections between psychological health and psychological disease.

The use of alcohol and its function in creative thinking has been discussed by Karlsson (1978) and others. Alcohol of course produces diminished observation and loss of memory, including at times the loss of whole classes of information necessary for adaptive functioning. However, it also loosens inhibitions, increases "inappropriate" associations, and leads to "cosmic" thoughts and utterances, all of which can be instrumental in certain types of creative activity. But of course alcohol can also be used for its damping effects when the cortical fires are burning too brightly. Research on creativity and the use of alcohol might profitably employ Pavlov's theories concerning cortical inhibition and excitation and their relationship to personality types.

Psychedelic or hallucinogenic (take your pick of the terms) drugs produce altered states of consciousness that clearly are the result of biochemical interventions affecting neural systems. These states result in temporary abrogation of certain perceptual constancies and thereby in novel experience, whether in a passive waking state or accompanied by active behavior that in turn leads to novel situations. Description of the effects of such drugs and their chemical nature, as well as speculation about the way they work, can be found in a summary by Barron, Jarvik & Bunnell (1964). Their effect specifically on creativity has been reviewed by Krippner (1977). In general, it appears that creativity as ability or achievement is little affected one way or another over the long term by such agents, though at the level of momentary direct experience they produce novelty and divergent thinking; their effect on creativity as attitude is difficult to assess, though important.

Perhaps these substances and their effects are best understood in relation to trance states and suggestibility. If someone in a good position to do so should suggest to you that you can do better at something, you probably will—about 10 to 20% better.

Testimony from recognized geniuses (see Ghiselin 1952, e.g.) show that intense motivation and experience in unusual states of consciousness are instrumental in what is later recognized by society as high creativity. The self-managed introduction of consciousness-altering substances may be a well-thought-out strategy on the part of some creative people; or it may simply be a compulsive method for achieving temporary regression in the service of the ego.

If the disposition to schizophrenia is inherited, is the component called thought disorder inherited too? Is the ability or tendency to think divergently inherited? Twin studies with normal subjects suggest on the whole that twin resemblances in verbal DT abilities do not show zygosity effects (Barron 1972; Pezzullo, Thorsen & Madaus 1972; Barron & Parisi 1977). However, those studies as well as the results obtained by Domino et al 1976, support the well-known distinction between verbal and figural abilities (which do seem to be inherited) in creativity. A refinement of design that would include sampling of co-twins of schizophrenic index cases as well as other family members seems in order.

PSYCHOBIOGRAPHY, PSYCHOHISTORY, AND THE LIFE-SPAN PERSPECTIVE

Pursuing a recognition in the early 1960s that biographical information provided good bases for predicting creative achievement, many investigators have developed and employed biographical inventories and a life-span approach in creativity research during the last 15 years. The heightened interest in the study of lives received an important impetus from the Henry A. Murray festschrift (*The Study of Lives* by White, 1963) and was evident in perspective-providing developmental reviews and theoretical work by

Arasteh (1968), Arasteh & Arasteh (1968, 1976), Wallach (1970), Gowan (1972, 1974), Kogan (1973), Landau & Maoz (1978), Shapiro (1975), Arlin (1976), Alpaugh, Renner & Birren (1976), and Runyan (1978); by methodological pioneering in the field by Simonton (e.g. 1975, 1976b, 1977, 1978); and by empirical studies cast in developmental terms (e.g. Dennis 1966; Roe 1965, 1972; Waterman, Kohutiz & Pulone 1977; Schultz, Hoyer & Kaye 1980). Studies of creativity and DT abilities in increasingly younger children (Dudek 1974, Starkweather 1976, Ward 1974, and many others) also indicated growing interest in the life-span perspective. So, too, did numerous studies of parental and home influences on the development of creative individuals (Nichols 1964, MacKinnon 1966, Datta 1967, Datta & Parloff 1967, Helson 1968b, Schaefer & Anastasi 1968, Anastasi & Schaefer 1969, Domino 1969, Heilbrun 1971, Barron 1972, Dewing 1973, Getzels & Csikszentmihalyi 1976, Grant & Domino 1976, Goertzel, Goertzel & Goertzel 1978, Domino 1979). The notoriously awesome problems of conducting longitudinal studies were taken on by several investigators (Helson 1967a; Owens 1969; Cropley 1972; Kogan & Pankove 1972, 1974; Schaefer 1972b,c, 1973; Torrance 1972b; Eiduson 1974; Getzels & Csikszentmihalyi 1976; Gough 1976b, 1979; Magnusson & Backteman 1978), who obviously realized that many fundamental questions regarding the psychology of creativity can only be approached from a developmental and longitudinal perspective.

At least two biographical inventories with empirically keyed creativity scales have been marketed—the Alpha Biographical Inventory, developed by C. W. Taylor and R. Ellison at the Institute for Behavioral Research in Creativity in 1966 (reviewed by Hemphill 1972 and Ward 1972) and the Biographical Inventory (Schaefer 1970a). These and similar inventories have been used in studies of artistic, scientific, and entrepreneurial creative achievement. Groups have included elementary school children (Ellison et al 1976); high school students (Schaefer & Anastasi 1968; Anastasi & Schaefer 1969; Schaefer 1969a; Walberg 1969a; Schaefer 1972b; Torrance, Bruch & Morse 1973; James et al 1974; Payne & Halpin 1974; Ellison et al 1976); professionals in engineering and scientific creativity (Buel 1965; McDermid 1965; Buel, Albright & Glennon 1966; Taylor & Ellison 1967; Tucker, Cline & Schmitt 1967; Owens 1969; Ellison, James & Carron 1970; Albaum 1976); and business managers (Barron 1969). Cross-validated correlations have typically ranged from the .30s to the high .50s with empirically keyed creativity scales developed from these inventories. Such creativity scales have also been used as creativity *criteria* against which other indices of interest have been correlated (e.g. Davis & Belcher 1971, Lacey & Erickson 1974, Suter & Domino 1975, Patel 1976, and Schaefer et al 1976).

The very factorial complexity (e.g. Morrison et al 1962; Payne & Halpin 1974) which gives these biographical scales their predictive power also creates serious interpretive difficulties if one attempts to derive theoretically pertinent meaning from them. While the inclusion of information about such factors as availability of cultural materials in the home, parental education, childhood hobbies, quality of education, perceived parental pressures and encouragements, previous creative activities, achievements and awards, current motivations, and current self-rated abilities certainly increases the predictive power of these scales, correlations between aggregations of such items and indices of creative achievement do not lend themselves to incisive interpretation. Such scales are factorially complex correlates of creative achievement, and as such should not be substituted for creative achievement indices. We believe that the maximum scientific value of such inventories will come from examining and reflecting upon the content of item-level correlates of creative achievement in particular settings and samples. By providing a wide range of information (particularly regarding situation and life-history factors often neglected in creativity research) biographical inventories have broadened our perspective in important ways. It would therefore be particularly disappointing if the inherent potentials of such inventories are lost in the tunnel-vision pursuit of large but theoretically unilluminating validity coefficients.

This line of work needs more attention, mostly because the items in a biographical inventory usually relate to life circumstance and can fill in some of the gaps in knowledge about *press* and about situational factors in general. Early foot in many professions, e.g., is based on money in the bank, and creativity is less a card of entry than an ability that might not otherwise find expression. The biographical inventory is especially important to the study of life's outcomes, and to the intersection of historical or socioeconomic conditions with stage of professional and personal development. Studies of cross-cultural and cross-generational effects on creativity are needed, such as the Barron & Young (1970) study of the descendants of immigrants from southern Italy to Rome and Boston respectively. Simonton (1975) has provided innovative systematic methods of generational analysis, with interesting results, for research on changes in creativity over long time spans. Goertzel, Goertzel & Goertzel (1978) have been less systematic methodologically but have given the field a major book, beguiling in its detailed consideration of creative lives. A rash of psychologically sensitive biographies ("psychobiographies") are evidence of new interest in a psychological, personological approach to the understanding of creative lives in their historical context. The study of such lives and careers does itself animate history and makes it more comprehensible. This is an area of study hardly begun. What is needed is a way of encoding observations from psychologically impressionistic and complex psychobiographies to yield data susceptible of analysis relevant to the life course and to historical process. The archives of research centers that have accumulated observations over the years are gold mines of data that can be used for such analyses given a reliable and standardized source of information about later significant events, outcomes if you will, in the lives of creative women and men. A good example of the pooling of such data from many sources is provided by the Murray Research Center for the Study of Lives, founded at Radcliffe College in 1979. Given the unusual difficulties and efforts involved in gathering rich psychological data on creative individuals, we hope that secondary analyses of such data, undertaken with increasingly sophisticated data-analytic techniques and from diverse conceptual perspectives, will become widespread in the 1980s. Such analyses could be greatly facilitated by the Murray Research Center and many other centers which have accumulated archives of unparalleled potential value for the study of creative people. Imaginative cooperation involving such centers and individual investigators who have accumulated valuable longitudinal data could provide very cost-effective bases of time-series data for secondary and meta-analyses. Social support for such centers in the form of money and endorsement from foundations is needed. The basic goal should be to understand integrity, excellence and creativity developmentally, especially in the later years. A new national center for such studies, not merely archival but newly initiated on the basis of our growing wisdom in these matters, is essential.

Literature Cited

Albaum, G. 1976. Selecting specialized creators: The independent inventor. *Psychol. Rep.* 39:175–79

Albaum, G., Baker, K. 1977. Cross-validation of a creativity scale for the Adjective Check List. *Educ. Psychol. Meas.* 37:1057–61

Al-issa, I. 1972. Stimulus generalization and overinclusion in normal and schizophrenic subjects. *J. Clin. Psychol.* 39:182–86

Alpaugh, P. K., Renner, V. J., Birren, J. E. 1976. Age and creativity: Implications for education and teachers. *Educ. Gerontol.* 1:17–40

Amos, S. P. 1978. Personality differences between established and less-established male and female creative artists. *J. Pers. Assess.* 42:374–77

Anastasi, A., Schaefer, C. E. 1969. Biographical correlates of artistic and literary creativity in adolescent girls. *J. Appl. Psychol.* 53:267–73

Anastasi, A., Schaefer, C. E. 1971. The Franck drawing completion test as a measure of creativity. *J. Genet. Psychol.* 119:3–12

Arasteh, A. R., Arasteh, J. D. 1968. *Creativity in the Life Cycle: II. An Interpretive Account of Creativity in Childhood, Adolescence and Adulthood.* Leiden, Netherlands: Brill

Arasteh, A. R., Arasteh, J. D. 1976. *Creativity and Human Development: An Interpretative and Annotated Bibliography.* New York: Schenkman

Arasteh, J. D. 1968. Creativity and related processes in the young child: A review of the literature. *J. Genet. Psychol.* 112:77–108

Arieti, S. 1976. *Creativity: The Magic Synthesis.* New York: Basic Books

Arlin, P. K. 1975. Cognitive development in adulthood: A fifth stage? *Dev. Psychol.* 11:602–6

Arlin, P. K. 1976. Toward a metatheoretical model of cognitive development. *Int. J. Aging Hum. Dev.* 7:247–53

Arlin, P. K. 1977. Piagetian operations in

problem finding. *Dev. Psychol.* 13: 297–98

Aronow, E. 1972. Comment on Raychaudhuri's "Relation of creativity and sex to Rorschach *M* responses." *J. Pers. Assess.* 36:303–4

Atwood, G. E., Tomkins, S. S. 1976. On the subjectivity of personality theory. *J. Hist. Behav. Sci.* 12:166–77

Bachtold, L. M., Werner, E. E. 1970. Personality profiles of gifted women: Psychologists. *Am. Psychol.* 25:234–43

Bachtold, L. M., Werner, E. E. 1972. Personality characteristics of women scientists. *Psychol. Rep.* 32:391–96

Bachtold, L. M., Werner, E. E. 1973. Personality characteristics of creative women. *Percept. Mot. Skills* 36:311–19

Backman, M. E., Tuckman, B. W. 1978. Review of the Remote Associates Test. In *The Eighth Mental Measurements Yearbook*, ed. O. K. Buros, pp. 369–70. Highland Park, NM: Gryphon

Baird, L. L. 1972. Review of the Remote Associates Test. In *The Seventh Mental Measurements Yearbook*, ed. O. K. Buros, pp. 825–29. Highland Park, NJ: Gryphon

Barron, F. 1955. The disposition toward originality. *J. Abnorm. Soc. Psychol.* 51:478–85

Barron, F. 1957. Originality in relation to personality and intellect. *J. Pers.* 25:730–42

Barron, F. 1969. *Creative Person and Creative Process.* New York: Holt, Rinehart & Winston

Barron, F. 1972. *Artists in the Making.* New York: Seminar

Barron, F., Egan, D. 1968. Leaders in innovators in Irish management. *J. Manage. Stud.* 5:41–60

Barron, F., Jarvik, M. E., Bunnell, S. 1964. The hallucinogenic drugs. *Sci. Am.* April:3–11

Barron, F., Parisi, P. 1977. Twin resemblances in expressive behavior. *Acta Genet. Med. Gemellol.* Spring

Barron, F., Young, H. B. 1970. Rome and Boston: A tale of two cities and their differing impact on the creativity and personal philosophy of southern Italian immigrants. *J. Cross-Cult. Psychol.* 1:91–114

Bennett, G. K. 1972. Review of the Remote Associates Test. See Baird 1972, p. 829

Bergum, B. O. 1973. Selection of specialized creators. *Psychol. Rep.* 33:635–39

Bergum, B. O. 1974. Self-perceptions of a graduate faculty whose publication rates are high or low. *Psychol. Rep.* 35:857–58

Bergum, B. O. 1975. Self-perceptions of creativity among academic inventors and non-inventors. *Percept. Mot. Skills* 40: 78

Binet, A., Henri, V. 1896. La psychologie individuelle. *Annee Psychol.* 2:411–65

Blaubergs, M. 1978. Personal studies of gifted females: An overview and commentary. *Gifted Child Q.* 22:539–47

Block, J. H. 1976. Issues, problems and pitfalls in assessing sex-differences: A critical review of *The Psychology of Sex Differences* (by E. E. Maccoby & C. N. Jacklin). *Merrill-Palmer Q.* 22:283–308

Block, J. H., Block, J., Harrington, D. 1975. *Sex-role typing and instrumental behavior.* Presented at Soc. Res. Child Dev. Meet., Denver

Bloomberg, M. 1973. Introduction: Approaches to creativity. In *Creativity*, ed M. Bloomberg, pp. 1–25. New Haven: College & Univ. Press

Buel, W. D. 1965. Biographical data and the identification of creative research personnel. *J. Appl. Psychol.* 49:318–31

Buel, W. D., Albright, L. E., Glennon, J. R. 1966. A note on the generality and cross-validity of personal history for identifying creative research scientists. *J. Appl. Psychol.* 50:217–19

Butcher, H. J. 1973. Intelligence and creativity. In *New Approaches in Psychological Measurement*, ed. P. Kline. New York: Wiley

Campbell, D. T. 1979. A tribal model of the social system vehicle carrying scientific knowledge. *Knowledge* 1:181–201

Carroll, J. B. 1976. Psychometric tests as cognitive tasks: A new "structure of intellect." See Resnick 1976, pp. 27–56

Carroll, J. B., Maxwell, S. E. 1979. Individual differences in cognitive abilities. *Ann. Rev. Psychol.* 30:603–40

Cattell, R. B. 1971. *Abilities: Their Structure, Growth, and Action.* Boston: Houghton Mifflin

Cattell, R. B., Eber, H. W., Tatsuoka, M. M. 1970. *Handbook for the Sixteen Personality Factor Questionnaire (16 PF).* Champaign, Ill: Inst. Pers. Ability Test.

Chambers, J. A. 1964. Relating personality and biographical factors to scientific creativity. *Psychol. Monogr.* 78

Chambers, J. A. 1969. Beginning a multidimensional theory of creativity. *Psychol. Rep.* 25:779–99

Chambers, J. A. 1973. College teachers: Their effect on creativity of students. *J. Educ. Psychol.* 65:326–34

Child, I. L. 1965. Personality correlates of esthetic judgment in college students. *J. Pers.* 33:476–511

468   BARRON & HARRINGTON

Claridge, G. 1972. The schizophrenias as nervous types. *Br. J. Psychiatry* 121:1–17

Cooper, H. M. 1979. Statistically combining independent studies: A meta-analysis of sex differences in conformity research. *J. Pers. Soc. Psychol.* 37:131–46

Corballis, M. C. 1980. Laterality and myth. *Am. Psychol.* 35:284–95

Cronbach, L. J. 1968. Intelligence? Creativity? A parsimonious reinterpretation of the Wallach-Kogan data. *Am. J. Educ. Res.* 5:491–511

Cropley, A. J. 1972. A five-year longitudinal study of the validity of creativity tests. *Dev. Psychol.* 6:119–24

Cross, P. G., Cattell, R. B., Butcher, H. J. 1967. The personality pattern of creative artists. *Br. J. Educ. Psychol.* 37:292–99

Csikszentmihalyi, M., Beattie, O. V. 1979. Life themes: A theoretical and empirical exploration of their origins and effects. *J. Hum. Psychol.* 19:45–63

Csikszentmihalyi, M., Getzels, J. W. 1973. The personality of young artists: An empirical and theoretical exploration. *Br. J. Psychol.* 64:91–104

Cunnington, B. F., Torrance, E. P. 1965. *Sounds and Images.* Boston: Ginn

Datta, L. E. 1963. Test instructions and identification of creative scientific talent. *Psychol. Rep.* 13:495–500

Datta, L. E. 1967. Family religious background and early scientific creativity. *Am. Social. Rev.* 32:626–35

Datta, L. E., Parloff, M. B. 1967. On the relevance of autonomy: Parent-child relationships and early scientific creativity. *Proc. 75th Ann. Conv. Am. Psychol. Assoc.,* pp. 149–50

Davis, G. A. 1975. In frumious pursuit of the creative person. *J. Creat. Behav.* 9:75–87

Davis, G. A., Belcher, T. L. 1971. How shall creativity be measured? Torrance tests, RAT, Alpha Biographical, and IQ. *J. Creat. Behav.* 5:153–61

Davis, G. A., Rimm, S. 1977. Characteristics of creatively gifted children. *Gifted Child Q.* 21:546–51

Del Gaudio, A. C. 1976. Psychological differentiation and mobility as related to creativity. *Percept. Mot. Skills* 43:831–41

Dellas, M., Gaier, E. L. 1970. Identification of creativity: The individual. *Psychol. Bull.* 73:55–73

Dennis, W. 1966. Creative productivity between the ages of 20 and 80 years. *J. Gerontol.* 21:1–8

Dewing, K. 1973. Some characteristics of the parents of creative twelve-year-olds. *J. Pers.* 41:71–85

Dobzhansky, T. 1964. *Mankind Evolving.* New Haven: Yale Univ. Press

Domino, G. 1969. Maternal personality correlates of sons' creativity. *J. Consult. Clin. Psychol.* 33:180–83

Domino, G. 1970. Identification of potentially creative persons from the Adjective Check List. *J. Consult. Clin. Psychol.* 35:48–51

Domino, G. 1974. Assessment of cinematographic creativity. *J. Pers. Soc. Psychol.* 30:150–54

Domino, G. 1976. Primary process thinking in dream reports as related to creative achievement. *J. Consult. Clin. Psychol.* 44:929–32

Domino, G. 1977. Homosexuality and creativity. *J. Homosex.* 2:261–67

Domino, G. 1979. Creativity and the home environment. *Gifted Child Q.* 23:818–28

Domino, G., Walsh, J., Reznikoff, M. 1976. A factor analysis of creativity in fraternal and identical twins. *J. Gen. Psychol.* 97:211–21

Dreistadt, R. 1968. An analysis of the use of analogies and metaphors in science. *J. Psychol.* 68:97–116

Dreistadt, R. 1974. The psychology of creativity: How Einstein discovered the theory of relativity. *Psychology* 11:15–25

Dudek, S. Z. 1968. Regression and creativity. *J. Nerv. Ment. Dis.* 147:535–46

Dudek, S. Z. 1974. Creativity in young children—attitude or ability? *J. Creat. Behav.* 8:282–92

Dudek, S. Z. 1975. Regression in the service of the ego in young children. *J. Pers. Assess.* 39:369–76

Dudek, S. Z., Hall, W. B. 1978–79. Design philosophy and personal style in architecture. *J. Altered States Consciousness* 4:83–92

Dykes, M., McGhie, A. 1976. A comparative study of attentional strategies of schizophrenics and highly creative normal subjects. *Br. J. Psychiatry* 128:50–56

Eiduson, B. T. 1974. 10-year longitudinal Rorschachs on research scientists. *J. Pers. Assess.* 38:405–10

Ellison, R. L., Abe, C., Fox, D. G., Coray, K. E., Taylor, C. W. 1976. Using biographical information in identifying artistic talent. *Gifted Child Q.* 20:402–13

Ellison, R. L., James, L. R., Carron, T. 1970. Prediction of R&D performance criteria with biographical information. *J. Ind. Psychol.* 5:37–57

Elton, C. F., Rose, H. A. 1974. Prediction of productivity from personality test scores. *J. Educ. Psychol.* 66:424–31

Farmer, E. W. 1974. *Psychoticism and person-orientation as general personality characteristics.* BSc thesis. Univ. Glasgow, Scotland

Fitzgerald, E. T. 1966. Measurement of openness to experience. *J. Pers. Soc. Psychol.* 4:655–63

Forisha, B. L. 1978a. Mental imagery and creativity: Review and speculations. *J. Ment. Imagery* 2:209–38

Forisha, B. L. 1978b. Creativity and imagery in men and women. *Percept. Mot. Skills* 47:1255–64

Frank, G. 1979. On the validity of hypotheses derived from the Rorschach: VI. *M* and the intrapsychic life of individuals. *Percept. Mot. Skills* 48:1267–77

Frederiksen, N., Ward, W. C. 1978. Measures for the study of creativity in scientific problem-solving. *Appl. Psychol. Meas.* 2:1–24

Freeman, J., Butcher, H. J., Christie, T. 1971. *Creativity: A Selective Review of Research.* London: Soc. Res. Higher Educ. 2nd ed.

Gall, M., Mendelsohn, G. A. 1967. Effects of facilitating techniques and subject-experimenter interaction on creative problem solving. *J. Pers. Soc. Psychol.* 5:211–16

Getzels, J. W., Csikszentmihalyi, M. 1976. *The Creative Vision: A Longitudinal Study of Problem Finding in Art.* New York: Wiley

Ghiselin, B. 1952. *The Creative Process.* Berkeley: Univ. Calif. Press

Gilchrist, M. 1972. *The Psychology of Creativity.* Melbourne: Melbourne Univ. Press

Glover, J. A. 1979. Levels of questions asked in interview and reading sessions by creative and relatively noncreative college students. *J. Genet. Psychol.* 135:103–8

Goertzel, M. G., Goertzel, V., Goertzel, T. G. 1978. *300 Eminent Personalities.* San Francisco: Jossey-Bass

Gordon, W. J. J. 1966. *The Metaphorical Way of Learning and Knowing.* Cambridge, Mass: Porpoise Books

Gotz, K. O., Gotz, K. 1973. Introversion-extraversion and neuroticism in gifted and ungifted art students. *Percept. Mot. Skills* 36:675–78

Gotz, K. O., Gotz, K. 1979a. Personality characteristics of professional artists. *Percept. Mot. Skills* 49:327–34

Gotz, K. O., Gotz, K. 1979b. Personality characteristics of successful artists. *Percept. Mot. Skills* 49:919–24

Gough, H. G. 1975. A new scientific uses test and its relationship to creativity in research. *J. Creat. Behav.* 9:245–52

Gough, H. G. 1976a. Studying creativity by means of word association tests. *J. Appl. Psychol.* 61:348–53

Gough, H. G. 1976b. What happens to creative medical students? *J. Med. Educ.* 61:348–51

Gough, H. G. 1979. A creative personality scale for the Adjective Check List. *J. Pers. Soc. Psychol.* 37:1398–1405

Gough, H. G., Woodworth, D. G. 1960. Stylistic variations among professional research scientists. *J. Psychol.* 49:87–98

Gowan, J. C. 1972. *Development of the Creative Individual.* San Diego: Knapp

Gowan, J. C. 1974. *Development of the Psychedelic Individual.* Buffalo: Creative Educ. Found.

Grant, T. N., Domino, G. 1976. Masculinity-femininity in fathers of creative male adolescents. *J. Genet. Psychol.* 129:19–27

Gray, J. J. 1969. The effect of productivity on primary process and creativity. *J. Proj. Tech.* 33:213–18

Greer, G. 1979. *The Obstacle Race: The Fortunes of Women Painters and Their Work.* New York: Farrar, Straus & Giroux

Groth, N. J. 1975. Success and creativity in male and female professors. *Gifted Child Q.* 19:328–35

Guilford, J. P. 1950. Creativity. *Am. Psychol.* 14:469–79

Guilford, J. P. 1967. *The Nature of Human Intelligence.* New York: McGraw-Hill

Guilford, J. P., Christensen, P. R. 1973. The one-way relation between creative potential and IQ. *J. Creat. Behav.* 7:247–52

Hall, W. B. 1972. A technique for assessing aesthetic predispositions: Mosaic construction test. *J. Creat. Behav.* 6:225–35

Hall, W. B., MacKinnon, D. W. 1969. Personality inventory correlates of creativity among architects. *J. Appl. Psychol.* 53:322–26

Harrington, D. M. 1972. *Effects of instructions to "Be creative" on three tests of divergent thinking abilities.* PhD thesis. Univ. Calif. Berkeley

Harrington, D. M. 1975. Effects of explicit instructions to "be creative" on the psychological meaning of divergent thinking test scores. *J. Pers.* 43:434–54

Harrington, D. M. 1979. *Creativity, analogical thinking and muscular metaphors.* Presented at Am. Psychol. Assoc. Meet., New York

Harrington, D. M. 1981. Creativity, analogical thinking and muscular metaphors. *J. Ment. Imagery.* In press

Harrington, D. M., Anderson, S. M. 1979. *Creative-self-concept, masculinity, femininity and three models of androgyny.* Presented at Am. Psychol. Assoc. Meet., New York

Harrington, D. M., Block, J. H., Block, J. 1974. *Measuring facets of creativity and intolerance of ambiguity in pre-school children with the Lowenfeld mosaic test.* Presented at West. Psychol. Assoc. Meet., San Francisco

Hasenfus, N., Magaro, P. 1976. Creativity and schizophrenia: An equality of empirical constructs. *Br. J. Psychiatry* 129:346–49

Hattie, J. A. 1977. Conditions for administering creativity tests. *Psychol. Bull.* 84: 1249–60

Hattie, J. A. 1980. Should creativity tests be administered under test-like conditions? An empirical study of three alternative conditions. *J. Educ. Psychol.* 72:87–98

Heilbrun, A. B. 1971. Maternal child rearing and creativity in sons. *J. Genet. Psychol.* 119:175–79

Helson, R. 1966a. Personality of women with imaginative and artistic interests: The role of masculinity, originality, and other characteristics in their creativity. *J. Pers.* 34:1–25

Helson, R. 1966b. Narrowness in creative women. *Psychol. Rep.* 19:618

Helson, R. 1967a. Personality characteristics and developmental history of creative college women. *Genet. Psychol. Monogr.* 75:205–56

Helson, R. 1967b. Sex differences in creative style. *J. Pers.* 35:214–33

Helson, R. 1968a. Generality of sex differences in creative style. *J. Pers.* 38:33–48

Helson, R. 1968b. Effects of sibling characteristics and parental values on creative interest and achievement. *J. Pers.* 36:589–607

Helson, R. 1970. Sex-specific patterns in creative literary fantasy. *J. Pers.* 38:344–63

Helson, R. 1971. Women mathematicians and the creative personality. *J. Consult. Clin. Psychol.* 36:210–20

Helson, R. 1973a. The heroic, the comic, and the tender: Patterns of literary fantasy and their authors. *J. Pers.* 41:163–84

Helson, R. 1973b. Heroic and tender modes in women authors of fantasy. *J. Pers.* 41:493–512

Helson, R. 1974. The inner reality of women. *Arts Soc.* 11:25–36

Helson, R. 1977. The creative spectrum of authors of fantasy. *J. Pers.* 45:310–26

Helson, R. 1977–78. Experiences of authors in writing fantasy: Two relationships between creative process and product. *J. Altered States Consciousness* 3: 235–48

Helson, R. 1978a. The imaginative process in children's literature: A quantitative approach. *Poetics* 7:135–53

Helson, R. 1978b. Creativity in women. In *The Psychology of Women: Future Directions in Research,* ed. J. Sherman, F. Denmark, pp. 553–604. New York: Psychol. Dimensions

Helson, R., Crutchfield, R. S. 1970a. Creative types in mathematics. *J. Pers.* 38: 177–97

Helson, R., Crutchfield, R. S. 1970b. Mathematicians: the creative researcher and the average PhD. *J. Consult. Clin. Psychol.* 34:250–57

Hemphill, J. K. 1972. Review of the *Alpha Biographical Inventory.* See Baird 1972, p. 1371

Hocevar, D. 1976. Dimensions of creativity. *Psychol. Rep.* 39:869–70

Hocevar, D. 1980. Intelligence, divergent thinking, and creativity. *Intelligence* 4:25–40

Holland, J. L., Baird, L. L. 1968. The preconscious activity scale: The development and validation of an originality measure. *J. Creat. Behav.* 2:217–25

Holloway, S., Torrance, E. P. 1977. The sounds and images test as a predictor of musical talent. *J. Creat. Behav.* 11:148

Horn, J. L. 1976. Human abilities: A review of research and theory in the early 1970s. *Ann. Rev. Psychol.* 27:437–85

Horn, J. L. 1977. Personality and ability theory. In *Handbook of Modern Personality Theory,* ed. R. B. Cattell, R. M. Dreger. Washington: Hemisphere

Institute for Behavioral Research in Creativity. 1966. *Alpha Biographical Inventory.* Greensboro, N.C.: Inst. Behav. Res. Creativity

Ironson, G. H., Davis, G. A. 1979. Faking high or low creativity scores on the Adjective Check List. *J. Creat. Behav.* 13:139–45

Jackson, D. N. 1967. *Personal Research Form Manual.* Goshen, NY: Res. Psychol. Press

Jackson, D. N. 1976. *Jackson Personality Inventory Manual.* Port Huron, Mich: Res. Psychol. Press

Jackson, D. N. 1978. Interpreter's guide to the *Jackson Personality Inventory.* In *Advances in Psychological Assessment,* Vol. 4, ed. P. McReynolds. San Francisco: Jossey-Bass

James, L. R., Ellison, R. L., Fox, D. G., Taylor, C. W. 1974. Prediction of artistic performance from biographical data. *J. Appl. Psychol.* 59:84–86

Jarvik, L. F., Chadwick, S. B. 1973. Schizophrenia and survival. In *Psychopathology: Contributions from the Social, Behavioral Sciences*, ed. M. Hammer, K. Salzinger, S. Sutton. New York: Wiley

Jones, W. H., Chernovetz, E., Hansson, R. O. 1978. The enigma of androgyny: Differential implications for males and females? *J. Consult. Clin. Psychol.* 46:298–313

Juhasz, J. B. 1972. An experimental study of imagining. *J. Pers.* 40:588–600

Kanner, A. D. 1976. Femininity and masculinity: Their relationships to creativity in male architects and their independence from each other. *J. Consult. Clin. Psychol.* 44:802–5

Karlins, M., Schuerhoff, C., Kaplan, M. 1969. Some factors related to architectural creativity in graduating architecture students. *J. Gen. Psychol.* 81:203–15

Karlsson, J. L. 1978. *Inheritance of Creative Intelligence: A Study of Genetics in Relation to Giftedness and its Implications for Future Generations.* Chicago: Nelson-Hall

Kasperson, C. J. 1978. Psychology of the scientist: XXXVII. Scientific creativity: A relationship with information channels. *Psychol. Rep.* 42:691–94

Katz, A. N., Poag, J. R. 1979. Sex differences in instructions to "be creative" on divergent and nondivergent test scores. *J. Pers.* 47:518–30

Keating, D. P., ed. 1976. *Intellectual Talent: Research and Development.* Baltimore: Johns Hopkins Univ. Press

Khatena, J. 1969. Onomatopoeia and images: preliminary validity study of a test of originality. *Percept. Mot. Skills* 31:86

Khatena, J. 1971a. Something about myself: A brief screening device for identifying creatively gifted children and adults. *Gifted Child Q.* 15:262–66

Khatena, J. 1971b. Evaluation and the creative potential in music. *Gifted Child Q.* 15:19–22

Khatena, J. 1975. Creative imagination, imagery and analogy. *Gifted Child Q.* 19:149–60

Khatena, J. 1978. Frontiers of creative imagination imagery. *J. Ment. Imagery* 2:33–46

Khatena, J., Torrance, E. P. 1976. *Manual for Khatena-Torrance Creative Perception Inventory.* Chicago: Stoelting

Kirton, M. J. 1976. Adaptors and innovators: a description and measure. *J. Appl. Psychol.* 61:622–29

Kirton, M. J. 1977a. Adaptors and innovators and superior-subordinate identification. *Psychol. Rep.* 41:289–90

Kirton, M. J. 1977b. *Manual of the Kirton Adaption-Innovation Inventory.* London: Natl. Fed. Educ. Res.

Kogan, N. 1973. Creativity and cognitive style. A life-span perspective. In *Life-Span Developmental Psychology: Personality and Socialization*, ed. P. B. Baltes, K. W. Schaie. New York: Academic

Kogan, N. 1974. Creativity and sex differences. *J. Creat. Behav.* 8:1–14

Kogan, N., Connor, K., Gross, A., Fava, D. 1980. Understanding visual metaphor: Developmental and individual differences. *Monogr. Soc. Res. Child Dev.* 45 (1, Serial No. 183)

Kogan, N., Morgan, F. T. 1969. Task and motivational influences on the assessment of creative and intellective ability in children. *Genet. Psychol. Monogr.* 80:91–127

Kogan, N., Pankove, E. 1972. Creative ability over a five-year span. *Child Dev.* 43:427–42

Kogan, N., Pankove, E. 1974. Long-term predictive validity of divergent-thinking tests: Some negative evidence. *J. Educ. Psychol.* 66:802–10

Korb, R., Frankiewicz, R. G. 1979. *Aptitudes, intellective styles, and personality characteristics as facilitators and differentiators of creativity.* Presented at Ann. Meet. Am. Psychol. Assoc., New York

Krantz, D. L., Wiggins, L. 1973. Personal and impersonal channels of recruitment in the growth of theory. *Hum. Dev.* 16:133–56

Krippner, S. 1977. Research in creativity and psychedelic drugs. *Int. J. Clin. Exp. Hypn.* 25:274–308

Lacey, L. A., Erickson, C. E. 1974. Psychology of the scientist: XXXI. Discriminability of a creativity scale for the Adjective Check List among scientists and engineers. *Psychol. Rep.* 34:755–58

Landau, E., Maoz, B. 1978. Creativity and self-actualization in the aging personality. *Am. J. Psychother.* 32:117–29

Lang, R. J., Ryba, K. A. 1976. The identification of some creative thinking parameters common to the artistic and musical personality. *Br. J. Educ. Psychol.* 46:267–79

Lemkau, J. P. 1979. Personality and background characteristics of women in male-dominated occupations: A review. *Psychol. Women Q.* 4:221–40

Lindauer, M. S. 1977. Imagery from the point of view of psychological aesthetics, the arts, and creativity. *J. Ment. Imagery* 2:343–62

Littlejohn, M. T. 1967. Creativity and masculinity-femininity in ninth graders. *Percept. Mot. Skills* 25:737–43

London, H., Exner, J. E. Jr., ed. 1978. *Dimensions of Personality.* New York: Wiley

Loshak, L. J., Reznikoff, M. 1976. Creativity and body image boundaries. *J. Pers. Assess.* 40:81–90

Lunneborg, C. E., Lunneborg, P. W. 1969. Architecture school performance predicted from ASAT, intellective, and nonintellective measures. *J. Appl. Psychol.* 53:209–13

Lynch, P. M. 1970. Creativity in Irish children. *J. Creat. Behav.* 4:53–61

MacKinnon, D. W. 1962a. The nature and nurture of creative talent. *Am. Psychol.* 17:484–95

MacKinnon, D. W. 1962b. The personality correlates of creativity: a Study of American architects. In *Proc. 14th Int. Congr. Appl. Psychol., Copenhagen, 1961,* ed. G. S. Nielsen, Vol. 2. Copenhagen: Munksgaard

MacKinnon, D. W. 1963. Creativity and images of the self. In *The Study of Lives,* ed. R. W. White, pp. 250–78. New York: Atherton

MacKinnon, D. W. 1965. Personality and the realization of creative potential. *Am. Psychol.* 20:273–81

MacKinnon, D. W. 1966. *Illustrative material for some reflections on the current status of personality assessment with special references to the assessment of creative persons.* Presented to graduate students, Dep. Psychol., Univ. Utah, Salt Lake City

MacKinnon, D. W., Hall, W. B. 1971. Intelligence and creativity. In *The Measurement of Creativity,* pp. 1183–88. *Int. Congr. Appl. Psychol., 17th, Liege, Belgium,* H. W. Peter, symp. chm. Brussels: EDITEST

Mackworth, N. H. 1965. Originality. *Am. Psychol.* 20:51–66

Magnusson, D., Backteman, G. 1978. Longitudinal stability of person characteristics: Intelligence and creativity. *Appl. Psychol. Meas.* 2:481–90

Martindale, C. 1977–78. Creativity, consciousness and cortical arousal. *J. Altered States Consciousness* 3:69–87

Martindale, C., Hasenfus, N. 1978. EEG differences as a function of creativity,

stage of the creative process and effort to be original. *Biol. Psychol.* 6:157–67

Maw, W. H., Maw, E. W. 1978. Nature and assessment of human curiosity. See Jackson 1978, pp. 526–71

McConaghy, N., Clancy, M. 1968. Familial relationships of allusive thinking in university students and their parents. *Br. J. Educ. Psychiatry* 114:1079–87

McDermid, C. D. 1965. Some correlates of creativity in engineering personnel. *J. Appl. Psychol.* 49:14–19

Mednick, S. A., Mednick, M. T. 1967. *Examiner's Manual: Remote Associates Test.* Boston: Houghton Mifflin

Meehl, P. E. 1962. Schizotaxia, schizotypy, schizophrenia. *Am. Psychol.* 17:827–38

Mendelsohn, G. A. 1976. Associative and attentional processes in creative performance. *J. Pers.* 44:341–69

Mendelsohn, G. A., Covington, M. V. 1972. Internal processes and perceptual factors in verbal problem solving: A study of sex and individual differences in cognition. *J. Pers.* 40:451–71

Milgram, R. M., Milgram, N. A. 1976. Creative thinking and creative performance in Israeli students. *J. Educ. Psychol.* 68:255–59

Milgram, R. M., Yitzhak, V., Milgram, N. A. 1977. Creative activity and sex-role identity in elementary school children. *Percept. Mot. Skills* 45:371–76

Morrison, R. F., Owens, W. A., Glennon, J. R., Albright, L. E. 1962. Factored life history antecedents of industrial research performance. *J. Appl. Psychol.* 46:281–84

Morse, J. A., Bruch, C. B. 1978. A comparison of sex roles of creative-productive versus non-productive women. *Gifted Child Q.* 22:520–25

Nichols, R. C. 1964. Parental attitudes of mothers of intelligent adolescents and creativity of their children. *Child Dev.* 35:1041–49

Nochlin, L. 1971. Why are there no great women artists? In *Women in Sexist Society,* ed. V. Gornick, B. K. Moran, pp. 480–510. Mentor Book, New Am. Libr.

Nochlin, L. 1979. Review of G. Greer's *The Obstacle Race. NY Times Book Rev.* 3 (Oct 28):46–47

Noppe, L. D., Gallagher, J. M. 1977. A cognitive style approach to creative thought. *J. Pers. Assess.* 41:85–90

Olsen, T. 1970. Silences: When writers don't write. *Women: A Journal of Liberation*

Olsen, T. 1978. *Silences.* New York: Delacorte

Owens, W. A. 1969. Cognitive, noncognitive and environmental correlates of mechanical ingenuity. *J. Appl. Psychol.* 53:199–208

Parloff, M. B., Datta, L., Kleman, M., Handlon, J. H. 1968. Personality characteristics which differentiate creative male adolescents and adults. *J. Pers.* 36: 528–52

Patel, K. 1976. Profiles of creative personality. *Psychologia* 19:173–83

Payne, D. A., Halpin, W. G. 1974. Use of a factored biographical inventory to identify differentially gifted adolescents. *Psychol. Rep.* 35:1195–1204

Pellegrino, J. W., Glaser, R. 1979. Cognitive correlates and components in the analysis of individual differences. *Intelligence* 3:187–214

Pezzullo, T. R., Thorsen, E. E., Madaus, G. F. 1972. The heritability of Jensen's level I and level II and divergent thinking. *Am. Educ. Res. J.* 4:539–46

Prentky, R. A. 1979. Creativity and psychopathology: A neurocognitive perspective. *Prog. Exp. Pers. Res.* 9:1–33

Raychaudhuri, M. 1966. Perceptual preference pattern and creativity. *Ind. J. Appl. Psychol.* 3:67–70

Raychaudhuri, M. 1967. *Studies in Artistic Creativity.* Calcutta: Rabindra Bharati

Raychaudhuri, M. 1971. Relation of creativity and sex to Rorschach *M* responses. *J. Pers. Assess.* 35:27–31

Raychaudhuri, M. 1972. Some thorny issues in cross-cultural research on creativity: A rejoinder to Aronow's comment. *J. Pers. Assess.* 36:305–6

Razik, T. A. 1965. *Creativity Studies and Related Areas.* Univ. Buffalo Found., NY

Rekdal, C. K. 1977. In search of the wild duck. *Gifted Child Q.* 21:501–15

Resnick, L. B. 1976. *The Nature of Intelligence.* Hillsdale, NJ: Erlbaum

Richards, R. L. 1976. A comparison of selected Guilford and Wallach-Kogan creative thinking tests in conjunction with measures of intelligence. *J. Creat. Behav.* 10:151–64

Rimm, S. 1976. *GIFT—An Instrument for the Identification and Measurement of Creativity.* PhD thesis. Univ. Wis. Madison

Rimm, S., Davis, G. A. 1976. GIFT: An instrument for the identification of creativity. *J. Creat. Behav.* 10:178–82

Roe, A. 1965. Changes in scientific activities with age. *Science* 150:313–18

Roe, A. 1972. Patterns in the productivity of scientists. *Science* 176:940–41

Rogolsky, M. M. 1968. Artistic creativity and adaptive regression in third grade children. *J. Proj. Tech. Pers. Assess.* 32:53–62

Rookey, T. J. 1971. *The Pennsylvania Assessment of Creative Tendency: Norms-Technical Manual.* Penn. Dep. Educ.

Rookey, T. J. 1974. Validation of a creativity test: The 100 students study. *J. Creat. Behav.* 8:211–13

Roslansky, J. D., ed. 1970. *Creativity: A Discussion at the Nobel Conference organized by Gustavus Adolphus College, St. Peter, Minnesota, 1970.* Amsterdam/London: North-Holland

Rossman, B. B. 1976. Art, creativity and the elephant: Some clues to artistic creativity among the gifted. *Gifted Child Q.* 20:392–401

Rossman, B. B., Horn, J. L. 1972. Cognitive, motivational and temperamental indicants of creativity and intelligence. *J. Educ. Meas.* 9:265–86

Rothenberg, A. 1973a. Word association and creativity. *Psychol. Rep.* 33:3–12

Rothenberg, A. 1973b. Opposite-responding as a measure of creativity. *Psychol. Rep.* 33:15–18

Rothenberg, A. 1979. *The Emerging Goddess: The Creative Process in Art, Science and other Fields.* Chicago: Univ. Chicago Press

Rothenberg, A., Greenberg, B. 1974. *The Index of Scientific Writings on Creativity. Creative Men and Women.* Hamden, Conn: Anchor Books

Rothenberg, A., Greenberg, B. 1976. *The Index of Scientific Writings on Creativity. General: 1566–1974.* Hamden, Conn: Anchor Books

Rothenberg, A., Hausman, C. R. 1976. Introduction: The creativity question. In *The Creativity Question,* ed. A. Rothenberg, C. R. Hausman, pp. 3–26. Durham, NC: Duke Univ. Press

Rotter, D. M., Langland, L., Berger, D. 1971. The validity of tests of creative thinking in seven-year-old children. *Gifted Child Q.* 15:273–78

Royce, J. R. 1980. Factor analysis is alive and well. *Am. Psychol.* 35:390–92

Runyan, W. M. 1978. The life course as a theoretical orientation: Sequences of person-situation interaction. *J. Pers.* 46:569–93

Schaefer, C. E. 1969a. The prediction of creative achievement from a biographical inventory. *Educ. Psychol. Meas.* 29:431–37

Schaefer, C. E. 1969b. The self-concept of creative adolescents. *J. Psychol.* 72:233–42

Schaefer, C. E. 1969c. Imaginary companions and creative adolescents. *Dev. Psychol.* 1:747–49

Schaefer, C. E. 1970a. *Biographical Inventory-Creativity.* San Diego: Educ. Ind. Test.

Schaefer, C. E. 1970b. A psychological study of 10 exceptionally creative adolescent girls. *Except. Child.* 36:431–41

Schaefer, C. E. 1971a. *Similes Test Manual.* Goshen, NY: Res. Psychol. Press

Schaefer, C. E. 1971b. Primary-process thinking in thematic fantasies of creative adolescents. *Personality* 2:219–25

Schaefer, C. E. 1971c. *Creativity Attitude Survey.* Psycholog. Educ.

Schaefer, C. E. 1972a. Primary process elements with Draw-a-Person protocols of creative young women. *Percept. Mot. Skills* 35:245–46

Schaefer, C. E. 1972b. Predictive validity of the Biographical Inventory Creativity: a five-year follow-up. *Psychol. Rep.* 30:471–76

Schaefer, C. E. 1972c. Follow-up study of a creativity scale for the Adjective Check List. *Psychol. Rep.* 30:662

Schaefer, C. E. 1973. A five-year follow-up of the self-concept of creative adolescents. *J. Genet. Psychol.* 123:163–70

Schaefer, C. E., Anastasi, A. 1968. A biographical inventory for identifying creativity in adolescent boys. *J. Appl. Psychol.* 52:42–48

Schaefer, C. E., Bridges, C. I. 1970. Development of a creativity attitude survey for children. *Percept. Mot. Skills* 31:861–62

Schaefer, C. E., Diggens, D. R., Millman, H. L. 1976. Intercorrelations among measures of creativity, openness to experience and sensation seeking in a college sample. *Coll. Stud. J.* 10(4):332–39

Schmidt, H. E. 1973. The identification of high and low creativity in architecture students. *Psychol. Afr.* 15:15–40

Schubert, D. S. P. 1973. Intelligence as necessary but not sufficient for creativity. *J. Genet. Psychol.* 122:45–47

Schultz, N. R. Jr., Hoyer, W. J., Kaye, D. B. 1980. Trait anxiety, spontaneous flexibility, and intelligence in young and elderly adults. *J. Consult. Clin. Psychol.* 48:289–91

Shapiro, E. 1975. Toward a developmental perspective on the creative process. *J. Aesthet. Educ.* 9:69–80

Shelton, J., Harris, T. L. 1979. Personality characteristics of art students. *Psychol. Rep.* 44:949–50

Showalter, E. 1971. Women writers and the double standard. In *Woman in Sexist Society,* ed. V. Gornick, B. K. Moran. New York: Basic Books

Simonton, D. K. 1975. Age and literary creativity: A cross-cultural and transhis-torical survey. *J. Cross-Cult. Psychol.* 6:259–77

Simonton, D. K. 1976a. Biographical determinants of achieved eminence: A multivariate approach to the Cox data. *J. Pers. Soc. Psychol.* 35:218–26

Simonton, D. K. 1976b. Philosophical eminence, beliefs, and zeitgeist: An individual-generational analysis. *J. Pers. Soc. Psychol.* 34:630–40

Simonton, D. K. 1977. Creative productivity, age, and stress: A biographical time-series analysis of 10 classical composers. *J. Pers. Soc. Psychol.* 35:791–804

Simonton, D. K. 1978. The eminent genius in history: The critical role of creative development. *Gifted Child Q.* 22:187–95

Singer, D. L., Rummo, J. 1973. Ideational creativity and behavioral style in kindergarten-age children. *Dev. Psychol.* 8:154–61

Smith, J. M., Schaefer, C.E. 1969. Development of a creativity scale for the Adjective Check List. *Psychol. Rep.* 25:87–92

Smith, M. L., Glass, G. V. 1977. Meta-analysis of psychotherapy outcome studies. *Am. Psychol.* 32:752–60

Sobel, R. S. 1978. Remote associates theory of creativity: Fifteen years later. *J. Suppl. Abstr. Serv.* MS 1735.

Spacks, P. M. 1972. *The Female Imagination.* New York: Avon

Stankov, L. 1980. Psychometric factors as cognitive tasks: A note on Carroll's new "structure of intellect." *Intelligence* 4:65–71

Stanley, J. C., George, W. C., Solano, C. H., eds. 1977. *The Gifted and the Creative.* Baltimore: Johns Hopkins Press

Stanley, J. C., Keating, D. P., Fox, L. H., eds. 1974. *Mathematical Talent: Discovery, Description and Development.* Baltimore: Johns Hopkins Press

Starkweather, E. K. 1976. Creativity research instruments designed for use with preschool children. In *Assessing Creative Growth: The Tests—Book One,* ed. A. M. Biondi, S. J. Parnes. Great Neck, NY: Creative Synergetics Assoc.

Stein, M. I. 1968. Creativity. In *Handbook of Personality Theory and Research,* ed. E. F. Borgatta, W. W. Lambert. Chicago: Rand McNally

Stein, M. I. 1974. *Stimulating Creativity.* New York: Academic. 2 vols.

Steiner, G. A., ed. 1965. *The Creative Organization.* Chicago: Univ. Chicago Press

Sternberg, R. J. 1977. *Intelligence, Information Processing, and Analogical Reasoning: The Componential Analysis of Human Abilities.* Hillsdale, NJ: Erlbaum

Sternberg, R. J. 1979. The nature of mental abilities. *Am. Psychol.* 34:214–30

Stolorow, R. D., Atwood, G. E. 1979. *Faces in a Cloud: Subjectivity in Personality Theory.* New York: Aronson

Stringer, P. 1967. Masculinity-femininity as a possible factor underlying the personality responses of male and female art students. *Br. J. Soc. Clin. Psychol.* 6: 186–94

Suler, J. R. 1980. Primary process thinking and creativity. *Psychol. Bull.* 88:144–65

Sussman, G., Justman, J. 1975. Characteristics of preadolescent boys judged creative by their teachers. *Gifted Child Q.* 19:310–16

Suter, B., Domino, G. 1975. Masculinity-femininity in creative college women. *J. Pers. Assess.* 39:414–20

Taft, R. 1971. Creativity: Hot and cold. *J. Pers.* 39:345–61

Taft, R., Gilchrist, M. B. 1970. Creative attitudes and creative productivity: A comparison of two aspects of creativity among students. *J. Educ. Psychol.* 61:136–43

Tan-Willman, C. 1974. Assessment and prediction of creativity in teaching. *Psychol. Rep.* 35:393–94

Taylor, C. W., ed. 1972. *Climate for Creativity.* New York: Pergamon

Taylor, C. W., Barron, F., eds. 1963. *Scientific Creativity.* New York: Wiley

Taylor, C. W., Ellison, R. L. 1967. Predictors of scientific performance. *Science* 155:1075–79

Taylor, I. A. 1975. A retrospective view of creativity investigation. See Taylor & Getzels 1975, pp. 1–36

Taylor, I. A., Getzels, J. W., eds. 1975. *Perspectives in Creativity.* Chicago: Aldine

Taylor, I. A., Sutton, D., Haworth, S. 1974. The measurement of creative transactualization: A scale to measure behavioral dispositions to creativity. *J. Creat. Behav.* 8:114–15

Torrance, E. P. 1966. *Torrance Tests of Creative Thinking.* Lexington, Mass: Personnel Press. Res. ed.

Torrance, E. P. 1967. The Minnesota studies of creative behavior: National and international extensions. *J. Creat. Behav.* 1:137–54

Torrance, E. P. 1969. Originality of imagery in identifying creative talent in music. *Gifted Child Q.* 13:3–8

Torrance, E. P. 1970. What kind of person are you? *Gifted Child Q.* 14:71–75

Torrance, E. P. 1972a. Creative young women in today's world. *Except. Child.* 38:597–603

Torrance, E. P. 1972b. Predictive validity of the Torrance Tests of Creative Thinking. *J. Creat. Behav.* 6:236–52

Torrance, E. P. 1974. *Torrance Tests of Creative Thinking: Norms-Technical Manual.* Lexington, Mass: Ginn

Torrance, E. P. 1979. *Cumulative Bibliography on the Torrance Tests of Creative Thinking.* Athens, Ga: Dep. Educ. Psychol.

Torrance, E. P., Alliotti, N. C. 1969. Sex differences in levels of performance and test-retest reliability of the Torrance Tests of Creative Thinking. *J. Creat. Behav.* 3:52–57

Torrance, E. P., Bruch, C. B., Morse, J. A. 1973. Improving predictions of the adult creative achievement of gifted girls by using autobiographical information. *Gifted Child Q.* 17:91–95

Torrance, E. P., Tan, C. A., Allman, T. 1970. Verbal originality and teacher behavior: A predictive validity study. *J. Teach. Educ.* 21:335–41

Trowbridge, N., Charles, D. C. 1966. Creativity in art students. *J. Genet. Psychol.* 109:281–89

Tucker, M. F., Cline, V. B., Schmitt, J. R. 1967. Prediction of creativity and other performance measures from biological information among pharmaceutical scientists. *J. Appl. Psychol.* 51:131–38

Urbina, S., Harrison, J., Schaefer, C., Anastasi, A. 1970. Masculinity-femininity and creativity as measured by the Franck Drawing completion test. *Psychol. Rep.* 26:799–804

Vernon, P. E. 1971. Effects of administration and scoring on divergent thinking tests. *Br. J. Educ. Psychol.* 41:245–57

Vernon, P. F. 1972a. Review of the Remote Associates test. See Baird 1972, pp. 829–30

Vernon, P. E. 1972b. The validity of divergent thinking tests. *Alberta J. Educ. Res.* 18:249–58

Vernon, P. E. 1978. Review of "Creativity Attitude Survey." See Bachman & Tuckman 1978, pp. 361–62

Vernon, P. E. 1979. *Intelligence: Heredity and Environment.* San Francisco: Freeman

Vernon, P. E., Adamson, G., Vernon, D. F. 1977. *The Psychology and Education of Gifted Children.* London: Methuen

Walberg, H. J. 1969a. A portrait of the artist and scientist as young men. *Except. Child.* 36:5–11

Walberg, H. J. 1969b. Physics, femininity and creativity. *Dev. Psychol.* 1:47–54

Wallach, M. A. 1970. Creativity. In *Carmichael's Manual of Child Psychology,* ed.

P. H. Mussen, 1:1211–72. New York: Wiley

Wallach, M. A., Kogan, N. 1965. *Modes of Thinking in Young Children.* New York: Holt, Rinehart & Winston

Wallbrown, F. H., Huelsman, C. B. Jr. 1975. The validity of the Wallach-Kogan creativity operations for inner-city children in two areas of visual art. *J. Pers.* 43:109–26

Wallbrown, F. H., Wallbrown, J. D., Wherry, R. J. Sr. 1975. The construct validity of the Wallach-Kogan creativity test for inner-city children. *J. Gen. Psychol.* 92:83–96

Ward, W. C. 1968. Creativity in young children. *Child Dev.* 39:736–54

Ward, W. C. 1972. Review of the *Alpha Biographical Inventory.* See Baird 1972, pp. 1371–73

Ward, W. C. 1974. Creativity (?) in young children. *J. Creat. Behav.* 8:101–6

Waterman, A. S., Kohutiz, E., Pulone, J. 1977. The role of expressive writing in ego identity formation. *Dev. Psychol.* 13:286–87

Welsh, G. S. 1975. *Creativity and Intelligence: A Personality Approach.* Chapel Hill, NC: Inst. Res. Soc. Sci.

Whipple, G. T. 1915. *Manual of Mental and Physical Tests. Part II: Complex Processes.* Baltimore: Warwick & York

White, R. W., ed. 1963. *The Study of Lives.* Reading, Mass: Addison Wesley

Wild, C. 1965. Creativity and adaptive regression. *J. Pers. Soc. Psychol.* 2:161–69

Winner, E., Gardner, H. 1977. The comprehension of metaphor in brain-damaged patients. *Brain* 100:717–29

Wispe, L. G. 1965. Some social and psychological correlates of eminence in psychology. *J. Hist. Behav. Sci.* 1:88–98

Woody, C., Claridge, G. S. 1977. Psychoticism and thinking. *Br. J. Soc. Clin. Psychol.* 16:241–48

Worthen, B. R., Clark, P. M. 1971. Toward an improved measure of remote associational ability. *J. Educ. Meas.* 8:113–23

Yamamoto, K. 1978. Review of "Creativity Attitude Survey." See Backman & Tuckman, pp. 362–63

Yarnell, T. D. 1971a. A common item creativity scale for the Adjective Check List. *Psychol. Rep.* 29:466

Yarnell, T. D. 1971b. Percentile norms for the Adjective Check List (ACL) creativity scale. *Psychol. Rep.* 29:675–78

Yu, M. 1977. *Personality Profile and Life Situation of Creative Female Professionals.* Presented at Meet. Can. Psychol. Assoc., Vancouver, B.C.

Zeldow, P. B. 1973. Replication and extension of the personality profile of "Artists in the Making." *Psychol. Rep.* 33:541–42

Ann. Rev. Psychol. 1981. 32:477–522

VISUAL NEURAL DEVELOPMENT[1]   ♦351

J. Anthony Movshon

Department of Psychology, New York University, New York, NY 10003

Richard C. Van Sluyters

School of Optometry, University of California, Berkeley, California 94720

CONTENTS

[1]Preparation of this manuscript was partly supported by grants to JAM from NIH (EY 2017) and NSF (BNS 76-18904), and to RCVS from NIH (EY 2193). Both authors are Alfred P. Sloan Research Fellows in Neuroscience.

We are grateful to Ms. Chris Nicholson for secretarial and editing assistance.

477

0066-4308/81/0201-0477$01.00

INTRODUCTION

In the middle of the journey of our life,
I came to myself within a dark wood where the straight way was lost.

—Dante, *The Divine Comedy, Inferno* I, 1

This review considers the development of function in the visual system of higher mammals, primarily through electrophysiological studies of neuronal properties in the geniculostriate visual pathway. Although we consider neuroanatomical and behavioral findings where they illuminate processes of functional development, we do not pretend to an even or orderly coverage of these areas. For surveys of material on neural development outside the scope of this review, several excellent sources are available (Jacobson 1978, Lund 1978). We assume a modest familiarity with the functional properties of the normal adult visual system; useful background material for this may be found in several recent reviews (Rodieck 1979, Van Essen 1979, De Valois & De Valois 1980, Lennie 1980).

Rather than execute a necessarily superficial survey of this whole area, we have chosen to direct most of our attention toward two basic questions that have been intensive areas for research and that remain unresolved: *First,* to what degree does normal visual neural development depend on adequate visual stimulation in early life? *Second,* in what way, and within what limits, can the environment act to modify visual neural function?

Though it may not seem wise to attempt to review topics embroiled in active controversy, we feel that these critical issues can be well defined and may benefit from dispassionate examination. Dispassionate does not, we hasten to add, mean unbiased or uncritical, and we apologize in advance to those of our colleagues who may feel that their views or findings are slighted here. But the number and variety of positions that find support in the literature are such that only the most neutral and pallid of reviews could hope to negotiate them without treading on a few toes.

Species   A review such as this could easily become an exercise in comparative physiology, for there seem to be substantial differences among species in the degree and manner in which the environment affects visual development. Since our interest is ultimately directed toward human development, our coverage would ideally concentrate on species similar in visual function to man. The large body of evidence on normal function in the macaque monkey would seem to make it the logical candidate; but there is little developmental literature on the monkey, and so for most important issues we will primarily consider data obtained from cats. While the cat's visual system differs in a number of important respects from the primate's (see Rodieck 1979, Van Essen 1979), it appears that in most ways visual development proceeds in the same manner and according to the same rules in the two species.

METHODOLOGY IN DEVELOPMENTAL STUDIES

All hope abandon, who enter here.

—Dante, *The Divine Comedy, Inferno* III, 9

Those who study development must contend with a host of problems that do not confront students of the adult visual system. It is often essential (and less often practical) to exercise tight control over many aspects of the rearing of subjects, and the peculiar problems of electrophysiological recording in young animals must be overcome.

Rearing

Virtually every study discussed below rests on assumptions about the conditions under which its subjects were reared. When one compares two animals raised differently, there is implicit the idea that in all respects other than the one being compared, the two animals are the same. But raising animals in abnormal visual environments (e.g. total darkness, special illumination, etc) inevitably results in other abnormalities. It is well known, for example, that animals raised in the dark tend to be at greater risk of infection, tend to gain weight less rapidly than their light-reared peers, and when ultimately removed from darkness, often show significant behavioral abnormalities probably unrelated to their visual deficits.

Even if these factors could be controlled, it is often difficult to be certain that the visual environment desired in a particular experiment was in fact obtained: sutured eyelids can open; the best fitting goggles can be knocked off or askew; mistakes can be made with darkroom doors. The possibility that significant alterations may result from accidents of this sort cannot be ruled out, but has never been effectively addressed.

Electrophysiology

While techniques of electrophysiological recording in adult animals are well understood and reliable, it is not clear that this is true in very young animals, where problems of three different kinds arise.

PHYSIOLOGY   It is widely assumed that the conventional situation adopted for CNS recording, in which the animal is paralyzed with a curariform neuromuscular blocking agent, artificially ventilated and lightly anesthetized, does not markedly affect visual unit properties. There is some support for this assumption in adult animals, where at least for levels of the system up to primary visual cortex it seems that unit properties are little different in awake and lightly anesthetized animals (Wurtz 1969, Noda et al 1971, Schiller et al 1976). So far as we are aware, no comparable evidence exists for young animals, and on general physiological grounds it seems likely that these are more susceptible to physiological stress than are adults. Therefore, much of the controversy discussed below concerning visual response properties in neonates is no doubt muddied by uncertainties about the physiological conditions during recording.

RECORDING   While recording methods developed for adults may be used in all but the youngest animals, problems arise from several sources. First, neurons are smaller in young animals, and this may alter the well-known sampling bias shown by microelectrodes. Second, since the skull and its sutures are not fully formed in young animals, the entire recording situation is often less stable, which may restrict the amount of data that can be obtained, especially from smaller, more difficult-to-isolate neurons.

VISUAL STIMULATION   In young kittens, if not in monkeys, the optical quality of the eye is much worse than in the adult. While recent evidence suggests that this is not an overwhelming problem (see below), it is clear that the highest retinal contrast levels obtainable in young animals are in some cases lower than the levels needed for effective stimulation, even in adult animals.

EXPERIMENTAL DESIGN   Developmental experiments present special problems of variability, both within and between animals, that require special attention to certain aspects of experimental design. In studies of the normal visual system, it is usual to consider data from a number of (presumably similar) adult normal animals; it is rare for data from different animals to differ significantly. Developmental studies often involve a number of rearing conditions, and the number of animals per experimental group is often small as a result. While most experiments tend to assume that the degree of interanimal variability is as low in specially reared animals as it is in normals, it is likely that the problems of rearing and recording alluded to above add significantly to the variance.

Suitable procedural controls for this problem include "blind" procedures in which the experimenter is unaware of the animal's history, and both a regular protocol for sampling from electrode penetrations and histological reconstruction at the end of the experiment that is sufficient to accurately localize the sites at which recordings are made. Ideally, comparisons should be made among animals from each of which data samples of identical size and neuroanatomical distribution have been taken. The abnormally weak and variable responses of many visual neurons in specially reared animals make it most desirable that objective methods (preferably involving randomly interleaved multistimulus experiments, e.g. Henry et al 1973) be used to study receptive field properties. This is not always practical, in that the greater reliability of data obtained in this way is paid for in the considerably reduced number of units that can be studied.

A perusal of the literature cited in this review will rapidly show how few studies (our own no less than others') satisfy these prescriptions and proscriptions.

Uses and abuses of statistics   Conventional parametric and nonparametric statistical techniques make strong assumptions about sample-independence that are clearly not jusified in dealing with neurophysiological data. An obvious example comes from the orientation and ocular dominance column structure of the visual cortex (Hubel & Wiesel 1977), which makes it probable that neurons recorded near one another have similar properties. To take distributions of these properties and subject them to conventional statistical treatment can as a result be grossly misleading. It is therefore most depressing to see the frequency with which this sort of error is made, and with which strong statements and inferences are based on flawed analyses. While it is not impossible to devise statistical techniques that take account of sample dependence, there has been no widespread serious attempt to apply these to questions of visual development.

NORMAL VISUAL DEVELOPMENT AND EFFECTS OF TOTAL DEPRIVATION

But so much the more malign and wild does the ground become
    with bad seed and untilled,
as it has the more of good earthly vigor.

—Dante, *The Divine Comedy, Purgatorio* XXX, 118

If one wishes to study the way in which development can be affected by environmental manipulations, it is essential to have sound data about the course of development in normal environments. A "normal" laboratory visual environment is, of course, in many ways different from a species' natural environment, but it is clearly worthwhile to know how visual function develops in animals raised in the laboratory setting when they are given full daily exposure to light and visual contour stimulation.

The grossly contrasting developmental manipulation is to deprive an animal of all light and pattern stimulation. Two methods are commonly used to produce this deprivation: complete dark-rearing and bilateral eyelid suture. While sporadic reports (discussed below) suggest that there may be some differences between dark-reared and binocularly lid-sutured animals, for most purposes these two rearing conditions appear to yield similar results. Comparing a deprived animal with a normal animal should give some indication of the overall range of effects developmental manipulations may be expected to produce, and allows us to consider the first of our two questions: to what degree does normal visual development depend on adequate stimulation in early life?

Visual Optics

NORMAL DEVELOPMENT   Neonatal monkeys and humans possess clear optic media. Although no quantitative measurements of image quality in the infant (or indeed mature) monkey eye are available, ophthalmoscopic examination gives the convincing impression that optical quality changes little after birth in these species. Since both men and monkeys can resolve spatial frequencies in excess of 40 c/deg (Campbell & Green 1965, De Valois et al 1974), it seems likely that optical quality per se does not significantly limit either development or developmental study. Young human infants show some definite abnormalities of accommodation (Braddick et al 1979), are often somewhat hypermetropic (Duke-Elder 1963), and tend to exhibit significant astigmatic refractive errors more often than adults (Mohindra et al 1978, Howland et al 1978); it is not unlikely that young monkeys show similar effects. But in general the effects of all these optical abnormalities are small compared to the differences in visual performance seen between infant and adult monkeys and humans.

Most of the following discussion centers, however, on the cat; in this species optical quality appears poor near birth and improves dramatically during precisely the period in which most neural developmental activity takes place. The main problem for the young kitten's image-forming apparatus is the persistence of the *tunica vasculosa lentis,* the vascular plexus that supplies the developing lens (Thorn et al 1976, Freeman & Lai 1978). The quality of other optical surfaces of the kitten eye also improves considerably over the first few weeks of life (Freeman & Lai 1978, Freeman et al 1978, Thorn et al 1976). Measurements of retinal image quality in young kittens, however, show that the effect of these imperfections is less than simple ophthalmoscopic inspection would suggest (Bonds & Freeman 1978, Derrington 1979). Even at the age of 16 days, image quality in the young eye is quite respectable; by 6 weeks or so, it is comparable to that seen in adults (Bonds 1974, Robson & Enroth-Cugell 1978). At all ages at which behavioral acuity measurements are possible, measured acuity is lower than that permitted by the optics (Mitchell et al 1976b, Bonds & Freeman 1978). Bonds' measurements suggest that light scatter, which is considerable even in the adult cat eye (Robson & Enroth-Cugell 1978), decreases more slowly than does simple image blur during development. Despite appearances, then, it seems that even in kittens, optical factors are probably not an important constraint on visual development. But it should be noted that the optical deficits in very young kittens are considerable and that it may be difficult to obtain an accurate estimate of refractive state in the young eye; in electrophysiological experiments, then, it is possible that image quality is degraded to a degree that affects the results.

EFFECTS OF DEPRIVATION   There is some evidence that eyelid suture (a commonly used deprivation procedure) can radically deform developing kitten and monkey eyes, causing large refractive errors (Wiesel & Raviola 1977, Wilson & Sherman 1977, Gollender et al 1979; but see also von Noorden & Crawford 1978 for a contradictory report). There is, however, no evidence that deprivation produced by other methods results in any significant optical deficits.

Retina

NORMAL DEVELOPMENT   The development of functional properties in the retina has until recently been little studied, a curious omission in view of the intense interest in cortical development. Even now, few studies describe retinal physiological development in any detail, and none of those in species other than cat.

Anatomically, the cat retina is immature at birth (Donovan 1966, Rusoff 1979); even in the central retina, fully adult morphology is apparently not seen until the third week, while the periphery may not be fully mature until some weeks later. Nonetheless, brisk visual responses may be recorded from retinal ganglion cells during the third week of life (Hamasaki & Flynn 1977, Rusoff & Dubin 1977, Hamasaki & Sutija 1979). Quantitatively, the responses of these neurons are less vigorous than those seen in adults, and their receptive fields are distinguished by weak or absent antagonistic surrounds. Until 4 to 5 weeks of age, it is difficult to classify cells as X or Y type by criteria used in adults (Enroth-Cugell & Robson 1966). Hamasaki & Sutija find that most of the cells they can classify in this way in young animals are Y cells, but Rusoff & Dubin's data show no major developmental difference between the two types. Oddly, Daniels et al (1978) report an opposite result for neurons in the lateral geniculate nucleus in kittens of the same ages; X cells there develop earlier than Y cells.

The receptive fields of ganglion cells in young kittens tend to be larger than those in adults. It is difficult to establish to what degree this is due to the weakness of antagonistic surrounds in these neurons, to what degree it is due to light scattered by the optics of the eye, and to what degree receptive field size is actually changing. In addition, the growth of the eye causes changes in the angular subtense of fixed distances on the retina. Rusoff & Dubin (1977) conclude that there is evidence of neural maturation until about 4 weeks of age; thereafter, changes in receptive field size seem to be accounted for by changes in eye size.

EFFECTS OF DEPRIVATION   We know of no evidence that visual pattern deprivation procedures produce significant effects on the properties of retinal cells, and there is some evidence that it does not (Sherman & Stone 1973, Kratz et al 1979a). We are unaware of any data on the properties of retinal cells in young monkeys, where the high quality of the optics would make interpretation and measurement much simpler.

Lateral Geniculate Nucleus (LGN)

NORMAL DEVELOPMENT   The principal developmental interest in the LGN has until recently been morphological. Wiesel & Hubel (1963a) reported that the responses of geniculate neurons in monocularly and binocularly deprived animals seemed for the most part normal, despite marked failure of cell growth in geniculate laminae connected to the deprived eye.

Much attention has subsequently been paid to this effect, and it will be considered in a later section of this review. Recently, however, more attention has been directed to possible effects of deprivation on LGN physiology and on its normal development.

Daniels et al (1978) studied the development of visual and electrical responsiveness in cat LGN neurons and found similar abnormalities in young animals to those reported above for retinal cells: reduced responsiveness and sensitivity to light, abnormally large receptive fields, and weak or absent antagonistic surrounds. Electrical responses in the young geniculate are grossly abnormal; this is doubtless due in large part to the fact that optic tract myelination is not complete in cats for some weeks after birth (Moore et al 1976). Daniels et al reported that most X cells in the LGN mature before Y cells; as mentioned earlier, this is not in agreement with the order reported in retina. Ikeda & Tremain (1978a) also report early development of geniculate X cells, though they make no specific comment about Y cells being absent. Ikeda & Tremain also reported improvement in the spatial resolution of LGN X cells that continues into the third month of life and that is greater than can be accounted for by the changes in eye size that seem to account for changes in retinal receptive field size. LGN development may significantly lag that of the retina, but since retinal resolution measurements are not available, this conclusion is necessarily tentative.

As in the retina, we are not aware of any data on development of geniculate properties in young monkeys; again, the quality of the optics would greatly ease experimental work in this species by comparison with the cat.

EFFECTS OF DEPRIVATION   The most-studied and most controversial effects of visual deprivation in the LGN are those consequent to monocular lid closure; we discuss these below in the context of partial deprivation effects because they seem to be secondary consequences of changes in geniculocortical projection patterns. Dark rearing or bilateral lid suture also appear to affect the LGN, though the available evidence suggests that the effects are subtle compared to those seen in cortex.

Wiesel & Hubel (1965a) reported that bilateral lid closure caused a marked shrinkage of cells in all layers of the cat LGN, but subsequent more extensive measurements by Guillery (1973) showed that this effect is relatively slight. Sherman et al (1972) and Kratz et al (1979b) reported that binocular deprivation reduced the proportion of Y cells recorded from cat LGN, although less dramatically than monocular deprivation did. These and other groups have reported relatively subtle effects of deprivation on the receptive field properties of LGN cells. While most cells appear normal, they may be quantitatively less sensitive than cells in normal LGN. In addition, Wiesel & Hubel (1963a) and Sherman et al (1972) report a small number of highly abnormal cells, with large, diffuse and insensitive receptive fields.

Visual Cortex

The visual cortex, particularly the striate cortex (area 17, V1), has in the last 10 years or so received more attention in developmental study than any other. While certain effects of deprivation may manifest themselves in the retina and LGN, it seems that it is in the cortex that the most profound and interesting developmental effects are to be seen.

NORMAL DEVELOPMENT   Cragg (1972, 1975a) studied the synaptic development of striate cortex, and reported that at the time of natural eye-opening (about 8 days), only a small fraction of the normal complement of synapses could be found. Between that time and the age of about 5 weeks, there is a burst of synaptogenesis; this is followed by a partial loss of synapses until adult levels are reached after the age of 3 months. Quantitatively, this change in synaptic density seems very much greater than the change in physiological properties measured over the same period; it is, however, not obvious how one should compare these two measures of development.

Receptive fields   Hubel & Wiesel (1963) studied the properties of a relatively small number of cells in area 17 of young kittens lacking visual experience. While they observed that many cells gave weak and erratic responses and lacked the degree of stimulus specificity seen in adult cortex, they reported that all the fundamental receptive field properties seen in the adult cortex—binocularity, orientation selectivity, and direction selectivity—could be seen in the naive cortex. They also reported recognizable examples of the major cell types seen in adults. This finding was challenged by Barlow & Pettigrew (1971; see also Pettigrew 1974), who claimed that most cells in visually inexperienced kittens lacked stimulus specificity, and that those cells showing stimulus preferences possessed only direction, rather than orientation, selectivity. These views represent two extremes, between which most subsequent claims have fallen. Most other reports on naive kitten cortex confirm Hubel & Wiesel's report that orientation-selective cells can be found (Sherk & Stryker 1976): these seem principally to be of the "simple" type, to be situated in cortical layer IV, and unlike most cells in young kittens, to be monocularly driven (Blakemore & Van Sluyters 1975, Buisseret & Imbert 1976, Fregnac & Imbert 1978, Derrington 1978, Bonds 1979). Some reports (e.g. Fregnac & Imbert 1978, Leventhal & Hirsch 1977) also suggest the intriguing possibility that these cells are preferentially sensitive to horizontal or vertical orientations. Most of these authors agree, however, that in very young animals many cells lack stimulus specificity, and a sizable minority of isolated neurons cannot be activated by visual stimuli.

Derrington (1978) reported that the spatial resolution and contrast sensitivity of cortical neurons improve markedly between 2 and 6 weeks; his data taken in conjunction with the LGN measurements of Ikeda & Tremain (1978a) suggest that at least the most sensitive cortical neurons at all ages faithfully relay all spatial information passed by the LGN. Until the age of 4 to 5 weeks, however, it is only a small minority of cortical neurons that do this.

Binocularity   Since binocular neurons are common in young kittens, it is natural to inquire about the development of the segregated ocular dominance structure present in adult cats (Hubel & Wiesel 1965, Shatz et al 1977, Shatz & Stryker 1978). In adult cats and monkeys, geniculate afferents devoted to the two eyes are segregated into discrete bands in layer IV; in this layer, cells tend to be monocularly driven (Hubel & Wiesel 1968, Shatz & Stryker 1978). While physiological recordings in young monkeys and kittens show evidence of the normal periodic variation in eye dominance seen in adults (Wiesel & Hubel 1974, Blakemore et al 1975a), recent anatomical evidence suggests that the segregation is much less pronounced in young animals and improves markedly in the first postnatal weeks (Rakic 1977, Hubel et al 1977, LeVay et al 1978, LeVay & Stryker 1979). These results, based on transneuronal transport of intraocularly injected amino acid label to the cortex, are weakened by the "leakiness" of axons and axon terminals in young animals—a great deal of "spillover" of the labeled material occurs in the LGN. LeVay et al (1978) attempt to measure and compensate for this spillover, and in so doing come to the conclusion that all the spillover affecting their results occurs in the LGN and none in cortex. They report that their physiological recordings show that layer IV neurons are frequently binocularly activated in young animals, but this result contradicts most other reports (see above). LeVay & Stryker (1979) report that the axonal arborizations of geniculate afferents in cortex lack the "puff" organization thought in adults to reflect ocular dominance bands (Ferster & LeVay 1978), but the presence of axonal branches does not, of course, indicate with certainty the presence of functional synapses.

On balance, the physiological evidence for ocular dominance columns in young animals, combined with the technical difficulties with the anatomical analysis attempted by LeVay and his colleagues, suggest that some segregation by ocular dominance is present in the cortex of young kittens without visual experience. A striking feature of the data presented by LeVay et al

(1978), although not remarked by the authors, is the very small number of cells dominated by the ipsilateral eye in the neonatal cortex. This is not inconsistent with other reports (e.g. Fregnac & Imbert 1978) and suggests that the phylogenetically more recent ipsilateral pathway might lag slightly in ontogeny.

In a finding consistent with the generally poor quality of receptive fields in young kittens, Pettigrew (1974) shows that the tight selectivity for binocular disparity typical of some cells in adult cortex (Pettigrew et al 1968) is absent in neonates. The development of disparity selectivity over the first few weeks closely matches the development of other receptive field properties (e.g. Derrington 1978, Bonds 1979), and is presumably a secondary consequence of it.

EFFECTS OF DEPRIVATION   The critical question that we address in this section concerns the effect of binocular deprivation (BD) on cortical receptive field properties. Inquiry here falls naturally into two parts: what is the effect of long-term visual deprivation, and how does the course of development differ between deprived and normally raised animals?

Long-term deprivation   Wiesel & Hubel (1965a) studied cortical unit properties in cats deprived of vision by bilateral lid suture for several months from the time of birth. They produced the most "favorable" report available on cortical function in animals raised in this way. They found that while at least one-quarter of the cells were unresponsive to visual stimuli, and another quarter had poorly defined and unselective receptive fields, most of the remaining neurons had relatively normal receptive field properties. Most subsequent studies have reported considerably more devastating effects of long-term BD than these. Several findings were common to almost all reports: fewer than one-fifth of cells have normal orientation selectivity; a somewhat higher proportion have direction selectivity; at least one-third of the cells are visually unresponsive; most responsive neurons remain binocularly activated, but most of the "normal" cells tend to be monocularly driven (Blakemore & Van Sluyters 1974, 1975; Kratz & Spear 1976; Leventhal & Hirsch 1977; Singer & Tretter 1976; Cynader et al 1976; Fregnac & Imbert 1978; Watkins et al 1978; Bonds 1979). In each report, the experimenters comment on the refractoriness and unreliability of neuronal responses in deprived cortex, and it is clear even though some proportion of cells can be likened qualitatively to those in adults, there are important quantitative effects on the sensitivity and statistical reliability of responses.

Pattern deprivation vs total deprivation   It is not clear whether there are important differences between cats raised in total darkness and cats deprived by binocular lid suture. Some diffuse light stimulation reaches the retina behind a sutured eyelid (Crawford & Marc 1976): cats can make luminance discriminations with an eye occluded in this way (Loop & Sherman 1977), and responses to visual stimuli can be recorded in the cortex while the lids are still closed (Spear et al 1978). Kratz & Spear (1976) point out that in most cases there is evidence for a loss of binocular interaction following bilateral lid closure, an effect apparently not seen after dark rearing; it must be noted that their results on this point are extreme by comparison with others in the literature. Differences between the two eyes in the pattern of diffuse stimulation they receive might decrease cortical binocularity by the kind of binocular competition mechanism discussed below. Against this view, however, stand the findings of Singer et al (1977) and Wilson et al (1977) that unequal diffuse light stimulation of the two eyes does not alter cortical binocularity.

Leaving binocularity aside, there is some evidence in the literature that dark-rearing may have more deleterious effects on cortical neurons than binocular lid suture: studies involving dark-reared animals usually find a higher proportion of unresponsive cells and a lower proportion of orientation-selective cells than studies involving bilateral eye closure (compare, for example, Pettigrew 1974, and Fregnac & Imbert 1978 with Wiesel & Hubel 1965a and Sherk & Stryker 1976). But in the absence of a well-controlled study of animals raised and recorded in the same laboratory, this is conjecture. The most parsimonious assumption is that most of the effects of BD, however produced, result from the absence of contoured visual patterns on the two retinas.

Time-course of deprivation effects   It is clear that BD grossly disrupts cortical function when comparison is made with normally reared adult cats. What is the nature of this effect? Does the cortex of a BD animal end up in a more severely abnormal state than it was near birth, or is there simply a failure of normal development that leaves the cortex "frozen" in its neonatal state? Or, indeed, is there any evidence for passive maturation? The natural way to approach these questions is to compare normally reared and BD animals over a range of ages, to establish when and in what way cortical properties in the two groups develop to the final adult state.

Several studies have pursued this approach, usually restricting their attention to animals younger than 6 to 8 weeks of age (Pettigrew 1974, Blakemore & Van Sluyters 1975, Fregnac & Imbert 1978, Bonds 1979, Derrington 1980). Most studies agree on the course of development beyond the age of about 4 weeks: after this time, cortical function in normal and deprived animals is clearly different. What remains unresolved is the question of the "starting point" for these developmental sequences, and thus the question of whether deprivation merely arrests development or causes atrophy. Those who find relatively large numbers of selective neurons in neonatal animals (Blakemore & Van Sluyters, Fregnac & Imbert, Bonds) report a slight decline in the quality of cortical function during deprivation. Those who find neonates to be in essence "undeveloped" (Pettigrew, Derrington) report little change with extended deprivation periods. Some results also suggest that there might be a brief period of passive maturation in BD animals. For example, Sherk & Stryker (1976), recording from 3½-week-old deprived kittens, report a very high proportion of orientation selective neurons. This age group is curiously poorly represented in most other studies, and it might be that passive maturation proceeds in both normal and BD animals until this time, after which development proceeds in normals while cortical function atrophies in deprived kittens. In addition, the anatomical observations of Cragg (1975b), which suggest that synaptic development is by no means abolished by deprivation, seem to argue against the idea that the cortex is simply "frozen" by deprivation.

Monkeys   Since most reports on neonatal cortex tend to support some notion of innate wiring, it seems likely that deprivation causes actual atrophy. The sparse evidence available from experiments on young monkeys tends to support this view. Wiesel & Hubel (1974) reported that the cortex of the neonatal monkey is rather adult-like, but that even animals deprived for relatively short periods have a noticeable proportion of abnormally unresponsive or unselective neurons. And Crawford et al (1975) found that about half the cells studied in a monkey that had been binocularly deprived early in life were unresponsive to visual stimulation. In broad outline, then, the properties of cortical neurons in young monkeys and the way in which deprivation affects those properties appear similar to those in kittens.

Does binocular deprivation preserve cortical plasticity?   Cynader et al (1976) found that relatively brief periods of visual experience in BD cats could restore large numbers of cortical cells to at least approximately normal function; this is in marked contrast to findings (discussed below) that similar recovery periods are ineffective in selectively deprived cats. Cynader (1979) presents evidence in favor of the intriguing idea that one of the effects of BD is to "freeze" in their neonatal state whatever mechanisms normally truncate the period of cortical plasticity; thus a 4- or 6-month-old BD animal might be as susceptible to environmental influence as a much younger normal animal. Cynader's evidence comes from experiments in which one eye of BD cats was opened at the age of 4 to 10 months; these animals showed shifts in cortical ocular dominance typical of younger monocularly deprived animals, and there is evidence that the effects can be seen within a few days or weeks of monocular experience. Since light-reared cats monocularly deprived at the same age show less change in cortical eye dominance, these results can be interpreted as evidence that deprivation extends the "critical period" for cortical development.

EFFECTS OF SELECTIVE DEPRIVATION

Ye that are of good understanding,
note the doctrine that is hidden under the veil of the strange verses.

—Dante, *The Divine Comedy, Inferno* IX, 61

In this section we turn to experiments involving more selective kinds of visual deprivation. A natural suggestion of the results of the complete deprivation experiments discussed above would be that selective kinds of visual deprivation might have selective effects. But how might these effects be mediated? It is possible to imagine that a particular kind of visual experience would be sufficient to induce development of a particular, presumably related, visual function, but that experience has no other effect than to "gate" otherwise normal development. However, there is abundant evidence from studies of several different kinds that selective experience exerts a much more active influence on development than this idea would suggest. Our second question is thus posed: in what way, and within what limits, does the visual environment act to modify neural function?

Monocular Occlusion

Wiesel & Hubel (1963b, 1965a) studied the cortical effects of periods of early unilateral eye closure in kittens. In marked contrast to the nonspecific atrophic changes that result from bilateral eye closure or dark rearing, monocular closure produces a pattern of physiological and anatomical changes in cortex that can only be explained by active modification of neural connection patterns. These cortical changes are accompanied by changes in LGN that appear to be secondary to changes in cortical afferent patterns.

VISUAL CORTEX   After a period of unilateral eye closure, Wiesel & Hubel found that the great majority of cortical neurons (which in normal or BD animals may be activated through either eye) responded to stimulation only when it was delivered through the nondeprived eye. This does not result from a simple atrophy of neurons connected to the deprived eye, since recordings from the cortex of monocularly deprived (MD) animals reveal no sizable regions devoid of active neurons and no marked increase in the number of neurons that cannot be activated visually. These findings have been widely replicated (e.g. Blakemore & Van Sluyters 1974, Olson & Freeman 1975, Kratz & Spear 1976, Movshon & Dürsteler 1977). Using special techniques to record from the small neurons of layer IV, Shatz &

Stryker (1978) showed that there remain significant numbers of neurons in this layer that retain functional contact with the deprived eye; this observation apart, there has been no important addition to Wiesel & Hubel's original findings. In monkeys, MD has effects similar in form and magnitude to those seen in cats (Baker et al 1974, Crawford et al 1975, Hubel et al 1977, Blakemore et al 1978a).

Eyelid suture both abolishes spatially patterned retinal stimulation and reduces the amount of light entering the eye by several log units, but it appears that it is the loss of spatial pattern that is critical to the effectiveness of deprivation. Depriving an animal of vision with a translucent contact lens is as effective as lid suture in changing cortical ocular dominance, even when care is taken to match the total flux entering each eye (Wiesel & Hubel 1965a, Blakemore 1976). Conversely, reducing the amount of light entering the eye without abolishing pattern vision does not significantly shift eye dominance toward the nonattenuated eye (Blakemore 1976).

Geniculocortical and intracortical effects   Two mechanisms appear to be involved in the cortical changes consequent to MD. The first involves a change in the sizes of the nonoverlapping ocular dominance bands devoted to the two eyes in layer IV. In MD animals, the bands devoted to the deprived eye fail to attain their normal extent, and the territory they eschew is invaded by enlarged bands devoted to the experienced eye (Hubel et al 1977, Shatz & Stryker 1978). Thus in layer IV, where geniculate terminals from each eye normally occupy about 50% of the available territory, the experienced eye comes to control 70–80%. This change alone, however, cannot explain the full extent of the cortical changes produced by MD. In normal animals, the eye that dominates a band of layer IV also dominates cells in layers above and below that band (Hubel & Wiesel 1965, 1968; Kennedy et al 1976; Hendrickson & Wilson 1979). In MD animals, however, virtually all cortical neurons outside layer IV respond only to stimulation of the experienced eye, even those that lie above and below the bands of remaining layer IV input from the deprived eye (Hubel et al 1977, Shatz & Stryker 1978). Thus a second mechanism, involving changes in intracortical rather than geniculocortical connectivity, must be involved. Further evidence for this comes from the fact that MD of late onset can cause significant overall changes in cortical ocular dominance without changing the size of layer IV ocular dominance bands (Hubel et al 1977).

A role for suppression?   The first of these deprivation mechanisms—the reallocation of terminal space in layer IV—can be simply viewed as a change in the pattern of afferents that changes the ocular dominance of cortical cells by changing the balance of their excitatory input from the two eyes. It is not clear that the second mechanism—changing intracortical connection patterns—operates so simply. There is evidence that in many cortical cells, inputs from the deprived eye are present but suppressed by a tonic inhibitory influence from the experienced eye. Kratz et al (1976) showed that removal of the experienced eye in adult MD cats caused an immediate increase in the proportion of cells that could be activated through the deprived eye. This finding has been confirmed by Hoffmann & Cynader (1977), Van Sluyters (1978), and Crewther et al (1978b), but remains controversial in view of negative findings by Harris & Stryker (1977), Blakemore & Hillman (1977) and Hawken et al (1978). A difficulty of interpretation arises, since the effects reported by Kratz et al are not dramatic, and the possibility exists that enucleating or otherwise inactivating an eye might have subtle effects other than purely visual ones on cortical responsiveness and on the probability of recording from different types of cell (see, for example, Crewther et al 1978b). Nevertheless, the body of evidence suggests that there is indeed a "release" phenomenon following enucleation; the natural explanation is that the experienced eye exerts a tonic inhibitory influence that is abolished when the eye is enucleated. There is evidence that the cells responding to the deprived eye after enucleation are found throughout cortex and are not confined to layer IV, suggesting that the effect must at least partly result from reorganization of intracortically relayed signals (Smith et al 1978).

Duffy et al (1976) reported that intravenous bicuculline (which blocks the action of GABA, a putative inhibitory neurotransmitter in cortex) causes a similar release effect. While this finding is consonant with the enucleation results, it must be noted that bicuculline has serious effects on structures outside the visual cortex and that the published data are not compelling. Singer (1977) reported on the basis of electrical stimulation experiments in deprived animals that intracortical inhibitory pathways appear less affected by MD than direct excitatory pathways. Also, Fiorentini & Maffei (1979) report that suitable averaging techniques reveal weak excitatory inputs from the deprived eye in a substantial proportion of neurons in MD cats. All these results are at least consistent with a role for a suppression mechanism in the cortical effects of MD, though none of them provide a basis for any detailed speculation on its nature or source.

Onset of deprivation effects   The effects of brief periods of eye closure have been studied by Hubel & Wiesel (1970), Olson & Freeman (1975), Movshon & Dürsteler (1977), and Shatz et al (1977). During the fourth week of life, as little as one day of MD has marked effects on cortical binocularity. The first effect to appear is a radical reduction in the proportion of binocularly activated cells; after longer deprivation periods, a shift in ocular dominance becomes obvious. The ocular dominance bands of layer IV become more sharply defined after brief periods of MD, without showing the changes in extent that occur after longer periods (Shatz et al 1977).

Sensitive period for deprivation effects   The cortex is susceptible to MD during the first 4 months or so of a kitten's life; deprivation after that time has little or no effect (Wiesel & Hubel 1965a,b; Hubel & Wiesel 1970; Cynader 1979). Hubel & Wiesel originally reported that the "sensitive period" did not begin until the beginning of the fourth week, but Van Sluyters & Freeman (1977) showed that some susceptibility to deprivation effects is present even during the second week. The most sensitive point in the sensitive period occurs during the fifth week; thereafter, effects of a constant deprivation period are less and less marked.

The effects of MD may be partly or completely reversed within the sensitive period if the sutured eye is opened and the open one sutured. This reversed MD is capable of reversing cortical ocular dominance completely if performed before the age of 5 weeks; delaying reversal beyond this time decreases the rate and then the extent of cortical dominance changes (Blakemore & Van Sluyters 1974, Movshon 1976, Berman & Daw 1977). Blasdel & Pettigrew (1978) reported that the effectiveness of deprivation reversal depended on the duration of the initial deprivation as well as on the age at which reverse suture took place; this is not in agreement with some other findings (compare Movshon 1976 and Van Sluyters 1978). Estimates of the sensitive period obtained from deprivation reversal experiments agree well with those obtained from experiments on induction of deprivation.

Hubel & Wiesel (1970) found that the effects of deprivation were not lessened by a subsequent period of binocular visual experience, even within the sensitive period, but Mitchell et al (1977) and Olson & Freeman (1978) showed that the deprived eye may regain considerable influence in this way. This recovery, like the recovery induced by reversed deprivation, involves only the relative balance of the two eyes' inputs in cortex—few binocularly activated cells are seen after recovery, and many of these have receptive field properties that are poorly matched in the two eyes (Blakemore & Van Sluyters 1974, Movshon 1976, Mitchell et al 1977). Reversed deprivation is also effective in reversing the effects of MD in monkeys (Blakemore et al 1978a, LeVay et al 1979).

Binocular competition   It is clear that the effects of MD are more extreme than one would predict from a knowledge of the effects of BD. This, combined with their results on kittens raised with artificial strabismus or alternate monocular occlusion (see below) prompted Hubel & Wiesel (1965) to propose that a developmental mechanism that depends critically on a competitive interaction between the two eyes operates in the cortex. This idea has proved most helpful in understanding the effects of a number of environmental manipulations that affect cortical binocular interaction.

The idea of binocular competition is usually couched in terms of a battle among geniculate afferents for terminal space in the cortex. Initially, LGN input from either eye is supposed to be potentially affective; over time, the input that more often activates the postsynaptic neuron comes to dominate that neuron. This idea is reminiscent of Hebb's (1949) model of learning in neural circuits; an ingenious biophysical explanation has been offered by Stent (1973).

The data available in 1965 did not fully specify a model of binocular competition, since there was no evidence that postsynaptic neurons needed to be involved for competitive effects to be seen. Four studies have recently attempted to answer this question by manipulating the visual input in such a way as to differentially activate pre- and postsynaptic elements.

Singer et al (1977) and Wilson et al (1977) devised a situation in which there would be asymmetric presynaptic activity but little or no postsynaptic activity: they raised animals under conditions of BD, but stimulated one eye with temporally modulated diffuse illumination. Since geniculate cells respond well to diffuse light but cortical cells do not, any ocular dominance shift would have to be due largely to presynaptic activity. Neither study reported a shift, and both concluded that postsynaptic involvement was a necessity.

Cynader & Mitchell (1977) and Rauschecker & Singer (1979) offered other evidence that cortical activity was necessary for ocular dominance to shift. Both groups stimulated one eye of kittens through a strong cylindrical lens that blurred contours of one orientation while correctly focusing those at the orthogonal orientation, by this means hoping to take advantage of the orientation selectivity of cortical cells to dissect cortical from geniculate-based effects. Cynader & Mitchell raised their kittens giving the other eye normal visual experience, while Rauschecker & Singer first deprived one eye and then reverse-sutured them, exposing the second eye through the cylindrical lens. Both groups sought, and found, an orientation-dependent change in ocular dominance: cells sensitive to the orientations correctly focused through the cylindrical lens tended to be dominated by the eye having the lens; cells sensitive to other orientations often were dominated by the other eye. Since only the postsynaptic cortical cells would distinguish on the basis of orientation, both groups again concluded that postsynaptic involvement was critical.

While the results of these four studies clearly suggest that the effects of MD occur primarily in cortex rather than in the LGN, it is less clear that they demonstrate that *postsynaptic* involvement is essential. If all cortical cells were orientation selective, binocularly driven and monosynaptically driven by LGN afferents, this conclusion would be inescapable; since they are not, however, it is not. All studies assume that the pattern selectivity of cortical cells (either their insensitivity to diffuse light or their orientation selectivity) and the convergence of binocular signals on these cells occur together; the analysis depends on pitting one of these properties against the other *across one synapse*. However, it appears that simple cells receiving direct geniculate input are often monocularly driven (Albus 1975, Shatz & Stryker 1978); only complex cells and simple cells outside layer IV tend to be binocularly activated. Thus it is conceivable that the results of these studies could be explained by two entirely presynaptic competitive interactions, first one between LGN fibers for control of layer IV, and then a second between the outputs of layer IV cells for control of cells in other layers. This bears an obvious conceptual similarity to the two mechanisms implicated in other MD studies (see above); as in those studies, definitive conclusions must await a laminar analysis of effects, with particular attention to the small cells of layer IV analyzed by Shatz & Stryker (1978). None of the four studies in question provides such an analysis.

Two other studies have partially pattern-deprived one eye. Eggers & Blakemore (1978) raised kittens with spherical blurring lenses over one eye; they observed a decrease in the spatial resolution of receptive fields driven through the blurred eye compared to those driven through the unblurred eye. Similar results, obtained in the LGN of kittens deprived by the rather less well-controlled means of chronic application of atropine by Ikeda & Tremain (1978b) suggest that, unlike the effects discussed above, these results may reflect changes in more peripheral parts of the visual pathway.

LATERAL GENICULATE NUCLEUS   Three effects of MD have been reported in the LGN. Cells in the deprived layers of the nucleus are smaller than those in experienced layers; Y cells are more rarely encountered in recording from deprived layers than in normal layers; there may be a spatial resolution deficit in X cells recorded in deprived layers.

Morphological effects   Wiesel & Hubel (1963a, 1965a; Hubel & Wiesel 1970) noticed that cells in deprived layers of the LGN tend to be 30–40% smaller in cross-sectional area than cells in experienced layers. Guillery (1973) and Garey et al (1973) showed that this results from a retardation of growth among cells connected to the deprived eye; cells connected to the open eye may grow faster and attain slightly larger size than cells in normal cats (Wan & Cragg 1976, Hickey et al 1977).

Wiesel & Hubel originally believed that the cell size differences were caused by a reduction in retinal signals afferent to the deprived LGN neurons and were unrelated to the changes they found in cortical binocularity. Subsequent work, however, strongly suggests that a binocular competition mechanism is involved in the LGN changes. The most parsimonious view appears to be that this is in fact the same competition mechanism seen in cortex, exerting retrograde effects in LGN.

Cell size differences are prominent only in regions of the LGN representing the binocular visual field. Guillery & Stelzner (1970) found no differences in cell size between cells representing the monocular segment of the visual field in MD animals, and Guillery (1972) made similar observations on cells representing a so-called "critical segment" of the visual field produced by making a retinal lesion in the nondeprived eye. Hickey et al (1977) reported some cell-size differences in the monocular segment of the LGN of long-term MD cats, but these changes are small in magnitude, late in onset, and generally similar to those seen throughout the LGN following BD (Guillery 1973, Hickey et al 1977). In monkeys, the difference between binocular and monocular segments of the LGN in their response to MD is somewhat less marked (von Noorden & Middleditch 1975), but cell growth seems more affected by BD in this species than in the cat (Headon & Powell 1978, Vital-Durand et al 1978).

The relative sizes of cells in the different layers of the LGN are well correlated with cortical ocular dominance, especially when changes in cortical dominance are effected in such a way as to change the size of the ocular dominance bands in layer IV (e.g. Sherman et al 1974, Garey & Dürsteler 1975, Dürsteler et al 1976, Movshon & Dürsteler 1977, Vital-Durand et al 1978). Moreover, the time course of the onset of LGN cell-size changes, and of their reversal by reversed deprivation, is indistinguishable from the time course of effects seen on cortical binocularity and ocular dominance column size (Dürsteler et al 1976, Wan & Cragg 1976, Cragg et al 1976, Movshon & Dürsteler 1977). Finally, abnormalities of LGN cell size are unaccompanied by changes in synaptic development that are normally associated with anterograde degeneration effects (Winfield et al 1976).

These findings are all consistent with the notion that LGN cell size is determined by the success with which a particular cell makes contact in the cortex; this success is often determined by a binocular competition mechanism (see above). Retrograde effects of this sort are well known in other neural systems (e.g. Lund 1978, Jacobson 1978).

It appears that all relay cells in the LGN are affected by deprivation but that larger cells show more marked effects than smaller ones (Hoffmann & Holländer 1978). By injecting HRP into areas 17 and 18 of MD cats, Garey & Blakemore (1977) and LeVay & Ferster (1977) showed that the large presumptive Y cells projecting to area 18 are much more affected by deprivation than the mixed population of cells projecting to area 17. In addition,

LeVay & Ferster (1977) and Lin & Sherman (1978) report some reduction in the number of labeled cells in deprived layers of the LGN following cortical injections.

Loss of Y cells Sherman et al (1972) reported that the frequency with which Y cells were encountered in recordings made from deprived LGN layers was much lower than it was either in normal animals or in the nondeprived layers of MD animals. This finding has been confirmed a number of times (Hoffmann & Cynader 1977, Hoffmann & Holländer, 1978, Sireteanu & Hoffmann 1979, Eysel et al 1979), and is not apparent in recordings made from the retina of MD animals (Sherman & Stone 1973).

While it is tempting to infer from these results that deprivation exerts a specific influence on the development of the retino-cortical Y pathway, several factors complicate the interpretation. Microelectrodes are more likely to record from large than from small cells, and deprivation causes marked cell-size changes in parts of the LGN coextensive with the zones in which Y cells are "lost" (see above). If the largest LGN cells are Y cells, and these are most changed in size after MD (LeVay & Ferster 1977, Garey & Blakemore 1977), then the Y cell "loss" could simply result from changes in recording probability. No definitive statement is possible on this point, since the determinants of microelectrode selectivity are not well understood: different laboratories using techniques that should produce similar results report wildly varying proportions of Y cells in LGN recordings, even in normal animals (cf Hoffmann et al 1972, So & Shapley 1979).

There is some evidence for a genuine loss of Y cells, or at least of functionally active Y cells, in BD animals where there is little abnormality of cell size (Sherman et al 1972, Kratz et al 1979b). Moreover, Kratz et al (1978), studying the medial interlaminar nucleus of the LGN (MIN), which contains almost solely Y cells, report large changes in recording probability and significant numbers of abnormal cells after MD. On the other hand, Eysel et al (1979), while confirming the Y cell loss in geniculate recordings, were unable to find any loss of Y cells in recordings made from the optic radiation between LGN and cortex. Recently Shapley & So (1980) have been unable to verify the Y cell loss, even in recordings made from LGN.

Certain other data are not easy to reconcile with an extensive Y cell loss. Area 18, which in cat receives its main LGN input from Y cells, is in some respects *less* affected by deprivation than area 17 (Singer 1978). In monkeys, where the Y cells are segregated into the magnocellular layers of the LGN (Dreher et al 1976), there is no evidence for special effects of MD on these layers (Headon & Powell 1973, von Noorden & Middleditch 1975). On balance, until more evidence is available about the cortical terminations of the X and Y pathways, and the way these terminations are affected by deprivation, it will be difficult to assess the significance of the reported selective effects of MD on Y cells.

Resolution deficits in X cells   Less well resolved even than the effects of MD on LGN Y cells is the status of reports that the spatial resolution of X cells (the other major cell type in the dorsal layers of the LGN) is markedly decreased by deprivation. Maffei & Fiorentini (1976a) claimed that LGN spatial resolution was roughly halved in deprived layers; while they did not classify their cells as X or Y, subsequent reports suggest that their results were due to changes in X cells rather than Y cells (Lehmkuhle et al 1978, 1980; Sireteanu & Hoffmann 1979).

The nature and magnitude of these changes are not well established. Maffei & Fiorentini and Lehmkuhle et al report resolution changes of about 50%, while Sireteanu & Hoffmann find a 30% difference between deprived and nondeprived layer A and no effects in layer A_1. Moreover, Derrington & Hawken (1980) and Shapley & So (1980) find no effect at all of deprivation on spatial resolution.

Kratz et al (1979a) report that retinal X cells are unaffected by deprivation, suggesting that, like the Y cell "loss," X cell resolution deficits in MD cats are of geniculate rather than retinal origin. This contrasts oddly with Ikeda & Tremain's (1979) report that an X cell resolution loss in esotropic strabismus (see below) is of retinal origin.

It is impossible to draw firm conclusions from these new and mutually contradictory reports. There is, however, a plausible optical reason for some of the resolution deficits in deprived cats. Lid suture, as mentioned above, causes deficits in eye growth and corneal formation that can produce high myopia in sutured eyes (Wiesel & Raviola 1977, Gollender et al 1979). While refractive errors are of course corrected during electrophysiological experiments, the powerful negative lenses needed cause a significant image minification. Rough calculations suggest that this might be as large as 20–25%, and could thus account for a significant portion of the effect reported. Unfortunately, none of the papers reporting resolution losses details the refractive state of the cats' eyes.

Summary   Monocular occlusion and its many variants are as well studied as any developmental manipulation. The main effects of these procedures are seen in cortex, with retrograde influences on the morphology and possibly the physiology of the LGN. Within cortex, two mechanisms seem to be involved, one that is a competition between geniculate afferents for terminal space in layer IV, and a second, possibly involving intracortical suppression, that exerts its primary influence outside layer IV.

Artificial Strabismus

Hubel & Wiesel (1965) described the changes in cortical function produced by raising kittens with their visual axes artificially misaligned in mimicry of the common human clinical condition of strabismus. Several months of divergent strabismus (exotropia, produced by disinserting the medial rectus muscle) beginning near birth reduces the proportion of cortical neurons receiving excitatory binocular input from around four-fifths to less than one-fifth; receptive field properties other than binocularity are apparently unaffected. These findings have been widely confirmed (Wickelgren-Gordon 1972; Yinon et al 1975; Yinon 1976a; Blakemore 1976; Ikeda & Tremain 1977; Blakemore & Eggers 1978, 1979; Van Sluyters & Levitt 1980) for both exotropic and esotropic (convergent) strabismus.

Cortical ocular dominance columns in strabismic cats are remarkably well defined both physiologically and anatomically (Hubel & Wiesel 1965, Shatz et al 1977). In fact, Hubel & Wiesel's observation of regular periodic variations in eye dominance in these animals led them to reexamine their data from normal animals and propose the existence of ocular dominance columns as a feature of normal cortical organization.

Interocular asynchrony   Hubel & Wiesel reasoned that misalignment of the visual axes causes an absence of synchrony in the signals falling on corresponding retinal points; this decorrelation of the signals in the cortical afferent pathways from the two eyes could cause connections to a cortical cell from the eye less effective in activating that cell to weaken and disappear through a competitive interaction of the sort discussed above. Additional evidence for this idea came from experiments in which kittens were alternately monocularly deprived, day by day: this alternate occlusion causes a breakdown in cortical binocularity indistinguishable from that seen after strabismus (Hubel & Wiesel 1965). Recently, Blasdel & Pettigrew (1979) tried to measure the amount of interocular asynchrony needed to disrupt cortical binocularity; they found that the alternating periods of occlusion each had to last many seconds before binocularity was disrupted. Blasdel & Pettigrew note that this seems rather longer than the period that Hubel & Wiesel's model would predict, but they did not systematically study the most important parameter for testing this model, the duration of the blank interval between stimuli delivered to the two eyes.

Alternatives to the interocular asynchrony hypothesis   Thus far, the evidence we have considered on factors causing a breakdown of cortical binocularity is all consistent with an idea that esssentially visual aspects of the rearing situation account for the effects observed. In recent years evidence of several kinds has accumulated that nonvisual influences on the development of binocular interaction may be of some importance. Ideas of this sort are as yet rather ill defined but fall into two groups: that somehow proprioceptive signals from the extraocular muscles can influence cortical binocularity; or that the effectiveness of visual signals in controlling behavior modulates some aspects of visual cortical development.

Evidence on the role of visuo-motor integration has come from experiments on the effects of torsional strabismus produced by rotating the eye surgically about its visual axis. Blakemore et al (1975b) found that unilateral 90° eye rotation caused a decrease in cortical binocularity similar to that observed after more usual forms of strabismus; this result, of course, can be readily understood within a binocular competition framework and has been replicated by Yinon (1975, 1976b). Oddly, if the unrotated eye is occluded by lid suture, the open, rotated eye fails to take control of sizable numbers of cortical neurons; rather, many cells become unresponsive or unselective and remain binocularly driven (Yinon 1975, 1976b, 1977a,b; Singer et al 1979b). One obvious possibility is that the eye rotation surgery, which is rather extreme, somehow disturbs the retina or optic nerve and thus compromises visual signals from the operated eye. Singer et al (1979b) attempted to control for this possibility by doing "sham" surgery on two kittens by disinserting all the extraocular muscles (a necessity in all eye rotations), but leaving the eyeball in its "normal" orientation in the orbit. In these kittens, eye dominance shifted toward the open, operated eye, as would be expected from conventional MD results.

Singer et al suggest that their results can best be explained by assuming that the degree to which visuo-motor integration is disrupted by an environmental manipulation importantly influences cortical development. Eye rotation, which is held to disrupt visuo-motor integration, thus leaves cortex relatively unaffected; sham rotation, held to be less disruptive, allows the cortex to respond in the usual way to abnormal experience. This scheme is, however, difficult to reconcile with behavioral data showing that kittens can execute complex visual-motor tasks using a rotated eye alone even if the normal eye was not occluded during development (Mitchell et al 1976a, Gordon et al 1979a, Peck et al 1979).

More direct evidence that altered visuo-motor function does not affect cortical development comes from the results of Freeman (1978), who subjected kittens to daily alternate monocular occlusion, allowing them normal mobility while one eye was open but restraining them while the other was open. This completely disrupts visuo-motor integration through the "passive" eye (Hein et al 1970), yet Freeman found no tendency for that eye to lose control of cortical neurons.

We thus return to the idea that the most parsimonious explanation of the failure of monocular occlusion to affect cortical dominance in eye-rotated cats is to be found in the hypothesis that the surgery is often locally disruptive, and that such cats are effectively subjected to a form of visual deprivation in the rotated eye. The eye rotation experiments thus become understandable within a conventional framework, without the necessity of postulating nonvisual influences. This notion finds further support in a brief report by Crewther et al (1978a), showing that ocular dominance in bilaterally eye-rotated kittens was identical to that found by others in normal or BD kittens. We should note that this is most certainly not the interpretation favored by these authors, who believe their results indicate it is the relative balance of proprioceptive signals from eye muscles in the two orbits that is critical.

This idea may be traced to a series of experiments by Maffei and his co-workers, in which the claim is presented that proprioceptive signals are of paramount importance in determining cortical ocular dominance (Maffei & Bisti 1976; Maffei & Fiorentini 1976b, 1977; Buisseret & Maffei 1977; Maffei 1978). In one experiment, kittens were made strabismic by disinserting muscles in one or both eyes. If the strabismus was asymmetric, cortical binocularity was lost, but symmetrically induced strabismus was ineffective. In a second study, unilateral strabismus was produced in kittens that were then given BD for some months; binocularity was lost in these kittens despite the fact that visual experience was apparently prevented. The findings of Crewther et al (1978a) discussed above, showing that bilaterally eye-rotated kittens have normal cortical binocularity, can be taken in conjunction with those of Blakemore et al (1975b) showing that unilateral eye-rotation kittens lose binocular cells, to provide support for the "proprioceptive imbalance" idea. And Freeman & Bonds (1979) showed that manipulation of the eye can increase the effectiveness of a brief period of MD in paralyzed kittens.

On closer examination, however, this idea seems less compelling. First, many of the findings upon which it is based have not proved to be replicable. Both Singer et al (1979c) and Van Sluyters & Levitt (1980) report that bilaterally produced strabismus is as effective as unilateral strabismus in reducing cortical binocularity. Van Sluyters & Levitt also failed to find a decrease of binocularity in strabismic kittens briefly deprived of vision; they further note that prolonged BD *alone* has been reported to reduce cortical binocularity (Wiesel & Hubel 1965a, Kratz & Spear 1976), allowing an alternative explanation for Maffei & Bisti's (1976) results.

Other results are also difficult to reconcile with the proprioceptive imbalance theory. Van Sluyters (1977, Van Sluyters & Levitt 1980; see also Smith et al 1979) has shown that an optical strabismus produced with prism-containing goggles is as effective as surgical strabismus in reducing cortical binocularity, despite the lack of involvement of proprioceptive mechanisms.

And others (e.g. Hirsch & Spinelli 1970, Shinkman & Bruce 1977, Blasdel & Pettigrew 1979) have presented results showing that other interocular stimulus differences, also unaccompanied by any obvious proprioceptive abnormality, can break down binocular connections. Conversely, Blakemore (1976) reported that exposure designed to match the visual images in the two retinae might preserve binocular connections in strabismic cats; the status of this observation is, however, doubtful (Blakemore 1976, p. 442).

It thus appears that interocular differences in patterned retinal stimulation are both *necessary* and *sufficient* to produce the full range of changes observed in the cortex of strabismic kittens, and that proprioceptive imbalance alone is not *sufficient* to produce these effects. It is more difficult to judge the *necessity* of proprioceptive abnormalities, since most procedures that involve disparate stimulation of the eyes result in a failure of eye alignment (e.g. Blake et al 1974) that might conceivably also involve changes in proprioceptive signals. But this is speculation, and in the absence of clear positive evidence it seems wise to doubt the importance of proprioceptive influences on cortical binocularity.

Anomalous retinal correspondence   Two reports claim a significant adaptive change in cortical receptive field properties following strabismus resembling the clinical condition of anomalous retinal correspondence, in which the oculocentric visual direction of the deviating eye is shifted so that it approaches that of the other eye. Buchtel et al (1975) immobilized one eye of adult cats and claimed to observe large compensatory shifts in the receptive field locations of cortical cells. However, the data are not presented in any detail, and the logic behind a fixed shift in receptive field position as compensation for a variable (noncomitant) strabismus is obscure. Shlaer (1971) raised kittens wearing goggles containing prisms that produced a small (about 2°) vertical misalignment of the visual axes. He claimed on the basis of a small sample of neurons that binocular cortical receptive fields had shifted position so as to compensate for about half this deviation; it is doubtful that Shlaer had sufficient information about eye movements in his recording situation to support this claim, even if his cats did not (as seems likely) make small vertical fusional eye movements to compensate for the prisms without altering retinal correspondence.

Van Sluyters (1977) examined these issues: he found that kittens raised with small vertical prismatic deviations showed normal cortical binocularity without a measurable shift in receptive field position; larger deviations reduced cortical binocularity, again without shifting the receptive fields of the few remaining binocular neurons.

There is one other report of an unusual change in receptive fields following strabismus. Singer et al (1979a) found that horizontal strabismus reduced the proportion of cells in striate cortex responding to vertical contours and horizontal image movements. They interpret these results in terms of the possible role of these cells in the control of fusional vergence eye movement, obviously absent in strabismic animals.

Strabismic amblyopia Humans with strabismus often have greatly reduced visual capacity in the deviating eye. An analog of this strabismic amblyopia was reported by von Noorden & Dowling (1970), who found that acuity was much reduced in the deviating eye of rhesus monkeys given artificial esotropia near birth. Examination of the LGN in these animals showed that cells in layers receiving input from the deviated eye were smaller than those connected to the normal eye (von Noorden 1973, von Noorden & Middleditch 1975), and recordings from visual cortex revealed that few cells could be activated through the deviated eye (Baker et al 1974). These findings are similar to those reported by others to follow monocular occlusion, and different in character from the reported consequences of strabismus in cats discussed above.

Evidence for strabismic amblyopia in the cat came from Jacobson & Ikeda (1979), who showed a severe resolution deficit in the deviating eye of esotropic cats. A correlate of this behavioral loss is found in the LGN where cells, especially X cells, show gross deficits in spatial resolution (Ikeda & Wright 1976). The severity of this loss decreases as age of onset of the strabismus increases, suggesting that esotropia simply arrests the development of geniculate X cell spatial resolution (Ikeda et al 1978). This resolution loss is reminiscent of that reported to occur in geniculate X cells following MD (see above), but differs in that it is restricted to X cells representing the central visual fields. Moreover, Ikeda & Tremain (1979) reported a similar loss of resolution in retinal *area centralis* X cells in esotropic cats, while the retina is apparently unaffected by MD (Kratz et al 1979a).

In addition to decreased acuity, esotropic cats have severely constricted nasal visual fields in the deviating eye (Ikeda & Jacobson 1977, Kalil 1977). A physiological correlate of this field loss is found in the LGN, where cells in layer A_1 ipsilateral to the deviating eye are smaller than cells in layer A or cells in the contralateral LGN (Ikeda et al 1977), and in the striate cortex where there is a tendency for the nondeviating eye to control an increased proportion of neurons (Kalil et al 1978).

The severe spatial resolution deficits Ikeda and co-workers find in the peripheral visual pathways are difficult to reconcile with reports that esotropia, like exotropia, reduces cortical binocularity without altering the spatial characteristics of receptive fields (Yinon 1976a; Blakemore & Eggers 1978, 1979; Kalil et al 1978). This apparent conflict may be resolved on the basis of a procedural difference. Ikeda's method for producing esotropia is idiosyncratic—she finds it necessary to extirpate two extraocular muscles, the nictitating membrane and connective tissue at the lateral canthus to produce a large-angle, long-duration deviation. Blakemore & Eggers simply disinserted a single muscle, the conventional method for producing artificial strabismus in cats (e.g. Hubel & Wiesel 1965, Kalil et al 1978, Van Sluyters & Levitt 1980). Indeed when Ikeda attempted to replicate her resolution deficits using the conventional surgical technique, she failed (Ikeda & Tremain 1979). It should also be noted that the techniques used in monkeys by von Noorden and his colleagues (see above) are also rather extreme; both his and Ikeda's methods appear likely to produce a serious ocular paresis as well as the simple deviation (without serious loss of ocular motility) that results from disinserting a single muscle.

Even if surgical differences can account for the different results obtained in esotropia, it is difficult to understand why even paretic strabismus should have even more serious effects on the retina and LGN than complete deprivation does (cf for example Ikeda & Wright 1976, Lehmkuhle et al 1980). Certainly Ikeda's suggestion that image blur resulting from accommodative errors in the deviating eye is the causative factor seems unlikely, and the possibility must be considered that the extreme nature of her surgical techniques can result in damage to the eye or orbital tissues sufficiently severe to cause pathological damage by itself.

Sensitive period for the effects of strabismus   Yinon (1976a), Van Sluyters (1977), and Ikeda et al (1978) have studied the age-dependence of the effects of artificial strabismus of various types in cortex and in LGN. From their results it appears that the "sensitive period" for the effects of strabismus is identical to that for monocular occlusion (see above).

Restricted Pattern Exposure

Neurons in the visual cortex have three properties absent in the LGN: binocularity, orientation selectivity, and direction selectivity (Hubel & Wiesel 1962, 1968). Experimental manipulation of binocular visual input by means of monocular occlusion, strabismus, and the like affects the development of binocularity in cortex; we now consider the effects of manipulations of visual pattern inputs upon cortical stimulus selectivity.

STRIPED ENVIRONMENTS   Blakemore & Cooper (1970) and Hirsch & Spinelli (1970, 1971) raised kittens in environments in which visual experience was limited to contours of a single orientation; both groups reported an alteration in the distribution of orientation preferences in cortex, with more cells preferring orientations near the experienced orientation than other orientations. This finding has recently been the center of some controversy, both over the magnitude and even the existence of the effect, and over its implications for mechanisms of cortical development.

The nature of stripe-rearing effects   There are important differences between the results of Blakemore & Cooper and Hirsch & Spinelli, which are obscured by the idiosyncratic method used by Hirsch & Spinelli to analyze cortical unit properties. Blakemore & Cooper found that in their kittens, cells having normal receptive field properties were recorded with a frequency and regularity not diminished from normal—the only important effect of stripe-rearing they noted was the altered distribution of orientation preferences. Hirsch & Spinelli, on the other hand, found that most cells in their animals were not selective for orientation. To be sure, those that *were* orientation selective matched the orientations used in rearing, but were a minority.

Interpretation of these differences is complicated by the fact that the two groups performed importantly different experiments. Blakemore & Cooper raised their kittens with both eyes open in cylinders painted with stripes— in this situation, rotation of the head and changes in gaze might significantly change the *retinal* orientation exposure. Hirsch & Spinelli used goggles to expose patterns to their otherwise dark-reared kittens—this procedure fixes retinal orientation more accurately than cylinder-rearing does, but removes any correlation between self-produced movements and changes in the retinal image. Moreover, Hirsch & Spinelli's kittens saw vertical contours through one eye and horizontal contours through the other. This led (presumably for simple reasons of uncorrelated binocular stimulation, see above) to a breakdown of binocularity in addition to a change in the cortical orientation preference.

Even when methodological differences are taken into account, there are real differences between the two groups' findings. These suggest two interpretations of the effects of stripe-rearing, which borrow from the cortical consequences of either MD or BD. Hirsch & Spinelli's results seem best explained by an "atrophy" model based on the results of BD experiments: in this model, cells that initially preferred orientations absent in the rearing situation are effectively deprived and show the same poverty of sensitivity and selectivity as cells in BD cats. Blakemore & Cooper's results, however, are more consistent with a "modification" model conceptually similar to the binocular competition idea used to explain the effects of MD: since in their results all cortical cells prefer orientations similar to those present in the rearing situation, it must be that neurons initially disposed to prefer other orientations are "captured" by the exposure, in a manner analogous to the capture of cortical territory by the open eye in an MD animal.

Neither report contained sufficient data or detail to distinguish between these models; this requires detailed information about the magnitude of the effect, and especially about the number and cortical distribution of cells that either prefer orientations different from the rearing orientation or prefer no orientation at all. The wide variation among the results of later studies makes a definitive answer elusive.

Blakemore and his co-workers have continued to report both very strong biases in the distribution of preferred orientations and a very small proportion of unresponsive or unselective neurons in stripe-reared animals of various kinds (Blakemore & Mitchell 1973; Blakemore 1974; Blakemore & Van Sluyters 1975; Blakemore 1976, 1977; Blakemore et al 1978b). This view has received limited support from other laboratories (Pettigrew et al 1973b).

Hirsch and his colleagues have continued to report sizable numbers of nonoriented or unresponsive neurons in stripe-reared cats (Spinelli et al 1972, Leventhal & Hirsch 1975, Stryker et al 1978).

Several other groups have reported biases in the distribution of cortical orientation preference following stripe-rearing that are neither as extreme as those found by Blakemore nor accompanied by as high a proportion of abnormal cells as found by Hirsch (Blasdel et al 1977, Flood & Coleman 1979, Gordon et al 1979b; see also Spencer 1974, Turkel et al 1975, Tretter et al 1975, Cynader et al 1975, Freeman & Pettigrew 1973).

Finally, two reports have claimed to find no orientation bias following stripe-rearing (Stryker & Sherk 1975, Fiorentini & Maffei 1978); one of these (Stryker & Sherk) is noteworthy for its use of "blind" experimental procedures and automated receptive field analysis techniques. Both these studies used cylinder-reared animals; no negative findings from goggle-rearing experiments have come to our notice.

Despite this plethora of reports, few address the questions of cortical functional architecture that are critical. Stryker et al (1978), who studied kittens reared in goggles in the manner of Hirsch & Spinelli, analyzed the sequences of preferred orientation encountered in their electrode penetrations according to the methods devised by Hubel & Wiesel (1974). This revealed that in the regions of the penetrations where receptive fields sensitive to orientations not seen during rearing would be expected, nonoriented and unresponsive cells were found. This is, of course, the result predicted by the "atrophy" model. On the other hand, Blakemore (1976) shows a penetration reconstruction that appears more consistent with a "modification" model. But few reports show distributions of orientation preference sufficiently tight to rule out explanations in terms of biased samples and "missed" cells during recording, and the available evidence appears to favor the "atrophy" model over the "modification" model of the effects of stripe rearing. This also has the virtue of parsimony, in that we may offer explanations of the effects of partially and completely restricted visual experience in essentially the same terms, postulating no special additional mechanism of plasticity to deal with stripe-rearing results.

OTHER UNUSUALLY PATTERNED ENVIRONMENTS   A third sort of explanation for the effects of early exposure to specific patterns proposed an even more extreme form of modification than that suggested by Blakemore & Cooper. In this scheme, cortical neurons are held before visual experience to be *tabulae rasae,* upon which the visual environment may imprint almost any stimulus preference. Evidence for this could most obviously come from the generation by visual experience of definite stimulus preferences in cortical cells for stimuli not preferred by cells in normal animals. Some anecdotal evidence of this kind emerged from stripe-rearing studies (Spinelli et al 1972, Pettigrew & Garey 1974, Spinelli 1978), but a more definite test would be to change the properties of a group of cortical cells in such a way that they are both indisputably mature and also different from cells seen in normal animals. Attempts of this sort were made by Pettigrew & Freeman (1973) and Van Sluyters & Blakemore (1973), who raised kittens in environments composed of small, randomly scattered spots of light, in the hope that cortical cells might develop a spot preference (rarely found in normal animals). While both reports claimed positive results, the data are sparse, normal control animals absent, and no quantitative measures of sensitivity (especially necessary for this sort of experiment) are shown. Moreover, Blakemore & Van Sluyters (1975) reinterpret their data in a more general context as consistent with the notion that experience of extended contour is necessary for normal cortical development; this emphasizes that evidence for cells both distinctive and mature in these kittens is lacking.

RESTRICTED EXPERIENCE OF IMAGE MOTION   Direction selectivity, like orientation selectivity and binocularity, appears in cats and monkeys at the level of the striate cortex. This property is present in neurons recorded from young kittens lacking visual experience (Hubel & Wiesel 1963, Barlow & Pettigrew 1971). Attempts of two kinds have been made to modify cortical direction selectivity: rearing animals under conditions of "directional deprivation" by giving them experience only of intermittently illuminated visual scenes, and attempting to bias the distribution of direction selectivity by exposing animals to patterns moving in only one direction.

Motion deprivation   Cynader et al (1973) and Olson & Pettigrew (1974) studied the effects of rearing kittens in an environment illuminated stroboscopically at a low rate (less than 1 Hz); the idea here is that ample experience of pattern will be available without retinal image motion. A simple prediction would be that cortical direction selectivity might be selectively impaired; in fact, very low rates of stroboscopic illumination appear to have effects as severe as total pattern deprivation, and animals raised in this environment have few orientation or direction selective cortical neurons. A more selective effect on directionality was reported by Cynader & Cherneko (1976), who raised their kittens in stroboscopic illumination at the rather higher rate of 8 Hz. This appears to leave the spatial receptive field properties of cortical cells unaltered, but radically reduces the proportion of directionally selective neurons.

Unidirectional rearing   Several groups have raised kittens in a controlled environment in which contours move in one direction only; despite the obvious problems of stimulus control posed by natural eye and head movements, all report positive results (Cynader et al 1975, Tretter et al 1975, Daw & Wyatt 1976). In these kittens, about three quarters of direction-selective neurons prefer movement in the experienced direction. Tretter et al used moving stripe environments in their study; not surprisingly, they report finding a bias in the distribution of preferred orientation as well as the directional bias. Initially more surprising is the similar finding of Cynader et al, who used moving "blobs" rather than stripes. However, if one considers that only the edges of the "blobs" oriented orthogonally or nearly orthogonally to the direction of movement were in fact in motion on the retina during rearing, this finding becomes explicable in conventional terms.

The effects of unidirectional rearing appear quantitatively less dramatic than the more extreme results reported to follow stripe-rearing, in that many cells remain functional with stimulus preferences different from those satisfied by the rearing environment. Given the problems of stimulus control during rearing (all directional rearing studies used free-field stimuli rather than goggles), it is difficult to ascribe strong significance to this difference.

SENSITIVE PERIOD FOR THE EFFECTS OF SPECIAL PATTERNS   Blakemore (1974) studied the effect of age on the effectiveness of periods of stripe-rearing; his data are consistent with the idea that the sensitive period for the induction of these effects is identical to that for the induction of the effects of monocular occlusion and strabismus (see above).

Daw and his colleagues have, however, provided some evidence that the sensitive period for the effects of unidirectional rearing ends rather earlier than that for the effects of MD (Daw & Wyatt 1976, Berman & Daw 1977).

Daw et al (1978) provide the most compelling evidence for this idea in an experiment that pits the reversal of lid suture against the reversal of unidirectional rearing; they show that reversed lid suture at the age of 5 weeks can reverse cortical ocular dominance, but that reversing the directional environment at the same time does not effectively reverse the cortical distribution of direction preference. If both manipulations are performed in the same kitten, cortical neurons are strongly dominated by the *second* eye to be open, but tend to prefer movement in the *first* direction seen; about 10% of cortical cells combine these two preferences.

Daw's results raise the interesting possibility that there may be different sensitive periods for the development of different neuronal properties; we may expect more studies of this sort (perhaps on sensitive periods for the development of disparity or spatial frequency selectivity) in the future.

Acute Conditioning of Cortical Unit Properties

Claims that very brief periods of abnormal visual experience can have marked effects on visual function have been made for a number of experimental situations, including monocular occlusion (Hubel & Wiesel 1970, Olson & Freeman 1975, Movshon & Dürsteler 1977, Freeman & Olson 1979); artificial strabismus (Van Sluyters 1977); stripe-rearing (Blakemore & Mitchell 1973); and unidirectional rearing (Tretter et al 1975). The effectiveness of a few hours or days of deprivation in awake, freely moving animals prompted a number of studies in which attempts were made to alter cortical unit properties acutely, during electrophysiological recording experiments (Pettigrew et al 1973a, Pettigrew & Garey 1974, Imbert & Buisseret 1975). The exciting prospect that the dynamics of cortical plasticity could be studied directly by this means has, however, receded in recent years.

There are several difficulties in evaluating the results of these studies. The initial reports contained rather little data and little evidence of awareness of the very large response variability in young animals. Moreover, several recent attempts to reproduce short-term conditioning effects have failed (Stryker & Sherk 1975; Freeman & Bonds 1979 and their note 2). For a time it seemed that a period of "consolidation" during which the mechanisms of plasticity would act to alter neural function might be needed (Pettigrew & Garey 1974, Peck & Blakemore 1975); subsequent work has shown, however, that a delay between brief exposure and recording dilutes rather than enhances the effects (Olson & Freeman 1975, Freeman & Olson 1979).

If brief periods of exposure are effective in awake, freely moving animals but not in immobilized, anesthetized ones, it is natural to examine the effects of anesthesia and paralysis separately. Freeman & Bonds (1979) report that brief exposure periods can be effective in anesthetized, paralyzed animals if artificial eye movements are provided, but it should be noted that their results are consistent with the idea that it is simply necessary that the animal be aroused during the exposure period. While it is not in doubt that brief periods of experience can be developmentally effective, the early promise that this fact could be used effectively to study mechanisms of plasticity has not been fulfilled.

Catecholaminergic Regulation of Cortical Plasticity

In a series of provocative papers, Kasamatsu & Pettigrew (1976, 1979; Pettigrew & Kasamatsu 1978; Kasamatsu et al 1979b) have advanced the hypothesis that the degree to which abnormal visual input can affect cortical function is determined by monoaminergic pathways originating in the brainstem (Moore & Bloom 1978, 1979). It is clear that factors other than purely visual ones influence cortical plasticity: most obviously, the susceptibility of the cortex to environmental influence varies with the age of the animal (see above). In addition, regulation of cortical plasticity by brainstem mechanisms could explain the apparent dependence of environmental modifiability on arousing or more specific ascending activity (see above).

Kasamatsu & Pettigrew's first observations suggested that intraventricular administration of 6-hydroxydopamine (6-OHDA), a neurotoxin specific to monoamine-containing neurons, prevented the cortical eye dominance shift after a period of monocular occlusion. This by itself is not conclusive, since 6-OHDA has many effects on brain function and behavior that could produce essentially pathological effects. Later they refined their techniques and used intracortical rather than intraventricular perfusion, which is anatomically highly specific (Kasamatsu et al 1979a); the results were similar.

Their second experiment (Pettigrew & Kasamatsu 1978, Kasamatsu et al 1979b) was more persuasive. They performed a pharmacological substitution study and showed that local cortical perfusion of norepinephrine (NE, the monoamine neurotransmitter they believe to be involved) could restore cortical modifiability even in the presence of intraventricular or intracortical 6-OHDA; Kasamatsu (1979) provided evidence that noradrenergic β-receptors mediate this effect. While some of Kasamatsu & Pettigrew's claims concerning the ability of intracortically perfused NE to extend the period of plasticity into adulthood (Kasamatsu et al 1979b), and the ineffectiveness of catecholamines in affecting cortical response to reversed lid suture (Ary et al 1979), seem less well founded, their experiments have demonstrated a mechanism that may regulate cortical modifiability. How this system operates, and whether it is merely one of several neural subsystems that modulate plasticity, are questions that await further study.

GENETIC AND ENVIRONMENTAL INFLUENCES ON VISUAL DEVELOPMENT

To a greater force, and to a better nature, you, free, are subject,
and that creates the mind in you, which the heavens have not in their charge.

—Dante, *The Divine Comedy, Purgatorio* XVI, 79

In our survey we have considered evidence from a variety of sources demonstrating that the visual environment plays a crucial role in the development of visual function. Despite some evidence for environmental effects on the retina and LGN, it is in the visual cortex that the most striking and interesting effects are seen.

A simple model of cortical development might regard the role of environmental influences in terms of the simple "functional validation" of connection patterns innately laid down. Thus the devastating effects of visual deprivation would represent a validation failure, and the partial development seen under conditions of partial visual deprivation would reflect a combination of normal development of connections adequately validated with the loss or atrophy of others. Certainly this model is consistent with the evidence that at least the skeleton of the normal organization of cortical receptive fields appears to be present before visual experience, with the effects of BD, and probably also with the effects of rearing in specially patterned environments. But it accounts less well for many of the changes seen after rearing under conditions that disrupt binocular function. For example, the clear capture of cortical territory by the open eye in an MD animal cannot reflect only a simple "deletion" of inappropriate connections; a compensatory expansion of other connections is certainly involved.

A second model would allow the environment more actively to guide the formation of functional connections; this model could be posed in a variety of versions differing in the range of guiding power permitted the environment. While current evidence suggests that this role is smaller than was thought a few years ago, we cannot consider it to be negligible.

A strong prediction of the "functional validation" model is that neurons in the visual cortex should either develop normal function or should fail in varying degrees to attain it—they should certainly *not* develop specific functional properties different from those innately laid down. Yet there is widespread evidence that cortical neurons can acquire unusual properties of a special kind: distinct but different stimulus specificities when stimulated through the two eyes. In normal cats, binocularly driven cortical neurons have closely matched receptive field properties in the two eyes (Hubel & Wiesel 1962). In particular, the preferred orientations in the two eyes never differ by more than 15° (Blakemore et al 1972, Nelson et al 1977). Yet cats raised under conditions in which the two eyes are never stimulated together sometimes possess abnormal cortical neurons having widely disparate orientation preferences in the two eyes (Hirsch & Spinelli 1971, Blakemore & Van Sluyters 1974, Leventhal & Hirsch 1975, Movshon 1976, Stryker et al 1978). These neurons may be few in number, yet their presence indicates that environmental influences can induce marked changes in neuronal properties. Indeed there is evidence that in some cases in which these neurons are found, wholesale changes in the functional architecture of the cortex can occur (Blakemore 1976, Movshon 1976).

On these grounds, a strictly constructed validation model may be rejected. But if the environment does have some shaping influence, what role does it play in normal animals? An appealing idea has its roots in the persistent involvement of binocular interaction in most areas in which extensive plasticity may be demonstrated, and in the apparent ease with which normal binocular function may be disrupted. This idea holds that mechanisms of binocular combination require a flexibility greater than innate predispositions can supply, and that the visual environment provides essential information that guides their development (Pettigrew 1978, Blakemore 1979). There is certainly ample evidence for modifiability of binocular connections, and it appears that effects even on receptive field properties other than binocularity are most clearly seen after rearing conditions that also affect binocularity (e.g. Hirsch & Spinelli 1971, Movshon 1976, Stryker et al 1978, Gordon et al 1979b).

It seems plausible, then, that the main structural plan of the cortex is innately drawn, but that the environment, in addition to validating that plan, actively contributes to the development of binocular function. But plausibility is not certainty—what *is* certain is that continued active research in this field will refine, and perhaps render obsolete, the concepts that are with us today.

Therefore the sight that is granted to your world penetrates within
    the Eternal Justice as the eye into the sea;
for though from the shore it sees the bottom, in the open sea it does not,
and yet the bottom is there but the depth conceals it.

—Dante, *The Divine Comedy, Paradiso* XIX, 73

Literature Cited

Albus, K. 1975. Predominance of monocularly driven cells in the projection area of the central visual field in cat's striate cortex. *Brain Res.* 89:341–47

Ary, M., Pettigrew, J. D., Kasamatsu, T. 1979. Manipulations of cortical catecholamines fail to affect suppression of deprived eye responses after reverse suture. *Invest. Ophthalmol. Visual Sci.* 18: ARVO Suppl., p. 136

Baker, F. H., Grigg, P., von Noorden, G. K. 1974. Effects of visual deprivation and strabismus on the response of neurones in the visual cortex of the monkey, including studies on the striate and prestriate cortex in the normal animal. *Brain Res.* 66:185–208

√Barlow, H. B., Pettigrew, J. D. 1971. Lack of specificity in neurones in the visual cortex of young kittens. *J. Physiol.* 218:98–101P

Berman, N., Daw, N. W. 1977. Comparison of the critical periods for monocular and directional deprivation in cats. *J. Physiol.* 265:249–59

Blake, R. M., Crawford, M. L. J., Hirsch, H. V. B. 1974. Consequences of alternating monocular deprivation on eye alignment and convergence in cats. *Invest. Ophthalmol.* 13:121–26

√Blakemore, C. 1974. Developmental factors in the formation of feature extracting neurons. In *The Neurosciences, Third Study Program,* ed. F. G. Worden, F. O. Schmitt, pp. 105–33. Cambridge, Mass: MIT Press

Blakemore, C. 1976. The conditions required for the maintenance of binocularity in the kitten's visual cortex. *J. Physiol.* 261:423–44

Blakemore, C. 1977. Genetic instructions and developmental plasticity in the kitten's visual cortex. *Philos. Trans. R. Soc. London Ser. B* 278:425–34

Blakemore, C. 1979. The development of stereoscopic mechanisms in the visual cortex of the cat. *Proc. R. Soc. London Ser. B* 204:477–84

Blakemore, C., Cooper, G. F. 1970. Development of the brain depends on the visual environment. *Nature* 228:477–78

Blakemore, C., Eggers, H. M. 1978. Effects of artificial anisometropia and strabismus on the kitten's visual cortex. *Arch. Ital. Biol.* 116:385–89

Blakemore, C., Eggers, H. M. 1979. Animal models for human visual development. In *Frontiers in Visual Science,* ed. S. J. Cool, E. L. Smith III, pp. 651–59. Berlin: Springer

Blakemore, C., Fiorentini, A., Maffei, L. 1972. A second neural mechanism of binocular depth discrimination. *J. Physiol.* 226:725–40

Blakemore, C., Garey, L. J., Vital-Durand, F. 1978a. The physiological effects of monocular deprivation and their reversal in the monkey's visual cortex. *J. Physiol.* 283:223–62

Blakemore, C., Hillman, P. 1977. An attempt to assess the effects of monocular deprivation and strabismus on synaptic efficiency in the kitten's visual cortex. *Exp. Brain Res.* 30:187–202

Blakemore, C., Mitchell, D. E. 1973. Environmental modification of the visual cortex and the neural basis of learning and memory. *Nature* 241:467–68

Blakemore, C., Movshon, J. A., Van Sluyters, R. C. 1978b. Modification of the kitten's visual cortex by exposure to spatially periodic patterns. *Exp. Brain Res.* 31:561–72

Blakemore, C., Van Sluyters, R. C. 1974. Reversal of the physiological effects of monocular deprivation in kittens: further evidence for a sensitive period. *J. Physiol.* 237:195–216

Blakemore, C., Van Sluyters, R. C. 1975. Innate and environmental factors in the development of the kitten's visual cortex. *J. Physiol.* 248:663–716

Blakemore, C., Van Sluyters, R. C., Movshon, J. A. 1975a. Synaptic competition in the kitten's visual cortex. *Cold Spring Harbor Symp. Quant. Biol.* 40, The Synapse, pp. 601–9

Blakemore, C., Van Sluyters, R. C., Peck, C. K., Hein, A. 1975b. Development of the cat visual cortex following rotation of one eye. *Nature* 257:584–86

Blasdel, G. G., Mitchell, D. E., Muir, D. W., Pettigrew, J. D. 1977. A physiological and behavioural study in cats of the effect of early visual experience with contours of a single orientation. *J. Physiol.* 265:615–36

Blasdel, G. G., Pettigrew, J. D. 1978. Effect of prior visual experience on cortical recovery from the effects of unilateral eyelid suture in kitten. *J. Physiol.* 272:601–19

Blasdel, G. G., Pettigrew, J. D. 1979. Degree of interocular synchrony required for maintenance of binocularity in kitten's visual cortex. *J. Neurophysiol.* 42:1692–710

Bonds, A. B. 1974. Optical quality of the living cat eye. *J. Physiol.* 243:777–95

Bonds, A. B. 1979. Development of orientation tuning in the visual cortex of kittens. In *Developmental Neurobiology of*

Vision, ed. R. D. Freeman, pp. 31–49. New York: Plenum

Bonds, A. B., Freeman, R. D. 1978. Development of optical quality in the kitten eye. *Vision Res.* 18:391–98

Braddick, O., Atkinson, J., French, J., Howland, H. C. 1979. A photorefractive study of infant accommodation. *Vision Res.* 19:1319–30

Buchtel, H. A., Berlucchi, G., Mascetti, G. G. 1975. Behavioural and electrophysiological analysis of strabismus in cats. In *Aspects of Neural Plasticity,* ed. F. Vital-Durand, M. Jeannerod. *INSERM* 43:27–44

Buisseret, P., Imbert, M. 1976. Visual cortical cells: their developmental properties in normal and dark-reared kittens. *J. Physiol.* 255:511–25

Buisseret, P., Maffei, L. 1977. Extraocular proprioceptive projections to the visual cortex. *Exp. Brain Res.* 28:421–25

Campbell, F. W., Green, D. G. 1965. Optical and retinal factors affecting visual resolution. *J. Physiol.* 181:576–93

Cragg, B. G. 1972. The development of synapses in cat visual cortex. *Invest. Ophthalmol.* 11:377–85

Cragg, B. G. 1975a. The development of synapses in the visual system of the cat. *J. Comp. Neurol.* 160:147–66

Cragg, B. G. 1975b. The development of synapses in kitten visual cortex during visual deprivation. *Exp. Neurol.* 46: 445–51

Cragg, B. G., Anker, R., Wan, Y. K. 1976. The effect of age on the reversibility of cellular atrophy in the LGN of the cat following monocular deprivation: a test of two hypotheses about cell growth. *J. Comp. Neurol.* 168:345–54

Crawford, M. L. J., Blake, R., Cool, S. J., von Noorden, G. K. 1975. Physiological consequences of unilateral and bilateral eye closure in macaque monkeys, some further observations. *Brain Res.* 84: 150–54

Crawford, M. L. J., Marc, R. E. 1976. Light transmission of cat and monkey eyelids. *Vision Res.* 16:323–24

Crewther, S. G., Crewther, D. P., Peck, C. K. 1978a. Maintained binocularity in kittens raised with both eyes rotated. *Invest. Ophthalmol. Visual Sci.* 17: ARVO Abstr. Suppl., p. 269

Crewther, D. P., Crewther, S. G., Pettigrew, J. D. 1978b. A role for extraocular afferents in post-critical period reversal of monocular deprivation. *J. Physiol.* 282:181–95

Cynader, M. 1979. Competitive interactions in postnatal development of the kitten's visual system. See Bonds 1979, pp. 109–20

Cynader, M., Berman, N., Hein, A. 1973. Cats reared in stroboscopic illumination: effects on receptive fields in visual cortex. *Proc. Natl. Acad. Sci. USA* 70:1353–54

Cynader, M., Berman, N., Hein, A. 1975. Cats raised in a one-directional world: effects on receptive fields in visual cortex and superior colliculus. *Exp. Brain Res.* 22:267–80

Cynader, M., Berman, N., Hein, A. 1976. Recovery of function in cat visual cortex following prolonged visual deprivation. *Exp. Brain Res.* 25:139–56

Cynader, M., Chernenko, G. 1976. Abolition of directional selectivity in the visual cortex of the cat. *Science* 193:504–5

Cynader, M., Mitchell, D. E. 1977. Monocular astigmatism effects on kitten visual cortex development. *Nature* 270:177–78

Daniels, J. D., Pettigrew, J. D., Norman, J. L. 1978. Development of single-neuron responses in kitten's lateral geniculate nucleus. *J. Neurophysiol.* 41:1373–93

Daw, N. W., Berman, N. E. J., Ariel, M. 1978. Interaction of critical periods in the visual cortex of kittens. *Science* 199:565–67

Daw, N. W., Wyatt, H. J. 1976. Kittens reared in a unidirectional environment: evidence for a critical period. *J. Physiol.* 257:155–70

Derrington, A. M. 1978. Development of selectivity in kitten striate cortex. *J. Physiol.* 276:46–47P

Derrington, A. M. 1979. Direct measurement of image quality in the kitten's eye. *J. Physiol.* 295:16–17P

Derrington, A. M. 1980. Effects of visual deprivation on the development of spatial frequency selectivity in kitten visual cortex. *J. Physiol.* 300:62P

Derrington, A. M., Hawken, M. P. 1980. Effects of visual deprivation on cat LGN neurones. *J. Physiol.* 300:61P

De Valois, R. L., De Valois, K. K. 1980. Spatial vision. *Ann. Rev. Psychol.* 31:309–41

De Valois, R. L., Morgan, H., Snodderly, D. M. 1974. Psychophysical studies of monkey vision III. Spatial luminance contrast tests of macaque and human observers. *Vision Res.* 14:75–81

Donovan, A. 1966. The postnatal development of the cat's retina. *Exp. Eye Res.* 5:249–54

Dreher, B., Fukada, Y., Rodieck, R. W. 1976. Identification, classification and anatomical segregation of cells with X-like properties in the lateral geniculate nucleus of old-world primates. *J. Physiol.* 258:433–52

Duffy, F. H., Snodgrass, S. R., Burchfield, J. L., Conway, J. L. 1976. Bicuculline reversal of deprivation amblyopia in the cat. *Nature* 260:256–57

Duke-Elder, S. 1963. *System of Ophthalmology, Vol. 3, Normal and Abnormal Development.* St. Louis: Mosby

Dürsteler, M. R., Garey, L. J., Movshon, J. A. 1976. Reversal of the morphological effects of monocular deprivation in the kitten's lateral geniculate nucleus. *J. Physiol.* 261:189–210

Eggers, H. M., Blakemore, C. 1978. Physiological basis of anisometropic amblyopia. *Science* 201:264–67

Enroth-Cugell, C., Robson, J. G. 1966. The contrast sensitivity of retinal ganglion cells of the cat. *J. Physiol.* 187:517–52

Eysel, U. T., Grusser, O. J., Hoffmann, K. P. 1979. Monocular deprivation and the signal transmission by X- and Y-neurons of the cat lateral geniculate nucleus. *Exp. Brain Res.* 34:521–39

Ferster, D., LeVay, S. 1978. The axonal arborizations of lateral geniculate neurons in the striate cortex of the cat. *J. Comp. Neurol.* 182:923–44

Fiorentini, A., Maffei, L. 1978. Selective impairment of contrast sensitivity in kittens exposed to periodic gratings. *J. Physiol.* 277:455–66

Fiorentini, A., Maffei, L. 1979. Responses of cortical neurones of monocularly deprived kittens: a re-examination. *J. Physiol.* 291:35P

Flood, D. G., Coleman, P. D. 1979. Demonstration of orientation columns with [^{14}C] 2-deoxyglucose in a cat reared in a striped environment. *Brain Res.* 173:538–42

Freeman, R. D. 1978. Visuomotor restriction of one eye in kitten reared with alternate monocular deprivation. *Exp. Brain Res.* 33:51–63

Freeman, R. D., Bonds, A. B. 1979. Cortical plasticity in monocularly deprived immobilized kittens depends on eye movement. *Science* 206:1093–95

Freeman, R. D., Lai, C. E. 1978. Development of the optical surfaces of the kitten eye. *Vision Res.* 18:399–407

Freeman, R. D., Olson, C. R. 1979. Is there a "consolidation" effect for monocular deprivation? *Nature* 282:404–6

Freeman, R. D., Pettigrew, J. D. 1973. Alteration of visual cortex from environmental asymmetries. *Nature* 246:359–60

Freeman, R. D., Wong, S., Zezula, S. 1978.

Optical development of the kitten cornea. *Vision Res.* 18:409–14

Fregnac, Y., Imbert, M. 1978. Early development of visual cortical cells in normal and dark-reared kittens: relationship between orientation selectivity and ocular dominance. *J. Physiol.* 278:27–44

Garey, L. J., Blakemore, C. 1977. Monocular deprivation: morphological effects on different classes of neurons in the lateral geniculate nucleus. *Science* 195:414–16

Garey, L. J., Dürsteler, M. R. 1975. Reversal of deprivation effects in the lateral geniculate nucleus of the cat. *Neurosci. Lett.* 1:19–23

Garey, L. J., Fiskin, R. A., Powell, T. P. S. 1973. Effects of experimental deafferentation on cells in the lateral geniculate nucleus of the cat. *Brain Res.* 52:363–69

Gollender, M., Thorn, F., Erickson, P. 1979. Development of axial ocular dimensions following eyelid suture in the cat. *Vision Res.* 19:221–23

Gordon, B., Moran, J., Presson, J. 1979a. Visual fields of cats with one eye intorted. *Brain Res.* 174:167–71

Gordon, B., Presson, J., Packwood, J., Scheer, R. 1979b. Alteration of cortical orientation selectivity: importance of asymmetric input. *Science* 204:1109–11

Guillery, R. W. 1972. Binocular competition in the control of geniculate cell growth. *J. Comp. Neurol.* 144:117–30

✓Guillery, R. W. 1973. The effect of lid suture upon the growth of cells in the dorsal lateral geniculate nucleus of kittens. *J. Comp. Neurol.* 148:417–22

Guillery, R. W., Stelzner, D. J. 1970. The differential effects of unilateral lid closure upon the monocular and binocular segments of the dorsal lateral geniculate nucleus in the cat. *J. Comp. Neurol.* 139:413–22

Hamasaki, D. I., Flynn, J. T. 1977. Physiological properties of retinal ganglion cells of 3-week-old kittens. *Vision Res.* 17:275–84

✓Hamasaki, D. I., Sutija, V. G. 1979. Development of X- and Y-cells in kittens. *Exp. Brain Res.* 35:9–23

Harris, W. A., Stryker, M. P. 1977. Attempts to reverse the effects of monocular deprivation in the adult cat's cortex. *Neurosci. Abstr.* 3:562

Hawken, M., Mark, R., Blakemore, C. 1978. The effects of pressure blinding in monocularly deprived cats. *Arch. Ital. Biol.* 116:448–51

Headon, M. P., Powell, T. P. S. 1973. Cellular changes in the lateral geniculate nucleus of infant monkeys after suture of the eyelids. *J. Anat.* 116:135–45

Headon, M. P., Powell, T. P. S. 1978. The effect of bilateral eye closure upon the lateral geniculate nucleus in infant monkeys. *Brain Res.* 143:147–54

Hebb, D. D. 1949. *The Organization of Behavior.* New York: Wiley

Hein, A., Held, R., Gower, E. 1970. Development and segmentation of visually controlled movement by selective exposure during rearing. *J. Comp. Physiol. Psychol.* 73:181–87

Hendrickson, A. E., Wilson, J. R. 1979. A difference in [¹⁴C] deoxyglucose autoradiographic patterns in striate cortex between Macaca and Saimiri monkeys following monocular stimulation. *Brain Res.* 170:353–58

Henry, G. H., Bishop, P. O., Tupper, R. M., Dreher, B. 1973. Orientation specificity and response variability of cells in the striate cortex. *Vision Res.* 13:1771–79

Hickey, T. L., Spear, P. D., Kratz, K. E. 1977. Quantitative studies of cell size in the cat's dorsal lateral geniculate nucleus following visual deprivation. *J. Comp. Neurol.* 172:265–82

Hirsch, H. V. B., Spinelli, D. N. 1970. Visual experience modifies distribution of horizontally and vertically oriented receptive fields in cats. *Science* 168:869–71

Hirsch, H. V. B., Spinelli, D. N. 1971. Modification of the distribution of receptive field orientation in cats by selective visual exposure during development. *Exp. Brain Res.* 13:509–27

Hoffmann, K. P., Cynader, M. 1977. Functional aspects of plasticity in the visual system of adult cats after early monocular deprivation. *Philos. Trans. R. Soc. London Ser. B* 278:411–24

Hoffmann, K. P., Holländer, H. 1978. Physiological and morphological changes in cells of the lateral geniculate nucleus in monocularly-deprived and reverse-sutured cats. *J. Comp. Neurol.* 177:145–58

Hoffmann, K. P., Stone, J., Sherman, S. M. 1972. Relay of receptive field properties in dorsal lateral geniculate nucleus of the cat. *J. Neurophysiol.* 35:518–31

Howland, H. C., Atkinson, J., Braddick, O., French, J. 1978. Infant astigmatism measured by photorefraction. *Science* 202:331–33

Hubel, D. H., Wiesel, T. N. 1962. Receptive fields, binocular interaction and functional architecture in the cat's visual cortex. *J. Physiol.* 165:559–68

Hubel, D. H., Wiesel, T. N. 1963. Receptive fields of cells in striate cortex of very young, visually inexperienced kittens. *J. Neurophysiol.* 26:994–1002

Hubel, D. H., Wiesel, T. N. 1965. Binocular interaction in striate cortex of kittens reared with artificial squint. *J. Neurophysiol.* 28:1041–59

Hubel, D. H., Wiesel, T. N. 1968. Receptive fields and functional architecture of monkey striate cortex. *J. Physiol.* 195:215–43

Hubel, D. H., Wiesel, T. N. 1970. The period of susceptibility to the physiological effects of unilateral eye closure in kittens. *J. Physiol.* 206:419–36

Hubel, D. H., Wiesel, T. N. 1974. Sequence regularity and geometry of orientation columns in the monkey striate cortex. *J. Comp. Neurol.* 158:267–94

Hubel, D. H., Wiesel, T. N. 1977. Functional architecture of macaque monkey visual cortex. *Proc. R. Soc. London Ser. B* 198:1–59

Hubel, D. H., Wiesel, T. N., LeVay, S. 1977. Plasticity of ocular dominance columns in monkey striate cortex. *Philos. Trans. R. Soc. London Ser. B* 278:377–409

Ikeda, H., Jacobson, S. G. 1977. Nasal field loss in cats reared with convergent squint: behavioural studies. *J. Physiol.* 270:367–81

Ikeda, H., Plant, G. T., Tremain, K. E. 1977. Nasal field loss in kittens reared with convergent squint: neurophysiological and morphological studies of the lateral geniculate nucleus. *J. Physiol.* 270:345–66

Ikeda, H., Tremain, K. E. 1977. Different causes for amblyopia and loss of binocularity in squinting kittens. *J. Physiol.* 269:26–27P

Ikeda, H., Tremain, K. E. 1978a. The development of spatial resolving power of lateral geniculate neurones in kittens. *Exp. Brain Res.* 31:193–206

Ikeda, H., Tremain, K. E. 1978b. Amblyopia resulting from penalisation: neurophysiological studies of kittens reared with atropinisation of one or both eyes. *Br. J. Ophthalmol.* 60:21–28

Ikeda, H., Tremain, K. E. 1979. Amblyopia occurs in retinal ganglion cells in cats reared with convergent squint without alternating fixation. *Exp. Brain Res.* 35:559–82

Ikeda, H., Tremain, K. E., Einon, G. 1978. Loss of spatial resolution of lateral geniculate nucleus neurones in kittens raised with convergent squint produced at different stages of development. *Exp. Brain Res.* 31:207–20

Ikeda, H., Wright, M. J. 1976. Properties of LGN cells in kittens reared with convergent squint: a neurophysiological demonstration of amblyopia. *Exp. Brain Res.* 25:63–77

Imbert, M., Buisseret, P. 1975. Receptive field characteristics and plastic properties of visual cortical cells in kittens reared with or without visual experience. *Exp. Brain Res.* 22:25–36

Jacobson, M. 1978. *Developmental Neurobiology.* New York: Plenum

Jacobson, S. G., Ikeda, H. 1979. Behavioural studies of spatial vision in cats reared with convergent squint: is amblyopia due to arrest of development? *Exp. Brain Res.* 34:11–26

Kalil, R. E. 1977. Visual field deficits in strabismic cats. *Invest. Ophthalmol. Visual Sci.* 16: ARVO Suppl., p. 163

Kalil, R. E., Spear, P. D., Langsetmo, A. 1978. Response properties of striate cortex neurons in cats raised with divergent or convergent strabismus. *Invest. Ophthalmol. Visual Sci.* 17: ARVO Suppl., p. 269

Kasamatsu, T. 1979. Involvement of the β-adrenergic receptor in cortical plasticity. *Invest. Ophthalmol. Visual Sci.* 18: ARVO Suppl., p. 135

Kasamatsu, T., Itakura, T., Jonsson, G. 1979a. Spread of catecholamines perfused into visual cortex: effective concentration for modification of cortical plasticity. *Neurosci. Abstr.* 5:629

Kasamatsu, T., Pettigrew, J. D. 1976. Depletion of brain catecholamines: Failure of ocular dominance shift after monocular occlusion in kittens. *Science* 194:206–9

Kasamatsu, T., Pettigrew, J. D. 1979. Preservation of binocularity after monocular deprivation in the striate cortex of kittens treated with 6-hydroxydopamine. *J. Comp. Neurol.* 185:139–62

Kasamatsu, T., Pettigrew, J. D., Ary, M. 1979b. Restoration of visual cortical plasticity by local microperfusion of norepinephrine. *J. Comp. Neurol.* 185:163–82

Kennedy, C., Des Rosiers, M. H., Sakurada, O., Shinohara, M., Reivich, M., Jehle, J. W., Sokoloff, L. 1976. Metabolic mapping of the primary visual system of the monkey by means of the autoradiographic ^{14}C-deoxyglucose technique. *Proc. Natl. Acad. Sci. USA* 73:4230–34

Kratz, K. E., Mangel, S. C., Lehmkuhle, S., Sherman, S. M. 1979a. Retinal X- and Y-cells in monocularly lid-sutured cats: normality of spatial and temporal properties. *Brain Res.* 172:545–51

Kratz, K. E., Sherman, S. M., Kalil, R. 1979b. Lateral geniculate nucleus in dark-reared cats: loss of Y cells without

changes in cell size. *Science* 203:1353–55

Kratz, K. E., Spear, P. D. 1976. Effects of visual deprivation and alterations in binocular competition on responses of striate cortex neurons in the cat. *J. Comp. Neurol.* 170:141–51

Kratz, K. E., Spear, P. D., Smith, D. C. 1976. Postcritical-period reversal of effects of monocular deprivation on striate cortex cells in the cat. *J. Neurophysiol.* 39:501–11

Kratz, K. E., Webb, S. V., Sherman, S. M. 1978. Studies of the cat's medial interlaminar nucleus: A subdivision of the dorsal lateral geniculate nucleus. *J. Comp. Neurol.* 180:601–14

Lehmkuhle, S., Kratz, K. E., Mangel, S. C., Sherman, S. M. 1978. An effect of early monocular lid suture upon the development of X-cells in the cat's lateral geniculate nucleus. *Brain Res.* 157:346–50

Lehmkuhle, S., Kratz, K. E., Mangel, S. C., Sherman, S. M. 1980. Spatial and temporal sensitivity of X- and Y-cells in dorsal lateral geniculate nucleus of the cat. *J. Neurophysiol.* 43:520–41

√Lennie, P. 1980. Parallel visual pathways. *Vision Res.* 20:561–94

LeVay, S., Ferster, D. 1977. Relay cell classes in the lateral geniculate nucleus of the cat and the effects of visual deprivation. *J. Comp. Neurol.* 172:563–84

LeVay, S., Stryker, M. P. 1979. The development of ocular dominance columns in the cat. *Soc. Neurosci. Symp.* 4:83–98

LeVay, S., Stryker, M. P., Shatz, C. J. 1978. Ocular dominance columns and their development in Layer IV of the cat's visual cortex: a quantitative study. *J. Comp. Neurol.* 179:223–44

LeVay, S., Wiesel, T. N., Hubel, D. H. 1979. Effects of reverse suture on ocular dominance columns in rhesus monkey. *Neurosci. Abstr.* 5:793

Leventhal, A. G., Hirsch, H. V. B. 1975. Cortical effect of early selective exposure to diagonal lines. *Science* 190:902–4

Leventhal, A. G., Hirsch, H. V. B. 1977. Effects of early experience upon the orientation sensitivity and the binocularity of neurons in the cat's visual cortex. *Proc. Natl. Acad. Sci. USA* 74:1272–76

Lin, C. S., Sherman, S. M. 1978. Effects of early monocular eyelid suture upon development of relay cell classes in the cat's lateral geniculate nucleus. *J. Comp. Neurol.* 181:809–32

Loop, M. S., Sherman, S. M. 1977. Visual discrimination during eyelid closure in the cat. *Brain Res.* 128:329–39

Lund, R. D. 1978. *Development and Plasticity of the Brain.* New York: Oxford Univ. Press

Maffei, L. 1978. Binocular interaction in strabismic kittens and adult cats deprived of vision. *Arch. Ital. Biol.* 116:390–92

Maffei, L., Bisti, S. 1976. Binocular interaction in strabismic kittens deprived of vision. *Science* 191:579–80

Maffei, L., Fiorentini, A. 1976a. Monocular deprivation in kittens impairs the spatial resolution of geniculate neurones. *Nature* 264:754–55

Maffei, L., Fiorentini, A. 1976b. Asymmetry of motility of the eyes and change of binocular properties of cortical cells in adult cats. *Brain Res.* 105:73–78

Maffei, L., Fiorentini, A. 1977. Oculomotor proprioception in the cat. In *Control of Gaze by Brain Stem Neurons, Developments in Neuroscience,* ed. R. Baker, A. Berthoz, 1:477–81. New York: Elsevier/North Holland Biomed. Press

Mitchell, D. E., Cynader, M., Movshon, J. A. 1977. Recovery from the effects of monocular deprivation in kittens. *J. Comp. Neurol.* 176:53–64

Mitchell, D. E., Giffin, F., Muir, D., Blakemore, C., Van Sluyters, R. C. 1976a. Behavioural compensation of cats after early rotation of one eye. *Exp. Brain Res.* 25:109–13

✓Mitchell, D. E., Giffin, F., Wilkinson, F., Anderson, P., Smith, M. L. 1976b. Visual resolution in kittens. *Vision Res.* 16:363–66

Mohindra, I., Held, R., Gwiazda, J., Brill, S. 1978. Astigmatism in infants. *Science* 202:329–31

Moore, C. L., Kalil, R., Richards, W. 1976. Development of myelination in optic tract of the cat. *J. Comp. Neurol.* 165:125–36

Moore, R. Y., Bloom, F. E. 1978. Central catecholamine neuron systems: anatomy and physiology of the dopamine systems. *Ann. Rev. Neurosci.* 1:129–69

Moore, R. Y., Bloom, F. E. 1979. Central catecholamine neuron systems: anatomy and physiology of the norepinephrine and epinephrine systems. *Ann. Rev. Neurosci.* 2:113–68

Movshon, J. A. 1976. Reversal of the physiological effects of monocular deprivation in the kitten's visual cortex. *J. Physiol.* 261:125–74

Movshon, J. A., Dürsteler, M. R. 1977. Effects of brief periods of unilateral eye closure on the kitten's visual system. *J. Neurophysiol.* 40:1255–65

Nelson, J. I., Kato, H., Bishop, P. O. 1977. Discrimination of orientation and position disparities by binocularly activated neurons in cat striate cortex. *J. Neurophysiol.* 40:260–83

Noda, H., Creutzfeldt, O. D., Freeman, R. B. Jr. 1971. Binocular interaction in the visual cortex of awake cats. *Exp. Brain Res.* 12:406–21

Olson, C. R., Freeman, R. D. 1975. Progressive changes in kitten striate cortex during monocular vision. *J. Neurophysiol.* 38:26–32

Olson, C. R., Freeman, R. D. 1978. Monocular deprivation and recovery during sensitive period in kittens. *J. Neurophysiol.* 41:65–74

Olson, C. R., Pettigrew, J. D. 1974. Single units in visual cortex of kittens reared in stroboscopic illumination. *Brain Res.* 70:189–204

Peck, C. K., Blakemore, C. 1975. Modification of single neurons in the kitten's visual cortex after brief periods of monocular visual experience. *Exp. Brain Res.* 22:57–68

Peck, C. K., Crewther, S. G., Barber, G., Johannsen, C. J. 1979. Pattern discrimination and visuomotor behaviour following rotation of one or both eyes in kittens and in adult cats. *Exp. Brain Res.* 34:401–18

✓Pettigrew, J. D. 1974. The effect of visual experience on the development of stimulus specificity by kitten cortical neurones. *J. Physiol.* 237:49–74

Pettigrew, J. D. 1978. The paradox of the critical period in striate cortical development. In *Neuronal Plasticity,* ed. C. Cotman, pp. 311–30. New York: Raven

Pettigrew, J. D., Freeman, R. D. 1973. Visual experience without lines: effect on developing cortical neurons. *Science* 182:599–601

Pettigrew, J. D., Garey, L. J. 1974. Selective modification of single neuron properties in the visual cortex of kittens. *Brain Res.* 66:160–64

Pettigrew, J. D., Kasamatsu, T. 1978. Local perfusion of noradrenaline maintains visual cortical plasticity. *Nature* 271:761–63

Pettigrew, J. D., Nikara, T., Bishop, P. O. 1968. Binocular interaction on single units in cat striate cortex: simultaneous stimulation by single moving slit with receptive fields in correspondence. *Exp. Brain Res.* 6:391–416

Pettigrew, J. D., Olson, C., Barlow, H. B. 1973a. Kitten visual cortex: short-term, stimulus-induced changes in connectivity. *Science* 180:1202–3

Pettigrew, J. D., Olson, C., Hirsch, H. V. B. 1973b. Cortical effect of selective visual experience: degeneration or reorganization? *Brain Res.* 51:345–51

Rakic, P. 1977. Prenatal development of the visual system in rhesus monkey. *Philos. Trans. R. Soc. London Ser. B* 278:245–60

Rauschecker, J. P., Singer, W. 1979. Changes in the circuitry of the kitten visual cortex are gated by postsynaptic activity. *Nature* 280:58–60

Robson, J. G., Enroth-Cugell, C. 1978. Light distribution in the cat's retinal image. *Vision Res.* 18:159–74

✓Rodieck, R. W. 1979. Visual pathways. *Ann. Rev. Neurosci.* 2:193–225

Rusoff, A. C. 1979. Development of ganglion cells in the retina of the cat. See Bonds 1979, pp. 19–30

Rusoff, A. C., Dubin, M. W. 1977. Development of receptive field properties of retinal ganglion cells in kittens. *J. Neurophysiol.* 40:1188–98

Schiller, P. H., Finlay, B. L., Volman, S. F. 1976. Quantitative studies of single-cell properties in monkey striate cortex. I. Spatiotemporal organization of receptive fields. *J. Neurophysiol.* 39:1288–1319

Shapley, R. M., So, Y.-T. 1980. Is there an effect of monocular deprivation on the proportion of X and Y cells in the cat lateral geniculate nucleus? *Exp. Brain Res.* 39:41–48

Shatz, C. J., Lindstrom, S., Wiesel, T. N. 1977. The distribution of afferents representing the right and left eyes in the cat's visual cortex. *Brain Res.* 131:103–16

Shatz, C. J., Stryker, M. P. 1978. Ocular dominance in Layer IV of the cat's visual cortex and the effects of monocular deprivation. *J. Physiol.* 281:267–83

Sherk, H., Stryker, M. P. 1976. Quantitative study of cortical orientation selectivity in visually inexperienced kitten. *J. Neurophysiol.* 39:63–70

Sherman, S. M., Guillery, R. W., Kaas, J. H., Sanderson, K. J. 1974. Behavioral, electrophysiological and morphological studies of binocular competition in the development of the geniculo-cortical pathways of cats. *J. Comp. Neurol.* 158:1–18

Sherman, S. M., Hoffmann, K. P., Stone, J. 1972. Loss of a specific cell type from the dorsal lateral geniculate nucleus in visually deprived cats. *J. Neurophysiol.* 35:532–41

Sherman, S. M., Stone, J. 1973. Physiological

normality of the retina in visually deprived cats. *Brain Res.* 60:224–30

Shinkman, P. G., Bruce, C. J. 1977. Binocular differences in cortical receptive fields of kittens after rotationally disparate binocular experience. *Science* 197:285–87

Shlaer, S. 1971. Shift in binocular disparity causes compensatory change in the cortical structure of kittens. *Science* 173:638–41

Singer, W. 1977. Effects of monocular deprivation on excitatory and inhibitory pathways in cat striate cortex. *Exp. Brain Res.* 134:568–72

Singer, W. 1978. The effect of monocular deprivation on cat parastriate cortex: Asymmetry between crossed and uncrossed pathways. *Brain Res.* 157:351–55

Singer, W., Rauschecker, J., Werth, R. 1977. The effect of monocular exposure to temporal contrasts on ocular dominance in kittens. *Brain Res.* 134:568–72

Singer, W., Rauschecker, J., von Grünau, M. 1979a. Squint affects striate cortex cells encoding horizontal image movements. *Brain Res.* 170:182–86

Singer, W., Tretter, F. 1976. Receptive-field properties and neuronal connectivity in striate and parastriate cortex of contour-deprived cats. *J. Neurophysiol.* 39:613–30

Singer, W., Tretter, F., Yinon, U. 1979b. Inverted vision causes selective loss of striate cortex neurons with binocular, vertically oriented receptive fields. *Brain Res.* 170:177–81

Singer, W., von Grünau, M., Rauschecker, J. 1979c. Requirements for the disruption of binocularity in the visual cortex of strabismic kittens. *Brain Res.* 171:536–40

Sireteanu, R., Hoffmann, K.-P. 1979. Relative frequency and visual resolution of X- and Y-cells in the LGN of normal and monocularly deprived cats: Interlaminar differences. *Exp. Brain Res.* 34:591–603

Smith, D. C., Spear, D., Kratz, K. E. 1978. Role of visual experience in postcritical-period reversal of effects of monocular deprivation in cat striate cortex. *J. Comp. Neurol.* 178:313–28

Smith, E. L., Bennett, M. J., Harwerth, R. S., Crawford, M. L. J. 1979. Binocularity in kittens reared with optically induced squint. *Science* 204:875–77

So, Y.-T., Shapley, R. M. 1979. Spatial properties of X and Y cells in the lateral geniculate nucleus of the cat and conduction velocities of their inputs. *Exp. Brain Res.* 36:533–50

Spear, P. D., Tong, L., Langsetmo, A. 1978. Striate cortex neurons of binocularly deprived kittens respond to visual stimuli through closed eyelids. *Brain Res.* 155:141–46

Spencer, R. F. 1974. *Influence of selective visual experience upon the post-natal maturation of the visual cortex of the cat.* PhD thesis. Univ. Rochester, NY

Spinelli, D. N. 1978. Neural correlates of visual experience in single units of cat's visual and somatosensory cortex. See Blakemore & Eggers 1979, pp. 674–88

Spinelli, D. N., Hirsch, H. V. B., Phelps, J., Metzler, T. 1972. Visual experience as a determinant of the response characteristics of cortical receptive fields in cats. *Exp. Brain Res.* 15:289–304

Stent, G. S. 1973. A physiological mechanism for Hebb's postulate of learning. *Proc. Natl. Acad. Sci. USA* 70:997–1001

Stryker, M. P., Sherk, H. 1975. Modification of cortical orientation selectivity in the cat by restricted visual experience: a reexamination. *Science* 190:904–6

Stryker, M. P., Sherk, H., Leventhal, A. G., Hirsch, H. V. B. 1978. Physiological consequences for the cat's visual cortex of effectively restricting early visual experience with oriented contours. *J. Neurophysiol.* 41:896–909

Thorn, F., Gollender, M., Erickson, P. 1976. The development of the kitten's visual optics. *Vision Res.* 16:1145–49

Tretter, F., Cynader, M., Singer, W. 1975. Modification of direction selectivity in neurons in the visual cortex of kittens. *Brain Res.* 84:143–49

Turkel, J., Gijsbers, K., Pritchard, R. M. 1975. *Environmental modification of oculomotor and neural function in cats.* Presented at Ann. Meet. Assoc. Res. Vis. Ophthalmol., Sarasota

✓Van Essen, D. C. 1979. Visual areas of the mammalian cerebral cortex. *Ann. Rev. Neurosci.* 2:227–63

Van Sluyters, R. C. 1977. Artificial strabismus in the kitten. *Invest. Ophthalmol. Visual Sci.* 16: ARVO Suppl., p. 40

Van Sluyters, R. C. 1978. Reversal of the physiological effects of brief periods of monocular deprivation in the kitten. *J. Physiol.* 284:1–17

Van Sluyters, R. C., Blakemore, C. 1973. Experimental creation of unusual neuronal properties in visual cortex of kittens. *Nature* 246:506–8

Van Sluyters, R. C., Freeman, R. D. 1977. The physiological effects of brief periods

of monocular deprivation in very young kittens. *Neurosci. Abstr.* 3:433

Van Sluyters, R. C., Levitt, F. B. 1980. Experimental strabismus in the kitten. *J. Neurophysiol.* 43:686–99

Vital-Durand, F., Garey, L. J., Blakemore, C. 1978. Monocular and binocular deprivation in the monkey: morphological effects and reversibility. *Brain Res.* 158:45–64

von Noorden, G. K. 1973. Histological studies of the visual system in monkeys with experimental amblyopia. *Invest. Ophthalmol.* 14:727–37

von Noorden, G. K., Crawford, M. L. J. 1978. Lid closure and refractive error in macaque monkeys. *Nature* 272:53–54

von Noorden, G. K., Dowling, J. E. 1970. Experimental amblyopia in monkeys. II. Behavioral studies in strabismic amblyopia. *Arch. Ophthalmol.* 84:215–20

von Noorden, G. K., Middleditch, P. R. 1975. Histology of the monkey's lateral geniculate nucleus after unilateral lid closure and experimental strabismus: further observations. *Invest. Ophthalmol.* 14:674–83

Wan, Y. K., Cragg, B. 1976. Cell growth in the lateral geniculate nucleus of kittens following the opening or closing of one eye. *J. Comp. Neurol.* 166:365–72

Watkins, D. W., Wilson, J. R., Sherman, S. M. 1978. Receptive-field properties of neurons in binocular and monocular segments of striate cortex in cats raised with binocular lid suture. *J. Neurophysiol.* 41:322–37

Wickelgren-Gordon, B. 1972. Some effects of visual deprivation on the cat superior colliculus. *Invest. Ophthalmol.* 11:460–67

Wiesel, T. N., Hubel, D. H. 1963a. Effects of visual deprivation on morphology and physiology of cells in the cat's lateral geniculate body. *J. Neurophysiol.* 26:978–93

Wiesel, T. N., Hubel, D. H. 1963b. Single-cell responses in striate cortex of kittens deprived of vision in one eye. *J. Neurophysiol.* 26:1003–17

Wiesel, T. N., Hubel, D. H. 1965a. Comparison of the effects of unilateral and bilateral eye closure on cortical unit responses in kittens. *J. Neurophysiol.* 28:1029–40

Wiesel, T. N., Hubel, D. H. 1965b. Extent of recovery from the effects of visual deprivation in kittens. *J. Neurophysiol.* 28:1060–72

Wiesel, T. N., Hubel, D. H. 1974. Ordered arrangement of orientation columns in

522   MOVSHON & VAN SLUYTERS

monkeys lacking visual experience. *J. Comp. Neurol.* 158:307–18

Wiesel, T. N., Raviola, E. 1977. Myopia and eye enlargement after neonatal lid fusion in monkeys. *Nature* 266:66–68

Wilson, J. R., Sherman, S. M. 1977. Differential effects of early monocular deprivation on binocular and monocular segments of cat striate cortex. *J. Neurophysiol.* 40:891–903

Wilson, J. R., Webb, S. V., Sherman, S. M. 1977. Conditions for dominance of one eye during competitive development of central connections in visually deprived cats. *Brain Res.* 136:277–87

Winfield, D. A., Headon, M. P., Powell, T. P. S. 1976. Postnatal development of the synaptic organisation of the lateral geniculate nucleus in the kitten with unilateral eye closure. *Nature* 263:591–94

Wurtz, R. H. 1969. Visual receptive fields of striate cortex neurons in awake monkey. *J. Neurophysiol.* 32:727–42

Yinon, U. 1975. Eye rotation in developing kittens: the effect on ocular dominance and receptive field organization of cortical cells. *Exp. Brain Res.* 24:215–18

Yinon, U. 1976a. Age dependence of the effect of squint on cells in kitten's visual cortex. *Exp. Brain Res.* 26:151–57

Yinon, U. 1976b. Eye rotation surgically induced in cats modified properties of cortical neurons. *Exp. Neurol.* 51:603–27

Yinon, U. 1977a. Inverted vision surgically induced in experienced cats: physiology of the primary cortex. *Exp. Brain Res.* 28:141–51

Yinon, U. 1977b. Inverted vision in adult cats: preservation of unidirectionality in cortical neurons. *Brain Res.* 120:164–66

Yinon, U., Auerbach, E., Blank, M., Friesenhausen, J. 1975. The ocular dominance of cortical neurons in cats developed with divergent and convergent squint. *Vision Res.* 15:1251–56

Ann. Rev. Psychol. 1981. 32:523–74
Copyright © 1981 by Annual Reviews Inc. All rights reserved

THE CENTRAL BASIS OF MOTIVATION: INTRACRANIAL SELF-STIMULATION STUDIES

♦352

M. E. Olds and J. L. Fobes

Division of Biology, California Institute of Technology,
Pasadena, California 91125

CONTENTS

523

0066-4308/81/0201-0523$01.00

INTRODUCTION

For the past quarter century two strategies have dominated the study of the physiological basis of motivation. One of these, reviewed here by Grossman (1979), directs its attention primarily to localization and characterization of "centers" considered to be implicated in the regulation of eating, drinking, and other activities pursuant to biological needs. The other approach, intracranial self-stimulation (SS), reviewed herein, focuses on a more general mechanism thought to modulate motivated behavior.

Prior to 1954, such an approach to the neural basis of motivational mechanisms was not thought possible. The findings of lesion studies had implicated particular subdivisions of the hypothalamus in the regulation of activities related to food, sex, and other biological needs. Complementary findings from stimulation studies had shown that complex behaviors such as eating or drinking could be elicited by stimulation of these discrete sites in the hypothalamus and nearby regions. It seemed, therefore, that an understanding of the neural control of those aspects of behavior which gave evidence of being motivational in nature required an understanding of the interaction of various subdivisions of the hypothalamus with one another, of the characteristic neural activity of these regions, of the type of input that modified the spontaneous activity, and of the built-in factors that were responsible for initiating and terminating their activity.

The shift in emphasis from the study of hypothalamic regulation of biological needs to the study of a relatively nonspecific motivational mechanism came about as a result of the discovery by Olds & Milner (1954) that rats given a brief electrical stimulus to their brains learned to perform a response under conditions of acquisition that were essentially similar to those existing for conventional rewards such as food. Yet the animals were not deprived and it was not obvious that some biological need was met by the brain stimulation. The significance of this finding lay in its implication of the possible existence of a specialized system whose activation yielded behavioral effects comparable to those seen in behaviors motivated by biological needs. If such a system existed, and if we could gain direct access to it by SS, thereby bypassing its normal physiological inputs, we were in a position to try to gain an understanding of the functional organization of the brain as it pertains to motivation and reinforcement. Further, this knowledge was expected to transcend the sum of the understanding gained about the individual hypothalamic circuits involved in feeding, drinking, and other specific behaviors related to biological needs.

Two volumes of proceedings recently published summarize the status of SS research up to the mid-1970s (Wauquier & Rolls 1976, Hall et al 1977). Both bear witness to the complexity of the issues, the difficulties encountered in attempts to answer the basic questions concerning the significance of the phenomenon, and the extraordinary range of topics wherein brain rewarding stimulation has found a niche. More recent reviews also cover special topics, and for completeness of coverage the reader is advised to consult these publications (Federation Proceedings 1979; Fibiger 1978; Routtenberg 1978, 1979; Stein 1978a,b; Wise 1978). The aim here is to highlight the directions that research in this field is taking and to evaluate what more we now know about the neural control of motivated behavior since the SS procedure was introduced in 1954.

Basic Issues

In the 25 years that have elapsed since the discovery of rewarding SS, a great deal of effort has been spent in trying to understand the phenomenon and its implications for functional brain organization. Although the issues have not changed, a shift in emphasis seems to have taken place from theoretical contributions to empirical concern for the anatomical constituents of the motivational mechanism. The issues in the field of SS research are of three types. The first concerns the nature of SS effects. Although we are not in a position to ask what the animal experiences when it obtains SS, we are able to compare the behavioral properties accompanying SS in various situations with those for conventional rewards in the same situations. Does SS have the same properties associated with behavior motivated by conventional rewards, or are there substantial differences that mitigate against the notion of SS tapping a central motivational-reinforcing mechanism? This issue was of great concern during the first decade of research with SS, but in recent years the interest in it has lagged, as though the matter had been settled to everyone's satisfaction. It might more accurately be considered to be in abeyance because no clear new approach has become available.

The second issue concerns the nature of the relationship between a general mechanism of reinforcement and the specific mechanisms believed to reside in the hypothalamus. What interaction is there between the activation of the general reward pathway and the activation of specific circuits? What is the neurophysiological relationship between conventional rewards and brain stimulation reward? For example, when probes supporting SS are in the hypothalamus, it is possible to argue that the effects of SS are equivalent to the effects that would be produced if these same circuits had been activated by conventional stimuli. Accordingly, so far as the hypothalamus is concerned, the brain stimulation produces accessibility to the circuits involved in the regulation of behavior to satisfy biological needs and may derive its motivating and reinforcing properties from the fact that it activates these circuits. But when probes supporting SS behavior are in structures remote from the hypothalamus, and we have little or no information about the involvement of these structures in motivation, it becomes more difficult to elaborate an interaction between the effects of conventional rewards and SS. Thus, demonstration that the distribution of reinforcing sites is widespread raised the question of the meaning of such a diffuse system so far as the particular "centers" in the hypothalamus and related regions were concerned.

The third issue received considerable attention at the beginning and continues to do so; this concerns the constituents of a central, diffusely distributed motivational-reinforcement pathway. It may be that this question has received the most attention during the last decade because methods have become available to anatomists that led to the discovery of new pathways, some of which overlapped substantially with the distribution of brain rewarding sites. Whatever the cause, the great interest in the question of the anatomical and pharmacological constituents of a central reinforcing mechanism dictates the emphasis given in the present review to this aspect of SS research.

BEHAVIORAL EFFECTS WITH SELF-STIMULATION AND CONVENTIONAL REWARDS

Results from the initial studies onward (see review in J. Olds 1962) made it quite clear that animals working for brain stimulation were highly motivated and quick to learn the response that produced the brain stimulation. Once the response was acquired, the outstandingly high incentive value of SS became readily apparent. Furthermore, an asymptote in performance was not readily attained: the more trials given, the more rapid the rate of responding to obtain SS as if, with time, the amount or quality of the reward improved. The rewarding effect that had initially been noted in an open field, and had subsequently been tested in an operant situation, could be obtained by stimulating regions in the diencephalon, including its ventral portion and limbic subdivisions (Olds et al 1960, Olds & Olds 1963). Also, the initial observations that had been made in rats were later confirmed in other species, including rabbits (Bruner 1966), cats (Roberts 1958), monkeys (Brady 1961), and humans (Heath & Mickle 1960).

One important aspect of the phenomenon was that the brain stimulus could be used in a learning situation with no biological deficit to energize the animal to behave and with no obvious reduction of a drive through biological satisfiers. The behavior of the animal illustrated reinforcement according to the empirical law of effect but still was not easily accommodated in the framework of prevailing theories of learning (Hull 1943), in which learning served to balance homeostatic mechanisms through drive reduction.

The similarities between brain rewarding stimulation and natural rewards noted in the situations in which the phenomenon was first studied served to a great extent to determine the framework for explanations of the phenomenon. It soon became apparent that, in addition to the similarities to conventional rewards, there were also differences between performance maintained by SS and that maintained by natural rewards. An explanation of these differences seemed of crucial importance if the SS phenomenon were to be viewed as evidence for the existence of a central mechanism of reinforcement.

Extinction and Partial Reinforcement

The most striking of these differences was observed when the brain stimulus was withheld after a period of SS. With conventional rewards—for example, food or water—the pattern of responding could be maintained for a rather long period after the reward was no longer given; that is, during extinction. In contrast to this pattern of gradual, protracted decay of responding, the pattern of extinction with SS was one of abrupt termination (Olds & Milner 1954; J. Olds 1955, 1962; Seward et al 1959).

Once the animals stopped responding during extinction, they seldom started up again spontaneously. Deutsch (1963, 1964; Howarth & Deutsch 1962; Deutsch & Howarth 1963) reported that his subjects seldom responded more than 30 times during extinction. This finding had also been reported by Seward and others (1959). Also, the more experience the animals had with SS, the more rapid was the falloff in response rate for SS when it was withheld. It seemed paradoxical that an animal shown by its behavior to be extraordinarily strongly motivated should cease so abruptly to respond. This peculiarity of SS was not restricted to a particular site or structure and it was not related to a particular pattern of responding. Whether the animal was self-stimulating at a very high rate in the posterior lateral hypothalamus or more slowly in the septal region mattered very little. If the stimulus was no longer available, the animal quickly ceased to work for it. Interestingly, however, the animal was easily brought back to its previously demonstrated highly motivated and hard-working state with a few experimenter-initiated brain stimuli. More recently it has been shown that subjects initiate SS spontaneously when the sessions run continuously for 24 hours or longer (Annau et al 1974).

Another difference between situations in which rats worked for natural rewards and those in which they worked for brain reward was revealed when the tests were carried out not in Skinner boxes, on a continuous schedule of reinforcement, but in runways or mazes (Gallistel 1966, 1967;

Panksepp et al 1968; Seward et al 1960; Wetzel 1963). In these latter situations the animal had to press the lever in the goal box to obtain the brain stimulus, and the scheduling of trials was an important factor in the rate of acquisition. When trials were spaced, the rate of acquisition was slow; when trials were massed, the rate of acquisition was rapid. This variable was of little significance in the acquisition of maze or runway learning with food as the reward. It was apparent, therefore, that brain stimulation-maintained behavior differed in this respect from behavior for a natural reward.

Other test situations brought out differences of a similar nature. For example, it is well known that animals can be trained to respond on a partial reinforcement schedule when food or water is the reinforcer. With respect to brain-rewarding stimulation, it was reported that training under partial reinforcement was very difficult (Sidman et al 1955, Brady & Conrad 1960, Brodie et al 1960, Keesey & Goldstein 1968).

These peculiarities, ranging from extinction and partial reinforcement responding to overnight decrement (J. Olds 1956, Seward et al 1960, Spear 1962, Wetzel 1963), and the need for priming to reestablish responding, all seemed to point to the fact that the high motivational level—so obvious when the animal was self-stimulating at high rates when each one of its responses was rewarded or when it was running mazes with massed trials —is a highly labile state. An interruption of performance seemed to result in the disappearance of the motivation, whereas in comparable situations with natural rewards, interruption of the consummatory behavior had little effect on the motivation which seemed to be of a robust nature capable of withstanding a variety of alterations in the animal's environment.

Other peculiarities of SS behavior were also reported. For example, the animals seemed not to be capable of satiation (J. Olds 1958); the brain reward appeared to have a higher incentive value than food for a hungry animal (Routtenberg & Lindy 1965), and sometimes approach and escape effects were derived from the same site (Bower & Miller 1958, Olds & Olds 1963). None of these peculiarities, however, matched in importance that which came to be attached to the pattern of extinction, or to the fact that the interruption of SS by partial reinforcement schedules or by insertion of delays between trials reduced the incentive value of SS to near zero.

Theories for Unusual Effects

The unusual properties of brain stimulation made one of two demands on the investigator: either the difference between the brain reward and conventional reward was too basic to view behavior accompanying SS as evidence for a central mechanism mediating behavior motivated by conventional rewards, or the difference could be explained in a context that accepted the notion of a central reward pathway.

Several theories were advanced to explain the peculiarities of brain-stimulation–maintained behavior: specifically, why the density of responding was low when the brain stimuli were spaced, why extinction was so rapid, and why, under appropriate conditions, the animal was as willing to escape the brain stimulus as to obtain it (Roberts 1958, J. Olds 1962, Ball & Adams 1965). The most influential of the theories was that advanced by Deutsch (1960, 1963; Deutsch & Deutsch 1966, 1973; Deutsch & Howarth 1963) and subsequently elaborated by Gallistel (1964, 1973). This theory proposed that the brain stimulus simultaneously activated two systems, a drive or motivational system that was the energizing factor responsible for the initiation of behavior, and a satisfying or reinforcing system that was responsible for the establishment of the connection between the response and the brain stimulus. The principal difference between the two components was the time course of the activation; the motivation component was active for a shorter period of time than was the reinforcing component. Hence, when a single train of electrical stimuli was given, the motivation produced decayed rapidly, whereas the reinforcement did not. To maintain the motivational system underlying SS, it was necessary to apply the brain stimulus at a rate that provided sufficient, continuous input. If activity in this system was allowed to die out, the experimenter had to initiate input to reestablish the motivation necessary to produce SS behavior.

Behavioral and neurophysiological evidence was advanced to support the theory (Howarth & Deutsch 1962, Deutsch 1964). For example, using runway situations, Gallistel (1966, 1967) obtained data supporting the notion that two systems underlay SS behavior and that they could be differentially manipulated. With physiological methods based on parameters to measure the refractoriness of neurons, these investigators showed that two types of neural elements appeared to be activated by the brain stimulus, and although these could not be separated at the behavioral level, they could be analyzed in terms of their physiological properties (see review in Gallistel 1973).

A considerable number of the SS investigations in the 1960s were directly concerned with the validity of Deutsch's proposed dual mechanisms. However, later work has reported resistance to extinction and behavior under partial reinforcement schedules that appear to be irreconcilable with Deutsch's approach (Herberg 1963a, Pliskoff & Hawkins 1963, Pliskoff et al 1965, Culbertson et al 1966, Deutsch & DiCara 1967, Gandelman et al 1968).

Resolution

The above work proceeded within the framework of motivational theory based initially upon drive and later upon incentive and reinforcement approaches that favor the examination of behavior viewed as the consequence of the conditions of reinforcement. SS behavior was subsequently examined in terms of factors such as the amount and quality of the reward, the delay between the response and the reward, and other aspects that were thought to be essential to the occurrence of the behavior. The gist of these studies was to indicate that the unique features of SS behavior were not intrinsic, but rather were due to the specific conditions of testing. When these conditions were altered to more closely match features present in situations in which conventional rewards were used, then the peculiarities with SS disappeared and behavior for the brain stimulus came to resemble the response patterns associated with natural rewards (Trowill et al 1969).

In more recent years the controversy has died down. It is not that the peculiar properties of SS behavior are no longer observed, but that they are no longer viewed by most workers as the basis for an intrinsic dichotomy between reinforcement by SS and reinforcement by natural stimuli. The evidence that SS behavior could be produced under partial reinforcement schedules such as FR-30 to 200 (Pliskoff et al 1965, Carey et al 1974), VI-30 sec to 10 min (Pliskoff et al 1965, Terman & Kling 1968, Schmidt et al 1977), or DRL-10 sec to 3 min (Pliskoff et al 1965; see also Beninger et al 1977, 1978) also served to reduce the need for theories to explain the difference between the brain stimulation effects and the effects of natural rewards in terms of the operation of special mechanisms. Additional evidence for basic similarity between the effects of the two types of rewards derived from studies in which brain stimulation was available for long periods in a situation where food and water were similarly available. The animal was free to obtain SS when it elected to do so. Under these conditions, the pattern of SS showed the same features of stop-go-rest as did the patterns of responding for food and water with which it competed. That is, there were periods of rest and periods of SS that were spontaneously initiated, just as there were periods of responding for food or water (Annau et al 1974).

It seems clear that the consensus reached with respect to the peculiar features of SS behavior is that it is qualitatively comparable to behavior observed with conventional rewards. This has been reflected in a sharp drop in studies directed to show whether priming is necessary, whether extinction is rapid, and whether the stimulus is capable of motivating responding under a variety of partial reinforcing schedules. Rather, research has been redirected to questions not of the likelihood of there being a central reinforcing mechanism, but of the relationship between such a mechanism and the regulatory activities known to take place when natural rewards guide behavior. That is, does SS influence the nervous system by acting on the same system as conventional rewards do?

BRAIN LOCI AFFECTED BY SELF-STIMULATION AND CONVENTIONAL REWARDS

One of the issues raised by the discovery of brain-stimulation–rewarded behavior was the nature of the relationship, if any, between the neural circuitry activated during SS and the neural circuitry known to be implicated in performance involving conventional rewards. SS can be obtained from a large number of sites at different brain levels (Olds & Olds 1963), and for some of these sites something was known about the structure's function. For other placements this was not the case. One structure that drew considerable attention from the beginning was the hypothalamus. It soon became clear that rewarding sites were more densely packed in this region than anywhere else, that animals worked at higher rates for SS there, and that the rate of acquisition, when hypothalamic stimulation was the reward, was more rapid than with stimulation in other structures. In terms of conventional rewards, an extensive body of literature on hypothalamic function assigned an essential role to this structure in motivation. How then, was this information to be integrated with results of SS?

Concepts of Physiological Regulation of Motivated Behavior

Two conceptual influences formed the background for research on the underlying physiology of SS. One derived from Hess's work in the 1930–1950 period (Hess 1957) and the other from the work of the physiologists Brobeck and Anand (Brobeck 1955, 1957; Anand & Brobeck 1951; Anand 1961). For the latter group, the advocated strategy for understanding the physiological basis of motivated behavior was to separate the behavior into its reflexive components and to study the neural basis of these constituents along with seeking the source of modulation that organizes these "elementary" components into an organized pattern. The complex behavior itself was conceived of as the sum of the individual reflexive constituents, integrated with one another through the influence of higher centers. One such center might be the hypothalamus, exerting facilitation or inhibition on lower level reflexive mechanisms.

Hess was concerned, however, not with the reflex components of motivated behavior and their organization into a hierarchical system, but rather with the "molar" aspects of behavior, its appetitive nature and its complexity shown in a natural setting. He reported that behaviors similar in duration, complexity, and other properties to behaviors observed in contexts with natural rewards could be elicited by direct electrical stimulation of discrete diencephalic sites. It was possible to elicit feeding, drinking, sexual behavior, or attack behavior by stimulation of particular brain areas. Although these stimulated sites were in close proximity to one another, the evidence indicated a separation or the coexistence of proximal, closely interdigitated aggregates of neurons whose activation by electrical means led to the expression of these "naturalistic" behaviors. It seemed likely, therefore, that these same neurons were active when the naturally occurring behaviors were observed.

These findings by Hess and others (Larsson 1954, Andersson & Wyrwicka 1957, Andersson et al 1958) resulted in the conception of hypothalamic and diencephalic regulatory circuits that were responsible for the "affective," appetitive properties of the behaviors we call motivated, and much subsequent effort was directed to obtaining evidence that these stimulation-elicited behaviors were amenable to modulation by the same factors that modulated the naturally occurring manifestations. The implication was that the mechanism thus activated was responsible for those aspects of behavior that had to do with its "voluntary" and appetitive character rather than with its reflexive character. Lower brainstem and spinal mechanisms might be responsible for some properties of motivated behavior, but those important to the understanding of the molar, naturalistic aspects of the motivated behavior resided at the diencephalic level or perhaps at even higher levels. The ultimate outcome of this orientation was the demonstration that there were sites that, when stimulated, led to the intake of food or water and others that appeared to inhibit intake (Miller 1958, Andersson et al 1960, Wyrwicka & Dobrzecka 1960, Hoebel & Teitelbaum 1962, Mogenson & Stevenson 1966, Mogenson 1969). Thus the conception emerged of complementary aggregates of neurons within the hypothalamus and related structures that worked in unison to produce the normal reactions associated with the pursuit of biological needs.

Overlap of Structures Important for Self-Stimulation and Homeostatic Regulation

So far as SS behavior was concerned, the evidence also pointed to the hypothalamus and related structures as playing a crucial role in the mediation of rewarding effects. It had been shown that rewarding effects could be obtained in the telencephalon and in the mesencephalon, yet the focus seemed to reside at the level of hypothalamus (J. Olds 1962, Olds & Olds 1963). Here the sites were more numerous and the effects produced were more rewarding. Was this because in the hypothalamus the rewarding brain stimulation activated the normal circuits associated with motivated behavior (J. Olds 1962; Valenstein 1969, 1970, 1976)?

From a more theoretical point of view, if a central reinforcing mechanism existed, it had to interact in some intimate fashion with the regulatory mechanisms that had been identified with other approaches in the hypothalamus. Either these special regulatory circuits were constituents of the reward pathway studied with SS behavior or they came under the modulatory influence of such a system. What needed to be done, therefore, was to show in what way sites that elicited, for example, feeding behavior when stimulated, were related to sites that supported SS behavior. How close was the overlap between the two effects? If the overlap was very close, it would be evidence that the rewarding brain stimulation was mediated through activation of the same circuits that were energized during brain stimulation-elicited behavior such as feeding. If the overlap was not close, then some explanation had to be found as to why the SS was capable of functioning in a manner similar to conventional reinforcers and yet did not depend for its effects on circuits for which there was strong evidence of regulation with natural rewards. The literature pertaining to this relationship has been reviewed in detail in recent years. It is extensive, covering the areas of feeding, drinking, sexual behavior, and temperature regulation, and we will deal only briefly with these data and with the implication of the work relating to hypothalamic functioning for conventional and SS rewards.

A persistent pursuit of this line of research was made by Hoebel (Hoebel & Teitelbaum 1962; Hoebel 1969, 1976, 1979). His detailed analysis of stimulation-induced behavior provides convincing evidence that such behavior is similar to naturally occurring behavior and is capable of being separately activated via electrical stimulation. In addition, he showed that the same factors that affect naturally occurring behavior involving food also affect the stimulation-induced behavior and the rate of responding for SS. In general, manipulations that alter the incentive value of food have comparable effects on SS. For example, food deprivation or insulin injections are accompanied by increased eating and SS with lateral hypothalamic placements. Similarly, ventromedial lesions result in overeating and increased SS, both of which return to normal levels on reaching the new weight plateau. Conversely, operations that decrease food intake, such as excessive body weight after forced feeding, stomach distention, or glucagon injections, likewise decrease SS. Similar evidence was produced for sexual behavior and drinking behavior (Herberg 1963b; Caggiula & Hoebel 1966; Mogenson & Stevenson 1966; Mogenson 1969, 1971, 1973; Caggiula 1970), offering support for functional differentiation of sites in the hypothalamus that reflected different regulatory circuits. These circuits could be activated by natural stimuli or by stimulation-induced behavior or by rewarding brain SS. But regardless of how the sites were activated, activation had basically the same effects on the behavior of the animal.

To maintain that conventional and SS rewards are mediated by common circuits, it was important to demonstrate that variables affecting behavior for conventional rewards affect stimulation-induced and SS behavior in the same direction. Moreover, a site associated with one type of natural behavior should be experimentally capable of separation from a site that induced another type. Thus, sites implicated in the regulation of food intake on the basis of stimulation-induced eating were thought to lead to more food intake under conditions of deprivation (but not to yield sexual or drinking behavior from the same site), and also to yield more SS behavior, which in turn was facilitated under food but not water deprivation.

However, a contrary line of evidence was produced by Valenstein (Valenstein et al 1968; Valenstein 1969, 1970, 1976). Valenstein and coworkers showed that stimulus-bound eating behavior obtained from one site could result in stimulus-bound drinking behavior from the same site under different experimentally induced circumstances. This seemed to demonstrate a fallacy in arguing in favor of distinct circuits at the hypothalamic level that could be activated separately and that reflected a functional organization responsible for the naturally occurring behaviors. For Valenstein, the rewarding effects of SS were real enough, but the notion that evidence for the circuitry underlying these effects could be obtained by showing a close overlap between the effects of stimulus-bound behavior and SS behavior seemed unrealistic. There appeared to be little likelihood that with the type of electrodes used and the current intensities applied the natural regulatory mechanisms would be activated in this way during SS or stimulus-bound behavior.

It would seem, therefore, that the effects produced by SS may or may not owe much to the fact that feeding, drinking, and so on have something to do with the normal activity of the neurons concerned. The view of Olds, Hoebel, and others is that rewarding effects of SS derive from the fact that these motivational mechanisms are activated in the hypothalamus. More recently there has been a shift away from the notion of regulatory centers in the hypothalamus, at least as all-inclusive regulators, and a corresponding shift from an emphasis on the overlap between SS sites and sites that induce stimulus-bound eating or drinking. Of course the data that show similar effects of manipulated variables on sites that induced feeding or drinking and SS, and the data showing differential distribution of these sites in the hypothalamus, still stand. The findings are clearly indicative of some overlap between homeostatic mechanisms in the hypothalamus and SS reward mechanisms. However, the view of a reward mechanism owing its properties to activities of hypothalamic homeostatic mechanisms may no longer be tenable and would in any event appear to be incomplete. Such an account says nothing about sites outside the hypothalamus that support SS. In recent years, the attention given to SS behavior within the framework of hypothalamic centers regulating motivational phenomena has given way to attention on other structures. That the two phenomena overlap at the level of the hypothalamus has been shown convincingly. Whether this means that the animal works for SS at hypothalamic sites because the stimulation produces experiences obtained with conventional rewards, and whether the neural control for both is exerted principally at the level of the hypothalamus, are questions not yet answered.

ANATOMICAL CONSTITUENTS OF THE REWARD PATHWAY

The importance of determining the physiological structures that support SS was recognized early and resulted in numerous mapping studies. The guiding principle for the implantation of electrodes was first to explore the diencephalon. Here it was shown, shortly after the discovery of rewarding effects in the septal region, that the ventral region yielded effects that were even more "rewarding." The results of a series of studies pointed unequivocally to the medial forebrain bundle (MFB) as an anatomical structure that supports SS behavior (J. Olds 1956, Olds & Olds 1963).

The Medial Forebrain Bundle

This structure, however, proved not to be as helpful as had initially been expected. It is a large tract of ascending and descending axons, some long, spanning the length of the brain, some short, extending no farther than a few millimeters in the diencephalon (Knook 1965, Nauta 1960, Millhouse 1969, Nauta & Haymaker 1969, Nauta & Domesick 1978). The fibers that make up this tract enter at each brain level and some leave the tract at each level. The MFB connects structures at each pole of the brain, and in the middle intersects with a major structure, the hypothalamus, as if functioning to relay messages from one end to the other via a connecting link. The early mapping studies demonstrated that probes implanted along the MFB supported SS behavior of a kind which suggested that this anatomical structure was the focus for the effect, the principal constituent of the circuit functioning to mediate reinforcement. The basis of this view was that the likelihood of obtaining SS behavior at this level was greater than at any other site explored thus far, the response rates were higher, and the period of training required to obtain high and stable rates over extensive periods was much shorter. However, the composition of this structure and the neural elements in it that were responsible for the reinforcing effect were not known and seemed technically difficult to unravel in view of the changing constituents of the structure at each brain level.

It seemed unreasonable to think that all the constituents in the MFB were responsible for the rewarding effect. This would make the circuit responsible for the effect almost coextensive with the whole brain, since so many structures in both forebrain and hindbrain send input to this tract and receive fibers from it. Another consideration was the variation in the pattern of behavior elicited along its trajectory; there were obvious variations in the nature of the rewarding effects as a function of the placement of the probes. In the anterior part of the tract the pattern of responding was slower than in the caudal end, was not accompanied by behavioral excitement, and did not suggest the presence of "mixed effects"—that is, positive and negative incentive properties. What we needed to know was the nature of the axons whose excitation led to effects sharing in common the property of reward, regardless of the site of excitation along the fiber tract.

An important feature of the anatomy of the MFB which seemed significant were the long axons, both ascending and descending, known to be major constituents of this tract. Self-stimulation behavior was obtained all along the tract, but in the late 1950s and early 1960s the origin of these long axons was not known. The anatomical evidence showed a picture of a compact bundle in the caudal end of the brain which gradually fanned out into the rostral regions. The distribution of SS sites in the MFB showed a more localized and stronger rewarding effect in the caudal regions, becoming gradually less localized and milder in the rostral regions. Here again, the SS data and the anatomical evidence appeared to point to the long axons as being responsible for the rewarding effect, but owing to the lack of knowledge concerning the localization of the cell bodies contributing this input to the MFB, even this correlation proved of little help in identifying the anatomical substrate for the behavioral effects.

Another puzzling matter related to the role of the hypothalamic nuclei that the MFB traversed. Not only were there aggregates of cells at the SS sites in the MFB at the diencephalic level, but in addition the anatomical studies revealed the presence of cells with short axons, which seemed not to be part of large cell groupings, which might be responsible for the rewarding effect. Finally, what was the functional significance for SS of the fact that a major structure such as the hypothalamus formed a linkage between extensive regions in the forebrain and hindbrain? It soon became evident that the correlation between SS sites and the MFB raised more questions than it answered because of the nature of the structure itself. The alternative implications were these: (a) that most of the structures contributing to this tract were responsible for the rewarding effect or that only some of them were and a way had to be found for identifying them; (b) that the hypothalamus, as the principal linkage between forebrain and hindbrain, was responsible and the mechanism was affected through its connections with fibers of the MFB; or (c) that the neurons with short axons found along the length of the MFB were responsible for the rewarding effect. No evidence was obtained in the early mapping studies to form the basis for a rational decision among these alternatives.

Mapping Studies

Olds (J. Olds 1962, 1976, 1977; Olds & Olds 1963) viewed the anatomical properties of the MFB and the focus of SS in this region as adding weight to the notion that SS behavior represented the activation of a central reinforcing mechanism. He argued that such a mechanism required a capacity to influence widespread, diffusely localized regions and that the MFB, by virtue of its morphology, seemed capable of doing so. The identification of the MFB as a major substrate for SS (J. Olds 1962, Olds & Olds 1965, Valenstein & Campbell 1966) influenced subsequent anatomical studies in two directions: the first was to test for rewarding sites in structures known to give or receive fibers from the MFB; the second was to explore the hypothalamus in detail for rewarding effects.

The picture that emerged from these mapping studies was of rewarding sites distributed from forebrain to midbrain. In the rat, SS was obtained in the olfactory bulbs (Phillips & Mogenson 1969), in the anterior forebrain areas (Routtenberg 1971, 1978, Routtenberg & Sloan 1972, Routtenberg & Santos-Anderson 1976, Mora 1978, Phillips & Fibiger 1978, Robertson & Mogenson 1978); in the amygdala (Wurtz & Olds 1963, Valenstein & Valenstein 1964, Hodos 1965); in the hippocampus (Ursin et al 1966); in the caudate (J. Olds 1960, Routtenberg 1971); and in the entorhinal, retrosplenial, and cingulate cortices (Stein & Ray 1959, Brady & Conrad 1960). In the ventral diencephalon, the reward sites tended to cluster in the lateral posterior hypothalamus (Olds & Olds 1963, Valenstein & Campbell 1966), though reward sites giving evidence of mixed effects were also found in the medial hypothalamus. In the brainstem, Olds & Olds (1963) reported reward sites in the ventral region, but it remained for Routtenberg and his colleagues (Routtenberg & Malsbury 1969, Huang & Routtenberg 1971) to demonstrate unequivocally that strong rewarding effects were to be found in the substantia nigra. In subsequent studies, it was also shown that rewarding effects were to be obtained from more dorsal regions (Olds & Peretz 1960), but these sites showed mixed effects and were sparsely distributed among sites that led to escape behavior.

In general, the same anatomical distribution of reward sites was shown in other species. In the cat, the caudate nucleus supported SS behavior (Justesen et al 1963), as did the MFB (Roberts 1958). In the monkey, SS sites were obtained in the amygdala, the caudate, and the putamen (Brady 1960, Brady & Conrad 1960), in the thalamus (Lilly 1960), in the basal tegmentum (Porter et al 1959), in the reticular formation (Brady 1960), and of course in the MFB (Brodie et al 1960). It was further reported that the MFB supported SS in the dog (Stark & Boyd 1963), in the dolphin (Lilly 1962), and in humans (Bishop et al 1963).

It was clear from these mapping studies that SS in the forebrain was very different from SS in the posterior lateral hypothalamus and the ventral tegmentum. The distribution of sites did not match known functional systems, such as the rhinencephalic system with its emphasis on the olfactory pathway, the limbic system (Papez 1937, Pribram & Kruger 1954, Nauta 1960), or the brainstem reticular activating system (Glickman 1960, Glickman & Schiff 1967). Each of these accommodated some reward sites but none accommodated all.

Moreover, a series of lesion studies served to underscore the diffuse nature of the anatomical pathway that subserved SS. Destruction of tissue in various limbic structures had little effect on SS in the MFB, yet if these structures send or receive axons to the MFB, it would seem that the elimination of these axons would eliminate, or at least strongly reduce, the rewarding effects. Destruction of axons in the MFB itself seemed to have little influence on SS behavior obtained in the same pathway. Some evidence was obtained, however, which showed that the site of the lesion and the time of testing for its effects on SS were crucial factors in judging whether or not there were lesion effects. Morgane (1961) and Boyd & Gardner (1967) showed that small lesions could produce large decrements in SS but that these decrements were not permanent and eventually the animals again responded for the brain stimulus. Valenstein (1966) interpreted the results of lesion studies as indicating that no particular pathway described with classical anatomical methods subserves SS, since no particular structure where the phenomenon had been demonstrated seemed essential to the maintenance of the behavior elsewhere. Olds & Olds (1969) reported, however, that extensive lesions caudal to the SS site in the MFB abolished SS for periods up to 8 weeks after destruction of tissue. This finding suggested that input caudal to the SS site in the MFB was responsible for the rewarding effects of stimulation in the MFB at the hypothalamic level.

The general consensus of the early mapping and lesion studies, looking toward classical anatomical systems as the substrate for reinforcement mechanisms, was that no such system was in fact the substrate, though the various systems contributed perhaps to the general effect. The focus remained on the MFB but the nature of the axons in this fiber tract responsible for the reinforcing effect remained elusive.

Studies of Neuronal Activity Related to Self-Stimulation

To understand self-stimulation behavior it seemed insufficient to analyze the phenomenon in behavioral terms, to explain it as the product of interaction among known functional systems mediating arousal, emotions, and homeostatic mechanisms, or to compile extensive maps of the distribution of rewarding sites. Rather, it seemed necessary, in addition to identifying the neurons that were directly and indirectly implicated in the behavior, to describe the neural action taking place at the relevant synapses during the behavior. Thus neurophysiological studies occupy a crucial place in the strategy to achieve understanding of the central organization that mediates motivational-reinforcing effects. In this review of the literature on SS, space does not permit discussion of the numerous studies that have been carried out and the achievements that have resulted from them. Therefore we have selected for review the work of three investigators as being illustrative of the goals of this line of research, of the strategies followed, and of the problems that beset interpretation of the data.

OLDS   This work took three directions. The first and simplest consisted in the recording of unit activity in the lateral hypothalamus in the rat prior to, during, and after feeding behavior (Hamburg 1971). When the rat was hungry, and before the animal found and ate the food pellets, the single neurons whose activity was recorded fired at relatively high spontaneous rates. This pattern was little changed during the consumption. However, after consumption—or rather in the intervals between consumption—the neurons stopped firing. The correlation between periods of unit suppression and intervals between food consumption was very strong. The high rate of firing before and during consumption did not seem to be the result of the high level of behavioral activity, nor was it obviously related during eating to some motor act of consumption. Instead, the firing pattern seemed to correlate with the motivation to eat, with the actual consummatory act, and then even more dramatically with the period of rest thereafter. This type of correlation between the output of a neuron in the lateral hypothalamus and a behavior pattern that alternated between food consumption and pauses seemed to provide strong evidence for the presence in the lateral hypothalamus of neurons related to "natural reward." Not all neurons in this region showed such a correlation, but a sufficient number of those sampled did support Olds' notion that hypothalamic neurons played a crucial role in the mediation of rewarding brain stimulation (J. Olds 1977).

The second approach looked for evoked action potentials produced by the rewarding stimulation (Ito & Olds 1971; Ito 1972, 1976). In this situation, single neural unit activity in a given region was first identified in the unanesthetized rat. The animal was also trained to self-stimulate at a posterior hypothalamic site. The idea was to determine whether the pattern of spontaneous output from the neuron was altered by each pulse of the electrical brain stimulus. As a rule, two types of changes are possible. The output can disappear for a period immediately following the first electrical pulse (in a time framework of milliseconds), then return before the next electrical pulse, and once again disappear and so on with each electrical pulse until the end of the train. Or the neuron can give an output that is time-locked to the application of each pulse in a train. In the first situation, the neural response to the rewarding brain stimulation is said to be inhibitory, and may have a rebound excitatory effect that precedes the application of the next pulse in the train. In the second situation, the neural response is said to be excitatory, and may be followed by a rebound inhibitory period before the application of the next pulse. The observation of such neural responses during SS behavior gave evidence of stimulus-locked neural activity possibly related to the rewarding effect of the stimulus. Interestingly, not many neurons in the various structures sampled—hippocampus, cortex, thalamus, brainstem—showed this kind of responsivity to SS; if many had, the correlation would be suspect on the grounds that the circuit mediating the rewarding effects included all structures sampled. Even when samplings of evoked action potentials were made in the hypothalamus itself, the number of cells showing the effect was rather small. Thus it was unlikely that the effect of the brain stimulus was spreading from the site of stimulation to activate neurons lying proximal to the site. Rather, the effect of the stimulus was local and its effect on neurons nearby indicated a specific relation to these neurons. This relation was consistent with the notion that the site of SS and the few neurons thus activated were part of a circuit that mediated reinforcing effects.

The third approach studied the capacity of neurons to alter their output as a result of learning (Disterhoft & Olds 1972, Olds et al 1972). It was reasoned that ideally it would be necessary to identify neurons suspected of being a part of a reinforcing system by their neural responses to natural reinforcers. A less compelling type of evidence, though more easily obtained, would be if neurons that did not initially show a response to a sensory stimulus, for example a tone, would respond to the tone when it came to signify that a natural reinforcer would follow. Neurons showing this type of plasticity would be candidates for inclusion in a system of elements mediating the reinforcing aspects.

Results were obtained with each approach and indicated some relation between the neurons sampled and reward, but considerably more evidence was needed in each case to spell out the nature of the relation and to rule out alternative interpretations of the effects observed. For instance, with the first approach the neurons fired before the act of eating and during eating, but the behavior of the animal during these two periods was highly complex and included a number of different motor acts. There was little hope of relating the pattern of firing to any of these acts. The neuron stopped firing after the animal ate, but was this related to a rewarding aspect or to some sensory or motor aspect of the situation? With the second approach the problems of interpretation stemmed from the fact that the electrical stimulus, though rewarding at the posterior hypothalamic site, did not distinguish between the rewarding elements it excited and the nonrewarding elements that happened to traverse the stimulated site. How could one know that the evoked action potentials or the suppressed neural output were not produced by stimulation of the elements *en passage* at the site of stimulation? With the third approach the problems that surfaced were related to the fact that too many neurons in too many structures showed altered responsivity owing to pairing of a sensory stimulus with a natural reinforcer. Here again the circuit mediating reinforcement would include too many elements, and some additional principle or more compelling evidence was necessary to link the observed neural activity with the rewarding properties of brain stimulation.

The task of identifying the neurons mediating the rewarding effects and the neural activity responsible for the effects therefore proved to be an extremely complex task. This was due to the fact that stimulation could never be specific to a functionally homogeneous set of elements and that neurons in "integrative" structures are spontaneously active, giving evidence of much plasticity but little indication of the sources of the plasticity.

ROLLS   Rolls has the same aim as Olds, namely to determine which neurons are activated during SS behavior or rewarding stimulation (Rolls 1975, 1976; Hall et al 1977). However, an integral part of his approach includes a second consideration; that is, what is the response to natural reinforcers of neurons activated during rewarding stimulation? He and his collaborators reported that SS evoked unit activity was recorded in the amygdala, in the mesencephalic reticular formation, in the prefrontal cortex, and in the hypothalamus. The experiments were carried out in rats, squirrel monkeys, and rhesus monkeys. In the hypothalamus the evidence for classifying the neural activity as reward-related was derived from three sources: 1. The neurons activated during rewarding stimulation of the lateral hypothalamus were shown also to be activated from other regions known to support SS behavior. Thus, hypothalamic neurons were activated not only by hypothalamic rewarding stimulation but also by rewarding stimulation in the orbitofrontal cortex in the nucleus accumbens and in the dorsomedial nucleus of the thalamus. 2. The neurons thus activated in the hypothalamus were also activated specifically by gustatory properties of food, while other neurons similarly linked to SS were activated by water. In other words, the activation by natural reward is specific with some neurons having a better response to food and others to water. Appropriate controls were carried out to show not only that the responses of these neurons to natural reinforcers were specific to one type of reinforcer per neuron, but that activation did not result from any motor act of the animal related to the consumption of the natural reward. However, there were neurons activated by the reward-ing stimulus in other regions, the globus pallidus, for example, in which the response to the natural rewards was not specific. And even in the hypo-thalamus not all neurons activated by the brain reward showed this type of response specificity to natural rewards. 3. The neural activity of these rewarding stimulation-related neurons showed changes that appeared to be related to the motivational state of the animal. For example, the neural activity evoked in these neurons by the presentation of a syringe that injected glucose decreased as a function of the number of times the animal received the glucose. Also, subsequent tests demonstrated that the recorded site itself supported SS, and that the rate of SS varied as a function of food deprivation. Here, then, was a concerted effort to demonstrate the connec-tion among various structures that support SS behavior. This was based on showing that they send input to neurons whose output is strongly influenced by rewarding stimulation and by specific natural rewards, and that the sites where the neurons are located are themselves SS sites.

In spite of the amount of evidence thus obtained and the strong indication that these neurons have something to do with reward from SS and conven-tional reinforcers, the evidence is less than compelling because of the com-plexity of test situations and because of the lack of information concerning all the sources of input to these neurons.

SEGAL   In this case the focus was not on hypothalamic neurons and their relation to natural rewards but on hippocampal neurons and the properties of the evoked unit activity in the CA1 and CA3 regions of this structure (Segal & Bloom 1976a,b). The aim was to find out whether any specific relation can be deduced from the properties of the evoked responses in the hippocampus.

The experiments were carried out in rats, and the SS site was in the region of the locus coeruleus, an area of interest for reasons to be discussed in the section on the neurochemical substrate of SS behavior. It is significant that selection was made of an SS site giving rise to the projection where unit activity was recorded. The purpose was to explore the nature of the relation-ship between the brain stimulus that was rewarding in the region of cell bodies and the evoked unit activity that was produced in the region of terminals from these cells. The neurons were morphologically identified as pyramidal cells, and the response consisted of long-term inhibition—a mini-mum of 300 msec—of the spontaneous activity. It was observed that the more rewarding the site the longer the duration of the inhibition in the hippocampus. On the other hand, the next behavioral response following the stimulus was offset by 200 msec; that is, before the inhibitory response had decayed. Accordingly, as was pointed out in a critical review of these findings (Hall et al 1977), under these conditions the inhibitory response was unlikely to have functioned as the cue for the next lever-pressing response that resulted in the brain stimulus being applied in the region of the locus coeruleus. Was it possible, then, that the neural response in the hippocampus mediated the rewarding properties of the stimulus and that the time-course of the rewarding properties ranged from 300 msec up? But here again the criteria that suggested themselves were in the nature of conventional reinforcers. At present there is no clear evidence that conventional rewards evoke an inhibitory response in the hippocampus of the type evoked by rewarding stimulation, whereas sensory stimuli, unrelated to reinforcement, do evoke such responses. Hence, even when the focus of interest shifted from the hypothalamus and frontal regions to the locus coeruleus and hippocampal pyramidal neurons, the results did not differ from those obtained in the hypothalamus. The shortcomings of these data also characterize the data obtained in the hippocampus.

Views on Self-Stimulation and Existing Functional Neural Systems

It is not possible within the limits of this review to discuss the many views advanced to explain SS in the context of existing functional mechanisms. We confine ourselves, therefore, to three examples, selected because of their influence on subsequent research. Some of the other views, such as those of Milner (1976, 1977) and Grastyan et al (1965), reflect an incorporation of SS within much broader conceptual frameworks.

OLDS   Olds conceived of two different systems in the brain that spanned its length and followed discrete, though closely interdigitated, pathways (J. Olds 1961, 1962, 1969; Olds & Olds 1962, 1963, 1964, 1965; Hall et al 1977). These systems were thought to mediate positive and negative effects, with SS leading to positive reinforcement following excitation of neural systems localized in the lateral hypothalamus (LH). In contrast, excitation of a periventricular system—the medial hypothalamic system (MH)—was found to be aversive and subjects would work to reduce its excitation. Some input to the MH is inhibitory and the MH itself is inhibitory to the LH. Hence activation of the inhibitory input to the MH could lead indirectly to reinforcement through disinhibition of the LH. The relations between MH and LH were considered to be unidirectional; the level of excitability in the MH could influence the activity of the LH, but the activity of the LH had little influence on the MH except by a rebound effect.

The specific process responsible for reinforcement in the LH was the excitation of interneurons that integrate activity between sensory input to the LH and motor output. The evidence provided by SS was interpreted to indicate that reinforcement could be achieved by activation of this system of neural elements—the LH interneurons and their output. It became obvious that during SS the animal sought not to reduce excitability but to increase it. It was therefore difficult to reason that the electrical stimulation achieved reinforcement by a reduction of excitability, especially in the context of views in which increased excitability reflected biological deficits (Hull 1943). For Olds, the SS phenomenon was taken to be clear evidence of a functional organization of the brain along hedonistic lines; interneurons mediated the hedonistic properties of stimulation. Olds further conceived that SS excited not only the interneurons but also cell groups specialized to mediate such functions as feeding. Thus, cell groups related to feeding (Hoebel & Teitelbaum 1962, Margules & Olds 1962), drinking (Mogenson & Stevenson 1966), or sexual behavior (Herberg 1963b, Caggiula & Hoebel 1966) could be excited at the same time as the interneurons, depending on the location of the probe.

ROUTTENBERG   Routtenberg (1968) conceived of three systems as the mediators of motivated behavior. The activation of the first system, Arousal I, whose anatomical origins were in the reticular midbrain, produced neocortical arousal and functioned as the organizer of behavioral responses. Activity in the second system, Arousal II, with its anatomical origins in the ventral tegmentum and projections to the hypothalamus, hippocampus, and septum, produced reward and incentive via an inhibitory action on system I. System I can influence System II (reward-incentive), but indirectly through the activation of a third, negative incentive system whose origins lie in the midbrain. Hypothalamic stimulation thus induced drive and the organization of responses via cortical activity, and reward together with incentive via influence on ventral tegmental activity.

VALENSTEIN   Valenstein (1969, 1970) disputed the notion that a brain stimulus activated specific hypothalamic homeostatic centers and showed that stimulation-elicited behavior at some such SS sites was not immutable. He conceived of the hypothalamus as consisting not of discrete aggregates within subdivisions, but of one general aggregate of cells whose motivational element resided in excitation. This in turn provided modulation, through descending pathways, of brainstem mechanisms of fixed action patterns. Reinforcement during SS was produced through feedback activity to the hypothalamus from the brainstem cell groupings responsible for the fixed action behavioral patterns and perhaps also from other cell groups responsible for learned patterns of behavior. His conception of a facilitation of motor output through feedback activity to the input for these motor systems provided a mechanism for reinforcement. That is, SS was reinforcing because of its capacity to activate motor outputs and the feedback excitation to the source responsible for their activation.

EVALUATION   The trouble with all of these views is that they fail to spell out the ways in which such systems might work except in the most general and speculative terms. However, for Olds' approach with the LH, the evidence indicates that there are cell aggregates that subserve homeostatic mechanisms, and there is also evidence for the existence of neurons embedded in the MFB whose morphological characteristics lend themselves more easily to classification as interneurons in the manner spelled out by Horridge (1968). In addition, there is evidence that the LH is a region that receives extensive polymodal sensory input. Reinforcement is conceived as activity in the output lines from the interneurons to the motor systems, and motivation is seen as activity in the output lines from the homeostatic cell groups to the motor systems subserving behaviors related to particular homeostatic mechanisms. It is significant that two categories of neurons are posited as being activated by SS and that each subserves motivation or reinforcement. How this is done is not spelled out in any detail.

Similarly, in Valenstein's view the cells of the hypothalamus have a function in reinforcement for two reasons: because they constitute an input to motor systems (as in Olds' view) and because the activity in the output systems feeds back to the hypothalamus itself to maintain activity. Thus, there is a closed loop whose activity constitutes reinforcement. Here again, few details are given to spell out the workings of the system, which is concerned with a hierarchy of controlling functions targeted mainly on brainstem and spinal motor mechanisms. Activity in the controlling function that encompasses the hypothalamus is reinforcing.

Routtenberg brings in several anatomical functional systems: ventral tegmentum, septum, hippocampus (mesolimbic system), reticular formation, and cortex system (mesocortical system), with the hypothalamus having a linkage role between midbrain and forebrain systems.

The shortcomings of these theories are that they do not give detailed descriptions of the systems that mediate the behavioral effects.

NEUROCHEMICAL CONSTITUENTS OF THE REWARD PATHWAY

Catecholamine Pathways

ANATOMICAL STUDIES   Interest in the catecholamine (CA) systems derived from several observations, one of which was that the course of some CA pathways was matched to a large degree by the distribution of reward sites. Another was that drugs which altered the central metabolism of CA-containing neurons profoundly altered SS in a predictable way. Since the alternative hypotheses of the anatomical substrate of SS discussed above —hypothalamic homeostatic centers, limbic system, and arousal midbrain pathways—failed to account for all SS sites uncovered or for the variety of effects accompanying SS at different brain levels, attention shifted to exploring the possibility that the CA systems constituted the substrate for the stimulation-induced rewarding effect.

The development that made possible this shift in the direction of research was the demonstration that some chemical constituents of central neurons —norepinephrine (NE), dopamine (DA), and 5-hydroxytryptamine (5-HT) (or serotonin as it is sometimes called)—could be visualized with a new technique. When brain tissue is exposed to formaldehyde vapors a reaction occurs which renders these substances fluorescent and thus visible under a microscope (Falck 1962, Falck et al 1962). Since these substances are contained in the perikarya of neurons, and in higher concentrations in the terminals of these neurons, it is possible to obtain a picture of their sites of origin and of their terminals (Dahlstrom & Fuxe 1964, Fuxe 1965). These chemicals are also contained in axons, but in smaller amounts, and hence special modifications of the methods were required which enhanced the content in the axons and thus made them visible. In recent years a variant of the fluorescent method with its greater sensitivity has been successfully used to demonstrate new subdivisions of these pathways and to visualize axons (Lindvall & Björklund 1974). The outcome of these methodological advances was the discovery of new anatomical pathways.

NOREPINEPHRINE SYSTEMS   The distribution of neurons containing NE, along with their terminals, permits the delineation of three systems (Dahlstrom & Fuxe 1964; Ungerstedt 1971; Moore 1973, 1975; Lindvall & Björklund 1974; Moore & Bloom 1979). Each has branches which, though innervating different structures, sometimes overlap in their regions of termination and join together during some part of their projection course. Of the three systems identified, two have been of great interest to investigators of SS. The first originates in the hindbrain in the region termed locus coeruleus (LC) because of the deep blue staining of cell bodies when Nissl stains are used. These cell bodies almost all contain NE and are tightly grouped within a very small area. Some of the cells have axons descending to the spinal cord and others have axons that ascend to the cerebellum and the cortex. The ascending axons, particularly those in the dorsal bundle which ascend to the cortex, have been the most intriguing because of their profuse branching. Single cells make connections with an extraordinarily large number of other cells through wide arborization of terminals innervating the cortex, septum, hippocampus, thalamus, hypothalamus, basal forebrain, and olfactory nuclei. Thus a small group of NE cells in the LC has the capacity to modulate the excitability level of a substantial part of the brain. A result deemed especially significant for SS was the fact that the ascending branch of this system is an important component of the MFB (Hall et al 1977). In the MFB it joins, in its rostral course, other systems containing CA. Before that junction, in caudal parts, it is distinct from the other systems.

In addition to the fluorescent method for visualizing these systems, other methods have become available to trace the course of anatomical systems. One such method, based on the transport of labeled amino acids, permits the tracing of pathways from the site of injection to remote sites, since the amino acids are taken up by the cell bodies and are transported to their terminals. With this technique, the relative density of innervation of different anatomical regions lying in the forebrain has been investigated. The results indicate that the amygdala, septum, and basal forebrain receive substantial input from the LC, as do the cortex and the hippocampus (Jones & Moore 1974, 1977; Jones et al 1977). The significance of this system for SS is that it contributes a substantial number of axons to the MFB, and hence to the forebrain, to innervate many structures known to support SS. But these structures also receive innervation from other CA-containing systems, and in the MFB the axons originating in the LC join other CA-containing systems. It is necessary, therefore, to determine whether the reinforcing properties of SS can be obtained in the parts where this system is distinct as well as in the region where the cell bodies lie.

The second NE system does not originate in such a tight group of cell bodies but instead in small aggregates of cell bodies in the hindbrain in a region ventral to the LC. The fibers of these ventral hindbrain cells come together in the central tegmental bundle, then merge again with other CA-containing fibers to enter the MFB. In the MFB this group of axons gives off collaterals to all of the hypothalamus, to the septum, and to other parts of the basal forebrain.

A third NE-containing system originates in the brainstem in the region of the raphe nucleus, ascends along a trajectory that traverses the central gray, and continues along the midline innervating medial thalamic nuclei (Lindvall & Björklund 1974). Another branch of this system innervates the dorsomedial nucleus of the hypothalamus and then ascends to the medial and midline thalamus. Not as much interest has been shown in this third system because many of the regions innervated, such as the medial thalamus, do not support SS. In the few sites where rewarding effects are obtained, they have mixed rewarding and punishing properties and the response rate is low. In the ventral tip of the central gray, rewarding effects have been obtained, more often stimulation produces escape behavior.

However, not all regions receiving input from the NE LC system support SS. The cingulate, entorhinal, and pyriform cortices are known to support SS (Routtenberg 1971, 1976), but other regions receiving innervation do not. In the hippocampus, some sites seem to be rewarding, but the meaning of reward has almost to be redefined because the behavior is so different in this region from what it is in the diencephalic MFB (Ursin et al 1966). More often than not, escape behavior is produced. In the amygdala, no effect is produced or escape behavior is obtained from most sites except for small circumscribed subdivisions (Wurtz & Olds 1963). Thus, it is not so much the structures innervated by the LC system that suggested this pathway as a possible substrate for SS as its substantial contribution to the MFB. For the ventral system, the evidence was better, since it contributed not only a substantial component to the MFB but also innervated the hypothalamus and the basal forebrain, regions known to support high to moderate SS. However, so far as the LC was concerned, of greatest significance to the issue of whether the NE-containing neurons constituted the neural substrate of reward was the fact that this nucleus contains NE cells almost exclusively. Therefore, it could be a crucial test site for assessing the role of the NE system.

DOPAMINE SYSTEMS   There are many DA systems in the mammalian brain (Dahlstrom & Fuxe 1964; Ungerstedt 1971; Jacobowitz & Palkovitz 1974; Palkovits & Jacobowitz 1974; Hall et al 1977) but here again only two have been of interest to investigators of SS because they contribute substantially to the composition of the MFB and innervate structures that support SS. One such DA system originates in the substantia nigra (SN), a region of the rostral brainstem. The other originates in the region medial to the SN and dorsal to the interpeduncular nucleus. In the SN, the DA-containing cell bodies are localized mainly in the zona compacta, and the axons of these cells course rostrally with other axons of the SN as the nigrostriatal bundle, traversing the dorsal lateral hypothalamus on their way to the striatum. A branch of this system also projects to the cingulate cortex (Berger et al 1974, 1976; Fuxe et al 1974; Lindvall & Björklund 1974). The course of this branch through the hypothalamus on the way to the striatum is via the MFB. It is noteworthy that the medial subdivisions of the striatum have been shown to support SS, as does the cingulate cortex (Routtenberg 1971, 1976; Phillips et al 1976). However, in both structures the response rates are mild, though they do not show the mixed effects of hippocampal or amygdaloid SS. It is the contribution to the MFB which raised the possibility that this system was a constituent of the anatomical substrate of reward.

The other DA-containing system of interest to SS originates in the tegmentum and innervates parts of the telencephalon. This system had great interest for researchers on affectivity because of its innervation of forebrain limbic structures. The axons originate in the tegmentum and join the nigrostriatal bundle in the lateral MFB to end in the amygdala, septum, nucleus accumbens, olfactory tubercule, and frontal cortex.

EVALUATION   The question, then, was whether these CA systems are the components of the MFB that are crucial to SS. One strategy was to test for SS at sites in the trajectory where the pathways are differentiated from one another and in regions where the cell bodies lie. For NE this is in the hindbrain at the level of the medulla and pons; for DA it is in the ventral midbrain. Several published reviews describe the contributions of various studies to the question of hindbrain SS (Crow 1972a,b 1976; German & Bowden 1974; Routtenberg 1976; Hall et al 1977; Fibiger 1978; Wise 1978). Only the salient features are presented here.

In 1969 Routtenberg and Malsbury reported that some probes in the superior cerebellar peduncle supported SS. Other workers (Crow 1972a,b; Ritter & Stein 1973; Breese & Cooper 1975, 1976; Ellman et al 1975; M. Olds 1976; Segal & Bloom 1976) reported that SS was obtained from the LC and nearby regions. Reviews of the anatomical results by Crow (1973) and by German & Bowden (1974) led these investigators to conclude that the NE neurons of this nucleus support SS, though the question of the basis for rewarding effects at nearby sites remained. Were the rewarding properties of these sites due to activation of the NE-containing cells in the LC? Crow (1972a,b) believed that SS in the peduncle was attributable to activation of the axons of the NE-containing cells of the LC. Alternatively, Amaral & Routtenberg (1975), Clavier & Routtenberg (1975) and Clavier et al (1976) have presented data pointing to the inadequacy of this view. With anatomical methods, they showed that lesions of the cerebellar peduncle led to a buildup of fluorescence in the LC (Clavier & Routtenberg 1974), based on the observation that interruption of axons results in a buildup of transmitter at the end proximal to the cell bodies. In this case, the finding seemed to support the observation that NE-containing neurons of the LC send their projections through the peduncle, and thus that these axons are probably excited during SS of the cerebellar peduncle. On the other hand, when these investigators made lesions in the LC itself to investigate its effect on SS in the cerebellar peduncle, the effect was minimal (Clavier & Routtenberg 1975). Thus at the peduncle site the contribution of LC axons was not a critical factor in producing rewarding effects. The problem of explaining hindbrain SS sites outside the LC therefore remained.

Moreover, there is disagreement about whether the LC itself supports SS (see review in Wise 1978). In general, on purely anatomical grounds, the exact site of stimulation is difficult to assess when the structure tested for rewarding effects is as small as the LC, and, because studies of SS vary in the stimulus parameters used, results are difficult to compare. Amaral & Routtenberg (1975) and Routtenberg (1976) reported that with fine wire electrodes and very low intensities of current they were unable to obtain rewarding effects in the LC and in the ventral pathway nearby where the NE cell groups are more dispersed. The reasoning behind their use of fine wires, low intensities of stimulation, and minimal animal training is that under these conditions only sites of unequivocal rewarding properties will be found; in such cases it would be possible to argue that the site responsible for the effects is highly localized (Routtenberg 1976). Of the many sites sampled at this brain level, a few proved to be rewarding, and these were near the superior cerebellar peduncle (Amaral & Routtenberg 1975). In a study using higher current intensities, but still almost no training, Simon et al (1975) also reported an absence of reward sites in the LC. Wise (1978) has recently reviewed data with respect to rewarding effects in the LC and concludes that some of the probes reported to support SS in the early studies of LC SS (Ritter & Stein 1973, Crow 1972a) probably did activate this nucleus. Probes that produced rewarding effects outside but near the LC probably excited axons ascending to the telencephalon, that is, the dorsal bundle. The negative results of Amaral & Routtenberg (1975) are explained as being due to stimulation of the caudal part of the LC (Wise 1978). This part sends projections to the cerebellum, whereas it is the excitation of the rostral subdivision, the part of the LC that sends projections to the telencephalon, that is responsible for the rewarding effects. Wise further points out that although there may be a correlation between the anterior LC and the dorsal bundle, which would explain rewarding effects in regions proximal to the LC, the evidence is not of a nature to suggest a causal relationship. Such evidence would have to show that SS in the dorsal bundle is eliminated by lesions of the LC, and that SS in the LC is eliminated by lesions of the dorsal bundle. The data available, based on electrolytic lesions or on lesions made with a neurotoxin specific to the NE-containing neural elements, indicate transient effects only; within a few days SS was reinstated. Surprisingly, the SS obtained in the MFB with this type of preparation was enhanced. This finding, together with the results of the lesion studies, leaves unresolved the question of the NE-containing neurons in the LC as the substrate for SS.

We have recently obtained data that support a role for NE but do not exclusively restrict the role to the NE neurons of the LC (Umemoto & M. Olds, unpublished data 1980). We used rats treated neonatally with the neurotoxin 6-hydroxydopamine (6-OHDA) to make specific lesions of NE-containing neurons, and two advantages are expected from this procedure. First, tests made in adult animals were likely to have taken place at a time when the processes initiated by the neurotoxin would have ceased; and second, because the destruction of NE terminals takes place during development, a compensatory mechanism is brought into play that results in highly elevated levels of NE in the pons-medulla region. We injected the neurotoxin bilaterally into the lateral ventricles in one type of preparation to obtain adult animals in which forebrain CA levels were depleted but hindbrain NE was elevated; in the other preparation we injected the neurotoxin bilaterally in the region of the LC. We tested for SS in the LC and in the MFB in the same animals. Those which received the toxin in the lateral ventricles showed an effect opposite to that usually found: SS in the MFB was difficult to obtain, the rates were low in spite of extensive training, and LC SS was dramatically high and required almost no training. These effects would seem to be due to the elevated NE levels in this region, since no similar elevation of 5-HT was observed. Dopamine does not innervate the hindbrain, and no elevation of DA has been reported with this approach (Sachs & Jonsson 1975). On the other hand, similar effects were produced by injections in the LC itself; the same high rates were obtained as in the animals that received the bilateral injections. On these grounds it could be argued that the NE neurons at this level are not necessary for SS. However, some neurons may have survived and formed new proximal projections, and nearby NE systems—the scattered NE-containing neurons described by Moore (Moore & Kromer 1978, Moore & Bloom 1979)—would also have had their terminals damaged and new proliferations would have formed. It may be that elevation of hindbrain NE levels owing to sprouting and supersensitive receptors activated by the surviving neurons form the basis for the SS effects, even though the injection site was in the LC. Our data demonstrate a relationship between NE at this brain level and rewarding effects, but do not indicate whether the NE-containing neurons of the LC alone are responsible for the effects. The data could be interpreted to indicate proliferation of the remaining LC cells or of NE-containing neurons in the other hindbrain systems. In either case, elevation of NE produced by neonatal injection of the neurotoxin produced dramatic increases in SS—resulting in a pattern more reminiscent of MFB SS than of LC SS.

Two questions therefore emerged from the mapping studies of the NE-containing cells in the LC: 1. How can SS at sites outside the LC be explained, especially sites such as those in the superior cerebellar peduncle, when destruction of the tissue in the LC has only minor effects on these sites? 2. How can the absence of rewarding sites in the LC studies of Routtenberg and his colleagues be explained when the same methods produce rewarding effects in the cerebellar peduncle? There appears to be agreement, however, that the SS in the LC is dramatically different from that in the MFB. To obtain SS in the LC, extensive training seems usually to be required, and current intensities may need to be adjusted to take into account the fact that stimulation of cell bodies may require a higher intensity than stimulation of fibers. Also, it has been observed repeatedly that LC SS produces little motor activity or behavioral activation compared to SS of the posterior lateral hypothalamus, and there is no evidence of mixed effects. In our laboratory we have obtained SS in the LC, but the sites are sparse and highly localized. One might reasonably argue, therefore, that the LC supports SS but that the pattern of SS differs dramatically from that in the diencephalon. As we have seen, other sites near the LC also support SS. The reward sites at this level are not clustered as the NE-containing cells are, but even with small probes of the type used by Routtenberg and with current intensities no higher than those used in the hypothalamus for the same type of electrodes, we observed SS in this nucleus and nearby. In recent work we obtained additional evidence implicating the NE-containing neurons of the hindbrain in SS, data that will be described in the section on pharmacological studies.

Routtenberg (1973, 1975) reported that the ventral NE-containing cell groups, which are widely dispersed over an extended region below the LC, though more highly localized according to earlier studies (Dahlstrom & Fuxe 1964, Ungerstedt 1971), also do not support SS. If these cells are in fact sparsely distributed, low level stimulation may never excite enough neurons to support SS. Counter to this finding is the evidence reported by Ritter & Stein (1974) and by Belluzzi et al (1975) (see reviews in German & Bowden 1974, Crow 1976) that stimulation of the ventral bundle supports SS. In other words, the axons of the sparsely distributed NE-containing cells do yield rewarding effects.

With respect to the SS in the periventricular gray region and in the dorsal and median raphe nuclei (Margules 1969, Routtenberg & Malsbury 1969, Ritter & Stein 1973, Simon et al 1973, 1975), Stein (Hall et al 1977) has maintained that it is the NE cells that mediate SS in this medial midbrain region. Yet certain inconsistencies remain: 1. SS in the dorsal raphe has been interpreted differently by some, even to mean that the 5-HT or DA or perhaps some other system may mediate rewarding effects (Clavier 1976, Crow 1976); 2. lesions of the LC do not affect SS sites in the cerebellar peduncle; and 3. other pathways, such as the gustatory pathway near the LC, take a course which could indicate that sensory systems mediate SS (Norgren 1976). Hence, the issue cannot be resolved on purely anatomical grounds, for localization of effects through visualization of electrode tips does not disclose the neural elements responsible for the effects, and the neural elements are not homogeneous at each site of stimulation.

SS has also been obtained in the SN (Routtenberg & Malsbury 1969, Prado-Alcala et al 1975) and in an area above the interpeduncular nucleus (Simon et al 1973, 1975; see reviews in Crow 1972a, 1976; German & Bowden 1974; Fibiger 1978) in which lie DA-containing cell bodies that give rise to the mesolimbic DA pathway. In both regions SS rates are high, required training periods are short, and the pattern of responding associated with stimulation of the MFB is matched in other aspects. In our own work we have obtained SS in the region of the LC, the dorsal raphe, and the zona compacta of the SN. It is relatively easy to obtain SS in the raphe and the SN; by comparison, it is difficult to obtain rewarding effects in the region of the LC. In experiments in which the animal was able to select the duration of the train, the differences between the durations selected in the LC and in the two other regions was striking (M. Olds 1975). At some LC sites the animal would remain on the lever for as long as one minute, and there was evidence neither of a mixed effect of the kind associated with posterior hypothalamic SS nor of seizure activity. In the dorsal raphe, on the other hand, the self-determined SS durations were extremely short (often less than 100 msec) and highly regular. The rewarding effects seemed to give way to aversive effects shortly after the onset of stimulation. The pattern in the SN was similar to that in the MFB. Whether these differential patterns could be explained in terms of the stimulation of NE- and DA-containing neurons is not apparent with evidence based solely on the location of the electrode tip.

It is clear that much information has been gained from these mapping studies. The picture of a reinforcing pathway has been extended to the hindbrain and has been broadened to include regions extending from the cortex to the pons and medulla, with evidence of properties other than those associated with diencephalic or telencephalic SS. However, compelling evidence that these systems mediate the rewarding effects has not been achieved, at least insofar as the anatomical studies were concerned, regardless of the electrode type or stimulation intensities used.

Pharmacological Studies

We noted in the previous section the overlap of projections of the CA systems with the distribution of rewarding sites for SS. Although a detailed analysis of rewarding sites in regions of origin of these CA projections to the MFB ultimately raised more questions than were answered, the correlational anatomical evidence was taken by some to support the CA theory of reward mediation (Crow 1972b, 1976; German & Bowden 1974). Just as the contribution of neurons to the MFB suggested that these systems might constitute the anatomical substrate for reinforcement, the effects of drugs related to CA metabolism suggested that their effects on SS resulted from action on CA and added further weight to the hypothesis that these neural systems constituted the substrate for reward.

The initial pharmacological studies showed that neuroleptics (compounds that interfere with CA transmission) such as chlorpromazine and reserpine reduced or eliminated SS (Olds & Travis 1960, Stein 1962). Similarly, compounds that promote CA-mediated neural transmission, such as D-amphetamine, enhanced SS (Stein 1964). Also, it was reported that alpha-methyl-para-tyrosine (α-MPT), a drug that inhibits tyrosine hydroxylase (the rate-limiting enzyme in the synthesis of NE) depressed SS— whereas monoamine oxidase inhibitors (compounds that inhibit the intraneuronal breakdown of CA) enhanced SS (Poschel & Ninteman 1966, Poschel 1969). On such grounds, Stein (1968) advanced the CA theory of reward. His view has influenced much of the research done on SS during the last 15 years, and as more data have been accumulated, more complexities and difficulties have been encountered. The history of this line of research has moved from initial testing of the CA hypothesis to testing the validity of the NE and DA hypotheses. Many of the difficulties have still not been resolved, and neither behavioral nor biochemical methods are available that unequivocally permit a direct attack on the problem. Hence, current investigation in this field include those who favor NE mediation, those who favor DA mediation, and those who favor a critical role for both amines. Some have come to view the CA hypothesis of reward on the same level, in terms of restricted applicability, with earlier hypotheses that focused on homeostatic or arousal mechanisms or on limbic systems.

The principal criticism of studies showing depressant effects on SS by drugs that interfere with CA metabolism derives from the fact that SS may be suppressed for reasons other than a reduction in the rewarding properties of stimulation. That is, the drugs can interfere with motor acts necessary to obtain SS, or can negatively affect sensory input or attention level, or can produce a mild illness or discomfort that is expressed in reduced rates of responding or even in complete elimination of SS. A criticism of drugs that enhance SS is that they may do so by raising arousal level of energization of the organism without raising the rewarding properties of stimulation. An additional criticism is that drugs have many effects even when they are said to be specific. Moreover, just as the anatomical studies resulted in data of a correlational nature, so too the pharmacological data are often correlational. The consequences of these criticisms have been to underscore the complexities inherent in identifying the pharmacological substrate of SS (Hall et al 1977, Fibiger 1978, Wise 1978).

THE NOREPINEPHRINE THEORY   Stein is the principal proponent of the NE theory of reward (Stein 1968, 1978a; Hall et al 1977; Stein & Wise 1973). In large part his recent work on this matter is based on initial results obtained with neuroleptics (1962) and D-amphetamine (1964), drugs believed to modulate SS because they either interfere with CA transmission or, in the case of amphetamine, render CA transmission more efficient. These findings served to initiate studies by Stein and coworkers and by investigators in other laboratories designed to determine whether the NE theory of SS is correct.

In addition to showing by mapping studies that SS could be obtained in the region of origin of the NE pathways, the strategy followed by Stein and his colleagues concerned the use of compounds that inhibit synthesis of NE (Wise & Stein 1969, Ritter & Stein 1973). The aim was to show that these compounds suppress SS, and that the suppression of responding can be restored by intraventricular administration of NE. Suppression was accomplished with α-AMPT, a drug that inhibits the synthesis of NE and DA (Ritter & Stein 1973), and later with disulfiram and diethyl-dithiocarbamate (DDC), two drugs that selectively inhibit the synthesis of NE by suppressing the action of dopamine-β-hydroxylase, the enzyme that converts DA to NE (Wise & Stein 1969). It was shown that after treatment with these drugs the infusion of NE in the ventricles restored previously suppressed responding. These data were taken as evidence that NE and not DA constituted the critical system for SS.

A different interpretation was placed on these findings by Roll (1970) on the basis of results obtained with α-AMPT, disulfiram, and DDC. She reported that when animals treated with these drugs were aroused by the experimenter and placed on the response lever, they responded with a few bursts, an observation she interpreted as indicating that the animals were sedated, not that they were no longer motivated to respond for the brain stimulus. In other words, the action of these drugs on SS could be explained by sedation rather than by alteration of the rewarding properties of the stimulus. Stein's answer to this line of argument has been that animals sedated with barbiturates can be made to respond for prolonged intervals even when they show flaccidity and obvious signs of sedation, whereas animals treated with α-AMPT do not appear to be sedated and behave during SS sessions in a fashion quite different from the barbiturate-treated rats (Stein 1964). We have confirmed these observations in experiments in which rats responding for SS in the MFB were treated with sodium pentobarbital or with α-AMPT. In the barbiturate situation the animals were incapacitated enough to stop responding, but if placed near the lever, or if the task was made easy enough, they responded steadily. In the other situation the animals did not appear to be incapacitated and no amount of priming would lead to steady responding. Instead, the pattern of the few responses elicited resembled the pattern of extinction associated with SS, where a few responses are emitted before the animal realizes that brain reward is no longer available. However, in our tests with disulfiram, the animals appeared sick, and therefore it is reasonable to assume that the discomfort was the basis for the suppression of responding.

The most important evidence against the NE theory came from the testing of two drugs that specifically inhibit the synthesis of NE but have fewer side effects than disulfiram or DDC. These two drugs, FLA-63 and U-14,625 were without effects on SS, even though the levels of NE in the brain were substantially reduced (Lippa et al 1973, Fuxe et al 1974, Stein et al 1976; reviews in Crow 1976, Fibiger 1978, and Wise 1978).

However, in this case it is possible to use the results of Franklin & Herberg (1974, 1975) to explain the ineffectiveness of the two compounds that deplete NE levels and yet have no effect on SS. The approach of these investigators relied on evidence that utilization of NE under normal circumstances is from newly synthesized NE available from a functional pool. But when this source is unavailable, as happens when synthesis is inhibited then utilization resorts to the storage pool. The reasoning was that FLA-63, the inhibitor of NE synthesis, was without effect on SS, even though levels of NE in the brain were reduced, because NE from the storage pool was still available. If this source was eliminated through pretreatment of the animals with reserpine, a drug that interferes with the storage of monoamines and thus causes their intraneuronal breakdown, then treatment with the synthesis inhibitor would eliminate both sources of NE. Under these circumstances SS should be depressed, as was in fact observed. Subsequent infusion of NE restored SS and these data have been interpreted as supporting the NE theory of reward.

But the criticism raised by many investigators against pharmacological studies of SS that show a depressant effect can be raised here; namely, that there may have been a subtle effect on the state of the animal that interfered with SS. Restoration of SS after NE may be due to elimination of some general effects or to a nonspecific change in the state of the animal (arousal) rather than to a direct effect on rewarding properties of SS.

A second approach used to obtain evidence for the NE theory focuses on showing that NE is utilized during SS. Stein & Wise (1969), for example, injected labeled NE via a push-pull cannula. Measurement in samples obtained during SS showed more radioactivity when rats were self-stimulating than when they were receiving noncontingent stimulation. Holloway (1975), though confirming Stein's results, showed that serotonin was similarly released during SS. Hence, these data cannot be viewed as indicating a critical role only for NE. More important, however, is the criticism of Fibiger (1978), who points out that the data are at best correlational. The effect on NE metabolism simply indicates that NE fibers or neurons were activated near the site of stimulation; they do not indicate that the neurons were responsible for the rewarding effect. This same argument has been made against the findings of unit activity evoked during SS by the stimulation. At each site of such stimulation the neural elements activated are heterogeneous and the problem is to find the critical element. Similarly, for biochemical studies the site of stimulation, most often in the MFB or the ventral tegmental area, includes NE as well as other systems. Therefore, it is not surprising that NE metabolism is altered through activation of the site, and the data do not support the argument that activation of NE is the sole process that produces the rewarding effect.

A third line of research used to support the NE theory relies on depletion of CA levels produced by intraventricular or intracerebral injection of the neurotoxin 6-OHDA. Breese et al (1971) and Breese & Cooper (1975) showed that intracisternal injection of 6-OHDA had no effect on MFB SS. However, in tests for SS at four sites in the same animal—MFB, SN, dorsal raphe, and LC regions—intraventricular 6-OHDA did depress SS in the MFB but there was some recovery, though never to the baseline level (M. Olds 1975). Repeated injections decreased the SS rate each time in MFB and SN placements, until responding was completely eliminated at these two sites. Responding was not eliminated in the dorsal raphe or in the region of the LC tested concurrently. It is well known that the biochemical effects of 6-OHDA in the adult animal are mainly a depletion in forebrain, and the effects become gradually smaller along a caudal trajectory. The effects on SS matched the pattern of biochemical effects. Here too, SS in diencephalon and rostral ventral mesencephalon was completely suppressed, whereas SS in the dorsal raphe and LC regions was not, indicating that the animal was not incapacitated. Quite the opposite was the case; the animals responded at higher rates in these caudal regions after 6-OHDA than before, suggesting that the accumulation of CA in the noninjured axons may have been responsible for facilitatory effects. Thus our own data clearly indicate that 6-OHDA can effectively suppress SS rates in the MFB and not be effective on more moderate rates in the LC, matching the pattern of depletion produced by the neurotoxin. Furthermore, NE injected in these rats restored high rates of SS in the MFB most effectively, and this compound was considerably more effective than DA, a finding consistent with earlier reports of SS restoration by NE (Stein & Wise 1969). However, 5-HT was also effective, though not as much so as NE. These data, because of the anatomical distribution of their effects and the effect of replenishment, are consistent with an NE theory of reward. On the other hand, there is the evidence of Clavier & Routtenberg (1975) that lesions of the dorsal bundle had little effect on SS in the LC, and vice versa.

Stein and coworkers have argued that the ventral NE system also supports SS, even though Amaral & Routtenberg (1975) failed to obtain SS in this system's region of origin in the hindbrain. Either knife cuts or 6-OHDA were used to lesion the ventral system for determining its effects on SS in the SN, a region where SS is supposed to be supported by activation of DA neurons (Belluzzi et al 1975). Under these conditions, the rate of SS in the SN was depressed, a finding interpreted as indicative that NE supports SS even at purportedly DA sites. However, this study was criticized on the grounds that knife cuts sectioned inputs to the SN from the ventral bundle and from other systems as well. Similarly, the dosage of 6-OHDA was too high to have made lesions in the ventral bundle only (Fibiger 1978). Therefore, reduction in SS at the SN was more likely to have been produced by destruction of tissue from several systems coursing through the SN than from the NE system, and these data are not seen as clearly supporting the NE theory of reward.

We have recently used adult animals to test the effects of 6-OHDA administered neonatally in either the lateral ventricles or in the LC. Given neonatally, this toxin markedly depletes CA in forebrain regions but increases NE levels in the hindbrain at the level of the LC (Taylor et al 1972, Sachs & Jonsson 1975, Jonsson & Sachs 1976, Peterson & Laverty 1976, Oke et al 1978, Bourgoin et al 1979). In treated animals we found MFB SS difficult to obtain, and when found the rates were low to moderate in a region generally acknowledged to yield the highest rates. In contrast, rates obtained in the LC were very high after minimal training. Although these data clearly support the NE theory of reward, the animals that received LC injections still yielded above normal SS whereas MFB SS was down. Animals treated with intraventricular 6-OHDA yielded few reward sites in the SN, whereas normal animals frequently yield reward sites in this region with high SS rates. Here again the evidence suggests that NE does play a role in LC and MFB SS, though a role for DA is not ruled out.

The failure of 6-OHDA LC lesions to eliminate SS in the same nucleus must still be explained. One could argue that the few remaining cells become supersensitive, or that the 6-OHDA injection produced sprouting of NE terminals from partly injured or noninjured NE neurons from other systems innervating the area of the LC lesions, or that the NE systems at this level are not the critical elements supporting SS. Clearly, more data are needed to resolve the question of why 6-OHDA given neonatally in the LC not only failed to eliminate SS but produced the same effect, though less dramatic, as the intraventricular 6-OHDA injection.

It is clear, however, that support for the NE theory of SS is based 1. on anatomical findings of SS in the LC and dorsal bundle and perhaps to some extent in the ventral central gray, 2. on studies of NE synthesis inhibitors, and 3. on biochemical studies of NE metabolism during SS. The anatomical data are correlational, however, and localization of probes is limited with available techniques, even if it were possible to assess at each site which of the heterogeneous elements in the region are crucial. The data relating to NE inhibitors are open to the criticism that some subtle behavioral malaise may have been induced which would be sufficient to reduce operant behavior of any kind because such behavior is highly drug-sensitive. Even when differential effects for varying rewards are shown (for SS, food or water), there is always the possibility that the difference in baseline rates explains the difference in drug effects rather than reflecting some special, specific action on a reward pathway. Furthermore, NE synthesis inhibitors that do not have side effects, yet produce a dramatic decrease in brain NE, have no effect on SS. Finally, there is the finding that lesioning the dorsal bundle does not affect LC SS and lesioning the LC does not affect SS in the dorsal bundle, the system at this level that is not interdigitated with the DA system. These findings taken together underscore the problems besetting the NE theory of reward.

Our own data with intraventricular 6-OHDA in adult animals demonstrated that MFB SS was also eliminated by a treatment that reduced forebrain NE and DA. SN SS was also eliminated, but not SS in the dorsal raphe and LC. This pattern of effects, which counters the argument of deficits in motor performance, matches the biochemical pattern of depletion produced in adult animals. Of course, deficits could be due to depletion of either NE or DA or both, except that intraventricular injection of NE was effective in reinstating SS whereas injection of DA was not. Our more recent data in the neonate further support the NE view, but here again is the need to explain data in animals that received LC injections. The literature thus indicates problems for the NE theory, especially in its restrictive version ascribing an exclusive role to NE. In any event, the data described above need to be accommodated within any other theory.

THE DOPAMINE THEORY   Evidence for the NE theory of reward was based mainly on the depressant action of NE synthesis inhibitors, on obtaining SS in the LC, on the facilitatory action of NE on MFB SS, and on the restoration by NE, but not by DA, of responding depressed by a variety of agents. Evidence for the DA theory derives principally (*a*) from anatomical data which show that SS can be obtained in the SN (a region that contains only DA neurons), in a region above the interpeduncular nucleus (the origin of the DA mesolimbic system); (*b*) from pharmacological data obtained with neuroleptics; and (*c*) from studies using 6-OHDA which show that permanent selective depletion of DA eliminates SS.

As we have seen, the first studies with neuroleptics used chlorpromazine and reserpine (Olds & Travis 1960, Stein 1962). However, the action of these drugs is not specific to DA, and in the case of reserpine the action is not via receptor blockage. These drugs did, however, depress MFB SS and implicate the CA systems. In more recent work, the drugs tested have been haloperidol, pimozide, and spiroperidol, three compounds shown to have specific DA-receptor blockage properties. In one of the first such studies, Wauquier & Niemegeers (1972, Wauquier 1976) showed that pimozide depresses SS in the MFB, and numerous subsequent studies have confirmed this finding (Liebman & Butcher 1973, Fibiger et al 1976, Fouriezos & Wise 1976). Similar effects have been obtained with other DA receptor blockers (Wauquier & Niemegeers 1972, Rolls et al 1974, Phillips et al 1975, Fibiger et al 1976, Wauquier 1976).

As with all drug-induced depressant effects on SS, the question can always be raised whether the action was on motor systems, on some other system, or on the reward system. This question is especially important in relation to the DA systems, since these are implicated in motor functions whereas NE systems are not. For this reason, several investigators have compared the effects of pimozide and spiroperidol on responses rewarded by brain stimulation, food, or water. Rolls and others (1974) tested spiroperidol under these conditions and the drug depressed lever responding for all three rewards. Also, responding for brain reward was shown to be depressed not only at a DA site but at nondopaminergic sites. Lever pressing for food and water was depressed, but consumption in the home cage was not, indicating that spiroperidol did not interfere with the motivation for food and water. This work has been regarded as supporting the view that the basis for the effect on SS was interference with motor performance and not the rewarding properties of stimulation. Phillips (1975) confirmed the finding that pimozide and haloperidol were effective at nondopaminergic reward sites as well as at DA sites, specifically the nucleus accumbens and dorsal noradrenergic bundle. Others have reported similar findings (Liebman & Butcher 1973, 1974).

In follow-up studies, Mora and coworkers (1975, 1976) investigated whether the effect of DA receptor blockers was due to the fact that the required response was too complex. It has been shown that these drugs induce sedation at high doses, and at lower doses tremors of the kind seen in Parkinsonian patients treated with DA agonists. It seemed possible, therefore, that the lever-pressing response made too many demands on the animal treated with this type of compound. Thus these investigators used lever-pressing or licking to obtain SS, and both responses were found to be depressed by spiroperidol. Regardless of the required task, the DA receptor blocker depressed SS. Evidence interpreted as supporting the DA theory of reward was also obtained by Rolls and colleagues (1974) in a study which showed that a low dose of spiroperidol depressed SS, whereas a much higher dose did not depress licking for water in thirsty animals. This finding indicates that the drug has an effect on SS at a dose that does not impair motor behavior for another reward, consistent with an interpretation of the drug's effect on rewarding properties of SS but not on motor systems.

The criticism leveled at these studies (Fibiger 1978) is that drug effects might vary owing to differences in baseline rates of licking for water or SS or bar-pressing for SS. It has been shown repeatedly that the action of many psychoactive drugs on operant responding is influenced by the baseline rate of the operant response (Kelleher & Morse 1968). Therefore it is conceivable that in these studies, where baseline rates were not controlled for similarity with different rewards, the differential drug effects were produced by differences in baseline rates. When rates were controlled, haloperidol was shown to have depressant effects equally on SS and responding for food reward, but not on the consumption of food (Fibiger et al 1976).

In general, the strategy has been to show that specific DA-receptor blockers have effects on SS at doses lower than those producing motor impairment or than those needed to influence operant behavior for other rewards. However, as pointed out by Fibiger (1978), the rate of responding for natural and brain rewards is different, and when the difference is controlled for, the effects of drugs are the same. Yet there are data to suggest that these compounds may have an effect on locomotor activity (Wise 1978). A different line of evidence to support the notion that DA may be responsible for rewarding effects of SS comes from comparisons of the pattern of responding after injection and during extinction (Fouriezos & Wise 1976; Wise 1976, 1978). In well-trained rats extinction is frequently rapid, with only a few responses given immediately after the current is turned off. The investigators reasoned that a drug that produces motor impairment would at low doses produce a gradual response decrease. Whereas if there were no motor impairment, but an absence of reward, the pattern of responding under the drug would be similar to the pattern during extinction. These authors obtained positive evidence for their view, and even showed that blocking access to the lever for a short period during pimozide treatment and then replacing the lever produced a burst of responding. This indicates that motor impairment was not the basis for lack of responding under pimozide. The criticisms based on the possibility of motor impairment that have been leveled at the NE theory also have been leveled at the DA theory. In addition, the question has been raised as to why DA-receptor blockers should be as effective at nondopaminergic SS sites as at DA sites.

A third approach used to argue for the DA theory derives from 6-OHDA. Breese and his coworkers (Cooper et al 1974; Breese & Cooper 1975, 1976; Hall et al 1977) showed that intracisternal or intraventricular injection of this compound was without effect on SS. On the other hand, when they pretreated animals with a compound that resulted in selective depletion of DA but not of NE, depressant effects on responding were produced. But here the same problem recurs: were depressant effects due to effects on some system other than the reward system?

One avenue used to answer this criticism has been to obtain differential effects on ipsilateral and contralateral sides of a unilateral lesion made with 6-OHDA injected locally in a specific aminergic pathway or in the ventricles (Phillips et al 1976, Clavier & Fibiger 1977). The reasoning is that on the ipsilateral side there should be depression of SS, owing to reduction or elimination of the rewarding properties. But on the contralateral side the depression should not occur, or at least should be less than on the other side. Thus, animals with SS electrodes implanted in both sides, and treated with 6-OHDA after pretreatment with the compound producing DA depletion only, were tested for these differential effects and positive results were obtained. Again, conflicting evidence is available (Ornstein & Huston 1975) which shows similar effects of treatment on ipsilateral and contralateral sides, once more raising the specter of motor impairment as the basis for depressant effects on SS.

Still another approach that has recently been interpreted as offering potential support for the DA theory concerns the use of amphetamine. In early studies of SS, Stein & Ray (1959) obtained evidence that D-amphetamine has a selective facilitatory effect on SS. They used a situation with two levers: the animal could press one lever to obtain SS, with its intensity starting high and decreasing stepwise, and could press the second lever to reset current at the initial intensity. When animals were treated with amphetamine, the stimulus intensity at which they pressed the reset lever decreased, indicating a lowering of threshold for obtaining rewarding effects of SS. Stein (1964) also showed that amphetamine facilitated SS tested at threshold levels of intensity but did not increase motor activity during extinction, again indicating that facilitatory effects were due not to behavioral stimulation but to an increase in rewarding properties of SS.

Recent work with amphetamine has shown that the two isomers D and L have unequal effects at different SS sites (Phillips & Fibiger 1973). The compounds were equally effective in the SN, a DA region, but the D isomer was more effective in the MFB, a region thought to be mainly noradrenergic. This approach was based on biochemical evidence that in a preparation of brain synaptosomes from the striatum the two drugs were equally effective in inhibiting uptake of DA by DA neurons. In a preparation of brain tissue excluding the striatum and thought to be principally NE in nature, D was more potent than L in inhibiting uptake of NE in NE neurons (Coyle & Snyder 1968). Thus it seemed that biochemical data could be used to gain insight into the respective roles of DA and NE at different SS sites. On these grounds, Phillips and Fibiger concluded that SS in the SN was based on activation of DA neurons and in the MFB on NE neurons.

However, the biochemical data have not been confirmed, and thus what remains is the observation that the two amphetamine isomers have different effects on SS at different sites (Fibiger 1978). Wise (1978) pointed out in a recent review of the literature that the actions of amphetamine are numerous and highly complex, and at present the action underlying its effect on SS is not understood.

To summarize, there is evidence for the DA theory, as there is for the NE theory, but objections can be raised against each. Additional research with methods permitting finer-grained analysis is required to resolve the issues. There is also the question of whether the theories would explain the SS obtained at each level of the brain and whether the theories have more merit than earlier ones in explaining particular sites of SS. In spite of negative arguments, evidence clearly indicates a role for these systems in SS, but we don't know where this influence comes in, and that is the root of the problem.

The Endorphins and Self-Stimulation Behavior

Recently a newly discovered system of neurons has been proposed as a critical factor in SS (Belluzzi & Stein 1977, Stein 1978b). The mammalian brain, it appears, contains opiate receptors and naturally occurring peptides with opiate-like properties that are the ligands for these receptors (Kuhar et al 1973; Hughes et al 1975; Pasternak et al 1975; Atweh & Kuhar 1977a,b,c,; Simantov et al 1977; Sar et al 1978). They are densely distributed in the hypothalamus, nucleus accumbens, ventral central gray, and LC, all regions where SS is obtained.

It has also been shown that morphine and other narcotic analgesics facilitate SS (Lorens & Mitchell 1973, Marcus & Kornetsky 1974, Lorens 1976, Esposito & Kornetsky 1977, Esposito et al 1979, Jackler et al 1979, Kornetsky 1979). This action is thought to be mediated by opiate receptors;

therefore effects on SS are interpreted to indicate the presence of opiate receptors on neurons activated during SS.

Another line of evidence shows that morphine and enkephalins have reinforcing properties. Self-administration of these compounds injected in the lateral ventricle of rats was reported by Stein and coworkers (Stein 1978a,b). Our own work (M. Olds 1979, Olds & Williams 1980) shows that morphine and DALA (a synthetic enkephalin with a longer action than the natural substance) support self-administration when injected at SS sites in the hypothalamus of rats.

Finally, naloxone, a specific antagonist of morphine, was used to suggest that enkephalins, and perhaps endorphins, play a role in SS on the evidence that naloxone depressed SS at various sites (Stein 1978a,b).

Much of the work with the enkephalins is still preliminary. Additional research is needed to spell out the role of these substances at various brain levels where SS has been obtained and to delineate their relationship to the catecholamine systems in modulating the rewarding properties of SS.

CONCLUSIONS

The evidence supports the view that in mammals the brain is organized along lines which include a functional system that mediates motivational-reinforcing properties of behavior. This evidence is comprised principally of data that show behaviors, similar to those seen in situations in which animals pursue natural rewards, can be obtained by direct stimulation of the brain. Even the idiosyncratic properties associated with these nonphysiologically induced behavioral patterns have been shown not to be absolute, but rather are related to testing situations or have been explained in terms of rapid onset and offset of the brain stimulus. The evidence also demonstrates that the sites are not homogeneously distributed in the brain, but instead are highly localized, though present at each brain level. These two sets of data have been the basis for presuming that the brain contains a reward mechanism, and that it can be activated electrically. For the first time it was possible to inquire into the nature of this system by identifying anatomical structures that make it up, transmitters that process information in it, and neural activity responsible for the behavioral effects.

The search for anatomical structures has met with both success and failure—success in the sense that the brain in several species has been explored extensively, and the results of these studies have given us rather detailed maps of where effects can be obtained. Rather than a system that includes one center or structure, a complex system is indicated that includes many structures, not all of which are equally important to the working of the whole system. The maps taken as a whole convey the notion that sites supporting SS are part of a system but not *what* system. Here the search has met with failure. The various systems presumed to constitute the substrate account for some of the sites but not all. Two difficulties attend mapping studies. As has been pointed out by Fibiger, the data are correlational. They tell us that a particular site is in a particular structure but we can't identify the elements excited by the brain stimulus. These elements are always heterogeneous, not only in the sense of including fibers and neurons but of fibers and neurons as part of a number of different systems. The problem, therefore, comes down to being able to dissect the anatomical constituents, excited either directly at the electrode tip or transsynaptically, that are responsible for rewarding effects.

To some extent, even with the present limitations of this approach, considerable progress has been made, for we have a much better conception than before of the extent and distribution of reward sites. But the new findings have raised new problems and require refinement of methods to achieve better resolution.

The investigations based on drugs have similarly met with success and failure. Here research has progressed from the use of drugs with effects on multiple systems to drugs that have better specificity. Considerable evidence implicating particular transmitter substances has been obtained, and here again the drugs are not ideal. The problem is somewhat analogous to that inherent in the anatomical approach—namely, even "specific" drugs have many effects, and these have to be analyzed before the modulation of self-stimulation behavior can be ascribed to a particular effect. The problem is compounded by interdigitation of the pathways containing various transmitters and by the likelihood that various transmitters implicated in SS work as a system, in balance with one another rather than in isolation. Just as there may not be any "centers" for mediating feeding, there may not be one transmitter for mediating the rewarding effects.

The same is true for neural activity; some types of neural action are more likely than others to relate to SS. This appears to be the case for inhibition, but is inhibition produced by excitation of reward fibers or of fibers *en passage?* Is it produced at all SS sites, or by particular sites in given structures?

The evidence shows enormous progress, if not in understanding the elements of the circuitry and how they relate to each other, at least in terms of having a working knowledge of that circuitry, of having an appreciation of the complexity of the task, and of the limitation of any particular approach. Clearly, much work is needed to fill the gaps and improve our technical armamentarium. What has been achieved is a conception of a functional system with its many working aspects, and this was within a framework that owes much to advances in molecular biology.

566   OLDS & FOBES

Literature Cited

Amaral, D. G., Routtenberg, A. 1975. Locus coeruleus and intracranial self-stimulation: a cautionary note. *Behav. Biol.* 13:331–38

Anand, B. K. 1961. Nervous regulation of food intake. *Physiol. Rev.* 41:677–708

Anand, B. K., Brobeck, J. R. 1951. Hypothalamic control of food intake in rats and cats. *Yale J. Biol. Med.* 24:123–40

Andersson, B., Kitchell, R. L., Persson, N. 1958. A study of central regulation of rumination and reticulo-ruminal motility. *Acta Physiol. Scand.* 46:319–38

Andersson, B., Larsson, S., Persson, N. 1960. Some characteristics of the hypothalamic 'drinking centre' in the goat as shown by the use of permanent electrodes. *Acta Physiol. Scand.* 50:140–52

Andersson, B., Wyrwicka, W. 1957. The elicitation of a drinking motor conditioned reaction by electrical stimulation of the hypothalamic 'drinking area' in the goat. *Acta Physiol. Scand.* 41:194–98

Annau, Z., Heffner, R., Koob, G. F. 1974. Electrical self-stimulation of single and multiple loci: long term observations. *Physiol. Behav.* 13:281–90

Atweh, S. F., Kuhar, M. J. 1977a. Autoradiographic localization of opiate receptors in rat brain. I. Spinal cord and lower medulla. *Brain Res.* 124:53–67

Atweh, S. F., Kuhar, M. J. 1977b. Autoradiographic localization of opiate receptors in rat brain. II. The brain stem. *Brain Res.* 129:1–12

Atweh, S. F., Kuhar, M. J. 1977c. Autoradiographic localization of opiate receptors in rat brain. III. The telencephalon. *Brain Res.* 134:393–405

Ball, G. G., Adams, D. W. 1965. Intracranial stimulation as an avoidance or escape response. *Psychon. Sci.* 3:39–40

Belluzzi, J. D., Ritter, S., Wise, C. D., Stein, L. 1975. Substantia nigra self-stimulation: dependence on noradrenergic reward pathways. *Behav. Biol.* 13:103–11

Belluzzi, J. D., Stein, L. 1977. Enkephalin may mediate euphoria and drive-reduction reward. *Nature* 266:556–58

Beninger, R. J., Bellisle, F., Milner, P. M. 1977. Schedule control of behavior reinforced by electrical stimulation of the brain. *Science* 196:547–49

Beninger, R. J., Laferriere, A., Milner, P. M. 1978. An investigation of responding on schedules of electrical brain-stimulation reinforcement. *Can. J. Psychol.* 32:106–15

Berger, B., Tassin, J. P., Blanc, G., Moyne M. A., Thierry, A. M. 1974. Histochemical confirmation for dopaminergic innervation of the rat cerebral cortex after destruction of the noradrenergic ascending pathways. *Brain Res.* 81:332–37

Berger, B., Thierry, A. M., Tassin, J. P., Moyne, M. A. 1976. Dopaminergic innervation of the rat prefrontal cortex: a fluorescence histochemical study. *Brain Res.* 106:133–45

Bishop, M. P., Elder, S. T., Heath, R. G. 1963. Intracranial self-stimulation in man. *Science* 140:394–96

Bourgoin, S., Adrien, J., Laguzzi, R. F., Dolphin, A., Bockaert, J., Hery, F., Hamon, M. 1979. Effects of intraventricular injection of 6-hydroxydopamine in the developing kitten. II. On the central monoamine innervation. *Brain Res.* 160:461–78

Bower, G. H., Miller, H. E. 1958. Rewarding and punishing effects from stimulating the same place in the rat's brain. *J. Comp. Physiol. Psychol.* 51:669–74

Boyd, E. S., Gardner, L. C. 1967. Effect of some brain lesions on intracranial self-stimulation in the rat. *Am. J. Physiol.* 213:1044–52

Brady, J. V. 1960. Temporal and emotional effects related to intracranial electrical self-stimulation. In *Electrical Studies on the Unanesthetized Brain,* ed. E. Ramsey, D. O'Doherty, pp. 52–77. New York: Hoeber

Brady, J. V. 1961. Motivational-emotional factors and intracranial self-stimulation. In *Electrical Stimulation of the Brain,* ed. D. Sheer, pp. 413–64. Austin: Univ. Texas Press

Brady, J. V., Conrad, D. 1960. Some effects of limbic system self-stimulation upon conditioned emotional behavior. *J. Comp. Physiol. Psychol.* 53:128–37

Breese, G. R., Cooper, B. R. 1975. Relationship of dopamine neural systems to the maintenance of self-stimulation. In *Neurotransmitter Balances Regulating Behavior,* ed. E. Domino, J. Davis, pp. 37–56. Ann Arbor: NPP Books

Breese, G. R., Cooper, B. R. 1976. Effects of catecholamine-depleting drugs and d-amphetamine on self-stimulation obtained from lateral hypothalamus and region of the locus coeruleus. See Wauquier & Rolls 1976, pp. 190–95

Breese, G. R., Howard, J. L., Leahy, J. P. 1971. Effect of 6-hydroxydopamine on electrical self-stimulation of the brain. *Br. J. Pharmacol.* 43:255–57

Brobeck, J. R. 1955. Neural regulation of food intake. *Ann. NY Acad. Sci.* 63:44–55

Brobeck, J. R. 1957. Neural control of hunger, appetite and satiety. *Yale J. Biol. Med.* 29:565–74

Brodie, D. A., Moreno, O. M., Malis, J. L., Boren, J. J. 1960. Rewarding properties of intracranial stimulation. *Science* 131:929–30

Bruner, A. 1966. Facilitation of classical conditioning in rabbits by reinforcing brain stimulation. *Psychon. Sci.* 6:211–12

Caggiula, A. R. 1970. Analysis of the copulation-reward properties of posterior hypothalamic stimulation in male rats. *J. Comp. Physiol. Psychol.* 70:399–412

Caggiula, A. R., Hoebel, B. G. 1966. "Copulation-reward site" in the posterior hypothalamus. *Science* 153:1284–85

Carey, R. J., Goodall, E. B., Procopio, G. F. 1974. Differential effects of d-amphetamine on fixed ratio 30 performance maintained by food versus brain stimulation reinforcement. *Pharmacol. Biochem. Behav.* 2:193–98

Clavier, R. M. 1976. Brain stem self-stimulation: catecholamine or non-catecholamine mediation. See Wauquier & Rolls 1976, pp. 239–50

Clavier, R. M., Fibiger, H. C. 1977. On the role of ascending catecholaminergic projections in intracranial self-stimulation of the substantia nigra. *Brain Res.* 131:271–86

Clavier, R. M., Fibiger, H. C., Phillips, A. G. 1976. Evidence that self-stimulation of the region of the locus coeruleus in rats does not depend upon noradrenergic projections to telencephalon. *Brain Res.* 113:71–81

Clavier, R. M., Routtenberg, A. 1974. Ascending monoamine-containing fiber pathways related to intracranial self-stimulation: histochemical fluorescence study. *Brain Res.* 72:25–40

Clavier, R. M., Routtenberg, A. 1975. Brain-stem self-stimulation attenuated by lesions of medial forebrain bundle but not by lesions of locus coeruleus or the caudal ventral norepinephrine bundle. *Brain Res.* 101:251–71

Cooper, B. R., Cott, J. M., Breese, G. R. 1974. Effects of catecholamine-depleting drugs and amphetamine on self-stimulation of brain following various 6-hydroxydopamine treatments. *Psychopharmacologia* 37:235–48

Coyle, J. T., Snyder, S. H. 1968. Catecholamine uptake by synaptosomes in homogenates of rat brain: stereospecificity in different areas. *J. Pharmacol. Exp. Ther.* 170:221–31

Crow, T. J. 1972a. A map of the rat mesencephalon for electrical self-stimulation. *Brain Res.* 36:265–73

Crow, T. J. 1972b. Catecholamine-containing neurones and electrical self-stimulation. A review of some data. *Psychol. Med.* 2:414–21

Crow, T. J. 1973. Catecholamine-containing neurones and electrical self-stimulation: 2. A theoretical interpretation and some psychiatric implications. *Psychol. Med.* 3:66–73

Crow, T. J. 1976. Specific monoamine systems as reward pathways. See Wauquier & Rolls 1976, pp. 211–38

Culbertson, J. L., Kling, J. W., Berkley, M. A. 1966. Extinction responding following ICS and food reinforcement. *Psychon. Sci.* 5:127–28

Dahlstrom, A., Fuxe, K. 1964. Evidence for the existence of monoamines containing neurons in the central nervous system. *Acta Physiol. Scand.* 62 (Suppl. 232): 1–80

Deutsch, J. A. 1960. *The Structural Basis of Behavior.* Chicago: Univ. Chicago Press

Deutsch, J. A. 1963. Learning and electrical self-stimulation of the brain. *J. Theor. Biol.* 4:193–214

Deutsch, J. A. 1964. Behavioral measurement of the neural refractory period and its application to intracranial self-stimulation. *J. Comp. Physiol. Psychol.* 58:1–9

Deutsch, J. A., Deutsch, D. 1966. *Physiological Psychology.* Homewood, Ill:Dorsey

Deutsch, J. A., Deutsch, D. 1973. *Physiological Psychology.* Homewood, Ill:Dorsey. 2d ed.

Deutsch, J. A., DiCara, L. 1967. Hunger and extinction in intracranial self-stimulation. *J. Comp. Physiol. Psychol.* 63: 344–47

Deutsch, J. A., Howarth, C. I. 1963. Some tests of a theory of intracranial self-stimulation. *Psychol. Rev.* 70:444–60

Disterhoft, J. F., Olds, J. 1972. Differential development of unit changes in thalamus and cortex of rat. *J. Neurophysiol.* 35:665–79

Ellman, S. J., Ackermann, R. F., Bodnar, R. J., Jackler, F., Steiner, S. S. 1975. Comparison of behaviors elicited by electrical brain stimulation in dorsal brainstem and hypothalamus of rats. *J. Comp. Physiol. Psychol.* 88:816–28

Esposito, R., Kornetsky, C. 1977. Morphine lowering of self-stimulation thresholds: lack of tolerance with long-term administration. *Science* 195:189–91

Esposito, R., McLean, S., Kornetsky, C. 1979. Effects of morphine on intracranial self-stimulation to various brain stem loci. *Brain Res.* 168:425–29

Falck, B. 1962. Observations on the possibilities for the cellular localization of monoamines with a fluorescent method. *Acta Physiol. Scand.* 197 (Suppl. 56): 1–25

Falck, B., Hillarp, N. A., Thieme, G., Torp, A. 1962. Fluorescence of catecholamines and related compounds condensed with formaldehyde. *J. Histochem. Cytochem.* 10:348–54

Federation Proceedings. 1979. 38:2445–76

Fibiger, H. C. 1978. Drugs and reinforcement mechanisms: a critical review of the catecholamine theory. *Ann. Rev. Pharmacol. Toxicol.* 18:37–56

Fibiger, H. C., Carter, D. A., Phillips, A. G. 1976. Decreased intracranial self-stimulation after neuroleptics or 6-hydroxydopamine: evidence for mediation by motor deficits rather than by reduced reward. *Psychopharmacology* 47:21–27

Fouriezos, G., Wise, R. A. 1976. Pimozide-induced extinction of intracranial self-stimulation: response patterns rule out motor or performance deficits. *Brain Res.* 103:377–80

Franklin, K. B. J., Herberg, L. J. 1974. Self-stimulation and catecholamines: drug-induced mobilization of the 'reserve'-pool reestablishes responding in catecholamine-depleted rats. *Brain Res.* 67: 429–37

Franklin, K. B. J., Herberg, L. J. 1975. Self-stimulation and noradrenaline: evidence that inhibition of synthesis abolishes responding only if the 'reserve' pool is dispersed first. *Brain Res.* 97:127–32

Fuxe, K. 1965. Evidence for the existence of monoamine neurons in the central nervous system. IV. Distribution of monoamine nerve terminals in the central nervous system. *Acta Physiol. Scand.* 64 (Suppl. 247):39–73

Fuxe, K., Hökfelt, T., Johansson, O., Jonsson, G., Lidbrink, P., Ljungdahl, A. 1974. The origin of the dopamine nerve terminals in limbic and frontal cortex. Evidence for meso-cortico dopamine neurons. *Brain Res.* 82:349–55

Gallistel, C. R. 1964. Electrical self-stimulation and its theoretical implications. *Psychol. Bull.* 61: 23–34

Gallistel, C. R. 1966. Motivating effects in self-stimulation. *J. Comp. Physiol. Psychol.* 62:95–101

Gallistel, C. R. 1967. Intracranial stimulation and natural reward: differential effects of trial spacing. *Psychon. Sci.* 9:167–68

Gallistel, C. R. 1973. Self-stimulation: the neurophysiology of reward and motivation. In *The Physiological Basis of Memory,* ed. J. Deutsch, pp. 176-267. New York: Academic

Gandelman, R., Panksepp, J., Trowill, J. 1968. The effect of lever retraction on resistance to extinction of a response rewarded with electrical stimulation of the brain. *Psychon. Sci.* 10:5–6

German, D. C., Bowden, D. M. 1974. Catecholamine systems as the neural substrate for intracranial self-stimulation: a hypothesis. *Brain Res.* 73:381–419

Glickman, S. E. 1960. Reinforcing properties of arousal. *J. Comp. Physiol. Psychol.* 53:68–71

Glickman, S. E., Schiff, B. B. 1967. A biological theory of reinforcement. *Psychol. Rev.* 74:81–109

Grastyan, E., Karmos, G., Vereczkey, G. K. L., Martin, J., Kellenyi, L. 1965. Hypothalamic motivational processes as reflected by their hippocampal electrical correlates. *Science* 149:91–94

Grossman, S. P. 1979. The biology of motivation. *Ann. Rev. Psychol.* 30:209–42

Hall, R. D., Bloom, F. E., Olds, J. 1977. Neuronal and neurochemical substrates of reinforcement. *Neurosci. Res. Prog. Bull.* 15:141–314

Hamburg, M. D. 1971. Hypothalamic unit activity and eating behavior. *Am. J. Physiol.* 220:980–85

Heath, R. G., Mickle, W. A. 1960. Evaluation of seven years experience with depth electrode studies in human patients. See Brady 1960, pp. 214–47

Herberg, L. J. 1963a. Determinants of extinction in electrical self-stimulation. *J. Comp. Physiol. Psychol.* 56:686–90

Herberg, L. J. 1963b. Seminal ejaculation following positively reinforcing electrical stimulation of the rat hypothalamus. *J. Comp. Physiol. Psychol.* 56:679–85

Hess, W. R. 1957. *Functional Organization of the Diencephalon.* New York: Grune & Stratton

Hodos, W. H. 1965. Motivational properties of long durations of rewarding brain stimulation. *J. Comp. Physiol. Psychol.* 59:219–24

Hoebel, B. G. 1969. Feeding and self-stimulation. *Ann. NY Acad. Sci.* 157:758–78

Hoebel, B. G. 1976. Brain-stimulation reward and aversion in relation to behavior. See Wauquier & Rolls 1976, pp. 335–72

Hoebel, B. G. 1979. Hypothalamic self-stimulation and stimulation escape in relation to feeding and mating. *Fed. Proc.* 38:2454–62

Hoebel, B. G., Teitelbaum, P. 1962. Hypothalamic control of feeding and self-stimulation. *Science* 135:375–77

Holloway, J. A. 1975. Norepinephrine and serotonin: specificity of release with rewarding electrical stimulation of the brain. *Psychopharmacologia* 42:127–34

Horridge, G. A. 1968. *Interneurons.* London: Freeman

Howarth, C. I., Deutsch, J. A. 1962. Drive decay: the cause of fast "extinction" of habits learned for brain stimulation. *Science* 137:35–36

Huang, Y. H., Routtenberg, A. 1971. Lateral hypothalamic self-stimulation pathways in *Rattus norvegicus. Physiol. Behav.* 7:419–32

Hughes, J., Smith, T. W., Kosterlitz, H. W., Fothergill, L. A., Morgan, B. A., Morris, H. R. 1975. Identification of two related pentapeptides from the brain with potent opiate agonist activity. *Nature* 258:577–79

Hull, C. L. 1943. *Principles of Behavior.* New York:Appleton-Century-Crofts

Ito, M. 1972. Excitability of medial forebrain bundle neurons during self-stimulation behavior. *J. Neurophysiol.* 35:652–64

Ito, M. 1976. Mapping unit responses to rewarding stimulation. See Wauquier & Rolls 1976, pp. 89–96

Ito, M., Olds, J. 1971. Unit activity during self-stimulation behavior. *J. Neurophysiol.* 34:263–73

Jackler, F., Steiner, S. S., Bodnar, R. J., Ackermann, R. F., Nelson, W. T., Ellman, S. J. 1979. Morphine and intracranial self-stimulation in the hypothalamus and dorsal brainstem: differential effects of dose, time and site. *Int. J. Neurosci.* 9:21–35

Jacobowitz, D. M., Palkovits, M. 1974. Topographic atlas of catecholamine and acetylcholinesterase-containing neurons in the rat brain. I. Forebrain (telencephalon, diencephalon). *J. Comp. Neurol.* 157:13–28

Jones, B. E., Halaris, A. E., McIlhany, M., Robert, Y. 1977. Ascending projections of the locus coeruleus in the rat. I. Axonal transport in central noradrenaline neurons. *Brain Res.* 127:1–21

Jones, B. E., Moore, R. Y. 1974. Catecholamine-containing neurons of the nucleus locus coeruleus in the cat. *J. Comp. Neurol.* 157:43–52

Jones, B. E., Moore, R. Y. 1977. Ascending projections of the locus coeruleus in the rat. II. Autoradiographic study. *Brain Res.* 127:23–53

Jonsson, G., Sachs, C. 1976. Regional changes in 3H-noradrenaline uptake,

catecholamines and catecholamine synthetic and catabolic enzymes in rat brain following neonatal 6-hydroxydopamine treatment. *Med. Biol.* 54:286–97

Justesen, D. R., Sharp, J. C., Porter, P. B. 1963. Self-stimulation of the caudate nucleus by instrumentally naive cats. *J. Comp. Physiol. Psychol.* 56:371–74

Keesey, R. E., Goldstein, M. D. 1968. Use of progressive fixed-ratio procedures in the assessment of intracranial reinforcement. *J. Exp. Anal. Behav.* 11:293–301

Kelleher, R. T., Morse, W. H. 1968. Determinants of the specificity of behavioral effects of drugs. *Ergeb. Physiol.* 60:1–56

Knook, H. L. 1965. *The Fibre Connections of the Forebrain.* Assen: Van Gorcum

Kornetsky, C. 1979. Functional, anatomical and pharmacological aspects of central motivational systems: a tribute to James Olds. *Fed. Proc.* 38:2445–73

Kuhar, M. J., Pert, C. B., Snyder, S. H. 1973. Regional distribution of opiate receptor binding in monkey and human brain. *Nature* 245:447–50

Larsson, S. 1954. On the hypothalamic organization of the nervous mechanism regulating food intake. *Acta Physiol. Scand.* 32 (Suppl. 115):1–63

Liebman, J. M., Butcher, L. L. 1973. Effects on self-stimulation behavior of drugs influencing dopaminergic neurotransmission mechanisms. *Naunyn-Schmiedebergs Arch. Pharmakol.* 277:305–18

Liebman, J. M., Butcher, L. L. 1974. Comparative involvement of dopamine and noradrenaline in rate-free self-stimulation in substantia nigra, lateral hypothalamus, and mesencephalic central gray. *Naunyn-Schmiedebergs Arch. Pharmakol.* 284:167–94

Lilly, J. C. 1960. Learning motivated by subcortical stimulation. See Brady 1960, pp. 78–105

Lilly, J. C. 1962. Operant conditioning of the bottlenose dolphin with electrical stimulation of the brain. *J. Comp. Physiol. Psychol.* 55:73–79

Lindvall, O., Björklund, A. 1974. The organization of the ascending catecholamine neuron systems in the rat brain as revealed by the glyoxylic acid fluorescence method. *Acta Physiol. Scand.* (Suppl. 412):1–48

Lippa, A. S., Antelman, S. M., Fisher, A. E., Canfield, D. R. 1973. Neurochemical mediation of reward: a significant role for dopamine. *Pharmacol. Biochem. Behav.* 1:23–38

Lorens, S. A. 1976. Comparison of the effects of morphine on hypothalamic and medial frontal cortex self-stimulation in the rat. *Psychopharmacology* 48:217–24

Lorens, S. A., Mitchell, C. L. 1973. Influence of morphine on lateral hypothalamic self-stimulation in the rat. *Psychopharmacologia* 32:271–77

Marcus, R., Kornetsky, C. 1974. Negative and positive intracranial reinforcement thresholds: effects of morphine. *Psychopharmacologia* 38:1–13

Margules, D. L. 1969. Noradrenergic rather than serotonergic basis of reward in the dorsal tegmentum. *J. Comp. Physiol. Psychol.* 67:32–35

Margules, D. L., Olds, J. 1962. Identical 'feeding' and 'rewarding' systems in the lateral hypothalamus of rats. *Science* 135:374–75

Miller, N. E. 1958. Central stimulation and other new approaches to motivation and reward. *Am. Psychol.* 13:100–8

Millhouse, O. E. 1969. A Golgi study of the descending medial forebrain bundle. *Brain Res.* 15:341–63

Milner, P. M. 1976. Models of motivation and reinforcement. See Wauquier & Rolls 1976, pp. 543–56

Milner, P. M. 1977. Theories of reinforcement, drive and motivation. In *Handbook of Psychopharmacology*, ed. L. Iversen, S. Iversen, S. Snyder, 7:181-200. New York: Plenum

Mogenson, G. J. 1969. Water deprivation and excessive water intake during self-stimulation. *Physiol. Behav.* 4:393–97

Mogenson, G. J. 1971. Stability and modification of consummatory behavior elicited by electrical stimulation of the hypothalamus. *Physiol. Behav.* 6:255–60

Mogenson, G. J. 1973. Hypothalamic limbic mechanisms in the control of water intake. In *The Neuropsychology of Thirst*, ed. A. Epstein, H. Kissileff, E. Stellar, pp. 119–42. New York: Winston

Mogenson, G. J., Stevenson, J. A. F. 1966. Drinking and self-stimulation with electrical stimulation of the lateral hypothalamus. *Physiol. Behav.* 1:251–54

Moore, R. Y. 1973. Telencephalic distribution of terminals of brainstem norepinephrine neurons. In *Frontiers in Catecholamine Research*, ed. E. Usdin, S. Snyder, pp. 767–69. New York:Pergamon

Moore, R. Y. 1975. Monoamine neurons innervating the hippocampal formation and septum: organization and response to injury. In *The Hippocampus, Vol. 1: Structure and Development*, ed. R.

Isaacson, K. Pribram, pp. 215–37. New York:Plenum

Moore, R. Y., Bloom, F. E. 1979. Central catecholamine neuron systems: anatomy and physiology of the norepinephrine and epinephrine systems. *Ann. Rev. Neurosci.* 2:113–68

Moore, R. Y., Kromer, L. W. 1978. The organization of central catecholamine neuron systems. In *Neuropharmacology and Behavior*, ed. B. Haber, M. Aprison, pp. 55–87. New York:Plenum

Mora, F. 1978. The neurochemical substrates of prefrontal cortex self-stimulation: a review and an interpretation of some recent data. *Life Sci.* 22:919–30

Mora, F., Rolls, E. T., Burton, M. J., Shaw, S. G. 1976. Effects of dopamine-receptor blockade on self-stimulation in the monkey. *Pharmacol. Biochem. Behav.* 4:211–16

Mora, F., Sanguinetti, A. M., Rolls, E. T., Shaw, S. G. 1975. Differential effects on self-stimulation and motor behavior produced by microintracranial injections of a dopamine-receptor blocking agent. *Neurosci. Lett.* 1: 179–84

Morgane, P. J. 1961. Medial forebrain bundle and "feeding centers" of the hypothalamus. *J. Comp. Neurol.* 117:1–26

Nauta, W. J. H. 1960. Some neuronal pathways related to the limbic system. See Brady 1960, pp. 1–16

Nauta, W. J. H., Domesick, V. B. 1978. Crossroads of limbic and striatal circuitry: hypothalamo-nigral connections. In *Limbic Mechanisms*, ed. K. Livingston, O. Hornykiewicz, pp. 75–94. London:Plenum

Nauta, W. J., Haymaker, W. 1969. Hypothalamic nuclei and fiber connections. In *The Hypothalamus*, ed. W. Haymaker, E. Anderson, W. Nauta, pp. 136–209. Springfield, Ill:Thomas

Norgren, R. 1976. Taste pathways to hypothalamus and amygdala. *J. Comp. Neurol.* 166:17–30

Oke, A., Keller, R., Adams, R. N. 1978. Dopamine and norepinephrine enhancement in discrete rat brain regions following neonatal 6-hydroxydopamine treatment. *Brain Res.* 148:245–50

Olds, J. 1955. Physiological mechanisms of reward. *Neb. Symp. Motiv.* 3:73–138

Olds, J. 1956. Runway and maze behavior controlled by basomedial forebrain stimulation in the rat. *J. Comp. Physiol. Psychol.* 49:507–12

Olds, J. 1958. Satiation effects in self-stimulation of the brain. *J. Comp. Physiol. Psychol.* 51:675–78

Olds, J. 1960. Differentiation of reward systems in the brain by self-stimulation techniques. See Brady 1960, pp. 17–51

Olds, J. 1961. Differential effects of drives and drugs on self-stimulation at different brain sites. See Brady 1961, pp. 350–66

Olds, J. 1962. Hypothalamic substrates of reward. Physiol. Rev. 42:554–604

Olds, J. 1969. The central nervous system and the reinforcement of behavior. Am. Psychol. 24:114–32

Olds, J. 1976. Reward and drive neurons: 1975. See Wauquier & Rolls 1976, pp. 1–27

Olds, J. 1977. Drives and Reinforcements. New York:Raven

Olds, J., Disterhoft, J. F., Segal, M., Kornblith, C. L., Hirsh, R. 1972. Learning centers of rat brain mapped by measuring latencies of conditioned unit responses. J. Neurophysiol. 35:202–19

Olds, J., Milner, P. 1954. Positive reinforcement produced by electrical stimulation of septal area and other regions of rat brain. J. Comp. Physiol. Psychol. 47:419–27

Olds, J., Olds, M. E. 1964. The mechanisms of voluntary behavior. In The Role of Pleasure in Behavior, ed. R. Heath, pp. 23–53. New York:Harper & Row

Olds, J., Olds, M. E. 1965. Drives, rewards, and the brain. In New Directions in Psychology, ed. F. Barron, 2:327–404. New York: Holt, Rinehart & Winston

Olds, J. Peretz, B. 1960. A motivational analysis of the reticular activating system. EEG Clin. Neurophysiol. 12:445–54

Olds, J., Travis, R. P. 1960. Effects of chlorpromazine, meprobamate, pentobarbital and morphine on self-stimulation. J. Pharmacol. Exp. Ther. 128:397–404

Olds, J., Travis, R. P., Schwing, R. C. 1960. Topographic organization of hypothalamic self-stimulation functions. J. Comp. Physiol. Psychol. 53:22–32

Olds, M. E. 1975. Effects of intraventricular 6-hydroxydopamine and replacement therapy with norepinephrine, dopamine, and serotonin on self-stimulation in diencephalic and mesencephalic regions in the rat. Brain Res. 98:327–42

Olds, M. E. 1976. Effectiveness of morphine and ineffectiveness of diazepam and phenobarbital on the motivational properties of hypothalamic self-stimulation behavior. Neuropharmacology 15:117–31

Olds, M. E. 1979. Hypothalamic substrate for the positive reinforcing properties of morphine in the rat. Brain Res. 168:351–60

Olds, M. E., Olds, J. 1962. Approach-escape interactions in rat brain. Am. J. Physiol. 203:803–10

Olds, M. E., Olds, J. 1963. Approach-avoidance analysis of rat diencephalon. J. Comp. Neurol. 120:259–95

Olds, M. E., Olds, J. 1969. Effects of lesions in medial forebrain bundle on self-stimulation behavior. Am. J. Physiol. 217:1253–64

Olds, M. E., Williams, K. N. 1980. Self-administration of D-ala-met enkephalinimide at hypothalamic self-stimulation sites. Brain Res. In press

Ornstein, K., Huston, J. P. 1975. Influence of 6-hydroxydopamine injections in the substantia nigra on lateral hypothalamic reinforcement. Neurosci. Lett. 1:339–42

Palkovits, M., Jacobowitz, D. M. 1974. Topographic atlas of catecholamine and acetylcholinesterase-containing neurons in rat brain. II Hindbrain. J. Comp. Neurol. 157:29–42

Panskepp, J., Gandelman, R., Trowill, J. A. 1968. The effect of intertrial interval on running performance for ESB. Psychon. Sci. 13:135–36

Papez, J. W. 1937. A proposed mechanism of emotion. AMA Arch. Neurol. Psychiatry 38:725–43

Pasternak, G. W., Goodman, R., Snyder, S. H. 1975. An endogenous morphine-like factor in mammalian brain. Life Sci. 16:1765–69

Peterson, D. W., Laverty, R. 1976. Operant behavioural and neurochemical effects after neonatal 6-hydroxydopamine treatment. Psychopharmacology 50:55–60

Phillips, A. G. 1975. Dopaminergic theories of reward: the role of the nigro-neostriatal system. Presented to East. Psychol. Assoc.

Phillips, A. G., Brooke, S. M., Fibiger, H. C. 1975. Effects of amphetamine isomers and neuroleptics on self-stimulation from the nucleus accumbens and dorsal noradrenergic bundle. Brain Res. 85:13–22

Phillips, A. G., Carter, D. A., Fibiger, H. C. 1976. Dopaminergic substrates of intracranial self-stimulation in the caudate-putamen. Brain Res. 104:221–32

Phillips, A. G., Fibiger, H. C. 1973. Dopamine and noradrenergic substrates of positive reinforcement: differential effects of d- and l-amphetamine. Science 179:575–77

Phillips, A. G., Fibiger, H. C. 1978. The role of dopamine in maintaining intracranial self-stimulation in the ventral tegmentum, nucleus accumbens and medial prefrontal cortex. *Can. J. Psychol.* 32: 58–66

Phillips, A. G., Mogenson, G. J. 1969. Self-stimulation of the olfactory bulb. *Physiol. Behav.* 4:195–97

Pliskoff, S. S., Hawkins, D. T. 1963. Test of Deutsch's drive-decay theory of rewarding self-stimulation of the brain. *Science* 141:823–24

Pliskoff, S. S., Wright, J. E., Hawkins, D. T. 1965. Brain stimulation as a reinforcer: intermittent schedules. *J. Exp. Anal. Behav.* 8:75–88

Porter, R. W., Conrad, D., Brady, J. V. 1959. Some neural and behavioral correlates of electrical self-stimulation in the limbic system. *J. Exp. Anal. Behav.* 2: 43–55

Poschel, B. P. H. 1969. Mapping of the rat brain for self-stimulation under monoamine oxidase blockade. *Physiol. Behav.* 4:325–31

Poschel, B. P. H., Ninteman, F. W. 1966. Hypothalamic self-stimulation: its suppression by blockade of norepinephrine biosynthesis and reinstatement by methamphetamine. *Life Sci.* 5:11–16

Prado-Alcala, R. A., Kent, E. W., Reid, L. D. 1975. Intracranial self-stimulation effects along the route of the nigrostriatal bundle. *Brain Res.* 84:531–40

Pribram, K. H., Kruger, L. 1954. Functions of the "olfactory brain." *Ann. NY Acad. Sci.* 58:109–38

Ritter, S., Stein, L. 1973. Self-stimulation of noradrenergic cell group (A6) in locus coeruleus of rats. *J. Comp. Physiol. Psychol.* 85:443–52

Ritter, S., Stein, L. 1974. Self-stimulation in the mesencephalic trajectory of the ventral noradrenergic bundle. *Brain Res.* 81:145–57

Roberts, W. W. 1958. Both rewarding and punishing effects from stimulation of posterior hypothalamus of cat with same electrode at same intensity. *J. Comp. Physiol. Psychol.* 51:400–7

Robertson, A., Mogenson, G. J. 1978. Evidence for a role for dopamine in self-stimulation of the nucleus accumbens of the rat. *Can. J. Psychol.* 32:67–76

Roll, S. K. 1970. Intracranial self-stimulation and wakefulness: effects of manipulating ambient catecholamines. *Science* 168:1370–72

Rolls, E. T. 1975. *The Brain and Reward.* Oxford:Pergamon

Rolls, E. T. 1976. The neurophysiological basis of brain-stimulation reward. See Wauquier & Rolls 1976, pp. 65–87

Rolls, E. T., Rolls, B. J., Kelly, P. H. Shaw, S. G., Wood, R. J., Dale, R. 1974. The relative attenuation of self-stimulation, eating and drinking produced by dopamine-receptor blockade. *Psychopharmacologia* 38:219–30

Routtenberg, A. 1968. The two-arousal hypothesis: reticular formation and limbic system. *Psychol. Rev.* 75:51–80

Routtenberg, A. 1971. Forebrain pathways of reward in *Rattus norvegicus. J. Comp. Physiol. Psychol.* 75:269–76

Routtenberg, A. 1973. Intracranial self-stimulation pathways as substrate for stimulus-response integration. In *Efferent Organization and the Integration of Behavior,* ed. J. Maser, pp. 263–318. New York:Academic

Routtenberg, A. 1975. Intracranial self-stimulation pathways as substrate for memory consolidation. *Nebr. Symp. Motiv.* 22:161–82

Routtenberg, A. 1976. Self-stimulation pathways: origins and terminations—a three-stage technique. See Wauquier & Rolls 1976, pp. 31–39

Routtenberg, A. 1978. The reward system of the brain. *Sci. Am.* 239:154–64

Routtenberg, A. 1979. Participation of brain stimulation reward substrates in memory: anatomical and biochemical evidence. *Fed. Proc.* 38:2446–54

Routtenberg, A., Lindy, J. 1965. Effects of the availability of rewarding septal and hypothalamic stimulation on barpressing for food under conditions of deprivation. *J. Comp. Physiol. Psychol.* 60: 158–61

Routtenberg, A., Malsbury, C. 1969. Brainstem pathways of reward. *J. Comp. Physiol. Psychol.* 68:22–30

Routtenberg, A., Santos-Anderson, R. 1976. The central role of prefrontal cortex in intracranial self-stimulation: a case history of anatomical localization of motivational substrates. In *Handbook of Psychopharmacology,* ed. L. Iversen, S. Iversen, S. Snyder, 8:1–24. New York: Plenum

Routtenberg, A., Sloan, M. 1972. Self-stimulation in the frontal cortex of *Rattus norvegicus. Behav. Biol.* 7:567–72

Sachs, C., Jonsson, G. 1975. Effects of 6-hydroxydopamine on central noradrenaline neurons during ontogeny. *Brain Res.* 99:277–91

Sar, M., Stumpf, W. E., Miller, R. J., Chans, K. J., Cuatrecasas, P. 1978. Immunohistochemical localization of enkephalin in rat brain and spinal cord. *J. Comp. Neurol.* 182:17–37

Schmidt, E., McCaleb, M., Merrill, H. K. 1977. Food and intracranial stimulation responding suppressed with regular-interval shock. *J. Exp. Anal. Behav.* 25:161–70

Segal, M., Bloom, F. E. 1976a. The action of norepinephrine in the rat hippocampus III. Hippocampal cellular responses to locus coeruleus stimulation in the awake rat. *Brain Res.* 107:499–511

Segal, M., Bloom, F. E. 1976b. The action of norepinephrine in the rat hippocampus IV. The effects of locus coeruleus stimulation on evoked hippocampal unit activity. *Brain Res.* 107:513–25

Seward, J. P., Uyeda, A., Olds, J. 1959. Resistance to extinction following cranial self-stimulation. *J. Comp. Physiol. Psychol.* 52:294–99

Seward, J. P., Uyeda, A., Olds, J. 1960. Reinforcing effect of brain stimulation on run-way performance as a function of interval between trials. *J. Comp. Physiol. Psychol.* 53:224–27

Sidman, M., Brady, J. V., Conrad, D. G., Schulman, A. 1955. Reward schedules and behavior maintained by intracranial self-stimulation. *Science* 122:830–31

Simantov, R., Kuhar, M. J., Uhl, G. R., Snyder, S. H. 1977. Opioid peptide enkephalin: immunohistochemical mapping in rat central nervous system. *Proc. Natl. Acad. Sci. USA* 74:2167–71

Simon, H., Le Moal, M., Cardo, B. 1973. Mise en évidence du comportement d'autostimulation dans le noyau raphé médian du Rat. *CR Acad. Sci. (Paris)* 277:591–93

Simon, H., Le Moal, M., Cardo, B. 1975. Self-stimulation in the dorsal pontine tegmentum in the rat. *Behav. Biol.* 13:339–47

Spear, N. E. 1962. Comparison of the reinforcing effect of brain stimulation on Skinner box, runway, and maze performance. *J. Comp. Physiol. Psychol.* 55:679–84

Stark, P., Boyd, E. S. 1963. Effects of cholinergic drugs on hypothalamic self-stimulation response rates of dogs. *Am. J. Physiol.* 205:745–48

Stein, L. 1962. Effects and interactions of imipramine, chlorpromazine, reserpine and amphetamine on self-stimulation: possible neurophysiological basis of depression. *Recent Adv. Biol. Psychiatry* 4:288–308

Stein, L. 1964. Self-stimulation of the brain and the central stimulant action of amphetamine. *Fed. Proc.* 23:836–50

Stein, L. 1968. Chemistry of reward and punishment. In *Psychopharmacology: A Review of Progress 1957–1967*, ed. D. Efron. PHS Publ. No. 1836, pp. 105–23. Washington DC: GPO

Stein, L. 1978a. Reward transmitters: catecholamines and opioid peptides. In *Psychopharmacology: A Generation of Progress*, ed. M. Lipton, A. DiMascio, K. Killam, pp. 569–81. New York: Raven

Stein, L. 1978b. Brain endorphins: possible mediators of pleasure and reward. *Neurosci. Res. Prog. Bull.* 16:556–67

Stein, L., Belluzzi, J. D., Wise, C. D. 1976. Norepinephrine self-stimulation pathways: implications for long-term memory and schizophrenia. See Wauquier & Rolls 1976, pp. 297–334

Stein, L., Ray, O. S. 1959. Self-regulation of brain stimulating current intensity in the rat. *Science* 130:570–72

Stein, L., Wise, C. D. 1969. Release of norepinephrine from hypothalamus and amygdala by rewarding medial forebrain bundle stimulation and amphetamine. *J. Comp. Physiol. Psychol.* 67:189–98

Stein, L., Wise, C. D. 1973. Amphetamine and noradrenergic reward pathways. See Moore 1973, pp. 963–68

Taylor, K. M., Clark, D. W. J., Laverty, R., Phelan, E. L. 1972. Specific noradrenergic neurons destroyed by 6-hydroxydopamine injection into newborn rats. *Nature New Biol.* 239:247–48

Terman, M., Kling, J. W. 1968. Discrimination of brightness differences by rats with food or brain-stimulation reinforcement. *J. Exp. Anal. Behav.* 11:29–37

Trowill, J. A., Panksepp, J., Gandelman, R. 1969. An incentive model of rewarding brain stimulation. *Psychol. Rev.* 76:264–81

Ungerstedt, U. 1971. Stereotypic mapping of the monoamine pathways in the rat. *Acta Physiol. Scand.* (Suppl. 367):1–122

Ursin, R., Ursin, H., Olds, J. 1966. Self-stimulation of hippocampus in rats. *J. Comp. Physiol. Psychol.* 61:353–59

Valenstein, E. S. 1966. The anatomical locus of reinforcement. In *Progress in Physiological Psychology*, Vol. 1, ed. E. Stellar, J. Sprague. New York: Academic

Valenstein, E. S. 1969. Behavior elicited by hypothalamic stimulation. A prepotency hypothesis. *Brain Behav. Evol.* 2:295–316

Valenstein, E. S. 1970. Stability and plasticity of motivation systems. In *The Neurosciences Second Study Program*, ed. F.

Schmitt, pp. 207–17. New York: Rockefeller Univ. Press

Valenstein, E. S. 1976. The interpretation of behavior evoked by brain stimulation reward. See Wauquier & Rolls 1976, pp. 557–76

Valenstein, E. S., Campbell, J. F. 1966. Medial forebrain bundle-lateral hypothalamic area and reinforcing brain stimulation. *Am. J. Physiol.* 210:270–74

Valenstein, E. S., Cox, V. C., Kakolewski, J. W. 1968. Modification of motivated behavior elicited by electrical stimulation of the hypothalamus. *Science* 159: 1119–21

Valenstein, E. S., Valenstein, T. 1964. Interaction of positive and negative reinforcing neural systems. *Science* 145: 1456–57

Wauquier, A. 1976. The influence of psychoactive drugs on brain self-stimulation in rats: A review. See Wauquier & Rolls 1976, pp. 123–70

Wauquier, A., Niemegeers, C. J. E. 1972. Intracranial self-stimulation in rats as a function of various stimulation parameters. II. The influence of haloperidol, pimozide and pipamperone on medial forebrain bundle stimulation with monopolar electrodes. *Psychopharmacologia* 27:191–202

Wauquier, A., Rolls, E., eds. 1976. *Brain Stimulation Reward.* New York: Elsevier

Wetzel, M. C. 1963. Self-stimulation aftereffects and runway performance in the rat. *J. Comp. Physiol. Psychol.* 56: 673–78

Wise, R. 1976. Evidence for involvement of a dopaminergic substrate in self-stimulation and in intravenous amphetamine self-administration. See Wauquier & Rolls 1976, pp. 205–7

Wise, R. A. 1978. Catecholamine theories of reward: a critical review. *Brain Res.* 152:215–47

Wise, R. A., Stein, L. 1969. Facilitation of brain self-stimulation by central administration of norepinephrine. *Science* 163:299–301

Wurtz, R. H., Olds, J. 1963. Amygdaloid stimulation and operant reinforcement in the rat. *J. Comp. Physiol. Psychol.* 56:941–49

Wyrwicka, W., Dobrzecka, C. 1960. Relationship between feeding and satiation centers of the hypothalamus. *Science* 132:805–6

Ann. Rev. Psychol. 1981. 32:575–627
Copyright © 1981 by Annual Reviews Inc. All rights reserved

EARLY VISUAL PERCEPTION[1]   ♦353

Bela Julesz and Robert A. Schumer

Bell Telephone Laboratories, Murray Hill, New Jersey 07974

CONTENTS

1.0 INTRODUCTION

Last year in this series, Russell & Karen De Valois (1980) undertook the difficult task of summarizing the many important findings that have accumulated in our field of specialty since the remarkable review by Sekuler (1974). Their bird's-eye view agrees to an astonishing degree with ours, and so we can afford to zoom in on a few select topics of strategic importance.

[1]Abbreviations used: AM, apparent movement; MTF, modulation transfer function; NP, neurophysiological atoms–perceptual molecules; PP, perceptual atoms–perceptual molecules; RDS, random-dot stereogram(s); RM, real movement; SF, spatial frequency.

0066-4308/81/0201-0575$01.00

576   JULESZ & SCHUMER

These topics have one guiding principle in common: they all deal with global percepts (perceptual molecules) that can be successfully decomposed into more elementary perceptual building blocks (perceptual atoms). Such an ambitious program has been carried out only recently in some relatively early stages of visual information processing.

This guiding principle sets us apart in important ways from the above-mentioned reviewers. We are interested in psychological models whose building blocks are themselves psychological units (perceptual channels, feature analyzers, etc) and whose existence is revealed by psychological methods alone. Thus we are interested mainly in research that tries to explain a perceptual phenomenon as an interaction of even more elementary psychological percepts. We call this *type PP* research. On the other hand, we regard attempts to describe a perceptual phenomenon by neurophysiological units as interesting, but rather speculative. We call such attempts *type NP* approaches, and include them in our review rather cautiously. We believe that the perceptual atoms of the psychologists are rather complex quantities for the neurophysiologist, and we know of very few instances where even a hypercomplex neural feature analyzer in the visual cortex could be correlated with the simplest percept.

We have focused our review on the most recent years, but have not refrained from citing earlier work when we feel that the impact of ideas that originated in the past are being, or perhaps only just coming to be, felt today.

1.1 Toward a Perceptual Atom Theory

That type PP problems are fundamental in perception is attested to by history, since the first model in visual perception was the three-color channel theory of Thomas Young in 1802, or of George Palmer in 1777 [whose publications are reprinted in a well-selected historical collection on color perception by MacAdam (1970)]. The opponent-color theory of Hering (1878), the first perceptual model of how the basic color channels interact, is also very old, even if only recently was the existence of these opponent-color channels hinted at by indirect neurophysiological evidence (Gouras 1970, De Valois 1973).

We believe that the benchmark of mature sciences is their ability to identify their basic elements ("atoms," "quarks," "genes," "phonemes," etc) and to explain their phenomena as the interaction of these elements. That Palmer introduced his atomistic theory of color perception years before Dalton proposed his atom theory to explain chemical reactions explains why this structuralist theory of color perception became the most scientific branch of psychology. [Interestingly, Dalton, who was the first to describe color blindness (see MacAdam 1970) believed in some aberrant

color filter over the retina, while Palmer had the correct explanation.]
Similar psychological atoms (channels) were discovered in other modalities
several decades ago, such as the "critical bands" in audition by Bekesy
(1929), or the elementary taste analyzers by Pfaffman (1941). Nevertheless,
in vision, if we discount color, it is curious that perceptual channels were
not postulated by a psychologist before the dawn of the neurophysiological
feature extraction era. For instance, the waterfall illusion discovered by
Purkinje (1820), and particularly the spiral aftereffect discovered by Plateau
(1850) (which cannot be attributed to scanning eye movements), were explained only recently by Sutherland (1961), and corroborated by Sekuler &
Ganz (1963) in terms of the selective adaptation of pools of cortical movement detectors (velocity channels). This is a most curious delay since Wohlgemuth (1911) proposed movement-channel adaptation for the movement
aftereffects several generations ago, and many of the pitch aftereffects in
audition had already been explained by Bekesy (1929) in terms of selective
adaptation of channels. [See the review of the recent history of the emergence of the channel concept for spatial frequencies (Julesz 1980b).] Except
for Wohlgemuth's theory, which was overlooked prior to Hubel & Wiesel
(1959), we are not aware of any channel-type explanations whatsoever for
the many perceptual phenomena, such as optical illusions, figural, tilt,
depth, motion aftereffects, etc for which channel concepts are now widely
used. Just a year before the discoveries by Kuffler (1953) and Barlow (1953),
the most up-to-date theory of figural aftereffects by Osgood & Heyer (1952)
was very different from the idea of feature detectors, emphasizing the role
of eye movements and positing unspecified neurons.

So it seems that type NP ideas—such as Sutherland's explanation of the
motion aftereffect in terms of cortical velocity detectors—had a revolutionary impact on visual perception. Nevertheless, when one wants to apply
type NP ideas in detail, such attempts are usually premature. For instance,
it was obvious after the discovery of Kuffler (and Hubel & Wiesel) units that
such single neural units cannot function as perceptual dot (bar) detectors.
After all, one of these neural units alone cannot distinguish between a
narrow dot (bar) with high contrast or a wider dot (bar) with a lower
contrast, while we can perceive the two cases properly. Therefore, one has
to assume that the perceptual system encodes the luminance distribution at
a given retinal position by multiple detectors with different receptive field
widths, as pointed out explicitly a long time ago (Julesz 1971, p. 12). This
type NP idea surfaced again in a more elaborate form, (Marr & Hildreth
1979) explaining why at least two channels are required to separate contours in machine vision, and "justifying" why Wilson & Bergen (1979)
found two channels for sustained or transient stimulation, respectively.
Indeed, after the discovery of multiple psychological channels tuned to

spatial frequencies (SF) by Campbell & Robson (1968), which is a type PP finding in its own right, a type NP idea becomes unnecessary in the framework of psychology.

However, recent neurophysiological findings (reviewed in Section 3.1.1) suggest that Hubel & Wiesel units are SF analyzers rather than bar detectors. Therefore, there is a possibility that the perceptual atom (SF channel) is also a neurophysiological atom (simple or complex cortical neuron). Thus a perceptual molecule (e.g. detection of a bar, thought to involve the pooling of SF channels) can be explained by both type PP and type NP models.

Recently we witnessed another type PP finding being explained by a type NP finding. Blakemore & Julesz (1971) found a perceived depth shift following depth adaptation in RDS which demonstrated the existence of a global stereopsis detector, although the neural site of such a highly global unit (pooling many disparity detectors in complex ways) was unknown. However, Gian Poggio has recently informed us that several of the binocular disparity sensitive units in area 17 of the monkey that fire for elongated bars having certain disparities (Poggio & Fischer 1977) continue firing when the same elongated bars are portrayed by a dynamic RDS without monocular cues. It remains to be seen whether all kinds of RDS are processed at such an early stage, particularly in the light of the ablation studies in the medial temporal cortex of monkey by Cowey & Porter (1979). The ablation had no effect on stereoacuity with line stereograms but impaired global stereopsis of RDS. Furthermore, Poggio's cyclopean neurons are orientation sensitive, contrary to some psychological evidence that the global stereopsis detectors are not orientationally tuned (Mayhew & Frisby 1978b).

In order to fully understand the problems of trying to model a percept by current neurophysiological findings, consider a study by Julesz & Hesse (1970). They made a computer movie in which areas of rotating "needles" perceptually segregated, provided the needles in adjacent areas rotated with different speeds. However, clockwise and counterclockwise rotating needle arrays of the same velocity did not segregate. If vertical needles moved laterally left-right or right-left, respectively, the adjacent areas segregated even when the oppositely moving needles had the same velocity. No knowledge of single electrode neurophysiology would permit an armchair theory of the striking difference in the global utilization of neuron pools shown by these tasks. The example shows the role of psychology in suggesting to neurophysiology what molar functions to look for. So the question of when a neurophysiological finding can be used to model a global percept critically depends on the psychological criterion. The reader is referred to a chapter, "The psychobiological silly season—or—what happens when neurophysiological data become psychological theories" (by Uttal in Nelson et al 1971).

While we will stress those rare instances when type NP models might be relevant, most global percepts in suprathreshold perception are still too complex for present-day single microelectrode neurophysiology. However, rapid progress in global neurophysiological techniques (e.g. radioactive glucose and similar metabolic markers) might bring neurophysiology into the realm of perception (Sokoloff et al 1977, Hubel et al 1978).

Early feature extractors must have evolved to enable the visual system to extract essential information without being swamped by the deluge of irrelevant input. In a sense, our interest in channels complements last year's review by Johansson, von Hofsten & Jansson (1980). The beautiful experiments by Johansson and his co-workers show how a minimum element set of a few dots attached to living creatures, and therefore having a complex structure, are adequate to evoke their complex spatiotemporal memory images. We are reviewing work that tries to clarify how a maximum element set of many dots (such as textures, gratings, dynamic arrays of dots, random-dot stereograms, etc) having a relatively simple structure can give rise to some unique global percepts with minimal load on memory. Particularly we are interested in those structures in usually unfamiliar stimuli that the early stages of the perceptual system are designed to extract.

Finally, early perception is rich in phenomena that permit the study of linearity/nonlinearity, probability summation/cooperativity, bottom up/top down processing, and psychoanatomy (i.e. skipping early stages operationally). We think that early perception is a model system to study these important and poorly understood phenomena, and serves as a link between spatial vision and cognition.

1.2 Personalia, Books, and Major Events

During this review period we lost Mike Fuortes, who used his immense neurophysiological knowledge to build one of the first sophisticated models of temporal mechanisms (Fuortes & Hodgkin 1964), and initiated a trend followed by Sperling & Sondhi (1968) and many others. His scholarship, advice, and warm personality will be remembered by many of us. Another tragic loss was the departure of Hans-Luke Teuber, whose work of correlating well-defined injuries of the nervous system with perceptual deficits had a unique interest for our area. A tribute to his leadership is the publication of Volume 8 of the *Handbook of Sensory Physiology* entitled *"Perception"* (edited by Held, Leibowitz & Teuber 1978) which he planned, solicited, and organized with great vigor. It contains important review articles by Braddick, Campbell & Atkinson (1978) and by Maffei (1978) on psychological and neural aspects of SF channels; by Sekuler, Pantle & Levinson (1978) on movement channels; by Stromeyer (1978) on form-color aftereffects; by Foley (1978) on distance perception; by Julesz (1978a) on global stereopsis and cooperative stereoscopic phenomena; by Ingle (1978) on shape recognition in vertebrates; by Dodwell (1978) on pattern and object perception; by

Coren & Girgus (1978) on optical illusions; by Oyama (1978) on figural aftereffects; by Yin (1978) on face perception; by Fox (1978) on visual masking; by Anstis (1978) on apparent movement; by Johansson (1978) on visual event perception; by E. J. Gibson (1978) on reading; by Dichgans & Brandt (1978) on visual-vestibular interactions; and chapters on visual deprivation (plasticity) by Blakemore (1978), Ganz (1978), and Hatwell (1978). Leaving out many other interesting chapters, we emphasize the chapter by Teuber (1978) on perceptual effects of cerebral lesions, one of his last published works.

Recently we lost J. J. Gibson, whose influence on perception, particularly his pioneering work on the importance of textures and adaptational aftereffects, set the tone for much research reviewed here. In his third book (1979), published just before his death, he elaborated on his theory of direct (immediate) perception. For a lucid discussion and critique of Gibson's ideas the interested reader should turn to Ullman's recent paper (1980). According to Ullman, describing the stimuli-percepts relation as "immediate" would be justified only if the relation had no meaningful decompositions into more elementary constituents. If we accept this summary of Gibson's basic concept, then our review of channels (elementary constituents) is contrary to the spirit of immediate perception. At the same time, Gibson's ideas of gradients and movement invariants of textures greatly influenced research in perception. This shows how rich and multifaceted a creative person's scientific heritage really is.

Another event was the long awaited publication of *Visual Coding and Adaptability,* edited by Harris (1980), that contains very relevant articles on developmental problems by Mitchell and Hein; on perceptual plasticity by Held and Harris; on physiological mechanisms by Robson and Teller; and on SF tuned channels by Graham, Julesz, Weisstein and Harris, and Weisstein. As a result of the careful work of Harris, the articles are self-supporting and complement each other, and serve as a lucid introduction to perceptual channels and plasticity.

An interesting symposium was organized by Kubovy & Pomerantz (1980) on "Perceptual Organization" where the contributors, leading researchers in acoustical and visual perception, were asked to go beyond their findings and give their opinion on the status and future of their fields. Among the contributors to this symposium were: Biderman, Graham, Hochberg, Julesz, Kahneman & Henik, Pomerantz, Pomerantz & Kubovy, Shaw & Turvey, and Shepard (see reference list).

Finally, the "Festschrift" commemorating the retirement of Lorrin Riggs, entitled *Visual Psychophysics and Physiology* (edited by Armington, Krauskopf & Wooten 1978), containing articles by many of his former students and coworkers, demonstrates the impact of Riggs, not only as a scientist but also as an educator.

2.0 THRESHOLD PERCEPTION

2.1 Spatial Frequency (SF) Channels

Within the scope of this chapter, the study of channels in spatial pattern vision has enjoyed the most vigorous attention in recent years. A diverse assortment of tasks have now shown that overall visual sensitivity to targets of different sizes or spatial frequencies is the envelope of the sensitivities of a number of mechanisms, each having narrower sensitivity than the observer as a whole. Important early developments in this area were reviewed with great clarity and insight by Sekuler (1974), and more recent and also excellent reviews may be found in Braddick et al (1978) and De Valois & De Valois (1980), who summarize many of the most recent results and trends.

In the earliest experiments on multiple channels, it was adequate just to show their existence convincingly (Pantle & Sekuler 1968, Blakemore & Campbell 1969, Graham & Nachmias 1971, Stromeyer & Julesz 1972). Recently, however, considerable effort has been devoted to solving the more exacting problems of how SF channels interact with each other at and above threshold, of describing the spatial structure of individual channels, and finally of showing how channels behave above threshold.

Sachs et al (1971) first pointed out that if each spatial frequency channel has its own independent source of noise and its own detector or threshold element, then when two or more mechanisms are activated by a stimulus, detection could be based on the response of either mechanism, and so psychometric functions should follow a form based on the probabilistic combination of the component psychometric functions. This combination, termed "probability summation," occurs because, like simultaneously flipping several coins and asking for at least one head, there are several independent chances to detect a single stimulus. The motive for studying probability summation has been to distinguish such purely statistical pooling effects from other, physiological pooling properties.

The study of probability summation has been made considerably easier by the introduction of an analytically convenient form for the psychometric function, or probability-of-seeing curve, by Brindley (1960), and first applied to grating detection by Quick (1974). Since the form appears to be replacing the traditional cumulative Gaussian curve as the standard psychometric function, we devote some space here to its character and to useful references. The expression for the probability of mechanism i detecting a stimulus is $P_i = 1 - 2^{-|R_i|^k}$, where R is a response measure proportional to stimulus intensity, energy, or contrast, and k controls the steepness of the function. The convenience of this expression derives from the fact that the product of a number of independent probabilities of failing to see a stimulus yields a sum in the lower exponent, and thus the overall probability of detecting a stimulus by at least one of j channels is $P_c = 1 - 2^{-\Sigma |R_i|^k}$. This simple expression yields a convenient prediction of the behavior of many independent channels acting at once. Also the function preserves its shape over changes in the number involved, consonant with the behavior of empirical psychometric functions, as noted by Green & Luce (1975). Useful examples of the application and interpretation of this function can be found in Quick (1974), Stromeyer & Klein (1975), Graham & Rogowitz (1976), Quick et al (1976), Graham (1977), Graham et al (1978), Watson (1979), Watson et al (1980) and Graham (1980b).

The identification of probability summation effects has clarified and unified a number of earlier results. When two widely separated frequencies are combined, threshold contrast for the compound is found to be somewhat less than that for the most detectable component; this has been explained by probability summation over independent mechanisms (Graham et al 1978). Similarly, Graham (1977, 1980b) has argued that the evidence of Kulikowski & King-Smith (1973) and of Shapley & Tolhurst (1973) for a large family of quite broadly tuned channels selective for lines, edges, etc, is invalid because apparent broad bandwidth could be due to probability summation among many narrower channels activated by broadband stimuli.

A more interesting application of probability summation involves decomposing a single SF channel into a number of independent spatial subunits. King-Smith & Kulikowski (1975) showed that the visibility of spatially extended stimuli could be understood as the probabilistic summation of independently activated local units, but they studied only extended stimuli that were composed of local elements widely spaced on the retina. With the idea of local spatial subunits in mind, Stromeyer & Klein (1975) suggested that the very narrow channel tunings of Sachs et al (1971) could be due to a subtle methodological artifact of the subthreshold summation experimental procedure. Frequencies close together, when added, produce spatial "beats" at the difference frequency when a system deviates from linearity. Indeed, if detection of a spatially extended pattern involves probability summation over spatial subunits, "beats," or regions of low contrast, will reduce the number of available subunits, causing an apparent reduction in sensitivity. How this artifact would lead to excessively narrow channel tuning estimates is discussed by Graham & Rogowitz (1976), Graham (1980b), Quick et al (1978), and Bergen et al (1979).

Such probability summation "over space" has been further suggested as the reason why adaptation to a spatial impulse fails to elevate threshold for gratings (Legge 1976). If detection of extended gratings is based on responses of many subunits, then only a few such subunits might be adapted by a spatially local bar stimulus. However, Weisstein et al (1977) have questioned whether a thin line is local or not, showing reductions in the perceived contrast of a grating when "masked" at 4° separations by a thin line, a somewhat strange result. Probability summation over space has also been suggested (Robson & Graham 1978, Bergen et al 1979) as the reason why a single grating becomes more detectable as the number of cycles presented is increased (Hoekstra et al 1974, Savoy & McCann 1975, Estevez & Cavonius 1976, Legge 1978).

Another important refinement to the channel model was first explicitly suggested by van Doorn et al (1972) and was incorporated into a detailed model of threshold vision by Limb & Rubinstein (1977). Since visual sensitivity is well known to vary across the retina (Hines 1976, Virsu & Rovamo 1979), each component of a spatially extended stimulus composed of different spatial frequencies might be detected at different retinal locations. Thus, there might be only one channel at any one retinal location, and evidence for independent detection of the components of a compound stimulus (Graham & Nachmias 1971) would then be explained just by a space-variant single channel model. Graham et al (1978) showed this objection to be wrong by using a new technique of multiplying a spatial sine wave by a spatial Gaussian. This results in a stimulus which is narrow in its SF content but also well localized in space. Graham et al were able to conclude that at each retinal location there must be more than one channel.

Wilson & Bergen (1979, Bergen et al 1979) have combined many of the above-mentioned refinements into a well-specified model of threshold vision. Their model postulates four mechanisms, though this number only reflects parsimony, being the least which gives a good fit to their data, and should not be taken as a rigorous claim in itself. Each mechanism varies in size and in sensitivity with changes in eccentricity, and probability summation over both mechanisms and space is incorporated. The model performs quite well in predicting the visibility of a variety of periodic and aperiodic simple and compound stimuli, though with 21 parameters (each well motivated) it would be surprising if good fits were impossible to achieve. Interestingly, the fairly broad channels Wilson & Bergen stipulate, almost 2 octaves wide, are too broad to explain the lack of subthreshold summation of two gratings even when inhomogeneity and probability summation are taken into account (Watson 1980, Watson & Nachmias 1980).

There is also evidence for the inhibition of inhibition (disinhibition), another type of nonlinearity, which, if valid, could make matters even more complex. Wilson, Phillips, Rentschler & Hilz (1979) had observers detect a test line in the presence of two slightly subthreshold flanking lines, and they report clear evidence of facilitation of detection at test-flank separa-

584   JULESZ & SCHUMER

tions larger than those at which inhibition of performance occurs. The authors of this paper have contrasting views in explaining this finding. Wilson and Phillips believe that only probability summation operates, while Rentschler and Hiltz assume disinhibition. It is intriguing that the same experimental data can be explained by two different nonlinear mechanisms, and it remains to be seen whether an experimental paradigm can be invented that distinguishes between them. Disinhibition has been shown to be important in suprathreshold vision, particularly in the tilt aftereffect (Carpenter & Blakemore 1973, Magnussen & Kurtenbach 1980). Perhaps even in threshold vision such a highly nonlinear effect is at work.

There is also evidence for inhibition between channels, which also would complicate the interpretation of studies of channel properties. Thomas et al (1979) showed that the discrimination of two gratings f_1 and f_2 requires lower contrast than the detection of a compound grating f_1+f_2. This could be due to inhibition between the channels detecting the two components, which would increase performance on the discrimination task and decrease performance on the detection of the compound. Evidence for interchannel inhibition, based on adaptation studies, has previously been presented by Tolhurst (1972) and De Valois (1977b). An alternative considered by Thomas et al to explain their results is that the noise within channels is correlated; this would have the same effect as interchannel inhibition. Again, it should be interesting to see if these interpretations can be distinguished experimentally. An incautious comparison of Thomas et al's result with Graham et al's (1978) finding, that a compound of two widely separated components can be detected at lower contrasts than can either of these components, leads to the seeming paradox that discrimination of f from $3f$ is easier than detection of f or $3f$ alone. This paradox might be due to the different psychophysical procedures and experimental settings used in these studies.

Many researchers interested in visual thresholds study a rather simple task: When does a Ganzfeld change into something else? The detection of deviation from a Ganzfeld might seem to require the lowest threshold, and one could assume that the identification of the SF of a grating, or discrimination between two gratings, would require larger contrasts. Therefore, the finding by Nachmias & Weber (1975) that two gratings in a 3:1 frequency ratio are discriminated as soon as they are detected, is a most interesting result. This suggests not only that each grating is detected by a separate channel, but also that the channels are "labeled," so that the patches that make up a grating are not just barely detected as being different from the surround, but the extent of a patch seems to selectively stimulate the proper SF channel.

2.2 Spatiotemporal Channels

While much of this research belongs to suprathreshold movement perception, recent advances permit us to review some spatiotemporal studies at threshold. Last year the spatiotemporal contrast detection threshold surface was measured in two independent laboratories. Koenderink & van Doorn (1979) found this surface to be bimodal with a peak at low SF and high temporal frequency, and another at high SF and low temporal frequency. They called their peaks "flicker" maximum and "pattern" maximum, respectively. Kelly (1979), who measured this surface under retinal stabilization, found only a unimodal shape and claimed that the "pattern" maximum is created by natural eye movements and disappears under stabilization. Earlier studies had already shown that the spatiotemporal threshold surface is not separable, thus $f(x,t) \neq f_1(x)f_2(t)$ (Robson 1966, Kelly 1966). This meant that such a surface could not be constructed by multiplying together a standard MTF curve with a standard flicker threshold (de-Lange) curve. Kelly's threshold surface is not cylindrical in shape (as a function of space and time) and therefore also is not separable.

These spatiotemporal MTF surfaces are only an envelope of many spatiotemporal frequency tuned channels. These were studied by Wilson & Bergen (1979), who found two kinds of channels for transient stimulation of grating patches and two kinds for sustained presentation. The channels sensitive to transient (higher temporal frequency) stimulation were sensitive to low SF, while those sensitive to sustained (low temporal frequency) stimulation were sensitive to high SF. Psychophysical evidence for such spatiotemporal interactions had earlier been provided by Robson (1966), van Nes et al (1967), Keesey (1972), Breitmeyer (1973), and Kulikowski & Tolhurst (1973). Breitmeyer & Julesz (1975) measured detection thresholds for gratings with rapid or gradual temporal onsets and decays. They found that for low SF gratings the rapid onset yielded lower detection thresholds than the gradual onset. However, no difference was found between rapid and gradual offsets. This asymmetry between onset and offset argues for spatiotemporal nonlinearity.

3.0 SUPRATHRESHOLD PERCEPTION

3.1 Contrast and Pattern Perception

Masking experiments with filtered noise or compound gratings use somewhat more sophisticated criteria than detecting departure from a Ganzfeld (i.e. the detection of something in nothing). They use a kind of dual criterion: When does the noise (spanning all possible signals) become a grating?

Therefore, it is interesting that Stromeyer & Julesz (1972), using one-dimensional filtered noise, corroborated the Blakemore & Campbell (1969) finding of critical bands obtained by adaptation. Neither study showed interactions between channels when their SF spectra differed by about two octaves. On the other hand, Henning et al (1975) used as a masker a compound grating composed of only three sinusoidal components instead of many, as in noise. They found that such a mask of high SF interfered with the detection of a sinusoidal grating two octaves lower in SF. Their finding is thus inconsistent with the hypothesis that the visual system spatially analyzes patterns in independent critical bands. They suggest the possibility that their data could be explained by a model that performs a squaring nonlinear distortion of high SF but not of low SF signals, but they regard such a model as being unlikely.

Rogowitz & Nachmias (1979) were able to reject this model since they found a failure of additivity of the effects of the putative distortion product and of a real grating at the distortion SF. Further, the masking effect differs depending on whether the components of the mask are added in sine phase or in cosine phase, though the distortion product is identical in both cases.

As was discussed in Section 2.1, even at absolute threshold for the detection of gratings there is evidence for nonlinear behavior. Obviously, suprathreshold vision must be even more nonlinear. Therefore, it is most surprising that for several suprathreshold phenomena quasilinear effects have been observed. Such linearity has been revealed either through the absence of SF cross-products (that is, through the independence of channels) or through linear input-output relations.

One suprathreshold phenomenon where the independence hypothesis seems to hold is the unmasking (recognition) of Harmon's famous block Lincoln picture when the "quantization noise" spectrum is filtered to be two octaves away from the image spectrum (Harmon & Julesz 1973). Julesz & Chang (1979) corroborated this finding. They combined a low-pass random-dot array with onefold symmetry and a high-pass array (two octaves apart in spectrum) with onefold symmetry but along an axis orthogonal to the first. Previously it had been shown that the sum of a horizontal and a vertical symmetric pattern (with overlapping spectra) appeared random (Julesz 1971). As expected from a multiple-channel theory, the sum of orthogonally symmetric filtered patterns in the Julesz & Chang study did not have a random appearance, but both the horizontal and vertical symmetry could be perceived simultaneously, provided the high-pass pattern was weighted in contrast about twice the low-pass pattern.

Other evidence for independent SF channels at suprathreshold levels was found in an apparent contrast matching task by Arend & Lange (1980), who repeated some suprathreshold contrast matching experiments of Hamerly et al (1977). Both groups found similar phase-insensitive mechanisms for contrast matching at 30x threshold, and Arend & Lange (1980) further found that the same gratings that fail to summate with one another in the determination of threshold also fail to summate above threshold in the determination of perceived contrast. It would be interesting to know the effect on contrast perception of the spatial "beats" which are present, since such "beats" in compounds made of nearby SF gratings appear to be important at threshold (as discussed in Section 2.1).

While this result is evidence of independence, it also appears to show a peculiar "peak response only" kind of nonlinearity, since compound gratings of widely separated components have the same apparent contrast as the larger component presented alone. It seems that contrast matching judgments utilize only the strongest response given by any active mechanism. Results of Ginsburg et al (1980), using contrast matching and magnitude estimation tasks, support this interpretation since they observed that the apparent contrast of a square wave grating is $4/\pi = 1.27$ times that of a sine wave at the same SF and physical contrast at contrasts ranging from 10% to 50%. Thus, the fundamental component of the square wave determines apparent contrast even though many higher harmonics are well above threshold. If one overlooks this perceptual disregard for higher SF components, other evidence for linearity in contrast perception was found by Ginsburg et al (1980). Perceived contrast was observed to be a linear function of physical contrast.

Using magnitude estimation, Cannon (1979) also showed that the perceived contrast of SF gratings is a linear function of physical contrast at large contrasts. However, he also replicated a finding of Georgeson & Sullivan (1975), who studied contrast matching, that the constant perceived contrast contour (across SF) flattens out above contrasts around 10–20%. This means that at low contrasts (less then 5%) contrast sensation is nonlinearly related to physical contrast, and the nonlinearity varies for different SF.

After reviewing evidence on suprathreshold linearity (or quasi-linearity) and independent SF channels, we mention several findings that show the contrary. Quick et al (1976), using a suprathreshold contrast matching task, found that the apparent contrast of a complex rating usually can be predicted from the apparent contrast of its components viewed alone, if contrast of these components is summed in a Pythagorean fashion: $C_{complex} = \Sigma C_i^2$. Mayhew & Frisby (1978a) extended the validity of this power law to monocular random-dot arrays with different spectra. They point out that a single-channel model is adequate to account for this power law of contrast summation for suprathreshold random textures. They kept the granularity (shape of the ellipsoid Fourier spectra) identical and changed only the orientation of the ellipsoid spectra, which permitted an easy matching between adjacent texture pairs for identical contrast; this is a rather difficult task for textures having widely differing spatial frequencies.

These studies might be reconciled with the previously cited results if the nonlinearities of contrast perception were confined to lower contrasts, as suggested by Cannon (1979). In this regard, it is interesting that the translation of stimulus contrast into channel response—the transducer function of SF channels—seems to be markedly nonlinear just above threshold (Nachmias & Sansbury 1974, Foley & Legge 1979). The contrast required to detect a grating is three to four times larger than the contrast difference required to discriminate two slightly above-threshold gratings. This can be explained if the transducer function is positively accelerated at low contrasts so that the discrimination task reflects performance on a steeper part of the transducer function (Stromeyer & Klein 1974, Van Meeteren 1978). Possibly a "linearization" of contrast sensation occurs only at medium to high contrasts.

3.1.1 Bars versus Gratings and Shifts in Attention

Recently considerable attention has been directed to the problem of whether bars or gratings are the elementary trigger features in visual perception. Since De Valois & De Valois (1980) devoted considerable space to this problem, we add only a few comments. Ever since Hubel & Wiesel (1959, 1962, 1968) discovered that cortical cells in the cat and monkey optimally respond to bars and edges, these neural units have often been regarded as bar or edge detectors. Campbell & Robson (1968) suggested a quasi-linear theory based on SF-tuned filters selective to sinusoidal gratings instead of seminaturalistic objects such as bars and edges. Neurophysiologists (Campbell et al 1969, Maffei & Fiorentini 1973; Movshon et al 1978) showed that the Hubel & Wiesel type bar and edge sensitive units were also sensitive to sinusoidal gratings. Indeed, Movshon et al found that the response of simple cells to narrow slits of light could be predicted quite well from their response to gratings. Nevertheless, in a psychological experiment, Sullivan et al (1972) reported that while adaptation to a grating selectively elevated thresholds for only nearby SF, adaptation to a bar adapted all bar widths nonselectively. They thus concluded that SF, and not bar width, is the "atom" of visual pattern mechanisms. Similar conclusions were presented in a neurophysiological study by Albrecht et al (1980), who reported that although visual cells in the macaque monkey's striate cortex are sensitive to bars, edges, and gratings, they are nevertheless far more selective for gratings of a given SF than for bars of a particular width.

We mentioned earlier that a Kuffler unit or Hubel & Wiesel unit alone cannot uniquely encode both contrast and stimulus width. So it is not surprising that if contrast and stimulus width are constrained (when only sinusoidal gratings are used), the trigger features become more precisely given. That does not mean, however, that in visual perception the "atom" is not a bar (edge) built up from several neurophysiological units. Indeed, Thomas (1970) and Macleod & Rosenfeld (1974) proposed psychophysical models based on size-specific rather than SF-specific mechanisms. Under the size-specific model the visual field is covered by small, overlapping regions (perceptual receptive fields), each sensitive to objects of a particular size (width).

In order to test which of the two perceptual models better describes suprathreshold phenomena, Frome et al (1979) undertook a modified version of the Blakemore & Sutton (1969) SF-shift experiment. Blakemore & Sutton had observers adapt to a sinusoidal grating before examining a grating of varying SF. They found that gratings higher in SF than the adapting grating appeared higher still, while gratings of lower SF appeared lower still (similar to the adaptation findings in the auditory domain of Bekesy 1929). Frome et al used a sinusoidal grating for adaptation but tested with a single bar. They found a perceived widening of the bar whether individual stripes in the grating were narrower than, equal to, or somewhat wider than the test bar, although they found perceived narrowing if the adapting grating's stripes were more than twice the width of the test bar. This finding argues against a size-specific model, according to which perceived widening should be experienced for a test stimulus wider than the adapting stimulus and perceived narrowing for a narrower test stimulus. Particularly, no size change should be experienced when the test and adaptation width agree, contrary to the observed finding. A SF model is consistent with the findings, since a bar has a broad spectrum, and adaptation to a grating reduces sensitivity to SF near the adapting frequency. Perceived widening of the bar should occur when there is relatively less response from the higher SF channels.

In another variant of this experiment Levinson & Frome (1979) used a square-wave grating as the test stimulus and found a Blakemore-Sutton kind of frequency shift of increased frequency while the individual bars of the grating (or a test square) always looked wider, a paradoxical result. This perceptual paradox is particularly strong in light of the finding of Frome et al that both gratings and bars are processed by SF channels. According to the authors, the only way to resolve this paradox is to evoke a selective attention mechanism. When observers attend to a single bar (or square) they can perceptually discount the rest of the visual field. Thus the spectrum of such a "perceptual window" convolutes with the spectrum of the bar, while for global grating perception no window is used.

A problem with many of the studies comparing bars with gratings is that a particular conception of "bar" is implicit, namely one having sharp edges. For example, Albrecht et al undoubtedly would have found greater selectivity for bar width if their "bars" had blurry edges, and it seems as reasonable for blurry bars to be considered as an alternative to gratings, in the search for the "atoms" of pattern vision, as for sharp bars.

In suprathreshold vision one-dimensional gratings and bars are very unnatural stimuli. One can expect many novel findings for two-dimensional stimuli both in the space and Fourier domains where gratings with different orientations can coexist. For instance, Heeley (1979) observed a SF-shift at orientations orthogonal to the adapting grating.

3.1.2 Globality versus Low SF Channels

The idea of the Gestaltists, that the holistic character of the stimulus influences its perception, is most provocative and hindered the structuralistic approach for a long time. Therefore, the proposal by Ginsburg (1975) to regard the low-SF channels as the "Gestalt analyzers" appears at first an interesting insight. Indeed, his low-pass filtering of optical illusions and Kanizsa figures seems to produce these global interactions and at the same time justify the existence of SF channels in vision.

In spite of the great heuristic appeal of this model, at its inception it had to face some contrary facts. For instance, most optical illusions are perceived even when portrayed by RDS, in spite of the fact that the binocular information can only exist at a much later stage than the site of filtering that Ginsburg proposes (Julesz 1971). Also, the illusory (virtual) contours in Kanizsa figures seem to disappear when binocular disparity is introduced (Gregory & Harris 1974). So the postulated low-SF channel must occur after the nonlinear operation of stereopsis. However, if stereopsis occurs as early as area 17 of the cortex, one could still assume that stereopsis may be processed at the same stage as SF filtering.

Therefore, the recent demonstration by Carlson et al (1980) is most illuminating. They portrayed illusory figures by small white dots having narrow black surrounding annuli (simulating a center-surround antagonistic Kuffler unit profile) in a gray background as shown in Figure 1. These Kuffler-dotted illusory figures give rise to strong illusory percepts in spite of the fact that they lack low-pass spectra. Indeed, the slightest blur makes these figures disappear completely. Thus the low-SF channels cannot respond to these Kuffler-dotted patterns, and therefore the globality of the Gestalt-like phenomena cannot be directly accounted for by low-pass filtering. Obviously, there must be some nonlinear operation that connects nearby space tokens (defined by high-SF channels) into enlongated lines as proposed by Marr (1976) in his "primal sketch" model, or as proposed in the texton model of Julesz (1980a). After such a nonlinear operation—a still

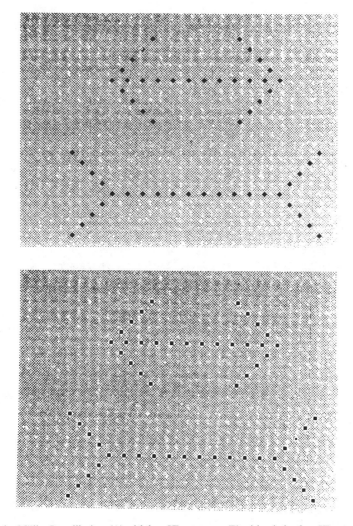

Figure 1 Müller-Lyer illusion: (A) with low SF spectrum; (B) with missing low SF spectrum (i.e. viewing from a distance makes the figures disappear). After Carlson et al (1980).

enigmatic process—one could postulate some linear low-pass filtering. Thus, globality without essential nonlinearities cannot explain perceptual phenomena.

3.1.3 The Problem of Phase

Suprathreshold vision is critically sensitive to phase (position) information. The slightest scrambling of the Fourier phase spectrum renders an image unrecognizable. Even in suprathreshold audition, where phase plays only a minor role, one can easily discriminate between a sharp click and white noise in spite of their identical power spectra.

The discovery of phase insensitivity in threshhold vision (Graham & Nachmias 1971) was a powerful motivation for models of multiple SF channels. The question naturally arises as to how these models should be extended to explain suprathreshold phase sensitivity. One possible answer is that each channel is labeled by a specific retinal locale. Another possible answer might be that within a critical band there is phase sensitivity even in threshold vision. Since the critical bands overlap, phase sensitivity might be exhibited through overlapping neighborhoods (i.e. with respect to phase sensitivity the visual system behaves like a manifold).

Notwithstanding the importance of phase in vision, we were able to find very little on this problem in the literature. Nachmias & Weber (1975), using a discrimination task, confirmed that the phase of an $f + 3f$ compound grating cannot be distinguished until somewhat above detection level contrast. Ross & Johnstone (1980), who used compound gratings with differences between the phase of the first and fifth harmonics, recently replicated this finding but only if the fundamental had a SF of 1 cycle/deg or higher. With a fundamental SF of 0.5 cycle/deg or less, phase sensitivity was found even at detection threshold. This might indicate that just one channel exists at very low SF.

Perhaps some of the phase insensitivity found with sinusoidal gratings is due to the artificiality of restricting stimuli to variations in one dimension only. Burr (1980) has found the relative phase threshold between an f and $3f$ grating to be as large as 30° (but constant for all SF for which both components can be seen). However, in two dimensions, sensitivity to vernier offsets is quite fine (e.g. 37 sec arc) for low SF (1 c/deg) cosine bars, as Krauskopf & Campbell have found (personal communication).

Very little is known about how a phase-insensitive system at threshold could become phase sensitive above threshold. One possibility is that above threshold there exist broad channels which are responsive to widely separated components. This was suggested by Nachmias & Weber (1975) to explain why the presence of a high contrast grating facilitates the detection of a grating at three times the inducing SF. Arend & Lange (1979) similarly showed phase sensitivity for the detection of an $f + 3f$ compound in the presence of a fixed $2f$ "mask." Taken together with narrowband phenomena in contrast matching (Arend & Lange 1980), this points to the existence of parallel broad and narrowband channels in suprathreshold vision, and rules out a scheme in which narrowband threshold channels act as an input stage to the broad channels.

In suprathreshold vision, there is some interesting evidence that particular phases of harmonically related SFs have preferred status in the visual system. Atkinson & Campbell (1974) found "monocular rivalry" in complex gratings formed by $f+3f$, that is, the lower and higher SF components alternated in the perceptual suppression of one another. However, these patterns proved most stable when the two components were in square wave or triangular wave phase. Furchner & Ginsburg (1978) further showed that a similar phase bias occurs when observers judge the appearance of such compound gratings. Finally, it may be possible to study the phase specificity of suprathreshold vision through adaptation techniques. De Valois (1977a) demonstrated different adaptation to two rectangular waveforms with identical power spectra but different phase spectra. In contrast to this finding, Jones & Tulunay-Keesey (1980) showed that adaptation to retinally stabilized counterphase flickering gratings generalizes across the relative phase of the test and adapting gratings, but this study may have been complicated by the fact that counterphase gratings seem to be detected by motion detectors (Sekuler et al 1978) which, of course, show no spatial phase sensitivity.

We will discuss further the problem of phase sensitivity in the next section in the context of texture discrimination, while we simply note here that recent results indicate that textural mechanisms are insensitive to the global phase spectrum but are sensitive to conspicuous local spatial information (Julesz & Caelli 1979). Foster & Mason (1980) attempted to refute even this more local claim for the case of figural perception. Their observers adapted to random arrays of micropatterns composed of T-like shapes or of disconnected perpendicular line segments and observed threshold elevation for the detection of a single T-shaped test figure. Adaptation was thus unselective for local cues, but this hardly seems surprising since threshold form vision is known to be phase-insensitive. Had they used a suprathreshold discrimination task instead of a detection task, it seems unlikely a phase-insensitive outcome would have resulted.

In summary, we know of no example in suprathreshold vision (except for contrast matching) where phase is ignored. How such an encoding of phase is carried out by the CNS is a mystery. Since we are not dealing with neurophysiological models, we only mention that no such neurophysiological mechanism has been found. Robson (1975) suggested that a mechanism using odd-symmetric and even-symmetric receptive fields could encode phase. However, as De Valois & De Valois (1980) point out, such a highly precise alignment of two receptive field centers has not yet been found, although, they add, neither has it been searched for by neurophysiologists.

3.2. Texture Discrimination: Beyond Autocorrelation

Preattentive or effortless texture discrimination (of side-by-side presented stochastic arrays without scrutinizing them) is an important link between spatial vision reviewed in the previous sections and the higher perceptual processes to be reviewed later. Indeed, Julesz (1962) observed that Markov texture pairs with identical second-order statistics (but different third- and higher-order statistics) usually could not be discriminated. Because the second-order probability distribution of color (luminance) values uniquely determines the autocorrelation function, hence the power spectrum, the indistinguishable iso–second-order textures have identical power spectra. Thus, it seemed, the preattentive visual system is insensitive to the phase (position) information. Since 1962, several non-Markov, two-dimensional texture classes were created with identical second-order statistics (see Figure 2) that were indistinguishable (Julesz et al 1973, Julesz 1975, Pratt et al 1978). [Some authors misunderstood the Julesz conjecture and mixed up second-order statistics with diagram statistics (that describe only adjacent samples); for details see Julesz 1978b].

In 1978 and since, several iso–second-order, even iso–third-order, texture classes were discovered that yielded strong texture discrimination based on local conspicuous features of quasi-collinearity, corner, closure, granularity, and connectivity (Caelli & Julesz 1978, Caelli et al 1978, Julesz et al 1978, Victor & Brodie 1978, Julesz 1980a). A typical distinguishable iso–third-order texture pair (that is also iso–second-order) (Julesz et al 1978) is shown in Figure 3, which demonstrates that texture granularity is a fourth-order statistical property. Figures 4A and 4B (Julesz 1980a) show iso–second-order texture pairs where discrimination is the result of conspic-

Figure 2   Indistinguishable texture pair with identical second-order statistics (hence identical power spectra). After Julesz (1980a).

uous local features of connectivity. Texture discrimination differs depending on whether the connected micropattern belongs to the target area or its surround. All these distinguishable iso–second-order texture pairs have identical Fourier amplitude (power) spectra and their phase spectra are both random (Julesz & Caelli, 1979).

Recently, Julesz (1980a) suggested that all these local, conspicuous features in distinguishable iso–second-order texture pairs can be reduced to only two features: elongated blobs (of given orientation, width, and length) and their terminators. He called these two fundamental textural atoms "textons." While Marr (1976) in his influential "primal sketch" model suggested the use of line segments and their terminators in machine vision, he borrowed these elements from existing neurophysiological results. The textons in iso–second-order textures, however, were discovered by psychological efforts of 18 years. It took that long to propose the modified-Julesz-conjecture: that preattentive texture discrimination cannot be performed globally by computing third- and higher-order statistics, but is the result of conspicuous feature differences in local texture elements (textons), or of differences in the first-order statistics of these textons.

Interestingly, Barlow (1953), who pioneered the notion that a receptive field might have behavioral significance, recently studied the detection of a rectangular random dot array surrounded by another with different probability distributions (Barlow 1978). To his surprise, detection performance did not change with the aspect ratio of the target rectangle, contrary to the fact that cortical cells are highly elongated. It appears that he used areas

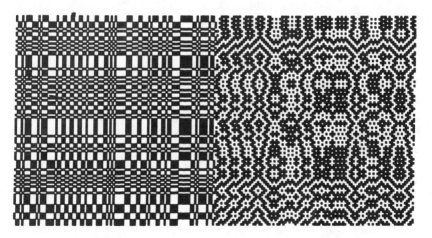

Figure 3 Distinguishable texture pair with identical third-order (hence identical second-order) statistics. Thus texture granularity is a fourth-order statistical property. From Julesz et al (1978).

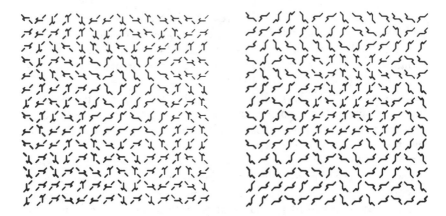

Figure 4 Distinguishable texture pair with identical second-order statistics (hence power spectra). (A) The unshared textons (terminators) belong to the target; (B) the unshared textons belong to the surround. From Julesz (1980a).

of random dots which were too large, and textons of elongated blobs manifest themselves only in small patches. Also, in Marr's primal sketch model real and virtual dipoles (between two place tokens) are treated equally, which led to incorrect predictions in texture discrimination (Marr 1977), as shown by Schatz (1978). It seems that in texture perception only three or more quasi-collinear place tokens act as real lines (Julesz 1980a).

In summary, texture discrimination is based on the number of unshared textons, but their exact positions are ignored (Caelli & Julesz 1979, Julesz 1980a). This position (phase) insensitivity to textons shows that texture perception is based on distributed attention. That attention is distributed in texture perception was first pointed out by Beck & Ambler (1972), who found that discrimination of T-s and *T*-s did not depend on set size, but discrimination of L-s and T-s did.

There is a large literature on simple perceptual discrimination (finding a set of target letters in a set of background letters) according to which the effect of set size (indicating serial or focal attention) can completely disappear with practice—it becomes a parallel attention process (Rabbitt et al 1979). Julesz & Burt (1979) systematically presented 2,3, . . .8 target micropatterns embedded in an array of iso–second-order dual micropatterns either dispersed or grouped (for 160 msec, followed by erasure). They found that (*a*) if detection is based on a critical texton that is present in the target micropattern but absent in the surround, then there is no difference in detectability between the dispersed or grouped conditions; (*b*) If the critical texton is absent in the target micropattern (and thus belongs to the surround), then the grouped condition is better perceived than the dispersed and probability of detection increases more rapidly with the number of target elements than in a. Furthermore, they found the presence of features (textons) in the target is more detectable than their absence, a finding noted in another texture paradigm by Beck (1973).

It is interesting that the perception of textons in the target area is a noncooperative process, but the perception of their absence in the target area is cooperative (defined here as better performance for the grouped than for the dispersed condition). A simple model based on pooled texton detector arrays of a critical size could explain these findings (Julesz & Burt 1979). Such a critical pooling (integration) area of textons has been suggested by Caelli & Julesz (1979), and earlier by Stevens (1978),—working on the perception of Glass patterns (Glass 1969, Glass & Switkes 1976)—who postulated the existence of integration areas covering about a dozen texture elements. The model by Julesz & Burt (1979) easily explains that the critical (unshared) texton in the few target micropatterns will activate one of the corresponding texton-detector arrays regardless of whether the micropatterns are dispersed or grouped. However, if the unshared texton belongs to the surround, then most of the texton detectors are activated and detection must be based on a significant deviation in the density of active texton detectors. Density reduction is greatest for the grouped condition.

Finally, Julesz & Burt (1979), using dual micropatterns with the same number of textons (see Figure 1), first found complete indiscriminability, but after several hundred trials discrimination became possible. Since in these experiments the foveal region was excluded and the brief exposure forced observers to keep their eyes on the center fixation point, the slow learning was restricted to the periphery. This learning was always based on detecting some existing texton that escaped attention prior to mastering the task. Such peripheral learning improvement was also observed by Johnson & Leibowitz (1979). This brings the texton theory close to some provocative findings by Treisman (1978), who found that the preattentive (parallel) system can easily cope with single (disjunctive) features, but only the attentive (serial) system can detect conjunction of features. Even after several hundred trials, RT for detecting conjunctions of "color" and "shape" still required a 27 msec/item slope, while single disjunctive features could be "overlearned," such that RT became independent of the number of items.

While the perceptual learning in the Julesz & Burt study was based on weak textons, formed by, say, the convex hull of the conspicuous textons in Figure 4, the conjunction targets of Treisman are conjunctions of textons, and thus more complex entities than textons. Conjunctions could be learned by the attentive (active) figure perception system, but not by the preattentive (passive) texture system. A detailed model of active and passive attention and perceptual learning was proposed by Shiffrin & Schneider (1977).

In all the iso–second-order textures either the surround or both the target and surround were composed of many micropatterns in *random* orientations [since only a few different (dual) micropatterns exist that can yield iso–second-order textures when placed in *parallel*]. So the perceptual grouping observed in parallel micropattern textures by Beck (1967), Pomerantz (1980), Martin & Pomerantz (1978) and others is not discussed here.

It should be stressed that the observation that in iso–second-order textures the phase information is often ignored does not mean that one can freely manipulate the phase. Indeed, if one were to manipulate the phase in a compound sinusoidal grating, trying to exploit the phase insensitivity Graham & Nachmias (1971) found for threshold detection, this would drastically alter the first- (and second-) order statistics. Indeed, the suprathreshold discrimination of such textures composed of compound gratings can be very strong, not so much because of phase change, but because of the conspicuous difference in their first-order statistics of luminance.

Finally, it should be noted that all the demonstrated strongly discriminable texture pairs had identical autocorrelation functions and thus power spectra. So any theory based on autocorrelation (Uttal 1975) is an oversimplification. A similar conclusion was reached by Uttal & Tucker (1977), who found that detection of dot targets in masking random dots increased with their complexity. However, this complexity scale, based on individual judgments, greatly deviated in some instances from a scale based on the autocorrelation of the dot patterns. Similarly, quasi-linear theories based on one-dimensional Fourier decompositions are unsuccessful because gratings have no terminators, and so such models fail to explain the strong discrimination in, say, Figure 4. Results of studies with patches of gratings might depend on how abruptly they taper off; the pendulum could swing back and perhaps in place of gratings local textons will be used again in vision research. The stimuli used by Wilson & Bergen (1979) and Regan & Beverley (1979) point toward this trend.

We noted that some authors misunderstood the nth-order statistics paradigm originally stated by Julesz (1962) for Markov textures and studied instead $n$gram transition probabilities. When they asked for the smallest n that could not yield discrimination of iso-$n$gram texture pairs, they really studied texture pairs with different second-order statistics, although the nearest neighboring dots up to a distance n had the same second-order statistics (Julesz 1978b, 1980c). This question—to what distance can the visual system detect correlation in a densely packed dot texture—is interesting in its own sake and was studied by Purks & Richards (1977) and Pollack (1973). The techniques of Gagalowicz (1979) permit such a study for non-Markov textures.

The above review of texture discrimination with stochastic constraints covers much of the perceptual literature. It is a profitable strategy to limit one's interest to texture discrimination instead of studying texture recognition and to impose stochastic constraints without which ad hoc variations result in unpredictable percepts. Obviously, in practical problems such as textural analysis of biomedical images or aerial photographs, one has to abandon many of these constraints. Zucker (1976) suggested generating more natural looking textures by periodic structures, and some interesting algorithmic texture generators that imitate "cellular" textures were described by Schachter et al (1978). There is a huge literature on machine segmentation of texture domains and their automatic identification in biomedical imagery that occurs in pathology, hematology, immunology, genetics, radiology, and nuclear medicine. Subsequent to the book *Picture Processing and Psychopictorics* (edited by Lipkin & Rosenfeld 1970), much of the recent literature on texture analysis for biomedical applications has been reviewed by Pressman et al (1979).

We mention only briefly some texture similarity experiments of one-dimensional synthetic textures composed of the sum of a few sinusoidal gratings with randomly selected amplitudes. Richards & Polit (1974) found that similarity between these textures was predictable by a four SF-channel model. Harvey & Gervais (1980), using multidimensional scaling, also found four channels underlying texture similarity. These channels were of the Wilson & Bergen (1979) type, but Harvey & Gervais suggested that the four channels interact in an opponent process manner. They conclude that texture perception is based on SF analysis rather than on feature extraction. Of course, one-dimensional textures do not exist in nature (even the bark of a tree is made up of elongated structures with many breaks), and as Julesz & Caelli (1979) showed, even highly conspicuous textures in two dimensions (e.g. Figure 4) can have identical Fourier amplitude spectra (since differences in terminator numbers do not reveal themselves in these spectra). This shows again the limitations of the SF-channel approach in visual perception. The discovery of textons argues rather for a feature extraction approach.

3.3 Cross-Correlation Channels in Depth and Movement

The importance of cross-correlation models in binaural audition was stressed by Licklider (1948) and Cherry (1953) and in insect vision by Reichardt (1957). Models in binocular vision, particularly in the global stereopsis of RDS, although related to cross-correlation, are more complex because areas of different disparities have to be segmented. However, there does exist a cross-correlation ion-like process in global stereopsis, as shown by measurements of the largest disparity jumps that can be correctly perceived as crossed or uncrossed (Tyler & Julesz 1980, Burt et al 1979). These disparity limits increase monotonically with target area up to target areas in excess of 100 deg^2, and can be over 2° arc, but of course observers do not see a dense surface at such enormous depth. They perceive only a slight depth jump of a cloud of dots toward or away from the observer.

This process is very different from actual global stereopsis, where a dense surface is perceived, and can be regarded as a precursor process. This might be similar to stereopsis with wide bars, as reported by Richards & Kaye (1974), who found that the maximum disparity for seeing bars in depth (though diplopic) increases as the square root of bar area (bar width), and can also be degrees of arc. As we mentioned, these cross-correlation-like processes are very different from the global stereopsis of dense surfaces, since a measure of sensitivity requiring detailed depth resolution showed improvement with increases in target area only up to 4 deg^2, the area of the fovea, where it reaches an asymptote (Schumer & Julesz 1980a).

This foveal asymptote for target area is also obtained when the task is to detect a change from correlation to uncorrelation or vice versa (Julesz & Tyler 1976; Tyler & Julesz 1976, 1978). The presentation time required to detect a transition from correlation to decorrelation (from order to disorder) was only 2 msec while from decorrelation to correlation (from disorder to order) it was 20 msec. Interestingly, changes from uncorrelation to negative correlation and vice versa were also perceived, which can be explained only if one assumes that simultaneously with a binocular fusion process a binocular rivalry process operates as well. This rivalry process favors the negative correlation the most. The strength of this rivalry process relative to that of the fusion process varied with observers, being 10% or less (even zero). Interestingly, the finding by Julesz & Miller (1975) that SF-filtered RDS can be fused while masking noise having a different spectrum can be in rivalry at the same time argues also for two different processes operating in parallel.

In an important paper, Lappin & Bell (1976) showed that sensitivity (d') for observing the direction of a stroboscopic movement jump in a random-dot cinematogram is inversely proportional to the square root of correlated target area. They proposed a signal detection model based on the output of a cross-correlation process (really autocorrelation, since the moving areas contained the same random dots). Julesz & Chang (1980) measured the maximum perceivable displacement in random-dot cinematograms in which 16 successive 10 msec frames contributed to movement. They obtained an increase with $(A)^{1/4}$ for maximum displacement. Thus if d', the response strength, is inversely related to d_{max}^2, the maximum displacement, the results could be related to the Lappin & Bell model. In Julesz & Chang's study $d_{max} > 25$ min arc (8 picture elements) was routinely achieved for 3°

x 3° target size. These results and those of Lappin & Bell are at variance with those of Braddick (1974), who found an asymptotic limit of d_{max} = 15 min arc. Some light was shed on these problems by Julesz & Chang, who found that without practice d_{max} for movement detection in a random-dot cinematogram increased as $(A)^{1/4}$, while for shape recognition in the same stimulus d_{max} seemed to be constant with area. However, with learning even d_{max} for shape recognition reached almost the same value as for movement detection. Note, however, that even though d_{max} for movement in random-dot cinematograms can be larger than the limit found by Braddick (1974), it is still an order of magnitude less than the limits found for apparent movement with monocularly recognizable forms, as discussed next.

3.4 Movement Perception

In Section 3.3, several experiments with random-dot cinematograms were reported. These can be regarded as studies of global movement perception, since the false target problem cannot be decided locally. Global movement perception tolerates only small displacements. On the other hand, local movement perception (for which the corresponding elements in successive frames can be locally determined by form recognition) tolerates large displacements. Since large displacements and highly central processes are hard to reconcile with the word "local" (although this terminology is used for global and local stereopsis by Julesz 1978a), we will use the terminology of Braddick (1974) and Anstis (1978) and call the global movement process short-range and the local one long-range.

Anstis, in his review, discusses the problem of the relationship between real movement (RM) and apparent movement (AM). We mention here only the theory of Braddick (1974), according to which AM is mediated by both the long- and short-range processes, while RM is mediated only by the short-range process. He finds that the short-range process and the long-range processes can be differentially studied using dichoptic presentation (Braddick & Adlard 1978). To summarize his results, for short-range movement motion perception precedes form perception (as in global stereopsis), while for long-range movement form perception precedes motion perception. For long-range movements, which occur only in AM, a form recognition mechanism labels some clusters of dots, and then the AM process looks for motion between similarly labeled clusters. While short-range AM has found wide application in television and movies, the phenomenon of long-range AM, interesting in its own right, does not seem to occur in real life situations. For an object in RM, the jumps in position between successive perceptual instants are never very large, but the tolerance of 15–30 min arc permits the processing of unexpected jumps. Recently, Petersik & Pantle (1979) juxtaposed short- and long-range processes. When they perturbed the local elements the short-range process gave way to the long-range process and a holistic, group movement was experienced. Burt & Sperling (1980) juxtaposed motion of arrays of dots successively presented in adjacent rows. They studied displacement and ISI (interstimulus intervals) and determined those relationships that best favor AM. Because they assumed a scaling invariance principle to derive their model, we return to this work in Section 3.6.

Other evidence shows that there are short-range AM processes beyond the cyclopean retina for stereopsis (Julesz & Payne 1968). A dynamic RDS target in depth could be successively presented in two different positions or orientations to produce AM, but at somewhat higher presentation rates (but less than the simultaneity rate) observers saw a single, stable percept at the average position of the two actual targets. For example, in the case of two tilted cyclopean gratings tumbling clockwise and counterclockwise, a single vertical grating is seen in standstill. In this experiment, AM must have taken place after stereopsis had identified the targets. Since this AM shows a stage, binocular standstill, not observed with luminance targets, it must be different from the AM observed when monocular identification is possible, and perhaps reflects a spatial averaging process in stereopsis which is overridden when the form of the moving surface is available to monocular pathways.

Many interesting studies on motion perception were reviewed by Sekuler et al (1978). They discuss the evidence for direction-specific movement channels and review both psychological and neurophysiological evidence. The chapter by Sekuler et al attests to the hectic activity in recent years. They review research using drifting and counterphase gratings, with and without retinal stabilization, and using random-dot arrays as adaptation and test stimuli, summarizing over 100 papers.

Direction-selective motion mechanisms appear to operate best at low SF and high temporal frequency, that is, at high velocities (Vel = TF/SF). Watson et al (1980) showed that the direction selectivity of mechanisms for movement begins to disappear at low target velocities. Under such conditions, targets moving in opposite directions summate their contrast in a compound detection task; also, discrimination of direction of individual components at low velocities is poor relative to detection. Both these results are expected of a single, directionally nonselective mechanism. That this result is not due to the use of low temporal frequencies alone, but depends on low velocity, is shown by Stromeyer et al (1979), who showed that test patterns of both quite low temporal and spatial frequency (thus of moderate velocity) give rise to direction-selective adaptation.

There is also evidence for a dichotomy between a flicker/motion sensitive system and a pattern sensitive system. The pattern system is most sensitive to high spatial but low temporal frequencies, while just the reverse is true for the flicker/motion system. Another difference is that the motion system is direction selective, while the pattern system is direction insensitive, even in its response to moving patterns. A typical finding in this regard is a recent report by Levinson & Sekuler (1980). They found direction-selective adaptation (to a moving dot array) when they tested (with dots) for threshold elevation using a flicker criterion, but found no directional selectivity when using a pattern threshold criterion. These results extend the findings of Keesey (1972), who found different thresholds for flicker and pattern detection. Although it may be possible at threshold to separate mechanisms for pattern and motion, Burr (1980) has recently shown that blur in moving dots disappears only when exposure duration is long enough for dot motion to be seen, indicating that motion mechanisms are also responsible for the analysis of the spatial form of the moving target.

An interesting question is how motion channels, which like SF channels have mostly been studied in threshold experiments, pool their outputs when operating above threshold. There is some evidence for quite broad pooling of information similar to the broad suprathreshold channels in the SF domain (Nachmias & Weber 1975). Levinson et al (1980) showed that above motion threshold (but below pattern threshold) two sheets of dots drifting in different directions are indiscriminable from a single sheet moving in the average direction, and this holds up to differences as large as 180°. The same conclusion can be reached from the elegant study of Riggs & Day (1980), who adapted to alternately presented orthogonally moving gratings and dot textures. They tested the aftereffect with a disk that contained two adjacent orthogonal gratings (or dots) at standstill, and found that the adjacent test gratings did not appear to separate and move orthogonally, but instead moved in unison according to the vectorial addition of the two aftereffect velocities.

An NP-model of the orthogonal movement aftereffects first reported by Brewster (1845) and studied by MacKay (1957, 1965) was presented by Georgeson (1976). He hypothesized that sustained cortical cells which are sensitive to the orientation of contours are antagonistically coupled to transient cells, in the same cortical hypercolumn, which themselves are sensitive to movement at right angles to those contours. According to MacKay & MacKay (1976) the experimental findings of Georgeson do not support this hypothesis since the sustained contour analyzers alone could account for his results. However, they acknowledge that some antagonism between visual channels for pattern and movement is an attractive NP-type model for orthogonal movement aftereffects.

A major event in motion perception was the publication of Ullman's book (1979), *The Interpretation of Visual Motion.* Here, within the framework of machine vision, Ullman proves an important theorem that "given three distinct orthographic views of four noncoplanar points in a rigid configuration, the structure and motion compatible with the three views are uniquely determined." This theorem gives the minimal requirements to recover a 3-D structure without phantom localizations. (There is only one possible misinterpretation: An object rotating by some angle α and its mirror image rotating by $-\alpha$ have the same orthographic projections.) Such a powerful theorem has many applications in movement studies, and Ullman discusses many of the movement illusions, from the Mach illusion to Ames's trapezoidal window, in the light of his theory.

Ullman's computational theory goes beyond autocorrelation although it still uses linear summation of local elements. In a recent paper, Lappin et al (1980) criticized this theory by showing that no linear summation of local processes can account for the perception of rigid three-dimensional objects. Lappin et al showed that a rotating sphere portrayed by a random-dot cinematogram (with many more than 4 dots) was vividly perceived, and this percept was dramatically degraded by the introduction of even a slight amount of decorrelation. However, this dramatic effect only held for the percept of a three-dimensional object and not for planar surfaces.

The role of stationary and transitory channels in foveal versus peripheral vision was suggested by MacKay (1964). Fixation upon one dot in a field of many randomly scattered dots leads to a loss of positional and detail information in the periphery: the random-dot textures become more uniform in size and appear almost regular. Nelson (1974) reported a similar perceptual reorganization while staring at an ant hill. He perceived either stationary gravel texture in the fovea or the moving ants in a wide peripheral area.

3.5 Global Stereopsis

During the 20 years since the introduction of RDS into psychology (Julesz 1960), this field has grown vigorously and arborized in several directions. Problems of false (phantom) target elimination, cooperativity, hysteresis effects, parallel versus serial models, disparity averaging, cyclopean MTF, hypercyclopean SF channels, problems of fusion, diplopia, and rivalry, clinical testing for stereoblindness, and isoluminance color stereograms are some of the main research activities.

That global stereopsis of RDS is basically different from that of classical targets has been known conceptually and experimentally since 1960. Indeed, the elimination of false localizations in RDS—a prodigious feat in random-line stereograms with vernier breaks (Julesz & Spivack 1967)—is not necessary in classical stereograms with conspicuous monocular cues. Furthermore, Fender & Julesz (1967) discovered a hysteresis effect under binocular retinal stabilization, and found 20 times larger cortical shifts for RDS than for simple line targets. This hysteresis for line targets was further corroborated for both nasal and temporal shifts by Diner (1978), and for RDS, under free viewing, a cortical shift in excess of 4° arc was measured by Hyson et al (1980). This stimulus complexity dependent hysteresis effect is the manifestation of a cooperative process at work.

This cooperativity was further corroborated by the findings that in ambiguous RDS, with several possible global states, a 4% unambiguous bias could initiate a disorder-order transition in a 50 msec brief flash, resulting in a single (the biased) global state (Julesz 1964), and this bias could exact its influence from 18 min arc disparity distance away (Julesz & Chang 1976). Since in 50 msec no vergence movements can be initiated and a 96% match for a serial search process would suffice, instead of the 100% match actually preferred by the stereopsis system, a parallel spring-coupled dipole model was proposed by Julesz & Chang (1976) in place of an earlier, serial cooperative model (Julesz 1971). This cooperative model eliminated false targets, found the biased organization, and exhibited hysteresis, a basic phenomenon of global stereopsis. Many other cooperative models of stereopsis have been proposed (Julesz 1963, Sperling 1970, Dev 1975, Nelson 1975, Marr & Poggio 1976, Mayhew & Frisby 1980b), but none of these explicitly exhibits hysteresis.

Most of these models assume that pools of binocular disparity detectors tuned to similar disparity values facilitate one another, while those tuned to values further apart are not combined or even inhibit each other. Such a global stereopsis unit is conceptually simple if one assumes that binocular disparity is encoded by a gamut of disparity detectors. Many relevant findings and models were reviewed by Julesz (1978a).

The false target problem has recently come under close scrutiny, derived from interest in the relation between luminance-domain channels and the mechanisms of stereopsis. An alternative to cooperative processing that has been considered, starting with the earliest demonstrations of random-dot stereopsis in 1960, is that large, spurious clusters in each random-dot image serve as conspicuous monocular cues which facilitate stereopsis (see Julesz 1961, discussion). Clusters could aid stereopsis in either of two distinct ways. First, it could be that conspicuous clusters help direct vergence eye movements and so cause the two stereo half-images to be brought into rough registration, whereupon finer disparity cues may be utilized. This view assumes that coarse features may be binocularly matched at quite large disparities.

The second possible benefit of coarse features has to do with their rarity. Large blobs in either eye's field may actually be unique within a reasonably large visual window, and so the false target problem for such blobs may be reduced to virtually nothing. Decisions about disparity in a local region based on large blobs might be made quite readily, and these decisions could then be used to influence finer disparity matches made on smaller, and possibly ambiguous, monocular features.

In addition, Richards (1977), using extremely narrow RDS targets in a tachistoscopic flash (violating the essence of RDS, which is the global distribution of information), found only a very small fusional area, and therefore argued that the false target problem might be rather overblown in the first place. His results, however, probably resulted from the use of targets too thin to be resolved by the stereoscopic system. Schumer & Julesz (1980b) recently showed that if the spatial configuration is optimized, discrimination thresholds of only a few minutes of arc at a pedestal of 50 min arc can be obtained with tachistoscopic RDS.

The critical issues, then, concern whether different size blobs are differentially utilized in stereopsis. Research on this question has tended to presume the translation of large blobs into low spatial frequencies, and of small features into high spatial frequencies. That SF channels might be utilized in stereopsis was demonstrated by Julesz & Miller (1975). They found that the fusion of a RDS made up of only a low SF spectrum is unaffected by high-frequency masking noise (and vice versa), but masking noise having a spectrum overlapping that of the stereogram disrupts stereopsis. Frisby & Mayhew (1977, Mayhew & Frisby 1978c) developed this idea into a particularly strong hypothesis (which Julesz and Miller cautiously avoided): binocular matches are made independently upon differently filtered images delivered by parallel and independent SF channels.

Mayhew & Frisby (1978c) tested this idea by studying contrast summation of two narrow bandpass filtered RDS with peak frequencies separated by a 4:1 ratio. They found that contrast threshold for stereopsis with the compound stereogram depended on the total power in the stereogram and not on the independent contrasts of the components, even taking probability summation into account. They conclude that there are probably early levels of stereopsis that are SF tuned, but that the final derivations of stable global percepts pool information over all of these channels. The early SF-tuned processes could be related to those binocular mechanisms shown to be SF-selective in threshold studies of dichoptic contrast summation (Blake & Levinson 1977) and masking (Legge 1979).

Surprisingly, neither of the stages in stereopsis seems to be orientation selective, since both masking and summation experiments with orientation filtered RDS show broad orientational interactions (Mayhew & Frisby

1978b,c). This conclusion was also drawn from the observation that the breaking up of diagonal connectivities in one half-image of a RDS impairs stereopsis no more than an equivalent amount of randomly introduced uncorrelation (Julesz 1964). These results are of special interest since physiologically identified candidates for fundamental disparity units are typically the orientation selective cortical receptive fields of visual areas 17 and 18 in cat and monkey as found by Pettigrew et al (1968), Hubel & Wiesel (1970), Poggio & Fischer (1977), von der Heydt et al (1978), Fischer & Krüger (1979), and Ferster (1979). However, the site of global stereopsis might not be only in area 17 (as Poggio's findings suggest) but might also be more central, for instance the medial temporal cortex, as the ablation studies in monkey by Cowey & Porter (1979) suggest. Interestingly, higher cortical areas show decreasing orientational tuning (Allman et al, in press). Some other early work on the neurophysiological basis of stereopsis was reviewed by Bishop (1973).

Particularly provocative is the view that channels tuned to lower SF code larger disparities while higher SF channels code small disparities and are capable of fine disparity resolution. Felton et al (1972) suggested such a connection when they reported that the bar width that gave the greatest disparity-specific adaptation increased with the adapting disparity, suggesting that broader bar widths are the strongest stimuli for those binocular mechanisms selective for large disparities. Richards & Kaye (1974) showed that the largest disparity for patent stereopsis increases with the width of the stimulus bars.

All these findings were incorporated into a new theory by Marr & Poggio (1979). They abandoned their earlier cooperative model and proposed a new model based on multiple SF channels associated with different disparity ranges, the use of vergence eye movements, and a buffer memory where the successful matches are stored. The key features of their model are that coarse SF channels encode large disparities, while fine SF channels encode only small disparities, and binocular matching takes place only between SF channels of the same coarseness. Furthermore, coarse channels control vergence movements and cause the left and right images to come within the codable disparity range of the fine channels, an idea earlier proposed by Sperling (1970).

Marr & Poggio assume SF channels to be the bar-masks of Wilson & Giese (1977) and compute the reponse of these channels to "white" noise, as might be used in a RDS. Marr & Poggio utilize zero crossings (the midpoints between adjacent light and dark patches) of the filtered image as the primitive matching elements because it allows them to use a powerful theorem by Logan (1977) that describes the distribution of zero crossings in a one-octave band-limited signal (Marr et al 1979). They find that only

5% of the time will a bar-mask filter with width w (of its excitatory region) contain two zero crossings, with the proviso that the gradients at the zero crossings have the same polarity. This proviso is essential since Julesz (1960) showed that contrast reversal of one stereo half-pair destroys stereopsis entirely. Thus, if binocular matches are made only within the disparity range $\pm w/2$, no false target will arise 95% of the time. After the largest blobs of w size are matched in the RDS, the vergence mechanism brings into the codable disparity range smaller SF channels that can match correspondingly smaller blobs without false targets.

This vergence movement-based scanning of the Marr-Poggio theory was disproved by Mayhew & Frisby (1979) and Schumer & Julesz (1980b). Mayhew & Frisby presented narrow-band filtered RDS for a brief flash. They claim to have refuted both the Felton et al (1972) proposal that low SF channels might feed only large disparity detectors and that high SF channels might feed only small ones, and the Marr-Poggio model based on this proposal. Both for filtered (10.8 c/deg center frequency) and unfiltered RDS, discrimination between 13' and 10.4' arc disparities was possible in less than 180 msec. Above 18' arc disparity even the unfiltered RDS required larger than 180 msec duration, indicating the need for vergence movements. Schumer & Julesz (1980b) found even stronger evidence against the Marr-Poggio theory. They presented a pair of dynamic RDS with ±50 min arc disparities for 100 msec with one of the pair having a sinusoidally corrugated surface in depth while the other was flat. Even at such large disparities (three times the limit set by Marr and Poggio, based on 5% false matches), observers could easily discriminate between flat and mildly corrugated surfaces. Perhaps the vergence mechanism of this theory could be replaced by a cortical shift mechanism, but the Fender & Julesz (1967) kind of binocular cortical shift mechanism works only for slow pulling rates. Even if some other cortical mechanism might be evoked, its neural realization is an enigma, while a cooperative model based on lateral facilitation and inhibition is conceptually simple. But more importantly, it is most unlikely that bar-mask filters of 50 min arc width abound in the central 10° or so of the visual field, and the coarsest filters Marr and Poggio assume are more than three times narrower. This restores the false target problem with full force.

Let us stress that for large disparity RDS (outside Panum's fusional area) vergence strategies of correct eye movements, which can greatly improve with learning, have a crucial role. Small disparity static and dynamic RDS, within Panum's fusional area, do not require vergence movements, and can be fused within 80 msec in foveal regions (Julesz et al 1976). Further, the slow emergence of cyclopean targets in RDS is not due to their complexity but only to the magnitude of disparity they contain. Stereopsis for large disparity RDS does, however, improve with practice (Ramachandran &

Braddick 1973, Frisby & Clatworthy 1975, Saye & Frisby 1975, Mac-cracken et al 1977). The memory for vergence eye movements contains two steps. In the absence of monocular contours one has to learn to voluntarily make large vergence movements and then learn not to make a sudden vergence but to do it slowly, so that the Fender-Julesz hysteresis range does not collapse. This "cerebellar" learning is very different from the behavior of the 2 1/2-D sketch memory Marr & Poggio propose for smaller dispari-ties.

So much space has been devoted to this model because it appeared to offer a "simpler" model of stereopsis than the cooperative model. However, this simplicity is illusory. Cooperativity (and hysteresis) is a much simpler notion than memory, based as it is on well specified nonlinear interactions. In favor of Marr and Poggio's theory it should be said that it shifted attention to the relationship between receptive field size and binocular disparity range and to how that relationship might bear on the elimination of false targets. Indeed, Burt et al (1979) observed markedly reduced limits for the maximum detectable brief depth-jump of a flat RDS in which large clusters of dots had been broken up. Schumer & Julesz (1980c) also found a large reduction in the maximum disparity pedestal at which stereopatterns (e.g. corrugated depth gratings) could be seen when clusters in the horizon-tal direction were broken up.

Thus, the evidence tends to favor the view that there exists an association between large disparities and low SF, though the complementary associa-tion between small disparities and high SFs, while logically plausible, lacks experimental support. Perhaps a connection between high SF channels and stereopsis is provided by a recently postulated disparity gradient limit of stereoscopic fusion by Burt & Julesz (1980), to be discussed in Section 3.6.

Mayhew & Frisby (1980a) proposed a model of global stereopsis based on simultaneous binocular matches and SF filtering. Disambiguation is based on possible matches in similar nonoriented SF filters followed by orientationally tuned nonlinear grouping processes. These nonlinear opera-tions over a large global area constitute again a cooperative model. Mayhew & Frisby (1980b) also challenge the zero crossing assumption of Marr & Poggio (1979). They generated a stereogram composed of a triangle wave grating paired with a phase-varying ramp grating. Stereo pairs of this type present interesting ambiguities about which elements are to be selected for left-right matches. Instead of the zero-crossing matches of Marr & Poggio (1979), the visual system seems to use the peaks of the luminance profiles.

Another interesting area of research that again illustrates a fundamental difference between global stereopsis of RDS and monocularly recognizable stereograms involves isoluminant color stereograms. While till 1971 it seemed futile to try to overcome the optical registration problems necessary to present isoluminance colored RDS (Julesz 1971), this technical feat was solved by Lu & Fender (1972). They showed that a 100x100 cell RDS with 40x40 cell center target would not yield depth around the isoluminance setting, even though the individual cells were clearly perceived in color and resolved in shape. This was the more curious since Ramachandran et al (1973) and Comerford (1974), who used monocularly recognizable stereograms, found stereopsis under isoluminance conditions. The complex optical problems of registration were made unnecessary by an ingenious invention by Gregory (1977), who confirmed both findings, i.e. no depth under isoluminance for RDS, depth under the same condition for classical stereograms. Finally, Ramachandran & Gregory (1978) showed that even stroboscopic movement perception would cease for random-dot cinematograms under isoluminance.

These findings were carefully retested by de Weert (1979), and he also concluded that for classical color line stereograms depth could not be eliminated at any luminance setting, while for cyclopean stereograms stereopsis could be made to disappear even when the setting deviated from isoluminance.

Whether these findings mean that the "cyclopean retina" is colorblind, or merely that RDS are more sensitive to a dramatic reduction of contrast than classical stereograms, is a problem worth studying. The first possibility is of special interest in light of findings that the cerebral cortex contains modules functionally specialized for color, depth, motion, etc (Zeki 1978).

Other interesting work related to stereopsis is reviewed in other sections, particularly in Section 4.0, on hypercyclopean channels. Here we stress only the maturity this field has achieved. We have reached a stage in the study of global stereopsis where models of great complexity and generality can be proposed and tested.

We hope that findings reviewed here also counter the opinion expressed by De Valois & De Valois (1980) ". . . that while Julesz random-dot stereograms are very useful analytic tools, they nonetheless constitute an artificially difficult problem for the visual system." That detailed depth resolution can be obtained in briefly flashed RDS in the order of about 1° arc disparities shows the robustness of this technique as well.

3.6 Scaling Invariance Principles in Depth and Movement Perception

To our knowledge, a scaling invariance principle was first stated by Tyler (1973) in the context of stereopsis of sinusoidally wiggling vertical lines. Disparity at the limit of fusion changed inversely with SF. Therefore, this limit did not change as the observation distance was varied, which defines the principle of scaling invariance. For stereograms composed of vertical lines wiggling in square wave fashion, however, Tyler (1975) failed to observe disparity scaling. The scaling principle also holds for global stereopsis (Tyler 1974, Burt et al 1978). For motion perception in random-dot cinematograms disparity scaling also holds, since Bell & Lappin (1973) increased the size of the picture elements together with that of the target area and did not observe any change in performance.

It is only recently that the deeper reason for the scaling principle has been understood for stereopsis. Burt & Julesz (1980) observed a fundamental and simple law for stereopsis that surprisingly was not explicitly stated before in mathematical terms, although qualitatively it had been noted from Helmholtz (1925) to Braddick (1970). When two dots at different distances from the observer and far from each other (in the x-y plane) can both be fused, then when the distance between the two is reduced while keeping their disparity constant, one of the two dots becomes diplopic. Burt & Julesz observed that if the disparity gradient (the ratio between the disparity difference and the distance) between the dots is larger than one, fusion ceases, even if the disparity difference is well within Panum's classical fusional area. For dot separations as small as 4' of arc, fusion was lost at 4' disparity, or less than one-third of the value reported by Ogle (1964) for the width of Panum's area in the fovea. Such a disparity gradient limit implies scaling invariance. This disparity gradient limit explains why two dots on a horizontal line cannot be fused so that the order of the dots is reversed in one eye with respect to the other. Such a "folding back" on itself of the fusion space results in a disparity gradient >2, outside the bounds for fusion. Similarly it explains why in Panum's limiting case one image must become diplopic since here the disparity gradient equals 2. This supports the argument by Kaufman & Lane (1979) that in Panum's limiting case depth is due to eye vergence rather than multiple fusion. Perhaps this principle of a disparity gradient limit elucidates why high SF channels (activated by nearby samples in the x-y plane) cannot encode large disparities between these samples.

The scaling invariance principle for movement perception was used as a guide by Burt & Sperling (1980) to derive a mathematical model of AM. They created an ambiguous display composed of dots, where apparent motion between dots could be perceived along many possible paths. For any given path, given by d_i and by t_i, the distance and time interval between successive elements of path P_i, they associated a stimulus strength S_i for motion. From scaling invariance, which they observed, it follows that S_i is a separable function of d and t, and they derive a logarithmic relationship between the t value where AM is equally likely to be perceived along paths i and j and d_i and d_j. They also observed that when successive elements along a path differ in orientation or size, the perceived motion along this path was not necessarily weaker than motion along a path composed entirely of identical elements. They account for their results by postulating motion analyzing channels in the visual system that are not feature selective and that differ in spatial but not in temporal characteristics. It is particularly interesting that the postulated motion-detecting channels are indifferent to element orientation, similar to the channels for global stereopsis as discussed in Section 3.4.

3.7 Depth and Movement

Our emphasis on stereopsis is based on its importance as a model system for cooperativity and as a tool for operationally skipping early stages, but not on its importance as the most powerful depth cue. Gibson (1950) emphasized that the most powerful depth cue was monocular movement parallax, since even one-eyed observers could estimate the direction in which an airplane was flying. Gibson proposed that the optical flow pattern was sufficient to determine the direction in which one was moving. In important papers, Lee (1974) and Nakayama & Loomis (1974) elaborated on Gibson's proposal and provided mathematical descriptions of the information available in optical flow patterns. Nakayama & Loomis also showed how a particular higher-order variable of optical flow might be extracted by velocity-sensitive neurons. Recently, Regan & Beverley (1978) proposed that changing-size tuned channels might locally extract information that would enable the visual system to construct global flow patterns without using distant interactions. Furthermore, Regan & Cynader (1979) found neurons in the cat cortex that operate only when a pair of nearby edges move in opposite directions, but are not sensitive to movement per se since they are not active when the edges move in the same direction. In a further observation, Regan & Beverley (1979) found that inspecting a radial flow pattern depressed visual sensitivity to changes in the size of a small test square, but only when the square was located near the focus of the adapting flow pattern. They regard this as evidence that their neurophysiological local channels tuned to expansion-contraction can find the fixed point in any global flow pattern. Once again, here is a rare case when a type PP model seems to be complemented by a type NP model.

Temporal factors in stereopsis were studied by Morgan (1975) and independently by Ross & Hogben (1975). They found a Pulfrich-like effect with AM in the horizontal direction (instead of RM as in the classical Pulfrich illusion). That dimming one eye's view was equivalent to retarding that view was first shown with dynamic RDS by Julesz & White (1969). In an AM study Burr & Ross (1979) presented spots of light moving stroboscopically against a background of dynamic noise. Binocular delay of the moving dots (without real binocular disparity, only disparity on the AM-generated interpolated positions) yielded vivid stereoscopic depth. Further, temporal delay combined additively with spatial disparity. The threshold temporal delay of 160 μsec corresponded to 2 sec arc virtual disparity (which is the smallest stereoacuity that can be achieved with real disparity under optimal laboratory conditions). Since frames were presented every 50 msec, the stereoscopic system could calculate delays of 0.25% of the presentation period!

Williams & Lit (1980) studied the Hess effect, a monocular analog of the Pulfrich effect. When images of a pair of vertically aligned targets of unequal luminance move horizontally across the retina of a stationary eye, the brighter target appears to lead the dimmer. This is an interesting phenomenon and could be studied with gratings having different SF, since the MTF of the human visual system dims gratings with higher SFs. Indeed, Campbell & Maffei (1979) observed that when two gratings were rotated with the same velocity, the one with the higher SF seemed to slow down, and at low contrast even appeared at a standstill, while the lower SF grating seemed to rotate.

4.0 HYPERCYCLOPEAN CHANNELS

The search for multiple channels, so successfully carried out a decade ago in the luminance domain, has lately brought similar findings beyond the "cyclopean retina" of Julesz (1971). Indeed, the study of aftereffects to adaptation, and of detection and discrimination thresholds following adaptation and during masking, that worked so admirably for the luminance stage, seem to work for the hypercyclopean stage as well.

Because cyclopean methodology skips earlier receptor and transducer stages and selectively stimulates the rich network of the CNS, it might reveal general properties of brain organization as a processor of information. Indeed, the many retinal and LGN stages specialized for processing luminance information are "blind" to the cyclopean information portrayed by RDS, particularly dynamic RDS (Julesz 1971, Ross 1974, Breitmeyer et al 1975).

Traditionally, research in vision and audition has examined how the prothetic continua of brightness (luminance) or loudness (pressure) are converted into the metathetic continua of spatial-extent, SF, or pitch (Stevens 1975). In cyclopean research the input variable is already a metathetic quantity (e.g. binocular disparity) and the output (e.g. segregated areas at a certain depth) also consists of metathetic quantities. It would therefore seem that problems of local-global interactions, nonlinearity-linearity, cooperativity-memory, etc could be more generally studied at the hypercyclopean level than at the hypocyclopean level.

It took only 4 years from the introduction of the random-dot stereogram methodology into psychology by Julesz (1960) until Papert (1964) produced a cyclopean figural aftereffect of tilt and found that RDS-produced edges yielded as large aftereffects as conventional edges. A similar cyclopean figural aftereffect of contour displacement was reported by Walker & Krüger (1972). The first three-dimensional repulsion aftereffect of perceived depth in RDS was observed by Blakemore & Julesz (1971), but they could not draw conclusions about the nature of the stereoscopic mechanisms involved because there are a number of underlying alternative mechanisms that could account for their findings. As has been pointed out by Ganz (1966), Blakemore & Sutton (1969), Anstis (1975) and Nelson (1975), the presence of figural aftereffects suggests the existence of two or more channels along which stimuli are represented. In this view an aftereffect is based on the imbalance in the overall response distribution following fatigue or adaptation of a subset of these channels. What is left unspecified by the Blakemore & Julesz finding is the specific nature of these stereoscopic channels.

A relevant study was performed by Tyler (1975), who reported aftereffects of tilt and size following prolonged viewing of a RDS portraying a corrugated sinusoid in depth (disparity grating). He also observed a perceived shift in the SF of a test disparity grating after adapting to a disparity grating of slightly different SF. Tyler inferred—by analogy to similar findings with luminance gratings by Campbell & Maffei (1971), Blakemore & Sutton (1969) and Blakemore et al (1970)—the existence of hypercyclopean channels selective for the orientation and SF of depth patterns. Schumer & Ganz (1979a) studied the subthreshold summation of disparity gratings with f and $3f$ corrugation frequencies and showed that at detection threshold each hypercyclopean channel is sensitive only to corrugated gratings of a specific frequency. Further, this threshold does not depend on the relative phase (spatial position) of the two disparity gratings. These cyclopean channels appear to interact with each other according only to probability summation. Schumer & Ganz also found that disparity gratings can selectively adapt stereoscopic channels tuned to the SF of disparity modulation. These channels are bandpass, but are more broadly tuned than the analogous channels in the luminance domain. The hypercyclopean channel bandwidth revealed by adaptation is 2-3 octaves (Schumer & Ganz 1979a), while hypocyclopean channel bandwidths measured by adaptation (Blakemore & Campbell 1969) and by filtered masking noise (Stromeyer & Julesz 1972) are about 1-1.5 octaves.

The masking noise paradigm was tried in the hypercyclopean domain by Tyler & Julesz (1978) using a narrowband compound disparity grating to mask a disparity grating. They found sharper critical bands than Schumer & Ganz, and thus the suprathreshold masking experiments reveal more global hypercyclopean channels in the spatial domain than do threshold experiments with adaptation. This is in contrast to the luminance masking experiments which yield similar critical bands to the values obtained by adaptation. Whether frequency beats "sharpen" the channel bandwidth estimates of Tyler & Julesz (1978) as was the case with "sharp" luminance channels (see Section 2.1) remains to be seen.

Both the adaptation and masking results with luminance gratings suggest antagonistic center-surround hypercyclopean receptive fields, which would explain the bandpass phenomena. Anstis et al (1978) observed a hypercyclopean Craik-O'Brien-Cornsweet illusion in which a spatial disparity transient causes a perceived global depth shift between two sides of a RDS surface which are actually of the same disparity. This also suggests lateral inhibitory interactions among pools of disparity units. Let us stress that the disparity-grating-frequency tuned hypercyclopean channels should not be confused with the SF-tuned channels in the luminance domain that are utilized in stereopsis, and which were discussed in Section 3.5.

Up to this point, the similarity between hypercyclopean-frequency-tuned channels and those in the luminance domain is striking. If these hypercyclopean channels were to be linear in disparity, then the Fourier transform of their SF tuning curve would give their disparity weighting function (receptive field profile) in the spatial domain. Indeed, a powerful depth (disparity) averaging effect in stereopsis helps to probe the linearity of this system in the disparity domain. The definition of linearity requires that if a hypercyclopean channel is stimulated by a spatiotemporal disparity signal that falls within its critical band, then another spatiotemporal disparity signal having the same average disparity distribution elicits the same output.

A number of studies with classical line stereograms have revealed disparity averaging (Tyler 1971, Richards 1972, Stigmar 1970, Foley 1976). Foley (1976, Birch & Foley 1979) showed that contributions to disparity averaging mechanisms are weighted according to the relative luminances of the target lines. Foley & Richards (1978) observed disparity averaging for binocular lines with disparities as great as 4° arc and for mixtures of nonsymmetric disparities. The averaging of signals from disparity detector pools is a phenomenon foreign to both known physiological findings as well as to psychophysically based models of stereopsis. All these models assume that disparity detectors, when activated, convey fixed disparity values to higher centers, though the hysteresis effect of Fender & Julesz (1967) clearly argues for an alternative interpretation.

Disparity averaging with RDS was first shown by Kaufman et al (1973), who presented the two combined half-images of a RDS to one eye, but a weighted mixture of the two half-images to the other eye, and varied the ratio of their brightnesses but kept their total brightness constant. As the ratio of the brightnesses varied (but was different from 1), depth was seen. Perceived depth depended on the disparity of the cyclopean target, but also increased linearly with the brightness ratio for smaller disparities (4-8 min arc). For slightly larger disparities (9-10 min arc), however, perceived depth jumped rapidly to full depth as soon as small imbalances in the half-field brightnesses were introduced.

Disparity averaging with RDS was studied in detail by Schumer (1979, Schumer & Ganz 1979b), using the technique of portraying multiple surfaces by even and odd rows of a RDS, respectively. He found that threshold for a corrugated sinusoid presented simultaneously and spatially overlapping with a flat surface was exactly twice the threshold for a corrugated sinusoid presented alone. This follows if the sinusoid and flat surface average to produce an effective stimulus with one-half the amplitude of the sinusoid alone. Further, disparity averaging was found to hold above threshold. The discrimination of a sinusoidal from a square wave disparity grating was first measured and found to occur well above detection threshold. It was then shown that in order to discriminate a sinusoid presented simultaneously with a flat surface from a square wave, the sinusoid again required twice the amplitude of the just-discriminable sinusoid when presented alone. Thus the combined surfaces were perceived according to disparity averaging.

What are the disparity limits of this averaging? The Kaufman et al (1973) study mentioned earlier showed linear weighting of disparity information up to about 8 min arc. Recently, Schumer & Julesz (1980d) used a different method to establish limits for disparity averaging. A split-screen display was used to test the discriminability of a sinusoidal disparity grating from a similar grating, but of twice the amplitude, and presented simultaneously with a flat RDS surface. As expected, discrimination was impossible at low amplitudes, but at about 4 min arc, the percept of the sine plus flat surface became discriminable by the presence of small protruding "nipples" at the peaks and troughs. This shows a sudden departure from the regime of disparity averaging and entry into a nonlinear domain of disparity processing.

Schumer & Julesz (1980b) measured forced-choice discrimination between flat and sinusoidal corrugated surfaces with large mean disparities (depth pedestals) using presentation times of 100 msec. Sensitivity was measured for a range of pedestal sizes and corrugation frequencies. It was found that the hypercyclopean MTF for disparity changes its shape (gets narrower) as the disparity pedestal increases, showing further the nonlinear behavior of the stereopsis system beyond the limits of disparity averaging. It is this nonlinear range between 4-50 min arc disparities where the nonlinear excitatory and inhibitory interactions between disparity detectors are taking place and where cooperative models of stereopsis are suggested.

We have seen how disparity domain interactions lead to hypercyclopean aftereffects, depth averaging, etc which Nelson (1977) described in a scholarly paper on "the plasticity of correspondence." The paper is a treasure chest of perceptual literature related to binocular vision, as is his earlier paper on a cooperative model of stereopsis (Nelson 1975). He discusses several new "induced effects" (based on vertical disparity) which are one of the most important plastic phenomena of stereopsis. Arditi (1979) studied the induced effect and noted that oblique structures in the stereograms are necessary to obtain it.

The selective stimulation of the cyclopean retina has yielded many hypercyclopean results that are analogous to hypocyclopean findings. This fact gives us confidence in the psychological methods used to explore both processing stages. This fact is also reassuring in that some general principles of brain functioning have been revealed that go far beyond luminance processing. On the other hand, hypercyclopean phenomena exhibit some complex properties—cooperativity and plasticity—that are less prevalent at earlier processing stages. They seem to be the next logical step to study. Furthermore, the ubiquitous microcomputer brings the real-time generation of dynamic RDS within the reach of any laboratory. That one can operationally skip several processing stages by psychological means alone —merely by utilizing binocularity—is a lucky break and should continue to be exploited by psychologists and neurophysiologists whenever possible.

5.0 EPILOGUE

We have focused on select topics that we feel constitute a new, unified trend in visual perception. We hope that our review has benefited from this unifying principle and shows where progress was made and what the unsolved problems might be. Among important findings and ideas that we could not review here are the interesting global theories of perception ranging from the brush-fire model of Blum (1973) to the relativistic model of movement foreshortening by Caelli et al (1978). Unfortunately, in these global theories the perceptual atoms are not defined, so they do not fit in our main theme. Also omitted is the Lie-algebra theory of Hoffman (1977, 1978) which is based on local operators, but these operators are so general that countless perceptual or neurophysiological atoms could be proposed as candidates, and those suggested by Hoffman are rather speculative, as discussed by Caelli (1977), Bruter (1977), Dodwell (1977), and Fregnac (1977).

The interesting field of perceptual constancies was also omitted except for scaling invariance in movement and depth perception. The crucial problems of foveal attention and eye movements were only hinted at, and temporal factors in vision were only briefly treated. While we discussed some top-down processes and learning phenomena, we only did so to emphasize that even in the earliest processing stages central processes do participate.

Within our own speciality we had to skip important work on binocular rivalry and binocular summation, infant perceptual development, amblyopia and stereoblindness, diagnosis of impaired stereopsis by evoked potentials elicited by dynamic RDS and random-dot correlograms, hemispheric localization and horopter problems in global stereopsis, psychoanatomic studies (the tracing of the information flow by RDS).

We hope that the work we reviewed gave a sense of the new collaborative spirit which appears to be infusing diverse areas of vision research that not long ago were pursued rather independently. It seems that this cohesion reflects more than some analogies between different descriptive levels, but rather signifies an appreciation of how these levels organize in an integrated system.

ACKNOWLEDGMENTS

We thank Mrs. Dorothy Caivano for her skillful assistance in typing and updating this manuscript and Mrs. Rhoda Iosso for helping with references and figures.

Literature Cited

Albrecht, D. G., De Valois, R. L., Thorell, L. G. 1980. Visual cortical neurons: are bars or gratings the optimal stimuli? *Science* 207:88–90

Allman, J. M., Baker, J. F., Newsome, W. T., Petersen, S. E. 1980. The cortical visual areas of the owl monkey: Topographic organization and functional correlates. In *Multiple Cortical Somatic Sensory-Motor, Visual and Auditory Areas and Their Connectivities,* ed. C. N. Woolsey. Clifton, NJ: Humana. In press

Anstis, S. M. 1975. What does visual perception tell us about visual coding. In *Handbook of Psychobiology,* ed. M. S. Gazzaniga, C. Blakemore. New York: Academic

Anstis, S. M. 1978. Apparent movement. See Held et al 1978, pp. 655–73

Anstis, S. M., Howard, I. P., Rogers, B. 1978. A Craik-O'Brien-Cornsweet illusion for visual depth. *Vision Res.* 18:213–17

Arditi, A. R. 1979. *An explanation of the induced size effect in binocular vision.* PhD thesis. New York Univ., NY

Arend, L. E., Lange, R. V. 1979. Phase-dependent interaction of widely separated spatial frequencies in pattern discrimination. *Vision Res.* 19:1089–92

Arend, L. E., Lange, R. V. 1980. Narrowband spatial mechanisms in apparent contrast matching. *Vision Res.* 20: 143–47

Armington, J. C., Krauskopf, J., Wooten, B. R., eds. 1978. *Visual Psychophysics and Physiology.* New York: Academic. 488 pp.

Atkinson, J., Campbell, F. W. 1974. The effect of phase on the perception of compound gratings. *Vision Res.* 16:337–44

Barlow, H. B. 1953. Summation and inhibition in the frog's retina. *J. Physiol.* 119:69–88

Barlow, H. B. 1978. The efficiency of detecting changes of density in random dot patterns. *Vision Res.* 18:637–50

Beck, J. J. 1967. Perceptual grouping produced by line figures. *Percept. Psychophys.* 2:491–95

Beck, J. J. 1973. Similarity grouping of curves. *Percept. Mot. Skills* 36:1331–41

Beck, J. J., Ambler, B. 1972. Discriminability of differences in line slope and line arrangement as a function of mask delay. *Percept. Psychophys.* 12:33–38

Bekesy, G. von. 1929. Auditory thresholds. Transl. E. G. Wever 1960. *Experiments in Hearing.* New York: McGraw-Hill

Bell, H. H., Lappin, J. S. 1973. Sufficient conditions for the discrimination of motion. *Percept. Psychophys.* 14:45–50

Bergen, J. R., Wilson, H. R., Cowan, J. D. 1979. Further evidence for four mechanisms mediating vision at threshold: sensitivities to complex gratings and aperiodic stimuli. *J. Opt. Soc. Am.* 69:1580–86

Biederman, I. 1980. On the semantics of a glance at a scene. See Kubovy & Pomerantz 1980

Birch, E. E., Foley, J. M. 1979. The effects of duration and luminance on binocular depth mixture. *Perception* 8:263–67

Bishop, P. O. 1973. Neurophysiology of binocular single vision and stereopsis. In *Handbook of Sensory Physiology*, ed. R. Jung, 7(3A):256–305. Berlin: Springer

Blake, R., Levinson, E. 1977. Spatial properties of binocular neurones in the human visual system. *Exp. Brain Res.* 27: 221–32

Blakemore, C. 1978. Maturation and modification in the developing visual system. See Held et al 1978, pp. 377–436

Blakemore, C., Campbell, F. W. 1969. On the existence of neurones in the human visual system selectively sensitive to the orientation and size of retinal images. *J. Physiol.* 203:237–60

Blakemore, C., Julesz, B. 1971. Stereoscopic depth aftereffect produced without monocular cues. *Science* 171:286–88

Blakemore, C., Nachmias, J., Sutton, P. 1970. The perceived spatial-frequency shift: Evidence for frequency-selective neurones in the human brain. *J. Physiol.* 210:727–50

Blakemore, C., Sutton, P. 1969. Size adaptation: A new aftereffect. *Science* 166: 245–47

Blum, H. 1973. Biological shape and visual science. *J. Theor. Biol.* 38(1):205–87

Braddick, O. J. 1970. Binocular fusion and perceptual processing. *Ophthalmol. Opt.* 10:993–1003

Braddick, O. J. 1974. A short-range process in apparent motion. *Vision Res.* 14:519–27

Braddick, O. J., Adlard, A. 1978. Apparent motion and the motion detector. In *Visual Psychophysics and Physiology*, ed. J. C. Armington, J. Krauskopf, B. R. Wooten. New York: Academic

Braddick, O. J., Campbell, F. W., Atkinson, J. 1978. Channels in vision: Basic aspects. See Held et al 1978, pp. 3–38

Breitmeyer, B. G. 1973. A relationship between the detection of size, rate, orientation and direction in the human visual system. *Vision Res.* 13:41–58

Breitmeyer, B. G., Julesz, B. 1975. The role of on and off transients in determining the psychophysical spatial frequency response. *Vision Res.* 15:411–15

Breitmeyer, B. G., Julesz, B., Kropfl, W. 1975. Dynamic random dot stereograms reveal an up-down anisotropy and a left-right isotropy between cortical hemifields. *Science* 187:269–70

Brewster, D. 1845. Notice on two new properties of the retina. *Trans. Br. Assoc.*, p. 8

Brindley, G. S. 1960. Two more visual theorems. *Q. J. Exp. Psychol.* 12:110–12

Bruter, C. P. 1977. On Hoffman's work. *Cah. Psychol.* 20:183–95

Burr, D. C. 1980. Motion smear. *Nature* 284:164–65

Burr, D. C., Ross, J. 1979. How does binocular delay give information about depth? *Vision Res.* 19:523–32

Burt, P., Julesz, B. 1980. A disparity gradient limit for binocular fusion. *Science* 208:615–17

Burt, P., Julesz, B., Kropfl, W. 1979. Disparity limits set by element and target shape in random-dot stereograms. *Invest. Ophthalmol. Visual Sci.* 18:174 (Suppl.)

Burt, P., Sperling, G. 1980. Time, distance, and feature trade-offs in visual apparent motion. *Psychol. Rev.* In press

Burt, P., Sperling, G., Julesz, B. 1978. The range of stereopsis. *J. Opt. Soc. Am.* 68:1365

Caelli, T. M. 1977. Criticism of the LTG/NP Theory of perceptual psychology. *Cah. Psychol.* 20:197–204

Caelli, T. M., Hoffman, W., Lindman, H. 1978. Subjective Lorentz transformations and the perception of motion. *J. Opt. Soc. Am.* 68:402–11

Caelli, T. M., Julesz, B. 1978. On perceptual analyzers underlying visual texture discrimination: Part I. *Biol. Cybern.* 28:167–75

Caelli, T. M., Julesz, B. 1979. Psychophysical evidence for global feature processing in visual texture discrimination. *J. Opt. Soc. Am.* 69:675–78

Caelli, T. M., Julesz, B., Gilbert, E. N. 1978. On perceptual analyzers underlying visual texture discrimination: Part II. *Biol. Cybern.* 29:201–14

Campbell, F. W., Cooper, G. F., Enroth-Cugell, C. 1969. The spatial selectivity of the visual cells of the cat. *J. Physiol.* 203:223–35

Campbell, F. W., Maffei, L. 1971. The tilt after-effect: A fresh look. *Vision Res.* 11:833–40

Campbell, F. W., Maffei, L. 1979. Stopped visual motion. *Nature* 278:192

Campbell, F. W., Robson, J. G. 1968. Application of Fourier analysis to the visibility of gratings. *J. Physiol.* 197:551–66

Cannon, M. W. Jr. 1979. Contrast sensation: A linear function of stimulus contrast. *Vision Res.* 19:1045–52

Carlson, C. R., Anderson, C. H., Moeller, J. R. 1980. Visual illusions without low spatial frequencies. *Invest. Ophthalmol. Visual Sci.* 19:165 (Suppl.)

Carpenter, R. H. S., Blakemore, C. 1973. Interactions between orientations in human vision. *Exp. Brain Res.* 18:287–303

Cherry, E. C. 1953. Some experiments on the recognition of speech with one and with two ears. *J. Acoust. Soc. Am.* 25:975–79

Comerford, J. P. 1974. Stereopsis with chromatic contours. *Vision Res.* 14:975–82

Coren, S., Girgus, J. S. 1978. Visual illusions. See Held et al 1978, pp. 549–68

√Cowey, A., Porter, J. 1979. Brain damage and global stereopsis. *Proc. R. Soc. London Ser. B* 204:399–407

Dev, P. 1975. Perception of depth surfaces in random-dot stereograms: A neural model. *Int. J. Man-Mach. Stud.* 7:511–28

De Valois, K. K. 1977a. Independence of black and white: Phase specific adaptation. *Vision Res.* 17:209–15

De Valois, K. K. 1977b. Spatial frequency adaptation can enhance contrast sensitivity. *Vision Res.* 17:1057–65

De Valois, R. L. 1973. Central mechanisms of color vision. See Bishop 1973, pp. 209–53

√De Valois, R. L., De Valois, K. K. 1980. Spatial vision. *Ann. Rev. Psychol.* 31:309–41

de Weert, C. M. M. 1979. Colour contours and stereopsis. *Vision Res.* 19:555–64

Dichgans, J., Brandt, T. 1978. Visual-vestibular interaction: Effects on self-motion perception and postural control. See Held et al 1978, pp. 755–804

Diner, D. 1978. *Hysteresis in human binocular fusion: A second look.* PhD thesis. Calif. Inst. Technol., Pasadena

Dodwell, P. C. 1977. Criteria for a neurophysiological theory of perception. *Cah. Psychol.* 20:175–82

Dodwell, P. C. 1978. Human perception of patterns and objects. See Held et al 1978, pp. 523–49

Estevez, O., Cavonius, C. R. 1976. Low-frequency attentuation in the detection of gratings: sorting out the artefacts. *Vision Res.* 16:497–500

Felton, T. B., Richards, W., Smith, R. A. 1972. Disparity processing of spatial frequencies in man. *J. Physiol.* 225:349–62

Fender, D. H., Julesz, B. 1967. Extension of Panum's fusional area in binocularly stabilized vision. *J. Opt. Soc. Am.* 57:819–30

Ferster, D. 1979. *Neurons sensitive to binocular depth in areas 17 and 18 of the cat visual cortex.* Soc. Neurosci. 9th ann. meet., Abstr. 783

Fischer, B., Krüger, J. 1979. Disparity tuning

and binocularity of single neurons in cat visual cortex. *Exp. Brain Res.* 35:1–8

Foley, J. M. 1976. Binocular depth mixture. *Vision Res.* 16:1263–67

Foley, J. M. 1978. Primary distance perception. See Held et al 1978, pp. 181–214

Foley, J. M., Legge, G. E. 1979. Contrast detection and discrimination. *Invest. Ophthalmol. Visual Sci.* 18:250–51 (Suppl.)

Foley, J. M., Richards, W. A. 1978. Binocular depth mixtures with non-symmetric disparities. *Vision Res.* 18:251–56

Foster, D. H., Mason, R. J. 1980. Irrelevance of local position information in visual adaptation to random arrays of small geometric elements. *Perception* 9:217–21

Fox, R. 1978. Visual masking. See Held et al 1978, pp. 629–54

Fregnac, Y. 1977. Contradictions between L.T.G. model and neurophysiology. *Cah. Psychol.* 20:209–11

Frisby, J. P., Clatworthy, J. L. 1975. Learning to see complex random-dot stereograms. *Perception* 4:173–78

Frisby, J. P., Mayhew, J. E. W. 1977. Global processes in stereopsis: some comments on Ramachandran and Nelson (1976). *Perception* 6:195–206

Frome, F. S., Levinson, J. Z., Danielson, J. T., Clavadetscher, J. E. 1979. Shifts in perception of size after adaptation to gratings. *Science* 206:1327–29

Fuortes, M. G. F., Hodgkin, A. L. 1964. Changes in time scale and sensitivity in the omatidia of Limulus. *J. Physiol.* 172:239–63

Furchner, C. S., Ginsburg, A. P. 1978. "Monocular rivalry" of a complex waveform. *Vision Res.* 18:1641–48

Gagalowicz, A. 1979. *Stochastic texture fields synthesis from a priori given second-order statistics.* Proc. Pattern Recognition and Image Processing Conf., Aug. 6–8, Chicago, pp. 376–81

Ganz, L. 1966. Mechanism of the figural aftereffects. *Perception* 73:128–50

Ganz, L. 1978. Sensory deprivation and visual discrimination. See Held et al 1978, pp. 437–88

Georgeson, M. A. 1976. Antagonism between channels for pattern and movement in human vision. *Nature* 259:413–15

Georgeson, M. A., Sullivan, G. D. 1975. Contrast constancy: deblurring in human vision by spatial frequency channels. *J. Physiol.* 252:627–56

Gibson, E. J. 1978. Perceptual aspects of the reading process and its development. See Held et al 1978, pp. 731–52

Gibson, J. J. 1950. *The Perception of the Visual World.* Boston: Houghton Mifflin

Gibson, J. J. 1979. *The Ecological Approach to Visual Perception.* Boston: Houghton Mifflin

Ginsburg, A. P. 1975. Is the illusory triangle physical or imaginary? *Nature* 257:219–20

Ginsburg, A. P., Cannon, M. W., Nelson, M. A. 1980. Suprathreshold processing of complex visual stimuli: Evidence for linearity in contrast perception. *Science* 208:619–21

Glass, L. 1969. Moire effect from random dots. *Nature* 243:578–80

Glass, L., Switkes, E. 1976. Pattern recognition in humans: Correlation which cannot be perceived. *Perception* 5:67–72

Gouras, P. 1970. Trichromatic mechanisms in single cortical neurons. *Science* 169:489–92

Graham, N. 1977. Visual detection of aperiodic spatial stimuli by probability summation among narrowband channels. *Vision Res.* 17:637–52

Graham, N. 1980a. Psychophysics of spatial-frequency channels. See Kubovy & Pomerantz 1980

Graham, N. 1980b. Spatial frequency channels in human vision: Detecting edges without edge detectors. See Harris 1980

Graham, N., Nachmias, J. 1971. Detection of grating patterns containing two spatial frequencies: A comparison of single-channel and multiple-channel models. *Vision Res.* 11:251–59

Graham, N., Robson, J. G., Nachmias, J. 1978. Grating summation in fovea and periphery. *Vision Res.* 18:815–25

Graham, N., Rogowitz, B. E. 1976. Spatial pooling properties deduced from the detectability of FM and quasi-AM gratings: a reanalysis. *Vision Res.* 16:1021–26

Green, D. M., Luce, R. D. 1975. Parallel psychometric functions from a set of independent detectors. *Psychol. Rev.* 82:483–86

Gregory, R. L. 1977. Vision with isoluminant colour contrast: 1. A projection technique and observations. *Perception* 6:113–19

Gregory, R. L., Harris, J. 1974. Illusory contours and stereo depth. *Percept. Psychophys.* 15:411–16

Hamerly, J. R., Quick, R. F., Reichert, T. A. 1977. A study of grating contrast judgement. *Vision Res.* 17:201–8

Harmon, L. D., Julesz, B. 1973. Masking in visual recognition: effects of two-dimensional filtered noise. *Science* 180:1194–97

Harris, C. S., ed. 1980. *Visual Coding and Adaptability.* Hillside, NJ: Erlbaum. In press

Harvey, L. O. Jr., Gervais, M. J. 1980. Visual texture perception and Fourier analysis. *Percept. Psychophys.* In press

Hatwell, Y. 1978. Form perception and related issues in blind humans. See Held et al 1978, pp. 489–520

Heeley, D. W. 1979. A perceived spatial frequency shift at orientations orthogonal to adapting gratings. *Vision Res.* 19:1229–36

Hein, A. 1980. The development of visually guided behavior. See Harris 1980

Held, R. 1980. The rediscovery of adaptability in the visual system: Effects of extrinsic and intrinsic chromatic dispersion. See Harris 1980

Held, R., Leibowitz, H. W., Teuber, H.-L., eds. 1978. *Handbook of Sensory Physiology,* Vol. 8: *Perception.* Berlin: Springer

Helmholtz, H. von. 1909. *Physiological Optics,* ed. Opt. Soc. 1925, transl. from 3rd German ed. Republished by Dover, NY

Henning, G. B., Hertz, B. G., Broadbent, D. 1975. Some experiments bearing on the hypothesis that the visual system analyses spatial patterns in independent bands of spatial frequency. *Vision Res.* 14:1039–42

Hering, E. 1878. *Zur Lehre vom Lichtsinn.* Vienna: Gerold's Sohn

Hines, M. 1976. Line spread function variation near the fovea. *Vision Res.* 16:567–72

Hochberg, J. 1980. Levels of perceptual organization. See Kubovy & Pomerantz 1980

Hoekstra, J., van der Goot, D. P. J., van den Brink, G., Bilsen, F. A. 1974. The influence of the number of cycles upon the visual contrast threshold for spatial sine wave patterns. *Vision Res.* 14:365–68

Hoffman, W. C. 1977. An informal, historical description (with bibliography) of the "L.T.G./N.P." *Cah. Psychol.* 20:135–74

Hoffman, W. C. 1978. The Lie transformation group approach to visual neurophysiology. In *Formal Theories of Visual Perception,* ed. E. L. J. Leeuwenberg, H. F. J. M. Buffart. New York: Wiley

Hubel, D. H., Wiesel, T. N. 1959. Receptive fields of single neurones in the cat's striate cortex. *J. Physiol.* 148:574–91

Hubel, D. H., Wiesel, T. N. 1962. Receptive fields, binocular interaction and functional architecture in the cat's visual cortex. *J. Physiol.* 160:106–54

Hubel, D. H., Wiesel, T. N. 1968. Receptive fields and functional architecture of monkey striate cortex. *J. Physiol.* 195: 215–43

Hubel, D. H., Wiesel, T. N. 1970. Cells sensitive to binocular depth in area 18 of the Macaque monkey cortex. *Nature* 255: 41–42

Hubel, D. H., Wiesel, T. N., Stryker, M. P. 1978. Anatomical demonstration of orientation columns in macaque monkey. *J. Comp. Neurol.* 177:361–80

Hyson, M. T., Julesz, B., Fender, D. H. 1980. Vergence eye movements and postulated cortical compensations during the fusion of horizontally misaligned random dot stereograms. In *Recent Advances in Vision*. Tech. Dig., OSA Meet., Sarasota, Fla.

Ingle, D. 1978. Mechanisms of shape-recognition among vertebrates. See Held et al 1978, pp. 267–96

Johansson, G. 1978. Visual event perception. See Held et al 1978, pp. 675–712

Johansson, G., von Hofsten, C., Jansson, G. 1980. Event perception. *Ann. Rev. Psychol.* 31:27–63

Johnson, C. A., Leibowitz, H. W. 1979. Practice effects for visual resolution in the periphery. *Percept. Psychophys.* 25: 439–42

Jones, R. M., Tulunay-Keesey, U. 1980. Phase selectivity of spatial frequency channels. *J. Opt. Soc. Am.* 70:66–70

Julesz, B. 1960. Binocular depth perception of computer-generated patterns. *Bell Syst. Tech. J.* 39:1125–62

Julesz, B. 1961. Binocular depth perception and pattern recognition. *London Symp. Inf. Theory, 4th*, ed. C. Cherry, pp. 212–24. London: Butterworth

Julesz, B. 1962. Visual pattern discrimination. *IRE Trans. Inf. Theory* IT-8 84–92

Julesz, B. 1963. Towards the automation of binocular depth perception (AUTO-MAP-1). *Proc. IFIPS Congr., Munich, 1962*, ed. C. M. Popplewell. Amsterdam: North-Holland

Julesz, B. 1964. Binocular depth perception without familiarity cues. *Science* 145: 356–62

Julesz, B. 1971. *Foundations of Cyclopean Perception*. Chicago: Univ. Chicago Press

Julesz, B. 1975. Experiments in the visual perception of texture. *Sci. Am.* 232: 34–43

Julesz, B. 1978a. Global stereopsis: Cooperative phenomena in stereoscopic depth perception. See Held et al 1978, pp. 215–56

Julesz, B. 1978b. Visual texture discrimination using random-dot patterns: Comments. *J. Opt. Soc. Am.* 68:268–70

Julesz, B. 1980a. Spatial nonlinearities in the instantaneous perception of textures with identical power spectra. In *The Psychology of Vision*, ed. C. Longuet-Higgins, N. S. Sutherland. *Philos. Trans. R. Soc. London* 290:83–94

Julesz, B. 1980b. Spatial frequency channels in one-, two-, and three dimensional vision: Variations on a theme by Bekesy. See Harris 1980, pp. 263–316

Julesz, B. 1980c. Figure and ground perception in briefly presented iso-dipole textures. See Kubovy and Pomerantz 1980

Julesz, B., Breitmeyer, B., Kropfl, W. 1976. Binocular-disparity–dependent upper-lower hemifield anisotropy and left-right hemifield isotropy as revealed by dynamic random-dot stereograms. *Perception* 5:129–41

Julesz, B., Burt, P. 1979. *Cooperativity of nearby micropatterns in texture discrimination*. Presented at Psychon. Soc. Meet., Phoenix

Julesz, B., Caelli, T. 1979. On the limits of Fourier decompositions in visual texture perception. *Perception* 8:69–73

Julesz, B., Chang, J. J. 1976. Interaction between pools of binocular disparity detectors tuned to different disparities. *Biol. Cybern.* 22:107–19

Julesz, B., Chang, J. J. 1979. Symmetry perception and spatial-frequency channels. *Perception* 8:711–18

Julesz, B., Chang, J. J. 1980. Perceptual learning in random-dot cinematograms. *J. Opt. Soc. Am.* In press

Julesz, B., Gilbert, E. N., Shepp, L. A., Frisch, H. L. 1973. Inability of humans to discriminate between visual textures that agree in second-order statistics—revisited. *Perception* 2:391–405

Julesz, B., Gilbert, E. N., Victor, J. D. 1978. Visual discrimination of textures with identical third-order statistics. *Biol. Cybern.* 31:137–40

Julesz, B., Hesse, R. I. 1970. Inability to perceive the direction of rotational movement of line segments. *Nature* 225:243–44

Julesz, B., Miller, J. E. 1975. Independent spatial frequency tuned channels in binocular fusion and rivalry. *Perception* 4:125–43

Julesz, B., Payne, R. A. 1968. Differences between monocular and binocular stroboscopic movement perception. *Vision Res.* 8:433–44

Julesz, B., Spivack, G. J. 1967. Stereopsis

based on vernier acuity cues alone. *Science* 157:563–65

Julesz, B., Tyler, C. W. 1976. Neurontropy, an entropy-like measure of neural correlation in binocular fusion and rivalry. *Biol. Cybern.* 22:107–19

Julesz, B., White, B. W. 1969. Short-term visual memory and the Pulfrich phenomenon. *Nature* 222:639–41

Kahneman, D., Henik, A. 1980. Perceptual organization and attention. See Kubovy & Pomerantz 1980

Kaufman, L., Bacon, J., Barroso, F. 1973. Stereopsis without image segregation. *Vision Res.* 13:137–47

Kaufman, L., Lane, B. C. 1979. Depth perception relative to convergence distance. *Invest. Ophthalmol. Visual Sci.* 18:174 (Supple.)

Keesey, U. T. 1972. Flicker and pattern detection: A comparison of thresholds. *J. Opt. Soc. Am.* 62:446–48

Kelly, D. H. 1966. Frequency doubling in visual responses. *J. Opt. Soc. Am.* 56: 1628–33

Kelly, D. H. 1979. Motion and vision. II. Stablized spatio-temporal threshold surface. *J. Opt. Soc. Am.* 69:1340–49

King-Smith, P. E., Kulikowski, J. J. 1975. The detection of gratings by independent activation of line detectors. *J. Physiol.* 247:237–71

Koenderink, J. J., van Doorn, A. J. 1979. Spatiotemporal contrast detection threshold surface is bimodal. *Opt. Lett.* 4:32–34

√Kubovy, M., Pomerantz, J. R., eds. 1980. *Perceptual Organization.* Hillside, NJ: Erlbaum. In press

Kuffler, S. W. 1953. Discharge patterns and functional organization of mammalian retina. *J. Neurophysiol.* 16:37–68

Kulikowski, J. J., King-Smith, P. E. 1973. Spatial arrangement of line, edge and grating detectors revealed by sub-threshold summation. *Vision Res.* 13: 1455–78

Kulikowski, J. J., Tolhurst, D. J. 1973. Psychophysical evidence for sustained and transient detectors in human vision. *J. Physiol.* 232:149–62

Lappin, J. S., Bell, H. H. 1976. The detection of coherence in moving random-dot patterns. *Vision Res.* 16:161–68

Lappin, J. S., Doner, J. F., Kottas, B. L. 1980. Minimal conditions for the visual detection of structure and motion in three dimensions *Science* 209:717–19

Lee, D. N. 1974. Visual information during locomotion. In *Perception: Essays in Honor of James J. Gibson*, ed. R. B.

MacLeod, H. L. Pick Jr. Ithaca: Cornell Univ. Press

Legge, G. E. 1976. Adaptation to a spatial impulse: implication for Fourier transform models of visual processing. *Vision Res.* 16:1407–18

Legge, G. E. 1978. Space domain properties of a spatial frequency channel in human vision. *Vision Res.* 18:959–69

Legge, G. E. 1979. Spatial frequency masking in human vision: Binocular interactions. *J. Opt. Soc. Am.* 69:838–47

Levinson, E., Coyne, A., Gross, J. 1980. Synthesis of visually perceived movement. *Invest. Ophthalmol. Visual Sci.* 19:105 (Supple.)

Levinson, E., Sekuler, R. 1980. A two-dimensional analysis of direction specific adaptation. *Vision Res.* 20:103–7

Levinson, J. Z., Frome, F. S. 1979. Perception of size of one object among many. *Science* 206:1425–26

Licklider, J. C. R. 1948. The influence of interaural phase relations upon the masking of speech by white noise. *J. Acoust. Soc. Am.* 20:150–59

Limb, J. O., Rubinstein, C. B. 1977. A model of threshold vision incorporating inhomogeneity of the visual field. *Vision Res.* 17:571–84

Lipkin, B. S., Rosenfeld, A., eds. 1970. *Picture Processing and Psychopictorics.* New York: Academic

Logan, B. F. Jr. 1977. Information in the zero-crossings of bandpass signals. *Bell Syst. Tech. J.* 56:487–510

Lu, S., Fender, D. H. 1972. The interaction of color and luminance in stereoscopic vision. *Invest. Ophthalmol.* 11:482–90

MacAdam, D. L. 1970. *Sources of Color Science.* Cambridge, Mass: MIT Press

Maccracken, P. J., Bourne, J. A., Hayes, W. N. 1977. Experience and latency to achieve stereopsis: a replication. *Percept. Mot. Skills* 45:261–62

MacKay, D. M. 1957. Moving visual images produced by regular stationary patterns. *Nature* 180:849–50

MacKay, D. M. 1964. Central adaptation in mechanisms of form vision. *Nature* 203:993–94

MacKay, D. M. 1965. Visual noise as a tool of research. *J. Gen. Psychol.* 72:181–97

MacKay, D. M., MacKay, V. 1976. Antagonism between visual channels for pattern and movement? *Nature* 263: 312–14

Macleod, I. D. G., Rosenfeld, A. 1974. The visibility of gratings: Spatial frequency channels or bar-detecting units? *Vision Res.* 14:909–15

Maffei, L. 1978. Spatial frequency channels. See Held et al 1978, pp. 39–66

Maffei, L., Fiorentini, A. 1973. The visual cortex as a spatial frequency analyzer. *Vision Res.* 13:1255–67

Magnussen, S., Kurtenbach, W. 1980. Adapting to two orientations: Disinhibition in a visual aftereffect. *Science* 207:908–9

Marr, D. 1976. Early processing of visual information. *Philos. Trans. R. Soc. London Ser. B* 275:483–524

Marr, D. 1977. Artificial intelligence—a personal view. *Artif. Intell.* 9:37–48

Marr, D., Hildreth, E. 1979. *Theory of edge detection.* MIT Artif. Intell. Lab. Memo No. 518

Marr, D., Poggio, T. 1976. Cooperative computation of stereo disparity. *Science* 194:283–87

Marr, D., Poggio, T. 1979. A theory of human stereopsis. *Proc. R. Soc. London Ser. B* 204:301–28

Marr, D., Ullman, J. M., Poggio, T. 1979. Bandpass channels, zero-crossings, and early visual information processing. *J. Opt. Soc. Am.* 69:914–16

Martin, R. C., Pomerantz, J. R. 1978. Visual discrimination of texture. *Percept. Psychophys.* 24:420–28

Mayhew, J. E. W., Frisby, J. P. 1978a. Suprathreshold contrast perception and complex random textures. *Vision Res.* 18:895–98

Mayhew, J. E. W., Frisby, J. P. 1978b. Stereopsis in humans is not orientationally tuned. *Perception* 7:431–36

Mayhew, J. E. W., Frisby, J. P. 1978c. Contrast summation effects in stereopsis. *Perception* 7:537–50

Mayhew, J. E. W., Frisby, J. P. 1979. Convergent disparity discriminations in narrow-band–filtered random-dot stereograms. *Vision Res.* 19:63–71

Mayhew, J. E. W., Frisby, J. P. 1980a. The computation of binocular edges. *Perception* 9:69–86

Mayhew, J. E. W., Frisby, J. P. 1980b. *Computational and psychophysical studies towards a theory of human stereopsis.* Special issue of *Artificial Intelligence* on computer vision (Monogr.)

Mitchell, D. E. 1980. The influence of early visual experience on visual perception. See Harris 1980. In press

Morgan, M. J. 1975. Stereoillusion based on visual persistence. *Nature* 256:639–40

Movshon, J. A., Thompson, I. D., Tolhurst, D. J. 1978. Spatial summation in the receptive fields of simple cells in the cat's striate cortex. *J. Physiol.* 283:53–77

Nachmias, J., Sanbury, R. 1974. Grating contrast: Discrimination may be better than detection. *Vision Res.* 15:899–910

Nachmias, J., Weber, A. 1975. Discrimination of simple and complex gratings. *Vision Res.* 15:217–23

Nakayama, K., Loomis, J. M. 1974. Optical velocity patterns, velocity-sensitive neurons, and space perception: a hypothesis. *Perception* 3:63–80

Nelson, J. I. 1974. Motion sensitivity in peripheral vision. *Perception* 3:151–52

Nelson, J. I. 1975. Globality and stereoscopic fusion in binocular vision. *J. Theor. Biol.* 49:1–88

Nelson, J. I. 1977. The plasticity of correspondence: after effects, illusions and horopter shifts in depth perception. *J. Theor. Biol.* 66:203–66

Nelson, T. M., Bartley, S. H., Bourassa, C. M., Ball, R. J. 1971. What is a channel? *J. Gen. Psychol.* 84:133–77

Ogle, K. N. 1964. *Researches in Binocular Vision.* New York: Hafner

Osgood, C. E., Heyer, A. W. 1952. A new interpretation of figural after-effects. *Psychol. Rev.* 59:98–118

Oyama, T. 1978. Figural aftereffects. See Held et al 1978, pp. 569–94

Pantle, A., Sekuler, R. 1968. Size-detecting mechanisms in human vision. *Science* 162:1146–48

Papert, S. 1964. Stereoscopic synthesis as a technique for localizing visual mechanisms. *MIT Q. Prog. Rep.* 73:239–44

Petersik, J. T., Pantle, A. 1979. Factors controlling the competing sensations produced by a bistable stroboscopic display. *Vision Res.* 19:143–54

Pettigrew, J. D., Nikara, T., Bishop, P. O. 1968. Binocular interaction on single units in cat striate cortex: Simultaneous stimulation by single moving slit with receptive fields in correspondence. *Exp. Brain Res.* 6:391–410

Pfaffman, C. 1941. Gustatory afferent impulses. *J. Cell Comp. Physiol.* 17:243–58

Plateau, J. A. F. 1850. Quatrieme note sur de nouvelles applications curieuses de la persistance des impressions de la retine. *Bull. Acad. Sci. Belg.* 16:254–60

Poggio, G. F., Fischer, B. 1977. Binocular interaction and depth sensitivity in striate and prestriate cortex of behaving Rhesus monkey. *J. Neurophysiol.* 40:1392–1405

Pollack, I. 1973. Discrimination of third-order Markov constraints within visual displays. *Percept. Psychophys.* 13:276–80

Pomerantz, J. R. 1980. Perceptual organization in information processing. See Kubovy & Pomerantz 1980

Pomerantz, J. R., Kubovy, M. 1980. Perceptual organization: An overview. See Kubovy & Pomerantz 1980

Pratt, W. K., Faugeras, O. D., Gagalowicz, A. 1978. Visual discrimination of stochastic texture fields. *IEEE Trans. Syst. Manage. Cybern.* 8:796–804

Pressman, N. J., Haralick, R. M., Tyrer, H. W., Frost, J. K. 1979. Texture analysis for biomedical imagery. In *Biomedical Pattern Recognition and Image Processing*, ed. K. S. Fu, T. Pavlidis. Berlin: Dahlem Konferenzen

Purkinje, J. A. 1820. Beiträge für nähren Kenntniss des Schwindles aus heautognostischen Daten. In *Purkyne's sebrana spisy* (opera omnia), ed. K. J. Lhotak, 2:15–37. Prague (1937)

Purks, S. R., Richards, W. 1977. Visual texture discrimination using random patterns. *J. Opt. Soc. Am.* 67:765–71

Quick, R. F. Jr. 1974. A vector-magnitude model of contrast detection. *Kybernetik* 16:65–67

Quick, R. F. Jr., Mullins, W. W., Reichert, T. A. 1978. Spatial summation effects on two-component grating thresholds. *J. Opt. Soc. Am.* 68:116–21

Quick, R. F. Jr., Hamerly, J. R., Reichert, T. A. 1976. The absence of a measurable "critical band" at low suprathreshold contrasts. *Vision Res.* 16:351–56

Rabbitt, P., Cumming, G., Vyas, S. 1979. Improvement, learning and retention of skills at visual search. *Q. J. Exp. Psychol.* 31:441–59

Ramachandran, V. S., Braddick, O. 1973. Orientation-specific learning in stereopsis. *Perception* 2:371–76

Ramachandran, V. S., Gregory, R. L. 1978. Does colour provide an input to human motion perception? *Nature* 275:55–56

Ramachandran, V. S., Rao, V. M., Vidyasagar, T. R. 1973. The role of contours in stereopsis. *Nature* 242:412–14

Regan, D., Beverley, K. I. 1978. Looming detectors in the human visual pathway. *Vision Res.* 18:415–21

Regan, D., Beverley, K. I. 1979. Visually guided locomotion: Psychophysical evidence for a neural mechanism sensitive to flow patterns. *Science* 205:311–13

Regan, D., Cynader, M. 1979. Neurons in area 18 of cat visual cortex selectively sensitive to changing size: Nonlinear interactions between responses to two edges. *Vision Res.* 19:699–711

Reichardt, W. 1957. Autokorrelations-Auswertung als Funktionsprinzip des Zentralnervensystems. *Z. Naturforsch.* 12:448–57

Richards, W. 1972. Response functions for sine- and square-wave modulations of disparity. *J. Opt. Soc. Am.* 62:907–11

Richards, W. 1977. Stereopsis with and without monocular contours. *Vision Res.* 17:967–70

Richards, W., Kaye, M. G. 1974. Local versus global stereopsis: Two mechanisms? *Vision Res.* 14:1345–47

Richards, W., Polit, A. 1974. Texture matching. *Kybernetik* 16:155–62

Riggs, L. A., Day, R. H. 1980. Visual aftereffects derived from inspection of orthogonally moving patterns. *Science* 208:416–18

Robson, J. G. 1966. Spatial and temporal contrast sensitivity functions of the human eye. *J. Opt. Soc. Am.* 56:1141

Robson, J. G. 1975. Receptive fields: neural representation of the spatial and intensive attributes of the visual image. In *Handbook of Perception*, ed. E. C. Carterette, M. P. Friedman, 5:81–112. New York: Academic

Robson, J. G. 1980. Neural images: The physiological basis of spatial vision. See Harris 1980. In press

Robson, J. G., Graham, N. 1978. Probability summation and regional orientation in sensitivity across the visual field. *Invest. Ophthalmol. Visual Sci.* 17:221 (Suppl.)

Rogowitz, B. E., Nachmias, J. 1979. Phase-dependent masking and facilitation: Evidence for the non-linear processing of amplitude-modulated gratings. *Eur. Conf. Visual Percept., Noordwijkerhout, The Netherlands*

Ross, J. 1974. Stereopsis by binocular delay. *Nature* 248:363

Ross, J., Hogben, J. H. 1975. Short-term memory in stereopsis. *Vision Res.* 14:1195–201

Ross, J., Johnstone, J. R. 1980. Phase and detection of compound gratings. *Vision Res.* 20:189–92

Sachs, M. B., Nachmias, J., Robson, J. G. 1971. Spatial-frequency channels in human vision. *J. Opt. Soc. Am.* 61:1176–86

Savoy, R. L., McCann, J. J. 1975. Visibility of low-spatial–frequency sine-wave targets: Dependence on numbers of cycles. *J. Opt. Soc. Am.* 65:343–49

Saye, A., Frisby, J. P. 1975. The role of monocularly conspicuous features in facilitating stereopsis from random-dot stereograms. *Perception* 4:159–71

Schachter, B. J., Rosenfeld, A., Davis, L. S. 1978. Random mosaic models for tex-

tures. *IEEE Trans. Syst. Man Cybern.*
8:694–702
Schatz, B. 1978. *The computation of immediate texture perception.* Comp. Sci. Dep. Rep. No. 152, Carnegie-Mellon Univ., Pittsburgh, Pa.
Schumer, R. A. 1979. *Mechanisms in human stereopsis.* PhD thesis. Stanford Univ., Stanford, Calif.
Schumer, R. A., Ganz, L. 1979a. Independent stereoscopic channels for different extents of spatial pooling. *Vision Res.* 19:1303–44
Schumer, R. A., Ganz, L. 1979b. Disparity averaging in random dot stereopsis. *J. Opt. Soc. Am.* 69:1479
Schumer, R. A., Julesz, B. 1980a. *Limited area integration of binocular disparity detectors in global stereopsis.* Presented at Topical Meet. Recent Adv. in Vision, Opt. Soc. Am., Sarasota, Fla., p. SB2
Schumer, R. A., Julesz, B. 1980b. Maximum disparity limit for detailed depth resolution. *Invest. Ophthalmol. Visual Sci.* 19:106–7 (Suppl.)
Schumer, R. A., Julesz, B. 1980c. Disparity limit in dynamic random-dot stereograms without low spatial frequencies. In preparation
Schumer, R. A., Julesz, B. 1980d. The range of disparity-averaging in random-dot stereograms. In preparation
√Sekuler, R. 1974. Spatial vision *Ann. Rev. Psychol.* 25:195–232
Sekuler, R., Ganz, L. 1963. Aftereffect of seen motion with a stabilized retinal image. *Science* 139:419–20
Sekuler, R., Pantle, A., Levinson, E. 1978. Physiological basis of motion perception. See Held et al 1978, pp. 67–96
Shapley, R. M., Tolhurst, D. J. 1973. Edge detectors in human vision. *J. Physiol.* 229:165–83
Shaw, R., Turvey, M. T. 1980. Coalitions as models for ecosystems: A realist perspective on perceptual organization. See Kubovy & Pomerantz 1980
Shepard, R. N. 1980. Psychophysical complimentarity. See Kubovy & Pomerantz 1980
Shiffrin, R. M., Schneider, W. 1977. Controlled and automatic human information processing: II. Perceptual learning, automatic attending, and a general theory. *Psychol. Rev.* 84:127–90
Sokoloff, L., Reivich, M., Kennedy, C., Des Rosiers, M. H., Patlak, C. S., Pettigrew, K. D., Sakurada, O., Shinohara, M. 1977. The [14C]deoxyglucose method for the measurement of local cerebral glucose utilization: theory, procedure, and normal values in the conscious and

anesthetized albino rat. *J. Neurochem.* 28:897–916
Sperling, G. 1970. Binocular vision: A physical and a neural theory. *J. Am. Psychol.* 83:461–534
Sperling, G., Sondhi, M. M. 1968. Model for visual luminance discrimination and flicker detection. *J. Opt. Soc. Am.* 58:1133–45
Stevens, K. A. 1978. Computation of locally parallel structure. *Biol. Cybern.* 29:19–28
Stevens, S. S. 1975. *Psychophysics: Introduction to its Perceptual, Neural, and Social Prospects.* New York: Wiley
Stigmar, G. 1970. Observations on vernier and stereo acuity with special reference to their relationship. *Acta Ophthalmol.* 48:979–98
Stromeyer, C. F. III. 1978. Form-color aftereffects in human vision. See Held et al 1978, pp. 97–142
Stromeyer, C. F. III, Julesz, B. 1972. Spatial frequency masking in vision: Critical bands and spread of masking. *J. Opt. Soc. Am.* 62:1221–32
Stromeyer, C. F. III, Klein, S. 1975. Evidence against narrow-band spatial frequency channels in human vision: The detectability of frequency modulated gratings. *Vision Res.* 15:899–910
Stromeyer, C. F. III, Klein, S. 1974. Spatial frequency channels in human vision as asymmetric (edge) mechanisms. *Vision Res.* 14:1409–20
Stromeyer, C. F. III, Madsen, J. C., Klein, S. 1979. Direction-selective adaptation with very slow motion. *J. Opt. Soc. Am.* 69:1039–41
Sullivan, G. D., Georgeson, M. A., Oatley, K. 1972. Channels for spatial frequency selection and detection of single bars by the human visual system. *Vision Res.* 12:383–94
Sutherland, S. 1961. Figural aftereffects and apparent size. *Q. J. Exp. Psychol.* 13:222–28
Teller, D. 1980. Locus questions in visual science. See Harris 1980
Teuber, H.-L. 1978. The brain and human behavior. See Held et al 1978, pp. 879–920
Thomas, J. P. 1970. Model of the function of receptive fields in human vision. *Psychol. Rev.* 77:121–34
Thomas, J. P., Barker, R. A., Gille, J. 1979. A multidimensional space model for detection and discrimination of spatial patterns. In *Modeling and Simulation,* Vol. 10: Proc. 10th Ann. Pittsburgh Conf., ed. W. G. Vogt, M. H. Mickle

Tolhurst, D. J. 1972. Adaptation to square-wave gratings: Inhibition between spatial frequency channels in the human visual system. *J. Physiol.* 226:231–48

Treisman, A. 1978. The psychological reality of levels of processing. In *Levels of Processing and Human Memory,* ed. L. S. Cermak, F. I. M. Craik. Hillside, NJ: Erlbaum

Tyler, C. W. 1971. Stereoscopic depth movement: Two eyes less sensitive than one. *Science* 174:958–61

Tyler, C. W. 1973. Stereoscopic vision: Cortical limitations and a disparity scaling effect. *Science* 181:276–78

Tyler, C. W. 1974. Depth perception in disparity gratings *Nature* 251:140–42

Tyler, C. W. 1975. Stereoscopic tilt and size aftereffects. *Perception* 4:187–92

Tyler, C. W., Julesz, B. 1976. The neural transfer characteristic (Neurontropy) for binocular stochastic stimulation. *Biol. Cybern.* 23:33–37

Tyler, C. W., Julesz, B. 1978. Binocular cross-correlation in time and space. *Vision Res.* 18:101–5

Tyler, C. W., Julesz, B. 1980. On the depth of the cyclopean retina. *Exp. Brain Res.* 40. In press

Ullman, S. 1979. *The Interpretation of Visual Motion.* Cambridge, Mass: MIT Press

√Ullman, S. 1980. Against direct perception. *Behav. Brain Sci.* In press

Uttal, W. R. 1975. *An Autocorrelation Theory of Form Detection.* Hillside, NJ: Erlbaum

Uttal, W. R., Tucker, T. E. 1977. Complexity effects in form detection. *Vision Res.* 17:359–66

van Doorn, A. J., Koenderink, J. J., Bouman, M. A. 1972. The influence of the retinal inhomogeniety on the perception of spatial patterns. *Kybernetik* 10:223–30

van Meeteren, A. 1978. On the detective quantum efficiency of the human eye. *Vision Res.* 18:257–67

van Nes, F. L., Koenderink, J. J., Nas, H., Bowman, M. A. 1967. Spatiotemporal modulation transfer in the human eye. *J. Opt. Soc. Am.* 57:1082–88

Victor, J. D., Brodie, S. E. 1978. Disciminimable textures with identical Buffon-needle statistics. *Biol. Cybern.* 31: 231–34

Virsu, V., Rovamo, J. 1979. Visual resolution, contrast sensitivity, and the cortical magnification factor. *Exp. Brain Res.* 37:475–94

von der Heydt, R., Adorjani, C., Hanny, P., Baumgartner, G. 1978. Disparity sensitivity and receptive field incongruity

of units in the cat striate cortex. *Exp. Brain Res.* 31–523–45

Walker, J. T., Kruger, M. W. 1972. Figural aftereffects in random-dot stereograms without monocular contours. *Perception* 1:187–92

Watson, A. B. 1979. Probability summation over time. *Vision Res.* 19:515–22

Watson, A. B. 1980. Summation of grating patches implies many frequency-selective detectors at one retinal location. *Invest. Ophthalmol. Visual Sci.* 19 (Suppl.):45

Watson, A. B., Nachmias, J. 1980. Summation of asynchronous gratings. *Vision Res.* 20:91–94

Watson, A. B., Thompson, P. G., Murphy, B. J., Nachmias, J. 1980. Summation and discrimination of gratings moving in opposite directions. *Vision Res.* 20:341–47 .

Weisstein, N., Harris, C. S. 1980. Masking and the unmasking of distributed representations in the visual system. See Harris 1980

Weisstein, N., Harris, C. S., Berbaum, K., Tangney, J., Williams, A. 1977. Contrast reduction by small localized stimuli: Extensive spatial spread of above-threshold orientation selective masking. *Vision Res.* 17:341–50

Williams, J. M., Lit, A. 1980. Luminance dependent latency as measured by the Hess effect. *Invest. Ophthalmol. Visual Sci.* 19:166 (Suppl.)

Wilson, H. R., Bergen, J. R. 1979. A four mechanism model for threshold spatial vision. *Vision Res.* 19:19–32

Wilson, H. R., Giese, S. C. 1977. The significance of frequency gradients in binocular grating perception. *Vision Res.* 16:983–90

Wilson, H. R., Phillips, G., Rentschler, I., Hilz, R. 1979. Spatial probability summation and disinhibition in psychophysically measured line-spread functions. *Vision Res.* 19:593–98

Wohlgemuth, A. 1911. On the after-effect of seen movement. *Br. J. Psychol.* Monogr. Suppl. (PhD thesis). Cambridge: Univ. Press

Yin, R. K. 1978. Face perception: A review of experiments with infants, normal adults, and brain-injured persons. See Held et al 1978, pp. 593–608

Zeki, S. M. 1978. Functional specialisation in the visual cortex of the rhesus monkey. *Nature* 274:423–28

Zucker, S. W. E. 1976. On the structure of texture. *Perception* 5:419–36

Ann. Rev. Psychol. 1981. 32:629–58
Copyright © 1981 by Annual Reviews Inc. All rights reserved

TEST THEORY AND METHODS ❖354

David J. Weiss[1]

Department of Psychology, University of Minnesota, Minneapolis, Minnesota 55455

Mark L. Davison

Department of Social, Psychological, and Philosophical Foundations of Education, University of Minnesota, Minneapolis, Minnesota 55455

CONTENTS

INTRODUCTION

This review is concerned with the approximate period January 1975 through December 1979, including a few papers published in early 1980. The focus of the review is on practical procedures for converting psycholog-

[1]Preparation of this paper was supported by Contracts N000–14–79–C–0324, NR150–431, and N000–14–79–C–0172, NR150–433 from the Personnel and Training Programs, Office of Naval Research to David J. Weiss; and by a National Academy of Education Spencer Fellowship to Mark L. Davison.

0066-4308/81/0201-0629$01.00

ical observations into numerical form, commonly referred to as "test theory." Both the theory and the resulting methodologies are reviewed. Excluded are procedures commonly used for attitude scaling, both unidimensional and multidimensional. However, some scaling methods which have relationships with or utility for testing in the ability and achievement domains have been included, even though they may technically be considered to be scaling methods. Also not included is the considerable literature on data analytic procedures such as factor analysis, multiple regression, most of the literature on structural equations analysis, and statistical procedures which are considered by some to be part of psychological measurement. The review also does not include the growing literature on problems of reliability of observations (e.g. interrater reliability) or such measurement approaches as functional measurement, which have had little application to the general problems of measuring individual differences. Thus, the review is concerned with procedures for the measurement of ability, aptitude, and other cognitive variables, and problems of estimating the precision and utility (validity) of measurements of this type. Due to space limitations the considerable literature on item response modes, including formula scoring, option weighting and alternative response modes, as well as literature on the measurement of change, moderator and suppressor variables, some alternative test models, nondichotomous test models, adverse impact of test fairness definitions, test fairness to women, and bias in test item content is not reviewed here; an extended version of this chapter which includes this and other literature is available from the authors.

CLASSICAL TEST THEORY AND METHODS

Classical test theory (CTT), which has its roots in work by Spearman in the early 1900s, now is approximating its seventy-fifth birthday. Despite Lumsden's (1976) critique of CTT, research related to it seems to continue unabated. Perhaps this attests to the usefulness of this approach to instrument construction, or perhaps it attests to the inertia that is built into a system of education and training that produces researchers who continue to perpetuate methodologies which, while useful, can be replaced by more coherent methodologies.

Reliability

Research on reliability estimation in CTT continues to focus on minor modifications of old standby coefficients. Thus, Huck (1978a) has modified Hoyt's analysis of variance reliability estimation procedure (originally developed in 1941) to better estimate the "true" reliability coefficient. The result is a higher reliability estimate by better specifying the error variance.

Kaiser & Michael (1977) show that "old faithful" Kuder-Richardson (K-R) Formula 20 can be estimated from factor scores derived from "Little Jiffy" factor analysis. In two closely related papers, Raju (1977, 1979) generalizes coefficient alpha (the general case of K-R 20 and equivalent to Hoyt's coefficient) to the reliability coefficient for a "test battery." While the development seems mathematically appropriate, Raju does not attempt to describe what the reliability of the test battery means; this lack of coherence is characteristic of much of the research on reliability coefficients in CTT. Is a test battery reliable when the tests are all highly intercorrelated? If so, of what use is such a test battery? What kind of standard error of measurement (SEM) can be derived from the reliability coefficient for a test battery? How would such a SEM be used and interpreted in any practical situation? These are some of the kinds of questions that need to be considered with regard to such a generalization of coefficient alpha.

CTT psychometricians seem to be playing "will the real lower bound please stand up?" This compulsion has been pursued by ten Berge & Zegers (1978), Jackson & Agunwamba (1977), Nicewander (1975), and Woodhouse & Jackson (1977). These papers "improve upon" work done by Guttman in the 1940s by attempting to better estimate the "true" reliability from a given data set. Nicewander (1975) shows a relationship between image factor analysis and one of Guttman's lower bounds. The search is extended by Jackson (1979) from internal consistency coefficients to split-half coefficients, even though the former are more appropriate for estimating internal consistency of a set of items. Methods for better estimating split-half reliability were further studied by Callender & Osburn (1977a,b), who developed an algorithm to generate the maximum split-half reliability for a set of test items. They go on to show that their sample based maximized split-half routine gives a better estimate of population reliability than do some of the internal consistency methods, but under the unrealistic conditions of tau equivalence—a linear relation between true scores on the two halves.

Of course the Spearman-Brown (S-B) formula, now well into middle age, is still a topic of research in CTT. Allison (1975) generalizes the formula to fractional length tests, and Feldt (1975) provides a formula for the situation in which the assumption of equal variances is not met. Like Callender and Osburn's approach, Feldt's coefficient makes the relatively strong assumption that true scores in the two subtests are perfectly correlated. Another sample-based optimization procedure is presented by Huck (1978b) in his solution to the problem of estimating reliability when items are equally difficult. The only really "new" reliability estimation procedure to appear during this period is a maximum likelihood factor analytic based method developed by Werts et al (1978).

Common to all these reliability estimation procedures, however, is a major weakness of CTT—the sample-based nature of all of the estimation procedures used for reliability. Thus, reliability estimates are specifically a function of the particular set of items and sample of individuals on which the data have been collected. The logical fallacy, of course, is that the translation of reliability coefficients into errors of measurement results in errors of measurement which are specific to a particular test administration event. Consequently, the same individual tested with two different groups of individuals may obtain two different errors of measurement and estimates of true score, based simply on the group of testees with which the person has been tested. This is a serious problem in CTT which cannot be solved adequately by sample-based methods for determining test scores or estimates of precision of measurement.

Nevertheless, CTT marches on. Much of the reliability research continues to concentrate on coefficient alpha, with a recent salutary trend toward methods for testing the significance of alpha or testing the difference in alpha coefficients from different groups. Pandey & Hubert (1975) compare several interval estimation procedures for coefficient alpha, while Joe & Woodward (1975) provide an approximate confidence interval for maximum coefficient aplha, which shows maximum alpha to be a function of the item intercorrelations for a set of test items. Woodward & Bentler (1978) provide a statistical lower bound population reliability which is useful in estimating population values of reliability from sample estimates which are usually higher due to sampling error. They use the sampling distribution of estimated alpha coefficients to obtain a new coefficient which better estimates the population reliability. Two new reliability coefficients and one old one are estimated by Sedere & Feldt (1977) in comparison to the theoretical distribution of alpha; these authors define conditions under which each of the estimates of reliability studied appears to be appropriate.

One of the most useful developments during this period is a test for alpha coefficients on independent samples (Hakstian & Whalen 1976) which is useful for comparing the alpha coefficients derived from different groups of individuals, such as individuals in different treatment conditions. Their development is supported by simulation data and is useful since it allows conclusions to be drawn about the effects of testing conditions on measurement precision, an area of research which has not received much attention in past years. Thus, although many authors have hypothesized the effects of testing conditions on precision/reliability of measurement, the lack of a statistical test for independent samples to compare such reliability coefficients has limited the conclusions to be drawn from such studies.

Another major problem with CTT has been in the confusion that it has engendered among the concepts of internal consistency, homogeneity, and unidimensionality. This is exemplified in the paper by Green et al (1977), in which homogeneity and unidimensionality are equated as follows: "homogeneous items have but a single common factor among them and are related to the underlying factor of ability or attitude in a linear matter" (p. 830), while internal consistency is defined as "interrelatedness but not necessarily unidimensionality." A related article by Terwilliger & Lele (1977) attempts to clarify the relationships among internal consistency, homogeneity, and Guttman's idea of reproducibility. These articles when taken together stand in sharp contrast to each other due to serious confusion that has developed in the reliability literature concerning these concepts. The confusion is exemplified by Green et al's equating of homogeneity and unidimensionality, while Terwilliger and Lele's use of homogeneity clarifies one use of the term.

Somewhere during the three-quarter century history of CTT the real purpose of reliability estimation seems to have been lost. Reliability coefficients in and of themselves have little utility for practical situations except for comparing their magnitudes in order to justify the use of measuring instruments. However, every reliability coefficient should be viewed only as a step toward estimating the precision of an individual score. In the history of other sciences, only psychometrics has developed the concept of reliability coefficients. In all other applications of measurement, e.g. physics and other sciences, precision of measurement is indexed by the probable deviation of an observed value from some true value, or by some confidence interval which is likely to include the true value. Thus, measurement of height is accurate to plus or minus some degree of error. Yet the preoccupation in psychometrics seems to be that of estimating reliability coefficients, with little attention paid to the problem of estimating the precision of an individual measurement or, conversely, the error of measurement. In the period under review, only two papers have been concerned with the standard error of measurement (SEM), the psychometric analog to the physical errors of measurement. Dudek (1979) revived some long-forgotten history of interpretations concerning the SEM, depending on whether the user of the measurement is concerned with estimating true score or placing an error band around an observed score. Kleinke (1979) demonstrates bias in some approximations to the SEM based on reliability coefficients, while Whitely (1979) is concerned with methods for estimating measurement error on highly speeded tests, an issue that previously had not been resolved adequately within the context of CTT.

Applications of reliability theory in experimental design and the analysis of experimental data have begun to receive some attention. Nicewander & Price (1978) extend the Overall & Woodward (1975, 1976) and Fleiss (1976) controversy to a discussion of the reliability of dependent variables and the power of significance tests. They indicate that reliability is not related to power for controlled experiments, and that under certain conditions both of the previous authors are correct. Their discussion focuses around the problem of an individual differences versus an experimental focus in the research design, since considerations of both between subjects variance and error variance are relevant to the reliability and power issue. Subkoviak & Levin (1977; Levin & Subkoviak 1977, 1978) and Forsyth (1978a,b) discuss the effects of measurement errors on the power of statistical tests. Careful reading of this interchange indicates that the nature of the experimental design plays some role in the effect of reliability on power, as does whether observed scores or true scores are being considered.

Generalizability Theory

Although not technically a part of CTT, generalizability theory is really only a generalization of Hoyt's basic idea of variance decomposition of a person by items response matrix. It is also heavily rooted in Tryon's "domain validity" theory. Although originally proposed by Cronbach et al in 1972, because of its complexity and the lack of procedures for estimating many of its parameters, generalizability theory had not been brought to practical status prior to the period under review. During this period, several developments in generalizability theory have occurred.

Kaiser & Michael (1975) derive Tryon's domain validity coefficient (which bears some striking similarities to Cronbach et al's generalizability coefficient) using minimal assumptions. It of course turns out to be a generalized version of the alpha coefficient—thus perpetuating what they characterize as "one of the favorite indoor sports of psychometricians" (p. 34)—but requires no assumptions about the means, variances, covariances, or structure of the items. McDonald (1978) draws relationships between the idea of "domain validity" and the concepts of generalizability theory, while Cardinet et al (1976) criticize applications of generalizability theory to educational measurement, and suggest examples of situations in which the variables on which differentiation is desired are opposite of those which are appropriate for typical generalizability analyses. While Joe & Woodward (1976) develop multivariate generalizability theory, estimating components of maximum generalizability and multifacet experimental designs with multiple dependent variables (which turn out to be multivariate extensions of the S-B formula), Brennan attempts to bring generalizability theory to the user (e.g. Brennan 1980a), develops algorithms and procedures for the estimation of variance components (e.g. Brennan 1975), and provides computer programs for implementing aspects of generalizability theory (Brennan 1980b).

Although generalizability theory appears to be a useful conceptualization, which has begun to reach practitioners for practical application, potential users of it should carefully consider some of its assumptions before
becoming too enamored with it. Rozeboom (1978) criticizes both Kaiser
and Michael and generalizability theory in terms of the conceptual existence
of a domain, and describes the logical impossibility of sampling from a
domain in order to make the assumptions necessary to generate both coefficient alpha and generalizability theory. He also indicates that domain validity provides no information about the domain, since it is strictly a function
of the number of items, and he further argues that domains are likely to be
multidimensional, while only the first dimension is estimated by domain
validity and the variance components of generalizability theory. Thus,
Rozeboom questions the implicit and explicit assumptions of generalizability theory and its predecessors, with some cogent criticisms which should
be carefully considered by persons who use this approach to the estimation
of measurement precision.

ALTERNATIVES TO CLASSICAL TEST THEORY

Because CTT has been unable to solve adequately a number of testing
problems during its history, several alternative test models have been
proposed. Criterion-referenced testing has developed and flourishes in an
attempt to solve the mastery testing problem. Latent-trait based test theories continue to be refined and applied to a wide range of problems for which
CTT is inadequate, and order-based test models which have developed
during the last few years show some promise for measuring certain kinds
of psychological variables.

Criterion-Referenced Testing

Popham (1975, p. 130) and Hambleton et al (1978a, p. 2) define a criterion-
referenced test (CRT) as one "used to ascertain an individual's status [the
individual's domain score] with respect to a well-defined behavior domain."
If this definition captured the sole essence of CRT, the term CRT would
be less appropriate than Hively's (Hively et al 1968) "domain-referenced
testing," Ebel's (1962) "content-referenced testing," or Osburn's (1968)
"universe-defined testing." Swaminathan et al (1974) point out that CRT
is used primarily to ascertain a student's standing with respect to a prescribed mastery (pass-fail) standard and hence the name CRT. In some
cases, *prior* normative information is used in setting the criterion (Pinney
1979; Popham 1978), a practice which blurs the distinction between norm-

and criterion-referenced testing but which helps avoid unrealistically high or low criteria.

Glass (1978), along with Burton (1978), Levin (1978), Linn (1978a), and Messick (1975), criticize the use of mastery criteria in testing because such criteria are necessarily arbitrary. In a well-reasoned response to Glass, Hambleton (1978) argues that the criteria are arbitrary, but in the best sense of the word—they are standards reflecting professional judgment and discretion. For all their faults, he argues, such criteria are still the best basis for educational decisions.

A number of technical issues have received minor attention. Wilcox (1976, 1979a) describes methods of deciding the optimal length for a CRT. Kingsbury & Weiss (1979a) and Spineti & Hambleton (1977) present computerized, adaptive CRT strategies which can reduce the number of items needed to make mastery decisions. Van der Linden (1979) argues that binomial test models, the models on which much of CRT theory rests, impose some unrealistic conditions on item characteristic curves. Lewis et al (1975) and Wilcox (1978a, 1979b,c) propose methods of estimating true domain scores on criterion-referenced tests.

Most of the CRT item analysis procedures are variations of conventional methods (Haladyna 1974, Lord 1977c, Mehrens & Lehmann 1978, Panell & Laabs 1979). For instance, Mehrens & Lehmann (p. 334) suggest pruning items on the basis of a discrimination index reflecting the difference between the item's difficulty in a pre- and post-instructional group. Several authors argue, however, that pruning items on the basis of difficulty or discrimination indices violates the very concept of CRT, defined as a test designed to assess an individual's status in a well-defined behavior domain (Levine 1976, Shoemaker 1974). Kwansa (1974) found that after items were pruned on the basis of conventional item statistics, the items remaining were not representative of the original domain. With the exception of Rovinelli & Hambleton (1977), the CRT critics of conventional item development procedures have been too glib about the problems in selecting items to be representative of a domain, problems exacerbated by the fact that the domain is often so vaguely defined.

One of the most frequently discussed problems in CRT is that of setting the criterion. Meskauskas (1976) reviews the suggested methods, covering several papers which appeared before the period of this review. Methods of setting the criterion which maximize subjective expected utility functions under various sets of assumptions have been proposed by Macready & Dayton (1977), Huynh (1976b), Huynh & Perney (1979), and Wilcox (1979d). Swaminathan et al (1975) and Wilcox (1977, 1979e) discuss a related problem, that of estimating the probability of false negative and false positive errors in making mastery decisions. Some decision makers, how-ever, may feel uncomfortable making the utility judgments which these criterion-setting methods require. Further, these methods for setting an observed mastery score require that there already exists a set criterion score either on a referral task or in terms of true scores, a requirement which begs the fundamental question in most cases.

Beginning with Swaminathan et al (1975), a number of coefficients of precision for CRT based on decision concepts have been proposed. Swaminathan et al proposed Cohen's kappa, which measures the consis-tency of decisions on two parallel tests, but can be estimated directly only if there are two test administrations. Huynh (1976a, 1979), Strasler & Raeth (1977), and Subkoviak (1976), discuss methods of estimating kappa from a single test administration. Algina & Noe (1978) and Subkoviak (1978) critically evaluate some of these single administration estimates.

Beginning with van der Linden & Mellenbergh (1978), the literature on decision-based coefficients of test precision starts winding toward a surpris-ing conclusion. Mellenbergh & van der Linden (1979) argue that tests should be evaluated not on the consistency of decisions across two occa-sions, but on the consistency between decisions based on the test and decisions which would be made if the true scores were known. With this consideration in mind, van der Linden & Mellenbergh (1978, Mellenbergh & van der Linden 1979), and Wilcox (1978b) propose a rescaling of Bayes risk as a decision-theoretic index of test quality. Bayes risk is the expected value of (decision) losses with respect to the joint distribution of random variables T (true scores) and X (observed scores) in a given population. Another decision-theoretic proposal is offered by Livingston & Wingersky (1979). Seemingly to their surprise and ours, van der Linden & Mellenbergh (1978) manage to show that their rescaling of Bayes risk is equal to the classical reliability coefficient if a linear or squared error loss function is assumed and if the regression of true on observed scores is assumed to be linear.

As van der Linden & Mellenbergh (1978) suggest, a measure of test precision should reflect the correspondence between decisions reached using true and observed scores. Coefficient kappa does not do so. Kappa and coefficients derived from Livingston (1972, Brennan & Kane 1977, Lovett 1977) are highly situation specific because they can vary a great deal de-pending on where the user sets the criterion. If the premise is accepted that a useful CRT must have a nonzero variance in the population for which it is intended, then the classical reliability coefficient may be a suitable index for CRT after all. It has a decision-theoretic interpretation, it does not depend on where the criterion is set, and it is readily understood by many users. The standard error is also a useful index of criterion-referenced test precision because it can be used to estimate the probability of misclassifying an examinee for any desired criterion level.

Criterion-referenced tests have been well represented in classrooms, if not in measurement texts, for as long as there has been education. CRT will continue to endure in the form of classroom exams, licensing exams, and tools of computer-aided instruction. Many of the recently developed psychometric methods for CRT may not endure so long. For example, because they require a previously set criterion score on a referral task or on the true score continuum, the methods of setting the criterion which are based on subjective expected utility theory largely beg the question. While kappa is gaining in popularity as a measure of test stability, it will not soon supplant variance-based indices of test precision. Sophisticated CRT methods of estimating true scores and setting test length can be expected to receive no more use than they have received in more conventional testing.

Latent Trait Test Theory

Latent trait test theories which have their roots in Thurstone's mental age scale in the mid-1920s and work by Mosier, Guttman, and Lazarsfeld (among others) in the 1940s have been applied and developed under several rubrics. Best known are item characteristic curve theory and more recently item response theory (IRT). The latter is used here because it emphasizes the psychologically based nature of these theories. In an attempt to make IRT more useful and widely understood, Hambleton & Cook (1977) provide a brief introduction to IRT in a special issue of the *Journal of Educational Measurement,* which includes examples of a number of IRT applications. A more comprehensive and relatively nontechnical review for the uninitiated is provided by Hambleton et al (1978b).

IRT models are usually differentiated by the number of parameters estimated for the items and the nature of the item characteristic curves (ICC). ICCs are usually assumed to be either normal or logistic ogives. Since there is a high degree of similarity between the two (although some differences in practical applications; e.g. Kingsbury & Weiss 1979b), that distinction will be ignored here, and the logistic ogive will be assumed. Thus, the basic differentiations among the models are in the number of parameters necessary to describe the shape and location of the ICC. The 1-parameter logistic (1PL) model—also known as the Rasch model, having been independently developed by the Danish mathematician—is a special case of general IRT in which test items are described only in terms of their difficulties while discriminations are assumed to be equal. The usual 2-parameter (2P) model (there is a special 2P case of the Rasch model) describes items by both their difficulties and discriminations, and the 3-parameter (3P) model adds a chance level or pseudo-guessing parameter as the third descriptor of the ICC.

1PL MODEL   The 1PL model has generated a substantial amount of research during the review period. As is characteristic of research on IRT models, much of the basic research has been focused on problems of item parameter estimation. Since the 1PL model parameter estimation procedure involves estimating only the difficulty parameters for items along with the ability parameters for individuals, these two parameters are usually estimated simultaneously. However, because of some mathematical problems, they can only be approximated under certain circumstances: Cohen (1979) provides a noniterative procedure for estimating ability and difficulty which gives similar values to the maximum likelihood procedures usually used for this purpose. Wright & Douglas (1977a,b) and Andersen & Madsen (1977) compare different procedures for estimating these parameters, and Andersen (1977) verifies that the number correct score is a minimal sufficient statistic in multiple-choice tests for estimating trait levels. He also demonstrates that the number correct score in the 1PL model is not a function of the item difficulties used in the test, while Kearns & Meredith (1975) provide Bayesian procedures for point estimates of 1PL model scores. Their procedure is an empirical Bayes procedure, which like all such procedures is sample dependent and only efficient with large sample sizes.

One important feature of the IRT models, and particulary the 1PL model, is that procedures are available for testing the fit of data to the models. However, there has been some question about the utility of tests that do fit the 1PL model. Wood (1978) fit the 1PL model to simulated coin tosses of 500 subjects on 50 variables, and demonstrated that lack of nonfit by itself is not good enough, since 94% of his randomly derived items fit the model. The problem is that some users of the 1PL model would be tempted to conclude on the basis of a lack of nonfit that the model does fit the data and use of the model would continue. However, Wood's data suggest that this would be inappropriate, since the true item discriminations were very low and setting them equal to 1 would result in inappropriate discrimination values and inappropriate values of the error of measurement for the testees. Thus, additional research is indicated on methods for testing fit of data to the 1PL model.

One of the major advantages of IRT models, including the 1PL model, is the promise of being able to measure individuals on the same ability scale, regardless of the difficulty of the subset of items on which they are measured. This invariance of ability estimates over item subsets implies the capability of IRT models to equate measurements from different tests, a problem which has not been adequately solvable with CTT (e.g. Slinde &

Linn 1977b). Thus, the usefulness of the 1PL model for vertical equating has been investigated by Slinde & Linn (1977a). Their data suggest problems in the use of the 1PL model for vertical equating, since they found mean differences in ability estimates based on high or low ability calibrations in their cross-validation groups, with greater differences for ability levels in the calibration groups that were farther apart. They suggest that perhaps more item parameters are necessary to do a good job of vertical equating. Gustafsson (1979) suggests that Slinde & Linn's results were caused by problems in their research design, although he does admit that there may be problems in vertical equating in the 1PL model if guessing exists. Slinde & Linn (1979a) then analyzed a different data set which did not have the problem Gustafsson suggested, but their results supported their earlier conclusions and suggest that guessing may be responsible for the problem. They do, however, concede that the 1PL model may be useful for equating in certain circumstances. This is confirmed by their later results (Slinde & Lind 1979b) which support the use of the 1PL model in vertical equating for relatively contiguous ability levels, but not for those which were further apart. Rentz & Bashaw (1977) also illustrate the use of the 1PL model for equating using a linking test of common items.

Because the 1PL IRT model promises measurement that is free of the influence of a specific group of testees or a specific subset of test items, in contrast to the sample-specific measurement of CTT, considerable research continues on these capabilities of the model, independent of the equating problem. Tinsley & Dawis (1975) found the 1PL easiness (difficulty) parameters to be invariant over samples of testees differing in ability level, but their results indicated that the easiness parameter estimates were no more invariant than the z-transformed porportion-correct difficulty values. Their data (Tinsley & Dawis 1977) also support the test-free characteristic of the 1PL model in that ability estimates for individuals did not differ substantially when they were based on item subsets of different difficulty levels selected from the same tests.

Dinero & Haertl (1977) studied the applicability of the 1PL model when item discriminations varied, generating testee response data from the 3P model and then fitting the 1P model. The results indicated that when the distribution of item discriminations was uniform, the 1P model did not fit the data, but when there were substantial numbers of items with similar discriminations (normal or skewed distributions of discriminations) the fit of the model was good. Whitely & Dawis (1976) found 1PL item difficulty parameter estimates to differ as a function of test context, thereby questioning the invariance characteristics of the 1PL model. Whitely (1977), in response to Wright (1977), agrees with Wood's later conclusion that the test of the fit of the model has little power for small samples and does not do well for sample sizes even up to 800; thus, fit studies should be interpreted cautiously.

The data on the robustness of the 1PL model are therefore equivocal, suggesting that the model may not work well equating scores of groups widely discrepant in ability, when guessing is present, or under some variations in item content. The interpretation of these results, however, is clouded by problems in determining the fit of the data to the model, and substantial additional research is necessary on this issue before questions of the invariance of the model can be investigated adequately. To handle the guessing problem, a 1PL model with guessing has been proposed (Keats 1974, White 1976, Colonius 1977).

2P AND 3P IRT MODELS   Being generalizations of the 1P model the applications and utility of these models are essentially the same. That is, they have the capability of providing sample-free measures of individuals, resulting in the same degree of "objectivity" as does the 1PL model. They also permit the measurement of individuals with any subset of items, although number correct score for these models does not convey the same information as it does for the 1PL model. Consequently, new scoring methods have been developed to implement these models (Bejar & Weiss 1979), as have additional methods for the estimation of item parameters (Wood et al 1976, Urry 1976).

One of the major advantages of IRT models is that the concept of reliability is not used. The consequence is that all the confusion that has been engendered with regard to reliability in CTT disappears, and issues of homogeneity, internal consistency, type of reliability coefficient, and lower bounds are eliminated. In place of reliability, IRT uses the concept of information/precision, which is inversely related to the standard error of measurement (or estimate) for a given level of a trait. Consequently, IRT permits the error of measurement to vary as a function of what is being measured, and information and its derivatives (e.g. the conditional standard error of measurement) index this change in precision of measurement as a function of the trait being measured. Samejima (1977b,c) differentiates various aspects of the information function, provides critiques of the concept of reliability, and develops the concept of weakly parallel tests—tests which have similar information functions but do not require the number of items, score categories, or other aspects of the tests to be similar. This redefinition of parallel tests permits not only the easier design of parallel tests for applied purposes, but the conceptual definition of parallel adaptive/tailored tests. Samejima also provides criticisms of the group dependence of the classical SEM (vs the SEM of IRT which is group independent).

As with the 1P model, an important problem is the development of accurate methods for estimating the parameters of test items. This is somewhat more complex in the 2P and 3P models since the problem becomes one of simultaneously estimating two or three parameters for each item, plus a trait level parameter for each person in the item calibration sample. Estimation procedures are described by Wood et al (1976) and Urry (1976); Jensema (1976) proposes a direct conversion method for estimating IRT parameters from the item parameters of CTT, while Schmidt (1977) evaluates a related graphical method of direct conversion; and Samejima (1977a) describes a method of estimating the parameters of ICCs when previous estimates of ability are available for a group of individuals. Ree (1979) compares four methods of estimating ICC parameters and concludes that no one of the procedures was consistently best, since the results obtained depended upon the characteristics of the data.

Like the 1P model, there have been several studies of the robustness of the 2P and 3P models under a variety of conditions. Ree & Jensen (1980) studied the effects of errors in item parameters on linear equating, while Hambleton & Cook (1980) studied the robustness of the models under a variety of conditions, as well as the effects of test length and sample size on estimates of the precision of IRT trait estimates. Reckase (1979) addresses his attention to the effects of multidimensionality in an item pool on item parameter estimates obtained in the 1P versus 3P models, while Lord (1975) solves an empirical problem of the correlation between difficulty and discrimination parameters by redefining the ability scale onto a different metric. In the application of 3P models to score equating and linking of items into larger pools, Marco et al (1980) examined the adequacy of IRT score equating models when sample and test characteristics are systematically varied; Yen (1980) studied the effects of context on item parameter and trait estimates. All these studies assist in gaining a better understanding of the potential of IRT models to perform adequately under a variety of situations.

The most frequent application of the 2P and 3P models has been to adaptive/tailored testing. Adaptive testing is the interactive administration of tests such that items are selected dynamically for each individual contingent upon the individual's responses to previous items. Adaptive testing requires immediate scoring of each response and some means of selecting the next item to be administered on the basis of response information and/or ability estimates determined for each individual on an item-by-item basis. Although adaptive testing does not require IRT (e.g. Weiss 1974, Vale & Weiss 1975, Waters 1977), IRT has served to facilitate the development and implementation of most adaptive testing strategies. The review period has seen considerable progress on adaptive testing and the implementation of the 2P and 3P IRT models. Three major conferences have provided a forum for the discussion of current research in this field (Clark 1975; Weiss 1978, 1980) while others (e.g. McBride 1977, Lord 1977a, Jensema 1977) have pursued basic research on the development and evaluation of a variety of adaptive testing strategies. These studies show, in general, that adaptive testing utilizing IRT is a viable methodology for the improvement of tests of ability and achievement, and it has considerable promise for the replacement of paper-and-pencil tests with computer-administered adaptive tests in the foreseeable future.

As might be expected, a few studies have been concerned with comparisons of IRT and CTT. Douglas et al (1979) compare CTT and IRT item analysis procedures by selecting items using traditional proportion-correct and item-total biserial correlations versus item selection based on 1PL procedures. Their data show that about half the items were selected in common by the two procedures, some were selected by neither and some by either. Their conclusion was that the two procedures define "different constructs," but there were no data to indicate which more adequately defined the trait desired. Lord (1977b) compares an IRT approach with three other approaches in the evaluation of the optimal number of choices in a test item. His results show that decreasing the number of choices per item while lenghtening the test proportionately decreases the efficiency for low ability testees and increases the efficiency for high ability testees; his data also show that reliability comparisons of the methods do not demonstrate differences, whereas comparisons in terms of information/efficiency describe differences in the operating characteristics of the different items.

NEW DEVELOPMENTS   One of the potentially most valuable contributions of IRT to psychological measurement is reflected in a series of papers relating the logic and procedures of IRT models to the mainstream of psychological measurement. One of the major deficiencies of CTT has been in the separation of its logic and methodology from the other methods of psychological measurement. The methods of CTT are unique to that approach, and have never been demonstrated to derive from or relate to any other models of psychological measurement. However, recent and important research has defined and described the continuity of the logic of IRT approaches with a variety of other approaches to psychological measurement. That IRT approaches are a special case of Thurstone's scaling techniques is well demonstrated by Brogden (1977), Andrich (1978d), and Lumsden (1980). Wainer et al (1978) analyze a data set by both Thurstone scaling methods and the 1PL model and demonstrate the similarity of the results. Perline et al (1979), and Brogden (1977) describe relationships between IRT models and additive conjoint measurement. Finally, an IRT model which implements the standard Likert successive integers attitude scaling approach has been developed (Andersen 1977, Andrich 1978a,b,c, Douglas 1978). Thus, by the use of IRT models, researchers can be assured of some continuity between test theory and other areas of psychological scaling.

A major advantage of IRT models is the possibility of determining whether a person (or item) is performing in accordance with the assumptions of the models. Since the models make very strong assumptions about the behavior of individuals, demonstration of model fit permits strong inferences to be made, and all of the power of the models can be put to practical use. Observed lack of fit for an individual permits the conclusion that the model is an inappropriate means of describing the behavior of that individual on that set of items, resulting in statements of the degree of person fit or indices of individual precision of measurement.

Most of the work on person fit has been done with the 1P model (e.g. Wright & Stone 1980), using a chi-square test of fit to the model predicted probabilities. Lumsden (1977, 1978) generalizes the issue to one of person reliability, defines the Person Characteristic Curve (PCC), and describes how the ICC and group reliability are functions of a series of PCCs. The PCC is renamed by Trabin & Weiss (1979) as the Person Response Curve (PRC) to emphasize the fact that it results from the responses of one individual to a set of test items; their empirical results of fitting observed to theoretical PRCs indicate an overwhelming fit of data from one group to the model, with the identification of a few individuals who appeared to have systematic lack of fit. Levine & Rubin (1980) call the problem one of measuring "appropriateness," and they define and study a series of person fit indices; their data illustrate the potential of some of their indices to identify lack of fit of individuals to IRT models. The further development of person fit indices may result in the identification of an important moderator variable to be used in prediction studies to improve predictive validity.

Order Models

Another new area of research which has surfaced during the last 5 years is the application of order-based models to the development of psychological measuring instruments. These models are based on the logical relationships among item responses and individuals utilizing items by persons dominance matrices. The methodologies have relationships with mathematical information theory (Krus & Ceurvorst 1979) and have their basic psychometric roots in Guttman's scalogram analysis (Bart 1976, Airasian et al 1975). The majority of research in order analysis has been in the field of attitude scaling, in the analysis of the structure of item/person matrices (Bart 1978, Krus 1977, 1978, Krus & Weiss 1976), and in the analysis of instructional hierarchies (Airasian & Bart 1975, Bart & Mertens 1979).

Dayton & Macready (1976); Davison (1980), and Davison & Thoma (1980) also describe methods for studying the internal structure of tests constructed around hypothesized item hierarchies.

Cliff (1979) translated the order model approach into a test theory which does not assume true scores, does not require prior item calibration data, and permits expressions of person consistency similar to the person fit approaches in IRT. He also applies order theory to adaptive testing (Cliff 1975, 1977, Cliff et al 1979, Cudek et al 1979), while Baker & Hubert (1977) propose some inference procedures and hypothesis testing procedures for order theory. Initial results of order theory seem promising, but additional research in test theory applications is necessary to determine the degree of sample specificity of this approach if it is to provide any advantages over classical test theory. Since order methods and IRT methods have their ancestry in Guttman's scalogram analysis, some thought should also be given to the relationships between the two methodologies.

VALIDITY

Content and Construct Validity

Two seemingly unrelated phenomena—the test fairness controversy (see below) and CRT—have heightened interest in content validity (Schoenfeldt et al 1976). Some believe that a content valid employment test or success criterion is inherently fair, while much of the CRT literature has emphasized the content validity of educational achievement tests to the exclusion of construct and criterion-related validity. The heightened interest in content validity has led to a controversy about when or whether any test can be judged soley on the basis of content validity.

Ebel (1975) argues that construct validity is not a concern if the behavior can be directly observed or the trait can be operationally defined. In opposition to the increased emphasis on content validity in educational testing, Messick (1975) argues that construct validity is as important for educational tests as for psychological tests and points out the logical difficulties associated with operational definitions. Guion (1977, 1978) presents his reservations about the increased emphasis on content validity in employment testing, including his concern that expert judgments about content validity are often made too glibly. He goes on to list six conditions which, in his opinion, a test must meet before it can be judged solely on the basis of its content validity, conditions which are much more stringent than those of Ebel (1975).

In the search for statistical procedures useful in studying aspects of construct validity, structural equation models have been applied to the study of multitrait-multimethod (MTMM) correlation matrices. According to Kalleberg & Kluegel (1975), the structural equations approach has the advantage that it (*a*) allows estimation of correlations between trait and method factors, (*b*) provides estimates of both trait and method factor influences on each measure, and (*c*) forces researchers to specify their assumptions. Mellenbergh et al (1979) note that structural equations models can be extended to the study of any test facet model, of which the MTMM model is one example and Guilford's structure of intellect model is another.

Avison (1978) and Schmitt (1978) point out that there is not just one but several structural equations models for studying MTMM matrices. Schmitt (1978) discusses the problem of choosing between possible models on the basis of their fit to the data, a problem which is only partially solved at present. It is not clear whether the choice of model substantially influences the conclusions reached. After reviewing alternatives to the structural equations approach, Schmitt et al (1977) conclude that the structural equations models provide the most detailed information about individual traits and methods. Davison (1978, 1979) has discussed methods of studying the interrelationships between subscales, each of which corresponds to an ordered stage in a developmental sequence. Applications of these techniques can be found in Davison et al (1980), Davison & Robbins (1978), and Davison et al (1978).

Criterion-Related Validity

How large a sample size is needed to study a test's predictive validity? This question is addressed by Cascio et al (1978) and Schmidt & Hunter (1977). Schmidt & Hunter argue that the sample sizes needed for predictive validity studies are often much larger than commonly recommended. Because the observed correlation is typically reduced by such influences as restriction in range and criterion unreliability, large sample sizes are needed to insure adequate power in statistical tests of predictive validity coefficients.

Schmidt & Hunter (1977) and Schmidt et al (1979) argue against the dominant belief that the predictive validity of selection tests is highly situation specific. Prior research has revealed considerable variation in the observed validity coefficients for the same test in several job settings. Schmidt and his coworkers argue that much of the variation is due to artifactual sources: including variation from one job setting to the next in criterion reliability, test reliability, range restriction, and criterion contamination. Because of the small sample sizes used in many validity studies, sampling error can also account for some of the variation. Schmidt & Hunter (1977) propose a Bayesian method of combining validity coefficients across studies on the same job family to arrive at pooled estimates of validity.

As Schmidt and his associates argue, a portion of the variation in a test's validity coefficient from study to study is due to artifactual sources and sampling error. But how much is due to those sources? Schmidt and his colleagues pile one untested assumption upon another to arrive at their estimates and to develop their Bayesian approach. However, the Bayesian alternative is only as good as the untested assumptions; and it presumes a satisfactory method of classifying tests into job families, something which does not now exist. Callender et al (1979) propose an alternative model which leads to smaller estimates of the artifactual variance and which leads to an alternative Bayesian approach.

While Schmidt's Bayesian model may not be the answer, his work raises an important issue. Given the often unavoidable limitations—particularly limitations of sample size—in job-specific validity studies, would pooled estimates sometimes be better? If so, under what conditions, and how should the several job-specific coefficients be pooled? A workable taxonomy of job families would need to be developed before job pooling could become accepted (Pearlman 1980).

Test Fairness

There are at least five major definitions of bias in selection. In general, no selection strategy can satisfy all of the fairness definitions. According to Cleary (1968, p. 115), a test is biased against members of a subgroup "if in the prediction of a criterion for which the test was designed, consistent nonzero errors of prediction are made for members of the subgroup." Einhorn & Bass (1971) define selection as fair if the least qualified persons who would be accepted from each subgroup have an equal chance of succeeding. Several authors define fairness in terms of ratios. Selection can be defined as fair if the ratio of the number selected to the number qualified is the same for all subgroups (Thorndike 1971), if the ratio of the number selected and qualified to the number qualified is the same for all groups (Cole 1973), or if the ratio of the number selected and qualified to the number selected is the same for all groups (Linn 1973). Petersen & Novick (1976) point out serious logical inconsistencies in the three ratio models.

Not all definitions of bias describe bias in selection. Jackson (1975) presumes that blacks and whites are equal in ability, and therefore any test is biased if the mean scores for blacks and whites are different. Mercer & Lewis (1978) have constructed a test which is fair according to Jackson's definition, by standardizing scores so that they have the same mean in minority and majority groups. Echternacht (1974), Ironson & Subkoviak (1979), and Scheuneman (1979) discuss performance-based measures of item bias. By eliminating items which contain bias as assessed by one of these performance-based measures, the most biased items in the test may be eliminated. After pruning such items, however, the test itself will be unbiased only if the average item in the original item pool was unbiased (Green 1978). Flaugher & Schrader (1978) found that pruning biased items did not substantially alter the mean difference between minority and majority students, and hence such methods of pruning items would likely not materially affect the adverse impact of selection decisions.

Empirical studies of tests for racial or ethnic minorities have focused heavily on blacks and to a lesser extent on Mexican Americans. There was much less research on Native Americans, Asian Americans, and non-Mexican, Hispanic populations. The most thoroughly researched setting was the college admission situation in which the predictors are high school grade point average (GPA) and scholastic admissions tests and the criterion is college GPA. Although there were numerous studies of employment selection, there was little consistency in the predictors and criteria employed. There are some general trends in the employment studies, but no conclusions can be drawn about specific jobs, tests, or criterion variables. As has been noted time and time again by authors in the area, the research strategies assume an unbiased criterion, when in practice there is no agreed upon standard by which to judge the criterion. Conclusions to be drawn from the research described below depend upon whether the criteria employed are believed to be biased.

It is commonly stated that traditional tests are less valid for minority applicants than for nonminorities. Such statements have given rise to the single-group and differential validity issues. Differential validity is said to exist when predictive validity coefficients are unequal in the minority and majority subgroups ($\rho_A < \rho_B$). When the predictive validity coefficient is greater than zero for only one subgroup ($0 = \rho_A < \rho_B$), then single group validity is said to exist. In her seminal work, Boehm (1972) defined single group and differential validity differently, but her definitions contain logical contradictions (Hunter & Schmidt 1978; Bartlett et al 1977).

In the area of employment selection, Bobko & Bartlett (1978), Boehm (1977, 1978), Gael et al (1975a,b), Hunter & Schmidt (1978), Hunter et al (1979), Linn (1978b), and O'Connor et al (1975) present and interpret the evidence pertaining to single group and differential validity. Particularly in later studies (Boehm 1977, Hunter et al 1979, Katzell & Dyer 1977, 1978, Linn 1978b, O'Connor et al 1975), authors conclude that the evidence against the single group validity hypothesis is overwhelming. Authors still differ on whether or not examples of differential validity occur more frequently than can be attributed to artifacts and sampling error. Most reviewers, however, conclude that examples of differential validity are rare and that when differences in validity do exist, they are usually small. Boehm (1977) found that the most methodologically sound studies reported the fewest examples of differential and single group validity. Bobko & Bartlett

(1978) and Linn (1978b) conclude that the single and differential group validity issues are secondary to the question of whether or not the performance of minorities is systematically underpredicted by tests. We strongly agree.

In the educational literature, examples of large differences in minority and majority validities are just as rare as in the employment literature. Wright & Bean (1974) found that the college GPAs of high SES students were somewhat better predicted than those of low SES students. Pfeifer (1976) found little difference in the predictability of whites and blacks. Breland (1978) and Wilson (1978) concluded that the traditional predictors of GPA are generally valid predictors for both majority and minority students. Flaugher (1978) argues that if educational examples of single group and differential validity are so hard to find, then they are probably not of much practical import.

While some researchers have been studying differential validity, others have been studying test fairness as defined by Cleary (1968) to determine if use of a common regression line for both majority and minority subgroups would result in over- or under-prediction of success for either group. Goldman and his coworkers (Goldman & Hewitt 1976, Goldman & Richards 1974, Goldman & Widawski 1976) generally found no evidence for bias in the prediction of college GPAs among blacks, whites, Chicanos, and Orientals. In the two exceptions (Goldman & Hewitt 1975, Goldman & Richards 1974), the authors found trivial differences between regression lines for Anglo and Mexican American samples. In another series of studies, Warren (1976) found only two instances in which regression lines were significantly different for Anglo and Mexican Americans. In one case, selection was biased in favor of Mexican Americans; in one case it was biased against them; and in both cases the bias was small. Cleary et al (1975) review several studies comparing regression lines for blacks and whites, concluding that when only standard courses are figured into the college GPA, differences in the regression lines are small and favor blacks more often than whites. Silverman et al (1976) found bias *in favor of* blacks. When differences exist, it is usually because the regression lines for the two groups have different intercepts, rather than because they have different slopes.

What can be concluded from these studies based on Cleary's definition of fairness? The evidence suggests that tests do not consistently underpredict the performance of minorities on traditional success criteria when a common regression line is used for both the majority and minority groups. This means that the tests are not more or less biased than the criteria they are designed to predict. The evidence could be said to overwhelmingly support the fairness of tests were it not for lingering doubts about the fairness of traditional success criteria. There is a pressing need to define what constitutes a fair criterion and then to evaluate traditional success criteria against that definition. Without further work on the criterion problem, a more definitive answer to the question of test fairness is impossible within the Cleary framework.

SUMMARY AND CONCLUSIONS

The period 1975 through 1979 has had considerable activity in test theory and its methods, covering a diverse range of topics. Because the main results and methods of CTT were developed and refined over the last 70 years or so, little progress was made in CTT, since there is little progress to be made. The period saw active work in developing alternatives to CTT. IRT models, particularly their applications to a variety of testing problems inadequately handled by CTT, have been the subject of considerable research activity. Methods and procedures for both the 1PL model and generalizations of the 1PL model to 2P and 3P models which assume more complex ICCs have been the objects of considerable amounts of research. Estimation procedures for these models have been refined and investigated, and the robustness of the estimation procedures and the models have been studied under a variety of circumstances. The result is the beginning of a better appreciation of the promise and limitations of these models and their areas of applications. Progress has been made in the development of equating procedures using IRT models and their applications to adaptive testing. An important new field of research that has developed as a result of the use of IRT models is the area of person fit, which has considerable promise for applications of psychological measurement in practical situations. In addition, the period has seen a needed integration between test theory approaches via IRT and other models of psychological measurement. More work is needed in this area to specify and describe the relationships of IRT models to other areas of psychological measurement in order to reintegrate psychological testing into the mainstream of psychology and its measurement procedures. And considerable research remains yet to be done on the development and refinement of IRT models and their range of applications.

There has been more research, and less speculation, about the utility of criterion-referenced tests during this period. Some technical advances have been made, but the problem of the arbitrariness of the cutting scores still remains a serious limitation to important applications of these methods. Order theory has developed as a possible viable approach to psychological testing, but considerable additional research is needed before it can be shown to have definite advantages over that of either CTT or IRT. No studies are yet available comparing order theory and IRT approaches on the same data sets. Issues of test fairness have received considerable attention. The literature has focused on problems of item and test bias and on test fairness in the study of differential validity. The problem of fairness of criteria remains yet to be addressed before the issue of test fairness can be resolved adequately. However, the search continues for selection devices other than tests which are likely to be less unfair. A realistic comparison of these approaches, however, would include evaluation of these alternatives on the same criteria used to evaluate the tests themselves.

Some progress was made in the area of validation by the use of structural equation models, particularly in the analysis of multitrait-multimethod matrices. The area of content validity was somewhat more adequately defined, but the issues still reduce to an unacceptable degree of individual judgment for the definition of content validity. Some research during the period has contributed to problems in the understanding of predictive validity.

Thus, like most other fields, progress comes slowly. Future research in test theory will make more progress if less emphasis is placed on relatively trivial research in classical test theory and the derivation of new formulas for already known concepts, and an emphasis is placed on the evaluation of alternative models which promise considerable improvement in the design, construction, and implementation of psychological measuring instruments.

Literature Cited

Airasian, P. W., Bart, W. M. 1975. Validating a priori instructional hierarchies. *J. Educ. Meas.* 12:163–74

Airasian, P. W., Madaus, G. F., Woods, E. M. 1975. Scaling attitude items: A comparison of scalogram analysis and ordering theory. *Educ. Psychol. Meas.* 35:809–19

Algina, J., Noe, M. J. 1978. A study of the accuracy of Subkoviak's single-administration estimate of the coefficient of agreement using two true-score estimates. *J. Educ. Meas.* 15:101–10

Allison, P. D. 1975. A simple proof of the Spearman-Brown formula for continuous length tests. *Psychometrika* 40:135–36

Andersen, E. B. 1977. Sufficient statistics and latent trait models. *Psychometrika* 42:69–81

Andersen, E. B., Madsen, M. 1977. Estimating the parameters of the latent population distribution. *Psychometrika* 42:357–74

Andrich, D. 1978a. A binomial latent trait model for the study of Likert-style attitude questionnaires. *Br. J. Math. Stat. Psychol.* 31:84–98

Andrich, D. 1978b. Application of a psychometric rating model to ordered categories which are scored with successive integers. *Appl. Psychol. Meas.* 2:581–94

Andrich, D. 1978c. A rating formulation for ordered response categories. *Psychometrika* 43:561–73

Andrich, D. 1978d. Relationships between the Thurstone and Rasch approaches to item scaling. *Appl. Psychol. Meas.* 2:451–62

Avison, W. R. 1978. Auxiliary theory and multitrait-multimethod validation: A review of two approaches. *Appl. Psychol. Meas.* 2:433–49

Baker, F. B., Hubert, L. J. 1977. Inference procedures for ordering theory. *J. Educ. Stat.* 2:217–33

Bart, W. M. 1976. Some results of ordering theory for Guttman scaling. *Educ. Psychol. Meas.* 36:141–48

Bart, W. M. 1978. An empirical inquiry into the relationship between test factor structure and test hierarchial structure. *Appl. Psychol. Meas.* 2:333–37

Bart, W. M., Mertens, D. M. 1979. The hierarchial structure of formal operational tasks. *Appl. Psychol. Meas.* 3:343–50

Bartlett, C. J., Bobko, P., Pine, S. M. 1977. Single-group validity: Fallacy of the facts. *J. Appl. Psychol.* 62:155–57

Bejar, I. I., Weiss, D. J. 1979. *Computer programs for scoring test data with item characteristic curve models.* Res. Rep. 79-1, Psychometric Methods Program, Dep. Psychol., Univ. Minn., Minneapolis. 84 pp.

Bobko, P., Bartlett, C. J. 1978. Subgroup validities: Differential definitions and differential prediction. *J. Appl. Psychol.* 63:12–14

Boehm, V. R. 1972. Negro-white differences in validity of employment and training selection procedures. *J. Appl. Psychol.* 56:33–39

Boehm, V. R. 1977. Differential prediction: A methodological artifact? *J. Appl. Psychol.* 62:146–54

Boehm, V. R. 1978. Populations, preselection, and practicalities. *J. Appl. Psychol.* 63:15–18

Breland, H. M. 1978. *Population validity and college entrance measures* (ETS RB-78–19). Princeton, NJ: Educ. Test. Serv.

Brennan, R. L. 1975. The calculation of reliability from a split-plot factorial design. *Educ. Psychol. Meas.* 35:779–88

Brennan, R. L. 1980a. Applications of generalizability theory. In *Criterion-Referenced Measurement: The State of the Art,* ed. R. A. Berk, pp. 186–232. Baltimore: Johns Hopkins Univ. Press

Brennan, R. L. 1980b. Handbook for Gapid: A Fortran IV computer program for generalizability analyses with single-facet designs. *Tech. Bull.* 34, Am. Coll. Test. Program, Iowa City

Brennan, R. L., Kane, M. T. 1977. An index of dependability for mastery tests. *J. Educ. Meas.* 14:277–89

Brogden, H. 1977. The Rasch model, the law of comparative judgment and additive conjoint measurement. *Psychometrika* 42:631–34

Burton, N. 1978. Societal standards. *J. Educ. Meas.* 15:263–71

Callender, J. C., Osburn, H. G. 1977a. A method for maximizing split-half reliability coefficients. *Educ. Psychol. Meas.* 37:819–25

Callender, J. C., Osburn, H. G. 1977b. An empirical comparison of coefficient alpha, Guttman's Lambda–2, and MSPLIT maximized split-half reliability estimates. *J. Educ. Meas.* 16:89–99

Callender, J. C., Osburn, H. G., Greener, J. M. 1979. *Small sample tests of two validity generalization models.* Presented at Ann. Meet. Am. Psychol. Assoc. NY

Cardinet, J., Tourneur, Y., Allal, L. 1976. The symmetry of generalizability theory: Applications to educational measurement, *J. Educ. Meas.* 13:119–35

Cascio, W. F., Valenze, E. R., Silbey, V. 1978. Validation and statistical power: Implications for applied research. *J. Appl. Psychol.* 63:589–95

Clark, C. L., ed. 1975. Proceedings of the first conference on computerized adaptive testing. Pers. Res. Dev. Cent. Rep. PS–75–6, US Civil Serv. Comm., Washington DC. 121 pp.

Cleary, T. A. 1968. Test bias: Prediction of grades of Negro and white students in integrated colleges. *J. Educ. Meas.* 5:15–24

Cleary, T. A., Humphreys, L. G., Kendrick, S. A., Wesman, A. 1975. Educational uses of tests with divadvantaged students. *Am. Psychol.* 30:15–41

Cliff, N. 1975. Complete orders from incomplete data: Interactive ordering and tailored testing. *Psychol. Bull.* 82:289–302

Cliff, N. 1977. A theory of consistency of ordering generalizable to tailored testing. *Psychometrika* 42:375–99

Cliff, N. 1979. Test theory without true scores? *Psychometrika* 44:373–93

Cliff, N., Cudek, R., McCormick, D. J. 1979. Evaluation of implied orders as a basis for tailored testing with simulation data. *Appl. Psychol. Meas.* 3:495–514

Cohen, L. 1979. Approximate methods for parameter estimates in the Rasch model. *Br. J. Math. Stat. Psychol.* 32:113–20

Cole, N. S. 1973. Bias in selection. *J. Educ. Meas.* 10:237–55

Colonius, H. 1977. On Keats' generalization of the Rasch model. *Psychometrika* 42:443–45

Cronbach, L. J., Gleser, G. C., Nanda, H., Rajaratnam, N. 1972. *The Dependability of Behavioral Measurements: Theory of Generalizability for Scores and Profiles.* New York: Wiley

Cudek, R., McCormick, D. J., Cliff, N. 1979. Monte carlo evaluation of implied orders as a basis for tailored testing. *Appl. Psychol. Meas.* 3:65–74

Davison, M. L. 1978. On a metric, unidimensional unfolding model for attitudinal and developmental data. *Psychometrika* 42:523–48

Davison, M. L. 1979. Testing a unidimensional, qualitative unfolding model for attitudinal or developmental data. *Psychometrika* 44:179–94

Davison, M. L. 1980. A psychological scaling model for testing order hypotheses. *Br. J. Math. Stat. Psychol.* In press

Davison, M. L., King, P. M., Kitchener, K. S., Parker, C. A. 1980. The stage sequence concept in cognitive and social development. *Dev. Psychol* 16:121–31

Davison, M. L., Robbins, S. 1978. The reliability and validity of objective indices of moral development. *Appl. Psychol. Meas.* 2:391–404

Davison, M. L., Robbins, S., Swanson, D. B. 1978. Stage structure in objective moral judgments. *Dev. Psychol.* 14:137–46

Davison, M. L., Thoma, S. J. 1980. CONSCAL: A FORTRAN program for testing structural hypotheses. *Appl. Psychol. Meas.* 4:8

Dayton, C. M., Macready, G. B. 1976. A probabilistic model for validation of behavioral hierarchies. *Psychometrika* 41:189–204

Dinero, T. E., Haertl, E. 1977. Applicability of the Rasch model with varying item discriminations. *Appl. Psychol. Meas.* 1:581–92

Douglas, F. M., Khalil, A. K., Farber, P. D. 1979. A comparison of classical and latent trait item analysis procedures. *Educ. Psychol. Meas.* 39:337–52

Douglas, G. A. 1978. Conditional maximum-likelihood estimation for a multiplicative binomial response model. *Br. J. Math. Stat. Psychol.* 31:73–83

Dudek, F. J. 1979. The continuing misinterpretation of the standard error of measurement. *Psychol. Bull.* 86:335–37

Ebel, R. L. 1962. Content standard test scores. *Educ. Psychol. Meas.* 22:15–25

Ebel, R. L. 1975. *Prediction? Validation? Construct validity?* Presented at Content Validity II, conf. at Bowling Green State Univ., July 18

Echternacht, G. 1974. A quick method for determining test bias. *Educ. Psychol. Meas.* 34:271–80

Einhorn, H. J., Bass, A. R. 1971. Methodological considerations relevant to discrimination in employment testing. *Psychol. Bull.* 75:261–69

Feldt, L. S. 1975. Estimation of the reliability of a test divided into two parts of unequal length. *Psychometrika* 40:557–61

Flaugher, R. L. 1978. The many definitions of test bias. *Am. Psychol.* 33:671–79

Flaugher, R. L., Schrader, W. B. 1978. *Eliminating differentially difficult items as an approach to test bias* (ETS RB–78–4). Princeton, NJ: Educ. Test. Serv.

Fleiss, J. L. 1976. Comment on Overall and Woodward's asserted paradox concerning the measurement of change. *Psychol. Bull.* 83:774–75

Forsyth, R. A. 1978a. A note on "Planning an experiment in the company of mea-surement error," by Levin & Subkoviak. *Appl. Psychol. Meas.* 2:379–83

Forsyth, R. A. 1978b. Some additional comments on "Planning an experiment in the company of measurement error." *Appl. Psychol. Meas.* 2:386–87

Gael, S., Grant, D. L., Ritchie, R. J. 1975a. Employment test validation for minority and nonminority telephone operators. *J. Appl. Psychol.* 60:411–19

Gael, S., Grant, D. L., Ritchie, R. J. 1975b. Employment test validation for minority and nonminority clerks with work sample criteria. *J. Appl. Psychol.* 60:420–26

Glass, G. V. 1978. Standards and criteria. *J. Educ. Meas.* 15:237–61

Goldman, R. D., Hewitt, B. N. 1975. An investigation of test bias for Mexican-American college students. *J. Educ. Meas.* 12:187–96

Goldman, R. D., Hewitt, B. N. 1976. Predicting the success of Black, Chicano, Oriental, and White college students. *J. Educ. Meas.* 13:107–18

Goldman, R. D., Richards, R. 1974. The SAT prediction of grades for Mexican-American versus Anglo-American students at the University of California, Riverside. *J. Educ. Meas.* 11:129–40

Goldman, R. D., Widawski, M. H. 1976. An analysis of types of errors in the selection of minority college students. *J. Educ. Meas.* 13:185–200

Green, B. F. 1978. In defense of measurement. *Am. Psychol.* 33:664–70

Green, S. B., Lissitz, R. W., Mulaik, S. A. 1977. Limitations of coefficient alpha as an index of test unidimensionality. *Educ. Psychol. Meas.* 37:827–38

Guion, R. M. 1977. Content validity—the source of my discontent. *Appl. Psychol. Meas.* 1:1–10

Guion, R. M. 1978. Scoring of content domain samples: The problem of fairness. *J. Appl. Psychol.* 63:499–506

Gustafsson, J. E. 1979. The Rasch model in vertical equating of tests: A critique of Slinde & Linn. *J. Educ. Meas.* 16:153–58

Hakstian, A. R., Whalen, T. E. 1976. A K-sample test for independent alpha coefficients. *Psychometrika* 41:219–31

Haladyna, T. M. 1974. Effects of different samples on items and test characteristics of criterion-referenced tests. *J. Educ. Meas.* 19:93–100

Hambleton, R. K. 1978. On the use of cut-off scores with criterion-referenced tests in instructional settings. *J. Educ. Meas.* 15:277–90

Hambleton, R. K., Cook, L. L. 1977. Latent trait models and their use in the analysis of educational test data. *J. Educ. Meas.* 14:75–95

Hambleton, R. K., Cook, L. L. 1980. The robustness of latent trait models and effects of test length and sample size on the precision of ability estimates. See Weiss 1980, pp. 349–64

Hambleton, R. K., Swaminathan, H., Algina, J., Coulson, D. B. 1978a. Criterion-referenced testing and measurement: A review of technical issues and developments. *Rev. Educ. Res.* 48:1–48

Hambleton, R. K., Swaninathan, H., Cook, L. L., Eignor, D. R., Gifford, J. A. 1978b. Developments in latent trait theory: Models, technical issues, and applications. *Rev. Educ. Res.* 48:467–510

Hively, W., Patterson, H. L., Page, S. H. 1968. A "universe defined" system of arithmetic achievement testing. *J. Educ. Meas.* 5:275–90

Huck, S. W. 1978a. A modification of Hoyt's analysis of variance reliability estimation procedure. *Educ. Psychol. Meas.* 38:725–36

Huck, S. W. 1978b. Handling "tied items" when using Lu's method of reliability estimation. *Educ. Psychol. Meas.* 38: 61–68

Hunter, J. E., Schmidt, F. L. 1978. Differential and single-group validity of employment tests by race. *J. Appl. Psychol.* 63:1–11

Hunter, J. E., Schmidt, F. L., Hunter, R. 1979. Differential validity of employment tests. *Psychol. Bull.* 86:721–35

Huynh, H. 1976a. On consistency of decisions in criterion-referenced testing. *J. Educ. Meas.* 13:253–65

Huynh, H. 1976b. Statistical considerations of mastery scores. *Psychometrika* 41: 65–78

Huynh, H. 1979. Statistical inference for two reliability indices in mastery testing based on the beta-binomial model. *J. Educ. Stat.* 4:231–46

Huynh, H., Perney, J. 1979. Determination of mastery scores when instructional units are linearly related. *Educ. Psychol. Meas.* 39:317–23

Ironson, G. H., Subkoviak, M. 1979. A comparison of several methods of assessing test bias. *J. Educ. Meas.* 16:209–26

Jackson, G. G. 1975. Comment on "Educational uses of tests with disadvantaged students." *Am. Psychol.* 30:88–92

Jackson, P. H. 1979. A note on the relation between coefficient alpha and Guttman's "split-half" lower bounds. *Psychometrika* 44:251–52

Jackson, P. H., Agunwamba, C. C. 1977. Lower bounds for the reliability of the total score on a test composed of non-homogeneous items. I: Algebraic lower bounds. *Psychometrika* 42:567–78

Jensema, C. J. 1976. A simple technique for estimating latent trait mental test parameters. *Educ. Psychol. Meas.* 36: 705–15

Jensema, C. J. 1977. Bayesian tailored testing and the influence of item bank characteristics. *Appl. Psychol. Meas.* 1:111–20

Joe, G. W., Woodward, J. A. 1975. An approximate confidence interval for maximum coefficient alpha. *Multivar. Behav. Res.* 10:93–98

Joe, G. W., Woodward, J. A. 1976. Some developments in multivariate generalizability theory. *Psychometrika* 41: 205–17

Kaiser, H. F., Michael, W. B. 1975. Domain validity and generalizability. *Educ. Psychol. Meas.* 35:31–35

Kaiser, H. F., Michael, W. B. 1977. Little Jiffy factor scores and domain validities. *Educ. Psychol. Meas.* 37:363–65

Kalleberg, A. L., Kluegel, J. R. 1975. Analysis of the multitrait-multimethod matrix: Some limitations and an alternative. *J. Appl. Psychol.* 60:1–9

Katzell, R. A., Dyer, F. J. 1977. Differential validity revisited. *J. Appl. Psychol.* 62: 137–45

Katzell, R. A., Dyer, F. J. 1978. On differential validity and bias. *J. Appl. Psychol.* 63:19–21

Kearns, J., Meredith, W. 1975. Methods for evaluating Bayes point estimates of latent trait scores. *Psychometrika* 40: 373–94

Keats, J. A. 1974. Applications of projective transformations to test theory. *Psychometrika* 39:359–60

Kingsbury, G. G., Weiss, D. J. 1979a. *An adaptive testing strategy for mastery decisions.* Res. Rep. 79–5, Psychometric Methods Program Dep. Psychol., Univ. Minnesota, Minneapolis

Kingsbury, G. G., Weiss, D. J. 1979b. *Relationships among achievement level estimates from three item characteristic curve scoring methods.* Res. Rep. 79–3, Psychometric Methods Program Dep. Psychol., Univ. Minnesota, Minneapolis

Kleinke, D. J. 1979. Systematic errors in approximations to the standard error of measurement. *Appl. Psychol. Meas.* 3: 161–64

Krus, D. J. 1977. Order analysis: An inferential model of dimensional analysis and scaling. *Educ. Psychol. Meas.* 37:587–601

Krus, D. J. 1978. Logical basis of dimensionality. *Appl. Psychol. Meas.* 2:323–31

Krus, D. J., Ceurvorst, R. W. 1979. Dominance, information, and hierarchical scaling of variance space. *Appl. Psychol. Meas.* 3:515–27

Krus, D. J., Weiss, D. J. 1976. Empirical comparison of factor and order analysis on prestructured and random data. *Multivar. Behav. Res.* 11:95–104

Kwansa, K. B. 1974. Content validity and reliability of domain referenced tests. *Afr. J. Educ. Res.* 1:73–79

Levin, H. M. 1978. Educational performance standards: Image or substance. *J. Educ. Meas.* 15:309–19

Levin, J. R., Subkoviak, M. J. 1977. Planning an experiment in the company of measurement error. *Appl. Psychol. Meas.* 1:331–38

Levin, J. R., Subkoviak, M. J. 1978. Correcting "Planning an experiment in the company of measurement error." *Appl. Psychol. Meas.* 2:382–85

Levine, M. 1976. The academic achievement test: Its historical context and social functions. *Am. Psychol.* 31:228–38

Levine, M. V., Rubin, D. B. 1980. Measuring the appropriateness of multiple-choice test scores. *J. Educ. Stat.* 4:269–90

Lewis, C., Wang, M., Novick, M. R. 1975. Marginal distributions for the estimation of proportions in *m* groups. *Psychometrika* 40:63–75

Linn, R. L. 1973. Fair test use in selection. *Rev. Educ. Res.* 43:139–61

Linn, R. L. 1978a. Demands, cautions, and suggestions for setting standards. *J. Educ. Meas.* 15:301–7

Linn, R. L. 1978b. Single-group validity, differential validity, and differential prediction. *J. Appl. Psychol.* 63:507–12

Livingston, S. A. 1972. Criterion-referenced applications of classical test theory. *J. Educ. Meas.* 9:13–26

Livingston, S. A., Wingersky, M. S. 1979. Assessing the reliability of tests used to make pass/fail decisions. *J. Educ. Meas.* 16:247–60

Lord, F. M. 1975. The 'ability' scale in item characteristic curve theory. *Psychometrika* 14:205–17

Lord, F. M. 1977a. A broad-range test of verbal ability. *Appl. Psychol. Meas.* 1:95–100

Lord, F. M. 1977b. Optimal number of choices per item—A comparison of four approaches. *J. Educ. Meas.* 14:33–38

Lord, F. M. 1977c. Some item analysis and test theory for a system of computer-assisted test construction. *Appl. Psychol. Meas.* 1:447–55

Lovett, H. T. 1977. Criterion referenced reliability estimated by ANOVA. *Educ. Psychol. Meas.* 37:21–29

Lumsden, J. 1976. Test theory. *Ann. Rev. Psychol.* 27:251–80

Lumsden, J. 1977. Person reliability. *Appl. Psychol. Meas.* 1:477–82

Lumsden, J. 1978. Tests are perfectly reliable. *Br. J. Math. Stat. Psychol.* 31:19–26

Lumsden, J. 1980. Variations on a theme by Thurstone. *Appl. Psychol. Meas.* 4:1–7

Macready, G. B., Dayton, C. M. 1977. The use of probabilistic models in the assessment of mastery. *J. Educ. Stat.* 2:99–120

Marco, G. L., Petersen, N. S., Stewart, E. E. 1980. A test of the adequacy of curvilinear score equating models. See Weiss 1980, pp. 167–96

McBride, J. R. 1977. Some properties of a Bayesian adaptive ability testing strategy. *Appl. Psychol. Meas.* 1:121–40

McDonald, R. P. 1978. Generalizability in factorable domains: "Domain validity and generalizability". *Educ. Psychol. Meas.* 38:75–79

Mehrens, W. A., Lehmann, I. J. 1978. *Measurement and Evaluation in Education and Psychology.* Chicago: Holt, Rinehart & Winston. 2nd ed.

Mellenbergh, G. J., Kelderman, H., Stijlen, J. G., Zondag, E. 1979. Linear models for the analysis and construction of instruments in a facet design. *Psychol. Bull.* 86:766–76

Mellenbergh, G. J., van der Linden, W. J. 1979. The internal and external optimality of decisions based on tests. *Appl. Psychol. Meas.* 3:257–73

Mercer, J., Lewis, J. F. 1978. *SOMPA: System of Multicultural Pluralistic Assessment (Ages 5–11).* New York: Psychol. Corp.

Meskauskas, J. A. 1976. Evaluation models for criterion-referenced testing: Views regarding mastery and standard setting. *Rev. Educ. Res.* 46:133–58

Messick, S. 1975. The standard problem: Meaning and values in measurement and evaluation. *Am. Psychol.* 30:955–66

Nicewander, W. A. 1975. A relationship between Harris factors and Guttman's sixth lower bound to reliability. *Psychometrika* 40:197–203

Nicewander, W. A., Price, J. M. 1978. Dependent variable reliability and the power of significance tests. *Psychol. Bull.* 85:405–9

O'Connor, E. J., Wexley, K. N., Alexander, R. A. 1975. Single-group validity: Fact or fallacy. *J. Appl. Psychol.* 60:352–55

Osburn, H. G. 1968. Item sampling for achievement testing. *Educ. Psychol. Meas.* 28:95–104

Overall, J. E., Woodward, J. A. 1975. Unreliability of difference scores. *Psychol. Bull.* 82:85–86

Overall, J. E., Woodward, J. A. 1976. Reassertion of the paradoxical power of tests of significance based on unreliable difference scores. *Psychol. Bull.* 83:776–77

Pandey, T. N., Hubert, L. 1975. An empirical comparison of several interval estimation procedures for coefficient alpha. *Psychometrika* 40:169–81

Panell, R. C., Laabs, G. J. 1979. Construction of a criterion-referenced diagnostic test for an individualized instruction program. *J. Appl. Psychol.* 64:255–61

Pearlman, K. 1980. Job families: A review and discussion of their implications for personnel selection. *Psychol. Bull.* 87:1–28

Perline, R., Wright, B. D., Wainer, H. 1979. The Rasch model as additive conjoint measurement. *Appl. Psychol. Meas.* 3:237–55

Petersen, N. S., Novick, M. R. 1976. An evaluation of some models for culture-fair selection. *J. Educ. Meas.* 13:3–29

Pfeifer, C. M. Jr. 1976. Relationship between scholastic aptitude, perception of university climate, and college success for black and white students. *J. Appl. Psychol.* 61:341–47

Pinney, G. W. 1979. Eighth graders below average in reading. *Minneapolis Tribune,* Nov. 11, 1979, p. 1B

Popham, W. J. 1975. *Educational Evaluation.* Englewood Cliffs, NJ: Prentice-Hall

Popham, W. J. 1978. As always provocative. *J. Educ. Meas.* 15:297–300

Raju, N. S. 1977. A generalization of coefficient alpha. *Psychometrika* 42:549–65

Raju, N. S. 1979. Note on two generalizations of coefficient alpha. *Psychometrika* 44:347–49

Reckase, M. D. 1979. Unifactor latent trait models applied to multifactor tests: Results and implications. *J. Educ. Stat.* 4:207–30

Ree, M. J. 1979. Estimating item characteristic curves. *Appl. Psychol. Meas.* 3:371–85

Ree, M. J., Jensen, H. E. 1980. The effects of sample size on linear equating of item characteristic curve parameters. See Weiss 1980, pp. 218–28

Rentz, F. R., Bashaw, W. L. 1977. The National Reference Scale for Reading: An application of the Rasch model. *J. Educ. Meas.* 14:161–79

Rovinelli, R. J., Hambleton, R. K. 1977. On the use of test specialists in the assessment of criterion-referenced test item validity. *Dutch J. Educ. Res.* 2:49–60

Rozeboom, W. W. 1978. Domain validity—Why care? *Educ. Psychol. Meas.* 38:81–88

Samejima, F. 1977a. A method of estimating item characteristic functions using the maximum likelihood estimate of ability. *Psychometrika* 42:163–91

Samejima, F. 1977b. A use of the information function in tailored testing. *Appl. Psychol. Meas.* 1:233–47

Samejima, F. 1977c. Weakly parallel tests in latent trait theory with some criticisms of classical test theory. *Psychometrika* 42:193–98

Scheuneman, J. 1979. A method of assessing bias in test items. *J. Educ. Meas.* 16:143–52

Schmidt, F. L. 1977. The Urry method of approximating the item parameters of latent trait theory. *Educ. Psychol. Meas.* 3:613–20

Schmidt, F. L., Hunter, J. E. 1977. Development of a general solution to the problem of validity generalization. *J. Appl. Psychol.* 62:529–41

Schmidt, F. L., Hunter, J. E., Pearlman, K., Shane, G. 1979. Further tests of the Schmidt-Hunter Bayesian validity generalization procedure. *Pers. Psychol.* 32:257–81

Schmitt, N. 1978. Path analysis of multitrait-multimethod matrices. *Appl. Psychol. Meas.* 2:157–73

Schmitt, N., Coyle, B. C., Saari, B. B. 1977. A review and critique of analyses of multitrait-multimethod matrices. *Multivar. Behav. Res.* 12:447–78

Schoenfeldt, L. F., Schoenfeldt, B. B., Acker, S. R., Perlson, M. R. 1976. Content validity revisited: The development of a content-oriented test of industrial reading. *J. Appl. Psychol.* 61:581–88

Sedere, M. V., Feldt, L. S. 1977. The sampling distributions of the Kristof reliability coefficient, the Feldt coefficient, and Guttman's Lambda-2. *J. Educ. Meas.* 14:53–62

Shoemaker, D. M. 1974. Toward a framework for achievement testing. *Rev. Educ. Res.* 44:127–47

Silverman, B. J., Barton, F., Lyon, M. 1976. Minority group status and bias in college and admissions criteria. *Educ. Psychol. Meas.* 36:401–7

Slinde, J. A., Linn, R. L. 1977a. An exploration of the adequacy of the Rasch model for the problem of vertical equating. *J. Educ. Meas.* 15:23–35

Slinde, J. A., Linn, R. L. 1977b. Vertically equated tests: fact or phantom? *J. Educ. Meas.* 14:23–32

Slinde, J. A., Linn, R. L. 1979a. A note on vertical equating via the Rasch model for groups of quite different ability and tests of quite different difficulty. *J. Educ. Meas.* 16:159–65

Slinde, J. A., Linn, R. L. 1979b. The Rasch model, objective measurement, equating and robustness. *Appl. Psychol. Meas.* 3:437–52

Spineti, J. P., Hambleton, R. K. 1977. A computer simulation study of tailored testing strategies for objective-based instructional programs. *Educ. Psychol. Meas.* 37:139–58

Strasler, G. M., Raeth, P. G. 1977. *An internal consistency estimate for criterion-referenced tests.* Presented at Ann. Meet. Natl. Counc. Meas. Educ.

Subkoviak, M. J. 1976. Estimating reliability from a single administration of a criterion-referenced test. *J. Educ. Meas.* 13:265–75

Subkoviak, M. J. 1978. Empirical investigation of procedures for estimating reliability for mastery tests. *J. Educ. Meas.* 15:111–16

Subkoviak, M. J., Levin, J. R. 1977. Fallibility of measurement and the power of a statistical test. *J. Educ. Meas.* 14:47–52

Swaminathan, H., Hambleton, R. K., Algina, J. 1974. Reliability of criterion-referenced tests. *J. Educ. Meas.* 11: 263–67

Swaminathan, H., Hambleton, R. K., Algina, J. 1975. A Bayesian decision-theoretic procedure for use with criterion-referenced tests. *J. Educ. Meas.* 12: 87–98

ten Berge, J. M. F., Zegers, F. E. 1978. A series of lower bounds to the reliability of a test. *Psychometrika* 43:575–79

Terwilliger, J. S., Lele, K. 1977. Some relationships among internal consistency, reproducibility and homogeneity. *J. Educ. Meas.* 16:101–8

Thorndike, R. L. 1971. Concepts of culture-fairness. *J. Educ. Meas.* 8:63–70

Tinsley, H. E. A., Dawis, R. V. 1975. An investigation of the Rasch simple logistic model: Sample free item and test calibration. *Educ. Psychol. Meas.* 35: 325–39

Tinsley, H. E. A., Dawis, R. V. 1977. Test-free person measurement with the Rasch simple logistic model. *Appl. Psychol. Meas.* 1:483–87

Trabin, T. E., Weiss, D. J. 1979. *The person response curve: Fit of individuals to item characteristic curve models.* Res. Rep. 79–7, Psychometric Methods Program Dep. Psychol., Univ. of Minn., Minneapolis. 36 pp.

Urry, V. W. 1976. Ancillary estimators for the item parameters of mental test models. *In Computers and testing: Steps toward the inevitable conquest,* ed. W. A. Gorham. Pers. Res. Dev. Cent. Rep. PS–76–1, US Civil Serv. Comm., pp. 14–18

Vale, C. D., Weiss, D. J. 1975. *A simulation study of stradaptive ability testing.* Res. Rep. 75–6, Psychometric Methods Program, Dep. Psychol., Univ. Minn., Minneapolis. 51 pp.

van der Linden, W. J. 1979. Binomial test models and item difficulty. *Appl. Psychol. Meas.* 3:401–11

van der Linden, W. J., Mellenbergh, G. J. 1978. Coefficients of tests from a decision theoretic point of view. *Appl. Psychol. Meas.* 2:119–34

Wainer, H., Fairbank, D., Hough, R. L. 1978. Predicting the impact of simple and compound life change events. *Appl. Psychol. Meas.* 2:315–24

Warren, J. R. 1976. *Prediction of college achievement among Mexican-American students in California* (ETS RB–76–22). Princeton, NJ: Educ. Test. Serv.

Waters, B. K. 1977. An empirical investigation of the stratified adaptive computerized testing model. *Appl. Psychol. Meas.* 1:141–52

Weiss, D. J. 1974. *Strategies of adaptive ability measurement.* Res. Rep. 74–5. Psychometric Methods Program, Dep. Psychol., Univ. Minn., Minneapolis

Weiss, D. J., ed. 1978. *Proceedings of the 1977 Computerized Adaptive Testing Conference.* Psychometric Methods Program, Dep. Psychol., Univ. Minn., Minneapolis. 443 pp.

Weiss, D. J., ed. 1980. *Proceedings of the 1979 Computerized Adaptive Testing Conference.* Psychometric Methods Program, Dep. Psychol., Univ. Minn., Minneapolis. 455 pp.

Werts, C. E., Rock, R. D., Linn, R. L., Joreskog, K. G. 1978. A general method of estimating the reliability of a composite. *Educ. Psychol. Meas.* 38:933–38

White, P. O. 1976. A note on Keats' generalization of the Rasch model. *Psychometrika* 41:405–7

Whitely, S. E. 1977. Models, meanings and misunderstandings: Some issues in applying Rasch's theory. *J. Educ. Meas.* 14:227–35

Whitely, S. E. 1979. Estimating measurement error on highly speeded tests. *Appl. Psychol. Meas.* 3:141–54

Whitely, S. E., Dawis, R. V. 1976. The influence of test context on item difficulty. *Educ. Psychol. Meas.* 36:329–37

Wilcox, R. R. 1976. A note on the length and passing scores of a mastery test. *J. Educ. Stat.* 1:359–64

Wilcox, R. R. 1977. Estimating the likelihood of false-positive and false-negative decisions in mastery testing: An empirical Bayes approach. *J. Educ. Stat.* 2:289–307

Wilcox, R. R. 1978a. Estimating true score in the compound binomial error model. *Psychometrika* 43:245–62

Wilcox, R. R. 1978b. A note on decision theoretic coefficients for tests. *Appl. Psychol. Meas.* 2:609–13

Wilcox, R. R. 1979a. Applying ranking and selection techniques to determine the length of a mastery test. *Educ. Psychol. Meas.* 39:13–37

Wilcox, R. R. 1979b. Achievement tests and latent structure models. *Br. J. Math. Stat. Psychol. MSP* 32:61–71

Wilcox, R. R. 1979c. An alternative interpretation of three stability models. *Educ. Psychol. Meas.* 39:311–15

Wilcox, R. R. 1979d. A lower bound to the probability of choosing the optimal passing score for a mastery test when there is an external criterion. *Psychometrika* 44:245–49

Wilcox, R. R. 1979e. On false-positive and false-negative decisions with a mastery test. *J. Educ. Stat.* 4:59–73

Wilson, K. M. 1978. *Predicting the long-term performance in college of minority and nonminority students: A comparative analysis in two collegiate settings* (ETS RB–78–6). Princeton, NJ: Educ. Test. Serv.

Wood, R. L. 1978. Fitting the Rasch model —a heady tale. *Br. J. Math. Stat. Psychol.* 31:27–32

Wood, R. L., Wingersky, M. S., Lord, F. M. 1976. *Logist: A computer program for estimating examinee ability and item characteristic curve parameters.* Res. Memo 76–6, Educ. Test. Serv., Princeton NJ

Woodhouse, B., Jackson, P. H. 1977. Lower bounds for the reliability of the total score on a test composed of non-homogeneous items. II: A search procedure to locate the greatest lower bound. *Psychometrika* 42:579–91

Woodward, J. A., Bentler, P. M. 1978. A statistical lower bound to population reliability. *Psychol. Bull.* 85:1323–26

Wright, B. D. 1977. Misunderstanding the Rasch model. *J. Educ. Meas.* 14:219–25

Wright, B. D., Douglas, G. A. 1977a. Best procedures for sample-free item analysis. *Appl. Psychol. Meas.* 1:281–95

Wright, B. D., Douglas, G. A. 1977b. Conditional versus unconditional procedures for sample-free item analysis. *Educ. Psychol. Meas.* 37:573–86

Wright, B. J., Stone, M. H. 1980. *Best test design.* Chicago: Mesa. 222 pp.

Wright, R. J., Bean, A. G. 1974. The influence of socioeconomic status on the predictability of college performance. *J. Educ. Meas.* 11:277–84

Yen, W. M. 1980. The effects of context on latent trait model item parameter and trait estimates. See Weiss 1980, pp. 197–217

Ann. Rev. Psychol. 1981. 32:659–704

INSTRUCTIONAL PSYCHOLOGY ❖355

Lauren B. Resnick[1]

Learning Research and Development Center, University of Pittsburgh, Pittsburgh, Pennsylvania 15260

CONTENTS

[1]The preparation of this review was supported by a grant from the National Institute of Education, United States Department of Education, to the Learning Research and Development Center. The opinions expressed do not necessarily reflect the position or policy of the National Institute of Education.

I wish to acknowledge the assistance of Mary S. Riley, who conducted an extensive and thoughtful search and classification of the literature for this review.

0066-4308/81/0201-0659$01.00

INTRODUCTION

An interesting thing has happened to instructional psychology. It has become part of the mainstream of research on human cognition, learning, and development. For about 20 years the number of psychologists devoting attention to instructionally relevant questions has been gradually increasing. In the past 5 years this increase has accelerated so that it is now difficult to draw a clear line between instructional psychology and the main body of basic research on complex cognitive processes. Instructional psychology is no longer basic psychology *applied* to education. It is fundamental research *on* the processes of instruction and learning.

Having become part of the mainstream, it is not surprising that instructional psychology is participating in the important shifts that are occurring in many other branches of psychology. Instructional psychology, like most research on human learning and development, is now largely cognitive; it is concerned with internal mental processes and how their development may be enhanced through instruction.

Three major trends in cognitive psychology are particularly relevant to the development of instructional psychology. First, there is a shift toward studying more and more complex forms of cognitive behavior. This means that many of the tasks and processes of interest to cognitive psychologists are ones that can form part of a school's curriculum. Psychological work on such tasks is naturally relevant to instruction. Second, a concomitant of increasing attention to complex tasks is a growing interest in the role of knowledge in human behavior. Much effort is now directed at finding ways to represent the structure of knowledge and at discovering the ways in which knowledge is used in various kinds of learning. As a natural outgrowth of this interest, there is new attention to meaningfulness and understanding as a normal part of the learning process rather than as a separate kind of learning to be contrasted with "rote" learning.

Finally, today's assumptions about the nature of learning and thinking are interactionist. We assume that learning occurs as a result of mental constructions of the learner. These constructions respond to information and stimuli in the environment, but they do not copy or mirror them. This means that instruction must be designed not to put knowledge into learners' heads, but to put learners in positions that allow them to construct well-structured knowledge. Several recent edited volumes (Klahr 1976; Anderson et al 1977b; Glaser 1978, 1981; Lesgold et al 1978; Snow et al 1980) lend weight to this characterization of instructional psychology as a part of cognitive science.

This review will concentrate on cognitive research in four broad areas that are of direct relevance to the school curriculum: reading, mathematics, science, and problem solving. In addition, it will include a growing body of literature on aptitude and intelligence. It will become clear that an enormous body of research must be considered, even though the chapter is limited to what might be termed the cognitive psychology of instruction. As a result, certain topics often considered part of the field—such as instructional design, instructional technology, and behavior modification—will not be included. At the end of the chapter, however, some of the steps that may be necessary to link cognitive instructional psychology more directly to practical educational concerns will be discussed.

READING

Reading is the instructional domain to which psychologists have attended for the longest time and in the greatest numbers. The sheer volume of books and articles on the psychology of reading makes an exhaustive review virtually impossible. It is more pertinent here to try to characterize the issues which psychologists are now addressing and to assess the relevance of psychological research and theory to reading instruction.

Trends in the psychology of reading can be followed by examining the various edited volumes in the field (Guthrie 1976, 1977; Freedle 1977, 1979; Just & Carpenter 1977; LaBerge & Samuels 1977; Reber & Scarborough 1977; Murray & Pikulski 1978; Resnick & Weaver 1979; Waller & MacKinnon 1979; Spiro et al 1980; Lesgold & Perfetti 1981). Until very recently little systematic work was being done on processes of reading comprehension. The vast bulk of research on reading was concerned with processes of word recognition, the early stages of reading acquisition, and difficulties in learning to read. This reflected a long history of pedagogical attention to oral reading, but the heavy emphasis on word recognition processes was a matter of concern to some, especially those who believed that too much instructional emphasis on "decoding" words might be detrimental to what they saw as the more fundamental processes of reading comprehension (e.g. Goodman & Goodman 1979, Smith 1979). The microprocesses of word recognition are still studied extensively. Now, however, debates over whether to emphasize decoding or comprehension in instruction are giving way to research on how the various processes of reading interact, both in skilled performance and in acquisition (e.g. Lesgold & Perfetti 1981). At the same time, an extensive body of research and theory in reading comprehension is stressing the active, constructive, and inferential character of reading.

Word Recognition

How people access the meanings of the printed words that make up a text remains the most heavily studied topic in the psychology of early reading. There is now an extensive body of research on how skilled readers recognize words, and growing attention is being directed to processes of word recognition in children as they learn to read. The number of experiments on word recognition and the variety of points of view are so great that the only sensible route into this topic is via the several recent reviews and interpretive integrations of the literature (e.g. Gibson & Levin 1975; Baron 1978, 1979; Brooks 1977; Coltheart et al 1977; Smith & Kleiman 1979; Barron 1981a,b; Katz & Feldman 1981). Some common problems permeate this work: (*a*) the unit of processing in word recognition, (*b*) the role of phonemic encoding in reading, and (*c*) the influence of surrounding semantic and syntactic context on word recognition.

THE UNIT OF PROCESSING   A long line of research has established what is known as the "word superiority effect"—i.e. letters are more easily (quickly) perceived in the context of a word than in isolation or in the context of a pseudoword. While this suggests that words are the basic unit of processing (Baron 1978), it remains possible that smaller units such as letters are basic, and the consistent redundancies of letter position and letter sequences, which the reader comes to rely on, may produce the apparent superiority of words over nonwords. Debate thus continues on the question of the unit of processing in reading. Some theorists (e.g., Gibson & Levin 1975, Adams 1979, LaBerge 1979, Smith & Kleiman 1979) explicitly allow for the possibility of processing several different units—ranging from the separate visual features of individual letters to letter groups (orthographic patterns), syllables, and whole words—in the course of skilled reading. Other theories are more exclusive, arguing that a particular unit must always be discriminated and then combined into higher level units. Venezky & Massaro (1979), for example, argue that spelling patterns or letter groups are always the basic units of encoding.

Since most experiments on the unit of processing have used skilled adult readers as subjects, the way in which processing units are acquired is not yet well understood. In any case, it is not possible to infer directly from current research the appropriate units for *teaching* beginning readers since attention to lower level units during instruction may be helpful in acquiring the higher level processing units that skilled readers presumably use (Juola et al 1979, LaBerge 1979, Venezky & Massaro 1979).

PHONOLOGICAL ENCODING AND LEXICAL ACCESS   Do readers pass directly from visual features to the meaning of a word, or does a phonological code mediate lexical access? Recent research has focused on very detailed analyses of the ways in which spelling patterns (orthography) reflect sound and meaning and how skill in using both kinds of information develops (Baron 1979, Venezky & Massaro 1979, Glushko 1981, Katz & Feldman 1981). Although most investigators have concluded that meaning can be accessed without phonological mediation, it seems that good readers are extremely sensitive to phonological information while poor readers have difficulty using this information (Barron 1981a). People with severe problems in learning (dyslexics) have particular difficulty with phonological processing (Vellutino 1977, Coltheart 1980). The speed of silent reading, together with the finding that people are able to understand written sentences even when they are required to simultaneously perform a vocalization task (Baddeley & Lewis 1981), suggest that if a phonological code is used by skilled readers it cannot be identical to the overt speech code. Baddeley and Lewis suggest that while vocalization may not be required in skilled reading, some kind of auditory imagery is necessary for many reading tasks. Several investigators have proposed that phonological encoding may occur *after* lexical access (Levy 1978, Danks & Fears 1979, Barron 1981b) and function to hold accessed words in working memory while subsequent words are processed and the meaning of the sentence determined.

As in the case of units of processing, there is no direct conclusion for reading instruction to be drawn from the presence or the timing of phonological encoding in skilled reading, since phonological information may be important in *learning* appropriate units of processing (Venezky & Massaro 1979, Barron 1981b, Glushko 1981). This would account for the correlation of phonological coding skill with general reading skill, even though such coding may not always be used by skilled readers.

CONTEXT   Several sources of evidence suggest that reading is an interactive process in which "top-down" information from the surrounding syntactic and semantic context, and "bottom-up" information from the visual stimuli combine to produce word recognition (Rumelhart 1977, Wildman & Kling 1978–79, Levy 1981, Rumelhart & McClelland 1981, Stanovich 1981). Oral reading errors, even in young readers, tend to be semantically and syntactically appropriate to the context (Stevens & Rumelhart 1975,

Goodman & Goodman 1977, Lesgold & Curtis 1981). Long hesitations or misreadings occur at points where word changes in a text produce syntactic or semantic anomalies (Danks & Hill 1981). People are faster at pronouncing a word in context than when the same word appears in isolation (J. R. Frederiksen 1981), and faster at pronouncing words when the preceding context is congruous with the word than when it is incongruous (Perfetti & Roth 1981, Stanovich 1981). Finally, research on "lexical decisions" shows that even with isolated words as stimuli, people are faster at deciding if a letter string is a word when it has been "semantically primed" by prior presentation of an appropriate superordinate category name or a related word; e.g. *parakeet* is processed faster after *bird* than after *mammal* (Becker & Killion 1977, Fischler 1977, Neely 1977, Tweedy et al 1977, Antos 1979). Sentences as well as single words can prime lexical decisions, for decisions are made faster on words that fit a previous sentence frame than on words that do not (Schuberth & Eimas 1977). Stanovich (1981) provides a review of data and a theoretical interpretation of contextual effects for both children and adults.

The establishment of context effects for word recognition leads naturally to the question of how readers process larger segments of text. Earlier research had established that people process words in clusters rather than in a linear word-at-a-time manner, that even in oral reading the eye scans ahead of the voice, and that the units of scanning are affected by the syntactic structure of the text (Gibson & Levin 1975). Recent work using computer-linked eye movement photography has been able to fill in our picture of this kind of meaning- and structure-dependent reading (Carpenter & Just 1977, Rayner 1978, McConkie 1979, Just & Carpenter 1981). These studies have shown that there are more and longer eye fixations and more regressions when texts less closely approximate normal English. In normal English fixations are longer on nonwords, infrequent words, or anomalous words inserted in a text. Further, wherever more time might be needed for semantic processing, longer fixations tend to be found. For example, fixations are longer on words requiring an inference to link them to a previously presented concept. Readers also tend to make regressive fixations to the referent of a pronoun.

The documentation of "top-down" processes has led some theorists to propose that early reading instruction should not focus on the print-sound (grapheme-phoneme) code, but instead upon the use of context and meaning to make and test inferences about words (e.g. C. H. Frederiksen 1979, Goodman & Goodman 1979, F. Smith 1979). However, research on the practical effects of code- versus language-oriented instruction generally tends to favor code instruction—at least in the first 3 years of instruction.

Early code instruction may be necessary because the phonological-code aspects of reading are harder to learn or less "natural" than the context-usage aspects of reading, and therefore are more dependent on instruction.

Sources of Difficulty in Learning to Read

CODING AUTOMATICITY   The interactive view of reading that derives from documentation of context effects and semantically sensitive scanning strategies raises in a new form a traditional issue in the psychology of reading: the relationship between skill in word recognition and skill in deriving meaning from text. While it is clear that there is more to reading than the sequential processing of individual words, there is also evidence that people who comprehend poorly have difficulty in recognizing words quickly (Perfetti & Lesgold 1979, Curtis 1980, J. R. Frederiksen 1981). In several analyses (LaBerge & Samuels 1974, Perfetti & Lesgold 1979, Perfetti & Roth 1981), fast or "automated" word recognition has been proposed as a necessary (although perhaps not sufficient) basis for reading comprehension, on the plausible assumption that limited working memory capacity is thus freed for higher-level semantic processing. The general argument is that unless word recognition is automated up to some minimal level, other processes important to comprehension cannot proceed because too much time and/or too much attentional capacity is used up in word recognition.

The apparent implication for instruction is that special training in fast word decoding should be offered to those having difficulty learning to read. One study (Fleisher & Jenkins 1978) has found that while practice on words presented out of context can significantly increase the speed of reading isolated words, this does not guarantee transfer to comprehension. Thus, at this time we lack an empirical demonstration of a *causal* relationship between automaticity in word recognition and reading comprehension. Such a causal relationship cannot be dismissed, however, because the studies conducted so far have not included extensive training in automaticity. In addition, immediate transfer to comprehension performance may be an inappropriate criterion to apply. It may be more sensible to look for evidence of easier *acquisition* of comprehension abilities when instruction or practice in those skills is provided.

PHONEMIC SEGMENTATION AND LINGUISTIC AWARENESS   A number of investigations have shown that children who have difficulty learning to read also have difficulty with aural phonemic segmentation—that is, they are unable to decompose the speech stream into separate phonemes (Menyuk 1976, Liberman & Shankweiler 1979). Programs for teaching phonemic segmentation have been proposed (see Liberman & Shankweiler 1979, Wallach & Wallach 1979). More extensive and well-controlled tests will be needed, however, to determine whether phonemic segmentation is best learned as a separate "prereading" skill or as part of a reading instruction program that explicitly links letters and sounds. Ehri (1979) has collected evidence on difficulties that young children have in identifying separate words in the speech stream. This and related aspects of "linguistic awareness" have come to be viewed as other important prerequisites or corequisites of early reading.

GENERAL LANGUAGE KNOWLEDGE   Claims that differences in general (oral) language abilities underlie difficulty in learning to read have frequently been made, particularly in attempts to account for correlations of social class and ethnic membership with reading skill (e.g. Shuy 1979). Most arguments linking oral language and reading have been fairly global, demonstrating differences in phonological or functional language patterns between social groups. Studies of individual differences in reading skill or individual difficulties in learning to read have been rare, and convincing theoretical accounts of the connection between specific language deficits and the acquisition of reading skill have been almost nonexistent. This has led some commentators to locate difficulties in reading acquisition less in the cognitive equipment of lower class or minority learners than in the differing instruction offered to children of different social groups (e.g. Gordon 1979) or in the system of expectations and rewards for schoolwork that operate in these groups (Entwisle 1979).

Reading Comprehension

THE ROLE OF INFERENCE   It is well established by now that both immediate and delayed recall of texts typically include material that is not actually in the text but is thematically related (e.g. Bransford & McCarrell 1974, Sulin & Dooling 1974, Thorndyke 1976, Brown et al 1977, Dooling & Christiaansen 1977, Kintsch & van Dijk 1978, Reder 1979). These findings make it clear that inferences beyond the explicit information in the text are a normal part of the reading process. However, the actual processes involved in making inferences and the way in which inference interacts with other processes of reading are only partially understood, and many questions are still unanswered.

Efforts to establish whether inferences occur at the time of initially reading the text or at recall (e.g. Kintsch 1974, Frederiksen 1975a,b, Singer 1976, Spiro 1977, Spiro & Esposito 1982) have yielded conflicting results, and there has not yet been an integrative analysis capable of resolving the differences and providing a credible account of all the findings. For the moment, research on the development of inferencing skills is also yielding conflicting findings. Some studies (e.g. A. L. Brown et al 1977, Kail et al 1977, Stein & Glenn 1979) find evidence of across-sentence inferences in children as early as second or third grade, while others show difficulty for children even as late as fourth or fifth grade (Paris & Upton 1976, Keeton 1977). Research on inference processes is also complicated by problems in deciding what should be counted as an inference from the text, as opposed to a plausible construction by the reader in order to meet a real or perceived task demand. Efforts such as those of Crothers (1978) to develop a typology of inferences and to embed these in a theory of text coherence may help in the development of an integrated theory of inference processes in reading.

Various studies have shown that the number and kind of inferences made depends upon the goal of the reader. For example, instructions that induce a mental set to apply the information in the text to solving certain problems increase the probability of inferences (Frederiksen 1972, 1975b; Spiro 1977). Instructions to simply recall, however, produce better recall of the explicit material.

Text structure and text processing The structure of the text can also affect the inferencing process. Well-organized passages in which the theme is presented at the beginning and temporal organization is clear induce more inferencing (Thorndyke 1977, Kieras 1978). Inferences important to the story line are particularly likely to be made (Goetz 1979). The findings on inference are in good accord with work on the role of importance in memory for prose, in which it has been demonstrated that superordinate ideas from a text are better remembered than subordinate ones (Meyer 1975, Smiley et al 1977, A. L. Brown & Smiley 1977) and that recall is clustered in ways that reflect hierarchical and superordinate relationships in the text (C. H. Frederiksen 1977).

An analysis of the local coherence relationships in a text provides the basis for the best developed and most extensively tested general model of reading comprehension that exists at this time (Kintsch 1974, Kintsch & van Dijk 1978). This work has its psychological origins in theories of memory, and also draws heavily on recent work in psycholinguistics on how old and new information is linked and processed. The model takes as its material to be processed the set of *propositions* derived from the text. The reader's task in understanding a text is to construct a mental representation of the propositional structure of the text, in which all propositions are linked via shared arguments. If the text does not specify the links between propositions, the reader must supply these links through inference. The difficulty of building this representation is affected by features of the text, such as the explicitness of the links between propositions. It is also affected by characteristics of the reader, such as the amount of text material one is able to process in a given processing cycle and the amount that can be held in short-term memory and carried into the next cycle.

Several empirical studies (Kintsch 1974, Kintsch et al 1975) have established both the utility of the propositional analysis that is at the heart of the model and the power of the model as a general account of localized sentence-to-sentence comprehension processes. Other studies (e.g. Garrod & Sanford 1977, Nash-Webber 1980) provide further evidence of the ways that referential relationships in texts affect the building of a coherent text representation. Kieras (1979) has formulated a computational model of reading that integrates information across sentences in a manner quite similar to that proposed in Kintsch and van Dijk's theory. This formalization represents an important first link between artificial intelligence models of reading and those deriving from a psychological memory tradition.

A potentially important instructional application of current work on text processing is the development of a better theory of what makes a text easy or difficult to understand. This question has long been of practical interest to educators, writers, and psychologists, and an extensive technology of "readability" measurement has developed over the years (Klare 1976). Existing readability formulas largely disregard questions of meaning, structure, and connectedness in the text; in most cases scrambled sentences or paragraphs earn the same readability score as properly ordered text. Recent work on readability seeks to explicate the effects of these characteristics of texts. Kintsch & Vipond (1979) and Miller & Kintsch (1980) have shown that the *propositional density* of the text (the number of propositions for a constant number of words), the number of *different arguments* (i.e. different concepts introduced), and the *cohesiveness* of the text (as defined by shared arguments between propositions) all affect readability. These effects follow logically from the models' descriptions of how readers build coherent representations of the text.

SPECIFIC KNOWLEDGE: SCHEMATA IN COMPREHENSION AND COMPOSITION   A second major theme in research on reading comprehension is the role that readers' prior knowledge plays in allowing them to interpret and understand a text. Central to virtually all of the work on prior knowledge is the notion of a *schema* as a framework for interpreting the text (R. C. Anderson et al 1977a, 1978; Rumelhart & Ortony 1977; Adams & Collins 1979; A. Collins et al 1980).

While schema theories vary in many potentially important details, they share certain general features. Schemata are general or "prototypic" knowledge structures. They specify certain kinds of information that are required for the prototypic situation or relationship to be filled out or "instantiated."

Reading comprehension proceeds, roughly speaking, by the reader's using the first part of the text to decide what schema is most likely to make sense of the text and then using that schema as a hypothesis for interrogating the text. This interrogation fills the schema's slots, thus completing the reader's mental model of the situation. The schema also serves as a filter that allows some information to be judged irrelevant and thus, presumably, not entered into the model (cf Hayes et al 1977).

Modern discussions of schema theory virtually always include reference to Bartlett's (1932) work on memory. Important links to recent work in artificial intelligence on the problem of language understanding (e.g. Schank & Abelson 1977, Winograd 1977) are also routinely noted. Each language understanding program tends to be capable of interpreting messages only in a relatively constrained area of knowledge. This is because the programs depend upon already stored knowledge for constructing sensible interpretations. Even the general planning knowledge that allows certain programs to go beyond stored scripts is actually knowledge of the kinds of goals, social actions, and relationships that are characteristic of certain kinds of situations and most likely to be expressed in narrative messages.

A number of empirical studies have demonstrated in a general way that prior knowledge works to constrain and enhance the process of reading comprehension. Early work on schemata showed that passages that subjects report to be incomprehensible, and for which recall is very low, become comprehensible and recallable when readers are told in advance what the theme of the story is. More recent work shows that the kinds of schemata people are most likely to activate because of their own background and interests can also influence how a passage is understood (R. C. Anderson et al 1977a, Waern 1977a,b), and directions to adopt a particular perspective can also affect what is learned and remembered from a text and what is rated important (Pichert & Anderson 1977); so can a story setting in which specific information is embedded (R.C. Anderson et al 1977a). Voss and his colleagues (Chiesi et al 1979, Spilich et al 1979) have shown that individuals with high prior knowledge of a topic remember more propositions from a text on that topic. They have suggested that prior knowledge aids readers in building and carrying in memory the macropropositions (Kintsch & van Dijk 1978) needed to make the story coherent. Other research (e.g. Thorndyke & Hayes-Roth 1979) is beginning to explore how schemata both facilitate and interfere with transfer of knowledge in learning from texts.

To a considerable extent today's work on the role of schemata in reading comprehension echoes an earlier line of work, introduced by Ausubel (1968) on the role of "advance organizers" in facilitating comprehension and retention of prose materials. A large body of empirical work has accumulated since Ausubel first proposed his theory on the effectiveness of advance organizers, and advance organizer research is still current. Several existing reviews (Barnes & Clawson 1975, Hartley & Davies 1976, Lawton & Wanska 1977, Mayer 1979) make it unnecessary to review this work in detail here. The kinds of organizers, the populations for study, and the conditions under which the organizers were used have varied widely. Given these variations, it is not surprising that conclusions about effectiveness of organizers have differed. It is clear that conditions exist under which provision of advance information relevant to the content of a text can indeed facilitate learning and retention of the material in the text. It has not been clear, however, what these conditions are or what the rules are for constructing advance organizers. A recent review by Mayer (1979) helps considerably because it specifies the conditions under which advance organizers can be expected to facilitate learning.

Story grammars   Several investigators have been exploring the ways in which highly schematized knowledge about "typical" sequences of events in narrative stories affects comprehension of this class of texts. A major branch of this work originated with a paper by Rumelhart (1975), in which he proposed that stories have a "deep structure" which, via a set of rewrite rules, becomes instantiated in a particular surface text structure. Understanding of stories, he suggested, depends on the reader's or listener's knowledge of both the paradigmatic base structures and the rules for expressing these structures in the surface text. Together these constitute a "grammar" for stories. Subsequently several investigators (Mandler & Johnson 1977, Thorndyke 1977, Stein & Glenn 1979) modified the grammar to make it applicable to a wider variety of stories, and other models of story structure have also appeared (e.g. Bower et al 1979). These grammars guide most of the current work.

A story grammar is actually a specification of a schema for a well-formed narrative story. The story schema specifies the types of information which should occur and the types of logical relationships that should link the parts. Several categories of information must occur, in order, in a well-formed story. Together these categories, in the specified order, make up an episode. Episodes themselves can be related with differing degrees of dependency. Another line of work on story schemata (Kintsch 1977, van Dijk 1977) develops from research in linguistics on the semantic structure of discourse. This work can also be viewed as an extension of the Kintsch and van Dijk theory of reading and text coherence. These findings account not only for local coherence, but for the overall coherence of the text via the building and linking of "macropropositions" (Kintsch & van Dijk 1978).

Story comprehension and recall are sensitive to the order in which categories of information are presented. People have difficulty recalling stories in which information is given in orders other than those specified in the grammar, and they tend to recall story information in the order predicted by the grammar, even when the text from which they learn the story uses a nonstandard order (Kintsch 1977, Kintsch et al 1977, Thorndyke 1977, Mandler 1978, Stein & Nezworski 1978, Bower et al 1979, Mandler & DeForest 1979, Stein & Glenn 1979). Young children are especially dependent on standard orders. There are also regularities in which categories of information in the story are most likely to be recalled, even when stories are presented in the standard sequence. Initiating events, attempts to achieve a goal, and consequences are nearly always remembered, while other categories, especially internal cognitive responses of the characters, have a low probability of recall. Further, if statements are added to the recall protocol that were not initially in the text, they are likely to fall into the initiating attempt and consequence categories (Mandler & Johnson 1977, Thorndyke 1977, Mandler 1978, Stein & Glenn 1979).

These findings suggest that certain categories are central to the structure of the story. However, some recent research (Black & Wilensky 1979) suggests that the semantic content, rather than form or placement of the information within the story, may be determining recall. Attempts to enlarge story research beyond simple demonstration of the reality of the grammars have been leading psychologists increasingly to a concern for the specific kinds of social knowledge held by children of different ages and stages of development. In particular, investigators have been examining development of the child's understanding of the relationship between motivations or intentions of characters and the outcomes of their actions (e.g. Austin et al 1977, Nezworski et al 1979, Bruce 1980, Goldman 1980, Stein & Goldman 1980, Bisanz & Voss 1981). The nature of inferences about both real-world and story situations is being explored in this research.

Written composition: Another application of schema theories   Written composition, the complement of reading comprehension, is just beginning to receive attention from psychologists, often working collaboratively with teachers of English (Button et al 1975, Frederiksen et al 1980, Gregg & Steinberg 1980). This work is marked by attention to the *processes* as opposed to the products of composition and by a general view of composition as a schema-driven problem-solving process. Flower & Hayes (1980a,b, Hayes & Flower 1980) have been comparing the processes of expert and novice adult writers within the context of an information-processing model of composition that identifies the three interacting stages: *planning* the structure, *translating* plans into text, and *reviewing* one's product. Bereiter & Scardamalia (1981) have been studying the development of composition skills in children, particularly emphasizing the difficulties of switching from the interactive mode of language production that characterizes conversation to the written mode in which the writer must generate language in the absence of an immediately responding audience. Bereiter and Scardamalia have found that the tasks of searching for appropriate content and planning a piece of writing are more effectively performed by children for narrative story compositions than for other genres of writing, since narratives are clearly the genre with which children have had the most experience. This finding suggests an important role for well-developed discourse schemata in the composition process.

INSTRUCTIONAL IMPLICATIONS OF RECENT COMPREHENSION RE-SEARCH   The view of reading comprehension stressed here is too recent to have yet generated many instructional applications. However, a few efforts to teach reading "strategies" have been made. In addition, an older line of work on questions and other adjuncts to texts may eventually be reinterpreted in light of today's more constructivist view of the reading process.

Teaching reading strategies   Various studies have shown that people adapt their reading to local features of the text. For example, reading rates are slower and there is more checking back at points in a text where ambiguous, inconsistent, or incoherent information is encountered (Kieras 1977). Eye movement data demonstrate additional processing activity at points where information from important clauses must be integrated and inferences made (Just & Carpenter 1981) and on parts of the text that are relevant to a particular kind of information the reader is trying to get from a passage (Rothkopf & Billington 1979). Skilled readers also adjust their reading rates to the general readability of the text (Bassin & Martin 1976, Coke 1976) and the kinds of information they seek to acquire (e.g. McConkie et al 1973, Samuels & Dahl 1975), and several studies cited above show that the number and types of inferences made depend upon the purpose for which a text is read. This evidence that skilled readers modify their processing to fit the demands of the reading situation has suggested the possibility of directly teaching reading strategies to less skilled people.

A number of investigators have instructed subjects to use a particular strategy during reading, and then have examined effects on comprehension and memory. Among the strategies that have been shown to improve performance are "imagining" the situation described in the text (e.g. Gustafsson 1977, Tirre et al 1980), generating sentences about story paragraphs (Doctorow et al 1978), generating questions about the text (Frase & Schwartz 1975), and elaborating and reorganizing material in the text

(Shimmerlik & Nolan 1976, Reder 1979). While simple strategies of this kind can be evoked by experimental instructions, the likelihood of using them under normal reading conditions must depend upon individuals' abilities to monitor their own comprehension as a basis for deliberately modifying processing (A. L. Brown, 1980). These abilities, which are at least partly a function of age, seem to depend critically on sensitivity to important relationships in a text.

There have been a few attempts to directly instruct self-monitoring skills. A. L. Brown, Campione & Barclay (1979) trained mildly retarded students on a set of strategies that included self-checking and estimating their own readiness to take a test. Larkin & Reif (1976) successfully taught a set of skills specific to learning quantitative relational concepts from physics texts and found transfer to concepts outside physics. Finally, Holley and associates (1979) increased comprehension of texts by teaching students to represent the concepts and relationships expressed in the text in a diagrammatic form similar to the network diagrams used by psychologists to represent the knowledge structures in long-term memory. These training efforts form part of a growing body of research on the possibility of improving general mental abilities through instruction, further discussed in the Intelligence and Aptitude section of this article.

Adjuncts to texts   When texts are used to teach a particular subject matter, various devices can be used to make learning more likely to occur (Rothkopf 1976). Work on adjunct aids, such as questions placed in various positions in the text, is more than a decade old. Several recent reviews (Anderson & Biddle 1975, Faw & Waller 1976, Rickards & Denner 1978) document and summarize the considerable body of empirical work in the area. In the more recent work there is more careful attention to the structure of the text in terms of importance and subordination relationships, density and distribution of information, and details of the relationships between texts and questions. Increasingly, distinctions are made between verbatim and paraphrase questions, or between rote and comprehension questions. There has also been an extension of the range of texts studied and the types of populations included (in particular, children and poor readers have been studied in addition to relatively well-educated adults).

While most research on adjunct aids has been on questions, a number of other adjuncts have also been studied. Among the adjuncts to texts that can, under certain conditions, aid learning of specific material are headings (Doctorow et al 1978), titles (Kozminsky 1977), and underlining and marking the text (Bausell & Jenkins 1977). An important extension of adjunct aid research has investigated the role of reading "goals" (i.e. advance specification of what kind of information to look for in the text) on learning and text processing (e.g. Rothkopf & Billington 1979, Rothkopf & Koether 1978, Gagne et al 1977, Geiselman 1977).

Despite repeated calls for theories that can account for questioning effects in terms of cognitive processes, there seems to have been only slight progress in this direction. The adjunct literature is still largely concerned with documenting which types of questions, in which positions in the text, and with what testing delays most affect learning. Attempts to explain these effects proceed largely in terms of "attending" or "set," which are constructs that invite but do not supply process explanations. A few authors have offered theoretical accounts of their findings to explain the ways in which text material is encoded and retrieved from temporary and long-term memory (e.g. R. C. Anderson & Biddle 1975, Rickards et al 1976, Kozminsky 1977, Andre & Womack 1978). In addition, a few recent studies have used measures such as reading times and eye movements (Reynolds et al 1979, Rothkopf & Billington 1979) or clustering in recall (Gagne et al 1977) to more directly assess processing when adjunct aids are present. At the moment, however, there has emerged no integrative account capable of linking questioning effects either to schema-theoretic theories of reading or to general propositional models of reading such as Kintsch and van Dijk's.

MATHEMATICS, SCIENCE, AND PROBLEM SOLVING

Over the past decade there has been a marked shift in the kinds of tasks studied by psychologists interested in human problem solving. Newell & Simon's (1972) landmark work described investigations that used puzzle-like tasks with well-defined structures. Today psychologists are studying loosely structured tasks whose solutions depend on a rich body of knowledge that problem solvers must bring with them from past experience. This shift within information-processing psychology has rendered much of the literature on problem solving relevant to the psychology of instruction, since the tasks now studied are often part of school, university, or technical curricula. Among the instructionally relevant task domains now being investigated are a number of topics in mathematics and physics, along with work on the learning and teaching of general problem-solving skills.

Mathematics

Mathematics is emerging as a prime topic in the cognitive psychology of instruction. This is partly because of its obvious importance in the school curriculum and partly because mathematicians' carefully formulated statements of the subject matter provide a well-defined arena for the study of psychological processes. Among the themes that characterize recent work on the psychology of mathematics are the relationships between computational skill and understanding, the role of mental representations in learning, and the ways in which new knowledge is constructed by learners. As in the field of reading comprehension, close associations and mutual influence exist between cognitive psychology and artificial intelligence. There is also growing communication between psychologists and researchers in mathematics education. Resnick & Ford (1980) provide a recent review of mathematics learning and instruction as studied by psychologists, and Begle (1979) reviews the empirical literature in mathematics education.

COMPUTATION   Calculation is traditionally at the heart of the elementary school mathematics curriculum, and psychologists' interest in the learning and teaching of calculation dates back at least to Thorndike's (1922) work on the *Psychology of Arithmetic.* Until recently, however, studies of calculation aimed to establish the relative difficulty of various types of problems, without attempting a psychological explanation of why some problems are more difficult than others. In the past decade cognitive psychologists have been testing detailed models of the processes involved in various kinds of computational problems. In the process they have begun to explore how the understanding of number and computational skill are related.

Arithmetic facts   Mathematics educators usually distinguish between knowing arithmetic "facts" (combinations of two numbers such as 3 + 5, 8 – 2, 9 X 4) and using these facts in complex calculations such as multidigit subtraction or long division. For many years, the "facts" were implicitly taken to be the most elemental units of calculation. It was assumed that they were memorized and then recalled on demand; in other words, that no reasoning went on in arriving at an answer. Recent work, however, has established quite clearly that these most basic of calculations can themselves be analyzed as psychologically complex events. Groen & Parkman's (1972) study is the point of reference for most of this work. These investigators showed that a model for simple addition, in which a counter is set to the larger of the two addends (regardless of whether it is presented first or second) and then incremented a number of times equal to the smaller addend, best accounted for the pattern of reaction times for problems with sums up to 10. This has become known as the *min* model because reaction time is a linear function of the minimum of the two addends. With respect to children, the finding has since been replicated and the model slightly refined in studies that have extended both the populations and the range of problems (Svenson 1975, Svenson et al 1976, Svenson & Broquist 1975). Groen & Resnick (1977) have further established that even when children are taught a simpler to learn (but less efficient to perform) procedure for addition they are likely to invent the *min* procedure for themselves after a number of weeks of practice. This is reminiscent of the process Krutetskii (1976) called "curtailment," in which children (especially the more mathematically able) develop shortcut procedures that are more efficient than the ones taught.

Counting models have been applied to other simple arithmetic tasks, such as subtraction (Woods et al 1975, Svenson & Hedenborg 1979) and addition with one of the addends unknown (Groen & Poll 1973). The validity of these models as accounts of mental calculation is supported by overt counting performances observed in informal problem-solving situations (Ginsburg 1977, Fuson 1981, Steffe & Thompson 1981); and they are by now widely accepted as accounts of children's arithmetic processes, at least during the early stages of acquisition. The picture is less clear for adults. Their reaction times fit the *min* model (Groen & Parkman 1972) but with a time value for each increment so small that it cannot be assumed to reflect actual mental counting. This could be accounted for by assuming that adults usually "look up" addition facts in a long-term memory store (which should produce a flat and fast reaction-time pattern), but occasionally forget a fact and then go through the incrementing procedure. Averaging across the look-up and incrementing trials would produce the fast value-per-increment that the data showed. However, Parkman (1972) found that the *min* model also fits two-digit multiplication in adults. It is implausible that multiplication is routinely performed by adults via incrementing (especially at the high speeds the data showed), and this has led to questioning the counting explanation for adult performance in addition as well. An alternative possibility is that memory stores are ordered so that look-up takes longer for some number facts than others. This would accord well with findings of Winkelman & Schmidt (1974), who found associative confusions between addition and multiplication, and Ashcraft & Battaglia (1978), who found that adults took an especially long time to reject as incorrect answers that differed from the correct answer by only 1 or 2. However, a detailed and plausible theoretical account of such an ordered memory store and its functioning has yet to be developed.

Calculation algorithms   Several investigations have established that when they make errors in extended calculations, children are likely to be systematically following incorrect algorithms rather than simply forgetting arithmetic facts (Menchinskaya & Moro 1975, Ginsburg 1977, J. S. Brown & Burton 1978). Systematic but incorrect arithmetic procedures have come to be called "buggy algorithms." Considerable recent effort has gone into explaining how these buggy algorithms arise (J. S. Brown & VanLehn 1981,

Resnick 1981). It is clear that they represent constructions or "inventions" by the learner (Resnick 1980), and this makes them a particularly apt domain in which to study the interaction between computational skill and understanding of mathematical concepts. This effort is complemented by observations of correct invented calculation procedures by children (Groen & Resnick 1977, Ginsburg 1981). These invented procedures reflect knowledge of the base-ten system of notation, principles of commutativity, and the possibility of partitioning and regrouping quantities to make use of heavily overlearned arithmetic knowledge.

Performance of mental calculation is a skill not explicitly called for in literate cultures. There is evidence that when required to do mental calculations, most adults attempt to perform them by imagining that the normal tools of calculation are present. Westerners go through steps much like those of written calculation (Hayes 1973, Hitch 1978), while expert Japanese abacus operators generate images of successive abacus displays (Hatano et al 1977, Hatano 1981). Mental arithmetic performed the same way as written procedures, however, create strains on short-term memory (Hitch 1978). It is therefore not surprising that adults who are expert at mental calculation do not attempt to mimic written procedures, but instead analyze numbers and their relationships in order to construct efficient mental strategies (Hunter 1968).

The mental representation of number   It is becoming clear from the findings on calculation procedures that a fully developed theory of arithmetic performance will have to include specification of the kinds of knowledge of numbers and their relationships that people hold in memory. Shepard, Kilpatric & Cunningham (1975) investigated number representations by asking adult subjects to give similarity ratings of all pairs of numbers from 0 to 9. Multidimensional scaling of these ratings revealed that the numbers tended to cluster according to magnitude, powers, and roots; prime and composite numbers were also distinguished, as were odd and even numbers. Judgments of numerical inequality can also be used to infer internal representations. Several studies have shown that both children and adults take longer to decide which digit (or dot display) is larger the closer the two quantities are in size (e.g. Sekuler & Mierkiewicz 1977, Potts et al 1978). This has been taken as evidence that quantity information is stored in analog form, so that difference judgments are made much as psychophysical judgments are (cf Holyoak 1978).

STORY PROBLEMS   Story problems are one of the most difficult topics in the school mathematics curriculum. This topic also links mathematics with language understanding. For both of these reasons, story problems have attracted more attention from psychologists than most other topics in mathematics. Earlier work established some of the "structural variables"—such as position of the unknown and number of actions required—that render story problems difficult, but did not clearly relate difficulty to the mental processes involved in solution. Soviet research (e.g. Mikhal'skii 1975) has given quite detailed accounts of processing difficulties but has not linked them explicitly to problem structure. More recent work has focused on the semantic relationships expressed in stories and the cognitive processes by which they are interpreted.

The most extensive research has been done on simple addition and subtraction problems. Results of studies done in several countries (Greeno 1980, Carpenter & Moser 1981, Fuson 1981, Nesher 1981, Vergnaud 1981) have suggested that a limited number of basic story "schemata" (e.g., combination of quantities, changing a quantity by adding or removing from it, comparing two quantities) are sufficient to characterize the situations described in all such problems. However, there are no simple one-to-one relationships between words used in a problem and the schema of the overall story. This analysis suggests three basic sources of difficulty in solving story problems. First, children may not yet have a good command of some of the basic schemata. This seems to be particularly the case for comparison schemata, which all of the cited studies show causing difficulty as late as third grade. Second, a solution strategy that attends to surface cues (e.g. key words such as "more" and "fewer") will often produce wrong answers. A third source of difficulty lies in the complexity of establishing a representation for an unknown which is in other than the final ("result") position of a story. This is particularly the case when the starting quantity is unknown and some change must be made to it. The subject must then modify the initial problem schema in order to infer the appropriate operation. A family of formal computational models (Greeno 1980) has been constructed which highlights the schema-driven character of story problem solution. Separate models that match performance at different levels of skill allow strong inferences about the kind of knowledge available at different points in the development of problem solving competence.

Only scattered studies exist for more complex story problems, but those that have examined the semantic schemata underlying problems have found sharp differences in ease of comprehending different schemata. These findings seem to parallel the better developed findings for addition and subtraction (Bourgeois & Nelson 1977). Several studies have also shown that skilled word-problem solvers are able to identify the underlying semantic schemata of algebra story problems (Krutetskii 1976, Hinsley et al 1977, Silver 1979) and use these structures to aid in problem solution. This is in contrast to a solution style that is sometimes recommended for teaching:

sentence-by-sentence direct translation into equations followed by solutions.

EARLY MATHEMATICAL KNOWLEDGE   Children's early concepts of number have received a large share of psychologists' attention, probably because of the centrality of the topic in Piaget's theory. For many years work on this topic sought to replicate the Piagetian finding that important aspects of number were not understood by children at the outset of school (or conversely, to show that number concepts could be acquired ahead of Piagetian schedule through training). The most recent research, however, represents a new kind of effort. It aims to discover the natural, untutored, mathematical competencies that children *do* possess. Gelman & Gallistel (1978) have analyzed number concepts into a set of specific principles (e.g. stable ordering of number names, cardinality, one-to-one correspondence), and have demonstrated that children 3 years of age show understanding of these principles when set sizes are very small. Greeno (1979) has developed a model that formally specifies the knowledge structures and processes that correspond to the Gelman and Gallistel counting principles.

Ginsburg (1977) has documented extensive informal knowledge of arithmetic on the part of preschool children, and Saxe (1979) has analyzed the developmental relationships between counting and other number skills. It has also been established that children—like adults—are able to "subitize" (quantify at a glance) small sets of up to three or four objects (Klahr & Wallace 1976). Brainerd (1979) presents data indicating that the natural growth of number concepts in children begins with concepts of ordinal relationships (embodied in counting and in transitive comparisons of quantity) rather than cardinality of sets (embodied in one-to-one comparisons of quantity), and that ability to perform addition and subtraction with small numbers actually develops before understanding of cardinality. The instructional implications, which are directly tested in some of Brainerd's experiments, run counter to the prescriptions for early mathematics teaching that are embedded in various "new math" programs; however, this remains a matter for debate.

The research just described is part of a new look at Piagetian constructs that is of potentially great relevance to instruction. Reanalyses of some of the classic Piagetian tasks have served to stress the fact that failure to perform a particular variant of the task does not necessarily signal complete incompetence with respect to basic concepts (Brainerd 1978). Apparently small changes in wording or physical presentation can substantially increase children's ability to perform tasks such as class inclusion (e.g. Trabasso et al 1978, Markman & Siebert 1976, Wilkinson 1976). Computational models of Piagetian task performance (Klahr & Wallace 1976) have also yielded evidence that unavailability of individual components of a task may produce failure, even though important semantic and logical relationships may in fact be grasped by the child. "Neo-Piagetian" interpretations of mathematics learning have also been proposed. For example, Case (1978) has interpreted failure on Piagetian tasks in terms of limited memory capacity that prevents young children from activating and coordinating several schemata simultaneously. He has shown that it is possible to build up a capacity for solving problems (such as unknown-first addition problems) that are normally very difficult for first graders, via instruction that simplifies the presentation to reduce the memory load. Another interpretation of Case's instruction is possible, however: namely that his "simplified" forms of the problem actually taught a schema for interpreting the problems, and it was acquisition of this schema rather than memory-load reduction that improved children's performance.

OTHER TOPICS IN MATHEMATICS   Other topics in mathematics are just beginning to receive attention from psychologists and other cognitive scientists. Currently published work on algebra (Shevarev 1975), largely descriptive in character, is based on extensive protocols of the behavior of individuals attempting to solve various kinds of problems.

Greeno (1978, Greeno et al 1979) developed computational models that match the essential characteristics of high school students' performances as they construct geometry proofs or perform geometry constructions. These models highlight the role of strategic knowledge specific to geometry (e.g. looking for vertical and corresponding angles or for side-angle-side patterns) in problem solving. This kind of strategic knowledge is not now taught in most geometry courses. The cognitive task analysis has thus yielded a direct suggestion for curriculum modification. The Greeno geometry data has been used as the basis for a computational program that acquires strategies of proof via practice on geometry problems (J. R. Anderson et al 1981). This work constitutes one of the most complete cognitive theories of learning available at present and signals one of the important agendas for cognitive-instructional psychology during the next decade: characterization of the processes of learning as well as of performance (see Anderson 1981 for a collection of "state of the art" papers in this area).

CONCRETE MODELS IN MATHEMATICS TEACHING   Mathematics educators have for several decades favored the use of concrete representations of mathematical concepts in the teaching of arithmetic (Resnick & Ford 1980). While it is established that the use of concrete materials often enhances learning, little is known about the processes that underlie these effects. Resnick (1981) has demonstrated that requiring step-by-step mappings between operations in a written form and operations in a physical representation enhances both written calculation skill and understanding of the mathematical principles that justify a written algorithm. However, without this enforced mapping children may simply learn an alternative means of calculation with the concrete materials. A parallel finding by Hatano (1981) shows that encouragement of mental imagery during abacus training is required if such training is to result in enhanced arithmetic performance without the abacus. In addition, Mayer (1975) found that use of a pictorial model which helped students "role play" what a computer would do as it received each command in a program helped students learn computer programming skills. Although some general principles for selecting representations for mathematics teaching have been suggested (Resnick 1976b, Fischbein 1977), there is as yet very little systematic work that explores which kinds of representations are most effective.

Science and Problem Solving

KNOWLEDGE STRUCTURES IN SCIENTIFIC PROBLEM SOLVING   Research on science learning and problem solving shares with mathematics a focus on the ways in which knowledge is organized and accessed and the ways in which domain-specific knowledge and general strategies of problem solving interact. The bulk of psychological research on science learning has concentrated on physics—especially mechanics. Several studies have shown a relationship between skill in solving physics problems and the kinds of knowledge structures possessed by the learner. Shavelson & Stanton (1975) developed a method for comparing the clustering of associations among physics terms in students' and professors' mental representations, and found that over the course of instruction students' cluster patterns moved closer to those of their instructors and to the structure presented in the instructional text. Thro (1978) replicated this finding and also showed that students who performed best on physics problems had clustering structures most closely matching the instructors' by the end of the course. In each of these studies, an important characteristic of the more advanced knowledge structures was their greater hierarchical organization.

A number of studies have shown that experts in various domains process information in larger chunks than novices (e.g. Reitman 1976, Chase & Simon 1973, Chi 1978). The substantive content of these chunks, however, has only recently been investigated. Chi et al (1980) have shown that when asked to sort and characterize physics problems (but not solve them), advanced graduate students in physics respond to the basic physics principles that can be abstracted from a problem; while undergraduates who have had one course in physics respond to the literal surface features of the problem. Larkin and associates (1980) have built computational programs that model the performance of novices and experts on problems in mechanics. The novice program begins by directly translating the verbal and diagrammatic information in the problem statements into algebraic formulas and then uses a "backward" (means-ends) strategy to work the problems. By contrast, the expert program uses information in its more extensive knowledge structure to build a "physical representation" of the problem and then works forward toward a solution. These contrasting novice-expert strategies are in good accord with data reported by Simon & Simon (1978) and Bhaskar & Simon (1977). Other work on knowledge structures in physics is also pointing to the importance of specific knowledge about the domain in successful reasoning (Clement 1979). In particular, there is an emerging body of work showing that students have strongly held and well-integrated beliefs about natural phenomena that can actually interfere with learning the modern scientific constructs taught in high school and college courses (e.g. Champagne et al 1980).

SCIENTIFIC REASONING   The question of when and how the ability to reason scientifically develops has concerned developmental psychologists as well as those more directly concerned with instruction in science. Efforts to teach the abilities involved in formal reasoning (e.g. Siegler & Liebert 1975, Lawson & Wollman 1976) have typically succeeded in teaching preadolescent children to perform some of the Piagetian formal reasoning tasks. Transfer has generally been limited, however, and there has been a recurrent finding that older children benefited more easily from instruction. Siegler (1976, 1978) has conducted a number of studies aimed at uncovering the source of this age-related ability to benefit from instruction. His analyses have demonstrated that children's responses to reasoning tasks are governed by rules, that these rules appear in an ordered developmental sequence, and that children unable to benefit from instruction that relied largely on feedback could be shown to have failed to encode (notice) certain key attributes (e.g. distance of weights on a balance scale). Teaching directed at increasing the encoding of these attributes substantially improved younger children's ability to benefit from the more general instruction. Rule- and task-structure based interpretations of development and instruction in performing various mathematical and scientific reasoning tasks have also been proposed by Spada (1978) and Scandura (1977).

TEACHING PROBLEM SOLVING   There have been a number of efforts to teach general problem-solving skills, often in conjunction with mathematics, science, and engineering courses (O'Neil 1978, Lochhead & Clement 1979, Schoenfeld 1979, Tuma & Reif 1980). For the moment, evidence favors the teachability of domain-specific skills, but wide generalizability of taught skills has yet to be demonstrated. This is what might be expected in light of the important role of domain-specific knowledge in problem solving that was noted above for physics (cf Greeno 1977). Nevertheless, strong arguments for continuing to explore the possibilities of teaching general strategies can be made (Simon 1980).

Work toward the development of automated tutoring programs (e.g. Stevens & Collins 1980) is perhaps the best current instantiation of a widely shared intuition that problem-solving activity in the context of rich knowledge structures will probably best serve both the general strategy and the specific subject matter goals of instruction. These programs are intended to query pupils in ways that force them to search their existing knowledge in order to answer questions for which answers are not immediately available. In the process, it is hypothesized, learners will acquire both more fully connected knowledge structures and an ability to use the querying strategies on their own. Most of the work on interactive tutoring to date, however, has focused on the problem of building the knowledge structures and questioning strategies that can guide the tutor's behaviors. As a result, little is now known about the actual effect on learners.

INTELLIGENCE AND APTITUDE

For many decades the concepts of intelligence and aptitude, particularly as expressed in tests of mental ability, played a central role in those branches of psychology concerned with the theory and practice of education. In the years immediately preceding the 1970s, interest in intelligence research waned. Despite increased sophistication in psychometric methods, progress in defining intelligence or in explaining the ability of intelligence tests to predict subsequent learning performance was limited (Estes 1974). In addition, changing conceptions of the origins of intelligence and of the ways in which environmental encounters could modify the phenotype were calling the older views (which were rooted in a conception of genetically determined, fixed intelligence) into question.

Recently, there has been an intense revival of research on the nature of intelligence, and this research has had a decidedly new look (Resnick 1976a, Sternberg & Detterman 1979, Friedman et al 1980, Snow et al 1980). In the more recent work there has been (a) a focus on defining intelligence rather than perfecting technological instruments for prediction; (b) an assumption that the definition would require characterization of intelligence and aptitudes in terms of cognitive processes or the actual processes of learning; and (c) an emphasis on how descriptions of individual differences in cognitive processing abilities might become the basis for adapting instruction to make it more effective for all individuals, rather than simply predicting success or failure in standard instructional situations (Glaser 1972). Some factor-analytic work still continues (e.g. Jarman & Das 1977, Horn 1979, Humphreys 1979), along with efforts to improve predictive testing by changing test administration procedures (e.g. A. L. Brown & French 1979, Carlson & Wiedl 1979). However, a new emphasis on discovering cognitive processes that underlie test performance has largely driven attention away from the factor-analytic method of study that characterized earlier efforts to define the nature of intelligence. Pellegrino & Glaser (1979) have made a useful distinction between a "cognitive correlates" and a "cognitive components" approach to the study of intelligence. The "correlates" approach uses an aptitude test as a criterion measure and seeks more elementary cognitive processes that are highly correlated with the test criterion. The "cognitive components" approach uses the test items as tasks to be analyzed in a search for the component processes of test performance itself. Research directly relating aptitude analyses to instruction has focused either on aptitude-treatment interactions (ATI) or on the possibility of training general learning strategies.

Cognitive Correlates of Aptitude

A major line of research seeks to identify basic cognitive processes that distinguish between high and low scorers on a particular aptitude test. The primitive processing parameters for study are drawn from the mainstream of basic research on cognitive processes, especially memory processes. This line of research was initiated by Hunt (1978), who suggests that verbal performance requires both the specific verbal knowledge that is called upon by the task and the exercise of certain mechanistic processes by which information is manipulated. According to Hunt's theory, individuals with less efficient mechanistic processes have to work harder at learning tasks involving verbal information. Over time this handicap produces relatively large individual differences in verbal skill and knowledge. The theoretical argument is buttressed by data from studies that have investigated the relationship between performance on laboratory information-processing tasks and scores on global measures of aptitude, such as IQ tests and college admission tests. Although early efforts (e.g. Hunt et al 1973) looked for associations with quantitative as well as verbal aptitude, the bulk of the work has focused on the correlates of either verbal ability or general intelligence measures that are heavily verbal in character. Findings concerning tasks and parameters associated with those measures can be briefly summarized as follows:

CODE ACCESS   The most robust finding in this literature concerns differences in the time needed to access name codes in long-term memory. Code access is defined as the difference between the time it takes to decide whether two stimuli have the same name (e.g. A = a) and the time it takes to decide whether they are physically identical (A ≠ a), or name identity time minus physical identity time (NI – PI). Stimuli in these experiments have been letters (Hunt et al 1975), pictures (Hunt 1976), homonyms (Goldberg et al 1977), and other symbols (Lyon 1977, Bisanz et al 1979). Subjects have ranged from children of varying mental abilities and ages to selected groups of university students. Across all of these variations, a fair summary is that the more verbally able need less time to access name codes (i.e. they show smaller NI–PI differences) than the less verbally able. Across studies there tends to be an increase in the NI–PI difference as one moves from high-verbal university students to young adults not in a university, to normal elementary school children, and finally to mildly retarded school children (Hunt 1978). A recent review of a number of studies on individual differences in code access (Carroll 1980) suggests that the apparent relationship of the NI–PI parameter may be an artifact of the fact that all of the tasks have a high loading on a perceptual speed factor, which is itself related to general mental ability (see also Jensen & Munro 1979 on the correlation of simple reaction time with IQ). However, this is likely to be debated in the literature for some time.

CATEGORY IDENTIFICATION   A task that appears to be a natural extension of NI–PI is deciding whether two presented nouns are members of the same taxonomic category (e.g. both pear and apple are fruits). Yet in the relatively small number of experiments in which this task has been used (Goldberg et al 1977, Hogaboam & Pellegrino 1978, Ford & Keating 1981), no consistent relationship with verbal ability as NI–PI has been shown.

SCANNING   Another parameter that has been shown to be associated both with differences in tested verbal ability and with age is time to search one's active memory store to determine if a particular item is in a brief list that has been memorized. Fast scan rates have been found to be associated with high verbal scores in university students (Hunt et al 1973). Decreases in scanning time over the 9- to 15-year age range also have been found (Keating et al 1980). Other scanning studies are reviewed by Sternberg (1975).

When a wide spread of ability is studied, the association with scanning emerges quite strongly. Thus, retardates and elderly people take longer per item of search than do typical high school students and adults, and particularly skilled mnemonists take even less time than normal adults. As scanning tasks are made harder, they discriminate better (Hunt et al 1975). However, in making the tasks harder other kinds of processing than simple scanning may be added, so that it is not completely clear what primitive process is being tapped.

Matching verbal descriptions with pictures   The time to comprehend descriptions such as "plus not above star" and decide whether they match a presented visual display is generally lower for high-verbal subjects (Hunt 1978), and the extra time needed to process phrases that contain a negation word ("no" or "not") has been found to be less for high- than for low-verbal subjects (Hunt et al 1975). A detailed look at individual differences in processing this task (MacLeod et al 1978) has revealed that a small number of subjects, who generate visual images and compare them with the picture rather than comparing verbal statements, do not show this effect. This points to the possibility that strategy differences and coding parameters may interact in a number of other task situations, although this has not as yet been examined.

Memory span   The number of items an individual is capable of recalling in a serial list has long been known to be correlated with mental age, and is a component of most IQ tests. A number of psychologists have developed theories of intelligence and mental development based on a span concept (e.g. Bachelder & Denney 1977, Bereiter & Scardamalia 1979). However, there is no convincing account now available concerning what mechanics of processing produce the association between mental age and memory span. For example, conflicting findings on whether memory for items or memory for order contributes most to the correlation between serial memory and intelligence have been reported (Cohen & Gowen 1978, Schwartz & Wiedel 1978, Hunt et al 1975). Increasing rehearsal efficiency has been proposed by many investigators (e.g. Belmont & Butterfield 1971, A. L. Brown 1974, Robinson & Kingsley 1977) as the source of better performance in the more intelligent. There is good evidence that retardates rehearse less than normally intelligent individuals. But it is not clear that rehearsal deficiencies can account for the correlation of memory span with mental age (Ellis 1978). Among recent studies challenging such an account are those that show that suppressing rehearsal does not change the size or order of individual differences (Lyon 1977). Evidence has also been found of *less* clustering in free recall for high- than low-verbal subjects (Hunt et al 1973) suggesting that high verbals rely more on passive memory processes. A potentially related line of investigation attempts to localize primacy and recency effects in memory deficits as a way of determining the extent to which low intelligent or developmentally young subjects are having difficulty in simply reading out information from the short term store; however, results continue to be conflicting (Huttenlocher & Burke 1976, Cohen & Sandberg, 1977, Cohen & Nealon 1979).

In summary, there seems to be enough evidence of individual and age differences in primitive parameters of mental processing that Hunt's notion that small differences in mechanistic processes could cumulate over time to produce considerable differences in verbal skill and knowledge seems plausible. However, it is important to note that, with the exception of the memory span work, a large portion of the findings clearly associating these parameters with individual differences comes from Hunt's own laboratory. Wider replication seems needed before strong conclusions about specific associations can be drawn. Moreover, odd findings such as those of Chiang & Atkinson (1976), showing interaction between sex and the *direction* of association of processing speed with measured aptitude, must eventually be accounted for. Recently, increasingly detailed analyses have shown that processes initially regarded as "primitives" are in fact made up of a number of separate components, with different rates of development (Hogaboam & Pellegrino 1978, Bisanz et al 1979), suggesting possibly different associations with intelligence. Finally, reanalyses and reinterpretations, such as Carroll's (1980) of data from various experimenters, virtually insure that debate over the nature of the relationship between the "primitives" of mental processing and traditionally measured mental ability will continue over the next several years.

Cognitive Components of Aptitude

Carroll (1976) and Simon (1976) first suggested the analysis of test items as cognitive tasks, and several research programs now focus on task analysis of traditional aptitude test items. Perhaps the most ambitious program in terms of the range of tasks studied is Sternberg's work on what he calls a "componential analysis" of intelligence (R. J. Sternberg 1977a,b, 1980b). Sternberg's analyses begin with a specification of the components hypothesized to be involved in the performance of a task. Several models are then specified, differing in the components called on, the sequencing of the components, the number of times each component needs to be executed, and the manner of execution (e.g. exhaustive or self-terminating searches). The models permit predictions of reaction time and error patterns under varying conditions of stimulus structure and task presentation.

Empirical tests of models generated for analogies, for example, have identified a "best fit" model and provided estimates of which processes absorbed most of the processing time. For verbal analogies, encoding of the stimulus terms accounted for about half of the solution time, while 30% of the time was spent on attribute comparison operations. For geometric analogies, attribute comparisons took much longer, both as a percentage of total time (57%) and in absolute terms. Sternberg has extended the analysis of analogies to children (Sternberg & Rifkin 1979, Sternberg & Nigro 1980), making it possible to chart developmental changes in the various components. The most important developmental observation was the greater tendency of children to rely on associations between the words in the analogy instead of analyzing all of the relationships. Other developmental work on analogies has also shown an early dependence on associative responding (Gentile et al 1977).

Other research on analogies performance is largely in agreement with Sternberg's findings on the importance of encoding. Some of the studies have further analyzed the encoding process itself, with particular attention to what aspects of the stimuli are encoded. For example, Mulholland, Pellegrino & Glaser (1980) showed that in geometric analogies individuals analyze stimuli in a systematic serial manner, so that latency of responding is a function of both the number of elements that must be encoded and the number of transformations necessary on each element (cf Royer 1978). They found a sharp increase in both reaction time and errors when multiple transformations on multiple stimuli had to be processed, suggesting that working memory limitations are important in analogy processing. For verbal analogies, studies by Pellegrino & Glaser (1980) and R. J. Sternberg (1977a,b) have all shown that individuals with high aptitude test scores specify more precisely the set of semantic features that relate the word pairs in an analogy, and that the extra time they spend on this process allows them to spend less time on subsequent decision and response processes.

Other test-like tasks that have been subjected to similar analysis include series completion (Pellegrino & Glaser 1980); syllogistic reasoning and transitive inference (Falmagne 1975, R. J. Sternberg 1980a, R. J. Sternberg et al 1980, Sternberg & Weil 1980); spatial abilities tasks such as mental rotation and visual comparison (Egan 1979, Cooper 1980); block designs (Royer 1977); and matrix tasks (Hunt 1974). Not all of this work has been explicitly oriented toward detecting individual differences. Instead, much has been inspired by the Piaget-generated debates over how and when various logical abilities develop in children, and over whether language or spatial representations are central (e.g. Osherson 1974, Falmagne 1975, Johnson-Laird & Wason 1977). We still have little cumulated knowledge about individual differences in processing. Nevertheless, from the perspective of a developing theory of aptitudes and individual differences, any systematic task analysis can be viewed as an important first step. This can be followed by attempts to relate performance models or parameters of specific processing components to individual differences. In fact, it seems likely that as efforts at detailed modeling of tasks proceed, individual differences will have to be considered if the data are to be sensibly interpreted. An interesting case in point is Cooper's (1980) study of visual comparison, in which subjects split naturally into two quite different subgroups, one using a holistic and one an analytic comparison strategy. The two strategies produced very different patterns of latencies, and the groups responded in predictably different ways to variations on task instructions and stimuli.

An emerging issue concerns the role of higher-level "executive" and "control" processes in accounting for individual differences in test performance. Some of the evidence for individual differences in executive and control strategies comes from findings showing that high aptitude individuals are more systematic in performing analogies (Sternberg 1977a,b, Glaser & Pellegrino 1980) and paper-folding and vocabulary tasks (Snow 1980) than low aptitude individuals. Increased attention to these higher-level processes can be expected in future research on the components of intelligence. This trend is paralleled by growing attention to executive and control processes in the work on aptitude training described below.

Aptitudes and Instruction

It is commonly assumed that characterization of the cognitive processes that underlie ability and aptitude differences will permit better adaptation of instruction to individual differences. Two complementary approaches to adaptation can be identified: (*a*) matching instructional treatments to individual processing capacities, and (*b*) training of aptitude-like processes so that learners will be better able to benefit from ordinary instruction.

APTITUDE MATCHING The scientific basis for aptitude matching as a strategy for adaptive instruction is the demonstration of an aptitude-treatment interaction (ATI)—that is, a finding that individuals with a particular aptitude profile progress further under one specified instructional treatment than another. Cronbach & Snow (1977) have provided an extensive review and critique of the ATI literature, and this has been supplemented by some recent reviews (Berliner & Cahen 1973, Snow 1977). Although the major interpreters of ATI research repeatedly stress the goal of reformulating traditional psychometric aptitude theory in terms of the cognitive processes that are implicated in aptitude test performance and in various instructional treatments (e.g. Snow 1978), virtually all existing ATI research is limited to comparisons of rather grossly defined instructional treatments for populations characterized in terms of test scores. The mediating cognitive processes are not assessed in detail. The result is that only the most general conclusions can be drawn about how to match treatments to abilities.

A recurrent finding is that structured treatments (tight sequencing, required responding, teacher control, instructions to process in a particular way, etc.) reduce the correlation between general intelligence and achievement. Low intelligence students do better under these conditions, which are interpreted as reducing the burden of information processing for the learner

(Snow 1977). This kind of instruction sometimes, but not always, suppresses performance of the more able. Despite efforts to distinguish between fluid and crystallized intelligence in ATI experiments, no consistent pattern of differences has emerged. Nor have other more specialized abilities shown consistent patterns of interactions with various treatments, despite many experimental efforts.

A cluster of cognitive styles and motivational traits have shown ATI's (Snow 1977), but various inconsistencies and anomalies in the findings warn against too simplified a conclusion concerning personality and style factors. Instead, a renewed effort to analyze these variables and related cognitive style constructs in terms of cognitive process seems to be needed (cf Goodenough 1976, Messick 1976).

Interactions between instructional treatments and characteristics of learners can also be sought by describing learners not in terms of aptitude traits but of level of knowledge (Mayer et al 1975). Tobias (1976) has reviewed a number of studies of achievement-treatment interactions. These studies tend to show that individuals who enter a course of instruction with little prior knowledge of the field make the best progress under highly structured teaching (as in programmed instructional formats), while those with prior knowledge do as well—and sometimes better—when they only read the material. These results echo the findings (see above) showing that advance organizers and other adjunct aids tend to be of benefit only when students do not already have some information about the topic. They also set in an interesting instructional context the research described above on novice-expert differences in knowledge structures and processing.

APTITUDE TRAINING   There has been much recent interest in the possibility of teaching aptitudes or learning skills. A few of the aptitude training efforts are directly linked to information-processing analyses of intelligence test tasks. In these studies (e.g. Whitely & Dawis 1974, Salomon & Achenbach 1974, Holzman et al 1976, Sternberg & Weil 1980) experimenters have taught knowledge and processing components identified in task analyses and/or specific algorithms for performing tasks such as series completion, syllogisms, or analogies. These studies show that performance on a class of tasks can be improved significantly by teaching their components. No effort has yet been made, however, to determine whether improved performance on the taught tasks also produces general improvement in ability, including transfer to other test-like tasks.

Until recently there was reason to be very cautious about expecting transfer from training on specific tasks. In work with retardates, several investigators had been able to show impressive immediate gains in performance on memory tasks by simply instructing individuals to rehearse the items on the memory lists or to engage in verbal elaboration (e.g. Butterfield et al 1973, A. L. Brown & Barclay 1976, Turnure et al 1976, Engle & Nagle 1979). In these studies, however, there was almost complete lack of transfer, even to only slightly modified tasks. More recently emphasis in training studies has begun to shift to "superordinate" (Belmont et al 1980) or "metacognitive" (Brown 1978) skills such as assessing one's own readiness for a test; and apportioning study time or deciding when to use rehearsal, imagery, or self-interrogation strategies (e.g. A. L. Brown & Campione 1977, Belmont et al 1978, Ross & Ross 1978, Borkowski & Cavanaugh 1979, Kendall et al 1980). After training both transfer and retention have improved. Several interesting papers (Belmont et al 1980, Brown & Campione 1980, Glaser & Pellegrino 1980) have suggested principles for developing general learning skills. These papers can best be thought of as outlining agendas for future research in the field.

Efforts to train intellectual skills have also been made for nonhandicapped populations. Dansereau and his colleagues (Dansereau et al 1979, Holley et al 1979, K. W. Collins et al 1980) have developed a learning-strategy program that includes strategies for comprehension and retention of text information, retrieval and utilization of information, and self-management of one's concentration and goal-setting behavior. The total program has shown a statistically significant but small effect, as measured by cognitive tests and student self-report. A particularly effective component of the training was a special strategy for analyzing texts, which is described above in the section on training reading strategies. Other training efforts have been conducted in the context of programs to increase mathematics and science problem-solving skills and are discussed above in the section on problem solving.

The apparent promise of training that focuses on executive or self-control strategies accords well with theories of intelligence that stress general strategies rather than specific capabilities as the hallmark of those who learn more easily (see especially Baron 1979, Wood 1979). Several investigators have proposed that the source of the ability to control one's own intellectual performance lies in social interactions in which an adult (acting in a formal or informal tutorial role) serves both as external controller and prompter of intellectual activity by the child and as a modeler of self-control strategies that the child can eventually manage alone (Wertsch 1978, Feuerstein 1979, A. L. Brown & Campione 1980). This view of the origins of intelligent self-monitoring is implicit in research efforts as divergent as shaping reasoning processes through computerized tutorial interactions (Stevens & Collins 1980) and characterizing social class differences in maternal teaching styles (Wood 1979).

A decade ago psychologists were actively engaged in developing and assessing intervention programs designed to compensate for social class differences in educational opportunity. Today this is no longer a very active area of study, perhaps partly because early evaluations of preschool interventions had generally reported that increases in IQ or related general measures of intellectual functioning dissipated within a year or two after the intervention had ended. Recent evidence, however, suggests that early interventions may have more lasting benefits than had earlier been thought. Reports on a 10-year follow-up of children who had participated in some of the preschool programs of the 1960s show higher rates of school success for these children than for controls (Darlington et al 1980). A 4-year follow-up on the effects of a special rehabilitation project for low income minority families where the mother's IQ was in the retarded range has also been reported. Children in the treated families show continuing normal IQs, while there were substantial retardation rates for a control sample (Heber 1980).

CONCLUSION

A richly detailed picture of the ways in which people perform many of the tasks central to education is beginning to emerge as a result of the research that has been reviewed here. Many of the emerging questions and directions for further research have been suggested in the course of the review. The task that remains is to consider how useful all of this might be to those concerned with the practical problems of education.

Even a diligent search for instructional implications of cognitive task analyses yields only the relatively general suggestions that have appeared in the course of this chapter. If one were to base prescriptions for instruction entirely on studies that included direct instructional interventions, the suggestions would have to be even more limited. For the moment, cognitive instructional psychology is a largely descriptive science, intent upon analyzing performance but not upon making strong suggestions for improving it. Can instructional psychology become a prescriptive science as well, able to guide processes of teaching as well as describe processes of learning?

In an earlier review of instructional psychology, Glaser & Resnick (1972) outlined five components of a prescriptive theory of learning: (a) description of the state of knowledge to be achieved, (b) description of the initial state in which the learner begins, (c) specification of actions which can be taken to transform the initial state, (d) assessment of specific instructional effects, and (e) evaluation of generalized learning outcomes. It seems fair to say that cognitive instructional psychology has focused most strongly up to now on components a and b. The largest amount of research has been devoted to describing the processes of skilled performers in various domains. With the growing body of work on children and the various expert-novice contrastive studies that have been reported, however, considerable progress is now being made in building descriptions of initial and intermediate states of competence.

With respect to component c, specifying the instructional acts that can help to transform learners' initial states, cognitive instructional psychology has been almost completely silent. Some of the investigators cited here have offered broad suggestions, such as reducing memory demands during the early stages of teaching a concept, linking syntactic rules to the semantic justifications for procedures, or helping students to acquire and organize large amounts of domain-specific information. A few studies have directly investigated the effects of such instruction in some limited domain. However, most of the instructional prescriptions to be gleaned from cognitive psychology must be viewed as very general principles, needing study and elaboration in multiple domains of learning. Meanwhile, instructional design theory (e.g. Merrill & Boutwell 1973, Markle 1978), which is directly concerned with prescribing interventions, has developed without much reference to cognitive psychology. As a step toward an eventual cognitively based instructional design theory, one of the most important things cognitive instructional psychologists might do is begin to describe in detail the cognitive processes involved in learning under various instructional conditions.

With respect to assessment of both specific and general outcomes (components d and e), it appears that instructional psychology now has most of the necessary tools in hand. In theory, at least, it is possible to use the descriptions of target and intermediate knowledge states, now being identified through cognitive task analysis, to create methods of measuring the success of instructional efforts. Greeno (1976) has suggested that descriptions of the knowledge structures of people competent in a domain might provide "cognitive objectives" for instruction. These would not supplant the behavioral objectives that have been guiding most systematic instructional design work, but instead would enrich them. Rather than treating performance on a specified set of tasks as themselves the objectives of instruction, it would become possible to treat task performances as indicators of the understanding and knowledge that are the deeper goals of education. Considered from the laboratory this point seems almost trivial, since this is exactly how most cognitive research proceeds in interpreting behavioral data. But the job of building a technology of mental measurement aimed at describing the content of individual knowledge and the processes by which it is used is not a simple one. Work toward such a new approach to educational assessment would do much to make instructional psychology a more prescriptive science.

Literature Cited

Adams, M. J. 1979. Models of word recognition. *Cognit. Psychol.* 11:133–76

Adams, M. J., Collins, A. 1979. A schema-theoretic view of reading. See Freedle 1979, pp. 1–22

Anderson, J. R., ed. 1981. *Cognitive Skills and Their Acquisition.* Hillsdale, NJ: Erlbaum. In press

Anderson, J. R., Greeno, J. G., Kline, P. J., Neves, D. M. 1981. Learning to plan in geometry. See Anderson 1981

Anderson, R. C., Biddle, B. W. 1975. On asking people questions about what they are reading. In *The Psychology of Learning and Motivation,* ed. G. Bower, pp. 89–132. New York: Academic

Anderson, R. C., Reynolds, R. E., Schallert, E. T. 1977a. Frameworks for comprehending discourse. *Am. Educ. Res. J.* 14:367–81

Anderson, R. C., Spiro, R. J., Anderson, M. C. 1978. Schemata as scaffolding for the representation of information in connected discourse. *Am. Educ. Res. J.* 15(3):433–40

Anderson, R. C., Spiro, R. J., Montague, W. E., eds. 1977b. *Schooling and the Acquisition of Knowledge.* Hillsdale, NJ: Erlbaum

Andre, T., Womack, S. 1978. Verbatim and paraphrased adjunct questions and learning from prose. *J. Educ. Psychol.* 70:796–802

Antos, S. J. 1979. Processing facilitation in a lexical decision task. *J. Exp. Psychol. Hum. Percept. Perform.* August: 527–45

Ashcraft, M. H., Battaglia, J. 1978. Cognitive arithmetic: Evidence for retrieval and decision processes in mental addition. *J. Exp. Psychol. Hum. Learn. Mem.* 4(5):527–38

Austin, V. D., Ruble, D. N., Trabasso, T. 1977. Recall and order effects as factors in children's moral judgments. *Child Dev.* 48:470–74

Ausubel, D. B. 1968. *Educational Psychology: A Cognitive View.* New York: Holt, Rinehart & Winston. 685 pp.

Bachelder, B. L., Denny, M. R. 1977. A theory of intelligence: I. Span and the complexity of stimulus control. *Intelligence* 1:127–50

Baddeley, A., Lewis, V. 1981. Inner active processes in reading: The inner voice, the inner ear and the inner eye. See Lesgold & Perfetti 1981

Barnes, B. R., Clawson, E. V. 1975. Do advance organizers facilitate learning? Recommendations for further research based on an analysis of 32 studies. *Rev. Educ. Res.* 45:637–59

Baron, J. 1978. The word-superiority effect: Perceptual learning from reading. In *Handbook of Learning and Cognitive Processes: Linguistic Functions in Cognitive Theory,* ed. W. K. Estes, Vol. 6. New York: Halsted

Baron, J. 1979. Intelligence and general strategies. In *Strategies of Information Processing,* ed. G. Underwood. London: Academic

Barron, R. W. 1981a. Reading skill and reading strategies: Use of visual and phonological information. See Lesgold & Perfetti 1981

Barron, R. W. 1981b. Some aspects of the development of visual word recognition. See Waller & MacKinnon 1981

Bartlett, F. C. 1932. *Remembering: A Study in Experimental and Social Psychology.* Cambridge, Mass: Univ. Press. 317 pp.

Bassin, C. B., Martin, C. J. 1976. Effects of three types of redundancy reduction on comprehension, reading rate, and reading time of English prose. *J. Educ. Psychol.* 68(5):649–52

Bausell, R. B., Jenkins, J. R. 1977. Effects on prose learning of adjunct cues and the difficulty of material cued. *J. Read. Behav.* 9:227–32

Becker, C. A., Killion, T. H. 1977. Interaction of visual and cognitive effects in word recognition. *J. Exp. Psychol.: Hum. Percept. Perform.* 3:389–401

Begle, E. G. 1979. *Critical variables in mathematics education: Findings from a survey of the empirical literature.* Washington DC: Math. Assoc. Am. Natl. Counc. Teach. Math. 165 pp.

Belmont, J. M., Butterfield, E. C. 1971. Learning strategies as determinants of memory deficiencies. *Cognit. Psychol.* 2:411–20

Belmont, J. M. Butterfield, E. C., Borkowski, J. G. 1978. Training retarded people to generalize memorization methods across memory tasks. In *Practical Aspects of Memory,* ed. M. M. Greeneberg, P. Morris, R. N. Sykes. London: Academic

Belmont, J. M., Butterfield, E. C., Ferretti, R. P. 1980. To secure transfer of training, instruct self-management skills. *Intelligence.* In press

Bereiter, C., Scardamalia, M. 1979. Pascual-Leone's M construct as a link between cognitive-developmental and psychometric concepts of intelligence. *Intelligence* 3:41–63

Bereiter, C., Scardamalia, M. 1981. From conversation to composition: The role of instruction in a developmental process. In *Advances in Instructional Psychology,* ed. R. Glaser, Vol. 2. Hillsdale, NJ: Erlbaum. In press

Berliner, D. C., Cahen, L. S. 1973. Trait-treatment interaction and learning. In *Review of Research in Education,* ed. F. N. Kerlinger, 1:58–94

Bhaskar, R., Simon, H. A. 1977. Problem solving in semantically rich domains: An example from engineering thermodynamics. *Cognit. Sci.* 1(2):193–215

Bisanz, G. L., Voss, J. F. 1981. Sources of knowledge in reading comprehension: Cognitive development and expertise in a content domain. See Lesgold & Perfetti 1981

Bisanz, J., Danner, F., Resnick, L. B. 1979. Changes with age in measures of processing efficiency. *Child Dev.* 50:132–41

Black, J. B., Wilensky, R. 1979. An evaluation of story grammars. *Cognit. Sci.* 3:213–30

Borkowski, J. G., Cavanaugh, J. C. 1979. Maintenance and generalization of skills and strategies by the retarded. In *Handbook of Mental Deficiency,* ed. N. R. Ellis. Hillsdale, NJ: Erlbaum

Bourgeois, R., Nelson, D. 1977. Young children's behavior in solving division problems. *Alberta J. Educ. Res.* 23(3):178–85

Bower, G. H., Black, J. B., Turner, T. J. 1979. Scripts in memory for text. *Cognit. Psychol.* 11:177–220

Brainerd, C. J. 1978. *Piaget's Theory of Intelligence.* Englewood Cliffs, NJ: Prentice-Hall

Brainerd, C. J. 1979. *The origins of the Number Concept.* New York: Praeger

Bransford, J. D., McCarrell, N. S. 1974. A sketch of a cognitive approach to comprehension. In *Cognition and the Symbolic Processes,* ed. W. B. Weimer, D. S. Palermo. Hillsdale, NJ: Erlbaum

Brooks, L. 1977. Visual pattern in fluent word identification. See Reber & Scarborough 1977

Brown, A. L. 1974. The role of strategic behavior in retardate memory. In *International Review of Research in Mental Retardation,* ed. N. R. Ellis, Vol. 7. New York: Academic

Brown, A. L. 1978. Knowing when, where, and how to remember: A problem of metacognition. See Glaser 1978

Brown, A. L. 1980. Metacognitive development and reading. See Spiro et al 1980

Brown, A. L., Barclay, C. R. 1976. The effects of training specific mnemonics

on the metamnemonic efficiency of retarded children. *Child Dev.* 47:70–80

Brown, A. L., Campione, J. C. 1980. Inducing flexible thinking: The problem of access. See Friedman et al 1980

Brown, A. L., Campione, J. C. 1977. Training strategic study time apportionment in educable retarded children. *Intelligence* 1:94–107

Brown, A. L., Campione, J. C., Barclay, C. R. 1979. Training self-checking routines for estimating test readiness: Generalization from list learning to prose recall. *Child Dev.* 50:501–12

Brown, A. L., French, L. A. 1979. The zone of potential development: Implications for intelligence testing in the year 2000. *Intelligence* 3:255–73

Brown, A. L., Smiley, S. S. 1977. Rating the importance of structural units of prose passages: A problem of metacognitive development. *Child Dev.* 48:1–8

Brown, A. L., Smiley, S. S., Day, J. D., Townsend, M. A. R., Lawton, S. C. 1977. Intrusion of a thematic idea in children's recall of prose. *Child Dev.* 48:1454–66

Brown, J. S., Burton, R. R. 1978. Diagnostic models for procedural bugs in basic mathematical skills. *Cognit. Sci.* 2:155–92

Brown, J. S., VanLehn, K. 1981. Toward a generative theory of bugs in procedural skills. In *Addition and Subtraction: Developmental Perspective,* ed. T. Romberg, T. Carpenter, J. Moses. Hillsdale, NJ: Erlbaum. In press

Bruce, B. 1980. Plans and social actions. See Spiro et al 1980

Butterfield, E. C., Wambold, C., Belmont, J. M. 1973. On the theory and practice of improving short-term memory. *Am. J. Ment. Defic.* 77:654–69

Button, J., Bergess, T., Martin, N., McLeod, A., Rosen, H. 1975. *The Development of Writing Abilities (11–18).* London: Macmillan

Carlson, J. S., Wiedl, K. H. 1979. Toward a differential testing approach: Testing-the-limits employing the Raven Matrices. *Intelligence* 3:323–44

Carpenter, P. A., Just, M. A. 1977. Reading comprehension as eyes see it. See Just & Carpenter 1977, pp. 109–39

Carpenter, T., Moser, J. 1981. The development of addition and subtraction problem solving skills. See Brown & VanLehn 1981

Carroll, J. B. 1976. Psychometric tests as cognitive tasks: A new "structure of intellect". See Resnick 1976a

Carroll, J. B. 1980. *Individual difference relations in psychometric and experimental cognitive tasks.* ONR Tech. Rep. 2, Thurstone Psychom. Lab., Univ. N. Carolina, Chapel Hill

Case, R. 1978. Piaget and beyond: Toward a developmentally based theory and technology of instruction. See Glaser 1978

Champagne, A. B., Klopfer, L. E., Anderson, J. H. 1980. Factors influencing learning of classical mechanics. *Am. J. Phys.* In press

Chase, W., Simon, H. A. 1973. Perception in chess. *J. Cognit. Psychol.* (4):55–81

Chi, M. T. H. 1978. Knowledge structures and memory development. In *Children's Thinking—What Develops?,* ed. R. S. Siegler. Hillsdale, NJ: Erlbaum. 371 pp.

Chi, M. T. H., Feltovich, P., Glaser, R. 1980. *Representation of physics knowledge by experts and novices.* ONR Tech. Rep. 2, Learn. Res. Dev. Cent., Univ Pittsburgh, Pa.

Chiang, A., Atkinson, R. C. 1976. Individual differences and interrelationships among a select set of cognitive skills. *Mem. Cognit.* 4:661–72

Chiesi, H. L., Spilich, G. J., Voss, J. F. 1979. Acquisition of domain-related information in relation to high and low domain knowledge. *J. Verb. Learn. Verb. Behav.* 18:257–74

Clement, J. 1979. Mapping a student's causal conceptions from a problem-solving protocol. See Lochhead & Clement 1979

Cohen, R. L., Gowen, A. 1978. Recall and recognition of order and item information in probed running memory, as a function of IQ. *Intelligence* 2(4):343–52

Cohen, R. L., Nealon, J. 1979. An analysis of short-term memory differences between retardates and nonretardates. *Intelligence* 3:65–72

Cohen, R. L., Sandberg, T. 1977. Relation between intelligence and short-term memory. *Cognit. Psychol.* 9:534–54

Coke, E. U. 1976. Reading rate, readability, and variations in task-induced processing. *J. Educ. Psychol.* 68:167–73

Collins, A., Brown, J. S., Larkin, K. M. 1980. Inference in text understanding. See Spiro et al 1980

Collins, K. W., Dansereau, D. F., Garland, J. C., Holley, C. D., McDonald, B. A. 1980. Control of concentration during academic tasks. *J. Educ. Psychol.* In press

Coltheart, M. 1980. Reading, phonological encoding and deep dyslexia. In *Deep Dyslexia,* ed. M. Coltheart, K. E. Patterson, J. C. Marshall, pp. 197–227. London: Routledge & Kegan Paul

Coltheart, M., Davelaar, E., Jonasson, J. T., Besner, D. 1977. Access to the internal lexicon. In *Attention and Performance,* Vol. 6, ed. S. Dornic. Hillsdale, NJ: Erlbaum

Cooper, L. A. 1980. Spatial information processing: Strategies for research. See Snow et al 1980, Vol. 1

Cronbach, L. J., Snow, R. E. 1977. *Aptitudes and Instructional Methods: A Handbook for Research on Interactions.* New York: Irvington. 574 pp.

Crothers, E. J. 1978. Inference and coherence. *Discourse Processes 1:51–71*

Curtis, M. E. 1980. Development of components of reading skill. *J. Educ. Psychol.* In press

Danks, J. H., Fears, R. 1979. Oral reading: Does it reflect decoding or comprehension? See Resnick & Weaver 1979, 3:89–108

Danks, J. H., Hill, G. O. 1981. *Interactive models of lexical access during oral reading.* See Lesgold & Perfetti 1981

Dansereau, D. F., Collins, K. W., McDonald, B. A., Holley, C. D., Garland, J., Diekhoff, G., Evans, S. H. 1979. Development and evaluation of a learning strategy training program. *J. Educ. Psychol.* 71(1):64–73

Darlington, R. B., Royce, J. M., Snipper, A. S., Murray, H. W., Lazar, I. 1980. Preschool programs and later school competence of children from low-income families. *Science* 208(4440):202–4

Doctorow, M., Wittrock, M. C., Marks, C. 1978. Generative processes in reading comprehension. *J. Educ. Psychol.* 70(2):109–18

Dooling, D. J., Christiaansen, R. E. 1977. Episodic and semantic aspects of memory for prose. *J. Exp. Psychol. Hum. Learn. Mem.* 3(4):428–36

Egan, D. E. 1979. Testing based on understanding: Implications from studies of spatial ability. *Intelligence* 3:1–15

Ehri, L. C. 1979. Linguistic insight: Threshold of reading acquisition. See Waller & MacKinnon 1979, pp. 63–114

Ellis, N. R. 1978. Do the mentally retarded have poor memory? *Intelligence* 2:41–54

Engle, R. W., Nagle, R. J. 1979. Strategy training and semantic encoding in mildly retarded children. *Intelligence* 3:17–30

Entwisle, D. R. 1979. The child's social environment and learning to read. See Waller & MacKinnon 1979

Estes, W. K. 1974. Learning theory and intelligence. *Am. Psychol.* 29(10):740–49

Falmagne, R. J., ed. 1975. *Reasoning: Representation and Process.* Hillsdale, NJ: Erlbaum

Faw, H. W., Waller, T. G. 1976. Mathemagenic behaviors and efficiency in learning from prose materials: Review, critique and recommendations. *Rev. Educ. Res.* 46:691–720

Feuerstein, R. 1979. *The Dynamic Assessment of Retarded Performers: The Learning Potential, Assessment Device, Theory, Instruments, and Technique.* Baltimore: Univ. Park

Fischbein, E. 1977. Image and concept in learning mathematics. *Educ. Stud. Math.* 8:153–65

Fischler, I. 1977. Semantic facilitation without association in a lexical decision task. *Mem. Cognit.* 5:335–39

Fleisher, L. S., Jenkins, J. R. 1978. Effects of contextualized and decontextualized practice conditions on word recognition. *Learn. Disabilities Q.* 1(3):39–47

Flower, L. S., Hayes, J. R. 1980a. The dynamics of composing: Making plans and juggling constraints. See Gregg & Steinberg 1980, pp. 31–50

Flower, L. S., Hayes, J. R. 1980b. Plans that guide the composing process. In *Writing: The Nature, Development and Teaching of Written Communication,* ed. C. Frederiksen, M. Whiteman, J. Dominic. Hillsdale, NJ: Erlbaum. In press

Ford, M. E., Keating, D. P. 1981. Developmental and individual differences in long-term memory retrieval: Process and organization. *Child Dev.* In press

Frase, L. T., Schwartz, B. J. 1975. Effect of question production on prose recall. *J. Educ. Psychol.* 67:628–35

Frederiksen, C. H. 1972. Effects of task-induced cognitive operations on comprehension and memory processes. In *Language Comprehension and the Acquisition of Knowledge,* ed. J. B. Carroll, R. O. Freedle, pp. 224–28. Washington DC: Winston

Frederiksen, C. H. 1975a. Acquisition of semantic information from discourse: Effects of repeated exposures. *J. Verb. Learn. Verb. Behav.* 14:158–69

Frederiksen, C. H. 1975b. Effects of context-induced processing operations on semantic information acquired from discourse. *Cognit. Psychol.* 7:139–66

Frederiksen, C. H. 1977. Semantic processing units in understanding text. See Freedle 1977, pp. 57–88

Frederiksen, C. H. 1979. Discourse comprehension and early reading. See Resnick & Weaver 1979, 1:155–86

Frederiksen, C. H., Whiteman, M., Dominic, J., eds. 1980. *Writing: The Nature, Development and Teaching of Written Communication.* Hillsdale, NJ: Erlbaum. In press

Frederiksen, J. R. 1981. Sources of process interactions in reading. See Lesgold & Perfetti 1981

Freedle, R. O., ed. 1977. *Discourse Production and Comprehension,* Vol. 1. Norwood, NJ: Ablex

Freedle, R. O., ed. 1979. *New Directions in Discourse Processing,* Vol. 2. Norwood, NJ: Ablex

Friedman, M., Das, J., O'Connor, N., eds. 1980. *Intelligence and Learning.* New York: Plenum. In press

Fuson, K. 1981. An analysis of the counting-on solution procedure in addition. See Brown & VanLehn 1981

Gagné, E. D., Bing, S. B., Bing, J. R. 1977. Combined effect of goal organization and test expectations on organization in free recall following learning from text. *J. Educ. Psychol.* 69(4):428–31

Garrod, S., Sanford, A. 1977. Interpreting anaphoric relations: The integration of semantic information while reading. *J. Verb. Learn. Verb. Behav.* 16(1):77–90

Geiselman, R. E. 1977. Memory for prose as a function of learning strategy and inspection time. *J. Educ. Psychol.* 69(5): 547–55

Gelman, R., Gallistel, C. R. 1978. *The Child's Understanding of Number.* Cambridge, Mass: Harvard Univ.

Gentile, J. R., Tedesco-Stratton, L., Davis, E., Lund, N. J., Agunanne, B. C. 1977. Associative responding versus analogical reasoning by children. *Intelligence* 1(4):369–80

Gibson, E. J., Levin, H. 1975. *The Psychology of Reading.* Cambridge, Mass: MIT Press

Ginsburg, H. 1977. *Children's Arithmetic: The Learning Process.* New York: Van Nostrand. 197 pp.

Ginsburg, H. 1981. The development of addition in the contexts of culture, social class, and race. See Brown & VanLehn 1981

Glaser, R. 1972. Individuals and learning: The new aptitudes. *Educ. Res.* 1(6): 5–13

Glaser, R., ed. 1978. *Advances in Instructional Psychology,* Vol. 1. Hillsdale, NJ: Erlbaum. 304 pp.

Glaser, R., ed. 1981. *Advances in Instruc-*

tional Psychology, Vol. 2. Hillsdale, NJ: Erlbaum. In press

Glaser, R., Pellegrino, J. 1980. Improving the skills of learning. *Intelligence.* In press

Glaser, R., Resnick, L. B. 1972. Instructional psychology. *Ann. Rev. Psychol.* 23:207–76

Glushko, R. 1981. Principles for pronouncing print: The psychology of phonography. See Lesgold & Perfetti 1981

Goetz, E. T. 1979. Inferring from text: Some factors affecting which inferences will be made. *Discourse Processes* 2:179–95

Goldberg, R. A., Schwartz, S., Stewart, M. 1977. Individual differences in cognitive processes. *J. Educ. Psychol.* 69(1):9–14

Goldman, S. R. 1980. Semantic knowledge systems for realistic goals. *Discourse Processes.* In press

Goodenough, D. R. 1976. The role of individual differences in field dependence as a factor in learning and memory. *Psychol. Bull.* 83(4):675–94

Goodman, K. S., Goodman, Y. M. 1977. Learning about processes by analyzing oral reading. *Harvard Educ. Rev.* 47:317–33

Goodman, K. S., Goodman, Y. M. 1979. Learning to read is natural. See Resnick & Weaver 1979, 1:137–54

Gordon, E. W. 1979. Implications for compensatory education drawn from reflections on the teaching and learning of reading. See Resnick & Weaver 1979, 2:299–319

Greeno, J. G. 1976. Indefinite goals in well-structured problems. *Psychol. Rev.* 83(6):479–91

Greeno, J. G. 1977. Process of understanding in problem solving. In *Cognitive Theory,* Vol. 2, ed. N. J. Castellan, D. B. Pisoni, G. R. Potts. Hillsdale, NJ: Erlbaum

Greeno, J. G. 1978. A study of problem solving. See Glaser 1978

Greeno, J. G. 1979. Preliminary steps toward a model of learning primary arithmetic. In *Explorations in the modeling of the learning of mathematics,* eds., K. C. Fuson, W. E. Geeslin. Monogr. from Georgia Cent. Study Learn. Teach. Math., Columbus, Ohio: ERIC/SMEAC Sci. Math. Inf. Anal. Cent.

Greeno, J. G. 1980. Some examples of cognitive task analysis with instructional implications. See Snow et al 1980, Vol. 2

Greeno, J. G., Magone, M. E., Chaiklin, S. 1979. Theory of constructions and set in problem solving. *Mem. Cognit.* 7(6):445–61

Gregg, L., Steinberg, E., eds. 1980. *Cognitive Processes in Writing: An Interdiscipli-*

nary Approach. Hillsdale, NJ: Erlbaum. 208 pp.

Groen, G. J., Parkman, J. M. 1972. A chronometric analysis of simple addition. *Psychol. Rev.* 79(4):329–43

Groen, G. J., Poll, M. 1973. Subtraction and the solution of open sentence problems. *J. Exp. Child Psychol.* 16:292–302

Groen, G. J., Resnick, L. B. 1977. Can preschool children invent addition algorithms? *J. Educ. Psychol.* 69:645–52

Gustafsson, J. 1977. Differential effects of imagery instructions on pupils with different abilities. *Scand. J. Educ. Res.* 21(4):157–79

Guthrie, J. T., ed. 1976. *Aspects of Reading Acquisition.* Baltimore: Johns Hopkins Univ. Press. 222pp.

Guthrie, J. T., ed. 1977. *Cognition, Curriculum, and Comprehension,* Newark, Del: Int. Read. Assoc.

Hartley, J., Davies, I. K. 1976. Preinstructional strategies: The role of pretests, behavioral objectives, overviews and advance organizers. *Rev. Educ. Res.* 46:239–65

Hatano, G. 1981. Learning to add and subtract: A Japanese perspective. See Brown & VanLehn 1981

Hatano, G., Miyake, Y., Binks, M. G. 1977. Performance of expert abacus operators. *Cognition* 5:57–71

Hayes, J. R. 1973. On the function of visual imagery in elementary mathematics. In *Visual Information Processing,* ed. R. G. Chase, pp. 177–214. New York: Academic

Hayes, J. R., Flower, L. S. 1980. Identifying the organization of writing processes. See Gregg & Steinberg 1980, pp. 3–29

Hayes, J. R., Waterman, D. A., Robinson, C. S. 1977. Identifying the relevant aspects of a problem text. *Cognit. Sci.* 1:297–313

Heber, R. F. 1980. Modification of predicted cognitive development in high risk children through early intervention. *Intelligence.* In press

Hinsley, D., Hayes, J. R., Simon, H. 1977. From words to equations: meaning and representation in algebra word problems. See Just & Carpenter 1977, pp. 89–106

Hitch, G. J. 1978. The role of short-term working memory in mental arithmetic. *Cognit. Psychol.* 10:302–23

Hogaboam, T. W., Pellegrino, J. W. 1978. Hunting for individual differences in cognitive processes: Verbal ability and semantic processing of pictures and words. *Mem. Cognit.* 6(2):189–93

Holley, C. D., Dansereau, D. F., McDonald, B. A., Garland, J. C., Collins, K. W. 1979. Evaluation of a hierarchical mapping technique as an aid to prose processing. *Contemp. Educ. Psychol.* 4: 227–37

Holyoak, K. J. 1978. Comparative judgments with numerical reference points. *Cognit. Psychol.* 10(2):203–43

Holzman, T. G., Glaser, R., Pellegrino, J. W. 1976. Process training derived from a computer simulation theory. *Mem. Cognit.* 4(4):349–56

Horn, J. L. 1979. Trends in the measurement of intelligence. *Intelligence* 3:229–40

Humphreys, L. G. 1979. The construct of general intelligence. *Intelligence* 3: 105–20

Hunt, E. 1974. Quote the raven? Nevermore! In *Knowledge and Cognition,* ed. L. Gregg, pp. 129–57. Hillsdale, NJ: Erlbaum

Hunt, E. 1976. Varieties of cognitive power. See Resnick 1976a, pp. 237–59

Hunt, E. 1978. Mechanics of verbal ability. *Psychol. Rev.* 85:109–30

Hunt, E., Frost, N., Lunneborg, C. 1973. Individual differences in cognition. A new approach to intelligence. In *The Psychology of Learning and Motivation,* ed. G. H. Bower, 7:87–120. New York: Academic

Hunt, E., Lunneborg, C., Lewis, J. 1975. What does it mean to be high verbal? *Cognit. Psychol.* 7:194–227

Hunter, I. M. L. 1968. Mental calculation. In *Thinking and Reasoning,* ed. P. C. Wason, P. N. Johnson-Laird. Baltimore: Penguin

Huttenlocher, J., Burke, D. 1976. Why does memory span increase with age? *Cognit. Psychol.* 8:1–31

Jarman, R. F., Das, J. P. 1977. Simultaneous and successive syntheses and intelligence. *Intelligence* 1:151–69

Jensen, A. R., Munro, E. 1979. Reaction time, movement time, and intelligence. *Intelligence* 3:121–26

Johnson-Laird, P. N., Wason, P. C. 1977. *Thinking: Readings in Cognitive Science.* Cambridge, Mass: Cambridge Univ.

Juola, J. F., Schadler, M., Chabot, R., McCaughey, M., Wait, J. 1979. What do children learn when they learn to read? See Resnick & Weaver, 2:91–107

Just, M. A., Carpenter, P. A. 1981. Inference processes during reading: Reflections from eye fixation. In *Eye Movements and Higher Psychological Functions,* ed. J. W. Senders, D. F. Fisher, R. A. Monty. Hillsdale, NJ: Erlbaum. In press

Just, M. A., Carpenter, P. A., eds. 1977. *Cognitive Processes in Comprehension.* Hillsdale, NJ: Erlbaum. 329 pp.

Kail, R. V., Chi, M. T. H., Ingram, A., Danner, F. W. 1977. Constructive aspects of children's reading comprehension. *Child Dev.* 48:684–88

Katz, L., Feldman, L. B. 1981. Linguistic coding in word recognition: Comparisons between a deep and a shallow orthography. See Lesgold & Perfetti 1981

Keating, D. P., Keniston, A. H., Manis, F. R., Bobbitt, B. L. 1980. Development of the search-processing parameter. *Child Dev.* 51:39–44

Keeton, A. 1977. Children's cognitive integration and memory processes for comprehending written sentences. *J. Exp. Child Psychol.* 23(3):459–71

Kendall, C. R., Borkowski, J. G., Cavanaugh, J. C. 1980. Metamemory and the transfer of an interrogative strategy by EMR children. *Intelligence* 4(3): 255–70

Kieras, D. E. 1977. Problems of reference in text comprehension. See Just & Carpenter 1977, pp. 249–69

Kieras, D. E. 1978. Good and bad structure in simple paragraphs: Effects on apparent theme, reading time, and recall. *J. Verb. Learn. Verb. Behav.* 17(1):13–28

Kieras, D. E. 1979. *Modelling reading times in different reading tasks with a simulation model of comprehension.* Tech. Rep. 2, Univ. Ariz., Tucson

Kintsch, W. 1974. *The Representation of Meaning in Memory.* Hillsdale, NJ: Erlbaum. 279 pp.

Kintsch, W. 1977. On comprehending stories. See Just & Carpenter 1977, pp. 33–62

Kintsch, W., Kozminsky, E., Streby, W. J., McKoon, G., Keenan, J. M. 1975. Comprehension and recall of text as a function of content variable. *J. Verb. Learn. Verb. Behav.* 14:196–214

Kintsch, W., Mandel, T. S., Kozminsky, E. 1977. Summarizing scrambled stories. *Mem. Cognit.* 5:547–52

Kintsch, W., van Dijk, T. 1978. Toward a model of text comprehension and production. *Psychol. Rev.* 85:363–94

Kintsch, W., Vipond, D. 1979. Reading comprehension and readability in educational practice and psychological theory. In *Perspectives on Memory Research,* ed. L. G. Nilsson, pp. 329–62. Hillsdale, NJ: Erlbaum

Klahr, D., ed. 1976. *Cognition and Instruction.* Hillsdale, NJ: Erlbaum. 361pp.

Klahr, D., Wallace, J. G. 1976. *Cognitive Development: An Information-Processing View.* Hillsdale, NJ: Erlbaum. 244 pp.

Klare, G. R. 1976. A second look at the validity of readability formulas. *J. Read. Behav.* 8(2):129–52

Kozminsky, E. 1977. Altering comprehension: The effect of biasing titles on text comprehension. *Mem. Cognit.* 5(4): 482–90

Krutetskii, U. A. 1976. *The Psychology of Mathematical Abilities on School Children.* Chicago: Univ. Chicago Press

LaBerge, D. 1979. The perception of units in beginning reading. See Resnick & Weaver 1979, 3:31–51

LaBerge, D., Samuels, S. J. 1974. Toward a theory of automatic information processing in reading. *Cognit. Psychol.* 6:293–323

LaBerge, D., Samuels, S. J., eds. 1977. *Basic Processes in Reading: Perception and Comprehension.* Hillsdale, NJ: Erlbaum. 370 pp.

Larkin, J. H., McDermott, J., Simon, D. P., Simon, H. A. 1980. Expert and novice performance in solving physics problems. *Science* 80(4450):1335–42

Larkin, J., Reif, F. 1976. Analysis and teaching of a general skill for studying scientific text. *J. Educ. Psychol.* 68(4): 431–40

Lawson, A. E., Wollman, W. T. 1976. Encouraging the transition from concrete to formal cognitive functioning—An experiment. *J. Res. Sci. Teach.* 13(5): 413–30

Lawton, J. T., Wanska, S. K. 1977. Advance organizers as a teaching strategy: A reply to Barnes and Clawson. *Rev. Educ. Res.* 47:233–44

Lesgold, A. M., Curtis, M. E. 1981. Learning to read words efficiently. See Lesgold & Perfetti 1981

Lesgold, A. M., Pellegrino, J. W., Fokkema, S. D., Glaser, R., eds. 1978. *Cognitive Psychology and Instruction.* New York: Plenum. 525 pp.

Lesgold, A. M., Perfetti, C. A. 1981. *Interactive Processes in Reading.* Hillsdale, NJ: Erlbaum. In press

Levy, B. A. 1978. Speech processes during reading. See Lesgold et al 1978, pp. 123–51

Levy, B. A. 1981. Interactive processing during reading. See Lesgold & Perfetti 1981

Liberman, I. Y., Shankweiler, D. 1979. Speech, the alphabet, and teaching to read. See Resnick & Weaver, 2:109–32

Lochhead, J., Clement, J., eds. 1979. *Cognitive Process Instruction.* Philadelphia: Franklin Inst. Press. 339 pp.

Lyon, D. R. 1977. Individual differences in immediate serial recall: A matter of mnemonics? *Cognit. Psychol.* 9:403–11

MacLeod, C. M., Hunt, E. B., Mathews, N. N. 1978. Individual differences in verification of sentence-picture relationships. *J. Verb. Learn. Verb. Behav.* 17:493–507

Mandler, J. M. 1978. A code in the node: The use of a story schema in retrieval. *Discourse Processes* 1:14–35

Mandler, J. M., DeForest, M. 1979. Is there more than one way to recall a story? *Child Dev.* 50:886–89

Mandler, J. M., Johnson, N. S. 1977. Remembrance of things parsed: Story structure and recall. *Cognit. Psychol.* 9:111–51

Markle, S. M. 1978. *Designs for Instructional Designers.* Champaign, Ill: Stipes

Markman, E. M., Siebert, J. 1976. Classes and collections: Internal organization and resulting holistic properties. *Cognit. Psychol.* 8:561–77

Mayer, R. E. 1975. Different problem solving competencies established in learning computer programming with and without meaningful models. *J. Educ. Psychol.* 67:725–34

Mayer, R. E. 1979. Can advance organizers influence meaningful learning? *Rev. Educ. Res.* 49:371–83

Mayer, R. E., Stiehl, C. D., Greeno, J. G. 1975. Acquisition of understanding and skill in relation to subjects' preparation and meaningfulness of instruction. *J. Educ. Psychol.* 68:331–50

McConkie, G. W. 1979. What the study of eye movement reveals about reading. See Resnick & Weaver 1979, 3:71–87

McConkie, G. W., Rayner, K., Wilson, S. J. 1973. Experimental manipulation of reading strategies. *J. Educ. Psychol.* 65(1):1–8

Menchinskaya, N. A., Moro, M. L. 1975. Questions in the methods and psychology of teaching arithmetic in the elementary grades. In *Soviet Studies in the Psychology of Learning and Teaching Mathematics,* ed. J. Kilpatrick, I. Wirszup, E. G. Begle, J. W. Wilson, 14:1–202. Stanford, Calif: Sch. Math. Study Group

Menyuk, P. 1976. Relations between acquisition of phonology and reading. See Guthrie 1976, pp. 89–110

Merrill, M. D., Boutwell, R. C. 1973. Instructional development: Methodology and research. In *Review of Research in Education,* Vol. 1, ed. R. Kerlinger. Illinois: Peacock

Messick, S., ed. 1976. *Individuality in Learning.* San Francisco: Jossey-Bass

Meyer, B. J. F. 1975. *The Organization of Prose and Its Effect on Recall.* Amsterdam: Elsevier

Mikhal'skii, K. A. 1975. The solution of complex arithmetic problems in auxiliary school. See Menchinskaya & Moro 1975, 9:1–100

Miller, J. R., Kintsch, W. 1980. Readability and recall of short prose passages: A theoretical analysis. *J. Exp. Psychol.: Hum. Learn. Mem.* In press

Mulholland, T. M., Pellegrino, J. W., Glaser, R. 1980. Components of geometric analogy solution. *Cognit. Psychol.* 12: 252–84

Murray, F. B., Pikulski, J. J., eds. 1978. *The Acquisition of Reading.* Baltimore: Univ. Park Press

Nash-Webber, B. L. 1980. Syntax beyond the sentence: Anaphora. See Spiro et al 1980

Neely, J. H. 1977. Semantic priming and retrieval from lexical memory: The roles of inhibitionless spreading activation and limited-capacity attention. *J. Exp. Psychol. Gen.* 106:1–66

Nesher, P. 1981. Levels of description in the analysis of addition and subtraction of word problems. See Brown & VanLehn 1981

Newell, A., Simon, H. A. 1972. *Human Problem Solving.* Englewood Cliffs, NJ: Prentice-Hall. 920 pp.

Nezworski, T., Stein, N. L., Trabasso, T. 1979. Story structure versus content effects on children's recall and evaluative inferences. Tech. Rep. 129, Northwestern Univ., Evanston, Ill.

O'Neil, H. F., ed. 1978. *Learning Strategies.* New York: Academic. 230 pp.

Osherson, D. 1974. *Logical Abilities in Children,* 3 Vols. Hillsdale, NJ: Erlbaum

Paris, S. G., Upton, L. R. 1976. Children's memory for inferential relationships in prose. *Child Dev.* 47:660–68

Parkman, J. M. 1972. Temporal aspects of simple multiplication and comparison. *J. Exp. Psychol.* 95(2):437–44

Pellegrino, J. W., Glaser, R. 1979. Cognitive correlates and components in the analysis of individual differences. *Intelligence* 3:187–214

Pellegrino, J. W., Glaser, R. 1980. Components of inductive reasoning. See Snow et al 1980, Vol. 1

Perfetti, C. A., Lesgold, A. M. 1979. Coding and comprehension in skilled reading and implications for reading instruction. See Resnick & Weaver 1979, 1:57–84

Perfetti, C. A., Roth, S. 1981. Some of the interactive processes in reading and their role in reading skill. See Lesgold & Perfetti 1981

Pichert, J. W., Anderson, R. C. 1977. Taking different perspectives on a story. *J. Educ. Psychol.* 69:309–15

Potts, G. P., Banks, W. P., Kosslyn, S. M., Moyer, R. S., Riley, C. A., Smith, K. H. 1978. Encoding and retrieval in comparative judgments. In *Cognitive Theory,* ed. J. N. Castellan, Vol. 3. Hillsdale, NJ: Erlbaum

Rayner, K. 1978. Eye movements in reading and information processing. *Psychol. Bull.* 85:618–60

Reber, A. S., Scarborough, D. L. 1977. *Toward a Psychology of Reading: The Proceedings of the CUNY Conferences.* Hillsdale, NJ: Erlbaum

Reder, L. M. 1979. The role of elaborations in memory for prose. *Cognit. Psychol.* 11:221–34

Reitman, J. S. 1976. Skilled perception in Go: Deducing memory structures from interresponse times. *Cognit. Psychol.* 8: 336–56

Resnick, L. B., ed. 1976a. *The Nature of Intelligence.* Hillsdale, NJ: Erlbaum. 364 pp.

Resnick, L. B. 1976b. Task analysis in instruction design: Some cases from mathematics. In *Cognition and Instruction,* ed. D. Klahr, pp. 51–80. Hillsdale, NJ: Erlbaum. 361 pp.

Resnick, L. B. 1980. The role of invention in the development of mathematical competence. In *Developmental Models of Thinking,* ed. R. Kluwe, H. Spada. New York: Academic. In press

Resnick, L. B. 1981. Syntax and semantics in learning to subtract. See Brown & VanLehn 1981

Resnick, L. B., Ford, W. W. 1980. *The Psychology of Mathematics for Instruction.* Hillsdale, NJ: Erlbaum. In Press

Resnick, L. B., Weaver, P. A., eds. 1979. *Theory and Practice of Early Reading,* Vols. 1–3. Hillsdale, NJ: Erlbaum

Reynolds, R. E., Standiford, S. N., Anderson, R. C. 1979. Distribution of reading time when questions are asked about a restricted category of text information. *J. Educ. Psychol.* 71:183–90

Rickards, J. P., Anderson, M. C., McCormick, C. B. 1976. Processing effects of common-word and number questions inserted in reading material. *J. Educ. Res.* 69:274–77

Rickards, J. P., Denner, P. R. 1978. Inserted questions as aids to reading text. *Instr. Sci.* 7:313–46

Robinson, J. A., Kingsley, M. E. 1977. Memory and intelligence: Age and ability differences in strategies and organization of recall. *Intelligence* 1:318–30

Ross, D. M., Ross, S. A. 1978. Facilitative effect of mnemonic strategies on multiple associate learning in EMR children. *Am. J. Ment. Defic.* 82:460–66

Rothkopf, E. Z. 1976. Writing to teach and reading to learn: A perspective on the psychology of written instruction. In *The Psychology of Teaching Methods,* ed. N. L. Gage, pp. 91–129. Chicago: Natl. Soc. Study Educ.

Rothkopf, E. Z., Billington, M. J. 1979. Goal-guided learning from text: Inferring a descriptive processing model from inspection times and eye movements. *J. Educ. Psychol.* 71(3):310–27

Rothkopf, E. Z., Koether, M. E. 1978. Instructional effects of discrepancies in content and organization between study goals and information sources. *J. Educ. Psychol.* 70(1):67–71

Royer, F. L. 1977. Information processing in the block design task. *Intelligence* 1:32–50

Royer, F. L. 1978. Intelligence and the processing of stimulus structure. *Intelligence* 2:11–40

Rumelhart, D. E. 1975. Notes on a schema for stories. In *Representation and Understanding: Studies in Cognitive Science,* ed. D. G. Brown, A. Collins, pp. 211–36. New York: Academic

Rumelhart, D. E. 1977. Understanding and summarizing brief stories. See LaBerge & Samuels 1977

Rumelhart, D. E., McClelland, J. L. 1981. Interactive processing through spreading activation. See Lesgold & Perfetti 1981

Rumelhart, D. E., Ortony, A. 1977. The representation of knowledge in memory. See Anderson et al 1977b, pp. 99–135

Salomon, M. K., Achenbach, T. M. 1974. The effects of four kinds of tutoring experience on associative responding. *Am. Educ. Res. J.* 11(4):395–405

Samuels, S. J., Dahl, P. R. 1975. Establishing appropriate purpose for reading and its effect on flexibility of reading rate. *J. Educ. Psychol.* 67(1):38–43

Saxe, G. B. 1979. Developmental relations between notational counting and number conservation. *Child Dev.* 50:180–87

Scandura, J. M. 1977. *Problem Solving: A Structural/Process Approach with Instructional Implications.* New York: Academic. 586 pp.

Schank, R., Abelson, R. 1977. *Scripts, Plans, Goals, and Understanding: An Inquiry into Human Knowledge Structures.* Hillsdale, NJ: Erlbaum. 248pp.

Schoenfeld, A. H. 1979. Explicit heuristic training as a variable in problem-solving performance. *J. Res. Math. Educ.* 10(3):173

Schuberth, R. E., Eimas, P. D. 1977. Effects of contexts on the classification of words and nonwords. *J. Exp. Psychol. Hum. Percept. Perform.* 3:27–36

Schwartz, S., Wiedel, T. C. 1978. Individual differences in cognition: Relationship between verbal ability and memory for order. *Intelligence* 2:353–69

Sekuler, R., Mierkiewicz, D. 1977. Children's judgments of numerical inequality. *Child Dev.* 48:630–33

Shavelson, R. J., Stanton, G. C. 1975. Construct validation: Methodology and application to three measures of cognitive structure. *J. Educ. Meas.* 12(2):67–85

Shepard, R. N., Kilpatric, D. W., Cunningham, J. P. 1975. The internal representation of numbers. *Cognit. Psychol.* 7:82–138

Shevarev, P. A. 1975. An experiment in the psychological analysis of algebraic errors. See Menchinskaya & Moro 1975, 12:1–60

Shimmerlik, S., Nolan, J. D. 1976. Reorganization and the recall of prose. *J. Educ. Psychol.* 68:779–86

Shuy, R. W. 1979. The mismatch of child language and school language: Implications of beginning reading instruction. See Resnick & Weaver, 1:187–207

Siegler, R. S. 1976. Three aspects of cognitive development. *Cognit. Psychol.* 8:481–520

Siegler, R. S. 1978. The origins of scientific reasoning. In *Children's Thinking: What Develops?* ed. R. S. Siegler, pp. 109–49. Hillsdale, NJ: Erlbaum

Siegler, R. S., Liebert, R. M. 1975. Acquisition of formal scientific reasoning by 10- and 13-year olds. *Dev. Psychol.* 11(3):401–2

Silver, E. A. 1979. Student perceptions of relatedness among mathematical verbal problems. *J. Res. Math. Educ.* 10(3):195–210

Simon, D. P., Simon, H. A. 1978. Individual differences in solving physics problems. See Siegler 1978, pp. 325–48

Simon, H. A. 1976. Identifying basic abilities underlying intelligent performance of complex tasks. See Resnick 1976a, pp. 65–98

Simon, H. A. 1980. Problem solving and education. See Tuma & Reif 1980

Singer, M. 1976. Context inferences in the

comprehension of sentences. *Can. J. Psychol.* 30:39–46

Smiley, S. S., Oakley, D. D., Worthen, D., Campione, J. C., Brown, A. 1977. Recall of thematically relevant material by adolescent good and poor readers as a function of written versus oral presentation. *J. Educ. Psychol.* 69(4):381–87

Smith, E. E., Kleiman, G. M. 1979. Theoretical issues and instructional hints. See Resnick & Weaver 1979, 2:67–90

Smith, F. 1979. Conflicting approaches to reading research and instruction. See Resnick & Weaver 1979, 2:31–42

Snow, R. E. 1977. Research on aptitudes: A progress report. In *Review of Research in Education,* ed. L. S. Shulman, Vol. 4. Itasca, Ill: Peacock

Snow, R. E. 1978. Theory and method for research on aptitude processes: A prospectus. *Intelligence* 2:225–78

Snow, R. E. 1980. Aptitude processes. See Snow et al 1980

Snow, R. E., Federico, P. A., Montague, W. E., eds. 1980. *Aptitude, Learning, and Instruction,* Vols. 1, 2. Hillsdale, NJ: Erlbaum. In press

Spada, H. 1978. Understanding proportionality: A comparison of different models of cognitive development. *Int. J. Behav. Dev.* 1:363–76

Spilich, G. J., Vesonder, G. T., Chiesi, H. L., Voss, J. F. 1979. *J. Verb. Learn. Verb. Behav.* 18:275–90

Spiro, R. J. 1977. Remembering information from text: The "state of schema" approach. See Anderson et al 1977, pp. 137–65

Spiro, R. J., Bruce, B. C., Brewer, W. F. 1980. *Theoretical Issues in Reading Comprehension: Perspectives from Cognitive Psychology, Linguistics, Artificial Intelligence, and Education.* Hillsdale, NJ: Erlbaum. In press

Spiro, R. J., Esposito, J. 1982. Superficial processing of explicit inferences in text. *Discourse Processes.* In press

Stanovich, K. E. 1981. Attentional and automatic context effects in reading. See Lesgold & Perfetti 1981

Steffe, L., Thompson, P. 1981. *Children's counting in the relationship to the conception of addition and subtraction.* See Brown & VanLehn 1981

Stein, N. L., Goldman, S. R. 1980. Children's knowledge about social situations: From causes to consequences. In *The Development of Friendship,* ed. S. R. Asher, J. M. Gottman. New York: Cambridge Univ. Press

Stein, N. L., Glenn, C. G. 1979. An analysis of story comprehension in elementary school children. See Freedle 1979, pp. 53–120

Stein, N. L., Nezworski, T. 1978. The effects of organization and instructional set on story memory. *Discourse Processes* 1:177–93

Sternberg, R. J. 1977a. Component processes in analogical reasoning. *Psychol. Rev.* 84(4):353–78

Sternberg, R. J. 1977b. *Intelligence, Information Processing, and Analogical Reasoning: The Componential Analysis of Human Abilities.* Hillsdale, NJ: Erlbaum

Sternberg, R. J. 1980a. Components of human intelligence. *Behav. Brain Sci.* In press

Sternberg, R. J. 1980b. Toward a unified componential theory of human reasoning. See Friedman et al 1980

Sternberg, R. J., Detterman, D. K., eds. 1979. *Human Intelligence: Perspectives on its Theory and Measurement.* Norwood, NJ: Ablex

Sternberg, R. J., Guyote, M. J., Turner, M. E. 1980. Deductive reasoning. See Snow et al 1980, Vol. 1

Sternberg, R. J., Nigro, G. 1980. Developmental patterns in the solutions of verbal analogies. *Child Dev.* 51:27–38

Sternberg, R. J., Rifkin, B. 1979. The development of analogical reasoning processes. *J. Exp. Psychol.* 27:195–232

Sternberg, R. J., Weil, E. M. 1980. An aptitude-strategy interaction in linear syllogistic reasoning. *J. Educ. Psychol.* 72:226–34

Sternberg, S. 1975. Memory scanning: New findings and current controversies. *Q. J. Exp. Psychol.* 27:1–32

Stevens, A. L., Collins, A. 1980. Multiple conceptual models of a complex system. See Snow et al 1980, Vol. 2

Stevens, A. L., Rumelhart, D. E. 1975. Errors in reading: An analysis using an augmented transition network model of grammar. In *Explorations in Cognition,* ed. D. A. Norman, D. E. Rumelhart, pp. 136–55. San Francisco: Freeman. 430 pp.

Sulin, R. A., Dooling, D. J. 1974. Intrusion of a thematic idea in retention of prose. *J. Exp. Psychol.* 103:255–62

Svenson, O. 1975. Analysis of time required by children for simple additions. *Acta Psychol.* 39:289–302

Svenson, O., Broquist, S. 1975. Strategies for solving simple addition problems: A comparison of normal and subnormal children. *Scand. J. Psychol.* 16:143–51

Svenson, O., Hedenborg, M. L. 1979. Strategies used by children when solving simple subtractions. *Acta Psychol.* 43:1–13

704   RESNICK

Svenson, O., Hedenborg, M., Lingman, L. 1976. On children's heuristics for solving simple additions. *Scand. J. Educ. Res.* 20:161–73

Thorndike, E. L. 1922. *The Psychology of Arithmetic.* New York: Macmillan

Thorndyke, P. W. 1976. The role of inferences in discourse comprehension. *J. Verb. Learn. Verb. Behav.* 15(4):437–46

Thorndyke, P. W. 1977. Cognitive structures in comprehension and memory of narrative discourse. *Cognit. Psychol.* 9(1): 77–110

Thorndyke, P. W., Hayes-Roth, B. 1979. The use of schemata in the acquisition and transfer of knowledge. *Cognit. Psychol.* 11(1):82–106

Thro, M. P. 1978. Relationship between associative and content structure of physics concepts. *J. Educ. Psychol.* 70(6): 971–78

Tirre, W. C., Manelis, L., Leicht, K. L. 1980. The effects of imaginal and verbal strategies on prose comprehension in adults. *J. Read. Behav.* 11:99–106

Tobias, S. 1976. Achievement treatment interactions. *Rev. Educ. Res.* 46:61–74

Trabasso, T., Isen, A. M., Dolecki, P., McLanahan, A. G., Riley, C. A., Tucker, T. 1978. How do children solve class-inclusion problems? See Siegler 1978

Tuma, D. T., Reif, F., eds. 1980. *Problem Solving and Education: Issues in Teaching and Research.* Hillsdale, NJ: Erlbaum. 212 pp.

Turnure, J., Buium, N., Thurlow, M. L. 1976. The effectiveness of interrogatives for promoting verbal elaboration productivity in young children. *Child Dev.* 47:851–55

Tweedy, J. R., Lapinski, R. H., Schvaneveldt, R. W. 1977. Semantic-context effects of word recognition: Influence of varying the proportion of items presented in an appropriate context. *Mem. Cognit.* 5:84–89

van Dijk, T. A. 1977. Semantic macro-structures as knowledge frames in discourse comprehension. See Just & Carpenter 1977, pp. 3–32

Vellutino, F. R. 1977. Alternative conceptualizations of dyslexia: Evidence in sup-

port of a verbal-deficit hypothesis. *Harvard Educ. Rev.* 47:334–54

Venezky, R. L., Massaro, D. W. 1979. The role of orthographic regularity in word recognition. See Resnick & Weaver 1979, 1:85–107

Vergnaud, G. 1981. A classification of cognitive tasks and operations of thought involved in addition and subtraction problems. See Brown & VanLehn 1981

Waern, Y. 1977a. Comprehension and belief structure. *Scand. J. Psychol.* 18(3): 266–74

Waern, Y. 1977b. On the relationship between knowledge of the world and comprehension of texts. *Scand. J. Psychol.* 18:130–39

Wallach, M. A., Wallach, L. 1979. Helping disadvantaged children learn to read by teaching them phoneme identification skills. See Resnick & Weaver 1979, 3:197–215

Waller, T. G., MacKinnon, G. E., eds. 1979. *Reading Research: Advances in Theory and Practice,* Vol. 1. New York: Academic. 262 pp.

Wertsch, J. V. 1978. Adult-child interaction and the roots of metacognition. *Q. Newsl. Inst. Comp. Hum. Dev.* 2:15–18

Whitely, S. E., Dawis, R. V. 1974. Effects of cognitive intervention on latent ability measured from analogy items. *J. Educ. Psychol.* 66(5):710–17

Wildman, D. M., Kling, M. 1978–79. Semantic, syntactic and spatial anticipation in reading. *Read. Res. Q.* 14:128–64

Wilkinson, A. 1976. Counting strategies and semantic analysis as applied to class inclusion. *Cognit. Psychol.* 8:64–85

Winkelman, J. H., Schmidt, J. 1974. Associative confusions in mental arithmetic. *J. Exp. Psychol.* 102(4):734–36

Winograd, T. 1977. A framework for understanding discourse. See Just & Carpenter 1977, pp. 63–88

Wood, D. J. 1979. Problem solving—the nature and development of strategies. See Baron 1979

Woods, S. S., Resnick, L. B., Groen, G. J. 1975. An experimental test of five process models for subtraction. *J. Educ. Psychol.* 67(1):17–21

CHAPTERS PLANNED FOR THE NEXT *ANNUAL REVIEW OF PSYCHOLOGY*

Volume 33 (1982)

AUTHOR INDEX

(Names appearing in capital letters indicate authors of chapters in this volume.)

A

Aardema, B., 386
Abate, F., 256
Abbas, P. J., 158, 177
Abe, C., 452, 464
Abelson, R., 334, 669
Abelson, R. P., 69, 104, 365
Abramowitz, S. I., 407
Abrams, B., 253, 254
Abramson, E. E., 427
Abramson, L. Y., 416, 418
Achenbach, T. M., 141, 690
Acker, S. R., 645
Ackermann, R. F., 549, 563
Acredolo, L. P., 125, 126
Adamopoulos, J., 369
Adams, D. W., 529
Adams, G. R., 142, 143
Adams, H. E., 424
Adams, M. J., 42, 662, 668
Adams, N. E., 412
Adams, R. N., 558
Adams, W. C., 361
Adamson, G., 449
Adelman, L., 71
Ades, H. W., 162
Adewole, A., 376
Adlard, A., 601
Adler, R., 336, 338
Adoni, H., 317
Adorjani, C., 607
Adrian, H. O., 170
Adrien, J., 558
Agras, W. S., 408
Agunanne, B. C., 688
Agunwamba, C. C., 631
Ahammer, I. M., 343
Ahlering, R. F., 384
Ahlgren, A., 136
Ahlm, K., 388
Aiken, L. S., 98
Ainsworth, M. D. S., 135
Airasian, P. W., 644
Ajzen, I., 65, 366, 368, 369, 371
Alafat, K. A., 390
Albaum, G., 453, 454, 464
Albrecht, D. G., 588
Albright, L. E., 464, 465
Albus, K., 496
Alder, V. A., 178
Alexander, C. N., 387
Alexander, J., 321, 329, 330
Alexander, R. A., 648
Alford, B. R., 179
Algina, J., 635-37
Al-issa, I., 461
Allal, L., 634
Allen, A., 372
Allen, E. A., 179

Allen, G. L., 126
Allen, J. B., 160
Allen, R. L., 312
Allen, R. P., 248, 250, 258, 260
Allen, T., 255, 257, 258
Allgeier, E. R., 386
Alliotti, N. C., 457
Allison, P. D., 631
Allman, J. M., 607
Allman, T., 457
Allport, F., 7
Alpaugh, P. K., 464
Alperson, J. R., 424
Altmann, D. W., 159, 164, 166, 169
Alwitt, L. F., 311, 333, 337
Amaral, D. G., 549, 550, 558
Ambler, B., 596
Amos, S. P., 452
Anand, B. K., 531
Anastasi, A., 447, 452, 453, 456-58, 464
Andersen, E. B., 639, 644
Anderson, C. H., 590, 591
Anderson, D. J., 177
Anderson, D. R., 311, 332-34, 337
Anderson, E., 221
Anderson, E. A., 387
Anderson, G., 414
Anderson, J. A., 24, 315
Anderson, J. H., 682
Anderson, J. R., 26-28, 37, 41, 680
Anderson, M. C., 668, 674
Anderson, N. H., 62, 71, 75, 108, 385, 386
Anderson, P., 483
Anderson, R., 390
Anderson, R. C., 102, 661, 668, 669, 673, 674
Anderson, R. W., 366
Anderson, S. D., 161, 162
Anderson, S. M., 458
Anderson, W. P., 289
Andersson, B., 532
Andison, F. S., 342
Andrasik, F., 424
Andre, T., 674
Andreasen, N., 415
Andreoli, V., 391
Andrews, D. F., 200, 223
Andrews, K. H., 366
Andrich, D., 643, 644
Angelborg, C., 171
Anglin, J. M., 31, 92, 93, 98
Angoff, C., 223

Anker, R., 497
Annau, Z., 527, 530
Anstis, S. M., 580, 601, 614, 615
Antelman, S. M., 556
Antoli-Candela, F. Jr., 178
Antos, S. J., 664
Aran, J.-M., 179
Arasteh, A. R., 464
Arasteh, J. D., 464
Archer, S., 143
Arditi, A. R., 617
Arend, L. E., 586, 587, 592
Arend, R. A., 135
Argyle, M., 426
Ariel, M., 510
Arieti, S., 419, 451
Arkin, R., 387
Arkin, R. M., 367
Arkkelin, D. L., 79
Arlin, P. K., 452, 464
Armington, J. C., 580
Armstrong, J. S., 72
Arnkoff, D., 412
Aronow, E., 451
Aronson, E., 128
Arrowood, A. J., 378
Ary, M., 511
Asakuma, S., 165
Asanuma, A., 162
Asarnow, J., 129
Aschenbrenner, K. M., 57
Ascher, D., 166
Ascher, L. M., 424
Ashcraft, M. H., 676
Ashcroft, J., 330, 331
Asher, S. J., 407, 413
Aslin, R. N., 121
Atanasoff, G., 284
Atkin, C. K., 312, 314, 319-21, 330, 336, 339-41, 345
Atkins, P. A., 314, 339
Atkinson, J., 482, 579, 581, 593
Atkinson, R. C., 687
Atlas, J. W., 282
Attneave, F., 105
Atweh, S. F., 563
Atwood, G. E., 459
Atwood, L. E., 326
Aubrey, R. F., 290
Auerbach, E., 500
Augustine, G. J., 254
Auh, T. S., 325, 326
Austin, J. G., 90
Austin, V. D., 671
Ausubel, D. B., 669
Avallone, V. L., 282

707

AUTHOR INDEX 713

E

Eagly, A. H., 358, 378, 389, 391
Easterbrooks, M. A., 135
Ebbesen, E. B., 81
Ebel, R. L., 635, 645
Eber, H. W., 455
Ebert, M. H., 259, 261
Echternacht, G., 647
Edelbrock, C. S., 141
Edelstein, A. S., 319
Edgar, P., 341
Edwards, D. W., 407
Edwards, W., 54, 58
Eells, W. C., 234
Egan, D., 458
Egan, D. E., 688
Egan, L. M., 314, 339
Egeth, H. E., 222
Eggermont, J. J., 178
Eggers, H. M., 496, 500, 504
Ehrenberg, A. S. C., 220, 225
Ehret, G., 173, 179
Ehri, L. C., 666
Eichman, P. L., 253
Eiduson, B. T., 451, 453, 464
Eignor, D. R., 638
Eimas, P. D., 664
EINHORN, H. J., 53-88; 55, 61-64, 66, 72, 73, 78, 79, 82, 647
Einon, G., 504, 505
Eisenberg, J. G., 341
Eisenberg-Berg, N., 137
Eiser, J. R., 359, 360, 388, 389
Eisler, R. M., 406, 426
Elberling, C., 155, 178
Eldredge, D. H., 155, 177, 178
Elkind, D., 143
Elliott, C. H., 428
Elliott, P., 315, 316
Ellis, A., 81
Ellis, H. C., 43
Ellis, N. R., 686
Ellison, R. L., 464
Ellman, S. J., 549, 563
Ellsworth, P. C., 375
Elman, D., 384
Elman, M., 260
Elms, A. C., 360
Elstein, A. S., 62
Elton, C. F., 453
Elwood, H., 314, 339
Emery, G., 418
Emmerich, W., 141
Endicott, J., 415
Engle, R. W., 691
Engström, B., 162
Engström, H., 162, 171
Enroth-Cugell, C., 483, 484, 588

Entwisle, D., 195
Entwisle, D. R., 666
Enzle, M. E., 390
Epley, E. A., 221
Epstein, L. H., 423
Erickson, B., 391
Erickson, C. E., 464
Erickson, J. R., 89
Erickson, P., 483, 499
Erikson, E., 142
Erre, J.-P., 179
Erreich, A., 96, 97
Erwin, J., 140
Esposito, J., 666
Esposito, R., 563
Estes, W. K., 28, 67, 78, 683
Estevez, O., 583
Ettema, J. S., 321, 333, 337, 345
Evans, E. F., 155-57, 160, 161, 166, 173-76
Evans, J. R., 282, 286
Evans, P., 11
Evans, S. H., 33, 691
Evenbeck, S., 392
Everitt, B., 192
Exner, J. E. Jr., 459
Eysel, U. T., 498
Eysenck, H. J., 308
Eysenck, M. W., 41

F

Fagan, J. F., 125
Fahlman, S. E., 23, 24
Fair, P. L., 367, 372
Fairbank, D., 643
Falck, B., 546
Falk, R., 78
Falmagne, R. J., 688
Fantz, R. L., 125
Farber, P. D., 643
Farkas, G. M., 424
Farmer, E. W., 461
Farnum, S. O., 287
Farquhar, A. B., 236
Farquhar, H., 236
Farquhar, J. W., 321, 329
Farran, D. C., 141
Faugeras, O. D., 594
Faulconer, B. A., 102
Fava, D., 451
Faw, H. W., 673
Fazio, R. H., 367, 370, 371, 373, 374, 377, 379, 381, 393
Fears, R., 663
Federico, P. A., 661, 683
Feigert, F. B., 319
Feighner, J. P., 415
Feinberg, B. M., 195, 231
Feinberg, S. E., 195, 220, 223, 236

Feingold, B. F., 253
Feiring, C., 134
Feldman, A., 126
Feldman, L. B., 662, 663
Feldman, R. S., 138
Feldt, L. S., 631, 632
Felton, T. B., 607, 608
Feltovich, P., 681
Fender, D. H., 605, 608, 610, 615
Ferguson, H. B., 255-57
Ferguson, J. M., 423
Ferguson, L. R., 143
Fernández, C., 155, 164, 172
Ferraro, J., 158
Ferretti, R. P., 691
Ferris, R. M., 254
Ferster, C. B., 265, 416
Ferster, D., 487, 497, 498, 607
Festinger, L., 362, 377
Fettiplace, R., 159, 168, 169
Feuerstein, R., 691
Fex, J., 166
Fibiger, H. C., 525, 537, 548, 549, 553, 555-58, 560-63; 0
Fiedler, L., 414
Fiedler, M. F., 118, 119
Field, D. E., 333
Field, T., 122
Fifield, M., 283
Figler, H., 282
Fillmore, C. D., 96
Findler, N. V., 27
Finlay, B. L., 480
Finney, J. W., 143
Fiorentini, A., 493, 499, 502, 507, 513, 588
Fischbein, E., 681
Fischer, B., 578, 607
Fischer, N. D., 166
Fischetti, M., 425
Fischhoff, B., 54, 57, 64, 67, 68, 73, 75, 76, 80-82
Fischler, I., 664
Fischoff, S., 376
Fishbein, M., 366, 368, 369, 371
Fishburn, P. C., 66
Fisher, A. E., 556
Fisher, E. B. Jr., 428
Fisher, N. I., 195
Fiske, D. W., 290
Fiskin, R. A., 496
Fitch, S. A., 143
Fitts, H., 426
Fitzgerald, E. T., 451
Fitzpatrick, T., 407
Flanery, R. C., 126, 127, 144
Flaugher, R. L., 648, 649
Flavell, J. H., 94, 129, 130
Flay, B. R., 364, 391, 392
Fleischman, M. J., 412
Fleisher, L. S., 665

SUBJECT INDEX

A

Abbreviated Conners Teacher
and Parent Rating Scale
see Tests and scales
Abortion
attitudes toward
and behavior, 371
Abstraction
and concepts
in learning and memory,
34–35
nature of
and categorization studies,
102–4
Accentuation theory
and attitude judgments,
388–89
Acetylcholine (ACh)
in cochlear physiology, 166
Achievement
and intelligence
in instructional
psychology, 689–90
Acquisition
role in evaluation
behavioral decision theory,
62–69
ACT Interest Inventory
see Tests and scales
Adaptation-Innovation
Inventory
see Tests and scales
Adaptive behavior
and new approaches to
theory, 14
Adenine nucleotide
in cochlear physiology, 166
Adjective Check List
see Tests and scales
Adolescence
developmental studies of,
142–43
hyperactive children during,
249
Adolescents
mass media effects on,
331–46
antisocial behavior, 340–42
attention and
comprehension,
332–35
political socialization,
338–40
prosocial effects, 342–44
responses to advertising,
335–38
sex-role socialization,
344–46
social cognition among, 140,
143

world conceptions of
and television effects,
328–29
Adoption studies
and behavioral genetics, 119
Adults
mass communication effects
on, 318–31
agenda setting, 322–26
campaigns and
development, 329–31
cultivation of beliefs,
322–26
gap hypothesis, 321–22
transmission of knowledge
and information,
318–21
Advertising
children's responses to
and mass media effects,
335–38
Affective processes
and development, 138
Age
and agenda-setting
hypothesis
in mass media studies, 326
bias against
in career interventions, 292
and newspaper usage, 313
and television use patterns,
311–12
prosocial effects, 344
Age differences
in creativity and personality,
455–56
in scanning ability, 685
Agenda setting
and choice and judgment
studies, 57, 68
and mass media effects,
322–26
Aggression
developmental studies of, 136
sex differences in, 136
on television
impact on children, 140,
308, 340–42
Aggressiveness
interpersonal
in hyperactives, 248
Alcohol abuse
among hyperactives, 249
Alcoholism
clinical treatment of, 427–28
Alcohol use
and attitude/behavior
studies, 368–69
and creative thinking, 460,
462
and dissonance theory, 380

Alpha Biographical Inventory
see Tests and scales
Altered states
of consciousness
and creativity studies, 441,
460, 462–63
Alternate Uses test
see Tests and scales
Alternatives
and choice
in current psychology, 8–9
Altruism
development in children, 138
American Sign Language
basic level categories of, 92,
97
Amphetamines
effects on self-stimulation,
554–55, 562–63
alpha-AMPT
effects on self-stimulation,
555–56
Amygdala
self-stimulation in, 537, 547,
549
Analogies tasks
and aptitudes, 687–88
Andrews' curves
in graphic data analysis,
226–28
Androgyny
psychological
and creativity, 457–58
Animal studies
amphibian and reptilian ear
in cochlear physiology,
154–80
cat and monkey visual
neurons, 477–513
neurophysiology of
self-stimulation, 523–65
Anorexia nervosa
clinical treatment of, 427
Anoxia
effects on endocochlear
potential, 164–65, 171
Anthropology
applying personal constructs
in, 8
influence on categorization,
91–92, 95
Anxiety
clinical treatment of, 412
sex differences in, 136
Anxiety management
and neuroses treatment, 422
Anxiety reduction
in developmental psychology
current views, 5
Approach-avoidance conflict
in choice, 70

733

Emotion
  Cognitive aspects of
    and development, 138
    in personality and social
      development, 134
Emotional response approach
  to attitude and covert
    behavior, 372
Employment testing
  construct validity in, 645–48
Encoding
  access
    and aptitude, 684–85,
      687–88
  phonological
    in word recognition
      studies, 663, 665
  visual
    and spatial frequency
      studies, 580, 593
Endolymph
  in cochlear physiology,
    162–65, 168
Endorphins
  and self-stimulation behavior,
    563–64
Enkephalins
  and self-stimulation behavior,
    564
Entertainment
  and mass media usage, 317
Environment
  in behavioral genetics studies,
    118–20, 143–44
  work
    and vocational research,
      296–97
Environmental control
  in habit disorder treatment,
    428
Environmental influence
  in psychopathology
    and treatment, 413, 422
  in visual development, 505–9,
    512–13
Environmental psychology
  and context studies, 6, 8, 14
Erythrosin (Red No. 3)
  role in hyperactivity, 254
Escape behavior
  and brain stimulation studies,
    547–48
Eserine
  in cochlear physiology, 166
Eskimos
  impact of television on, 329
ESP
  and current trends in
    psychology, 11
Etharcrynic acid
  and endocochlear potentials,
    164–65

Ethnic variables
  in psychotherapy, 414
Evaluation
  in behavioral decison theory,
    62–63, 69–71
Event perception
  and contextualism, 17–18
Evoked action potentials
  in self-stimulation studies,
    539
Evoked response audiometry
  conference proceedings on,
    155
Evolutionary biology
  and choice, 8–9
Evolutionary theory
  and behavioral decision
    making, 58–59
EXPAK
  scatterplot display of, 214
Expectancy value models
  and attitude change studies,
    385–86
Experience
  and attitude change studies,
    370–71
Experience Inquiry
  see Tests and scales
Experience Inventory
  see Tests and scales
Experimental psychology
  history and current trends,
    3–4, 6–8
  and humanistic psychology,
    10
Eysenck Personality Inventory
  see Tests and scales

F

Face perception
  and categorization studies,
    105
  in visual studies, 580
FACES
  in graphical data analysis,
    222–23, 227–28, 230,
    235
Factor analysis
  in aptitude and instruction,
    684
Fairness
  in testing, 645, 647–50
Family social relations
  and child development,
    138–40, 143
Family studies
  and developmental
    behavioral genetics,
    118–20, 143–44
  and vocational research, 287

Fault trees
  in probability estimation
    and decision theory, 57, 67
Feature extractors
  in visual perception, 577, 579
Feingold's diet
  in hyperactivity studies,
    253–54
Field dependence
  and individual uniqueness, 8
Figure-ground perception
  and acquisition
    in behavioral decision
      theory, 63–65, 67–68
Firstborns
  developmental studies of,
    137, 141
Floating fourfold circular
  display (3FCD)
    in graphical data analysis,
      223
Flooding
  as neuroses treatment,
    422–23
Fluorescent method
  for tracing reward pathways
    in self-stimulation studies,
      546–47, 549
Frequency analysis
  see Cochlear physiology
Friendship
  and peer relations, 139
Fuzzy logic
  and concepts
    in learning and memory,
      32–33

G

GABA
  in visual development
    studies, 493
Galvanic skin response (GSR)
  and arousal
    in hyperactivity, 256
Gambling
  in conflict and choice studies,
    75–76
Gap hypothesis
  and mass media knowledge,
    321–22, 330–31
Gender
  and television use, 311–12
Generalizability theory
  in classical test theory,
    634–35
General systems theory
  and contextualism, 17
  and theory of living systems,
    14–16
Genetics
  behavioral

and test performance
theory of, 688–89
Infancy
developmental studies of,
120–23
Infants
abstraction in, 34
attachment among
and peer relations, 135–36
categorization abilities of,
94–95
social responsiveness of
heritable influences in, 120
and sound/picture response,
332
spatial abilities of, 127–28
visual development of, 482
Inference
in reading comprehension
studies, 666–68
Information integration theory
and attitude change, 385
Information processing
and career decision making,
299
deficits in
among autistic children,
269–70
and divergent thinking
abilities
in creativity studies, 445
of mass media programming,
308, 318
Information-processing model
of written composition
in instructional
psychology, 671–72
Information processing theory
and attitude change studies,
358
and changes in psychology,
4–5
Information scales
see Tests and scales
Informed consent
and clinical psychology,
407
Inhibition
and abstraction
in concept learning, 35
Ink Blots test
see Tests and scales
Inoculation theory
and resistance to persuasion,
361–62
Inside-out plots
in graphical data analysis,
222, 225–27
Insomnia
clinical treatment of, 412,
423–24
Instructional psychology,
659–93

intelligence and aptitude,
683–92
aptitudes and instruction,
689–92
cognitive components,
687–89
cognitive correlates,
684–87
mathematics, 674–81
reading, 661–74
comprehension, 666–74
difficulty in learning,
665–66
word recognition, 662–65
science and problem solving,
681–83
Intelligence
and aptitude
in instructional
psychology, 683–92
and creativity, 444–52
and divergent thinking
abilities, 446–50
models of intellect, 444–45
other special abilities,
450–52
rated or perceived
intelligence, 446
traditional measures of
intelligence, 445–46
current research on, 5, 7–8
as focus of behavioral
genetics, 118–19
Intention
and attitude/behavior
studies, 368–69
Interaction
and attributes
in categorization theory,
108
Interest inventories
see Tests and scales
Interpersonal communication
and agenda-setting effect
of mass media, 326
and attitude change, 380
Interpersonal model
in treatment of depression,
419–20
Interpersonal skills
in habit disorder treatments,
428
Interracial behaviors
and attitude studies, 367, 369
Intuitive responses
and optimal models
in behavioral decision
theory, 59–61
IQ
and mother-infant
interactions, 141
tests
see Tests and scales

Item response theory (IRT)
and latent trait test theory,
638–44, 650

J

Jackson Personality Inventory
see Tests and scales
Judgment
and choice processes, 53–83
acquisition, 62–69
conflict, 71–77
environment vs problem
space, 57–59
evaluation/action, 69–71
intuitive responses, 59–61
learning/feedback, 77–80
methodological concerns,
80–83
optimal decisions, 55–61
strategies and mechanisms
of, 61–77
task, 55–57, 62
Judgmental effects
in attitude change studies,
387–89
accentuation theory,
388–89
perspective theory, 388
Jury judgments
and attitude studies, 385

K

Kanamycin
in cochlear studies, 173–74
Knowledge
transmission of
and mass media effects,
318–21
KYST/INDSCAL
scatterplot display of, 214

L

Language
acquisition
and cognitive development,
132–33
and categorization of natural
objects, 92–93, 97
and credibility judgments
in attitude studies, 391
deficits in autism, 268–70,
272
development
recent reviews of, 131–34
understanding
and difficulty in learning
to read, 665–66, 669,
672
and mathematics
instruction, 677–79

CUMULATIVE INDEXES

CONTRIBUTING AUTHORS, VOLUMES 28–32

CHAPTER TITLES, VOLUMES 28–32